COMPUTER SECURITY HANDBOOK

COMPUTER SECURITY HANDBOOK

Fifth Edition

Volume 2

Edited by

SEYMOUR BOSWORTH

M.E. KABAY

ERIC WHYNE

WILEY

John Wiley & Sons, Inc.

Library of Congress Cataloging-in-Publication Data:

Computer security handbook. 5th ed. / edited by Seymour Bosworth, M.E. Kabay, Eric Whyne.
    p. cm.
  Includes index.
  ISBN 978-0-471-71652-5 ((paper) (set)) – ISBN 978-0-470-32722-7 ((vol 1)) – ISBN 978-0-470-32723-4 ((vol 2)) 1. Electronic data processing departments–Security measures. I. Bosworth, Seymour. II. Kabay, Michel E. III. Whyne, Eric, 1981–
  HF5548.37.C64 2009
  658.4'78–dc22

                                                     2008040626

Printed in the United States of America

10 9 8 7 6 5 4 3 2 1

CONTENTS

PART IV   PREVENTION: HUMAN FACTORS

PART V   DETECTING SECURITY BREACHES

PART VI   RESPONSE AND REMEDIATION

PREFACE

Computers are an integral part of our economic, social, professional, governmental, and military infrastructures. They have become necessities in virtually every area of modern life, but their vulnerability is of increasing concern. Computer-based systems are constantly under threats of inadvertent error and acts of nature as well as those attributable to unethical, immoral, and criminal activities. It is the purpose of this *Computer Security Handbook* to provide guidance in recognizing these threats, eliminating them where possible and, if not, then to lessen any losses attributable to them.

This *Handbook* will be most valuable to those directly responsible for computer, network, or information security as well as those who must design, install, and maintain secure systems. It will be equally important to those managers whose operating functions can be affected by breaches in security and to those executives who are responsible for protecting the assets that have been entrusted to them.

With the advent of desktop, laptop, and handheld computers, and with the vast international networks that interconnect them, the nature and extent of threats to computer security have grown almost beyond measure. In order to encompass this unprecedented expansion, the *Computer Security Handbook* has grown apace.

When the first edition of the *Handbook* was published, its entire focus was on mainframe computers, the only type then in widespread use. The second edition recognized the advent of small computers, while the third edition placed increased emphasis on PCs and networks.

Edition	Publication Date	Chapters	Text Pages
First	1973	12	162
Second	1988	19	383
Third	1995	23	571
Fourth	2002	54	1,184
Fifth	2009	77	2,040

The fourth edition of the *Computer Security Handbook* gave almost equal attention to mainframes and microcomputers.

This fifth edition has been as great a step forward as the fourth. With 77 chapters and the work of 86 authors, we have increased coverage in both breadth and depth. We now cover all 10 domains of the Common Body of Knowledge defined by the International Information Systems Security Certification Consortium (ISC)^2:

1. Security Management Practices: Chapters 10, 12, 13, 14, 15, 19, 10, 31, 43, 44, 45, 46, 47, 48, 49, 50, 51, 54, 55, 62, 63, 64, 65, 66, 67, 68, 74, 75, 76

2. Security Architecture and Models: Chapters 1, 2, 3, 8, 9, 24, 26, 27, 51
3. Access Control Systems and Methodology: Chapters 15, 19, 28, 29, 32
4. Application Development Security: Chapters 13, 19, 21, 30, 38, 39, 52, 53
5. Operations Security: Chapters 13, 14, 15, 19, 21, 24, 36, 40, 47, 53, 57
6. Physical Security: Chapters 4, 13, 15, 19, 22, 23, 28, 29
7. Cryptography: Chapters 7, 32, 37, 42
8. Telecomm, Networks, and Internet Security: Chapters 4, 5, 6, 13, 14, 15, 16, 17, 18, 20, 21, 24, 25, 26, 27, 30, 31, 32, 33, 34, 35, 41, 48
9. Business Continuity Planning: Chapters 22, 23, 56, 57, 58, 59, 60
10. Law, Investigations, and Ethics: Chapters 11, 12, 13, 31, 42, 61, 63, 64, 69, 70, 71, 72, 73

In addition to updating every chapter of the fourth edition, we have added chapters on:

- History of Computer Crime
- Hardware Elements of Security
- Data Communications and Information Security
- Network Topologies, Protocols, and Design
- Encryption
- Mathematical Models of Information Security
- The Dangerous Information Technology Insider: Psychological Characteristics and Career Patterns
- Social Engineering and Low-Tech Attacks
- Spam, Phishing, and Trojans: Attacks Meant to Fool
- Biometric Authentication
- Web Monitoring and Content Filtering
- Virtual Private Networks and Secure Remote Access
- 802.11 Wireless LAN Security
- Securing VoIP
- Securing P2P, IM, SMS, and Collaboration Tools
- Securing Stored Data
- Writing Secure Code
- Managing Software Patches and Vulnerabilities
- U.S. Legal and Regulatory Security Issues
- The Role of the CISO
- Developing Classification Policies for Data
- Outsourcing and Security
- Expert Witnesses and the *Daubert* Challenge
- Professional Certification and Training in Information Assurance
- Undergraduate and Graduate Education in Information Assurance
- European Graduate Work in Information Assurance and the Bologna Declaration

We have continued our practice from the fourth edition of inviting a security luminary to write the final chapter, "The Future of Information Assurance." We are pleased to include a stellar contribution from Dr. Peter G. Neumann in this edition.

SEYMOUR BOSWORTH
Senior Editor
January 2009

ACKNOWLEDGMENTS

Seymour Bosworth, Senior Editor   I would like to give grateful recognition to Arthur Hutt and Douglas Hoyt, my coeditors of the first, second, and third editions of this *Handbook*. Although both Art and Doug are deceased, their commitment and their competence remain as constant reminders that nothing less than excellence is acceptable. Mich Kabay, my coeditor from the fourth edition, and Eric Whyne, our new third editor, continue in that tradition. I would not have wanted to undertake this project without them.

We mark with sadness the passing of our friend and colleague Robert Jacobson, who contributed to Chapter 1 (Brief History and Mission of Information System Security) and wrote Chapter 62 (Risk Assessment and Risk Management). Bob was a significant and valued contributor to the development of our field, and we miss his cheerful intelligence. We also miss Diane Levine, who contributed so much to both the third and fourth editions. She wrote four chapters in the third edition and six in the fourth. We are honored to continue to list her as a coauthor on five updated chapters in the fifth edition.

Thanks are also due to our colleagues at John Wiley & Sons: Tim Burgard as Acquisitions Editor, Stacey Rympa as Development Editor, Natasha Andrews-Noel as Senior Production Editor, and Debra Manette as Copyeditor and Joe Ruddick as Proofreader. All have performed their duties in an exemplary manner and with unfailing kindness, courtesy, and professionalism.

M. E. Kabay, Technical Editor   The contributions from my faculty colleagues and from our alumni in the Master of Science in Information Assurance (MSIA) program at Norwich University are noteworthy. Many of the *Handbook*'s authors are graduates of the MSIA program, instructors in the program, or both.

I am immeasurably grateful to Sy for his leadership in this project. In addition to the inherent value of his decades of experience in the field of information security, his insightful editorial comments and queries have forced everyone on the project to strive for excellence in all aspects of our work. He is also fun to work with!

Our coeditor Eric Whyne has loyally persevered in his editorial tasks despite ducking bullets in the war in Iraq, where he has served honorably throughout most of the project. Our thanks to him for his service to the nation and to this project.

Our authors deserve enormous credit for the professional way in which they responded to our requests, outlines, suggestions, corrections, and nagging. I want to express my personal gratitude and appreciation for their courteous, collaborative, and responsive interactions with us.

Finally, as always, I want to thank my beloved wife, Deborah Black, light of my life, for her support and understanding over the years that this project has taken away from our time together.

Eric Whyne, Associate Editor   There is an enormous amount of work put into a text of this size. The diligent and gifted authors who have contributed their time are some of the brightest and most experienced professionals in their fields. They did so not for compensation but because they love the subjects which they have put so much effort into mastering. The *Computer Security Handbook* will continue its tradition of being a collection point for these labors so long as there are great minds in love with the challenging problems of computer security and willing to devote their time to sharing solutions.

At the time I started on the project, I was a Marine Officer working in the data communications field in Ramadi, Iraq. I worked the night shift and spent my afternoons perched in a folding chair, under the relatively cool Iraq winter sun, writing correspondence and doing first-past edits of the chapters of the *Handbook*. Upon my return to the United States, my spare evenings along the North Carolina coast were dedicated to the *Handbook* as I worked my day job as the Marine Corps Anti-Terrorism Battalion Communications Officer. Since then I have deployed once more to Iraq as an advisor to the Iraqi Army. Everywhere I have gone, and with every job I have held, I have been able to apply and refine the principles covered in this *Handbook* and in previous versions. From the most high-tech cutting-edge, multiplexed satellite communications system used in military operations in Iraq, to the relatively mundane desktop computer networks of offices in the United States, to the ancient weathered computers the Iraqi Army totes around with them and ties into the power grid at any opportunity, computer security is critical to the accomplishment of the most basic tasks these systems are used for.

Unarguably, the exchange of information and ideas has been the largest factor in the shaping and betterment of our world throughout history. Having spent the last year of my life living as a local in a third-world country, that fact is fresh on my mind. In that spirit, computers are recognized as the most powerful and universally applicable tool ever devised. This book's purpose is to help you ensure that your computers remain powerful and successfully applied to the tasks for which you intend them to be used.

I am grateful to Sy Bosworth and Mich Kabay for their faith in bringing me into this project, and for their guidance and leadership along the way. They are both great people, and it has been an honor and a joy to work with them.

INTRODUCTION TO PART IV

PREVENTION: HUMAN FACTORS

Human factors underlie all the mechanisms invented by technical experts. Without human awareness, training, education, and motivation, technical defenses inevitably fail. This part details a number of valuable areas of knowledge for security practitioners, including these chapters and topics:

43. **Ethical Decision Making and High Technology.** A strategy for setting a high priority on ethical behavior and a framework for making ethical decisions

44. **Security Policy Guidelines.** Guidelines for how to express security policies effectively

45. **Employment Practices and Policies.** Policy guidelines on hiring, managing, and firing employees

46. **Vulnerability Assessment.** Methods for smoothly integrating vulnerability assessments into the corporate culture

47. **Operations Security and Production Controls.** Running computer operations securely, and controlling production for service levels and quality

48. **E-Mail and Internet Use Policies.** Guidelines for setting expectations about employee use of the Web and e-mail at work

49. **Implementing a Security Awareness Program.** Methods for ensuring that all employees are aware of security requirements and policies

50. **Using Social Psychology to Implement Security Policies.** Drawing on the science of social psychology for effective implementation of security policies

51. **Security Standards for Products.** Established standards for evaluating the trustworthiness and effectiveness of security products

CHAPTER 43

ETHICAL DECISION MAKING AND HIGH TECHNOLOGY

James Landon Linderman

43.1 INTRODUCTION: THE ABCs OF COMPUTER ETHICS

43.1.1 Why an Ethics Chapter in a Computer Security Handbook?

In an information age, many potential misuses and abuses of information create privacy and security problems. In addition to possible legal issues, ethical issues affect many groups and individuals—including employees and customers, vendors, consultants, bankers, and stockholders—who have enough at stake in the matter to confront and even destroy an organization over ethical lapses. As is so often the case, consciousness raising is at the heart of maintaining control.

In this chapter, the term "ethics" refers to a system of moral principles that relate to the benefits and harms of particular actions and to the rightness and wrongness of motives and ends of these actions. The major sections cover principles of ethics, tests to help recognize ethical and unethical behavior, and approaches to help ensure good ethical conduct.

43.1.2 How Much Time Do You Have for This Chapter?

Section 43.2 requires only one minute to read, but it forms the foundation of this chapter and of a lifelong concern for one of the most important requisites of a valued career and of a civilized society. Ethics matters, and here are the ABCs:

Section 43.2 **A**wareness (a one-minute primer)

Section 43.3 **B**asics (a 10-minute summary)

Section 43.4 **C**onsiderations (a 100-minute study)

Section 43.5 **D**etails (a lifetime of ongoing commitment)

43.2 AWARENESS.

The sections that follow distill some of the most important issues.

43.2.1 Principle 1: Ethics Counts.

Increasingly, society is holding individuals and organizations to higher ethical standards than in the past; for example, in recent years, many countries have passed privacy legislation, conflict-of-interest restrictions for public officials, and full-disclosure laws for candidates for a variety of public offices. People, individually and collectively, really want to trust others. Two corollaries to the principle that ethics counts are:

1. Good ethical standards are usually good for business.
2. Violations of ethics are almost always bad for business.

In other words, good ethical behavior usually is appreciated by society, and bad ethical behavior almost always is frowned on and punished—sooner or later.

43.2.2 Principle 2: Ethics Is Everybody's Business.

A second important principle is that good ethics flourishes best when everyone works at it, both in practicing good ethics and in holding others to do so. The reverse of this is also true: Those who practice bad ethics, or choose to ignore the bad ethics of others, are truly part of the problem. Ethics is inescapably everybody's business.

43.2.3 A Test: Put Yourself in Another's Shoes.

One of the best evaluators of whether certain behavior is ethical or not invites you to put yourself in the other person's shoes and ask the role-reversal question: "What if I were on the receiving end of the behavior in question?" This variant of the time-honored golden rule translates to "If I wouldn't like it done to me I probably shouldn't do it to others."

43.2.4 An Approach: Disclose!

One of the best guidelines to help ensure good ethical behavior is to let your stakeholders in on what you are doing or are about to do. Good ethics flourishes in the light of day; bad ethics ultimately relies on concealment. Disclosure buys you two forms of peace of mind: First, you're being openly honest; second, if others do not like it, you have at least given them the opportunity to express their concerns.

For example, consider organizational policy about managers reading employee e-mail. Almost any policy (anywhere from aggressive intervention to complete hands off) is likely to be ethical if and only if employees are made aware of it.

43.3 BASICS.   The expansion of Section 43.2 that follows elaborates on the basic principles enunciated there.

43.3.1 Principle 3: Stakeholders Dictate Ethics.   Stakeholders are defined as any individuals or groups with something at stake in the outcome of a decision. In the world of business, stockholders are almost always stakeholders; employees, customers, suppliers, and even competitors are often stakeholders too. How a decision harms or benefits stakeholders is a major ethical consideration. Effects on stakeholders are so important that the best place to start looking at the ethics of a decision is to identify stakeholders and just what it is they have at stake. Decisions will invariably affect individuals and groups, often in opposite ways: Some may stand to gain, others to lose or suffer. The effects and trade-offs raise the principal ethics concerns.

43.3.2 Principle 4: Traditional Principles Still Apply.   Recent generations are not the first to raise questions and develop ideas about ethics, although the concept of business ethics has been mocked as an oxymoron and only recently promoted in academia as a valuable area of study. High technology has complicated some issues, but these fundamental principles still apply:

- The Golden Rule ("Do unto others as you would have them do unto you") and its variants have already been mentioned. These principles remain timeless and fundamental.
- Consideration of the interplay of duties, rights, and responsibilities remains important. When making ethical decisions, we normally examine the legal, professional, and customary constraints on behavior that apply to our situation.
- Traditional reasons for good ethical behavior, such as religious principles, egoism, utilitarianism, and altruism, still provide us with a useful taxonomy for discussions about ethics.

The point is that even though modern technology has created new opportunities for unethical behavior and new motivations for good ethical behavior, it has not been necessary to develop new principles to deal with ethics. For example, many of the principles (including politeness) governing the behavior of door-to-door sales still apply to Internet push technology.

43.3.3 More Tests.   In Section 43.2.3, we suggested the "other's shoes test" as an excellent evaluator of whether certain behavior is ethical or not. Here we introduce three other tests. The first two are negative in the sense of suggesting that behavior is inappropriate; the third is positive and suggests that the behavior in question is ethical.

1. The "mom test" asks how your mom (spouse, children, best friend, etc.) would react if aware of your actions. If you would be embarrassed having someone close to you know what is going on, the odds are pretty good it is unethical.
2. The "eye-team test" takes this a step further and considers the results of exposing your actions to the whole world as part of an investigative team broadcast. Again, the more embarrassment, the more likely the unethical nature of the actions.

3. The "market test" asks you to think about openly publicizing your actions as a competitive customer relations strategy. Never mind whether such a marketing strategy is actually feasible; if such exposure could impress others favorably, chances are you are on solid ethical ground.

43.3.4   A Guideline Approach: Ask!   Section 43.2.4 endorsed disclosure as one of the best guidelines to help ensure good ethical behavior. This simply means letting your stakeholders in on what you are doing, or about to do. Having done so, it then becomes an appropriate guideline to ask those stakeholders for their permission (or acquiescence, or at least acknowledgment) before you proceed. This can be in the form of allowing stakeholders to opt out of certain policies. Many stakeholders prefer an opt-in approach rather than a default assumption of acceptability, particularly if that assumption is nonintuitive or otherwise obscure.

An example of this approach to ethical behavior is the legally enforced requirement in many countries to ask customers for permission to use their personally identifiable information for purposes other than the original defined functions. Typically, customers have either to opt out of information sharing or opt in to such use of their information.

In other cases, stakeholders such as employees or shareholders may disagree with the ethical implications of proposed actions. They can then argue against the proposals to the extent possible. The ultimate option for such stakeholders is to withdraw; employees can resign and shareholders can sell their shares. If the proposed actions are perceived as illegal, critics can become whistle-blowers and report the suspected illegality to law enforcement and regulatory officials.

43.3.5   Another Guideline Approach: An Ethics Officer.   Designating an individual to serve as a full- or part-time ethics officer in an enterprise is a powerful proactive way to help ensure good ethical behavior. Many large organizations now consider this a position on the top management team. But even small organizations can formally delegate such responsibilities on a part-time basis; they need not require much time and energy of the individual involved. In all cases, the common objectives include:

- Clear management commitment to good business ethics, including adequate resources to support this position
- Organizational recognition that this individual has appropriate authority and responsibility, and is a conduit of information into and within the organization
- Hassle-free avenues of access to this person

43.4   CONSIDERATIONS.   This section discusses some issues of management style in promulgating and enforcing ethics.

43.4.1   Principle 5: Ethics Need Not and Should Not Be a Hassle.   The last thing one wants with business ethics is hassle. An organization's ethics policies should not be obscure, complicated, onerous, or an obstacle to getting things done. The keys to avoiding hassles include:

- Clear and straightforward articulation of ethics policies
- Consciousness raising as a prime objective of ethics policies

- Clear, comfortable, and safe access to interpretation, for example, by an ethics officer
- Consistency in promulgation, education, application, and enforcement

Employees should not have to guess what constitutes acceptable behavior, nor should they be encumbered by anxiety, guilt, or fear. Individuals should be able to gain clarification on matters before, during, or after events without delay and without fear of being considered a nuisance. Questions about ethics issues deserve unbiased answers, without the presumption that there has been a breach of ethical conduct or that ulterior motives are involved.

Whenever an individual is uncomfortable with a situation or a potential situation, whether he or she is directly involved or not, and particularly if "whistle blowing" implicates others or even organizational policy, that discomfort needs to be addressed. Even if the individual is wrong and should not be concerned, the discomfort should be dispelled. If the individual is right and there is a legitimate concern, the organization should resolve the issue in a way that does not put the whistle-blower on the spot but rather indicates support for such disclosure.

43.4.2 Principle 6: Ethics Policies Deserve Formality. Like other important policies, an organization's ethics policies deserve formality:

- Clear documentation
- Clear motivation
- Clear sanctions
- Clear management support at every level, including the top

Anything less than the foregoing suggests confusion at best, and lip service at worst. Formality should not mean bureaucracy or piles of manuals. Consistent with the fifth principle of avoiding hassles, documentation should be brief and clear, and directed at simplifying matters rather than complicating them. The preparation and presentation of policies should reflect a process of thoughtful, high-priority consideration.

A corollary of this principle is peer participation. Policies that ultimately rely on organizational support are best developed and disseminated with peer involvement.

43.4.3 Principle 7: Ethics Policies Deserve Review. Perhaps the only thing as dangerous as ignorance when it comes to policy is complacency. This is as true of ethics policies as it is of any other organizational policy. In particular, to assume everyone in an organization is on board with policy is naive at best. Review offers a type of preventive maintenance whereby policies and their promulgation are reconsidered with an eye to improvement.

Any organizational policy requires subscription on the part of the members of the organization. Understanding of, and compliance with, any policy suffers a dangerous tendency to lapse when a policy simply gathers dust. Even an occasional mention and discussion of ethical issues or principles during meetings can breathe new life into old policy.

Just as a corollary of Principle 6 was peer participation in the formalization of policy, so is peer involvement a corollary of policy review. Such peer review not only facilitates fresh insights into policy, but the process itself represents a powerful educational opportunity.

43.4.4   Principle 8: Anticipate.   Few people relish the prospect of a serious breach of organizational ethics, particularly if matters reach the point of embarrassing publicity or even legal action. It is better to contemplate the worst scenarios in advance rather than to deal with them without preparation and after the fact. Wishful thinking often deters an organization from including appropriate issues in formal policy. This must not be permitted to happen.

It is better to address tough issues head on than to take anything for granted. The two best ways of doing so are to:

1. Have comprehensive policies that cover any foreseeable eventuality.
2. Have a full- or part-time ethics officer in place to stay on top of things.

43.4.5   The Smell Test.   Sometimes the other tests discussed (other's shoes, mom, eye-team, market) can result in fuzzy or ambiguous analysis. It may be hard to put yourself in someone else's shoes, especially if different individuals would have widely different reactions to your behavior. And sometimes your family and friends, the general public, or your customers could be neutral or divided in their reactions. The so-called smell test does not require quantitative or even qualitative estimations; it simply relies on your intuition as to whether the behavior in question "smells fishy." In other words, if you catch yourself seeking justifications, or feel a bit uncomfortable even thinking about the implications, the ethics may be as bad or poor as they smell.

43.4.6   An Approach: Stock Taking.   Where can an organization start with all this if it has not already done so? Things usually start with a concerned individual (you?) doing some stock taking and consciousness raising. Questions for you and others in your organization to consider follow. If you like the answers, then your organization is ethically aware. If you do not like the answers, your organization must deal with the issues you have uncovered.

- If you felt that a fellow employee was misusing company resources or harassing someone, is it obvious what you should do? Is there someone in the organization you could comfortably talk with?
- Do you have the sense that top management in your organization is aware of ethics issues? Do you have the sense that they care?
- Do you know if your organization monitors employee e-mail or computer usage? How much personal business, such as e-mail and net surfing, is permissible on company time?
- How important is quality to your company's products and services? Are marketing claims consistent with quality?
- What, if any, information does your company capture about customers, suppliers, or employees without their permission? Without even their knowledge? What, if any, information does your company provide to entities outside the organization about customers, suppliers, or employees without their permission? Without even their knowledge?
- Does your organization fully comply with license arrangements and payments for software and hardware?

- Are customers, suppliers, and employees always treated with dignity and respect? How would a stakeholder (e.g., a new employee) become aware of organizational ethics policies?

For each of these questions, the issue of how one knows must be raised. Ambiguous, confusing, or unreliable knowledge of what is or is not going on should raise red flags of concern. Discomfort with such knowledge may be symptomatic of underlying problems with ethics.

The stock taking just suggested should translate into action steps for your organization. Here are a few suggested actions to get started.

- Ask some of your peers to consider the same stock-taking questions, and compare their thoughts with yours.
- Itemize and prioritize any concerns.
- Make an appointment with someone fairly high up in management to discuss those concerns. If you are that someone, make an appointment with two or three peers and with subordinates who represent the staff.
- Examine the feasibility of appointing a full- or part-time ethics officer while considering the downside of not having one.
- Ask your internal or external auditors to consider an audit of your ethics policies the next time they do a financial or operational audit.

43.5 CONCLUDING REMARKS.   As with security awareness, ethical awareness needs freshness and repetition.

43.5.1 How to Keep Up.   One of the best ways for individuals and organizations to keep up with matters of good ethics is to spread the job around. Do not try to shoulder the effort alone; it will likely overwhelm any one individual, and collective thinking is valuable in these matters. Without abrogating individual responsibilities, charging the right person with the job of ethics officer will certainly help to keep the enterprise on an appropriate ethical course. A growing number of periodicals, both professional and of general interest, include articles involving ethics. Reading and then discussing them with your peers can be invaluable. Additionally, there has been an increase in the number of Web sites addressing ethical issues. See Section 43.6.

43.5.2 Why to Keep Up.   Keeping on top of organizational ethics is important because it is the right thing to do. Contemporary business practice embraces the idea of an extended value chain where entities such as customers and suppliers, traditionally seen as outside organizational boundaries, are now viewed as partners. Strategic alliances are being formed with these entities, and keeping business partners satisfied and confident is now a strategic necessity. Souring the relationship by a breach of ethics is completely inconsistent with sound business practices. Even if customers and suppliers are not formally viewed as business partners, they are still essential to doing business and are not to be taken for granted. At the very least, given the range of alternative choices available today, unfair exploitation and other forms of unethical practice expose an organization to outright abandonment.

Finally, in the spirit of total quality management, whereby everyone in the enterprise is seen to contribute to its success or failure, your enterprise can be said to be counting on you. The converse may also be true: Your job and your future career may well depend on the success of your enterprise. The good ethics of your organization reflect favorably on you and your colleagues, but bad ethics will have an opposite effect.

43.6   FURTHER READING.   A list of a few books and Web sites that will be helpful to readers seeking further discussion of ethical decision making in general, and ethics in business and high technology follows.

Australian Institute of Computer Ethics. www.businessit.bf.rmit.edu.au/aice/index. htm.

Barger, R. N. "In Search of a Common Rationale for Computer Ethics," 1994; www.nd.edu/˜rbarger/common-rat.html.

Computer Ethics Institute. www.computerethicsinstitute.org.

Cavazos, E., and G. Morin. *Cyberspace and the Law: Your Rights and Duties in the On-Line World.* Cambridge, MA: MIT Press, 1996.

Computer & Information Ethics Resources on Center for Applied Ethics, University of British Columbia. www.ethicsweb.ca/resources/.

Computer Ethics. "Cyberethics." http://cyberethics.cbi.msstate.edu/.

Computer Ethics. "ThinkQuest." http://library.thinkquest.org/26658/?tqskip=1

Cyber Citizen Partnership. Information Technology Association of America (ITAA) & Department of Justice (DoJ). www.cybercitizenpartners.org/.

Cyberangels. www.cyberangels.org/.

Cyberspacers (kids' site). www.cyberspacers.com/home.html.

EpistemeLinks. Philosophy Resources on the Internet—Computer Ethics. http:// tinyurl.com/33kduz.

Ethics and Information Technology (journal). www.springer.com/computer/ programming/journal/10676.

Floridi, L. "Information Ethics: On the Philosophical Foundations of Computer Ethics." Version 2.0, 1998; www.wolfson.ox.ac.uk/˜floridi/ie.htm.

Forester, T., and P. Morrison. *Computer Ethics: Cautionary Tales and Ethical Dilemmas in Computing.* Cambridge, MA: MIT Press, 1990.

Institute for Global Ethics. www.globalethics.org/.

Johnson, D. O. *Computer Ethics*, 3rd ed. New York: Prentice Hall, 2000.

Kabay, M. E. "Hacker Tips Published in Wall Street Journal." Network World Security Strategies, August 28, 2007; www.networkworld.com/newsletters/sec/2007/ 0827sec1.html.

Kabay, M. E. "Ethical Decision-Making: Identifying the Ethical Issue," Network World Security Strategies, August 30, 2007; www.networkworld.com/ newsletters/sec/2007/0827sec2.html.

Kabay, M. E. "Ethical Decision-Making: Using Formal and Informal Guidelines," Network World Security Strategies, September 4, 2007; www.networkworld.com/ newsletters/sec/2007/0903sec1.html.

Kabay, M. E. "Ethical Decision-Making: Principles, Rights and Duties, and Intuitive Cues," Network World Security Strategies, September 6, 2007; www. networkworld.com/newsletters/sec/2007/0903sec2.html.

Kabay, M. E. "Incident Response: Don't Lie," Network World Security Strategies, October 23, 20/07; www.networkworld.com/newsletters/sec/2007/1022sec1. html.

Kallman, E. A., and J. P. Grillo. *Ethical Decision Making and Information Technology: An Introduction with Cases*, 2nd ed. New York: McGraw-Hill, 1996.

Lessig, L., D. Post, and E. Volokh. "Cyberspace Law for Non-Lawyers." Published via e-mail, 1997; www.ssrn.com/update/lsn/cyberspace/csl_lessons.html

Online Ethics Center for Engineering and Science. http://onlineethics.org/.

Orlando, J., and M. E. Kabay. "Social Engineering in Penetration Testing: Cases," Network World Security Strategies, October 25, 2007; www.networkworld.com/newsletters/sec/2007/1022sec1.html.

Project NEThics at the University of Maryland. www.inform.umd.edu/CompRes/NEThics/ethics.

Schumacher, P., and M. E. Kabay. "Social Engineering in Penetration Testing: Intimidation," Network World Security Strategies, November 8, 2007; www.networkworld.com/newsletters/sec/2007/1105sec2.html.

Schumacher, P., and M. E. Kabay., "Social Engineering in Penetration Testing: Overload and Fascination," Network World Security Strategies, November 13, 2007; www.networkworld.com/newsletters/sec/2007/1112sec1.html.

Spinello, R. *Case Studies in Information and Computer Ethics.* New York: Prentice Hall, 1996.

Tavani Bibliography of Computing, Ethics, and Social Responsibility, Mississippi State University. http://cyberethics.cbi.msstate.edu/biblio.

University of British Columbia Centre for Applied Ethics. www.ethics.ubc.ca

Web Wise Kids. www.webwisekids.com/.

SECURITY POLICY GUIDELINES

M. E. Kabay and Bridgitt Robertson

44.1 INTRODUCTION. This chapter reviews principles, topics, and resources for creating effective security policies. It does not propose specific guidelines except as examples. Many of the chapters in this *Handbook* discuss policy; a few examples are listed next:

Chapter 23 provides an extensive overview of physical security policies.

Chapter 25 discusses local area network security issues and policies.

Chapter 38 reviews software development policies.

Chapter 39 surveys quality assurance policies.

Chapter 45 provides guidance on employment policies from a security standpoint.

Chapter 47 includes policies for improving operations security and production.

Chapter 48 reviews specific recommendations for e-mail and Internet usage.

Chapter 49 looks at methods for enhancing security awareness.

Chapter 52 offers policies for secure application design.

Chapters 56 through 59 deal with policies for emergency response, backup, and recovery.

Chapter 61 presents policies for working effectively with law enforcement.

Chapter 66 discusses effective methods for developing security policies in specific organizations.

44.2   TERMINOLOGY.   One of the preeminent leaders in security policy development, Charles Cresson Wood, has emphasized that when developing policy, it helps to segregate information that has different purposes. Specifically, one should create different documents for policy, standards, and procedures.[1]

44.2.1   Policy.   The term "policy" is defined as the rules and regulations set by the organization. Policies are laid down by management in compliance with applicable law, industry regulations, and the decisions of enterprise leaders. Policies are mandatory; they are expressed in definite language and require compliance. Failure to conform to policy can result in disciplinary action, termination of employment, and even legal action. Familiar examples of policy include requirements for background checks when hiring employees, the obligation to follow laws governing the duplication of proprietary software, and restrictions on the use of corporate vehicles for private purposes.

Security policy governs how an organization's information is to be protected against breaches of security; examples include policies on identification and authentication, authorization for specific kinds of access to specific data, responsibilities for data protection, limitations on the use of corporate resources for e-mail and Internet access, and restrictions on installation of programs on corporate systems. Policies are the basis for security awareness, training, and education; they are a necessary underpinning for security audits. Without policies, it is impossible to demonstrate due diligence in the protection of corporate assets.

Policies are focused on the desired results, not on the means for achieving those results. The methods for achieving policies are defined in the next sections on controls, standards, and procedures.

44.2.2   Controls.   When developing a framework for implementing security policies, controls are the measures used to protect systems against specific threats. For example, a policy might stipulate that all production systems must be protected against unauthorized modification of data by programmers; a specific control that could be named in the policy might be that test data extracted by programmers from the production databases must be anonymized to protect confidential data.

44.2.3   Standards.   A standard in computing can be an accepted specification for hardware, software, or human actions. An example of a technical standard is the transmission control protocol/Internet protocol (TCP/IP) that governs how systems can be interconnected into the Internet.

Standards can be de facto when they are so widely used that new applications routinely respect their conventions; an example is the Hewlett-Packard interface bus

(HP-IB), which became so popular that it was eventually turned into a de jure standard when the Institute of Electrical and Electronics Engineers (IEEE) based its formal IEEE-488 standard on the HP-IB. In contrast, the Centronix parallel interface, although equally popular and universally used, remains proprietary.

In a corporate environment, the term "standard" refers to specific technical choices for implementing particular policies. For example, a corporate policy might stipulate that strong identification and authentication, selected by the technical staff, must be used when gaining access to restricted data; the corresponding standard might specify that a particular brand and model of a microprocessor-equipped smart card should be used in satisfying access control restrictions. Typically, standards are of concern to those who must implement policies; not all standards need be made known to all personnel. Standards also must change in response to a changing technical environment; typically standards change much more rapidly than policies.

44.2.4 Procedures.   Procedures prescribe how people are to behave in implementing policies. For example, a policy might stipulate that all confidential communications from employees traveling outside the enterprise must be encrypted; the corresponding standard might define the proprietary virtual private network (VPN) software and hardware needed to implement that policy; and the corresponding procedure would explain in detail each step required to initiate a secure connection using that particular VPN.

44.3 RESOURCES FOR POLICY WRITERS.   If one is setting out to create policy *de novo* (i.e., without a preexisting policy document), it is critically important to use an existing policy template. Creating policies without guidance from experienced policy writers is a time-consuming, frustrating job that can consume thousands of hours of time, cause dissension within the enterprise, and leave everyone so disgusted that the policies end up turning into *shelfware*: stored, but never used. There are several well-recognized resources for helping policy writers structure their work, avoid pitfalls, and save enormous amounts of time. In the review that follows, readers will find information about these resources:

- ISO 17799
- CobiT®
- CERT-CC documentation
- NSA Security Guidelines
- U.S. Federal Best Security Practices
- RFC2196
- IT Baseline Protection Manual
- Commercial policy guides

44.3.1 ISO/IEC 17799:2005.   An increasingly popular standard for writing and implementing security policies, especially in Europe, is ISO/IEC 17799:2005, which is based on the old BS7799.

The British Standard 7799 (BS7799) originated in the U.K. Department of Trade and Industry as a code of practice; it was formally renamed the BS7799 in February 1995. BS7799 was not adopted quickly in Great Britain because it was not flexible enough, it used a simplistic security model, and there were more pressing issues, such as the imminent arrival of the Y2K problem.[2] In addition, BS7799 was a proprietary standard for which users had to pay the equivalent of several hundred dollars before accessing the full documentation.

Version 2 of BS7799 was published in May 1999, and that year also saw the establishment of formal certification and accreditation methods. At that point, the International Organization for Standardization (ISO) began the process of defining BS7799 as an international standard; ISO 17799 was published in 1999. In 2005, the standard was renamed as ISO/IEC 17799:2005 in collaboration with the International Electrochemical Commission (IEC).[3]

With the increasing interest in security, ISO 17799 certification has been established as a goal for many organizations throughout the world. Major consultancies have trained their auditing staff for compliance with ISO 17799; e-commerce is also a driving force behind the push for certification. One possible motivation is the experience of the ISO 9000 (quality) certification process in the 1980s; certification soon became a competitive edge and then a competitive requirement to maintain and develop market share.

In the context of policy development, ISO 17799 offers a convenient framework to help policy writers structure their project in accordance with an international standard. The abstract from the ISO follows.

ISO/IEC 17799:2005 establishes guidelines and general principles for initiating, implementing, maintaining, and improving information security management in an organization. The objectives outlined provide general guidance on the commonly accepted goals of information security management. ISO/IEC 17799:2005 contains best practices of control objectives and controls in the following areas of information security management:

- security policy;
- organization of information security;
- asset management;
- human resources security;
- physical and environmental security;
- communications and operations management;
- access control;
- information systems acquisition, development and maintenance;
- information security incident management;
- business continuity management;
- compliance.

The control objectives and controls in ISO/IEC 17799:2005 are intended to be implemented to meet the requirements identified by a risk assessment. ISO/IEC 17799:2005 is intended as a common basis and practical guideline for developing organizational security standards and effective security management practices, and to help build confidence in interorganizational activities.

The full text of ISO 17799 is available in electronic format or on paper from the ISO for 202 Swiss francs. In addition, a variety of guides are available to help organizations to develop ISO 17799-compliant policies with minimal rewriting.[4]

44.3.2   CoBiT.   The *Control Objectives for Information and related Technology* (CoBiT) provide a business-oriented set of standards for guiding management in the sound use of information technology.[5] CoBiT was developed by volunteers working under the aegis of the IT Governance Institute (ITGI), which was itself founded by the Information Systems Audit and Control Association (ISACA).

CobiT is an information technology (IT) governance framework and supporting tool set that allows managers to bridge the gap between control requirements, technical issues, and business risks. CobiT enables clear policy development and good practice for IT control throughout organizations. CobiT was first published by ITGI in April 1996. ITGI's latest update— CobiT 4.1— emphasizes regulatory compliance, helps organizations to increase the value attained from IT, highlights links between business and IT goals, and simplifies implementation of the CobiT framework. CobiT 4.1 is a fine-tuning of the CobiT framework and can be used to enhance work already done based on earlier versions of CobiT. When major activities are planned for IT governance initiatives, or when an overhaul of the enterprise control framework is anticipated, it is recommended to start fresh with CobiT 4.1. CobiT 4.1 presents activities in a more streamlined and practical manner so continuous improvement in IT governance is easier than ever to achieve.[6]

CobiT documents are available free (with registration) through download as PDF files in English, French, German, Hungarian, Italian, Japanese, Korean, and Russian.[7] The extensive *Frequently Asked Questions* provide detailed guidance for managers beginning their study of the standard.[8] ISACA also provides an interactive, Web-enabled version of CobiT that allows registered users to "construct and download [their] own, personalized version of CobiT for use on the desktop in MS Word or Access format."[9] Different levels of detail are available for visitors, ISACA members, and purchasers. ISACA also offers training courses in its "CobiT Campus"[10] as shown:

- CobiT Awareness Course (2 hours, self-paced e-learning)
- CobiT Foundation Course (8 hours, self-paced e-learning or 14 hours, classroom)
- CobiT Foundation Exam (1 hour, online 40 questions)
- IT Governance Implementation Course (14 hours, classroom)
- CobiT for Sarbanes-Oxley Compliance (5 hours, self-paced e-learning)

44.3.3   Informal Security Standards.   In addition to the formal standards just discussed, several sets of guidelines have garnered a degree of acceptance as the basis for exercising due diligence in the protection of information systems. These informal standards include:

- CERT-CC security improvement modules
- Security guidelines handbook from the U.S. National Security Agency (NSA)
- RFC2196 from the Internet Engineering Task Force
- IT baseline protection manual from the German Information Security Department

44.3.3.1   CERT-CC® Documentation.   The Computer Emergency Response Team Coordination Center (CERT-CC)® at the Software Engineering Institute (SEI) of Carnegie Mellon University (CMU) has compiled a series of security improvement modules (www.cert.org/certcc.html) on these topics:

Vulnerability Remediation
- Current Vulnerability Work
- Vulnerability Notes Database

CSIRT Community
- CSIRT Development
- National CSIRTs

Secure Coding
- Secure Coding Project Page
- Secure Coding Standards

Artifact Analysis

In addition, CERT expert Julia H. Allen published an excellent guide in 2001 that has retained its value.[11] Chapter headings for this 480-page text are listed next.

1. The CERT Guide to System and Network Security Practices
2. Securing Network Servers and User Workstations
3. Securing Public Web Servers
4. Deploying Firewalls
5. Setting Up Intrusion Detection and Response Preparation
6. Detecting Signs of Intrusion
7. Responding to Intrusions

Appendix A: Security Implementations
Appendix B: Practice-Level Policy Considerations

44.3.3.2 NSA Security Guidelines. The National Security Agency (NSA) of the United States has published a freely available *Security Guidelines Handbook*.[12] The preface describes it in this way:

> This handbook is designed to introduce you to some of the basic security principles and procedures with which all NSA employees must comply. It highlights some of your security responsibilities, and provides guidelines for answering questions you may be asked concerning your association with this Agency. Although you will be busy during the forthcoming weeks learning your job, meeting co-workers, and becoming accustomed to a new work environment, you are urged to become familiar with the security information contained in this handbook.

This set of employee policies is tailored to the needs of the high-security NSA, but it provides useful information that all organizations can adapt to their own requirements. According to the table of contents, these topics are included:

Initial Security Responsibilities
- Anonymity
- Answering Questions about Your Employment
- Answering Questions about Your Agency Training
- Verifying Your Employment
- The Agency and Public News Media

General Responsibilities

- Espionage and Terrorism
- Classification
- Need-to-Know
- For Official Use Only
- Prepublication Review
- Personnel Security Responsibilities
- Association with Foreign Nationals
- Correspondence with Foreign Nationals
- Embassy Visits
- Amateur Radio Activities
- Unofficial Foreign Travel
- Membership In Organizations
- Changes in Marital Status/Cohabitation/Names
- Use and Abuse of Drugs
- Physical Security Policies
- The NSA Badge
- Area Control
- Items Treated as Classified
- Prohibited Items
- Exit Inspection
- Removal of Material from NSA Spaces
- External Protection of Classified Information
- Reporting Loss or Disclosure of Classified Information
- Use of Secure and Non-Secure Telephones

Helpful Information

- Security Resources

44.3.3.3 *U.S. Federal Best Security Practices.*

The United States Federal Chief Information Officers (CIO) Council has created a Best Practices Committee that provides extensive free documentation for policy makers.[13] The committee is defined in this way:

> The Best Practices Committee (BPC) is established by the CIO Council Charter to serve as a focal point for promoting information management/information technology (IM/IT) best practices within the federal government. The BPC brings together a team of IT professionals committed to identifying the most successful of IM/IT practices being implemented in industry, government, and academia, and sharing them with agency CIOs as best practices, to be considered for emulation throughout the Federal government. It is about sharing the successes of others, and *not reinventing the wheel*. It is about constantly learning and applying working models to reduce complexity and achieve results. It is also about cost avoidance and sound stewardship of the taxpayers' dollars.

There is an extensive collection of documents freely available in PDF format for downloading.[14] Some of the topics in the collection of particular interest for this chapter's context include:

- Best Practices
- Enterprise Architecture
- IT Security/Privacy
- GAO Reports
- IT Related Laws and Regulations

44.3.3.4   RFC2196 (Site Security Handbook).   The Internet Engineering Task Force (IETF) has an extensive list of informational documents called Requests for Comments (RFCs) governing all aspects of the Internet.[15] One document of particular value to any organization trying to improve its security practices is the classic *Site Security Handbook*, RFC2196, edited by B. Fraser of the Software Engineering Institute at Carnegie Mellon University, the same body that hosts the CERT-CC.[16] The *Handbook* has this structure:

Introduction
- Purpose of this Work
- Audience
- Definitions
- Related Work
- Basic Approach
- Risk Assessment

Security Policies
- What is a Security Policy and Why Have One?
- What Makes a Good Security Policy?
- Keeping the Policy Flexible

Architecture
- Objectives
- Network and Service Configuration
- Firewalls

Security Services and Procedures
- Authentication
- Confidentiality
- Integrity
- Authorization
- Access
- Auditing
- Securing Backups

Security Incident Handling

- Preparing and Planning for Incident Handling
- Notification and Points of Contact
- Identifying an Incident
- Handling an Incident
- Aftermath of an Incident
- Responsibilities

Ongoing Activities

Tools and Locations

Mailing Lists and Other Resources

References

44.3.3.5 *IT-Grundschutz Catalogues.* The German government's computer security arm, the *Bundesamt für Sicherheit in der Informationstechnik*, has published a useful set of guidelines since 1997, the *IT-Grundschutzhandbuch*. Originally known in English as the *IT Baseline Protection Manual*, the most recent version as of this writing was published in 2005 and is available free in English as the *IT-Grundschutz Catalogues*.[17] The work is freely available in PDF in German, English, Swedish, and Estonian.

In general, each module presents concepts, threats and vulnerabilities, and countermeasures. This work is easy to understand and provides a sound basis for effective information security protection.

44.3.4 Commercially Available Policy Guides. There are several commercially available policy templates that save time when developing new policies or improving existing policies. Three of particular value are discussed next.

44.3.4.1 *Charles Cresson Wood's* ISPME. The most widely used commercially available collection of security standards is the work by Charles Cresson Wood, *Information Security Policies Made Easy* (*ISPME*). The text includes a CD-ROM for easy access to the text so that users can avoid tedious retyping of existing materials.

Wood integrates the perspectives of both management and technical staff when making recommendations. He was one of the original promoters of information security as a way to achieve a competitive advantage and a coauthor of the first computer crime investigation manual. He was one of the first to advocate and document integration of information resource management concepts with information security activities, use of head-count ratio analysis to determine appropriate levels of information security staffing, an information security document life cycle for planning and budgeting purposes, and network management tools to achieve consistent and centralized systems security. He has also developed and successfully marketed two unique software packages that automate information security administration activities. In addition, he evaluated and recommended U.S. Government policies on open versus classified cryptographic research for Frank Press, President Carter's technology advisor.

One of the outstanding features of *ISPME* is that Wood explains every policy and sometimes provides opposing policies for use in different environments. His text is not only a set of templates but an excellent basis for teaching security principles by looking at the practice of security.

44.3.4.2 *Tom Peltier's* Practitioner's Reference. Tom Peltier is the Year 2001 Hall of Fame Award Recipient from the Information Systems Security Association (www.issa.org). The citation (www.peltierassociates.com/) provides the background that explains why Peltier is so highly regarded in the field of security:

> Tom Peltier is in his fifth decade working with computer technology. During this time he has garnered numerous industry honors for sharing his experiences with follow professionals. Because of his work he was given the 1993 Computer Security Institute's (CSI) Lifetime Achievement Award. In 1999, the Information Systems Security Association (ISSA) bestowed on him its Individual Contribution to the Profession Award, and in 2001 he was inducted into the ISSA Hall of Fame. Tom was also awarded the CSI Lifetime Emeritus Membership Award.

Peltier's policy text is *Information Security Policies and Procedures*. He provides you with the tools you need to develop policies, procedures, and standards. He demonstrates the importance of a clear, concise, and well-written security program. His examination of recommended industry best practices illustrates how they can be customized to fit any organization's needs.

44.3.4.3 SANS Resources. The System Administration and Network Security (SANS) Institute is well known for the excellent security resources it makes available to members and the general public.

44.3.4.3.1 Security Essentials Courses. The SANS Security Essentials Courses (www.sans.org/training/description.php?tid=672) provide a solid foundation for understanding the issues underlying security policies. Level 524, *Security Policy & Awareness* (www.sans.org/training/description.php?tid=368), highlights this objective:

> This course is designed to offer an individual a comprehensive approach to understanding security awareness and developing security policy. Business needs change, the business environment changes, and critical systems are continually exposed to new and developing vulnerabilities. Security awareness training is an effective business strategy that reduces the overall risk to an organization, therefore minimizing user-related faults and errors that lead to destructive and costly security incidents. Security awareness and policy development and assessment are a never-ending process.

44.3.4.3.2 Free Resources. The SANS Institute offers many free resources. For details, see www.sans.org/free_resources.php?utm_source=web-sans&utm_medium = ImageReplace&utm_content=Main_resource_button_green&utm_campaign=Home Page&ref=3601. Topics include:

- Reading Room: Over 1,600 computer security white papers in over 70 categories
- Top 20: The Twenty Most Critical Internet Security Vulnerabilities
- Newsletters: Latest Security News

44.4 WRITING THE POLICIES. How should one write security policies? Should they be suggestions? Orders? Positive? Negative? This section affirms that policies should be definite, unambiguous, and directive. In addition, all policies should have (preferably optional) explanations for the reasons behind them.

44.4.1 Orientation: Prescriptive and Proscriptive. Security policies should be written with clear indications that all employees are expected to conform to them. Language should be definite and unambiguous (e.g., "All employees must . . . "

or "No employees shall . . . .") Some policies require people to do something—these are *prescriptive* (e.g., "Employees must follow the password procedures defined by the Information Protection Group at all times.") Other policies prohibit certain actions—these are *proscriptive* (e.g., "No employee shall make or order illegal copies of proprietary software under any circumstances.")

44.4.2 Writing Style.   Each policy should be short. Simple declarative sentences are best; writers should avoid long compound sentences with multiple clauses. Details of implementation are appropriate for standards and procedures, not for policies. Policies can refer users to the appropriate documents for implementation details; for example, "Passwords shall be changed on a schedule defined in the *Security Procedures* from the Information Protection Group."

For more details on developing policy, see Chapter 45 in this *Handbook*.

44.4.3 Reasons.   Few people like to be ordered about with arbitrary rules. Trying to impose what appear to be senseless injunctions can generate a tide of rebellion among employees. It is far better to provide explanations of why policies make sense for the particular enterprise; however, such explanations can make the policies tedious to read for more experienced users. A solution is to provide optional explanations. One approach is to summarize policies in one part of the document and then to provide an extensive expansion of all the policies in a separate section or a separate document. Another approach is to use hypertext, as explained in Section 44.6.3 of this chapter.

44.5 ORGANIZING THE POLICIES.   Policies are distinct from the sequence in which they are presented. It is useful to have two distinct presentation sequences for policies: topical and organizational.

44.5.1 Topical Organization.   Security involves a multitude of details; how one organizes these details depends on the purpose of the policy document. The most common format puts policies in a sequence that corresponds to some reasonable model of how people perceive security. For example, employees can look at security with a rough correspondence to the physical world. Under this model, one might have a policy document with a table of contents that looks like this:

Principles
Organizational Reporting Structure
Physical Security
- Servers
- Workstations
- Portable computers

Hiring, Management, and Firing
Data Protection
- Classifying information
- Data access controls
- Encryption
- Countering industrial espionage

Communications Security

- Perimeter controls
- Web usage and content filtering
- E-mail usage and privacy
- Telephone and fax usage

Software

- Authorized products only
- Proprietary (purchased) software
- Development standards
- Quality assurance and testing

Operating Systems

- Access controls
- Logging

Technical Support

- Service-level agreements
- Help desk functions

44.5.2 Organizational.   The complete set of policies may be comprehensive, concise, and well written, but they will still likely be a daunting document, especially for nontechnical staff. To avoid distressing employees with huge tomes of incomprehensible materials, it makes sense to create special-purpose documents aimed at particular groups. For example, one could have guides like these:

- General Guide for Protecting Corporate Information Assets
- Guide for Users of Portable Computers
- A Manager's Guide to Security Policies
- Human Resources and Security
- Network Administration Security Policies
- Programmer's Guide to Security and Quality Assurance
- The Operator's Security Responsibilities
- Security and the Help Desk

Each of these volumes or files can present just enough information to be useful and interesting to the readers without overwhelming them with detail. Each can make reference to the full policy document.

44.6   PRESENTING THE POLICIES.   What options do policy makers have for publishing their policies? This section discusses printing them on paper versus publishing them electronically.

44.6.1   Printed Text.   Policies are not inherently interesting. Large volumes full of policies quickly become shelfware. Short paper documents, however, are familiar to people; they can be carried around, or placed at hand for easy reference anywhere.

Reference cards, summary sheets, stickers, and posters are some of the printed media that can be useful in security awareness, training, and education programs. Printed text, like its electronic versions, provides the opportunity for typeface and color to be used in clarifying and emphasizing specific ideas. However, printed copies of policies share a universal disadvantage: They are difficult to update.

Updating dozens, hundreds, or thousands of individual copies of policy documents can be such a headache that organizations simply reprint the entire document rather than struggle with updates. Updates on individual sheets require the cooperation of every user to insert the new sheets and remove the old ones; experience teaches that many people simply defer such a task, sometimes indefinitely, and that others have an apparently limited understanding of the sequential nature of page numbers. Badly updated policy guides may be worse than none at all, especially from a legal standpoint. If an employee violates a new policy that has been promulgated verbally, but available manuals fail to reflect that new policy, it may be difficult to justify dismissal for wrongdoing.

44.6.2 Electronic One-Dimensional Text. Despite the familiarity and ubiquity of paper, in today's world of near-universal access to computers in the work environment, there is a place for electronic documentation of policies. Such publication has enormous advantages from an administrative standpoint. All access to the policies can be controlled centrally, at least in theory. Making the current version of the policies (and subsets of the policies, as explained in Section 44.5.2) available for reference on a server obviates the problem of updating countless independent copies and avoids the normal situation when using paper: chaotic differences among copies of different ages.

How can one cope with employees stubbornly determined to have their own local copies of the policies on their workstations? One solution to this problem of enforcing a single version is to alert every user to changes in the central copy, or to send every user copies of the appropriate documents by e-mail, with a request to replace their copies of lower version number. Although this solution is not perfect, it does help to keep most people up to date.

44.6.3 Hypertext. Perhaps the most valuable contribution from electronic publication of policies is the availability of hypertext. Hypertext allows a reader to jump to a different section of text and then come back to the original place easily. On paper, forward and backward references are cumbersome, and most readers do not follow such links unless they are particularly keen on the extra information promised in the reference. In electronic files, however, additional information may be as easy to obtain as placing the cursor over a link and clicking.

The most important function of hypertext for policy documents is to provide definitions of technical terms and explanations of the reasons for specific policies.

Some users are more comfortable with printed policies. Hypertext, like other formats of text, generally permits users to print out their own copies of all or part of their policy documentation. Many of the tools also allow annotations by users on their own copy of a file.

44.6.3.1 HTML and XML. The most widely used hypertext format today is Hypertext Markup Language (HTML). Its variant Extensible Markup Language (XML), provides additional functionality for programmers, but from the user's perspective, the hyperlinks are the same. A simple click of the mouse in a Web browser (e.g., Microsoft Internet Explorer, Netscape Communicator, or Firefox) branches to a different page. More sophisticated programming allows the use of frames and, with

JAVA or ActiveX, pop-up windows. Navigation buttons allow the user to move backward to a previous page or forward to another page. Links also can be used to open new windows so that several pages are visible at once. All of these techniques allow users to move freely through a text with full control over the degree of detail they wish to pursue.

44.6.3.2 Rich Text Format and Proprietary Word Processor Files.
Some people prefer to use word processor files for hypertext. As long as everyone uses the same word processing software, this approach can work acceptably. For example, it is usually possible to insert a hyperlink to a section of a single document, to a location in a different file on disk, or to a page on the Web. Some word processors, such as Microsoft Word and Corel WordPerfect, allow one to insert pop-up comments; floating the cursor over highlighted text brings up a text box that can provide definitions and commentary.

In addition to explicit links, Microsoft Word and other modern word processing programs can display a table of headings that allows instant movement to any section of the document.

Rich text format (RTF) is a general format for interchanging documents among word processors, but the results are not always comparable. For example, a comment created using Microsoft Word shows up as a pop-up box with a word or phrase highlighted in the text; the same comment and marker read from an RTF file by Corel WordPerfect shows up as a balloon symbol in the left margin of the document.

44.6.3.3 Portable Document Format.
Adobe Acrobat's portable document format (PDF) provides all the hyperlinking that HTML offers, but it does so in a form that is universally readable and that can be controlled more easily. The free Acrobat reader is available for multiple operating systems from www.adobe.com. PDF documents can be locked easily, for example, so that no unauthorized changes can be made. In addition, unlike HTML and word processor documents, PDF files can be constructed to provide near-perfect reproduction of their original appearance even if not all the fonts used by the author are present on the target computer system. To create PDF files, one uses the Acrobat product; the installation adds two printers to the printer list. The Acrobat PDFWriter program produces relatively crude output that does not always look identical on all systems, but the Acrobat Distiller program produces highly controllable output with uniform properties. Adobe Acrobat also allows one to create a detailed table of contents for documents.

44.6.3.4 Help Files.
Help files also provide hypertext capability. In the Windows environment, one can create help files using utilities such as Help & Manual from www.ec-software.com or AnetHelpTool from www.anetsoft.com/aht32/en/product_descr.htm. Entering the search string "create help files" into a search engine such as Google (www.google.com) brings up many pages of such tools. Windows Help files can be distributed easily to any Windows user because they are relatively small, and they are loaded almost instantly by the Help subsystem. In addition, users are permitted to add their own notes to such documents and can easily print out sections if they wish.

44.7 MAINTAINING POLICIES.
No fixed policy document can cover all eventualities. The information security field changes constantly, and so must policies. Information security is a process much like total quality management: For success, both require a thoroughgoing integration into corporate culture.

Above all, some named individuals must see maintaining security policies as an explicit part of their job descriptions. Hoping that someone will spontaneously maintain security policies is like hoping that someone will spontaneously maintain financial records. However, as explained in Chapter 45 of this *Handbook*, security policies should represent the best efforts of people from throughout the organization, not the arbitrary dictates of just one person.

44.7.1 Review Process.   An information protection working group can meet regularly—quarterly is a good frequency to try—to review all or part of the policies. Employees can be encouraged to suggest improvements in policies or to propose new policies. The working group can identify key areas of greatest change and work on those first, leaving minor policy changes to subcommittees. Members of the working group should discuss ideas with their colleagues from throughout the enterprise, not just with each other. Every effort should contribute to increasing the legitimate sense of involvement in security policy by all employees, including managers and executives.

44.7.2 Announcing Changes.   Drafts of the new versions can be circulated to the people principally affected by changes, so that their responses can improve the new edition. Truly respectful inquiry will result in a greater sense of ownership of the policies by employees, although few of them will rejoice in the new policies. Some employees will see new security policies merely as a mild irritant, while others may view them as a tremendous obstacle to productivity and a general nuisance.

Ideally, major changes in policy should be described and explained in several ways. For example, a letter or e-mail (digitally signed, for security) from the president, chair of the board of directors, chief officers, or chief information security officer can announce important changes in policy and the reasons for the changes. A brief article in the organization's internal newsletter, or a spot on the intranet, can also provide channels for communicating the policy decisions to everyone involved.

Finally, the updated policies can be made available or distributed to all employees using some of the channels discussed in Section 44.6.

44.8 SUMMARY.   These 10 recommendations will help in preparing to create and implement security policies:

1. Distinguish among policies, controls, standards, and procedures.
2. Use all resources from government, industry bodies, and commercial organizations in preparing to create policies.
3. Use unambiguous prose when defining policies: Tell people what to *do* and what *not* to do.
4. Use short sentences.
5. Give reasons for policies.
6. Provide different views of policies—topical and organizational.
7. Provide several ways of reading the policies, including printed text, electronic text, and hypertext.
8. Review and improve or adapt policies regularly.
9. Circulate drafts showing changes in policies to interested participants before publishing them.
10. Announce major changes using high-level authorities within the enterprise.

44.9   FURTHER READING

Allen, J. H. *The CERT® Guide to System and Network Security Practices*. Reading, MA: Addison-Wesley, 2001.

Barman, S. *Writing Information Security Policies*. Indianapolis: New Riders, 2002.

Boran, S. "IT Security Cookbook," 2003; www.boran.com/security/index.html.

Clarke, R. "Best Practice Guidelines: Controls over the Security of Personal Information," 1993; www.anu.edu.au/people/Roger.Clarke/DV/PDSecy.html.

Egan, M. and T. Mather. *The Executive Guide to Information Security: Threats, Challenges, and Solutions*. Reading, MA: Addison-Wesley. 2004.

Flynn, N. *The E-Policy Handbook: Designing and Implementing Effective E-Mail, Internet, and Software Policies*. Herndon, VA: AMACOM, 2001.

INFOSYSSEC. "Security Standards, Laws and Guidelines," 2008; www.infosyssec.org/infosyssec/secstan1.htm.

NSA. "NSA Security Guidelines Handbook," Fort Meade, MD: National Security Agency Central Security Service, 2002; www.tscm.com/NSAsecmanual1.html.

Overly, M. E. *E-Policy: How to Develop Computer, E-Policy and Internet Guidelines to Protect Your Company and Its Assets*. Herndon, VA: AMACOM, 1998.

Peltier, T. R. *Information Security Policies and Procedures: A Practitioner's Reference*, 2nd ed. Boca Raton, FL: Auerbach, 2004.

RUsecure. *Information Security Policies: Securing Information in the Digital Age*. Macclesfield (Cheshire), U.K.: RUsecure Information Security, 2001; www.information-security-policies.com/index.htm.

Wood, C. C. *Information Security Policies Made Easy*, version 10. Houston: Information Shield, 2005; www.informationshield.com/ispmemain.htm.

44.10   NOTES

1. C. C. Wood, *Information Security Policies Made Easy,* version 10. Houston: Information Shield, 2005; www.informationshield.com/ispmemain.htm.

2. *ISO 17799 Information Security Portal,* www.computersecuritynow.com/.

3. ISO/IEC 17799:2005, "Information Technology—Security Techniques—Code of Practice for Information Security Management"; www.iso.org/iso/iso_catalogue/catalogue_tc/catalogue_detail.htm?csnumber=39612.

4. Sites that provide free evaluation versions of policy guides include: "Information Security Policy World," www.information-security-policies-and-standards.com/, and "Computer Security Policy Directory," www.computer-security-policies.com/index.htm.

5. IT Governance Institute, "CobiT 4.1" (PDF), 2007; www.isaca.org/AMTemplate.cfm?Section=Downloads&Template=/MembersOnly.cfm&ContentFileID=14002 (free, but registration required).

6. ISACA, "CobiT 4.1 Brochure," 2007; www.isaca.org/Content/NavigationMenu/Members_and_Leaders/COBIT6/Obtain_COBIT/COBIT4.1_Brochure.pdf.

7. ISACA CobiT downloads: www.isaca.org/Content/NavigationMenu/Members_and_Leaders1/COBIT6/Obtain_COBIT/Obtain_COBIT.htm.

8. CobiT FAQ: www.isaca.org/Content/NavigationMenu/Members_and_Leaders1/COBIT6/FAQ6/COBIT_FAQ.htm.

9. CobiT Online: www.isaca.org/Template.cfm?Section=COBIT_Online&Template=/ContentManagement/ContentDisplay.cfm&ContentID=15633.

10. CobiT Campus: www.isaca.org/Template.cfm?Section=Home&CONTENTID=19542&TEMPLATE=/ContentManagement/ContentDisplay.cfm.

11. J. H. Allen, *The CERT® Guide to System and Network Security Practices* (Reading, MA: Addison-Wesley, 2001).

12. NSA, "NSA Security Guidelines Handbook" (Fort Meade, MD: National Security Agency Central Security Service, 2002); www.tscm.com/NSAsecmanual1.html.

13. CIO Council BPC; www.cio.gov/index.cfm?function=bpstatement.

14. CIO Council Documents: www.cio.gov/index.cfm?function=documents.

15. IETF RFCs: www.ietf.org/rfc.html.

16. B. Fraser, "Site Security Handbook," IETF RFC 2196, 1997; www.ietf.org/rfc/rfc2196.txt?number=2196.

17. BSI, "IT-Grundschutz Catalogues," Bundesamt für Sicherheit in der Informationstechnik (German Federal Office for Information Security), 2005; www.bsi.de/english/gshb/index.htm.

EMPLOYMENT PRACTICES AND POLICIES

M. E. Kabay and Bridgitt Robertson

45.1 INTRODUCTION. Crime is a human issue, not merely a technological one. True, technology can reduce the incidence of computer crimes, but the fundamental problem is that people can be tempted to take advantage of flaws in our information systems. The most spectacular biometric access control in the world will not stop someone from getting into the computer room if the janitor believes it is "just to pick up a listing."

People are the key to effective information security, and disaffected employees and angry ex-employees are important threats according to many current studies. For example, the 2007 CSI Computer Crime and Security Survey, published by the Computer Security Institute, reported on responses from 494 participants in a wide range of industries, nonprofits and government agencies; the authors stated:

> Insider abuse of network access or e-mail (such as trafficking in pornography or pirated software) edged out virus incidents as the most prevalent security problem, with 59 and 52 percent of respondents reporting each respectively.[1]

The same report indicated that about 64 percent of the respondents believed that insiders accounted for at least some of their cybercrime losses:

- 27 percent agreed with estimates of "up to 20 percent"
- 11 percent estimated 21 to 40 percent
- 11 percent estimated 41 to 60 percent
- 10 percent estimated 61 to 80 percent
- 5 percent estimated 81 to 100 percent

Finally, the CSI reported that "respondents indicated a jump in insider abuse of network resources from 42 to 59 percent."

This chapter presents principles for integrating human resources (HR) management and information security into corporate culture.[2]

45.2 HIRING.   The quality of employees is the foundation of success for all enterprises; it is also the basis for effective information security.

45.2.1 Checking Candidate's Background.   Hiring new employees poses a particular problem; growing evidence suggests that many people inflate their résumés with unfounded claims. According to Edward Andler, author of *The Complete Reference Checking Handbook*, "cheating on résumés has become distressingly common. And many people are getting by with it, which appears to be making others follow suit." His research shows that up to 10 percent "seriously misrepresent" their background or work histories. A research project run by the Port Authority of New York and New Jersey used an advertisement asking for electricians who were expert at using "Sontag Connectors." They received 170 responses claiming such expertise, even though there was no such device.[3]

Reviewers should be especially careful of vague words such as "monitored," and "initiated." During interviews or background checking, HR staff should find out what the candidate did in specific detail, if possible. All references should be followed up, at least to verify that the candidates really worked where the résumé claims they did.

Unfortunately, there is a civil liberties problem when considering someone's criminal record. Once people have suffered the legally mandated punishment for a crime, whether fines, community service, or imprisonment, discriminating against them in hiring may be a violation of their civil rights. Can one exclude convicted felons from any job openings? From job openings similar to areas in which they abused their former employers' trust? Are employers permitted in law to require that prospective employees approve background checks? Can one legally require polygraph tests? Drug tests? Personality tests?

In some jurisdictions, "negligent hiring" that results in harm to third parties is being punished in civil litigation. Imagine, for example, that a firm were to hire an active criminal hacker as a system administrator without adequate background checking and interviews; if the hacker were then to use his position and corporate resources to break into or sabotage another organization's systems, it is reasonable to suppose that the victim could claim damages from the criminal's employer on the basis of negligent hiring. In addition, "negligent retention" could hold an employer liable when an employee, who may pose a risk to coworkers or the public, is not terminated immediately.

Employers should consult their corporate legal staffs to ensure that they know, and exercise, their rights and obligations in the specific legal context of their work.

Even checking references from previous employers is fraught with uncertainty. Employers may hesitate to give bad references for incompetent or unethical employees for fear of lawsuits if their comments become known, or if the employee fails to get a new job. Today, one cannot rely on getting an answer to the simple question "Would you rehire this employee?"

Ex-employers must also be careful not to inflate their evaluation of an ex-employee. Sterling praise for a scoundrel could lead to a lawsuit from the disgruntled new employer.

For these reasons, a growing number of employers have corporate policies that forbid discussing a former employee's performance in any way, positive or negative. All one gets from a contact in such cases is "Your candidate did work as an Engineer Class 3 from 1991 to 1992. I am forbidden to provide any further information."

It is commonplace in the security field that some people who have successfully committed crimes have been rewarded by a "golden handshake" (a special payment in return for leaving) and sometimes even with positive references. The criminals can then move on to victimize a new employer. However, no one knows how often this takes place.

To work around such distortions, interviewers should question candidates closely about details of their education and work experience. The answers can then be checked for internal consistency and compared with the candidate's written submissions. Liars hate details: It is so much harder to remember which lie to repeat to which person than it is to tell the truth.

There are commercial services specializing in background checking (e.g., www.virtualhrscreening.com). They provide the necessary forms to allow employers to query credit records and other background information www.virtualhrscreening.com/forms.htm). Companies such as Kroll and Securitas Security Services also conduct extensive background checks.

Another way to conduct an employee background check can be done for free, via powerful search engines, such as Google. By entering someone's name into one of these search engines, there is a good possibility that some aspect of the applicant's life will be retrieved. Of particular interest might be a search of messages from a particular blog to see what information is being disseminated.

Experienced employees should interview the candidate and compare notes in meetings to spot inconsistencies. A director of technical support at a large computer service bureau questioned a new employee who claimed to have worked on a particular platform for several years—but did not know how to log on. Had he chatted with any of the programmers on staff before being hired, his deception would have been discovered quickly enough. Ironically, had he told the truth, he might have been hired anyway.

45.2.2 Employment Agreements. Before allowing new employees to start work, they should sign an employment agreement stipulating that they will not disclose confidential information or trade secrets of their previous employers. Another clause must state that they understand that the new employer is explicitly *not* requesting access to information misappropriated from their previous employer, or from any other source. The Uniform Trade Secrets Act, which is enforced in many jurisdictions in the United States, provides penalties that are up to triple the demonstrated financial damages, plus attorney's fees, caused by such data leakage. One high-profile case involved three employees who were found guilty of stealing and trying to sell Coca-Cola secrets to its rival Pepsi.[4]

45.3 MANAGEMENT. Security is the result of corporate culture; therefore, management practices are critically important for successful information protection.

External attacks through Internet connections, and damage from malicious software, are certainly important threats; nonetheless, insider damage due to errors and omissions as well as through dishonesty or a desire for revenge are still major problems for information security.[5] These problems are compounded when there are collaborative threats involving insiders working with those outside the enterprise.

45.3.1 Identify Opportunities for Abuse.   Security managers do not have to be paranoid, they just have to act as if they are paranoid. Managers must treat people with scrupulously fair attention to written policies and procedures. Selective or capricious enforcement of procedures may constitute harassment. If some individuals are permitted to be alone in the printer room as salary checks are printed, while other employees of equivalent rank must be accompanied, the latter can justifiably interpret the inconsistency as an implicit indication of distrust. Such treatment may move certain employees to initiate grievances and civil lawsuits, to lay complaints under criminal statutes for discrimination, or even to commit vengeful acts.

45.3.2 Access Is Neither a Privilege Nor a Right.   When management removes access rights to the network server room from a system analyst who has no reason to enter that area, the response may be resentment, sulking, and abuse. People sometimes treat access controls as status symbols; why else would a CEO who has no technical training demand that his access code include the tape library and the wiring closet? Managers can overcome these psychological barriers to better security by introducing a different way of looking at vulnerabilities and access. After identifying an opportunity for a particular employee to use the system in unauthorized ways, one should turn the discussion into a question of protecting the person who has unnecessary access against undue suspicion. For example, an employee having more access to secured files than is required is put at risk. If anything ever did go wrong with the secured files, that employee would be a suspect. There is no need to frame the problem in terms of suspicion and distrust.

With these principles in mind, managers should be alert to such dangers as permitting an employee to remain alone in a sensitive area, allowing unsupervised access to unencrypted backups, or having only one programmer who knows anything about the internals of the accounting package.

As for language, it would be better to stop referring to access *privileges*. The very word connotes superiority and status—the last things management should imply. Access is a function and a responsibility, not a privilege or a right; it should be referred to simply as *access functions* or *access authorizations*.

45.3.3 The Indispensable Employee.   In many areas of information processing, redundancy is generally viewed as either a bad thing or an unavoidable but regrettable cost paid for specific advantages. For example, in a database, indexing may require identical fields (items, columns) to be placed in separate files (data sets, tables) for links (views, joins) to be established. However, in managing personnel for better security, redundancy is a requirement. Without shared knowledge, and our organization is at constant risk of a breach of availability.

Redundancy in this context means having more than one person who can accomplish a given task. Another way of looking at it is that no knowledge should belong to only one person in an organization. Putting the keys to the kingdom in the hands of one employee invites disaster.

Unique resources always put systems at risk; that is why companies such as Tandem, Stratus, and others have so successfully provided redundant and fault-tolerant computer systems for critical task functions, such as stock exchanges and banking networks. These computer systems and networks have twin processors, channels, memory arrays, disk drives, and controllers. Similarly, a fault-tolerant organization will invest in cross-training of all its personnel. Every task should have at least one other person who knows how to do it—even if less well than the primary resource. This principle does not imply that managers have to create clones of all their employees; it is in fact preferable to have several people who can accomplish various parts of any one person's job. Spreading knowledge throughout the organization makes it possible to reduce the damage caused by absence or unavailability of key people.

It is dangerous to allow a single employee to be the only person who knows about a critical function in the enterprise. Operations will suffer if the key person is away, and the enterprise will certainly suffer if this unique resource person decides to behave in unauthorized and harmful ways. Managers should ask themselves if there is anyone in their department whose absence they dread. Are there any critical yet undocumented procedures for which everyone has to ask a particular person?

A client in a data center operations management class volunteered the following story. There was a programming wizard responsible for maintaining a key production program; unfortunately, he had poor communication skills and preferred to solve problems himself rather than to train and involve his colleagues. "It'll be faster for me to do it myself," he used to say. During one of his rare vacations, something went wrong with "his" production program, shutting down the company's operations. The wizard was in the north woods, out of reach of all communications; the disaster lasted until he returned.

Not only does the organization suffer, but also the indispensable persons suffer from the imbalance of knowledge and skill when no one else knows what they know. Some indispensable employees are dedicated to the welfare of their employer and of their colleagues. They may hesitate to take holidays. If their skills are needed from hour to hour, it becomes more difficult for them to participate in committee meetings. These are the people who wear beepers and cannot sit undisturbed even in a two-hour class. If the indispensable employees' skills affect day-to-day operations, they may find it hard to go to off-site training courses, conferences, and conventions. Despite their suitability for promotion, indispensable people may be delayed in their career change because the organization finds it difficult or expensive to train their replacements. In extreme cases, newly promoted managers may find themselves continuing to perform specialized duties that ought to be done by their staff. Sometimes even a VP of Operations is the only person who can make changes to a production system that should be performed by a programmer three or four levels down.

A particular kind of indispensability occurs when an employee becomes the de facto technical support resource for a particular software package or system. Without authorization from their managers, these employees can find themselves in difficulty. They may be fired because their productivity drops too low according to their job descriptions, which do not include providing undocumented technical support to other people. They may burn out and quit because of overwork and criticism. Or they may cause resentment among their colleagues and neighbors by declining to help them, or by complaining about overwork. Alternatively, they may enjoy the situation, and manage to meet all the demands on their time quite successfully, until others in the information technology department begin to feel threatened, and someone either complains to the higher-ups or begins spreading nasty comments about these unauthorized support technicians.

Looking at this situation from a management point of view, there are problems for the recipients of all this free aid. The longer they persist in getting apparently free help from their unofficial benefactor, the longer they can avoid letting upper management know they need help. Then when the bubble bursts and the expert becomes unavailable, managers are confronted with a sudden demand for unplanned resources. In most organizations, unexpected staffing requirements are difficult to satisfy. Managers have a hard time explaining how it is that they were unable to predict the need and to budget for it.

Sometimes persons continue to be indispensable because of fear that their value to their employers resides in their private knowledge. Such employees resent training others. The best way to change their counterproductive attitude is to set a good example; managers should share knowledge with them and with everyone else in their group. Education should be a normal part of the way everyone in the enterprise works. Managers can encourage cross-training by allocating time for it. Cross-training can be a factor in employee evaluations. Current topics from the trade press and academic journals, for example, can be discussed in a journal club, or at informal, scheduled meetings, where people take turns presenting the findings from recent research in areas of interest.

Reluctance to explain their jobs to someone else may also mask unauthorized or illegal activity. Take, for example, the case of Lloyd Benjamin Lewis, assistant operations officer at Wells Fargo Bank in Beverly Hills, California. He arranged with a confederate outside the bank to cash fraudulent checks for up to $250,000 each on selected legitimate accounts at Lewis's branch. Using a secret code stolen from another branch, Lewis would scrupulously encode a credit for the exact amount of the theft, thus giving the illusion of correcting a transaction error. Lewis stole $21.3 million from his employer between September 1978 and January 1981, when he was caught by accident. For unknown reasons, a computer program flagged one of his fraudulent transactions so that another employee was notified of an irregularity. It did not take long to discover the fraud, and Lewis was convicted of embezzlement. He was sentenced to five years in a federal prison.[6]

Because Lewis was obliged to be physically present to trap the fraudulent checks as they came through the system, he could not afford to have anyone with him watching what he did. Lewis would have been less than enthusiastic about having to train a backup to do his job. If anyone had been cross-trained, the embezzlement would probably not have continued so long, or have become so serious.

45.3.4 Career Advancement.   In a topic related to avoiding indispensability, managers can improve the security climate through accepted principles of good human resources management, such as career advancement for all employees. By promoting individuals to new responsibilities, managers can also increase the number of people with expertise in critical functions. As managers carry out their regular employee performance reviews, they should include discussions of each person's career goals. Here, based on a summary by employment expert Lee Kushner, are some practical questions to discuss with employees as part of their interviews.[7]

1. What are your long-term plans?
2. What are your strengths and weaknesses?

3. What skills do you need to develop?

4. Have you acquired a new skill in the past year?

5. What are your most significant career accomplishments, and will you soon achieve another one?

6. Have you been promoted over the past three years?

7. What investments have you made in your own career?

8. Are you being impatient?

When managers support individuals' interests and aspirations, they foster a climate of respect and appreciation and concurrently support positive feelings about the organization.

45.3.5 Vacation Time. In the example presented in Section 45.3.3, Lloyd Benjamin Lewis took his unauthorized duties (stealing money from his bank) so seriously that during the entire period of his embezzlement, about 850 days, he was never late, never absent, and never took a single vacation day in over two years. Any data center manager should have been quite alarmed at having an employee who had failed to be absent or late a single day in more than two years. The usual rule in companies is that unused vacation days can be carried over for only a limited time, and then they expire. This is intended to be an incentive to take vacation time; for normal, honest employees, it probably works fine. For dishonest employees who have to be present to control a scam, losing vacation days is intolerable.

Every employee should be required to take scheduled vacations within a definite—and short—time limit. No exceptions should be permitted. Excessive resistance to taking vacations should be investigated to find out why the employee insists on being at work all the time.

Unfortunately, this suspicious attitude toward perfect attendance causes problems for the devoted, dedicated, and honest employee. An innocent person can get caught up in a web of suspicion precisely because of exceptional commitment. One may be able to avoid difficulties of this kind by: (1) making the reasons for the policy well known to all employees so no one feels singled out; (2) relying on the judgment, discretion, and goodwill of the investigating manager to avoid hurt feelings in their most loyal employees; and (3) switching such an employee's functions temporarily to see if anything breaks.

45.3.6 Responding to Changes in Behavior. Any kind of unusual behavior can pique the curiosity of a manager. Even more important from a security management standpoint, any consistent change in behavior should stimulate interest. Is a normally punctual person suddenly late, day after day? Did an employee start showing up regularly in hand-tailored suits? Why is a usually charming person snarling obscenities at subordinates these days? What accounts for someone's suddenly working overtime every day, in the absence of any known special project? Is a competent person now producing obvious errors in simple reports? How is it that a formerly complacent staffer is now a demanding and bitter complainer?

With so much of the enterprise's financial affairs controlled by information systems, it is not surprising that sudden wealth may be a clue that someone is committing a computer crime. A participant in an information systems security course reported that an accounting clerk at a government agency in Washington, DC, was arrested for massive embezzlement. The tip-off? He arrived at work one day in a Porsche sports car and boasted of the expensive real estate he was buying in a wealthy area of the capital region—all completely beyond any reasonable estimate of his income.

Not all thieves are that stupid. A healthy curiosity is perfectly justified if you see an employee sporting unusually expensive clothes, driving a sleek car after years with a rust bucket, and chatting pleasantly about the latest trip to Acapulco when that person's salary does not appear to explain such expenditures. Unsolicited inquiries into people's private lives, however, will usually win no friends. There is a delicate line to walk, but ignoring the issue does not make it disappear.

The other kind of change—toward the negative—also may indicate trouble. Why is the system manager looking both dejected and threadbare these days? Is he in the throes of a personal debt crisis? In the grip of a blackmailer? Beset with a family medical emergency? A compulsive gambler on a losing streak? On humane grounds alone, one would want to know what is up in order to help; however, a manager concerned with security would be compelled to investigate. In these days of explosive rage, and ready access to weapons, ignoring employees with a dark cloud hovering over their heads may be irresponsible and dangerous.

Any radical change in personality should elicit concern. If the normally relaxed head accountant now has beads of sweat on her forehead whenever you discuss the audit trails, perhaps it is time to look into her work more closely. Why does a good family man begin returning from long lunches with whiskey on his breath? A formerly grim manager now waltzes through the office with a perpetual smile on his face. What happened? Or what is happening?

All of these changes should alert managers to the possibility of changes in the lives of their employees. Although these changes do indeed affect the security of an organization, they also concern managers as human beings who can help other human beings. Mood swings, irritability, depression, euphoria—these can be signs of psychological stress. Is an employee becoming alcoholic? A drug addict? Abused at home? Going through financial difficulties? Having trouble with teenagers? Falling in love with a colleague? Of course managers cannot help everyone, and in some cases, help should involve qualified mental health professionals; but at least everyone can express concern and support in a sensitive and gentle way. Such discussions should take place in private, and without alarming the subject or exciting other employees. At any time, a manager should feel free to involve the HR or personnel department. They will either have a psychologist or trained counselor on staff or be able to provide appropriate help in some other way, such as an employee crisis line.

There are sad cases in which employees have shown signs of stress but have been ignored, with disastrous consequences: suicides, murders, theft, and sabotage. Be alert to the indicators and take action quickly.

Australian human resources expert Laura Stack offers this analysis of signs of extreme stress:

> People don't normally all of a sudden flip out; they give off early warning signals. Luckily, managers can observe signs of stress in employee behaviour, beginning with milder signs and culminating in desk rage. Be observant for the following stress stages:
>
> Physical stage: Headaches, illness, fatigue.
>
> Social stage: Negativity, blaming things on others, missed deadlines, working through lunch.
>
> Cerebral stage: Clock-watching, errors in assignments, minor accidents, absentmindedness and indecisiveness.

Emotional stage: Anger, sadness, crying, yelling, feelings of being overwhelmed, depression.

Spiritual stage: Brooding, crying, wanting to make drastic changes in life, not relating well with people, distancing themselves from personal relationships.[8]

The manager's job in probing behavioral changes is difficult; one must walk the thin and possibly invisible line between laissez-faire uninvolvement, risking lifelong regrets or even prosecution for dereliction of duty, and overt interference in the private affairs of the staff, risking embarrassment and possible prosecution for harassment.

Written policies will help; so will a strong and ongoing working relationship with the HR staff. Making it clear to all employees that managers are available for support, but are also expected to investigate unusual behavior, will also help avoid misunderstandings.

45.3.7 Separation of Duties. The same principles that apply to the control of money should apply to control of data. Tellers at a bank, when someone deposits a large check, will always go to a supervisor and have that person look the check over and initial the transaction. When bank tellers empty the automatic teller machines at night and fill the cash hoppers, there are always two people present. In most organizations, the person who creates a check is not the person who signs it.

In well-run information systems departments, with good operations security, data entry is distinct from validation and verification.[9] For example, a data entry supervisor can check on the accuracy of data entry but should not be allowed to enter a new transaction without having a direct supervisor check the work. There is no excuse for allowing the data entry supervisor to enter a transaction and then, effectively, to authorize it. What if the entry were in error—or fraudulent? Where would the control be?

In quality assurance for program development, the principles of separation of duty are well established. For example, the person who designs or codes a program must not be the only one to test the design or the code.[10] Test systems are separate from production systems; programmers must not have access to confidential and critical data that are controlled by the production staff. Programmers must not enter the computer room if they have no authorized business there; operators must not modify production programs and batch jobs without authorization.[11]

Managers should consider giving up access to functions that have been delegated to two or more subordinates. Maintaining such access could cause more problems than it solves, but in an emergency, access and control could easily be restored. This attitude exemplifies the concept of separation of duties.

In early 1995, the financial world was rocked by the collapse of the Barings PLC investment banking firm. The Singapore office chief, Nicholas Leeson, was accused of having played the futures market with disastrous consequences.[12] The significant point is that he managed to carry out all the orders without independent overview. Had there been effective separation of duties, the collapse would not have occurred.

Another shocking example occurred when a system administrator at UBS PaineWebber, upset about the poor salary bonus he received, deployed malicious code on the company's network. But before quitting his job, he wrote a program that would delete files and wreak havoc on the company's network. By creating a logic bomb, he was able to impact over 1,000 servers and 17,000 individual workstations. Additionally, buying puts against UBS, he would profit from that attack.

A related approach is called dual control. As an example of dual control, consider the perennial problem of having secret passwords not known to managers who sometimes need emergency access to those passwords. This problem does not generally apply to ordinary users' passwords, which normally can be reset by a security administrator without having to know the old password. This temporary password should be changed to a truly secret string by the user, after a single logon. However, to guard against the absence of the only person who has the root password for a system, possibly because the others are on vacation, it is advisable to store a written copy of the root password in a truly opaque envelope, seal it, sign the seal, tape over the seal with nonremovable tape, and then store the envelope in a corporate safe. The principle of dual control dictates that such a copy of the root password should be accessible only if two officers of the organization simultaneously sign for it when taking it out of the corporate safe.

In conclusion, managers should think about the structure of control over information as they design security policies, so that the safeguards afforded by separation of duties or dual control are present throughout all systems.

45.3.8 No Unauthorized Security Probes.   In general, all managers—not just security officers—should always be looking for vulnerabilities and opportunities for improving security. However, no one should ever *test* production systems for vulnerabilities without the full cooperation of the corporate information protection group, and only with authorization of the right executives. Written approval for explicit tests of security are informally known as *get-out-of-jail cards* because without them, employees can go to jail for unauthorized probes of system security.

The case of Randal Schwartz, a consultant to Intel Corporation in Beaverton, Oregon, is a salutary example for employees of the dangers of unauthorized security probes. He was convicted of hacking his way into Intel Corporation computer networks in what he claimed was an effort to point out security flaws while he was working there as a consultant. The would-be security expert failed to notify his employers of his intentions and forgot to get authorization for stealing passwords and making unauthorized changes in system software. He was convicted of three felony counts in July 1995 and was fined $68,000 in restitution as well as being put under five years of probation and having to perform 480 hours of community service.[13]

A counterexample to warn managers of misplaced zeal in suppressing cooperation with law enforcement is the case of Shawn Carpenter, a network intrusion detection security analyst at Sandia National Laboratories. He was fired by publicity-shy administrators when he worked with law enforcement officials to track down extensive penetrations of U.S. national security assets. An investigation code-named TITAN RAIN began in late 2003.[14] Carpenter noted a flood of expert hacker activity focusing on data theft from a wide range of national security interests. Carpenter discovered that "the attacks emanated from just three Chinese routers that acted as the first connection point from a local network to the Internet."[15] Carpenter worked with U.S. Army Counterintelligence and FBI investigators to learn more about the attacks and the attackers. Carpenter never used Sandia's or government-owned equipment or network resources in his investigations. Administrators applied Sandia Internal Directive 12 ISNL ID012 which "specifically prohibits employees from speaking with local, state or Federally-elected officials." In 2007, Carpenter was awarded $4.3 million for wrongful termination.[16]

45.4 TERMINATION OF EMPLOYMENT.   Taking our security mandate in the widest sense, we have to protect our employer and ourselves against potential damage from unethical, disgruntled, or incompetent employees, and against the legal consequences of improper firing procedures. Common sense and common decency argue for humane and sensitive treatment of people being fired and those who are resigning. Firing people is a stressful time for everyone concerned, and it usually leads to increased security risks.[17] Managers should do everything in their power to ensure a courteous, respectful, and supportive experience when terminating employment.

45.4.1 Resignations.   Potentially the most dangerous form of employment termination is a resignation. The problem is summed up in the caption of a cartoon where a savage attack is in progress against a medieval town that is in flames; a clan war chieftain confronts a singed and dirty warrior. "No, no, Thor! Pillage, THEN burn!" Like the war chieftain, employees rarely resign without planning. An employee may have an indefinite period during which the action is imminent, while the employer may remain unaware of the situation. If the employee has bad feelings toward, or evil designs on, the current employer, there is a period of vulnerability frequently unknown to management. Dishonest or unbalanced employees could steal information or equipment, cause immediate or delayed damage using programmatic techniques, or introduce faulty data into the system.

The policies discussed in previous sections of this chapter should reduce the risks associated with resignations. The manager's goal should be to make resignations rare and reasonable. By staying in touch with employees' feelings, moods, and morale, managers can identify sources of strain and perhaps resolve problems before they lead to resignations and their associated security risks.

45.4.2 Firings.   Firings appear to give the advantage to employers, but there may be complications.

45.4.2.1 Timing.   One advantage is that the time of notification to a fired employee can be controlled to minimize effects on the organization and its business. For example, employers might find it best to fire an incompetent, or no longer acceptable, employee before beginning an important new project or after a particular project has finished.

Some people argue that to reduce the psychological impact on other employees, they should fire people at the end of the day, perhaps even before a long weekend. The theory is that the practice gives everyone a cooling-off period outside working hours. These managers say they do not want the buzz of conversation and speculation that often follow a firing to intrude on the workday. This policy fails to regard the psychological stress to employees who have a ruined weekend and no way of responding constructively to their potentially catastrophic loss of a regular income.

A better approach to this stressful task is to fire people early on Monday morning in order to provide an unrushed exit interview and, if appropriate, job counseling to help the employee prepare for job hunting. In this scenario, the regrettable necessity (from the manager's point of view) of terminating employment is buffered by professionals in the HR department, who can give the departing employee a sense of hope and some practical as well as emotional support in this difficult time. A humane attitude is particularly important during downsizing, or when plants are closed, and many people are being fired—one of the worst experiences possible for both employees and managers, and an event that has serious security implications.

In one large company, the personnel department asked their information security staff to suspend the access codes for more than 100 people who were to be fired at 18:00 on Tuesday. On Wednesday at 08:00, the security staff began receiving phone calls asking why the callers' logon IDs no longer worked. It turned out that the personnel staff had failed to inform the terminated employees on time. The psychological trauma to both the employees who were fired and to the security staff was severe. Several security staff members were sent home in tears to recuperate from their unfortunate experience. The harm done to the fired employees was even more serious, and the effect on morale of the remaining employees was a disaster. There could well have been violence in that situation.

45.4.2.2 Procedures upon Termination.   In both resignations and firings, security consultants unanimously advise instant action. Not for them the leisurely grace period during which employees wind down their projects, or hand them off to other staff members. Security officers are a hard lot, and they usually advise this scenario: In a formal exit interview, and in the presence of at least two managers, an officer of the employer informs the employee politely that his or her employment is at an end. During the exit interview, the officer explains the reasons for termination of employment. The officer gives the employee a check for the period of notification required by law or by contract, plus any severance pay due. Under supervision, preferably in the presence of at least one security guard, the employee is escorted to the accustomed work area and invited to remove all personal belongings and place them in a container provided by the employer. The employee returns all company badges, IDs, business cards, credit cards, and keys, and is then ushered politely outside the building.

At the same time all this is happening, all security arrangements must be changed to exclude the ex-employee from access to the building and to all information systems. Such restrictions can include:

- Striking the person's name from all security post lists of authorized access
- Explicitly informing guards that the ex-employee may not be allowed into the building, whether unaccompanied or accompanied by an employee, without special authorization by named authorities
- Changing the combinations, reprogramming access card systems, and replacing physical keys if necessary for all secure areas to which the individual used to have authorized access
- Removing or changing all personal access codes known to have been used by the ex-employee on all secured computer systems, including microcomputers, networks, and mainframes
- Informing all outside agencies (e.g., tape storage facilities and outsourced functions) that the ex-employee is no longer authorized to access any of the employer's information or to initiate security or disaster recovery procedures
- Requesting cooperation from outside agencies in informing the employer if ex-employees attempt to exercise unauthorized functions on behalf of their former employer

The task is made more difficult by seniority, or if the ex-employee played an important role in disaster recovery or security. The employer should be assiduous in searching out all possible avenues of entry resulting from the person's position of responsibility and familiarity with security procedures.

In one story circulating in the security literature, an employee was fired without the safeguards just suggested. He returned to the workplace the next Saturday with his station wagon and greeted the security guard with the usual friendliness and confidence.

The guard, who had known him for years, was unaware that the man had been fired. The ex-employee still had access codes and copies of keys to secure areas. He entered the unattended computer room, destroyed all the files on the system, and then opened the tape vault. He engaged the guard's help in loading all the company's backup tapes into his station wagon. The thief even complained about how he had to work on weekends. This criminal then tried to extort money from the company by threatening to destroy the backup tapes, but he was found by police and arrested in time to prevent a disaster for his ex-employer.

This story emphasizes the importance of reaching *everyone* who needs to know that an employee no longer works for the enterprise.

45.4.2.3 *Support in Involuntary Terminations.*

Security does sometimes prevent a farewell party, one obvious sign of friendliness. The problem with a farewell party at work is that employees leaving under a cloud may feel humiliated when other people get a party but they do not. Generally it makes sense to treat all departing employees the same, even if the termination is involuntary.

However, nothing stops a humane and sensitive employer from encouraging employees to arrange an after-hours party even for people who have been fired. If a *resignation* is on good terms, however, the employer may even arrange a celebration, possibly during working hours and perhaps at company cost, without having to worry about possible negative repercussions.

A firing, or a resignation on poor terms, has two psychological dangers: effects on the individual concerned of embarrassment, shame, and anger, and effects on the remaining staff of rumors, resentment, and fear. Both kinds of problems can be minimized by publishing termination procedures in organization documents provided to all employees; by requiring all employees to sign a statement confirming that they have read and agreed to the termination procedures; and by consistent application of the termination procedures.

The personal shock of being fired can be reduced by politeness and consideration consistent with the nature of the reasons for being fired, although even nasty people should not be subject to verbal or physical abuse, no matter how bad their behavior. Their treatment should be consistent with that meted out to other fired employees, and there should be generous severance arrangements, if possible.

Organizational turmoil can be reduced by convening organization-wide or departmental meetings to brief remaining employees on the details of a significant termination. Open discussions, including how people feel about the rupture of relationships, can be helpful. The remaining employees may have to suffer grief, as a process, not a state. Grief is a normal and healthy response to disruption of relationships (e.g., death of a loved one, divorce, and even the loss of a coworker). Some people value social relationships more than other aspects of their work, and they may be especially affected by firings. Grief involves stages of denial, anger, mourning, and recovery. Trying to forestall such responses by denying that people legitimately have feelings is foolish and counterproductive. It is far better to encourage those who are upset to voice their feelings, and to engage in constructive discussion, than to clamp down in a futile attempt to suppress discussion.

45.4.2.4 *Style of Termination.*

The way an organization handles job termination affects more than internal relations; it also influences its image in the outside world. Prospective employees will think twice about accepting job offers from an organization that mistreats departing employees. Clients may form a negative impression of a company's stability if it abuses its own people. Investors also may look askance at a firm that gets a reputation for shoddy treatment of employees. Bad relations among managers and employees are a warning sign of long-term difficulties.

45.4.2.5   Legal Issues.   There is another dimension to employment termination that depends on local laws and the litigation environment. The United States, for example, is said to be one of the most litigious nations on the planet, perhaps because of the high number of lawyers compared with the total population.

The list that follows is not legal advice; for legal advice, consult an attorney. However, simple experience does teach some principles, even without going to law school. Here are some pragmatic guidelines for preventing legal problems related to firings for cause:

- Build a solid, documented case for firing someone before acting.
- Keep good records, be objective, and get the opinions of several trustworthy people on record.
- Offer the delinquent employee all reasonable chances to correct his or her behavior.
- Give the employee clear feedback long before considering firing.

Timing is important in employee relations, as it is in almost everything else we do. In particular, if an employee is found to be behaving improperly or illegally, there must be no marked delay in dealing with the problem. Such persons could sue the employer and individual managers. They could argue in court that the very fact that there was a delay in firing them was proof that the firing was due to other factors such as personality conflicts, racism, or sexism. A well-defined procedure for progressing through the decision will minimize such problems.

The critical legal issue is consistency. If rules such as those just described for the day of the firing are applied haphazardly, there could easily be grounds for complaining of unfairness. Those to whom the rules were strictly applied would justifiably feel implicitly criticized. How would we feel if we were singled out by having guards check what we took home from our desk—if everyone else got a party and two weeks' notice? Such inconsistency would be grounds for legal proceedings for defamation of character. The company might lose and it might win, but what nonlawyer wants to spend time in court?

Another issue that arises in connection with firings and resignations involves nondisclosure agreements. All such agreements must be included in a contract signed before the prospective employee begins work; it is almost impossible to force an existing employee to sign such an agreement.

Managers, the legal department, and the personnel department should study the necessity and feasibility of instituting a legally binding contractual obligation to protect their company's confidential information for a specified period of time after leaving. One typically does not impose indefinite gags on people, as one year seems to be normal. (However, there are exceptions. Oprah Winfrey insists that all employees who work at Harpo sign a lifelong confidentiality agreement, which an Illinois appeals court upheld when a former employee tried to write a book about the media mogul.) For this measure to be meaningful, the initial employment contract should stipulate that departing employees must reveal their new employer, if there is one at that time.

Noncompetition agreements require the employee to refrain from working for direct competitors for perhaps a year after termination of employment. The key to a successful clause here is that there be a strict, operational definition of "direct competitors." Because this limitation can be an onerous impediment to earning a living, many jurisdictions forbid such clauses.

45.5 SUMMARY.   Some of the key recommendations from this chapter follow.

Hiring

- Investigate the accuracy of every likely job candidate's résumé.
- Perform background investigations when hiring for sensitive positions.
- Arrange for experienced staff members to interview candidates and discuss inconsistencies.
- Require signing of a legally appropriate employment contract.

Ongoing Management

- Identify and resolve opportunities for abuse.
- Assign access functions on the basis of need, not social status.
- Identify indispensable employees, and arrange for cross-training of other staff.
- Require employees to take their vacations, or to rotate their job functions periodically, so as to assure operational continuity and as a possible indication of fraud.
- Note and respond to sudden changes in behavior and mood; involve human resources as appropriate.
- Enforce separation of duties and dual control for sensitive functions.
- Do not engage in, or tolerate, unauthorized probes of system security.

Termination of Employment

- Provide an opportunity for fired employees to receive counseling and support.
- Ensure that the HR department collaborates with the information technology group to take all appropriate security measures when anyone leaves the employment of the enterprise.
- Ensure that firings do not cause long-term morale problems.
- Follow the guidance of corporate counsel to avoid wrongful dismissal suits.
- Use legally appropriate nondisclosure and noncompetition clauses in employment contracts.

In summary, information security depends on coordination with HR personnel to ensure consistent policies for hiring, ongoing management, and termination of employment.

45.6 FURTHER READING

Armstrong, M. *A Handbook of Human Resource Management Practice*, 10th ed. London, UK: Kogan Page, 2006.
Bologna, J. *Handbook on Corporate Fraud: Prevention, Detection, Investigation.* Boston: Butterworth-Heinemann, 1993.

Dresang, D. L. *Personnel Management in Government Agencies and Nonprofit Organizations*, 5th ed. London, UK: Longman, 2008.

Mathis, R. L., and J. H. Jackson. *Human Resources Management*, 9th ed. Cincinnati: South-Western Publishing, 1999.

McNamara, C. "Human Resources Management," 2007, www.mapnp.org/library/hr_mgmnt/hr_mgmnt.htm.

NAPA (National Academy of Public Administration: Human Resources Management Consortium), 2008, www.napawash.org/pc_human_resources.

NOLO. "Human Resources," 2008. Includes links to "Hiring Employees," "Personnel Policies & Practices," "Preventing Discrimination," "Ensuring Privacy in the Workplace," "When Workers Leave," "Firing Employees," and other topics; www.nolo.com/resource.cfm/catid/cb627bad-f421-4af1-ae5c9d84021bb999/111/259/.

SHRM (Society for Human Resource Management). White Papers, 2008, www.shrm.org/hrresources/whitepapers_published/toc.asp.

45.7   NOTES

1. R. Richardson, (2007). "CSI Computer Crime and Security Survey," Computer Security Institute, 2007, www.gocsi.com/forms/csi_survey.jhtml (free; registration required).

2. For guidance on setting policies, see Chapter 44 in this *Handbook*; for details of e-mail and Internet usage policies, see Chapter 48; for security awareness advice, see Chapter 49; for applications of the principles of social psychology in reinforcing a culture of security, see Chapter 50.

3. Peter Levine, quoted in www.virtualhrscreening.com/background/whybackground.htm.

4. Department of Justice Press Release, "Jury Finds Former Coke Employee Guilty in Conspiracy to Steal and sell Coca-Cola Trade Secrets," February 2, 2007, http://atlanta.fbi.gov/dojpressrel/pressrel07/tradesecrets020207.htm.

5. See Chapter 10 in this *Handbook* for more details on understanding computer crime statistics.

6. "Around the Nation: 2d Man Pleads Guilty in Wells Fargo Case," *New York Times,* August 12, 1981, p A.10 (fee required), http://tinyurl.com/5byd6c.

7. L. J. Kushner, "Career Management 101 for Information Security Pros," *Information Security,* June 29, 2006, http://searchsecurity.techtarget.com/generic/0,295582,sid14_gci1196912,00.html.

8. L. Stack, "Employees Behaving Badly: Combating Desk Rage," *Human Resources,* October 5, 2004, www.humanresourcesmagazine.com.au/articles/C6/0C0251C6.asp?Type=60&Category=903.

9. See Chapter 47.

10. See Chapter 39.

11. See Chapter 47.

12. Nicholas Leeson official Web site: www.nickleeson.com/biography/index.html.

13. S. Pacenka, "Computer Crime?" *State of Oregon v. Randal Schwartz*, Washington County Circuit Court C94-0322CR, 2007. Complaint brought by Mr. Schwart's client, the Intel Corporation; www.lightlink.com/spacenka/fors/.

14. I. Winkler, "Guard against Titan Rain Hackers," *Computerworld,* October 20, 2005, www.computerworld.com/securitytopics/security/story/0,10801,105585,00.html.

15. N. Thornburgh, "The Invasion of the Chinese Cyberspies (and the Man Who Tried to Stop Them)," *TIME*, August 29, 2005, www.time.com/time/magazine/printout/0,8816,1098961,00.html.

16. J. Vijayan, "Reverse Hacker Wins $4.3M in suit against Sandia Labs: Shawn Carpenter used his own hacking techniques to probe outside breach," *Computerworld,* February 14, 2007, www.computerworld.com/action/article.do?command=viewArticleBasic&articleId=9011283.

17. S. Terlap and E. Morath, "Final Day at Ford Bittersweet for Scores of Salaried Workers," *Detroit News,* March 1, 2007, http://detroitnews.com/apps/pbcs.dll/article?AID=/20070301/AUTO01/703010359/1148.

VULNERABILITY ASSESSMENT

Rebecca Gurley Bace

46.1 SCOREKEEPER OF SECURITY MANAGEMENT. Information security has, over time, evolved from a collection of esoteric security issues and technical remedies to its current state, in which it is more tightly integrated with the area of enterprise risk management. One effect of this move from technology to management discipline is the growth in the deployment and use of vulnerability management (and its primary technical constituent, vulnerability assessment [VA]) systems. These systems are considered fundamental to modern information security practice and have matured in architecture, features, and interfaces to accommodate the changing landscape of modern enterprises.

46.1.1 What Is Vulnerability Management? Vulnerability management is a process of assessing deployed IT systems in order to determine the security state of the system. It includes the determination of corrective measures to mitigate issues identified that represent exposures for the enterprise, and managing the application of those measures. Vulnerability assessment is the key technology component of vulnerability management. However, there is a synergy between VA and the other elements of vulnerability management such that these elements drive what features are supported by VA technology.

The vulnerability management process is often defined in terms of four key functions. They are:

1. **Inventory.** Before an examiner can determine the extent of testing, one must identify all systems resident within the domain of interest. At this time, the operating system platforms and functions associated with each system are articulated and documented.

2. **Focus.** Once an examiner has an idea of the systems that reside within the network, he must determine what information he (or his assessment tools) needs to see in order to find those vulnerabilities that are relevant to him and the enterprise. Some include the tuning of vulnerability assessment tools as a part of this step.

3. **Assess.** The examiner runs any tests (both automated and manual) necessary to identify vulnerabilities resident on the systems. She then assesses the results of these tests. Finally, she evaluates (and ranks) the actual risk to her organization's systems security, making that judgment guided by security policy and current risk management criteria.

4. **Respond.** Finally, the examiner must execute procedures that act on the results of the assessment in order to address the problems identified.

Now that we have laid the cornerstones of the vulnerability management process, let us proceed to the technology particulars of vulnerability assessment.

46.1.2   What Is Vulnerability Assessment?   Vulnerability assessment is the analysis of the security state of a system on the basis of system information collected on demand. The four-step strategy for VA follows.

1. Sample a predetermined set of target system attributes (e.g., specific parameters for particular firewalls).

2. Place the sampled information in a data store.

3. Organize and compare the data store to a reference set of attributes.

4. Document and report the differences between the data store and the reference set.

46.1.3   Where Does Vulnerability Assessment Fit in Security Management?   Vulnerability assessment and its parent function, vulnerability management, are key elements of virtually all modern system security management strategies. There are many reasons for the popularity and acceptance of these functions, including:

- When systems are first deployed, VA allows you to baseline the security state of those systems.

- When security breaches are suspected, VA may allow you to quickly identify likely paths of attack and, furthermore, determine whether they have been exercised.

- When new vulnerabilities are reported, VA can allow you to identify systems that are subject to the vulnerabilities so that you can patch or otherwise address the exposures.

- The results of individual VAs can be archived and used to document the security state of systems at a specific time. This is often used to satisfy regulatory audit or other oversight requirements.

Although VA and vulnerability management are accepted as important system security functions, they are not sufficient to protect systems from all security threats. Such measures should be included in a more comprehensive security strategy that includes security policy and procedural controls (see Chapters 44, 45, 47, 48, 49, 50, 51, 52, and 53 in this *Handbook*), network firewalls and other perimeter defenses (Chapter 26), strong identification and authentication mechanisms (Chapters 28 and 29), access control mechanisms (Chapter 32), file and link encryption (Chapters 7, 32, 33, 34, and 36), file integrity checking (Chapters 3, 7, 39, 40, 41, 47, and 53), physical security measures (Chapters 22 and 23), and security training and education (Chapters 74 and 75). There are references and insight into building the rest of a comprehensive security strategy throughout this book.

46.1.4 Brief History of Vulnerability Assessment.   Early vulnerability assessment systems (VASs) include the COPS (Common Open Policy Services) system, developed in the late 1980s by Eugene H. Spafford and Daniel Farmer at Purdue University.[1] COPS was a UNIX-targeted credentialed vulnerability assessment product that gained wide acceptance in security circles. The initial freeware version of the Internet Security Scanner (ISS) was also released in the early 1990s, as was Farmer's and Wietse Venema's vulnerability assessment software, SATAN (Security Administrator Tool for Analysing Networks).[2]

Subsequent trends of note include the advent of open source tools for performing various forms of VA (e.g., NESSUS,[3] which provides vulnerability scanning capabilities, and NMAP (Network Map),[4] which provides an inventory of the systems on a specific network, along with the network services resident on those systems). Also of note is the move of VA to the network "cloud" (i.e., the vulnerability assessment is actually performed over the network, controlled by the security administrator over a Web interface, with results stored off site.)

46.2 TAXONOMY OF VULNERABILITY ASSESSMENT TECHNOLOGIES.
VA products snapshot the security state of systems, diagnosing problems that indicate that the system is vulnerable to specific attacks.

VA performs an examination of key indicators within systems that are known to correspond to security vulnerabilities. Some consider some types of VAS a special case of a host-based, interval-based intrusion detection process and describe it in terms of the intrusion detection process model outlined in Chapter 27.

46.2.1 Vulnerability Assessment Strategy and Techniques.   As noted, there is a four stage high-level strategy for conducting VA: sample, store, compare, and report. This four-stage process becomes quite complex when fleshed out to cover the full range of vulnerabilities that are commonly exploited by modern adversaries. A standard VA process may involve the use of any or all of these techniques:

Network scanning. Maps network nodes and associated services by use of a "port scanner." This articulates issues at a network and network services layer of abstraction. See Section 46.2.2 of this chapter.

Vulnerability scanning. Takes the port-scanning functions of network scanners to the next level by testing for operating system and application software system vulnerabilities resident on hosts connected to the network. See Section 46.2.3.

Password cracking. Identifies weak passwords (see Chapter 7 in this *Handbook*).

Log review. A feature rooted in the earliest production computing platforms, log review remains one of the most powerful means of identifying weaknesses in systems (see Chapters 15, 18, 21, 25, 28, 36, 29, 40, 47, 53, 56, 57, 61, and 63 in this *Handbook*). Log review is mentioned throughout this book.

Integrity checking. Uses checksums, hash totals, and digital signatures to allow quick and reliable detection of tampered files and system objects (see Chapters 3, 7, 39, 40, 41, 47, and 53 in this *Handbook*).

Virus detection. Scans for known viruses infecting systems (see Chapter 16 in this *Handbook*).

War dialing. Scans enterprise systems for unauthorized modems (see Chapter 4 in this *Handbook*).

War driving. Scans enterprise systems for unauthorized wireless LAN connections (see Chapter 15 in this *Handbook*).

Penetration testing. Reenacts attackers' behavior in order to gain access and thereby test technical and procedural security measures.[5] See Section 46.3 of this chapter.

As many of these techniques are complex enough to merit a full chapter of their own, we focus on only three of them in this chapter: network scanning, vulnerability scanning, and penetration testing.

46.2.2   Network Scanning.   Network scanners run a function called a *port scanner,* which uses a feature of ICMP, part of TCP/IP, in order to identify hosts available in a specified network address range. The port scanner then scans identified systems for open network ports and associated services.

Some network scanners use inference and other techniques to make intelligent guesses about the operating systems being run on open systems. These inferences are based on the combinations of active ports observed on a specific host (e.g., if Port 80 is open on a given host, it is likely running a web server.) Some scanners listen to ports for traffic that provides additional information about the system connected to that port. One example of this type of surveillance is called *banner grabbing*, and can provide a great deal of detail about the connected system.

As a primary security policy decision involves specifying what systems are allowed on an enterprise network, network scanners provide a vital piece of information for VA. They also provide collateral information regarding the connected systems on a network, which is critical for tuning and refining the VA process. It is important, however, to understand that although the operation of a network scanner is automated, the identification of vulnerabilities discovered by network scanning is not. There is minimal, if any, decision support in network scanning products—some will identify certain port numbers as associated with a known Trojan attack. Therefore, it is important that the results from a network scanner be evaluated by someone familiar with the assessed network and associated security policy.

46.2.3 Vulnerability Scanning.

Vulnerability scanning is the heart of traditional VA systems. In some ways vulnerability scanning appears to be the same as port scanning, but it differs in a critical way: It takes the additional step not only of collecting data regarding traffic, connections, and system attributes but of analyzing the data to determine whether they match a known vulnerability. Many systems (credentialed; see Section 46.2.4.1) also attempt to correct the vulnerabilities identified in the scan, either with human interaction or automatically.

As vulnerability scanning usually targets specific hosts, it often conducts a deeper inspection than network scanners, identifying software versions, specific software applications, and configuration attributes of systems. The policy checks available to host-based vulnerability scanners can include usage patterns for software.

Perhaps the most valuable feature of vulnerability scanners is the current database of known vulnerabilities. Virtually all commercial offerings in this area include updates to these vulnerability databases as a core feature of the product. Many products offer features that assist security managers in configuring scanners to fit their environments, including a wide variety of configuration, reporting, and support features.

Vulnerability scanners can perform extremely fine-grained security assessment, in far more detail than network port scanners. However, this degree of detail comes at a price. Vulnerability scanners are typically slower and more resource greedy than network port scanners. The range of available assessment techniques is usually richer for vulnerability scanners; some (e.g., DDoS testing) can disrupt the normal operation of an enterprise network. False positive rates (i.e., vulnerabilities spotted where none exist) can be high for many vulnerability scanners, requiring more human intervention. Finally, as the value of the vulnerability scanner resides in its vulnerability database, it is critical that the database be updated frequently. A vulnerability scanner with a noncurrent database leaves users open to compromise.

46.2.4 Assessment Strategies.

As in intrusion detection systems, VASs have features that allow differentiation between individual systems. The primary descriptors for VASs involve the information sources and how those information sources are generated.

46.2.4.1 Credentialed Monitoring.

Credentialed monitoring approaches for vulnerability assessments are those that utilize system data sources such as file contents, configuration information, and status information. This information is gained from nonintrusive sources; that is, it is gained by performing standard system status queries and inspection of system attributes. These sources are accessible only when the entity gathering them has legitimate access to the system (i.e., the entity possesses access credentials). In UNIX systems, this information is gathered at the host or device level; therefore, *credentialed approaches* are also *host-based* approaches. As many modern operating systems (e.g., Windows) handle status information differently, often providing it in the form of Application Programming Interfaces (APIs), the *credentialed = host-based* equivalence does not always apply in those environments.

46.2.4.2 Noncredentialed Monitors.

Noncredentialed monitoring approaches are those approaches that stage system attacks and record target system responses to the attacks. These approaches are much more intrusive than credentialed attacks and do not assume (nor do they require) any legitimate access to the target system; they are launched from an attacker's perspective. Noncredentialed approaches are often called *active* approaches and have detection and monitoring features that complement those of credentialed approaches. In particular, noncredentialed approaches are usually superior for diagnosing vulnerabilities associated with network services. As noted, in UNIX systems, noncredentialed assessments are usually considered *network-based* assessments. For instance, network scanning is a noncredentialed monitoring process. It bears repeating that here, as in credentialed approaches, the equivalence relationship does not necessarily apply in Windows and other modern operating system environments that provide status information in API form.[6]

46.2.5   Strengths and Weaknesses of VAS.   Knowing that security point products (e.g., firewalls, NIDS, and access-control systems) that defend particular features of a security perimeter cannot be perfect in the dynamic world of network and system attack, VASs serve an important function in the overall strategy for protecting information assets.

A list of the benefits associated with vulnerability analysis follows.

- VASs conserve time and resources, as they allow even nonexpert personnel to check systems automatically for literally thousands of problems, any one of which might result in an intrusion.
- VASs can be extremely helpful in training security novices to make systems more secure.
- VASs can be updated to reflect new knowledge of vulnerabilities found by vendors and researchers.
- VASs can be configured to address specific vulnerabilities and configurations affected by regulatory requirements. They are a critical component in IT security regulatory compliance.
- As VASs are used in more environments as a part of a risk management regime, they are helpful for benchmarking the security state of systems in order to document progress toward a protection goal.
- VASs are systematic and therefore consistent. These attributes allow them to be used as quality assurance measures for network or security managers. Many security professionals routinely recommend that operational security policies include provisions for using VASs to check systems for problems after major changes have occurred (as might be the case whenever software is updated or system recovery is required).

Weaknesses in vulnerability assessment include these:

- Although vulnerability assessment is necessary for system security, it is not in and of itself sufficient to secure a system.
- Many VASs serve only to diagnose problems, not to correct them. They are part of a more comprehensive vulnerability management process. User follow-through is still required.
- If the VASs are not kept up to date, they may mislead users into underestimating the risk of penetration.
- VASs can negatively impact the performance of an operational network. It is critical to balance demand for the network with the performance hits associated with running some types of VAS.

- As in many other knowledge-based security tools, VA can be used for either productive or malicious purposes. In the hands of a security manager, VA is a valuable diagnostic technique. In the hands of an attacker, VA may optimize efforts to identify targets of attack and provide insight as to exactly how those targets might be compromised.

46.2.6 Roles for Vulnerability Assessment in System Security Management. Vulnerability assessment products can be used at several points in the system security management life cycle.

First, when a new program is put into place, a VA can baseline the security state of the system. This application is particularly valuable in establishing the case for a security program, as it provides hard evidence that security problems exist.

Next, when an operational system changes (as might be the case when software updates are installed or new equipment is connected), a VA can help. It can find specific security vulnerabilities that occur as side effects of such changes.

Finally, when security incidents occur or are suspected, VA results can assist investigators in diagnosing possible paths of entry for attackers, locating artifacts of attacks (such as backdoors or Trojan horses), and identifying the system resources affected by an attack so that they can be restored to their original states.

46.3 PENETRATION TESTING. Even the best designed VA scan is not a complete test of a system's security against a specific threat or adversary. When one considers whether illicit access to an information system might allow an attacker to inflict significant damage to an organization, VA of the systems yields, at best, a partial answer. Penetration testing expands the scope of VA to include the physical, personnel, and procedural controls that would be targeted by an adversary in an attack. This is done manually, by a penetration test team. Although many think of penetration tests as no-holds-barred hacker exercises, they should be thoroughly planned and staged with a great deal of forethought and consideration. In this section, we discuss the various techniques employed by penetration test teams and about the serious issues that arise in the context of penetration testing.

46.3.1 Penetration Test Goals. As mentioned, the goal of penetration testing is to conduct a realistic test of adequacy of security measures for a given enterprise system. In particular, several goals are associated with penetration-testing activities:

- Penetration testing is intended to model real-world attacks as closely as possible.[7] Note that this differs from the goals of VA in this way: Vulnerability assessment is carried out within the policy context of the target system being assessed. In penetration testing, testers take the assessment outside this context, allowing security planners to make realistic judgments about whether operational systems are adequately protected from specific threats at a particular point of time.

- Penetration testing allows the testing of simultaneous levels of security measures at once. This is useful in situations when the complexity of fielded systems (and the measures employed to protect them) surfaces questions about conflicting goals of security and availability and other operational conflicts.

- Penetration testing allows one to better identify potential access paths to critical information or system assets that other VA techniques failed to locate.

- Penetration testing should be carried out in a way that does not jeopardize normal business activity. As it is by definition carried out on operational systems in live environments, this is a critical requirement.

- Finally, as in the general case of VA, penetration testing often serves as a dramatic demonstration of security issues to senior management, helping win buy-in for funding security initiatives. This means that testing should produce unambiguous results that balance business and technical considerations.

46.3.2 Attributes of Penetration Testing.

As mentioned, there is a wide range of possible activities that can fit into the general classification of penetration testing. As an exhaustive set of penetration test cases can be extremely expensive (and furthermore jeopardize normal business operations), it is critical to specify exactly what assets a penetration test team is to target and the techniques it is allowed to employ in its test activity.

Examples of attributes commonly associated with penetration testing include:

- **Testing models.** Penetration testing can be conducted in the total absence of system information (also known as *zero knowledge* test scenarios) or, at the other end of the spectrum, with the test team provided with full documentation for both the systems and organization alike (*full knowledge*). Some security experts believe that the best penetration tests provide for a test team that is equipped not only with full knowledge of the systems involved, but also full risk modeling information for the enterprise.[8]

- **Scope of penetration testing.** Penetration testing can include physical and communications exploits as well as system exploits. It can be designed to allow social engineering attacks, and, if so, specify to what degree these attacks will proceed.

- **Assumed level of sophistication of penetration testers.** As in the real world of attackers, the sophistication of penetration team activities can vary widely. Novice attackers are usually less targeted than more expert attackers (i.e., marked more by shotgun or brute-force techniques, which are usually easier to detect). Expert attackers usually do more target surveillance and make far better uses of the information gathered. Finally, the goals of novice versus expert attackers usually differ, with experts usually focusing more on the business impact of attacks while novice attackers often settle for more visible targets (e.g., system defacement or other trophies of successful attack.)

46.3.3 Social Engineering.

As penetration testing usually tests procedural and physical security measures in combination with classic system protection, social engineering techniques are often included in the testing resources available to penetration test teams.

Social engineering is defined as the use of any of a number of techniques to induce employees or other authorized personnel to divulge confidential information that can then be used to gain illicit access to systems. Many of these techniques are used in classic criminal enterprise—thus their use in the context of penetration testing should be both constrained and accompanied by administrative measures to protect the testing team. For instance, before any social engineering techniques are used in a penetration test, the team should have signed statements from the client organization explicitly permitting the use of such techniques; the client staff should also be prepared for the use of social engineering techniques in the context of security testing.[9]

Examples of specific social engineering techniques sometimes used in security testing include:

- **Piggybacking.** A test team member, in business attire, follows an authorized employee through badge-accessible door.
- **Shoulder surfing.** A test team member, in business attire, loiters with organization employees outside an entrance, looking over their shoulders as employees enter a key code to unlock the door.
- **Faux service.** Test team members, attired as service technicians, appear in an employee's office and ask for access to a system; if the employee resists, the test team makes veiled bureaucratic threats.
- **Dialing for passwords.** Test team members, equipped with internal phone lists and an internal phone line, call employees, posing as system maintenance personnel, asking for password information.
- **Bribery.** A test team member poses as a representative of a competitor, approaches an employee of the organization, and offers a significant bribe ($50,000) for information enabling an attack.[10]
- **Overload.** Multiple members of the test team converge on an employee who can enable access to controlled area. Team members demand so many decisions of the employee that they start forcing simple decisions, (such as enabling access). In a common utilization of this technique, team members lock out specific accounts (by exceeding the number of failed logins) multiple times, then pressure system administrators to change the password to the account to a known value "until we have time to deal with this access issue properly."
- **Fascination.** Multiple members of the test team stage a play involving an employee charged with maintaining access control or another security function. The object of the play is to compel the employee to act in a fashion that is at odds with his or her security responsibility.
- **Bullying.** In this, perhaps most extreme, technique, a test team member pulls rank on an employee (e.g., in military situations, presents himself as a senior officer) demanding that the employee honor a direct order to violate security policy.[11]

46.3.4 Managing Penetration Testing. Given the relatively unconstrained spirit associated with penetration testing, it is critical that the process be managed properly. Some of the requisite management considerations mirror those of the more generic process of VA. Independent oversight is required for the conduct of VA; it is especially critical to the success of penetration testing. Test scenarios should be documented and approved in advance by at least two representatives of the organization being tested, and the employees of the organization should be prepared for testing, especially when social engineering techniques are included in the scope of penetration testing.

This set of agreements and preparation for testing is key to balancing the need to perform realistic and relevant VA (including penetration testing) with the need to minimize the impact of such testing on normal business operations.

As human systems and constructs are as much a part of business operations as information systems, minimizing impact involves consideration of the ethics of social engineering. The first ethical tenet asserts that social engineering tests should not cause psychological distress to test subjects. Most employees are conscientious with regard to security and other company policies and may consider being targeted by social engineering tests as a breach of trust. Their reactions to that perceived breach may range from anger to resignation, or to a lawsuit.

Another ethical tenet states that those who fail social engineering or other penetration tests should not be subject to humiliation; this requires that test results be treated as confidential information. Finally, testers should not rely unduly on verbal misrepresentation or acting to achieve the goals of testing[12] —the objective of such testing is to establish whether security measures are appropriate and effective for the organization, not to score a win for the test team at all costs. To leave a tested organization in worse condition than the test team found it is a hollow victory for all involved.

46.4   FURTHER READING

Foster, J. C. *Writing Security Tools and Exploits.* Norwell, MA: Syngress, 2005.

Hurley, C. *Penetration Tester's Open Source Toolkit*, Vol. 2. Norwell, MA: Syngress, 2006.

Hurley, C. *Wardriving & Wireless Penetration Testing.* Norwell, MA: Syngress, 2006.

Manzuik, S., A. Gold, and C. Gatford. *Network Security Assessment: From Vulnerability to Patch.* Norwell, MA: Syngress, 2006.

Van Der Walt, C., H. D. Moore, R. Temmingh, H. Meer, J. Long, C. Hurley, and J. Foster. *Penetration Tester's Open Source Toolkit.* Norwell, MA: Syngress, 2005.

46.5   NOTES

1. D. Farmer and E. H. Spafford, "The COPS Security Checker System," *Proceedings of the Summer USENIX Conference,* Anaheim, CA, June 1990, pp. 165–170, www.deter.com/unix/papers/cops.pdf.

2. D. Farmer and W. Venema, "Improving the Security of Your Site by Breaking into It," Internet white paper, 1993, www.porcupine.org/satan.

3. www.nessus.org.

4. www.insecure.org/nmap.

5. J. Wack, M. Tracy, and M. Souppaya, "Guideline on Network Security Testing," NIST Special Publication 800-42, National Institute of Standards and Technology (October 2003), http://csrc.nist.gov/publications/nistpubs/800-42/NIST-SP800-42.pdf.

6. A. Shostack and S. Blake, "Towards a Taxonomy of Network Security Assessment Techniques." *Proceedings of 1999 Black Hat Briefings,* Las Vegas, NV, July 1999, www.blackhat.com/presentations/bh-usa-99/AdamS/shostack-blackhat.pdf.

7. Siemens Insight Consulting, "Penetration Testing," April 2006, www.insight. co.uk/files/datasheets/ Penetration%20Testing%20(Datasheet).pdf.

8. G. McGraw, "Is Penetration Testing a Good Idea?" *Network Computing,* July 1, 2005, www.networkcomputing.com/showArticle.jhtml?articleID=164901611.

9. M. E. Kabay, "Social Engineering in Penetration Testing—Planning," *Network World Security Strategies*, November 1, 2007, www.networkworld.com/ newsletters/sec/2007/1029sec2.html.

10. M. Fisher and M. E. Kabay, "Penetration Testing, Part 3," *Network World Security Strategies,* February 11, 2003, http://www.networkworld.com/ newsletters/sec/2003/0210sec1.html.

11. P. Schumacher and M. E. Kabay, "Social Engineering in Penetration Testing—Intimidation," *Network World Security Strategies*, November 8, 2007, www.networkworld.com/newsletters/sec/2007/1105sec2.html.

12. J. Orlando and M. E. Kabay, "Social Engineering in Penetration Testing: Analysis," *Network World Security Strategies,* October 30, 2007, www.networkworld.com/newsletters/sec/2007/1029sec1.html.

CHAPTER **47**

OPERATIONS SECURITY AND PRODUCTION CONTROLS

M. E. Kabay, Don Holden, and Myles Walsh

47.1 INTRODUCTION. Despite the enormous increase in individual computing on personal computers and workstations in the years since the first edition of this *Handbook* was published in 1975, many mainframe computers and their networks are still used for enterprise computing in applications devoted to the core business of the enterprise. This chapter focuses on how to run vital computers and networks safely and effectively.

Readers with a military background will note that operations security in the civilian sector is different from the OPSEC (a military acronym for "operational security") designation used in military discourse. As defined by the Joint Chiefs of Staff of the United States military, "OPSEC seeks to deny real information to an adversary, and prevent correct deduction of friendly plans."[1]

In determining what operations security and production controls are required for any system, a thorough risk analysis should be conducted; you will find references throughout this *Handbook*. For a quick analysis, it may be helpful to use a few other common military acronyms and list the threats from their perspectives.

> **EMPCOA**—enemy's most probable course of action. What is the most likely course of action an attacker will take against your systems?
>
> **EMDCOA**—enemy's most dangerous course of action. What is the worst possible thing an attacker could accomplish?

Weighing these as part of a risk analysis can help tremendously to decide how to employ limited resources. The acronym "METT-TC," which is essentially a larger version of the engineering triad of cost, time, and quality, may help. There are various versions of the METT-TC acronym, but perhaps the most useful stands for mission (what we need to do), equipment (what we have), time (by when we need to do it), troops (whom we have to do it), terrain (where are we doing it), and culture (the possible cultural considerations). Each part of our METT-TC analysis should be self-evident, except for perhaps culture. Ignoring the management, political, and community cultures of the locations in which to install security controls is a frequent mistake, with usually dire consequences for both security and the careers of security professionals.

It is critical to be able to define precisely the terms associated with operations security and production controls before engaging in a discourse about them.

47.1.1   What Are Production Systems?   A *production system* is one upon which an enterprise depends for critically important functions. Examples include systems for handling accounts receivable, accounts payable, payroll, inventory, manufacturing systems, real-time process control, data entry systems, Web-based client interfaces for e-commerce, critical information systems, portable data handling systems, and management information systems.

47.1.2   What Are Operations?   *Operations* consist of the requirements for control, maintenance, and support of production systems. Operations staff are responsible for such functions as:

- Integrating new software systems into an existing configuration
- Running programs and batch jobs to update databases and create reports
- Installing new versions of production programs
- Maintaining production databases for maximal efficiency
- Managing backups (creation, labeling, storage, and disposal)
- Responding to emergencies and recovering functionality
- Mounting storage volumes of tapes, cartridges, or disks in response to user or program requests

- Handling special forms for particular printouts (e.g., check blanks)
- Managing all aspects of production networks, such as configuring routers, bridges, gateways, wireless propagation, and firewalls

47.1.3   What Are Computer Programs?   A *computer program* is a set of instructions that tells a computer what to do to perform a task. Computer programs may be acquired, or they may be internally developed. Internally developed programs are stored in computer systems in two basic forms. Source programs are in the form in which they were written (coded) by computer programmers. The statements in source programs are in languages such as COBOL, Visual BASIC, C++, or Java. Source language programs are kept in files and stored on disk folders called source libraries or program libraries. Executable programs have been converted from source code, by compilation or interpretation, into a program that the computer can execute. Executable programs may be maintained in two separate forms: object and load. An object program is a partially executable module that must be linked to other executable modules, such as input/output modules, to become a load module. As load modules, the programs are said to be in executable form. Executable programs are kept in production libraries, from which they are called when needed. Acquired programs are generally in object and load form. The source code is proprietary to the organization that developed it and is rarely given to the acquiring enterprise.

When internally developed programs have to be changed, programmers work with copies of the source programs. The copies are stored in another type of library, referred to as programmer libraries. The programmers make changes to their copy of the source programs, and go through a process of recompiling and testing until the modified program is working properly. When acquired programs require changes, often a contract to make the modifications is issued to the organization from which the programs were acquired. In some situations, internal programmers generate new programs and interfaces to the original acquired programs. The same libraries are used: source libraries for source code, production libraries for executable modules, and programmer libraries for work in progress. These libraries need to be protected. Loss or damage can entail huge costs and considerable inconvenience; recovering them can require a long time and great expense.

47.1.4   What Are Procedures?   Procedures are sets of statements that tell a computer what to do in certain situations. They are unlike programs in that they are not compiled. Stored in files or databases, they are invoked as needed. Procedural statements are made up of operational commands and parameters. The operational commands tell the computer what to do, and the parameters tell the computer which entity to act upon. Job Control Language (JCL) is an example of a procedural language. Procedural language statements often are used in database management systems and in security software products.

47.1.5   What Are Data Files?   Everything stored and maintained in a computer system takes the form of a file. Programs, procedures, information, all are stored in files, using the concept of a file in its broadest sense; that is, a collection of related items. This usage has become most apparent with the ubiquitous personal computer (PC). Data files, as distinguished from program files and other types, are those that store information. In a PC environment, data files may be called documents. Documents are created by word processors, spreadsheet programs, graphics generators, and other application programs. In mainframe and midsize computer environments, data files are those created and maintained by applications such as payroll, accounting, inventory, order entry, and sales.

Some data files are transient; that is, they are created, used, and deleted within a short period of time. If lost or damaged, they can be reconstructed quickly, with little difficulty. There is usually no need to protect transient files. Other files, such as master files or organizational databases (groups of files that are linked to one another), contain information that is vital, confidential, or virtually irreplaceable. These files, generated by PCs, mainframes, and midsize computer systems, must be protected by security software and backup procedures, to ensure against loss, destruction, theft, and unauthorized disclosure.

47.2   OPERATIONS MANAGEMENT.   The processes for effective and efficient management of operations have direct benefits on information assurance. In particular, these aspects of operations management are of special value for improving and maintaining security:

- Separation of duties
- Defining the role of the security officer or security administrator
- Limiting access to the operations center
- Defining secure change-control processes
- Careful controls over externally supplied software
- Managing quality assurance and quality control.

47.2.1   Separation of Duties.   Separation of duties is a key control that should be applied to development and modification of programs. In enterprises where there are systems and programming departments that create and maintain custom programs, each individual programmer is assigned a user ID and a password. In these enterprises, where programs are developed and maintained internally, changes are constantly made to programs in order to meet changing business requirements. Modified executable programs, after recompilation and testing by programmers, are moved from their libraries into production libraries. Modified source programs are moved into source libraries. The programmers are responsible for keeping the source libraries current, while computer operations, or some other functional group separated from programming, may be responsible for maintaining the production libraries. When an updated executable program is transferred from the programmer's library to the production library, a transmittal is included, signed off by a manager in the programming department.

A particular consequence of the separation of duties is that a member of the operations staff should always be involved in the functional analysis and requirements definition phases for changes to production programs. The operations perspective is not always clear to programmers, and such issues as logging, backout, and recovery, as discussed later in this chapter, need to be brought to their attention early in the development and maintenance cycles.

47.2.2   Security Officer or Security Administrator.   Contemporary enterprises typically include a mix of mainframes, midsize computers, and local area networks (LANs) comprised of hundreds or thousands of workstations, PCs, terminals, and other devices, all interconnected with one another, and with the same mix in other enterprises throughout the world via the Internet. A department, or an individual in smaller enterprises, has the responsibility for providing and maintaining the security of files, databases, and programs. The title that is often associated with this function is information security officer. This individual or department has the mandate to carry out the security policy as set down by the senior management of the enterprise. The security officer is empowered to allow or to disallow access to files, databases, and programs. In the language of the security officer, procedures are set up and maintained that establish relationships among individuals, programs, and files. Users, programmers, and technicians are granted privileges for full access, update only, or even read only. The security officer has the power to change or to revoke privileges.

47.2.3   Limit Access to Operations Center.   Physical access to the operations center grants a person enormous power to disrupt production systems. Such access must be tightly controlled.

47.2.3.1   *Need, Not Status, Determines Access.*   A fundamental principle for effective security is that access to restricted areas is granted on the basis of roles. Employees whose roles do not justify access should be excluded from autonomous access to production systems. In particular, high-placed executives, such as the president, chief executive officer, chief financial officer, chief operating officer, chief technical officer, and all vice presidents, should examine their own roles and determine if they should be able to enter the operations center unaccompanied; in most cases, such access is unjustified. Limiting their own access sets an important model for other aspects of security policy and demonstrates that need, not social status or position within the corporate hierarchy, determines access to restricted areas.

47.2.3.2   *Basic Methods of Access Control.*   As explained in Chapter 28 in this *Handbook*, access control depends on identification and authentication (I&A). I&A can be based on:

- What one has (tokens such as physical keys or smart cards)
- What one knows (user IDs and passwords or passphrases)
- What one is (static biometric attributes such as fingerprints, iris patterns, retinal patterns, and facial features)
- What one does (dynamic biometrics such as voice patterns, typing patterns, and signature dynamics)

For more information on biometric authentication, see Chapter 29.

A typical arrangement for secure access to an operations center may involve keypads for entry of a particular code or card readers programmed to admit the holders of specific magnetic-stripe or smart card. If the operations center is a 24-hour operation with full-time staffing, the presence of operators provides an additional layer of security to preclude unauthorized access. Remote monitoring of sensitive areas increases security by discouraging unauthorized access or unauthorized behavior and speeds up the response to possible sabotage. For extensive discussion of physical and facilities security, see Chapters 22 and 23.

47.2.3.3   *Log In and Badge Visitors.*   Visitors to a facility that houses sensitive systems should be logged in at a controlled entrance and provided with visitor badges. In high-security applications, an additional login may be required when entering the operations center itself. To encourage return of visitor badges, some security policies require the visitor to deposit a valuable document, such as a driver's license, with the security guards at the main entrance. The effectiveness of visitor badges depends entirely on the use of badges by all personnel at all times; if *not* wearing a badge is acceptable and common, a malicious visitor could simply hide a visitor badge to pass as an authorized employee.

The time of login and of logout can be valuable forensic evidence if malfeasance is detected. However, such records can be shown to be reliable only if the guards responsible for keeping the logs consistently verify the completeness and correctness of all information written into the logs.

47.2.3.4 *Accompany Visitors.* No unaccompanied visitors should be permitted to circulate in the operations center or in the facility housing such a center. In high-security facilities, someone must even accompany the visitor to the washroom and wait for the visitor outside the door.

If a consultant or temporary employee is to work on a project for longer than a day, it may be acceptable to grant that person a restricted pass for low-security areas; however, high-security areas, such as the operations center, would still require such a person to be accompanied.

47.2.4 Change-Control Procedures from the Operations Perspective.
When programmers have made changes to production programs and all documentation and testing procedures are complete, the new versions are formally turned over to the operations staff for integration into production.

47.2.4.1 *Moving New Versions of Software into Production.* Operations managers and staff must meet these demands when moving new versions of software into production:

- Identification—tracking which software is in use
- Authorization—controlling changes
- Scheduling—minimizing disruptions to production
- Backups—ensuring that all requisite information is available to restore a prior state
- Logging—keeping track of data input for recovery, and of errors for diagnosis of problems
- Backout—returning to a prior production version in case of catastrophic errors

47.2.4.1.1 Identification. Knowing precisely which versions of all production software are in use is the basis of production controls. Every module must have a unique identification that allows immediate tracking between executable code and source code; all changes to a particular module must be fully documented by the programming group. Unique identifiers allow the quality assurance process to ensure that the only modules that go into production are those that have been properly tested.

Most production shops use a three-level numbering scheme to track versions. Typically, version *a.b.c* (e.g., 7.13.201) is defined in this way:

- *c* changes every time anything at all—even a spelling mistake—is changed.
- *b* changes when program managers decide to group a number of fixes to errors into a new version for release to production.
- *a* changes when significant new functions are added; often the source code is completely renumbered if the changes are great enough.

The version number of object code must match the number of its source code. All object code should include internal documentation of its version number so that the version can be ascertained instantly, without having to consult possibly inaccurate external documentation.

47.2.4.1.2 Authorization. Strict procedures must be in place to preclude rogue programmers from introducing modified code into the production suite. In addition to the dangers of introducing untested or undocumented changes, allowing any individual to modify production processes without verification and authorization by an appropriate chain of responsibility can allow hostile code, such as Trojan horses and backdoors, to be introduced into the systems.

47.2.4.1.3 Scheduling. Implementing any new version of a production system requires careful planning and scheduling. Operations staff must prepare for changes in all aspects of production that depend on the system in question; for example, there may be requirements for new printer forms, additional magnetic tapes, and other supplies that must be ordered in advance. New requests for operator intervention, or changes in status and error messages during production, necessitate appropriate documentation and training. Effects on other programs may require special preparations that must take into account the scheduling requirements of the other systems that are affected. In addition, new versions of software often are implemented immediately after major production jobs, such as end-of-year or quarterly processing, to maintain consistency within an accounting period. For all these reasons, scheduling is critically important for trouble-free operations.

47.2.4.1.4 Backups. When modifying production systems, operations staffs usually take one or more complete backups of the software and data to be modified. This procedure is essential to allow complete restoration of the previous working environment should there be catastrophic failure of the new software and data structures.

47.2.4.1.5 Logging. To allow recovery or backout without losing the new data and changes to existing data that may have been carried out using new software and data structures, all production programs should include a logging facility. Logging keeps a journal of all information required to track changes in data and to regenerate a valid version of the data by applying all changes to an initial starting condition. Logging requires synchronization with backups to avoid data loss or data corruption. Special requirements may exist when a new version of the production system involves changes to data structures; in such cases, applying the information about changes to the older data structures may require special-purpose application programs. Since programmers sometimes forget about such possibilities, operations staff should be prepared to remind the programming staff about such requirements during the design phases for all changes.

47.2.4.1.6   Backout and Recovery.   Sometimes a new version of production software is unacceptable and must be removed from the production environment. This decision may be made immediately, or it may occur after a significant amount of data entry and data manipulation has taken place. In either case, operations should be able to return to the previous version of a production system without data loss. This process involves restoring the earlier complete operating environment, with software and data in synchrony, and then using log files to repeat the data input and data modifications from the moment of changeover to the moment of fallback.

Not all of the changes that were made using a new version will necessarily be applicable to the previous data; for example, if new fields were added to a database, the data stored in those fields would not be usable for an older, simpler data structure. Similarly, if fields were removed in the newer database, recovery will involve providing values for those fields in the older database. All of these functions must be available in the recovery programs that should accompany any version change in production systems.

47.2.4.2   Using Digital Signatures to Validate Production Programs.

If an unauthorized intruder or a disgruntled employee were discovered to have gained access to the production libraries, it would be necessary to determine if there had been unauthorized modifications to the production programs.

Date and time stamps on programs can record the timing of changes, but many operating environments allow such information to be modified using system utilities that read and write directly to disk without passing through normal system calls. In those instances, there would be no time stamp or log entry.

One approach that has been used successfully is to apply checksums to all production components. Checksum software applies computations to programs as if the codes were simply numbers; the results can be sensitive to changes as small as a single bit. However, if the checksums are computed the same way for all programs, access to the checksum utility could allow a malefactor to change a module and then run the checksum utility to create the appropriate new checksum, thus concealing the evidence of change. To make such subterfuge harder, the checksums can be stored in a database. Naturally, this database of checksums itself must be protected against unauthorized changes. Storing checksums may make unauthorized changes more difficult to disguise, but it also extends the chain of vulnerabilities.

A better way of determining whether object code or source code has been modified is to use digital signatures. Digital signatures are similar to checksums, but they require input of a *private key* that can, and must, be protected against disclosure. Verifying the digital signature may be done using a corresponding *public key* that can be made available without compromising the secrecy of the private key. For more information on public and private keys, see PKI and certificate authorities in Chapter 37 of this *Handbook.*

When digital signatures are used to authenticate code, it may be possible to validate production systems routinely, provided that the process is not too arduous to be accomplished as part of the normal production process. For example, it should be possible to validate all digital signatures in no more than a few minutes, before allowing the daily production cycle to start.

47.2.5   Using Externally Supplied Software.   Production often uses software from outside the organization; such software may be commercial off-the-shelf (COTS) programs or it may consist of programs modified for, or written especially for, the organization by a software supplier. In any case, external software poses special problems of trust for the production team. There have been documented cases in which production versions of software from reputable software houses have contained viruses or Easter eggs (undocumented features, such as the well-known Flight Simulator in MS-Excel versions, which pops up a graphic landscape that includes a monitor showing the names of the Excel development team). In addition, some consultants have publicly admitted that they deliberately include Trojan horse code (undocumented malicious programming) that allows them to damage data or inactivate the programs they have installed at client sites if their fees are not paid.

In large data centers, it may be possible to run quality assurance procedures on externally supplied code. Such tests should include coverage monitoring, in which a test suite exercises all the compiled code corresponding to every line of source code. However, it is rare that an operations group has the resources necessary for such testing.

The trustworthiness of proprietary external software written or adapted especially for a client ultimately may depend on the legal contracts between supplier and user. Such legal constraints may not prevent a disgruntled or dishonest employee in the supplier organization from including harmful code, but at least they may offer a basis for compensation should there be trouble.

47.2.5.1   *Verify Digital Signatures on Source Code If Possible.* If externally supplied code is provided with its source library as well as with compiled modules, operations should try to have the supplier provide digital signatures for all such programs. Digital signatures will permit authentication of the code's origins and may make it harder for malefactors to supply modified code to the user. In addition, the digital signatures can support nonrepudiation of the code (i.e., the supplier will be unable credibly to claim that it did not supply the code) and therefore the signatures may be useful in legal action, if necessary.

47.2.5.2   *Compile from Source When Possible.* Wherever possible, it is highly desirable to be able to compile executables from source code on the target machine. Compiling from source allows quality assurance processes to check the source for undocumented features that might be security violations and to couple the executables tightly to the verified source. In addition, compiling on the local system ensures that all calls to system routines will be satisfied by linking to executables such as dynamic link libraries (DLLs) supplied in the current version of the operating system.

However, compilation on a local system has additional implications that complicate implementation of new applications: Because the system routines being linked to the compiled code may not be identical to those used during the manufacturer's quality assurance tests, the customer organization must plan for its own quality assurance testing.

Operations staff should express this preference for source code clearly to the person or group controlling acquisition of external software. For more information about writing secure code, see Chapter 38 in this *Handbook*; for information about secure software development and quality assurance, see Chapter 39.

47.2.6 Quality Control versus Quality Assurance.   Throughout this chapter, quality assurance has been mentioned as an essential underpinning for operations security. *Quality assurance* refers to the processes designed to ensure and to verify the validity of production programs. However, another aspect of quality concerns the operations group: the quality of output. The process of verifying and ensuring the quality of output is known as *quality control.*

47.2.6.1 *Service-Level Agreements.*   Unlike mathematical truth, there is no absolute standard of quality for computing operations. Every organization must define the level of quality that is suitable for a particular application. A commonly quoted principle in programming and operations is that there is a complex relationship among quality, cost, and development time: Increasing quality increases both cost and development time; shortening development time increases cost, if quality is to be maintained. It follows that every system should include a definition of acceptable performance; such definitions are known as *service-level agreements* (SLAs).

SLAs typically include minimum and maximum limits for performance, resource utilization, and output quality. The limits should be expressed in statistical terms; for example, "The response time measured as the time between pressing ENTER and seeing the completed response appear on screen shall be less than three seconds in 95 percent of all transactions and shall not exceed four seconds at any time." SLAs may define different standards for different types of transactions if the business needs of the users so dictate.

47.2.6.2 *Monitoring Performance.*   Computer-system performance depends on four elements:

1. Access time and speed of the central processing unit(s) (CPU)
2. Access time and speed of mass storage (disks)
3. Access time and speed of fast memory (RAM)
4. Application design

In addition, network performance depends on communications-channel bandwidth and traffic.

Operations groups should monitor performance to ensure that the requirements of the SLAs are met. There are two approaches to such monitoring: (1) analysis of log files and (2) real-time data capture and analysis.

Log files that are designed with performance analysis in mind can capture the precise times of any events of interest; for example, one might have a record in the log file to show when a particular user initiated a read request for specific data and another record to show when the data were displayed on the user's screen. Such level of detail is invaluable for performance analysis because the data permit analysts to look at any kind of transaction and compute statistics about the distribution of response times. In turn, these data may be used for trend analysis that sometimes can highlight problems in program or data structure, design, or maintenance. For example, an excessively long lookup time in a data table may indicate that the system is using serial data access because it had been designed without an appropriate index that would permit rapid random access to the needed records.

Another approach to performance monitoring and analysis is to use real-time monitors that can alert operations staff to abnormal performance. For example, an application program may be designed to calculate response times on the fly; the results may be displayed numerically or graphically on a *dashboard* for the operations staff. Values falling below a specified parameter may signal an abnormal condition, using color or sound to alert the operators to the drop in performance. Such *integrated performance metrics* allow the fastest possible response to performance problems.

Even if the application programs lack integrated performance metrics, it is sometimes possible to use system-level online performance tools to analyze system activity. In one instance, for example, a software supplier had promised a response time of 10 seconds or less for all transactions, but one particular operation was taking 43 minutes. Using the online performance tool, it quickly became obvious that the transaction in question was generating an enormous amount of disk I/O (read and write operations). Investigation revealed that the program design was forcing 80,000 random-access reads in a particular data set to locate a few target records. Installing and using an appropriate index and compacting the data set to provide rapid access to blocks of related records reduced response time to 6 seconds.

47.2.6.3 *Monitoring Resources.*

Consistent monitoring of resource utilization is one of the most valuable roles of the operations staff. Data center operations should include regular analysis of system log files to track changes in the number of files, amount of disk free space available, number of CPU cycles consumed, number of virtual memory swap operations, and less esoteric resource demands, such as numbers of lines or pages printed, number of tape mounts requested, number of backup tapes in use, and so on. These data should be graphed and subjected to trend analysis to project when particular resources will be saturated if the trend continues. Operations can then reduce demand either by improving aspects of production (e.g., optimizing programs to require fewer resources) or by increasing available resources (e.g., installing a memory upgrade).

Another level of analysis focuses on specific users and groups of users. Each functional group using the production systems should be analyzed separately to see if there are discontinuities in their trends of resource utilization. For example, a specific department might show a relatively slow and stable rise in CPU cycles consumed per month—until the rate of increase suddenly increases tenfold. If such a rate of increase were to continue, it could surpass all the rest of the system demands combined; operations therefore would investigate the situation before it caused problems. The cause of the discontinuity might be a programming error; for example, there might be a logical loop in one of the programs or a repeated computation that ought to have its result stored for reuse. However, the change in slope in CPU utilization might be due to introduction of new programs with a rapidly growing database; in such cases, operations would have to act to meet heavy new demands.

Disk space is often a key resource that can cause problems. If users fail to clean up unwanted files, disk space can disappear at an astounding rate. This problem is exacerbated by poor programming practices that allow temporary work files to remain permanently in place. Systems have been designed with tens of thousands of sequentially numbered "temporary" work files that had no function whatsoever after a production run was completed but that were accumulated over several years.

One of the methods widely used to reduce resource waste is *chargeback*. Using system and application log files, system administration charges the users of particular systems a fee based on their use of various resources. Sometimes these chargebacks are viewed as "funny money" because they are an accounting fiction—no money changes hands. However, requiring managers to budget carefully for computing resources can greatly improve attention to mundane housekeeping matters such as cleaning up useless files. If the chargeback system extends to aspects of program performance such as number of disk I/Os, it can even influence programmers to optimize their design and their code appropriately. Optimization is appropriate when the total costs of optimization are less than the savings in resources and the increases in productivity that result from optimization efforts, measured over the lifetime of the application.

47.2.6.4 *Monitoring Output Quality.*

The final component of quality control is the meticulous monitoring of everything that is produced in the data center and sent to users or clients. Although much printing is now performed on local printers controlled by users, in many situations the operations group is responsible for documents such as payroll checks, invoices, and account status reports. Every operations group must explicitly assign responsibility for verifying the quality of such output before it leaves the data center. Operators should keep careful logs that record various types of error (e.g., torn paper, misaligned forms, or poor print quality) so that management can identify areas requiring explicit attention to improve quality.

47.3 PROVIDING A TRUSTED OPERATING SYSTEM.

The operating system (OS) is usually the single biggest and most important example of externally supplied software in a data center. Because the OS affects everything that is done in production, it is essential to know that the software is trustworthy. To this effect, operations staff use procedures to ensure that *known-good* software is always available to reinstall on the system.

47.3.1 Creating Known-Good Boot Medium.

The simple principle that underlies known-good operating software is that there shall be an unbroken chain of copies of the OS that have never run any other software. That is, operations will create a boot medium (tape, cartridge, CD-ROM) immediately after installing known-good software.

For example, if boot-medium V1B0 is defined as version 1 of the OS as it is delivered from the manufacturer, its installation would require specific settings and parameters for the particular configuration of the system. Immediately after installing V1B0, but before running any other software, operations would create medium V1B1 and set it aside for later use if V1B0 had to be replaced.

47.3.2 Installing a New Version of the Operating System.

Continuing this example of how to maintain known-good operating software, it might become necessary to install a new version of the operating system—say, version 2 on medium V2B0. Before using V2B0, operations would reinstall the current known-good OS, say from V1B1. Only then would V2B0 be installed, and the new boot medium V2B1 would be created immediately.

47.3.3 Patching the Operating System.

Often, when it is necessary to modify a small part of the OS, rather than installing a whole new version, manufacturers ask users to *patch* the OS. The patch programs modify the compiled code in place. If checksums or digital signatures are in use to maintain OS integrity, these codes will have to be regenerated after the patch is applied. However, to maintain a known-good status, applying a patch should follow a rigid sequence:

1. Load the current known-good software from the appropriate medium (e.g., V2B1).
2. Install the patch.

3. Immediately create a known-good boot medium before running any other software (in our example, this medium would be V2B2).

For extensive discussion of managing patches for production systems, see Chapter 40 in this *Handbook*.

47.4   PROTECTION OF DATA

47.4.1   Access to Production Programs and Control Data.   Just as the operations center needs restricted access, so do production programs and data. From a functional point of view, there are three categories of people who might be allowed access to programs and data on which the enterprise depends: users, programmers, and operations staff.

47.4.1.1   Users.   The only people who should have read and write access to production *data* are those users assigned to the particular systems who have been granted specific access privileges. For example, normally only the human resources staff would have access to personnel records; only the finance department staff would have full access to all accounts payable and accounts receivable records. Managers and other executive users would have access to particular subsets of data, such as productivity records or budget figures. Of course, *no* user should ever have write access to production *programs*.

47.4.1.2   Programming Staff.   Programmers create and maintain production programs; they naturally have to be able to access the versions of those programs on which they currently are working. However, programmers must not be able to modify the programs currently used in *production*. All changes to production programs must be documented, tested, and integrated into the production environment with the supervision of quality assurance, operations, and security personnel.

Programmers need to be able to use realistic data in their development, maintenance, and testing functions; however, programmers should *not* have privileged access to restricted data. For example, programmers should not be allowed to read confidential files from personnel records or to modify production data in the accounts payable system. Programmers can use extracts from the production databases, but particular fields may have to be randomized to prevent breaches of confidentiality. Programmers generally resent such constraints, but usually an effective process of education can convince them that maintaining barriers between production systems and systems under development is a wise policy.

47.4.1.3   Operations Staff.   Much as the programmers are responsible for developing and maintaining systems, so the operations staff are responsible for using and controlling these systems. Operations staff perform tasks such as scheduling, error handling, quality control, backups, recovery, and version management. However, operations staff should not be able to modify production programs or to access sensitive data in production databases.

47.4.2   Separating Production, Development, and Test Data.   For obvious reasons, testing with production data and production programs is an unacceptable practice, except in emergency situations. Therefore, programmers who develop new programs or modify existing programs must perform tests using their own libraries.

These are frequently referred to as test libraries. Experienced programmers keep copies of the source programs for which they are responsible as well as copies of some of the files that are used by the programs and subsets of others in their own test libraries. To avoid security violations, such copies and subsets should be anonymized to the degree necessary to protect confidentiality. For example, a system using personnel data might substitute random numbers and strings for the employee identifiers, names, and addresses.

It is important to include time stamps on all files and programs, including both production and test versions. This practice serves to resolve problems that arise about program malfunctions. If all programs and files have time stamps, it can be helpful in determining whether the most current version of the load program is in the production library and whether test files and production files have been synchronized.

Final testing prior to production release may entail more formal review by an independent quality assurance section or department; the quality assurance group may also control transfers of programs to the production library.

47.4.3   Controlling User Access to Files and Databases.   Access to files has to be controlled for two reasons:

1. There is confidential information in files that is not to be made accessible to everyone.

2. There are other files that are considered auditable.

The information in these files may be confidential, but that is not the reason for controlling access to them. The information in these files must be controlled because changing it is illegal. An example would be an enterprise's general ledger file once the books have been closed. Changing the information in these files gave birth to the pejorative phrase "cooking the books." The original copies of these files are developed on the computer that handles the day-to-day transactions of an enterprise. Some time after the month-end closing of the books, copies of these files are archived. In this form they are the recorded history of the enterprise and cannot be changed. Storing this chiseled-in-stone historical information, combining details and summaries in database format, so as to be accessible for the purpose of analysis is known as data warehousing.

In most large enterprises, these files are created on mainframe and midsize computers, although as the speed and storage capacity of microcomputers continue to increase, these files are beginning to appear on microcomputer database servers in LANs. In any event, controlling user access to files is performed in several ways depending on what types of access are allowed. Remote access to online production databases and files is often done over leased lines—dedicated communication facilities paid for on a monthly basis as opposed to dial-up or switched lines paid for on a when-used basis. Access control may be readily accomplished through the use of front-end security software modules, which in turn feed into database and file handling software and finally into the application software. For example, in an environment using a software product for handling queries and updates of online databases and files, a number of different security software products could be installed. Such products use what are called rules or schemas to validate user IDs and passwords, to authorize types of transactions, and to allow access to files and databases.

Many information system installations allow remote communications for many kinds of transactions. Various individuals, including sales representatives entering order information and traveling executives wishing to access current information from databases or files, use public networks, such as wired or wireless Internet service providers at hotels, airports, and coffee shops. This type of access increases the potential for security breaches. The usual practice today is to use *virtual private networks* (VPNs), which consist of encrypted channels between the portable equipment and the enterprise networks. Even so, some inadequate implementations of VPNs allow cleartext transmission of the initial logon information, allowing the identification and authentication data to be captured and used for unauthorized access. Poorly secured network access also allows *man-in-the-middle* attacks on the user's traffic.

For more information about encryption, see Chapters 7 and 37 in this *Handbook*; for more about network and communications security, see Chapters 5, 25, 32, 33, and 34.

47.5 DATA VALIDATION.   Just as it is essential to have trusted operating systems and application software for production, the operations group must be able to demonstrate that data used for production are valid.

Validation controls normally are carried out dynamically throughout data entry and other processing tasks. Some validity checks are carried out automatically by database software; for example, inconsistencies between header records and details may be reported as errors by the database subsystems. Bad pointers are usually flagged immediately as errors by the database software; examples include:

- Pointers from a particular master record to a detail record with the wrong key value or to a nonexistent location

- Forward or backward pointers from a detail record to records that have the wrong key value for the chain or that do not exist at all

However, many errors cannot be caught by database subsystems because they involve specific constraints particular to the application rather than errors in the database itself. For example, it may be improper to allow two chemical substances to be mixed in a processing vat, yet there is nothing in the data themselves that the database software would recognize as precluding those two values to be recorded in the input variables. The programmers must include such restrictions in edit checks; often these relations among variables can be coded in a data dictionary. If the programming environment does not allow such dependencies, the programmers must incorporate the restrictions in lookup tables or in initialization of variables.

From a production point of view, operations staff must run appropriate validation programs created by the database suppliers and by the application programmers to assure the quality of all production data. The next sections review in more detail what is involved in such validation programs.

47.5.1 Edit Checks.   Operations should have access to diagnostic programs that scan entire databases looking for violations of edit criteria. For example, if a field is designated as requiring only alphanumeric characters but not special characters such as "#" and "@," then part of the diagnostic sweep should be checking every occurrence of the field for compliance with those rules. Similarly, range checks (greater than, less than, greater than or equal, equal, less than or equal, between) are a normal part of such scans. Lookup tables listing allowed and forbidden data and combinations of data provide further sophistication for more complex relations and restrictions. In any case, the role of operations staff is to run the diagnostics and identify errors; correction of the errors should fall to authorized personnel, such as the database administrators.

Diagnostic programs should provide detailed information about every error located in the production files. Such details include:

- Configurable view of the record or records constituting an error, showing some or all of the fields
- Unique identification of such records by file name or number, record number, and optionally by physical location (cylinder, sector) on disk
- Error code and optional full-text descriptions of the error, including exactly which constraints have been violated

A diagnostic program should, ideally, also allow for repair of the error. Such repair could be automatic, as, for example, insertion of the correct total in an order-header, or manual, by providing for the database administrator to correct a detail record known to be wrong.

47.5.2 Check Digits and Log Files.   Another form of verification relies on check digits. Programs can add the numerical or alphanumeric results of data manipulations to each record or to groups of records when transactions are completed properly. Finding records with the wrong check digits will signal inconsistencies and potential errors in the processing. Check digits are particularly useful to identify changes in production databases and other files that have been accomplished through utilities that bypass the constraints of application programs. For example, most databases come with a relatively simple ad hoc query tool that permits lookups, serial searches, views, and simple reporting. However, such tools often include the power to modify records in compliance with database subsystem constraints, but completely free of application program constraints. An even more powerful type of utility bypasses the file system entirely, and works by issuing commands directly to the low-level drivers or to the firmware responsible for memory and disk I/O. In the hands of the wrong people, both database and system utilities can damage data integrity. However, it is usually difficult for the users of these utilities to compute the correct checksums to hide evidence of their modifications. A diagnostic routine that recomputes checksums and compares the new values with the stored values can spot such unauthorized data manipulations immediately.

A similar technique for validating and repairing data uses database and application log files to record information such as before and after images of modified records. Such log files also can include special marker records to flag different steps in complex transactions; these flags can allow diagnostic programs to identify precisely when transactions have been interrupted or subjected to other forms of failure. Using these log files, it is often possible to identify which defective transactions need to be removed, repeated, or completed.

Commercial data-integrity software is available for a wide range of platforms and databases. Searching on "data integrity software" in the Google search engine (www.google.com) locates many references to such products.[2]

For more information on integrating security into application design, see Chapter 52 in this *Handbook*. For more about log files and other monitoring and control systems, see Chapter 53.

47.5.3 Handling External Data.   Before using data provided by external organizations, operations should routinely check for data purity. Diagnostic routines from the programming group should be available to check on all data before they are used in batch processing to update a production database. The same principles of data validation used in checking production databases should apply to all data received from clients, suppliers, governments, and any other organization. Special validation programs can and should be written or obtained to test the data received on any medium, including tapes, cartridges, removable discs, CD-ROMs, DVDs and data communications channels.

47.6 CONCLUDING REMARKS. Up until the mid-1980s, the world of mainframes and minicomputers differed from that of PCs. However, from the mid-1980s and into the millennium, these worlds have merged. LANs have proliferated, the Internet has changed the way business is conducted, and bridges, routers, and gateways make it possible for information to move among computer platforms, regardless of type. Security requirements are now universal in scope. Numerous layers of software and hardware separate the user and the technician from the information to which they require access. These layers themselves contribute to security because they require some technical skill to get at the information. As this is being written in 2008, computer literacy is increasing rapidly. Children are taught to use computers in grade school, and tens of millions of workers routinely use PCs or workstations daily, so the security provided by the technology is not as significant as it once was.

Security is also an economic issue. If an individual with the requisite skill is determined to gain access to online files or databases, it is extremely expensive to prevent such access. Even with high expenditures, success in achieving complete security is never guaranteed. Nevertheless, if the value of the information and its confidentiality justifies additional expense, there are software products available that employ complex schemes to support security. When necessary, information security can be extended down to the field level in records of online files and databases.

Other related security measures, such as physical protection, communication security, encryption of data, auditing techniques, system application controls, and other topics, are covered in other chapters of this *Handbook*. No one measure can stand alone or provide the ultimate protection for security, but with a proper balance of measures, the exposures can be contained and managed.

47.7 FURTHER READING

Baumann, W. J., J.T. Fritsch, and K. J. Dooley. *Network Maturity Model: An Integrated Process Framework for the Management, Development and Operation of High Quality Computer Networks.* Parker, CO: Outskirts Press, 2007.

Benyon, R., and R. Johnston *Service Agreements: A Management Guide.* San Antonio, TX: Van Haren Publishing, 2006.

Blanding, S. *Enterprise Operations Management Handbook*, 2nd ed. Boca Raton, FL: Auerbach, 1999.

Cisco. "Cisco Data Center Management." White paper, 2004. Available: www.cisco.com/web/about/ciscoitatwork/downloads/ciscoitatwork/pdf/Cisco_IT_Operational_Overview_Data_Center_Management.pdf or http://tinyurl.com/5vl2n6.

McCrie, R. *Security Operations Management*, 2nd ed. Upper Saddle River, NJ: Prentice-Hall, 2006.

47.8 NOTES

1. United States Joint Chiefs of Staff, "Information Operations," Joint Publication 3–13, 2006, p. II-2. Available: www.dtic.mil/doctrine/jel/new_pubs/jp3_13.pdf.

2. The site http://dmoz.org/Computers/Software/Databases/Data_Warehousing/Data_Integrity_and_Cleansing_Tools listed 45 such tools at the time of writing (May 2008).

E-MAIL AND INTERNET USE POLICIES

M. E. Kabay and Nicholas Takacs

48.1   INTRODUCTION.[1]   The Internet offers every enterprise exciting opportunities to find timely information and to reach potential clients. This very power brings with it risks of damaging corporate and professional reputations. Nontechnical problems in cyberspace include bad information, fraud, loss of productivity, and violations of civil and criminal law as well as violations of the conventions of proper behavior established by custom in cyberspace.

In addition, widespread abuse of Internet access while at work is forcing recognition that clear policies are essential to guide employees in appropriate use of these corporate resources. The consensus in our profession—despite the dreadful lack of hard statistics—is that something like two-thirds of all the damage caused to our information systems is from insiders who are poorly trained, careless, or malicious. (For a detailed discussion of security statistics, see Chapter 10 in this *Handbook.*) For example, a study published in late 2005 reported that:

> Sixty-nine percent of 110 senior executives at Fortune 1,000 companies say they are "very concerned" about insider network attacks or data theft, according to a study by Caymas Systems, a network security technology firm based in San Jose, Calif. And 25 percent say they are so concerned they can't sleep at night, Sanjay Uppal, a vice president at Caymas Systems, told eSecurityPlanet.[2]

A McAfee-sponsored survey in Europe showed that (in the words of the Department of Homeland Security *Daily Open Source Infrastructure Report*[3]):

> Workers across Europe are continuing to place their own companies at risk from information security attacks. This "threat from within" is undermining the investments organizations make to defend against security threats, according to a study by security firm McAfee. The survey, conducted by ICM Research, produced evidence of both ignorance and negligence over the use of company IT resources. One in five workers let family and friends use company laptops and PCs to access the Internet. More than half connect their own devices or gadgets to their work PC and a quarter of these do so every day. Around 60 percent admit to storing personal content on their work PC. One in ten confessed to downloading content at work they shouldn't. Most errant workers put their firms at risk through either complacency or ignorance, but a small minority are believed to be actively seeking to damage the company from within. Five percent of those questioned say they have accessed areas of their IT system they shouldn't have while a very small number admitted to stealing information from company servers.[4]

Another topic of growing significance is saturation by floods of e-mail sent by well-intentioned employees who do not know how to use e-mail effectively.

Finally, some of the information in this chapter may help security administrators involve their users in a more active role by giving them take-home messages that can help them protect their own families and friends. Getting employees to care about security for their families is a good step to involving them in corporate security.

For more information on effective security awareness and corporate culture change, see Chapters 49 and 50 in this *Handbook.*

48.2   DAMAGING THE REPUTATION OF THE ENTERPRISE.   When someone posts information to the Net, the message header normally indicates who the sender is. In particular, all employees using a corporate e-mail account identify their employer in every posting. It follows that when an employee—for example, joe@acme.com—misbehaves on the Net, it is likely that everyone seeing the misbehavior will associate it with the employer, regardless of futile attempts to dissociate the employee from the employer by statements such as "The opinions above are not necessarily those of my employer."

Employees can embarrass their employers by using their corporate e-mail identifiers in these ways:

- **Flaming.** Launching rude verbal attacks on others.
- **Spamming.** Sending "junk" e-mail, unsolicited advertising and sales promotions, to multiple, often unrelated, Usenet groups and mailing lists and to people's e-mail addresses without their permission. Often called "spam," it should be spelled in lowercase or as "Spam" to respect the Hormel Corporation, owners of the SPAM^{TM} trademark (all uppercase is the luncheon meat).[5]
- **Mail-bombing.** Sending many e-mail messages to a single e-mail address to annoy its user, or in extreme cases, to cause a denial of service.

In addition, employees can violate laws, send out embarrassing content via e-mail, implicate their employers in personal affairs, and spread falsehoods with actionable consequences.

48.2.1 Violating Laws.   Employees may engage in illegal activities that can seriously compromise their employer; examples include:

- Industrial espionage
- Stock manipulation
- Criminal hacking, unauthorized penetration of other systems
- Sabotage, denial of service attacks
- Vandalism, defacement of Web sites
- Creating, transmitting, or storing child pornography
- Sending threats (e.g., of harm to the President of the United States)
- Credit card fraud, using stolen or fraudulently generated credit card numbers for purchases made using corporate resources

Corporate Internet usage policies should explicitly forbid any of these actions.

48.2.2 Ill-Advised E-mail.   There have been too many cases of foolish use of e-mail in recent years. Employees have created a hostile working environment by sending internal e-mail with lewd or hateful jokes and images; staff members have insulted their bosses or their employees in e-mail that later became public; people have made libelous accusations about other workers or about competing companies. All of these uses are wholly inappropriate for a medium that takes control of distribution away from the originators and produces records that can be backed up and archived for indefinite periods of possible retrieval.

Common sense dictates that anything sent via e-mail should not be illegal or even embarrassing if it were published in a newspaper.

Users should also be aware that it is a poor idea to insult people using e-mail. Sending *flames* that belittle, ridicule, and demean other people is likely to generate more of the same in response, and flaming is an ugly practice that distorts standards for public and private discourse. If a user or employee chooses to respond to a rude or demeaning e-mail, he or she should refrain from replying with the same rude or demeaning tone. Employees should work to maintain the moral high ground by refraining from obscenity, profanity, and vulgarity in written as well as in oral discourse. Not only is this a good habit in general, but it also avoids the possibility of enraging total strangers who may be physically or electronically dangerous. These best practices also apply to the home and family life. Criminal hackers have been known to damage credit ratings, participate in identity theft to rack up large bills in the victims' names, and even tamper with phone company accounts. In one notorious prank, hackers forwarded all incoming phone calls for the famous security expert Donn Parker, who is quite bald, to a hair restoration business.

Anonymizers are services that strip identifying information from e-mail and then forward the text to the indicated targets. However, even anonymizers respond to subpoenas demanding the identity of people involved in libel or threats. The Web site called *annoy.com* consistently posts messages that will annoy a substantial number of people as an exercise of United States First Amendment rights; however, even that service once had a particularly clear message on its refusal to tolerate abuse:

> **WARNING**
> It has come to our attention that certain people have been using annoy.com to deliver what some might consider to be threats of physical violence or harm to others.
>
> Do not mistake our commitment to freedom of speech for a license to abuse our service in this manner.
>
> We plan to cooperate fully with law enforcement agencies in whatever efforts they make to find you and punish you—even if it's some renegade authoritarian dictatorship. . .Free speech and annoy.com are not about harassment and definitely not about harm or violence. If you think for a second we will allow cowardly idiots to spoil our free speech party you are making a mistake. A huge mistake.

In the case of USENET, a global Internet discussion system, a message is forever: There are archives of USENET messages stretching back for a decade. Sending abusive or degrading messages online may not permanently damage a person's reputation, but it is not likely to *improve* anyone's prospects for getting or keeping a good job, especially if the sender's e-mail address refers back to a corporate affiliation.

48.2.3 Inappropriate Use of Corporate Identifiers.   Considerable controversy exists as to whether corporate policy should forbid corporate IDs for any personal use on the Internet. There is little reason for posting messages to newsgroups in the .alt hierarchy, and especially not to groups catering to or sympathetic to criminal activity. If employees of an organization want to participate in vigorous political discussion, conversations about sexual activity, and any other topic unrelated to their work, they are free to do so using their own Internet identities. Employers pay for corporate e-mail identities; people who want to post opinions about, say, basket weaving techniques should pay for their own access and leave their employer out of the postings.

The risks of damaging an organization's reputation by violating netiquette are high. Some abusers have themselves been abused by angry and unscrupulous Internauts. In one notorious early case, back in 1994, a naive executive spammed the Net—he posted messages in a couple of dozen newsgroups. In retaliation, his company's 800-number was posted to phone-sex discussion groups in the .alt hierarchy, resulting in thousands of irate and expensive phone calls by seekers of aural sex. Regular customers were unable to get through, and some staff resigned because of the offensive calls. The executive nearly lost his job.

An additional risk is that employees will inadvertently post company-confidential information to what they erroneously perceive as closed, private groups. Competitors or troublemakers can then exploit the information for competitive advantage or publicize it to harm the enterprise. Even if a discussion group or mailing really is closed, nothing prevents a participant from using or disseminating confidential information without permission. By the time the breach of security is discovered, it can be too late for remediation.

48.2.4 Blogs, Personal Web Sites, and Social Networking Sites.
Should employers be concerned about the creation of blogs and personal Web sites by employees? There have been cases in which employees made unwise or frankly derogatory comments about their current employers, with predictable consequences. It is much better to prevent such conflicts by establishing clear policies for employees that explicitly ban mention of the employer's name in personal publications and media such as blogs and Web sites. A variation can require corporate approval by the public relations or communications departments before material is published. Such policies are commonplace for control over what employees publish in interviews, newsletters, and other publications.

Some employees likely have personal pages in social-networking sites such as Facebook, Friendster, and MySpace. The same issues arise when employees make reference to their employer by name: How do employers feel about seeing a half-naked engineer waving a bottle of beer pictured on a Web page that displays their corporate name? Employment agreements can, and should, stipulate limitations on the use of corporate identity. Further complicating the matter is the growth of professional social networking sites such as LinkedIn. These sites encourage posting a "digital resume," which includes basic information about an individual's employment history. Much like personal networking sites, companies must set clear expectations on use and periodically monitor compliance through searches and visual inspection.

48.2.5 Disseminating and Using Incorrect Information.
The Internet and in particular the World Wide Web are in some ways as great a change in information distribution as the invention of writing 6,000 years ago and the invention of movable type 600 years ago. In all these cases, the inventions involved *disintermediation*: the elimination of intermediaries in the transmission of knowledge. Writing eliminated the oral historians; one could read information from far away and long ago without having to speak to a person who had personally memorized that knowledge. Print allowed a far greater distribution of knowledge than handwritten books and scrolls, eliminating an entire class of scribes who controlled access to the precious and rare records. The Net and the Web have continued this trend, with a radical increase in the number of people capable of being publishers. Where publishing once required printing presses, capital, and extensive administrative infrastructure, or at least relatively expensive mimeographs (1950s), photocopiers (1960s), and printers (1970s), today an individual can publish material relatively inexpensively, if not free. Many Internet Service Providers (ISPs) offer free Web-hosting services and places for people to join electronic communities of every imaginable type. Even if the individual does not have access to the Internet at home, and follows work policies on use, free access can be obtained from local libraries or the increasing number of free Internet hot spots.

Web pages can lead to visibility unheard of even a decade ago. For example, one young exhibitionist named Jennifer Kaye Ringley put up a Web site to display images of her home taken through Web-enabled cameras (Webcams); this "jennycam.org" site received up to *half a million hits per day* while it was in operation. Another young woman decided to put up a Web site devoted to one of her favorite literary characters, Nero Wolfe, in the mid-1990s. Within a few years, her site was so well respected that she was hired by a Hollywood filmmaker as a technical consultant on a series of Nero Wolfe movies. The fees she was paid, despite offering to help for free, helped her get through her Ph.D. studies in social psychology. It would have been virtually impossible for her to achieve this recognition by trying to publish her own hard-copy fan magazine; the paper might have reached a few hundred people, but the Web site reached many thousands.

Unfortunately, all of this disintermediation has negative implications as well as positive ones. Freedom from publishers has liberated the independent thinker from corporate influence, editorial limitations, and standards for house style. However, this freedom also liberated many people from responsible reporting, adequate research, and even the rudimentary principles of spelling and grammar. The dictum "Don't believe everything you read" is even more important when reading Web-based information. Individuals may publish incorrect versions of technical information (e.g., health sites that claim that massaging parts of the earlobe can cure many known diseases), unsubstantiated theories about historical and natural events (e.g., the Tungska Impact of 1908 was caused by an antimatter meteorite), and off-the-wall revisionist history (e.g., slavery in the United States was good for black people, and Hitler never persecuted Jews).

48.2.6   Hoaxes.   Pranksters have been using e-mail to fool gullible people for years using a particular sort of incorrect information: deliberate *hoaxes*. A hoax is a mischievous trick based on a made-up story. There are two major kinds of hoaxes circulating on the Internet: urban myths and false information about viruses. The archives in the urban myths Web sites are full of hilarious hoaxes, some of which have been circulating for years. Why don't they die out?

The problem is the nature of the Internet. Information is not distributed solely from a centrally controlled site; on the contrary, anyone can broadcast, or rebroadcast, any kind of data at any time. There is neither reliable creation dates nor obligatory expiry dates on files, so those receiving a five-year-old document may have no obvious way of recognizing its age, and they almost certainly have no simple way of identifying obsolete or incorrect information. All they see is that the document has been sent to them recently, often by someone they know personally.

48.2.6.1   Urban Myths.   Here are some notorious examples of the bizarre and sometimes disturbing urban myths that are thoroughly debunked on the Snopes.com Web site:

- **Expensive cookies.** Someone claims that a Neiman-Marcus employee charged $250 to a credit card for the recipe to some good chocolate chip cookies. This story has been traced to a false claim dating back to 1948 in which a store was accused of charging $25 for the recipe to a fudge cake.
- **Do not flash your car lights.** In a gang-initiation ritual, hoodlums drive down a highway with their car lights off. Innocent drivers, flashing their lights as a reminder, would become the new target victims, usually resulting in their deaths by the gang.
- **Watch out for poisoned needles.** Insane, vengeful druggies leave needles tipped with HIV+ blood in movie theater seats, gas pump handles, and telephone change-return slots.

- **Lose your kidneys.** The victim visits a foreign city, goes drinking with strangers, and wakes up in the morning in a bathtub of ice with two neat incisions through which both kidneys have been removed.

- **Poor little guy wants postcards.** Craig Shergold is just one of the many real or imaginary children about whom well-meaning people circulate chain letters asking for postcards, business cards, prayers, and even money. Shergold was born in 1980; when he was nine, he was diagnosed with brain cancer, and friends started a project to cheer him up—they circulated messages asking people to send him postcards so he could be listed in the *Guinness Book of World Records.* By 1991, he had received 30 million cards and an American philanthropist arranged for brain surgery, which worked: Shergold went into remission. The postcard deluge did not. By 1997, the local post office had received over *250 million* postcards for him, and he was long since sick of the whole project.

- **Wish you would stop Making a Wish.** Around the mid-1990s, some prankster inserted false information about the Make-a-Wish Foundation into the outdated chain letters concerning Shergold. The unfortunate organization was promptly inundated with e-mail and postal mail, none of which was in any way useful or relevant to its work.

48.2.6.2 Virus Myths. One category of hoaxes has become a perennial nuisance on the Net: virus myths. There is something wonderful about the willingness of gullible, well-meaning people to pass on ridiculous news about nonexistent viruses with impossible effects. One of the most famous is the Good Times "virus," which appeared around 1994. The myth and numerous variants have been circulating uninterruptedly for years. Every few years, there is a new outburst as some newcomers to the Internet encounter an old copy of the warnings and send it to everyone they know.

The original very short warning was as follows, including the incorrect punctuation:

> Here is some important information. Beware of a file called Goodtimes.

> Happy Chanukah everyone, and be careful out there. There is a virus on America Online being sent by E-Mail. If you get anything called "Good Times", DON'T read it or download it. It is a virus that will erase your hard drive. Forward this to all your friends. It may help them a lot.

The Good Times virus claimed that downloading a document or reading a document could cause harm; at that time, such a claim was impossible. Ironically, within a couple of years, it did in fact become possible to cause harm via documents because of the macro-language capabilities of MS-Word and other programs enabled for scripting. Over the rest of the 1990s, foolish people modified the name of the imaginary virus and added more details, sometimes claiming impossible effects such as destruction of computer hardware.

By 1997, the warnings were so ridiculous that an anonymous author distributed the following Monty Pythonesque satire:

> It turns out that this so-called hoax virus is very dangerous after all. Goodtimes will re-write your hard drive. Not only that, it will scramble any disks that are even close to your computer. It will recalibrate your refrigerator's coolness setting so all your ice cream goes melty. It will demagnetize the strips on all your credit cards, screw up the tracking on your television and use subspace field harmonics to scratch any CDs you try to play.

> It will give your ex-girlfriend your new phone number. It will mix Kool-aid into your fish tank. It will drink all your beer and leave dirty socks on the coffee table when company comes over.

It will put a dead kitten in the back pocket of your good suit pants and hide your car keys when you are late for work.

Goodtimes will make you fall in love with a penguin. It will give you nightmares about circus midgets. It will pour sugar in your gas tank and shave off both your eyebrows while dating your girlfriend behind your back and billing the dinner and hotel room to your Discover card.

It will seduce your grandmother. It does not matter if she is dead, such is the power of Goodtimes, it reaches out beyond the grave to sully those things we hold most dear.

It moves your car randomly around parking lots so you can't find it. It will kick your dog. It will leave libidinous messages on your boss's voice mail in your voice! It is insidious and subtle. It is dangerous and terrifying to behold. It is also a rather interesting shade of mauve.

Goodtimes will give you Dutch Elm disease. It will leave the toilet seat up. It will make a batch of Methamphetamine in your bathtub and then leave bacon cooking on the stove while it goes out to chase gradeschoolers with your new snowblower.

Unaware people circulate virus hoaxes because they receive the hoax from someone they know. Unfortunately, a personal friendship with a sender is no guarantee of the accuracy of their message. Some awfully nice people are gullible, well-meaning dupes of social engineers. Transmitting technical information about viruses (or any apprehended danger) without verifying that information's legitimacy and accuracy is a disservice to everyone. It makes it harder for experts to reach the public with warnings of real dangers, and it clutters up recipients' e-mail in-baskets with alarming information of limited or no use whatever.

48.2.6.3   Junk E-mail.   Unsolicited commercial e-mail (UCE) is derisively known as *junk* e-mail and also as *spam*. Junk e-mail is spawned by foolish (in the early days) or criminal (today) people who send out thousands or millions of identical messages to unwilling recipients. Junk e-mail clogs victims' in-baskets and wastes their time as they open these unwanted messages and take a few seconds to realize that they are junk. Junk e-mail containing pornographic images or advertising pornography may be highly offensive to the recipients. Junk may even push people's e-mail systems over their server limits if they are not picking up their messages regularly; in such cases, wanted e-mail may bounce because the mailbox is full. Today, junk e-mail is the primary vector for social engineering attacks such as *phishing* designed to trick recipients into compromising their privacy or their identification and authentication codes. (See Chapter 20 in this *Handbook* for more details of spam, phishing, and other tricks.)

Most junk e-mail uses forged headers; that is, the senders deliberately put misleading information in the From and Reply fields to avoid receiving angry responses from the victims of their criminal behavior. Forging e-mail headers is illegal in the states of Massachusetts, Virginia, and Washington. In these states, if the perpetrators are identified, it can lead to court cases and financial penalties for each message involved in the fraud.

In one famous, groundbreaking case, college student Craig Nowak sent out a few thousand junk e-mail messages and followed the instructions in his spam kit by putting a made-up Reply address using "@flowers.com" without checking to see if there really was such a domain. Indeed there was, and the owner of this reputable floral delivery service, Tracy LaQuey Parker, was none too pleased when her system was flooded with over 5,000 bounce messages and angry letters from customers saying that they would never do business with her again. She sued the student for damages and was awarded over $18,000 by a judge who said he wished he could have been even more punitive.[6]

In general, spam has become a mechanism for tricking unaware vendors into paying for illusory marketing services. It is sad to see e-mail advertising for Chinese industrial piping being sent to North American university professors; the victims are the hard-working Chinese industrialists who have been cheated by assurances from criminals promising to send their advertising to willing and well-qualified recipients.

Much of the remaining junk is sent out in the hope that a significant proportion of the recipients of the misspelled, absurd claims will be gulled into sending money—or their e-mail addresses—to drop boxes. For more information about such social engineering attacks, see Chapters 19 and 20 in this *Handbook*.

If you are involved in an e-mail discussion group, especially an unmoderated group, about a specific topic, do not post e-mail to members of the list on a subject that is outside the topic area. A typical class of inappropriate posting is an appeal for support of a worthy cause that has no, or only a tenuous, relation to the subject area. For example, someone might appeal for support to save whales in a discussion group about gardening: bad idea. The reasoning is "They like plants; probably environmentally sensitive; likely to be interested in conservation; therefore they will be glad to hear about whales." The problem is that such reasoning could be extended to practically any topic, disrupting the focus of the group. Such messages often cause angry retorts, which are typically sent by naive members to the entire list instead of only to the sender of the inappropriate mail. Then the angry retorts cause further angry responses about burdening the list with useless messages and soon the gardening group is mired in dissension and wasted effort, generating bad feeling and distrust.

As suggested in the preceding paragraph, if you see inappropriate messages on an e-mail list you care about, do not reply to the entire list; reply *nicely* and only to the sender, with possibly a copy to the moderator, if there is one. The reply should be temperate and polite.

48.2.6.4 *Chain Letters and Ponzi Schemes.* A particularly annoying form of junk e-mail is the chain letter. Some chain letters include ridiculous stories about terrible diseases and accidents that have befallen people who refused to forward the message. Others focus on getting victims to send money to someone at the top of a list of names, while adding their names to the bottom of the list, before sending it on to a specified number of recipients. Depending on the length of the list and the amount to be sent to the person on top, the theoretical return could be in the hundreds of thousands of dollars. In practice, only the originators of the scheme profit. After a while, all possible participants have been solicited with disappointing results, and the chains are broken in many places.

Another type of pyramid is known as a Ponzi scheme, which is an investment swindle in which high profits are promised and early investors are paid off with funds raised from later ones. The scam is named after Charles Ponzi (1882?–1949), a speculator who organized such a scheme in 1919 and 1920. The Ponzi scheme tricked thousands of people in Boston when Ponzi guaranteed a 50 percent profit on contributions in 45 days and a doubling of value in 90 days. The con man claimed he was redeeming 1-cent Spanish postal certificates for 6-cent U.S. stamps—a claim ridiculed by financial analysts at the time. Nonetheless, Ponzi took in around $15 million in 1920 dollars and stole around $8 million, paying out the rest to the early participants in order to develop credibility. Six banks collapsed because they invested their depositors' funds in the scheme. Ponzi eventually served over three years in jail but escaped in 1925.[7]

The modern-day e-mail Ponzi scheme typically includes passionate assurances from vaguely identified people about how skeptical they were about the scheme, but how they succumbed to curiosity, participated in the scheme, and earned vast amounts of money (e.g., $50,000) within a couple of weeks. The letters often include assurances that everything is legal and point to nonexistent postal information phone lines or claim "As Seen on TV" at various points in the letter.

These letters instruct the victim to send a small amount of money (typically $1 or $2) to a short list of about four people to receive their "reports." The victim is then instructed to add his or her name and address to the list, while removing the first one, before sending a copy of the new letter to as many people as possible. Some letters go through computations involving such assumptions as "Imagine you send out a hundred, a thousand, or ten thousand messages and get a mere 1%, 2%, or 10% response" and then promise enormous returns. In fact, the "reports" are nothing but one-page, meaningless blurbs about chain letters. The scammers are trying to get around regulations such as the U.S. Post Office's bar against fraudulent uses of the mail.

Here is the exact text of a letter sent on December 1, 2000, by V. J. Bellinger of the Operations Support Group of the United States Postal Inspection Service in Newark, New Jersey. It has some interesting information that should be helpful to readers attempting to convince employees (or family and friends) that such chain e-mail involving postal addresses is illegal.

> A chain letter or a multi-level marketing program is actionable under the Postal Lottery, False Representation, and/or Mail Fraud Statutes if it contains three elements: prize, consideration and chance. Prize is usually in the form of money, commissions, or something else of value that the solicitation claims you will receive. Consideration is the required payment to the sponsor in order to obtain the prize. Chance is determined by the activities of participants over whom the mailer has no control. These types of schemes constitute lotteries are barred from the mails because they violate the following statutes: Title 18, United States Code, Sections 1302 and 1341 and Title 39, United States Code, Section 3005.
>
> In attempts to appear legal, many chain letter or multi-level marketing mailings offer, for a fee, a product, or "report." However, since the success of the program is dependent on the number of people willing to participate, all three elements that constitute a violation continue to be present.
>
> The promoter of this scheme has been advised of the potential violations involved and has been requested to discontinue this type of mailing activity. . ..

A superficially similar phenomenon is known as multilevel marketing. In this non-fraudulent, legitimate system of selling products and services, people are encouraged to recruit distributors from among their friends and acquaintances, but the emphasis is on the value of the products. No one claims that anyone is going to become wealthy without work, and there is no demand for investments. The products have an established market, and the company makes money through sales, not through recruitment.

48.2.6.4.1   Practical Guidelines

- Do not participate in any scheme that relies on forwarding large numbers of letters or e-mail messages to everyone you know or to strangers.
- Differentiate between pyramid frauds and legitimate multilevel marketing systems: The former emphasize enrolling participants, whereas the latter emphasize the value of products and services.
- Do not participate in alleged multilevel marketing systems if they require substantial investments.

- If you are interested in a multilevel marketing operation:
  - Check out the owners and officers.
  - Talk to people who have bought the products to see if they are happy with their purchases.
  - Contact your local Better Business Bureau to see if there have been any complaints.
- Do not send money to suspected pyramid frauds.
- Work with your colleagues to demonstrate how a pyramid fraud takes money from a growing number of later victims and shifts it to people who participate earlier in the fraud. Reinforce the fact that fraud is illegal, even though the prospect of early participation might seem to yield results.

48.2.6.5 *Get-Rich-Quick Schemes.* Other get-rich-quick schemes on the Net play on the victims' wishful thinking, their lack of skepticism, and usually on a lack of common sense. There have been claims that you can earn a quarter of a million dollars a year by grooming poodles in your home. Or that you can become a millionaire by working four hours a week, sending out promotional literature for products you do not even have to sell. Often, dangerous people promulgate some such schemes; for example, some extremist militia groups have been charging people hundreds of dollars to learn how to defraud the government by claiming liens on government property and then pledging the nonsensical liens as collateral for loans. Other criminals circulate programs for generating fraudulent credit card numbers and using them to steal goods. In other cases, criminals charge money to teach victims how to falsify their bad credit records so they can obtain yet more fraudulent credit, all the while claiming that their criminal methods are 100 percent legal.

From a corporate standpoint, such chain letters and schemes waste bandwidth and pose a potential for serious embarrassment when enterprise resources are used to spread the nonsensical material. However, corporate security can win favor with users by helping them avoid the pitfalls of such fraud, even when using their own computer systems. The benefits are particularly strong when helping employees to teach their own children how to avoid this kind of trouble.

To illustrate the trouble kids can get into using these techniques, consider the case of Drew Henry Madden. In 1996, this 16-year-old Australian boy from Brisbane, just after leaving school, started defrauding businesses using stolen and forged credit card numbers. He stole $18,000 of goods and, in February 1997, pled guilty to 104 counts of fraud and was sentenced to a year in jail. However, investigators uncovered additional fraud, and it turned out that he had stolen an additional $100,000 in goods and services. In October 1997, he pled guilty to another 294 counts of fraud and was given an additional suspended sentence. His defense attorney blamed poor security for the losses: "Madden started with very minor credit card fraud, but it escalated alarmingly, because the safeguards were so inadequate." Despite the youngster's unusual revenue stream, his mother appeared to have accepted his globetrotting ways and massive purchases of lottery tickets without comment. At one point, she told reporters, "If we were a wealthy family he'd be at a private school, where his talents could be directed properly."

A relatively new kind of fraud on the Internet is the diploma mill. These organizations pretend to be educational institutions; actually, they are one or more fraudulent individuals who sell bogus diplomas purporting to represent recognized degrees but that fool no one but the purchaser. While diploma mills are not accredited, the lack of accreditation does not automatically implicate a school as a fraudulent entity.

48.3   THREATS TO PEOPLE AND SYSTEMS.   One particular class of e-mail deserves a special mention: threats. Threatening e-mails may target people, systems, organizations, or the processes that these entities rely on. As with the other types of illegal activity on the Internet, proper education, awareness, and response can limit the number of future victims.

48.3.1   Threats of Physical Harm.   Anyone who receives threats through e-mail has a right, and possibly a duty, to inform local law enforcements officials. In today's climate of fear and violence, any threat warrants attention. In addition to the distress such messages can generate, they may be warning signs of serious trouble. In particular, threats about violence at work, at school, or against any definable group may be the early warning that allows authorities to step in to defuse a potentially explosive situation.

Sending threatening e-mail is not an acceptable joke or a minor prank, especially if the threat involves violence. Some people, believing that they can mask their real identity, have foolishly sent death threats to the White House; because the Secret Service is obligated by law to investigate *all* threats to the president and the first family, agents show up within a few hours to interrogate the miscreants. For example, youngsters in the tenth grade at Profile High School in Bethlehem, New Hampshire, sent death threats to the White House Web site from their school computers. The messages were traced within minutes by the Secret Service, the children were suspended from school, and they lost their Internet privileges for the next two years.

48.3.2   Pedophiles Online.   This section applies primarily to training users for protection of their children.

"Pedophilia" is defined as sexual arousal in response to contact with or images of prepubescent children. Some pedophiles misrepresent themselves as youngsters in chat rooms or via e-mail and trick children into forming friendships with what they believe are peers. In one notorious case, Paul Brown Jr., a 47-year-old man, misrepresented himself as a 15-year-old boy in e-mail to a 12-year-old girl in New Jersey. The victim's mother stumbled onto the long-range relationship when she found sitting on her own doorstep a package from her daughter to a man she did not know; the child had put the wrong postage on it and the post office had sent it back. Opening the package, she found a videotape that showed her daughter cavorting naked in front of the family video camera. The distraught mother searched her daughter's room and discovered a pair of size 44 men's underpants in one of the child's bureau drawers.

Brown was arrested in February 1997. Police found correspondence with at least 10 other teenage girls across the country, through which Brown convinced his young victims, some as young as 12, to perform various sexual acts in front of cameras and to send him the pictures and videotapes. He pleaded guilty in June to enticing a minor into making pornography. In August 1997, at his sentencing hearing, one of his many victims told the court that she had suffered ridicule and humiliation as a result of her entrapment and had left her school to escape the trauma. She accused Brown of emotional rape. Displaying an astonishing interpretation of his own behavior, Brown said at his sentencing hearing, "It was just bad judgment on my part." Using good judgment, the court sentenced him to five years of incarceration.

In March 2000, Patrick Naughton, a former executive of the INFOSEEK online company, pled guilty to having crossed state lines to commit statutory rape of a child. In August, FBI officials said that Naughton had been providing help in law enforcement investigations of pedophilia on the Net. In return for his cooperation, prosecutors asked the court for five years of probation (instead of a possible 15 years in prison), counseling, a $20,000 fine (instead of the maximum $250,000), and an agreement not to have "unapproved" contact with children and to stay out of sex chat rooms online.

The problem of Internet-enabled pedophile stalking has reached international dimensions. In January 1999, police forces around the world cooperated to track and close down a worldwide ring of pedophiles trafficking in child pornography through the Net. In June 2000, child safety experts warned the U.S. congressional committee on child online protection that with the average age of online users declining (children between the ages of two and seven are among the fastest-growing user cohorts on the Internet), children increasingly are put at risk by their careless or ignorant online activities. Parry Aftab, a children's advocate, told committee members that 3,000 children were kidnapped in the United States last year after responding to online messages posted by their abductors. A recent survey of teenage girls found 12 percent had agreed to meet strangers who had contacted them online.

48.3.3 Viruses and Other Malicious Code.   As of 2008, the WildList (www.wildlist.org) reports over 2,000 distinct forms of malicious program code commonly circulating in cyberspace. There are many more types recorded by antivirus researchers, but they have not been seen infecting significant numbers of user computers. Most of these harmful programs are limited to antivirus laboratories and to the computers of virus hobbyists—people who derive pleasure from playing with danger. For more information about viruses and other malware, see Chapters 16, 17, 18, and 41 in this *Handbook*.

Employers should have policies clearly forbidding the creation, exchange, and storage of malicious software on corporate systems.

48.3.4 Spyware and Adware.   In December 1999, computer scientist, cybercrime investigator, and writer Richard Smith became curious about a program called *zBubbles* that he had installed on his system to improve online shopping. Created by Alexa, a subsidiary of e-tailer Amazon.com, the program provided competitive information about alternative and possibly cheaper sources for particular products. However, Smith discovered that there was more going on than met the eye.

Smith monitored his own Internet traffic while he was using zBubbles by using a packet sniffer, a tool that displays details of every piece of information being transmitted through a network connection. He found that zBubbles was sending a steady stream of information about him and his surfing habits to Alexa, including his home address, the titles of DVDs he had browsed on Buy.com, and the details of an airline ticket he had verified online. In addition, the program even continued to send information regularly to Alexa's servers even when Smith was not using his browser. It was learned that zBubbles was not the only program sending information back to its makers.

Many programs are available that, once installed, report on the Web sites you visit, which banner advertisements you click, what products you search for, and any other information the programs have been designed to acquire. Even widely used downloading software, such as NetZip, has been shown to report to its providers on the names of every file downloaded by each user.

Sometimes these programs are informally known as "E.T." applications, in a reference to Steven Spielberg's movie of that name, in which an extraterrestrial strives to "phone home"—exactly what the spyware programs are doing.

The term "spyware" is applied to any technology that transmits information without the knowledge of its user. Several programs distributed without charge through the Internet secretly collect information about the user, monitor user behavior, and then send those data to advertisers. The more general class of monitoring software that collects information for use by advertisers is known as *advertising-supported software* or *adware.* These programs allow freeware to make money for its creators by generating revenue based on how many users transmit information to the advertisers about their habits.

Although defenders of the advertising-supported programs claim that they are harmless, privacy advocates argue that the issue is control: Do users know what these programs are doing, or are they collecting and transmitting information covertly? Some adware comes with complicated contracts containing complex legal language to bury the fact that they will monitor and report user behavior. Worse yet, many such contracts explicitly authorize the software supplier to alter the privacy conditions without notification and, preposterously, instruct the user to check the contracts on the Web frequently. No one has the time to monitor countless suppliers to see if privacy conditions have been altered, especially if there is no attempt to highlight changes.

Another issue is that some spyware modules have used *stealth* technology characteristic of viruses, Trojan horses, and other malicious software. For example, some adware (e.g., TSADBOT) installs itself as a system process and is not listed in the Windows task list. Therefore, it cannot easily by aborted by a user. TSADBOT also resists removal; even if the carrier product is uninstalled, TSADBOT persists. If a user's firewall blocks outbound transmission by the TSADBOT process, the spyware initiates attempts to reach its target at a rate of 10 per second, potentially leading to central processing unit (CPU) and network resource overload.

Spyware, like any software, can contain errors that cause system problems. In particular, components of the Aureate/Radiate spyware have been shown to cause system instability and crashes.

One of the most egregious cases of spyware erupted in 1999, when it was discovered that CometCursor, a supplier of cute cartoon-character cursors aimed at children, was sending information back to its servers about what the children were browsing on the Net. According to some attorneys, this kind of covert data gathering about children may be a violation of the U.S. federal Child Online Privacy Protection Act.

Several free software programs have been written to help users identify and remove spyware. In addition, personal firewalls can usually identify and block unauthorized outbound communications; the free version of ZoneAlarm, for example, does so effectively. Today's antimalware programs (e.g., Norton Antivirus) include antispyware functions. There are also many specialized programs available that run in the background to monitor and thwart attempts to install spyware and adware; examples include Lavasoft's Ad-Aware and Computer Associates' PestPatrol.

48.4   THREATS TO PRODUCTIVITY.   Some activities and phenomena are nuisances to employers principally because of their noxious effects on productivity and their abuse of corporate resources. Junk e-mail and mailstorms, for example, are a problem because they saturate resources, not because they cause specific harm to the organization or to its employees. However, chain letters, get-rich-quick schemes, online auctions, online gambling, excessive online shopping, and Internet addiction can be directly harmful to employees and others.

48.4.1 Inefficient Use of Corporate E-mail. The next sections focus on problems caused by mistakes in the use of e-mail—mistakes that can cause annoyance, inefficiency, and potential disruption of critical business processes.

48.4.1.1 Forwarding E-mail to Personal Accounts. Employees may be tempted to forward their corporate e-mail traffic to their personal e-mail addresses for convenience, or when they have no convenient way of accessing their corporate e-mail system from outside the office. Such forwarding should be forbidden by policy unless virtual private networks (VPNs) or other strongly encrypted channels are used for the employee's private e-mail.

E-mail and other traffic on the Internet have no inherent confidentiality. In theory, anyone capable of intercepting TCP/IP packets anywhere during transmission can breach confidentiality. Thus, again in theory, anyone with access to the equipment of Internet Service Providers, Internet backbone transmission lines, and even to the public switched telephone network can intercept packets. With downlink footprints from satellite relays amounting to square miles, practically anything can in theory be intercepted from much of the traffic circulating on the Internet.

However, in practice, reported breaches of confidentiality have almost all resulted from data access at the end points, not in transit. Insider attacks and breaches of server security have been responsible for most of the data interceptions that have reached the press and the courts.

A practical impediment to effective interception of meaningful data in transit is the datagram routing that underlies the Internet: Datagrams are packets of information with origin and destination information; store-and-forward transmission allows these datagrams to be sent through the Internet via different routes from other packets in a message stream. Routing tables can be updated in real time to reflect changes in traffic density or availability of specific links to other destinations on the Internet, so there is no guarantee that packets from the same message will travel the same route or arrive in the proper sequence (sequence numbers allow reassembly of the original message). Therefore, seizing individual packets at random anywhere other than the origin and destination of packets is unlikely to result in very much result for the effort.

Nonetheless, best practices do recommend that encryption be used for communication of sensitive data; therefore, many organizations install Virtual Private Networks (VPN) for communication with established trading partners. VPN software is also available for "tunneling" through the Internet from a remote workstation over nonsecure communications lines. A simple example of such a link-encryption function is the Web-based e-mail services that use SSL to establish a secure link to the e-mail server (i.e., they use https instead of just plain http). The user can pick up e-mail from the corporate server without having it forwarded in the clear to an insecure external e-mail service. Some of the e-mail products include facilities for direct communication between a secure e-mail server and the users' e-mail client.

Using "VPN tunneling software" as a search string in the Google search engine brings up hundreds of hits, many of them for specific products and data sheets, so readers will be able to find a solution that fits their needs.

48.4.1.2 Mislabeling the Subject Line. Many people make the mistake of creating new messages to a correspondent by finding any old message from that person and replying to it. The problem is that these people usually leave the old subject intact,

resulting in ridiculous situations such as finding a critically important message in July in an e-mail labeled "Birthday party 12 May."

Not all e-mail messages are created equal; some are destined for the trash heap, if not of history, at least of the e-mail system. That decision is sometimes made automatically as a function of the subject line. For example, a user adds the subject line of a joke to an e-mail filter, resulting in future messages with that subject ending up in the junk mail folder. Someone replies to the joke message with important information, and the mail filter sees the subject and automatically moves the message to the recipient's junk mail folder. The recipient may never see the important information, as most people do not actively monitor their junk folders.

Another problem with mislabeled subjects occurs when someone embeds more than one distinct topic in an e-mail message whose subject line implies otherwise. For example, suppose an e-mail message subject reads "Next week's meeting" but the sender includes an urgent request for action today on some critical issue; there is a good chance the receiver may not open the message right away if other messages seem more important.

Employees should make their subject line as descriptive as possible without turning it into a paragraph. Some e-mail systems truncate subject lines in the display of messages that a user sees; it makes sense to put keywords at the front of the subject. Encourage staff to use prefixes such as "MSIA:" or "SGS:" to help organize their messages. Using standard formats in subject lines can help too. For example, faculty and staff in the MSIA program at Norwich University refer to an issue in a particular seminar by using the form "MSIA c.s" in their subject line, where c represents the class (e.g., 24 for students starting in December 2009) and s represents the seminar number.

As for confidentiality, consider that using the To and CC ("carbon copy"—a bit of historical detritus) fields in e-mail makes all recipient addresses visible to all recipients. This situation is usually helpful in internal e-mail because team members can see who has gotten the message, but it can be annoying in external e-mail. Why should a list of dozens, or even hundreds, of names of strangers be distributed freely among them, without the explicit permission of all concerned? Who knows where that information will end up? Use of the BCC ("blind carbon copy") field can eliminate the ability of recipients being able to see all of the intended recipients for the original message. This extra step is a good piece of e-mail etiquette, whether the message is business or personal. The BCC field is also useful for internal e-mail when the list of recipients is very large, but it is not important for people to know exactly who received the message.

These simple suggestions can make e-mail more effective as a communications tool.

48.4.1.3 *First e-Impressions.*   When you receive an e-mail message from a stranger, do you care whether it has spelling mistakes and grammar mistakes? What about offensive language and off-color humor? Does the context matter? For example, do you apply the same standards to e-mail referring to business matters as to informal communications about a hobby?

Researchers at the University of Chicago have been investigating the effects of e-mail on perceptions of character. Psychologist Nicholas Epley and colleagues examined oral exchanges on conversational topics by phone between randomly selected people using six assigned questions. They then transcribed the oral conversations and used exactly the same answers for the written, e-mail version of the question and answer sessions.[8]

Their results were interesting. The questioners had been given false biographical sketches of the people they were communicating with, indicating substandard intelligence or normal intelligence, as well as different pictures showing neat people or slobs. Subjects who used the phone to listen to the prescribed responses had favorable impressions of their interlocutor's intelligence, regardless of the bios and pictures. In contrast, "Via e-mail, however, students held onto their first impressions, continuing to assume their partners had substandard intelligence, for example, if that's what the biographical sketch indicated."

If this research is confirmed, the lesson is that when using e-mail, first impressions really do count. Professionals should carefully review e-mail messages for acceptable writing, including word choice, punctuation, capitalization, and spelling.

48.4.1.4 E-mail Disclaimers. Author MK recently received a 30-word e-mail message from a very nice reader in Britain and noticed that his e-mail system added the following astonishing disclaimer, which is quoted in its sonorous totality, including British spelling, after scrubbing it of identifying details:

> This e-mail, its contents and any files or attachments transmitted with it are intended solely for the addressee(s) and may be legally privileged and/or confidential. Access by any other party is unauthorised without the express written permission of the sender.
>
> If you have received this e-mail in error you may not copy or use the contents, files, attachments or information in any way nor disclose the same to any other person. Please destroy it and contact the sender on the number printed above, via the <Name of Bank> switchboard on +44 (0) nnnn nnnnnn for <place1> and + 44 (0) nnnn nnnnnn for <place2> or via e-mail by return.
>
> Internet communications are not secure unless protected using strong cryptography. This e-mail has been prepared using information believed by the author to be reliable and accurate, but <Name of Bank> makes no warranty or representation, express or implied, as to its accuracy or completeness and is not liable to you or to anyone else for any loss or damage in connection with any transmission sent by the Bank to you over the Internet. <Name of Bank> makes no warranty that any information or material is free from any defects or viruses.
>
> In particular <Name of Bank> does not accept responsibility for changes made to this e-mail after it was sent. If you suspect that this e-mail may have been amended or intercepted, please contact the sender in the manner stated above. If this transmission includes files or attachments, please ensure that they are opened within the relevant application to ensure full receipt. If you experience difficulties, please refer back to the sender in the manner stated above.
>
> Any opinions expressed in this transmission are those of the author and do not necessarily reflect the opinions of the Bank and may be subject to change without notice.
>
> Please note that for the purposes of this document all references to <Name of Bank> or the Bank shall be taken to mean <Name of Bank> (place) Limited or any other member of the <Bigger> Bank Group. Nothing in this transmission shall or shall be deemed to constitute an offer or acceptance of an offer or otherwise have the effect of forming a contract by electronic communication.

MK commented in his response, "Did you know that your message has 30 words (152 bytes including spaces) whereas your disclaimer has 367 words (2,177 bytes)? That's the lowest signal-to-noise ratio (6.5 percent useful information out of the total and a 1:73 signal:noise ratio) I've ever seen outside a copy-of-copy-of-copy chain. Please congratulate your attorneys on using maximum of bandwidth for minimum content!"

Cluttering up e-mail messages this way is a waste of bandwidth. It is worse in offices where people copy entire messages without editing the contents, resulting in copy-of-copy-of-copy chains that spread like cancerous eruptions through in-baskets throughout the organization. Some well-meaning folks even include the detailed headers in their copies.

As a matter of courtesy and good sense, when one replies to a message, it is a simple matter to strip nonessentials out of the copy of the original. Senders can use ellipses (... for cuts within a sentence, ... for cuts crossing sentence boundaries) to signal gaps, but usually one or two snips are enough to clean up the copy so that the reader can get the gist of the conversation without having to wade through reams of superfluous stuff. Unfortunately, this recommendation does not seem to be used much in practice.

48.4.1.5 *Centralized Distribution Lists.*

Organizations may grow large enough that there is significant turnover among the staff. Not only do new staff members periodically join the group, but also staff members move from one functional group to another; for example, a staff member may change from being an assistant director in one program to being an administrative director in another. Occasionally, staff members may leave the group altogether.

A primitive way of maintaining distribution lists is to name a "Keeper-of-the-Lists" to maintain the list of all staff members; however, there is no link between the file and the mailing lists that each member of the group must maintain to be able to distribute e-mail to appropriate individuals or groups. The independent files are almost certain to diverge from a centralized and accurate list. For example, a message that should be sent to all current employees may end up missing several new members and including staff members who no longer work in the target group.

Trying to make many people maintain their own copies of several distribution lists is a hopeless cause: Even with the best will in the world, people will inevitably forget to update their lists and therefore:

- Some mailings will miss legitimate recipients.
- Some people will receive messages they have no business reading.

There are at least four solutions that would rectify such a problem.

1. One can implement a central e-mail sever (e.g., Microsoft Exchange Server), switch all users to a centrally controlled e-mail client (e.g., Microsoft Outlook), and define corporate distribution lists maintained by the Keeper-of-the-Lists. All users will automatically access the one and only distribution list for each group without manual intervention.

2. One can install widely available list-server software to allow centralized creation and maintenance of specific lists; for example, SGS-ALL, SGS-DIRECTORS, MSIA-STAFF, MSIA-INSTRUCTORS, and the like create lists that all employees can use in addressing e-mail.

3. One can switch all users to any e-mail client that supports exportable mailing lists. Updated corporate distribution lists can then be sent to all users. However, this solution still requires manual intervention by users: Everyone has to replace an old list by the new list.

4. One can create a discussion group on a public server (e.g., Yahoo Groups) to define closed groups. These groups provide automatic access to mailing lists. Unfortunately, this approach has serious problems:
   - There are security concerns about using such groups for corporate communications.
   - It seems inappropriate to put a necessary production application on a free resource completely out of the control of the organization.

48.4.1.6   HTML E-mail.   One of the six fundamental attributes of information that we protect is integrity, one aspect of which is consistency with the originally stored data (see Chapter 3 in this *Handbook*). When someone goes to the trouble of producing an elegantly formatted memorandum, or other document, and sends it out to recipients, everyone would like to preserve data integrity by seeing the same appearance on all the systems sharing that document.

Unfortunately, sending formatted messages as e-mail messages (as distinct from attachments) does not guarantee preservation of the exact appearance of the source material.

Attractive, well-formatted e-mail messages with boldface, italics, different point sizes, and the like usually get transmitted as HTML (hypertext markup language) to recipients' mailboxes, where most people's e-mail clients (Eudora, Netscape, Outlook, etc.) allow the funny-looking code to be reconstituted into something similar to the original.

The word "similar" is mentioned rather than "exactly like" because HTML does not necessarily control the final appearance of text on a recipient's system. The codes refer to types, not exact matches, of fonts; thus a sender might want to use, say, 24-point Arial as a Heading 1 display but a particular recipient might have defined Heading 1 as, say, Times Roman 14 point. A two-page original document may appear to be a three-page document to one recipient and a one-page document to another.

More significantly, though, many people turn off HTML e-mail for security reasons. All such formatted e-mail gets converted automatically into plain ASCII text. A correspondent once sent author Kabay a message that read: "Note: The on-line course evaluation system may be used from room, lab and home—anywhere Internet access is available. / Overview: . . . . Failure to complete a course evaluation will result in a 'hold' being placed on the student's final grades."

The fragment of message that follows shows the result of MS-Outlook auto-conversion of the original formatted HTML message to ASCII:

```
Note: The on-line course evaluation system may be used
from room, lab and home ? anywhere Internet access is
available.

Overview: . . . . Failure to complete a course
evaluation will result in a ?hold? being placed on the
student?s final grades.
```

In the conversion process, the original apostrophes turned into question marks ("?hold?") because the sender was using "curly" quotation marks instead of the straight ones in the word-processing package or e-mail editor. If one cares to prevent this peculiarity when using MS-Word, one has to turn off the option in the {Tools | AutoCorrect | AutoFormat As You Type} screen by unchecking the box labeled {"Straight quotes" with "smart quotes"}.

In addition, it looks like a dash character may have been in the text in the first section (labeled "Note"). One can turn that conversion off in the same menu by unchecking {Hyphens (–) with dash . . .}.

A much simpler solution to prevent the mess is simply to send unformatted ASCII text in all outbound messages by selecting that option in one's e-mail package.

Some people try to send files that should look the same on a recipient system and the originating system by attaching word processing documents: for example, Word DOC files, WordPerfect WPD files, or Rich Text Format (RTF) files (and so on).

Unfortunately, even these attempts do not necessarily work as planned, since lack of shared fonts, different default paper sizes (different countries may use different sizes), and different printing margins (resulting from installation of different printers) may cause the documents not to look precisely the same on all systems.

So if the exact appearance of a message one is sending via e-mail is critically important, one should send the content *and* its format in a way that is (largely) platform independent; for example, Acrobat PDF (Portable Document Format) files. Although even they do not necessarily result in perfect rendition of the author's intentions across systems, PDF files are far more likely to succeed than the other methods mentioned. One can create PDF files in a number of ways; some systems have Adobe Acrobat installed so that one can either "print" to an Acrobat driver to create the PDF files or even just click a toolbar button to do so from within the word processor. MS-Office 2007, for example, provides the ability to Save as PDF in all of its major components. Other packages exist that are less expensive (and generally less feature-rich) than the full Adobe Acrobat software, but nonetheless allow users to create PDF files easily. One can type "create PDF" into a Web search engine to find lots of choices.

48.4.1.7 Distribution Lists in E-mail.
Recently a nice lady in the human resources (HR) department at our university sent out a note to a dozen people reminding us that we had not yet finished signing up for our new medical insurance coverage.

Unfortunately, she put all the e-mail addresses into the CC (carbon copy) line where they were visible to everyone in the list. Predictably, someone on the list composed a response to her, hit Reply All, and sent some mildly personal information about the state of her medical concerns to all the recipients on the original list, none of whom had any interest in her problems.

Luckily, there was not a lot of private information in that message, but it did prompt the realization that many people unthinkingly use the CC line for addresses to a distribution list and that many people unthinkingly use Reply All for replies to every e-mail message.

The combination can lead to embarrassing violations of confidentiality; when the HR department staff use CC instead of BCC (the Blind Carbon Copy function that conceals the distribution list), the Reply All function can inadvertently violate privacy.

In this case, there was no particularly sensitive material revealed, but a different case could easily violate HIPAA (Health Information Portability and Accountability Act) and the university's rules on employee confidentiality.

Once employees understand the issue, they will learn not to use CC for distribution lists when the intention is to communicate with individuals; by default, everyone should use the BCC list unless there is a need to stimulate group discussion of an issue or it is important for the members of the group to know who received the message.

It is important not to dismiss this issue as too easy or too obvious to bother with. "Against stupidity, the gods themselves contend in vain," wrote Friedrich von Schiller in his *Maid of Orleans* (Die Jungfrau von Orleans) in 1801. Nonetheless, the CC + Reply All habit becomes a covert channel for release of confidential information for people who refuse to keep an address book, and simply look up any old e-mail and Reply All to it as a lazy way of sending a new message.

If you doubt the seriousness of the problem, take some time to look through your own archives of e-mail and count how many obvious cases there are of e-mails with inappropriate subject lines and inappropriate distribution lists sitting in your received folders. Unfortunately, you may be dismayed by the results of your research.

48.4.1.8 *Effective Use of BCC.* As discussed, the problems caused by CC are worse when the recipients do not know each other. One often receives messages from technically unsophisticated correspondents who put dozens of e-mail addresses in the CC field even though many of the recipients are total strangers to each other. Such exposure of e-mail addresses always makes security staff nervous; who knows whether everyone on the list is trustworthy? Even if the list is not misused for outright spam, people often Reply All with useless information, effectively adding people to discussion lists that they never wanted to be on.

One particularly annoying habit is to Reply All with a comment stemming from some initial message. People then generate a series of increasingly long messages including copies of all the previous copies of the ostensibly clever repartee, driving some users to generate an addition to their junk mail filters.

The habit of using Reply All is annoying enough when a reply does not in fact have to go to everyone on the original distribution list. However, Reply All is a positive menace if it is coupled with the abhorrent practice of using an existing e-mail message as a shortcut to creating a new one with a completely different topic, as discussed in Section 48.4.1.2.

48.4.1.9 *Managing Private E-mail at Work.* What is wrong with using corporate e-mail for jokes, invitations, and the like? One issue is the waste of bandwidth. Some people find the quality of the jokes, hoaxes, and cheering sessions low enough to be irritating. Worst yet, the tolerance level for what is considered appropriate in the workplace may vary by individual, requiring the utmost care and consideration for everyone. Another problem arises with politically sensitive messages, such as announcements or viewpoints that some members of a group may find offensive. Why should everyone in the group be subjected to a barrage of unsolicited e-mail just because they work somewhere?

The question also raises some valuable and instructive points about appropriate-use policies for e-mail. Corporations must have a formal written policy on appropriate use of official e-mail. Managers should frame clear written policies that any of the staff members can easily consult for guidance about suitable and unsuitable content for personal messages using corporate mailing addresses. Such policies will reduce possible disappointments and resentments resulting from decisions based on unwritten expectations. In addition, any hint of discrimination based on particular political or religious biases will have to be scrutinized to ensure that the organization is not subject to legal repercussions.

An easy tool that employees can develop is a voluntary mailing list of nonwork e-mail addresses for nonwork e-mail. A Yahoo group http://groups.yahoo.com/, for example, offers many benefits over an informal list in the CC: or To: field. Jokes and the like can thus be distributed only to willing recipients, since joining can be purely optional. However, employees must always remember that any activities occurring on company equipment, or using company computing resources, may be viewed by authorized parties and could potentially hurt their reputation or, even worse, set them up for legal problems.

48.4.2 Mail Storms. A peculiar kind of junk e-mail is sent by accident. These flurries of unwanted messages are called *mail storms*.

Most of us belong to mailing lists; many of us have more than one e-mail address; some of us use autoforwarding to shift e-mail from one address to another automatically;

and a few of us use automated responses on our e-mail accounts to let correspondents know when we are out of the office or unable to respond quickly.

All of these factors can contribute to mail storms.

48.4.2.1 Autoforwarding.

A mail storm occurs when computers begin sending mail to each other without human intervention. Sometimes mail storms can become a denial of service by saturating communications channels and other resources. The e-mail–enabled worms such as Melissa, the I-love-you message, and others, are examples of malicious software programs whose authors deliberately wrote them to create mail storms.

In a simple situation, an employee leaving on vacation decides to receive company e-mail using a personal account on an ISP with a global presence. By setting an auto-forward command on the company account, all incoming mail was sent to the personal e-mail account. Unfortunately, on the remote tropical island where the vacationer spent two weeks, it was impossible to access the worldwide ISP without paying a surcharge of $6 a minute for long-distance service to the nearest dial-up node. This proved too expensive, and no e-mails were received or sent.

Meanwhile, the company account dutifully forwarded every message it received to the proper personal account—which had a tiny storage limit of 250 messages. That limit was reached within a few days. At that point, every inbound message generated a bounce informing the sender that the recipient's mailbox was full.

The very first full-mailbox message sent to the company account was autoforwarded back to the vacationer's personal mailbox. That copy of the full-mailbox message generated a second mailbox-full message, which then got bounced back to the company account, and so on without letup. Eventually, even the company mailbox filled up, and then the two e-mail systems continued chattering at each other indefinitely. The number of e-mail messages that can be generated by this kind of infinite loop is a function of the latency of the positive feedback system that the user has accidentally created. For example, if it takes exactly one minute for a bounce message to be returned to the originating site, then each message causing an initial error can create 60 additional messages per hour. However, every new message from another sender that arrives at the originating mailbox will generate its own new set of bouncing messages in infinite loops. It is not uncommon to see tens of thousands of messages accumulating in the recipient's mailbox if nobody notices the loops with traffic mounting steadily into hundreds or thousands of messages per hour bouncing between the accounts. Eventually the mail servers can crash because of the overwhelming traffic; system administrators then have to turn off the autoforwarding and block mail from the affected accounts.

An out-of-office message can inadvertently create mail storms through a *race condition* (see Chapter 39 in this *Handbook*). For example, two employees both enable out-of-office messages, and one sends an e-mail to the other before leaving the e-mail client. A mail storm will result.

48.4.2.2 Poorly Configured List Servers.

The user of an autoresponder may belong to a list where the From address is actually the broadcast address that sends a response to the entire list. The very first automated out-of-office response to the list will generate a message to everyone on that list, producing an infinite sequence of to-and-from messages. This situation is very embarrassing for the list administrator and intensely annoying for everyone else.

48.4.2.3 *Human Error.* Something analogous to a mail storm results from thoughtless behavior when using a public list. A typical instance occurs when a list member posts to an entire list comments relevant only to one individual. For example, a member asks for a reprint of an article and another answers on the list: "I'll send you a reprint tomorrow." Several thousand unwilling readers now know about this projected e-mail message. One of these irritated people posts a message saying "Did you really have to post that message to the entire list?" This second message is so irritating that at least one other person posts a third message to the entire list, criticizing the originator of the second letter for criticizing the writer of the first. This useless tempest of e-mail continues via the public list, creating thousands of copies of useless information.

Another form of inconsiderate behavior is to quote entire messages when responding to e-mail. Only the fragments of text that have elicited a response should be copied to the new message. This principle is particularly important on public lists, where messages have been observed containing the entire text, including Internet headers, for up to seven levels of previous messages. Often the amount of new information contained in messages posted to Usenet groups is extremely small; the rest was quotations of quotations of quotations.

48.4.3 Buying on the Web. Employers may decide to allow reasonable (however they decide the term) use of corporate resources for non–work-related activities, including buying services and products through the Internet. However, it is in the interests of employers to educate employees to avoid becoming victims of criminals. An employee distraught over the loss of significant sums due to foolish credulity will not be as productive as usual; in any case, no one wants to see friends and colleagues cheated.

Buying from known merchants through the Web can be as satisfying as buying in their stores. If you know the organizations selling goods and services, there is no more reason to be worried about buying from them through a Web connection than buying from them over the phone or in person at a store. Web sites belonging to recognized merchants or organizations, such as nonprofit charities, are trustworthy, especially if they show any of several symbols representing compliance with various standards of security for customer data. Some of the safety seals in common use include:

Network Solutions
Network Solutions is an independent, initiative dedicated to building users' trust and confidence on the Internet and accelerating growth of the Internet industry. Potential buyers won't spend time on a site unless they know from whom they're getting information or who's really selling the goods and services . . ..Big stores and long-recognized brands are recognized in the physical world, but what about online? In the anonymous world of the Web, consumers want to be certain about the site they're visiting, to know that the business behind the site is real. Identity is the foundation for trust . . ..Without identity, legitimacy will always be suspect. Network Solutions validates the status of a business before issuing an SSL SiteSafe Certificate. This authorizes the business to display a closed padlock, the https secure designation, and a clickable seal for more information. Under limited circumstances, the company guarantees up to $1 thousand for a single loss due to a mis-issued SSL Certificate or Site Confirm Seal. The program is intended to alleviate users' concerns about online privacy and security, while meeting the specific business needs of each licensed Web site.[9]

48.4.3.1 *Dynamic Pricing.* One controversial technique that some firms have been studying is *dynamic pricing.* Dynamic pricing presents different prices to different customers. By building a profile of a specific customer's buying habits, vendors can inflate prices for people who appear to be more willing to buy higher-priced goods and lower prices for those who are cost-conscious. Many brick-and-mortar stores do the same, in that stores in some parts of town may cater to richer people than in other areas; similarly, some chains of stores have been documented as charging higher prices to poor people in ghettos than in suburbs, in part because there is less competition in poor neighborhoods and the cost of doing business may be higher there. A different kind of dynamic pricing occurs in the airline industry, where seats on planes vary in price according to when they are booked and how many seats are expected to be sold. However, unlike these examples, dynamic pricing on the Web resembles traditional automobile sales, where research confirms that women and racial minorities are consistently offered higher prices than the deals for white males. In both automobile sales and dynamic pricing on the Web, the fundamental difference from the normal free-market model is that the prices are varied secretly so that only the victim of the predatory pricing sees the offered price. Without mechanisms for sharing information among purchasers, this model of pricing seems to put the buyers at an immense disadvantage with respect to the seller. It will be interesting to see how it develops over time.

48.4.3.2   Privacy.   Another key area of concern when buying products on the Web is privacy. Many consumers prefer their buying habits to remain their own business. Receiving unwanted paper mail or e-mail, because of past purchases, seems intrusive and irritating to them; they classify all such promotions as junk mail. Other consumers appreciate the convenience of receiving targeted information about new products and special sale prices for items they have previously bought. In either case, it is important to pay attention to the privacy policies offered by online vendors. Marketers must decide whether to set up their systems on an opt-in or opt-out basis. If marketers choose the former, then all individuals actually must *agree* to have information about themselves included on lists that may be used within the organization or sold to or traded with third parties. If the system is set up for opt-out, then everyone's information may be freely disclosed, except for those who specifically state that they do not want the list keepers to do so. These are broad general outlines; the privacy policy of each organization must be spelled out in detail. Some sites such as online bookstores and music services may keep detailed records of what each person buys from them and even what items are simply looked at. These Web sites can then tailor their sales presentations to products that are appropriate to each customer's interests. Amazon.com, for example, tries to be helpful to visitors by suggesting books that may interest the returning visitor based on previous behavior. However, one of the unexpected consequences of customer profiling is that the practice may reveal more than users would wish; if you watch one of your employees enter such a Web site and discover that the predominant theme is, say, weapons and techniques of terrorism, you might want to have some serious discussions with your human resources staff. A less positive application of profiling caused a flurry of interest when information about the purchasing habits of employees of specific companies was accidentally made available to those companies' competitors.

Another issue often raised in discussions of privacy involves "cookies." Cookies are small text files that a site stores on a visitor's hard disk to store information that can be used the next time the user visits the site. Properly defined cookies can be used only by the site that deposited them. The information stored can include the sequence of Web pages the visitor saw, or personal identifiers that allow the Web software to recognize the visitor so that the Web site can build up a preference profile for each visitor or client and to enable those cheery greetings like "Welcome back, Bob! We have a special deal for you on the newest title in *The Real Man's Guide to Heavy*

Artillery series!" Cookies also may be used to accumulate items in a shopping cart; without cookies, each purchase would have to be concluded separately.

In general, cookies are harmless. If you do not like the idea of having identifiers stored on your system, you can block cookies in your browser settings, block them globally or on a site-by-site basis using a personal firewall, or install cookie sweepers that get rid of all cookies whenever you activate them.

For a review of legal aspects of privacy in cyberspace, see Chapter 69 in this *Handbook*.

48.4.3.3 *Online Auctions.* The theory behind an auction is that the competition for an object or service helps participants determine a fair price. This process can be corrupted in a real-world, physical auction if the seller conspires with confederates to bid up the price artificially. Unfortunately, this is even easier online, where anyone can have as many identities as he or she wants. The ease with which browsers and e-mail systems allow forged headers and forged identifiers means that sellers can inflate the price of their own offerings.

The Federal Trade Commission of the United States reports that online auctions cause the largest number of complaints they receive annually about fraud.

This theoretical discussion does not even begin to address such questions as whether the auctioned items really exist, are as described, or will ever be delivered. A case of such fraud occurred on eBay, where Robert Guest of Los Angeles admitted in court in July 1999 that he defrauded victims of about $37,000 by offering goods for auction via eBay but failed to deliver anything. The customers of Mr. Guest certainly found out the hard way that they were being cheated, but it appears that they could not have known in advance that he was untrustworthy. Although eBay maintains a system whereby potential bidders can see reviews and comments posted by earlier customers of each seller, new sellers such as Mr. Guest have no record, and anyone with a bad record can assume a new identity.

eBay has further responded to these concerns by suggesting the use of escrow services and by warning its users that it does not guarantee the legitimacy of the transactions it facilitates.

There are also concerns about the legality of some of the items put up for auction. Someone offered items made from endangered species, in violation of the Convention on International Traffic in Endangered Species. The products included dried feet of elephants and gorillas caught in snares and allowed to die excruciating deaths before being hacked into pieces. In the United States, buying, selling, and possessing such contraband can lead to arrest, prosecution, fines, or imprisonment.

More ludicrously, someone put up a human kidney for sale through eBay in September 1999 and received bids of up to $5.8 million. The auction service canceled the sale because selling human organs is a federal felony punishable by up to $250,000 in fines and at least five years in jail. A week later eBay had to shut down an auction for an unborn human baby. Prices for the supposed baby had risen into the $100,000 range before eBay shut down that auction. Finally, a fool or a prankster—it is unclear which—tried to sell 500 pounds of fresh marijuana online. The auction was shut down after 21 hours, during which prices offered had reached $10 million. In August 2001, a couple offered to name their baby in accordance with the wishes of a high bidder. That auction, too, was ended prematurely.

Most of the bids probably were not legitimate. It is unlikely that everyone who bid for kidneys, pot, and babies really expected to pay for what they were bidding on. They may have been treating the auction like a video game, with no element of reality.

Situations such as these invite other abuses, and ordinary users are often at a loss as to how to proceed.

Even if the items being offered for sale online are ordinary things such as software or physical products, they may have been obtained illegally. Online auctions are a frequently used channel for fencing stolen goods.

Corporate users should probably not be using Internet auctions to buy or sell products, except in those closely guarded, industry-specific sites that have proven their worth. Certainly, employees should not be using corporate Internet access to engage in such activities for their private purposes.

48.4.4   Online Gambling.   It is hard to imagine that any enterprise would authorize employees to gamble online using corporate resources, but providing employees with the following guidance may be a valuable service.

48.4.4.1   Fraud and Error.   In 1998, the Arizona lottery discovered that no winning number in its Pick 3 game had ever included even one numeral 9.[10] It turned out that the pseudo–random number generator algorithm had an elementary programming error that generated only the digits 0 through 8. All those who had used a 9 in their lottery numbers felt justifiable anger—especially when they were told they could have a refund, but only if they had kept their old losing tickets.

The Arizona lottery used a simulated random process to provide the illusion to gamblers that they were betting on a physical process such as balls mixing together in a barrel and falling out of a tube. One of the problems with the Arizona simulation is similar to a genuine vulnerability in proprietary (i.e., secret) cryptographic algorithms. As cryptographers have stressed over many decades, the security of an encryption scheme should not depend on the secrecy of its algorithm. Had the lottery algorithm been exposed to public scrutiny, its flaws would have been detected sooner. For example, in the 1980s, there was much excitement over a new encryption scheme called the knapsack algorithm; after extensive examination by cryptographers, it proved to be flawed. It is conceivable that someone detecting the flaw in the Arizona lottery might have made bets with a higher probability of winning than those of uninformed people, but exposing the algorithm and its implementation to scrutiny before it went into production would have made that less likely.

These examples demonstrate that electronic gambling, as in older, conventional types, is subject to more than the rules of chance. Lack of conformity to good security practices lays both the gambler and the "house" open to abuse and to inadvertent errors.

48.4.4.2   Lack of Control.   Physical gaming devices are located in real-world establishments under the nominal control of regulatory and law enforcement officials. Even so, they are always adjusted for a certain predetermined payout. Gambling based on the results of actual sports events or contests is validated by external news reports, although the contests themselves can be rigged. But there is no basis for a gambler to trust the results of computer-generated pseudo–random numbers displayed on a browser screen.

Most individual gamblers will never know if a long-range analysis of the pseudo–random numbers would support their hopes for fairness in the odds. No one is keeping track of these data except the people making money from the participants, and they are not distributing the results.

The disclaimer at one Internet gambling portal, findinternetcasino.com, is not very encouraging:

> Although every attempt has been made to ensure fairness and security toward the player at each of the links that can be found in the directories, FindInternetCASINO® cannot be held responsible if discrepancies occur between an Online Gambling operation and you, the player, after following a link from this WWW site. Consult your local authorities prior to registering with any online wagering service. U.S. Citizens: The information at this site is for entertainment and news purposes only. Use of this information in violation of any federal, state or local laws is prohibited.

48.4.4.3 Legal Issues.   In some jurisdictions, betting online is illegal. In the United States, for example, it is already illegal to use interstate telecommunications to place bets; in addition, Internet betting is illegal in the United States even if the host is outside the United States. At the same time, due to ambiguities in the current laws and the inability to clearly enforce them, the use of overseas betting sites has driven this business to a total of over $15.5 billion a year, over half of that income coming from the United States. The ambiguities stem from a lack of a clear definition on what constitutes "illegal online gambling." This resulted in certain groups of individuals believing that they were exempt from the law, poker players being the most common. In addition, online horse-racing receives a specific exemption from the law, but without accompanying clarification on whether the wagering process constitutes online gambling.

Unfortunately, in the United Kingdom and many other countries, online gambling is for the most part legal. This creates numerous conflicts of interest, and international tension, between various betting companies in legalized countries, all advertising to Americans eager to risk their money for a chance at a big payout. It appears that until clear definitions are included in the law, the blurred line between legal and illegal gambling activities using online resources will continue.[11]

48.4.5 Internet Addiction.   Any activity can become the basis of compulsive exaggeration. A small proportion, around 5 percent, of Internet users may qualify as addicted to any of these computer-mediated activities:

- An uncontrollable desire to find and organize more and more information about an enormous range of topics
- Excessive involvement in games, gambling, and buying things on the Internet
- Excessive concentration on relationships mediated through e-mail and chat rooms, to the detriment of real-life relationships
- Involvement in long sessions of viewing pornography, or of being sexually stimulated via e-mail, chat rooms, pornographic sites, or sexual-fantasy games

None of these activities is a suitable use of corporate computing resources, and employees should be alerted to the policies prohibiting such activities at work. In addition, everyone should be aware of the dangers of Internet addiction.

The issue here is what constitutes *excessive* involvement in these activities. Professional psychologists such as Dr. Kimberly Young have identified some of the diagnostic criteria for these disorders, including these based on her *Internet Addiction Test*:[12]

- Regularly staying online longer than intended
- Often neglecting obligations to spend more time online

- Consistently preferring to spend time online instead of with one's partner
- Frequent complaints by friends and family about excessive Internet use
- Suffering consequences at school or at work because of time spent online
- Giving e-mail a higher priority than other important issues
- Concealing the extent of Internet usage
- Turning to the Internet as a substitute for dealing with disturbing issues
- Feeling that life without the Internet would be devoid of meaning and pleasure
- Getting angry when disturbed during Internet usage
- Losing sleep due to late-night Internet activity
- Yearning to be back online

Those who feel uncomfortable about their level of involvement with the Internet would do well to take this test offered by Dr. Young, and, if several of their answers are positive, to seek counseling to prevent possibly tragic consequences of untreated addiction.

48.4.6   Online Dating and Cybersex.   As in other topics in this chapter, it is unlikely that corporate policy would allow users to engage in online dating and cybersex. Nonetheless, in line with the overall orientation of this chapter, the next sections will help employees understand the issues in these online activities.

48.4.6.1   *Dating Online.*   Thousands of sites on the Web specialize in helping people meet each other. In a sense, chat rooms and bulletin board systems are ways for people with similar interests to communicate about their hobbies and lifestyles. There are also sites that specialize in helping people find others who match particular profiles. Some of these sites are free; others charge fees for participation. Dating service sites usually explicitly restrict participation to people over 18 years old, and most of them depend on possession of a credit card as their sole mechanism for authenticating age. It is very difficult to exclude teenagers, or even younger children, from such sites if they have access to credit card numbers.

Parents, teachers, and employers who want to get a sense of what is going on can type "online dating" in the search field of a search engine such as Google (www.google.com) and then visit a few of the sites. If children post information about themselves in such a cyberspace locale, even with false information claiming that they are adults, there is a real risk of attracting unsavory characters or perhaps ordinary people who can become angry at being tricked into exposing their feelings to an imposter.

48.4.6.2   *Sex Talk Online.*   In addition to matchmaking, users of the Internet also can get involved in *cybersex*. People chatting online can describe themselves or each other in sexual interactions that are inappropriate for youngsters. Such online chat also has been implicated in a number of divorces, since many spouses find it wholly inappropriate that their beloved is getting sexually excited with a stranger via the Internet.

In August 2001, a 15-year-old girl from Massachusetts was alleged to have been kept captive for at least a week during which she was repeatedly sexually abused by the couple who had brought her to Long Island. According to the criminal complaint, she was also "loaned out" for two days to another man and further abused. The couple had met the teenager in an Internet chat room, where their conversation was explicitly sexual.

Employers should ensure that no one in their employ, none of their colleagues or employees, and none of their children could engage in these activities, whether using corporate resources or home computers.

48.4.6.3 Traffic in Women.

A number of sites on the Web, particularly some situated in the former Soviet bloc, advertise services for introducing men to willing candidates for marriage. The evidence is strong that much of the information communicated about the supposedly nubile and marriage-oriented women is false. Many of the pictures are taken from public Web sites and include actresses and people who have posted their photos on social networking groups. Sometimes the same picture has dozens of names associated with it. Much as in the phone-based sex-talk services, people claiming to be youthful, attractive, persons of marriageable age may be nothing of the sort, and may be copy/pasting responses from prepared scripts. When men travel to visit their potential mates, they can be charged high rates for the privilege of taking their dates to expensive restaurants. Some of the women who actually do go through with marriages later divorce their hapless victims in what appears to be a systematic fraud.

48.4.7 Games and Virtual Reality.

Some enterprises allow their employees to play games at various times during the day—usually low-usage times such as lunch, or before and after the normal workday. However, some Internet-enabled multiuser games can consume enormous bandwidth; the shoot-'em-up ("first-person shooter," or FPS) game called Quake was notorious in its day for saturating all available connectivity.

When helping employees understand how to negotiate the perils of the Internet, you might recommend that parents read reviews of video games before allowing their young children to play them. Some games have astonishing levels of graphic violence ("Brilliant Bleeding! Detailed Decapitations!") and unusual values ("Win points by burning as many residents to death as possible!"). This latter example is based on a notorious case in which a video-game vendor was apparently surprised by the public wave of revulsion over a game that glorified arson. Some military and police shoot-'em-up games explicitly take points off for hitting innocent bystanders; others do not. Some games use graphic nudity; others are more modest. The main point is that relying on the judgment of eight-year-olds to choose their own entertainment may be unwise.

From a corporate perspective, it would be unusual to find employers encouraging the use of local or networked games during working hours; however, some may allow use of their resources in off-hours, assuming the corporation does not maintain around-the-clock operations. However, issues of suitability persist; some games may contribute to a hostile work environment and lead to complaints and lawsuits from offended employees.

A development that started in the 1990s has become a potentially valuable tool in the first decade of the 21st century: virtual reality or virtual worlds such as Second Life (http://secondlife.com/) or Gaia (www.gaia.com/). These services use controllable representations called *avatars*, which allow some degree of expressiveness when communicating. Participants see a representation of a three-dimensional world, complete with viewpoint and perspective, that includes their interlocutors in a shared virtual reality that can be creative and fun. Some companies are using resources in these virtual worlds for advertising, delivery of services (e.g., training and education), and internal remote meetings or training. Organizations must determine appropriate policies about the use of such services.

48.5   LEGAL LIABILITY.   This section briefly reviews some of the legal issues that may arise as a result of misuse of e-mail and Internet resources. For more detailed information, see Chapters 63, 64, 69, 70, 71, and 72 in this *Handbook*.

48.5.1   Libel.   Some people have taken advantage of the freedom to publish whatever they want by crossing the boundaries of libel. For example, the self-styled "reporter" Matt Drudge went too far in postings on his electronic scandal sheet in 1997, when he made unsubstantiated accusations about White House advisor Sidney Blumenthal's marriage. Professional journalists pounced on him for shoddy journalism. Blumenthal and his wife filed a $30 million libel suit against Drudge even after he apologized for failing to verify the gossip he disseminated. Drudge then claimed that public White House support for Blumenthal amounted to a threat against free speech.

In another notorious case, Walter Cronkite, whom polls revealed to be the most respected man in the United States in the 1980s, was appalled to discover a page of lies about him on the Web in 1997. A 28-year-old programmer, Tim Hughes, invented and posted a scurrilous story about Cronkite's becoming enraged at the author, shrieking imprecations at Hughes and his wife, boasting about his own infidelity, and spitting in their spice cake at a Florida restaurant. In addition, the anti-Cronkite Web page included falsified photographs purporting to show Cronkite at a Ku Klux Klan meeting. Cronkite threatened to sue for libel; Hughes took the page down and weakly protested that it was all a joke.

The effect of this kind of misinformation on children or immature employees, untrained in critical thinking and lacking in skepticism about information on the Internet, can be damaging.

Another source of information is the Usenet—that collection of thousands of discussion groups on every conceivable topic. These discussion groups fall into two major classes: moderated and unmoderated. In a moderated group, messages are passed through a *moderator* who decides either to post them for participants or to delete offensive or otherwise inappropriate messages. Not all moderated groups are reliable, and not all unmoderated groups are unreliable. However, many unmoderated groups distribute unsubstantiated information from people who appear to derive their major pleasure in life by insulting other participants and by making outrageous statements about any topic that comes up. Everyone should be trained to recognize emotional and inflammatory language, and should be encouraged to apply skeptical analysis to all statements, especially to those published in rants.

In the first decade of the 21st century, *blogs*—commentaries published on the Web by individuals or groups—have exploded into common awareness. The same principles of critical evaluation apply to blogs as to any other source of disintermediated information.

48.5.2   Stolen Software, Music, and Videos.   Organizations cannot permit employees to download and make illegal copies of intellectual property of any kind. Security policies must explicitly address these issues; security monitoring must explicitly control for abuse of corporate resources in such activities. The risks to organizations by tolerating such violations of law are severe. For more details of intellectual property law, see Chapter 11 in this *Handbook*.

48.5.3   Plagiarism.   A different kind of fraud involving intellectual property occurs when people misrepresent someone else's work as their own. Older students know intellectually that this is supposed to be bad, but for young children, the issue is completely abstract. The problem today is that plagiarism is easier than ever and harder for teachers to detect.

Academic guidelines try to make it clear to students that copying other people's work without attribution is called *plagiarism* and is severely frowned on. Plagiarism includes not only direct quotation without indications of origin but also paraphrasing that merely shuffles the ideas around a little or substitutes synonyms for the original words. In many institutions, plagiarism is grounds for suspension or expulsion. In all cases, plagiarism defeats the purpose of writing assignments by eliminating the opportunity for critical thinking and creative expression. Few plagiarists remember what they have copied from others after they hand their material in.

Assuredly, students have traded term papers and other assignments for centuries. However, the availability of electronic documents and of the World Wide Web has enormously increased both the fund of material that can be plagiarized and the ease of copying. Worse still, some people are profiting from easy accessibility by selling papers specifically for plagiarism and even writing papers to order. In one study by Peggy Bates and Margaret Fain of the Kimbel Library at Coastal Carolina University, the authors easily located over 100 sites on the Web selling or donating papers to students for plagiarism.[13]

To combat this problem, science has come to the aid of beleaguered instructors by providing automated similarity analysis of any paper submitted electronically. The system uses a bank of more than 100,000 term papers and essays as well as documents located on the Web; analysis uses pattern recognition to measure similarities among different documents and to estimate the probability of plagiarism. According to the turnitin.org documentation:

> Our system is now being used in the majority of universities in the United States and the U.K., as well as a large number of schools around the world. Many of these institutions, among them UC Berkeley and the fifty-eight member schools of the Consortium of Liberal Arts Colleges, an association of the most respected liberal arts schools in the US, have chosen to ensure the academic integrity of all their students by selecting institution-wide subscriptions to our service. Other universities, such as Harvard and Cornell, have elected to make use of our system on a departmental or single-instructor basis.

Plagiarism is also a risk to the enterprise; having employees misuse other people's or other organization's materials without attribution can lead to lawsuits, embarrassing publicity, and serious financial penalties.

48.5.3.1 Practical Guidelines

- Discuss plagiarism clearly at work, at home, and at school.
- Use examples to illustrate the difference between plagiarism and a legitimate use of other people's work.
- Encourage children to practice summarizing information in their own words.
- Practice writing references to quoted material.
- Have a student submit a sample term paper to the turnitin.org analysis program for an automatic *Originality Report.*
- Discuss how antiplagiarism sites analyze documents to measure similarities and help teachers identify plagiarism.

48.5.4 Criminal Hacking and Hacktivism.

As discussed in Chapter 45 in this *Handbook*, it is important that all employees understand and agree that using corporate systems for unauthorized access to computers and networks is grounds for dismissal, and possibly criminal prosecution. In particular, no employee should ever imagine that testing for security weaknesses in the enterprise's systems without authorization is a contribution to security.

The motivation for illegal actions does not mitigate the seriousness of computer trespass. Employees should be informed explicitly that regardless of the excuse, no violations of law will be tolerated. For example, hacking into systems in another country to support a war effort is not excusable; nor is destroying child pornography sites a good idea. Cybervigilantes can destroy evidence needed for prosecution.

48.5.5 Creating a Hostile Work Environment.

In today's society, there are numerous activities and language constructs that individuals of a certain race, gender, sexual orientation, national origin, religious affiliation, or other legally protected characteristics may find offensive. Any type of harassment, most especially comments or actions based on these protected characteristics, toward another employee may create a hostile work environment. The two most common situations created by a hostile work environment are:

1. A reduction or loss of productivity due to the harassment, whether physical, verbal, or psychological

2. A reduction in salary, bonus, job level, responsibilities, or other components of compensation due to one or more of the legally protected characteristics

Although there are no formal laws barring "hostile work environments," Title VII of the Civil Rights Act of 1964 covers these types of situations. These laws are written in such a way that an individual comment or action does not usually constitute harassment. Rather, a pattern of frequent, severe, and pervasive abuse may constitute a hostile work environment. It is important to distinguish between "quid pro quo" harassment, where an employee is required to tolerate such harassment in order to maintain job status or compensation levels, and a hostile work environment. Both are very serious and potentially illegal activities, but this section focuses on the hostile environment.[14]

Employers are obligated by law to set appropriate expectations around employee behavior, and confidentially and swiftly to investigate any complaint of harassment from an employee. Employees are granted some legal protections such that retaliation by an employer for "sounding the alarm" on a hostile environment is illegal.

These issues become even more important when office romances occur. Although many employers forbid couples from working together in the same department, in part to avoid any perception of favoritism or future harassment cases, should the romance fail, there is still the potential for romantically linked coworkers to create a hostile environment for others. In this case, employers have an obligation to define in policy that coworkers should maintain a professional relationship while on company business. Even though two individuals may feel that their words or actions are seemingly innocuous, it is the perception of others around them that creates the basis for a harassment complaint. The best solution is to keep personal lives out of the office, which is a difficult but appropriate recommendation for everyone.

48.5.5.1 Hate Groups.

Another source of concern for employers and parents is the easy accessibility of hate literature on the Web. Hatemongers have taken full advantage of the largely unregulated nature of the Net to spread their pernicious messages. One can find Web sites devoted to hatred of every imaginable identifiable group. Race, ethnicity, religion, gender, sexual orientation, immigration status, and political ideology—anything can spark hatred in susceptible personalities. Unfortunately, some of the hate groups have been quite successful in recruiting young people through the Web; they publish propaganda such as pro-Nazi revisionist history that may fool uncritical people into believing their rants. Neo-Nazi and racist skinhead groups have formed hate-rock groups that take advantage of kids' enthusiasm for very loud music with aggressive lyrics.

Employers cannot tolerate the slightest involvement of their employees in such activities using corporate resources. Aside from their possible personal revulsion at such hatemongering, managers also should be aware that toleration of intolerance can lead to a hostile work environment in which targets of hate or contempt can legitimately appeal to the courts for compensatory and punitive damages. Employees must understand and agree that using any corporate resources for participation in hate groups is a serious infraction of Internet usage policy.

According to the Simon Wiesenthal Center, there are over 2,300 Web sites advocating hatred, of which over 500 are extremist sites hosted on American servers but authored by Europeans; most European countries have strict antihate laws. Using more stringent criteria, the Hate Watch group estimates more than 500 extremist hate sites on the Web; it distinguishes between hate propaganda and those pages that consist largely of racial epithets, dismissed as mere graffiti.

The Southern Poverty Law Center monitors 500 active hate organizations in the United States. It has regularly reported on the growing number and stridency of such sites. In comments about the center's paper for the United Nations Commission on Human Rights, spokesperson Mark Potok said at a conference in 2000:

> A few years ago, a Klansman needed to put out substantial effort and money to produce and distribute a shoddy pamphlet that might reach a few hundred people. Today, with a $500 computer and negligible other costs, that same Klansman can put up a slickly produced Web site with a potential audience in the millions.[15]

A fundamental reality is that human beings are gregarious. They find it very easy to affiliate with others to form *in-groups,* groups to which they feel entitled to belong. Unfortunately, defining in-groups naturally means it is equally easy to define *out-groups*: groups to which we *do not* want to belong. Grade school and high school cliques are examples of in- and out-groups. A wealth of study in social psychology confirms the validity of the universal impression that we tend to inflate our esteem for in-groups and to reduce our respect and liking for out-groups. However, research also shows that social norms against discrimination can reduce hostility toward out-groups; thus it seems likely that parental and teacher articulation of norms of tolerance can significantly reduce children's susceptibility to the blandishments of hate groups.

48.5.5.2 Pornography. Pornography—even with the most restrictive definitions—is widespread on the Internet. Observers of Net culture have commented that the sure-fire way of telling if new technology is going to be a success on the Internet is to see how quickly pornographers can apply it. For example, the appearance in July 2000 of the first WAP (wireless application protocol) pornography sites signaled the adoption of WAP technology into the mainstream. Although the sites offered only tiny grainy images of naked Japanese models, sociologists said that the same expected sequence of rapid technological advances had occurred with photography and video cameras.

48.5.5.2.1   Prevalence of Porn.   Some studies of Internet traffic have claimed that more than half of the total Net bandwidth is used for transfer of pornography or solicitations for purchase of pornography.

48.5.5.2.2   Trickery.   Pornographers use various tricks to get people onto their Web sites:

- Using a different domain, like the old whitehouse.com, which used to take advantage of interest in "whitehouse.gov" by showing porn (it is now a site for political commentary).
- Misspellings, such as the now-inactive micosoft.com, which traded on the likelihood of mistyping "Microsoft.com."
- Junk e-mail invitations with innocent-looking labels for URLs that do not match the actual link but instead take the viewer to a pornography site.
- Padding porn-site metatags (normally invisible text used to describe a Web site) with inoffensive keywords that place the site high on search engine lists where they can appeal to children.
- Disabling normal features of a browser to trap victims in the porn site. One perpetrator who was shut down by the Federal Trade Commission (FTC) actually ran Java applets that disabled the back arrow and defeated the ability to close the browsers. People trapped in porno-hell had to reboot their computers to get out.

Porn sites are notorious for using deceit to defraud their victims. One widely used scam is to demand a credit card number from a visitor as proof of their age (it is nothing of the sort), then to charge the card even though the site clearly states that there is a period of free use.

In 1996, viewers of pornographic pictures on the sexygirls.com site were in for a surprise when they got their next phone bills. Victims who downloaded a *special viewer* were actually installing a Trojan horse program that silently disconnected their connection to their normal ISP and reconnected them (with the modem speaker turned off) to a number in Moldova in central Europe. The long-distance charges then ratcheted up until the user disconnected the session—sometimes hours later, even when the victims switched to other, perhaps less prurient, sites. Some victims who stayed online for a long time paid more than $1,000 in long-distance charges. In February 1997 in New York City, a federal judge ordered the scam shut down. An interesting note is that AT&T staff spotted the scam because of unusually high volume of traffic to Moldova, not usually a destination for many U.S. phone calls. In November 1997, the FTC won $2.74 million from the Moldovan telephone company to refund to the cheated customers —or the ones willing to admit to having been cheated.

Both of the scams just described relied in part on the reluctance of porn-seeking victims to admit to their socially disapproved interest. Few victims were willing to pursue the matter until the damages mounted into the thousands of dollars.

48.5.5.2.3   Filtering.   An entire industry has grown up to try to shield (or block) children from seeing pornography or other materials deemed offensive by their parents or by the makers of the blocking software. The popular blocking systems are reviled by many free-speech advocates, and often ridiculed for what are described as clumsy, keyword-oriented algorithms. The classic examples of ludicrous blocking include trapping access to any site that uses the word "breast"—including even possibly this very page if you are reading it on the Web. Other simple-minded traps have blocked users from accessing information pages for geographical locations ending in the old British suffix "-sex" such as Wessex, Sussex, Middlesex, and so on. The village of Scunthorpe in England was blocked by software used by a major Internet service provider because its internal filters prevented anyone from using "vulgar" words in their mailing address.

Some of the blocking software products use hidden assumptions about the unsuitability of a wide range of topics, including abortion rights, civil rights, political ideology, and gay liberation. Any parent is entitled to express opinions about any topic; however, parents will want to check on whether a particular program is imposing its makers' political agenda by stealth. In the workplace, employers who use broad-spectrum blocking software may interfere with legitimate research by their employees.

48.5.5.2.4 Monitoring.   A different approach to interfering with the nefarious deeds of pornographers is to install monitoring software on the computers that employees use at work or that children will use at home. These products keep a log, or audit trail, that allows employers and parents to see exactly what users have been doing with their computers.

In the family context, most important, however, is the principle that machines and programs cannot by themselves teach values. Instead of relying only on passive barriers or on snoopware, parents would do well to make surfing the Internet a family activity rather than a private hobby. When kids express interest in pornography—because our popular culture is full of sexual innuendo that children read, hear, and see—it makes sense to discuss the issues rather than try to pretend that they do not exist. One approach for reducing the power of the forbidden fruit offered by pornographers is to explain to children in a supportive and nonpunitive way why sexual exploitation and degradation are bad for people. Children who stumble on porn sites by accident or at their friends' houses may be better prepared to cope with the sometimes disturbing images and words if their parents have prepared them for this aspect of today's world.

48.5.6 Archiving E-mail.   Organizations must remember that e-mail may be demanded as evidence in court cases. There is a fiduciary duty to maintain business records appropriately for each type of business, and that obligation extends to electronic records. Policies should stipulate how long e-mail records should be maintained. Destruction of e-mail should never be selective, especially if there is an anticipated threat of legal action. Selective destruction of particular records, or premature wholesale destruction of e-mail, may be interpreted by the courts as grounds for charges of interference with the judicial process.

For details of backup and archiving policies, see Chapter 57 in this *Handbook*.

48.6 RECOMMENDATIONS.   This section summarizes some practical recommendations for employees and their families.

48.6.1 Protecting Children

- Explain the dangers of communicating with strangers via the Net in the same terms that you discuss the dangers of talking to strangers anywhere else.
- Alert children to the questionable identity of anyone they meet exclusively through the Net or via e-mail. Discuss the possibility that people are not what they claim to be in their online persona.

- It is important that children feel confident of a supportive response from their parents when raising these issues. Establish a calm atmosphere so that children will not fear your reactions if they are troubled by what they encounter online. Worst of all would be to punish a child for reporting a disturbing incident.

- Tell children not to give their address to strangers they meet electronically.

- Children should not send pictures of themselves to strangers.

- Make a practice of discussing online relationships in a friendly and open way at home. Show interest in the new friends without expressing hostility or suspicion; ask to participate in some of the online chats and e-mail correspondence. Invite your children to sit in with you during your own online interactions.

- If a child feels that another child met online is becoming a good friend, parents should contact the child's parents by phone and, eventually in person, before allowing contacts.

- If a child wants to meet someone encountered on the Internet, be sure that a parent is involved at all stages. Never let a child meet anyone in the real world whom he or she has met only on the Net. Any attempt to induce a child to meet the correspondent alone or secretly should be reported to local police authorities for investigation.

- Make it clear that anyone who suggests hiding an online relationship from the child's parents is already doing something wrong.

- Make it clear to your children that no one has the right to send them age-inappropriate, sexually suggestive, or frankly pornographic materials, whether written or pictorial. Suggestions on the Internet that children engage in virtual sex play or sexual fantasies should be reported to parents right away. Making, transmitting, and storing child pornography is a felony; report such cases to local police authorities at once.

- Children receiving a request for anything unusual (e.g., a request for a piece of clothing or for nude pictures) should immediately report the incident to their parents. Teachers and other caregivers can adapt these principles for the specific circumstances of their relationship with the children they are taking care of.

48.6.2 Threats

- Employers, parents, and teachers should clearly enunciate policies preventing anyone—including children—from uttering threats of violence or other harm, even in e-mail messages or chat rooms.

- Employees should be instructed to report all threats directed at them, or at others, to the security officers in their organization; similarly, parents, teachers, or librarians should ensure that children know to report any threats immediately to the appropriate adult.

48.6.3 Hate Sites

- To protect children against the wiles of these hateful people, the most important step is to discuss the issue of hate speech and hate groups with them openly. Parents may even want to visit some of the sites listed below *with your kids* to give them a sense of the problem and possible countermeasures.

- Discuss your children's feelings about out-groups in their own lives; for example, encourage them to speak freely, without fear of punishment or reprimand, about whatever groups they do not like. Then pursue the discussion with explanations of such issues as cultural differences, history, or whatever else you feel will help your children gain perspective on their own feelings and behavior. Of course, this positive attitude cannot be applied to hate groups or similar outlaws.

- Provide positive social role models for children with respect to hate groups. Speak out firmly in opposition to intolerance rather than sit silently by when bigots display their hatred for other groups.

48.6.4 Pornography

- Place young children's Internet-access computers in a family area of the home rather than in their bedrooms.

- Interact with your children while they are using the Internet; treat the Web browser like a window on the world, and be present to help your children interpret that world in a way consistent with your values.

- Talk with your children about the existence and nature of pornography; as they reach puberty, assure them that there is nothing wrong with being interested in sex but that pornography is not a healthy way of learning about wholesome, loving relations.

- Warn your children about some of the tricks used by pornographers to get traffic on their Web sites, such as telling them to download special readers. Tell them about the Moldovan porn scam.

- Discuss the issue of junk e-mail that advertises porn sites. Warn children that no one should ever click on a URL from any kind of junk e-mail because it can easily be a trick to get them into dangerous territory.

- Teach your children to keep an eye on the actual URL that appears in the browser window; any discrepancy between the visible URL shown on a page and the actual URL should alert them to the possibility of fraud.

- Explain that pornographers sometimes charge for access to their sites without permission; be sure your children understand how dangerous it would be to give your credit card number to these people for any reason.

48.6.5 Internet Addiction

- Know the warning signs of Internet addiction and self-monitor.

- Discuss Internet addiction and its warning signs with your employees and your children.

- Encourage open discussion of feelings about the Net, so that children feel free to turn to you for help if they become uncomfortable or unhappy about their own experiences on the Net.

48.6.6 Online Dating

- Do not build online profiles or give out addresses, phone numbers, or school names.

- Do share e-mail accounts with your children, and oversee their messages.

- Keep the computer in a family room where children's activities can be monitored.
- Remember that people may lie when describing themselves online.
- Do not allow children to meet online users without permission, and make all meetings in public places with adult supervision.
- Forward copies of suggestive or obscene messages to your Internet service provider.
- Find ways to block objectionable material.
- Discuss online dating with kids so they understand what is involved.
- Ensure that kids understand why it is inappropriate and even dangerous for them to masquerade as adults in online dating services.
- Do not rush into face-to-face contact; you need to be sure that you are meeting someone who is on the level, not an imposter who has ulterior motives.
- You may want to take advantage of anonymizing services offered by some dating sites to avoid handing out your real e-mail address to complete strangers.
- Be suspicious of anyone who tries to pressure you in any way, including demanding money or insisting on a meeting, before you feel confident of the person's good intentions.
- As you are getting to know someone online, ask questions about lots of things you are interested in—for example, hobbies, politics, religion, education, birth date, family background, and marital history and status.
- Keep the answers you receive and beware of people who provide inconsistent or contradictory information as they are communicating with you—any lie is a danger signal.
- Be suspicious of anyone who seems to be too good to be true; if someone matches you on every single preference or interest you mention, try mentioning the very opposite of what you said earlier in the communications and see if the person agrees with *that* too. Trying too hard to please by lying may mark a manipulative and potentially dangerous personality.
- Be honest about yourself; state your own interests and characteristics fairly, including things you think might be less attractive than stereotypes and cultural norms dictate. A mature, good person will not necessarily be turned off if you do not look like a movie star, or if you do not play four musical instruments perfectly, or if you lisp.
- If you get to the point of exchanging pictures, be sure that you see the person in a wide variety of situations and with other people; some online daters send false pictures to misrepresent themselves.
- Talk to the person you are getting interested in over the phone; be suspicious if the person resists such a request for a long time or always has excuses for not being available when you have agreed to talk.
- Listen carefully to how the person sounds on the phone, and be suspicious if you now receive information that contradicts something the person wrote to you about. Any lie should alert you to potential problems.
- Before you agree to meet, get your date's full name, address, and telephone number. Be suspicious if the person refuses to give you a home number: Could he or her have a spouse or a current live-in friend that he or she is trying to deceive? Call the home number a couple of times to see if someone else answers.

- Give the person's information, and the exact details of where and when you are going to meet, to friends and family. Do not ever accept a date with someone who wants to keep the location and time a secret. Be sure the meeting place is well lighted and in a public place such as a coffee shop.

- Do not allow a stranger to pick you up at your house, and be sure you can get home by yourself.

- Before considering further involvement, for safety's sake think about having a background check done on the person you like, using a professional service such as whoishe.com or whoisshe.com.

48.6.7   Online Games

- Learn to play some of the games your kids are enthusiastic about. Take the time to immerse yourself in the imaginary worlds they play in, and study the underlying values that are being communicated by the game creators.

- Use published reviews from online or other media that reflect your own family's values before allowing games into your home.

- Accompany your children to the stores when buying video games. Check for parental warning labels. Talk to the salespeople if you think they are reliable.

- Know the characteristics of your hardware and software before buying recently released games. Do not buy a new game only to discover that it does not run on your obsolescent system. A disappointed child can apply intense pressure to spend money on a new system. Some games are computationally intensive and require expensive, advanced computer hardware and modern sound systems, complete with a high-powered amplifier driving woofers and subwoofers.

- Try making game playing an opportunity for family fun or parent-child bonding instead of the isolating experience games can sometimes be. See if you can all have fun with puzzle- and exploration-oriented games such as *Myst* and *Riven*, neither of which involves violence, and both of which are visually beautiful.

48.6.8   Online Purchases

- Before spending a considerable amount of money on a new online merchant's site, do some basic research into the site's reliability. Check the company's reputation; see if it belongs to the Better Business Bureau (BBB), and contact the appropriate chapter of the BBB to see if there have been complaints about the vendor.

- Do a Web search using a good search engine, such as Google, to see if there are any up-to-date reports about customer experience on the site you are interested in.

- Pretend that you already have a problem and look for the customer service pages. Are there clear instructions on how to communicate problems? Would you have the choice of e-mail, letters, or phone communications? If you have the time, you may even want to try calling customer service and find out just how they handle calls. If you hit a company that hangs up on you when its lines are busy ("We are sorry, but all our agents are busy; please call back later."), you might want to give serious thought as to whether it is safe doing business with them.

- Read the company's return policy; how does it handle breakage in transit, or defective goods? Does it offer guarantees on delivery time? What happens if the company is out of stock on a specific item—does it ship partial shipments or wait for everything to be ready? When out of stock, does it charge your credit card immediately, or only after the shipment is made? If it splits your shipment, does it charge extra for delivery of the later parts?

- Read the site's privacy policy. If the text is practically invisible 6-point yellow on white, be suspicious. Look for weasel-words in the clauses that say, for instance, that their policies can be changed at any time without notice. You must check the site regularly to see if the policy has changed, but this is unrealistic. Instead, look for firm, clear assurances that your personal information will not be sold, traded, or given away without your permission. Usually Web site owners state that they may have to divulge information to partnering organizations that handle such normal functions as billing and order fulfillment. There can be little objection to this provided the partners are bound by acceptable security policies.

- Keep a detailed record of your transactions. Use the browser functions to save copies of, or print out, the relevant Web pages with descriptions of the products, prices, a summary of your order, the order number, promised delivery date, and method of shipment.

48.6.9 Online Auctions

- Before becoming involved with online auctions, research the value of goods you are interested in buying. Check bricks-and-mortar stores, online retail outlets, and comparative shopping sites that provide you with specific prices.

- Examine the policies and costs on shipping, warrantees, and refunds.

- Set your upper limit before you get involved in an auction. Do not be influenced by the value other people appear to place on a particular product or service, and certainly do not be caught up in a bidding frenzy.

- Do not treat online auctions as a competition you have to win.

- Look for auction services that provide a guarantee of support if you are cheated in a transaction. For example, check for language in the terms of service that covers losses up to a suitable limit. Check for insurance policies, costs, terms, and limits. Use search engines to evaluate the trustworthiness of the service you are thinking of using.

- If possible, use a service that provides an escrow function so that you pay money to the service and then release it only when the product is received in good condition.

- Use the browser functions to print documents, and save Web pages to disk at every stage of each transaction.

48.6.10 Online Gambling

- Do not gamble with money you cannot afford to lose.
- Do not gamble online, except at well-known sites.
- If you do gamble online, do not gamble with money at sites hosted outside your own country.
- Do not give your credit card number to online gambling centers that are outside your own country.
- Before you gamble online, do some research to find out if there have been complaints about that casino. Contact your Better Business Bureau, or equivalent, and

see if you can find friends or acquaintances who have played on the site you are considering.

48.6.11   Preventing Malware Infections

- Keep your virus strings up to date (automatic daily updates are good).
- Do not download or use software that purports to help you break the law or cheat people and businesses.
- Do not download or use software that has been copied without permission or in violation of license restrictions. That is software piracy, copyright infringement, or plain theft.
- Do not execute software that anyone sends you through e-mail even if you know and like the person who sent it to you. Just because the person is nice does not mean he or she is qualified to inspect programs for safety.
- Before sending someone an attachment such as a picture or any other kind of file by e-mail, let your recipient know what to expect via a preliminary message; if you do not know the person personally, send an e-mail requesting permission to send the attachment.
- Never open attachments you have received without advance notice, regardless of who sent them or what the subject line or text says. Be especially suspicious of generic subjects such as "FYI" without details or "You'll like this." If you are really curious about the attachment, phone or e-mail the supposed sender to find out whether it is legitimate. However, remember that you should not run programs you receive as attachments, regardless of what the sender thinks.
- Do not forward programs, even reliable programs, to anyone; instead, tell your friends where to download useful programs from a trustworthy source, such as a legitimate Web site.
- Before sending anyone an MS-Word document as an attachment, save the document as an RTF file instead of as the usual DOC file. RTF files do not include document macros and therefore cannot carry macro-viruses.
- Disable automatic execution of macros in MS-Word using the Tools | Macros | Security menu and select the High option, which restricts macro execution to digitally signed macros from trusted sources. If the default value is not changed, there is no security against macros.
- Use the options offered by your e-mail client to shut off automatic opening or execution of attachments.
- Do not circulate virus warnings; if you insist on doing so, personally check their validity on any of a number of virus-information and hoax sites on the Web.

48.6.12   Guarding against Spyware

- Before installing freeware or adware, read the terms and conditions carefully to see if they currently include language permitting automatic transfer of information to the supplier or to third parties. Be aware that these contracts often include language authorizing the supplier to change the terms and conditions at any time and without notifying you.

- Install and use a spyware scanner and removal program, such as the free Ad-Aware program from Lavasoft, PestPatrol from Computer Associates or ZoneAlarm firewall.

- If you are particularly irritated by spyware, install a real-time spyware monitor and blocker such as those just mentioned.

- Support legislative attempts to force software manufacturers to disclose their use of spyware.

48.6.13 Junk E-mail

- Do not buy products or services from anyone who has sent you junk e-mail. If the company is unprofessional or inconsiderate enough to use such methods of advertising, it does not deserve either your business or your trust.

- Do not assume that the From address is correct, because often it is either nonexistent or, worse, fraudulently misrepresents the origin by pointing to a legitimate business that is completely innocent of wrongdoing. Never bombard the owner of a From address with multiple copies, or even one copy, of abusive e-mail. Such messages, known as *mail-bombs,* will probably reach the wrong target—some innocent addressee.

- Never respond to the address listed for removal from an e-mail distribution list unless you initiated the contact or are confident that you know the organization that sent you the message (e.g., publications you already subscribe to). Since bounces (returned e-mail due to bad addresses) never reach them and there is no incremental cost for sending out addresses to unwilling people, these operators really do not care how you feel about the junk they send. Therefore, the unethical people who send junk e-mail use the REMOVE function primarily to harvest correct e-mail addresses so they can sell them to someone else.

- Even if you trust the organization that sent you a junk e-mail, never click on a link contained in the message. Instead, visit the company's Web site and request removal from their official contact address, which any reputable company has.

- Do not visit the URLs listed in junk e-mail messages. Some of them are deliberately mislabeled and may bring you to offensive Web sites.

- If you *really* feel angry about a particular e-mail and it has a dropbox (a real address in the body of the message where you are supposed to reply), then if you have nothing better to do, you may want to send a copy of the spam to the appropriate address (usually in the form abuse@ISPname.domain where you have to fill in the variables *ISPname* and *domain*) address running the dropbox. However, the chances are high that your message will be one of hundreds or thousands of similar reports.

- Do not send any junk e-mail yourself. Encourage those around you (friends, neighbors, children) not to send junk e-mail either.

48.6.14 Mail Storms.   Here are some simple suggestions for reducing the likelihood of mail storms:

- Minimize the use of automated responses on your e-mail accounts.
- If you do autoforward your e-mail, do not let your target mailbox fill up.

- If you are receiving autoforwarded e-mail from your primary mailbox, do not autoforward back to the original mailbox.
- E-mail system administrators should receive exception reports identifying accounts with excessive numbers of e-mail messages or excessive traffic, so that they can investigate for mail storms.
- Firewalls that inspect the content of e-mail messages should be able to react to an excessive number of bounce messages from a single originating address by deleting the traffic or informing the system administrator of a likely mail storm.
- Managers of unmoderated lists should configure a From address different from the address that participants use to post messages to the list.
- Users of list servers who want to send personal messages should reply to the sender, not to the entire list.

48.6.15   Detecting Hoaxes.   Key indicators that a message is a hoax:

- Use of exclamation marks. No official warning uses them.
- Use of lots of uppercase text, typical of youngsters.
- Misspellings and bad grammar.
- No date of origination or expiration.
- Inclusion of words like "yesterday" when there is no date on the message.
- References to official-sounding sources such as Microsoft, Computer Incident Advisory Capability (CIAC), Computer Emergency Response Team Coordination Center CERT-CC) but no specific document URLs for details. URLs for a site's home page do not count.
- No valid digital signature from a known security organization.
- Requests to circulate widely. No such request is ever made in official documents.
- Claims that someone is counting the number of e-mail messages containing copies of the hoax.
- Threats about dire consequences if someone "breaks the chain" by refusing to forward the message.
- Claims of monetary rewards that make no sense. For example, the Disney organization will send you $5,000—for forwarding an e-mail message.
- Use of complicated technical language such as "n-th dimensional infinite complexity control loops" that do not make sense.
- Claims of damage to computer hardware from viruses or other computer software.

48.6.16   Get-Rich-Quick Schemes

- Remind everyone to use common sense: Earning lots of money with little or no effort usually results in uncovering something impossible or illegal.
- Teach users the mantra of the skeptic: "If it sounds too good to be true, it usually is."
- Explain how dangerous it is to get involved with criminal schemes like using stolen or falsified credit cards. Talk about the victims of such fraud: Everyone who pays higher interest rates on unpaid credit card bills and innocent shopkeepers who lose merchandise to e-commerce crooks.

- Especially when talking to children, discuss Internet-mediated theft in the same terms as you discuss shoplifting. Explain how commerce works; point out that everyone suffers from all kinds of theft, including electronic shoplifting.

48.6.17   Hacking

- Contact your local FBI office and find out if they can send a speaker to your company or to a local meeting of a professional security association for a discussion of computer crime.
- If you or specific authorized staff (e.g., from the security group) do visit Web sites that support criminal hacking, be sure to use a personal firewall and set the parameters to deny access to personal information and to refuse cookies and active code (ActiveX, Java) from such sites.

48.7   CONCLUDING REMARKS.   This chapter focuses specifically on the use and abuse of Internet and e-mail resources. However, it becomes clear that both of these technologies are simply extensions of the human being behind the computer. Whether it is pornography, online gambling, deceitful e-mails, or simply posting inappropriate material to a public Web site, the potential for damage to an individual, family, or organization is high. Taking a proactive stance through education and awareness is one major tool to combat these deceptive and unethical practices.

Employers have an ethical, and in many cases legal, responsibility to develop and implement policies around the appropriate use of the Internet and e-mail at work. Unfortunately, simply putting the policies out for employee consumption is not enough. Employers must continually remind employees about both the dangers of misuse and the potential consequences to their employment. And when an employee chooses to violate the policy, employers must have a clearly defined process for encouraging proper behavior.

The scope of impact for these issues does not simply end when the employees leaves the office. Because of the widespread use of Internet and e-mail into nearly every facet of our lives, taking the message home to the family is an important responsibility for everyone. Child predators use the Internet to prey on unsuspecting or naive children, in an effort to exploit them for whatever immoral activity they wish. Parents then have an obligation to put their own family policies in place regarding what is, or is not, acceptable use of the Internet and e-mail in the home.

Unfortunately, there is no easy answer to the problems described in this chapter. Both the Internet and e-mail are neither good nor bad. They only become good or bad by the users and their actions. As technology continues to increase in speed, and in the ability to store more data in less space, everyone must take an active role in protecting each other at the corporate level and in the home.

48.8   FURTHER READING

Blanpain, R., and M. Van Gestel. *Use and Monitoring of E-mail, Intranet, and Internet Facilities at Work: Law and Practice*. The Hague: Kluwer Law International, 2004.

Cavanaugh, C. *Managing Your E-Mail: Thinking Outside the Inbox*. Hoboken, NJ: John Wiley & Sons, 2003.

Criddle, L. *Look Both Ways: Help Protect Your Family on the Internet*. Redmond, WA: Microsoft Press, 2006.

Flynn, N., and R. Kahn. *E-Mail Rules: A Business Guide to Managing Policies, Security, and Legal Issues for E-Mail and Digital Communication.* New York: AMACOM, 2003.

Goldsmith, J., and T. Wu. *Who Controls the Internet? Illusions of a Borderless World.* New York: Oxford University Press, 2006.

Holtz, S. *Corporate Communications: A Guide to Crafting Effective and Appropriate Internal Communication.* New York: AMACOM, 2004.

Jovin, E. *E-mail Etiquette for Business Professionals.* New York: Syntaxis Press, 2007.

Spinello, R. A. *Regulating Cyberspace: The Policies and Technologies of Control.* Westport, CT: Quorum Books, 2002.

Willard, N. E. *Cyberbullying and Cyberthreats: Responding to the Challenge of Online Social Aggression, Threats, and Distress*, 2nd edition. Champaign, IL: Research Press, 2007.

48.9 NOTES

1. Parts of this article are based on materials originally published by M. E. Kabay in his *Network World Security Strategies* column and in older writings. To avoid cluttering the text with nonessential endnotes, no quotation marks or references are provided for such material.

2. Gaudin, "Insider Threats Giving IT Execs Nightmares," *eSecurityplanet,* November 4, 2005; www.esecurityplanet.com/prevention/article.php/3561761.

3. www.dhs.gov/iaipdailyreport.

4. J. Leyden, "The Enemy Within: Geeks, Squatters and Saboteurs Threaten Corporate Security," *The Register,* December 15, 2005; www.theregister.co.uk/2005/12/15/mcafee_internal_security_survey/.

5. There are several copies of the Monty Python SPAM skit available on YouTube. The skit shows two customers overwhelmed by a menu consisting largely of SPAM—with Vikings singing a rousing chorus of "spam, Spam, SPAM!" in the background.

6. *Parker v. C. N. Enterprises Order,* District Court of Travis County, Texas. Final Judgment; http://legal.web.aol.com/decisions/dljunk/parkero.html.

7. Information on the Ponzi scheme is taken from *The People's Chronology* copyright © 1995, 1996 by James Trager; published by Henry Holt & Co. and made available through the Microsoft Encarta 2007 CD. All rights reserved.

8. C. Tran, "Reading Is Believing." *ScienceNow,* July 19, 2005; http://sciencenow.sciencemag.org/cgi/content/full/2005/719/1 (by subscription only).

9. From the NetworkSolutions Web site: www.networksolutions.com/ssl-certificates/index.jsp OK now.

10. A. Hamilton, "Arizona Lottery Pick 3 Random Number Bug," *RISKS Forum Digest* 19, No. 83 (1998); http://catless.ncl.ac.uk/Risks/19.83.html#subj5.

11. E. Werner, "Feds Say Vague Law Makes Ban on Internet Gambling Tough to Enforce," Associated Press, April 2, 2008; www.startribune.com/politics/national/congress/17227309.html.

12. K. Young, "Internet Addiction Test," 2008, Center for Internet Addiction Recovery, www.netaddiction.com/resources/internet_addiction_test.htm.

13. P. Bates and M. Fain, "Cheating 101: Paper Mills and You," 2000; www.coastal.edu/library/papermil.htm.

14. A. Larson, "Sexual Harassment Law," Law Offices of Aaron Lawson (September 2003): www.expertlaw.com/library/employment/sexual_harassment.html#FN1.

15. M. Potok, "Internet Hate and the Law: The First Amendment Protects Most Hateful Speech on the World Wide Web, but There Are Exceptions," *Southern Poverty Law Center Intelligence Report* 97 (Winter 2000); www.splcenter.org/intel/intelreport/article.jsp?aid=288.

CHAPTER **49**

IMPLEMENTING A SECURITY AWARENESS PROGRAM

K. Rudolph

49.1   INTRODUCTION.   Even the best security process will fail when implemented by the uninformed. Information technology security awareness is achieved when people know what is going on around them, can recognize potential security violations or suspicious circumstances, and know what initial actions to take. Security awareness is the result of activities, tools, and techniques intended to attract people's attention and to help them focus on security. Because people play an integral role in protecting an organization's assets, security awareness among staff, contractors, partners, and customers is a necessary and cost-effective countermeasure against security breaches. Effective awareness programs motivate people and provide measurable benefits. Prerequisites for implementing a security awareness program successfully include senior-level management support, an in-place security policy, measurable goals, and a plan for reaching those goals. Attention-getting awareness materials tailored to the audience and to the technology yield maximum program impact. This chapter contains practical information on design approaches for an awareness program, including its content, techniques, principles, tools, measurement approaches, and evaluation techniques.

49.2   AWARENESS AS A SURVIVAL TECHNIQUE.   In recent years, awareness of security concerns worldwide has increased. Business, government organizations, and individuals are conducting a significant part of their activities electronically. Electronic information (corporate and personal data) often can be easily accessed, copied, and distributed. Increased use of information technology (IT) and the Internet has resulted in increased risks and increased regulatory requirements. Public awareness of the risks of inappropriate, unwanted, or illegal access, use, and disclosure of data has also increased. Security, once perceived as the responsibility of the IT department, is now an issue at the board of directors' level.

More, more advanced, and more connected digital technologies have brought new threats and vulnerabilities. An insider or visitor could take away entire databases concealed in a pocket on a thumb drive. As of early 2008, these small, portable memory devices can hold up to 100 GB in a configuration the size of a business card.[1] Professional hackers are now being commissioned for specific security attacks. The following are some of the trends that are growing in popularity with criminals: malicious code, phishing, blended attacks, search engine poisoning, exploitation of application systems vulnerabilities, mobile device viruses, and target-specific attacks.

Changes in mobile devices, wireless networks, and cybercrime methods mean that the success or even survival of an organization may depend on personnel understanding and following the requirements for protecting information assets.

Security awareness is the individual's understanding that security is important and that everyone has a role in ensuring the security of information and information technology. The two questions at the heart of a security awareness program are:

1. Would the individual recognize a potential security problem?
2. Would that person take appropriate action?

In the animal kingdom, awareness—being alert to danger signals and responding quickly—can be the difference between survival and death. Bats and dolphins use sonar to detect and avoid dangers, while cats use whiskers and keen senses of hearing, smell, and night vision to probe their environments. Being alert to danger signals and responding quickly is also important for organizations. An organization's staff can similarly function as its detection instruments, automatically recognizing things that are out of place and reflexively taking preventive and mitigating actions. Awareness activities can build and support this reflexive behavior.

Awareness among an organization's staff (including contractors, third-party partners and vendors, and, in some cases, customers) is a cost-effective security countermeasure; that is, one that costs less than the impact that it addresses. When determining the cost effectiveness of controls, a general rule is that prevention costs less than cure. "Controls designed to prevent breaches from occurring are more cost-effective than those designed to identify and/or correct breaches after the fact—the main reason being that preventive controls reduce or eliminate the impact costs."[2] The cost of security controls can include up-front expenses (e.g., purchase price, maintenance, or license fees), implementation and management costs, and costs associated with using or operating the controls. "Cutting-edge high technology security controls are, generally speaking, substantially more expensive across all three categories than low-tech service or procedural controls."[3] Security consultant Hal Tipton calls security awareness "the most valuable yet the most overlooked and underfunded mechanism for improving the implementation of information security."[4]

Members of an organization's workforce are often the first to be affected by a security incident. Their compliance with security policy can make or break a security program. A staff that is security-aware can detect and prevent many incidents and mitigate damage when incidents do occur. To reap these benefits, awareness must be a critical part of an organization's security program.

Many industries, as well as the U.S. Government, are finding that security education and awareness are no longer optional.[5] In the United States, the Federal Information Security Management Act (FISMA), the Health Insurance Portability and Accountability Act (HIPAA), the Sarbanes-Oxley Act (SOX), and the Gramm-Leach-Bliley Act (GLBA) require the federal government, the healthcare industry, and financial institutions, respectively, to provide mandatory security awareness for staff. Various U.S. states have passed laws that supplement the federal laws. Also, the European Union follows a Data Protection Directive that addresses the access, use, and disclosure of personal information. "As this type of legislation becomes reasonable and customary, negligence and due diligence law come into play. Therefore, security awareness training is likely to become mandatory for all industries."[6]

49.2.1   Awareness versus Training.   Learning is a continuum; it starts with awareness, builds to training, and evolves into education.[7] Rebecca Herold, security consultant and author, explains that "[a]wareness is typically the 'what' component of your education strategy for influencing behavior and practice; training is typically the 'how' component to implement security and privacy."[8]

Security awareness differs from security training in purpose, approach, and results. Awareness has the following characteristics:

- It is intended to focus attention on security and to change attitudes. Awareness sets the stage for training by changing individual perceptions and the organizational culture so that security is recognized as critical. "Awareness activities are intended to allow individuals to recognize Information Technology (IT) security concerns and respond accordingly."[9]
- Learning tends to be short term, immediate, and specific.
- Learners are information recipients.
- It reaches broad audiences with multiple, attractive, attention-getting techniques.

Training exhibits different characteristics:

- It is more formal than awareness. The purpose of training is to build knowledge and skills to facilitate job performance.
- Training takes longer and involves producing skills and competency for those involved in functional specialties other than IT security (e.g., management, systems design, and acquisition).
- It is provided selectively based on an individual's roles (job functions) and needs.
- Learners have an active role.

49.2.2   IT Security Is a People Problem.   In 1952, UNIVAC, the first commercial computer, was used to predict the outcome of the U.S. presidential election. Early in the evening, based on input of the first returns, the computer predicted a landslide for Eisenhower. Walter Cronkite refused to report these results because he did not find them credible. Some people went as far as to suggest that they reprogram the computer to provide a different result. In the end, Eisenhower did win by a landslide, which led some to remark that the problem with computers is people.

IT security used to be viewed as a technology problem. Sophisticated hardware and software solutions are still used to control access, detect potential intrusions, and prevent fraud. Yet security incidents are occurring with increasing frequency. The reality is that computer security is both a human and a technological problem: People do not perform work consistently; they get tired and may perform tasks erratically; they may get angry (at the organization, their spouse, their boss, or at work in general) and intentionally try to disrupt or compromise operations; they may cause system failures by independently "improving" business processes; or they just do not follow established policies and procedures. As security author Donn B. Parker points out, some employees believe that "they can work faster and better by not making backups, using pirated software, failing to securely store sensitive information, endangering information, and secretly sharing the organization's sensitive information with competitors over the Internet in return for favors."[10] Connecting computers into networks significantly increases risk because network security depends on the cooperation of every user. A single individual who allows a desktop or laptop computer to be compromised places every interconnected system and its associated assets at risk.

"Computers alone don't implement information security policies and standards—human beings purchase and configure the systems, switch on the control functions, monitor the alarms, and run them."[11] In addition, people are more perceptive and adaptive than hardware or software components. Thus, if properly trained and motivated, they can be the strongest and most effective security countermeasure. Investments in technology to improve information security must be accompanied by investments in people. An awareness program is a needed complement to technical controls, not an alternative.

49.2.3 Overnight Success Takes Time. Like exercise, security awareness requires time and repetition. If the audience is bombarded with the total awareness arsenal at one time, it becomes overwhelmed and rejects or fails to assimilate much of the information presented. Information overload is a common mistake in awareness programs. If the same volume of information is presented over an extended time, information retention and assimilation into daily business processes are increased.

Effective awareness programs are long-term activities that bring about gradual improvement. Management must consistently support the security program and not change approaches from year to year for the sake of change. Awareness activities must consistently reinforce the awareness message rather than replacing it with each new management interpretation. An effective security awareness program uses techniques similar to those used for a social marketing campaign, repeating a consistent message (e.g., "Don't drink and drive," "Buckle up," "Smoking kills," "Loose lips sink ships") and may need two to five years to produce measurable results.[12]

49.3 CRITICAL SUCCESS FACTORS. A security awareness program needs a successful launch for maximum impact. Critical program elements include:

- An information security policy that establishes the security rules of behavior for the organization
- Senior-level management support and buy-in to demonstrate the importance of security
- Destinations and road maps to guide and monitor program activities
- Visibility and audience appeal to ensure that all subgroups within the workforce are addressed

49.3.1 In-Place Information Security Policy.

Security objectives must be embodied in policies that clarify and document management's intentions and concerns. Policies are an organization's laws. They set expectations for employee performance and guide behaviors. An effective information security policy includes statements of goals and responsibilities and delineates what activities are allowed, what activities are not allowed, and what penalties may be imposed for failure to comply.

Effective information security policies show that management expects a focus on security. Well-defined security policies make it easier to take disciplinary action against those who compromise security. Established policies are also useful in dealing with personality types who will not do something until management tells them to.

A cohesive information security awareness policy, tailored to the organizational culture, gives the total information security program credibility and visibility. It shows that management recognizes that security is important and that individuals will be held accountable for their actions. As Daryl White, chief information officer for the U.S. Department of the Interior, said, "You can't hold firewalls and intrusion detection systems accountable, you can only hold people accountable."[13]

An awareness policy should address three basic concepts:

1. Participation in the awareness program is required for everyone, including senior management, part-time and full-time staff, new hires, contractors, or other outsiders who have access to the organization's information systems. For example, new hires might be required to receive an information security awareness orientation briefing within a specific time frame (e.g., 30 days after hire) or before being allowed system access. Existing employees might be required to attend an awareness activity or take a course within one month of program initiation and periodically thereafter (e.g., semiannually or annually). Existing employees might also be required to refresh their security awareness when the organization's IT environment changes significantly.

2. Everyone will be given sufficient time to participate in awareness activities. In many organizations, security policy also requires that employees sign a statement indicating that they understand the material presented and will comply with security policies.

3. Responsibility for conducting awareness program activities is assigned. The program might be created and implemented by one or a combination of: the training department; the security staff; or an outside organization, consultant, or security awareness specialist.

49.3.2 Senior-Level Management Support.

Senior management must be committed to information security and must visibly demonstrate that commitment by example (e.g., signing the launch memo that introduces an awareness program or activity, participating in awareness activities, and encouraging others to do so), by providing an adequate budget, and by supporting the security staff. Organizational leaders must understand and support the program as well as provide oversight. Recent years have shown a significant shift in responsibilities from a compliance officer or committee to the highest levels of an organization.

For example, ChoicePoint Inc., a data broker, was duped by thieves (social engineers) into turning over private data on more than 160,000 people. On January 26, 2006, the Federal Trade Commission (FTC) and ChoicePoint reached a $15 million settlement, which included $10 million in fines. This is the largest civil penalty imposed by the

FTC to date. In addition, ChoicePoint is required to submit to independent audits of its procedures every two years for the next 20 years.[14] U.S. Senator Charles E. Schumer, who introduced a data security bill in 2005, said that "the settlement was not punitive enough."[15]

Poor security measures can be costly: in damage to the organization's brand or reputation, in impact on operations, and in actual and potential lawsuits. The media will not hesitate to report on any type of security threat or breach. Stories such as this one are a wake-up call. This new story highlights the need for senior executive commitment to the security function.

Senior managers should see information security as a way to protect the organization's reputation. It protects customer confidence and market valuations, and it delivers a competitive edge. Security is not just about reducing risk. In today's e-commerce environment, effective information security can increase business and profits. Top management should believe that security is not solely a risk avoidance measure (like an insurance policy). Security and awareness programs should be seen as an e-business supporter and enabler.

49.3.3 Example.   Senior management must lead by example. If senior managers do not take security seriously, the program will lack credibility. For example, if the security policy prohibits employees from bringing software from home for use on the organization's PCs and senior executives are seen using personal software on their office system to evaluate their stock portfolios, employees will perceive the policy as inconsistent, unfair, and not universally applicable.

49.3.4 Budget.   Demonstrated, documented top-management support prevents middle managers from denying requests to fund information security. Managers often do not allocate employee time for security awareness activities because they do not see a direct connection to the bottom line for which they are held accountable.

Some security analysts recommend that 40 percent of an organization's security budget be spent on awareness measures.[16] The National Institute of Standards and Technology (NIST) offers four approaches to identifying funding requirements for awareness and training programs. These are:

1. Percent of overall training budget
2. Allocation per user by role
3. Percent of overall IT budget
4. Explicit dollar allocations by component based on overall implementation costs[17]

49.3.5 Security Staff Backing.   Senior managers must stand behind the organization's policies and the security staff charged with enforcing those policies. This is especially important in areas where security and convenience conflict, such as enforcing a control that removes system access for users whose records show that they have not completed a required awareness refresher activity.

49.3.6 Reward for Good Security Behaviors.   Often, management wants to treat security as a core requirement. Managers may believe that security is part of everyone's job and no special recognition or incentives should be provided. This approach does not work well because security tends to be outside the normal business process. For example, if everyone only does what they are supposed to do, then we really do not need security controls. Unfortunately, if we do not have effective controls, we find out that there is noncompliance only after something bad happens (e.g., customer data are compromised).

Managers who treat security as a core requirement and do not explicitly promote and identify good or poor compliance are generally assuming that they will be able to identify noncompliance from the information they receive from normal businesses activity. This is not a correct assumption. For example, customer data may be compromised with no impact on the business process.

For a number of years, government agencies held the same perception, that security was a core function and did not give it any special emphasis. This changed as the number of incidents and their impact grew. The increase in security losses resulted in legislation requiring that agencies maintain security awareness and training programs. This resulted in improved security environments.

One of the key issues that managers need to learn and understand is that security is a special concern that must be emphasized routinely if assets are to be adequately protected. Security should be integrated with performance appraisals. "Personnel become motivated to actively support information security and privacy initiatives when they know that their job advancement, compensation, and benefits will be impacted. If this does not exist, then an organization is destined to depend only upon technology for information security assurance."[18]

49.3.7   Destination and Road Maps.   Ideally, the goals (destination) of an awareness program should be specific, realistic, and measurable. Victor Basili of the University of Maryland developed an approach for metrics where the metric is created as the final step of a process called Goal-Question-Metric.[19] He recommends defining a goal, for example: "Goal—decrease inappropriate Web site visits." Next, create a question that will indicate whether the goal is being met or not: "Are staff continuing to visit Web sites that they should not?" Then, and only then, create a metric that will support the goal. The metric would be the number of attempts to access inappropriate Web sites, such as illegal or pornographic material. This information can be extracted from Web filtering products. This offers several benefits:

- It's an automated metric.
- It's easy to collect.
- It will give an idea of what the organization's users are doing.

Reaching an identified security awareness destination is easier with a road map or plan. An anecdotal story about Abraham Lincoln tells of his statement that if he had eight hours to chop down a tree, he would spend the first six sharpening his ax. Lack of planning usually means that time is spent reacting to events rather than being proactive and prepared. It takes great effort to chop down a tree with a dull ax. Similarly it is much harder to create, manage, or measure the effect of an unplanned awareness program than a planned program with defined objectives, assigned responsibilities, and management direction.

As with Lincoln sharpening his ax, planning promotes awareness activities that are carefully designed to elicit specific, positive responses. Plans should also be flexible to address changes in organizational structure, organizational objectives, and applicable threats and vulnerabilities. This flexibility should also allow incorporation of particularly relevant current events. For example, an awareness activity might emphasize the offering of rewards by Microsoft for help in capturing virus writers as evidence that security issues are getting high-level attention.

The security awareness plan should contain these elements:

- A description of the organization and its IT culture (culture is the instinctive behavior of individuals within an organization), including assigned roles and responsibilities
- The status of the organization's current efforts (can include baseline)
- An approach to ensure senior management support
- A determination of awareness needs (topics)
- Program goals and metrics
- A description of how staff will be motivated
- A description of methods and materials to be acquired, created, and/or modified
- A schedule showing actions to be completed and who is responsible for ensuring their completion (including program evaluation and updates)

A baseline will establish where the organization stands with regard to its security awareness efforts and program. It may be that the baseline is zero and a program has not been implemented. In that case, the organization may take a survey to find out how people in the organization view security and how familiar they are with security policies. The results of the survey would become the baseline. Where a program has been implemented, the organization may choose to document the level of awareness so that over time other measurements can be taken to show changes.

A security awareness program should be an ongoing effort. Some organizations offer a security awareness orientation to new employees and regular reinforcement for all employees at various times throughout the year. Doing so provides spaced repetition of the material and reinforces learning. Some organizations address security awareness on a monthly basis with newsletters, posters, screen savers, contests, surveys, and online modules. Other organizations offer awareness courses that are updated annually and provide reinforcement at various times, such as on November 30, International Computer Security Awareness Day. NIST SP 800-50[20] presents a detailed awareness approach for establishing and maintaining a security program, including an appendix with a sample awareness and training program plan template.

49.3.8   Visibility and Audience Appeal.   An effective awareness program cultivates a professional, positive, and visible image. A visible program demonstrates the value of the awareness activities, raises employee morale, and encourages the support of the general workforce. The more methods used to spread the message, the more visible the program will be. An awareness program that uses computer-based courses, posters, acknowledgment statements, newsletters, contests, and videos will reach more people than a program that consists of posting security policies to the organization's intranet and sending a memo advising staff to read the policies.

Security awareness programs that show the organization's concern for employees' IT security well-being at home (for telecommuters and others who use computers at home) and while traveling are better received than programs that ignore such issues. This is because the radio station that most people are tuned to is "WII FM," or *What's in It for Me*? Whether the target audience is all end users or senior management, showing them how they will personally benefit from improved security awareness contributes to program success. Viewing security as a service with the entire organization as a customer highlights the importance of marketing security to management and staff.

Common mistakes in security awareness programs include not fitting the program to the environment, using unmodified educational materials, and having no consideration for the learner.[21] Learners should be able to relate to the awareness materials and apply the materials to their jobs. Organizations should build awareness programs around their business environment instead of purchasing ready-made awareness materials or copying a program from another organization without modifying it.

Joseph A. Grau, former chief of the Information Security Division at the Department of Defense Security Institute, believed in the importance of marketing security and often pointed out that customers actually pay for security services. For example, managers pay for enforcing the requirement to lock a classified document in a safe rather than leaving it on a desk, with labor hours. Other methods of payment are in the form of energy, attention, and concern for security matters, such as taking time to identify and report a potential security incident. Even egos are part of the payment for security when "scientists, researchers, technical specialists, engineers, and management personnel must refrain from communicating their successes to friends, family, and peers to protect sensitive, company private, or classified information."[22]

49.4   OBSTACLES AND OPPORTUNITIES.   Starting an awareness program is not as easy as one might expect. Although senior managers seem to recognize the benefits of an awareness program when asked, they may still be reluctant to devote financial resources and staff time to it. It is relatively easy to identify the cost of an awareness program, but it is difficult to quantify its benefits. This is a primary reason why the U.S. Government has made maintenance of a computer security awareness program mandatory.[23]

The basic challenges faced when starting and maintaining an effective awareness program include gaining management support, gaining union support (where applicable), overcoming audience resistance, and addressing the diffusion of responsibility.

49.4.1   Gaining Management Support.   Management provides essential ingredients to a security awareness program: credibility, supervision, resources, and advocacy. Credibility comes when management complies with the security rules. If managers do not comply, then there is no reason to expect anyone else to comply. Employees will generally follow the lead of their managers, who must be role models for good security. When managers are seen to ignore policies, their subordinates quickly imitate the managers' behavior. The problem then spreads throughout the organization.

Given that most security incidents stem from errors and omissions, managers should review performance records. They should analyze each incident that causes a loss or damage to identify the cause. Certain employees may be associated with unusually high or low rates of specific problems. Analysis can reveal learning opportunities that can benefit the entire group. Managers should let workers know that they are being monitored.

Management allocates resources for the awareness program, visibly demonstrating that their support for the program is genuine. Managers must use rewards and penalties to reinforce or change behavior. They should emphasize and reward job performance that supports the positive objectives of security, profitability (for companies), productivity, and growth of the organization. Managers must also support the program by supporting the security staff and showing that computer security is good business. If management does not show that awareness has a positive return, it will be difficult to justify consistent funding. To assist management in these tasks, it is important to keep management informed, speak their language, and provide proof of impact.

49.4.2   Keep Management Informed.   Managers need enough information to allow them to understand security concerns, make informed comments, and respond knowledgeably to questions. To get this information to management, identify management reporting and communication mechanisms, such as progress reports, management briefings, and program reviews, and contribute information on security awareness program activities. Include updates with metrics that show performance measured against program goals.[24]

Timing can also be important as support for security is strongest after a breach when the costs of poor security become apparent. Such costs can be summed in a dollar loss, which includes the cost to notify those affected, customer dissatisfaction and defection, investigations, lawsuits, and other losses incurred by the breach. In many cases, the cost of a breach quickly exceeds security program costs. It is important for management to be careful not to react in such a way that gives the impression that incident clean-up is recognized, but ongoing compliance is not.

49.4.3   Speak Their Language.   To communicate with management, the IT staff concerned with awareness should consider these issues:

- Present realistic information rather than either overstating threats or fears. Be careful not to provide a false sense of security by overemphasizing positive aspects in an attempt to keep the program from being seen as a problem child.

- Present reasonable suggestions for solutions, along with problems and concerns.

- Prepare a written and verbal presentation so that if the allotted time is cut, you will be able to condense the verbal presentation and leave the written one, thereby delivering the complete message.

- Remember the budget—include costs involved and where possible reflect the anticipated benefits (e.g., fewer violations, increased compliance, better audit findings, reduction in misuse of IT assets or personnel time).

- Remember the ecology—ecology is the study of the relationship between organisms (users, systems, etc.) and their environment (hardware, physical access control, etc.). "The ecological aspects of security assert that you cannot afford to focus on one portion of the system without keeping track of the impact of each decision on the health of the ecosystem."[25] Be aware of the impact of the program on the entire organization and its mission. Management concerns include the amount of time that staff spend away from their jobs to satisfy administrative requirements.

- Management resistance is often based on expending funds on something perceived as a low priority or on concerns about balancing security with operational needs. Although the time and effort to build a strong security program are not trivial, it is far less by comparison with the time and effort required to deal with just one serious incident. For example, in 2007, the FTC "received over 800,000 consumer fraud and identity theft complaints. Consumers reported losses from fraud of more than $1.2 billion."[26] Using effective security awareness to avoid being targeted by class-action lawsuits for loss of control over personally identifiable information is a rational strategy.

- Some security professionals recommend pointing out that insurance policies require continuous funding but are not often used; however, few organizations choose to forgo those costs.[27] Another incentive for organizations is that many contracts require information security programs—especially when the contract is with the federal government or if it deals with intellectual property belonging to customers (e.g., contracts for hardware or software design services).

49.4.4   Gaining Union Support.   John Ippolito, CISSP and coauthor of NIST SP 500-16, says in correspondence with this author: "Mention unions when developing an awareness program and the response ranges from a quizzical look to a sneer. People with a quizzical look have generally never worked with a union and fail to see their role in an awareness program. Those who sneer at the mention of union participation have typically had past efforts blocked by union action."

Unions can be a partner or an impediment to an awareness program or anything in between. Often their role depends on how they are approached. Unions look after the best interests of their membership. An awareness program is trying to communicate computer security roles and responsibilities to that membership. Thus, union and program objectives, although different, are not in conflict. To gain union support, sell (present) your program as being in the best interests of union membership. Tips to accomplish this objective include:

- Bring in the union representatives early in the program development phase. Union representatives do not like to be ignored, especially when their membership is involved. If union representatives are presented with a fully developed program, their first response may be to think that it is detrimental to the membership; otherwise you would have given them more of an opportunity to contribute to its development. This thinking may then result in a micro-review, in which union representatives look for anything, no matter how small, that might be interpreted as contrary to the interests of union members.

- Be sure that the representatives understand that the objective of the computer security awareness program is to create within the workforce an understanding that there is a problem (i.e., the potential for a security incident) that can adversely affect the ability of their membership to get their job done. Thus, program participation is beneficial to their members, and it will help them reduce operating costs without staff reductions.

- Make it clear that the awareness program creates no new responsibilities. The awareness program is intended to help the workforce members recognize potential problems and follow existing security procedures. Ask the union representatives for examples of work situations that might be appropriate to highlight potential security issues.

- Be careful when suggesting any employee testing. Unions often interpret testing, especially when results are recorded, as a management mechanism used to limit the ability of their members to advance. Even a simple pass/fail test can create a union issue as the union will seek clarification about what happens if a person does not pass the test. At the awareness level, recording test or quiz results can be counterproductive and can create anxiety. The best approach is often to ask challenging questions and allow for safe failure, in which students can learn from their mistakes without penalties. Often a goal of an awareness program is to take away some of the fear and ignorance that have traditionally surrounded IT security by allowing people to learn in a nonthreatening environment.

49.4.5   Overcoming Audience Resistance.   Another common obstacle is audience resistance. A story about a millionaire who threw a large pool party at his mansion illustrates this issue. The pool contained four alligators, and the millionaire announced that he would give $100,000 or a new Ferrari to anyone who would swim the length of the pool. A large splash immediately followed his announcement. The crowd watched a man frantically swimming to the other end. "Well done!" said the millionaire. "Which will you have, the money or the car?" The wet and angry man answered, "I don't care about your prize; I just want to know who pushed me." This is how some end users feel about mandatory awareness courses and activities. It does not matter how good the activity or reward; they just do not want to be told that they have to do it.

In many organizations, a positive approach is more effective than a negative one. Programs that rely on *FUD* (motivation by fear, uncertainty, and doubt) or use negative phrases such as "failure to attend" may not be as effective, because such statements are viewed by some employees as challenges, whereas others see them as empty threats. In addition, such statements can be offensive to those employees who are always cooperative. It is often better "to encourage participation, expect compliance, and deal with the no-shows later."[28]

An awareness program must address the total organization. This includes the naive user, the new user, the power user, and even those who think that computer security is worthless and does not apply to them. Given this audience diversity, the content must be structured so that the same level of awareness can be communicated using a variety of techniques. For example, password protection might be best communicated to the naive user through a computer-based war story, whereas the same concepts might be best communicated to the power user with a brief statement of the organizational requirements on a poster or reminder memo.

Although the basic technology components may be similar from one organization to the next, the manner in which they are configured is often different, as is the terminology used to refer to them. For example, some organizations use the term "desktop" and others the term "workstation" to refer to the computer installed at an end user's location. These seemingly trivial differences can make a one-size-fits-all awareness approach fail.

49.4.6   Addressing the Diffusion of Responsibility.   One result of addressing the entire organization with a single message is a diffusion of responsibility. When people are in a group, responsibility for acting is diffused. The security awareness program must convey that each individual is responsible for taking action to prevent or report breaches, regardless of how many others may have noticed the same symptoms or other factors.

To illustrate the diffusion of responsibility, researchers conducted an experiment where a student alone in a room staged an epileptic fit. When there was just one person listening next door, that person rushed to the student's aid 85 percent of the time. However, when subjects thought there were four others also overhearing the seizure, they came to the student's aid only 31 percent of the time. In another experiment, people who saw smoke seeping out from under a doorway reported it 75 percent of the time when they were on their own but only 38 percent of the time when they were in a group.[29] Providing individual reinforcement in addition to group activities may mitigate this diffusion of responsibility.

49.5   APPROACH.   Raising awareness is similar to social marketing, which uses advertising techniques to inform the public of societal concerns, such as the campaigns to reduce smoking or decrease the use of alcohol on college campuses.

49.5.1   Awareness as Social Marketing.   The marketing concepts of message, product, and market apply in a security awareness campaign. The message is the need for security, the product is the practice of security, and the market is all employees. Communication is the essential tool, and the information disseminated becomes the foundation on which behavioral change is built.

Research and planning are essential and should result in a clear strategy that:

- Defines program objectives.
- Identifies primary and secondary audiences.
- Defines information to be communicated.
- Describes approaches that fit the organizational culture and structure.
- Describes benefits that accrue to the audience.

Research may be conducted by observation, surveys, tests, and interviews. Review help-desk statistics and trends for indications of actual and potential security incidents and evidence of training needs. For example, a large number of password resets might indicate that password procedures need to be reviewed or that users need additional training. Ask the staff how they would break into the system—the people closest to the system ought to know its vulnerabilities and should be thinking about how to fix them. Ask them to consider such questions as "Are security breaches predictable?"

Pretest materials before distributing them. Pretesting provides evidence that materials are reaching your target audience with the intended message. It can also avoid embarrassing situations, such as occur after distributing a poster on which punctuation or the lack of punctuation changes the message (e.g., "Slow Work Zone" instead of "Slow, Work Zone"). Pretesting may be accomplished using focus groups, providing materials to a single unit within the organization or through group or individual interviews. In all cases, the evaluation should include a set of multiple choice or ranking questions with one or two open-ended questions. This analysis approach facilitates data comparison and aggregation. The question set should be structured to determine the message received and the level of experience (novice, beginner, user, power user) required to understand the material and receive the intended message. The questions should also be structured to avoid leading the respondent.

49.5.2   Motivation.   An organization truly dedicated to security will develop an effective security motivation program along with or as a part of a continuing awareness effort. It should use the following motivators:

- Anticipation and receipt of rewards
- Fear and experience of penalties

Other (less controllable) motivators include: character, loss experience (self and others), professional and company loyalty, self-interest (protection of personal investment and reputation), desire to excel beyond peers, and convenience.

M. E. Kabay writes of a security officer who experimented with reward and punishment in implementing security policies. Workers were supposed to log off their terminals when leaving the office, but compliance rates were only 40 percent. In one area, the security officer put nasty notes on terminals that were not logged off and reported offenders to their bosses. In another area, the security officer identified those users who had logged off and left a chocolate candy on there keyboards. After one month, compliance in the punished area had risen to 60 percent. Compliance in the area that received the candy had reached 80 percent. (For fuller discussion, see Chapter 50 in this *Handbook*.)

An awareness program seeks to change attitudes and behaviors that may have been practiced for a long time in company procedures or become habits that are now part of the organizational culture. Change (positive or negative) is often met with resistance simply because people do not like change. An awareness program must consider this natural workforce resistance to change by appealing to complementary attitudes or preferences. For example, the practice of password sharing with new employees to "get them on the system sooner" may be widespread. By showing that people are respected and recognized in the organization for protecting system access, rather than placing system assets at risk, the awareness campaign may change this behavior.

Security consultant Parker said:

> I see poor security in every organization no matter how good the information security staff, awareness program, and technical controls may be, because of the lackadaisical, unsustainable performance of the organization's staff and managers to make the bothersome safeguards and security practices effective. They give lip service to security; they have bursts of security efforts when they are being watched or have suffered a loss, but support ultimately deteriorates for lack of a natural, ongoing motivation in the face of the overpowering pressure of job performance and finding the convenient way to do things. In contrast, computers maintain security, because security is built into their performance (if users and administrators do not tamper with it).

His conclusion was that security should be built into the performance of people as well as into the performance of our computer systems.[30]

Rewards and penalties are the traditional job performance motivators in any employee/employer or contractual relationship. They are useful for motivating security as well. Rewards usually involve praise and recognition, job advancement, and financial benefits (often in the form of specific bonuses for exemplary behavior). Rewards could also be prizes for exemplary security performance (e.g., winning a competition among groups for the fewest guard-reported or auditor-reported security lapses). Rewards could include recognition letters, pins, plaques, additional leave, or car parking privileges.

Penalties often involve the loss of perks, position, or remuneration; leave without pay; being fired; or legal action. A security consultant tells of a manager who publicly posted the name of anyone who revealed a password, and required everyone in the group to immediately change their passwords. This produced peer pressure to keep passwords secret because no one liked having to learn a new one.

Studies of what workers want from their jobs were conducted in the 1940s and repeated in the 1980s and 1990s. Managers identified good wages, job security, and promotion/growth opportunity as the primary reasons that their employees worked. When workers and supervisors were asked to rank a list of motivators from 1 to 10 in order of importance to workers, workers rated "appreciation for a job well done" as their top motivator; supervisors ranked it eighth. Employees ranked "feeling in on things" as being second in importance; their managers ranked it last at number 10.[31]

Security controls are generally viewed as an impediment to getting work done. The workforce needs to be motivated to comply through an awareness message that makes it clear that the need for security has been balanced against its impact on business processes. This message must be carried forward to system designers so that they also understand that cumbersome controls that are too disruptive to business processes will create an environment hostile toward security and are an incentive to bypass controls to meet schedules and production objectives.

Making security a part of employees' job performance will remove the conflict between job performance and security constraints. If we do not add security of information to the motivators of job advancement and financial compensation, there will be conflict, and we will continue to have superficial security.

Human resources (HR) departments often strive to keep the appraisal process from being diluted with too many evaluation subjects, and especially those that have less tangible means of performance measurement, such as security. Security consultant Parker tells of an HR manager who believed that security should be treated the same as nonsmoking, using the Internet and telephones for personal purposes, and parking regulations. The rules are posted, and if you do not follow them, you suffer penalties up to the severest one of losing your job. The reward for obeying the rules is that you get to keep your job.

The HR manager

> failed to see the significance of information security for the organization, its strategic value, and possible conflict with other job performance. We need top management support to convince HR and line managers to incorporate security providing both rewards and penalties. These motivational efforts should be the objectives of security plans presented to top management until they are achieved.[32]

Audience perceptions and cultural characteristics are factors that may be used in structuring motivational materials. Some of these factors are shown next.

- People want to conform to the organizational performance norm (i.e., they generally do not want to stand out in a crowd). Thus, show that security compliance results in positive feedback, whereas prosecution of violators is noisy and intended to cause embarrassment.

- People are superstitious. That is one reason they pass on chain letters and often open or read e-mails with a subject line that indicates bad luck will follow if they do not continue the chain. Motivate your audience to change their perception of the superstition and alert them to its use as a tactic of criminals.

- People are curious. That is the primary reason why so many virus attacks are successful. People open an e-mail because the subject line makes them curious about the message contents. For example, the message "Your Account is Over-drawn," will make many people open a message to see what account or how much over. Awareness techniques can take advantage of people's curiosity by creating multilevel messages, such as this one patterned on the Burma Shave model of stretching a message over a series of signs:

> Hackers send e-mail
> With subjects enticing
> To open the message
> And the virus it's hiding

Fear is often used as a motivator; however, the primary value of scare tactics is to attract audience attention. Learning communicated through fear is generally retained only in the short term. People follow messages communicated through fear, but their compliance quickly falls off when nothing bad happens. For example, if the message is *"Open an e-mail attachment and you may get a virus that destroys your hard disk,"* every time an e-mail attachment is opened and nothing happens, the fear associated with this message is reduced. Eventually, opening an e-mail attachment will be performed without concern—until a virus actually does strike.

Therefore, fear should not be used as a primary motivator. However, if you do decide to use fear as a motivator, be prepared to back it up with consequences and publicity regarding every security incident. Although you may use fear to attract attention, a more effective delivery approach will have a positive spin. There should be more emphasis on how security measures can help your audience get the job done than on how many days they will be suspended if they fail to comply. Demonstrate that the courage and independence it takes to resist appeals from friends and coworkers to share copyrighted materials illegally are rewarded (i.e., those who follow the rules are seen as praiseworthy and not as weaklings).

Employees rarely see that their changed security practices result in any change in risks. Risk reduction efforts will be eroded if workers see that the security they support has little bearing on the kinds of losses that occur. If employees see inconsistencies of intense security at some times and little or no security at others, this will also detract from risk reduction efforts. Workers who ask, "Why are we locking the doors but leaving the windows open?" will not be motivated to increase security.

It is better to motivate staff with rewards for the positive and measurable objective of due diligence than with the negative approach of risk reduction.

Due diligence involves using generally accepted good practices, meeting the requirements of laws and regulations, achieving security effectiveness relative to others' efforts (including competitors), and satisfying the demands of customers and shareholders. It is achieved by benchmarking, using security products and services, and using the current common body of safeguard knowledge. Due diligence is a more tangible objective than risk reduction.

Failure to properly tailor motivating techniques to your audience often results in these problems:

- **Loss of the audience's attention.** The awareness message is never communicated; thus, workforce behavior remains unchanged.

- **Alienation of the audience**. The awareness message is communicated, but the workforce perceives the message as an incentive to work against security objectives.

- **Trying to do too much.** Awareness is not training or educating. If the awareness audience is bombarded with everything that a security officer or system administrator should know about security, the awareness message will be lost and the audience turned off. Like an exercise program, awareness material is best when delivered in small increments, over an extended time frame, and is targeted to establishing the basic understanding that there is a security problem.

49.6 CONTENT. Awareness is intended to change individuals' behaviors so that they recognize potential security incidents and react appropriately. Awareness materials are generally broad in coverage but limited in depth (i.e., awareness covers a lot of ground but does not dig very deep holes). Using such materials avoids encroaching on training, which is in-depth but is also role based (i.e., provides the security training specific to an individual's organizational responsibilities).

The NIST recommends these 27 topics for security awareness programs:

- password use and management,
- protection from malicious code,
- policy (implications of noncompliance),
- unknown e-mail attachments,
- Web use,
- spam,
- data backup and storage,
- social engineering,
- incident response,
- shoulder surfing (watching over someone's shoulder as he or she types),
- changes in system environment,
- inventory and property transfer,
- personal use and gain issues,
- hand-held device security issues,
- encryption and transmission of sensitive data,
- laptop security while on travel,
- personally owned systems and software at work,
- timely application of system patches,
- software license restriction,
- supported or allowed software on organization systems,
- access control, individual accountability,
- user acknowledgment statements,
- visitor control and physical access to spaces,
- desktop security,
- protection of information throughout the life cycle,
- and e-mail list etiquette.[33]

To avoid overwhelming the audience, NIST also recommends that these topics be explained one or a few at a time: "Brief mention of requirements (policies), the problems that the requirements were designed to remedy, and actions to take are the major topics to be covered in a typical awareness presentation."[34]

Rebecca Herold lists 59 topics for security awareness and training and 20 target audiences, including customer privacy advocates, executive management, mid-level managers, IT personnel, all personnel, new personnel, customer service and call centers, and trainers. Topics to be addressed include security of third-party access, security in job definitions and performance appraisals, business continuity planning, backups and logging, personal information privacy, electronic commerce, and mobile and remote computing.[35]

At the most basic level, an awareness program should address two questions appropriate to every audience:

1. What does a security incident look like?
2. What do I do about it (security)?

"All individuals in the workforce are important to fulfilling organizational goals" is a message that needs to be communicated through an awareness program. People need to be reminded of the value of their work because they often do not understand how their work contributes to the business process. In addition, organizations provide their workforce with significant assets in the form of equipment, software, and data. Compromise or loss of these assets could cause significant harm to the organization's solvency and make it subject to legal liability due to data compromise.

Individuals often are the first to detect security incidents. The actions they take or fail to take subsequently determine the level of damage. Further, individual compliance with established security policies and procedures can make or break a security environment. For example, an individual leaving an unattended desktop connected to the corporate network places all the interconnected assets at risk.

49.6.1 What Do Security Incidents Look Like?   What do security incidents look like? What does a criminal look like? Both questions have no single answer. There is no single criminal profile, and there is no single set of characteristics that fits a security incident.

An awareness program needs to communicate that individuals are not expected to report only verified security incidents. The determination as to whether a particular event is or is not a security incident is an after-the-fact decision made by the technical staff after evaluating the event, its cause, and impact. Individuals are expected to report anything that "might be" a security incident. Thus, the awareness materials should explain that individuals should report erratic or abnormal system behavior or such occurrences as phone calls from "equipment vendors" asking for user passwords, unusual processing slowdowns, dial-in circuits that are always busy, or anything else that appears strange or differs from the normal processing environment.

49.6.2 What Do I Do about Security?   Individuals should be made aware of how to react to incidents (e.g., a call that the individual suspects is from a social engineer, an unknown visitor in the work area, a suspected viruses, or a bomb threat). Tip sheets with "Recognize—React" information or bulleted lists explaining "What You Can Do" for various security topics is useful. Explaining the role of the entire workforce (i.e., it is everybody's responsibility) in security comprises the bulk of the awareness program. The material communicated must be coordinated with organizational policies, and it must be limited in depth—do not cross over into training, or you will lose your audience. The material should also be tailored to the organization's technical architecture and configuration (e.g., do not explain the threats to wireless communications if wireless is not present; do not talk about mainframe security when there is no mainframe).

49.6.3 Basic Security Concepts.   Risks, threats, and vulnerabilities are basic concepts of security that must be generally understood so that security and the individual's relation to security can be placed in its proper perspective.

- **Risk.** The entire workforce should generally understand the concept of risk. The basic understanding that should be communicated is that no useful system is without risk and that security controls provide reasonable levels of protection, not absolute protection. Thus, it is critical that individuals report anomalies that may indicate an attack or security incident.

- **Threat.** A threat is always present, and neither the individual nor the organization can affect when or if a threat will affect or attack the organization (i.e., threats are always there, and you cannot change that). This is a simple but often misunderstood concept. Awareness programs need to address threats so that the workforce will understand that systems operate in an unfriendly environment and that is why it is so important for everyone to help maintain and strengthen the security environment.

- **Vulnerabilities**. Threats cannot have an impact on a system unless there is vulnerability. Vulnerabilities include failure to change passwords, update or patch operating systems, or report potential incidents; lack of a surge suppressor; verbose information broadcasts on networked servers; and many others. Individuals can identify vulnerabilities (e.g., a desktop without a surge suppressor). Awareness material should provide examples of how to identify vulnerability and the reporting process to ensure that the vulnerability is addressed.

49.6.4   Technical Issues.   Technical issues are the specific threats, system components, controls, or control techniques that should be considered for inclusion in an awareness program. The following are examples:

- Access control and passwords: password creation, change, resets, deletion.
- Social engineering: include specific examples of scripts that might be used.
- Malware: how it can damage an information system, and how the organization handles viruses, hoaxes, and spam.
- Data sensitivity, including privacy issues: vulnerability of payroll, medical, and personnel records.
- Data handling: including transmission (wireless or hard-wired), storage, and backups.
- Appropriate use of the Internet: including the World Wide Web, peer-to-peer file sharing, and e-mail.
- Mobile computing: for those who work from home or on travel.
- Home PCs: how security is important at home as well.
- Laptops, PDAs, handheld devices, and mobile phones

Each item included should be tailored to the specific user environment and organizational policy.

49.6.5   Reporting.   The primary responsibility of all individuals within the workforce is to comply with security policies and procedures and report potential vulnerabilities and potential security incidents. This section presents the topics that should be addressed regarding reporting in an awareness program.

- **Who.** Individuals within the workforce should be given the contact information, such as telephone and pager numbers, e-mail, and Web site URLs (addresses) of the security staff, the incident response team, and help desk personnel.
- **What.** The most critical information is who is reporting the incident; its symptoms, date, and time; and actions taken. Other types of information that are helpful when reporting a suspected problem include the affected system(s) or site(s), hardware and operating system, duration of incident, connections with other systems that were active, damage, and assistance needed.
- **When.** Users need to know that, with security events, time is of the essence. Reporting the problem immediately can often prevent or limit the scope and severity of the damage. Users should know not to delay reporting.
- **How.** Workers should be given instructions for reporting suspected problems by telephone or by e-mail using a system that is not suspected of being under attack.

49.7 TECHNIQUES AND PRINCIPLES. Presentation of awareness materials is crucial. If the employee's reaction is "I knew that" or "so what?" the program is not effective. Desired responses include:

- "I never thought of it that way."
- "That surprises me!"
- "That's a great idea!"
- "I'd almost forgotten about that . . . ."
- "I can use this."

49.7.1 Start with a Bang: Make It Attention Getting and Memorable. Experienced, in-demand speakers do not start a presentation with a long, dry, boring introduction that lists every law, regulation, policy, standard, guideline, or other requirement that relates to information security. If there were such a thing as a deadly sin in an awareness program, it would be to bore the audience. For an awareness message to be effective, the audience must identify with the idea, concept, or vision.

49.7.2 Appeal to the Target Audience. A U.S. Critical Infrastructure Assurance Office publication states: "The level of security awareness required of a summer intern program assistant is the same as that needed by the Director, Chief, or Administrator of the agency,"[36] and U.S. federal employees must attain this security awareness within 60 days of starting work. Although workers at all levels need to have security awareness, the methods for effectively reaching different employees with the awareness message may need to be different. It is easier to hit the bull's-eye when one can focus on a specific target.

There are different audiences within all organizations, with different characteristics based on their needs, roles, and interests:

- **Needs.** Audiences with similar needs will have similar levels of computer knowledge and experience. End users with minimal computer experience may be intimidated by and not respond well to technical jargon. Analogies and examples are more appropriate for audiences with little in-depth computer expertise.
- **Roles and interests.** Awareness programs that appeal to the existing values and motivations of the target audience will be more successful than ones that try to

change them. End users are usually interested in getting their job done with as little obstruction as possible. They are usually interested in knowing about the effect of security on their workload, delays, and job performance evaluations. Managers are usually interested in the bottom line and measurable results. They want to know "How much will this security control cost?" and "What kind of benefits will it bring?" Technical staff should receive materials with correct technical term usage. Otherwise, they may conclude that the information is beneath them or that it has been prepared by persons who lack technical knowledge.

To create an awareness program, first identify the audiences and conduct research to find out what they know and what questions about security they ask most often. Surveys and questionnaires can be used to reveal the starting level of awareness of security issues. They will also be useful for measuring progress after the awareness program is implemented.

Historical information can provide clues about what the audience knows and does not know. Asking the question "What security-related problems have the organization experienced?" may reveal information that can be used to tailor the awareness program.

49.7.3 Address Personality and Learning Styles.   Trainers often describe three primary learning styles: auditory, visual, and kinesthetic. An auditory learner picks up information from hearing or reading it and is effectively reached by lectures and written material. A visual learner wants to see what is being taught and prefers diagrams, charts, and pictures. A kinesthetic learner responds well to tactile input and wants to walk through the steps or learn by physically doing the task.

Yet personality styles are arguably more important than learning styles. Some people will not follow a procedure until they understand the reason for it. To reach these people, present the "whys." If an exercise is included as part of an awareness course, once a question is answered, give learners the choice of trying again or receiving the answer. Some people learn best and have better retention when they figure out something for themselves. Others just want to see the result and move on to the next topic or exercise.

49.7.4 Keep It Simple: Awareness Is Not Training.   Awareness efforts should be simple. An objective of an awareness program is to take away the fear and ignorance that have traditionally surrounded information security. Effective awareness activities make people recognize that there is a problem and that they are part of the solution.

49.7.5 Use Logos, Themes, and Images.   Attention is a prerequisite to learning. This was recognized at least 80 years ago: "The person who can capture and hold attention is the person who can effectively influence human behavior."[37] Awareness activities and materials should be designed to attract attention in a positive way. Clever slogans and eye-catching images contribute to the program's success.

Well-designed security logos and mascots can be a source of pride and a showpiece for the organization. Images have greater impact than words. Color and design, as well as the uniqueness of the image, add to its effectiveness. The careful use of animated images in presentations, computer- and Web-based courses, and screen savers can enhance the message. A Web-based course used by many U.S. Government organizations opens with the words "What would happen if someone changed your data?" The words are an animated image that changes a few characters at a time until the message becomes completely unreadable: "Wyad ciunx safper ef stmxune khopgel joor deko?" This image makes a dramatic point about data integrity and availability.

Themes can be used to unite several concepts into a related message. The theme of "Prevention Is Better than Cure" would be appropriate for organizations that process medical data. Give-away items, such as first-aid kits with security slogans and contact information imprinted on them, could tie in to a medical theme, as could the concepts of virus checking software and backups being similar to health insurance cards in that they must be current to be of value.

The U.S. Nuclear Regulatory Commission (NRC) celebrates International Computer Security Day each year with a different theme. The theme of a recent celebration was "Keep It Clean"; an NRC computer security officer (CSO) dressed as Mr. Clean (complete with a bald head and gold hoop earring) passed out antivirus software to employees who attended the event. A large, signed color photograph of the official Mr. Clean was on display. Another year, the celebration introduced the agency's new security mascot, Cyber Tyger. Cyber Tyger was featured on posters, on the cover of the antivirus software CD, and on buttons. Again, one of NRC's CSOs arrived in costume and delighted the visitors. In other years the themes have been "It's a Bug's Life" and "PC Doctor," in which a "sick" PC was wheeled into the lobby on a gurney while the CSO, dressed in surgical scrubs and mask, explained the symptoms of a virus infection to visitors.

Awareness posters can be developed around a common theme, with common design elements, or a phrase or logo. A staged campaign of posters might include a series with numbers on them; for example, "85" on one and "3 million" on another. No explanation of the numbers would be given, and a mystery would develop. Later, new posters could explain that 85 is the number of reported incidents at the organization in the past year and that 3 million is the number of dollars of lost business from a distributed denial of service attack.

49.7.6 Use Stories and Examples: Current and Credible. Stories about real people and real consequences (people being praised, disciplined, or fired) are useful in presentations and courses. Sources of stories include individuals who have been with the organization for a long time and have a "corporate memory," news events, Internet special-interest bulletin boards, and security personnel who attend special interest group meetings and conferences.

The stories should relate to situations and decisions the audience may face. Stories about hackers accessing medical records would be useful to organizations that process medical data, whereas stories about fraud or identity theft would be of interest to personnel involved in the financial industry or the accounting function of an organization.

Awareness material must be fresh and not stale. Chef Oscar Gizelt of Delmonico's Restaurant in New York said, "Fish should smell like the tide. Once they smell like fish, it's too late." If awareness material is not changed frequently, it too begins to smell old and becomes boring or less credible.

Credibility is crucial for an awareness program to be effective. The message should be clear, relevant, and appropriate to the real world. If the audience is required to use 15 different passwords as a part of day-to-day functions, prohibiting them from writing their passwords may not be as realistic as providing strategies for protecting the written list.

49.7.7 Use Failure.   "Expectation failure" is an important learning accelerator.[38] People often do not pay attention to information they are expecting to hear or see. When an employee takes a computer-based awareness quiz and gets an answer wrong, he or she pays more attention. Yet failure should be safe and private. For this reason, computer-based awareness questions and quizzes should provide immediate feedback but should not record answers. At the awareness level, it is more important to give staff members something to think about than to have them get every answer correct. To remove anxiety, inform staff members that their answers will not be recorded.

49.7.8 Involve the Audience: Buy-In Is Better than Coercion.   People who have contributed to the awareness program with suggestions, contest entries, or focus group testing are more likely to accept and follow security controls. This assumes that feedback is given for every suggestion submitted. No feedback implies no management interest.

Awareness activities that are active and involve the audience are more memorable than passive ones. Whether in person, on a poster, or through a Web-based awareness course, involving the audience with questions such as "Did you know . . .?" and "What would you do if . . .?" is an effective awareness technique.

Trivia questions and unexpected or counterintuitive facts are good attention getters. For example, asking this question,

> In the United States, which of the following activities is illegal?
>
> **A.** Creating a virus that spreads through e-mail
> **B.** Disrupting Internet communications
> **C.** Failing to make daily backups of data

usually results in people choosing the first answer. The question is designed to provoke thought, because creating a virus is not actually illegal. Releasing a virus is, but that is not one of the answers. The correct answer is "Disrupting Internet communications." The question is designed to get people to think about security in new ways.

Another good awareness technique is to use unusual or psychologically compelling questions designed to engender thought. Such questions can be given during live presentations or over the Web. For example, logic professor Rick Garlikov suggested the following sequence of questions to help end users realize that it is not only the probability of a bad thing happening but also the damage that could occur that determines how much precaution is needed.

Start out asking the audience, "How many of you see security as just being a nuisance to your doing your real work?" If people raise their hands, call on them and ask "How so?" or "In what way?" or "Why is that?" Then see what they say, and go from there with "What if. . .?" types of questions.

Ask how many believe that "an ounce of prevention is a pain in the neck" or "an ounce of prevention is a lot of trouble."

Agree that we all hate to take precautions when risk does not seem likely. However, there are two factors in determining the potential damage caused by any risk situation: probability and impact. Most people only take probability into account. Offer to try a Socratic demonstration to show that probability is not the only factor to take into account:

Ask, "How many of you would play Russian roulette?"

We assume most / all will not. If someone does say he would play, ask why. See whether his reason makes any sense. If not, just laugh and go on.

Ask those who won't play, "Why not?"

Presumably someone will say something like "You can get killed," or "It's not good odds."

Then say, "Yes, and the odds are one in six, which are not good odds. But, I'll tell you what, let's make the odds a lot better. We'll just put one bullet in one chamber of one of 100 revolvers, so that your odds will only be 1 in 600. And we will sweeten the pot by letting you win $10 if the gun does not go off when you shoot it at your head? Now how many will play?"

If some would play under those conditions, ask them why, and let others agree or disagree.

The point is that, no matter how much you increase the odds, the risk is not worth the game because you have too much to lose and not nearly enough to gain.

To wrap up this line of questions, explain: "The idea is that it is not just the odds that matter; it is what you can win versus what you can lose, along with the odds that need to be taken into account.

"So even if the risk of being hacked might be small, what will it cost you or your company if it happens?

"What is the cost in trying to prevent it by just being a little more careful in ways we will teach you—such as changing your password more frequently, or being suspicious of anyone's needing your password, or never hooking up a modem just to have slightly more convenience, and so on?"

49.7.9   Make It Memorable.   Well-crafted awareness material is like a piñata: When the audience breaks it open, it should be full of surprises. An activity that often results in wonderful surprises and learning is role playing. Role playing (live or by means of computer- or Web-based simulations) is an excellent way to show the target audience what is expected of them. At a recent security educators' conference, two educators did an impromptu role play of a worker dealing with a boss who wanted to tailgate—to follow the employee through a secure door that had been opened with the employee's card key. The audience was entertained and learned by example how to handle such a situation and how to teach others to do the same. Audience members will remember the role play long after they have forgotten material presented on slides.

To attract attention in an awareness campaign, Richard Heron, manager of Information Security for the Royal Bank of Canada in Sydney, Australia, handed out fortune cookies with security messages in them. He bought 20 boxes of fortune cookies, printed some key security messages (regarding passwords, not discussing confidential company information in public, etc.) on strips of paper, placed the security messages into the 400 cookies (using plastic gloves), took them to work, and handed them to the 300+ bank employees.

He describes these benefits of this approach: getting his message across in a memorable way, having the opportunity to meet and talk with staff so that they know who he is and how to reach him with security concerns, sharing his message in a positive nonconfrontational way, and sparking employees' interest and discussions about security. He found that staff began to query others: "What message did you get? I got 'If you fail to plan, you plan to fail.'" In the future he plans to include 10 messages in red or gold paper that will entitle the 10 recipients to win a prize.

49.7.10 Use Competition.   Several federal organizations use a Web-based awareness course that is updated annually. Each year, the course shows the number of people in each area and office who are registered to take the course and the percent who complete it, also by area and office, in a real-time bar chart with animations. The office or area that reaches a 100% completion rate first wins a trophy that stays with that area's security officer for the entire year. All course takers can view the contest from any page in the course. In addition, the course includes a poster idea contest with monthly winners, whose ideas are rendered by a professional artist and then provided in downloadable PDF format. A grand winner is picked from the 12 monthly winners, and that poster is printed in an 11×17 format and provided to the organization. All winning posters display the name and office of the winners. The program allows end users to earn from one to three gold stars on their course completion certificates by answering bonus questions. Additionally, the first 10% of course takers to complete the course receive a certificate that has a blue rosette at the top with the words "First ten percent."

Some organizations also have teams of people whose job is to break into their own systems. These penetration testers leave tracks in the system audit trails, and system, network, or LAN administrators who find and report the "intrusions" win T-shirts that say "I caught the test team," and coffee mugs or other prizes. An additional benefit realized by the organizations is that some of the administrators also caught real intrusion attempts during this activity.

For organizations with competitive business units, managers might volunteer their groups to participate in penetration testing performed by an outside firm that uses social engineering techniques in person and via phone and e-mail to test the group's resistance to such attacks. The group with the best result would be given recognition and rewards.

49.7.11 Incorporate User Acknowledgment and Sign-Off.   A technique for getting people to pay attention is to hold them personally responsible for their actions and choices. Many organizations have established policies requiring that individuals' system access be removed if participation in documented awareness orientations or refreshers is not recorded for them by the end of each fiscal year.

"Noisy prosecutions," which publicly shame security policy violators, are an excellent way to discourage security breaches. An example would be listing violators on the organization's intranet. Organizations may be reluctant to report security incidents out of concern for losing public confidence. Reporting incidents, however, allows trends to be tracked and may result in faster identification and response to problems.

49.7.12 Use Analogies.   Analogies, metaphors, and similes help learners associate new concepts with their previous knowledge or experience. These figures of speech create pictures that connect the teacher and learner to the same idea. The famous U.S. trial lawyer, Gerry Spence, says, "Words that do not create images should be discarded."[39] Saying that an organization that has a firewall but does not prevent users from installing modems in their desktop PCs is "like putting a steel door on a straw house" allows readers to visualize the concept.

Analogies can make complex topics easier to understand. They form a bridge between what the learners already know and the new concept or idea that the learners are expected to understand. For example, a common analogy used to explain password protection techniques is that passwords are like toothbrushes (change them often; never share). Another analogy is that passwords are like bubble gum (strongest when fresh;

should be used by an individual, not a group; and if left lying around, will create a sticky mess). A memorable analogy, especially if accompanied by an illustration, is that passwords are like long underwear: They should be long and mysterious, should protect the owner, should be used by one person and not a group, and should be changed periodically.

The more creative or unusual the analogy, the more likely it is to be remembered. For example, sensitive data are like prescription medicines: They should be used only by those who need them and who are authorized to have them; they should not be transferred, sold, or given to those for whom they are not authorized; and they can cause damage if they are given to people who do not have a legitimate need for them. Cars, medieval castles, and American Indian and European folklore, among other topics, have been used successfully to present information security concepts.

49.7.13   Use Humor.   Humor is an effective attention getter and can be used to motivate people and influence an organization's culture. It also helps people relax, which facilitates learning. Here are two rules for using humor in awareness presentations, courses, and materials:

1. Use humor that is relevant and complements or augments the message. Humor must be used for a purpose; otherwise it is a distraction and will cause a loss of credibility.
2. Do not use humor that will offend your audience. Avoid sexist, ethnic, religious, political, and bathroom humor. Do not make fun of something that cannot be changed, such as a physical or social characteristic.

It is often more acceptable to use humor involving oneself or those in positions of power, such as management and auditors. For example, a presenter might say "The auditor is the one who arrives after the battle and bayonets the wounded" to an audience of managers. Or a consultant for disaster recovery sites might explain about having a one-page disaster plan: "The plan is simple. It has only two steps: First, I always keep a copy of my resume up to date; and second, I store a backup copy in a secure, off-site location." The possibility of having this use of humor backfiring should be considered carefully.

Sources of humor include:

- Cartoons, especially those that deal with organizational and technology humor
- Humorous definitions; for example, "the Arnold Schwarzenegger virus —it'll be back"
- Security-related poems or lyrics written to the tunes of popular songs or in a specific style, such as an information security rap
- A security haiku, a 17-syllable poem composed in three lines of 5, 7, and 5 syllables, such as:

  Computer virus,
  destroyer of files, survives
  through lack of scanning.

- David Letterman–style "Top Ten" lists, such as the Top Ten excuses for not making a backup or for not reporting a suspected incident

49.7.14   Show Consequences.   Some organizations send memos to all staff that describe specific examples of personnel who have violated policy. The memos cover a set time period—for example, the previous quarter—and include the number of individuals; the nature of the violations; and the penalties, such as loss of Internet privileges or two months without pay (also displayed in dollars, based on the average salary).

49.7.15   Use Circumstances.   Current events can be an excellent source of material and can add credibility to an awareness program. Several Internet security and technology sites offer subscriptions to electronic security alerts and news clippings. Some organizations have established a "news hawk" program in which rewards are given to the first employee to bring in a new relevant story that can be used as part of the awareness program. This is also a good technique to gain buy-in from the end user community.

49.8   TOOLS.   When choosing tools to convey an awareness message, three questions should be addressed:

1. What tools are most appropriate for the message?
2. What methods are most likely to be credible to and accessible by the target audience?
3. Which methods (and how many methods) are feasible, considering the available budget and the time frame?

Using as many methods and tools as possible, with a consistent message, reinforces the message and increases the likelihood that the audience will be exposed to it often enough or long enough to absorb it.

49.8.1   Web-Based Courses.   Pentasafe conducted a survey of security awareness practices in 45 countries, in two parts—one for managers and one for workers. The findings were provided in the Security Awareness Index Report.

One of the findings was that there are proven ways to increase awareness.[40] The most effective method was a Web or computer-based course. Courses are usually designed to be viewed with a Web browser. Courses can be hosted on Web sites on the Internet, on the organization's intranet, or in CD or DVD format on individual computers.

Web-based awareness courses are useful for staff members who are geographically dispersed and who need to take the refresher or course at a time that is convenient for them. Such courses are especially well suited for use by individuals who have diverse backgrounds and experience with technology. Online courses offer these advantages over traditional place-based and instructor-led training:

- Feedback is immediate, so learners do not build on early misunderstandings. Well-designed Web-based training takes cultural and personality differences into account and reassures timid trainees while allowing more confident ones to progress at a faster pace. "Why" buttons or links, "How" buttons, "Show me an example" buttons, and "Give me an alternative" buttons can be set up to let learners with different needs and personalities use the course to learn in ways that are comfortable for them.

- Because a Web-based awareness course can be taken at any time, it is convenient for the trainees. It does not have to be scheduled, so those with variable or hectic schedules can arrange to take the course at a time that is good for them.
- Web-based courses allow users to make mistakes and learn from them in a safe, nonthreatening environment.
- Web-based courses are flexible and can be customized to accommodate learners with different levels of experience and different interests. By placing detailed information in subordinate, linked pages, users are able to choose between the "need to know" main pages and the "nice to know" hyperlinked pages.
- Web-based courses can reduce costs and training time. Placing updates to courses on the Web eliminates the work involved with distributing the current version and materials to multiple locations. This can be more efficient and consistent because the content has been reviewed, edited, and tested to make it clear and concise.
- Web-based courses are self-paced, so that more experienced users can race through without getting bored while novice users can ponder and explore.

Exciting and effective Web-based courses should have these characteristics:

- Start with a bang. Begin with a story, an image, a headline, or something that immediately engages the learner's attention. Courses should never start with a dull "why you need this training..." introduction. Writer Paul O'Neil offers some excellent advice to writers that applies to creators of awareness programs: "Always grab the reader by the throat in the first paragraph, sink your thumbs into his windpipe in the second, and hold him against the wall until the tagline."
- Be goal-based, allowing learners to choose how and when they will meet the course requirements.
- Be active and involve learning by doing.
- Address multiple learning styles and personalities. Appealing to multiple senses increases retention. Appealing to different personality styles ensures that the message will reach a wider audience.
- Challenge the learner's beliefs and expectations and allow learners to fail in interesting and safe ways.
- Use scenarios, examples, and analogies—people learn best from real situations where they can relate the learning to prior knowledge.
- Provide feedback, such as immediate answers to questions. Feedback is essential to motivation and performance.
- Be memorable. People tend to remember things that are unusual or unexpected or that carry a visceral impact. Repetition also contributes to how memorable an idea is.
- Include stories. Stories grab people's attention. Organizations should collect stories about security incidents, security heroes, mistakes made, and lessons learned.
- Be accessible. Guidelines for creating Web pages that are accessible to people with vision or hearing impairments are published by the World Wide Web Consortium (W3C). To be accessible, the Web pages should not rely on vision or sound alone to impart meaning. For example, all graphics should be labeled with text that explains the graphic, and the contrast between the text and the background should be maximized.

A potential problem to watch for in Web-based courses is the tendency to get carried away by the technology. Just because an awareness course could have three dozen animated, singing computers decorating the pages does not mean that it should. The technology must be used appropriately; bigger buildings do not make better scholars, and more impressive technology does not necessarily result in a better learning experience. A Web-based course that is overloaded with animations and graphics that do not relate to course content or that has a poorly designed user interface will set the awareness program back.

49.8.2 Compliance Agreements.   The most effective security awareness offerings after computer-based instruction, according to the Security Awareness Index report, were:

- Tracking whether workers read policies or not
- Requiring a compliance statement
- Requiring full time employees (FTEs) to read policies
- Making policies available in electronic format
- Require workers to read policies annually
- Requiring a compliance statement prior to issuing a user ID[41]

49.8.3 Performance Appraisals.   Including security awareness activities and behaviors (such as participating in awareness courses, reading newsletters, attending events, having no infractions found, or reporting vulnerabilities or incidents) in job descriptions and performance appraisals motivates staff to actively support the organization's security program.

49.8.4 Checklists, Pamphlets, Tip Sheets.   Brochures, pamphlets, and comic books can be targeted to specific audiences. Recognize and react sheets that list signs of an incident and the steps for the end user to take are useful. Checklists of behaviors organized by topic are often useful.

49.8.5 Memos from Top Management.   Memos and alerts concerning security issues can be distributed to staff. Memos signed by top management are more effective than memos signed by less recognizable personnel. If appropriate, to attract attention, consider stapling a facial tissue to stressful memos, such as ones that may be perceived as adding inconvenience or an additional burden on users.

49.8.6 Newsletters.   Publications, such as newsletters and magazines in paper and electronic format, may be devoted to security or may contain articles on security-related events or items of interest. Newsletters should be tailored to the organization's industry or business. They should also be short, two to four pages, and should use attention-getting graphics, headlines, and white space to appeal to readers. Interaction with the audience can be created by encouraging questions to be answered in future newsletters or including contests, and inviting the readers to submit news items, tips, trivia, or reviews of security books or products.

49.8.7 In-Person Briefings (and Brown-Bag Lunches).   At a brown-bag lunch, people who attend security-related workshops, conferences, or seminars can share a summary of the information presented with those who did not attend. Guest speakers can present material on current topics or their areas of expertise.

49.8.8 Contests.   Contests are a good way to motivate people. Vince Lombardi, former head coach of the Green Bay Packers, understood this. He once said, "Winning isn't everything. It's the only thing." After criticizing him for this statement, some of his critics put together a new kind of baseball league for children in a Texas community: "It was like the Little League—the same ball, same bat, same number of innings, same playing field—everything was the same except that they didn't keep score. The idea was that there wouldn't be any losers because nobody would know who won." The game lasted one and a half innings. After that "the kids went across the street to play sand lot ball where they could keep score."[42]

Security trivia contests, poster contests, security fact or fiction contests, first group to complete a security activity contest, and the like are all ways to increase audience participation and motivation.

The Federal Information Systems Security Educators' Association (FISSEA) has an annual contest for security awareness Web sites, posters, and trinkets. Membership in this organization is open to government and business internationally. Security educators and staff could be encouraged to enter this contest.

49.8.9 Intranet and/or Internet.   Security awareness activities that use the Internet or an intranet offer the advantages of ease of use, scalability (can be used for various audience sizes and in distributed locations), accountability (can capture use statistics, quiz or test scoring, and other metrics), accommodation of individual learning rates, and even interaction among members of a community or among students and instructors.

Web sites (public or private) can be used in these ways:

- As a research tool for gathering information
- To present policies and other documents
- To post alerts
- To collect data for security awareness surveys or incident reporting
- For self-assessments to identify at-risk security practices
- For anonymous reporting of security concerns
- For Webcasts of security conferences or presentations

49.8.10 Posters.   A poster series with themes or related designs can be used to highlight specific security issues. A poster should be colorful and should present a single message or idea. Using a professional artist to design the posters will increase their impact. Posters should be larger than standard letter size to stand out and gain attention. They should be changed or rotated regularly and placed at eye level in many locations. Posters can be printed on both sides of the paper, saving paper and shipping costs for organizations with multiple locations. Exhibit 49.1 is an example of such a poster.

49.8.11 Awareness Coupons and Memo Pads.   Awareness coupons as shown in Exhibit 49.2 are rewards given out to people for following security policy.

EXHIBIT 49.1   Sample Poster

Source: © Native Intelligence, Inc. Artwork by Charles A. Filius.

EXHIBIT 49.2   Security Coupons

Source: © Native Intelligence, Inc. Artwork by Charles A. Filius.

EXHIBIT 49.3   Security Memo

Source: © 2006 NativeIntelligence.com

When a recipient displays the coupon or tells others about it, people think more about security, thus enhancing awareness.

Security memo pad reminders (see Exhibit 49.3) are also good tools and are used in the same way as the awareness coupons.

49.8.12   Videos.   Videos can be delivered on DVDs, VHS tapes, CD-ROMs, or over the Web in various formats including podcasts (videos formatted to play on iPods or other portable media players). Most security awareness videos are less than 20 minutes long. They can be used at orientation briefings and brown-bag lunches for staff where popcorn can be provided in bags preprinted with security messages. Videos are useful starting points for discussions and for briefings. They provide a consistent message throughout the organization and can be shown to staff at distributed locations, saving instructor travel time and costs. They can also be used to demonstrate cost effectively the impact of security failures such as a fire at a data center, or how sensitive data were found in the trash. Security awareness videos are available commercially for various fees and from the U.S. Government often at no charge or for a nominal fee.

Although they are effective training tools, videos have their drawbacks. They can be expensive to produce, with costs averaging $4,000 or more per finished minute.

In addition, as rapidly as technology and threats change, videos can quickly become outdated. An option is to produce an awareness video in digital format in segments that allow for updates as the environment or organizational needs change.

49.8.13 Trinkets and Give-Aways.   Various give-away items can be imprinted with a security slogan and contact information, such as security staff phone numbers or the organization's security Web site address. Give-aways that the recipient places in a visible location increase the exposure time of the message. Examples of give-away items are:

- Pencils, pens, and highlighters: "Report security breaches—it's the 'write' thing to do."
- Erasers: "Wipe out password sharing."
- Notepads: "Note who should be in your area and challenge strangers."
- Frisbees: "Our information security program is taking off."
- Mouse pads and inserts: Mouse pads may be specially printed or have removable paper inserts, making the cost to change the message far less than the cost of printing new mouse pads.
- Key chains: "You are the key to information security."
- Flashlights: "Keep the spotlight on security."
- Cups or mugs: "Awareness—the best part of SecuriTEA" (when the campaign has explained that TEA stands for training, education, and awareness).
- Magnets, buttons, and stickers: "Stick with security."
- First-aid kits: "Be prepared for security."
- Rulers and calculators: "Security counts."
- Calendars with security images and messages.
- Candy bars with wrappers printed with security messages.
- Coasters, toys, hand exercisers, informational cards, posters, virus scanning software, and screen savers.
- Fortune cookies with a security message (see Exhibit 49.4)

Larger, more expensive items, such as T-shirts, tote bags, and gift certificates, can be used as prizes for raffles at security events. The more useful, beautiful, or cleverly designed the item, the greater the likelihood that it will be kept.

49.8.14 Screen Savers.   Screen savers are a graphic form of communication and, like posters, should be eye-catching for maximum impact. Involving a professional artist will improve message delivery. Screen savers should contain contact information for the organization's security and incident-handling functions. Animations or trivia questions and answers may make the screen saver more interesting. Screen savers should be updated periodically to keep the message fresh. Commercially produced security screen savers are available, as are screen savers that can be easily tailored to deliver a security message.

Exhibit 49.4 Security Awareness Cookies
Source: © Native Intelligence, Inc.

49.8.15 Sign-On Screen Messages. With some systems, it is possible to add a text message to the log-on or sign-on screen. These messages should be short, to the point, and changed frequently.

49.8.16 Surveys and Suggestion Programs. Surveys, suggestion programs, and contests help achieve buy-in. Contests to suggest or name a security mascot, to provide poster ideas, or even ways to improve security can boost morale and contribute to team spirit. At presentations, speakers can tape prizes or awards under seats in the front row to encourage people to come early and sit up front.

49.8.17 Inspections and Audits. Inspections and audits raise awareness among the staff being reviewed, at least for the duration of the inspection. Additional audits and inspections, although useful techniques, create a negative perception. Another technique, called "SBWA" for *security by wandering around*, identifies staff members doing something correctly. A security staff member can tour the work area at the end of the day and leave certificates of congratulations, thank-you notes, or trinkets on the desks of people who have locked all sensitive information in cabinets before leaving. Randomness is more effective than regularly scheduled inspections. Another possibility would be to have the security personnel periodically demonstrate social engineering by attempting to smooth-talk users into providing their passwords. People who refuse would be rewarded. The number of people who fall for the scheme might be used as an example for the next awareness session.

49.8.18 Events, Conferences, Briefings, and Presentations. Participation in events, such as the Computer Security Day[43] on November 30, or in any of the various information security conferences, raises awareness. Here are other events that can contribute to awareness:

- A "Grill Your Security Officer Cook-Out" where food is served and staff are encouraged to bring any questions about security to the security officer.
- Lectures by dynamic speakers. A boring speaker will hurt the program's credibility, but a talented professional speaker can be eye-opening. Sometimes personnel are more accepting of information presented by an independent subject matter expert. Some organizations sponsor a monthly lecture series or lunch presentations on relevant topics.
- Security awareness briefings. Briefings are typically given to senior executives who have little time to spare and to new arrivals who need an overview of the organization's information security awareness policy before being granted system access.

49.9 MEASUREMENT AND EVALUATION. Security consultant Hinson has compared security to the brakes in a car. The brakes slow you down, but they also make it possible for you to go a lot faster.[44] A good metrics program takes time to set up, but once you have it set up and working well, it can save you time in the long run by making your program more effective. Metrics aid in decision making. Without a solid metrics program, it is hard to know whether the program is effective, or if the organization should spend more money on doing the same thing, or if the resources would be better used elsewhere. As with any tool, it is important to know how to use metrics. Metrics are best used when they compare measurements over time to a baseline.

The field of security metrics is evolving, and different organizations have put forth different tools, different guidance, and different frameworks for evaluating IT security. For example, various organizations use metrics based on ISO 17799; NIST—SP 800-55, FITSAF; CoBIT; PCI; HIPAA; GLBA; SOX; SANS; FISMA; or combinations of these documents. Few organizations use common metrics or even a common vocabulary. Also, many of the tools and guidance for measuring IT security metrics only consider security awareness as a small portion of overall security program metrics. Often the questions asked about security awareness programs are high level and not specific. A 2004 survey by the Robert Frances Group found that only 40 percent of respondents felt that their IT security measurement practices were effective.[45]

It is easy to collect quantitative measures of data, such as such as the number of virus infections, data compromises, or program costs. A common measurement is the number of people who participated in awareness orientations and refreshers. This figure can be determined through attendance sheets, course registrations or completion notifications for online courses, and signed user "acceptance of responsibilities" statements. Another common metric is seat time—how long this person spent in front of a computer, clicking through the screens, soaking up the knowledge that was there. Attendance and seat time can indicate that a program is not effective, but they are not the best measurements of how effective an awareness program is. Better measurements focus on what end users are doing and measure user behaviors that are a part of normal business operations. More valuable measures address user perceptions, activities, and especially behaviors.

49.9.1 Changes in Behavior. Past studies have shown that internal users still represent the greatest threat to security—through accidental or intentional behavior. End user security behaviors can be grouped into categories such as good, bad, and ugly. In this approach, *good behavior* complies with the letter of the law or better, the spirit of the law. *Bad behavior* includes *naive mistakes or dangerous tinkering*—for example, sharing a password, deploying a wireless network gateway that allows noncompany personnel to use the company's network, setting up a packet-spoofing application to test one's programming ability, or setting up a network monitoring scanner on one's PC. *Ugly behavior* consists of *detrimental misuse* or *intentional destruction*—for example, someone builds a special script that disables other users' terminal sessions, forges e-mail header information to make it look like someone else sent a message, uses a file decryption program to discover the contents of a file containing trade secrets, or intentionally introduces a Trojan horse program into the network.[46]

These behaviors can be measured through surveys, observation, help desk and incident reports, manual tests or audits, and software. As an example, Exhibit 49.5 and

Security Awareness Program Metrics Internal User Behaviors *Examples to be tailored should be based on goals and then questions.*	G · B · U*	Survey	Observation	Help Desk Incid. Rpts	Manual Tests or Audits	Software (Automated)
% of users recognizing a security event scenario	G	✓				
% of users susceptible to social engineering (compare mid-week at mid-day to Friday afternoon)	B				✓	
% of users revealing their password when tested	B				✓	
% of users activating a "test virus"	B				✓	
% of security incidents having human behavior as a major factor / involving behaviors covered in awareness materials	BU			✓		
Storage of unauthorized file content on desktop or network resources, such as audio, video, or other multimedia files	B					✓
Number of attempts to access inappropriate/blocked Web sites	B					✓
Non-public information found in dumpsters outside of facilities	B		✓			
% of systems having unapproved software installed	BU				✓	✓
% of systems having unapproved hardware installed	B				✓	✓
% of e-mails (random sample) with inappropriate content	B				✓	
% of passwords visible or in common locations (e.g., under lamp)	B		✓			
% of PCs logged on and unattended	B		✓			
% of laptops, portable devices/media, sensitive data unsecured	B		✓			
% of laptops, portable devices/media stolen (office/travel)	B			✓		
Number of attempts to use unauthorized resources, e.g., VPN	B					✓
% of e-mails sent via Internet containing non-public/sensitive data that are not encrypted	B				✓	
% of users wearing badges with picture facing out	G		✓			
% of monitors positioned to be easily seen from hallways, doors, or windows (especially on the ground floor)	B		✓			

EXHIBIT 49.5   Awareness Metrics, continued as exhibit 49.6

Source: © 2005 Native Intelligence, Inc.

Security Awareness Program Metrics Internal User Behaviors *Examples to be tailored should be based on goals and then questions.*	G · B · U*	Survey	Observation	Help Desk Incid. Rpts	Manual Tests or Audits	Software (Automated)
% of users who challenge unknown visitor with no access badge	G		✓	✓		
% of users who open a test e-mail with a questionable subject	B				✓	✓
% of users activating a "test virus"	B				✓	✓
% of users who click a link in a test e-mail (instead of typing the URL into their browsers)	B				✓	✓
% of users responding to a test e-mail via an "unsubscribe" link	B				✓	✓
% of crackable user passwords	B				✓	✓
% of user systems having spyware or malware installed	B				✓	✓
Number of incidents of unauthorized use of administrator privileges	U			✓	✓	
% of users sending Internet e-mail to multiple recipients who do not use the BCC field	B				✓	
% who have actively acknowledged policies / security responsibilities	G					✓
Number of major findings from internal and external security audits	B				✓	
% viewing optional security materials in online courses	G					✓
% participating in contests, suggestion programs, bonus questions	G					✓

* G·B·U = Good, Bad, or Ugly
G: Good behavior complies with the 'letter of the law' or better, the 'spirit of the law,' e.g., not releasing non-public information inappropriately, discovering and reporting a security vulnerability.
B: Bad behavior includes **naive mistakes** or **dangerous tinkering** – e.g., sharing a password, deploying a wireless network gateway that allows non-company personnel to use the company's network, setting up a packet spoofing application to test one's programming ability; or setting up a network monitoring scanner on one's PC.
U: Ugly behavior consists of **detrimental misuse** or **intentional destruction** – e.g., someone builds a special script that disabled other users' terminal sessions, forges e-mail header information to make it look like someone else sent a message, uses a file decryption program to discover the contents of a file containing trade secrets, or intentionally introduces a Trojan horse program into the network.

(Behavior categories inspired by "Analysis of End User Security Behaviors" – by Jeffrey M. Stanton, Kathryn R. Stam, Paul Mastrangelo, and Jeffrey Jolton, July 12, 2004.)

EXHIBIT 49.6   Awareness Metrics, continued from 49.5

Source: © 2005 Native Intelligence, Inc.

Exhibit 49.6 illustrate a table showing measurable end user security behaviors, whether the behaviors are good, bad, or ugly, and how they could be measured.

Also, personal statements, such as feedback solicited from a survey or Web-based course question that asks "What aspects of your behavior have you changed as a result of recent awareness activities?" can be used to measure behavioral change. Adding a yes-or-no checkbox to help desk or incident reporting forms that asks "Was this issue addressed in security awareness materials or courses?" can help identify areas that need additional emphasis in awareness materials.

49.9.2   Audience Satisfaction.   Audience satisfaction can be measured after the fact with course or presentation evaluations or surveys about the awareness program. "Smiley face" evaluations, where the audience is asked to rate the program or activity on a scale, measure how well the audience liked the course, activity, or materials. User feedback may be requested on the presentation's relevance and effectiveness. Asking for suggestions is also a good approach. The volume and content of suggestions provided are good indicators of message impact.

49.9.3   Audience Involvement.

Attendance statistics from sign-in sheets, head counts, or evaluations or the number of trinkets given away at an event can be used to measure involvement in presentations and events. Web-based courses can measure the number and percent of people who started and completed the course and the amount of time spent on modules and pages and can record feedback questions and answers provided.

If contests are used, the number and quality of entries can be measured.

49.9.4   Learning or Teaching Effectiveness.

Pre- and post-surveys and tests are useful in determining what the audience remembered and therefore in tailoring more effective future programs. Unless a preprogram test or preliminary survey is conducted, objectively measuring improvement is difficult, if not impossible. However, subjective measurement, such as surveying users on what they learned, is also useful and does not require a pretest.

49.9.5   Audience Performance.

This type of evaluation goes beyond the learner to gather input from an outside evaluator, such as a supervisor, security practitioner, incident response team, or help desk personnel. Follow-up interviews, walk-through testing, help desk and incident reporting statistics, and audit findings can be used to measure improvements in awareness and job performance.

For example, before presenting an awareness campaign on password construction and management, a password-cracking program could be run to identify passwords that are subject to guessing or compromise. The same program could be run after the awareness activities and the results compared. Or an evaluator could walk though the work areas at lunchtime, looking for terminals that are unattended but not logged off. The same inspection could be performed at various times after the awareness program is initiated. Similarly, a survey of attitudes and specific knowledge could be taken before awareness efforts are initiated. Staff might be asked to whom they should report an incident or if they may take older versions of upgraded software home for use once newer versions have been licensed by the organization. Similar questions could be asked at intervals after the awareness program is implemented and the results compared. Regardless of the specific measurement used, a comparison baseline is needed. Data for the baseline should be gathered before the awareness program is implemented.

As with any awareness campaign, a security awareness effort requires repetition and consistency from year to year to achieve and maintain the desired impact and changes in workforce behavior.

49.10   CONCLUSION.

Awareness among an organization's staff is vital to maintaining the integrity of data and systems. Although organizations often view computer security as a technological problem and use sophisticated hardware and software solutions to control access, detect potential security incidents, and prevent fraud, the reality is that computer security is as much a people problem as a technological problem. End users are closer to potential problems; therefore, they need to be aware of potential risks, threats, vulnerabilities, and their own security responsibilities.

People are major contributors to the IT security problem, and they are also crucial to its solution. People are perceptive and adaptive, and if trained and motivated to be aware, they can be the strongest and most effective security countermeasure. Individuals often are the first to detect security incidents. The actions they take or fail to take determine the level of damage. An aware workforce often can compensate for deficiencies in technical controls. The intent of the awareness program is to make recognition of and reaction to security threats a reflexive behavior.

Awareness takes time. It also requires the organization to have an in-place information security policy, the support of the senior-level managers, and clear goals and plans for achieving awareness. The importance of establishing measurable goals cannot be overestimated and is critical to obtaining support and funding.

The goal of an awareness program is often to change attitudes and behaviors that may be embedded in long-term procedures or habits. To effect awareness, the program must appeal to the audience and be tailored to the workforce and to the technology of the organization. The primary message of a security awareness program should be that security is everyone's responsibility and that individuals need to be able to recognize and respond to suspected security incidents. End user security behaviors should be included in security awareness metrics. Actions taken by end users make a significant difference, thus, a well-trained and motivated workforce is a critical and necessary security control.

49.11   GLOSSARY

Awareness—being conscious of what is going on around one; security awareness specifically focuses attention on security. Security awareness is the individual's understanding that security is important and that everyone has a role in ensuring the security of information and information technology.

Awareness campaign—the activities associated with conveying a specific awareness message (e.g., telling people "log off when away from your computer").

Awareness program—the planned implementation and control of a mix of awareness activities over a period of time, with measurable goals and multiple topics. An awareness program may encompass several campaigns.

Education—the process of integrating all security skills and competencies into a common body of knowledge, adding a multidisciplinary study of concepts, issues, and principles.

End user (also computer user or user)—any person who uses an information system.

Focus group—a small group of end users (or of individuals from the target audience) who review and discuss awareness activities, courses, products, and the like, often under the guidance of an awareness material developer or training specialist.

FUD factor—the effects of *f*ear, *u*ncertainty, and *d*oubt (FUD).

Malicious code (also malware)— hardware, software, or firmware that is intentionally included in a system for an unauthorized purpose (e.g., a Trojan horse).

Orientation briefing—a presentation that provides new employees, contractors, and the like. with basic security information and information on the organization's security policies and programs. Usually these presentations are conducted on arrival or shortly thereafter.

Refresher—an awareness activity, such as a briefing, intended to reinforce and update awareness of security controls and policies and to remind individuals of their security responsibilities.

Safe failure—the opportunity to learn from mistakes privately, such as with a computer simulation or course.

Security basics and literacy—a transitional stage between awareness and training.

Social engineering—social methods (e.g., threats, misrepresentations) that deceive a victim so that the victim does what the attacker wants him or her to do. Often the goal is to get the victim to provide private or sensitive information, such as account numbers or passwords. An example of a social engineering attack is the use of "phishing" e-mails.

Social marketing—an approach to security awareness using attraction and persuasion techniques designed to encourage a group of people to alter old ideas, understand and accept new ideas, and value their new awareness enough to change attitudes and take positive actions to improve IT security.

Target audience—a specified audience or demographic group for which a security awareness message is designed.

Threat—anything that can potentially harm a system or its associated assets (hardware, software, data, operations). Threats may be man-made or natural occurrences. Awareness programs do little to address threats; instead, they seek to reduce vulnerabilities.

Training—the process of producing relevant and needed security skills and competency. Security awareness is the "what"; training is the "how."

Vulnerability—a weakness in automated system security procedures, administrative controls, physical layout, internal controls, and so forth, which could be exploited by a threat to gain unauthorized access to information or disrupt critical processing. A goal of security awareness programs is to reduce behavior-related vulnerabilities.

49.12 FURTHER READING

Corporate Executive Board. "Trends in IT Security Threats." Corporate Executive Board, 2005. Catalog No.: IEC13EKU9P.

Schneier, B. *Beyond Fear*. New York: Copernicus Books, 2003.

Trowbridge, J. "An Overview of remote Operating System Fingerprinting," 2003; www.sans.org/rr/papers/42/1231.pdf.

Wilson, M., ed., D. E. de Zafra, S. I. Pitcher, J. D. Tressler, and J. B. Ippolito. "Information Technology Security Training Requirements: A Role- and Performance-Based Model," National Institute of Standards and Technology Special Publication 800-16, 1998; http://csrc.nist.gov/publications/nistpubs/800-16/800-16.pdf.

49.13 NOTES

1. "Buffalo 100 GB USB Flash Drive. (Now We Definitely Need USB 3.0)," 2008; www.everythingusb.com/buffalo_shd-uhr100gs_100gb_flash_drive_13962.html.

2. IsecT, Ltd. "Human Factors in Information Security," 2003; www.noticebored.com/NB_White_paper_on_human_factors_v5.pdf.

3. IsecT, Ltd., "Human Factors in Information Security."

4. R. Herold, *Managing an Information Security and Privacy Awareness and Training Program.* Boca Raton, FL: Auerbach Publications, 2005.

5. T. Ludwig, "Think Secure: Building Your Security-Minded Workforce," Getronics white paper, 2005; https://gsuonline.com/documents/Thinksecurewhitepaper .pdf.

6. Ludwig, "Think Secure."

7. M. Wilson and J. Hash, "Building an Information Technology Security Awareness and Training Program," National Institute of Standards and Technology Special Publication 800-50; http://csrc.nist.gov/publications/nistpubs/800-50/ NIST-SP800-50.pdf.

8. Herold, *Managing an Information Security and Privacy Awareness and Training Program.*

9. Wilson and Hash, "Building an Information Technology Security Awareness and Training Program."

10. D. Parker, "Motivating the Workforce to Support Security Objectives: A Long-Term View," 2002; www.iwar.org.uk/comsec/resources/sa-tools/ Motivation-for-Information-Security.pdf.

11. IsecT, Ltd., "Human Factors in Information Security."

12. R. Zimmerman, *Social Marketing Strategies for Campus Prevention of Alcohol and Other Drug Problems.* Washington, DC: Higher Education Center for Alcohol and Other Drug Prevention, 1997; www.higheredcenter.org/pubs/ soc-marketing-strat.pdf.

13. D. Verton, "Federal Agency Faces Judicial Ultimatum," 2002; www .computerworld.com/securitytopics/security/story/0,10801,69937,00.html.

14. FTC, "The Federal Trade Commission's Settlement with ChoicePoint," 2006; updated March 18, 2008; www.ftc.gov/choicepoint.

15. T. Zeller, "U.S. Settles with Company on Leak of Consumers' Data," *New York Times,* January 27, 2006; www.nytimes.com/2006/01/27/business/27choice.html.

16. P. McBride, "How to Spend a Dollar on Security," *Computerworld,* November 9, 2000; www.computerworld.com/securitytopics/security/story/0,10801, 53651,00.html.

17. Wilson and Hash, "Building an Information Technology Security Awareness and Training Program."

18. Herold, *Managing an Information Security and Privacy Awareness and Training Program.*

19. V. Basili, G. Caldiera, and H. D. Rombach, "The Goal Question Metric Approach." In Encyclopedia *of Software Engineering,* pp. 528–532 (New York: John Wiley & Sons, 1994); www.cs.umd.edu/~basili/publications/technical/T87.pdf.

20. Wilson and Hash, "Building an Information Technology Security Awareness and Training Program.

21. Herold, *Managing an Information Security and Privacy Awareness and Training Program.*

22. Hall, K., and the SE SIG Steering Committee "A System for Gaining Management Support for Your Safeguards and Security Awareness Program," 2002; www.orau.gov/se/Products/SE%20SIG%20Gaining%20Mgmt%20Support.doc.

23. The Federal Information Security Management Act of 2002, Section 3544, "Federal Agency Responsibilities"; www.fedcirc.gov/library/legislation/FISMA.html.

24. Hall and the SE SIG Steering Committee "A System for Gaining Management Support for Your Safeguards and Security Awareness Program."

25. R. Bace, *Intrusion Detection* (Indianapolis: Macmillan Technical Publishing, 2000).

26. Federal Trade Commission "Consumer Fraud and Identity Theft Complaint Data: January–December 2007" (February 2008); www.ftc.gov/opa/2008/02/fraud.pdf.

27. Bace, *Intrusion Detection*.

28. Hall and the SE SIG Steering Committee, "A System for Gaining Management Support for Your Safeguards and Security Awareness Program."

29. J. Darley and B. Latane, "Bystander Intervention in Emergencies: Diffusion of Responsibility," *Journal of Personality and Social Psychology* 8 (1968):377–383.

30. Parker, "Motivating the Workforce to Support Security Objectives."

31. B. Nelson, "The Top Ten Ironies of Motivation," Nelson Motivation, Inc., 2002; http://nelson-motivation.stores.yahoo.net/toptenirofmo.html.

32. Parker, "Motivating the Workforce to Support Security Objectives."

33. Wilson and Hash, "Building an Information Technology Security Awareness and Training Program."

34. Wilson and Hash, "Building an Information Technology Security Awareness and Training Program."

35. Herold, *Managing an Information Security and Privacy Awareness and Training Program.*

36. Office of Personnel Management regulation: 5 CFR Part 930, RIN 3205-AD43.

37. H. Overstreet, *Influencing Human Behaviour* (New York: Norton & Company, 1925).

38. R. Schank, *Virtual Learning* (New York: McGraw-Hill, 1997).

39. G. Spence, *How to Argue and Win Every Time* (New York: St. Martin's Press, 1995).

40. PentaSafe, "Security Awareness Index Report Worldwide State of Security Awareness," (2002); http://security.ittoolbox.com/pub/AM101502a.pdf.

41. PentaSafe. "Security Awareness Index Report Worldwide State of Security Awareness."

42. C. Coonradt, *The Game of Work*. Park City: Game of Work, 1997.

43. www.computersecurityday.org/.

44. G. Hinson, *Business Case for an Information Security Awareness Program.* Noticebored, LLC, 2007; http://noticebored.com/NB_generic_business_case_for_infosec_awareness_program.pdf.

45. C. Robinson, "Collecting Effective Security Metrics," Robert Frances Group, 2004; www.task.to/events/presentations/Required%20Security%20Metrics%20-%20statistics.pdf.

46. J. Stanton, K. Stam, P. Mastrangelo, and J. Jolton, "Analysis of End User Security Behaviors," July 12, 2004; http://sise.syr.edu/StantonC&Spublished.pdf.

CHAPTER **50**

USING SOCIAL PSYCHOLOGY TO IMPLEMENT SECURITY POLICIES

M. E. Kabay, Bridgitt Robertson, Mani Akella, and D. T. Lang

50.1 INTRODUCTION[1]. Most security personnel have commiserated with colleagues about the difficulty of getting people to pay attention to security policies—to comply with what seems like good common sense. They shake their heads in disbelief as they recount tales of employees who hold secured doors open for their workmates—or for total strangers, thereby rendering million-dollar card-access systems useless. In large organizations, upper managers who decline to wear their identification badges discover that soon no one else will either. In trying to implement security policies, practitioners sometimes feel that they are involved in turf wars and personal vendettas rather than rational discourse.

These problems reflect the social nature of human beings; however, they also reflect the fact that although people involved in information systems security and network management have a wide variety of backgrounds, many lack training in social or organizational psychology.

Security policies and procedures affect not only what people do, but also how they see themselves, their colleagues, and their world. Despite these psychosocial issues, security personnel pay little or no attention to what is known about social psychology. The established principles of human social behavior have much to teach in any attempts to improve corporate and institutional information assurance (IA).

IA specialists concur that security depends on people more than on technology. Another commonplace is that employees are a far greater threat to IA than outsiders.

It follows from these observations that improving security necessarily involves changing beliefs, attitudes, and behavior, both of individuals and of groups. Social psychology can help us understand how best to work with human predilections and predispositions to achieve our goals of improving security:

- Research on social cognition looks at how people form impressions about reality. Knowing these principles, we can better teach our colleagues and clients about effective security.

- Work on attitude formation and beliefs helps to present information effectively, and so convince employees and others to cooperate in improving security.

- Scientists studying persuasion and attitude change have learned how best to change people's minds about unpopular views, such as those regarding the security community.

- Studies of factors enhancing prosocial behavior provide insights on how to foster an environment where corporate information is willingly protected.

- Knowledge of the phenomena underlying conformity, compliance, and obedience can help to enhance security by encouraging compliance and by protecting staff against social pressure to breach security.

- Group psychology research provides warnings about group pathology and about hints for working better with groups in establishing and maintaining IA in the face of ingrained resistance.

This chapter reviews well-established principles of social psychology that help security and network management personnel implement security policies more effectively. Any recent introductory social psychology college textbook will provide ample references to the research underpinning the principles applied here to security policy implementation.[2]

50.2   RATIONALITY IS NOT ENOUGH.   IA policies sometimes evoke strong emotions. People can get very angry about what they perceive as interference with their way of getting their work done. From the perspective of the traditional information security professional, information security is still perceived as a technical problem, but as recent research reveals, it is more of a management problem, and the prevalent security culture offers insight into how management handles this problem.

To put the discussion in context, here is a definition of rationality from a respected academic, Jonathan Baron: rationality is "the kind of thinking we would all want to do, if we were aware of our own best interests, in order to achieve our goals."[3]

Applying this definition to the concept of security, it seems to imply that rational thought would direct us to what appears to be the best compromise between what we perceive as our security needs and what appears to be the most convenient process.

50.2.1 Schema.   Psychologists use the word "schema" to summarize the complex picture of reality upon which we base our judgments. The schema is what social psychologists call the way people make sense of their social interactions. IA practitioners must often change their colleagues' schemata.

Schemata are self-consistent views of reality. They help us pay attention to what we expect to be important and to ignore irrelevant data. They also help us organize our behavior. For example, our schema for relations at the office includes polite greetings, civil discussions, written communications, and businesslike clothes. The schema excludes obscene shrieks, abusive verbal attacks, spray-painted graffiti, and colleagues dressed in swim suits. It is the schema that lets people know what is appropriate or inappropriate in a given situation.

Unfortunately, security policies and procedures conflict with most people's schemata. Office workers' schemata includes sharing office supplies ("Lend me your stapler, please?"), trusting their team members to share information ("Take a look at these figures, Sally"), and letting their papers stay openly visible when they leave their desks.

Sharing user IDs, showing sensitive information to someone who lacks the appropriate clearance, and leaving workstations logged on without protection are gross breaches of a different schema—that of the IA specialist. Think about access controls: Normal politeness dictates that when a colleague approaches the door we have just opened, we hold the door open for the person; when we see a visitor, we smile politely—after all, it might be a customer. In contrast, access-control policies require that we refuse to let even well-liked colleagues piggyback their way through an access-card system; security policies insist that unbadged strangers be challenged or reported to security personnel. Common sense tells us that when the chief executive officer (CEO) of the company wants something, we do not oppose it; yet good IA dictates that we train computer room operators to forbid entry to anyone without documented authorization—including the CEO.

Sometimes people subvert IA by systematically getting around the rules because their normal social schema supersedes the security schema. It is not uncommon for naive staff to give keys or the door lock combination for access into secured areas to regularly schedule outside delivery and maintenance persons. Such delivery people are rarely subjected to security checks, and yet their potential for intentional or inadvertent damage is great; nonetheless, the naive staff members are acting without authorization, subverting normal security controls, and entrusting the safety and security of corporate resources to relative unknowns: Why? Are they deliberately violating security policy with evil intent? Of course not: The employees are simply acting in a friendly fashion and extending trust that might be appropriate in other circumstances—but they are using the wrong schema for a high-security corporate environment. In contrast, an IA specialist's schema in the same circumstances includes all the potentially untrustworthy friends of those outsiders. Until the security administration group alters the employees' perception of the appropriateness of the security regulations, the conflict between different schemata will continue to cause security violations and fuel resentment on all sides.

Indeed, a common response to attempts at enforcing existing policies and procedures, or to new security rules, is a charge of paranoia leveled against security personnel. Other accusations include authoritarian behavior and undue interference with job functions. These responses usually indicate a conflict between accepted norms of behavior and the need to change behavior to conform to security principles. They imply that social and cultural needs and behavior were not accounted for in the design of the principles. They also indicate a need for security personnel to understand that basic social graces and accepted norms of social activity conflict with the basic needs of security—and that the employees violating security rules are not inherently bad people.

Some redesign might allow for better security by recognizing that security rules can violate accepted social norms. For example, in the case of security-locked doors, one could allow for relatively free access to common areas (thus allowing people to hold the door for colleagues following them) while forbidding such actions in secured locations. A posted explanation of both the reasons for, and consequences of, the policy explicitly addressing the difference between the needs of normal politeness and the needs of high security could lead to better adherence to stated policy. The text might read something like this:

> This is a high-security area. Preventing anyone from entering without swiping their owned access card is not rude: it's common sense. Entering secured areas without using each employee's access card could put employees who did not use their access cards to enter at risk in an emergency if security staff didn't know that they were still in the secured areas. You are welcome to exercise normal politeness by holding the doors open for your colleagues and badge-wearing visitors in the nonsecured areas.

If we persist in assuming that we can influence our colleagues to change their perception of IA solely by informing, cajoling, nagging, or browbeating them, we will continue to fail. IA must be integrated into the corporate culture by changing our colleagues' schemata, a process that needs to use all of the techniques that social psychology can teach us.

A simple measure of this reality is to be found in the persistent avoidance practiced by many U.S. Government agencies in applying the information security program requirements of the Federal Information Security Management Act of 2002 (FISMA). It took almost five years and a series of undesirable security incidents before the various agencies woke up to the reality of the need to implement appropriate protection.[4] Another illustration of the reluctance to implement security policies is the Veterans Affairs debacle in the late 2000s involving loss of control over personally identifiable information on unencrypted disk drives.[5]

50.2.2 Theories of Personality.   One of the most pervasive obstacles to cooperation in organizations is interpersonal conflict. Many conflicts are rooted in differences of *personality style*. For example, one widely used set of categories for describing people's personalities uses this schema:

- Extroversion
  - High: active, assertive, energetic, outgoing, talkative
  - Low: quiet, reserved, shy, silent, withdrawn
- Agreeableness
  - High: affectionate, appreciative, kind, soft-hearted, sympathetic
  - Low: cold, fault-finding, hard-hearted, quarrelsome, unfriendly
- Conscientiousness
  - High: efficient, organized, planful, responsible, thorough
  - Low: careless, disorderly, frivolous, irresponsible, slipshod

- Emotional stability
  - High: calm, contented, stable, unemotional
  - Low: anxious, moody, nervous, tense, worrying
- Openness or culturedness
  - High: imaginative, insightful, intelligent, original, wide interests
  - Low: commonplace, shallow, simple, narrow interests, unintelligent

The adjectives used in this summary are positive for the "high" side of each trait and negative for the "low" side. However, the assumption that different personality types are easily characterized as superior and inferior seriously interferes with respectful communications among colleagues. For example, people with "low" characteristics might view the preceding summary in this way:

- Extroversion
  - High: nervous, aggressive, excitable, pushy, chattering
  - Low: dignified, respectful, unassuming, attentive, self-sufficient
- Agreeableness
  - High: clinging, gushy, soft-headed, knee-jerk reactive, uncritical
  - Low: stately, analytical, rational, principled, reserved
- Conscientiousness
  - High: obsessive, compulsive, unspontaneous, pompous, slavish
  - Low: free, spontaneous, creative, fun, youthful, having perspective
- Emotional stability
  - High: frozen, ambitionless, boring, dead
  - Low: vibrant, romantic, alive, strong, sensible
- Openness or culturedness
  - High: flaky, theoretical, complicated, off-the-wall, dilettante
  - Low: earthy, smart, grounded, focused, practical

In discussing corporate culture change, leaders must be on guard to defuse conflicts based on the misperception that one particular response or view of an issue is necessarily good and another necessarily bad. The conflict may be rooted in personality styles rather than in problems of understanding. If the security working group proposes that all employees must challenge anyone in the secured areas who is not wearing a badge, some people—those who have low extroversion, for example—may have a great deal of difficulty with the concept that they should tell anyone else what to do, especially a manager of a higher rank than their own. Arguing only over the reasons why such a policy would be *useful* would sidestep the fundamental problem: that the required behavior is in direct conflict with possibly lifelong and firmly held views on appropriate behavior.

Security personnel must remember that failure to comply with policy is not necessarily the result of a bad attitude. When it becomes obvious that conflicts are rooted in personality, security personnel will have to try to arrive at a useful compromise. Instead of requiring that everyone confront the unbadged individual personally, the security policies could include a proviso allowing for individuals to choose simply to inform security personnel immediately.

Role-playing exercises sometimes can defuse a problem in accepting security policies by desensitizing resistant personnel. Going through the motions of what they fear or dislike sometimes can help them come to realize that the proposed change in behavior is not as bad as they originally thought. Returning to the example of confronting violations of security, many people have difficulty imagining that they could tell a superior in the management hierarchy not to *piggyback*. This term, like "hitchhiking" and "tailgating," describes entering through a secured door that has been opened by someone else using a valid access code or token. Going through exercises in which each person pretends in turn to be the upper manager and then the challenger helps to break down resistance to this particular security policy. Trainers can emphasize that the challenge must be seen using a different schema from the normal situation:

- It is socially acceptable to apply security policies within the organization.
- Higher-status employees can encourage lower-status employees by articulating their support for the policy and showing that they are not offended by the request.
- Participants of all hierarchical levels can introspect to see that they themselves do not feel offended when they are politely asked to use their badge during the role-playing exercise.

In general, leaders of the security team responsible for implementing security policies should be on the lookout for conflicts of style that interfere with the central task of making the enterprise more secure. If an individual likes short, direct instructions without chitchat about nonessentials, the security team member should adapt and stick to essentials; if an individual is known to like getting to know a stranger and wants to spend a few minutes learning about family background, it should not be opposed. Communicating ideas in a way that is likely to be acceptable is more important than imposing one's own interpersonal style preferences on others.

Above all, security personnel—and management in general—ought to be doing a great deal more *listening* and a great deal less *commanding*.

Some important psychological issues for security leaders to consider include:

- Digital security is extremely complicated, and the explanations can be very technical—both attributes that are unfavorable to fostering management attention.
- Most security incidents stem from insiders rather than from outsiders prevention requires consistent nagging—not something management or anyone else normally regards favorably.
- Success in digital security (in fact, all of security) is best shown by having *nothing* happen, which is a tough thing to measure and tougher to sell. So the personal payoff for a well-executed security strategy is often little to nothing—and no management executive wants to put up *nothing* as a true measure of success.

The practical implications of these observations include:

- Discussions of IA should be down-to-earth and practical whenever possible.
- Awareness can be achieved by more positive means than nagging.
- One can create metrics of success by using security games and competitions that are fun as well as informative and effective at maintaining security awareness.

Here is an abstract of an article on the general manager's contribution to security:

Few senior executives pay much attention to computer security. They either hand off responsibility to their technical people or bring in consultants. But given the stakes involved, an arm's-length approach is extremely unwise. According to industry estimates, security breaches affect 90% of all businesses every year and cost some $17 billion. Fortunately,. . .senior executives don't need to learn about the more arcane aspects of their company's IT systems to take a hands-on approach. Instead, they should focus on the familiar task of managing risk. Their role should be to assess the business value of their information assets, determine the likelihood that those assets will be compromised, and then tailor a set of risk abatement processes to their company's particular vulnerabilities. *This approach, which views computer security as an operational rather than a technical challenge, is akin to a classic quality assurance program in that it attempts to avoid problems rather than fix them and involves all employees, not just IT staffers.* The goal is not to make computer systems completely secure—that's impossible—but to reduce the business risk to an acceptable level.[6]

We have italicized the key sentence in the quote to emphasize the critical role of changing corporate culture in successful security management.[7]

50.2.3 Explanations of Behavior.   In practice, trying to change corporate culture can be a frustrating and long-drawn-out project. One aspect of this process that security group leaders should monitor closely is the interpretation of employee behavior (called *attribution* theory in the social psychology literature) by members of the security team. In general, people can be viewed as interpreting (i.e., explaining) other people's behavior according to two independent dimensions: *internal or external* and *stable or unstable*. Here are some explanations of why Betty has failed to log off her session for the fourth time this week before leaving the office:

- **Internal, stable.** "That's just the way she is—she never pays attention to these rules."
- **Internal, unstable.** "She's been under strain lately because her child is sick—that's why she's forgotten."
- **External, stable.** "The system doesn't respond properly to the logoff command."
- **External, unstable.** "This week, the system has not been responding properly to the logoff command."

This simple four-way classification is useful for leaders in understanding and avoiding classic errors of attribution. Such attribution errors can cause conflicts between the security staff and other employees, or even among employees with different degrees of compliance to policy.

50.2.4 Errors of Attribution.   Some well-established misinterpretations of others' behavior can interfere with the acceptance of security policies. Such errors interfere with the ability of security personnel to communicate the value of security policies. Security group leaders should sensitize their staff to the consequences of these errors.

50.2.4.1 Fundamental Attribution Error.   The most important error people use when explaining other people's behavior is to assume that a person's actions are stable, internal features; a typical example of this error is the naive belief that an actor's personality is essentially what that person portrays in performance. Anyone who has ever experienced surprise at the demeanor and speech of a favorite actor who is being interviewed has committed the *fundamental attribution error*. Some actors who play bad characters in fictional situations have even been verbally and physically assaulted by viewers who cannot resist the fundamental attribution error, and who genuinely believe that the actors are as bad as the nasty people they portray. The abstract of a conference presentation in 2008 summarized some significant findings illustrating this point:

> Two studies attempted to document the occurrence of the psychological phenomenon known as the fundamental attribution error (FAE) in the audiovisual medium. The FAE refers to the human tendency to attribute people's behavior to internal attributes more than external factors. In Study 1, we demonstrated that in the audiovisual medium, viewers tend to attribute an actor's behavior in television dramas to the actor's personality, ignoring the existence of a script dictating the actor's behavior. Study 2 replicated this finding, and also demonstrated that the tendency to make the FAE is related to the degree to which the person reports being transported into the narrative of the TV drama. Furthermore, we showed that the tendency to attribute character traits to the actor is not diminished following exposure to the same actor playing two opposing roles. The last scene viewed was found to determine the evaluation of the actor's characteristics.[8]

In security work, being on guard against the fundamental attribution error helps to smooth relations with other employees. For example, if a security group member sees an employee, Jill, who is not wearing her badge, it is easy to assume that she never wears her badge and is refusing to wear it because of a character flaw. The security officer may act according to these assumptions by being harsh or unfriendly in correcting Jill's behavior. The harshness generates resentment, and Jill may come to associate security with unpleasant people, thus reducing the likelihood that she will comply with policy or encourage others to do so.

In fact, however, most people's behavior is far less stable and internal than unstable and externally based. For example, if the security officer simply smiled and pointed gently to the lack of a badge instead of jumping to conclusions, he might discover that Jill's lack of a badge today was due simply to her having taken her jacket off just before an urgent call from the vice president, interrupting her normal procedure of moving the badge from jacket to shirt pocket. Thus, her lack of a badge would not be stable behavior at all—it would be a temporary aberration of no long-lasting significance. A solution would be to get used to clipping the badge to her trousers or her skirt instead of her jacket or her blouse. Similarly, just by asking nicely, the security officer might learn that Jill normally does wear her badge, but today her four-year-old son took it off her jacket to play with it, without his mother's noticing the change. In this example, Jill's behavior is externally based and has nothing to do with character. The kindly interactions between Jill and the security guard *increase* the sense of social relation and make it more likely that she will remember the incident positively and comply with the security policy in the future.

In summary, by being aware of the fundamental attribution error, security personnel can be trained to adopt a less judgmental, or quick-draw, mentality that can alienate other employees and damage security programs.

50.2.4.2 *Actor-Observer Effect.*   The *actor-observer effect* consists of interpreting one's own behavior as appropriate unstable, externally motivated responses to environmental conditions, whereas other people's behavior is viewed in the light of the fundamental attribution error as stable, internally motivated expressions of character

traits. Becoming aware of this tendency helps security personnel resist the fundamental attribution error.

50.2.4.3 Self-Serving Bias.
The counterpart of the actor-observer effect is the *self-serving bias*, which fools people into believing that their own behavior is due to stable, internal aspects of their character. Security officers who are unaware of this dangerous error may come to feel that they are in some sense superior to other people who do not know as much about security as they do or who do not comply as fully as they do with security policy. The officers may have failed to integrate the fact that hours of training and coaching by their security group leaders are at least as responsible for their own knowledge of, and compliance with, security policies as any innate superiority.

By bringing this kind of erroneous thinking to light during training and supervision of security staff, managers can help reduce the conflicts that naturally result from an air of assumed superiority.

50.2.4.4 Salience and Prejudice.
When people are asked to guess which person in a group is the most influential (or least influential) person, social psychologists find that whichever person stands out the most, for whatever reason, is more often attributed with the special properties in question. Such effects apply to any characteristic that the psychologists ask about: most (or least) intelligent, aggressive, sympathetic, and so on. This phenomenon is known as the *salience effect*.

An application of the salience effect might occur if security officers see a group of employees who are violating security policies. A natural and counterproductive tendency is to leap to the conclusion that the tallest or shortest, the thinnest or fattest, the whitest or blackest person in the group must be to blame. This error can result in unfair treatment of perfectly innocent people.

This problem of misinterpreting salience is exacerbated by prejudice; for example, imagine there were an identifiable group called the "Ogunians" (as far as we can determine, there is no such group) who traditionally wear, say, a seven-sided symbol of their identity. If an anti-Ogunian security officer sees a noncompliant group where one of the members is wearing the characteristic heptagon of Ogun, it may be hard for the officer to resist blaming the noncompliance on the Ogunian even if, in fact, the Ogunian was waiting to use a valid access card in full compliance with security policy.

Worse, people can be so strongly influenced by expectation—part of their schema—that they actually misperceive a situation altogether. For example, in some classic experiments studying prejudice in the 1950s, psychologists showed subjects a drawing of two people, one light-colored and the other dark-colored, standing in a tramway car. One was holding a knife. When questioned about the image afterward, white subjects consistently reported that the black figure had been holding the knife, but actually it was the white figure in the drawing who had the knife.

Thus, even observation itself can be twisted by prejudice and expectations; for example, if the anti-Ogunian security officer sees a group of people passing through an open doorway into a secured area without using their badges, the officer may incorrectly report that it was the fault of an Ogunian even if there was no Ogunian in the group. Such a mistaken report would not only infuriate innocent Ogunians and possibly cause general Ogunian resentment or hostility toward "security," but it also could mislead the security group itself into trying to correct the behavior of the wrong person or people.

Similarly, any minority—whether in terms of gender, gender orientation, religion, race, or disability—can be the focus of a prejudiced security officer's blame when a group disobeys policy. Security leaders should make their staff aware of the danger of applying this erroneous method of explaining group behavior. In many organizations, such discrimination is a violation of corporate policy and may even be illegal. In any case, prejudice is not constructive and must be monitored and overcome.

50.2.5 Intercultural Differences.

Many countries in the world are experiencing changes in their population due to immigration. Especially in areas where people have heretofore been largely homogeneous, cultural, religious, and racial diversity can lead to interpersonal and intergroup conflicts. Such conflicts may be based in part on prejudice, but they also may be the result of differing values and assumptions.

This definition of culture helps define the discussion:

Culture as Mental Programming

Every person carries within him- or herself patterns of thinking, feeling, and potential acting that were learned throughout their lifetime. Much of it has been acquired in early childhood, because at that time a person is most susceptible to learning and assimilating. As soon as certain patterns of thinking, feeling, and acting have established themselves within a person's mind, he or she must unlearn these before being able to learn something different, and unlearning is more difficult than learning for the first time.

Using the analogy of the way computers are programmed, this book will call such patterns of thinking, feeling and acting *mental programs,* or ... *software of the mind.* ...

A customary term for such mental software is *culture.*[9]

Security personnel engaged in the process of corporate culture change should be sensitive to the possibility that people with different real-world cultural backgrounds can respond differently to proposed security policies. For example, in 2001 the fundamentalist extremists of the Taliban in Afghanistan decreed that non-Muslim people would have to wear badges in public.[10] One can imagine that a Hindu Afghan refugee in the United States who is told to wear a badge for security reasons might have an unexpectedly emotional response to the order. Before pressuring (or becoming hostile to) anyone who seems to be resisting a policy, it is valuable to inquire about the person's beliefs and attitudes and to explain the foundation for the policies in question. Especially where there are intercultural differences, such inquiry and discussion can forestall difficulties and dissension and assuage unexpected, culturally rooted anxiety.

Security professionals need to be acutely aware of the cultural differences of individuals in their target audiences. For example, in some cultures (mostly the new world and western), reality is directly related to facts and verifiable calculations. Other cultures may put a stronger emphasis on personal feelings, intuition, and culturally ingrained beliefs into their comprehension of reality. Hence different people may not share the same understanding of reality or implement policies by the same principles unless they make their assumptions known, and discuss them with the intention of coming to agreement.

When considering culture, the changing dynamics of modern society also need to be accounted for. Any modern city or leading public institution today is a complex combination of people from different cultural and social backgrounds. Working together for large parts of their active days together as a group leads to a melting pot situation, with all the individual cultures and social leanings being added into the mix and emerging as a (mostly) different culture. The individuals then take this new culture back home, where it mixes in with their family and friends' contributions, resulting in often more modifications and variation. The organization itself is constantly changing, as people join and leave. All of this leads to culture being a dynamic phenomenon, albeit not as rapidly changing as the technology front. Hence, any security policy or framework needs to be able to account for and accommodate this changing paradigm if it has to be successful in securing the enterprise.

50.2.6   Framing Reality.   How can we make the corporate culture more supportive of IA?

Schemata influence what we perceive. For example, an employee refuses to take vacations, works late every night, is never late, and is never sick. A model employee? Perhaps, in one schema. From the security point of view, the employee's behavior is suspect. There have been cases where such people have been embezzlers unable to leave their employment: Even a day away might result in discovery of their crimes. Saint or sinner? Our expectations determine what we see.[11]

To change the schema so that people take IA seriously, we should provide participants in training and security awareness with real-life examples of computer crime and security breaches, so that security policies make obvious sense rather than seeming to be arbitrary.

Schemata influence what we remember. When information inconsistent with our preconceptions is mixed with details that fit our existing schemata, we selectively retain what fits and discard what conflicts. When we have been fed a diet of movies and television shows illustrating the premise that information is most at risk from brilliant hackers, why should we remember the truth: that carelessness and incompetence by authorized users of information systems cause far more harm than evil intentions and outsiders ever do?

Instructors should emphasize the practical side of IA by showing how policies protect all employees against false accusations, prevent damage to the organization's reputation and profits, and even play a role in national security. This is especially true where business touches the technical infrastructure on which we all depend.

Most important of all, teaching others about IA cannot be an occasional and haphazard affair. Before attempting to implement policies and procedures (aside from emergency measures that are needed at once), we should ensure that we build up a consistent view of IA among our colleagues. In light of the complexity of social cognition, our usual attempts to implement security policies and procedures seem pathetically inept. A couple of hours of lectures followed by a video, a yearly ritual of signing a security policy that seems to have been written by Martians—these are not methods that will improve security. These efforts merely pay lip service to the idea of security.

According to research on counterintuitive information, people's judgment is influenced by the manner in which information is presented. For example, even information contrary to established schemata can be assimilated if people have enough time to integrate the new knowledge into their worldviews. It follows that nonemergency security policies should be introduced over a long time, not rushed into place.

An effective IA program includes frequent reminders of security. To change the corporate culture, practitioners should use methods such as a security corner in the corporate publication, security bulletins detailing the latest computer crime or security breach that has hit the news, contests for identifying the problems in realistic scenarios, and write-in columns to handle questions about policies. IA has to become part of the framework of reality, not just an imposition from management.

In every security course or awareness program, instructors and facilitators should explicitly address the question of corporate culture, expectations, and social schemata.

Do not rely solely on intellectual discourse when addressing a question of complex perceptions and feelings. Use simulations, videos, and role-playing exercises to bridge the gap between intellect and emotion.

Address the feelings and perceptions of all participants as they learn about the counterintuitive behaviors that improved security will demand. Encourage learners to think about how they might feel and respond in various situations that can arise during the transition to a more secure environment. For example, ask participants to imagine:

- Asking colleagues not to step through a secured entrance without passing through the access-control system with their own identity
- Telling their boss that they will not copy software without a license to do so
- Questioning a visitor or employee who is not wearing an identity badge[12]

50.2.7 Getting Your Security Policies Across.   What are some ways to change our colleagues' schemata so that they become more receptive to IA policies?

- **Initial exposure.** Preliminary information may influence people's responses to information presented later. For example, merely exposing experimental subjects to words such as "reckless" or "adventurous" affects their judgment of risk-taking behavior in a later test.

  It follows that when preparing to increase employee awareness of security issues, presenting case studies is likely to have a beneficial effect on participants' readiness to examine security requirements.

- **Counterexamples**. Preexisting schemata can be challenged by several counterexamples, each of which challenges a component of the schema. For example, prejudice about an ethnic group is more likely to be changed by contact with several people, each of whom contradicts a different aspect of the prejudiced schema.

  It follows that security awareness programs should include many realistic examples of security requirements and breaches. In a counterexample, students in college IA courses have commented on the unrealistic scenario in a training video they were shown: a series of disastrous security breaches occurring in the same company. Based on the findings of cognitive social psychologists, the film would be more effective for training if the incidents had been dramatized as occurring in different companies.

  In practical terms, practitioners should stay current and update their materials. Many IA publications provide useful case studies that will help make awareness and training more effective.

- **Choice of wording.** Perceptions of risks and benefits are profoundly influenced by the wording in which situations and options are presented. For example, experimental subjects responded far more positively to reports of a drug with "50 percent success" than to the same drug described as having "50 percent failure."

  It follows that practitioners should choose their language carefully during security awareness campaigns. Instead of focusing on reducing failure rates (violations of policy), we should emphasize improvements in our success rates. Unfortunately, some rates cannot be expressed in positive terms; for example, it is not easy to measure the success rate of security measures designed to foil attacks on systems.

Judgments are easily distorted by the tendency to rely on personal anecdotes, small samples, easily available information, and faulty interpretation of statistical information. Basically, we humans are not always rational processors of factual information. If security awareness programs rely strictly on presentation of factual information about risks and proposed policies and procedures, they are likely to run up against a stubborn refusal to act logically. Security program implementation must engage more than the rational mind. We must appeal to our colleagues' imagination and emotion as well. We must inspire a commitment to security rather than merely describing it.

50.2.8   Reward versus Punishment.   When enforcing security policies, too many organizations focus entirely on punishing those who break the rules. However, everything we know about modifying behavior teaches us to use reward rather than punishment. Punishing people who do not comply with security rules often generates resentment and hostility that carry over into future interactions. Instead of seeing information assurance as a benefit to the organization and to their interests, victims of harsh treatment can resist even well-intentioned, sensible changes in security policies simply because of the emotional overlay associated with the embarrassment and frustration generated by criticism and penalties.

In addition to avoiding negativity and push-back, reward may simply work better than punishment at changing behavior. For example, a security officer from a large corporation experimented with reward and punishment in implementing security policies. Employees were supposed to log off their mainframe terminals when leaving the office, but compliance rates were only around 40 percent. In one department, the security officer used the usual techniques recommended in the literature and common among security professionals; for example, she put up nasty notes on terminals that were not logged off, changed the passwords on delinquent accounts, and humiliated violators by forcing them to report to their bosses for authorization to obtain a new password. However, in a different department, she simply left a Hershey's Chocolate Kiss on the keyboard of every terminal whose user had indeed logged off before leaving. After one month of these two strategies, compliance rates in the department subject to punishment had climbed to around 60 percent. Compliance in the department getting chocolates had reached around 80 percent—and there feelings toward security were much more favorable than the norm.

This case illustrates some of the benefits of reward:

- Compliance rates were significantly higher than in the group subjected to punishment.
- Attitudes (see Section 50.3) are more likely to be positive.
- Costs can be lower because small rewards delivered en masse may be much cheaper and quicker to apply than administrative procedures applied one by one through management intervention

50.3   BELIEFS AND ATTITUDES.   Psychologists distinguish between beliefs and attitudes. A *belief* refers to cognitive information that need not have an emotional component. An *attitude* refers to an evaluation or emotional response. Thus, a person may believe correctly that copying a large number of proprietary software packages without authorization is a felony while nonetheless having the attitude that it does not matter to him. A rational employee may *believe* that malware can be downloaded onto company computers through unauthorized software available on unvetted Web sites (and thus answer a questionnaire evaluating security awareness correctly) yet have the *attitude* that the risk is negligible—and cheerfully go on downloading unauthorized software at work.

50.3.1   Beliefs.   Beliefs can change when contradictory information is presented, but some research suggests that it can take up to a week before significant shifts are measurable. Other studies suggest that when people hold contradictory beliefs, providing an opportunity to articulate and evaluate those beliefs may lead to changes that reduce inconsistency.

These findings imply that corporate security must explore the current structure of beliefs among employees and managers. Questionnaires, focus groups, and interviews may not only help the security practitioner, they actually may help move the corporate culture in the right direction. The *Hawthorne Effect* is the name given to improvements in measured behavior resulting simply from employee responses to being studied; done correctly, honestly, and nonpunitively, inquiring into employee beliefs and attitudes may communicate a genuine interest by management in improving security policy and practice with input from everyone involved.

50.3.2   Attitudes.   An attitude, in the classical definition, is a learned evaluative response, directed at specific objects, which is relatively enduring and influences behavior in a generally motivating way. The advertising industry spends over $50 billion yearly to influence public attitudes in the hope that these attitudes will lead to changes in spending habits—that is, in behavior.

Research on classical conditioning suggests that attitudes can be learned even through simple word association. If we wish to move our colleagues toward a more negative view of computer criminals, it is important not to portray computer crime using positive images and words. Movies that show criminal hackers as pleasant, smart, physically attractive, and likable people may do harm by minimizing the seriousness of industrial espionage and cybervandalism. When teaching security, we should avoid praising the criminals we describe in case studies.

Studies of how attitudes are developed consistently show that rewards and punishments are important motivators of behavior. Studies show that even apparently minor encouragement can influence attitudes. A supervisor or instructor should praise any comments that are critical of computer crime or that support the established security policies. Employees who dismiss security concerns, or who flout the regulations, should be challenged on their attitudes, not ignored. Such challenges are best carried out in private to avoid causing embarrassment to the skeptics and possibly generating resistance due to pride or a sense of machismo.

50.3.3   Changing Attitudes toward Security.   Persuasion—changing someone's attitudes—has been described in terms of communications. The four areas of research include:

1. **Communicator variables.** Who is trying to persuade?
2. **Message variables.** What is being presented?
3. **Channel variables.** By what means is the attempt taking place?
4. **Audience variables.** At whom is the persuasion aimed?

50.3.3.1   Communicator Variables.   Attractiveness, credibility, and social status have strong effects immediately after the speaker or writer has communicated with the target audience; however, over a period of weeks to a month, the effects decline until the predominant issue is message content. We can use this phenomenon by identifying the senior executives most likely to succeed in setting a positive tone for subsequent security training. We should look for respected, likable people who understand the issues and sincerely believe in the policies they are advocating.

One personality style in particular can threaten the success of security policies: the *authoritarian personality*. A body of research suggests that some people, often those raised by punitive parents highly concerned with social status, become rigidly devoted to conventional beliefs, submit to authority, exercise authority harshly themselves, and are hostile to groups they perceive as unpopular. An authoritarian person might make a terrible security officer. Such an officer might derive more satisfaction from ordering people around and punishing them than from long-term success in implementing security policies.

50.3.3.2   Message Variables.   Fear can work to change attitudes only if judiciously applied. Excessive emphasis on the terrible results of poor security is likely to backfire, with participants in the awareness program rejecting the message altogether. Frightening consequences should be coupled immediately with effective and achievable security measures.

Some studies suggest that presenting a balanced argument helps convince those who initially disagree with a proposal. Presenting objections to a proposal and offering counterarguments is more effective than one-sided diatribes. Popular training videos from the Software & Information Industry Association use this technique: they show people such as "college students, college faculty and publishers of all types of media discuss[ing] the legal and ethical implications of copying other people's works" and fairly present the arguments of copyright violators before rebutting them.[13]

Modest repetition of a message can help generate a more positive response. Thus security awareness programs that include imaginative posters, mugs, special newsletters, audio and videotapes, and lectures are more likely to build and sustain support for security than occasional intense sessions of indoctrination. The use of multiple communications channels (discussed in the next section) also increases the effectiveness of the message.

50.3.3.3   Channel Variables.   The channel through which we communicate has a strong effect on attitudes and on the importance of superficial attributes of the communicator. In modern organizations, most people assume that a meeting is the ideal way to communicate new information. However, the most effective medium for convincing someone to pay attention to any topic is face-to-face persuasion. Security training should include more than tapes and books; a charismatic teacher or leader can help generate enthusiasm for—or at least reduce resistance to—better security.

In addition, security educators should not introduce new ideas to decision makers in a meeting. There is too much danger of confounding responses to policy with nonpolicy matters rooted in relationships among the participants. It is not uncommon for one executive to oppose a new policy simply because another has supported it. A good way to introduce security policies is to have individual meetings with one executive at a time in order to explain the issues and proposals and to ask for support.

Psychologists testing cognitive response theory have studied many subtle aspects of persuasion. Experiments have shown that rhetorical questions, such as "Are we to accept invasions of our computer systems?" are effective when the arguments are solid but counterproductive when arguments are weak. Security officers should not ask rhetorical questions unless they are certain that almost everybody will inevitably have the same answer—the one the security officers are looking for.

Consideration of facts and logical arguments, as the central route to persuasion, has been found to lead to more lasting attitudes and attitude changes than the peripheral influences from logically unrelated factors, such as physical attractiveness of a speaker.

50.3.3.4   *Audience Variables.* As mentioned, questionnaires and interviews may help cement a favorable change in attitude by leading to commitment. Once employees have publicly avowed support for better security, some will begin to change their perception of themselves. Specific employees should be encouraged to take on various areas of public responsibility for IA within their work group. These roles should periodically be rotated among the employees to give everyone the experience of public commitment to improved security.

To keep up interest in security, regular meetings of enthusiasts to discuss recent security news can keep the subject fresh and interesting. New cases can help security officers explain policies with up-to-date references that will interest their fellow employees and motivate managers to pay attention to security policies.

50.4   ENCOURAGING INITIATIVE. The ideal situation would be for everyone actually to help enforce security policies. Actually, however, some people are cooperative and helpful whereas others—or even the same people in different circumstances—are reluctant and suspicious about new policies. What can we do to increase cooperation and reduce rejection?

50.4.1   Prosocial Behavior. Studies of people who have come to the aid of others can help to encourage everyone in an organization to do the right thing. Some people intervene to stop crimes; others ignore crimes or watch passively. Social psychologists have devised a schema that describes the steps leading to prosocial behavior:

1. People have to notice the emergency or the crime before they can act. Thus, security training has to include information on how to tell that someone may be engaging in computer crime.

2. The situation has to be defined as an emergency—something requiring action. Security training that provides facts about the effects of computer crime on society and solid information about the need for security within the organization can help employees recognize security violations as emergencies.

3. Everyone must take responsibility for acting, but the larger the number of people in a group confronted with an emergency, the slower the average response time. Larger groups seem to lead to a *diffusion of responsibility*; each person feels that someone else is more responsible for dealing with the emergency. Another possible factor is uncertainty about the social climate; people fear appearing foolish or overly emotional in the eyes of those present. To overcome this effect, a corporate culture must be established that rewards responsible individual behavior, such as reporting security violations.

4. Once responsibility for solving a problem has been accepted, appropriate decisions and actions must be taken. Clearly written security policies and procedures will make it more likely that employees act to improve security. In contrast, contradictory policies, poorly documented procedures, and inconsistent support from management will interfere with the decision to act.

Another analysis proposes that people implicitly analyze costs of helping and of not helping when deciding whether to act prosocially. The combination of factors most conducive to prosociality is low cost for helping and high cost for not helping.

Security procedures should make it easy to act in accordance with security policy. There should be a hot line for reporting security violations, and anonymity should be respected if desired. Psychological counseling and follow-up should be available if people feel upset about their involvement. Conversely, failing to act responsibly should be a serious matter; personnel policies should document clear and meaningful sanctions for failing to act when a security violation is observed. Penalties would include critical remarks in employment reviews and, where appropriate, even dismissal.

One method that does *not* work to increase prosocial behavior is *exhortation*; merely lecturing people in the abstract about what they ought to do has little or no positive effect.

Significantly, the general level of stress and pressure to focus on difficult tasks with seemingly impossible deadlines can greatly reduce the likelihood that people will act on their moral and ethical principles. Security is likely to flourish in an environment that provides sufficient time and support for employees to work professionally. Offices where everyone responds to a continuing series of apparent emergencies will not be likely to pay attention to security violations.

Some findings from research confirm common sense. For example, guilt motivates many people to act more prosocially. This effect works best when people are forced to assume responsibility. Thus, enforcing standards of security using reprimands and sanctions can indeed increase the likelihood that employees subsequently will act more cooperatively; however, as suggested earlier, punishment should not replace reward.

In addition, mood affects susceptibility to prosocial pressures. Bad moods make prosocial behavior less likely, whereas good moods increase prosociality. A working environment in which employees are respected is more conducive to good security than one that devalues and abuses them.

Even cursory acquaintance with other people makes it more likely that we will help them; it thus makes sense for security supervisors to get to know the staff from whom they need support. Encouraging social activities in an office (e.g., lunchtime discussion groups, occasional parties, and charitable projects) enhances interpersonal relationships and can improve the climate for effective security training. *Management by walking around* is an excellent practice at many levels, including fostering at least the first stage of interpersonal relationship among coworkers.[14]

50.4.2 Conformity, Compliance, and Obedience.   These days, many people react negatively to the words "conformity," "compliance," and "obedience," but ignoring social phenomena will not help security practitioners to attain their goals. Despite the unpopularity of this subject area, it is valuable to understand how people can work together in reinforcing security policies. The next sections look at how to increase conformity with a culture of cooperation for increased security, compliance with rational security rules, and a bias toward obedience to IA authorities in security matters.

50.4.2.1   *Social Pressure and Behavior Change.* Turning a group into a community provides a framework within which social pressures can operate to improve an organization's IA. Most people respond to the opinions of others by shifting their own opinions, sometimes unconsciously, toward what statisticians call the *mode*—the most popular opinion. Security programs must aim to shift the normative values, the sense of what one should do, toward protecting confidentiality, possession or control, integrity, authenticity, availability, and utility of data.

An informal survey conducted by Mani Akella, a coauthor of this Chapter, at three leading financial firms on Wall Street resulted in these inferences from a test group of 80 respondents:

- Older employees prefer to model their reactions based on common group preferences even if some of the reactions go against their own gut feeling. The rationale here seems to be that the group provides anonymity and even insulates them from management reaction. Younger employees, however, tend to buck the group trend when they disagree with proposed concepts.

- Leadership has a large role to play—and the group modifies its reactions very quickly to adapt to leadership changes. If the leader likes to follow a specific path and not ask questions, the entire group tends to let issues lie and not disturb the even tenor of the organization for fear of disturbing the leader, even at the cost of risking serious potential security lapses (see Section 50.5.4 on groupthink). If the leader fosters a dynamic, open, and collaborative environment with a measured adaptability to evolving threats, however, the group enlivens itself with innovation and puts out additional effort to stay abreast (or even ahead) of the current threat landscape.

- When the leaders challenge the individuals to greater achievement without threats of punitive reaction, the *group* reacts with positive response. Leadership can create a security environment that can exceed the enterprise's security expectations by encouraging the individual to increase productivity and to reward oneself with greater job satisfaction. Security, like most other organizational management efforts, is all about people. Responsible, satisfied, and aware personnel naturally lead to better overall security for the organization.

50.4.2.2   *Changing Expectations.* As has been evident in public campaigns aimed at eliminating drunken driving, it *is* possible to shift the mode. In the United States in the mid-twentieth century, many people believed that driving while intoxicated was amusing; today, a drunken driver is a social pariah. High school children used to kill themselves in large numbers on the nights of their high school proms; today, many children spontaneously are arranging for safe rides home. Between 1982 and 2006, the percentage of people killed due to alcohol intoxication in traffic fatalities in the United States fell from 60 percent to 41 percent.[15] In much the same way, we must move toward making computer crime as distasteful as public drunkenness.

The trend toward similar behavior increases when people within the group like or admire each other. In addition, the social status of an individual within a group influences that individual's willingness to conform to group standards. High-status people (those liked by most people in the group) and low-status people (those disliked by the group) both tend to be more autonomous and less compliant than people liked by some and disliked by others. Therefore, security officers should pay special attention to those outliers during instruction programs. Managers should monitor compliance more closely at both ends of the popularity range. If security practices are currently poor, and allies are needed to change the norm, working with the outliers to resist the majority's anti-security bias may be the most effective approach. The most popular people may be disastrous agents of rebellion if they do not sign on to the security program; paradoxically, the most unpopular people may be helpful if they can be persuaded to comply.

50.4.2.3 Norm of Reciprocity.

According to social psychologists, the norm of reciprocity indicates that, in social relations, favors are usually returned. Even a small, unexpected, unsolicited, or even unwanted gift increases the likelihood that we will respond to requests. For example, members of various religious cults often hand out flowers or books at airports, knowing that the norm of reciprocity will increase the frequency and amount of donations from basically uninterested passersby.

A security awareness program that includes small gifts, such as an attractive mug labeled "SECURITY IS EVERYONE'S BUSINESS" or an inexpensive but useful booklet summarizing security policies, can help get people involved in security. The combination of such programs with rewards for compliance can be a powerful tool for improving security.

Combining a token of appreciation with direct personal contact starting with the statement "I need your help" followed by a frank exposition of the security situation can be positive at all levels. This approach works at multiple levels—establishing personal relations, building on the norm of reciprocity, and changing the schema.

50.4.2.4 Incremental Change.

The foot-in-the-door technique suggests that a small initial request should be followed by an even larger second one. Political field workers, for example, know that they can start small by asking people to let them put candidate stickers in their window; then they ask to put a candidate's poster on their lawn; eventually they can ask for volunteer time or money. Every compliance with a request increases the likelihood that the person will agree to the next step in an escalating series. It is as if agreeing to one step helps to change the targets' sense of themselves. To reduce discomfort about their beliefs and their behavior (what psychologists call *cognitive dissonance*), people change their beliefs to conform with their behavior.

Employees can be asked personally to set a good example by blanking screens and locking terminals when leaving their desks. Later, once they have begun the process of redefining themselves ("I am a person who cares about computer security"), they can be asked for something more intense, such as participating in security training by asking others to blank their screens and lock their terminals—or rewarding those who do with the famous chocolate tidbit. By applying the same methods to various tasks, the corporate culture can change so that a majority of people feel personally committed to good security practices.

Some security specialists have proposed that we should not ask the audience to think. The reasoning is that each incremental policy step should not require the target audience to reason or explain behavior. Rather, focus on building conditioned reflexes to specific environmental and usage factors. The organization and the security team should be more assured of a common and predictable reaction to any security threat from each individual internal person. However, a countervailing view is that every behavior proposed to improve security *must* be grounded in an understandable schema. In other words, although one need not force the members of the audience to *articulate* the rationale, the rules must make sense if they are to be integrated, remembered, and applied in the long term.

50.5   GROUP BEHAVIOR.   Some groups of people are referred to as teams, while others are called gangs. Social psychological insights into group behavior can improve success rates for IA policies.

50.5.1   Social Arousal.   Studies on the behavioral effects of being in groups produced contradictory results; sometimes people did better at their tasks when there were other people around, and sometimes they did worse. Eventually, psychologists realized that the presence of other people is *socially arousing*; that is, people become more aware both of their own behavior and of social norms when they are in groups. Social arousal *facilitates well-learned habits, but it inhibits poorly learned habits*. Thus, when trying to teach employees new habits to improve security, it is counterproductive to put them into large groups. Individualized learning (e.g., by means of computer-based training and videotapes) can overcome inhibitory effects of groups in the early stages of behavioral change.

50.5.2   Locus of Control.   Another factor that interferes with implementation of security policies is the *locus of control*. People do not like feeling that they have no control over their environment. For example, in a classic experiment reported in social psychology textbooks, two equivalent teams of people were both subjected to loud and disruptive noise coming through a loudspeaker in their work area. One group had no control whatever over the noise, whereas the other had a large button with which they could stop the noise at once. The group with the stop button did noticeably better at their complex task than the other group—yet in no case did anyone actually press the button. Simply feeling that they *could* exert control, if they wanted to, significantly altered the performance of the experimental subjects.

   Similarly, in studies of healing among older patients, three groups were defined: (1) controls, (2) people given a plant in a pot, and (3) people given a plant in a pot plus instructions to water it regularly. The third group did significantly better than the second in their recovery. Once again, the sense of control over the environment appeared to influence outcomes.

   In security policy implementation, experience confirms that those organizations with the most participation and involvement by all sectors do best at developing and implementing information protection plans. A common phrase that refers to this phenomenon is "buy-in," as in: "The different departmental representatives felt that they could genuinely buy into the new policies because they had fully participated in framing them."[16]

50.5.3   Group Polarization.   Another branch of research into group psychology deals with group polarization. Groups tend to take more extreme decisions than would individuals in the group acting alone. In group discussions of the need for security, polarization can involve deciding to take more risks—by reducing or ignoring security concerns—than any individual would have judged reasonable. Again, one-on-one discussions of the need for security will generally be more effective in building a consensus that supports cost-effective security provisions than will large meetings.

50.5.4   Groupthink.   In the extreme, a group can display groupthink, in which a consensus is reached because of strong desires for social cohesion. When groupthink prevails, evidence contrary to the received view is discounted; opposition is viewed as disloyal; dissenters are discredited. Especially worrisome for security professionals, those people in the grip of groupthink tend to ignore risks and contingencies. To prevent such aberrations, the leader must remain impartial and encourage open debate. Respected security consultants from the outside could be invited to address the group, bringing their own experiences to bear on the group's requirements. After a consensus—not the imposition of a dominant person's opinions—has been achieved, the group should meet again and focus on playing devil's advocate to try to come up with additional challenges and alternatives.

In summary, security experts should pay attention to group dynamics and be prepared to counter possible dysfunctional responses that interfere with acceptance of IA policies.

50.6 TECHNOLOGICAL GENERATION GAPS. In our society there are growing societal gaps between the social groups that grew up interacting in real-world communities (unwired), groups that grew up with the Internet (wired), and the newest group growing up with the always-on technology of our complex and content-rich wireless social networks.

- **The unwired generation.** In today's "always-on" world of ubiquitous wireless communications, we sometimes forget about the unwired generation, those born in the early 1960s or before, who grew up actually playing outside with their friends and communicating face to face. For these employees, online discussion groups, streaming video training, blogs, and e-mail may not be as effective as with other, more technological groups. The unwired generation frequently sees the use of impersonal technology in training as an indicator of management apathy toward a topic that is not worth taking the time for real-world interaction. To this generation, if security training is important, someone should take the time to deliver it face to face. The unwired generation is also the most susceptible to many of the social psychology techniques and pitfalls discussed in this chapter.

- **The wired generation.** Those born from the early 1960s to the late 1970s comprise the wired generation. This transitional generation grew up at the dawn of the Internet from 300 baud dial-up access to ISDN. From MS DOS to Windows 98 and from Cobol to C++, this generation is the bridge from the real world to the cyber world. This generation is also the generation currently coming to power in both business and government. Although accustomed to meeting face to face for important business, the wired generation lives by e-mail and cell phones, tolerating both the unwired and wired methods of communicating and learning.

- **The always-on generation.** Those born after 1980 comprise the always-on generation. This generation grew up with high-speed Internet, cell phones, video games, portable electronics, and online virtual communities. This is the connected, networked, MySpace generation. It is this generation that seems to confound traditional security screening and implementation policy.

Although the unwired and wired generations shared psychological roots in the real world, the always-on generation has two homes: the real world and the cyber world. With instant messaging (IM) and cellular wireless, this generation moves in and out of cyberspace as the previous generation moved between the worlds of work and home. Moreover, like the previous generations, the always-on generation has different psychological and sociological frameworks for their worlds—a serious information assurance concern.

To the unwired and wired generations, personal communication meant face to face. To the always-on generation personal, communication means IM, e-mail, and digital phones. In addition, social interaction often means blogs, Web pages, message boards, and wikis. Add to this the fact that the always-on generation has a keen ability to quickly transfer information between their tightly integrated worlds, and you have the ingredients for a security officer's nightmare.

Recognizing these differences and reacting accordingly can pay sizable dividends in both security compliance and general management success. As a first step, one can ensure that security teams include members from more than the oldest generation in the enterprise; younger people may be able to act as intermediaries or translators between increasingly disparate cultures.

50.7   SUMMARY OF RECOMMENDATIONS.   This chapter has reviewed the major findings of social psychology that can help to improve IA programs. These ideas can prove useful to readers who think about social psychology as they work to implement security policies:

- Recognize that IA policies often conflict with the schema for trusting, polite behavior in situations outside the work arena.
- Train IA personnel to recognize that failure to comply with security policies may be rooted in many other factors than simply bad attitude.
- Listen more than you command.
- Teach security personnel to avoid the classic errors of attribution when trying to understand their colleagues' motivations.
- Openly discuss and counter prejudice before it causes conflicts.
- Take intercultural differences into account when setting and implementing security policies.
- Before attempting to implement policies and procedures, ensure a consistent view of IA among colleagues.
- Whenever possible, security policies should be introduced over a long time, not rushed into place.
- Presenting case studies is likely to have a beneficial effect on participants' readiness to examine security requirements.
- Security awareness programs should include many realistic examples of security requirements and breaches.
- Attempt to inspire a commitment to security rather than merely describing it.
- Emphasize improvements rather than reduction of failure.
- Create a new concern for corporate security by exploring the current structure of beliefs among employees and managers.
- Never portray computer crime using positive images and words.
- Praise any comments that are critical of computer crime or that support the established security policies.
- Employees who dismiss security concerns or flout the regulations should be challenged on their attitudes, not ignored.
- Identify the senior executives most likely to succeed in setting a positive tone for subsequent security training and engage their cooperation to act as role models.

- Examples of frightening consequences used in awareness and training materials should be coupled immediately with descriptions of effective and achievable security measures to forestall such consequences.
- Presenting objections to a proposal and offering counterarguments is more effective than one-sided diatribes.
- Security awareness programs should include many, frequent, and preferably novel and entertaining reminders of security issues.
- In addition to tapes and books, rely on a charismatic teacher or leader to help generate enthusiasm for better security.
- Encourage specific employees to take on public responsibility for IA within their work groups.
- Rotate security roles periodically.
- Security training should include information on how to tell that someone may be engaging in computer crime.
- Build a corporate culture that rewards responsible behavior, such as reporting security violations.
- Develop clearly written security policies and procedures.
- Security procedures should make it easy to act in accordance with security policy.
- Treat failures to act in accordance with security policies and procedures as very serious matters.
- Enforcing standards of security can increase the likelihood that employees will subsequently act more cooperatively.
- A working environment in which employees are respected is more conducive to good security than one that devalues and abuses them.
- Get to know the staff from whom you need support.
- Encourage social activities in the office.
- Pay special attention to social outliers during instruction programs.
- Monitor compliance more closely at both ends of the popularity range.
- Work with the outliers to resist a group's anti-security bias.
- Include small gifts in your security awareness program.
- Start improving security a little at a time, and work up to more intrusive procedures.
- Before discussing security at a meeting, have one-on-one discussions with the participants.
- Remain impartial, and encourage open debate in security meetings.
- Bring in experts from the outside when faced with groupthink.
- Meet again after a consensus has been built, and play devil's advocate.
- Recognize the generational technology gaps in our culture and communicate accordingly; therefore, include people from different generations in your security teams.

None of these suggestions is essential; none of them is appropriate in all situations. However, building on the accumulated experience and wisdom of social psychologists will support the smooth integration of information assurance into any corporate culture. We hope that readers will explore the literature of social and organizational psychology and will try out new ideas that will enrich the field of information assurance in years to come.

50.8   FURTHER READING

Adler, N. J., and A. Gunderson. *International Dimensions of Organizational Behavior*, 5th ed. Cincinnati, OH: South-Western College Publications, 2007.

Greenberg, J. *Managing Behavior in Organizations*, 5th ed. Upper Saddle River, NJ: Prentice-Hall, 2008.

Kinicki, A. *Organizational Behavior*, 4th ed. New York: McGraw-Hill, 2008.

Kowert, P. *Groupthink or Deadlock: When Do Leaders Learn from Their Advisors?* Albany, N: State University of New York Press, 2002.

Lesko, W. A. ed. *Readings in Social Psychology: General, Classic, and Contemporary Selections*, 7th ed. New York: Allyn & Bacon, 2008.

Mills, J. H. *Understanding Organizational Change*. New York: Routledge, 2009.

Myers, D. G. *Social Psychology*, 9th ed. New York: McGraw-Hill, 2006.

Senior, C., and M. Butler. *Social Cognitive Neuroscience of Organizations*. Hoboken, NJ: Wiley-Blackwell, 2008.

Smith, E. R., and D. M. MacKie. *Social Psychology*, 3rd ed. Philadelphia: Taylor & Francis, 2007.

50.9   NOTES

1. This chapter is based on original work by M. E. Kabay as a contributed paper at the Sixteenth National Computer Security Conference organized in 1993 by the National Computer Security Center. That work was updated over the years and became a chapter in the third edition of this *Handbook*. It has been updated for this edition with contributions from colleagues teaching and studying in the MSIA program at the School of Graduate Studies at Norwich University.

2. No specific references to the scholarly literature of social psychology research are included in this chapter except for quoted materials. For details of the information presented, consult any college-level introduction to social psychology.

3. J. Baron, *Thinking and Deciding* (Cambridge, UK: Cambridge University Press, 1994).

4. Government Accountability Office, "Information Security: Emerging Cybersecurity Issues Threaten Federal Information Systems," United States Government Accountability Office Report GAO-05-231 (May 2005); www.gao.gov/new.items/d05231.pdf.

5. M. E. Kabay, "The VA Data Insecurity Saga." (2008), www2.norwich.edu/ mkabay/infosecmgmt/vasaga.pdf.

6. R. D. Austin and C. A.R. Darby, "The Myth of Secure Computing," *Harvard Business Review* (June 2003); http://harvardbusinessonline.hbsp.harvard.edu/b01/en/common/item_detail.jhtml?id=4031&referral=2340.

7. For an in-depth discussion of the manager's role in IA, see Chapter 63 in this *Handbook*; for a discussion of the role of the chief information security officer, see Chapter 65.

8. N. Tal-Or and Y. Papirman, "The Fundamental Attribution Error in Attributing Fictional Figures' Characteristics to the Actors." Paper presented at the annual meeting of the International Communication Association, Sheraton New York, New York, NY, April 13, 2008; www.allacademic.com/meta/p13476_index.html.

9. G. Hofstede and G. J. Hofstede, *Cultures and Organizations: Software of the Mind,* 2nd ed. (New York: McGraw-Hill, 2004).

10. S. Salahuddin, "Taliban Defend Yellow Badges for Non-Muslim Afghans," Reuters, May 23, 2001; www.afghanistannewscenter.com/news/2001/may/may23c2001.html.

11. See Chapter 45 in this *Handbook* for a discussion of such an example.

12. For more ideas on effective security-awareness programs, see Chapter 49.

13. SIIA Resource eStore: www.siia.net/estore/10browse.asp?Category=Anti-piracy.

14. See FUTURECents, "Management by Walking Around,"www.futurecents.com/mainmbwa.htm; and R. Amis, "Time Again for Management by Walking Around?" *IT Manager's Journal,* January 15, 2006; www.itmanagersjournal.com/ feature/ 10227.

15. MADD, "Total Traffic Fatalities vs. Alcohol Related Traffic Fatalities—1982–2006," Mothers Against Drunk Driving, http://maddtx.org/stats/ 11882.

16. See Chapter 66 in this *Handbook* for a discussion of the importance of widespread participation in security-policy development.

SECURITY STANDARDS FOR PRODUCTS

Paul Brusil and Noel Zakin

51.1   INTRODUCTION.   Standards provide for uniformity of essential characteristics of products and product-related procedures. Standards allow consumers to have a better understanding of what they purchase. This section provides a general introduction to standards: who creates standards, what types of features and capabilities are standardized, why standards are important, and what types of standards apply to products.

In later sections, attention turns to standards associated with testing and evaluation of products. The nonstandard approaches confronting and befuddling consumers, as well as the issues arising from nonstandard approaches, are contrasted with the confidence obtained by using a universal, internationally accepted standard for product testing and evaluation. The common standard allows the consumer to understand with greater certainty the security and assurance features offered by a product. Increased software quality assurance became of top concern to U.S. Government agency chief information security officers (CISOs) as attention turned to the Federal Information Security Management (FISMA) Act.[1]

51.1.1   Value of Standards.   Many parties benefit from standards: customers, vendors, testing houses, and more.

Customers find standards helpful in several ways. Standards help specify their needs for various security functionalities and the degrees of assurance they require in the products they buy. Standards help customers understand what security functionality and assurances that a product builder claims to provide. Standards help consumers select commercial off-the-shelf products that they can trust will conform to their security and assurance requirements and that, as needed, interoperate with comparable products. Customers under the mandates of the security-relevant regulations imposed by the Health Insurance Portability and Accountability Act (HIPAA) and the Sarbanes-Oxley Act (SOX) often look to establishing due diligence by leveraging products that have established trust in their security and assurance functionality in a standard way.

Vendors find standards helpful in several ways. Use of standards provides evidence that vendors have migrated their product development to a paradigm wherein security is built-in from the start. Use of standards provides evidence that security is not some afterthought that is patched or bolted on. Use of standards shows that security is the foundation on which a vendor is building a product. Use of standards helps open global marketplaces to vendors. By using standard, third-party verification of security capabilities, vendors are making their products either stand out from or be comparable to their competitors.

51.1.2 Purpose of Product Assessment.

Trust in the electronic processing, storage, and interactions among customers, business partners, suppliers, service organizations, and governments is key to electronic economy and electronic government models. The need for trust will only increase as new IT paradigms and technologies proliferate, mutate business and IT support models, and introduce new risks and vulnerabilities. For electronic business models and electronic government models to succeed, all e-business and e-government players need confidence in the IT products used by interacting players as well as in the intervening IT infrastructure. Recent federal government administrations have recognized the importance of establishing trust in IT. They have issued directives and guidance to elevate awareness of the central, critical nature of IT and to help to preserve trust in national IT infrastructures.[2]

IT "systems" are often composed of many individual products. Methods for establishing trust in products do not necessarily work for establishing trust in systems. Methods of establishing trust in IT systems exist. They include, for example, the U.S. Department of Defense (DoD) DITSCAP and NIST C&A, as mentioned earlier. Also, while the Common Criteria approach is basically focused on establishing trust in individual products, there is ongoing research into the potential use of the Common Criteria paradigm as a way to establish trust in systems of individual IT products.

Such systems-focused, trust-development methods tend to be employed only by large enterprises. Furthermore, the problem of establishing a quantitative measure of trust in a very large, heterogeneous system like a national IT infrastructure is not yet well understood. At a minimum, it requires coordination and cooperation among all who contribute to or use the infrastructure. Although still argued among security professionals, many believe a step in the right direction is to build IT systems with products and components that are individually assessed to be trustworthy, with some specified degree of confidence. What is most difficult, however, in a product assessment is to test its security aspects in an environment that perfectly mimics the environment in which the product is to be used.

Another key notion besides trust is the notion of risk management. When electronic relationships are established between parties, there are quantifiable risks associated with such relationships.

Risks are quantifiable in many ways. For example, they can be quantified in terms of the types of possible adverse events. They can be quantified in terms of the likelihood of different types of adverse events and by the value of what is to be protected by IT security solutions during an adverse event. They can be quantified in terms of the consequences of adverse events, such as the liability that may be exposed via compromises, or the entities that may be hurt by compromises.

Risks then can be mitigated in a number of possible ways. For example, risks can be mitigated by using products that reduce the occurrence or impacts of the adverse events of most concern. When assets of increasing value need to be protected, risks can be reduced by using products that have increased assurance. Risks also can be mitigated by using products that decrease the specific, deleterious liabilities and undesired consequences of greatest concern. Being able to specify the risks of concern, and security solutions that mitigate those risks, is a powerful strategy uniquely held by the Common Criteria paradigm.

Linking notions of trust together with notions of risk reduction makes for an even more powerful strategy. Establishing trust among interacting electronic parties that all parties are using products with appropriate security quality is akin to the role of face-to-face handshakes in older business models. In the e-business marketplace, trust, like the old handshake, is key to increased revenues via increased business transaction volumes. Furthermore, by mitigating risks, business losses and costs can be reduced. When trust enhancement is coupled with risk management, the resulting increased revenues, combined with decreased losses and lower costs, make for significant profit multiplication.

The Common Criteria paradigm is a standards-based product assessment strategy that provides for both establishing appropriate levels of trust in products and for specifying and mitigating risks of most concern. Indeed, the Common Criteria paradigm appears to be the only strategy available today for simultaneously establishing trust and managing risk in products.

Various ways have been developed and used over the years to build confidence about the quality of security implementations. The focus of such efforts includes establishing trust via one or both of two perspectives: (1) that a product performs its claimed security functionality completely and correctly and (2) that the product builder's processes (from design, to development, to delivery, to maintenance) are sound. Typically, trust is established either by testing just the implementation or by evaluating both the product and its implementer.

Not all approaches to establishing trust via product assessment necessarily address trust via assessment of implemented security functionality as well as by assurance of the soundness of the builder's abilities and processes. Furthermore, many of the testing and evaluation approaches are not based on standards.

51.1.3 Sources of Standards.   Formal standards relevant to information assurance (IA) are created, published, and maintained by "recognized" standards bodies. There are various recognized standards including technology-specific working groups associated with professional organizations like the IEEE (Institute of Electrical and Electronic Engineers) and the IETF (Internet Engineering Task Force). Standards are also created by working groups associated with recognized country-specific national standards bodies, such as the ASC (American Standards Committee, formerly ANSI) in the United States or BSI (British Standards Institute) in the United Kingdom. Such national standards bodies create either country-specific standards, or they collaborate and harmonize with other peer national standards bodies to create international, globally applicable standards such as those associated with ISO (Organization of International Standardization).

Recognized organizations within national governments also create standards. For example, the National Institute of Standards and Technology (NIST)—a U.S. federal agency under the U.S. Department of Commerce—creates and issues standards called FIPS (Federal Information Processing Standards). FIPS often, but not always, apply just to the U.S. federal government. Indeed, a 2005 amendment to the Federal Acquisition Regulation to implement the IT security provisions of the FISMA requires all federal procurements to adhere to pertinent FIPS. NIST also publishes Special Publications that may recommend standard best practices for use government-wide. Along similar lines, the U.S. DoD publishes standard directives. Such directives, for example, specify what must be done by DoD entities to meet a need or what constraints DoD organizations must follow when purchasing IT products.

National governments also form bodies to collaborate and to harmonize international standards for use by governments within several nations. The Common Criteria Project is an example of such a cross-government standardization body. Standards developed by this particular cross-government standards body are also fed to recognized international standards bodies like International Standards Organization (ISO) to create even broader-reaching standards.

Technology-specific consortia, such as the OMG (Object Management Group), and industry-specific consortia, such as the Smart Card Security Users Group and TeleManagement Forum, have large, broad-based, international membership. Often they are considered to be creators of informal standards for use within specific industries or technology sectors.

Smaller consortia or individual entities also claim to create "standards," but, such efforts are generally not accepted by broad constituencies as legitimate, recognized standards.

51.1.4 Classes of Security Standards. Standards are developed to provide mutually recognized specifications for various reasons. For example, like FIPS 140 related standards, they can specify security requirements, product evaluation methods, and product validation concepts. Like the Common Criteria (Sections 51.6 and 51.7), standards can specify the security functionality, or assurance characteristics, to be incorporated into products as well as test methods to use when evaluating products. Other standards can specify interoperable profiles of security capabilities. Standards can also specify how to become a product tester or how to assess the capabilities of vendors. Like ISO 17799[3] and NIST SP 800-53,[4] standards can specify guidelines or best practices for users assembling and using secure components. Like the DITSCAP (replaced by DIACAP in November 2007)[5] for U.S. DoD, and the NIACAP[6] and NIST Certification & Accreditation[7] (C&A) methodologies for U.S. federal civilian departments and agencies, standards can specify how to certify and how to accredit systems composed of secure products and secure components. Or, like DoD's 8500.1[8] and 8500.2,[9] they can be standard policy and policy implementation directives, respectively, for what types of products DoD must procure. Various standards are described throughout this book. This chapter focuses on those standards associated with assessing products.

51.1.5 Products for Which Standards Apply. There are two classes of products of interest in this chapter: "security" products and "security-enabled" products. Security products directly provide security services or prevent penetrations. Security products include, for example, intrusion detection products and firewalls. Security-enabled products are secured products that do not exist solely to provide security services; instead they provide other services that are protected. Examples include operating systems, database management systems, and virtual private networking gear that incorporate security functionality such as identification and authentication or IPsec (IP security) to protect either the product or the services provided by the product.

51.1.6 Breadth of Product-Oriented Standards. In today's heterogeneous, multidisciplinary, multitechnology, multiparty, interconnected information technology (IT) environments, different types of security standards for products are essential for a variety of reasons.

Standards exist to provide consistent ways to stipulate security needs and requirements in both security products and secured products. Other standards specify the security functionality appearing within products. Standards like IPsec not only specify security functionality, but they also foster interoperability of separately built security implementations. Yet other standards specify security-related software interfaces, naming conventions, and data structures such as for Common Object Request Broker Architecture (CORBA) middleware products. In aggregate, standards promote consistent security, end to end as well as across different business domains and computing environments.

Standards also exist to govern the testing of products. As security products become just as popular attack targets as secured products themselves, it is essential that vendors and buyers of security and security-enhanced products determine what security requirements a product addresses and how well it meets those requirements. Conformance testing demonstrates whether an implementation includes the functionality stipulated in a functional standard. However, conformance of different products to the same functional standard does not necessarily ensure that these products will interoperate. Interoperability testing can assure secure interoperation between comparable products built by autonomous vendors or products used between autonomous parties. Conformance implies only that interoperability is possible; but interoperability needs to be verified by pair-wise testing. Standards exist to specify how to examine conformance of implementations to functional standards and how to assure the interoperability of implementations that must meet the same functional standard.

Interoperating, conformant, secured products and security products cannot necessarily be trusted to provide or to support sound security, or to mitigate the risks of greatest concern. Key to developing trust is to build confidence that products mitigate the risks of concern, that products are properly built and behave according to specification, and that products do no more or no less than advertised. Standards like the Common Criteria exist for establishing and testing the degree to which risks and vulnerabilities are mitigated to a specified level of confidence. These standards exist to specify and to test that the quality of security associated with products used by interacting parties are comparable.

Furthermore, yet other standards (within the suite of Common Criteria standards) exist to accredit organizations to conduct conformance, trust, or interoperability testing in a standard way.

51.1.7   Focus of This Chapter.   A major goal of standardization efforts is to evolve toward an IT-driven economy where security products, and secured products, approach plug-and-play status. They should be comparably trusted, purchased from multiple competing vendors, and mixed, matched, and integrated to provide requisite secure, trusted IT infrastructures that reduce the risks of greatest concern.

Although several different categories of security-relevant standards should be considered, standards associated with developing product trust are especially important in the electronically interwoven world.

This chapter focuses on such trust-enhancing standards. It summarizes various historical and current approaches for developing product trust. It spotlights the internationally recognized Common Criteria paradigm that provides a standard way for stipulating (1) the risks of concern, (2) the security functional requirements that must be met in order to mitigate stated risks, and (3) the security assurance requirements that must be met to provide confidence that products are built with desired quality. According to this paradigm, risks and protection requirements are stipulated so that security solutions can be tested in a standard way, via testing laboratories that are accredited (in a standard way), to be able to verify (in a standard way) product compliance with stipulated standard security functional, and security assurance, requirements. The limitations of this paradigm are also summarized.

51.2 NONSTANDARD PRODUCT ASSESSMENT ALTERNATIVES.   For completeness, a variety of the product assessment approaches that are not dependent on standard, internationally recognized, security testing and evaluation approaches are listed here. They include:

- Vendor self-declarations (Section 51.2.1)
- Customer in-house assessments (Section 51.2.2)
- Consortium-based assessments (Section 51.2.3)
- Informal evaluations via open-source code development (Section 51.2.4)
- Informal assessments via hacking (Section 51.2.5)
- Assessments by magazines and trade press publications (Section 51.2.6)
- Commercial assessments using nonstandard methods (Section 51.2.7)

There are shortcomings to most of these approaches. Many do not offer much value. One of the basic shortcomings is that lack of reliance on standards makes for difficulty in comparing the product assessment results:

- of different products
- for products tested and evaluated via different approaches
- for products tested and evaluated by different testing facilities that all purportedly use the same product assessment approach

51.2.1 Vendor Self-Declarations.   One of the initial approaches to providing trust is based on the notion of vendor self-declarations. A vendor can unilaterally claim that a specific product meets the security needs of a class of customers and that an appropriate amount of customer-desired confidence can be placed in the product's implemented security features. In part, the confidence associated with this approach is implicitly tied to the past reputation of a vendor or to the customer's past experience in dealing with the vendor. If the vendor's reputation or customer's experiences are good, there is some sense that the vendor may have again done an adequate job of implementing security. This approach is prevalent when no independent testing and evaluation facilities exist. The problem with this approach is that it lacks measurable ways of quantifying the degree of trust that can be associated with a product. It also lacks measurable ways of comparing the relative degrees of trust that can be associated with different products.

With the typical torrent of upgrades and revisions to products, this approach may have some merit in establishing a degree of confidence in products that have been changed since the version of the product that may have undergone rigorous security testing and evaluation. If a vendor is known to have good security engineering capabilities—such as can be assessed, in part, by standard Capability Maturity Model approaches (see Section 51.4.1)—and if the vendor can provide reasonable evidence as to the nature of the upgrade or revision since the product version that underwent rigorous assessment, then there can be some qualitative (albeit, quantitatively unknown) degree of confidence about the upgraded or revised product. Under these conditions, customers who have innate trust in the vendor can believe that the quality of the changed product is similar to the quality of the version of the product that was formally assessed.

51.2.2 Proprietary In-House Assessments. Product consumers can develop the requisite substantial technical expertise in-house to test and to evaluate specific security-enhanced products directly. Alternatively, consumers can contract a private evaluator, such as one of the big consulting houses or systems integrators, to do such testing and evaluation. Often their approaches are unique and proprietary.

Some financial institutions have used the in-house assessment approach. Financial institutions as a whole are very careful to make sure that products they use are trustworthy. The security, integrity, and soundness of all products and systems supporting financial institutions must be consistent and verifiable. These institutions fear that any breach of IT security anywhere within their systems will result in a loss of confidence in the entire institution, not just in the specific, subverted IT product.

Many financial institutions developed their own internal security specifications and evaluation processes as well as an evaluation methodology to quantify, to compare, to approve, and to certify general security aspects of competing products. One of the consequences of this approach was that it required substantial, costly duplication of testing infrastructure across the financial industry as well as the costly duplication of vendor testing efforts for those products that were candidates for purchase by multiple customers. With each financial entity funding the establishment of its own testing program, the aggregate testing expenses were raised across all entities within the financial industry.

Furthermore, as the volume of financial devices, such as credit card platforms, operating systems, and thousands of applications, continues to increase dramatically, in-house resources are finding it difficult to keep up. They have found this kind of do-it-yourself, in-house testing approach to be a tremendous undertaking in terms of development, implementation, legitimacy demonstration, maintenance, and rejustification. They have found it to be expensive, time consuming, resource intensive, hard to maintain, always open to interpretation and to debate, and always in need of justification to regulators and principals in new markets.

51.2.3 Consortium-Based Assessment Approaches. Many consortium-directed approaches exist, or have existed, to demonstrate product interoperability, or conformance of a product to stated security features or to specific security technology standards.

In the Internet world, the notion of implementation bake-offs among trial (pre-product) implementations of emerging IETF standards has been a mainstay in the community for quite some time. For example, in 2005 the IETF initiated a series of IPsec VPN Interoperability Workshops upon culmination of the Internet Key Exchange Version 2 (IKEv2) standard. Vendors of IKEv2-based pre-products gathered in a common testing facility to test the functionality and interoperability of their pre-products against those of their competitors. Initial test scenarios focused on basic functionality and secure tunnel maintenance.

Other consortia use either their own or standard testing approaches. Such consortia include, for example, the VPN Consortium, SPOCK, and the Smart Card Security Users Group.

51.2.3.1 *Virtual Private Network Consortium.* The *Virtual Private Network (VPN) Consortium* (www.vpnc.org/) developed an approach for demonstrating conformance of a product to a specific security standard. The VPN Consortium conducts testing of the IPsec (IP SECurity) and Secure Sockets Layer (SSL) implementations built by its consortium members.

In the early 2000s, the consortium provided three specific profiles of conformance tests of VPN products implementing the IETF's IPSec standard. For each type of test profile, predefined tasks had to be performed successfully against two different reference test gateways. Due to the nonexhaustive set of tests, passing a VPN Consortium conformance test provided only indications that tested products conform, in limited part, to various standard parts of the IPsec standard. Such tests also provided indications that interoperability may be possible with other products that pass the same tests under the same environmental situations.

The consortium now focuses on interoperability testing. It conducts two classes of IPsec interoperability tests: Basic Interoperability and AES Interoperability. The types of capabilities being tested, and the profiles by which tested systems are set up for each class of interoperability testing, are specified. The tests help assure VPN users that IPsec systems set up according to the specified profile are generally interoperable with other IPsec systems also set up according to the same profile.

The consortium also provides interoperability testing for profiled uses of SSL implementations.

Plans for other interoperability profiles and details on products that have passed the VPN Consortium's testing, and received conformance certification logos or interoperability certification logos, can be obtained at www.vpnc.org.

There is speculation that other telecommunications-oriented consortia (e.g., the WiMAX Forum) that are currently focusing on conformance and interoperability testing of communication technology may expand to include testing of security capabilities associated with telecommunication gear (wireless security capabilities in the case of the WiMAX Forum).

51.2.3.2 Security Proof of Concept Keystone (SPOCK). The *Security Proof of Concept Keystone* (SPOCK) (http://csrc.nist.gov/nissc/1996/papers/NISSC96/paper068/seminar.PDF) was a joint government-industry consortium sponsored by the National Security Agency (NSA). It developed and conducted product-specific, loose conformance and performance verification tests in government environments to demonstrate a vendor's or system integrator's stated claims about implemented security features and performance. Recently, the SPOCK program consolidated with other NSA initiatives, such as the Capabilities Presentation Program (www.nsa.gov/ia/industry/indus00022.cfm?MenuID=10.2.2) and the Information Assurance Technical Framework Forum. These other initiatives are focused on presenting and discussing IA products, IA-enabled products and IA solutions among U.S. Government agencies, industry, and academia.

51.2.3.3 Smart Card Security Users Group. Although proprietary, in-house approaches were used by individual financial institutions to assess thousands of financial IT products, components, and systems, the financial community banded together as a whole in the *Smart Card Security Users Group*. Through this group, financial institutions use a single standard—the Common Criteria (see Sections 51.6 and 51.7)—for product assessments and to avoid duplication of their individual product assessment efforts. Benefits of such an alliance include:

- Financial institutions can replace their internal, custom product assessment approaches with a common, universally accepted approach.
- They can pool their resources to address common security testing and evaluation needs by using standards-based, Common Criteria security specification and testing schemes recognized across all major financial players.

- They can develop profiles of security requirements for the various common elements of smart cards (e.g., chips, operating systems, applications, crypto engines).

- They can develop common test suites to unify the current hodgepodge of fragmented customer-specific and vendor-specific testing of smart cards.

- They can outsource security testing and evaluation to competent, accredited testing laboratories whose expertise can be used by all financial institutions.

The alliance produced a Common Criteria profile of standard security functional requirements and assurance requirements for smart cards. This standard requirements profile was validated and certified by an independent, accredited security testing laboratory (www.cse-cst.gc.ca/services/ccs/scsug-v30-e.html), and it is now used across the financial community. Consumers within the financial industry reference the profile to state their requirements. Vendors reference the profile to indicate what they built.

Accredited testing laboratories use standard methods to test individual products once for the entire financial community (not once per financial institution). The standard tests assess a vendor's claim that its product meets the standard requirements profile.

With known confidence, a financial institution can then purchase any product from the pool of assessed products that have been independently certified to comply with the Smart Card Security Users Group requirements profile. Increasingly, smart cards and smart card components must be evaluated according to this basic Common Criteria paradigm as a necessary precursor to purchase by a financial institution.

51.2.4   Open Source Approach.   A widely used approach in software development is the Open Source model. According to this approach, software is made publicly available for inspection, for modification of flaws and inefficiencies, and for potential upgrading of capabilities and features. In theory, by the continuous and collective—but uncoordinated and seemingly semirandom—efforts of potentially thousands of autonomous software developers and testers, the public review will improve the quality of the software over time.

The downside of the open source approach is that the degree of trustworthiness achieved by the process is unmeasurable.

To help identify security issues in open source code, the U.S. Department of Homeland Security initiated the Vulnerability Discovery and Remediation Open Source Hardening Project. In this project, new approaches for finding critical defects in complex software code sets will be developed and used to test open source code to isolate defects and root causes.

However, the trustworthiness of a product is more than just improved code. Although the open source code will have some degree of trustworthiness developed by the open source process, the incorporation of such code into a product still leads to other factors that influence trustworthiness in the product. Product trustworthiness also depends on vendor processes, such as the quality of design, the protection provided to security features during the delivery of a product from the vendor to the consumer, vendor strategies for maintaining or upgrading security in the face of new threats, and so on.

Vendors such as IBM, Red Hat Enterprise Linux, and Trusted Computer Solutions, as well as Novell, SuSE, and IBM teams are relying on the standard Common Criteria testing and evaluation approach to assess their Linux software products running in Intel hardware environments. The benefit of tying an open source technology development such as Linux with a Common Criteria evaluation is that mass-market consumers in all industries can purchase a highly secure, trusted operating system at no additional price than that of the previous unsecured Linux. (With much of the R&D associated with the security aspects of Linux provided by the aggregate of the open source community, the vendor has essentially no security R&D costs to amortize over the sales of products.)

51.2.5 Hacking.   De facto assurance of the underlying security in a product can arise from those who actively probe new products for security flaws. Such probing may arise from internally sanctioned security probing or from unsanctioned, unexpected probing by individuals of ill will. Hacking approaches (ethical or otherwise) do not necessarily follow a consistent or comprehensive approach to evaluating the quality of the security functions and services that are implemented. Hence, the level of assurance achieved is unknown and typically very low.

51.2.6 Trade Press.   Many trade press publications and magazines conduct reviews of products that pertain to security. Products are tested in ad hoc environments and against ad hoc criteria that vary from product to product and magazine to magazine. Such magazines may rely on consultants, staff, or private labs to review products. Some reviews may focus on examining quantitative product details other than security, such as performance or throughput of a product. Tests performed often fall short of assessing the real security aspects of a product. Some reviews rate qualitative parameters, such as product "innovativeness." Because of the potential lack of quantified testing rigor and potential dissimilarity of evaluation metrics, comparisons of trade press reviews from different sources are difficult. Perhaps most important, no evaluations are made of the confidence (assurance) that can be associated with the soundness of the security implementation.

Examples of publications that provide reviews of security products include *Information Security Magazine* (www.infosecuritymag.com), *Secure Computing Magazine* (www.scmagazine.com/), *Network Computing* (www.networkcomputing.com), and *InfoWorld* (www.infoworld.com).

51.2.7 Initial Third-Party Commercial Assessment Approaches.   Initial commercial approaches provided relatively low-confidence, so-called surface-level testing that generated a "brand mark" for vendors' product brochures and advertisements. Such commercial activities began at a time when there needed to be a lower-cost—albeit lower confidence—alternative to expensive, lengthy, economically inappropriate government evaluations such as the so-called *Orange Book* evaluations (see Section 51.5.1). These commercial assessment activities were also available to support trade press surveys and magazine reviews of products.

Such nonstandard, third-party approaches are still prevalent. There is a certain qualitative amount of risk reduction achievable by these approaches. They are typically based on simple, one-size-fits-all testing that usually provides minimal, cursory checks of some of the implemented security functions. Some of these tests focus on product details other than security, such as performance or throughput. No evaluation is made of the confidence (assurance) that can be associated with the soundness of the security implementation. Instead, these are "black box" approaches wherein products are examined based only on their outputs relative to stimuli. These approaches have no assessment capabilities based on the fundamental design of the product, or of the engineering principles used by the vendor to build the product.

Many vendors, nonetheless, undergo these types of commercial testing because of the pressures from their competitors' products being so tested. Testing costs are reasonable, but such testing provides no inputs (e.g., evaluation reports) to consumers that can be analyzed to differentiate products. More comprehensive products are not examined for any of their differentiating capabilities. Instead, such check-mark testing programs merely provide a common-denominator assessment floor for products.

Typical vendor reaction to these types of "branding" programs is that the check marks are often not very good and are often distracting nuisances.[10] Vendors also indicate that unlike more rigorous testing paradigms, such as that based on the Common Criteria, these check-mark branding programs do not have processes to help improve the quality of the product under test. Unlike Common Criteria testing labs, many vendors do not see check-mark testing labs as strategic partners looking to improve the product under test.

Examples of these types of product assessment approaches include the West Coast Labs Check Mark Program, the ICSA Labs Certified Program, and the Spywaretesting.org initiative.

51.2.7.1 Check Mark Program.   The Check Mark program is a private testing service provided by West Coast Labs (www.westcoastlabs.org/). Although touted to use "standard" testing criteria in a "standard" testing approach, the Check Mark program—in truth—establishes private criteria and a private testing methodology that are not recognized by legitimate standards bodies such as ISO. West Coast's private criteria and testing approaches apply to certain types of computer security products, such as antivirus products, firewall products, and VPN products. The criteria are designed to achieve a very basic level of protection against a number of common hostile attacks. West Coast Labs tests products against the applicable Check Mark criteria and, if successfully tested, produces a certificate which shows that specific releases of products meet specific Check Mark criteria.

51.2.7.2 ICSA Labs Certified.   Another well-known, commercial product branding service is the product-certification program (www.icsalabs.com/icsa/topic.php?tid=fdghgf54645-ojojoj567) conducted by ICSA Labs (www.icsalabs.com), which was part of Cybertrust and is currently an independent division of Verizon Business.[11]

The ICSA approach is similar to the West Coast Labs testing approach. Product performance is tested against specified criteria to assess whether the product can resist the types of common threats and risks specified in the testing criteria. Product testing is typically a checklist-oriented approach geared for nonexpert testers. Testing criteria are developed for a number of classes of products, such as firewalls and antivirus (AV) software. While Check Mark uses "private" testing criteria, ICSA uses so-called public criteria. These "public" criteria are, however, nonstandard like those of Check Mark since they are created outside the recognized national or international standards-development communities. Instead, ICSA's testing criteria are developed via "invited participation."

Products that pass ICSA criteria are entitled to display the ICSA brand mark. Products that fail are reported to their vendors with detailed analysis of the criteria they failed.

Unlike the West Coast certificate, once products are awarded an ICSA certificate, vendors take on the obligation to self-check and to self-declare continued certification of evolutions of the specific version product that passed ICSA testing. Spot checks by ICSA are used to verify that currently shipping products still can pass the ICSA tests.

51.2.7.3 StopBadware.org Initiative.   In early 2006, a small number of antispyware product vendors, testing houses, and academics started an initiative to publicize malicious spyware and adware and to create common, third-party spyware testing methods, evaluation criteria, and common spyware samples.[12] At the time of the writing of this chapter (June 2008), the Web site was still active (www.stopbadware.org/home) and included alerts and reports, a clearinghouse for researchers and users, information for end users and Webmasters, and ways to get involved in fighting "badware." Time will tell if the initiative will be useful and will gain momentum.

51.3   SECURITY ASSESSMENT STANDARDS FOR PRODUCTS.   In contrast to the informal, nonstandard product assessment approaches just discussed, standards exist for assessing various aspects of security associated with products. Standards exist to assess the overall quality and soundness of the builder of a product (see Section 51.4). Security assessment approaches based on these standards can yield generalized conclusions that "good" vendors build "good" products. Other standards (see Section 51.5) are used to assess both the quality of product builders and the quality of their products. These standards can be used to quantify how well "good" vendors build "good" products (with identifiable and demonstrable assurance levels), how much "better" specific vendors can build even "better" products (with identifiable and demonstrable, generally higher assurance levels), and how comprehensive are the security functionalities within the specific classes of products these vendors build.

51.4   STANDARDS FOR ASSESSING PRODUCT BUILDERS.   Some standards apply specifically to developers of security products. These standards include the Capability Maturity Model (see Section 51.4.1) and ISO 9000 (see Section 51.4.2) standards.

51.4.1   Capability Maturity Model.   Standards exist to measure the software and security competency of any type of organization including vendors that build security-oriented products.

A standard for assessing the competency of software developers is the *Capability Maturity Model* (CMM).[13] The "Capability Maturity Model for Software" is a family of Software, Systems Engineering, and Product Development Capability Maturity Models[SM] (CMMs[R]).

The *Systems Security Engineering Capability Maturity Model* (SSE-CMM) approach uses such standards. It can be used as a way to assess the soundness of a security product builder's engineering practices during the many stages of product development, such as during:

- Product requirements capture and analysis
- Product concept definition including accurate translation of security requirements into product requirements
- Product architecting
- Product design
- Product implementation

A security product developer can demonstrate competence in building products by means of recognized, so-called capability maturity assessments of the developer's software and security engineering processes. Security-enhanced products built by organizations with demonstrated expertise and maturity can merit greater trust than products built by organizations that do not demonstrate mature, competent, software design, and security engineering capabilities.

The SSE-CMM establishes a framework of generally accepted security engineering principles and a standard way of measuring (and improving) the effectiveness of an organization's security engineering practices. The SSE-CMM describes the essential characteristics of, and provides tools for, assessing an organization's security engineering process that must exist to ensure good security engineering. These characteristics are graded by a set of security metrics that assess specific attributes about a vendor's processes, and the security effectiveness of the results of vendor's processes.

When the level of the SSE-CMM security metrics associated with a specific builder shows the builder to have mature security engineering capabilities, and effective security engineering practices, then confidence is increased that the builder can build sound security products.

Trust in, and assurance about, a product can be inferred to some degree for measurably competent vendors that use sound security engineering processes as assessed by the SSE-CMM. The quantitative comparability of assurance developed via the SSE-CMM approach to the assurance developed via other approaches such as evaluation of assurance requirements stipulated from the Common Criteria (CC) paradigm is currently unknown and is the subject of investigation. For now, it appears possible to assess the assurance of a vendor's capability to build quality products by both the SSE-CMM and CC approaches; but, perhaps both approaches should be integrated to form a more comprehensive assurance assessment model.

Further information about how the SSE-CMM approach can be used is available at the International Systems Security Engineering Association Web site (www. sse-cmm.org).

51.4.2   Quality (ISO 9000).   The ISO 9000 standard is used as a guide to conduct a broad, high-level, horizontal assessment of the quality of systems and of the competence of an organization across all its facets.[14] Although not specific to organizations that build security products, it does provide some amount of basic information about the potential for quality and repeatability in an organization's ability to meet its mission. In fact, derivative standards, such as in the Common Criteria, in part inspired by ISO 9000, are used to accredit the quality associated with security testing laboratories.

51.5   COMBINED PRODUCT AND PRODUCT BUILDER ASSESSMENT STANDARDS.   Some standards evaluate both developers and their security products. The next sections review the history of sunsetted national standards (see Section 51.5.1) and the emergence of widely accepted, replacement, international standards (see Section 51.5.2) for evaluating both developers and their products.

51.5.1   Competing National Criteria Standards.   To introduce consistency in describing the security features and levels of trust of a limited set of security-enhanced products, and to facilitate comprehensive testing and evaluation of such products, the U.S. DoD developed the *Trusted Computer System Evaluation Criteria* (TCSEC).[15] The TCSEC— oft-called the *Orange Book*—defined a small set of classes (C1 to A1) of increasing security functionality and increasing assurance applying to operating systems. The TCSEC was extended to networking devices[16] and database management systems.[17] Government in-house evaluations were offered first, followed by comparable, government-sponsored commercial evaluation services.

Partly because of large testing delays and costs, other countries developed other criteria that were more flexible and adaptable to accommodate rapidly evolving IT. The *Information Technology Security Evaluation Criteria* (ITSEC) arose from the combined inputs of earlier German criteria, French criteria, and U.K. confidence levels.[18] The *Canadian Trusted Computer Product Evaluation Criteria* (CTCPEC) were then developed as a combination of the TCSEC and ITSEC approaches. The U.S. Federal Criteria development then attempted to combine the CTCPEC and ITSEC with the TCSEC.

With growth of the international market for trusted IT products, competing criteria had the potential to fracture the market. Efforts began to harmonize the various criteria into common criteria that would be standards-based and internationally accepted. The result was a single, wide-ranging, widely accepted, Common Criteria. These standard criteria provide a fully flexible, highly tailorable approach to the standardization of security functionality, evaluation assurance requirements, specification, and testing of implementations. U.S., national government policy (DoD 8500.1) sunsetted the *Orange Book* TCSEC approach and now points to requiring DoD (DoD 8500.2) and potentially civilian agencies (President Bush's "National Strategy") to use the Common Criteria approach[19] instead.

51.5.2 Emergence of Common Criteria Standard.   Out of the old, cumbersome, and costly *Orange Book* approach, and out of the experiences, lessons, and analyses of the other national criteria, a new, commercially driven strategy emerged for testing products, and demonstrating confidence that their security features behave properly. This best-of-all-previous-breeds strategy is based on a new, international standard—referred to as the Common Criteria (CC). Version 1.0 of the CC was published in 1996 followed by Version 2 in 1998. Version 2 was subsequently standardized by the ISO as International Standard 15408.[20] The international community began transitioning to version 3 in 2006 according to a stipulated transition schedule (www.niap-ccevs.org/cc-scheme/cc_docs/).

The CC strategy resolves differences among the earlier competing national criteria and accompanying certification and accreditation strategies, and integrates the best aspects of its predecessors. The CC strategy offers a single, internationally recognized approach for specification and evaluation of IT product security. This approach is widely useful within the entire international community.

In contrast to the preceding, nonstandard approaches to establishing trust in products (see Section 51.3), the Common Criteria paradigm presents a fundamentally new strategy that overcomes shortcomings of these other approaches. It provides a recognized, reliable, internationally maintained mechanism to develop trust that:

1. Security requirements are specified correctly.

2. Vendors do not misunderstand the requirements.

3. Vendors design and manufacture products that address the requirements and provide risk integrity.

The CC provides an unprecedented, fully flexible process for specifying and testing security requirements for any and all classes, and specific instances, of existing or future IT products.

Unlike all the other approaches, the CC also provides a way to specify assurance requirements and to evaluate how well they are met. Assurance requirements are extremely important and are typically not considered in other product assessment approaches. Assurance requirements are the essential ingredients in establishing confidence in implementations of security and in providing the level of trust necessary for economies and governments to rely on new e-business and e-government models. Trust is established by gaining confidence that the security functionalities claimed to be implemented to address specific security functional requirements (1) are effective in satisfying specified security objectives and (2) are implemented correctly and completely. It is also established by ensuring that product developers have sound processes and take specified actions accompanying the life cycle of the product they build, test, deliver, and maintain.

The Common Criteria also establishes a method to develop common tests and evaluation methods and to use them to verify the security aspects of products in competent, accredited laboratories. Assessments of security products are composed of both analysis and testing of the product. Use of standard evaluation criteria and standard evaluation methodology leads to repeatable, objective test and evaluation results. Furthermore, independent review and validation of Common Criteria–based testing and evaluation is available to boost consumers' confidence even further. Well-respected consulting houses have concluded that Common Criteria evaluation provides a substantial improvement over the testing practices used by many vendors today that result in seriously undertested software.[21] The Common Criteria specification and testing approach is equally applicable to any and all types of products, such as products that implement security technologies (e.g., crypto boxes, firewalls, or audit tools) as well as products that are either security-enabled (e.g., messaging or Web e-commerce packages) or security relevant (e.g., operating systems or network management systems).

The CC is today's unified choice for developing trust in products. The Common Criteria paradigm provides an extra level of due diligence. It improves and differentiates products and allows buyers to compare products objectively. It is accepted by mutual agreement in most of the world's largest IT-building and IT-buying countries.

51.6   COMMON CRITERIA PARADIGM OVERVIEW.   This section introduces the Common Criteria (CC) paradigm. The underlying scheme, the associated processes, and the underlying standards are summarized.

The remainder of this chapter goes into detail. Section 51.7 describes the standards associated with defining profiles of customer security requirements and vendor solutions, while Section 51.8 describes how these standards are used. Section 51.9 describes standards associated with defining testing and evaluation[22] methodology, while Section 51.10 describes the agreement for allowing products to be tested in any country and sold within any other country with no further testing. Section 51.11 describes the scheme used within the United States to support this agreement fostering the recognition and sale of tested products across national borders, while Section 51.12 gives a sense of the numbers and types of products within the marketplace of CC-tested products.

51.6.1   CC Scheme.   The Common Criteria paradigm is a multipurpose scheme for:

- Stipulating security requirements that can be used in product procurements
- Specifying companion security solutions in products

- Testing products according to product-tailored—but standard—criteria and testing methodologies using accredited, third-party, commercial testing laboratories
- Independently validating test results
- Providing certificates to tested and validated products that obviate any need for further product retesting in all countries that mutually recognize each other's commercial testing capabilities and testing results

The benefits of the CC paradigm are many. It forces consumers to be thorough in analyzing and understanding:

- Their security requirements
- The threats and vulnerabilities that products need to handle
- The security policies—both organizational as well as legal and/or regulatory—that apply
- The environment in which products are to work
- Assumptions about the environment that are pertinent to the security offered or needed by a product

It forces vendors and consumers to understand thoroughly:

- The products they build or buy
- Whether and how products address customer security requirements and mitigate stipulated threats and vulnerabilities
- How vendors validate their claims about meeting requirements and mitigating threats and vulnerabilities

51.6.2 Common Criteria Paradigm Process.   The path to trustworthy products begins by consumers using a standard methodology, standard language, and a catalog of standard security requirements to develop security profiles tailored to the types of products they want. The profiles stipulate the security functional needs. They also stipulate the confidence or assurance desired in products as well as in product builders' processes from product design through maintenance.

Next, product builders use the same standard methodology, language, and catalog to define their products' security specifications. They define product security specifications in terms of both security functionality and security assurance about the product and the builders' processes. The builders' specifications show how their products meet stated consumer security functionality and assurance needs. Builders' specifications may also show how their products meet any additional builder-claimed security features that go beyond the consumers' stated needs.

Then an international agreement on how such products should be tested comes into play. This so-called Mutual Recognition Arrangement (MRA) outlines in broad terms the scheme of processes and procedures that individual countries should follow in order to have Common Criteria–based testing performed once in any country and accepted internationally.

In the United States, the Common Criteria Evaluation and Validation Scheme (CCEVS) is just such a national scheme developed in accordance with the MRA. The MRA allows CCEVS-based testing results in the United States to be recognized by all the major IT building and buying countries in the world. The CCEVS is the only way available in the United States that is recognized across national borders to demonstrate security and assurance requirements conformance of products evaluated in the United States (See Section 51.11 for CCEVS details.)

51.6.3 Standards that Shape the Common Criteria Paradigm.   Several international standards shape the CC paradigm. These include formal standards that provide for a thorough, step-by-step discipline to define the security requirements of consumers and to define the security capabilities of products. There are also standards that define processes, procedures, rules, and infrastructure for testing products and validating test results.

The "Common Criteria for Information Technology Security Evaluation" is the ISO standard geared toward the part of the paradigm pertaining to profiling security requirements and product specifications.

The Common Evaluation Methodology is an informal international standard, maintained by a board of experts that pertains to product testing methods and evaluation actions.[23]

The "Arrangement on the Mutual Recognition of Common Criteria Certificates in the Field of Information Technology Security" document, colloquially called the Mutual Recognition Arrangement (MRA) or the Common Criteria Recognition Arrangement (CCRA), is a treaty-level international agreement among a growing number of national bodies for the purpose of recognizing and accepting testing performed in other signatory nations.[24]

The Common Criteria Evaluation and Validation Scheme is organized and managed, and operates according to concepts, specified in an informal standard[25] developed by the U.S. MRA signatories.[26] Other CCEVS documents detail CCEVS procedures and provide guidance to submitters of products to be tested, to test labs and to test validators (see www.niap-ccevs.org/cc-scheme/policy/ccevs/guidance_docs.cfm).

The CCEVS also uses standards that pertain to accrediting prospective testing laboratories. An ISO standard is used for stipulating testing laboratory competency.[27] Another ISO standard further refines these general requirements for IT testing laboratories.[28] Countries also define technology-specific refinements and extensions to lab competency requirements. In the United States, for example, an NIST standard stipulates more specific laboratory competency requirements pertaining to security assessment procedures and to CC security proficiency of lab staff.[29]

In aggregate, the CCEVS-specified and CCEVS-used standards define the processes and procedures used within the United States to test, to validate, and to certify products recognized under the terms of the MRA. Other similar national schemes for using the CC exist in other countries.

51.7 DETAILS ABOUT THE COMMON CRITERIA STANDARD.   As described in Section 51.8.1, the ISO 15408 CC standard identifies the models for two types of security profiles, the methodology for developing such profiles, as well as the structures for each of these types of profiles. The CC standard also provides catalogs of security and assurance requirements (discussed here in Sections 51.7.2 and 51.7.3 respectively) of known validity that can be used, mixed, and matched to express the security requirements of virtually any type of IT product or system.

51.7.1 Models for Security Profiles.   The CC standard defines the language and structures for two types of security profiles and the methodology to create such profiles.

One type of security profile is the Protection Profile (PP). A PP is used to stipulate the generic, product-neutral profile of security requirements for some class of IT product, such as a firewall or a telecommunications switch. Two types of security requirements can be stipulated: functional requirements and assurance requirements. Functional requirements define desired security behavior. Assurance requirements provide the basis for establishing trust. PPs are typically developed by prospective consumers or by consortia of IT buyers or sellers. PPs are developed to create standard sets of security requirements that meet the needs of prospective buyers.

The second type of profile structure is the Security Target (ST). An ST is a product-specific stipulation of the security requirements addressed by a specific product along with information as to how the implemented product meets the stated security requirements. As stipulated in its accompanying ST, a specific product may claim conformance to one or more Protection Profiles. For example, a turnkey healthcare information system product can claim it conforms to a DBMS PP, an operating system PP, a PKI PP, and a firewall PP. Alternatively, a specific product may claim conformance to product-specific security requirements enumerated solely within the ST. A specific product can alternatively claim conformance to both a PP (or several PPs) as well as to additional product-specific security requirements enumerated within the ST.

The purpose of testing and evaluation of a product is to confirm that the product meets the product-specific requirements and evaluation criteria contained in the product's ST.

51.7.2 Security Functional Requirements Catalog.   The CC standard contains a catalog of security functional requirements organized according to a taxonomy of several different classes of security functional requirements, such as the Audit class, the Identification and Authentication class, and the Security Management class.

Each class has several families of functional security requirements, each family of which differs in emphasis or rigor in the way the security objectives of the parent class are considered. For example, the Audit class includes families of requirements that pertain to different aspects of auditing, such as audit data generation and audit event storage.

Each family of security functional requirements typically contains several individual, more specialized, elemental security functionality requirements components. These components are the specific security functional requirements that can be stipulated within a PP or ST as a desired security functionality. For example, the Audit Data Generation family of security functional requirements contains a component that pertains to audit record generation and another component that pertains to the linkage between a user and an auditable event.

To foster versatility and evolution, the CC also permits any new security requirements that do not appear in the taxonomies of standard requirements to be created using the CC's standard language. If additional requirements become popular, future versions of the CC standard may incorporate such additional requirements directly into the CC catalogs.

51.7.3 Security Assurance Requirements Catalog.   The CC standard also contains a catalog of assurance requirements organized according to a taxonomy of several assurance classes, such as classes pertaining to assurance requirements associated with (a) configuration management of the product, (b) design, development, delivery, and operation of the product, and (c) maintaining assurance throughout the product's life cycle. Two assurance classes contain assurance requirements applicable to the evaluation of PP or ST profiles.

The taxonomy of assurance requirements is refined in terms of a number of families of requirements within each assurance requirements class. Furthermore, a number of hierarchical assurance requirements components are contained within each family of assurance requirements.

51.7.3.1 *Packaged Levels of Assurance.*   Assurance requirements are bundled into one of seven predefined levels of assurance called Evaluation Assurance Levels (EALs). Higher assurance level bundles (e.g., EAL4) contain more rigorous packages of component assurance requirements than lower level bundles (e.g., EAL1). EALs form a rising scale of objective measures of risk reduction.

The names associated with the EALs provide a sense of the increasing assurance:

EAL1: Functionally Tested

EAL2: Structurally Tested

EAL3: Methodically Tested and Checked

EAL4: Methodically Designed, Tested, and Reviewed

EAL5: Semi-Formally Designed and Tested

EAL6: Semi-Formally Verified Design and Tested

EAL7: Formally Verified Design and Tested

EALs provide a monotonically increasing scale that balances the increasing levels of confidence that can be obtained with the increasing cost and decreasing feasibility of conducting the testing and evaluation necessary to develop a specific, higher level of confidence. EALs range upward from the entry-level EAL1 to a stringent EAL7.

At the low end, EAL1 can be used to support the contention that baseline due care has been exercised with regard to protection of personal information and to establish some confidence in correct operation of a product in an environment where the threats to security are not considered very serious. In the middle range, EAL4 specifies more rigorous assurance requirements, such as automated configuration management, and development controls that are supported by a life-cycle model. At the highest extreme, EAL7 requires a formally verified design and extensive formal analysis. EAL7 may be applicable to certain highly specific, perhaps one-of-a-kind products, targeted for extremely high-risk situations or where the high value of the assets being protected justifies the extraordinary costs of an evaluation to this level of confidence.

Typical commercial products can be expected to fall in the range from EAL1 to EAL4.

Typically, an EAL package is stipulated within a PP or an ST. Alternatively, a PP or ST may, instead, stipulate either (a) individual component assurance requirements from the assurance requirements catalog, or (b) a specific EAL plus additional specific assurance requirements from the assurance requirements catalog.

51.7.4 Comprehensiveness of Requirements Catalogs.   The taxonomies of both types of security requirements—functional and assurance—are broad, and both catalogs of security requirements are deep: Hundreds of individual, selectable security requirements are defined. Furthermore, the CC was designed to accommodate evolution of its security requirements catalogs as technologies and security needs evolve. New security requirements that are specified according to the CC language, but that are outside the current CC catalogs, can become potential candidates for new,

internationally agreed-on, security requirements to be incorporated into later versions of the standard CC catalogs.

Given the breadth, depth, and changeability of possible security requirements that can be stipulated within PPs or STs, the Common Criteria provides the ability to stipulate the requirements and products of virtually an unlimited number of existing and yet-to-be-conceived security product needs (PPs) and security product solutions (STs).

51.8 USING THE CC TO DEFINE SECURITY REQUIREMENTS AND SECURITY SOLUTIONS.   The CC provides a standard way to stipulate (a) the risks of concern, (b) the security functional requirements that must be met in order to mitigate stated risks, and (c) the security assurance requirements that must be met to provide the confidence desired that products are built with desired quality. Consumers develop PPs to specify their needs to their suppliers. Product developers create STs to specify how implemented security functions and assurance measures meet consumers' needs.

The CC defines the structures and content requirements for constructing PPs and STs. The topics of content are summarized in Sections 51.8.1 and 51.8.2, respectively, with examples drawn from a PP for a Private Branch Exchange (PBX) style of telecommunications switch (www.niap-ccevs.org/pp/draft_pps/archived/pbxpp.pdf).

Benefits of PPs and STs are given in Section 51.8.3. A summary of the state of profile development in the community is given in Section 51.8.4

51.8.1 Protection Profile Construction and Contents.   PPs enumerate the IA security functional and assurance requirements that an organization considers appropriate and valuable for a specific type of product in a specific threat environment. Each PP states the security problem that a PP-compliant product is intended to solve and stipulates the security requirements that are known to be useful and effective in meeting specific security objectives.

PPs should be created to be realistic in their ability to be met by a variety of potential products, each of which can have its high-level security specifications documented in an ST. Care must be taken to make sure PPs are achievable, generally with commercially available technology.

Guidance for developing PPs is available.[30] For PPs in the government sector, principles for developing U.S. Government PPs are available (www.niap-ccevs.org/cc-scheme/policy/ccevs/scheme-pub-3.pdf), along with manuals to help select security requirements appropriate for environments with specific classes of robustness needs (www.niap-ccevs.org/pp/ci_manuals.cfm).

The main contents of a PP include statements about:

1. The threats and vulnerabilities to which a product will be exposed
2. The security environment within which a product is to reside
3. The security objectives to be met by a product
4. The security requirements to be addressed by a product
5. The rationale that is provided to justify all decisions and choices made in developing the content within a PP

51.8.1.1 Threats and Vulnerabilities.   A PP must identify the expected threats and vulnerabilities against which a prospective product must be protected.

As needed, threat and vulnerability analyses should be conducted. In the PBX case, threats and vulnerabilities include, for example:

- Theft of telecommunications services
- Hijacking of resources within the PBX to commit cyber crime or cyber espionage
- Unauthorized use and modification (or destruction) of processes, system software, applications, and databases embedded within the product

51.8.1.2   Security Environment.   The intended operational environment within which a product is to reside must be described in terms of both its IT and non-IT aspects. Assumptions about the product's usage, administration, and management should be enumerated. All policies to which the product must comply within the intended environment should be enumerated. Such policies include all applicable laws and regulations as well as any organizational policies or rules with which the product must comply. All natural-language expressions of the environment, threats, policies, and assumptions must be codified via CC terminology and put into the PP. In the PBX case, the environment includes the types of PBX users and administrators, the types of PBX interfaces, and the types of interconnectivity expected with other telecommunications gear.

51.8.1.3   Security Objectives.   The PP must identify the realistic and achievable security objectives that must be established for both the product and the environment within which the product is to reside. The security objectives should indicate which threats are to be countered by the product and which are to be countered by the IT and non-IT environments in which the product is to operate, and to be administered and managed. The security objectives should indicate with which of the organizational policies the product will comply and which organizational policies the environment will address. All stipulated security objectives should be traceable back to the underlying stipulations of threats, policies, and assumptions.

51.8.1.4   Security Requirements.   A compatible set of security functional requirements components should be selected and refined from the CC catalogs to meet the stipulated security objectives and to thwart specified threats. The security functional requirements also should be selected to support the stipulated security policies, under the stipulated assumptions pertaining to the operational and administrative environment. The security functional requirements should specify functionality that will meet each security objective stipulated for the product as well as functionality that will meet each security objective that applies to the IT part of the environment in which the product is to reside.

In the PBX case, 50 security functional requirements components were selected from seven classes of security functional requirements, including, for example, Audit (Class FAU), Cryptographic Support (Class FCS), Authentication Handling (Class FIA), and Protection of Security Functions (Class FPT). The requirements components selected for the Audit Class include components that stipulate what the PBX must audit, what information must be logged, who can access logs, and what are the rules for monitoring, operating, and protecting logs.

Likewise, security assurance requirements should be selected from the catalog of assurance requirements. Specific assurance requirements components, or a specific EAL package, should be selected to provide the desired level of assurance that the security objectives within the PP have been met. The desired level of assurance and the cost to attain such assurance should be balanced against factors, such as (1) the value of the resources to be protected, (2) the risk and extent of possible losses, (3) the level of confidence desired, and (4) any reasonably expected cost and delay factors that may accompany the development, and any subsequent testing, evaluation, and validation of a product at a specific level of assurance.

In the PBX case, over 100 assurance requirements components were selected from seven assurance requirements classes to demonstrate that:

- Product design and configuration are good.
- Adequate protection is provided during the design and implementation of the product.
- Vendor testing on the product is of a specified depth and breadth.
- Security functionality is not compromised during product delivery.
- There is a specified quality and appropriateness in the product manuals that pertain to product installation, maintenance, and use.

Standard CC requirements components may be used exactly as defined in the CC; or, when appropriate, they may be tailored through the use of permitted, standard operations in order to meet a specific security policy or to counter a specific threat. Through such operations, (1) options within the standard CC requirements may be selected; (2) quantifications within specific CC security requirements may be assigned; and (3) any refinements to CC requirements may be made. Any such tailoring that is not completed within a PP may be completed within an ST that claims conformance to the PP.

51.8.1.5 Rationale.
Rationale should be provided for all decisions and choices made in developing all of the PP content. Rationale should justify how selected security functional and assurance requirements components are suitable to counter the enumerated threats. Rationale should justify how selected requirements components comply with the enumerated policies or how they handle the enumerated assumptions stipulated for the environment. The rationale should provide a mapping between stipulated requirements and stated security objectives and then back to the original, underlying, driving needs as stated in terms of threats, policies, assumptions, and the environment in which a product is to reside.

51.8.2 Security Target Construction.
Product developers create STs to document detailed information about the security aspects of products they build. An ST is required when a specific product is submitted for CC-based testing; the product-specific ST provides the basis and evaluation criteria against which testing and evaluation of the product are performed. STs also may be used for conveying detailed information to consumers about the security functionality of, and assurance associated with, a specific product and the configuration in which a product has been formally tested.

STs contain a description of the environment within which the product described via an ST is intended to operate. That is, an ST enumerates the (a) threats to the product, (b) policies, laws, and regulations with which the product is claimed to conform, and (c) assumptions about the security aspects of the IT and non-IT environment within which the product is intended to be used. STs delineate the security objectives that the builder of a specific product claims are addressed by the product. STs also enumerate the security requirements that the product builder claims are addressed by the product as well as those requirements to be addressed by the environment within which the product is intended to operate.

Part of an ST is very much like the PP to which an ST may be compliant. Some PP-compliant STs will merely reference the associated PP rather than repeating the PP contents within the ST.

However, the ST goes further than a PP because it also specifies the security functions offered by the product to meet each of the stated security requirements in the ST. It also specifies the assurance measures taken by the product builder to meet all the stated assurance requirements in the ST.

Furthermore, a product builder may claim in the ST that the specific product conforms to one or more PPs. If so, the ST can claim that the product it describes addresses the security functional and assurance requirements stipulated in each of the PPs to which the product is claimed to be conformant. As appropriate, the ST may refine PP-stipulated security requirements that are generic or product-neutral in the PP. The ST can thus specifically tailor to the product any general requirements that may appear in a PP. The ST also may add security requirements over and above any PPs to which the product claims to be conformant.

Rationale is provided for all decisions and choices made in developing the ST content. Rationale justifies how selected security functional and assurance components (a) are suitable to counter the enumerated threats, (b) comply with the enumerated policies, and (c) handle the enumerated assumptions stipulated for the environment. Rationale also justifies how implemented security functions meet stated security functional requirements and how the assurance measures used meet the stated security assurance requirements. Rationale justifies all claims made in an ST about the PPs with which the product conforms. In essence, the rationale provided demonstrates that the ST contains an effective and suitable set of countermeasures and that this set of countermeasures is consistent, complete, and cohesive.

51.8.3 Benefits of PPs and STs.   For potential consumers of security-relevant products, PPs provide a standard and flexible way to help organize requirements capture and analysis. PPs provide a standard and flexible way to transform security needs and policies into unambiguous, widely recognized, exactly tailored, product-neutral, security requirements for the desired security functional behavior and assurance levels for *any class of desired IT product.*

PPs provide a standards-based mechanism to convey clearly an organization's, or a market sector's, security needs to suppliers, vendors, and business partners. Indeed, PPs associated with broad aspects of critical infrastructure may be approved as recognized standards. PPs provide the bases for standard, requirements-based testing and evaluation in that stated assurance requirements impact the requisite depth and breadth of testing and evaluation.

As for STs, by examining an ST, consumers can verify completely and unambiguously whether the claimed security functionality of a product and the claimed assurance associated with the product are consistent with consumers' requirements. Comparing product-specific STs with PPs of interest fosters a common buyer/seller understanding of security needs and security capabilities and confidence in products. By comparing the STs of products, consumers are better able to compare the security features of competing products. Consumers are able to understand what types of tests and evaluations that a specific product underwent. They also are able to determine whether the configuration in which a product was tested is consistent with the environment into which the product will be deployed. Through these types of benefits, consumers can shorten their acquisition cycles for security-relevant products.

Furthermore, vendors' and suppliers' marketing can improve by using a product's ST to show how a specific product matches customer security requirements.

Evaluators in CC testing laboratories also benefit by being able to understand the scope of the product-specific evaluation that needs to be performed on a specific product. That is, claims made within the ST are subject to evaluation by a testing laboratory.

51.8.4   Extant PPs and STs.   PPs have been created, and are being created, for many classes of products and technology. Of some note is the registry of U.S. Government PPs that have been validated by CC testing labs operating under the CCEVS. Over 25 classes of PPs are available and stipulate security needs for products and technology such as:

- Antivirus
- Biometrics
- Certificate management
- Role-based access control
- Firewalls (packet-filtering firewalls and application-filtering firewalls)
- Intrusion detection/prevention systems
- DBMSs
- Public key infrastructure/key management Infrastructure
- Operating systems

Also, PPs support specific needs of specific industries. For example, a PBX PP, telecom switch PP, and Voice over IP firewall PP apply to the telecommunication industry's needs. PPs for smart cards, smart card components (chips, operating systems, applications, crypto-engine, etc.), and Certificate Issuing and Management Systems apply to the financial industry. An Industrial Control System PP www.isd.mel.nist.gov/projects/processcontrol/SPP-ICSv1.0.pdf) expresses the needs of the 600 member enterprises within the Process Control Security Requirements Forum.

Since PP development is decentralized by its very nature of being customer specific or industry specific, no single registry of completed PPs (or PPs under development) exists. For example, in the United States, the several government PPs are listed at www.niap-ccevs.org/cc-scheme/pp/. There are comparable national registries in other countries. Commercial customers or vendors also develop PPs (such as for Windows and Linux), but knowledge of the existence of such PPs tends to arise in a haphazard fashion (often as products are entered into CCEVS testing and evaluation).

STs exist for at least all products that have undergone CC-based testing. Tested products that have further undergone testing validation by a CC Validation Body are listed on the Web sites of the several national bodies and national schemes associated with the CC paradigm. Thus, at least the products listed, for example, on the CCEVS Validated Products List (www.niap-ccevs.org/cc-scheme/vpl/) have associated STs. Many other products also have associated STs. But it is difficult to develop centralized listings of all such products since not all products that have undergone CC-based testing have necessarily been tested at accredited CC testing laboratories; and products that have been tested by such testing labs have not necessarily had their testing validated and listed by a CC national validation body.

51.9   COMMON TEST METHODOLOGY FOR CC TESTS AND EVALUA-
TIONS.   According to the Common Criteria paradigm, testing and evaluation either of CC profiles or of products claiming conformance to CC profiles are conducted as structured and formal processes. That is, evaluators use a standard methodology to carry out a series of standard testing and evaluation activities. The standard methodology and assessment activities are defined in the Common Evaluation Methodology (CEM) standard.

The CEM standard provides a common base for independent, autonomous CC testing laboratories to assess CC profiles and vendor products in the same ways. Use of the CEM by all CC testing labs provides a common floor of confidence in similar products that may have been assessed by different CC testing labs.

Because the CEM is internationally recognized, the use of customer-unique or country-unique assessment is minimized if not avoided all together. Assessment costs are minimized, since vendors need only prepare for one testing campaign rather than for a battery of different testing campaigns conducted against different customer-specific, or country-specific, assessment criteria.

51.10   GLOBAL RECOGNITION OF CEM/CC-BASED ASSESSMENTS.
To fortify assessment consistency, and the use of standard CEM-based CC testing and evaluation in CC testing labs that may be in different countries, many countries have banded together to declare their mutual recognition of CEM-based assessment regardless of the country in which a CC testing lab is located. The goal is to allow CC profiles or products claiming conformance to CC profiles to be tested once in a competent, consistent, credible way by any CC testing lab anywhere in the world so that product suppliers can sell CEM/CC-assessed products everywhere in the world, without any further reassessments by different countries or different buyers.

The "Common Criteria Arrangement on the Mutual Recognition of the Common Criteria Certifications in the Field of Information Technology Security," often called just the Mutual Recognition Arrangement (MRA), is the official multicountry declaration that different countries will recognize the CEM/CC-based assessments that may be conducted by CC testing labs in each others' jurisdictions.

The MRA identifies the several conditions necessary for mutual recognition of CEM/CC-based assessments by CC testing labs. The MRA requires the use of the CC and CEM as the basis for evaluation criteria and evaluation methods. The MRA stipulates that each country must have a national scheme for supporting CEM/CC-based assessments by accredited, quality-consistent CC testing labs and that each country must establish an accredited validation body to validate and to certify the results of CC testing labs in the country.

Each country's validation body is responsible for defining and maintaining each country's national scheme for mutually recognizing CEM/CC-based testing, evaluation, national validation, and national certification of CE/CC-assessed CC profiles or vendor products. Each country's validation body is responsible for achieving correct, consistent, credible, and competent application of the CC and CEM within the country.

51.11   EXAMPLE NATIONAL SCHEME: CCEVS.   The U.S. national scheme
is called the *Common Criteria Evaluation and Validation Scheme* (CCEVS). The CCEVS operates under the authority of the U.S. CCEVS Validation Body. The CCEVS

Validation Body operates under the terms of the MRA as well as additional national requirements.

The purpose of the CCEVS is twofold. The CCEVS establishes, and maintains the quality of, the CC-based security testing, validation, and certification infrastructure in the U.S (see Section 51.11.1). It also defines the policies, procedures, processes, and sequence of events for using this infrastructure for testing, evaluating, validating, and certifying products and profiles in the United States (see Section 51.11.2). More about the CCEVS is available at www.niap-ccevs.org/cc-scheme/defining-ccevs.cfm.

51.11.1 Maintaining the Testing Infrastructure. The CCEVS defines the organizational entities associated with, and the processes and procedures for establishing and maintaining, an MRA-recognized, U.S. Government–overseen, commercial security testing infrastructure for conducting CC-based testing in the United States. Both products' security claims and the proper construction of customer security requirements profiles can be assessed via this infrastructure.

This infrastructure depends on the availability of multiple, accredited, independent, commercial, fee-for-service, security testing laboratories, a government oversight body, and government certificate issuing authorities.

The labs, called CC Testing Labs (CCTLs), are accredited by the U.S. Department of Commerce's National Voluntary Laboratory Accreditation Program (NVLAP). NVLAP uses standards and guidance established by the CCEVS. Information about the process and benefits of accrediting laboratories appears elsewhere.[31] Accreditation fosters commonality of testing across all CCTLs. Lists of CCEVS-accredited CCTLs (www.niap-ccevs.org/cc-scheme/cctls/) or labs in the process of seeking accreditation (www.niap-ccevs.org/cc-scheme/cctls/?candidate) are maintained by the CCEVS Validation Body. Lists of official CCTLs around the world (www.commoncriteriaportal.org/labs.html) and accredited under different national schemes are available at the Common Criteria Portal (www.commoncriteriaportal.org/).

The CCEVS Validation Body provides the services of U.S. government oversight of the testing infrastructure and its operation. It also provides the service of validating the results of product or profile testing and issuing certificates to tested products or profiles that have been validated.

51.11.2 Using the Testing Infrastructure. A discussion of the basic processes associated with using the testing infrastructure follows.

Organizations seeking analysis and assessment of PPs, STs, and products claiming conformance to such profiles select and contract with accredited labs (CCTLs) of their choice.

CCTLs provide impartial, standardized, third-party analysis and assessment of such profiles and products. CCTLs use appropriate, common CEM test methods that are standard across all test labs. These methods are tailored to security requirements or to security claims about a product. These common test methods are used to verify in a standard way that a product under test complies with the builders' claims about (1) the security features of a product and (2) the processes associated with the development and life cycle of the product.

The cost to conduct an evaluation varies dramatically, depending on the complexity of the product and the EAL claim to be assessed. CCTL fees to evaluate simple, low-EAL products can be on the order of tens of thousands of dollars, whereas CCTL fees to evaluate complex, moderately high EAL products can cost a million or more.

The costs to evaluate many products fall between these extremes. Similarly, time to complete an evaluation may range from a couple to several months.

The CCEVS Validation Body provides independent, standardized, government oversight of the security analysis and assessment activities of the accredited labs. It ensures consistency across CCTLs and therefore promotes comparability of testing and evaluation results across all CCTLs.

The CCEVS Validation Body can be used as an independent body to validate the testing results generated by a CCTL. Such additional validation, if pursued, establishes even greater confidence and trust in the product under test. Under the authority of NSA and NIST, the CCEVS Validation Body issues MRA-recognized certificates to successfully assessed and validated products and CC profiles. These certificates confirm that the conclusions of the testing lab were consistent with the evidence presented and that there are no factors which would invalidate the evaluation. The certificate applies only to the product that was evaluated, not future versions of that product. However, an assurance maintenance scheme (discussed later) allows future versions of the certified product to maintain certification.

The CCEVS Validation Body also maintains lists of profiles and products that have been validated and certified in the United States (see Section 51.12).

Detailed information about preparing for, conducting, and validating testing appears elsewhere.[32]

51.11.3   Maintaining Certification in an Evolving Marketplace.   Validated products that claim conformance to the CC AMA Assurance Maintenance class of assurance requirements, and that have been altered or upgraded since the time of their original CC evaluation, can undergo a mutually recognized assurance maintenance scheme process[33] to maintain their CC certification at the same level of assurance. Certification retention depends on (a) the vendor pursuing all the assurance maintenance activities stipulated in the CC AMA assurance requirements, (b) the vendor submitting a Security Impact Analysis (SIA) that in part provides an audit of the vendor's assurance maintenance activities, and (c) acceptance of the SIA by the CCEVS Validation Body. Otherwise, the revised product must undertake a new CC evaluation. Practical information about the assurance maintenance process is available elsewhere.[34]

51.12   VALIDATED PROFILES AND PRODUCTS.   CC profiles successfully validated under the CCEVS are placed on a national registry of PPs (www. niap-ccevs.org/cc-scheme/pp/). Profiles under development in the United States and not yet validated are also listed (www.niap-ccevs.org/pp/draft_pps/) in an attempt to help avoid duplication of effort by independent organizations that may wish to develop similar PPs. A complete list of profiles validated around the world by all national schemes is available at the Common Criteria Portal (www.commoncriteriaportal.org/ products.html).

Products successfully validated under the CCEVS are placed on a Validated Products List (www.niap-ccevs.org/cc-scheme/vpl/). The list is sorted by product type, assurance level, product name, and vendor name. Common Criteria certificates issued for IT products apply only to the specific versions and releases of those products for which a validated CCTL assessment took place. An evaluated product will remain on the Validated Products List for three years, after which time it will be moved and indefinitely listed on a historical evaluated products list (www.niap-ccevs.org/ cc-scheme/vpl/archived/). This archival list contains validated products that are no longer commercially available. A list of products currently undergoing evaluation within the CCEVS is also maintained (www.niap-ccevs.org/cc-scheme/in_evaluation/).

A complete list of the hundreds of products evaluated across all national schemes, along with their associated PPs, is available at the Common Criteria Portal (www.commoncriteriaportal.org/products.html). Similar to the CCEVS, other national schemes maintain lists of products currently under evaluation within each national scheme.

Many of the market leading vendors in many areas of technology have validated products, and many of the most prevalent areas of technology are supplied by validated products. Vendors include major players such as Apple, BMC, Cisco, CA, HP, IBM, Juniper, Microsoft, Oracle, Sun, Sybase, Symantec, Xerox, and many more. The technologies for which validated products are available include proprietary and open source operating systems, network and security management equipment, certificate management components, firewalls, IDSs/IPSs, copiers, web servers, messaging gear, AV gear, VPN gear, and many more.

Validated products are getting significant traction in the government marketplace. Certain commercial industries—for example, the process control and financial industries—also are attracted to validated products. Although there are still consumers and vendors who believe that the CC paradigm is complicated, inefficient, or costly, the many who do build and buy validated products see the CC paradigm as the best, proactive way to improve the security and assurance of products bought and sold in the marketplace.

51.13   BENEFITS OF CC EVALUATION.   CC-based testing under the aegis of a national scheme benefits both manufacturers and their customers.

51.13.1   Helping Manufacturers.   CC-based accredited testing directly helps product manufacturers, and thereby also indirectly benefits product consumers, in a number of ways.

Reliance on standards broadens potential markets. It is important that security evaluations of IT products be carried out in accordance with recognized standards and procedures. The use of standard IT security evaluation criteria, and IT security evaluation methodology, contributes to the repeatability and objectivity of the results. The use of standards tends to increase the product appeal to various, nonrelated customer constituencies.

CC-based testing under an MRA-recognized national scheme helps manufacturers penetrate global markets. It provides access to the MRA, and products and profiles so tested and validated can be recognized internationally within all countries, without needing to undergo any additional testing.

It helps manufacturers penetrate specific domestic markets. In the United States, for example, national government policy (NSTISSP #11 and DoD 8500) requires procurement and use of products that are CCEVS certified.[35] According to this policy, U.S. DoD and civil agencies working for DoD must purchase only CCEVS-certified products whenever products are needed for environments pertaining to matters of national security. The civil sector government agencies also are encouraged to purchase such products for all other applications.

CC-based testing helps manufacturers lower costs by providing a pool of private, accredited, competitive security testing labs that have consistent testing quality and competence. Even when selecting the least expensive testing lab, manufacturers do not have to worry about sacrificing the quality of the testing services they receive.

By avoiding any further testing or retesting beyond that performed by the selected testing lab, manufacturers are spared enormous and costly country-specific or
customer-specific testing campaigns. Lower testing costs can increase product profit
margins or lower product prices or both.

An analysis of the CCEVS paradigm reveals some deficiencies to be addressed. The
cost and time duration of evaluations may be addressed through tax credit incentives
and development of so-called Common Criteria Lite concepts. Also, as vendors begin
to leverage the lessons they learn from CC-based testing into their own development
processes, it seems plausible that some sort of "self-certification program, subject to the
same rigorous evaluation and audit requirements as the third-party evaluation program,
may reduce the cost and time burdens of third-party evaluations."[36] There have also
been criticisms that certified products can cost more than uncertified versions,[37] but a
consensus seems to be growing that the CC scheme is overwhelmingly positive.[38]

51.13.2   Helping Consumers.   CC-based testing directly benefits product
consumers in a number of ways.

It provides consumers an impartial, high-quality assessment of a security profile,
or a security-focused IT product, since it is an assessment that is conducted by an
independent entity. The fact that testing by accredited testing labs is done according
to standards gives consumers a strong sense that testing is objective and not slanted to
benefit the product that was tested.

CC-based testing is a first step to helping consumers understand what features are
offered by products, whether products comply with certain stated security requirements,
and how trustworthy such products should be considered.

Because the CC paradigm has overcome many of the limitations of other approaches
to developing trust in products, products tested by CCTLs are, arguably, among the
most trustworthy products available. CCEVS lessons reveal that tested products tend
to be more trustworthy. Indeed, statistics[39] show that nearly a third of products tested
were improved by identification and elimination of security flaws that could have been
exploited by attackers. Even a greater percentage of tested products were improved by
adding or extending security functionality.

With products that can be trusted, customers will be able to reduce their product acquisition costs by eliminating acceptance testing that duplicates testing already
performed on a product by an accredited testing lab.

Furthermore, such as the case with Linux CCEVS certification, vendors of CC-tested
products often choose not to increase the price of their product after it is evaluated
and certified. Instead, such vendors are looking to increased sales to cover the costs of
product certification.

51.14   CONCLUDING REMARKS.   Early efforts to test the security features of
products were lacking in many aspects. Not many evaluated the assurance associated
with products. Product comparisons typically were "apples-to-oranges" comparisons,
and consumers had no common way to articulate their security and assurance needs.
The Common Criteria changes these dynamics.

The experience gathered from ongoing security requirements, profiling, and security
product testing efforts has consistently shown the Common Criteria paradigm to be
a powerful, flexible, standards-based mechanism. It is a mechanism that facilitates
defining IT security and assures confidence requirements tailored to users' specific
needs. It facilitates stipulating IT product security specifications that are compliant
to requirements. It facilitates testing and test verification of products to show they are

correct, complete, well built, and compliant to their security specifications. It facilitates worldwide recognition of tested, CC-specified IT products and systems.

The CC paradigm is effective. It improves product quality by forcing a meticulous and clear focus on security, by forcing a rigorous security design and development discipline, and by forcing a testing campaign that is appropriate to the normal operation of the product or system, so as to verify that the implemented security is correct, complete, and compliant under normal operations.

The CC paradigm helps users understand what risks and vulnerabilities are important (via PPs) and what risks and vulnerabilities are addressed by products (via STs). It helps users understand what level of protection and confidence they want (via PPs) and what level of protection and confidence are provided by products (via STs). It also may help shorten users' product acquisition cycles since PPs can be used as procurement specifications, and since users can minimize their own acceptance testing efforts.

The CC paradigm can provide due diligence evidence. By providing a way to demonstrate the traceability of the security aspects of a product back to user requirements as well as to applicable policies, laws, and regulations, the CC paradigm can minimize users' exposure to potential penalties for noncompliance to security-relevant laws or regulations.

The CC paradigm helps vendors describe and demonstrate what level of security they designed and built into their products. It helps vendors show that they understand and meet consumer requirements and that they have nothing to hide. Consumers know exactly what they get in CC-specified and CC-validated products.

Even products that do not undergo evaluation benefit, as vendors that have undertaken CC-based evaluations have improved their overall product development, delivery, and support processes, and accordingly have reduced their overall likelihood to produce security defects and vulnerabilities. Products that are more secure because of the culture and environment in which they were built all tend to increase the overall assurance in all kinds of IT infrastructures.

The high and consistent testing and verification standards that the CC paradigm provides worldwide allow vendors to outsource the security testing, validation, and certification of their products anywhere in the world. The standards allow testing costs to be capped because they limit the number of necessary security (re)evaluations to only one. The standards allow builders to implement security products anywhere in the world and to test security products anywhere in the world; and, correspondingly, the use of these standards allow users to buy products with confidence from anywhere around the world.

The CC paradigm improves product quality and therefore helps to differentiate products in terms of verified quality. It facilitates expansion of a stable set of quality products from which to build integrated systems. It raises the level of confidence, credibility, and trust in products as well as in vendors and their product design, development, testing, and maintenance processes.

Most important, the CC paradigm assures that better-engineered, more acceptable products are available from vendors who prepare for and undergo rigorous, independent, CC-based evaluations.

51.15 NOTES

1. "Federal Information Security Management Act of 2002" (colloquially, Title III of the E-Government Act of 2002), U.S. Public Law 107-347, Section III, Dec 2002. (Available via http://csrc.nist.gov/sec-cert/ca-library.html)

2. Bill Clinton, "Critical Infrastructure Protection," Presidential Decision Directive/ NSC-63, PDD-63, B The White House, Washington, DC, May 22, 1998, http://fas.org/irp/offdocs/pdd/pdd-63.htm. "Defending America's Cyberspace— National Plan for Information Systems Protection," Version 1.0, The White House, 2000. George W. Bush, "The National Strategy to Secure Cyberspace," The White House, Washington, DC, February 2003, www.whitehouse.gov/pcipb/.

3. "Information Technology—Security Techniques—Code of Practice for Information Security Management," ISO/IEC 17799 (2005), http://webstore.ansi.org/ ansidocstore/product.asp?sku=ISO%2FIEC+17799%3A2005.

4. Ron Ross et al., "Recommended Security Controls for Federal Information Systems," Special Publication 800-53, National Institute of Standards and Technology, Department of Commerce (December 2007), http://csrc.nist.gov/ publications/nistpubs/800-53-Rev2/sp800-53-rev2-final.pdf

5. Department of Defense Instruction, "DoD Information Technology Security Certification and Accreditation Process (DITSCAP)," 5200.40, December 30, 1997, http://iase.disa.mil/ditscap/i520040.pdf.

6. National Security Telecommunications and Information Systems Security Instruction (NSTISSI) No. 1000, "National Information Assurance Certification and Accreditation Process (NIACAP)" (April 2000), www.cnss.gov/Assets/pdf/ nstissi_1000.pdf.

7. NIST Special Publication 800-37, "Guide for the Security Certification and Accreditation of Federal Information Systems (May 2004), http://csrc.nist.gov/ publications/nistpubs/800-37/SP800-37-final.pdf.

8. Department of Defense Directive 8500.1, "Information Assurance (IA)," October 24, 2002, www.acq.osd.mil/ie/bei/pm/ref-library/dodd/d85001p.pdf.

9. Department of Defense Instruction 8500.2, "Information Assurance (IA) Implementation," February 6, 2003, www.niap-ccevs.org/cc-scheme/policy/dod/ d85002p.pdf.

10. Personal communications with several keynote speakers at the First International Common Criteria Conference, National Information Assurance Partnership, Baltimore, MD, May 2000.

11. "Verizon Business Completes Cybertrust Acquisition" July 9, 2007, www. verizonbusiness.com/us/about/news/displaynews.xml?newsid=22913&mode= vzlong&lang=en&width=530&root=/us/about/news/releases/&subroot=release. xml&langlinks=off.

12. Greg Keizer, "Google, Sun, Lenovo, Others Out to Shame Spyware." *TechWeb Network,* January 25, 2006; www.techweb.com/wire/ebiz/177103886.

13. Carnegie Mellon University Software Engineering Institute, "Capability Maturity Model for Software," CMU/SEI-91-TR-24, 1991. The model is described at www.sei.cmu.edu/cmm/. See also www2.umassd.edu/SWPI/ processframework/cmm/cmm.html.

14. "International Standards for Quality Management," 2nd ed., ISO 9000 (1992).

15. U.S. Department of Defense, "Trusted Computer System Evaluation Criteria" (TCSEC), DOD5200.28-STD (December 1985).

16. National Computer Security Center, National Security Agency, "Trusted Network Interpretation of the Trusted Computer System Evaluation Criteria" (TNI), 9800 Savage Rd., Ft. Meade, MD 20755, July 31, 1987.

17. National Computer Security Center, National Security Agency, "Trusted Database Management System Interpretation of the Trusted Computer System Evaluation Criteria," NCSC-TG-021, 9800 Savage Rd., Ft. Meade, MD 20755, April 1991.

18. Office for Official Publications of the European Communities, "Information Technology Security Evaluation Criteria" (ITSEC), Luxembourg (1991).

19. National Security Telecommunications and Information Systems Security Committee (NSTISSC), "Advisory Memorandum on the Transition from the Trust Computer System Evaluation Criteria to the International Common Criteria for Information Technology Security Evaluation," NSTISSAM Compusec/1-99, http://niap.nist.gov/cc-scheme/nstissam_compusec_1-99.pdf, NSTISSC Secretariat, National Security Agency, 9800 Savage Rd., Ste. 6716, Ft. Meade, MD 20755-6716, March 11, 1999.

20. "Common Criteria for Information Technology Security Evaluation," Version 2, ISO/IEC International Standard (IS) 15408-1 through 15408-3, ISO/IEC JTC1 SC27 WG3, 1999. Updates and future drafts are available: www.niap-ccevs.org/cc-scheme/cc_docs/.

21. W. Rishel, "ISO 15408 for Security and Privacy in Healthcare," Research Note, Technology, T-10-5507, Gartner Group, March 2, 2000.

22. The terms "testing" and "evaluation" are a source of ambiguity and discrepancy in the community. In this chapter the terms "testing," "evaluation," and "testing and evaluation" are used interchangeably.

23. Common Evaluation Methodology Editorial Board, "Common Methodology for Information Technology Security Evaluation: Evaluation Methodology," Version 3.1 (September 2007). Updates and future drafts are available.

24. "Mutual Recognition of the Common Criteria Certifications in the Field of Information Technology Security," initially signed October 5, 1998; updated as "The Arrangement on the Recognition of Common Criteria Certificates in the field of Information Technology Security" (May 2000), www.niap-ccevs.org/cc-scheme/cc-recarrange.pdf, and as updated periodically with new signatory countries: www.niap-ccevs.org/cc-scheme/ccra.cfm.

25. NIAP/Department of Commerce, National Institute of Standards and Technology, Computer Security Division, "Common Criteria Evaluation and Validation Scheme for Information Technology Security—Organization, Management and Concept of Operations," Scheme Publication #1, Version 2. Available from NIAP/Department of Commerce, Room 426, NN, 100 Bureau Drive, Mail Stop 8930, Gaithersburg, MD 20899-8930 (May 1999). http://www.niap-ccevs.org/cc-scheme/policy/ccevs/scheme-pub-1.pdf

26. These signatories are the NSA and the NIST operating together in a joint program called the National Information Assurance Partnership (NIAP); www.niap-ccevs.org/.

27. ISO/IEC Guide 25, "General Requirements for the Competence of Calibration and Testing Laboratories" (1990). www.fasor.com/iso25/.

28. ISO/IEC Technical Report 13233, "Information Technology Interpretation of Accreditation Requirements in Guide 25 Accreditation of Information Technology and Telecommunications Testing Laboratories for Software and Protocol Testing Services." Can be purchased online: www.iso.org/iso/iso_catalogue/catalogue_tc/catalogue_detail.htm?csnumber=21468.

29. NIST Handbook 150-20 "Information Technology Security Testing—Common Criteria," (www.niap-ccevs.org/cc-scheme/policy/ccevs/HB150-20.pdf), a technology-specific extension to J. L. Cigler and V. R. White, eds., NIST Handbook 150, "National Voluntary Laboratory Accreditation Program—Procedures and General Requirements," U.S. Department of Commerce, Technology Administration, National Institute of Standards and Technology (Washington, DC: U.S. Government Printing Office, 1994); http://ts.nist.gov/Standards/Accreditation/upload/nist-handbook-150.pdf

30. Technical Report ISO/IEC TR 15446, "Information Technology—Security Techniques—Guide for the Production of Protection Profiles and Security Targets" (July 2004), (http://isotc.iso.org/livelink/livelink/fetch/2000/2489/Ittf_Home/PubliclyAvailableStandards.htm). Look under ISO/IEC TR 15446:2004.

31. Seymour Bosworth and M. E. Kabay, *Computer Security Handbook,* 4th ed. (New York: John Wiley & Sons, 2002), Chapter 27, Section 27.9.7, Section 27.4.7 New York.

32. Bosworth and Kabay, *Computer Security Handbook,* 4th ed., Chapter 27, Section 27.9.8.

33. Common Criteria project, "Assurance Continuity: CCRA Requirements," CCIMB-2004-02-009, Version 1.0 (February 2004), www.niap-ccevs.org/cc-scheme/cc_docs/assur_con_v1.pdf.

34. Soheila Amiri, "The Purpose and Value of Common Criteria Assurance Maintenance (AMA)," CyberGuard Corp., Fort Lauderdale, FL (May 2004) (www.cyberguard.com/download/white_paper/en_cg_AMA.pdf).

35. National Security Telecommunications and Information Systems Security Committee, "National Policy Governing the Acquisition of Information Assurance (IA) and IA-Enabled Information Technology (IT) Products," National Security Telecommunications and Information Systems Security Policy (NSTISSP) No. 11, NSTISSC Secretariat, National Security Agency, 9800 Savage Rd., Suite 6716, Ft. Meade MD 20755-6716 (January 2000). (Updated as NSTISSP No. 11, Revised Fact Sheet, "National Information Assurance Acquisition Policy" (July 2003); www.cnss.gov/Assets/pdf/nstissp_11_fs.pdf.) Also, National Security Telecommunications and Information Systems Security Committee, "Advisory Memorandum for the Strategy for using the National Information Assurance Partnership (NIAP) for the Evaluation of Commercial Off-the-Shelf (COTS) Security Enabled Information Technology Products," NSTISSAM Inforsec/2-00, February 8, 2000, www.cnss.gov/Assets/pdf/nstissam_infosec_2-00.pdf. Available from NSTISSC Secretariat, National Security Agency, 9800 Savage Rd., Suite 6716, Ft. Meade MD 20755-6716.

36. National Cyber Security Partnership, Technical Standards and Common Criteria Task Force, "Recommendations Report" (April 2004), www.cyberpartnership.org/init-tech.html.

37. P. Wait, "Energy Contract Stirs Conflict: Deal Raises Questions about Evaluation Process, Common Criteria's Value," *Government Computer News,* May 14, 2006; www.gcn.com/print/25_12/40754-1.html#.

38. W. Jackson, "Mary Ann Davidson: In Defense of Common Criteria," *Government Computer News,* October 8, 2007; www.gcn.com/print/26_26/45166-1.html#.

39. Rutrell Yasin, "NIAP Chief Touts Common Criteria," *Federal Communications Week*, October 27, 2004; http://archives.neohapsis.com/archives/isn/2004-q4/0097.html.

INTRODUCTION TO PART V

DETECTING SECURITY BREACHES

No matter how well we implement security mechanisms, we are facing human opponents who may counter our best efforts until we can respond appropriately. How do security and network administrators find out if there has been a breach of security? How can they evaluate their own defenses before they are penetrated? This part includes chapters on:

52. **Application Controls.** Application-software security and logging
53. **Monitoring and Control Systems.** System logging and data reduction methods
54. **Security Audits, Standards, and Inspections.** Measuring compliance with explicit policies and with industry standards
55. **Cyber Investigation.** Organizing effective digital forensic studies of observed or suspected security breaches, for internal use, and for cooperation with law enforcement

APPLICATION CONTROLS

Myles Walsh

52.1 PROTECTION IN APPLICATION DEVELOPMENT. In computer installations where systems development takes place, there are technologies that tend to enhance security. These technologies, together with mandatory organizational procedures and standards, force analysts and programmers to adhere to guidelines when they are developing in-house applications or systems to be marketed. This chapter reviews some of the methods programmers use to prevent and identify problems involving data corruption or unavailability.

One of the underpinnings of modern programming is the technology known as the database management system (DBMS). Many applications are developed using this technology. A contemporary RDBMS supports relational databases. Relational databases themselves are based on an underlying technology developed in the 1960s and implemented through the remainder of the twentieth century. It seems certain that the technology will continue to be used for the foreseeable future.

RDBMSs are sets of programs that provide users with the tools to perform these tasks:

- Create database structures (file or table layouts, and screens or forms).
- Enter information into the structures.
- Establish cross-references among the files or tables.

- Manipulate (sort, index, and summarize) the information in the structures.
- Import information from nonrelational database structures and export information to nondatabase structures. This must allow for interfaces between applications using an RDBMS and applications using conventional files structures.
- Provide for the security and the integrity of the database.

Many DBMSs also include the tools to create a data repository. Data repositories, expanded versions of data dictionaries that store information about databases, are documentation databases that include descriptive information about all the resources included in an information systems environment. Data dictionaries are often integrated with an RDBMS, and, if used as intended, force documentation standards in information systems environments. Common file or table structures, common program modules, and common field definitions contribute significantly to the reduction of confusion and of communication breakdowns in an enterprise.

There are two primary methods of organizing files and databases for access and processing: batch and online. Protection of online files and databases requires additional planning when the systems using them are being designed, and special precautions when they are being used. Protection of batch files is more straightforward because the creation of backup copies is an inherent part of the batch process.

Another issue is data validation during data entry or during data transfer from older systems. Every attempt should be made to ensure that data are entered or transferred and validated expeditiously. Failure to get correct data into a system quickly delays the creation and display of the information, the very purpose of almost all systems. When improper attention is directed to validation of the data as it enters the system, incorrect information is created by the system. The acronym "GIGO" (garbage in, garbage out) has become part of the national lexicon of everyday language. Unfortunately, there are some techniques that, when improperly used, contribute to the creation of incorrect information; examples include prototyping, joint application development (JAD), and rapid application development (RAD). By definition, a prototype is a model that is put together to demonstrate that the concept of a proposed system is valid. Basically, prevalidated test data are used to test the concept. However, too often a successfully tested prototype system is put into production without adequate validation procedures. The same situation can arise with RAD and JAD projects, which can tempt practitioners to implement new software products without considering their impact on other systems within an organization.

For related topics, see Chapter 38 in this *Handbook* on writing secure code, Chapter 39 on software development and quality assurance, Chapter 40 on managing software patches, and Chapter 47 on operations security and production controls.

52.2   PROTECTING ONLINE FILES.   Data can be damaged through hardware problems, errors in software, and problems during concurrent access by two or more users or processes.

52.2.1   Types of Data Corruption.   Data corruption implies incorrect data. Corruption can occur because of physical factors or logical errors in programs.

Physical corruption occurs through breakdown or other failures of hardware such as computers and network equipment, especially of mass-storage devices such as magnetic disks, tapes and cartridges, and optical drives. Data corruption during transmission can occur through electromagnetic perturbations of communications cables and radio-frequency noise that affects wireless transmission. Fiber optic cables are susceptible to cross-talk and to disruption caused by physical bends or kinks in the cables; CD-ROM (compact-disk read-only memory), CD-WORM (write-once, read-many), and CD-RW (read-write) disks are susceptible to dirt and abrasion. In addition to problems in the transmission or storage media, improper settings, or the effects of wear in the equipment, can cause errors. Examples include misalignment of magnetic heads on disks and tapes; bad contacts in wireless transmission equipment, causing noise; and improper positioning of lasers in optical media. See Chapters 22 and 23 for extensive discussion of physical factors that can cause data corruption.

Logical corruption occurs through programming errors such as incorrect sums, bad arithmetic formulas, incorrect logical conditions, bad data in look-up tables, out-of-bounds conditions allowing reading and writing in the wrong areas of memory, and the effects of malicious software.

It is sometimes possible to identify the source of errors by examining their characteristics. For example, physical corruption characteristically shows data written inappropriately across blocks rather than in single fields defined by software applications. Such physical corruption usually has no relationship with the damaged records other than physical proximity on the disk; therefore, a cardinal sign of physical corruption is damage to files from completely different applications—a block of database records contiguous to a block of text files, for example.

In contrast, logical corruption characteristically shows errors in the same field in multiple records. Another class of logical errors shows bad values for boundary conditions (e.g., the smallest or largest possible value) but correct data within the range. Such errors rarely cross application boundaries unless there is a logical relationship among the damaged files; for example, an error in a spreadsheet (almost always due to input or programming errors by the user) may propagate to text files if object linking and embedding (OLE) are used to insert the spreadsheet results into the document. Other documents will remain unaffected by such logical errors. For more extensive discussion of logical errors, see Chapter 39 on software development and quality assurance.

52.2.2 Database Management Subsystems.   In the 1960s, representing complex systems, such as those based on accounting records, forced programmers to define their own file structures to represent relationships among the data; for example, an order header file would be linked to the corresponding order detail records through hard-coded relationships in the application programs. Each programmer or programming team had to define its own data access paths and code them explicitly. Coordinating access to multiple individually named files caused headaches for programmers. For example, it was easy to make errors such as forgetting to increment counters representing how many detail records corresponded to a master (index) record (i.e., line counts in order headers disagreeing with the actual number of detail lines). Because there was no particular protection for the files in such systems, it was easy to replace or delete individual files by mistake, leading to massive logical corruption. Deletion of header records could leave a fragment of inaccessible details in associated files. Programs had to keep pointers up to date for forward and backward chaining. Backups sometimes failed through operator error when not all related files were included. Furthermore, every system had its own unique methods for managing the data, causing maintenance and learning headaches.

The late 1960s saw many large programming shops defining their data access methods by using library routines that all programmers could share, but there was still a heavy investment in learning the new rules whenever a programmer changed jobs.

In the early 1970s, the programming field saw explosive growth in implementation of database management subsystems, where the interface to the database controlled utility functions such as indexing, pointing, and chaining. A typical DBMS would protect all files, now called *data sets,* against accidental erasure, and would force all reads, writes, appends, and locks to be mediated by the DBMS routines. Such interfaces usually provide for identification and authorization codes to control access to the data. In addition to these barriers to accidental or uncontrolled access, a DBMS also typically provides backup utilities to ensure that all data sets are copied together and to prevent accidental restoration of the wrong version of a data set. A DBMS also often provides ad hoc query tools that can substitute for specially written programs to accomplish simple requests; some also have more powerful report functions for formatting output with headers, footers, and calculations. Finally, a DBMS usually provides logging facilities to keep records of different types of access to the database.

The most important rules enforced by a DBMS are *referential integrity* to prevent common logical data corruption, automatic *uniqueness constraints* to preclude duplicate and conflicting records, and *locking* for safe concurrent access.

- **Referential integrity.** Referential integrity in DBMS design ensures that every dependent record has a primary key value that matches an existing primary key in the master file. In an order database, for example, order numbers in a header file (often called the order master) are the primary keys. Each order header record contains unique information about an order, such as customer number, date placed, total price of materials, taxes, and shipping costs. The order detail file contains the dependent records, each of which can be located using its order number as the primary key. Each detail record contains information about a specific part of the corresponding order, such as an item number, quantity ordered, price, extended price, and special charges or discounts. If an order header record is to be deleted, all the order detail records must be deleted first; otherwise, the detail records would be left with no way to locate them through their primary key value. Similarly, no detail record can be added unless the master record with the same primary key already exists.

- **Uniqueness constraints.** A modern DBMS allows configuration of nonrepeating primary keys; for example, in an order database, the order number would typically be a nonrepeating or unique key, because there should never be two orders with the same identifying number. Setting the uniqueness property would preclude adding a second header record with the same value in the order number field as another order.

52.2.3   Lock on Update.   When more than one user accesses a database, it is possible to experience conflicts over the use of specific records. A classic example occurs in an inventory database, where there are 15 units of part 1 in the inventory. User Albert needs to take 5 units of part 1 out of inventory, leaving a total of 10. The inventory program reads the inventory record for part 1 and modifies record 1 to show only 10 units. However, if, while this is going on, user Betty needs 3 units of part 1, the inventory record still shows 15 units available because user Albert has not yet updated that record. After user Albert's program completes its update, the record shows 10 units available, but after user Betty's program overwrites that record to show 12 available units for part 1, the inventory total is off by 5 units. This situation is an example of a *race condition* as described in Section 39.4.1.6 of Chapter 39 in this *Handbook.*

To avoid this kind of logical corruption, a DBMS provides facilities for *locking* parts of the database. In the inventory example, user A's program would lock the inventory record for part 1 (or the entire inventory data set) until the update is completed. That way, user B's program would have to wait for user A's program to *unlock* the data before being able to act on the inventory record.

The obvious symptom of a bad locking strategy is a discrepancy between the database value and the real-world value. However, such a discrepancy is not by itself proof of logical corruption, because the same divergence could arise from events in the real world not reflected in the database. In the inventory example, the actual inventory may have been reduced by theft or increased by an unrecorded addition of materials.

52.2.3.1 *Unconditional versus Conditional Locking.* There are two types of locking strategy: *conditional* locking and *unconditional* locking. Conditional locking attempts to obtain a lock, but if the required record or the entire data set is already locked, the DBMS returns control to the calling program with a status indicator of this condition. The application program can then be written to loop until the lock is obtained. The unconditional lock request hangs the program until the lock is granted. The DBMS or the operating system provides automatic queuing using a first-in, first-out queue.

52.2.3.2 *Deadlocks.* Unconditional locking carries risks if multiple resources are locked by programs. For example, if program A unconditionally locks resource 1 and program B locks resource 2, trouble will occur when program A then attempts to lock resource 2 while program B tries to lock resource 1. Neither program will release the resource it has locked until it is released, and so both will wait forever or until one of the programs is forcibly terminated. Such a situation is known as a *deadlock* or more colorfully as a *deadly embrace*. If programmers insist on using unconditional locking, the deadlock prevention strategy is to ensure that all programs accessing the database must lock resources in the same order (e.g., lock 1, then lock 2) and must unlock in the reverse order (unlock 2, then unlock 1).

Other strategies are to keep transactions as short as possible and to avoid the necessity for operator interactions that would keep the records locked for long periods of time.

52.2.4 Two-Phase Commit. Sometimes many records or data sets must be locked for complex transactions to be completed. For example, in a hospital's clinical systems database, discharging a patient could require modifications in data sets such as the patient-master, treatment-detail, nursing assignment master and details, doctor assignment master and details, and data sets for the financial functions. Locking everything that might be needed and waiting for a human being to enter all the appropriate data could take seconds to minutes, during which time all the affected records would be locked and unavailable to everyone else on the system. In the extreme, if an operator were to leave in the middle of a transaction, other users could be blocked out of large parts of the database for an indeterminate length of time, even for hours. The delays resulting from such locking around human intervention led to the principle that no transaction can be allowed to lock around a human intervention.

Another problem with locking around human intervention is that a system failure could terminate processing while the database was in an inconsistent state. For example, in the inventory case, the DBMS might have updated the order detail by adding an item but not yet updated the order header to show the new total cost of the order. To reduce the likelihood of such an occurrence, a DBMS can support the two-phase commit as an aid to making changes as fast as possible and thus reducing the window of vulnerability for interruption. In the two-phase commit, the DBMS obtains copies of all the records needed when the operator begins a transaction. Once the operator has taken all necessary steps for completing the transaction, the DBMS locks and reads all the changed records again and compares the current values with the initial values; if there are no differences, the DBMS makes all the required changes and immediately unlocks all the records. However, if the current values have been modified since the operator requested the initial copies, then some other process has been active and so the DBMS reports that verification is needed. The operator typically is given the choice of how to proceed; for example, if there are no items left in inventory, the order may have to be delayed or canceled, whereas if there are enough items, the operator need merely reinitiate the transaction with the new initial values.

52.2.5 Backup Files and System Logs.

When information in an online file or database is updated, the old information—that is, the information that was in the record before the change was made—is overlaid; unless steps are taken, it disappears without a trace. For this reason, many DBMSs allow an image of the original record to be copied to the transaction log file. In other cases, where the exact history of a particular group of records must be preserved, as with insurance and medical data, an application may append new records but not delete old ones.

If online files and databases were never damaged or lost, data loss would be of no concern. However, in an imperfect world, steps must be taken so that damaged or lost online files and databases can be recovered. For further details of data backup and recovery, see Chapter 57 in this *Handbook*.

In order to recover online files and databases, it is first necessary to make periodic backup copies and to make log copies of records that have been updated in the time between making the backups. How often a backup copy is made depends on how dynamic the files or databases are. In most enterprises, a significant number of total or partial files and databases are copied daily. It is not uncommon for computer operations departments to spend several hours each day doing backups. Whenever a backup copy of a file or database is created, there are two correct copies at that point in time. To explain how online file and database backup and system logging work, think of a single online file. The file is taken off-line and is no longer accessible to online transactions at 4 A.M., and a copy is made. Both copies of this file are identical at that time. At 6 A.M. the original file is put back online, and transactions recorded during that interval are run to update that file. From that point on, with each update transaction, the differences between that file and its backup increase.

At 2 P.M., if for some reason the file is no longer usable, the backup file is then eight hours behind. At this point, the log file becomes critical in the restoration process. The log file is in sequence by time and contains copies of the updated records both before and after update was performed. It also contains copies of the transaction record.

52.2.6 Recovery and Restart.

After it has been determined that an online file or database has been corrupted or destroyed, a procedure known as recovery and restart is initiated. The first step in this procedure is to copy the backup to create a new original. The next step uses the log file to reapply, in time sequence, all the transactions that had been executed since the backup copy was made.

Contemporary database systems have files that cannot be taken off-line. They are online 24 hours a day, seven days a week. In order to make backup copies, parts of the database are copied periodically (dynamic backup). Conceptually, a database can be broken up into parts. Each part can be backed up separately at different time periods. A number of schemes can be devised to back up some of the records. For example, copy to a backup file every fifth record of the database in one time period, say records 5, 10, 15, 20, and so on. A bit later, copy to another backup file records 1, 6, 11, 16, 21, and so on. If a conflict occurs between copying the record for backup and a transaction attempting to update the record, have an appropriate procedure established to let one or the other take place first. Recovery and restart, as well as backout procedures, work the same way, with the additional complexity of establishing priorities for which gets done first when conflicts occur. Even though these conflicts increase complexity, they are resolved when the procedures for recovery, restart, and backout are created.

52.2.7 Backout.   The log file is also used in a process known as backout. This process is initiated when online update transactions fail to complete after making incomplete or partial updates to files or databases. For example, an update transaction in which there are additions to three fields in three separate files is supposed to take place. After making two out of the three updates, the transaction terminates abnormally because of a program malfunction. Eventually the program gets corrected, but something has to be done to undo the two partial updates. Otherwise, when the program is fixed and the transaction is rerun, those two updates would be reapplied, which would result in erroneous duplication. The backout procedure is initiated for those transactions that, if they had not completed properly, would generate errors.

Recovery using log files requires marking the start and end of every transaction; if the log file records show a transaction start without the corresponding transaction end, recovery processes can recognize the transaction as incomplete. Such markers correspond to what are called *checkpoints* in the program design.

52.2.8 Roll-Forward Recovery.   Another approach to recovery is to start from a known good state and redo all transactions that are known to have been accomplished correctly. This roll-forward recovery requires a database backup and a transaction log file to be synchronized, so that the first record in the transaction log file represents the first transaction immediately following a database backup. With these data in hand, it is possible to reconstruct all the modifications up to, but not including, the last complete transaction. All incomplete transactions are discarded, although the recovery program typically prints out all the details available for transactions that were not completed.

52.2.9 Distributed Databases.   A distributed database is one that is stored in different databases on different computer platforms. Databases can be distributed over many sites, using several different architectures.

The simplest and most susceptible to failure is the single database server that houses the database and shares its contents among several local area networks. Whenever the server or the database is off-line, or during a crash, all clients lose access to the database. The backup and recovery of a single server database follows the procedures described earlier.

A second architecture is the replicated database server, in which there are duplicate copies of the database on multiple servers. This type of system allows clients to access information from any of several copies of the database. With a replicated server environment, clients still can have access to the database when one of the servers is off-line. Such replicated systems usually have an additional benefit of being able to balance transaction traffic so as to keep any one server from being overwhelmed. The trade-off is the database synchronization process that increases the complexity of the replicated server architecture. Although the backup and recovery of a distributed database also can follow the procedures described earlier, it is complicated by the synchronization requirement.

A third architecture is known as a partitioned database server, in which specific subsets of a database are on two or more database servers. There could be a marketing database on one server, an accounting and finance database on a second server, and an inventory database on a third server. Because it is generally not possible to have mutually exclusive subsets of databases, synchronization must still be part of this architecture. Backup and recovery of partitioned databases requires application of the procedures just described for each of the subsets.

There is another distributed architecture known as federated database servers. This architecture is used in support of databases on two or more servers, made up of ordinarily incompatible storage models such as hierarchical and relational models, supported by different DBMSs. With the federated architecture, a single unified database definition, or schema, is created and stored on a combined database server. That server acts as an interface between application programs and the databases residing on the other servers. Queries and other transactions are sent to the combined database server, which translates these into queries and transactions to the underlying databases. Responses then return from the underlying databases to the unified schema to formulate a response to the user. Backup and recovery procedures such as those described earlier are used for the underlying databases.

Although federated database architecture can be complex and expensive to maintain, it can be less complex and less expensive than the process of supporting application programs for each of the underlying DBMSs. Federated architecture is often used in the implementation of data warehouses, which are used to extract information from multiple internal databases, as well as external databases, to support management decision making.

52.3   PROTECTING BATCH FILES

52.3.1   Backup File Creation.   The protection of files that are updated by batch processing programs is automatic, because the file is completely recopied and the original is left in the form it was in before the program executed. Therefore, each processing cycle leaves its own backup. The name "batch processing" comes from the idea of sequentially processing transactions in a group. There are always two or more files involved: the master file that is being updated and one or more transaction files that contain the information used to update the master. The process copies master file records that have no update activity into a new master file, updates the master records that do have activity and copies them into the new master file, and does not copy those master records that are flagged as deletions in the activity file. When the process completes, there are at least three files: the original master, the activity file(s), and the new master. Backups are the original master and the activity file(s). In the next processing cycle, the new master becomes input, together with that cycle's activity file(s). If a problem is encountered with the master file, the prior cycle's master file and all subsequent activity files can be used to generate an updated master. Keeping two or three generations of master and activity files is a common practice. The term "generation" is often applied to the batch processing cycles—generation 0, generation 1, generation 2—or as *grandfather*, *father*, and *son*. Recently these latter terms have been replaced by "grandparent," "parent," and "child."

52.3.2   Audit Controls.   Another security measure applied when working with batch files involves using control totals to ensure that the batch process has executed with accuracy. Specific controls may include counts of records. There also may be control totals of the values in specific fields of the input records to compare with totals in the output, after processing additions and subtractions. For example, in a payroll system, information from time cards is submitted to a computer for processing. Along with the time cards is a transmittal that contains a count of the time cards, and totals of all the straight time and overtime hours compiled by the department that originated the time cards. A procedure is run in which the control totals on the transmittal are checked against the totals actually input from the time cards, to ensure correctness before initiating the payroll process. If discrepancies are encountered, they need to be investigated and corrected before taking the next step in processing the payroll.

52.4   ENSURING THAT INFORMATION IN THE SYSTEM IS VALID.   The next sections present a brief overview of validation; for more extensive coverage of this topic, see Chapter 47 in this *Handbook* on operations security and production controls.

52.4.1   Validation Controls.   Whether an application updates its files by means of batch or online processing, or by some combination of both, validation of input is paramount. The term "GIGO" (garbage in, garbage out) is not heard as often as it used to be, yet it is as true as ever. Most contemporary systems use online files and databases, with information entered interactively, allowing for validation at the source. Several specific validation techniques have been applied to reduce the amount of incorrect information input into files and databases.

52.4.1.1   Methods for Identifying Input Errors and Unauthorized Modifications.   Data input errors are common. Fours and nines, ones and sevens, and sixes and zeroes can easily be mistaken for one another. Operators can leave out a digit or insert an extraneous one. Transposition is another type of mistake that is made from time to time. For example, an order entry operator may key in 3286 instead of 3826 (a transposition error), or perhaps 7790 instead of 7796 (a transcription error). Such errors would be reported when the check-digit calculation produces a number that differs from the input check digit. A check digit is an extra digit that is added to a generated variable as a suffix. For example, a five-digit stock number could have an extra digit; the sixth digit or check digit, as it is called, is calculated by applying an algorithm (performing some arithmetic) on the first five digits, resulting in a single-digit result. To minimize input errors, check digits can be used on any variables that are program-generated: for example, part numbers, employee numbers, and codes of various types. For more on check digits, see Chapter 4.

A single check digit can sometimes conceal the existence of double or multiple input errors in an input string because of the relatively simple arithmetic schemes. More complex versions of the check digit generate a sequence of digits called a *check sum,* which provides greater power to help identify input errors or fraud; credit card numbers typically include a four-digit check sum.

An extension of the check sum, the hash total, is a common tool for identifying logical or physical data corruption. A hash total is simply the meaningless sum of numerical values, such as part numbers, rather than the meaningful sum of quantities. Recalculation of a hash total can usually indicate if the data have been corrupted since the last time the hash total was computed.

A digital signature is a cryptographically generated value based on an encryption key. Applying the same digital signature process to the data should generate an identical signature. In addition, as described in Chapters 7 and 37 in this *Handbook*, using the public key cryptosystem allows one to verify the authenticity as well as the integrity of signed data.

52.4.1.2 *Range Checks.*

Range checks offer another way of validating information at its source. In situations where quantities and currency values are being entered, lower and upper limits can be established. For example, a range check could be used on quantity ordered to ensure that the value entered is within specific bounds, such as no less than 10 or no more than 60 of a certain item. Although not completely error proof, such limits can at least eliminate obvious errors and reduce those not so blatant. Range checking with values of 10 and 40 will eliminate the extra 0 error, where an operator enters 100 or 600, or 1 or 4.

52.4.1.3 *Validity Checks Using Tables.*

Using tables of values or valid codes is one of the best ways to ensure that only correct information is entered into files and databases. In contemporary files and databases, data type is specified as a property of the field during the design phase, and these properties can be used to make sure that text information is not entered into numeric fields and vice versa. Properties are also used to filter out invalid data configurations. Although impossible to filter out misspelled last names and other open-ended types of information, it is possible to filter out invalid state codes. A table containing the 51 (DC is the 51st) valid state codes can be used to ensure that none but those 51 can be entered. Other such entities (e.g., department codes, product codes or types, and price classes) are primary candidates for table validation.

With tables, it is also possible to make combination tables. For example, if a certain product code fell within a specific range, then only four price classes would be allowable. To be concrete, when a product code falls within the 600 to 699 range, then the price class could only be R, PR, OC, and CD. Such tables are used to validate information as it is initially entered into files and databases. Entry of invalid information, whether intentional or inadvertent, is inhibited.

Tables of forbidden combinations are particularly important in real-time control systems for processes that can go seriously wrong as a result of bad inputs. For example, in December 1992, an explosion at a chemical plant in the Netherlands was traced to a data input error that could have been prevented by an edit check that verified a table of forbidden chemical mixtures. An excerpt from a report discussing the event by Meine van der Meulen of The Netherlands Organization for Applied Scientific Research, Department of Industrial Safety, states:

> The accident started with a typing error in a prescription by a Laboratory worker. Instead of tank 632 he typed tank 634. In tank 632 there was stored resin feed classic (UN-1268) and normally used in the batch process. In tank 634 DCDP (dicyclopentadiene) was stored. The operator, who had to check if the tank contents was equal with the prescription, filled the reactor with the wrong chemicals.
>
> . . .a heavy explosion occurred which caused the death of 3 firemen of the works fire brigade and injured 11 workers [including] 4 firemen of the works fire brigade. The damage was estimated at several [10s] of millions NL guilders.[1]

Tables generally should be used only for information that is relatively static, because of the need for maintenance. Frequent table maintenance can lead to errors that have a cascading effect. If a table is incorrect, then all the information supposedly validated by that table could be incorrect throughout the files and databases.

52.4.2 Diagnostic Utilities. Production programs need to operate on verifiably correct data. Every production program should include diagnostic utilities to scan databases for logically impossible values or deviations from reality. For example, a diagnostic routine might check to be sure that every header total matches the total computed from the linked line item values. Because older data may have been accepted under older range-validation rules, all records should be checked to ensure that they conform to the current range constraints. Similarly, any other logical constraints in an application system should be explicitly addressed in the diagnostic program. The output from the program should give all the details appropriate for identifying and correcting the incorrect data. For example, instead of simply indicating

```
BAD VALUE IN PRICE FIELD, RECORD 1234
```

the output should explain something like

```
PRICE FOR ITEM 1234 = $45.67 WHICH EXCEEDS CONFIGURED
LIMIT OF $40.00 SHOWN IN INVENTORY MASTER RECORD 78999
```

52.5 CONCLUDING REMARKS. In another application of the 80/20 rule, 20 percent of the design and development work is expended in handling 80 percent of the data (the normal and the correct) going through a system, whereas 80 percent of the design and development work is expended for handling 20 percent of the data (the errors, the exceptions, and the unusual situations) going through the system. It is safe to say that more effort should be expended on validation, and on backup and recovery procedures, than is spent on those processes that handle validated data and the routine tasks of application processing.

Failure to include adequate backup and recovery procedures will jeopardize the operational integrity of an entire organization. The reliability of contemporary computer hardware together with built-in redundancy makes outages due to equipment failure less likely. Unfortunately, the same cannot be said for software and procedures. In any case, operational systems do fail, although rarely. Adequate backup and recovery processes and procedures have to be put in place to handle system failures. These processes and procedures range from disaster recovery to single system or application recovery. To ensure that sites, enterprises, and applications can be brought back after failures requires that control processes and procedures be put in place during the design and development process and kept up to date as the situation requires.

52.6 FURTHER READING

Post, G. V. *Database Management Systems: Designing and Building Business Applications*. New York: McGraw-Hill, 2004.

Romney, M. B., and P. J. Steinbart. *Accounting Information Systems*, 11th ed. Upper Saddle River, NJ: Prentice Hall, 2008.

Shelley, G. B., T. J. Cashman, and H. J. Rosenblatt. *Systems Analysis and Design*, 4th ed. Boston: Course Technology, 2001.

Sommerville, I. *Software Engineering*, 8th ed. Boston: Addison Wesley, 2006.
Stair, R. M., and G. W. Reynolds. *Principles of Information Systems*, 5th ed. Boston: Course Technology, 2001.

52.7 NOTE

1. Meine van der Meulen, "Large Accident at CINDU Plant in The Netherlands (additional info)," RISKS 14, No. 22, January 4, 1993.

CHAPTER 53

MONITORING AND CONTROL SYSTEMS

Caleb S. Coggins and Diane E. Levine

53.1   INTRODUCTION.   Monitoring and control (M&C) systems address security events through prevention, detection, and response. When aligned with security policy and appropriately implemented, these systems enable organizations to analyze trends, manage security incidents, and mitigate risk. Automation will play an important role as organizations seek to improve the efficiency and usability of real-time monitoring, controls, and secure log management. Although the scope of M&C systems may vary in size and complexity, the central components remain the same: data collection, data reduction, and system response.

Data collection includes log file generation and storage. Computer systems use *log files* to store records of events. Logged information includes system time, relevant users, affected systems, and the actions performed. *Data reduction* aggregates and correlates data into an easily understood and usable format. These information *dashboards* enable information managers and operators to understand quickly the state of the infrastructure, without the historically time-consuming process of manually reviewing individual log files. *System response* includes alert notification, corrective actions, and recovery procedures. The response may be automated or may involve feedback through a human-machine interface (HMI). The future viability of an information infrastructure relies on the effectiveness of these components.

53.1.1 Prevention, Detection, and Response.

In an idealistic scenario, automated systems would intelligently anticipate, detect, and prevent all problems from negatively impacting systems and business processes. However, not all problems merit costly security systems or dedicated sensors. For practical purposes, organizations must deploy cost-effective sensors and controls necessary to mitigate unacceptable risk. *Prevention* refers to the system's ability to prohibit an undesirable action. Common tools used in network security include in-line intrusion prevention systems (IPSs), intrusion detection systems (IDSs), and unified threat management (UTM) appliances. Deploying these systems at choke points and at the network edge restricts the scope of worm propagation and other undesirable network communications. In the physical security realm, single-person mantraps prevent individuals from tailgating into secure facilities.[1]

Detection refers to the ability to identify attacks and other security concerns through sensory input. Systems rely on automated detection mechanisms and human observation. M&C systems must have reliable detection mechanisms in order to manage security events and provide meaningful metrics on the state of the information infrastructure. Proactive detection may involve the authorized use of a vulnerability scanner by penetration testers. Reactive detection includes the identification of an attacker who performed a denial of service (DoS) attack on an enterprise network.[2]

Response refers to the output of M&C systems. A monitoring system may detect a malicious script disabling the host-based firewall on all of the workstations in the internal network, then log the activity and send an administrative alert to an operator or centralized correlation engine. A control system, however, would correct the firewall state or possibly even prohibit someone from making the change in the first place. Additional human response may occur after the administrative alert or dashboard refresh, such as escalation to an incident response team or implementing new controls to protect workstation integrity.[3]

Failure to detect and report security breaches may have legal ramifications, as many states require security breach notification.[4] Implementing *defense in depth* (layered defenses) increases the likelihood of threat detection, incident prevention, and response. AC power loss at a secure facility and a nonresponsive battery or generator backup may render a closed-circuit television (CCTV) system incapable of detecting a physical attack. An additional layer, such as physical security guards, can provide a degraded level of monitoring while technicians restore power and monitoring systems to normal functionality.[5]

53.1.2 Controlling versus Monitoring.
Monitoring refers to the observation, logging, and reporting of systems, components, and events. Data collected from monitoring systems may identify intruders, locate system vulnerabilities, confirm operational status, and provide confirmation that controls are online and in place. M&C systems operate in two modes, *continuous* and *batch*.

1. **Continuous mode** provides ongoing measurement and compliance assurance. Systems that operate in real-time, continuous mode present a more accurate, up-to-the-second view of an organization's operational environment.

2. **Batch mode** takes place at specific points in time. An annual audit often utilizes batch mode analysis, to evaluate system controls and scan for noncompliant processes.

Control refers to what we can manipulate and audit. Rather than merely observing and recording information about an unauthorized change in the operational environment, controls can restrict such activities based on predefined configurations and processes. Control systems ensure that the operational environment reflects stated policies and standards. The Control Objectives for Information and Related Technology (COBIT) section AI1.9 and ISO17799 section 9.7 identify the need to monitor system access and use (see Chapters 44 and 54 in this *Handbook* for discussion of these standards).

Organizations that depend on passwords for authentication should establish policies and draft procedures to meet those requirements. If the standard includes a 12-character minimum password length, with specific complexity requirements, then password controls would prohibit users from generating a 5-character password such as *PASS1*.[6]

Auditors inspect the operational environment to ensure controls meet regulatory requirements and that they reflect stated policies and standards. Typically, auditors evaluate a sample of control sets at scheduled intervals. These point-in-time, manual efforts provide insight into the infrastructure's degree of compliance. However, they do not provide the same level of efficiency as integrating automation into a framework that supports continuous information assurance.

The environment directly impacts system security. Temperature, humidity, air quality, and other variables may introduce unscheduled system failures in a work environment. Such variables outside our control that directly affect our information infrastructure require monitoring. Computer system management applications monitor internal components as well as temperature and voltage levels. Most organizations may not be able to control the temperature of an overheating processor or a lack of electricity provided by the utility company, but sensory thresholds in a monitoring application may trigger automated scripts or notify local personnel to initiate a system shutdown.

Organizations decide to implement systems with monitoring or control capabilities for a number of reasons including cost, logistical difficulties, and intentional design. For organizations with a nascent security program and incomplete understanding of the operational environment, monitoring can even provide a means of transition to future controls. As part of a cultural shift, monitoring can baseline current activities such as Internet usage and gradually introduce filtering controls to enforce security policies.

53.1.3   Control Loop.   For most environments, humans remain in the control loop. The *control loop* consists of the controller, the target system, a two-way communication path, and the transmitted data. The control loop is considered a closed loop when the process is automated and does not require human interaction; an open loop involves human interaction. The requirements of the system determine the loop type. When gas pipeline sensors detect a sudden decrease in pressure, an automated control system may need to perform an immediate lockdown to isolate the leak and send alert notifications. Leaving the loop open and waiting for human response may result in significant product loss and possibly in environmental and legal difficulties. In the case of operating system patch deployment, an open loop would allow a system to interrogate hosts, determine patch levels, and report status for further review and action. A supervisor could then approve specific patches to particular systems, after sufficient lab testing and coordination with system stakeholders.

53.1.4   Defining the Scope and System Requirements.   For M&C systems to operate effectively, management must clearly define the scope and system requirements. The *scope* specifically refers to the relevant processes and the people who interact with the computing environment. In order to monitor the Research and Development (R&D) Department for network communications regarding intellectual property, the scope may include IT/IS support staff, shared network resources, and existing processes to communicate with remote sites and external departments. The *system requirements* refer to the capabilities necessary to perform the desired functions of M&C. The requirements for monitoring R&D may include the need for real-time packet captures, an algorithm to identify intellectual property, automated alerts, and a reasonably secured collection device. Installing a network test access port (TAP) on the network uplink and then writing the captured traffic to a data collector for future analysis may seem logical. However, if a site survey identifies the use of undocumented cellular modems, unencrypted wireless hot spots, and personal e-mail accounts for sensitive communications, the network TAP will fail to address the original goal. In this case, the system requirements could expand to include control elements, such as network access control (NAC), mandatory IPSec communication policies, and security awareness training for R&D personnel.

53.2   CHANGE AND SECURITY IMPLICATIONS

53.2.1   Regulations, Policies, and Frameworks.   Compliance requirements and an organization's security program influence the implementation of M&C systems. Regulations may require access controls to restrict information to authorized users and sufficient monitoring to detect unauthorized attempts to gain access to information resources. In response to HIPAA, an organization may need to integrate additional log review procedures as well as appropriate measures to control all systems and processes that touch or potentially transfer personally identifiable information (PII). A public company that regularly generates financial reports needs adequate controls, to ensure accurate reporting. A security policy may reference the need to comply with Sarbanes-Oxley (particularly Section 404). The scope of an M&C system would then need to include computing resources, information process flows, and personnel with access to the financial information system. M&C systems should reflect the expectations of an organization's security policy and should fit into a relevant framework, such as COBIT. Utilizing a control framework provides logical management of M&C systems. The framework enables management to further understand enterprise processes and determine the need for risk mitigation or acceptance. PO9.7 in COBIT identifies control systems as part of the safeguard selection portion of risk management.

53.2.2 Change Management.   M&C systems enhance an organization's ability to identify and manage change in the information infrastructure. Knowing when authorized and unauthorized changes occur can improve problem resolution and can help in attack identification. In a data center environment, centralized system monitors track operational status. If database servers suddenly stop responding to network requests, a monitoring system could alert site staff to investigate the issue immediately. The cause may trace back to the remote exploit of a known vulnerability or to an unscheduled patch installation on production database servers during peak business hours. In either case, the information reported enables management to assess the situation and to implement corrective actions to reduce the likelihood of future attacks or procedural oversights.[7]

53.2.3 Configuration Protection.   When new systems are deployed or legacy systems are brought up to specific compliance levels, configuration concerns surface. Although policy-based standards may correctly define the appropriate configurations to protect the information assets, failure to consistently apply configuration templates or checklists introduces unnecessary complexity to vulnerability management. To address this challenge, M&C systems can centrally identify anomalies and bring systems back into compliance using predefined criteria. The PCI Data Security Standard (DSS) requires file integrity detection and alerting. However, an organization may also find it advantageous to deploy a system that will not only detect and alert, but also will automatically remediate, integrity discrepancies, and will quarantine the noncompliant files.

In industrial control systems (ICSs), programmable logic controllers (PLCs) store and run ladder logic programs to control hardware devices in the field. Programmers or automation specialists update these programs using specialized software for industrial networks. Modifying the program will directly affect the output of the actuators connected to the PLC. For that reason, the program must be protected from malicious and accidental alteration. Incorrectly modifying a tank sensor's set point to a value greater than the tank's capacity could result in product loss, requiring manual override. Using a password to protect the running program and layered network defenses, such as a network IPS, contribute to configuration protection in this scenario.

53.2.4 Performance Considerations.   Like all systems, M&C systems require resources to operate. Depending on the operational model, these resources may come from the same host system, a network connection, or a remote device. Failing to gauge the performance impact of a monitoring system could leave the operational environment in a degraded state. Additionally, deploying new systems during peak times in a business cycle may disrupt normal operations. Installing an enterprise file integrity monitoring system and performing a baseline on production systems during peak hours could lead to overutilization of system resources and could halt critical production jobs. Changes in M&C require planning and coordination with relevant business units and technical staff, to ensure that new systems meet both the business needs and the technical requirements to operate efficiently.

53.3   SYSTEM MODELS

53.3.1   Internal, One to One, One to Many, and Distributed.   M&C systems fit into four general models: internal, one to one, one to many, and distributed. The type of model used depends on the complexity of the system and the type of information required. These models may include autonomous systems as well as those that require human interaction.

1. An *internal system* is one of the simplest forms of M&C; it monitors or controls itself. A single server or network device may monitor processor utilization or other system components, to evaluate system performance issues. From a control perspective, an internal system may prohibit specific actions, such as unauthorized attempts to modify system files or to log on locally to the system.

2. The *one-to-one model* enables one system to monitor or control another independent system. This would be fairly costly, if heavily implemented in large environments. However, it can be quite useful in specific, high-availability situations that require failover. A network firewall, or critical server, would continually monitor and mirror the configuration and session information of the primary system. Once the primary system faults, the monitoring system would assume production functions, to avoid significant disruptions to the business environment. Another example may involve a two-node array of Internet proxy servers. Each server can monitor the other one and trigger an alert when a system faults. Until the system issue is resolved, the array may operate in degraded mode.

3. The *one-to-many model* is most common in enterprise environments. A central monitor and control system remotely manages a number of systems. From a central point, all targets may be interrogated and updated, without the need for manual, one-to-one changes. Centralized M&C can also reduce cost by simplifying M&C functions of multiple resources at various sites. This model also improves audit efficiency, as fewer systems must be reviewed to analyze changes throughout the information infrastructure.

4. The *distributed* model involves sensors and controls dispersed throughout the environment. The control elements may operate independently or remotely with input from a central control system. Each system feeds information to a central collector for secure log management, reporting, and data reduction. For organizations attempting to manage heterogeneous devices, a distributed model enables staff to implement the best M&C components for specific systems while still maintaining the ability to aggregate data into a centralized repository. This level of aggregation provides a wider view of change in the infrastructure.

53.3.2   Automation and the Human–Machine Interface.   Automation enables M&C systems to collect sensory information and to initiate a response, without the need for human interaction. Many information systems operate round the clock and

generate large volumes of event logs. Delegating to operations staff the task of manually reviewing thousands of event logs, and correlating events into meaningful information would be impractical. The purpose of M&C systems is to obtain meaningful intelligence from target systems and to report and correct anomalies. By automating data collection and reduction, managers and staff can review event summaries and respond to situations that have not already been automatically controlled.

The *human-machine interface* (HMI) is the point at which an operator communicates with a monitoring or control system. In industrial environments, HMI middleware transforms system activities into interactive screens, with enough capabilities for staff to perform specific job functions. The presentation of data is an important factor for HMI. Operators must have the ability to perform their job functions and to maintain adequate situational awareness, without access to unnecessary elements of a system. If the HMI interface runs on a standard personal computer, the operator should not be permitted to use the system to watch DVD movies or to participate in personal file-sharing networks on the Internet.

The time-saving value of automation has also been realized in autonomous vehicles, such as those implemented by the U.S. Department of the Navy. Unmanned undersea vehicles (UUVs)[8] reflect the distributed model, performing autonomous actions, with information exchange through a sensor grid within the Global Information Grid (GIG).[9] These systems can monitor environmental variables, detect threats such as unexploded ordinance, respond to change, and communicate with system owners. Much like intrusion detection and prevention systems in a network environment, UUVs can perform functions that may be unsuitable for direct human interaction. Both can perform continuous monitoring and collect a large volume of information that could not be collected through manual efforts. Also, similar to intrusion prevention systems in a network environment, a UUV may detect a threat, alert nearby UUVs, and report status back via the GIG. For network IPSs with worm-throttling capabilities, wormlike activities may be detected and cross-reported to additional sensors for rapid anomaly detection and containment.

53.3.3 Snapshots versus Real Time.   *Snapshots* provide a point-in-time view of a target system. Auditors use these for regularly scheduled audits. Scanning the environment on a monthly basis to confirm compliance can also unearth security trends within an environment. Trend reports identify security performance over time. An organization may notice a sharp decline in vulnerabilities after an external audit. Over time, without a stable vulnerability management program, the number of vulnerabilities will return to preaudit levels. Snapshots do not provide immediate or ongoing information on changes or corrective actions made to production systems. Additionally, snapshots will not verify that a control is working all of the time, only during the time that the snapshot was taken. If frequent changes impact a critical system during unexpected intervals, real-time M&C may be necessary. Real-time M&C can also address regulatory requirements and point the way toward proactive security.

Real-time monitoring refers to persistent, ongoing observation of a target. *Real-time control* refers to a control system's ability actively to influence its target. Industrial environments depend on information gathered through real-time M&C. When liquefied natural gas (LNG) travels through an LNG terminal,[10] operators should not have to wait until the tanker is empty in order to confirm that any of the product successfully transferred to the storage tanks. An M&C system can continually monitor the volume of product leaving the vessel, compare that data to the volume entering the storage container, trigger alerts if a leak is detected, and initiate a shutoff to avoid product loss. When allocating and distributing resources to meet demand, real-time monitoring provides overseers with an immediate understanding of the areas of need. In a network environment, this may include peak network usage during an accounting cycle or daily floods of lunchtime Internet traffic. In industrial areas, real-time monitoring can detect where electric grid managers should route additional power resources to meet demand, how much to pull from reserves, as well as when to implement rolling blackouts to maintain grid integrity.[11]

For Internet-facing Web sites, real-time monitoring would identify a distributed denial of service (DDoS) attack and alert staff. With real-time control, a network security device could throttle down or block the attack traffic. For nonmalicious traffic floods, the Web site host might utilize an intelligent load balancer and geographically dispersed reserve systems to redirect requests to available resources. DS13.3 in COBIT identifies the need for adequate event logging to analyze activities over time. However, without well-planned, automated processes, and data reduction, the volume of data generated from snapshots and real-time activities will overwhelm staff. Through centralized data collection and reduction, security auditors can evaluate the results of both real-time and snapshot reporting. This combination can identify general trends, ensure that M&C systems continually operate, and preserve evidence of a real-time attack.

53.3.4   Memory Dumps.   Memory dumps are representations of the data in memory. Memory dumps are used most typically after a system failure, but they are also useful in forensic research when investigators want the maximum amount of information possible from the system. There are two approaches to obtaining copies of memory: online, using diagnostic utilities while the system is running, and off-line, from magnetic storage media to which memory regions are copied.

53.3.4.1   *Diagnostic Utilities.*   Diagnostic utilities are system software routines that that can be used for debugging purposes. Also known as *debug* utilities, these programs run at maximum privilege (*root* or *supervisor* level, or their equivalents) and allow the privileged user to see or modify any portion of memory. The utilities usually print or display the contents of memory regions in a variety of formats such as binary, octal (base 8), or hexadecimal (base 16), with conversion to ASCII for easier readability. The utilities generally can provide immediate access to memory structures such as terminal buffers that allow the analyst to see what specific users are typing or seeing on their screens, file buffers that contain data in transit to or from specific open files, spoolers (print buffers), and program-specific regions such as data stacks. Because debug utilities also allow modification of memory regions, they are to be used with the utmost circumspection; for security reasons, it is wise to formulate a policy that no debug utility with root access can be run without having two people present. In high-security operations, the output of debug utilities should be logged to paper files for proof that no unauthorized operations were carried out using these programs. Access to privileged debug programs should be tightly controlled, such as by strict access-control lists or even by encryption using restricted keys.

53.3.4.2   *Output to Magnetic Media or Paper.*   One method of doing a memory dump and follow-up analysis is by copying the data from memory onto magnetic media such as tape, removable disks, or rewriteable CDs. Although it was once practical to print the entire contents of memory to paper, the explosive growth of memory sizes makes such printing impractical in today's systems. In 1980, for example, a large multiuser minicomputer might have 1 megabyte of RAM available, so that the printout was a quite manageable, half-inch-thick stack of paper. At the time of this writing, however, when it is common to see PCs with 256 megabytes of RAM, a single printout of the entire contents of memory could be several feet thick.

Copying memory to a static storage medium is, therefore, preferred for memory dumps following system crashes.

53.3.4.3 Navigating the Dump Using Exploratory Utilities.
On production systems using reliable operating systems, crashes are rare and are generally explored thoroughly to identify the causes of the anomaly. Generally after creating a dump it is necessary to study it looking for the problem and then correcting it. For large-memory systems, exploratory utilities are used to speed the search for problems in the dump by allowing the analyst to find any named system table or other memory region.

53.3.4.4 Understanding System Tables.
System tables are directories of system data where each datum is identified by an assigned label, by its position in the table, or by pointers from other tables. An understanding of system tables is essential in analyzing system problems.

Regardless of the details of the operating system and the system-specific names of tables, some of the important system tables include:

- **Process control table,** Pointers to the process tables for each process that is running on the system or that was running when the copy of memory was obtained
- **Process tables.** Detailed information about each process, with pointers to all the tables for that particular process
- **Data stacks.** All the variables used by specific processes
- **Buffers.** Data in transit to or from files and devices, such as disks and terminals
- **Memory management tables.** Lists of available memory blocks
- **Interprocess communications tables.** For example, information about resources locking or any logical flags used by multiple processes

Working with someone who understands the detailed structure of the operating system tables can be critically important for security work in which investigators must determine exactly what happened during an intrusion or other unauthorized use of a system.

53.3.4.5 Security Considerations for Dump Data.
Memory dumps must be secured while in use and destroyed when appropriate. The dump contains the totality of a system's information in memory, including such data as:

- Passwords that had just been typed into terminal buffers for use in changing logons or for accessing restricted subsystems and applications
- Encryption keys
- Confidential data obtained from restricted files and not authorized for visualization by operations staff (e.g., medical data from personnel files)
- Financial data that could be used in frauds
- National security information restricted to higher levels of clearance than the system administration

53.4   TARGETS AND METHODS.   This section provides an overview of the general classes of logging; Section 53.5 discusses specific types of log file records and their applications in system management, security management, and forensic analysis.

53.4.1   Overview.   Targets and methods used to perform control and monitoring vary, based on the business scope and the target system functions. Targets include process flow, job scheduling, network connectivity, environmental measurement, system state assurance, system component status, process activities, configuration settings, file system information, and access control. Current regulations may include only a subset of an organization's information systems in the scope of compliance. Changes to the infrastructure and compliance requirements are inevitable. It is important to implement scalable and flexible M&C in order to accommodate future needs.

53.4.2   Process Flow and Job Scheduling.   Some organizations use a combination of mainframe and distributed system resources. The mainframe group may use a particular batch job scheduler to process and monitor job status and output. Other distributed systems throughout the organization might use their own schedulers and logging capabilities. The complexity of this design, however, does not facilitate enterprise-wide monitoring and auditing. A centralized job scheduler may be necessary to monitor and control job flow. The centralized system will need to connect to disparate systems to collect job status and initiate commands. For management, an enterprise view of job scheduling can identify unnecessary complexity and redundancy, leading to future process improvement. When shifting to a central job scheduling system, it may seem desirable to shift the entire environment immediately or possibly to revert to a central mainframe. However, a gradual migration to centralized M&C would be a more ideal method of change.

53.4.3   Network Connectivity.   *Network connectivity* refers to the devices, protocols, and communication media (wired or wireless) used in a computing environment. A network operations center will want to monitor the status of network links, health indicators of critical devices, and data streams traversing the network. In a layered environment, physical access to the network cabling may be secured in cable raceways and network closets or at distribution points. Devices will be up to date and configured according to best practices. Unnecessary protocols will be controlled by blocking or routing suspicious traffic to network black holes and honeynets for further intrusion analysis. Network intrusion prevention systems (IPSs) can identify a communications anomaly, block the communication exchange, log the event, and trigger an administrative alert. Prevention requires planning and sufficient controls to deny an attack from achieving its goal. A method to implement M&C for sensitive network nodes may involve moving nodes to isolated segments, deploying in-line network IPSs, and utilizing host-based security agents. Additional enterprise security assessment tools may also scan, report, generate tickets, propose remediation measures, and analyze security trends over time.

In addition to monitoring general network connectivity, some networks are specifically deployed for the purpose of M&C. Legacy industrial systems now integrate common Ethernet networking elements into mechanical, electromechanical, and electronic environments. Wireless continues to emerge as an alternative means of M&C. The Zigbee[12] specification utilizes the IEEE 802.15.4 standard to provide ad hoc, local networking connectivity. Zigbee is primarily used for M&C. In a plant floor or outdoor facility, additional cabling for M&C systems may be infeasible. A potential solution may be to integrate inexpensive, robust Zigbee control points. Organizations that continue to rely on dial-up modems and standard wired telephone communications may have a need to implement line taps or to detect rogue taps, within the bounds of the law. For geographically dispersed sites, satellite and leased-line network connections bring sites together to manage M&C data centrally.

53.4.4 Environmental Concerns.   Some environmental variables are easier to monitor than control. Whether we are using Zigbee to transmit sensory information or a software package to measure AC voltage irregularities, environmental measures provide additional situational awareness for information systems and staff. Humidity, temperature, smoke, and leaking water directly impact computing systems in a data center. Dedicated air-conditioning units and dehumidifiers can monitor and control humidity and temperature. Indeterminate sources of smoke or water leakage may be difficult to control with automated response, but monitoring and alert notification may trigger corrective procedures by staff in order to mitigate risk.

As part of a business continuity plan, it may become necessary for an organization to monitor and prepare for environmental threats such as floods, structural collapse, and power loss. A monitoring system, with early warning capability, could notify staff to report to an alternate work site or to prepare for contingency operations. In the event that an environmental threat disrupts control systems, staff must be capable of manual override. The EPA recommends familiarity with manual operations, in the event of a supervisory control and data acquisition (SCADA) system failure.[13] In addition to manual override, integrating redundant M&C systems with seamless failover can decrease the likelihood of operational disruptions.

53.4.5 System State.   The *system state* refers to a collection of critical variables on the target system. In industrial control systems, the system state may reflect the overall picture of an electrical grid, or it may reduce to whether a single valve is open or closed. A monitoring system may need to track running processes in memory, services, open port connections, system files, hardware status, and log data. When an antivirus application process fails to start, resulting in a subsequent malware infection, the monitoring system can trigger an alert so that staff or an automated control system can isolate the infection. One method of monitoring the system state is to run an *agent* on the host system. Software agents monitor a predefined list of items and report status on a regular basis to a central monitoring hub. When the agent fails to respond or "check in," the monitoring system can issue an alert to investigate the issue.

Host intrusion prevention systems (HIPS) protect the system state of nodes in a network environment. HIPS analyze activities based on signature and heuristic detection routines. They provide a reasonable means of Monitoring and Control (M&C), with the potential for centralized reporting and attack correlation. For postmortem analysis, memory dumps can be useful in analyzing problems with the system state. If a network monitoring system detected botnet-related activity originating from a system in human resources, capturing the live system state may be advantageous to an investigation. As part of the evidence collection process of forensics, controlling and preserving the system state requires specialized training and tools such as Helix.[14]

53.4.6 System Components.   Monitoring applications can track the usage and overall performance of system components, including CPU, memory, and storage media. Operating systems also have built-in tools to monitor components and store results in log files. Inventory management systems collect component-level information as well as software information as configured by operations staff. Six months after an equipment refresh, an audit may identify systems operating with only half of the originally purchased memory. The logged information will help to determine the scope of the issue.

Monitoring the performance of system components can also identify changes in business need or system abuse. With the deployment of a new Web portal, existing Web proxy servers may no longer be capable of handling the heavier load. Logged performance data would corroborate the need to expand the infrastructure or add additional capacity to existing systems. Performance set points trigger alerts when components depart from normal operating levels. The alerts may identify externally driven changes, such as voltage drops, or internal limits, such as maximum memory utilization. Heavy resource utilization on a historically idle PC running HMI may even point to misuse of the system for non-SCADA related activities, such as Internet surfing or video playback.

System component monitors most often attempt to identify overutilized CPUs, heavy memory consumption, and full storage media. However, identifying routinely under-utilized resources gives management the ability to reallocate resources to areas of need rather than purchase unnecessary additions to the infrastructure. Disk quotas control the allowable amount of usable media for users and applications. To protect a system from unintentional or malicious overutilization, quotas should be reviewed as part of a layered strategy. Virtual machines use storage, memory, and processor quotas to control the resources utilized on a host system. With large virtualization environments, an enterprise virtual manager system may be necessary to ensure adequate load balancing across all of the virtual system hosts as well as to determine if additional tuning is required to improve virtual machine performance.

53.4.7   Process Activities.   A *process* refers to a running program in a computing device. Processes may initiate at the system or user level and may contain multiple threads. M&C processes can prevent malware infections and can identify abnormal process activities. Antivirus systems typically address this area. The SQL Slammer worm targeted a vulnerable process over a network connection, injecting code into memory without writing to disk storage.[15] In addition to process monitoring, network traffic analysis and network IPSs could mitigate this type of activity. Using enterprise monitoring tools to aggregate critical process information on a number of systems will help to identify application issues, such as runaway processes.

Monitoring process activities can also play a role in software metering. Organizations may want to identify application usage for different departments, in order to avoid deploying unnecessary applications and paying higher licensing fees. Agents can centrally report elapsed time for target processes, for data aggregation, and for management report generation. For performance tuning and resource evaluation, agents can monitor CPU time for running programs. High CPU time would indicate high utilization of CPU resources. For behavior modification, organizations may choose to monitor and control unauthorized applications. Blocking the execution of known applications by file name or hash value can limit the level of follow-up required to locate and kill remote processes. Monitoring for uncategorized or unapproved processes may further help in identifying the cause of performance degradation on remote systems.

53.4.8   File System.   File system activities provide a wealth of auditing information. File systems store log data ranging from application errors to unauthorized authentication attempts. Just like IDS logging, file system logging requires performance tuning to aggregate the data and to avoid data loss. Logging every file access attempt and data modification on a system will quickly fill up an event log. If system owners configure the log file to overwrite when full, critical events may be lost. The volume of log entries also impacts network resources. A constant flow of file system activity log entries may create a network bottleneck and disrupt the data collection process. Focusing on critical system files, sensitive data, and configuration settings will decrease the number of log entries and provide a more targeted set of results.

The configuration files for operating systems and applications require layers of protection to avoid unauthorized modification. Much like the layers to be discussed in Section 53.5.4, regarding log record security, Access Control Lists (ACLs), encryption, digital signatures, and checksums can play a critical role in protecting objects within the file system. Attempts to bypass M&C systems may begin with configuration files and settings. End users attempting to bypass Internet Web filters may reconfigure their Web browsers to use a rogue proxy server. Attackers attempting to modify the configuration of a poorly secured Web server may leverage the security lapses to target additional systems connected to the internal network. Controlling changes to configuration settings via system policies and HIPS will mitigate these kinds of attacks.

53.4.9   Access Controls.   Access control is a central part of security management and compliance efforts. Organizations often rely on more than one stand-alone system for identification and authentication, including applications, network operating systems, and building security. As a result, they face significant challenges while attempting to communicate, aggregate, and manage access control events. Adding and removing staff to a secure environment may involve badge identification, security tokens, and passwords. An M&C system targeting access control will need to ensure that unauthorized personnel not have access to any physical or digital resources. Management may first need to develop a process flow with support from operations staff and business stakeholders.

Aggregating access logs and detailing failed login attempts and multiple user instances aid in the identification of system abuse. When users log on to network resources, they establish a *session* with the target system. Multiple sessions for the same user, at multiple sites, may indicate that a user account has been compromised or is being shared. Depending on the level of importance, this information may surface in an exception report, trigger an administrative alert, or result in an automated account lockout. Similarly, a series of invalid login attempts may reach a threshold and automatically disable the user account for a predefined period of time. This control minimizes the effort required to actively monitor system accounts while ensuring that attackers are not able to perform a brute-force attack on the credentials of an authorized user.

53.5   LOG MANAGEMENT

53.5.1   Log Generation.   A *log file* contains a record of events. This record is the basic building block for centralized M&C systems. These files serve as a digital audit trail for system activities. Operating systems and applications may contain built-in logging capabilities. However, logging is not always enabled, or it may even require additional tools to convert the output into a usable or aggregated form. The system monitors activities and writes relevant information as a log file entry. Operating system log files track application issues, access attempts, and system-wide problems. Thresholds and file sizes can be adjusted to meet the requirements of the environment. It may be unnecessary to write a log entry every time a user successfully opens or closes a file on an internal workgroup file server, but doing so would be necessary to enable success and failure auditing for users attempting to log on to a sensitive financial system.

Transaction logs take logging one step further, by storing copies of the actual changes made to a system. They have a fixed size, automatically generating a new file for future transactions. Most common in database applications, transaction logs can be used to rebuild a corrupt database. Using a known-good database backup and all of the transaction logs prior to the failure, databases can be rolled forward to a reliable point in time. Transaction logs should be actively monitored, as they can quickly consume large amounts of storage. Normally, committed transaction logs are purged after a successful backup. Other log types, such as Web site traffic, may automatically generate new log files once per day; these logs may not contain entire Web site transactions, but they will identify the visitor based on predefined criteria. The key here is the flexibility in determining what will be monitored and what format will work best for log generation.

Data retention policies must clearly define how long data should be retained, according to legal requirements and internally driven policy. Log file archiving and storage become problematic over time. System-level log files may reach maximum size and overwrite existing log data or trigger a system shutdown. Centralized log management systems may slow to a crawl when querying a relational database for data to export to a flat file. Log collection and analysis systems must be scalable enough to process large volumes of data that will increase in size and number over time. A system designed to handle an average load of 10GB per day, with a 12-month retention cycle, may require compression technology to manage efficiently a 200GB-per-day average load during the next fiscal year.

53.5.2 Types of Log File Records. A *log file* (sometimes known as an *audit trail*) traditionally contains records about transactions that have updated online files or otherwise represent events of interest (e.g., logging on to the system or initiating a process). Some database or application log files also may contain copies of records that were affected before or after the logged transaction. There are a number of different types of log file records, and each contains a specific kind of information. Typically, all the operating system log records are stored in files with a maximum configured size, and that are identified by monotonically increasing file numbers. When the file fills up, the operating system opens another one with the next number in sequence as its identifier. Because log file records of different types have different sizes, on some operating systems the log file is defined with a variable record length.

53.5.2.1 System Boot. The system boot log record contains information on booting up, or starting, the machine. Since this is related to a specific activity and generally to a specific area of the hardware or media, information on the boot can prove helpful when the boot fails and analysis needs to take place.

53.5.2.2 System Shutdown. The system shutdown log record contains information on when the system was shut down and by whom. This information can be invaluable when attempting to analyze a problem or find a saboteur. On systems that include emergency shutdowns (e.g., by calling routines such as *suddendeath* when system parameters fall outside the range of allowable values), the shutdown record may contain specific information about the cause of the emergency shutdown.

From a security standpoint, trustworthy system boot and system shutdown records can prevent a malefactor from concealing a shutdown followed by unauthorized boot to a diagnostic subsystem that would allow file manipulations without log records to track the operations. The boot records would show an unexplained gap between shutdown and boot.

53.5.2.3 Process Initiation. A *process* begins when a specific program is loaded and run by a particular user at a particular time. Log records for process initiation show when the various processes were initiated and who initiated them. These files provide a method of tracking employee activity as well as monitoring events that occur. In addition, such records allow cost recovery using chargeback at different rates for different programs or for program launches at different times of day. More important, the record of which programs were executed by whom at which times can be invaluable in forensic research.

53.5.2.4 Process Termination. When reviewing the process termination log record, an administrator will be able to tell when each process completed or was terminated for some other reason. Some systems may provide more information, such as why an unscheduled or abrupt termination occurred, but not all process termination log records provide that information. Process termination records typically include valuable statistical information such as:

- Which process spawned or forked the process in question
- Identification of any processes spawned by the processes
- Number of milliseconds of CPU used
- Number of files opened and closed by the process
- Total number of input/output (I/O) operations completed by the process
- Total size of the memory partitions allocated to the process
- Maximum size of the data stack
- Number and maximum size of extra data segments in memory
- How many swaps to virtual memory were needed during the existence of the process
- Maximum priority assigned to the process for scheduling by the task manager

53.5.2.5 Session Initiation. A *session* consists of the communications between a particular user and a particular server during a particular time period. Whenever a user logs on to a system and initiates a session, a record of that event can be found in the session initiation log record. Frequent review of these records provides important information to alert administrators that an intruder is in the system. For instance, if an administrator knows that an authorized user is on vacation and the session initiation log file shows that a session was initiated for that particular user's ID, chances are significant that an unauthorized party used the system via a borrowed or stolen user ID. These records are particularly valuable during forensic work.

53.5.2.6 Session Termination. When a session terminates, for whatever reason, a copy of the time when it terminated is generally stored in the session termination log record. Much like the process termination record, the session termination record can include a great deal of aggregated information about the activities carried out during the session, such as total I/O, total number of processes launched and terminated, total number of files opened and closed, and so forth.

53.5.2.7 Invalid Logon Attempts.   The invalid logon attempt file can prove invaluable in cases where logon attempts do not succeed. In some instances, the file can tell if the user attempted to log on with an incorrect password, if the user exceeded the allowed number of failed attempts, or if the user was attempting to log on at a seemingly unusual time. These log records can provide important information in cases where an administrator is attempting to track specific actions to a user or to ascertain if the logon failure was due to a simple error or to an attempted impersonation by an unwanted outsider. In hardwired networks, where every device has a unique identifier, the records usually include a specific identifier that allows administrators to track down the physical device used for the attempted logons.

53.5.2.8 File Open.   The file open log record provides information on when each specific file was opened and by which process; in addition, the record generally records the mode in which the file was opened: for example, exclusive read and write, exclusive read, exclusive write with concurrent read, append only, or concurrent read and write.

53.5.2.9 File Close.   The file close log record gives an administrator information regarding when the file was closed, by which process, and by what means. The file usually captures information on whether the user specifically closed the file or whether some other type of interruption occurred. The records usually include details of total read and write operations, including how many physical blocks were transferred to accomplish the total number of logical I/O operations.

53.5.2.10 Invalid File Access Attempts.   An important log record in the M&C effort, the invalid file access attempt shows the administrator when and to which files there were invalid file access attempts. The records generally show which process attempted the I/O and why it was refused by the file system (e.g., attempted write to a file opened for read-only access, violation of access control list, or violation of file-access barriers).

53.5.2.11 File I/O.   Whenever information is placed into, read out of, or deleted from a file (input/output), the information regarding those changes is captured in the file I/O log. As mentioned earlier, the log includes images of a record before and after it was accessed. The I/O log can be used in file recovery after system or application crashes. Coupled with transaction-initiation and termination records, such data can be used for automatic roll-back or roll-forward recovery systems.

The activities recorded here can prove especially helpful when trying to validate actions that were taken and to attribute them to specific individuals. Detailed logs are typical for databases, where a subsystem provides optional logging of all I/O. Application log records, designed and programmed by application developers, also typically allow administrators to enable such detailed logging.

53.5.2.12 System Console Activity.   The system console activity file provides information on any actions that originate from or are viewed at the system console. Typically, the system console includes not only logon and logoff records but also special requests, such as printer form mounts, specific tape or cartridge mounts, comments sent to the console by batch jobs, and free-form communications from users. The console file records all such activity as well as every command from the system operator, and the system responses to those commands. These records provide an excellent tool for investigators tracking down the specific events in a computer incident.

53.5.2.13   Network Activity.   Network activity files provide valuable information on activity taking place on the network. Depending on the sophistication and settings of the system an administrator is using, the information derived can be plentiful or scant. Specific devices may generate their own records on network activity; for example, routers, gateways, and firewalls may all keep their own log files. However, typically these are circular files in which records to be entered after the file is full are shifted to the start of the file, where they overwrite the oldest records. In forensic work, it is essential to capture such data before the information of interest is obliterated. Unfortunately, in many systems, the volume of network activity is so high that log files contain only the most recent minutes of traffic.

53.5.2.14   Resource Utilization.   A review of the resource utilization log records will show all of the system's resources and the level of utilization for each. By monitoring this file, administrators frequently make important decisions regarding modifying system configuration or expanding the system.

53.5.2.15   Central Processing Unit.   The CPU file shows the capacity and usage of the central processing unit for whichever system is being used and monitored. Based on this information, administrators can monitor when usage is heaviest and the CPU is most stressed, and can decide on utilization rules and requirements as well as on possible CPU upgrades. As in all log file analyses, any outliers (unusual values) and any unexpected change in usage can be investigated. Global CPU utilization records can be compared with the sum of CPU usage collected from process termination records; discrepancies may indicate stealth operation of unauthorized processes, such as malicious software.

53.5.2.16   Disk Space.   The log records for disk space show the amount of disk space originally available on a system, the amount of disk space used (and generally what type of files it is being used for), and the amount of disk space that remains free and available. Comparison of total disk space utilization with the total space allocated to all files can reveal problems such as *lost disk space* (i.e., space allocated to files that were never closed properly; such space is unusable by the file system because there are no pointers indicating that the disk sectors are actually supposed to be free). Such unallocated sectors or clusters also may be where malefactors hide data they have stored without authorization by bypassing the file system.

53.5.2.17   Memory Consumption.   Important information on the amount of memory in a system and the amount actually being used can be obtained from the memory consumption log records. Such records typically also include information on virtual memory usage. Therefore, they can provide warning of *thrashing* conditions, where memory segments are being copied to disk and read back from disk too often. Details of memory consumption may be useful in tracking down unauthorized processes such as worms.

53.5.2.18   System Level versus Job Level.   Different levels of monitoring, logging, and auditing may take place. Some of this may be preprogrammed, but in most environments it is possible to select the log records and related reports that are desired. For instance, a regular system level audit log may be produced at intervals, just to provide information that the system is up and running without any extraordinary problems. But an in-depth job level audit may take place more frequently, in order to monitor the specific job and ensure that it is running correctly and providing the information needed.

53.5.3 Automation and Resource Allocation
The importance and value of log management cannot be overemphasized. Utilizing secure, well-organized log management systems to monitor and respond to events can lower the administrative effort required to manage an infrastructure. With the growing demands of compliance and costs associated with data retention, it is important to include log management within the scope of the enterprise data retention policy. E-discovery laws and postmortem attack analysis rely on efficient access to accurate log information. Logs require system resources, ranging from media storage to CPU cycles and memory utilization. Trade-offs must be considered when setting aside potential business-generating resources for the purpose of infrastructure management.

Manually reviewing millions of log files on various systems, in different time zones and inconsistent formats, is unrealistic for staff. For geographically dispersed sites, real-time log transfers may be delayed due to limited bandwidth available via slow links. Not all logged information is of equal value. Some data records may tie directly to compliance issues, while others provide noncritical benefits to daily operations. Based on policy, management must determine what types of data must be aggregated and reduced in order to monitor and to ensure ongoing compliance. This is part of the scope definition process of M&C systems. Planners and implementers must not only scope current requirements but must ensure that the log management plan will scale to address future regulations and internal security requirements.

53.5.4 Log Record Security
An organization must protect its log records from unauthorized access and modification. The four most common methods of log record security are: access control lists, checksums, encryption, and digital signatures. Combining these methods, based on the system requirements, can adequately protect most log data. Attackers with unfettered access to unencrypted e-mail log files could download copies of the files and search them for sensitive information as well as modify or delete message content directly from the target server. This type of attack threatens every element of the Parkerian hexad.[16] In addition to the common concerns of confidentiality breaches and loss of data integrity, unauthorized access to log files may provide an attacker with additional information on the network environment. Vulnerability scanners may run at scheduled intervals and log detected issues to a central database. Leveraging aggregated data, an attacker can more efficiently compromise a network environment and evade detection routines accustomed to high-footprint reconnaissance.

Operating system and application-level access control lists (ACLs) restrict access to files. Some log files may be written to write-once, ready-many (WORM) media for auditors or legal staff. Operations staff may have no legitimate need to access such data. However, they may need to ensure that the communication flow operates continually. Databases can implement even more granular controls on specific records and fields, to avoid unnecessary information disclosure. Physical access controls to the media while in storage or in transit must also be considered when planning a M&C system for log data. Properly implemented ACLs can limit the level of log data exposure to authorized personnel and system processes.

Organizations subject to PCI DSS are required to implement integrity controls on log data. Historically, 32-bit cyclic redundancy checks (CRCs) generated checksums to guard against file alteration. Today, stronger cryptographic checksums, such as those generated by the SHA-2 family, provide a more reasonable level of integrity assurance.[17] Checksums do not require constant human interaction. For tamper protection, a monitoring system may baseline a system and store copies of files or their hash equivalents for periodic or real-time file comparison. Changes to logs or other critical files could then be centrally reported for manual investigation. A control system could automatically quarantine the unauthorized file and restore a copy of the original file.

Digital signatures use public key cryptography to provide data integrity and non-repudiation. These build on standard cryptographic checksums because they not only confirm file integrity but also identify who or what entity is providing that assurance. This becomes significant when controlling software distribution. Many organizations download third-party software updates over the Internet. To ensure package integrity, vendors can digitally sign the files to ensure that the recipient received an unaltered software update. For organizations that must submit reports to external recipients, such as government offices, digital signatures can decrease the paper trail and provide a more efficient, digital means of meeting regulatory requirements.

Encryption must be considered for log data in transit and at rest. Encrypting entire log files reduces the ability to view or alter the contents. It also increases the resource usage on the target system during the encryption process. Like checksums, the keys required for decryption should be stored in a secure location, to increase the difficulty in defeating the control. Utilizing whole-disk encryption and then transferring a log file over a network in plaintext is not a consistent method of log security. Establishing secure network links, such as implementing IPSec, provides end-to-end link security. A combination of network and system-level encryption may be necessary to secure log files and other sensitive information properly.

The chain of custody should also be considered when planning a log management system. Some log data may need to be used in court. Without a verifiable audit trail, the contents may be inadmissible. A documented chain of custody for media transfers between staff and sites can validate physical controls. Implementing cipher block chaining (CBC) can further protect against unauthorized changes to log data. The previous log file ciphertext would XOR with the current plaintext to create a new value for encryption operations. This concept can also be useful for record sets within log files and database applications, as it will identify record deletions and other data modifications. See Chapter 7 in this *Handbook* for more information on cryptography.

53.6 DATA AGGREGATION AND REDUCTION

53.6.1 Centralized Data Stores.
Systems generate logs in a variety of formats that are not always easy to access. The first phase in data aggregation is ensuring that logging is working properly on the target system. The second phase, gradually connecting logging points to a centralized data store, leverages existing logging mechanisms to create an enterprise view of events. Centralized data storage provides a single point of analysis and audit, without the time-consuming process of manually interrogating individual systems throughout the environment. Log data must be communicated in a secure manner. An agent-based system needs to establish a secure communication channel with the primary collector, to avoid distributing log details to an unauthorized

collector. This security measure may be built into the aggregating application, or it may utilize IPSec over controlled network links.

A major problem with large volume data stores, processing time, creates a conflict between complete log processing and incident response time. Depending on the resources available, it may be more economically advantageous to store secured log data in compressed archives while using agent-based monitoring only to report critical security issues or operational problems to central storage. The time and effort to log, parse, and report on every data block received by the central collector may exceed internal security policy requirements and the perceived cost benefit. Filtering out noncritical events and alerts would then be part of the baselining process for the central M&C system. Storing and analyzing entire log files may serve as a secondary (slower) monitoring mechanism, while the security specific alerts are handled on an immediate basis.

53.6.2 Filtered Queries.   The volume of log file records can be overwhelming and generally impossible for operations staff to review individually and on a regular basis. Centrally storing the data does not change the infeasibility of the task. It does however lend itself toward improved data reduction. Transforming raw data into a meaningful, reduced form can minimize the noise and enable staff and automated processes to target higher-priority activities. Running filtered queries against log records can provide more immediate results on potential attacks or system issues. A scheduled query may list all failed logon attempts. Additional filtering may drill down to a set of computing assets (e.g., servers processing credit card data) or user types such as root-level accounts. Another more specific query may only list network traffic anomalies between the R&D Department and an array of Internet proxy servers.

53.6.3 Analyzing Log Records.   Log records can be valuable to the system administrator, but only if they are put to use. Properly using a log file requires monitoring and reviewing its records and then taking actions based on the findings. Such analysis typically uses utilities provided by the supplier of the operating system or by third parties, such as commercial software companies or freeware distributors.

53.6.3.1 Volume Considerations.   Someone must make a decision regarding how big log files should be. Such a decision is generally made by the system administrator and is based on what is considered useful and manageable. If money is involved—for instance, if additional storage capacity is needed—the chief technology officer (CTO), chief information officer (CIO), chief operating officer (COO), system auditor, and a variety of other staff members might be called on to review the activities and volumes of the logs and to participate in any decisions regarding expenditures for new equipment. However, in the three decades preceding this writing in 2008, disk space costs have fallen about 40 percent per year compounded annually—from approximately $488,000 per gigabyte to approximately $0.29 per gigabyte in constant dollars, so disk space is not much of an issue anymore.[18] More important is that log files, like any file, may be left in an inconsistent state if the system crashes; closing a log file and opening a new one in the series is a prophylactic measure that ensures that less information will be lost in disk I/O buffers if there is a system crash.

53.6.3.2 Archiving Log Files.   Archiving is a very important part of making and using log files. Every company needs to decide how long to keep its log files and where to keep them. Decisions of this nature sometimes are made based on space considerations, but more frequently are made based on legal requirements within specific industries. Some companies may decide to keep materials for a year or two, while others may be mandated by law to retain archived log files for seven or eight years.

The decisions regarding the archiving of log files should never be made arbitrarily; in every instance a careful review and check of company, legal, and industry requirements should be conducted. Based on the findings of that review, a written policy and procedures should be produced. Every company needs to tell its employees what these policies and procedures are, so they can be aware of what materials are being kept, where they can be found, and how they can be accessed.

53.6.3.3 Platform-Specific Programs for Log File Analysis.
Many operating systems are in existence, and although there are certain similarities in how they function, there are also differences. Special training on each specific operating system may be necessary in order to do a correct analysis of the platform-specific log files it generates.

53.6.3.4 Exception Reports.
The volume of log file records can be overwhelming. For example, a multiuser system with 10,000 users per day (e.g., a large automated banking application) could generate millions of records of the logons, logoffs, file openings, file closings, and record changes alone. Exception reports allow the analyst to focus on specific characteristics (e.g., withdrawals of more than $200 from ATMs at a specific branch between 2:00 A.M. and 3:00 A.M. on last Tuesday night) or on statistical characteristics, such as the largest withdrawals in the network at any time. Such tools greatly simplify detection and analysis of anomalies and are particularly helpful in tracking down criminal behavior or other unauthorized activities.

53.6.3.5 Artificial Intelligence.
In our current advanced electronic society, artificial intelligence (AI) programs have been developed that actually can check user profiles for unusual and suspicious activities and generate an alert and a report whenever these types of activities are noticed. Because of the preprogrammed artificial intelligence and the parameters set, instead of having to launch the program and monitor it, the system launches the program on a regular basis and collects the data. Anything of an unusual nature causes an alert to be generated.

53.6.3.6 Chargeback Systems.
Chargeback systems, such as internal billing services and those used by external service bureaus, prove valuable in monitoring and tracing system activities through their logs. In some states and cities, legislation requires that these types of services keep accurate logs for audit purposes. The original records are used not only for tracking but also in court cases as evidence. In most situations, both internal and external services are the secondary "proof" of transactions, while the initial system logs provide the primary proof.

The log file records provide the basis for sophisticated billing algorithms that encourage rational use of resources. In addition, because unexpected changes in expenses can stimulate interest by accounting staff and managers, billing systems sometimes can help identify unauthorized usage, such as online gambling, excessive downloads from the Internet, and installation of unauthorized code for processing, using idle time on a computer.

53.6.4 Dashboards.
Dashboards consolidate information into a relevant and easily understood summary. Text, visual, and auditory elements may be employed, depending on management needs and system capability. Dashboards build on

Web-based technology with a database backend to present a high-level overview of operational status at near-real-time refresh rates. Charts, graphs, LED-style indicators, system visualizations, and alert banners enhance the dashboard experience when used in moderation. Employees typically reference dashboards from a standard Web browser or on a large video screen mounted in a common area.

Department and management-specific dashboards should also be considered when implementing specialty M&C systems. Depending on the sensitivity of the information, rotating the dashboards on common screens or within the Web portal itself may provide an opportunity to increase employee awareness of company-wide and department-specific performance. Associates may learn from Internet security sources, the current level of business risk, of current operational performance (e.g., system uptime, and product generated, or sales volume), or even of the current state of cybersecurity.[19]

Rather than implement dashboards, some organizations continue to rely on a myriad of system consoles to monitor and control specific elements within an infrastructure. As a result, they miss out on the benefits of quickly understanding the state of the environment by leveraging enterprise data reduction tools through a ubiquitous Web interface. System management consoles often cater more to technical operations staff than to upper management. Some vendors attempt to provide all-in-one consoles for various system management tasks. However, they generally do not provide a broad, holistic view of the business environment. As a result, system management consoles and dashboards will likely continue to coexist for the foreseeable future.

53.7 NOTIFICATIONS AND REPORTING

53.7.1 Alerts. Log management must include layers of automation to reduce the time required to review and respond to events in the environment. How an M&C system deals with alerts will directly impact the security of the target system. Overwhelming operators with too many alerts will result in slower problem-response time as well as the potential to ignore critical issues. The purpose of alerts is to improve responsiveness to major issues, such as a leaking pipeline or multisite network outage. Alerts may be configured at specific set points, so that a responder will be notified only when the attack threshold is reached. Elements that are controlled in the environment may have a higher threshold for alert notification. A sudden influx of malware from the Internet may be immediately detected and filtered at the network edge. Notifying operations staff of a large volume of malware may be useful. However, spamming security administrators with alerts on every blocked attack would be an inefficient use of alert notification resources.

Additionally, the means of alert notification play an important role in business continuity and disaster recovery. Out-of-band monitoring systems may detect a network equipment error that could not otherwise be detected by the failing device itself. For alert recipients, multiple notification means may be necessary. E-mail, pager, cell phone, and SMS messaging are the most common forms. Alert visualization is another valuable means for operators actively monitoring the environment. Similar to the dashboard concept, visualization can reduce data collected from sensors into a visual map, with graphical indicators to identify system issues. A combination of dashboard-style alert monitoring and targeted message delivery may provide the best coverage for issues of high importance.

In industrial environments, operators utilize HMI tools to maintain situational awareness with field equipment. HMI uses virtual buttons and other visual elements to simplify industrial functions. If alerts are frequently generated for noncritical activities, staff will clear the alert list and ignore them over time. Ignoring alerts for critical issues can directly impact production and lead to costly repairs. In this situation, a management dashboard could display performance statistics that may trigger a field investigation into the root cause of declines in production performance.

53.7.2 Trend Analysis and Reporting. Data aggregation, reduction, and correlation lay the foundation for trend analysis. Data related to compliance requirements can be analyzed to determine the pace of security improvements within the organization. Further analysis may identify the level of consistency of an internal security program as well as the true drivers of audit compliance. If system vulnerabilities and business risk continually peak in between scheduled external audits, management will need to investigate the root cause of this unstable, cyclic behavior.

Chargeback refers to the ability to charge for the use of IT services. Some organizations include these costs in the overhead of doing business rather than billing individuals and departments. Regardless of the financial preference, enabling chargeback monitoring in an environment provides an understanding of how information resources are used. If the Marketing Department utilization has grown from 40 to 70 percent of the Internet bandwidth, and the Help Desk use has expanded from 30 to 50 percent of the grid computing resources, the trends may encourage management to realign resources to meet business demand or investigate resource abuse. Monitoring resource utilization and demand can also benefit development and testing cycles, so that production resources are properly allocated.

Exception reports focus on specific data anomalies, such as employee expense reports that suddenly exceed USD $3,000. Managers may want to employ continuous monitoring of the financial system to evaluate exception report trends. In addition to misuse and fraud, exception reports can identify system problems. Generating exception reports for systems that regularly operate below acceptable performance levels may point to a failing component. Management, at an industrial site that regularly fails to account for missing product, may uncover procedural issues that result in wasted material or defective equipment that must be repaired to resolve the ongoing product loss. Exception reports may also identify an isolated issue or a widespread problem. If change management recorded the replacement of hardware on five pipeline segments and they all started leaking at the same time, aggregated log data and exception reports would support the need for hardware and procedural reviews. Or an exception report, based on sensor data collected in November 2002 along the Denali Fault,[20] may correlate with an environmental issue (e.g., earthquake) that would possibly explain the cause of an equipment malfunction.

53.8   MONITORING AND CONTROL CHALLENGES

53.8.1 Overview. Legacy systems do not always possess sufficient M&C for today's business and regulatory requirements. The art of retrofitting security into a legacy system requires overcoming physical, technical, and psychosocial barriers. Physical barriers range from wired ICS installations to wireless mobile communications. Technical issues include learning to detect and monitor unique communication protocols and managing systems that historically operated in isolated locations with little or no security oversight. Psychosocial challenges are often the most difficult. Organizations and business sectors unaccustomed to mature M&C systems typically deny the need for such systems. Rationalization attempts generally include denial that an attacker would ever target their systems, claims that the business is running well, and concerns that additional changes or complexity will likely disrupt production. Security awareness training can address these misperceptions, while pointing to the lack of M&C data available to support any claims that operations is running as efficiently and securely as it should.

53.8.2   Industrial Control Systems.   Industrial control systems (ICSs) operate in a number of industries, including oil, water, and power. ICSs are generally divided into distributed control systems (DCSs) and supervisory control and data acquisition (SCADA). DCSs are more commonly associated with processes such as oil refining. SCADA systems involve more human interaction via HMI, and they collect data from a number of remote devices. Some systems contain elements of both DCS and SCADA. Security issues have increased, due to network connectivity and perceived risk to the critical infrastructure of the United States. These systems are expected to continue to integrate on a global scale, with improved, centralized data aggregation and reporting. Management will find value not only in aggregating their own organization's data but in collaborating in industry forums to implement more stable, interoperable, and secure industrial M&C systems. Like mainframes, SCADA systems no longer operate in an isolated environment. Technicians dial in with a modem or through a virtual private network (VPN) tunnel over the Internet to manage a PLC remotely. Remote sites often communicate via leased lines, satellite, and dial-up modems. Some industrial sites utilize Zigbee wireless equipment rather than installing standard cabling to monitor and control remote devices.

M&C challenges for these systems include authentication, network security, configuration protection, and physical security. Historically, authentication has not been required to use a PC to communicate directly with a PLC over a SCADA network. Some vendors now attempt to build authentication into the HMI. However, the network protocols used in SCADA (e.g., MODBUS/TCP, DNP3) can still send unsolicited messages to the PLC to execute arbitrary commands. Configuration protection is typically associated with the running program on a PLC, which may have a weak or nonexistent password. From the operator standpoint, HMI usually runs on an unpatched PC with application-level security controls. These controls can be bypassed by attacking the improperly secured, underlying operating system. Physical security remains a challenge, as equipment may not be located in a secured area, or operators may lack adequate security awareness training to implement proper security procedures. Fortunately, these M&C systems may leverage existing information security resources to mitigate risk in a layered architecture. NIST SPEC PUB 800-82 clearly describes the security landscape surrounding these systems. Network firewalls, intrusion prevention systems, and more robust physical security would all contribute to a more secure SCADA environment. Vulnerability detection tools now target SCADA protocols, with the goal of detecting vulnerabilities and mitigating risk. Developing more secure communication protocols, and establishing configuration protection guidelines, would further improve the authentication weaknesses in SCADA deployments.

53.8.3   Mobile Computing.   As we continue to integrate mobile and distributed computing systems, the complexity and difficulty required to secure systems increases. We have more variables to address. Information flows even further from the traditional network perimeter. With advances in deperimeterization, M&C systems must ensure that data remains secure while in transit and at rest, as determined by organizational policy. Mobile technologies communicate over wireless links, invisible to traditional M&C systems. Some wireless devices require centralized system management but rarely connect to the corporate network. Mobile encryption and mandatory VPN connectivity help to control data storage and transmission. With centralized policies, these systems ensure consistent data communications throughout an organization.

Radio-frequency identification (RFID) monitoring systems wirelessly identify and collect information from the target system. NIST 800-98 describes the technological benefits and risks related to implementing this technology. M&C systems often collect sensitive information. The privacy issues inherent in RFID will require thorough risk assessment, to avoid potential data loss. Tagging all of an organization's employees with RFID badges that contain PII subject to HIPAA regulations would be unwise, as the RFID tags could potentially be accessed from over one meter away, without the holder's knowledge. From an inventory perspective, RFID tags provide a means to automate site audits of company assets or to collect asset information without manually writing it down. To avoid compromise, the device standards use integrity checks (CRC) and require a password to render them nonresponsive.

53.8.4 Virtualization. Organizations use a variety of computing equipment to meet their business needs. Some equipment may remain underutilized, while critical database servers require additional disk space and working memory. Virtualization provides the ability to slice and pool computing resources into more efficient, targeted, and often portable business resources. Virtual systems generally consist of physical hardware, a virtualization interface (VI), and a virtual machine (VM). The VM may be an application or an entire operating system. Since the VI oversees the VMs, we must implement appropriate M&C at the VI layer as well as within and around the VMs.

Users of a virtualized operating system may not be able to detect that it is virtualized. For example, a Web hosting company may wish to provide dedicated virtual servers to its customers without the additional expense of dedicated hardware. In this situation, the organization could deploy FreeBSD servers, implement a degree of virtualization using "jails"[21] to provide a high level of compartmentalized, system-level access to customers. An operator with root access to a jailed environment should not see the processes executed by other jails nor the underlying system hosting the jails. However, the host system owner may monitor or control elements of the host system as well as those within jailed environments. Additional monitoring of the host system may also be necessary, to detect jailbreak attempts.

Another type of virtualization, *paravirtualization*, utilizes a *hypervisor* as the VI between the hardware and the VM. Rather than create identical jailed environments, a hypervisor can be used to support more than one type of guest VM, such as Ubuntu, Fedora, and PC-BSD. This configuration is possible because the hypervisor handles all communications (hypercalls) between the hardware and the VMs. Along the same lines as a FreeBSD host with jails, the hypervisor can monitor and control activities within and around the VMs with varying degrees of transparency to the VM user. The capability of stealth VM monitoring makes virtualization a useful monitoring tool for honeypot research. For a greater level of system assurance, organizations will need tools to detect and prevent attacks against the hypervisor.

Portability, an advantage of virtualization, poses a challenge for M&C systems. VMs can migrate from one hardware device to another frequently, while the integrity of an off-line VM is unknown. In a managed, virtualized infrastructure, performance degradation issues detected in the VI may trigger VMs to migrate from one physical server to a less utilized resource. An unstable VM may also be manually forced off-line and rapidly redeployed using a backup virtual disk, without disrupting other VMs sharing the same physical hardware. Tracking these moving targets requires reliable access to the virtual pool of resources, documentation mapping virtual to physical resources, as well as a clearly defined policy for virtual system provisioning. For example, an organization with policies that require clear separations between confidential and public systems should prohibit the same hypervisors from managing both payroll applications and public kiosk VMs on the same hosts.

53.9 SUMMARY.   Monitoring and control systems protect our business environments from undesirable events and operational inefficiency. We may never control every element of our information systems. However, we must be able to identify what needs to be monitored and what must be controlled. Regulations and internal policies define those needs. Frameworks, such as COBIT, provide a means to organize controls into specific objectives. The selection of an appropriate system model is based on scope and the business requirements. Human interaction plays a critical role in many legacy systems. However, to meet the growing need for reporting and continuous assurance, organizations must integrate automation into M&C systems. Even with automation, unique challenges surface in industrial controls, mobile computing, virtual systems, grid computing, and other network environments. In these situations, we must return to the fundamental questions of M&C:

- What are the compliance and internal policy requirements?
- What systems, components, or processes need to be monitored or controlled?
- What model will be used to monitor or control the target?
- Where will the data be stored?
- How will the data records be secured?
- What kind of data reduction and reporting is required?
- Who or what will respond to detected issues?
- What measures exist to protect M&C systems from compromise?

Monitoring, control, and auditing interrogate information systems, identify problems, initiate corrective measures, and generate meaningful information on the state of our infrastructure. The systems may involve human interaction or function in an automated, closed-loop format. Systems generate log files based on system activities, store them in secure locations, and enable aggregators to collect and reduce the data into actionable information. Although log aggregation improves the analysis process, the resources required to store and manipulate the data can become problematic. Not all events are useful. In order to manage reasonable data volumes, only specific activities should be logged or collected by the central management system. Log file data provides a means to analyze events historically at any measured point in time—a necessary part of infrastructure management. Organizations need to understand the value of assets, align business with regulatory requirements, and find new ways to leverage M&C to improve operational performance.

53.10 REFERENCES

Control Objectives for Information and Related Technology (COBIT): www.isaca.org/cobit.

ISO/IEC 17799:2005: www.iso.org/iso/en/prods-services/popstds/informationsecurity.html.

Karygiannis, T., B. Eydt, G. Barber, L. Bunn, and T. Phillips. NIST Special Publication 800-98. *Guidelines for Securing Radio Frequency Identification (RFID) Systems.*

U.S. Department of Commerce, April 2007, http://csrc.nist.gov/publications/nistpubs/800-98/SP800-98_RFID-2007.pdf.

Payment Card Industry Data Security Standard (PCI DSS): www.pcisecuritystandards.org.

Sarbanes-Oxley Act of 2002. 15 U.S.C. 7201. Public Law 107-204. 107th Congress; www.sec.gov/about/laws/soa2002.pdf.

Stouffer, K., J. Falco, and K. Kent. NIST Special Publication 800-82. *Guide to Supervisory Control and Data Acquisition (SCADA) and Industrial Control Systems Security*. U.S. Department of Commerce, September 2006, http://csrc.nist.gov/publications/drafts/800-82/2nd-Draft-SP800-82-clean.pdf.

53.11   NOTES

1. For more information on intrusion detection systems and unified threat management appliances, see Chapter 27 in this *Handbook*.

2. For more information about DoS attacks, see Chapter 18 in this *Handbook*.

3. For more information on incident response, see Chapter 56 in this *Handbook*.

4. Legislation on Notice of Security Breaches. National Conference of State Legislatures, www.ncsl.org/programs/lis/cip/priv/breach.htm.

5. For more information on physical and facilities security, see Chapters 22 and 23 in this *Handbook*.

6. See Chapter 28 in this *Handbook* for discussion of identification and authentication.

7. For more information on software development and quality assurance, see Chapter 39 in this *Handbook*; for information on managing software patches, see Chapter 40.

8. U.S. Department of Navy, "The Navy Unmanned Undersea Vehicle (UUV) Master Plan," November 9, 2004, www.navy.mil/navydata/technology/uuvmp.pdf.

9. Department of Defense Directive No. 8100.1, "Global Information Grid (GIG) Overarching Policy," September 19, 2002, www.defenselink.mil/cio-nii/docs/d81001p.pdf.

10. Federal Energy Regulatory Commission, "Existing LNG Terminals," www.ferc.gov/industries/lng/indus-act/terminals/exist-term/everett.asp.

11. Consortium for Electric Reliability Technology Solutions, "Demand-Response, Spinning-Reserve Demonstration—A New Tool to Reduce the Likelihood of Outages," News release, July 26, 2006, http://certs.lbl.gov/press/press-7-26-06.html.

12. Zigbee Alliance: www.zigbee.org/.

13. U.S. Environmental Protection Agency, "Suggested Pre-Hurricane Activities for Water and Wastewater Facilities," www.epa.gov/safewater/hurricane/pre-hurricane.html.

14. Helix by e-Fense: www.e-fense.com/helix/.

15. CERT® Advisory CA-2003-04 MS-SQL Server Worm, January 27, 2003, www.cert.org/advisories/CA-2003-04.html.

16. See Chapter 3, page 3 in this *Handbook*.

17. J. Wack, M. Tracy, and M. Souppaya, NIST Special Publication 800-42, *Guideline on Network Security Testing*, U.S. Department of Commerce, October 2003, http://csrc.nist.gov/publications/nistpubs/800-42/NIST-SP800-42.pdf.

18. An HP7925 120MB disk drive cost $25,000 in 1980, about $36,366 in 2008 currency. The cost per GB in 1980 was ~$488,000 in 2008 dollars. In 2008, a Hitachi 7K1000 1 terabyte drive for sale at consumer stores costs ~$300, or about $0.29/GB. The ratio of the change in cost today versus in 1980 is ~6×10^{-7}. Taking the 28th root of the change gives an annual cost change of ~60 percent per year (40 percent decline per year compounded annually).

19. Talisker Security Wizardry, The Computer Network Defence Internet Operational Picture, http://securitywizardry.com/radar.htm.

20. U.S. Geological Survey, Fact Sheet 017-03, "The USGS Earthquake Hazards Program in NEHRP—Investing in a Safer Future," by J. R. Filson, J. McCarthy, W. L. Ellsworth, and M. L. Zoback. Last modified May 17, 2005. http://pubs.usgs.gov/fs/2003/fs017-03/

21. For more information on jails, see Chapter 15 of the FreeBSD Documentation Project's *FreeBSD Handbook*, contributed by Matteo Riondato: www.freebsd.org/doc/en_US.ISO8859-1/books/handbook/jails.html.

CHAPTER **54**

SECURITY AUDITS, STANDARDS, AND INSPECTIONS

Donald Glass, Chris Davis, John Mason, David Gursky, James Thomas, Wendy Carr, and Diane Levine

54.1   INTRODUCTION.   Traditional auditing focused on reviewing organizational financial records and controls to validate the accuracy and integrity of financial data. External auditors typically focused on material or macro-level issues, and internal auditors focused primarily on transaction-level controls, protecting assets, and validating information adequacy and validity. However, changes in the regulatory environment over the past several years have caused a significant increase in the scope and depth of these responsibilities.

This chapter focuses on these areas:

- Sarbanes-Oxley 404 (SOX), Gramm-Leach-Bliley Act (GLBA), and Health Insurance Portability and Accountability Act (HIPAA) compliance
- Auditing standards, such as ISO 17799 and ISO 27001
- Statement of Auditing Standards (SAS) 70 audits, both Type I and Type II
- Technical guidelines for performing audits

With the changed environment, the extent, focus, reliance, and quality of the audit work has increased significantly in quantity, depth, and reliance. Thus, the current business environment, whether global or domestic, increasingly requires routine, periodic security audits, and inspections that include:

- Regulatory compliance; for example, SOX, HIPAA, and GLBA
- Ensuring that threats to (and weaknesses of) the organization's mission-critical and key systems are recognized and addressed
- Ensuring that the organization is not unwittingly posing an IT-related risk or threat to other organizations, whether related, foreign, competitor, peer, or unrelated

These audits typically address networks, host systems, Internet-related connectivity, protection and detection devices, physical premises, and policy-related items on a recurring basis, since a static posture may unwittingly leave the organization vulnerable.

Often these reviews and audits may be regarded by an organization's management as falling into one of two categories:

1. A cost of doing business, one required by a regulator or governmental law
2. A "nice to have (but don't spend too much money)"

Both categories, particularly the latter, tend to ignore the value added by such reviews, since the expense is often the primary (or only) criteria evaluated by senior management. Yet the impetus of the regulatory mandates has seemingly pushed many of the latter into the former; this is due in part to SOX drastically reducing an auditor's "gray area"—that is, exceptions are not clearly either right or wrong or being considered reportable and compliant—since minor exceptions can result in management test failures.

To this end, the training of information technology (IT), information assurance (IA), and information security (IS) management and staff are focusing increasingly on not only the EDP environment but also the technology of compliance, the regulatory environment, and the regulatory impact on technology and business. To that end, numerous undergraduate and graduate programs have been developed in universities and colleges around the world to train students in the discipline of EDP and compliance auditing.

54.2   AUDITING STANDARDS.   Auditing standards and practices assist organizations in meeting regulatory requirements and provide industry guidance for performing due diligence, certification, and ensuring stakeholder security. Standard-setting entities may include international organizations, federal and state levels of government, and industry-specific groups or associations whose focus includes regulatory compliance. Guiding principles and information published by these entities may be required or, at the very least, provide managers with the newest information regarding industry advances. Managers must not only be aware of new developments in auditing methodology; they must also be adept in identifying and applying the best solution available to their unique physical and logical architecture.

54.2.1   Introduction to ISO.   ISO[1] (International Organization for Standardization) is a nongovernmental cooperative of international members who work together to create, identify, and publish industry standards as they relate to business and technology. Membership is comprised of member bodies, correspondent members, and subscriber members. A member body is a group that represents the accepted standards of a specific country. Correspondent members represent a country that does not yet have fully developed standards,while subscriber members represent countries with negligible economies.[2] Level of membership determines technical and policy participation and voting privileges, but members all are equally represented in international standardization and are encouraged to contribute.

Standards are developed based on industry interest; needs of vendors, governments and consumers; and initiatives of the ISO where it sees market interest. Once the idea of a standard has been recognized by the ISO, member committees begin the process of defining the technical requirements necessary for the standard. Committee members include technical experts representing countries interested in the potential new standard. Once the technical requirements have been defined, interested members and countries work toward agreement on detailed specifications for the standard. When final details have met committee approval, a draft of the international standard is released for review. Final release of an official ISO standard[3] requires approval of two-thirds of the members who participated in the development process and 75 percent of all members who vote.[4]

Standards established by ISO are not regulatory in and of themselves, but are meant to represent best practice guidance that is globally consistent for a given trade or line of business. Universal acceptance and implementation of ISO standards and guidance further elevates them as identifiers of distinction within a given industry. Similar to worldwide recognition of ISO 9000 and ISO 14000 as standards for Quality and Environmental Management (respectively), ISO 27000 series is quickly becoming accepted as the measurement of excellence in Information Security Management.

British Standard 7799, representing best practices for information security, was first published in February 1995. This three-part standard encompasses security objectives and controls as well as the development methodology necessary to create an information security management system (ISMS).[5]

- BS7799: Part 1, Best Practices for Information Security Management
- BS7799: Part 2, Defines specifications for information security management systems
- BS7799: Part 3, Guidelines for information security risk management

The information security management system as created by BS7799 and further improved on by ISO 17799 and ISO/IEC 27000 is a means to ensure the best environment not only for security practices but also for objective auditing and assessments. An organization's interpretation of, and adherence to, the ISMS model can be a major indicator of the security climate of the organization as well as of management's support of policies and procedures. Programs that support ISMS functions must be promoted and used by management to demonstrate their significance to employees and to encourage participation. Audits typically consist of a planning phase, the actual audit process, and the final report to the audit committee. Audits or assessments that are performed in an ISMS environment will be revealed in the final reporting. Documented ISMS policies and programs, security climate of both management and employees, and adherence to doctrine are not only necessary for an information security management system to be effective, but will ensure a successful audit process.

In the past few years British Standard 7799 has been adapted for translation by ISO into ISO 17799 and the ISO 27000 series, and it continues to evolve as a widely accepted standard for information security management and for operational procedure guidance. Both agencies (and their collective members) understood the need for a comprehensive program that addressed the risk management and auditing needs of organizations while defining a framework for programs and policies to support this concept. Partial or full implementation of these standards not only prepares organizations for audits and risk assessments but can also help them meet regulatory requirements.

In December 2000, BS7799 Part 1 (Best Practices for Information Security Management) was revised and released as ISO 17799.[6] The ISO 17799 standard is comprised of 10 domains:

1. Business continuity planning
2. System access control
3. System development and maintenance
4. Physical and environmental security
5. Compliance
6. Personnel security
7. Security organization
8. Computer and operations management
9. Asset classification and control
10. Security policy

In 2005, ISO completed a cooperative effort with the International Electrotechnical Commission to release ISO/IEC 17799:2005. This release, entitled *Information Technology—Security Techniques—Code of Practice for Information Security Management,* added objectives and controls for information security management and updated the previous release to include advances in technology (mobile and wireless) and in applications and uses of the Internet.[7]

While BS7799 and ISO 17799 established widely implemented guidance for the information security management systems standard, the evolutionary path of their published standards has made them nearly obsolete. The ISO/IEC 27000 set of standards not only incorporates the guidance of BS7799 and ISO 17799[8] but also provides a more thorough explanation and understanding of each domain by partitioning them into distinctly separate standards.

54.2.2   ISO/IEC 27001.   Information and network security has been a concern since the early days of worms and viruses; however, it has only been in the past 10 to 15 years that structures have been defined to integrate security with network use and risk management. Introduction of BS7799 and its acceptance by ISO have given administrators the long-needed tools to identify and manage these domains. Additionally, regulations such as the Sarbanes-Oxley Act of 2002, the Gramm-Leach-Bliley Act, Health Insurance Portability and Accountability Act, and the Federal Information Security Management Act have set down compliance requirements that are more easily achievable with a comprehensive information security management system in place.

BS7799 Part 2, after collective revision, was adopted as ISO 27001 in October 2005 and represents ISMS requirement standards for entire organizations (not systems).[9] ISO/IEC 27001:2005, titled *Information Technology—Security Techniques—Information Security Management Systems—Requirements*, is only one standard in the ISO/IEC 27000 series. All standards included in the ISO/IEC 27000 family are:

- ISO/IEC 27000: Fundamentals and Vocabulary
- ISO/IEC 27001: ISMS—Requirements (revised BS7799 Part 2:2005)
- ISO/IEC 27002: Code of Practice for Information Security Management
- ISO/IEC 27003: ISMS Implementation Guidance (under development)
- ISO/IEC 27004: Information Security Management Measurement (under development)
- ISO/IEC 27005: Information Security Risk Management (based on and incorporating ISO/IEC 13335 MICTS Part 2 [under development])
- ISO/IEC 27006: Requirements for Bodies Providing Audit and Certification of Information Security Management Systems[10]

ISO/IEC 27001 (ISMS Requirements) closely models the Organization for Economic Cooperation and Developments (OECD)[11] guidance on the security of information systems and networks, and is driven by the Plan-Do-Check-Act (PDCA) cycle.[12]

The PDCA cycle, developed by W. Edwards Deming in the 1950s, asks managers to view business processes as being in a constant feedback loop.[13] This method allows managers to be involved more thoroughly in the entire change control and improvement process.

Organizations may implement some or all of the standards of ISO/IEC 27001, or take their program a step further by applying for ISMS certification. Certification provides both auditors and stakeholders with the assurance that a comprehensive program is in place for information security and business systems. Whether an organization seeks recognized ISMS certification or not, there are several advantages to adopting the objectives and controls outlined in ISO/IEC 27001. As stated earlier, having a comprehensive ISMS program in place can greatly contribute to compliance in other areas. An ISO/IEC 27001 certificated ISMS will ensure compliance with the whole range of information security–related legislation, including HIPAA, GLBA, and FISMA regulations, as well as the conditions for a successful Sarbanes-Oxley Section 404 report.[14]

54.2.3 Gramm-Leach-Bliley Act.   The Financial Services Modernization Act of 1999, more commonly known as the Gramm-Leach-Bliley Act, regulates the security of consumers' personal financial information and nonpublic personal information (NPI). Major provisions of the GLBA address privacy requirements for information, disclosures of personal and financial information to third parties, rules regarding the safeguarding of information, and protections against the use of pretexting to illegally acquire personal information.[15] Financial information may include names of financial institution customers, account numbers, and information related to balances and transactions. NPI may include date of birth, Social Security number, drivers' license number, financial account numbers, balances, home address, telephone numbers, and so on.

GLBA also governs the disclosure of such information to third parties. Institutions that are affected by GLBA must disclose to customers, in the form of a privacy notice, when and how their information is released. Additionally, institutions must provide for customers the opportunity to opt out of having their information shared with some third parties. Customers may not use the opt-out privileges to stop the release of their information to law enforcement agencies that are performing an authorized investigation.

GLBA regulations also protect consumers against the increasingly used form of social engineering called "pretexting." Pretexting is the act of using false statements or impersonation to obtain access to the information of another individual. An example would be a perpetrator calling a financial institution and pretending to be an authorized account holder requesting to make a funds transfer by telephone. In the absence of face-to-face verification of a drivers' license or some other token, banks are allowing such transactions to occur after the caller has verified some "known" information, be it date of birth, address, Social Security number, and so on. GLBA makes the act of pretexting illegal and encourages institutions to use more stringent methods for confirming a customer's identity.

Internal auditing to determine compliance with GLBA protects organizations and ensures the proper handling of NPI. Because mishandling or unauthorized release of NPI can lead to incidents of fraud and identity theft, institutions that are required to use and maintain such information must be very diligent in their security processes. Periodic audits of business and network processes that control the storage, transmission, and use of NPI will aid in alerting organizations to weaknesses in their security and will document due diligence efforts in the protection of customer information. For more on GLBA see Chapter 64 in this *Handbook*.

54.2.4   Auditing Standards Conclusion.   Today, organizations are more actively participating in risk management than ever before. In cases where organizations have the assets available, they may choose to combine compliance, auditing, and risk management departments into a working cooperative. Needlessly duplicating efforts to meet overlapping compliance and regulatory requirements can be a waste of both time and resources for all involved.

Managers also have a better understanding that damage from threats (both internal and external) may result in losses to operations and reputation, and exposure to legal recourse. Auditing systems and processes give a certain degree of assurance to management, administrators, regulators, and stakeholders that an organization is prepared for this damage. Benefits derived from performing periodic and event-based audits include:

- Identifying threats to information assets (which assist in accurate risk analysis estimates, and can justify security expenditures)
- Reducing costs by identifying optimal configurations for operations and network systems
- Assisting in structuring internal assurance programs and policies
- Increasing the integrity of organizations by certification and compliance with industry security standards[16]

Incorporating the guidance of applicable auditing standards can provide evidence of both due diligence and a proactive security climate within an organization. Attaining certification status further substantiates this sincerity while also going a long way toward meeting regulatory compliance. Whether an organization chooses partial or full implementation or certification, the stakeholders, in the end, will be the actual beneficiaries of a more secure system.

54.3 SAS 70 AUDITS.   Both public companies and government agencies have been under constant pressure to improve efficiencies and to reduce operational costs. In addition, public companies are being driven by investors and shareholders to improve profitability, which has resulted in a move toward outsourcing. This move is not limited to public companies; now government agencies are starting to embrace outsourcing as a method to contain costs. Executive officers of organizations that are considering outsourcing must understand both the benefits and the risks, in addition to how they can mitigate the risk to an acceptable level for their organizations.

With the drive for more companies to focus on their core competencies, these types of business functions are being outsourced:

- Customer service and help desk
- Data processing
- Human resources and benefit plans
- Web hosting
- Claims processing
- Financial and accounting

54.3.1 Introduction to SAS 70 Audits.   An SAS 70 audit is the primary method of ensuring that a company being considering for outsourcing meets security requirements. In addition to being used for outsourcing, SAS 70 can be utilized when partnering with companies that may have access to your IT resources and data. In this section, the two types of SAS 70 audits and their components are described.

Terminology associated with SAS 70 audits:

Service organization—the company that will process information or transactions on behalf of the user organization

Service auditor—retained by the service organization to conduct an SAS 70 audit and provide a certification of audit results

User organization—the company that outsourced services and is the customer of the service organization

Users' auditors—either an internal or external auditing group that provides auditing services to the user organization

The SAS 70 (Statement on Auditing Standard 70) is a standard that was developed by the American Institute of Certified Public Accountants (AICPA), titled *Reports on the Processing of Transactions by Service Organizations.* The SAS 70 defines the professional standards that are used by the service auditor that will be assessing the internal controls that a service organization has implemented.

An SAS 70 audit is an authoritative guidance that allows a service organization to disclose its control processes and activities to potential customers and to external

Exhibit 54.1   Types of SAS 70 Audits

SAS 70 Report Content	Type I	Type II
Independent service audits report	Included	Included
Service organizations description of controls	Included	Included
Information provided by the independent service auditor; includes a description of the service auditor's tests of operating effectiveness and the results of those tests	Optional	Included
Other service relevant information	Optional	Included

auditors; the information is stated in a standard reporting format. There are two different types of SAS 70 audits, known as Type I and Type II, as illustrated in Exhibit 54.1.

A critical difference between an SAS 70 Type I audit and Type II is that a Type I audit may list hundreds of different controls but they are not tested, whereas a Type II audit will test these controls and report on their effectiveness. Because of this testing, Type II audits are more costly but provide a detailed report.

An SAS 70 audit starts with the service auditor conducting an initial assessment and evaluation of the processing system and of the transaction systems processing controls, and a review of the policies and procedures that govern IT system and processes. Next, the auditor will develop a statement of work (SOW), that will be presented to the service organization with completion date, details of the audit, and cost.

An SAS 70 audit team will be managed by a CPA, normally a partner in the accounting firm conducting the audit. This individual will be the primary interface with the customer executive management and will certify the audit results. Two other key people on the audit team are the technical audit lead and the application lead; these are the people who do the actual auditing. The technical lead is responsible for evaluation and testing of systems and network devices. On a typical Solaris or Microsoft server, 200 to 300 items will be tested or reviewed, averaging four to five hours per server. The application lead will test and evaluate applications like Oracle, Net-Backup, and SAS to determine if good security practices are being followed for installation, configuration, and operations; the review of applications can take from days to weeks to complete, depending on complexity.

In addition to reviewing hardware and software configurations, IT policies and procedures have to be evaluated, reviewed, and verified. Management, including system and network administrators, will be interviewed to determine how they do certain tasks. For example, who approves a user account request form, and how does the form flow through the approval process? In addition, system or application administrators will be asked to explain what they do from the time they receive an account request form until the account is created. The auditor will use the information gathered from the interviews to determine if account polices and procedures are being followed and if they are adequate for the customer's environment.

A brief overview of what an auditor would review for a user request policy and how the results would be reported follows.

- **Policy statement.** All users who require a new computer account, or modification to an existing account, on any system at the Company will be required to complete User Account Request Form UA-09.

- **Polices and procedures.** User Account Request Policy "IT-23 November 1, 2006." All requests for a new account or for modification of an existing account must be submitted on a UA-09 Form.

- **Test procedure.** Conduct a statistical sample of user request forms and review the forms for proper authorized signatures and completeness. Interview authorized signers for compliance with user request policy; ensure that users are only given roles consistent with their job position's "least privileges."

- **Test results.** Collect statistical samples of user request forms and interview the supervisors of the individuals making the requests to determine that least privileges needed to perform their job have been requested and approved. Check forms for completeness and accuracy of information.

- **Analysis of test results.** The auditor will provide both the positive test results and negative results with commentary. A sample of a positive or negative test results:

  - **Positive test result.** All forms that were reviewed were completed in accordance with User Account Request Policy "IT-23 November 1, 2006," and all interviews indicated that all policies and procedures were correctly followed. No discrepancies were found.

  - **Negative test result.** After reviewing the User Account Request Form and interviewing supervisors and authorized signers, it was determined that User Account Request Policy "IT-23 November 1, 2006" was not followed. Users were given privileges beyond what was required to perform their job.

Exceptions and findings are reported in the final SAS 70 report sent to management in these ways:

- If the auditor deems that it is relevant, an exception is reported, including a description of the exception.

- The auditor will consider any mitigating controls or any management responses to the exception.

- If, in the auditor's opinion, the finding has an impact on the control objectives, then it would be reported with a qualified opinion and potential impact, if not it would be reported as an exception.

The final document that an SAS 70 will provide is the conclusion and summary report, which will clearly state whether the description of the controls is accurately and fairly presented. The report will also state whether the controls were adequately designed to meet their control objectives. The report for a Type II audit would also include the results of tests that were performed and would evaluate whether they provide reasonable assurance that controls were operating correctly during a period of time, normally no less than six months.

54.3.2 Cost and Benefits of SAS 70 Audits.   Whether your organization is a service provider or an outsourcing company, it must understand the cost and benefits of an SAS 70 audit and if an SAS 70 provides the information assurance required. If the company is a small service organization, and a user organization is requesting an SAS 70 audit, serious consideration will be required to determine whether to keep that customer or drop it. An initial audit SAS 70 audit can cost from $25,000 to over $1 million, in addition to the annual cost to keep the audit current. User organizations

Exhibit 54.2   Pros and Cons for Service and User Organizations

	Service Organization	User Organization
Independent assessment of controls	Pro	Pro
Lower cost for evaluation of controls	Con	Pro
No additional review of controls required	Con	Con
SAS 70 audits are forward looking	Con	Con
SAS 70 audits must be continuously reviewed and updated	Con	Pro
SAS 70 audits increase the value of services	Pro	Pro
Disruption to service organization is reduced by eliminating user organization auditors from visiting service organization to conduct audit	Pro	Pro
The SAS 70 audit can be used to build a strong working relationship between organizations	Pro	Pro
Audit results can provide opportunities for improvements	Pro	Pro

have quickly embraced the SAS 70 audit because of the Sarbanes-Oxley Act (SOX) and Gramm-Leach-Bliley (GLB) requirements.

SAS 70 has adopted the Committee of Sponsoring Organizations of the Tread-way Commission (COSO) as its standard for reviewing internal controls. The COSO definition of internal control is "a process, effected by an entity's board of directors, management and other personnel, designed to provide reasonable assurance regarding the achievement of objectives." Also, COSO is the same standard that Sarbanes-Oxley Section 404 has adopted for how to review internal controls.

The SAS 70 has pros and cons for both the service organization and user organization that need to be understood so that management can do a cost-benefit analysis (see Exhibit 54.2).

54.3.3   SAS 70 Audits Conclusion.   In conclusion, an SAS 70 audit is not a 100 percent guarantee of assurance that all security-related controls and processes have been correctly designed and implemented. But it provides a high-level of confidence that risk have been assessed and mitigated. The SAS 70 audit results can also provide information about areas for further investigation. The major benefit of an SAS 70 audit is that it can be used to meet the reporting requirements for SOX Section 404 reporting.

54.4   SARBANES-OXLEY

54.4.1   Introduction.   This section focuses on the practicalities of SOX compliance in the real world and introduces concepts that the practitioner is sure to encounter.

Sarbanes-Oxley is the financial reporting act enacted into U.S. law in July 2002. It is the U.S. federal government's response to a number of major public company accounting failures, most infamous of which where Enron and WorldCom.

Simply put, SOX is designed to reduce fraud and conflicts of interest while increasing financial transparency and public confidence in the market. The act is intended to encourage honesty and integrity in financial reporting and to place responsibility directly with owners, managers, and executives. The act requires that the executive officers certify that they are "responsible for establishing and maintaining internal controls" and "have designed such internal controls to ensure that material information relating to the company and its consolidated subsidiaries is made known to such officers by others within those entities, particularly during the period in which the periodic reports are being prepared." SOX allows for the possibility of both civil litigation and criminal prosecution.[17] Thus, noncompliance is likely to result in considerable fines, imprisonment, or both for those who fail to ensure the accuracy of their organization's financial reporting.

Bearing in mind that SOX currently applies only to publicly traded companies, many companies have delisted themselves from the U.S. stock exchange, or reverted to private status, to avoid inclusion in the act. More significantly, many non-U.S.-held companies now find themselves covered by SOX because they or their subsidiaries are listed on the U.S. stock exchange. As such, compliance is necessary for the entire organization, not just the listed subsidiary. Thus, from humble beginnings, the act now has global market penetration.

Although in this case regulation may be the driver for good governance, it should remain just that: the driver. It is in the best interests of an organization to design and implement a comprehensive governance program, to assess and implement internal processes and controls, and to set targets beyond that of mere regulatory compliance. Additionally, the entire compliance effort should be repeatable, as compliance is not a one-off activity; rather it will be repeated annually for the life of the organization (or until such time as the law is materially revised or repealed).

54.4.2 Section 404. SOX consist of a number of sections, most beyond the scope of this discussion. From an information assurance professional's viewpoint however, Section 404 is most significant. It is the area that directly addresses the impact of information technology on financial reporting and the adequacy and effectiveness of associated internal controls. With widespread reliance on IT for financial and operational management systems, it is now accepted within industry that adequate and effective internal controls are necessary, particularly for systems supporting significant business processes.[18]

54.4.3 Achieving Compliance. SOX compliance should be approached by first ensuring identification of key processes within the organization, how they are implemented and controlled, and the methods for reporting on their success or failure. It is important to provide coverage across the entire system life cycle, and internal processes must include projects, design, architecture, system development, delivery, and operations. An auditor will be looking for no more than the assessment of core processes, the adequacy of associated controls, and whether those processes were followed, and controls executed, as stated. For more on SOX issues and regulations see Chapter 64 in this *Handbook*.

54.4.3.1 Control Framework. Fortunately, the hard work of choosing a controls and assessment framework has already been done. The Securities and Exchange

Commission (SEC) mandates the use of the internal control framework recommended by COSO,[19] and the Public Company Accounting and Oversight Board (PCAOB) supports the SEC's choice as detailed in its Auditing Standard No. 2, *An Audit of Internal Control Over Financial Reporting Performed in Conjunction with an Audit of Financial Statements.*

54.4.3.2 COSO. A detailed description of the framework suggested by COSO is beyond the scope of this chapter. The recommended reading section lists a number of very useful resources from which to learn more. According to COSO, the core elements of internal control[20] are:

- Control environment
- Risk assessment
- Control activities
- Information and communication
- Monitoring

54.4.3.3 CoBiT. By extension, a practical framework from which to derive key processes and controls for SOX compliance activities is ISACA's CoBiT (Control Objectives in Information Technology) framework. CoBiT is a comprehensive framework for management of the governance of risk and control of IT, comprising 4 domains, 34 IT processes, and 215 control objectives.[21] Although it has a wider purpose than simply addressing SOX compliance, CoBiT removes much of the guesswork by suggesting 12 out of the 34 available standard processes for inclusion in a SOX implementation:

1. Acquire and maintain application software. (AI2)
   The provision of line of business applications, whether custom or off the shelf, should be congruent with business requirements.
2. Acquire and maintain technology infrastructure. (AI3)
   Technology infrastructure should underpin the delivery of services required by the business and follow organizational standards.
3. Enable operations. (AI4)
   Support effective use of technology through knowledge transfer, agreed service levels, and properly integrated solutions.
4. Install and accredit solutions and changes. (AI7)
   Ensure that supplied systems are fit-for-purpose prior to delivery and that they function as expected postinstallation.
5. Manage changes. (AI6)
   Provide an effective, formal change management system to reduce errors and defects that may impact successful operations and business processes.
6. Define and manage service levels. (DS1)
   Align key business processes with delivery of technology in a set of meaningful service definition documents, with a mechanism for reporting to stakeholders on performance and achievement of service levels.
7. Manage third-party services. (DS2)
   Ensure the delivery of essential third-party services to support business activities while remaining transparent with regard to cost, benefits, and risks.

8. Ensure systems security. (DS5)
   Maximize the integrity and availability of systems and the confidentiality of data stored thereon while minimizing the impact of vulnerabilities through the application of effective security policies, standards, and procedures.

9. Manage the configuration. (DS9)
   Maintain an accurate and readily accessible repository of application and system configuration information, baseline standards, and variations thereof.

10. Manage problems and incidents. (DS8, DS10)
    Provide formal problem and incident management for all operations, including identification of issues, root cause analysis, and end-to-end problem resolution.

11. Manage data. (DS11)
    Provide tried and tested backup, recovery, and disposal systems.

12. Manage the physical environment and operations. (DS12)
    Control access to facilities and to computing assets, to reduce the likelihood of business disruption resulting from data leakage or theft of assets.

Specific analysis may require the addition of further processes, and within each process, the addition or removal of specific controls to further tailor the framework for each organization. It is important to ensure that process and control selection is agreed with the internal audit function and external auditors before committing to a particular framework.

54.4.3.4 Testing.
Of equal importance to process and control selection is the agreement of the testing plan and schedule, especially the number of tests and the associated sample sizes.

For most organizations, resources are not unlimited. It is likely that staff will be asked to assume responsibility for some portion of SOX activity in addition to their regular workload. Thus, achieving a balance between compliance and the number of controls associated with each process is critical because it is the controls that will be tested throughout the year, with the test results supporting the SOX certification process. A reduction in the number of tests or sample sizes can directly affect the integrity and quality of the results and positively affect staff efficiency and productivity. Although testing will likely be seen as onerous, much of the control activity should be considered business as usual, and thus the day-to-day processes should yield much of the evidence required for testing.

This section focuses on the importance and impact of IT on the wider goal of SOX compliance, but not all processes, even within an IT organization are technical. Many are activities such as director-level meetings, incident boards, recovery forums, project risk meetings, and so on, and all may be part of a process that is included under SOX and must therefore be tested.

Testing typically falls into two categories: examination and discussion. Examination requires that a representative sample of evidence showing that a control is operating properly is collated and verified as accurate. Discussion requires that understanding of the process and associated controls be confirmed on a one-to-one or group basis among responsible staff. Sample sizes will depend on the test population and the frequency of sampling, and probably on the importance of the statistical accuracy of the results.

54.4.4 Audit and Certification.
There will be at least two independent audit processes at work: internal and external. Internal audit will occur at the culmination of

EXHIBIT 54.3 Typical Annual SOX Schedule

Period*	Activity
January/February	Create and agree on controls and associated tests, certification schedule, and testing plan based on agreed processes
March to August	Execute testing (typically by process)
September	Retest where necessary
October	Internal audit
November/December	External audit, produce certificates, publish management letter

* The actual dates for compliance activities will vary with each organization and its respective financial years and filing deadlines.

SOX testing, as a final quality assurance checkpoint that the organization is compliant. Any identified gaps at must either be remediated or officially acknowledged within a formal risk process prior to the arrival of the external auditors.

54.4.4.1 External Audit. External audit will occur close to the end of the year and is the final test of compliance. It is not acceptable to wait until the external audit function identifies a gap before carrying out remediation activities. Any areas of noncompliance at this stage will be officially reported and may be included in the final management letter.

54.4.4.2 Schedule. Certification requirements vary by organization, although obviously at least an annual certificate will be required. Many organizations certify quarterly or monthly as part of some other SOX-related or controls process, and use those certificates to supplement their final annual declaration (see Exhibit 54.3).

54.4.5 Sarbanes-Oxley Conclusion. SOX compliance activities should not stand alone within the organization. They should be considered part of a wider risk-management program, preferably one supported by an embedded, proactive, risk-aware control culture. Further, it is never recommended to execute a compliance program with the goal of simply meeting regulatory requirements. In reality, a program that is designed from the outset to exceed the current regulation, and be adaptable to changes to existing or entirely new regulation, represents a much smarter investment.

54.5 ADDRESSING MULTIPLE REGULATIONS FOR INFORMATION SE-CURITY. Federal regulations and industry standards increasingly recognize the need to address controls related to information security. However, because of continual advances in technology and the diversity of equipment and structures available for use, regulations and standards have continued to be vague in stating specifically how security configurations should be implemented, tested, and monitored. Although there are many different clients from diverse industries, with various regulations, legislation, or industry specific standards, all of them have a fundamental source of their best practices.

During the 1980s, the Defense Computer Security Center began to create a series of standards related to securing computer systems for governmental and subcontracted entities. The series of documents relating to the configuration, auditing, and securing of systems is commonly referred to as the "Rainbow Series" due to the fact that each text in the series is a different color.[22] Systems that have followed the procedures of the series are considered "trusted" systems, due to the rigid requirements for following the configuration criteria contained within this series. The Rainbow Series documents have evolved to meet the demands of processing and computer systems of today; however, the fundamentals of how to secure and audit systems and information have remained semiconstant and have begun to be defined as "best practices."

The term "best practices" is vague, but the concept comprises a set of standards, experiences, and after-action reports (lessons learned) that are intended to help meet the information security controls most commonly expected of trusted organizations. These best practices were derived from standards that were developed for secure or "trusted" systems. Today, information assurance best practices have evolved from the rigid requirements of the Rainbow Series standards. Best practices can now be found contained within various documents including:

- Auditing checklists that can be obtained from the Information Systems Audit and Control Association (ISACA)
- Defense Information Systems Agency's Security Technical Implementation Guides (DISA-STIG)
- National Security Agency's Network Applications Team of the Systems and Network Attack Center (NSA)
- National Institute of Standards and Technology (NIST) Computer Security Division's Special Publication 800 Series documents

Another way to address the multiple regulations is to incorporate one of the more comprehensive frameworks, such as Control Objectives for Information and related Technology (CoBIT), Information Technology Infrastructure Library (ITIL®), and the International Standards Organization (ISO) 27000 series, with many relying on the others for ensuring that the information security areas have appropriate controls. Sections relevant to information security vary on the types of framework that should be incorporated but have value in that they identify areas that should have manual or technology controls pertinent to those areas.

For example, the Federal Information Security Management Act of 2002, the Sarbanes-Oxley Act of 2002, and the Health Insurance Portability and Accountability Act of 1996 all address security policy, logical access controls, and methods for the handling and storage of sensitive information.

In the past, if help was needed to classify information, the *Yellow Book,* or the CSC-STD-003-85, was the reference or standard. Once information was appropriately classified, an information security classification policy was developed by the organization and was applied to securing that data in information systems.

Today, legislative and industry specific requirements sometimes define what is critical or sensitive information; for many organizations looking for answers, the starting reference is the NIST SP 800-60, *Guide for Mapping Types of Information and Information Systems to Security Categories.* For many organizations, the National Institute of Standards and Technology Special Publications (NIST–SP) 800 series is a great location to start.

54.5.1 Publicly Available Security Publications.   The NIST Special Publication 800-53 Revision 1[23] is the "Recommended Security Controls for Federal Information Systems." The purpose of Special Publication 800-53 is to provide guidelines for selecting and specifying what should be security controls for information systems

supporting the executive agencies of the federal government. The guidelines have been developed to help achieve secure system requirements by:

- Facilitating a more consistent, comparable, and repeatable approach for selecting and specifying security controls for information systems
- Providing a recommendation for minimum security controls for information systems categorized in accordance with FIPS 199,[24] *Standards for Security Categorization of Federal Information and Information Systems*
- Providing a stable yet flexible catalog of security controls for information systems to meet current organizational protection needs and the demands of future protection needs based on changing requirements and technologies
- Creating a foundation for the development of assessment methods and procedures for determining security control effectiveness

The guidelines provided in Special Publication 800-53 are applicable to all federal information systems[25] with the exception of systems designated as national security systems as defined by 44 U.S.C. Section 3542.[26] The guidelines have been broadly developed from a technical perspective to complement similar guidelines for national security systems. This publication is intended to provide guidance to federal agencies implementing FIPS 200,[27] *Minimum Security Requirements for Federal Information and Information Systems*. In addition to the agencies of the federal government, the state, local, tribal governments, and private-sector organizations that comprise the critical infrastructure of the United States are also encouraged to use these guidelines as appropriate.

The security controls in Special Publication 800-53 have been developed using inputs from a variety of sources including NIST Special Publication 800-26, Department of Defense (DoD) Policy 8500, Director of Central Intelligence Directive (DCID) 6/3, ISO/IEC Standard 17799, General Accounting Office (GAO) Federal Information System Controls Audit Manual (FISCAM), and Health and Human Services (HHS) Centers for Medicare and Medicaid Services (CMS) Core Security Requirements. The security controls cover these topic areas:[28]

- Risk assessment
- Certification, accreditation, and security assessments
- System services and acquisition
- Security planning
- Configuration management
- System and communications protection
- Personnel security
- Awareness and training
- Physical and environmental protection
- Media protection
- Contingency planning
- Maintenance
- System and information integrity
- Incident response
- Identification and authentication

- Access control
- Accountability and audit

54.5.2 Federal Information Systems Management Act (FISMA).
FISMA affects almost all governmental entities and was created as part of the E-Government Act (Public Law 107-347)[29] passed by the 108th Congress in 2002 and signed into law by then President George W. Bush. The resolution recognized the importance of information security to the economic and national security interests of the United States. Title III of the E-Government Act entitled the FISMA[30] to require each federal agency to develop, document, and implement an agency-wide information assurance program which would provide security controls for the information and systems that support the operations and assets of the agency. This measure should also include security controls for information- handling services or systems that are provided, or managed, by third-party agencies, contractors, or other sources.

FISMA defined what should be included in an information security program to be effective:

- Periodic assessments of risk, including the magnitude of harm that could result from the unauthorized access, use, disclosure, disruption, modification, or destruction of information and information systems that support the operations and assets of the organization (Many corporate entities may refer to this as a business impact analysis [BIA].)
- Policies and procedures that are based on the information provided by risk assessments, that would cost-effectively reduce information security risks to an acceptable level, and that would ensure that information security is addressed throughout the life cycle of each organizational information system
- Subordinate plans for providing adequate information security for networks, facilities, information systems, or groups of information systems, as appropriate
- Security awareness training to inform personnel (including contractors and other users of information systems that support the operations and assets of the organization) of the information security risks associated with their activities and their responsibilities in complying with organizational policies and procedures designed to reduce these risks
- Periodic testing and evaluation of the effectiveness of information security policies, procedures, practices, and security controls will be performed, with frequency determined by the level of risk, but no less than annually
- A process for planning, implementing, evaluating, and documenting remedial actions to address any deficiencies in the information security policies, procedures, and practices of the organization
- Procedures for detecting, reporting, and responding to security incidents
- Plans and procedures to ensure continuity of operations for information systems that support the operations and assets of the organization

FISMA, along with the Paperwork Reduction Act of 1995 and the Information Technology Management Reform Act of 1996 (Clinger-Cohen Act), explicitly emphasizes a risk-based policy for cost-effective security. In supporting and reinforcing this legislation, the Office of Management and Budget (OMB) through Circular A-130,

Appendix III, Security of Federal Automated Information Resources,[31] requires executive agencies within the federal government to:

- Plan for security
- Ensure that appropriate officials are assigned security responsibility
- Periodically review the security controls in their information systems
- Authorize system processing prior to operations and periodically thereafter

These management requirements presume that responsible agency officials understand the risks and other factors that could adversely affect their objectives. Moreover, these officials must understand the status of their security programs, and the security controls planned or in place to protect their information and information systems, in order to make informed judgments and investments that appropriately mitigate risk to an acceptable level.

The ultimate objective is to conduct the day-to-day operations of the agency and to accomplish the agency's stated missions with security commensurate with level of risk, while acknowledging the magnitude of harm that could result from the unauthorized access, use, disclosure, disruption, modification, or destruction of information. As a key element of the FISMA Implementation Project, NIST also developed an integrated Risk Framework[32] that effectively brings together all of the FISMA-related security standards and guidance, in order to promote the development of comprehensive and balanced information security programs by agencies.[33]

54.5.3 Risk Framework

Step 1. Categorize the information system and the information resident within that system based on impact. (FIPS 199iii and NIST SP 800-60[34])

Step 2. Select an initial set of security controls for the information system based on the FIPS 199 security categorization and apply tailoring guidance, as appropriate, to obtain a starting point for required controls. (FIPS 200 and NIST SP 800-53)

Step 3. Supplement the initial set of tailored security controls based on an assessment of risk and local conditions, including organization-specific security requirements, specific threat information, cost-benefit analyses, and special circumstances. (NIST SP 800-53 and SP 800-30[35])

Step 4. Document the agreed-on set of security controls in the system security plan, including the organization's justification for any refinements or adjustments to the initial set of controls. (NIST SP 800-18[36])

Step 5. Implement the security controls in the information system.

Step 6. Assess the security controls using appropriate methods and procedures to determine the extent to which the controls are implemented correctly, operating as intended, and producing the desired outcome with respect to meeting the security requirements for the system. (NIST SP 800-53A[37])

Step 7. Authorize information system operation based on a determination of the risk to organizational operations, organizational assets, or to individuals resulting from the operation of the information system and the decision that this risk is acceptable. (NIST SP 800-37[38])

Step 8. Monitor and assess selected security controls in the information system on a continuous basis including documenting changes to the system, conducting security impact analyses of the associated changes, and reporting the security status of the system to appropriate organizational officials on a regular basis.[39]

54.5.4 Multiple Regulations and Information Security Audits Conclusion.

The National Institute of Standards and Technology special publications are a great place for many organizations to start asking the right questions about securing their information. Those readers who have worked on a Sarbanes-Oxley audit have seen that the FISMA Risk Framework has many of the same requirements and steps as the Committee of Sponsoring Organizations of the Treadway Commission (COSO)[40] framework has. COSO is used by the Public Company Accounting Oversight Board (PCAOB)[41] for meeting audit objectives in Sarbanes-Oxley 404 audits.

Although NIST and other standards and technical configuration documents may be more stringent than what any specific organization requires to maintain compliance, they are a good starting place for ensuring that all facets of the relevant technology will meet many, if not all, of the legislative security requirements during an audit.

54.6 TECHNICAL FRAMEWORKS FOR IT AUDITS.

The best IT auditors struggle with the reality of acceptable risk and vague controls, looking for solid frameworks to help with their audit. Great research and a good framework can help determine the questions for many of the unique or new audits that have not been faced in the past. Three useful models, as discussed next, can be applied from a high-level perspective to make sure that all of the relevant questions have been covered. In addition to models, general best practices help round out the technical bases to make sure the audit reveals any material weaknesses in key controls.

54.6.1 Framework 1: People, Processes, Tools, and Measures.

The first useful framework—People, Processes, Tools, and Measures (PPTM)—is simple conceptually, but its wide scope digs quickly into often-overlooked critical processes and important controls. Take a randomly picked application about which nothing is known, and apply PPTM concepts to the application to understand it and to develop a series of controls to test, and useful information to gather.

1. **People** build the application, input data into the application, and use the output or storage of the data handled by the application. People are a component that touches or uses the application, and as such should have controls that govern the interaction. For example, how are the people authenticated or authorized as administrators or users of the application?

2. **Processes** surround the operations of the application. What processes govern standard operating practices, and how can they be validated?

3. **Tools** are the physical controls, such as other applications that might interface with the application or ensure the quality or validation of the application. Other types of tool controls include checking the platform that the application uses. What physical controls existed during the implementation or are currently in operations to make sure the application is in a secure environment?

4. **Measures** are often-overlooked metrics, although they represent some of the most useful data in thorough audits. They can verify that the application is performing its function in support of its assigned business role. For example, metrics can

report on the operating efficiency of an application and how well it might scale to meet customer needs over time.

54.6.2 Framework 2: STRIDE.   STRIDE encompasses six areas of risk common to different technologies. Similar to how PPTM is used, STRIDE will help in understanding how the area of risk might play a role in the technology to be audited and then in finding the controls that alleviate that risk. The keepers of OWASP, the Open Web Application Security Project at www.owasp.com, provide an excellent example of applying STRIDE to Web applications.

1. **Spoofing** describes the risk of any user assuming the identity of another user or masking directly or indirectly the attributes of another user. For example, a user logging onto a banking Web site should generally not be able to assume another user's identity.

2. **Tampering** with data describes the need for input validation, process validation, and output validation. The integrity of the data should be preserved at all times, and in some cases protected from tampering, with encryption or by independent verification.

3. **Repudiation** describes a scenario where a user can suggest that a transaction never occurred. Poor audit trails lead to this situation. Nonrepudiation is the control that protects against repudiation. It includes signing a message with date and time as a unique, unduplicatable moment.

4. **Information** disclosure describes the additional controls to prevent information from leaving the system to unauthorized parties or programs.

5. **Denial** of service describes a condition where the application or technology could be maliciously or inadvertently removed from service. If this is a concern, controls should be in place such as redundant systems, backups, and measures to prevent denial-of-service events.

6. **Elevation** of privilege describes the situation where a user maliciously or inadvertently gains administrative rights.

54.6.3 Framework 3: PDIO.   PDIO—Plan, Design, Implement, and Operations—borrows from Cisco System's project management processes and describes the life cycle of a technology. The usefulness of this framework can be very powerful, especially when combined with PPTM. Administrators address people, processes, tools, and measures at each step in a project's planning, designing, implementation, and operations. PDIO can be viewed from a macro perspective to understand an entire new project or from a microperspective to understand each smaller element. The big-picture understanding of an audit is the mark of a great result that provides incredibly valuable—and useful—information to customers so that they can strengthen their controls.

54.6.4 General Best Practices.   This short list of common best practices should help with additional controls for testing. This is especially helpful during an audit of a new technology that does not yet have an appropriate audit program.

1. **Apply defense in depth** so that you have layered controls.

2. **Use a positive security model**. By default, deny actions and allow only a trusted or benign subset of available options. Negative security models trust everything by default and attempt to discover when to block offending behavior.

3. **Fail safely** so that people, equipment, data, and business processes are safe from harm.

4. **Run with least privilege** to prevent users from escalating their privileges above what is necessary to do their job.

5. **Avoid security by obscurity.** Try to hide data or options. Security by obscurity is setting up the technology for compromise.

6. **Keep security simple.** Overly complex systems are difficult to administer and often end up not secured.

7. **Detect intrusions and keep logs.** There should be an audit trail for everything important.

8. **Never trust infrastructure and services**, especially those coming from a third-party managed solution, where there might be different security policies and practices from the originating organization.

9. **Establish secure defaults.** Default to safe values and actions over defaulting to less secure values and actions. Another common mistake is not to specify an important value, causing issues later for the technology or application.

10. **Use open standards** because they are tested more thoroughly than proprietary technologies. Encryption in Digital Rights Management is an example where several purportedly secure private ciphers or cryptographic systems have been broken.

54.6.5 Technical Frameworks Conclusion.   The use of frameworks can be a valuable asset when approaching a technical audit, allowing quick determination of those areas where the audit is going to be most demanding and where compliance can be most effective.

54.7   FURTHER READING

Cascarino, R. E. *Auditor's Guide to Information Systems Auditing*. Hoboken, NJ: John Wiley & Sons, 2007.

Champlain, J. J. *Auditing Information Systems*. Hoboken, NJ: John Wiley & Sons, 2003.

Davis, C., M. Schiller, and K. Wheeler. *IT Auditing: Using Controls to Protect Information Assets*. New York: McGraw-Hill Osborne Media, 2006.

Gallegos, F., D. P. Manson, S. Senft, and C. Gonzales. *Information Technology Control and Audit*, 2nd ed. Boca Raton, FL: Auerbach, 2004.

Hunton, J. E., N. A. Bagranoff, and S. M. Bryant. *Core Concepts of Information Systems Auditing*. Hoboken, NJ: John Wiley & Sons, 2003.

ITGI. *Managing Enterprise Information Integrity: Security, Control and Audit Issues*. ISACA, 2004; www.isaca.org/Template.cfm?Section=Published_by_ISACA_and_ITGI&Template=/Ecommerce/ProductDisplay.cfm&Productid=574.

Lahti, C. B., and R. Peterson. *Sarbanes-Oxley Compliance Using COBIT and Open Source Tools*, 2nd ed. Burlington, MA: Syngress Publishing, 2007.

Moeller, R. *COSO Enterprise Risk Management: Understanding the New Integrated ERM Framework*. Hoboken, NJ: John Wiley & Sons, 2007.

Shostack, A., and A. Stewart. *The New School of Information Security*. Addison-Wesley Professional, 2008.

Tarantino, A. *Manager's Guide to Compliance: Sarbanes-Oxley, COSO, ERM, COBIT, IFRS, BASEL II, OMB's A-123, ASX 10, OECD Principles, Turnbull Guidance, Best Practices, and Case Studies*. Hoboken, NJ: John Wiley & Sons, 2006.

Umar, A. *Information Security and Auditing in the Digital Age: A Practical and Managerial Perspective.* Middlesex, NJ: NGE Solutions, 2004.

54.8   NOTES

1. ISO is not an abbreviation of International Organization for Standardization but instead a shortened form of the Greek ISOS, meaning "equal." The term was chosen to be understood in all translations and speak to the organizations' intent of equal representation for all members regardless of their national economic status or country's level of development.

2. International Organization for Standardization, *ISO Membership.* Retrieved on February 5, 2007, from www.iso.org/iso/en/aboutiso/isomembers/index.html.

3. All approved standards continue to be subject to periodic review to ensure timely update of industry requirements and technologies.

4. International Organization for Standardization, *How Are ISO Standards Developed?* Retrieved on February 5, 2007, from www.iso.org/iso/en/stdsdevelopment/whowhenhow/how.html.

5. An ISMS includes any components necessary to maintain information assurance (to include, policies, plans, processes, roles, responsibilities etc.).

6. C & A Systems Security Limited, *BS 7799 Compliance and Management.* Retrieved on February 5, 2007, from www.securitypolicy.co.uk/bs-7799/index.htm.

7. International Organization for Standardization, *Improved ISO/IEC 17799 Makes Information Assets Even More Secure.* Retrieved on February 5, 2007, from www.iso.org/iso/en/commcentre/pressreleases/archives/2005/Ref963.html.

8. Effective April 2007, ISO 17799 was renamed ISO/IEC 27002.

9. Prasanna Ramakrishnan, "Information Security Management Systems" (2003). Retrieved on February 5, 2007, from www.cccure.org/Documents/ISMS/isms.pdf.

10. International Register of Information Security Management System Certificates, *ISMS Standards for ISO 27000.* Retrieved on February 5, 2007, from www.iso27001certificates.com.

11. OECD in an international cooperative committed to sharing information and developing accepted standards on economic and social issues related to trade, education, development, and science.

12. IT Governance Ltd., *Information Security Standards ISO 27001.* Retrieved on February 5, 2007, from www.itgovernance.co.uk/iso27001.asp.

13. IT Governance Ltd., *Information Security and ISO 27001 – An Introduction.* Retrieved on February 5, 2007 from www.itgovernance.co.uk/files/Infosec_101v1.1.pdf.

14. IT Governance Ltd., *ISO 27001 in North America.* Retrieved on February 5, 2007, from www.itgovernance.co.uk/page.27001.

15. U.S. Senate Committee on Banking, Housing and Urban Affairs, Financial Services Modernization Act (1999), http://banking.senate.gov/conf/grmleach.htm.

16. Corsaire, "Penetration Testing Guide" (2005), www.penetration-testing.com.

17. 15 U.S.C. § 7241 (Section 302) (civil provision), www4.law.cornell.edu/uscode/html/uscode15/usc_sec_15_00007241—-000-.html; 18 U.S.C. § 1350 (Section 906) (criminal provision), www4.law.cornell.edu/uscode/html/uscode18/usc_sec_18_00001350—-000-.html.

18. A significant business process is one that accounts for a certain portion of an organization's balance sheet. The actual threshold for inclusion will vary by organization.

19. Committee of the Sponsoring Organizations of the Treadway Commission, www.coso.org.

20. "Internal Control—Integrated Framework," COSO, March 1, 2006. Retrieved March 5, 2007, www.coso.org/publications/executive_summary_integrated_framework.htm.

21. CoBiT is freely available to members of ISACA and is also available free to nonmembers with a simple registration, www.isaca.org/Template.cfm?Section=COBIT6.

22. US DOD CSC, "Rainbow Series" (1980), available at www.fas.org/irp/nsa/rainbow.htm.

23. NIST, "Recommended Security Controls for Federal Information Systems," Special Publication 800-53 Revision 2 (December 2007), http://csrc.nist.gov/publications/nistpubs/800-53-Rev2/sp800-53-rev2-final.pdf.

24. NIST, "Standards for Security Categorization of Federal Information and Information Systems (February 2004)," FIPS 199, http://csrc.nist.gov/publications/fips/fips199/FIPS-PUB-199-final.pdf.

25. A federal information system is an information system used or operated by an executive agency, by a contractor of an executive agency, or by another organization on behalf of an executive agency.

26. NIST, "Guideline for Identifying an Information System as a National Security System (August 2004)," Special Publication 800-59, http://csrc.nist.gov/publications/nistpubs/800-59/SP800-59.pdf.

27. NIST, "Minimum Security Requirements for Federal Information and Information Systems (March 2006)," FIPS -200, http://csrc.nist.gov/publications/fips/fips200/FIPS-200-final-march.pdf.

28. NIST, "Federal Information Security Management Act (FISMA) Implementation Project," http://csrc.nist.gov/groups/SMA/fisma/index.html.

29. E-Government Act of 2002, www.usaid.gov/policy/egov/egov_2002.pdf.

30. Federal Information Security Management Act of 2002 (FISMA), 44 U.S.C. § 3541, *et seq.,* www4.law.cornell.edu/uscode/html/uscode44/usc_sec_44_00003541—-000-.html.

31. OMB, Circular A-130—Revised, Transmittal Memorandum No. 4, "Memorandum for Heads of Executive Departments and Agencies; Subject: Management of Federal Information Resources," www.whitehouse.gov/omb/circulars/a130/a130trans4.html.

32. NIST, "FISMA Risk Management Framework," http://csrc.nist.gov/groups/SMA/fisma/framework.html.

33. NIST, "FISMA Detailed Overview," http://csrc.nist.gov/groups/SMA/fisma/overview.html.

34. NIST, "Draft Guide for Mapping Types of Information and Information Systems to Security Categories: Volume 1: Guide for Mapping Types of Information and Information Systems to Security Categories; Volume 2: Appendices (November 2007)," SP 800-60 Revision 1, http://csrc.nist.gov/publications/PubsDrafts.html#SP-800-60-Rev.%201 and http://csrc.nist.gov/publications/PubsDrafts.html#SP-800-60-Rev.%201.

35. NIST, "Risk Management Guide for Information Technology Systems (July 2002)," SP 800-30, http://csrc.nist.gov/publications/nistpubs/800-30/sp800-30.pdf.

36. NIST, "Guide for Developing Security Plans for Federal Information Systems (February 2006)," SP 800-18 Revision 1, http://csrc.nist.gov/publications/nistpubs/800-18-Rev1/sp800-18-Rev1-final.pdf.

37. NIST, "Draft Guide for Assessing the Security Controls in Federal Information Systems (December 2007)," SP 800-53A, http://csrc.nist.gov/publications/PubsDrafts.html#SP-800-53-A.

38. NIST, "Guide for the Security Certification and Accreditation of Federal Information Systems (May 2004)," SP 800-37, http://csrc.nist.gov/publications/nistpubs/800-37/SP800-37-final.pdf.

39. NIST SP 800-37 and SP 800-53A.

40. AICPA, COSO publications (AICPA 2007), www.coso.org/publications.htm and www.cpa2biz.com.

41. PCAOB, Standards Board (2003–2006), available at www.pcaobus.org/index.aspx.

CYBER INVESTIGATION[1]

Peter Stephenson

55.1 INTRODUCTION. Cyber investigation (also widely known as *digital investigation*) as a discipline has changed markedly since publication of the fourth edition of this *Handbook* in 2002. In 1999, when *Investigating Computer Related Crime*[2] was published, practitioners in the field were just beginning to speculate as to how cyber investigations would be carried out. At that time, the idea of cyber investigation was almost completely congruent with the practice of computer forensics. Today (as this is being written in April 2008), we know that such a view is too confining for investigations in the current digital environment.

Cyber investigation today is evolving into a discipline that is not only becoming commonplace in information technology but is also finding acceptance by both law enforcement and the forensic science community. The American Academy of Forensic Science, for example, now recognizes the forensic computer-related crime investigator as a legitimate discipline within its general category of membership.[3]

This chapter defines cyber investigation and examines some of its forensic components. It discusses a useful cyber investigation approach called end-to-end digital investigation (EEDI). Finally, the chapter explores some forensic tools and considers their usefulness both practically and theoretically.

55.1.1 Defining Cyber Investigation.

Rogers, Brinson, and Robinson[4] approach the definition of cyber forensics in an ontology ("the question of how many fundamentally distinct sorts of entities compose the universe"[5]); it can also be viewed as a taxonomy ("the practice or principles of classification"[6]). Although their descriptive schema is not complete, it is informative. Most important, Rogers's approach recognizes that there is no simple definition of cyber investigation; ontology and taxonomy are therefore particularly useful in clarifying meaning and structure for such a field.

The *Rogers cyber forensic ontology* consists of five layers. Ontology generally contains classes, sub-classes, slots, and instances. These elements also contain constraints and relations. Rogers's five layers can be considered to be a superclass with two classes and four nested subclasses. He does not define the other elements in his paper. The Rogers schema is easy to extend, however, to a proper ontology using a tool such as Protégé.[7] For our purposes, we will refer to his model as the *Rogers taxonomy*.

The core of the Rogers taxonomy as a definition resides in the relationships inherent in the various subclasses. Exhibit 55.1 presents the taxonomy as a hierarchy with two major classes, Profession and Technology.

Starting with *cyber forensics* at the top and with two classes represented in columns, the farther to the right in each class, the more granularity one adds to the characterization. Ontology supports understanding by providing a collection of characteristics that describe a concept; each class and nested subclass adds characteristics to that concept and contributes to a functional definition of cyber forensics. At the same time, concepts *not* included help to constrain the description and increase the precision of the ontological definition.

55.1.2 Distinguishing between Cyber Forensics and Cyber Investigation.

Cyber investigation uses the tools of *cyber forensics* as part of investigative procedures. The Digital Forensics Research Workshop (DFRWS)[8] in 2001 developed a useful framework for digital investigation,[9] a version of which appears in Exhibit 55.2.

Although this framework appeared in 2001, it has not been improved on markedly in the intervening years.[10]

55.1.3 DFRWS Framework Classes.

The DFRWS framework is a matrix. The columns are called *classes* and the cells are called *elements*. In the class descriptions that follow, the quoted italicized descriptions are taken verbatim from the original publication.[11]

The DFRWS framework classes contain key elements that are under constant review by the digital forensics community. The continuity among the classes is important; for example, the Preservation class continues as an element of the Collection, Examination, and Analysis classes. This indicates that *preservation* of evidence (as characterized by

○ Profession
  ➢ Law
    ❖ Enforcement
      ✓ Evidence
      ✓ Collection/Analysis
    ❖ Courts
      ✓ Laws
      ✓ People
  ➢ Academia
    ❖ Research
      ✓ Discipline definition
      ✓ Problem solving
    ❖ Education
      ✓ Contributions
      ✓ Professional outcome
  ➢ Military
    ❖ Offensive
      ✓ Passive
      ✓ Active
    ❖ Defensive
      ✓ Proactive
      ✓ Reactive
  ➢ Private sector
    ❖ Industry
      ✓ System admins
      ✓ Legal contact
    ❖ Consulting
      ✓ Data recovery
      ✓ Forensic analysis
      ✓ Expert witness consultant

○ Technology
  ➢ Software
    ❖ Analysis tools
      ✓ Proprietary
      ✓ Open-source tools
    ❖ Operating systems
      ✓ Proprietary OS
      ✓ Open-source OS
      ✓ Open source
    ❖ File systems
      ✓ Windows
      ✓ UNIX/Linux
      ✓ Mac
  ➢ Hardware
    ❖ Large-scale digital devices
      ✓ Clusters
      ✓ Grids
    ❖ Small-scale digital devices
      ✓ Cell phones
      ✓ PDAa
      ✓ SSD Operating software
    ❖ Computers
      ✓ Desktops
      ✓ Laptops
      ✓ Servers
      ✓ Tablets
    ❖ Storage devices
      ✓ Thumb drive
      ✓ Digital music player
      ✓ External music player
      ✓ External hard drives
    ❖ Obscure devices
      ✓ Gaming devices
      ✓ Recording devices

EXHIBIT 55.1   Rogers Cyber Forensics Taxonomy

case management, imaging technologies, chain of custody, and time synchronization) is an ongoing requirement throughout the digital investigative process. Thus *preservation* is "a guarded principle across 'forensic' categories."[12] Traceability, likewise, is a guarded principle, but not across all forensic categories. The next topics discuss each of the DFRWS framework classes in more detail. Elements marked with an asterisk (*) in the discussions are *required* in all cyber investigations.

55.1.3.1 Identification Class.   The DFRWS defines the Identification class in this way:

Determining items, components and data possibly associated with the allegation or incident. Perhaps employing triage techniques.[13]

EXHIBIT 55.2 DFRWS Digital Investigation Framework

Identification	Preservation	Collection	Examination	Analysis	Presentation
Event/Crime detection	Case management	Preservation	Preservation	Preservation	Documentation
Resolve signature	Imaging technologies	Approved methods	Traceability	Traceability	Expert testimony
Profile detection	Chain of custody	Approved software	Validation techniques	Statistical	Clarification
Anomalous detection	Time synchronization	Approved hardware	Filtering techniques	Protocols	Mission impact statement
Complaints		Legal authority	Pattern matching	Data mining	Recommended countermeasure
System monitoring		Lossless compression	Hidden data discovery	Timeline	Statistical interpretation
Audit analysis		Sampling	Hidden data extraction	Link	
		Data reduction		Spatial	
		Recovery techniques			

The Identification class describes the method by which the investigator is notified of a possible incident. Since about 50 percent of all reported incidents have benign explanations,[14] processing evidence in this class is critical to the rest of the investigation. Likewise, as it is the first step in the EEDI process, it is the only primary evidence not corroborated directly by other primary evidence. Therefore, a more significant amount of secondary evidence is needed to validate the existence of an actual event.

The author has adopted the next definitions of the individual framework classes for the purposes of EEDI. The DFRWS has, as of this writing, not developed such definitions. Elements marked with an asterisk (*) are required elements within the DFRWS class. The elements of the Identification class are:

- **Event/crime detection.**[*] This element implies direct evidence of an event. An example of such direct evidence is discovery that a large number of credit card numbers have been downloaded from a server.

- **Resolve signature.** This applies to the use of some automated event detection system, such as an intrusion system or antivirus software program. The system in use must make its determination (of the presence of an event of interest) by means of signature analysis and mapping.

- **Profile detection.** Like signature resolution, profile detection usually relies on some automated event detection system. However, in this instance, the event will be characterized through matching with a particular profile as opposed to an explicit signature. Signatures generally apply to an individual event. Events, however, may come together in an *attack scenario* or *attack profile*. Such a profile may consist of a number of events, a pattern of behavior, or pattern of specific results of an attack.

- **Anomalous detection.** Again, like the preceding two elements, this usually relies on a detection system. However, in the case of anomalous detection, the event is deduced from the detection of patterns of behavior outside of the observed norm. Anomalies can include the presence of unusual behavior but also, as in the classic Sherlock Holmes case of the dog that "did nothing in the night-time," the absence of expected behavior.[15]

- **Complaints.** This element relies on the direct reporting of a potential event by an observer. This person may observe the event directly or simply the end result of the event.

- **System monitoring.** System monitoring explicitly requires some sort of intrusion detection, antivirus, or similar system in place. It is less specific than other elements requiring a specific action (e.g., anomaly, profile of signature detection) and may be used together with another element of this class.

- **Audit analysis.** This element refers particularly to the analysis of various audit logs produced by source, target, and intermediate devices.

55.1.3.2 Preservation Class.   The Preservation class deals with those elements that relate to the management of items of evidence. The DFRWS describes this class as "a guarded principle across 'forensic' categories." The requirement for proper evidence handing is basic to the digital investigative process as it relates to legal actions.

The DFRWS defines this class as "[e]nsuring evidence integrity or state."

- **Case management.*** This element covers the management of the investigative process by investigators and digital forensic examiners. Typical in this element are investigator notes, process controls, quality controls, and procedural issues.

- **Imaging technologies.** This element is separate from the elements in the Collection class in that it does not refer to specific hardware, software, or techniques. The imaging technologies element refers to the *technology* used for imaging computer media. For example, physical imaging or bitstream backup may be considered an appropriate imaging technology whereas a logical backup would not be. The term "imaging" as used here is rather broad. It encompasses not only the technology used to create an image of computer media but also the technology used to extract such items as logs from a device. In this case, the log might be extracted from a bitstream image or it might be read out of the device to a peripheral as a result of a keystroke command issued by the investigator.

- **Chain of custody.*** This element refers to the process of limiting access to and subsequent alteration of evidence. In most jurisdictions chain of custody rules require that the evidence custodian be able to account for all accesses or possible accesses to items of evidence within his or her care from the time it is collected until the time it is used in a legal proceeding,

- **Time synchronization.*** This element refers to the synchronizing of evidence items to a common time base. Since logs and other evidence are collected from a number of devices during the conduct of an investigation, it is clear that those devices can differ from each other in terms of time base. If all devices are in a single time-synchronized network, they will not, of course, differ. However, that rarely is the case, and some effort must be made to obtain a common time base for all devices. There are two approaches one might take. The first is to adjust all times on evidence to a common device. The second is to use a common time zone (TZ), such as Universal Time (UT) or Greenwich Mean Time (GMT), as a baseline. No evidence is modified. The investigator simply notes the variance of a particular log or other piece of digital evidence from the predetermined time standard. This also is referred as *normalizing* time stamps.

55.1.3.3 Collection Class.
The Collection class is concerned with the specific methods and products used by the investigator and forensic examiner to acquire evidence in a digital environment. As has been noted, the Preservation class continues as an element of this class. With the exception of the legal authority element, the elements of this class are largely technical.

The DFRWS defines this class as "[e]xtracting or harvesting individual items or groupings."

- **Approved methods.*** This element refers to the techniques used by the forensic examiner or investigator to extract digital evidence. The concept of being *approved* refers to the general acceptance in courts of the techniques and training or certifications of the individual performing the evidence collection. The most rigorous test of methods and technologies is the *Daubert* test. (For more information on expert testimony, see Chapter 73 in this *Handbook*.) However, due largely to the immaturity of digital forensic science, most court tests have not had this level of rigor applied. For this reason, those elements in this class that relate to approval derive their authority from cases where the technique, technology, or product has been challenged in a court of the same level as the case in question and has survived the test.

- **Approved software.** This element addresses the specific software product used to collect evidence. The discussion of the approval process in the last bullet point applies. There is an issue specifically involving software used for digital forensic data collection. In order for a software program to be considered approved, it must be identical in every way to the software that has survived either a *Daubert* hearing or a court challenge. That means that the software source code must be in every way identical in both instances of the program. Failing that, the program may need to undergo its own court testing. For the purposes of the framework and subsequent EEDI procedures, however, a program that has any differences (e.g., version level, bug fixes, source code changes, etc.) from the program tested originally is not considered to be approved software.

- **Approved hardware.** This element describes the hardware, if any, used to collect evidence. Usually this is not an issue unless the hardware is designed specifically for use in a digital forensic evidence collection environment. To a lesser extent, the caveats of sameness that apply to approved software apply to approved hardware. The hardware device used must in every way be identical to instances of the device that have survived court challenges. The approved hardware element does not apply to simple computers, disks, or other media used by the examiner to collect evidence unless the device was developed explicitly for digital forensic evidence collection and contains special unique features for use in that environment only.

- **Legal authority.*** The legal authority element is the only element of this class that is nontechnical. In most jurisdictions, some legal authority is required prior to extracting information from computer media. This authority could be a policy, a subpoena, or a search warrant, for example. Failure to comply with applicable laws may render the evidence collected useless in a court of law.

- **Lossless compression.** This element refers to the compression techniques, if any, used by backup, encryption, or digital signature software used to collect and/or preserve evidence. If the software program uses compression, it must be proven to be lossless, that is, to cause no change whatever upon the integrity of the evidence on which it is used.

- **Sampling.** If sampling techniques are used to collect evidence, it must be shown that the technique causes no degradation of the evidence collected, or, if it has, that the effects can be demonstrated clearly and unambiguously. It must also be shown that the sampling method is valid (generally accepted by the mathematical community) and that the conclusions that may be drawn from the sample are defined clearly.

- **Data reduction.** When techniques and/or programs (such as normalization) are used to reduce data that contain or may contain evidence, it must be shown that such techniques or programs produce valid, repeatable, provable results that do not affect, in any way whatever, the evidence being collected. For example, using data reduction directly on evidence would alter the evidence and would not be acceptable. However, using such methods or tools on a *copy* of the evidence would have no direct affect on the evidence. Its affect on the analysis of the evidence (the validity of conclusions, e.g.) is an issue for the Examination and Analysis classes.

- **Recovery techniques.** This element refers to the recovery of data that may contain evidence from a digital device. It specifically describes the methods used by the forensic examiner to extract evidence using approved hardware, software, and methods. Whereas the elements of approved hardware, software, and methods refer to the naming (or brief description of) the element and the connection between the element and the appropriate court test by which it is approved, "recovery techniques" describes in detail the actual process used to recover the evidence. By extension, when nonforensic methods are used to collect information (e.g., traditional investigation methods such as interviewing), we consider these techniques also to be recovery techniques and we apply the same rules to them (e.g., approved methods, legal authority, etc.) as we would in a digital environment. However, we apply the rules in the context of the technique used.

55.1.3.4   Examination Class.   The Examination class deals with the tools and techniques used to examine evidence. The DFRWS gives describes the Examination class in this way: "Closer scrutiny of items and their attributes (characteristics)." It is concerned with evidence discovery and extraction rather than the conclusions to be drawn from the evidence (Analysis class). Whereas the Collection class deals with gross procedures to collect data that may contain evidence (such as imaging of computer media), the Examination class is concerned with the examination of those data and the identification and extraction of possible evidence from them. Note that the Preservation class continues to be pervasive in the Examination class.

- **Traceability.**[*] This element is, arguably, the most important element in the EEDI process. It is the traceability and continuity of a *chain of evidence* throughout an investigation that leads to the credibility and correctness of the conclusions. According to the DFRWS, "[t]raceability (cross referencing and linking) is key as evidence unfolds."

- **Validation techniques.** This element refers to techniques used to corroborate evidence. Evidence may be corroborated in a variety of ways. Traditionally, evidence is corroborated by other, relevant evidence. However, digital evidence may stand on its own merit if its technical validity can be established. For example, a fragment of text extracted from an image of a computer disk may be shown to be a valid piece of evidence through various technical validation techniques. Its applicability or usefulness as an element of proof in an investigation may be open to interpretation, but that it is *valid* data would not be in dispute. A log, however, if extracted from a device that had been penetrated by a criminal hacker, would require additional corroboration (validation) to show that the hacker had not altered its contents.

- **Filtering techniques.** When dealing with evidence acquired from certain types of digital systems (such as intrusion detection systems), it is not uncommon to find that the gross data have been filtered for expediency by the system. Although many intrusion detection experts would agree that filtering at the source (the incoming data flow from sensors) is not as appropriate as filtering the display while preserving the original data, such source filtering does occur. This element requires that the investigator and/or forensic examiner determine and describe the filtering techniques used, if any, and apply the results of that description to the determination of the validity of the data as evidence. Another application of filtering is the extraction of potential evidence from a gross data collection[16] such as a bit-stream image of digital media. Some digital forensic tools use filters to extract data of a particular type, such as graphical images. This element requires that the filtering technique be defined clearly and understood by the investigator or forensic examiner. These tools may also use the filtering technique of matching a known hash value to digital items on a gross data collection. Items that match the known hash are presumed to be the same as the item for which the hash value was originally generated. Again, the techniques and tools applied must be clearly understood by the investigator or the forensic examiner.

- **Pattern matching.** This element addresses methods used to identify potential events by some predetermined signature or pattern. Examples are pattern-based intrusion detection systems and signature-based virus checkers. When the pattern or signature is unclear, ambiguous, or demonstrates a large number false positives or negatives, the evidence and conclusion following from it are open to challenge.
- **Hidden data discovery.** This element refers to the discovery of evidence that is hidden in some manner on computer media. The data may be hidden using encryption, steganography, or any other data-hiding technique. It may also include data that have been deleted but are forensically recoverable.
- **Hidden data extraction.** This element addresses the extraction of hidden evidence from a gross data collection.

55.1.3.5 Analysis Class.
This class is described by the DFRWS as "[f]usion, correlation and assimilation of material for reasoned conclusions."

The Analysis class refers to those elements that are involved in the analysis of evidence collected, identified, and extracted from a gross data collection. The validity of techniques used in analysis of potential evidence impact as directly the validity of the conclusions drawn from the evidence and the credibility of the evidence chain constructed therefrom. The Analysis class contains, and is dependent on, the Preservation class and the Traceability element of the Examination class.

The various elements of the Analysis class refer to the means by which a forensic examiner or investigator might develop a set of conclusions regarding evidence presented from the other five classes. As with all elements of the framework, a clear understanding of the applicable process is required. Wherever possible, adherence to standard tools, technologies and techniques is critical.

The link element is the key element used to form a chain of evidence. It is related to traceability and, as such, is a required element.

55.1.3.6 Presentation Class.
DFRWS describes the Presentation class in this way: "Reporting facts in an organized, clear, concise and objective manner."

This class refers to the tools and techniques used to present the conclusions of the investigator and the digital forensic examiner to a court of inquiry or other finder of fact. Each of these techniques has its own elements, and a discussion of expert witnessing is beyond the scope of this chapter. However, for our purposes, we will stipulate that the EEDI process emphasizes the use of timelines as an embodiment of the clarification element of this class. For more information on expert witness testimony, see Chapter 73 in this *Handbook*.

55.2 END-TO-END DIGITAL INVESTIGATION.
The end-to-end digital investigation process takes into account a structured process including the network involved, the attack computer, the victim computer, and all of the intermediate devices on the network. Structurally, it consists of nine steps:

1. Collecting evidence

2. Analysis of individual events

3. Preliminary correlation

4. Event normalizing

5. Event deconfliction

6. Second-level correlation (consider both normalized and nonnormalized events)

7. Timeline analysis

8. Chain of evidence construction

9. Corroboration (consider only nonnormalized events)

55.2.1   Collecting Evidence.   A formal definition of the term "evidence collection" is:

> The use of approved tools and techniques by trained technicians to obtain digital evidence from computer devices, networks and media. By "approved" we mean those tools and techniques generally accepted by the discipline and the courts where collected evidence will be presented.[17]

The collection of evidence in a computer security incident is time sensitive. When an event occurs (or when an expected event fails to occur), we have the first warning of a potential incident. An event may not be, by itself, particularly noteworthy. However, taken in the context of other events, it may become extremely important. From the forensic perspective, we want to consider all relevant events, whether they appear to have been tied to an incident or not. Events are the most granular elements of an incident.

We define an incident as a collection of events that lead to, or could lead to, a compromise of some sort. That compromise may include unauthorized change of control over data or systems; disclosure or modification of a system or its data; data or system destruction of the system; or unauthorized alterations in availability or utility or its data. An incident becomes a crime when a law or laws is/are violated.

Collecting evidence from all possible locations where it may reside must begin as soon as possible in the context of an incident. The methods vary according to the type of evidence (forensic, logs, indirect, traditionally developed, etc.). It is important to emphasize that EEDI is concerned not only with digital evidence. Gathering witness information should be accomplished as early in the evidence collection process as possible. Witness impressions and information play a crucial role in determining the steps the forensic examiner must take to uncover digital evidence.

Critical in this process are:

- Images of effected computers
- Logs of intermediate devices, especially those on the Internet
- Logs of effected computers
- Logs and data from intrusion detection systems, firewalls, and so on

55.2.2   Analysis of Individual Events.   An alert or incident is made up of one or more individual events. These events may be duplicates reported in different logs from different devices. These events and duplications have value both as they appear and after they are normalized. This analysis step examines isolated events and assesses what value they may have to the overall investigation and how they may tie into each other.

55.2.3 Preliminary Correlation.

The formal definition of the term "correlation" is:

> The comparison of evidentiary information from a variety of sources with the objective of discovering information that stands alone, in concert with other information, or corroborates or is corroborated by other evidentiary information.

Preliminary correlation examines the individual events to correlate them into a *chain of evidence*. The main purpose is to understand in broad terms what happened, what systems or devices were involved, and when the events occurred.

The term "chain of evidence" refers to the chain of events related in some consistent way that describes the incident. The relationship may be temporal or causal. Temporal chains are also called timelines. Essentially they say "This happened, *then* that happened." Causal relationships imply cause and effect. They say "That happened *because* this happened."

The term "chain of evidence" must not be used as a synonym for "chain of custody," which this chapter defines in the discussion of the Preservation class of the DFRWS framework.

55.2.4 Event Normalizing.

The formal definition of "normalization" is:

> The combining of evidentiary data of the same type from different sources with different vocabularies into a single, integrated terminology that can be used effectively in the correlation process.

Some events may be reported from multiple sources. During part of the analysis (timeline analysis, e.g.), these duplications must be eliminated. This process is known as normalizing. EEDI uses both normalized and nonnormalized events.

55.2.5 Event Deconfliction.

The formal definition of "deconfliction" is:

> The combining of multiple reportings of the same evidentiary event by the same or different reporting sources, into a single, reported, normalized evidentiary event.

Sometimes events are reported multiple times from the same source. An example is a denial-of-service attack where multiple packets are directed against a target and each one is reported individually by a reporting resource. The EEDI process should not count each of those packets as a separate event. The process of viewing the packets as a single event instead of multiple events is called deconfliction.

55.2.6 Second-Level Correlation.

Second-level correlation is an extension of earlier correlation efforts. However, at this point, views of various events have been refined through normalization or deconfliction. For example, during the process of deconfliction or normalization, we have simplified the collection of events to eliminate redundancies and/or ambiguities. The resulting data set now represents the event universe at it simplest (or nearly simplest). These events (some of which actually may be compound events, i.e., events composed of multiple subevents) now represent the building blocks with which we may build chains of evidence.

55.2.7 Timeline Analysis.

In this step, normalized and deconflicted events are used to build a timeline using an iterative process that should be updated constantly as the investigation continues to develop new evidence. The entire process is iterative: Event analysis, correlation, deconfliction, and timeline analysis are repeated in sequence as required.

55.2.8   Chain of Evidence Construction.   Once there is a preliminary timeline of events, the process of developing a coherent chain of evidence begins. Ideally, each link in the chain, supported by one or more pieces of evidence, will lead to the next link. That rarely happens in large-scale network traces, however, because there often are gaps in the evidence-gathering process due to lack of logs or other missing event data.

Such problems do not invalidate this step, however. Although we may not always be able to construct a chain of evidence directly, we can nonetheless infer missing links in the chain. Now, an inferred link is not evidence: It is more properly referred to as a *lead*. Leads can point us to valid evidence and that valid evidence can, at some point, become the evidence link. Thus again, the iterative process of refinement of evidence makes it perfectly reasonable to start with a chain that is part evidence and part leads and refine it into an acceptable chain of evidence.

A second approach to handling gaps in evidence is to corroborate the questionable link very heavily. If all corroboration points to a valid link, it may be acceptable. For most purposes, however, the former approach is best.

55.2.9   Corroboration.   In this stage, we attempt to corroborate each piece of evidence and each event in our chain with other, independent evidence or events. For this process, we use the noncorrelated event data as well as any other evidence developed either digitally or traditionally. The best evidence is that which has been developed digitally and corroborated through traditional investigation or vice versa. The final evidence chain consists of primary evidence corroborated by additional secondary evidence. This chain will consist of both digital and traditional evidence. The overall process does not differ materially between an investigation and an event postmortem except in use of the outcome.

55.3   APPLYING THE FRAMEWORK AND EEDI.   The important issue in application is evidence management. Both the framework and EEDI help the investigator manage evidence. They do not substitute for good investigative techniques. The incident may or may not be a criminal act; even if it is such an act, it may not be treated as one. No matter. The approach to investigating is essentially the same in either case. In order to understand how these investigative tools might apply, it is useful to begin with a generalized framework for understanding the execution of a cyber incident.

55.3.1   Supporting the EEDI Process.   Experienced traditional investigators often resist a process-based approach to investigation. However, in numerous interviews with such investigators, the author determined that what these investigators do by habit and experience is almost exactly the same process discussed in this chapter. Thus it is convenient to view the DFRWS framework and EEDI as tools that investigators can use to apply past physical investigation experience to the more complicated requirements of digital investigation.

55.3.2   Investigative Narrative.   The investigative narrative typically consists of the investigator's notes. The EEDI process supports the construction of an investigation around an investigative framework. For the purposes of this chapter, we use the DFRWS framework shown in Exhibit 55.2. The framework includes the basic areas where investigative and forensic controls are required. Once the narrative is complete, it can be translated into a more structured evidence support and management process using the framework and EEDI.

For example, under the Collection class, we find reference to approved software, hardware, and methods. This indicates that the forensic software, hardware, and methods used by the investigator or digital forensic examiner must meet some standard of acceptance within the investigative community. That standard usually refers to court testing. Should the investigator or forensic examiner not adhere to that standard, the evidence collected will be subject to challenge. At critical points in the investigation, such as the collection of primary evidence, such a lapse could jeopardize the outcome materially.

Again, the framework does not necessarily alter the generalized investigative techniques of experienced investigators and forensic examiners. Rather, it adds a dimension of rigor and quality assurance to the digital investigative process. It also ties the functions of the forensic examiner and the investigator tightly together, ensuring that the chain of evidence is properly supported, developed, and maintained.

55.3.3 Intrusion Process.   Today (2008), there are many ways in which an attack can occur. There has been a shift since about 2000 in types of incidents from manual hacking to automated malware-generated attacks. The sources of these attacks vary widely over time, and there is no definitive pattern to how they work. Today's assaults typically are some form of blended attack. Examples are botnets, spam, Trojan horses, rootkits, worms, and other malware. (See Chapters 2, 13, 15, 16, 17, and 18 in this *Handbook* for more details of attack methods.)

A *blended attack* is one in which various intrusion techniques are combined to deliver a payload. The payload can be a malicious outcome, such as damaging the target computer, or it can be more subtle, such as a spybot that harvests personal information and calls home periodically to deliver its collected information.

Regardless of the intrusion technique—manual hacking or automated malware—there is a generalized pattern of activities associated with a cyber attack. These steps are:

- **Information gathering.** Information gathering usually does not touch the victim. During this phase, the attacker selects his or her target, researches it, and determines such things as expected range of IP addresses exposed to the Internet. There is an exception to not touching the victim: Sometimes an attacker performs a scan of a block of IP addresses to determine whether there are any vulnerable devices in the IP block. This is what security professionals usually call a *script-kiddie* attack. The usual use for this step, however, is to select a victim for a targeted attack.

- **Footprinting.** Footprinting is the act of scanning a block of addresses owned by a victim for those that are on line and may be vulnerable. The attacker is obtaining the *footprint* of the victim's presence online.

- **Enumerating.** "Enumerating" refers to the analysis of exposed addresses for potential weaknesses. In this step, the attack may grab banners to determine the versions of various services running on the target. The objective is to understand what the victim is running on exposed machines. Once that information is gathered, the attacker can select potentially successful exploits based on published vulnerabilities. Although this process will leave a footprint on the target, it is likely to remain hidden in thousands of lines of logs (as in the footprinting phase). If these two steps (footprinting and enumerating) are performed carefully, they will not trigger most intrusion detection systems.

In a fully automated attack, such as one resulting from some form of social engineering (phishing, e.g.), these two steps are replaced by research that focuses on people and their access methods (e.g., e-mail addresses). (For more information on social engineering, see Chapter 19 in this *Handbook*; for more on phishing, see Chapter 20.)

- **Probing for weaknesses.** In this step, the attacker may perform a vulnerability scan or some more stealthy probes to determine specific exploitable vulnerabilities. In an automated attack, this phase may consist of attempting to seduce large numbers of targets to give up important information that can be used in the next step. In this case, the probes consist of social engineering attempts.

- **Penetration.** This is the entry phase. It is essentially the same no matter if the attack is manual or automated. Only the penetration technique changes. The objective always is to reach inside of the victim system.

- **Backdoors, Trojans, rootkits, and so on.** In this phase, the attacker deposits the payload. The objective may be to reenter the target at some later date, plant some malware, or take the system down with a denial-of-service attack. Most experts seem to agree that denial-of-service attacks are on the decline. The objective of today's intruders is more frequently stealing information than damaging systems. (For more about denial-of-service attacks, see Chapter 18 in this *Handbook*.)

- **Cleanup.** In a traditional hack, this step is where the attacker removes tools from the target, alters logs, and performs other actions to cover his or her tracks and obscure his or her presence from system administrators and forensic analysts. In an automated attack, the tasks are similar and have similar objectives, but the techniques are a bit different and the forensics required to find evidence are a bit different.

55.3.4   Describing Attacks.   Three factors lead to a successful attack:

1. The attacker can access the target.
2. There is a significant vulnerability to attack, and that vulnerability can be identified by the attacker.
3. The attacker needs to have effective command and control and the prospects for attribution are minimized.

It is important to be able to describe a cyber event in clear terms. There are several attack taxonomies and descriptive languages available to help do that. However, these tools, while useful, are inconsistent with each other (there is no universally accepted descriptive language or taxonomy) and are often unnecessarily complicated for smaller investigations. The author recommends Howard's common language (see Chapter 8 in this *Handbook*)[18] as a good starting point for something simple and concise. Before applying a common language, however, there are several questions that need to be asked.

- **Description of the attack.** This is a narrative describing how the attack appeared when analyzed: What is happening? What service is being targeted? Does the service have known vulnerabilities or exposures?

- **Type of attack.** Is it benign, an exploit, a denial-of-service attack or reconnaissance?
- **Attack mechanism.** This is a narrative describing how the attack was carried out: How did the attacker do it?
- **Correlations.** How does this attack compare with other similar attacks? Are there any other attacks happening at the moment that might help trace/explain the attack?
- **Evidence of active targeting.** Is the attack leveled against one or more specific targets, or is it a generic "blast"?
- **Severity.**

  Severity = (Target Criticality + Attack Lethality) − (System Countermeasures + Network Countermeasures)

  Severity formula values usually are from 1 to 5 with 5 representing the highest measure. These computations are for heuristic purposes only and do not purport to be rigorous metrics.

In answering these questions, the analyst may apply the common language (or other formal approach) as appropriate.

There are also 10 generalized questions about the incident that need to be resolved early in the investigation. These can form an informal template for early interviews.

1. What is the nature of the incident?
2. How can we be sure that there even was an incident?
3. What was the entry point into the target system? Was there only one?
4. What would evidence of an attack look like? What are we looking for?
5. What monitoring systems were in place that might have collected useful data before and during the incident?
6. What legal issues need to be addressed (policies, privacy, subpoenas, warrants, etc.)?
7. Who was in a position to cause/allow the incident to occur?
8. What security measures were in place at the time of the incident?
9. What nontechnical (business) issues may have impacted the success or failure of the attack?
10. Who knew what about the attack, and when did they know it?

55.3.5 Strategic Campaigns.   The steps in an attack are, largely, tactical. This is what may be expected from an attacker during an individual attack. Often the tactical attacks are part of larger strategic campaigns. Examples are spam, identity theft carried out by organized groups, and politically motivated cyber war. There are three important differences between a tactical attack and a strategic campaign:

1. Single objective versus ongoing objectives
2. Low-hanging fruit versus sustained effort to penetrate
3. Trivial versus complicated targets and objectives

Attacks may be part of campaigns. However, just because a company experiences a tactical attack does not mean that it is part of a sustained campaign. Campaigns have distinct phases:

1. Mapping and battle space preparation
2. Offensive and defensive planning
3. Initial execution
4. Probes, skirmishes
5. Adjustment and sustainment
6. Success and termination

55.4   USING EEDI AND THE FRAMEWORK.   Once we understand how attackers attack, we can see how EEDI and the framework can help us. The first, and most obvious, application of EEDI is the application of the investigative process to identify the results of each of the attack phases above. The act of collecting evidence, for example, may lead us to performing a forensic analysis of the target computer. When we do that, we will want to refer to the framework to ensure that we have not missed some important task. We may apply each step of the EEDI process to each step of the attack process to gather, correlate, and analyze evidence of an attack.

- **Collecting evidence.** Perform appropriate log collection, forensic imaging, and so on. Conduct interviews. There are 10 classes of evidence that the investigator should collect:

  1. Logs from monitoring devices
  2. Logs from hosts and servers
  3. Firewall and router (especially edge router) logs
  4. Interviews with involved personnel
  5. Interviews with business and technical managers
  6. Device configuration files
  7. Network maps
  8. Event observation timelines
  9. Notes of relevant meetings
  10. Response team notes and observations

- **Analysis of individual events.** Consider each of the events revealed by the collection and analysis of evidence in step one. Look for evidence of enumeration, penetration, and cleanup.

- **Preliminary correlation.** Tie together events from logs so that a smaller evidence set emerges. Consider each step of the attack process that applies to the device or system under analysis. Generate a straw-man chain of evidence.

- **Event normalizing.** The first and most important aspect of normalizing is time stamping. It is unlikely that all of the involved devices are on the same time tick. In this step, some allowance for differences in time zones and clocks must be made. Other normalizing tasks include combining different reports of the same events.

- **Event deconfliction.** This simply is an extension of event normalizing.

- **Second-level correlation.** This is a further refinement of the evidence and the straw-man chain of evidence. Here an important task is correlating log events,

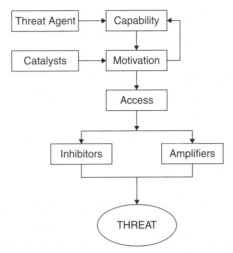

EXHIBIT 55.3   Jones's Threat Delivery Model

media forensic results, and results of interviews into a clear chain of evidence. This chain should be both causal and temporal, although the emphasis on the temporal chain is in the next step. This step is distinguished from the next two steps by level of detail. This correlation should offer significant detail. The next steps refine that detail making the results more comprehensible to laypeople.

- **Timeline analysis.** Refine the level of detail in the temporal chain of evidence.

- **Chain of evidence construction.** Refine the level of detail in the causal chain of evidence.

- **Corroboration.** Apply as much corroboration to evidence associated with each step of the attack process as you can.

55.5   MOTIVE, MEANS, AND OPPORTUNITY: PROFILING ATTACKERS.

Attacks, even automated ones, are performed by people. In order to understand attacks, we must understand the people who deliver them. We call those people *threat agents* because an attack simply is the delivery of a threat against a target. The act of delivering a threat is described concisely by Jones.[19] His model appears in Exhibit 55.3.

According to Jones, the threat agent first must have the capability of delivering the threat: The attacker must have access to the threat and know what to do with it. An example is an attacker who delivers a virus to a target system. The virus is the threat, and the attacker is the threat agent.

The threat agent then must be motivated to carry out the attack. However, just because motivation exists does not mean that a wily attacker will deliver the threat immediately. Usually there needs to be a catalyst which tells the attacker that, for whatever reason, the time has come to attack.

The next step in the process, access, is the first place that we can manage the attack. Denying the threat agent access to the target denies the threat agent the ability to deliver the threat. However, assuming that the attacker can obtain access, the effectiveness of the attack is now determined by the amplifiers and inhibitors present in the target system. These steps have direct analogs in the notion of motive, means, and opportunity, as Exhibit 55.4 shows.

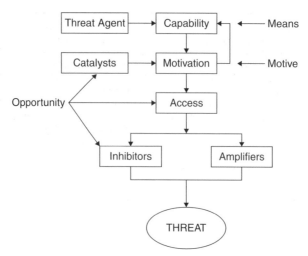

EXHIBIT 55.4 Jones's Model Showing Motive, Means, and Opportunity

55.5.1 Motive. Motive is critically important to understanding an attack. Why an attacker attacks often helps us understand the attack and, ultimately perhaps, who the attacker is. Traditional profiling matches evidence to known perpetrator profiles to understand the perpetrator. We do the same thing in cyber investigation.

An attacker with the motive of stealing personally identifiable information for the purpose of identity theft or credit card fraud may have an entirely different motive from a disgruntled employee who performs the same act to get even with his or her employer. In the former case, the attacker is motivated strictly by financial gain. In the latter, the attacker is motivated by a need for revenge.

Understanding the motivation helps us to determine the level of threat. In the former case, since the motivation is financial, the threat is significant and potentially far reaching because the attacker could attempt to maximize financial return. In the latter case, the threat could be somewhat less because, having stolen the information, the attacker might be likely to publicize his or her act in order to get the revenge desired. This might result in extortion attempts or leaks to the media but not in the attempt to sell or profit from the theft through sale of the information.

Additionally, analysis of motivation can help determine if the attacker is likely to be an individual or is part of a group. Groups tend to have somewhat different motivations from individuals, and they manage their attacks differently. There are several classes of threat agents, and each one has its own unique motive set. A summary appears in Exhibit 55.5.

The FBI, prior to 1995, described motive in general terms in its adversarial matrix.[20] Although this matrix needs updating for current trends and technology, it still is amazingly accurate and provides useful guidelines to the investigator. The behavioral characteristics appear in Exhibit 55.6, which is drawn from a British source.[21] This equates, approximately, to motive.

Jones also describes a motivation taxonomy:

- Political
- Secular

- States
  - Theft of intellectual property
  - Disruption
- Organized crime and terrorists
  - Money laundering
  - Theft of trade secrets for resale
  - Disruption
- Competitors
  - Competitive advantage
- Cyber mercenaries
  - Personal gain
- Gangs, new-age gangs
  - Financial gain
- Lone hackers and hacker "clubs"
  - Peer respect and power
  - Occasionally knowledge
- Disgruntled employee
  - Revenge
  - Personal gain

EXHIBIT 55.5   Types of Threat Agents and Their Motivations

- Crime
- Personal gain
- Revenge
- Financial
- Knowledge or information

EXHIBIT 55.6   Adversarial Matrix Behavioral Characteristics

Category of Offenders	Motivation	Personal Characteristics	Potential Weaknesses
Crackers			
Groups	Intellectual challenge; peer group fun; in support of a cause	Highly intelligent individuals, counterculture orientation	Do not consider offenses crimes, talk freely about actions
Individuals	Intellectual challenge; problem solving; power; money; in support of a cause	Moderately to highly intelligent	May keep notes and other documents of actions
Criminals			
Espionage	Money and a chance to attact the system	May be crackers operating in groups or as individuals	Become greedy for more information and then become careless
Fraud/Abuse	Money or other personal gain; power	Same personal characteristics as other fraud offenders	Become greedy and make mistakes
Vandals			
Strangers	Intellectual challenge; power; money	Same characteristics as crackers	May become too brazen and make mistakes
Users	Revenge against organization; problem solving; money	Usually have some computer expertise	May leave audit trail in computer logs

- Peer recognition
- Power
- Curiosity
- Religion
- Terrorism
- Competitive advantage
- Belief

55.5.2 Means.   Means is a very important part of the profile. In cyber investigation, we generally equate means directly to the tools and techniques used in the attack. Indirectly we relate means to skill level of the attacker. We live in an Internet-enabled society. That state of affairs extends to computer-related crime. Relatively unskilled threat agents can deliver moderately sophisticated attacks simply because the means is readily available on the Internet to enable their actions. Analysis of evidence for indications of skill level helps us to eliminate suspects.

A word on investigative process is in order here. Although it may seem as if the right approach to an investigation is to focus on the probable perpetrator, in reality, it is far more productive, initially at least, to focus on those who absolutely could *not* be the perpetrator. This is an extension of the Sherlock Holmes' admonition: "It is an old maxim of mine that when you have excluded the impossible, whatever remains, however improbable, must be the truth."[22] The point here is that it is far more efficient to eliminate those who could not have participated in the attack. In cyber investigations, doing this becomes even more important because of the huge universe of possible participants in a network-based attack.

The FBI adversarial matrix of operational characteristics appears in Exhibit 55.7. Exhibit 55.8 extends the operational characteristics and includes specific tools, techniques, and support required. These equate, approximately, to means.

55.5.3 Opportunity.   The Jones threat model describes the notion of opportunity. Considered with means, opportunity helps determine whether an attacker is a credible threat agent. Opportunity not only reflects Jones' threat model, it includes such things as knowledge of the victim system. The insider threat is an important piece of the opportunity puzzle. In this case, an insider can be the attacker him- or herself or a confederate of the threat agent. Besides insider help, the attacker may have the support of a group of some sort, such as a hacker gang, drug gang, or organized crime group.

55.6 SOME USEFUL TOOLS.   The usual tools for digital investigation include tools for:

- Computer forensic imaging and analysis
- Network forensic/log aggregation and analysis
- Malware discovery
- Media imaging (without analysis)
- Network discovery
- Remote (over-the-network) computer forensic analysis and imaging

EXHIBIT 55.7 FBI Adversarial Matrix of Operational Characteristics

Category of Offenders	Planning	Level of Expertise	Tactics/Method Used
		Crackers	
Groups	May involve detailed planning	High	Each target computers via computer networks, exchange information with other crackers and groups
Individuals	Study networks before attempts are made	Medium to high, Experience gained through social networks	Use networks but more likely to use trial and error online than to do careful research and planning, use BBSs share accounts on other systems
		Criminals	
Espionage	Same characteristics as crackers	High	May contract with crackers to conduct information and data collection
Fraud/Abuse	Careful planning prior to crime	Medium to high, although is typically more experienced at fraud than at computer programming	May use more traditional intrusion methods, such as wiretapping and trapdoors, will break into systems using basic methods
		Vandals	
Strangers	Not much planning, more a crime of opportunity	Varies	Looks around until able to gain access to system
Users	May involve detailed planning and execution	Varies, may have high level of expertise	Trapdoors and Trajon horse programs, data modification

These tools are well known in the cyber forensic community and do not warrant further elucidation here.[23] Specific products come and go so it is not appropriate to provide that level of detail here.

In addition, there are some nonstandard tools that can make the EEDI process much easier. These include:

- Link analysis
- Attack-tree analysis
- Modeling
- Statistical analysis

Unlike the standard tools, these specialized requirements bear explanation. Again, however, specific products come and go. Where examples are provided, the specific

Exhibit 55.8 FBI Adversarial Matrix Resource Characteristics

Category of Offenders	Training Skills	Minimum Equipment Needed	Support Structure
Crackers			
Groups	High level of informal training	Basic computer equipment with modem	Peer group support
Individuals	Expertise gained through experience	Basic computer equipment with modem	BBS, information exchanges
Criminals			
Espionage	Various level of expertise	Basic computer equipment with modem, in some cases, uses more sophisticated devices	Support may come from sponsoring intelligence agency
Fraud/Abuse	Some programming experience	Computer with modem or access to target computer	Peer group support, possible organized crime enterprise
Vandals			
Strangers	Range from basis to highly skilled	Basic computer equipment with modem	Peer group support
Users	Some computer expertise, knowledge of programming ranges from basic to advanced	Access to targeted computer	None

product that generated the example will be listed along with its source at the time of writing.

55.6.1 Link Analysis. In this author's view, link analysis is the single most useful technique for cyber investigators. Link analysis allows the investigator to analyze large data sets for nonobvious relationships. Link analysis is used in the investigation of complicated criminal activities, such as fraud, drug-related activities and groups, terrorist acts and groups, and organized crime. It is used far less commonly in analysis of cyber crime, but it should be integrated into cyber investigations.

The core theory behind link analysis is that pairings of related items (e.g., people and addresses, source and destination IP addresses, hacker aliases and real names, etc.) can be analyzed to find relationships that are not immediately obvious. We do that by testing for associations in suitable pairs of data sets.

An example of such an analysis is an analysis of hackers and groups. We might start by pairing hacker aliases and real names. These can be collected in a simple spreadsheet in columns with the first column as hacker aliases. Through research, the real names of some of the hackers may be discovered and be placed into their own column next to their associated aliases. Next, research may reveal hacks associated with individual aliases or, perhaps, real names. These go into their own column in the same row with their associated hackers. Finally, perhaps the groups with which the hackers are associated can provide useful connections. These groups are researched and placed in their own column on the rows associated with the hackers who are members.

The link analyzer accepts the input two columns at a time and iteratively analyzes the relationships. Some of the things that the analysis might reveal are multiple aliases for the same hacker, multiple hackers participating in the researched hacks, and membership in various hacker groups. In turn, membership in a particular hacker group may imply participation in individual hacks by members of the group who were not initially reported as being involved.

A more difficult problem to solve is the relationship between attack source IP addresses and target addresses. Often these relationships are *clustered*. In link analysis language, a *cluster* is

> a group of entities that are bound more tightly to one another by the links between them than they are to the entities that surround them.[24]

Since the entities within a cluster are more tightly interconnected within the cluster than they are with entities outside of the cluster, these clustered entities usually represent activities of interest.

Applying this concept to a large log from a firewall, we might take all of the denied connections, place their source and destination addresses in the link analyzer, and look for relationships. That might yield a complicated pattern such as the one shown in Exhibit 55.9.

This map can be simplified by performing a cluster analysis as shown in Exhibit 55.10.

The clustering operation on the data in Exhibit 55.9 reveals the cluster in Exhibit 55.10. This simplified analysis in turn shows two interesting relationships:

1. It quickly identifies the IP addresses that are broadcasting.
2. It clearly shows several IP addresses that are receiving a lot of traffic as well as the sources of that traffic.

The cluster map in Exhibit 55.10 is far easier to read than the map in Exhibit 55.9. Considering that the original log had several thousand entries, this is a much improved way to see nonobvious relationships; it is much easier than reading the log data or manipulating a spreadsheet.

55.6.2 Attack-Tree Analysis.

Attack-tree analysis is a technique for analyzing possible attack scenarios on a compromised network. Its purpose is to hypothesize the attack methodology and calculate the probabilities of several possible scenarios. Once these probabilities are calculated, the investigator can hypothesize where to look for evidence. In a complicated attack on a large distributed network, having a set of these models on hand can be a big help. The analyst prepares various attack-tree models in advance and then modifies them to be consistent with the facts of a particular incident. This limits the number of high-probability attack paths and simplifies the evidence discovery process.

55.6.3 Modeling.

"Attack modeling" is a broad term that refers to all of the techniques used to simulate attack behavior. The author uses Coloured Petri Nets (CPNets).[25] CPNets are a graphical representation of a mathematical formalism that allows the modeling and simulation of attack behavior on a network. To use CPNets effectively, the investigator must understand the enterprise in terms of its *security-policy*

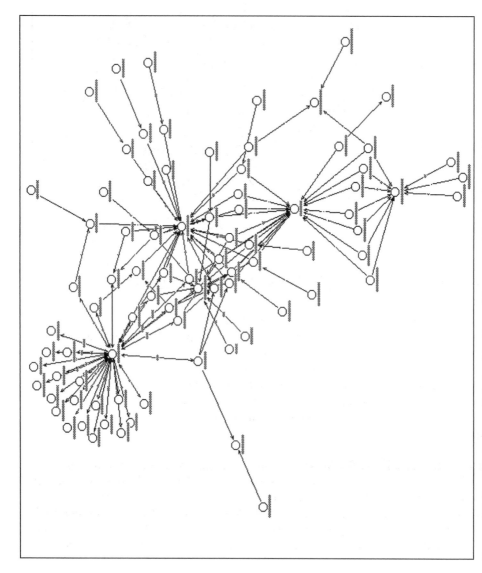

Exhibit 55.9 Link Analyzer Relationship Map of Source and Destination IP Addresses

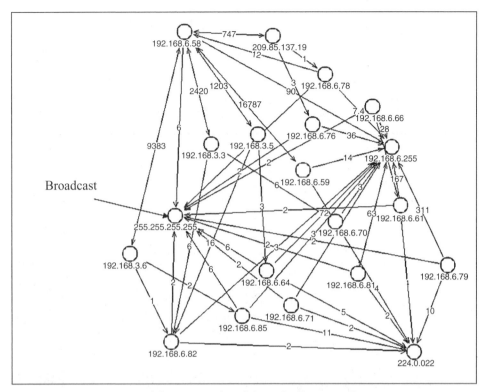

EXHIBIT 55.10   Map in Exhibit 55.9 Reduced through Cluster Analysis

domains. The author defines security-policy domains in this way: "A security policy domain, E_p, consists of all of the elements, **e,** of an enterprise that conform to the same security policy, **p**."[26]

The policy domains are represented along with the communications links between them in a graphical chart. Once the mathematical definitions of the domains and the communications conditions that exist between them have been defined, the behavior of the attack can be simulated. The simulations assist the investigator in tracing the attack source.

55.7   CONCLUDING REMARKS.   In this chapter, we discussed a structured approach to cyber investigation along with some of the tools and techniques that support such an approach. Nordby[27] suggests that reliable methods of inquiry possess the characteristics of "integrity, competence, defensible technique and relevant experience." The nature of cyber investigation and cyber forensics supports this through rigor, underlying models and frameworks, and investigators who adhere to those characteristics.

55.8   FURTHER READING

Brown, C. L. T. *Computer Evidence: Collection & Preservation.* Hingham, MA: Charles River Media, 2005.

Carrier. B. *File System Forensic Analysis.* Upper Saddle River, NJ: Addison-Wesley, 2005.

Carvey, H. *Windows Forensics and Incident Recovery.* Upper Saddle River, NJ: Addison-Wesley, 2004.

Farmer, D., and W. Venema. *Forensic Discovery*. Upper Saddle River, NJ: Addison-Wesley, 2005.

Jones, K. J., R. Beijtlich and C. W. Rose. *Real Digital Forensics: Computer Security and Incident Response*. Upper Saddle River, NJ: Addison-Wesley, 2005.

Marcella, A., and D. Menendez. *Cyber Forensics: A Field Manual for Collecting, Examining, and Preserving Evidence of Computer Crimes*, Second Edition. Boca Raton, FL: Auerbach, 2007.

Steel, C. *Windows Forensics: The Field Guide for Corporate Computer Investigations*. Hoboken, NJ: John Wiley & Sons, 2006.

55.9 NOTES

1. Much of this chapter is excerpted with minor edits from P. Stephenson, "Structured Investigation of Digital Incidents in Complex Computing Environments," PhD diss., Oxford Brookes University, 2004, available in the British Library.

2. P. Stephenson, *Investigating Computer Related Crime* (New York: CRC Press, 1999).

3. American Academy of Forensic Science, 2008: www.aafs.org/default.asp? section_id=membership&page_id=how_to_become_an_aafs_member#General.

4. M. Rogers, A. Brinson, and A. Robinson, "A Cyber Forensics Ontology: Creating a New Approach to Studying Cyber Forensics," *Journal of Digital Investigation* (2006): S37–S43.

5. *Microsoft® Encarta® 2008*, "Metaphysics" [DVD] (Redmond, WA: Microsoft Corporation, 2008).

6. *Microsoft® Encarta® 2008 Dictionary* [DVD] (Redmond, WA: Microsoft Corporation, 2008).

7. Open-source ontology editor available from http://protege.stanford.edu/.

8. Digital Forensic Research Workshop: http://dfrws.org/.

9. DFRWS attendees, "A Road Map for Digital Forensic Research," Report from the First Digital Forensic Research Workshop, August 7–8, 2001, Utica, NY. Available: Air Force Research Laboratory, Rome Research Site, Rome, NY, http://dfrws.org/2001/dfrws-rm-final.pdf.

10. There have also been attempts to relate cyber investigation to the generalized Zachman Enterprise Architecture Framework: J. A. Zachman, "A Framework for Information Systems Architecture," *IBM Systems Journal* 26, No. 3 (1987), www.research.ibm.com/journal/sj/263/ibmsj2603E.pdf.

11. DFRWS attendees, "Road Map for Digital Forensic Research."

12. DFRWS attendees, "Road Map for Digital Forensic Research."

13. The DFRWS definitions in these sections are from Digital Forensics Research Workshop, "Day 1-DF-Science, Group A Session 1 (D1-A1), Digital Forensic Framework," Work notes for the 2003 Digital Forensics Research Workshop, August 6, 2003. For more information on the DFRWS Framework, see DFRWS attendees, "Road Map for Digital Forensic Research."

14. Author's experience over 20 years of conducting incident response.

15. A. C. Doyle, "Silver Blaze." In: *The Memoirs of Sherlock Holmes* (London: Newnes, 1893).

16. A gross data collection is a file or files containing data collected from a digital source that may contain individual evidentiary data.

17. This and other formal definitions appear in Stephenson, "Structured Investigation of Digital Incidents in Complex Computing Environments."

18. See Chapter 8, Sections 8.1 to 8.6, in this *Handbook*.

19. Andrew Jones describes a cyber threat delivery model in his paper "Identification of a Method for the Calculation of Threat in an Information Environment," unpublished (April 2002, revised 2004).

20. D. Icove, K. Seger, and W. VonStorch, *Computer Crime: A Crimefighter's Handbook* (Sebastopol, CA: O'Reilly & Associates, 1995.

21. Stephenson, "Structured Investigation of Digital Incidents in Complex Computing Environments."

22. A. C. Doyle, *The Sign of Four* (London: Blackett, 1890).

23. For more details, see the recommendations for further reading.

24. i2 Limited "About Clusters," Analyst's Notebook v6 Help file, August 9, 2005; www.i2.co.uk.

25. Coloured Petri Nets at the University of Aarhus: www.daimi.au.dk/CPnets.

26. P. Stephenson and P. Prueitt, "Towards a Theory of Cyber Attack Mechanics," First IFIP 11.9 Digital Forensics Conference, 2005.

27. S. H. James and J. J. Nordby, *Forensic Science: An Introduction to Scientific and Investigative Techniques* (Boca Raton, FL: CRC Press, 2003).

INTRODUCTION TO PART VI

RESPONSE AND REMEDIATION

What are the options when security breaches or accidents occur? How do we prepare for trouble so that we can minimize the consequences and respond quickly and effectively? This part includes these chapters and topics:

56. **Computer Security Incident Response Teams.** Planning and rehearsing responses to a wide variety of security problems—in advance instead of on the fly

57. **Data Backups and Archives.** The essential tool for all forms of recovery

58. **Business Continuity Planning.** Systematic approach to analyzing the priorities for orderly recovery when anything interrupts the smooth operation of the organization

59. **Disaster Recovery.** Planning for rapid, cost-effective return to normal after a crisis is over

60. **Insurance Relief.** Using modern insurance services to reduce the consequences of disasters

61. **Working with Law Enforcement.** Establishing relations with all levels of law enforcement before there is a crisis, and coordinating efficiently and effectively to support investigation and prosecution of criminals

COMPUTER SECURITY INCIDENT RESPONSE TEAMS[1]

Michael Miora, M. E. Kabay, and Bernie Cowens

56.1   OVERVIEW.   No matter how good one's security, at some point a security measure will fail. Knowing that helps organizations to plan for security in depth, so that a single point of failure does not necessarily result in catastrophe. Furthermore, instead of trying to invent a response when every second counts, it makes sense to have a competent team in place, trained, and ready to act. The value of time is not constant. Spending an hour or a day planning, so that an emergency response is shortened by a few seconds, may save a life or prevent a business disaster.

An essential element of any effective information security program today is the ability to respond to computer emergencies. Although many organizations have some form of intrusion detection in place, far too few take full advantage of the capabilities those systems offer. Fewer still consistently monitor the data available to them from automated intrusion detection systems, let alone respond to what they see.

The key is to make beneficial use of the knowledge that something has happened, that something is about to happen, or that something is perhaps amiss. Intrusion detection systems can be costly to implement and maintain. It therefore makes little business sense to go to the trouble of implementing an intrusion detection capability if there is not, at the same time, a way to make use of the data produced by these systems.

Computer emergency quick-response teams are generally called *computer security incident response teams* (CSIRTs, the abbreviation used in this chapter) or *computer incident response teams* (CIRTs). Sometimes one sees the term "computer emergency response team" (CERT), but that term and acronym are increasingly reserved for the Computer Emergency Response Team Coordination Center (CERT/CC®) at the Software Engineering Institute of Carnegie Mellon University, as explained in Section 56.1.3 of this chapter.

CSIRTs can provide organizations with a measurable return on their investment in computer security mechanisms and intrusion detection systems. Intrusion detection can indicate that something occurred; CSIRTs can do something about that occurrence. Often their value to an organization can be felt in more subtle ways as well. Many times computer emergencies and incidents cast an organization in an unfavorable light, and they can erode confidence in that organization. Efficient handling of computer emergencies can lessen the erosion of confidence, can help speed the organization's recovery, and in some cases can help restore its image. In addition, CSIRT postmortems (see Section 56.7) can provide information for process improvement (as discussed in Section 56.7.2).

When an incident occurs, the intrusion detection system makes us aware of the incident in one manner or another. We make use of this knowledge by responding to the situation appropriately. "Appropriately" can mean something different in different situations. Therefore, a well-trained, confident, authoritative CSIRT is essential.

Intrusion detection systems are not the only means by which we learn about incidents. In a sense, every component of a system and every person who interacts with the system forms a part of the overall defense and detection system. End users are often the first to notice that something is different. They may not recognize a particular difference as an incident; however, proper awareness and training will encourage them to report such situations to those who can make a determination and act on the information.

56.1.1 Description. CSIRTs are multifaceted, multitalented groups of individuals who are specially trained and equipped to respond quickly and effectively to computer emergencies.

CSIRTs come in a variety of forms and compositions. For example, while some teams are static, established groups, others are assembled dynamically to fit a specific mission or to deal with specific emergencies. Often the most effective teams are characterized as a mixture of these two approaches. These teams generally have a standing core membership made up of both technical and nontechnical members. When a situation arises that must be addressed by the CSIRT, additional members with specific skills are added to meet the requirements of handling the incident in progress. Once the incident is resolved, the team reverts to its core membership status.

56.1.2 Purpose. CSIRTs provide the first reaction to an incident. Their immediate goal should be to take control of a situation in order to contain the scope of a potential compromise, to conduct damage control, and to prevent the possible spread of a compromise to adjacent systems. Containing the scope of compromise is also synonymous with preventing or reducing loss.

Maintaining a dedicated CSIRT at the ready, 24 hours a day is a costly proposition from many perspectives. Virtually any organization today, no matter its mission, will be hard pressed to justify funding such a team only to have the team stand by awaiting an emergency. The cost of maintaining a team of highly trained resources, with only emergency response roles, is a most difficult issue to overcome. Therefore, it is important to make use of team members and their skills during nonemergency periods. In many organizations, the teams have important security and awareness roles as integral parts of their charters. Carefully selected, these additional roles can benefit team readiness while at the same time providing tangible and often visible value to the organization.

For example, some CSIRTs spend their nonemergency days and nights monitoring security issues and developments for the latest trends, threats, and countermeasures. They analyze threat data and prepare reports for various levels of the organization on such topics as virus protection, password security, and emerging technology. Members of the team spend a significant amount of time and effort developing and maintaining leading-edge technical skills. They hone their response skills and procedures through continuous training. Training often is conducted in the classroom and through dry runs using a variety of response scenarios.

Often, response teams provide and maintain awareness programs for the organization. This serves several purposes. First, awareness programs benefit an organization by pointing out risks and ways to avoid them. Next, delivering awareness programs makes the team members more visible. As a result, should something unusual or out of the ordinary occur, members of the organization are not only more likely to notice it, they are also more likely to report the information, so that it winds up in the hands of the response team.

The teams respond to emergencies or incidents. An incident does not always indicate something unwanted; it also can be something that is merely unexplained, or out of the ordinary. A response acts not only to defend, or to fight back, or to prevent further damage, but also to discover more information or to verify facts—in essence, it is part investigation and part education. To keep in step with the rapid pace of change in technology, quick response teams must be learning constantly. These teams should strive to remain abreast of each new development and technology that impacts, or has the potential to impact, the systems under their care. Therefore, responding to incidents, whether actual attacks or benign anomalies, should be seen as opportunities to sharpen the CSIRT's skills. This need is also served by the additional responsibilities the team holds in nonemergency times, typically including ongoing security research and evaluation.

If locks and other preventive measures were foolproof, intrusion detection and incident response would be unnecessary. Banks put huge vault doors, time locks, and other seemingly impenetrable defenses into their buildings. But they recognize that these measures are insufficient to prevent completely any loss of their money or other valuables. So they also install alarm systems to detect when one of the defensive barriers has been breached. But that knowledge is of little value if no one hears the alarm or, if having heard it, does not act on the information. Therefore, organizations also put into place guards, night watchers, and others, including law enforcement, to monitor systems and to respond. CSIRTs are the response part of the secure + monitor + detect + respond equation. Because connected systems are under constant passive and active attack virtually 24 hours a day, emergency response teams are a necessary part of the security equation.

56.1.3 History and Background.   CSIRTs can be traced back to one of the more notorious computer incidents of the late twentieth century. The infamous Morris Worm incident of November 2, 1988, wreaked havoc by disabling a significant portion, by some estimates as much as 10 percent, of the Internet. As organization after organization attempted to deal with the worm, it quickly became apparent that a coordinated response to such incidents would have helped to lessen the impact and speed recovery. There was no central place to report or disseminate information about the attack. Internally, few organizations were equipped with teams dedicated to responding to such attacks. As a result, they wasted time and resources duplicating efforts to identify the source of the attack, to formulate countermeasures, and finally to eradicate the worm.

At that time, the most common response was simply to disconnect from the Internet. That same response would carry unacceptable losses of revenues, confidence, and performance for today's commercial enterprises. As more commercial organizations, government agencies, and individuals became dependent on Internet-connected systems, the criticality of the need for teams capable of responding to emergencies quickly and effectively increased.

The Morris Worm incident and several other attacks on the Internet in November and December 1988 highlighted the need for a coordinated response to widespread computer emergencies. As a result, in December 1988, under the direction of the Defense Advanced Research Projects Agency (DARPA), security experts established the Computer Emergency Response Team Coordination Center (CERT/CC®) at the Software Engineering Institute of Carnegie Mellon University in Pittsburgh, Pennsylvania. The role of the CERT/CC was to coordinate communication among organizations during computer emergencies. Their role has since expanded dramatically to include, among other things, assisting with the establishment of other CSIRT teams, acting as a clearinghouse for threat and vulnerability data, and providing training and education programs relating to security incident handling. Many entities, both public and private, have since that time adopted CSIRT's incident-handling procedures.[2]

Since its inception, CERT/CC has provided invaluable services to the world community of Internet users and especially to system and security administrators. In addition to the archives of security alerts and incident analyses available online and via free e-mail subscriptions, CERT/CC provides free electronic textbooks of great quality. One of these is the famous *Handbook for Computer Security Incident Response Teams (CSIRTs)* edited by Moira J. West-Brown and colleagues, and which is now in its second edition.[3] We strongly recommend this work to anyone concerned with establishing and managing a CSIRT.

West-Brown et al. describe the functions of the CSIRT in this way:

> For a team to be considered a CSIRT, it must provide one or more of the incident-handling services: incident analysis, incident response on site, incident response support, or incident response coordination.

They explain in detail all aspects of these functions, and they summarize their research on the range of services that CSIRTs actually provide, whether by themselves or in cooperation with other teams in the information technology sector. They provided a "List of Common CSIRT Services" as Table 4 in their *Handbook for CSIRTs*; we have reformatted it here:

- Reactive Services
  - Alerts and warnings
  - Incident handling
    - ◊ Incident analysis
    - ◊ Incident response on site
    - ◊ Incident response support
    - ◊ Incident response coordination
  - Vulnerability handling
    - ◊ Vulnerability analysis
    - ◊ Vulnerability response
    - ◊ Vulnerability response coordination
  - Artifact handling
    - ◊ Artifact analysis
    - ◊ Artifact response
    - ◊ Artifact response coordination
- Proactive Services
  - Announcements
  - Technology watch
  - Security audits or assessments
  - Configuration and maintenance of security tools, applications, and infrastructures
  - Development of security tools
  - Intrusion detection services
  - Security-related information dissemination
- Security Quality Management Services
  - Risk analysis

- ○ Business continuity and disaster recovery planning
- ○ Security consulting
- ○ Awareness building
- ○ Education and training
- ○ Product evaluation or certification

The only problematic term in this list is "artifact," which the authors define as "any file or object found on a system that might be involved in probing or attacking systems and networks or that is being used to defeat security measures. Artifacts can include but are not limited to computer viruses, Trojan horse programs, worms, exploit scripts, and toolkits" (p. 28).

The specific combination of functions that a CSIRT will provide will be a function of personnel and budgetary resources, and of the maturity of the team. It is wise to focus a completely new CSIRT on essential services such as incident handling and analysis as their first priority. With time and experience, the team can add functions, such as coordinating with other security teams, with computer and network operations in the more proactive services, and with the security quality services that will lead to long-term reduction in security incidents and to lower damages and costs from such incidents.

56.1.4 Types of Teams. The exact composition of a CSIRT depends on factors such as the size, type, complexity, budget, and location of its sponsoring organization. Some organizations might be able to justify and support a full-time, dedicated, in-house CSIRT with the very latest technology and training. Others might improvise teams once an incident occurs, or they might even hire outside expertise to handle computer emergencies on their behalf. Still others might use a combination of these approaches by having core CSIRT staff who can be augmented by other people as needed to manage incidents.

One viable alternative to developing in-house quick response teams is to take advantage of outsourced services in this area. Outsourced incident-handling services are becoming increasingly popular, and many security companies offer them to their customers. In some cases, this might be the most practical option for companies that lack the resources or desire to develop in-house response capabilities. Outsourcing computer emergency quick response efforts can be an effective, albeit somewhat costly, alternative to developing in-house response teams, for both short- and long-term incident handling.

However, for many organizations, establishing their own incident response capabilities can provide significant advantages. Internal teams generally know the organization and understand its goals, issues, and requirements. Outsourced responses are often mechanical and standardized. Vendors can take longer to respond since they are normally located off site and might even be a considerable distance away. Vendors may undergo frequent staff turnover, which can mean that those assigned to respond to incidents at an organization might be unfamiliar with that organization or its mission. As a result, outsiders might require precious time to "ramp up" before dealing effectively with a current incident or situation. The connected nature of today's organizations, and modern monitoring technologies, may make up for distance in some ways, but there is no substitute for an expert on site.

Some organizations are fortunate enough to have implemented formal, standing CSIRTs whose members are dedicated primarily to monitoring systems, preventing intrusions, and responding to computer emergency incidents. These teams are superior to ad hoc or outsourced teams in their ability to respond quickly with customized procedures acting from a deep and current knowledge base.

56.2   PLANNING THE TEAM.   Not every organization has a CSIRT already in place; not all CSIRTs are structured and managed in the most appropriate ways for an organization's specific needs. This section presents systematic approaches for rational design and implementation of a CSIRT.

Establishing a CSIRT is a complex process that must be given careful thought and must be based on comprehensive planning. Before establishing a CSIRT, the organization needs to determine exactly what it expects to accomplish. From this, the organization can decide on specific goals for the team, and perhaps most important, it can decide on policies that apply to the team. The team should be conceived and defined in terms of the organization to which it belongs. That is, the team should be tailored to achieving a specific mission. Clarity, vision, and focus are vital planning elements that ultimately will determine the success or failure of the CSIRT. Skimping during the planning stage will ensure failure. Devoting some extra effort to planning in this stage will help improve the chances of success.

56.2.1   Mission and Charter.   The CSIRT should include members from every sector of the organization; key members include operations, facilities, legal staff, public relations, information technology, and at least one respected and experienced manager with a direct line to top management. The CSIRT should establish good relations with law enforcement officials and should be prepared to gather forensic evidence. The organization should have a policy in place on how to decide whether to prosecute malefactors if they can be identified. The CSIRT should be prepared to respond not only to external attacks but also to criminal activities by insiders. Proper logging at the operating system level and from intrusion-detection systems can be useful to the CSIRT. The CSIRT plays an important role in disaster prevention, mitigation, and recovery planning.

Organizing people to respond to computer security incidents is worth the effort not only when an incident occurs but also because the analysis and interactions leading to establishment of the CSIRT bring benefits even without an emergency. A CSIRT can provide opportunities for improving institutional knowledge, contributing to continuous process improvement and offering challenging and satisfying work assignments to technical and managerial staff, thus contributing to reduced turnover. A well-trained, professional, courteous CSIRT can improve relations between the entire technical support infrastructure and the user community. The team and its members often serve as key elements of business continuity and disaster recovery teams.

A clear, written mission and a charter establishing the CSIRT are essential to its success. These documents should establish why the team exists and what the organization expects from the team at a high level. Although the current security landscape provides compelling reasons for establishing an incident response capability, identifying organization-specific goals and expectations for the team remains an essential task.

Effective policies are essential for any organization. The CSIRT's mission and charter should be based on organizational policies, especially information security policies. Establishing a team without having appropriate policies in place is ineffective and can put the team at odds with its own organization. Without formal policies upon which to base computer emergency response activities, the team can have no legitimate basis for deciding on courses of action that support the organization. During an incident,

CSIRT decisions can be unpopular. Disconnecting systems from the Internet could prevent some, or perhaps all, of the organization from carrying out its mission. Without established policies both to define and to defend those decisions, often the team is viewed as an adversary.

Without this clear definition of mission and an idea of what can be expected from the CSIRT, internal cooperation and support for the team will be difficult to obtain and even more difficult to sustain. Without internal cooperation, the team's effectiveness will be diminished, which could exacerbate the impact of an incident or prevent the team from handling an incident in a timely manner.

The overarching goal of responding to an incident should always be to prevent further damage and to restore systems and operations to normal as expeditiously as possible, consistent with organizational policies. The CSIRT members must have a clear sense of the strategic and operational priorities of the organization, just as members of business continuity and disaster recovery teams do. Without a clear idea of what the organization expects the team to accomplish, the team is likely to waste the limited time and resources it usually has available.

For more information on business continuity planning, see Chapter 58 in this *Handbook*; for discussion of disaster recovery, see Chapter 59.

56.2.2 Establishing Policies and Procedures.   As the U.S. Government Defense Information Systems Agency (DISA) training course on CD-ROM about CSIRTs succinctly puts it, "policies and procedures are not merely bureaucratic red tape."[4] They are the scaffolding on which one can establish clear understanding and expectations for everyone involved in incident response. These living, evolving documents are (quoting the CD-ROM notes) tools that provide guidance on:

- Roles and responsibilities
- Priorities
- Escalation criteria
- Response provided
- Orientation

Policies are the statements of desired goals; procedures are the methods for attaining those goals. Policies tend to be global and relatively stable; procedures can and should be relatively specific, and can be adapted quickly to meet changing conditions and to integrate knowledge from experience. Policies cannot be promulgated without the approval and support of appropriate authorities in the organization, so one of the first steps is to identify those authorities. Another step is to gain their support for the policy project.

All policies and especially CSIRT policies should be framed in clear, simple language so that everyone can understand them, and they should be made available in electronic form. Hypertext can make policies more understandable by providing pop-up comments or explanations of difficult sections or technical terms. Similarly, procedures show how to implement the policies in real terms. For example, a policy might stipulate: "All relevant information about the time and details of a computer incident shall be recorded with regard for the requirements of later analysis, and for possible use in a legal proceeding." That policy might spawn a dozen procedures describing exactly how the information is to be recorded, named, stored, and maintained through a proper chain of custody. For example, one procedure might start: "Using the Incident-Report form in the CSIRT Database accessible to all CSIRT members, fill in every required field. Use the pull-down menus wherever possible in answering the questions." Again, as the DISA CD-ROM points out, these procedures should minimize ambiguity and should help members of the team to provide a consistent level of service to the organization. A glossary of local acronyms and technical terms can be helpful as part of these procedures.

Whenever policies and procedures are changed in a way that may affect users, it is important to let people know about the changes so that their expectations can be adjusted. The DISA course recommends using several channels of communications to ensure that everyone gets the message; for example, send e-mail, use phone and phone messages, send broadcast voicemail, announce the changes at staff meetings, and use posters and Web sites.

For more information on promulgating security policies, see Chapters 44 and 50 in this *Handbook*.

56.2.3 Interaction with Outside Agencies and Other Resources. No CSIRT can operate in a vacuum in an interconnected world. At some point, teams and their sponsors will require interaction with outside agencies, and even with other CSIRTs. Rather than wait until an emergency is under way, the team should establish and document contacts such as:

Internal Contacts

- **Management.** The team should establish and maintain management contacts who hold sufficient authority to make the tough business decisions that will inevitably arise during an emergency situation.

- **Systems.** The CSIRT should have a working relationship with those responsible for operating and maintaining the organization's information systems. These contacts will be necessary to allow CSIRT members appropriate system access during an emergency response situation.

- **Applications.** As with systems personnel, the CSIRT should have preestablished contact with those who manage and maintain applications. These individuals will be able to provide CSIRT members with access to application logs, documentation, and with access to accounts during an emergency.

- **Business units.** CSIRT members should be familiar with and have established contacts with the various organizational business units they support. Having such contacts ahead of time will facilitate decision making and will avoid delays in gaining access to appropriate business personnel during an emergency.

External Contacts

- **CERT/CC.** The CERT/CC can provide valuable advice and assistance to the response team during an attack. Knowing before an emergency whom to contact, and how to reach them, will speed the process.

- **Consultants.** Often, organizations will rely on outside consultants to augment technical skills and knowledge. Therefore, it is important that the organization be able to contact these consultants during an emergency, in the event their expertise is required to respond to or to resolve a situation. Planning for such emergency contact ahead of time will avoid delays in responding to an emergency.

- **Vendors.** Responding to an emergency may require specialized information about hardware or software features and about specifications that might be available only from a vendor. Additionally, backup systems or software may need to be acquired in order to return systems to operational status during or after an incident.

- **Law enforcement.** Law enforcement agencies today frequently have specialized units capable of assisting an organization in tracing and identifying the perpetrator of an attack. However, it is important that law enforcement contacts be made in advance so that the organization can make sound decisions about whom to notify and how best to use such assistance.

- **Utilities.** Obviously, electrical power and similar infrastructure services are essential to any organization. Power outages and similar emergencies can have a devastating effect on operations. Maintaining contact with local utilities will help the organization plan for and mitigate impact from power outages. In the event of an outage, team members will know whom to contact, and they can gather information about the cause and duration of an outage more quickly.

- **Internet service providers.** Typically, vital connectivity is provided to the organization by one or more Internet service providers (ISPs). In many cases, ISPs are the first line of defense against some types of Internet-originated attacks, such as distributed denial of service. In addition, if an organization is attempting to track a suspected intruder, the Internet service provider will be pivotal. It is therefore vitally important that the CSIRT have preestablished contacts within the organization's ISPs in order to avoid wasting precious response time trying to get assistance during an emergency.

- **Other CSIRTs.** Other CSIRTs may well have faced the situation or emergency that another team might be facing. Other CSIRTs can provide advice and assistance, and some may even share resources and expertise to help an organization respond to an emergency. There is also an opportunity to share knowledge and conduct joint training with other teams.

56.2.4   Establish Baselines.   In order to be able to spot that which is out of the ordinary, the CSIRT must determine what "normal" looks like. False incidents have occurred because the observer did not have adequate knowledge to realize that the event was actually normal. Emergency response teams called into action without well-documented baselines, or detailed activity logs, must work very hard to determine whether the event is normal.

In either case, whether the triggering event turns out to be false or genuine, resources and time will have been wasted by this identification effort. A good baseline can reduce the resources expended on false positives, and can hasten the response to real events.

56.3   SELECTING AND BUILDING THE TEAM.   An effective CSIRT is comprised of these elements, dictated by the incident at hand:

- People
- Skills
- Knowledge
- Equipment
- Access
- Authority

The makeup of the team has everything to do with how effective and responsive it will be in an emergency. Careful selection of team members at the outset will provide for an effective, cohesive group with the right skills, authority, and knowledge to deal properly with a range of known and unknown incidents.

Frequently, the first inclination is to select the most technically knowledgeable individuals available as members of the team. While technical ability is essential to a CSIRT, this should not be the overriding characteristic. Given aptitude and motivation, appropriate technical skills can be learned. Indeed, during the course of an incident situation, adept handlers can draw on the technical expertise of people, either internal or outside, to augment their own skills and knowledge.

Maturity and the ability to work long hours under stress and intense pressure are crucial characteristics. Integrity in the response team members must be absolute, since these people will have access and authority exceeding that given them in normal operations.

Exceptional communications skills are required because, in an emergency, quick and accurate communications are needed. Inaccurate communications can cause the emergency to appear more serious than it is and therefore escalate a minor event into a crisis. Conversely, proper communications can galvanize others into immediate and effective activity, without creating a panic reaction.

56.3.1 Staffing.   The CSIRT may be a permanent, full-time assignment for a fixed group of experts, or it may be a part time role formed dynamically as conditions require. In either case, or for any of the intermediate arrangements, certain fundamentals will dictate the choice of staff members.

The DISA course on CSIRT management also addresses the question of the technical level required by CSIRT staff. The course authors suggest using a scale from 1 to 10, with 1 representing the novice or support staff and 10 representing the technical wizard: Individuals in the 1-to-3 technical range should be sufficient to handle the initial triage process, which involves separating service request into categories, and directing them to the appropriate team member.

Information requests can be handled by team members in the 1-to-5 range. For example, a support staff person can send out publications, while someone with greater expertise would be required to address questions about identifying spoofed e-mail.

Team members in the 5-to-8 technical range are necessary to respond to actual incidents. This response can involve technical analysis and communicating with compromised sites, with law enforcement technical staff, and with other CSIRTs. In handling incidents that represent new attack types, it may be necessary to call "wizards" to help understand and analyze the activity.

Vulnerability handling requires the most proficient personnel, falling into the 8-to-10 range. These individuals must be able to work with software vendors, CSIRTs, and other experts to identify and resolve vulnerabilities. Many CSIRTs do not have access to this level of technical expertise.

CSIRT staff with the psychological flexibility to allow them to adapt quickly to changing requirements will do better than people who resist change or resent ambiguity. Ideally, the team will include problem-solvers with an intuitive grasp of the differences between observation and assumption, hypothesis, and deduction. As always, team players committed to getting the problem solved will contribute more than people interested in acquiring personal credit for achievements. Having at least one person on the team with a penchant for meticulous note taking is a real benefit (see Sections 56.4.5.2 and 56.5.6).

56.3.2   Involve Legal Staff.   As with any crisis event, every action carries with it a potential legal implication. This is especially true in a situation where an evidentiary chain may be required. Even if evidence is not a primary concern, due diligence requires that accurate records be kept of the incident costs, including response team costs, and of the scope of compromise and effect.

The corporate legal staff must play an important role in developing response team procedures, in training the response team, and in crisis resolution.

56.4   PRINCIPLES UNDERLYING EFFECTIVE RESPONSE TO COMPUTER SECURITY INCIDENTS.   Some general considerations underlie effectiveness for all incident-handling teams.

56.4.1   Baseline Assumptions.   The primary consideration in responding to any emergency situation must be given to preventing loss of human life. Following that, a comprehensive information security program will have included the identification and classification of the most sensitive data and systems. This classification should provide a clear prioritization of what should be protected first, in the event of an emergency. For example, a business's survival might depend on the confidentiality and integrity of some intellectual property, such as engineering diagrams. After the safety of personnel, those drawings, and the systems on which they are stored, would be the obvious first priority for protection. A network intrusion that threatened an e-mail server located on a separate network segment would likely not warrant immediately disconnecting the entire network from the Internet. If the particular server containing the company's engineering drawings, or the network segment on which it sits, were under direct attack, however, an appropriate first response might well be to disconnect from the Internet.

In any case, there must be an unambiguous sense among the CSIRT that those responsible for taking actions in good faith will not suffer reprisals as a result of taking those actions. For example, based on facts in evidence at one time or another, a member of the team might decide to disconnect an operational system from the Internet because it appears to be under attack or compromised. Should this turn out to be a false alarm of some sort, the individual authorizing the action should suffer no reprisal or sanction by taking what he or she believed was a legitimate action to stop, or to respond to, an attack.

With appropriate plans in place before incidents happen, recovery can be effected much more quickly and with less residual damage.

Appropriate responses depend on the systems involved, and should be documented and agreed to before those systems are connected to the Internet. If a router, or a firewall protecting the outer perimeter of the network, becomes compromised, it may be necessary to disconnect the entire system in order to contain the situation.

If a Web server in an isolated part of the network becomes compromised, though, disconnecting only that system should be sufficient. However, any business-related activities carried out using that server might no longer be available. A loss of revenue or image might result from disconnecting the server. Business units and others that depend on these systems must be made aware of, and must agree to accept, the impact of proposed responses the CSIRT might take during an incident.

Planned responses, combined with the authority and confidence to execute them, can save the organization both time and money. As an example, if every incident requires the presence of senior business managers or executives, those leaders must be taken away from their normal duties during rehearsals and during actual events. If the CSIRT leader on duty or on call, finds the incident to be routine, and if the incident has been well planned for, a simple notification of the facts can be sent to appropriate senior-level personnel, leaving them free to attend to their normal duties and to participate only in a major event at their appropriate level of management.

Planned, preapproved responses can speed reaction times, enhance security, and lessen impact of a given breach or incident. In most cases, the CSIRT leader will follow a series of commonsense steps to handle an incident from identification through resolution. As the leader progresses through each step, he or she may choose from one of the preapproved responses to handle the incident, or the situation may require the involvement of other people and resources for resolution. In either case, the basic flow of events should be similar to this list:

- **Triage.** Deciding how to direct calls for help or reports of a computer security incident
- **Technical expertise.** Assembling the different kinds of knowledge required to support an effective response
- **Tracking incidents.** Ensuring appropriate documentation to save time and reduce errors
- **Critical information.** Laying the ground rules for collecting the kinds of data needed for effective decisions
- **Telephone hotline.** Establishing protocol for real-time notification and response

56.4.2 Triage.   The word "triage" itself comes from a French root meaning "to sort." In medicine, triage is "prioritization of patients for medical treatment: the process of prioritizing sick or injured people for treatment according to the seriousness of the condition or injury."[5] Similarly, anyone receiving calls about computer security incidents must be able to classify the call right away, so that the right resources can be called into play. As the DISA course on CSIRT management suggests:

The triage process recognizes and separates

- new incidents,
- new information for ongoing incidents,
- vulnerability reports,
- information requests, [and]
- other service requests.[6]

We have altered the order of the original list to reflect a decreasing rank of importance for these factors in communicating and acting upon calls.

Triage is common to ordinary help desks as well as to emergency hotlines. In general, there are two models for staffing the phones for such front-line functions: the "dispatch" model and the "resolve" model.[7]

1. The *dispatcher* has just enough technical knowledge to collect appropriate information about an incident and to assign a team member for investigation; the alternative is to assign someone with more expertise to answer the phone so that response can be even faster.

2. However, the *resolve* model risks wasting resources because the more experienced staff member may end up doing largely clerical work instead of focusing on applying expertise to problem analysis and resolution.

To support triage, staff members need explicit training on data collection and priorities. They need to record: who is calling; how to reach that person; what the caller thinks is happening; what the caller has observed; how serious the consequences are; how many people or systems are affected; whether the incident is in progress or is over, as far as they know; and how the caller and others are responding. The CSIRT procedures should include guidance on assigning priorities to incidents; factors can include security classifications (e.g., SECRET or COMPANY CONFIDENTIAL data under attack), type of problem (e.g., breach of confidentiality, data corruption, loss of control, loss of authenticity, degradation of availability or utility), possible direct costs (e.g., personnel downtime, costs of recovery, or loss of business), possible indirect costs (e.g., damage to business reputation or legal liability) and so on, as appropriate for each organization.

Readers may find the work of John Howard relevant for such analysis; Dr. Howard has established a useful taxonomy for discussing computer security incidents that can serve as a framework for establishing priorities.[8] See Chapter 8 in this *Handbook.*

We recommend an automated system for capturing information on all calls to the CSIRT. Using keywords "helpdesk software" and also "help desk software" in an online search brings up dozens of options for such programs. Readers with modest skills in database design can also create their own using a program such as MS-Access, but it may take a good deal of time to improve the home-grown system so that it matches commercial or freeware versions based on extensive experience of the user community. However, with appropriate locking strategies to permit safe concurrent access and with well-designed automated reports, your CSIRT can know and control the priorities of all the open incidents under investigation at any time.

For more about management perspectives on triage, see Section 56.6.3.

56.4.3   Technical Expertise.   The DISA CD-ROM course starts by classifying technical expertise in approximate ranges:

- **Low**, suitable for the triage function which involves determining who should best handle a specific call
- **Medium**, appropriate for answering requests for information
- **High**, suitable for technical problem-solving
- **Expert**, suitable for handling problems that others have been unable to resolve and especially for issues involving vulnerability analysis and real-time response to attacks

As the DISA writers point out, "Vulnerability handling requires your most proficient personnel. . . . These individuals must be able to work with software vendors, CIRTs, and other experts to identify and resolve vulnerabilities. Many CIRTs don't have access to this level of technical expertise."

56.4.4   Training.   Teams that have no experience responding to incidents are of little value to an organization. Predictably, computer emergency responses by untrained or inexperienced teams result in loss or destruction of evidence, legal exposure by failing to properly protect individual rights, and failure to properly document and learn from the experience. To be most effective, training must be iterative (learn, exercise, review, analyze, repeat) and should involve as many realistic scenarios as possible, so that the CSIRT becomes exposed to a wide variety of potential emergency situations.

56.4.4.1 Rehearse Often. Experience can be gained only by responding to incidents or through training with simulated attacks. While the time and resources required to practice responding to incidents might be costly, more costly still is the potential damage resulting from an uncontained or poorly handled breach of the system.

An excellent opportunity to practice response procedures, and to develop response teams, occurs during periodic security assessments, including penetration testing. Penetration tests simulate external and internal attacks on a system and offer a real yet controlled environment in which to exercise, train, and evaluate a CSIRT. The simulation is especially effective when an outside, independent team is engaged to conduct the penetration test and security assessment. With proper coordination, the test can provide an opportunity for the team to observe, and react to, many different types of incidents.

56.4.4.2 Perform Training Reviews. At the conclusion of any training exercise, it is important to reassemble the team as soon as possible, not only to review management's view of its performance but to reveal its own perspectives as well. Each of the participants should be asked what went right and what went wrong. Were necessary resources (information, decision makers, tools, software, equipment) unavailable when the team needed them? Did the team have, or was it able to obtain in a timely manner, the physical and system access it needed? Did it have the right documentation and access to other company personnel? Were systems for communicating among the team and with other company or external personnel adequate and efficient?

Video cameras are a useful tool for recording events during the training sessions; many employees will have such equipment available and can make inexpensive recordings that can be analyzed during the training reviews.

See Section 56.7.1 on postmortem analysis of real incidents for more ideas that can be applied to training reviews.

56.4.5 Tracking Incidents. This section focuses on some of the advantages, requirements, and tools for incident tracking. First, we establish why documentation in general is so important.

56.4.5.1 Will This Have to Be Done Again? When one of the authors (MK) joined Hewlett-Packard (Canada) Ltd. in 1980, he arrived on the job armed with a small, green, hard-covered Daytimer® book prominently labeled LOGBOOK in big black letters. From his first day as a member of the systems engineering organization, he wrote down what he learned; he logged how he spent his time. When he met clients, he took notes. When he installed new versions of the MPE operating system, he kept a chronological record of everything he did—including mistakes. When he taught courses, he kept a list of questions he could not answer right away.

Pretty soon, people began asking him what he thought he was doing, writing a novel?

His colleagues may have been puzzled by what they perceived as a mania for record keeping, but he was equally astonished that record keeping was not a normal part of their way of doing work. The reason for automatically kept records was his years in scientific research, where logbooks with hard covers, numbered pages, and even waterproof paper were just usual parts of doing serious work. The idea of doing anything of importance without keeping a concurrent record simply did not occur to anyone in research. One could not reproduce an experiment without knowing exactly what sequence one had used in accomplishing the steps. Even adding salts to solutions had to be done in a particular order.

So he just kept on keeping his little green logbooks.

56.4.5.2 Why Document?
Documentation, far from being a sterile exercise done to conform to arbitrary requirements of nameless, faceless superiors, should be a vital part of any intellectual exercise. Documentation is simply writing down what we learn: the crucial step in human history that changed traditional cultures into civilizations. By keeping a record independent of any specific individual, we liberate our colleagues and our successors from dependence on our physical availability. Documentation is our assurance that work will continue without us; a kind of immortality, if you will.

We document what we do as a part of systematic problem solving. Writing forces us to identify the problem in words, instead of being content to define it in vague, unclear ideas. Writing down each idea we are in the process of testing helps us notice the ideas we missed the first time we tackled the problem. Keeping notes helps us pay attention to what we are doing.

Documenting what we do also helps us during training—both our own and that of the people we are helping to learn technical skills. Trainees can review their own notes on how to do something instead of relying entirely on someone else's description. If taking notes is viewed as a chance to engage one's mind more thoroughly in what we are learning, it can be stimulating and even fun.

Finally, accurate records can be a boon in legal wrangles. In a case one of us (MK) experienced, upper management seriously considered legal procedures against a supplier for supposed breach of contract. Careful records of exactly when meetings were held, and with whom, permitted us to analyze the problem and to resolve the issues by collaboration instead of by confrontation. Such records, if kept consistently, in good times and bad, can be accepted in a court of law as evidence—but only if everything points to a steady pattern of record keeping as events unfold. Records made long after a problem occurs are worthless.

56.4.5.3 Keep Electronic Records.
The best way of keeping records on specific problems is an easy–to–use database. Such records help team members remember and share information that can help in solving new problems as they arise. With easily accessible records, it is possible to solve problems without the presence of specific team members. Such shared knowledge speeds problem resolution, improves the competence of all team members with access to the knowledge base, and provides a sound basis for training and integration of new team members. Sharing knowledge can be a liberation for key members of any organization by sparing them from the sense of obligation to be present at all times; it also supports management policies that enforce security principles by requiring employees to take vacation time. For a discussion of the dangers of allowing any employee to become indispensable, see Chapter 45 in this *Handbook* on employment practices and policies.

56.4.5.4 Advantages for Technical Support and CSIRTs.
Keeping track of all of technical support calls is essential for effective incident handling. Having

details available to all members of the CSIRT in real time, and for research and analysis later, serves many functions:

- **Communication among team members.** Having the details written down in one place means that team members can pass a case from one to another and share data efficiently.
- **Better client service.** Callers become frustrated when they have to repeat the same information to several people in a row; a good incident-tracking system reduces that kind of irritation.
- **Documentation for effective problem solving.** A good base of documented experience can help find the right procedure and the right solution quickly.
- **Institutional memory.** When experience is written down and accessible, the organization's capacity to respond quickly and correctly to incidents improves over time.
- **Follow-up with clients.** Managers can use the incident database to prepare management reports and to follow-up with specific clients to understand and resolve difficulties or complaints.
- **Forensic evidence.** Detailed, accurate, and correctly time-stamped notes can be a deciding element in successful prosecution of malefactors.

56.4.5.5   Requirements.   Some of the more obvious requirements of any incident-handling system are:

- A unique identifier for each case.
- Dates and times for all events.
- Who currently controls the case: it should be instantly obvious who is in charge of solving the problem.
- Keywords.
- Contact information: Every person in the case should be listed with office phone, cell phone, e-mail, and fax numbers.
- Handover of control: Whenever someone takes over control of the case, that handover should be noted in the record.
- Technical details including
  - Diagnostics.
  - Tests of hypotheses.
- Resolution: What was the outcome? When was the case closed?
- Search facilities: Full-text search capabilities.
- Knowledge base: Ability to integrate vendor-supplied entries to speed research.
- Industry-standard database engine: Easy to learn, maintain, and improve.
- Accept input from comma-separated value (CSV) files: Import data from other systems.

56.4.5.6   Tools.   There is a wide range of software available for tracking incidents. One can build one's own, but then proper documentation and training materials must also be created, because turnover is a constant problem for CSIRTs. In addition, unless analysts have experience with the CSIRT function, they are likely to miss useful features that have accumulated over the years in products used by thousands of people.[9] Well-respected open-source tools are listed in the "Further Reading" section of this chapter.

All such tools can be complex. To prevent people from fumbling about in an emergency, a budget must be established adequate for staff training in implementation of the selected tool.

56.4.5.7 Get the Global Picture.

When gathering information about an incident, staff members should establish a clear picture of what people were doing when they realized that there was a problem. For example, it may be important to know that someone was accessing a rarely used account and noticed that a file was not available because someone else had it open. Those details will help to characterize the attack and to provide clues that may lead to additional valuable data. However, the CSIRT investigator should also ask why the contact was accessing the rarely used account; it takes only a minute, but getting a wider picture may give the analyst another perspective that can also lead to new clues. In the scenario just sketched, one could imagine that a system administrator had become curious about some unexpected resource utilization in a supposedly dormant account. This simple fact might lead to additional exploration of system log files and questions about whether any other dormant accounts had sparked curiosity. So, in general, it is worthwhile to explore the situation more broadly at first, rather than driving down the very first avenue that presents itself in the initial questions.

For more information on using log files for analysis of problems, see Chapter 53 in this *Handbook*.

56.4.5.8 Distinguish Observation from Assumption.

As the CSIRT member listens to the observations of other staff members, it is critically important to distinguish facts—that is, personal observations—from assumptions. Assumptions are ideas taken for granted or statements that are accepted without proof. For example, imagine the serious consequences of hearing someone say, "And so then they must have exploited a flaw in the firewall and then they. . ." and simply writing that assumption down as if it were a tested and validated explanation of the events. Such an assumption could profoundly distort the investigation, putting people's efforts onto the wrong track and diverting their attention from a more fruitful line of inquiry. Hearing such a statement, one should write down, "And so perhaps they exploited a flaw in the firewall and. . ." or "Bob thinks that they exploited a flaw in the firewall and. . ."

56.4.5.9 Distinguish Observation from Hearsay.

Everyone has played the child's game of whispering a sentence to another person and then hearing the distorted version that come out the other end of a long chain of transmission without error correction. CSIRT staff must always distinguish between first-person observations ("I read the log file and found. . .") and hearsay ("Shalama read the log file and she found. . ."). Team members should not trust hearsay: They must check it out themselves by tracking down the source of the information. Even when someone is reporting a personal observation to a CSIRT member, it is important to weigh the cost of verifying the observation (when possible) against the consequences of branching off into the wrong part of the solution space.

56.4.5.10 Distinguish Observation from Hypothesis.

Sometimes when people are careless or untrained, they do not distinguish between what they *saw* and an idea that might *explain* what they saw. In the previous example about a supposed flaw in a firewall, the person speaking seemed to take the flaw for granted; that was an assumption. A similar problem can occur when someone thinks that *maybe* there is a flaw in the firewall and then proceeds as if that were true without testing the hypothesis. "And so maybe they exploited a flaw in the firewall, so we should patch all the holes right away." Putting aside for the moment the advisability of patching holes in firewalls, merely hypothesizing an exploit does not make it true. Maybe it is a good thing to patch the firewall, but it does not follow that it is the top priority right now simply from having thought of the idea. CSIRT staff should be careful to think about what they are hearing and should note explicitly when people are proposing explanations rather than reporting facts.

56.4.5.11 Challenge Hypotheses.

When CSIRT members develop hypotheses about what is happening in a breach of security, they have to do two things: see if the ideas are consistent with observation but also test those ideas to see if they are flawed.

Trying to show that an idea is *correct* is a natural response when solving problems. Especially when the clock is ticking and a critical process is stopped, the immediate need is to get the system running immediately, no matter what it takes. Unfortunately, doing something and having the system work afterward does not automatically mean that the solution being proposed actually fixed the problem—that is the fallacy known as *post hoc, propter hoc* (after the fact, because of the fact). It is possible that what we think fixed the problem simply preceded a change of state related to some other factor. The supposed fix may have nothing to do with the solution or may be only part of the solution. Even under pressure, technical support teams with experience go beyond the immediate fix to see if there are other factors that need to be controlled for long-term stability of the system.

In analyzing the behavior of a compromised system, the CSIRT is usually less concerned with restart than with forensic analysis. Who did what to which parts of the system? What do the log files tell us about the incident? How could the attacker have gotten in? What might (s)he have changed?

For that kind of analysis, it is especially important to find ways of testing our ideas before we go down a long chain of reasoning that may be flawed at its very start. Thus, just as in quality assurance, try to come up with ways of showing that our explanation is *wrong*. If we fail to disprove a hypothesis using genuine, thoughtful, intelligent tests of our ideas, maybe we have got something useful after all. In practice, the principle teaches us to go a step further when solving problems. Instead of stopping the testing as soon as we find supportive evidence, we can make it a habit to ask "Yes, but what if . . . ?"

56.4.6 Telephone Hotline.

Users should be trained and encouraged to call the telephone hotline—usually the help desk line—to report anomalies or suspected breaches of security. The help desk operator can route the call to the appropriate persons, including the CSIRT monitor.

Returning for a moment to the advice on staffing the CSIRT as discussed in Section 56.3.1, there are some additional requirements for the people involved in the CSIRT concerning their interpersonal relations. Not only should managers look for, and ensure, adequate technical knowledge, they should also enhance interpersonal skills and disciplined work habits.

CSIRT members inevitably work with some users who are stressed by the problems they are facing. It is no help to have a technical wizard who so offends the users that they stop cooperating with the problem-resolution team. Sometimes CSIRT staff members forget that their job includes not only resolving a technical issue but also keeping the clients as happy as possible under the circumstances—and the use of the word "clients" is deliberate here.

Here are some of the most irritating responses to users we have run across in several decades of technical support and client support followed by our comments in brackets:

- "No one has ever complained about this before." [So what? If the problem is real, we should thank the user for reporting it, not make veiled criticisms that imply that the problem cannot be real.]
- "I don't have time for this now." [That is a time management problem for the CSIRT, not for the client. Take responsibility for getting the right person to take charge of the problem in real time.]
- "Why don't you try calling . . .?" [Same comment as last one.]
- "That's not my problem." [Just plain rude as well as irresponsible.]
- "Why don't you reload the operating system and call me back if it happens again?" [Significant risk and time cost for the client; often the first-line suggestion of the terminally incompetent technician.]
- "Just format your hard disk and see if it happens again." [Even worse than the previous suggestion if it is just a casual suggestion to get the client off the phone for now.]
- "Don't get mad at me—I just work here." [A professional will understand that there is a difference between criticism directed at the organization or its procedures versus a direct *ad hominem* attack. The former should be taken seriously and passed on to people who can evaluate the seriousness of the criticism; the latter can be unacceptable and should be passed on to a manager who can explain the need for civility even under stress.]

56.5   RESPONDING TO COMPUTER EMERGENCIES.   This section offers specific recommendations and comments on a structured response plan to help develop a systematic approach to CSIRTs.

56.5.1   Observe and Evaluate.   A response team leader must assess the situation as quickly as possible, based on available information. The leader should make a preliminary estimate of the type of incident, its scope, the people involved, and the data or systems affected, and then begin formulating first responses. This is the point at which the team leader or other responsible person orders a move from a state of standby monitoring to one of active monitoring, focused on the particular event or events. It is important to maintain standby and baseline monitoring activities during an actual incident, because the obvious event might well be a ruse designed to divert attention from a more serious attack.

If proper planning has taken place, the team leader usually will be able to direct a specific course of action in response to a particular incident. The leader can choose from a menu of planned responses while drawing on only those resources necessary to execute that particular response. Doing this minimizes the impact on staff at all levels and allows the incident to be dealt with efficiently and effectively. However, the more unique or complex the situation, the more likely it is that a complete team response may be required.

Responses, the players involved, and the audience are obviously different when considering a data center–type situation as opposed to a user-reported situation. Often, formal handling procedures are preestablished for data centers that generally are staffed by more technical personnel. The CSIRT can expect a higher level of response from data center personnel and will likely be able to communicate instructions more concisely and with more assured compliance.

Dealing with individual users, however, requires a greater degree of sensitivity and understanding. In most cases, the CSIRT will be moving quickly and enthusiastically when handling an incident, since this is what the team has trained so long and hard to do. Individual users often are stressed or bewildered when confronted by a computer emergency incident serious enough to warrant a response team. In these situations, users tend to be nervous rather than excited or confident. This can cause communication problems, especially when a team member converses with users over a phone. Instructions become garbled, or may not be carried out exactly as desired.

Team members must be trained to communicate clearly and calmly when dealing with individual users who may not have exceptionally well-developed technical skills. This is especially important when giving end users instructions over the phone or via some remote means. A calm, careful conversation will lessen the amount of stress the individual feels while helping to ensure that the CSIRT member's instructions are carried out properly. Proper compliance with instructions can make or break an incident investigation, especially when forensic issues are to be considered, as in the case of known or suspected criminal activity. Failure to maintain the state of an attacked system properly can thwart any subsequent attempt at a successful prosecution.

56.5.2 Begin Notification.   Once the team leader establishes that an incident is in fact in progress, notification must begin to appropriate individuals within the organization, consistent with the type of situation. Notification and actions should be carried out, whenever possible, according to existing plans.

In some cases, the CSIRT leader might be able to identify the incident as one calling for a prearranged response. The leader, having the authority and confidence to carry out such a preapproved response, will notify those appropriate to the incident and carry out the contemplated actions. In other cases, the situation might not be so clear, and the notification process might include additional personnel with authority to decide on various courses of action.

56.5.3 Set Up Communications.   Team members, especially when dealing with remote or multiple sites, must be able to communicate easily and securely with one another as well as with management representatives. Team members need to be able to communicate data, status updates, actions, responses, and similar events. Communications should flow securely to the designated CSIRT leader for coordination. The team leader must be able to direct and advise other team members, but the potentially sensitive nature of an incident may require that these communications be handled out of band and through secure means. "Out of band" in this case refers to communication methods that are neither part of nor connected to the system believed to be under attack. For example, in communications regarding an attack, the use of unencrypted e-mail that might be intercepted by an attacker, or by other unauthorized parties, should be avoided whenever possible.

56.5.4   Contain.   The CSIRT's next course of action is to contain the incident. The goal is to limit the scope of any compromise as much as possible, by isolating the system under attack from other systems in order to prevent the problem, attack, or intrusion from spreading. Containment might involve steps such as disconnecting systems from the Internet. However, doing so might limit the organization's ability to catch an intruder who is currently active on the system. The priority level assigned to intruder identification and prosecution is a part of the mission and charter of the team, modified by the specific action plans in use for a particular incident.

56.5.5   Identify.   Once the team has taken steps to contain the incident as much as possible, it should focus on identifying exactly what happened, why it happened, and how it happened, and then identify steps that can be taken to prevent a recurrence. This effort also might involve identifying who, if anyone, was or still is involved in the incident or attack.

56.5.6   Record.   All CSIRTs should be trained to document everything during an incident. No event or detail is too small to record when responding to computer emergencies. Always try to answer "Who? What? Where? How? When? Why?" This is especially true when dealing with criminal activity, when there is an expectation that the intruder will be prosecuted. Keeping accurate records of what happened and the team's actions can prove pivotal in the organization's ability to identify positively the cause or source of an incident and to prevent similar incidents in the future.

   In the case of criminal activity, with an expectation of prosecution, a legal representative should be kept informed so that appropriate forensic measures may be ordered at appropriate times.

56.5.7   Return to Operations.   For most business managers and executives, restoring operations is of paramount importance. Frequently they will pressure the EDP people and the CSIRT to put off all other activities and to direct all resources to that end. Except in extreme cases, that pressure should be resisted, and the orderly carrying out of all preceding steps must be assured. As soon as possible, the CSIRT should assist operations personnel with bringing systems back online and returning them to full operating capacity. In some cases, hard drives, logs, and even entire systems may need to remain off-line until detailed forensics examinations can be completed. In these situations, backup systems should be used to bring systems and operating capabilities back online.

56.5.8   Document and Review.   While all CSIRT members should keep careful notes at all times, it is important to remember that formal procedures to document incidents and resulting actions is vital to the overall success of the incident response effort. This documentation can form the basis for new approaches, procedures, policies, awareness programs, and similar changes. Documenting successes and failures can provide the organization with a realistic view of its security posture and of its capability to respond to emergencies, and in some cases can justify the expenditure of additional funds on training or technology. This effort also ensures that the data captured can be used by the CSIRT to learn and to sharpen skills.

56.5.9   Involving Law Enforcement.   The decision to involve law enforcement, or even when to involve law enforcement, in an incident response is one that must be given careful consideration. While most organizations recognize the benefit of a close relationship with law enforcement, involving such agencies when responding to a computer emergency can have consequences beyond those that are immediately evident.

Clearly, local and national law enforcement agencies have a great deal to offer when establishing CSIRTs and developing incident handling capabilities. It is not uncommon these days to find that many law enforcement agencies have specialized units dedicated to computer crimes and issues. They can be a valuable resource, likely to have a wealth of threat data on hand. For this reason, it is important to partner with appropriate agencies to take advantage of their experience and to establish relationships. Knowing whom to contact in an emergency not only will save time and frustration, but may mean the difference between merely repelling an attack or catching and successfully prosecuting the perpetrator, which could help prevent future attacks.

Local laws and statutes may dictate specific notification requirements that an organization is obliged to follow in the event an actual or suspected incident occurs. Careful review of local laws, statutes, and ordinances should be undertaken to ensure that the organization complies with notification requirements and other legal requirements.

When there is a choice to be made, the organization must weigh carefully the decision to involve law enforcement, and especially the question of when to do so. In most cases, formally involving law enforcement means that the organization may have to turn control of the incident and subsequent investigation over to the agency whose jurisdiction it is to investigate the crime.

While most professional law enforcement agencies will work with an organization to minimize any adverse impact on normal operations, this may not always be feasible. Because the goals of law enforcement often are different from those of others, especially of commercial enterprises, law enforcement agencies may not consider the impact of their response on the organization under attack.

Since law enforcement's mission is to investigate criminal activity, its focus will naturally be on identifying, tracking, and locating the intruder. This can, in some cases, result in seizure and removal for forensic purposes of systems and data, even systems that may be critical to the continued operation of the organization. In the case of a business, this might well mean the loss of necessary servers or workstations while an investigation is under way, with a possibly devastating effect.

Indeed, decisions about a preferred response may be taken out of the hands of managers and executives when law enforcement enters into an incident response situation. A commercial business might focus on identifying the vulnerability that made the attack possible, protecting against that vulnerability, and restoring systems to full operating capability. If, during the course of these efforts, the perpetrator can be identified, law enforcement will be informed, but such identification is rarely the overriding objective of the business. For law enforcement, however, identification and prosecution of the perpetrator is the primary objective. Establishing contact with appropriate law enforcement agencies before the organization is forced to respond to an incident will help the CSIRT plan when to notify law enforcement and how most effectively to align both sets of objectives when dealing with an incident.

For more details of working with law enforcement agencies and personnel, see Chapter 61 in this *Handbook*. For additional discussion of data collection for forensic applications, see Section 56.6.9 in this chapter.

56.5.10   Need to Know.   Protecting information about an incident in progress is essential, not only to a successful response but because it can have serious legal, privacy, and other ramifications as well. Those charged with handling an incident must use out-of-band communications, such as cellular telephones, pagers, and encrypted e-mail systems not connected to the system under attack, to ensure that knowledge of the incident is restricted to those who need to know about it. Attackers could intercept team communications if passed through in-band or normal channels and use that information to cover their tracks or even to prolong an incident.

Responding to incidents always involves gathering information about systems, users, activities, and events. In most cases, sensitive system and even personal information may be collected. During the course of their response and investigation, members of the team frequently make assumptions about the identities of those responsible for the incident, These assumptions are based on data that are continually being collected, refined, modified, and frequently changed during the course of an emergency response. Should an unproven or interim assumption that a particular individual was involved in the incident be made public, that individual's reputation might become needlessly tarnished, and the organization might well find itself facing legal proceedings as a result.

It is therefore essential that the CSIRT disseminate information about the incident according to a strict need-to-know policy. Limiting knowledge about an incident will help ensure that sensitive information remains in the hands of those who need it to perform their duties.

56.6   MANAGING THE CSIRT.   All the work that goes into creating a CSIRT can be wasted if managers fail to lead. Sloppy management can result in degraded performance, alienation of the client base, staff frustration, sabotage, and employee turnover. Management plays a key role in the formation, operation, and support of a CSIRT. Ideally, teams should be composed not only of technical personnel, but also of managers with sufficient authority to assist the team in taking actions that contain an incident and that protect data and systems from further compromise. Outside of incident handling, management support for planning, establishing and enforcing policies, and preauthorizing responses is essential. Most important is management support of the CSIRT. Without solid backing from the highest levels of management, the CSIRT will be frustrated in its attempts to carry out its mission.

56.6.1   Professionalism.   The DISA course wisely emphasizes the importance of professional behavior by all members of the CSIRT. The authors write:

> The survival of your CIRT may well depend upon using a Code of Conduct, which will earn the trust and respect of the commands you support. The conduct of any single team member reflects upon the entire CIRT organization. If the commands don't trust your CIRT, they won't report to you. It is important, therefore, not only to have a Code of Conduct, but also to shake it out and dust it off every once in a while. Remind team members what it is and why it is important . . . and use it.[10]

Here are some of the practical recommendations from that course (although we have put them in our own words for the most part):

- Write down the rules—a code of conduct—that represent your ideals of courteous, professional service to your clients.
- Train the team to understand and apply the code.
- Review the code periodically with the team.
- Speak clearly and avoid technobabble.
- Tell people exactly what you intend to do.
- Never hesitate to say "I don't know—but I'll find out."

- Do not criticize other people in your interactions with clients.
- Respect the confidentiality of your clients.
- Be respectful of your callers; do not belittle them or make them feel bad.

Notice how consistently we refer to clients; this usage emphasizes that both technical support teams and CSIRTs all perceive users as people to whom we owe service. There is no benefit to allowing an adversarial relationship between the technical support team or a CSIRT and the client base. Managers must not allow a gulf to develop between the CSIRT and the client community; leaders should clamp down on disparaging terms and derogatory comments about users. Team members must understand why such language is harmful.

Managers should identify CSIRT members with a chip on their shoulders; they must not adopt defensive, arrogant, or aggressive attitudes toward the users. If a computer-security incident can be traced to procedural errors (i.e., the procedures themselves rather than user error are causing problems), the person reporting the problem should be thanked for the information, not criticized for having experienced or identified the problem.

No one in a CSIRT has ever regretted being professional.

56.6.2 Setting the Rules for Triage.   As we mentioned in Section 56.4.2, "triage" in French means "sorting." In emergency medicine, the term was applied to the process of prioritizing treatment for patients arriving at trauma hospitals near combat zones in World War I. The same concept has been applied to help desks. For example, the "Help desk triage policy" from Courtesy Computers illustrates how a help desk team can categorize problems to ensure that important issues receive faster service than less important problems.[11] Importance is defined in terms of the number of users affected, the effects on mission-critical functions, and the costs of downtime or of less-than-optimal functions. The five priority levels suggested in the document are typical of the kind of triage categories established in many help desk departments (adapted from a table in the Courtesy Computers document):

Priority 1
- Issues of the highest importance; mission-critical systems with a direct impact on the organization (Examples: widespread network outage, payroll system, sales system, telecom system, etc.)
- Contact: Immediate–5 minutes
- Resolution: 30 minutes

Priority 2
- Single user or group outage that is preventing the affected user(s) from working (Examples: failed hard drive, broken monitor, continuous OS lockups, etc.)
- Contact: 15 minutes
- Resolution: 1 hour

Priority 3
- Single user or group outage that can be permanently or temporarily solved with a workaround (Examples: malfunctioning printer, PDA synchronization problem, PC sound problem, etc.)

- Contact: 30 minutes
- Resolution: Same day

Priority 4

- Scheduled work (Examples: new workstation installation, new equipment/software order, new hardware/software installation)
- Contact: 1 hour
- Resolution: 1–4 days

Priority 5

- Nonessential scheduled work (Examples: office moves, telephone moves, equipment loaners, scheduled events)
- Contact: Same day
- Resolution: 5 days

The particular structure and specific timelines are merely examples, not blanket recommendations. Every organization must determine its own version of such a table.

In his helpful overview, "CIRT —Framework and Models," Ajoy Kumar summarizes the functions of triage in this way:

Triage: The actions taken to categorize, prioritize, and assign incidents and events.[12]

It includes the following sub-processes:

- Categorize events.
- Correlate various events. Personnel involved in such teams typically also belong to Forensic teams.
- Prioritize events.
- Assign events for handling and response.
- Communicate information to "Respond" process for further handling.
- Re-assign (and close) events not belonging to CIRT.

The DISA training materials suggest three broader categories of interactions with help desks and CSIRTs: "incidents, vulnerabilities, and information requests."[13]

1. Incidents involve breaches of security
2. Vulnerabilities include reports of security weaknesses (and may be reported as part of an incident)
3. Information requests often are managed using lists of frequently asked questions (FAQs).

The DISA instructors go on to define factors that can help CSIRTs prioritize incidents:

- The sensitivity and/or criticality of the data affected
- The amount of data affected
- Which host machines are involved
- Where and under what conditions the incident occurred
- Effects of the incident on mission accomplishment

- Whether the incident is likely to result in media coverage
- Number of users affected
- Possible relationships to other incidents currently being investigated
- The nature of the attack
- Economic impact and time lost
- Number of times the problem has recurred; and even
- Who reports the incident.[14]

On this last point, the DISA writers point out that the organizational rank of someone calling in an incident *may* bear on its priority—but that it may be wise to cross-check the report with a security expert who can speak to whether the report is sound. Sometimes a high-level manager's sense of urgency may be rooted more in his sense of self-importance than in operational requirements.

In summary, it is important to establish a sound basis for staff members of the CSIRT to carry out triage effectively. Once the rules for evaluating incidents have been clarified, staff members should practice analyzing a number of cases to train themselves in applying the rules consistently. Role-playing exercises, based on historical records or on made-up examples, can provide an excellent and enjoyable mechanism for staff members to establish a common standard for this difficult and sensitive task.

For additional ideas on using ideas and lessons from social psychology in managing security personnel, see Chapter 50 in this *Handbook*.

56.6.3 Triage, Process, and Social Engineering.

Sometimes staff (or even managers) question the value of strict adherence to policy. Policy is sometimes seen as the expression of unnecessary rigidity—an inability to respond quickly to changing or unexpected circumstances. However, in CSIRT management, knowing and adhering to well-thought-out policies and following a reliable process are particularly valuable, not only for information gathering, data recording, and analysis, but also to maintain strict security.

One of the well-known tricks used by criminal hackers and spies is to simulate urgency that supports demands for violations of normal security restrictions. For example, criminals will call a relatively low-status employee such as a secretary and pressure him into violating standard protocols to obtain the password of his boss by claiming extreme circumstances of great urgency. The criminal may escalate the pressure to outright bullying by threatening the employee with punishment.

A criminal determined to penetrate security barriers can manufacture an incident that leads to involvement of the CSIRT. Allowing such a person to apply pressure for violations of protocol is an invitation to compromise. Worse, such deviations from well-tried and well-justified procedures can add to the embarrassment caused by the compromise; it is bad enough to have someone breaking through our security without having to admit that we helped.

For additional information on social engineering, see Chapters 19 and 20 in this *Handbook*.

56.6.4 Avoiding Burnout.

Much of the discussion that follows applies equally to CSIRTs and to help desks; in a sense, one can view the CSIRT as a specialized help desk. Many CSIRTs are specialized subsets of the help desk team.

Any organization, even one with a relatively small CSIRT or a small help desk, can suffer spikes in demand. Ordinary business cycles can influence network usage; for example, universities often see perfectly normal but large increases in call volumes at registration times as new students forget their passwords, try to connect unverified laptops to the university network, or get blocked for violating appropriate-use policies. At any site, a denial-of-service attack, a plague of computer virus infections, or an infestation of computer worms can cause a flood of calls.

Another trend is the ironic observation that the better a CSIRT (or help desk team, although the focus will continue on CSIRTs) becomes at handling problems, the more readily members of its community will turn to it to report problems or ask for help. Thus the better the CSIRT does its job, the heavier its workload can become, at least for a while. According to the DISA course:

> As a new CSIRT grows and the workload increases, and especially on those teams that provide 24-hour emergency response, burnout becomes quite common. By studying the issue, one national CSIRT determined that a full-time team member could comfortably handle one new incident per day, with 20 incidents still open and actively being investigated.[15]

Staff members who face increasing workloads may become stressed. Working long periods of overtime, missing time with family and friends, perhaps even missing regular exercise and food—these factors may lead to increased errors and turnover if people are forced to accept increasingly demanding conditions for long periods.

One of the most valuable organizational approaches to preventing burnout is to rotate staff from the IT group through the CSIRT function on a predictable schedule. For example, one can assign people to the CSIRT for three- or six-month rotations.

Such rotations require especially good training programs and particularly good documentation, to maintain efficiency as new people come on duty; in addition, the assignments must be staggered so that the CSIRT does not have to cope with large numbers of newcomers all at once. Ideally, there would not be more than one switch of personnel a week.

How should existing assignments be transferred within the CSIRT? *Difficult* existing cases should be transferred to staff members who have been on duty for a few weeks, not to the incoming staff member (even one with experience on the CSIRT). The incoming CSIRT member should be given a chance to get into (or get back into) the rhythm of the job before being hit with the most intractable problem or the most ornery client.

Every incident must have a case coordinator—the person who monitors the problem, aggregates information from varied resources, and serves as the voice of the CSIRT for that incident. When transferring responsibility for a case from one case coordinator to another, managers should ensure that the previous coordinator prepares clients for the transition and introduces the new coordinator to the key client contacts to ensure a smooth transition of control. Clients often come to depend on the person they have been working with to resolve an incident; an unexpected change can be unsettling and disturbing.

56.6.5 Many Types of Productive Work.   The DISA course writers suggest:

> Allow team members to allocate time away from high stress incident response assignments and pursue broader interests in areas such as tool development, public education and presentations, research, and other professional opportunities.[16]

CSIRT members, by the nature of their work, will have a great deal to contribute to the awareness, training, and education of their colleagues.

In the technical support group for Hewlett-Packard Canada in the 1980s, managers exercised great care in preventing consistent overwork. In emergencies, employees all pitched in—including managers—to resolve the problem for clients; however, the policy on allocation of time was strictly enforced under normal circumstances. Everyone kept careful records of time worked—a habit everyone can usefully follow—so that managers could analyze where the burden was distributed, and to provide statistical information for load balancing and personnel planning. Employees who violated the policy that no more than 70 percent of their time in the system engineering group should be spent on billable hours were warned to ease off; the rationale was that it was *necessary* to maintain constant training and time for administration and just for thinking, to ensure long-term productivity of their specialists.

56.6.6 Setting an Example.   The behavior of managers can greatly influence morale, motivation, and dedication among team members. For example, supervisors and upper managers can greatly motivate staff by pitching in to support them during emergencies or extraordinary demands, even if only by their presence. Making the CSIRT a stimulating and enjoyable duty that people *want* to be on is one of the best approaches to avoiding burnout and ensuring reliable response to computer-related problems.

56.6.7 Notes on Shiftwork.   As discussed in Section 56.6.4, rotating assignments among CSIRT members can be an excellent idea. However, frequent changes in work schedules that involve changes in sleep cycles are *not* a good idea; for example, weekly changes in shift from day to night schedules can seriously disrupt the natural circadian wake/sleep cycle and have been shown to increase the rate of errors and accidents.[17] One authoritative resource states that there are "adverse health and safety effects to working shifts[:]"

> A shiftworker, particularly one who works nights, must function on a schedule that is not natural. Constantly changing schedules can:
>
> - upset one's circadian rhythm (24-hour body cycle),
> - cause sleep deprivation and disorders of the gastrointestinal and cardiovascular systems,
> - make existing disorders worse, and
> - disrupt family and social life.[18]

Scientific studies throughout the world have long shown that shiftwork, by its very nature, is a major factor in the health and safety of workers; LaDou writes in his abstract:

> Daily physiologic variations termed circadian rhythms are interactive and require a high degree of phase relationship to produce subjective feelings of wellbeing. Disturbance of these activities, circadian desynchronization, whether from passage over time zones or from shift rotation, results in health effects such as disturbance of the quantity and quality of sleep, disturbance of gastrointestinal and other organ system activities, and aggravation of diseases such as diabetes mellitus, epilepsy and thyrotoxicosis.[19]

The U.S. National Institute for Occupational Safety and Health has published a monograph about shiftwork that contains this advice for improving shiftwork schedules:

- Avoid permanent (fixed or non-rotating) night shift.
- Keep consecutive night shifts to a minimum.
- Avoid frequent shift changes—provide enough stability to let employees adapt to their schedule.
- Plan some free weekends.
- Avoid several long days of work followed by four- to seven-day "mini-vacations"— such schedules are stressful because of the radical shifts of diurnal cycles in the two phases.
- Keep long work shifts and overtime to a minimum.
- Consider different lengths for shifts.
- Examine start-end times to fit in better with life in the external world; for example, making it possible for parents on night shift to see their children before they leave for school.
- Keep the schedule regular and predictable.
- Examine rest breaks.[20]

56.6.8 Role of Public Affairs.
The nature of interconnected systems today all but guarantees that any incident will become obvious to partners, customers, clients, and others. In many cases, the organization will be compelled to advise its constituents continuously of the status of any outage or degradation of services resulting from an incident, and the causes behind it. Therefore, it is crucial that information released for general consumption be properly screened and cleared prior to release. It is equally important that such information be released through a single source, such as the public affairs office. Restricting release of incident-related information through the public affairs office, or other designated point, will help ensure that frequent, straightforward communications with stakeholders can take place, while at the same time controlling rumors and misinformation. This simple step can do much to lessen anxiety about an incident and to reassure members, partners, and customers that the situation is well in hand and will be resolved.

56.6.9 Importance of Forensic Awareness.
As implied in Section 56.5.9, depending on the specific incident, the organization may desire not only to control the incident, but also to trace and prosecute the perpetrators in the case of known or suspected criminal activity. It is therefore highly advisable that members of the CSIRT receive thorough training in procedures for collecting and preserving evidence. Mishandling of evidence can result in an inability to take successful legal action against an attacker or to recover damages following an incident. Computer forensics and evidence handling should be high on the CSIRT's list of training topics. Chapters 2 and 34 of this *Handbook* contain additional material on computer forensics and working with law enforcement.

56.7 POSTINCIDENT ACTIVITIES.
One of the most important principles of management in general, and operations management in particular, is that fixing a problem has two aspects: the short term and the long term. One must be able to solve problems quickly enough to be effective; that is, the speed of solution must be appropriate to the consequential costs of delay. However, we should not figuratively

wipe our hands in satisfaction and walk away from a problem resolution without thinking about why it happened, how we fixed it, and whether we can do better to avoid repeats and to improve our response.[21]

The CSIRT's efforts do not end once the incident is resolved. Instead, the team should take a reasonable period to rest and recover. Then, while the details are still fresh in the team members' minds, they should examine the incident from start to finish, both formally and informally, asking questions such as "What happened? What went right? What went wrong?" This way, the team will learn from each incident and become more efficient and confident when handling new incidents in the future.

At the conclusion of each incident, the team should be assembled and a formal debriefing and review of the incident should be carried out. This debriefing should include a complete review of the team and its handling of the incident, including its adherence to policy and its technical performance. Each team member should be individually debriefed following the incident. Their recollections, thoughts, ideas, and reactions as to how the incident was handled, and how the team performed, should be documented and preserved. A management team might debrief members, and team members might debrief each other, or they might even debrief themselves using a checklist or form. Regardless of the method, the CSIRT members themselves are the best source of data about the weaknesses and strengths of the team, and that data must be captured if the team is to improve and grow in skills and confidence.

Once individual impressions are captured, it is often effective to assemble the team as a group for an incident postmortem session. Starting from the beginning of the incident, the team should examine whether it had adequate, workable policies on which to base its actions and decisions. The group should jointly evaluate each aspect of the team, its composition, skills, authority, and step-by-step handling of the incident. A list of lessons learned and action items for improvements should result from this review.

Data collected during this review process should form the basis for improving the team. This information provides input to what should be a continuous cycle involving planning, preparation, training, responding, and evaluating. Shortfalls in training, skills, equipment, access, policies, and authority will become evident through this process. These shortfalls can be corrected to improve the team's ability to respond effectively to incidents in the future.

The next sections provide additional insights into how to learn from the CSIRT's experiences.

56.7.1   Postmortem.   As a matter of standard operating procedure, every technical support person and the CSIRT must schedule time to analyze the underlying factors that led to the problem they have just resolved. This analysis will likely involve operational staff outside the CSIRT; these are the people with line expertise who will be able to contribute their intimate knowledge of technical details that contributed to this security breach. These discussions can often lead to practical recommendations for improvement of the security architecture, such as its topology or firewall placement, operational procedures such as monitoring standards or vulnerability patching, and technical details such as configurations or parameter settings.

Similarly, it is a commonplace in discussions of disaster recovery and business continuity planning that every practice run, or real-life incident, should be analyzed to see where we have made errors or achieved less than our goals in performance.

Managers must ensure that these analyses are not perceived as (or worse, really are) finger-pointing exercises for apportioning blame. In a column for *Network World*, M. E. Kabay has explained the concepts of "egoless work"; the postmortem analysis of an incident must be ego-free.[22] Managers can set the tone by responding positively to what might otherwise be perceived as criticism; "That's a good point" and "Very good observation" are examples of positive, encouraging responses to observations such as "We were too slow in getting back to the initial caller given that she clearly stated that the entire department was off-line." The meeting should focus on ways to improve the response, given the insights resulting from detailed analysis of successes and failures during an incident.

The other aspect that sometimes gets lost in such postmortems is exploring the reasons for the problems. If we do not pay attention to underlying causes, we may fix specific problems, and we may improve particular procedures, but we will likely encounter different consequences of the same fundamental errors that caused those particular problems. We must pursue the analysis deeply in order to identify structural flaws in our processes, so that we can correct those problems and thus reduce the likelihood of entire classes of problems.

The U.S. National Institute of Standards and Technology *Computer Security Incident Handling Guide* specifically recommends a postincident analysis in section 3.4. We quote the authors' list of suggested questions verbatim:

- "Exactly what happened, and at what times?
- How well did staff and management perform in dealing with the incident? Were the documented procedures followed? Were they adequate?
- What information was needed sooner?
- Were any steps or actions taken that might have inhibited the recovery?
- What would the staff and management do differently the next time a similar incident occurs?
- What corrective actions can prevent similar incidents in the future?
- What additional tools or resources are needed to detect, analyze, and mitigate future incidents?"[23]

The authors also recommend these actions (paraphrasing and summarizing):

- Invite people to the postmortem with an eye to increasing cooperation throughout the organization.
- Plan the agenda by polling participants before the meeting.
- Use experienced moderators.
- Be sure the meeting rules are clear to everyone to avoid confusion and conflict.
- Keep a written record of the discussions, conclusions, and action items.

On this last point, we add that all action items should indicate clearly who intends to deliver precisely what operational result, to whom, in which form, and by when.

56.7.2 Continuous Process Improvement: Sharing Knowledge within the Organization.

On page 3-23 of the *Computer Security Incident Handling Guide*, the authors make a series of recommendations on how to capitalize on the knowledge gained through systematic analysis of incidents.[24] We are commenting briefly on each of their suggestions (which are shown in quotation marks).

- "Reports from these meetings are good material for training new team members by showing them how more experienced team members respond to incidents." The incident reports that were used for discussion in the analytic meetings should be made available, perhaps as appendices, in a single report document so that all of the information about a specific incident or series of incidents can be accessed at one time. In what follows, such a dossier is referred to as the *follow-up report*.

- "Another important post-incident activity is creating a follow-up report for each incident, which can be quite valuable for future use." The general principle is that without documentation, we lose the opportunity for increasing institutional knowledge. If we do not record what we have learned, transmission depends on luck: the haphazard contacts of people who need to know something with those who can help. Without documentation and efficient indexing, information transferred becomes an inefficient, random process of querying and guesswork. Informal knowledge sometimes remains limited to a few people or even a single individual; without these key resources, the information is unavailable. If the holders of undocumented information leave the organization, their knowledge is usually lost to the group.

- "First, the report provides a reference that can be used to assist in handling similar incidents." Why waste time reinventing solutions that have already been found? Why make the same errors and cause the same problems that have already been located and that could be avoided?

- "Creating a formal chronology of events (including time-stamped information such as log data from systems) is important for legal reasons, as is creating a monetary estimate of the amount of damage the incident caused in terms of any loss of software and files, hardware damage, and staffing costs (including restoring services)." One of the most important kinds of information for managing security is the cost estimate. Rational allocation of resources depends on knowing how often problems occur, and how much they cost, so that we can spend appropriate amounts of money for equipment, and for the time of our employees and consultants to prevent such problems.

- "This estimate may become the basis for subsequent prosecution activity by entities such as the U.S. Attorney General's office." Estimates of monetary consequences are also essential for civil torts in the calculation of restitution.

- "Follow-up reports should be kept for a period of time as specified in record retention policies." As the *Guide*'s authors discuss in their section 3.4.2, historical records become increasingly useful as they provide a statistical base for analyzing and predicting phenomena. The costs of saving such data (which have relatively small volumes) have dropped to virtually nothing given the huge digital storage capacities of today's archival media, and their extremely low cost.

56.7.3 Sharing Knowledge with the Security Community. One of the most valuable contributions we can make to each other is information sharing. The Computer Emergency Response Team Coordination Center (CERT/CC) offers an overview of why and how to report security incidents in its "Incident Reporting Guidelines."[25] The CSIRT experts summarize the types of activity on which they would appreciate receiving reports; reasons for reporting security incidents; the variety of people and agencies who can benefit from such reports; extensive guidelines on what to include in the reports; and how to reach the CERT/CC securely.

The section "Why should I report an incident?" has these headers (and a paragraph or so of explanation of each point):

- You may receive technical assistance.
- We may be able to associate activity with other incidents.
- Your report will allow us to provide better incident statistics.
- Contacting others raises security awareness.
- Your report helps us to provide you with better documents.
- Your organization's policies may require you to report the activity.
- Reporting incidents is part of being a responsible site on the Internet.

Another way of contributing to the field is to speak at conferences. For example, the Forum of Incident Response and Security Teams (FIRST) organizes conferences, technical colloquia, and workshops.[26] The 19th Annual FIRST Conference on Computer Security Incident Handling was held in Seville, Spain, on June 17–22, 2007.[27] That year the focus was "Private Lives and Corporate Risk: Digital Privacy—Hazards and Responsibilities," and the conference included sessions on a wide range of topics suitable for technical, managerial, and legal staff at all levels. The conferences are open to all, not just members of FIRST, and organizers want participants to:

- Learn the latest security strategies in incident management
- Increase your knowledge and technical insight about security problems and their solutions
- Keep up-to-date with the latest incident response and prevention techniques
- Gain insight on analysing network vulnerabilities
- Hear how the industry experts manage their security issues
- Interact and network with colleagues from around the world to exchange ideas and advice on incident management best practices.

Readers should think about contributing papers to such conferences. Anyone who has spoken at technical conferences will confirm that there is no better way to solidify one's expertise than marshaling information into a clear presentation and speaking before one's peers. Feedback from interested participants can improve not only the current presentation but also the process being described. Intelligent, enthusiastic interchange among practitioners of goodwill with varied experiences, and from different environments, is not only productive of new ideas, it is immense fun.

The FIRST event includes "Lightning Talks" which are described as "short presentations or speeches by any attendee on any topic, which can be scheduled into conference proceedings with the approval of the organisers." Participants with hot news can thus present their findings or their ideas without necessarily having to prepare a long lecture or submitting their work many months in advance.

Other conferences, such as those organized by the Computer Security Institute (CSI),[28] MIS Training Institute (MISTI),[29] and RSA Security,[30] among many others, usually offer opportunities for discussions of CSIRT management. Readers, if they can, should take advantage of these opportunities by registering for the calls for participation (CFPs) and responding to one or two a year.

56.8 CONCLUDING REMARKS. CSIRTs are an effective organizational tool for responding to computer emergencies. However, to be effective, these teams must be carefully planned, built, trained, and supported. Proper planning and the establishment of a clear set of organizational objectives for the CSIRT are key to ensuring success. Teams that are well planned, well trained, confident, and that possess the authority and training to execute their stated mission, ultimately can provide a real return on investment for an organization. This return often can be measured in terms of limiting the impact and cost, both tangible and intangible, of a computer emergency.

56.9 FURTHER READING

Brownlee, N., and E. Guttman. "Expectations for Computer Security Incident Response," RFC 2350. IETF (June 1998), www.ietf.org/rfc/rfc2350.txt.

CERT/CC. "Resources for Creating, Managing and Improving Your CSIRT," 2001, www.CSIRT.org/csirts.

Cerberus Helpdesk: http://cerberusweb.com/.

Donald A-M. "Good, but There's More . . ." Commentary on J. Ward, "Evaluate Help Desk Call-Tracking Software with These Criteria," *TechRepublic*, April 15, 2003; http://tinyurl.com/4bcve.

Help Desk Institute: www.thinkhdi.com/.

HelpMaster Pro Suite: www.prd-software.com.au/prd/help-desk-products/.

Open Source Ticket Request System (OTRS): http://otrs.org/.

Request Tracker (RT): www.bestpractical.com/rt/.

TrackIt!: www.itsolutions.intuit.com/Track-It.asp.

Ward, J. "Evaluate Help Desk Call-Tracking Software with These Criteria," *TechRepublic*, April 10, 2003, http://articles.techrepublic.com.com/5100-1035_11-5030618.html.

Ward, J. "Product Review: HEAT PowerDesk, Call Center Tracking Software,. *TechRepublic*, May 20, 2003, http://articles.techrepublic.com.com/5100-1035_11-5034947.html.

Ward, J. "Product Review: HelpMastercall, Center Tracking Software," *TechRepublic*, April 24, 2003, http://techrepublic.com.com/5100-6270-5034721.html.

56.10 NOTES

1. Parts of this chapter, which is a major revision of the corresponding chapter in the *Computer Security Handbook*, Fourth Edition, are based on a long series of articles published over several years by M. E. Kabay in his *Network World Security Strategies* newsletter. To avoid cluttering the text with unnecessary endnotes and quotation marks, there are no further specific references to particular sources in the *Network World* series on CSIRT management.

2. www.cert.org.

3. M. J. West-Brown, D. Stikvoort, K.-P. Kossakowski, G. Killcrece, R. Ruefle, and M. Zajicek, *Handbook for Computer Security Incident Response Teams (CSIRTs),* 2nd ed. (Pittsburgh, PA: Computer Emergency Response Team Coordination Center [CERT/CC™], Carnegie Mellon University Software Engineering Institute, 2003); www.cert.org/archive/pdf/csirt-handbook.pdf.

4. DISA, "Introduction to Computer Incident Response Team (CSIRT) Management, v1.0" (CD-ROM), Defense Information Systems Agency, 2001. Available free for download as ZIP file with permission of the DISA Information Assurance Support Environment at www2.norwich.edu/mkabay/infosecmgmt/disa_cirtm_cdrom.zip.

5. Microsoft® Encarta® Reference Library 2008.

6. DISA, "Introduction to Computer Incident Response Team (CSIRT) Management."

7. B. Czegel, *Running an Effective Help Desk,* 2nd ed. (New York: John Wiley & Sons, 1998).

8. J. D. Howard, "An Analysis of Security Incidents on the Internet, 1989–1995," PhD diss., Department of Engineering and Public Policy, Carnegie Mellon University, Pittsburgh, PA, April 1997; www.cert.org/research/JHThesis/Start.html.

9. For an extensive list of articles on this topic, use the *Network World* search function: http://search.networkworld.com/query.html?qt=help+desk&

10. DISA, "Introduction to Computer Incident Response Team (CSIRT) Management, v1.0."

11. Help Desk Triage Policy, Courtesy Computers, www.courtesycomputers.com/Best%20Practices/help%20desk%20triage.doc.

12. A. Kumar, "CIRT—Framework and Models." SecurityDocs.com, January 31, 2005; www.securitydocs.com/library/2964.

13. DISA, "Introduction to Computer Incident Response Team (CSIRT) Management."

14. DISA, "Introduction to Computer Incident Response Team (CSIRT) Management."

15. DISA, "Introduction to Computer Incident Response Team (CSIRT) Management."

16. DISA, "Introduction to Computer Incident Response Team (CSIRT) Management."

17. T. Dawson and A. Aguirre, "How Work Schedules Impact the Costs, Risks and Liabilities of Extended Hours Operations; Recommendations for Improvement," Circadian Technologies Inc. white paper, 2005. Available free (registration required) from www.circadian.com/contactforms/workfactorsform.php.

18. Canadian Centre for Occupational Health and Safety, "Rotational Shiftwork," 1998, www.ccohs.ca/oshanswers/work_schedules/shiftwrk.html.

19. J. LaDou, "Health Effects of Shift Work," *Western Journal of Medicine* 137, No. 6 (December 1982,; www.pubmedcentral.nih.gov/articlerender.fcgi?artid=1274227.

20. R. R. Rosa and M. J. Colligan, "Plain Language about Shiftwork," U.S. Department of Health and Human Services, Public Health Service, Centers for Disease Control and Prevention, National Institute for Occupational Safety and Health, 1997, www.cdc.gov/niosh/pdfs/97-145.pdf.

21. M. E. Kabay, "On Not Knowing," 2004, www2.norwich.edu/mkabay/opinion/index.htm.

22. M. E. Kabay, "Egoless Work: Take Your Ego out of the Equation," *Network World Security Strategies Newsletter,* February 2, 2006, www.networkworld.com/newsletters/sec/2006/0130sec2.html.

23. T. Grance, K. Kent, and B. Kim, *Computer Security Incident Handling Guide*, NIST Special Publication SP800-61, 2004, http://csrc.nist.gov/publications/nistpubs/800-61/sp800-61.pdf.

24. Grance, Kent, and Kim, *Computer Security Incident Handling Guide*.

25. www.cert.org/tech_tips/incident_reporting.html.

26. www.first.org/.

27. www.first.org/conference/2007/.

28. www.gocsi.com/netsec/.

29. www.misti.com/default.asp?Page=70.

30. www.rsaconference.com/2008/US/.

CHAPTER **57**

DATA BACKUPS AND ARCHIVES

M. E. Kabay and Don Holden

57.1 INTRODUCTION. Nothing is perfect. Equipment breaks, people make mistakes, and data files become corrupted or disappear. Everyone, and every system, needs a well-thought-out backup and retrieval policy. In addition to making backups, data processing personnel also must consider requirements for archival storage and for retrieval of data copies. Backups also apply to personnel, equipment, and electrical power; for other applications of redundancy, see Chapters 23 and 45 in this *Handbook*.

57.1.1 Definitions. *Backups* are copies of data files or records, made at a moment in time, and primarily used in the event of failure of the active files. Normally, backups are stored on different media from the original data. In particular, a copy of a file on the same disk as the original is an acceptable backup only for a short time; the *.bak, *.bk!, *.wbk, and *.sav files created by programs such as word processors are examples of limited-use backups. However, even a copy on a separate disk loses value as a backup once the original file is modified, unless *incremental* or *differential* backups also are made. These terms are described in Section 57.3.3. Typically, backups are taken on a schedule that balances the costs and inconvenience of the process with the probable cost of reconstituting data that were modified after each backup; rational allocation of resources is discussed in Section 57.8.

Deletion or corruption of an original working file converts the backup into an original. Those who do not understand this relationship mistakenly believe that once they have a backup, they can safely delete the original file. However, before original files are deleted, as when a disk volume is to be formatted, there must be at least *double backups* of all required data. Double backups will ensure continued operations should there be a storage or retrieval problem on any one backup medium.

This chapter uses these abbreviations to denote *data storage capacities*:

KB = kilobyte = 1,024 bytes (characters) (approximately 10^3)

MB = megabyte = 1,024 KB = 1,048,576 bytes ($\sim 10^6$)

GB = gigabyte = 1,024 MB = 1,073,741,824 bytes ($\sim 10^9$)

TB = terabyte = 1,024 GB = 1,099,511,627,776 bytes ($\sim 10^{12}$)

PB = petabyte = 1,024 TB = 1,125,899,906,842,624 bytes ($\sim 10^{15}$)

EB = Exabyte = 1,024 PB = 1,152,921,504,606, 846,976 bytes ($\sim 10^{18}$)[1]

Archives—Although backups are used to store and retrieve operational data chronologically, data archives are used to store data that is seldom or no longer used but, when needed for reference, compliance (e.g., Federal Drug Administration (FDA), Health Insurance Portability and Accountability Act of 1996 (HIPAA), Securities and Exchange Commission (SEC)), or legal actions such as *e-discovery* (turning over electronic evidence in a legal proceeding), must be retrieved in a quick, logical mode. Some new data storage management systems combine both backup and this expanded archival capability.

Continuous Data Protection (CDP)—The Continuous Data Protection Special Interest Group (CDP SIG) of the Storage Networking Industry Association (SNIA) defines CDP as:

> a methodology that continuously captures or tracks data modifications and stores changes independent of the primary data, enabling recovery points from any point in the past. CDP systems may be block-, file- or application-based and can provide fine granularities of restorable objects to infinitely variable recovery points. So, according to this definition, all CDP solutions incorporate these three fundamental attributes:
>
> 1. Data changes are continuously captured or tracked
> 2. All data changes are stored in a separate location from the primary storage
> 3. Recovery point objectives are arbitrary and need not be defined in advance of the actual recovery.[2]

Virtual Tape Library (VTL)—A disk-based system that emulates a tape library, tape drives, and media. These systems are used in disk-based backup and restore operations.[3]

57.1.2   Need.   Backups and storage archives are used for many purposes:

- To replace lost or corrupted data with valid versions
- To satisfy audit and legal requirements for access to retained data
- In forensic examination of data to recognize and characterize a crime and to identify suspects
- For statistical purposes in research
- To satisfy requirements of due care and diligence in safeguarding corporate assets
- To meet unforeseen requirements

57.2   MAKING BACKUPS.   Because data change at different rates in different applications, backups may be useful when made at frequencies ranging from milliseconds to years.

57.2.1   Parallel Processing.   The ultimate backup strategy is to do everything twice at the same time. Computer systems such as HP NonStop and Stratus use redundant components at every level of processing; for example, they use arrays of processors, dual input/output (I/O) buses, multiple banks of random access memory, and duplicate disk storage devices to permit immediate recovery should anything go awry. Redundant systems use sophisticated communications between processors to ensure identity of results. If any computational components fail, processing can continue uninterrupted while the defective components are replaced.

57.2.2   Hierarchical Storage Systems.   Large computer systems with terabytes or petabytes of data typically use a *hierarchical storage system* to place often-used data on fast, relatively expensive disks while migrating less-used data to less expensive, somewhat slower storage media such as slower magnetic disks, optical media, or magnetic tapes. However, users need have no knowledge of, or involvement in, such migration; all files are listed by the file system and can be accessed without special commands. Because the secondary storage media are stored in dense cylindrical arrays, usually called *silos,* they may have total capacities in the PB per silo, with fast-moving robotic arms that can locate and load the right unit within seconds. Users may experience a brief delay of a few seconds as data are copied from the secondary storage units back onto the primary hard disks, but otherwise there is no problem for the users. This system provides a degree of backup simply because data are not erased from the silo media when they are copied to magnetic disk on the system, nor are data removed from disk when they are appended to the secondary storage; this data remanence provides a degree of temporary backup because of the duplication of data. For more information on disk-based storage systems, see Chapter 36 in this *Handbook.*

57.2.3   Disk Mirroring.   There are several methods for duplicating disk operations so that disk failures cause limited or no damage to critical data. Continuous data protection (CDP) provides infinitely granular recovery point objectives (RPO), and some implementations can provide near instant recovery times (RTO). This is because CDP protection typically is done on a write transaction by- write transaction basis. Every modification of data is recorded, and the recovery can occur to any point, down to the demarcation of individual write operations.

57.2.3.1   RAID.   Redundant arrays of independent (originally *inexpensive*) disks (RAID) were described in the late 1980s and have become a practical approach to providing fault-tolerant mass storage. The falling price of disk storage has allowed inexpensive disks to be combined into highly reliable units, containing different levels of redundancy among the components, for applications with requirements for full-time availability. The disk architecture involves special measures for ensuring that every sector of the disk can be checked for validity at every input and output operation. If the primary copy of a file shows data corruption, the secondary file is used and the system automatically makes corrections to resynchronize the primary file. From the user's point of view, there is no interruption in I/O and no error.

RAID levels define how data are distributed and replicated across multiple drives. The most commonly used levels are described in Exhibit 57.1.[4]

57.2.3.2   Storage Area Network and Network Area Storage.   A storage area network (SAN) is a network that allows more than one server to communicate with more than one device via a serial Small Computer System Interface (SCSI) protocol. SANs share devices via the SCSI protocol, running on top of a serial protocol such as Fibre Channel or Internet SCSI (iSCSI). They offer multiple servers access to raw devices, such as disk and tape drives.

Network-Attached Storage (NAS) effectively moves storage out from behind the server and puts it directly on the transport network. Unlike file servers that have SCSI and local area network (LAN) adapters, a NAS appliance offers multiple servers access to a file or file system via standard file-sharing protocols: Network File System (NFS), Common Internet File System (CIFS), Direct Access File System (DAFS), or others. One NAS disadvantage is that it shifts storage transactions from parallel SCSI connections to the production network. Therefore, the backbone LAN has to handle both normal end user traffic and storage disk requests, including backup operations. For more information on SAN and NAS, see Chapter 36.

57.2.3.3   Workstation and Personal Computer Mirroring.   Anyone who has more than one computer may have to synchronize files to make them the same on two or more computers. In addition to the simple matter of convenience, synchronizing the computers provides excellent backup, which supplements daily incremental backups (i.e., backups of all the files that have changed since the previous incremental backup) and periodic full backups. The inactive synchronized computers serve as daily full backups of the currently active computer. For example, the Laplink Gold and Microsoft SyncToy products (see also Section 57.3.4.4) unfailingly check files on the source and target machines and allow one to choose how to transfer changes:

- *Clone* the target machine using the source machine as the standard (i.e., make the target identical to the source).
- Add all new files from the source to the target without deleting any files on the target.
- Add all new files from either machine to the other without deleting files.

Software solutions also can provide automatic copying of data onto separate internal or external disks. There are dozens of such utilities available, many of them free.[5]

RAID Features and Performance

Comparison of RAID levels from the RAID Advisory Board.

Common Name	Description	Disks (cost)	Data Reliability	Data Transfer	Maximum I/O Rate
0 Disk Striping	Data is distributed across disks in the array. No redundant info provided.	N	Lower than single disk	Very high	Very high for read and write
1 Mirroring	All data replicated on N separate disks. N is almost always 2.	2N 3N etc.	Higher than RAID 2, 3, 4, or 5. lower than 6	R: higher than single disk W: similar to single disk	R: up to 2x single disk W: similar to single disk
2	Data are protected by Hamming code. Redundant information distribued across m disks (m = number of data disks in array).	N+m	Much higher than single disk; comparable to RAID 3, 4, or 5	Highest	Similar to 2x single disk
3 Parallel Transfer Disks with Parity	Each data sector is subdivided and distributed across all data disks. Redundant information normally stored on dedicated parity disk.	N+1	Much higher than single disk; comparable to RAID 2, 4, or 5	Highest	Similar to 2x single disk
4	Data sectors distributed as with disk striping. Redundant information stored on dedicated parity disk.	N+1	Much higher than single disk; comparable to RAID 2, 3, or 5	R: similar to disk striping W: much lower than single disk	R: similar to disk striping W: much lower than single disk
5	Data sectors distributed as with disk striping. Redundant information interspersed with user data.	N+1	Much higher than single disk; comparable to RAID 2, 3, or 4	R: similar to disk striping W: lower than single disk	R: similar to disk striping W: usually lower than single disk
6	As RAID Level 5, but with additional independently computed redundant information	N+2	Highest	R: similar to disk striping W: lower than RAID 5	R: similar to disk striping W: much lower than RAID 5

EXHIBIT 57.1 RAID Levels

Source: Used with kind permission of Alan Freedman, *Computer Desktop Encyclopedia* (Point Pleasant, PA: Computer Language Company, 2008), www.computerlanguage.com.

Examples include:

- SureSync software, which runs on Windows 2003, XP, and Vista, and which can replicate and synchronize files on Windows, MAC and Linux.
- NFTP 1.64, which runs on Windows, OS/2, BeOS, Linux, and Unix; it includes "transfer resume, automatic reconnect, secure authentication, extensive firewall and proxy support, support for many server types, built-in File Transfer Protocol (FTP) search, mirroring, preserving timestamps and access rights, control connection history."[6]
- UnixWare Optional Services include Disk Mirroring software for what was originally the Santa Cruz Operation (SCO) Unix.
- Double-Take software goes beyond periodic backup by capturing byte-level changes in real time and replicating them to an alternate server, either locally or across the globe.

Early users of software-based disk mirroring suffered from slower responses when updating their primary files because the system had to complete output operations to the mirror file before releasing the application for further activity. However, today's software uses part of system memory as a buffer to prevent performance degradation. Secondary (mirror) files are nonetheless rarely more than a few milliseconds behind the current status of the primary file.

57.2.4 Logging and Recovery.   If real-time access to perfect data is not essential, a well-established approach to high-availability backups is to keep a log file of all changes to critical files. *Roll-forward* recovery requires:

- Backups that are synchronized with log files to provide an agreed-on starting point
- Markers in the log files to indicate completed sequences of operations (called *transactions*) that can be recovered
- Recovery software that can read the log files and redo all the changes to the data, leaving out incomplete transactions

An alternative to roll-forward recovery is *roll-backward* recovery, in which diagnostic software scans log files and identifies only the incomplete transactions and then returns the data files to a *consistent state*. For a detailed discussion of logging, see Chapter 53 in this *Handbook*.

MS Windows XP and later versions include the *System Restore* function.[7] System Restore uses a disk buffer of at least 200 MB to store several time-stamped copies of critical executable files and settings, including system registry settings, when users install new software or patches. Users can also create restore points themselves. Users can thus return their operating system to a state consistent with that of a prior time. In addition, Windows offers a device driver rollback function for a single level of driver recovery.[8]

57.2.5 Backup Software.   All operating systems have utilities for making backups. However, sometimes the utilities that are included with the installation sets are limited in functionality; for example, they may not provide the full flexibility required to produce backups on different kinds of removable media. Generally, manufacturers of removable media include specialized backup software suitable for use with their own products.

There are so many backup products on the market for so many operating environments that readers will be able to locate suitable candidates easily with elementary searches. When evaluating backup software, users will want to check for these minimum requirements:

- The software should allow complete control over which files are backed up. Users should be able to obtain a report on exactly which files were successfully backed up and detailed explanations of why certain files could not be backed up.
- Restore operations should be configurable to respect the read-only attribute on files or to override that attribute globally or selectively.
- Data compression should be available.
- A variety of standard, open, (not proprietary) data encryption algorithms should be available.
- Backups should include full directory paths on demand, for all files.
- Scheduling should be easy, and not require human intervention once a backup is scheduled.
- Backups must be able to span multiple volumes of removable media; a backup must not be limited to the space available on a single volume.
- If free space is available, it should be possible to put more than one backup on a single volume.
- The backup software must be able to verify the readability of all backups as part of the backup process.
- It should not be easy to create backup volumes that have the same name.
- The *restore* function should allow selective retrieval of individual files and folders or directories.
- The destination of restored data should be controllable by the user.
- During the restore process, the user should be able to determine whether to overwrite files that are currently in place; the overwriting should be controllable both with file-by-file confirmation dialogs and globally, *without* further dialog.

57.2.6   Removable Media.   The density of data storage on removable media has increased thousands of times in the last half century. For example, in the 1970s, an 8-inch word-processing diskette could store up to 128 KB. In contrast, at the time of writing (April 2008), a removable disk cartridge 3 inches in diameter stored 240 GB, provided data transfer rates of 30 MB per second, and cost around $100. Moore's Law predicts that computer equipment functional capabilities and capacity double every 12 to 18 months for a given cost; this relationship definitely applies to mass storage and backup media.[9]

57.2.6.1   External Hard Disk Drives.   Many styles of portable, removable stand-alone disk drives with Universal Serial Bus (USB) and FireWire connections are available at relatively low cost. For example, a USB 2.0 portable unit measuring 1.8 centimeters (cm) × 12.4 cm × 7.9 cm, with 250 GB capacity, and weighing 155 gm cost $143 in April 2008; it fit easily into a briefcase or a purse to provide backup and recovery for travelers with laptop computers.

For office or higher-volume applications, a 2 TB Western Digital MyBook USB 2.0/Firewire 400/Firewire 800 external hard drive cost $526. The 17.4 cm × 15.9 cm ×

10.4 cm device weighed 1.9 kilograms, had its own power supply, and allowed for RAID 1 configuration or for RAID 0 striping for higher throughput.

Such devices make it easy to create one or more encrypted clones (exact copies, although not necessarily bit-for-bit copies)[10] of all of one's laptop or tower computer data, and can allow one to synchronize the clones as often as necessary. The disadvantage compared with using multiple independent storage media is that if the unit fails, all the backup data are lost.

57.2.6.2   Removable Hard Disk Drives.   Hard disk cartridges offer small businesses and home offices a convenient removable storage medium for backups. For example, the Odyssey system from Imation uses disks that are about 6.4 to 8.9 cm in diameter, with capacities ranging from 40 GB to 120 GB, that fit an external docking station with a USB 2.0 interface, or internal units that fit in a standard floppy disk drive on a personal computer. In May 2008, the 120 GB disk cartridges cost $230 each and the drive unit cost about $200.[11]

In 2002, a number of disk manufacturers formed the Information Versatile Disc for Removable Usage (iVDR) Consortium to standardize the characteristics of hard disk cartridges, making it as easy to slip a disk drive into a reader slot on a computer as it used to be to slip a floppy disk into a floppy disk drive. The consortium aimed to establish at least three shapes of removable cartridges:

1. iVDR: 110 millimeters (mm) $\times$ 80 mm $\times$ 12.7 mm
2. iVDR Mini: 67 mm $\times$ 80 mm $\times$ 10 mm
3. iVDR Micro: 50 mm $\times$ 50 mm $\times$ 8 mm

The first iVDR product was the 160 GB Hitachi Maxell Removable Hard Disk Drive iV, introduced in March 2007; the first consumer appliance using iVDR disks was the Hitachi Wooo high-definition plasma television set. Industry analysts predicted that iVDR disks would quickly reach 0.5 TB capacities, allowing for storage of 5,000 commercial movies per disk and providing an attractive storage medium for data backups and archives.

57.2.6.3   Optical Storage.   Many systems now use optical storage for backups. Compact disk read-write (CD-RW) disks are the most widely used format; each disk can hold approximately 700 MB of data. However, single-layer DVDs can store 4.7 GB, while dual-layer DVDs can store 8.5 GB on media that cost less than a dollar per disk. Write parameters in the optical drivers allow users to specify whether they intend to add to the data stored on disks or whether the disks should be closed to further modification at the end of the write cycle. Internal and external optical read/write drives cost less than $100.

Blu-ray discs™ (BDs) are an optical disk alternative to the DVD format that won out over the competing High Definition (HD) DVD standard in 2008. Single-layer BDs can store 25 GB in the same size disk as CDs and DVDs; dual-layer BDs store 50 GB.

An upcoming technology to monitor is the holographic disk, with storage capacities of up to 1.6 TB. However, at the time of writing in April 2008, these devices were still relatively expensive: around $180 per disk and $18,000 per disk drive.[12]

Large numbers of CDs, DVDs, and BDs are easily handled using *jukeboxes* that apply robotics to access specific disks, from collections of hundreds or thousands, on demand. Network-capable jukeboxes allow for concurrent access to multiple disks;

stand-alone models suitable for home or home office use are also available at lower cost.

57.2.6.4 Tape Cartridge Systems.   The old 9-track, reel-to-reel 6,250 bytes-per-inch (bpi) systems used in the 1970s and 1980s held several hundred MB. Today's pocket-size tape cartridges hold GBs. For example, the industry leader in this field, a Sony LTO3 cartridge, has 400 GB native and 800 GB compressed maximum storage capacity per cartridge and a transport speed of 80 MB/s native and 160 MB/s compressed data transfer. Cartridges have mean-time-between-failure (MTBF) of 250,000 hours with 100 percent duty cycles and can tolerate 1 million tape passes. All such systems have streaming Input/Output (I/O) using random access memory (RAM) buffers to prevent interruption of the read/write operations from and to the tapes and thus to keep the tape moving smoothly to maximize data transfer rates.

Although this buffering is effective for directly attached tape systems, this is not effective for backing up data over a LAN. When backing up data over a LAN, users will probably experience *shoeshining* of the tape drive (rapid back-and-forth movement of the tape), which reduces the effective throughput rate significantly. For example, a 50 MB per second (ps) tape drive, receiving a data stream at 25 MBps, does not write at 25 MBps. Rather it fills a buffer and writes short bursts at 50 MBps. The mechanical motion of the tape moves empty tape over the read/write head after the data transfer ends. The tape motor then stops, rewinds to reposition the tape at the appropriate place on the tape for continued writing, and prepares itself to write another short burst at 50 MBps. This repositioning process of stopping, rewinding, and getting back up to speed is called *backhitching*. Each backhitch can take as long as a few seconds. Frequent backhitching is called *shoeshining* because the tape activity mimics the movement of a cloth being used to shine shoes. The farther one operates from the designed throughput rate, the less time one spends writing data and the more time backhitching. A 50 MBps tape drive that is receiving data at 40 MBps will actually write at 35 MBps because it is spending at least 20 percent of its time shoeshining. Similarly, a data stream at 30 MBps will actually be written at 20 MBps, a 20 MBps data stream at 10 MBps, and a 10 MBps data stream at less than 1 MBps.

In conjunction with automated tape library systems, holding many cartridges and capable of switching automatically to the next cartridge, tape cartridge systems are ideal for backing up servers and mainframes with TBs of data. Small library systems keep 10 to 20 cartridges in position for immediate access, taking approximately 9 seconds for an exchange. These libraries have approximately 2 million mean exchanges between failures, with MTBF of around 360,000 hours at 100 percent duty cycle.

The large enterprise-class library systems such as the 8-frame Spectra Logic's T950 can be configured with up to 10,050 slots and 120 LTO (Linear Tape-Open, the open-software alternative to DLT or Digital Linear Tape) drives. The 8-frame T950 offered a native throughput of 14.4 GB/second using LTO-4 drives. These library systems can encrypt, compress, and decrypt data using the strongest version of the Advanced Encryption Standard (AES), to meet regulatory and security compliance requirements. As another example, the Plasmon Ultra Density Optical (UDO) Library offered up to 19 TB of archival storage capacity for enterprise systems at a price of about $100,000.

57.2.6.5 Virtual Tape Library.   Virtual tape libraries (VTLs) that are used for backup emulate tape drive and library functions and can provide a transition to an integrated disk-based backup and recovery. These units (e.g., the IBM Virtual Tape Server introduced in 1997) provide backward compatibility for older production systems by using optical, or modern high-capacity magnetic disk storage but presenting the data as if they were stored on magnetic tapes and cartridges. VTLs can use existing storage architecture and can be used remotely. Naturally, their throughput is far greater than the older tape-based backup systems.

57.2.6.6 *Personal Storage Devices: Flash Drives.*   USB flash drives have become ubiquitous due to the decline in price and the vast amount of data that they can store. Cheap multi-MB and multi-GB USB flash drives (also called memory sticks and thumb drives) are available at drugstores, are given away at conferences, and are available in a variety of forms, such as pens, pocketknives, dolls, and even sushi. Other personal devices can also be used to store large amounts of data. These include music players, personal digital assistants, and mobile phones. Although these devices can provide a convenience for the user who wants to transfer large amounts of data, they pose a serious security risk to businesses since sensitive company data can be easily removed, against company policy. Although some USB flash drives have built-in encryption to protect the contents from being exposed if the device is lost or stolen, most flash drives and other personal devices store data in unencrypted form—a serious problem if the device is lost or stolen. Some companies have implemented technical means to block the use of USB flash and other devices from downloading data from corporate PCs. Just as these devices can download data from a computer, they can also be a vector for transferring malware to a computer and to a network. User policies and education are the primary defenses to supplement technical controls.

Flash drives are sometimes recommended as a backup medium for end-users. However, they suffer from a number of disadvantages:

- They are usually physically small and therefore easy to misplace or lose.
- They are relatively fragile (e.g., their enclosures break easily if struck and are not water resistant).
- They are expensive per storage unit compared with magnetic or optical media.

57.2.6.7 *Millipede: A Future Storage Technology.*   IBM research scientists have developed *Millipede*, a method of storing data using an atomic force microscope to punch nanometer-sized depressions in thin polymer films.[13] The storage density is about 100 GB per square cm.

57.2.7 Labeling.   Regardless of the size of a backup, every storage device, from diskettes to tape cartridges, should be clearly and unambiguously tagged, both electronically and with adhesive labels. Removable media used on Windows systems, for example, can be labeled electronically with up to 11 letters, numbers, or the underscore character. Larger-capacity media, such as cartridges used for UNIX and mainframe systems, have extensive electronic labeling available. On some systems, it is possible to request specific storage media and have the system automatically refuse the wrong media if they are mounted in error. Tape library systems typically use optical bar codes that are generated automatically by the backup software and then affixed to each cartridge for unique identification. Magnetic tapes and cartridges have electronic labels written onto the start of each unit, with specifics that are particular to the operating system and tape-handling software.

An unlabeled storage medium or one with a flimsily attached label is evidence of a bad practice that will lead to confusion and error. Sticky notes, for example, are not a good way to label diskettes and removable disks. If the notes are taken off, they can get lost; if they are left on, they can jam the disk drives. There are many types of labels for storage media, including printable sheets suitable for laser or inkjet printers and using adhesive that allows removal of the labels without leaving a sticky residue. At the very least, an exterior label should include this information:

- Date the volume was created (e.g., "2010–09–08")
- Originator (e.g., "Bob R. Jones, Accounting Dept.")
- Description of the contents (e.g., "Engineering Accounting Data for 2010")
- Application program (e.g., "Quicken v2010")
- Operating system (e.g., Windows VISTA Enterprise)

Storing files with *canonical names* (names with a fixed structure) on the media themselves is also useful. An example of a canonical file much used on installation disks is "READ.ME." An organization can mandate these files as minimum standards for its storage media:

- ORIGIN.mmm (where *mmm* represents a sequence number for unique identi-fication of the storage set) indicating the originating system (e.g., "Accounting Workstation number 3875-3" or "Bob Whitmore's SPARC in Engineering")
- DATE.mmm showing the date (preferably in year-month-day sequence) on which the storage volume was created (e.g., "2010–09–08")
- SET.mmm to describe exactly which volumes are part of a particular set; contents could include "SET 123; VOL 444, VOL 445, VOL 446"
- INDEX.mmm, an index file listing all the files on all the volumes of that particular storage set; for example, "SET 123; VOL 444 FIL F1, F2; VOL 445 FIL F3, F4; VOL 446 FIL F5"
- VOLUME.nnn (where *nnn* represents a sequence number for unique identification of the medium) that contains an explanation such as "VOL 444 SET 123 NUMBER 1 OF 3"
- FILES.nnn, which lists all the files on that particular volume of that particular storage set; for example, contents could include "SET 123, VOL 444, Files F1, F2, F3"

Such labeling is best handled by an application program; many backup programs automatically generate similar files.

57.2.8 Indexing and Archives.   As implied earlier, backup volumes need a mechanism for identifying the data stored on each medium. Equally important is the capacity to locate the storage media where particular files are stored; otherwise, one would have to search serially through multiple media to locate specific data. Although not all backup products for personal computers (PCs) include such functionality, many do; server and mainframe utilities routinely include automatic indexing and retrieval. These systems allow the user to specify file names and dates, using wild-card characters to signify ranges and also to display a menu of options from which the user can select the appropriate files for recovery.

This file-level indexing, though, is not sufficient for retrieving unstructured content such as word processing documents, e-mails, instant messages, diagrams, Web pages, and images that may be required for regulators, business research, and legal subpoenas (e-discovery). The Federal Rules of Civil Procedure (FRCP) specifically address discovery and the duty to disclose evidence in preparation for trial.[14] Recent changes to FRCP specifically address electronic data. Due to the cost of locating and retrieving data for litigation, companies are changing the way they manage the life cycle of data. For instance, the cost to do a forensics search of one backup tape to locate e-mails that contain certain relevant content can be $35,000 per tape. In some recent cases, a search of e-mail tapes has involved over 100 tapes. Companies are now implementing archiving systems to address this requirement.

A method of providing fast access to fixed content (data that are not expected to be updated) is *content-addressed storage* (CAS). CAS assigns content a permanent place on disk. CAS stores content so that an object cannot be duplicated or modified once it has been stored; thus, its location is unambiguous. EMC's Centera product first released in 2002 is an example of a CAS product.

When an object is stored in CAS, the object is given a unique name that also specifies the storage location. This type of address is called a content address. It eliminates the need for a centralized index, so it is not necessary to track the location of stored data. Once an object has been stored, it cannot be deleted until the specified retention period has expired. In CAS, data is stored on disk, not tape. This method streamlines the process of searching for stored objects. A backup copy of every object is stored to enhance reliability and to minimize the risk of catastrophic data loss. A remote monitoring system will notify the system administrator in the event of a hardware failure.

Combined archiving and backup systems can reduce the amount of stored data by reducing the amount of duplicate data, thereby reducing the storage cost and time to retrieve or restore data files.

57.3   BACKUP STRATEGIES.   There are different approaches to backing up data. This section looks at what kinds of data can be backed up and then reviews appropriate ways of choosing and managing backups for different kinds of computer systems. Some of the challenges that a backup strategy should address are:

- Rapid growth of electronic data
- Shrinking time for backing up data
- Increasing backup costs
- Performance bottlenecks
- Compliance and legal discovery

57.3.1   Selecting the Backup Technology.   Initially, computers used directly attached tape drives for long-term storage and then centralized tape libraries. With the decline in price of disk drives, their reduced form factor, and high reliability, it is now feasible to use disks in addition to or in place of tapes. Two alternatives to tape backups are the disk-to-disk and disk-to-disk-to-tape.

1. *Disk to Disk (D2D).* Current backup software supports writing to a disk file as if it were another backup device. One way to do this is by emulating a tape device, allowing the disk file or "virtual tape" to integrate into the existing software architecture. D2D backup uses these virtual tapes to save backup data by writing to virtual tape libraries, and then restores the backup data by reading from the

VTL. Disk to disk takes advantage of random access, high-volume manufacturing, disk reliability, RAID, and familiar technology.

2. ***Disk to Disk to Tape (D2D2T).*** Another approach to backup and archive is a hybrid that uses both disk and tape backup media. With a disk to disk to tape (D2D2T), data are initially copied to backup storage on a disk storage system and then periodically copied again to a tape storage system (or possibly to an optical storage system). Many businesses still back up data directly to tape systems. For high-availability applications, where it is important to have data immediately accessible, a secondary disk can provide faster restoration if the data on the primary disk becomes inaccessible (e.g., a server failure or data corruption). The time to restore data from tape may be unacceptable. However, tape often is used for off-site backup and restoration in case of a disaster, because tape is a more economical alternative for long-term storage and is more portable.

57.3.2   Exclusive Access.   All backup systems have trouble with files that are currently in use by processes that have opened them with write access (i.e., which may be adding or changing data within the files). The danger in copying such files is that they may be in an *inconsistent state* when the backup software copies their data. For example, a multiphase transaction may have updated some records in a detail file, but the corresponding master records may not yet have been posted to disk. Copying the data before the transaction completes will store a corrupt version of the files and lead to problems when they are later restored to disk.

Backup software usually generates a list of everything backed up and of all the files *not* backed up; for the latter, there is usually an explanation or a code showing the reason for the failure. Operators always must verify that all required files have been backed up and must take corrective action if files have been omitted.

Some high-speed, high-capacity backup software packages provide a buffer mechanism to allow high-availability systems to continue processing while backups are in progress. In these systems, files are frozen in a consistent state so that backup can proceed, and all changes are stored in buffers on disk for later entry into the production databases. However, even this approach cannot obviate the need for a minimum period of quiescence so that the databases can reach a consistent state. In addition, it is impossible for full functionality to continue if changes are being held back from the databases until a backup is complete; all *dependent* transactions (those depending on the previously changed values of records) also must be held up until the files are unlocked.

57.3.3   Types of Backups.   Backups can include different amounts and kinds of data:

- *Full* backups store a copy of everything that resides on the mass storage of a specific system. To restore a group of files from a full backup, the operator mounts the appropriate volume of the backup set and restores the files in a single operation.
- *Differential* backups store all the data that have changed since a specific date or event; typically, a differential backup stores everything that has changed since the last full backup. The number of volumes of differential backups can increase with each additional backup. To restore a group of files from a differential backup, the operator needs to locate the latest differential set and also the full backup upon which it is based to ensure that all files are restored. For example, suppose

a full backup on Sunday contains copies of files A, B, C, D, and E. On Monday, suppose that files A and B are changed to A' and B' during the day; then the Monday evening differential backup would include only copies of files A' and B'. On Tuesday, suppose that files C and D are changed to C' and D'; then the Tuesday evening backup would include copies of files A', B', C', and D'. If there were a crash on Wednesday morning, the system could be rebuilt from Sunday's full backup (files A, B, C, D, and E), and then the Tuesday differential backup would overwrite the changed files and restore A', B', C', and D', resulting in the correct combination of unchanged and changed files (A', B', C', D', and E).

- *Incremental* backups are a more limited type of differential backups that typically store everything that has changed since the previous full or incremental backup. As long as multiple backup sets can be put on a single volume, the incremental backup requires fewer volumes than a normal differential backup for a given period. To restore a set of files from incremental backups, the operator may have to mount volumes from all the incremental sets plus the full backup upon which they are based. For example, using the same scenario as in the explanation of differential backups, suppose a full backup on Sunday contains copies of files A, B, C, D, and E. On Monday, suppose that files A and B are changed to A' and B' during the day; then the Monday evening incremental backup would include only copies of files A' and B'. On Tuesday, suppose that files C and D are changed to C' and D'; then the Tuesday evening backup would include copies only of files C' and D'. If there were a crash on Wednesday morning, the system could be rebuilt from Sunday's full backup (files A, B, C, D, and E) and then the Monday incremental backup would allow restoration of A' and B' and the Tuesday incremental backup would restore C' and D', resulting in the correct combination of unchanged and changed files (A', B', C', D', and E).

- *Delta* backups store only the portions of files that have been modified since the last full or delta backup; delta backups are a rarely used type, more akin to logging than to normal backups. Delta backups use the fewest backup volumes of all the methods listed; however, to restore data using delta backups, the operator must use special-purpose application programs and mount volumes from all the delta sets plus the full backup upon which they are based. In the scenario used earlier, the delta backup for Monday night would have records for the changes in files A in delta-A and records for the changes in file B stored in file delta-B. The Tuesday night delta backup would have records for the changes in files C and D stored in files delta-C and delta-D, respectively. To restore the correct conditions as of Tuesday night, the operator would restore the A and B files from the Sunday night full backup, then run a special recovery program to install the changes from the delta-A and a (possibly different) recovery program to install the changes from delta B. Then it would be necessary to load the Tuesday night delta backup and to run recovery programs using files C and D with corresponding files delta-C and delta-D, respectively.

Another aspect of backups is whether they include all the data on a system or only the data particular to specific application programs or groups of users:

- *System* backups copy everything on a system.
- *Application* backups copy the data needed to restore operations for particular software systems.

In addition to these terms, operators and users often refer to *daily* and *partial* backups. These terms are ambiguous and should be defined in writing when setting up procedures.

57.3.4   Computer Systems.   Systems with different characteristics and purposes can require different backup strategies. This section looks at large production systems (mainframes), smaller computers used for distributed processing (servers), individual computers used primarily by one user (workstations), and portable computers (laptops) or handheld computers and personal digital assistants (PDAs).

57.3.4.1   Mainframes.   Large production systems using mainframes, or networks of servers, routinely do full system backups every day because of the importance of rapid recovery in case of data loss (see Chapters 42 and 43 of this *Handbook*). Using high-capacity tape libraries with multiple drives and immediate access to tape cartridges, these systems are capable of data throughput of up to 2 TB per hour. Typically, all backups are performed automatically during the period of lowest system utilization. Because of the problems caused by concurrent access, mainframe operations usually reserve a time every day during which users are not permitted to access production applications. A typical approach sends a series of real-time messages to all open sessions announcing "Full Backup in xx minutes; please log off now." Operations staff have been known to phone offending users who are still logged on to the network when backups are supposed to start. To prevent unattended sessions from interfering with backups (as well as to reduce risks from unauthorized use of open sessions), most systems configure a time-out after a certain period of inactivity (typically 10 minutes). If users have left their sessions online despite the automatic logoff, mechanisms such as forced logoffs can be implemented to prevent user processes from continuing to hold production files open.

In addition to system backups, mainframe operations may be instructed to take more frequent backups of high-utilization application systems. Mission-critical transaction-processing systems, for example, may have several incremental or delta backups performed throughout the day. Transaction log files may be considered so important that they are also copied to backup media as soon as the files are closed. Typically, a log file is closed when it reaches its maximum size, and a new log file is initiated for the application programs.

57.3.4.2   Servers.   Managers of networks with many servers have the same options as mainframe operations staff, but they also have increased flexibility because of the decentralized, distributed nature of the computing environment. Many network architectures allocate specific application systems or groups of users to specific servers; therefore, it is easy to schedule system backups at times convenient for the various groups. In addition to flexible system backups, the distributed aspect of such networks facilitates application backups.

Web servers, in particular, are candidates for high-availability clones of the entire Web site. Some products provide for regeneration of a damaged Web site from a read-only clone, one that includes hash totals allowing automatic integrity checking of all elements of the exposed and potentially damaged data on the public Web site.[15]

57.3.4.3   Workstations.   Individual workstations pose special challenges for backup. Although software and backup media are readily available for all operating systems, the human factor interferes with reliable backup. Users typically are not focused on their computing infrastructure; taking care of backups is not a high priority for busy professionals. Even technically trained users, who are aware of the dangers, sometimes skip their daily backups; many novice or technically unskilled workers do not even understand the concept of backups.

If the workstations are connected to a network, then automated, centralized, backup software utilities can protect all the users' files. However, with user disk drives containing as many as 500 GB of storage, and with the popularity of large files such as pictures and videos, storing the new data, let alone the full system, for hundreds of workstations can consume TBs of backup media and saturate limited bandwidths. It takes a minimum of 29 hours to transfer 1 TB over a communications channel running at 10 MB (100 Mb) per second. There are also privacy issues in such centralized backup if users fail to encrypt their hard disk files. In addition, it is impossible to compress encrypted data, so encryption and backup software should always compress *before* encrypting data.

57.3.4.4 *Laptop Computers.*

A laptop computer is sometimes the only computer a user owns or is assigned; in other cases, the portable computer is an adjunct to a desktop computer. Laptop computers that are the primary system must be treated like workstations. Laptops that are used as adjuncts—for example, when traveling—can be backed up separately, or they can be synchronized with the corresponding desktop system.

Synchronization software, such as LapLink, offers a number of options to meet user needs:

- A variety of hardwired connection methods, including cables between serial ports, parallel ports, SCSI ports, and USB ports.

- Remote access protocols allowing users to reach their computer workstations via modem, or through TCP/IP connections via the Internet, to ensure synchronization or file access.

- Cloning, which duplicates the selected file structure of a source computer onto the target computer; cloning deletes files from the target that are not found on the source.

- Filtering, which prevents specific files, or types of files, from being transferred between computers.

- Synchronization, in which all changes on the source computer(s) are replicated onto the target computer(s). One-way synchronization updates the target only; two-way synchronization makes changes to both the target and the source computers.

- Compression and decompression routines to increase throughput during transfers and synchronizations.

- Data comparison functions to update only those portions of files that are different on source and target; for large files, this feature raises effective throughput by orders of magnitude.

- Security provisions to prevent unauthorized remote access to users' computers.

- Log files to record events during file transfers and synchronization.

Windows systems can also use the simple and free SyncToy software.

In addition to making it easier to leave the office with all the right files on one's hard disk, synchronization of portable computers has the additional benefit of creating a backup of the source computer's files. For more complete assurance, the desktop system may be backed up daily onto one or two removable drives, at the same time that the portable computer's files are synchronized. If the portable is worked on overnight, all files should be synchronized again in the morning.

57.3.4.5 *Mobile Computing Devices.* Another area that is often overlooked is mobile computing devices: Smart phones and Personal Digital Assistants (PDAs), including Palm, BlackBerry, daVinci, iPAQ, Axim and Rex. These devices often contain critically important information for their users, but not everyone realizes the value of making regular backups. Actually, synchronizing a PDA with a workstation has the added benefit of creating a backup on the workstation's disk. Security managers would do well to circulate an occasional reminder for users to synchronize or back up their PDAs to prevent data loss should they lose or damage their valuable tool. Some PDA docking cradles have a prominent button that activates instant synchronization, which is completed in only a minute or two. BlackBerries can be backed up using Desktop Manager or a wireless connection.

57.3.5 Testing. Modern backup software automatically verifies the readability of backups as it writes them; this function must not be turned off. As mentioned earlier, when preparing for any operation that destroys or may destroy the original data, two independent backups of critical data should be made, one of which may serve as the new original; it is unlikely that exactly the same error will occur in both copies of the backup. Such risky activities include partitioning disk drives, physical repair of systems, moving disk drives from one slot or system to another, and installation of new versions of the operating system.

57.4 DATA LIFE CYCLE MANAGEMENT. Data management has become increasingly important in the United States with electronic discovery and with the passage of laws, such as the Gramm Leach Bliley Act (GLBA), Health Insurance Portability and Accountability Act (HIPAA), and the Sarbanes-Oxley Act (SOX), that regulate how organizations must deal with particular types of data. (For more on these regulations, see Chapter 64 in this *Handbook*.) Data life cycle management (DLM) is a comprehensive approach to managing an organization's data, involving procedures and practices as well as applications. DLM is a policy-based approach to managing the flow of an information system's data throughout its life cycle, from creation and initial storage, to the time when it becomes obsolete and is destroyed. DLM products automate the processes involved, typically organizing data into separate tiers according to specified policies, and automating data migration from one tier to another, based on those policies. As a rule, newer data, and data that must be accessed more frequently, are stored on faster but more expensive storage media, while less critical data are stored on cheaper but slower media.

Having created a backup set, what should be done with it? And how long should the backups be kept? This section looks at issues of archive management and retention from a policy perspective. Section 57.5 looks at the issues of physical storage of backup media, and Section 57.6 reviews policies and techniques for disposing of discarded backup media.

57.4.1   Retention Policies.   One of the obvious reasons to make backup copies is to recover from damage to files. With the 2006 changes to the Federal Rules for Civil Procedures (FRCP), the corporate legal staff should provide advice regarding the retention period of certain data in order to comply with legal and regulatory requirements and to avoid potential litigation. In all cases, the combination of business and legal requirements necessitates consultation outside the information technology (IT) department; decisions on data retention policies must involve more than technical resources. Backup data may be used to retrieve files needed for regulatory and business requirements; the next section looks at archive systems as a more effective method of storing and retrieving data needed for business and legal purposes.

The probability that a backup will be useful declines with time. The backup from yesterday is more likely to be needed, and more valuable, than the same kind of backup from last week or last month. Yet each backup contains copies of files that were changed in the period covered by that backup but that may have been deleted since the backup was made. Data center policies on retention vary because of perceived needs and experience as well as in response to business and legal demands. The next sample policy illustrates some of the possibilities in creating retention policies:

- Keep daily backups for 1 month.
- Keep end-of-week backups for 3 months.

If your company does not have a data archive system, or if the backup system does not include archival features, you may need to keep the backup media for longer periods:

- Keep end-of-month backups for 5 years.
- Keep end-of-year backups for 10 years.

With such a policy in place, after 1 year there will be 55 backups in the system. After 5 years, there will be 108, and after 10 years, 113 backups will be circulating. Proper labeling, adequate storage space, and stringent controls are necessary to ensure the availability of any required backups. The 2006 changes to the FRCP may require the corporate legal staff to advise retention of certain data for even longer periods, as support for claims of patent rights, or if litigation is envisaged. In all cases, the combination of business and legal requirements necessitates consultation outside the IT department; decisions on data retention policies must involve more than technical resources and may include engineering, accounting, human resources, and so on.

57.4.2   Rotation.   Reusing backup volumes makes economic and functional sense. In general, when planning a backup strategy, different types of backups may be kept for different lengths of time. To ensure even wear on media, volumes should be labeled with the date on which they are returned to a storage area of available media and should be used in order of first in, first out. Backup volumes destined for longer retention should use newer media. An expiry date should be stamped on all tapes when they are acquired so that operations staff will know when to discard outdated media.

57.4.3   Media Longevity and Technology Changes.   For short-term storage, there is no problem ensuring that stored information will be usable. Even if a software upgrade changes file formats, the previous versions are usually readable. In

1 year, technological changes such as new storage formats will not make older formats unreadable.

Over the medium term—up to 5 years—difficulties of compatibility do increase, although not catastrophically. There are certainly plenty of 5-year old systems still in use, and it is unlikely that this level of technological inertia will be seriously reduced in the future.

Over the longer term, however, there are serious problems to overcome in maintaining the availability of electronic records. During the last 10 to 20 years, certain forms of storage have become essentially unusable. As an example, the AES company was a powerful force in the dedicated word processor market in the 1970s; 8-inch disks held dozens or hundreds of pages of text and could be read in almost any office in North America. By the late 1980s, however, AES had succumbed to word processing packages running on general-purpose computers; by 1990, the last company supporting AES equipment closed its doors. Today it would be extremely difficult to find the equipment for reading AES diskettes.

The problems of obsolescence include data degradation, software incompatibilities, and hardware incompatibilities.

57.4.3.1 Media Degradation. Magnetic media degrade over time. Over a period of a few years, thermal disruption of magnetic domains gradually blurs the boundaries of the magnetized areas, making it harder for I/O devices to distinguish between the domains representing 1s and those representing 0s. These problems affect tapes, diskettes, and magnetic disks and cause increasing parity errors. Specialized equipment and software can compensate for these errors and recover most of the data on such old media.

Tape media suffer from an additional source of degradation: The metal oxide becomes friable and begins to flake off the Mylar backing. Such losses are unrecoverable. They occur within a few years in media stored under inadequate environmental controls and within 5 to 10 years for properly maintained media. Regular regeneration by copying the data before the underlying medium disintegrates prevents data loss.

Optical disks, which use laser beams to etch bubbles in the substrate, are much more stable than magnetic media. Current estimates are that CD-ROMs and CD-RW and DVD disks will remain readable, in theory, for at least a decade, and probably longer. However, they will remain readable in practice if, and only if, future optical storage systems include backward compatibility.

USB flash drives have largely replaced floppy diskettes and zip disks as a means of storing or transporting temporary data. Flash drives, similar to flash memory, have a finite number of cycles of writing and erasing before slowing down and failing. Typically, this is not an issue, as the number of cycles is in the hundreds of thousands.

57.4.3.2 Software Changes. Software incompatibilities include the application software and the operating system.

The data may be readable, but will they be usable? Manufacturers provide backward compatibility, but there are limits. For example, MS-Word 2007 can convert files from earlier versions of Word—but only back to version 6 for Windows. Over time, application programs evolve and drop support of the earliest data formats. Database programs, e-mail, spreadsheets—all of tomorrow's versions may have trouble interpreting today's data files correctly.

In any case, all conversions raise the possibility of data loss since new formats are not necessarily supersets of old formats. For example, in 1972, RUNOFF text files on mainframe systems included instructions to pause a daisy-wheel impact printer so the operator could change daisy wheels—but there was no requirement to document the desired daisy wheel. The operator made the choice. What would document conversion do with that instruction?

Even operating systems evolve. Programs intended for Windows 3.11 of the early 1990s do not necessarily function on Windows VISTA in the year 2008. Many older operating systems are no longer supported and do not even run on today's hardware.

Finally, even hardware eventually becomes impossible to maintain. As mentioned, it would be extremely difficult to retrieve and interpret data from word processing equipment from even 20 years ago. No one outside museums or hobbyists can read an 800 bpi 9-track $\frac{3}{4}$-inch magnetic tape from the very popular 1980 HP3000 Series III minicomputer. Over time, even such parameters as data encoding standards (e.g., Binary Coded Decimal (BCD), Extended Binary Coded Decimal (EBCDIC), and American Standard Code for Information Interchange (ASCII)) may change, making obsolete equipment difficult to use even if they can be located.

The most robust method developed to date for long-term storage of data is COM (Computer Output to Microfilm). Documents are printed to microfilm, appearing exactly as if they had been printed on paper and then microphotographed. Storage densities are high, storage costs are low, and, if necessary, the images can be read with a source of light and a simple lens or converted to the current machine-readable form using optical character recognition (OCR) software.

57.5   SAFEGUARDING BACKUPS.   Where and how backup volumes are stored affects their longevity, accessibility, and usability for legal purposes.

57.5.1   Environmental Protection.   Magnetic and optical media can be damaged by dust, mold, condensation, freezing, and excessive heat. All locations considered for storage of backup media should conform to the media manufacturer's environmental tolerances; typical values are 40 to 60 percent humidity and temperatures of about 50 to 75° F (about 10 to 25° C). In addition, magnetic media should not be stacked horizontally in piles; the housings of these devices are not built to withstand much pressure, so large stacks can cause damaging contact between the protective shell and the data storage surface. Electromagnetic pulses and magnetic fields are also harmful to magnetic backup media; mobile phones, both wireless and cellular, should be kept away from magnetic media. If degaussers are used to render data more difficult to read before discarding media (see Section 57.6), these devices should never be allowed into an area where magnetic disks or tapes are in use or stored.

57.5.2   On-Site Protection.   It is obviously unwise to keep backups in a place where they are subject to the same risks of destruction as the computer systems they are intended to protect. However, unless backups are made through telecommunications channels to a remote facility, they must spend at least some time in the same location as the systems on which they were made.

At a minimum, backup policies should stipulate that backups are to be removed to a secure, relatively distant location as soon as possible after completion. Temporary on-site storage areas that may be suitable for holding backups until they can be moved off-site, include specialized fire-resistant media storage cabinets or safes, secure media storage rooms in the data center, a location on a different floor of a multifloor building, or an appropriate location in a different building of a campus. What is *not* acceptable is to store backup volumes in a cabinet right next to the computer that was backed up.

Even worse is the unfortunate habit of leaving backup volumes in a disorganized heap on top of the computer from which the data were copied.

In a small office, backups should be kept in a fire-resistant safe, if possible, while waiting to take the media somewhere else.

57.5.3   Off-Site Protection.   As mentioned, it is normal to store backups away from the computers and buildings where the primary copies of the backed-up data reside.

57.5.3.1   *Care during Transport.*   When sending backup media out for storage, operations staff should use lockable carrying cases designed for the specific media to be transported. If external firms, specializing in data storage, pick up media, they usually supply such cases as part of a contract. If media are being transported by corporate staff, it is essential to explain the dangers of leaving such materials in a car: In the summer cars can get so hot that they melt the media, whereas in winter they can get so cold that the media instantly attract harmful water condensation when they are brought inside. In any case, leaving valuable data in an automobile exposes them to theft.

57.5.3.2   *Homes.*   The obvious, but dangerous, choice for people in small offices is to send backup media to the homes of trusted employees. There are a number of problems with this storage choice:

- Although the employee may be trustworthy, members of that person's family may not be so. Especially where teenage and younger children are present, keeping an organization's backups in a private home poses serious security risks.
- Environmental conditions in homes may be incompatible with safe long-term storage of media. For example, depending on the cleaning practices of the household, storing backups in a cardboard box under the bed may expose the media to dust, insects, cats, dogs, rodents, and damage from vacuum cleaners. In addition, temperature and humidity controls may be inadequate for safe storage of magnetic media.
- Homeowner's insurance policies are unlikely to cover loss of an employer's property and surely will not cover consequential losses resulting from damage to crucial backup volumes.
- Legal requirements for a demonstrable chain of custody for corporate documentation on backup volumes will not be met if the media are left in a private home, where unknown persons may have access to them.

57.5.3.3   *Safes.*   There are no *fireproof* safes, only *fire-resistant* safes. Safes are available with different degrees of guaranteed resistance to specific temperatures commonly found in ordinary fires (those not involving arson and flame accelerants). Sturdy, small safes of 1 or 2 cubic feet are available for use in small offices or homes; they can withstand the heat during the relatively short time required to burn a house or small building down. They can withstand a fall through one or two floors without breaking open. However, for use in taller buildings, only more expensive and better-built safes are appropriate to protect valuable data.

57.5.3.4 *Banks.*   Banks have facilities for secured, environmentally controlled storage of valuables. Aside from the cost of renting and accessing such boxes, the main problem for backup storage in banks is that banks are open only part of the day; it is almost impossible to access backups in a safe deposit box after normal banking hours. In any case, it is impossible to rent such boxes with enough room for more than a few dozen small backup media. Banks are not usable as data repositories for any but the smallest organizations and should not be considered as a reasonable alternative even for them.

57.5.3.5 *Data Vaults.*   Most enterprises will benefit from contracting with professional, full-time operations that specialize in maintaining archives of backup media. Some of the key features to look for in evaluating such facilities include:

- Storage areas made of concrete and steel construction to reduce risk of fire
- No storage of paper documents in the same building as magnetic or optical media storage
- Full air-conditioning including humidity, temperature, and dust controls throughout the storage vaults
- Fire sensors and fire-retardant technology, preferably without the use of water
- Full-time security monitoring including motion detectors, guards, and tightly controlled access
- Uniformed, bonded personnel
- Full time, 24/7/365 data pickup and delivery services
- Efficient communications with procedures for authenticating requests for changes in the lists of client personnel authorized to access archives
- Evidence of sound business planning and stability

References from customers similar in size and complexity to the inquiring enterprise will help a manager make a wise choice among alternative suppliers.

57.5.3.6 *Online Backups.*   An alternative to making on-site backup copies is to pay a third party to make automatic backups via high-speed telecommunications channels and to store the data in a secure facility. Some firms involved in these services move data to magnetic or optical backup volumes, but others use RAID (see Section 57.2.3.1) for instant access to the latest backups. Additional features to look for when evaluating online backup facilities:

- Compatibility of backup software with the computing platform, operating system, and application programs
- Availability of different backup options: full, differential, incremental, and delta
- Handling of files that are held in an *open* state by application programs
- Availability and costs of sufficient bandwidth to support desired data backup rates
- Encryption of data during transmission and when stored at the service facility
- Strong access controls to limit access to stored data to authorized personnel
- Physical security at the storage site, and other criteria similar to those listed in Section 57.5.3.5

- Methods for restoring files from these backups, and the speed with which it can be accomplished

In a meta-analysis of 24 reviews of a total of 39 online backup services, ConsumerSearch concluded in 2007 that the best online backup service was MozyPro; other useful services included iBackup and Box.net.[16]

A related topic is the converse of online backups: backing up online services such as Gmail and AOL, where critical data reside on a server out of a user's control. For an e-mail service, use an e-mail client configured to access the service using Post Office Protocol (POP) or Internet Message Access Protocol (IMAP) (see Chapter 5 in this *Handbook*), or use scripting languages to extract data from the server to a hard disk.[17]

57.6   DISPOSAL.   Before throwing out backup media containing unencrypted sensitive information, operations and security staff should ensure that the media are unreadable. This section looks at the problem of data scavenging and then recommends methods for preventing such unauthorized data recovery.

57.6.1   Scavenging.   Discarded disk drives with fully readable information have repeatedly been found for sale by computer resellers, at auctions, at used-equipment exchanges, on eBay, and at flea markets and yard sales.[18] In a formal study of the problem from November 2000 through August 2002, MIT scientists Simson Garfinkel and Abhi Shelat bought 158 used disk drives from many types of sources and studied the data they found on the drives. Using special analytical tools, the scientists found a total of 75 GB of readable data. They wrote:

> With several months of work and relatively little financial expenditure, we were able to retrieve thousands of credit card numbers and extraordinarily personal information on many individuals. We believe that the lack of media reports about this problem is simply because, at this point, few people are looking to repurposed hard drives for confidential material. If sanitization practices are not significantly improved, it's only a matter of time before the confidential information on repurposed hard drives is exploited by individuals and organizations that would do us harm.[19]

Computer crime specialists have described unauthorized access to information left on discarded media as scavenging, browsing, and Dumpster-diving (from the trade-marked name of metal bins often used to collect trash outside office buildings).

Scavenging can take place within an enterprise; for example, there have been documented cases of criminals who arranged to read *scratch tapes,* used for temporary storage of data, before they were reused or erased. Often they found valuable data left by previous users. Operations policies should not allow scratch tapes, or other media containing confidential data, to be circulated; all scratch media, including backup media that are being returned to the available list, should be erased before they are put on the media rack.

Before deciding to toss potentially valuable documents or backup media into the trash can, managers should realize that in the United States, according to a U.S. Supreme Court ruling, discarded waste is not considered private property under the law. Anything that is thrown out is fair game for warrantless searches or inspection by anyone who can gain access to it, without violating laws against physical trespass. Readers in other jurisdictions should obtain legal advice on the applicable statutes.

Under these circumstances, the only reasonable protection against data theft is to make the trash unreadable.

57.6.2 Data and Media Destruction.   Most people know that when a file is erased or purged from a magnetic disk, most operating systems leave the information entirely or largely intact, only removing the pointers from the directory. *Unerase* utilities search the disk and reconstruct the chain of *extents* (areas of contiguous storage), usually with human intervention to verify that the data are still good.

57.6.2.1 Operating System Erase.   Multiuser operating systems remove pointers from the disk directory and return all sectors in a purged file to a disk's free space map, but the data in the original extents (sections of contiguous disk space) persist until overwritten, unless specific measures are taken to obliterate them.

Formatting a disk is generally believed to destroy all of its data; however, even formatting and overwriting files on magnetic media may not make them unreadable to sophisticated equipment. Since information on magnetic tapes and disks resides in the difference in intensity between highly magnetized areas (1s) and less-magnetized areas (0s), writing the same 0s or 1s in all areas to be obliterated merely reduces the signal-to-noise ratio. That is, the residual magnetic fields still vary in more or less the original pattern—they are just less easily distinguished. Using highly sensitive readers, a magnetic tape or disk that has been zeroed will yield much of the original information.

57.6.2.2 Field Research.   Garfinkel and Shelat reported on the many failed attempts to destroy (*sanitize*) data on disk drives, including erasure (leaves data almost entirely intact), overwriting (good enough or even perfect but not always properly applied), physical destruction (evidently, renders what is left of the drive unusable), and degaussing (using strong magnetic fields to distort the magnetic domains into unreadability).

With regard to ordinary file-system formatting, the authors noted:

> most operating system format commands only write a minimal disk file system; they do not rewrite the entire disk. To illustrate this assertion, we took a 10-Gbyte hard disk and filled every block with a known pattern. We then initialized a disk partition using the Windows 98 FDISK command and formatted the disk with the format command. After each step, we examined the disk to determine the number of blocks that had been written. . . . Users might find these numbers discouraging: despite warnings from the operating system to the contrary, the format command overwrites barely more than 0.1 percent of the disk's data. Nevertheless, the command takes more than eight minutes to do its job on the 10-Gbyte disk—giving the impression that the computer is actually overwriting the data. In fact, the computer is attempting to read all of the drive's data so it can build a bad-block table. The only blocks that are actually written during the format process are those that correspond to the boot blocks, the root directory, the file allocation table, and a few test sectors scattered throughout the drive's surface.[20]

57.6.2.3 Clearing Data.   One way of *clearing* data[21] on magnetic media is to overwrite several passes of random patterns. The random patterns make it far more difficult, but not impossible, to extract useful information from the discarded disks and tapes. For this reason, the U.S. Government no longer allows overwriting of classified media to obliterate data remanence when moving media to a lower level of protection. Small removable thumb drives of 2 GB, and Advanced Technology Attachment (ATA) disk drives of 15 GB or more can use a secure erase to purge data.[22] ATA drives have secure erase in their firmware. Secure erase for thumb drives can be downloaded from the University of California, San Diego (UCSD) CMRR site.[23]

Degaussers can be used to remove data remanence physically. A degausser is a device that generates a magnetic field used to sanitize magnetic media. Degaussers are rated based on the type (i.e., low energy or high energy) of magnetic media they can purge. Degaussers operate using either a strong permanent magnet or an electromagnetic coil. These devices range from simple handheld units suitable for low-volume usage to high-energy units capable of erasing magnetic media either oxide or metal based, up to 1,700 Oersteds (Oe). These devices remove all traces of previously recorded data allowing media to be used again. The U.S. Government has approved certain degaussers for secure erasure of classified data. Degaussing of any hard drive assembly usually destroys the drive, as degaussing also erases firmware that manages the device. There are other downsides to using degaussers.

Enscence Data Technology, a firm specializing in secure data destruction, has argued that software overwriting alone is not trustworthy because the choice of algorithm may be inadequate and because certain portions of the drive may not be overwritten at all. Degaussing is unreliable and even dangerous; sometimes drives are damaged so that they cannot be checked by users to evaluate the completeness of data wiping—even though expert data recovery specialists may be able to extract usable data from the degaussed disks. The strong magnetic fields can also unintentionally damage other equipment. Outsourcing degaussing introduces problems of having to store drives until pickup, losing control over data, and having to trust third parties to provide trustworthy records of the data destruction. Physical shredders are expensive and usually offered only by outside companies, leading to similar problems of temporary storage, relinquishing control, and dubious audit trails. Enscence Data Technology's *Digital Shredder* is a small, portable hardware device that provides a wide range of interfaces called *personality modules* that allow a variety of disk drives to be wiped securely. The design objectives, quoting the company, were to provide:

1. Destruction of data beyond forensic recovery
2. Retention of care, custody, and control
3. Certification and defendable audit trail
4. Ease of deployment
5. Ability to recycle the drive for reuse.

The unit can wipe up to three disks at once. It includes its own touch screen; offers user authentication with passwords to ensure that it is not misused by unauthorized personnel; provides positive indications through colored light-emitting diodes (LEDs) to show the current status of each bay; can format drives for a range of file systems; and can be used to reimage a drive by make bitwise copies from a master drive in one bay to a reformatted drive in another.

Another solution is physical destruction[24] of magnetic or optical backup media before they are discarded. For end user departments, operations and security staff can provide identifiable secure collection receptacles (typically black) throughout the enterprise. Discarded media can be erased or destroyed by appropriate staff on a regular schedule. Hard disks, tapes, optical disks, and floppy disks can be cut into pieces, melted with oxyacetylene torches, crushed in large compactors, and incinerated, although proper incineration requires specialized equipment to prevent atmospheric release of toxic by-products. Some commercial companies specialize in secure destruction of sensitive records and can provide bonded pickup services, or mobile destruction units, that move from enterprise to enterprise on a regular schedule and handle paper as well as magnetic and optical media.

Disk Costs, Variable

   a. Disks/Backup   _____

   b. Purchase Cost/Disk   _____

   c. Disk Cost/Backup (a*b)   _____

Time Costs, Variable

   d. Hours/Backup Disk   _____

   e. Total Disks/Backup   _____

   f. Total Hours/Backup (d*e)   _____

   g. Operator Cost/Hour (Salary + Benefits) _____

   h. Time Cost/Backup (f*g)   _____

Total Variable Costs/Backup (f+h)   _____

Fixed Costs

   i. Monthly costs of storage space, racks, insurance, transportation, hardware rental and maintenance, software rental and maintenance, cost of time to combine daily backups into weekly, weekly into monthly, etc.   _____

   j. Number of Backups/Month   _____

   k. Fixed Cost/Backup (i/j)   _____

Total Variable and Fixed Costs/Backup (f+h+k) _____
Annualized Costs

   l. Backups/Year   _____

   m. Total Variable and Fixed Costs/Backup (f+h+k) _____

   n. Total Cost/Year (l*m)   _____

Exhibit 57.2 Calculating Costs of Backup

57.7 COSTS. All data center managers should be able to answer questions about the costs of the backups being made on their systems. Exhibit 57.2 presents the factors that should be included in a simple spreadsheet when calculating costs of backups, with disks as an example of backup media.

57.8 OPTIMIZING FREQUENCY OF BACKUPS. Suppose a manager asks the security and operations staff these questions:

- "If backups are so important that you do a daily full backup, why don't you do a full backup twice a day?"
- "If taking a daily full backup is good enough for you, why don't you save money by doing a full backup only every other day?"

To answer such questions, managers must be able to adjust the frequency of backups to the perceived risk. One of the ways of approaching a rational allocation of resources when faced with random threats is to calculate the *expected value* of a strategy. The expected value is the average gain (if it is a positive quantity) or loss (if it is negative) that participants will incur in a process that involves random events. When this technique applies to losses over an entire year, it is called the *annualized loss expectancy*. Insurance companies use this approach to balance the costs of premiums against the disbursements to customers.

For backups, the principle is summarized by this equation:

$$E(x) = P(u)^*C(u) - P(n)^*C(n)$$

Where:

$x =$ Some particular strategy, such as doing a daily full backup.

$E(x) =$ Expected value or cost of the strategy.

$P(u) =$ Probability of having to use the backup within a single day; for example, 1 chance in a 1000 or 0.001.

$C(u) =$ Money saved by not having to redo all the work that would otherwise be lost if there were no backup; for example, the cost of paying for reconstruction of the previous day's data (e.g., \$9,000) + avoidance of lost business, wasted salary, and other expenses during 3 hours of downtime during reconstruction (e.g., \$30,000) for a savings of \$39,000 per incident when the backups are available.

$P(n) =$ Probability of not having to use the backups at all in a given day $= 1 - P(u) = 0.999$.

$C(n) =$ Cost of making and storing a daily backup that will not be used (e.g., \$50).

The expected value of doing a single daily full backup using the figures used in the last example is

$$E(x) = (0.001^*\$39,000) - (0.990^*\$50) = \$39 - \$49.95 = -\$10.95$$

In other words, the daily full backup has an average cost of about \$11 per day when the likelihood of its use is factored into the calculations. This is equivalent to a self-insurance strategy to prevent larger disasters by investing money in preventive mechanisms and measures for rapid and less expensive recovery than possible without the backups.

If one adjusts the frequency of backups, the calculated loss expectancy can be forced to zero or even to a positive number; however, no self-insurer can make a profit from loss-avoidance measures. Nonetheless, adjusting the frequency and costs of backup strategies using the suggested factors and calculation of loss expectancies can help a data center manager answer questions from management about backup strategies in a rational manner. Since no one can estimate precisely how much a disaster costs or compute precise probabilities of having to use backups for recovery, these figures can serve only as rough guidelines.

In many organizations, the volume of changes follows a seasonal pattern. For example, 80 percent of all orders taken might come in two two-month periods spaced half a year apart. Registration for colleges occurs mostly in the autumn, with another bulge in January. Boat sales and ski sales follow seasonal variations. Despite this obvious variability, many organizations follow the same backup schedule regardless of date. It makes sense to adjust the frequency of backups to the volatility of data, since operations can schedule more frequent backups when there are many changes and fewer when the data are relatively stable.

57.9   CONCLUDING REMARKS.   Backups are an essential component of operational security, and they play a crucial role in business resumption and disaster recovery. Backup policies should be developed rationally as a function of the specific requirements of each application, and of each computer system. Because conditions change, backup policies should be adjusted as needed to reflect changing requirements. Decisions on keeping archival copies of data should include consideration of legal requirements. Backup policies should include provisions for the full life cycle of the backup media, including acquisition, rotation, storage, and destruction.

57.10   FURTHER READING

Borg-Breen, J., and L. Phelan. "A Proactive Approach to e-Discovery," *Network World Security* (2007); www.networkworld.com/news/tech/2007/100607-proactive-approach.html.

Brown, D. *1StepBackup for Windows—The BOOK: Windows Computer Backup in ONE Easy Step.* Scotts Valley, CA: CreateSpace, 2008.

Connor, D. "E-discovery Appliances Find Crucial Documents," *Network World Data Center* (2007); www.networkworld.com/news/2007/013007-ediscovery-appliances.html.

Ensconce Data Technology. "Avoiding Self-Inflicted Security Breaches Through Effective Hard Drive Sanitization" (2006); www.deadondemand.com/assets/documents/avoiding_self_inflicted_security_breaches.pdf.

Harris, N. *I5/OS V5r4 Virtual Tape: A Guide to Planning and Implementation.* IBM, 2006.

Kabay, M. E. "Disk Data Remanence, Part 2: Digital Shredder," *Network World Security Strategies* (2007); www.networkworld.com/newsletters/sec/2007/0806 sec1.html.

Kissell, J. *Real World Mac Maintenance and Backups.* Berkeley, CA: Peachpit Press, 2006.

Little, D. B., and D. A. Chapa. *Implementing Backup and Recovery: The Readiness Guide for the Enterprise.* Hoboken, NJ: John Wiley & Sons, 2003.

Markham, R. "Retention Management: the Holy Grail of Records Management," Forrester Research (2006); www.forrester.com/Research/Document/Excerpt/0,7211,39336,00.html.

Mullins, R. "Baltimore Utility Power Up with e-Discovery Program." *Network World Data Center* (2007); www.networkworld.com/news/tech/2007/100607-proactive-approach.html.

Preston, W. C. *Backup and Recovery.* Sebastopol, CA: O'Reilly, 2007.

Wendt, J., and J. Konkle. "Where Encryption Fits Best," *Storage* (November 2007); http://searchstorage.techtarget.com/magazineFeature/0,296894,sid5_gci1281599,00.html.

Wendt, J. "New Role for Tape Libraries," *Storage* (September 2007); http://searchstorage.techtarget.com/magazineFeature/0,296894,sid5_gci1272873,00.html.

57.11   NOTES

1. According to a 1998 proposal from the International Electrotechnical Commission, the preferred prefixes should be KiB for kibibytes, MiB for mebibytes, GiB for gibibytes, and TiB for tebibytes to distinguish them from the powers-of-10 notations using kilo (10^3), mega (10^6), giga (10^9), and tera (10^{12}), but this

suggestion has not been accepted by the technical community. See NIST Reference on Constants, Units and Uncertainty. http://physics.nist.gov/cuu/Units/binary.html.

2. SNIA CDP SIG, Continuous Data Protection Special Interest Group (2008),; www.snia.org/forums/dmf/programs/data_protect_init/cdp/.

3. SNIA, "Virtual Tape Library Buyer's Guide" (2006); www.snia.org/about/resources/VTL_BuyersGuide_V1_20061025.pdf.

4. For more extensive discussion of RAID levels, see IBM Technote, "About RAID levels and ClearCase" (2008); www-1.ibm.com/support/docview.wss?uid=swg21149421.

5. 3D2F.com Software Directory, "Automatic Folder File Free Software" (2008); http://3d2f.com/tags/software/automatic/mirror/folder/file/

6. 3D2F NFTP download, http://3d2f.com/programs/5-339-nftp-download.shtml.

7. M. Wise, "Windows XP Systems Restore," *Windows & .NET Magazine* (September 2002); http://technet.microsoft.com/en-us/library/bb490854.aspx.

8. Microsoft TechNet, "How to Roll Back a Device Driver, for the IT Pro" (2001); http://technet.microsoft.com/en-us/library/bb457021.aspx.

9. In 1980, an HP7925 120 MB drive the size of a washing machine cost $25,000—about $213,333 per GB in 1980 dollars. In 2008, a Seagate 1 TB drive the size of a paperback book cost $237—about $0.23 per GB in 2008 dollars or roughly $0.07 in 1980 dollars. The compounded annual rate of decline in the cost of disk storage over 28 years was thus about 0.58 per year—pretty close to Moore's Law. See Intel Museum, "Moore's Law" (2008); www.intel.com/museum/archives/history_docs/mooreslaw.htm.

10. Bit-for-bit copies are used in forensic analysis (see Chapter 55 in this *Handbook*) and include the entire contents of a storage medium, including control information and unused areas, in exactly the original layout found on the source device. In contrast, the term "clone" implies that all functional data are replicated but does not require identical distribution of those data on the physical media. Thus a bit-for-bit copy will include bad sectors and deleted files but a clone will not.

11. Odyssey Removable Hard Disk Storage System, www.imation.com/products/odyssey/index.html.

12. A. Weiss, "Data Storage, the Next Generation," *ACM netWorker* 11, No. 3 (2007): 26–33. Available online from the ACM Digital Library, http://portal.acm.org/.

13. P. Vettiger, et al., "The 'Millipede'—More than One Thousand Tips for Future AFM Data Storage," *IBM Journal of Research and Development* 44, No. 3 (2000): 323–340; www.research.ibm.com/journal/rd/443/vettiger.pdf.

14. Federal Rules of Civil Procedure, www.law.cornell.edu/rules/frcp/.

15. SiteVault Site Backup Utility, www.site-vault.com/.

16. ConsumerSearch, "Online Backup Services Reviews: Reviewing the Reviews" (2007); www.consumersearch.com/www/internet/online-backup-services/.

17. G. Trapani, "Geek to Live: Back up Gmail with fetchmail," *Lifehacker* (2007); http:// lifehacker.com / software / gmail / geek-to-live—back-up-gmail-with-fetch mail-235207.php.

18. Parts of this section are taken and modified from M. E. Kabay, "Disk Data Remanence, Part 1: The Problem," *Network World Security Strategies* (2007); www.networkworld.com/newsletters/sec/2007/0730sec2.html.

19. S. L. Garfinkel and A. Shelat, "Remembrance of Data Passed: A Study of Disk Sanitization Practices," *IEEE Security & Privacy* (January/February 2003); www.computer.org/portal/cms_docs_security/security/v1n1/garfinkel.pdf.

20. Same as endnote 19 (Abbreviated).

21. Clearing information is a level of media sanitization that would protect the confidentiality of information against a robust keyboard attack. Simple deletion of items would not suffice for clearing. Clearing must not allow information to be retrieved by data, disk, or file recovery utilities. It must be resistant to keystroke recovery attempts executed from standard input devices and from data scavenging tools. For example, overwriting is an acceptable method for clearing media. Most media can be cleared with one overwrite. (NIST SP800-88 Rev. 1)

22. Purging information is a media sanitization process that protects the confidentiality of information against a laboratory attack. A laboratory attack would involve a threat with the resources and knowledge to use nonstandard systems to conduct data recovery attempts on media outside their normal operating environment. This type of attack involves using signal processing equipment and specially trained personnel. (NIST SP800-88 Rev. 1)

23. www.cmrr.ucsd.edu/about.

24. Destruction of media is the ultimate form of sanitization. After media are destroyed, they cannot be reused as originally intended.

CHAPTER **58**

BUSINESS CONTINUITY PLANNING

Michael Miora

58.1 INTRODUCTION. We are in an age where businesses and governments are turning in increasing numbers to high-technology systems, and to the Internet, to gain and maintain their competitive advantage. Businesses of all types are relying on high-technology products to build, promote, sell, and deliver their wares and services—as are government, educational, and nonprofit enterprises. All of these are dependent on technology to maintain their income, image, and profitability. business continuity planning (BCP) is the process of protecting organizations from the deleterious effects on their missions that can result from outages in information systems.

The goal of BCP is to protect the operations of the enterprise, not just the computing systems. Prudent planning is not restricted to computer or telecommunications systems but is enterprise-wide. There lies the key difference between the traditional hot sites and service providers and the newer, self-contained and supported backup and recovery capabilities. Without the people, procedures, and connectivity to keep the enterprise going, there is little point in restoring systems.

The enterprise has evolved to this dependency through the continual redefining of the word "fast" and the growing expectation of having access to information anywhere and at any time. In the 1960s and 1970s, fast turnaround meant a week or, with luck, a few days. In the 1980s, fast was redefined to mean *today*—the 1980s brought lower-cost computing and the beginning of high-speed communications. For the 1990s, fast meant *now*. The 1990s brought the Internet, intranets and extranets, with distributed systems, sophisticated client/server architectures, and high-speed communications.

Today, information is predominantly collected and sent electronically, often without human intervention. Analyses have been automated and streamlined, strengthened by user-friendly tools and by expert systems. Data are requested, sent, and analyzed in minutes; reports are generated automatically; and presentations can be created, edited, and delivered in near–real time. Moreover, access to information is provided almost equally fast to internal corporate personnel, to business partners and allies, and to customers and consumers.

It should be self-evident to business owners and other stakeholders that planning is an important function and that no enterprise, large or small, should be without a plan. However, as shown in Exhibit 58.1, this is not the case. Regardless of the size of the enterprise, full readiness to handle disruptions is not universally achieved. For larger enterprises, only one-third of companies claim to be fully prepared. For smaller companies, the number is larger, but the validity of some of these responses may be questioned, given that this result is based on self-assessments reported to a survey organization.

At least one partial explanation for this lack of preparedness goes to the heart of how BCP is understood in the business community. It is not clearly understood that the goal of BCP is to protect the business, not simply its equipment or information; at least one goal of this chapter is to show that the focus of the planning should be on business issues.

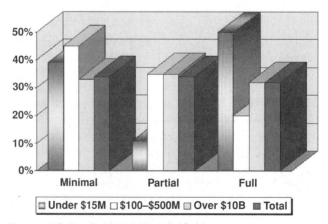

Exhibit 58.1   Corporate Preparedness
Source: BC Management, "2003 Benchmark Study Results."

58.1.1 Enterprise Risks and Costs. The overall risk is to the continued survival of the enterprise. A company weakened by a disaster, and without adequate preparation, may be unable to recover before failure or a hostile takeover occurs. In the 1970s, formal business continuity plans did not exist; only data backup and recovery procedures, with some disaster recovery planning for large systems, was considered. Today, companies without active and tested enterprise contingency plans are likely to fail in the event of a disaster. Such failures may have dire consequences for the board and corporate officers, whose lack of due diligence is demonstrated by the absence of planning. The need for planning may be well recognized, but protected companies are still in the minority.

There is abundant evidence that unprotected companies suffer greatly during major outages. In investment trading, time is crucial, yet many investment firms did not have a plan in place until late 1993, when a major hot-site provider first built a contingency trading facility in New York. Companies protected by disaster recovery plans can control their losses, holding them down to reasonable levels. Experts in the field believe that companies without such plans are likely to suffer significantly greater losses, with consequences so critical that almost 50 percent of firms that do not recover within 10 days never will recover.

R. A. Elbra, the author of "Contingency Planning," a technical report published in 1989 for the National Computing Center (London), demonstrated that if a critical system was inoperable without suitable backup for as few as six days, the cumulative loss could amount to 200 percent of the net daily income produced by that system. After 12 days, the cumulative loss could be 800 percent of the net daily income, as shown in Exhibit 58.2. In the years since that report was published, the reliance by large and small enterprises on their systems has grown significantly. As greater portions of corporate revenues are closely tied to systems and connectivity, these numbers take on even greater significance.

Even today, few industries have strict disaster recovery or business continuity planning regulations. The banking industry is subject to such regulations for portions of its systems only. Even Sarbanes-Oxley has minimal requirements, although there are other U.S. federal and state laws that lay requirements on financial services organizations. The Health Insurance Portability and Accountability Act (HIPAA) contains security and privacy elements that make Business Continuity Plans even more important than before, although full BCP is not a specific requirement.

EXHIBIT 58.2 Fiscal Losses Caused by Disasters

There are many examples of serious downtime, including one instance of a construction crew repairing a nearby roadway and mistakenly damaging the power lines feeding a nearby set of buildings. Repairs required parts that delayed completion of repairs for almost 48 hours. One of the affected companies was an electrical supply company with revenues of approximately $50 million annually. The company felt safe because it had a plan that included reciprocal agreements to share spare computer time with other companies using similar equipment. Unfortunately, the company was unable to secure as much time as it expected because some of the other companies had changed equipment since the agreements were made, some were too busy with their own processing, and some simply did not abide by their agreements. To the chagrin of management, the replacement capability was limited to 30 percent of normal processing. Management reported that this outage cost the company over $250,000 in lost and unrecoverable sales. Although managers were unsure of their market share losses, they did know that two major customers subsequently split their orders between the affected company and another supplier. Although this is not a headline-grabbing disaster, it did significantly affect this financially healthy company.

A less healthy company might have been bankrupted by such a loss. Even surviving businesses experience significantly lower profits for the two-year period following a disaster. Reconstruction costs usually exceed insurance allowances and typically involve uninsured costs for modernization. Insurance premiums usually rise, and advertising budgets increase, to repair the corporate image. The largest problems, however, are due to productivity declines and inefficient operations caused by production restarts, debugging efforts, and the need to retrain newly hired staff to replace employees who departed in fear of corporate collapse or layoffs.

Cantor Fitzgerald, a bond company with a major office in the World Trade Center, lost 733 workers in the North Tower on September 11, 2001. The company's disaster recovery plans and mirroring sites enabled it to be back in action and taking orders just 47 hours after that loss. This was especially noteworthy because of the range of the disaster and the fact that the tragic loss of life included approximately 150 information technology workers.

Management's voice is needed to address another key issue. During natural disasters, employees at all levels of the corporate structure will make family and home their top priority. The successful recovery plan considers the need for employees with recovery responsibilities to ascertain first the condition of their own homes and families. Corporate management can make it clear to all employees that people come first. Recovery plans must provide participants with the time and the means to reach their loved ones. Once people are satisfied that families and homes are safe, then they can turn their full attention to corporate recovery.

58.1.2 Types of Disasters.   Many different threats can lead to disasters. Exhibit 58.3 lists a small sampling of these potential threats. It is neither feasible nor desirable to design a strategy for each of these disasters. It is more important to consider the effects of each applicable potential threat. For example, a bomb threat may deny access to the building or to the local area for a time. A small fire may deny access to an entire building for a day and to a small portion of the building for a few months. All threats can then be grouped by their levels of impact. Exhibit 58.4 lists one hierarchical structure that maps the levels of impact to a predefined duration of outages.

Identifying disaster threats and grouping them into disaster types fulfills a planning need. Each disaster type is associated with an outage duration, which is the length of

♦ Accidents	♦ Equipment Problems
♦ Airports	♦ Fire
♦ Arson	♦ Flood
♦ Blackout	♦ Forced Evacuation
♦ Bomb Threat	♦ Hurricane
♦ Building/Facility Inaccessibility	♦ Ice Storms
♦ Chemical Spills	♦ Key Resource Loss
♦ Civil Disorders	♦ Labor Disputes
♦ Civil Disturbances	♦ Malicious Damage
♦ Computer Compromise	♦ Municipal Services Stoppages
♦ Computer Virus	♦ Postal Service Disruption
♦ Construction Damage	♦ Power Loss or Fluctuation
♦ Construction Obstruction	♦ Riot
♦ Data Diddling	♦ Security Breach
♦ Data Loss	♦ Strike
♦ Disgruntled Employee	♦ Terrorism
♦ Drug Abuse	♦ Tornado
♦ Earthquake	♦ Toxic Spills
♦ Elevator Failure	♦ Vandalism
♦ Embezzlement	♦ Volcano
♦ Environmental Control Failure	♦ Water

EXHIBIT 58.3 Disaster Threats

Area Affected	Duration of Outage
Partial Building	Less than 1 Day
	1–3 Days
	4–7 Days
	Week to Month
	More than Month
Full Building	Less than 1 Day
	1–3 Days
	4–7 Days
	Week to Month
	More than Month
Multi-Building (Campus Facility)	Less than 1 Day
	1–3 Days
	4–7 Days
	Week to Month
	More than Month
Local Area (Immediate)	Less than 1 Day
	1–3 Days
	4–7 Days
	Week to Month
	More than Month
Region	Less than 1 Day
	1–3 Days
	4–7 Days
	Week to Month
	More than Month

EXHIBIT 58.4 Levels of Impact and Durations

downtime expected, and with a set of predefined outage durations, such as indicated in Exhibit 58.4. Therefore, each disaster type can be mapped to specific corporate functions that will be affected.

For example, a bomb threat may affect an entire building, but only for a fraction of a day. If this is so, then protecting against a bomb threat requires protecting only those corporate functions performed in that building whose survival time is one day or less. A toxic spill caused by a nearby train derailment may disrupt an entire facility, or campus of buildings, for several days. Protecting against a toxic spill requires protecting all functions whose survival time is less than several days. A regional disaster such as an earthquake, flood, or hurricane, however, disrupts operations for a longer period, and may prevent quick recovery anywhere within the affected area.

Business continuity plans need to be developed in a modular fashion so that modules can be activated depending on the disaster type. Assessing the expected duration of a disaster provides a means of determining which functions should be scheduled for recovery initiation; assessing the level of impact provides a mechanism for determining what type of recovery should be performed on each function. These are the two major factors that need to be identified promptly after a disaster: estimated duration and expected level of impact.

On September 11th 2001, there were many companies whose complete operations were destroyed; In one case, all of the staff perished. Yet, the companies that had made business continuity and disaster recovery in advance did recover, some with no discernable long-lasting impact to the client base or long-term profitability. The companies that survived and flourished and preplanned, pre-staged and up-to-date hot sites, either through an external provider of internally.

The key point is that planning for specific threats is not necessary. Planning for types of outages is more efficient and more effective. It may not matter whether the building is damaged by fire or water, or terrorist attack but the extent of damage and the duration of the outage are important, for those factors determine the types of recoveries to make. Traditionally, enterprise risks were calculated on a per-threat basis. Each threat was analyzed to determine the percentage probability of that threat occurring within a period. Those probabilities were then summed over all possible threats. The resulting figure was a representation of probability of some disaster having a significant impact on business operations over a period such as a year. The disadvantage of this method is that it misleads management into believing that the probabilities are so small as to be insignificant. A different and more streamlined analysis is more useful for the disaster recovery process. It is called the Generalized Cost Consequence model (GCC) and is described in Section 58.5.2.

58.1.3 Recovery Scenarios.   Recovery scenarios are the planned steps to be followed when disaster strikes. These scenarios are designed based on the various threat levels of impact and durations. All recovery scenarios are built in three phases, or sequences, of activities as shown in Exhibit 58.5.

The beginning sequence evaluates an emergency to determine the effect of the event on the enterprise. This can be an unhurried, deliberate activity when there is sufficient notice of an approaching problem. An example of this is a hurricane, where weather reports contain warnings days in advance, and additional information can be evaluated as it becomes available. In contrast, the pace is highly fast and frenetic during an evacuation due to fire, flood, or earthquake. Achieving a safe position is always the first consideration; following that are the other steps: determining the disaster type and declaring a disaster; activating the disaster recovery teams; making legal, regulatory,

Beginning Sequence	Middle Sequence	End Sequence
Evaluate Emergency Determine Disaster Type Declare Disaster Initiate Recovery Procedures Activate Teams Make Notifications	Restore Critical Functions Business Function Recovery Command Center Control Based on Disaster Type Activate Hot Sites Ongoing Damage Assessment Monitoring and Control	Restore Normal Operations Full Damage Assessment Salvage Operations Reconstruction/Restoration One or Two Relocations Data Reconciliation Data Synchronization

EXHIBIT 58.5   Phases of Recovery

and other notifications; and establishing command and control centers. This beginning sequence often involves top corporate management.

The middle sequence includes most of the major recovery activities. Whereas the beginning sequence determines the type of disaster in progress, this sequence provides procedures to the various functional groups based on the type of disaster in progress. One key element of the middle sequence is to perform ongoing damage assessments and maintain contact with salvage operations. Knowledgeable information technology personnel should be available to review salvage possibilities and rebuilding plans for information equipment.

The end sequence restores normal operating conditions. This phase of recovery is the least predictable of all, and is linked to disaster type and to specific threats. Therefore, this phase is planned in more general terms than the two preceding sequences. In the end sequence, detailed damage assessment is performed. Salvage operations for vital records, information equipment, data, and general facility equipment take place. Reconstruction or relocation activities are specified and executed. Finally, normal operations are restored. Often the end sequence includes two facility relocations. The first relocation moves operations from the emergency operations centers, including the command center, hot sites, work area recovery centers, and other off-site workplaces, to a longer-term interim operating area. This longer-term operating area may be a cold site or other temporary work area. The second relocation is from the interim facility back to the reconstructed, or to a newly constructed, permanent home.

Completion of the recovery plan occurs when normal operations are restored. Ending the formalized recovery procedures before then may introduce errors and may compromise integrity in the final move to the permanent facility. In this final move, large processing equipment is torn down and moved, just as it was during the initial disaster declaration, only in a more deliberate manner. Temporary operations may require use of the reserve systems as backup in case the move encounters problems. Often much of the equipment at the interim site is required at the permanent site.. Finally, data reconciliation, the merging of data from different operating environments, and data synchronization require planning and careful implementation to prevent the destruction and replacement of good data with erroneous information.

The traditional disaster recovery strategies include hot sites for data centers and emergency services for employees. These sites have been effective and continue to be necessary, but not sufficient. New strategies are needed to consider the new ways of doing business: mobile computing, real-time sales and service support, client/server architectures, extensive telecommunications, real-time process controls, and online customer service support. Preplanned recovery capabilities can resurrect functions that depend on huge databases and large systems in hours rather than days. Connectivity can be restored in minutes, and the client base need never know that a disaster has occurred. Business can continue, no matter what has happened, so long as proper recovery precautions have been taken.

58.2   DEFINING THE GOALS.   Defining the specific goals of a business continuity plan is a multistep process that correlates what is important to the enterprise with what the enterprise does, and is tempered by what is possible. A general goal for a plan may be stated in this way: Protect critical business functions so they will continue meeting minimum corporate objectives cost effectively during times of crises and disasters. This general statement describes (BCP) goals for many companies. Before building a plan, however, specific goals must be conjectured by the planner, evaluated by the planning team or steering committee, and validated by corporate management.

This section describes the specific elements and steps of defining the goal of the recovery and continuity plan, and identifying the specific objectives required to meet that goal. Succeeding sections describe how to determine the criticality and time sensitivity of various corporate business functions, how to gain and keep commitments from management, and how to define what protections are needed for each business function.

A business continuity plan may have many specific goals. For example, a central order entry and production scheduling system may reside at corporate headquarters or at the corporate sales office, while manufacturing may be dispersed geographically and by product across many facilities. One possible objective of the plan for such an enterprise is to maintain production levels at some fraction of normal levels even if the corporate center is damaged or destroyed.

A California manufacturer of custom filters devised exactly such an objective. For the vast majority of the firm's products, normal operating procedures were for a five-day cycle from order to shipment. Order entry was performed at corporate headquarters. Full material requirements planning (MRP) of all North American manufacturing sites, including purchasing, control, scheduling, and shipping, was performed on the same system. Corporate management determined that the company could not survive for more than a short time unless overall plant production capacity was maintained at 50 percent of normal levels. Production of less than 50 percent would make it infeasible for the company to survive more than two weeks. Production of more than 50 percent but less than 100 percent of normal levels would severely reduce or eliminate profits but would not cause corporate failure. The clear goal of this plan was to protect the functions required to meet the objective of achieving a minimum of 50 percent of normal levels.

The firm performed an analysis of products and revenues. It considered the quantity and cost of the various filters made, the resulting manufacturing load, and the customer base. Although the overall requirement was to maintain a manufacturing load of at least 50 percent of normal, the firm also wanted to make certain that major customers were served and that large contract commitments were met. All of these requirements were incorporated into the final BCP. In another case, a major electronics manufacturer provided free, seven-day, 24-hour customer service and technical support to all customers. Two facilities in the United States provided support to customers worldwide. This support was a major competitive advantage and was believed to be a major contributing factor to the reputation and exceptional customer loyalty enjoyed by the manufacturer. During normal operations, the call center guidelines were:

- All incoming calls must be answered by the third ring.
- Average waiting times must be less than two minutes.

- Maximum waiting times would not exceed six minutes without operator intervention. Moreover, busy signals should not exceed one caller in 500. Communications systems linked technical support personnel with technical databases.

These were strict criteria for the company's service-level objectives, and traffic engineering studies carefully monitored busy signals and queuing delays to prevent violations of call center guidelines. Trunk lines were added or removed, and staff members were rescheduled to maintain this level of support, which far exceeded industry standards. The major goal for the call center business continuity plan was to maintain service-level objectives at a predefined minimum degradation level. The allowable queuing delay was increased significantly, and the busy signal allowance was increased slightly. A special message would play apologizing for any inconvenience, but all customers still would be served. The planning project identified what capabilities were needed to meet these requirements. The goal of this plan was to provide the backup capabilities needed to meet the reduced service-level objectives using a combination of the preexisting surviving call center and some emergency capability for the damaged or destroyed call center.

Corporate goals are independent of means and systems; they are stated in business terms. Top management must make decisions about what needs to be protected and how protected it needs to be. Often, though, this is an iterative process in which management designs some preliminary decisions and instructs analysts to confirm or refine those thoughts. The disaster recovery planning process includes steps to do just that during the business impact analysis (BIA) phase.

The goals of the plan are associated with the products and services that the enterprise or operating unit provides. In cases where the facility to be protected is a support facility, such as the corporate headquarters of a manufacturing conglomerate, the services provided are in support of the overall corporate operations, perhaps including banking and other support activities. In these cases, although the services are somewhat removed from actual production, they are still imperative to continuing production. Building the plan requires goals that are more specific in nature than those in the examples above. In this methodology, these lower-level goals are referred to as the plan objectives.

The BCP objectives are closely coupled with specific business functions and are not adequately defined until the conclusion of the business impact analysis. In order to begin this definition process, however, first the recovery problem must be constrained by defining the scope of the disaster recovery plan.

58.2.1   Scope.   The scope of the plan is the definition of the environment to be protected. Before performing detailed analyses and interviewing management, decisions must be made regarding who and what is to be included in the plan. Specifying the systems, equipment, procedures, locations, and support capabilities that require protection identifies the scope. The corporate environment consists of people, information, facilities, and equipment. The plan focuses on a subset of the people, some of the information, selected facilities, and specific equipment. That constitutes the scope of the BCP. Stated more simply, no matter what the size or complexity of the enterprise, planning is performed on one part of the enterprise at a time.

The scope must be established in order to define the goals of the plan. However, during the planning process, the scope will be refined and redefined as the analysis progresses. Which facility is involved? Is part of a building being protected, such as the data center or the shop floor? Is it the entire facility, including a campus of buildings that fall into the scope of the plan? To perform a BIA, users must focus on the business elements that reside or utilize the people, information, facilities, and equipment that are in scope. However, sometimes it becomes clear during the analysis that the scope must be broadened or can be restrained to protect business functions adequately.

In a world of tight budgets, compressed schedules, and phased implementations, BCP usually is performed in stages. Perhaps the computer and telecommunications systems are protected first, followed later by other office support equipment such as copiers and hard copy files. No matter which elements are chosen for implementation, the scope must be clearly documented. For computer systems, the current systems in use must be identified. Hardware and software must be described in detail. Special equipment must be identified.

In the planning process, it sometimes becomes clear that important items have been excluded from the plan. Where those newly uncovered requirements prove to be critical, they must be included, but for all others, a well-defined scope will prevent creeping requirements that increase cost and lengthen implementation schedules. Requirements identified as desirable but not absolutely necessary can be recorded in an ongoing project log and scheduled for implementation in a later phase. It is better to put into place a plan that leaves out some capabilities while meeting basic objectives than to allow the planning scope to expand, thereby risking long delays or project abandonment. A clearly defined scope enables the planning team to communicate to management precisely what is and what is not protected or included in the planning process.

Major scope issues and disagreements sometimes can be resolved in this early phase of the planning project. If not, resolution of these issues is best delayed until the conclusion of the BIA, since that process reveals hidden functional interdependencies. For example, research and development (R&D) functions usually are longer-term projects that can be delayed without major impact on the enterprise. In many plans, R&D functions are relegated to low priority. Consider, however, the case of a customer service technical representative discussing the status of a custom-manufactured product with a key customer who is unhappy with the delivered prototype. If R&D technical personnel are required to resolve such issues, and resolution has an impact on production schedules, then R&D may be elevated to a higher priority. The BIA process usually reveals and prioritizes such hidden interdependencies.

58.2.2 Correlating Objectives to Corporate Missions and Functions.
It usually falls on the information systems and technology department to build the BCP. Naturally, then, most plans focus first on computers and telecommunications. While there is nothing intrinsically wrong with starting that way, it must be just the first step of the analysis. The danger is the potential for myopic views of corporate functions; corporate computer and telecommunications systems may be required for the successful execution of critical business functions, but usually they are only part of many needed capabilities. Desktop paper files, telephones, personal phone directories, and copying machines may be just as important as access to the corporate database or to some tailored vertical application. The list of functions and equipment to be investigated must be complete or the resulting plan will be inadequate.

The BIA provides a formal methodology for ranking business functions by criticality and time sensitivity. The process includes interviews with key personnel from each business function included in the scope of the planning project. There are two dangers inherent to an information technology–based approach to disaster recovery planning.

1. Business functions that do not use information systems may be inadvertently overlooked.
2. Noncomputer support structures and systems may not be recognized and, therefore, not brought into the protection definition process.

When the information systems department leads the disaster recovery project, it will naturally base the plan on a systems-based knowledge of the enterprise. The accounting department, a traditional heavy user of computer systems, will naturally be included among the functions that potentially need protection. Similarly, all other functions that use computers in their normal activities will likely be included in any list of functions requiring analysis. All organizational elements that use computer systems will be recognized and included precisely because they use computers and therefore are known to the systems department. However, there are many important functions that may not regularly use computers or may use them in ways that are only minimally visible to the systems people.

Mailroom operations are frequently omitted because often they are not computer users. Planning personnel are clearly well aware that mail operations exist; they just might forget to include them in the planning process even though mail operations are important to every organization. Planning mailroom recovery and continuation is simple before a disaster but very difficult after the fact.

Facilities management, maintenance, and plant engineering organizations are seldom intensive computer users in their daily activities. Nevertheless, in normal circumstances, operations in a large facility would deteriorate quickly without these functions. During a disaster, these are the people who can rapidly determine the nature and breadth of facility damage. They are the people who need to be instantly available to evaluate damage, hasten repairs, and estimate duration of outages. They are also the individuals who are often left off the disaster recovery team lists and phone rosters. Similarly, security forces are needed when building damage leaves valuable equipment and other assets vulnerable to theft or vandalism. They may be needed to protect employees who are working during civil disturbances or other such incidents. Corporate communications and public relations departments are also frequent computer systems users, but they are not very visible to the systems department as unique functions, although their contributions to a successful recovery are often essential.

The safest way to compile a list of business functions is to work from three documents: an organization chart, a corporate phone directory, and a list of corporate operations budget line items (see Exhibit 58.6). Using these three lists, the planner can develop a comprehensive list of business functions and can identify the manager or supervisor of each function. That comprehensive list should include every function performed, regardless of the perceived importance of that function. Criticality and time sensitivity will be determined during the BIA; leaving off any functions can lead to inaccurate BIA results.

Working from that comprehensive list, a second list should be compiled that includes or excludes each business function based on the defined scope of the BIA. When doubt exists, the function should be included. The BIA will be the final filter for out-of-scope functions. Therefore, for each function in the list, the planner must determine which of the included elements are relevant to the function under evaluation. Although this

EXHIBIT 58.6   Building and Filtering the List of Functions

may seem to be a complicated process, it is usually straightforward. The golden rule is: When in doubt, include the function. It can always be excluded later if analysis shows that the function is really out of scope.

58.2.3 Validating Goals.   A full disaster recovery plan must consider the contribution of each element of the organization to the overall corporate goals. Clearly, no single area is dispensable, for if it were, it would have been discarded already. Properly defined goals are independent of specific functions as they are stated in global terms. Validating the goals requires examining each function to determine how it contributes to the corporate objectives. It is necessary to distinguish between the importance of a function toward meeting specific disaster recovery goals and the overall importance of a function to an enterprise.

Even functions that are not relevant to any specific disaster recovery goals may be crucial to the overall operation of the enterprise. The BCP focuses on protecting selected corporate functions for a specified period of time, but it is a mistake to assume that a function whose importance to recovery goals is low is not important to the enterprise in the longer run. For example, during a crisis, the corporate tax accounting function often can cease operations with little impact to the enterprise. If this is true, then the continuation requirements for that department are minimal, and the recovery timeline can be extended. Clearly this does not mean that the corporate tax accounting function is unimportant. Other examples of longer-term requirements include fulfilling regulatory and legal requirements.

The goals of the BCP are associated with the products and services of the enterprise and are expressed in business terms. Validating those goals requires presenting management with options for levels of protection and their associated costs. Gross estimates are possible at the outset; refined presentations require a complete BIA. The goals should be clearly defined and presented to management. Although these goals are not addressed specifically by each procedure in the ultimate BCP, they drive the entire recovery strategy development. A clear and concise description of the goals must be presented to management and approved by them. After this approval, the disaster recovery planners can attempt to attain those goals. During the strategy development, other alternatives may appear and may be added for ultimate management consideration, but the initial goals become the operational baseline against which strategies and costs can be measured.

58.2.4 Mapping Goals to Recovery Phases. There are three phases to the recovery process:

1. Continuation activities
2. Resumption activities
3. Restoration activities

The continuation activities are those specific tasks and procedures that enable a very limited set of functions to continue operating with little or no interruption. The resumption activities provide for resuming a full, or almost full, range of business functions, even if that resumption means using backup methods and temporary operating procedures. The restoration activities are those that bring back a normal operating environment in a permanent facility.

The continuation and resumption activities occur during the middle sequence of activities and are the activities that must meet the short-term recovery goals that are within the domain of the recovery plan. The restoration activities occur during the end sequence and may include some long-term goals. The long-term goals may include decisions about rebuilding versus relocating and other major decisions that are beyond the province of BCP construction.

Each goal should be assigned to one of these three sets of activities. This assignment is based primarily on timeline considerations: what must be continued quickly versus what can wait a short while, and what can be delayed for the longer term. In the call center example, the number of rings, the allowable queuing delays, and the busy signal allowance were measurements of service levels. They constituted the goals for the recovery plan. After an interruption, the levels of service can be restored to normalcy gradually, as a function of time since the disaster. Stated differently, with each passing day, the level of service should improve. Therefore, the goal of the continuation activities may be for service within some stated parameters, and the goal of the resumption activities would be for improved levels of service. Normal levels may await the restoration activities.

Clearly, the same level of service can be attained at lower cost if the timing requirements are loosened. That is the reason it is important to assign each goal to a particular set of activities. Exhibit 58.7 illustrates a potential mapping of service levels to activity sets. In the first hours following a disaster, the continuation activities maintain a minimum required level of functionality, with some increases over time. The resumption activities dramatically increase functionality immediately and then bring functionality, over time, to an almost normal condition. The restoration function, shown as two bars to represent temporary and permanent facilities, achieves full levels of service.

EXHIBIT 58.7   Service Levels Mapped to Recovery Activities

58.2.5   Emergency Issues.   A good plan includes provisions for ensuring the *safety* of all employees potentially affected by a disaster. This is especially true for employees working on site when a disaster occurs. Life safety issues include health and safety preparedness, shelter and care of employees caught in the enterprise facilities during a disaster, and search and rescue teams for employees in imminent danger. Some of these protections are required by various local, state, and federal regulatory agencies. Others are not mandated but are nonetheless important to the survival of the employees and the business.

Public relations is an important issue during any disaster. More than one enterprise has realized too late that neglecting the media can induce a second, even greater disaster than the original one to which the media was responding. Even a small fire can make major news in the local community. The public relations aspect includes recovery actions. For example, one chemical company suffered a minor fire but refused to inform the media on the status of cleanup operations. The result was predictable: The media reported that a fire had potentially released toxic chemicals into the local environment and that the company had refused to comment. That report did more to damage the reputation of this chemical company than did the fire that caused the spill, which was not in fact toxic, and was brought under control within hours of the fire.

58.3   PERFORMING A BUSINESS IMPACT ANALYSIS.   The business impact analysis comprises the heart of the planning process. It is here that the recovery planner determines what is important for inclusion into the BCP and what is not relevant to that effort. The BIA determines how far to go in protecting the people, information, and equipment that constitute the organization and its functions so that all survive to flourish another day.

The BIA assesses how unavailability of each system would affect the enterprise. The BIA is a multistep process that may be performed over a period of weeks or months, depending on the availability of various corporate personnel. Often the BIA may be a first effort to determine the total cost and the schedule required for a full plan. In all cases, the BIA should precede any other planning activities since it will help determine the direction and strategies for prevention, mitigation, and recovery.

58.3.1   Establishing the Scope of the Business Impact Analysis.   To succeed, a project must be well defined in terms of work effort and work product. Just as the BIA helps bound the recovery problem in precise recovery terms so that the project may be successful, the BIA subproject also must be understood in terms of the work required and the product of the analysis. This requires establishing the scope of the BIA by deciding what equipment the BIA will investigate and what people to interview.

The BIA begins with an inventory process to catalog the various equipment and capabilities to be protected. As systems evolve to meet ever-increasing customer demands, equipment and management responsibilities change along with them. For example, a mainframe shop with large local area networks (LANs) and wide area networks (WANs) may be managed by the information technology department, whereas smaller LANs may be managed by individual departments such as accounting or engineering.

Without a comprehensive and constantly updated list of systems across departments and functional areas, systems can evolve quickly with little or no overall corporate knowledge. For the recovery planner, this means the plan will be incorrect at its outset, or will grow obsolete quickly.

The inventory should describe in detail the general hardware and software used in each included system, paying particular attention to special-purpose equipment, such as imaging equipment, custom equipment, and uncommon equipment.

The inventory must include communications links and equipment. A connectivity map showing LAN and WAN equipment and connections is useful; a cabling diagram with gateways, routers, bridges, firewalls, proxy servers, and other communication equipment is also important. General telephony diagrams and summaries of lines and capacities are required to bring voice communications systems into the recovery process.

The inventory provides an opportunity to decide what level of office equipment and supplies (e.g., paper, writing implements, staplers, note pads) should be protected by the recovery plan. Although staplers seldom will be critical, certain printed business forms might well require off-site storage for quick recovery. Boxes of corporate checks, for example, should be stored securely off site.

Security access controls and special alarm systems should be included in the inventory, along with current procedures for maintaining them. There have been instances of a recovery hampered by inaccessibility to the building caused by active alarm and access control systems. Inclusion of such systems into the inventory helps ensure that they will help rather than hinder the recovery process.

58.3.2   Interview Process.   The best source of information about the work performed by the enterprise is the enterprise's own labor force. Corporate executives understand and control corporate goals; managers understand and control operations. Front-line supervisors and workers perform the daily tasks that bring revenue to the enterprise, and these are the people who have the knowledge needed for the BIA. The recovery planner must collect that information, understand it, and translate it into terms meaningful for disaster recovery planning. Exhibit 58.8 shows the three steps of interviewing.

The first step is to compile a list of all the departments that fall within the scope of the BIA. The term "department" is used here to describe an organizational entity that may not correspond with a specific organization chart position or with the use of the term within the enterprise. The term is meant to convey a functionally complete unit

Summarize All
Departments

List All Functions in
the Department

List All Functions
by Rank

EXHIBIT 58.8   Three Steps of Interviewing

performing a task or a series of related tasks. It might well be that people from different organization chart departments work more closely with one another than they do with people in their own departments.

For example, the accounting department of an organization may handle all corporate accounting functions, including accounts receivable (A/R), accounts payable (A/P), general ledger (G/L), and payroll. However, for the purpose of the planning project, the planner may choose to group accounting into two departments: accounting and payroll. In this way, payroll can be separated from its organizational component and combined with other portions of the enterprise that provide the payroll data, and with which the payroll department interacts daily.

Once the list of departments is complete, the next step is to choose an individual in each department to be the primary interview candidate. Because the primary interviewee from each department will perform two functions—(1) identify all of the high-level functions performed within that department and (2) describe in detail many of those functions—that person should be an experienced and knowledgeable member of that department. It is neither necessary nor desirable to assign this interview position to a senior manager. Management interviews should be scheduled for a later phase that requires management insight. The first interviews should focus on daily task structures and purposes.

The recovery planner guides the interview. The first step of the interview is to describe the department in terms of its overall function and to list all the high-level functions performed. For example, in the accounting department, the high-level functions usually include accounts payable, accounts receivable, general ledger, and payroll. It may include corporate tax preparation, or that may be a completely separate function. It may include financial reporting for the Securities and Exchange Commission (SEC) and other filings, or a different department may perform those functions.

A corporate human resources department may include employee records, benefits management, payroll distribution, time sheet processing, and other common functions. For the planning project, the payroll distribution and time sheet processing functions may be more closely allied with the accounting department than with the human resources department.

During the interview process, the department expert will likely want to describe functions at a detailed level. For example, in the financial reporting area, the expert may want to list each and every report produced. While it may be useful for the planner to learn about the production of these reports, the BIA should categorize all related reporting functions into one function. Therefore, there is no function called 10K Reports, but there may be an overall SEC Reporting function. It is not possible to list all functions or potential functions here, but Exhibit 58.9 lists some examples. Each department should include several to a dozen functions. If a department contains only one function, it may be combined with another department, or it may be divided into lower-levels functions. If a department includes too many functions, then either the functions should be combined into a higher level, or that department can be divided into two departments.

The primary purpose of these interviews is to provide the information necessary to perform a matrix analysis that ranks all enterprise functions for recovery capabilities and timelines. An important secondary purpose is to raise corporate awareness of the recovery planning goals and preparations. During this interview process, the planner

Common Functions
◆   Accounts Payble
◆   Accounts Receivable
◆   Cash Accounting
◆   Customer Service
◆   Financial Analysis
◆   Financial Consolidation
◆   Financial Reporting
◆   General Ledger
◆   Inventory
◆   Invoicing
◆   Marketing Support
◆   Order Entry
◆   Parts Inventory
◆   Payroll
◆   POS, ATM and Related
◆   Process Control
◆   Purchase Order Generation
◆   SEC Reporting
◆   Tax
◆   Vital Records
◆   Work-In-Progress

EXHIBIT 58.9   Examples of High-Level Functions

can explain that the overall purpose of the planning project is to protect employees and the business functions they perform. This is the opportunity to promulgate disaster preparedness as a normal and necessary part of the corporate business posture.

58.3.3 Describing the Functions.   Once the functions have been listed, the interviewer must collect summary information about each function. This functional summary will be included in the BIA document so that it will be clear to the reader precisely what the function entails. The description of no more than one or two paragraphs prevents misunderstandings and helps focus discussions during the interview. Along with the summary description, the interviewer can further describe the function by identifying the key and alternate individuals responsible for performing that function. These are not the managers of the functional areas; these are the people who do the work on a daily basis, enter the data, and perform the function. Each function should be associated with those individuals and with the functional area manager, and the information should be recorded in a matrix format.

This matrix format provides a single place to record all the nonnarrative information about the function. The matrix, which also will include quantitative data, will be combined with the narrative descriptions and some analysis to become the BIA document. The descriptions of each function identify the function clearly, assess the survivability factors of the function, and associate the function with the various existing corporate capabilities. The sections that follow describe the information to be collected about each function and suggest ways to encourage objectivity, even when collecting subjective quantification information. Exhibit 58.10 shows a blank, sample matrix.

58.3.4 Definition of Departments and Functions.   The first column is entitled *Department,* such as Financial Reporting, Central Distribution Center, A/P, Merchandising, Planning, Distribution, and Purchasing. Although these are not necessarily equal in number or scope, they are units that need to be analyzed as groups. When unsure of organizational entities, the planner can use the organization chart as a starting point. The department title can always be modified and the functions expanded as the need arises during the development of the BIA.

The second column is the *Functions* list. The functions are the high-level groups of activities performed within the department. Each function is a group of activities related to a single purpose. In the accounting department, for example, there is an accounts payable function, which may include activities such as receiving invoices, requesting payment approval, scheduling payment, and printing checks. Although these

Department	Functions	Key Person	Key Alternate	Survival Days	Criticality	Ops Impact	Ranking Factor	No. Users	Category	Department Head	System Elements

EXHIBIT 58.10   Blank, Sample BIA Matrix

detailed tasks are very important, they need not be described individually since they all follow a single thread and timeline. The aim of the BIA is to establish the time and processing needs; therefore, any series of tasks that occur in a closely connected chain can be addressed together. Exhibit 58.11 pictorially depicts the relationship between departments and functions.

Another example of a department is the distribution center of a warehousing operation. This may include functions commonly known as receiving, processing, shipping, quality control, and inventory control. Some of these are aggregates of lower-level tasks. Processing is a function that includes "pulls," "moves," and "put-aways." If shipping, receiving, and processing are performed using the same resources according to a similar timeline, then they can be grouped as one function. Often the BIA calls this the Shipping and Receiving function. If inventory control is an outcome or natural by-product of the Shipping and Receiving function, then it need not be addressed individually. If inventory control includes special functions apart from the Shipping and Receiving function, however, it can be addressed separately.

One example of inventory as a separate function is regulated inventories. For example, alcohol storage requires careful scrutiny according to regulations of the Bureau of Alcohol, Tobacco, and Firearms. Inventories must be documented according to length of storage time, source, destination, and quantities. In this case, inventory control is a special function with its own resource and timeline requirements. Another example of inventory control as a separate function is the isolated customs areas in import and export centers, where inventory must be controlled according to source, arrival time, destination, departure time, and shipper.

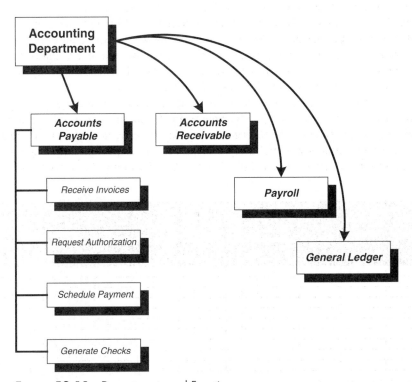

EXHIBIT 58.11   Departments and Functions

If functions are defined too tightly, which means at too low a level of detail, then there will be a great many functions, thereby hiding the true set of functions requiring analysis. This will result in a large set of functions that are so interrelated that they cannot reasonably be separated for individual analysis. If the functions are defined too loosely, which means at too high a level, then there will be too few functions, thereby hiding the timelines and forcing all functions to be rated as time critical. During the interview process, it is likely that the definition of functions will be refined and redefined several times. The functional area experts should guide the definitions, with the recovery specialist helping formulate the ideas.

58.3.4.1 Key Person, Key Alternate, and Department Head.   The third column in exhibit 58.12 identifies the *Key Person* for each function. The key person is typically neither a manager nor a supervisor. Rather, the key person normally performs the task at hand. For example, in the accounting department's time-keeping function, the key person is the individual who collects and enters or validates the time-keeping information. For the treasury department, bank transfer function, this is the individual who calls or connects to the banking system to perform the transfers and manage accounts—in other words, the person who will be responsible for performing the function during a crisis when little supervision, help, or direction is available. The manager may not know the phone numbers to dial, the people to talk to, or the keystrokes required to perform the function, but the key person must know these things, for that person may be working in virtual isolation immediately following a disaster.

The key person becomes an important member of the recovery team when that function is identified as a time critical, or Category I, function. In those cases, the key person receives training, special backup and communications equipment, and extra responsibilities. The key person is the enterprise's first line of defense against disasters.

The *Key Alternate Person*, identified in the fourth column, is the backup to the key person. When possible, the key alternate should be as well equipped and well trained as the key person. In practice, however, this is seldom feasible. The key alternate should be an employee who is as familiar with the tasks to be performed as the key person.

The eleventh column identifies the *Department Head*. This is the one individual who is held accountable for performance of all the functions listed for the department. The department heads for the various departments recorded in the matrix may report at different levels on the organization chart; this is an acceptable situation so long as each department head has direct management control of all functions listed for the department.

58.3.4.2 Survival Time.   The fifth column records the *Survival Days* as reported by the interviewee and discussed with the disaster recovery planner. The survival days are the length of time the enterprise can withstand the lack of a function with minimal impact. This length of time is measured in whatever units are appropriate to the enterprise, which may be minutes, hours, or months. This length of time is the maximum allowable downtime for the function, after which the enterprise begins to suffer serious repercussions. This measure does not determine the importance of the function to the enterprise; it only measures the time sensitivity of the function. Payroll, for example, is most often very time sensitive, affecting operations after only one or two days.

It may be possible to postpone tax accounting functions because there are alternative actions possible. Missing a filing deadline is avoidable by using past data and making reasonable, informal estimates of changes. Overpayments have few or no consequences. Underpayments may result in modest penalties and interest. Typically,

Range	Description
1 to 2	"Nobody would notice." Very minor inconvenience.
3 to 4	Minor inconvenience, virtually no fiscal impact.
5 to 7	Greater inconvenience, monetary impact.
8 to 9	Major problems, significant monetary impact.
10	"Out of business."

Exhibit 58.12   Criticality Ratings and Descriptions

payroll checks are generated close to the distribution date, with little spare time. However, most organizations can develop backup payroll procedures that can compress payroll processing into one or two days so that there is no delay in payroll distribution. Obtaining this information may require exploring past instances when the function had been postponed. The delay may have been due to illness, vacation, system downtime, or management direction. Inquiring about the effect of the delay may help refine the estimate of allowable down time for the BIA.

58.3.4.3   Criticality.   The *Criticality* of a function, recorded in the sixth column, measures the magnitude of the immediate effect on the enterprise of function loss beyond the survival time. If payroll processing has been determined to have a one-day survival time, then criticality is the effect on the enterprise of payroll processing delays beginning on the second day and continuing from there. If tax accounting has been assigned an allowable down time of 30 days, then its criticality is the affect on the enterprise after 30 days.

Criticality is a measure of time-phased impacts. The criticality of a function is loosely based on fiscal impact to the enterprise. It is not identical with fiscal loss because indirect impacts are also important. A corporate image of reliability and strength may be lost forever if functional capabilities are not restored. NASA's *Challenger* disaster had an effect far beyond any fiscal estimate. The space program suffered a setback and a long delay. Some believe that NASA's loss of funding in subsequent years was attributable to this disaster. The value of lives lost in the disaster is, of course, immeasurable.

A major telephone common carrier once lost a major switching station, thereby causing all of its customers to be without long-distance phone capability for a significant time in the middle of a business day. Although the company lost only a relatively modest amount of money due to lost calls, the damage to its reputation lives on. Its loss of business is irreparable: Many of its dedicated customers decided to double-source their long-distance providers and now split their services between this company and its major competitor. This event constituted a permanent, unrecoverable loss of market share.

The Criticality column records an estimate of the impact of loss once the survival period has been exceeded. It is an estimate because it is not the result of a detailed analysis but rather is provided by the interviewee based on heuristic analyses and experience. The interviewee is asked to rank each function on a scale of 1 to 10, where 1 is the least critical, and 10 is the most critical. Exhibit 58.12 summarizes these level criticality ratings and provides brief descriptions. The recovery planner provides this information to the interviewee and solicits a response. These criticality ratings are subjective, so the planner and the expert must work together to attempt to smooth out individual prejudices and opinions as much as possible. However, the ratings are designed to work with the operational impact measure (described in Section 58.3.4.4) to minimize this problem.

On the rating scale, a value of 10 is the highest level of criticality possible. This value should be accepted only if it is clear that virtually all corporate functions will come to a standstill. Frequently, the payroll function for hourly employees fits this criterion. Hourly, unionized employees may be specifically barred from working by union rules if the enterprise cannot provide a paycheck within some number of hours after the checks are due. In the case of a manufacturing company, this could mean that all production, receiving, shipping, and related functions cease. This is tanta-mount to a company shutdown. The phrase "out of business" from the summary table (Exhibit 58.12) fits this scenario. This phrase does not mean that the company ceases to exist; it means only that company operations cease until this function is restored.

The criticality range 8 to 9 often is used to signify that loss of a function will not drive an enterprise to close its doors but will cause severe damage or loss of confidence. Missed deliveries, loss of customer service functions, lower quality, and similar effects warrant a rating in this range. Functions such as corporate communications (e.g., press releases, customer relations, and shareholder notices), banking functions, some accounting filings, and order entry are examples of functions in this range.

The range of 5 to 7 is probably the criticality rating used most often. This range indicates considerable fiscal effect and significant inconvenience. If such a function were not recovered in time, the effect would be felt but would not be a major corporate event. Perhaps the significant difference between the range of 5 to 7 and the range of 8 to 9 can be summarized in this way: The former is an internal event that would be an internal problem. The latter would be reportable in annual reports and may require media involvement or public advertisements to explain the outage. The higher range has significance beyond corporate walls. Some functions that often meet the lower criteria are accounts payable, various reporting functions, and low-priority government regulatory requirements.

The criticality range of 3 to 4 identifies loss of a function as a minor inconvenience, with little or no monetary impact. Various filings, audits, and internal support functions often can be delayed, with no impact other than the need to perform the work later when functional capability is restored. These are not unimportant functions, but they are functions that can be delayed for a fixed interval with minimal impact on corporate operations. Examples of such functions are certifications, some SEC filings, electronic data processing (EDP) audit, financial audit, internal consulting, corporate directories, and ongoing training programs. Although these are important functions, sometimes significant to overall corporate survival, often they can be delayed without major problems.

The 1- to 2-criticality level indicates that loss of the function would be barely noticeable for the short term and would cause minimal inconvenience. Although these may be important, often regulated, functions, often they are fairly time independent. Examples include former employee tracking functions, claims management, charitable contributions, and equal employment opportunity/affirmative action plans. Although these are not necessarily level 1 to 2 functions in all companies, often they are functions that can be delayed for a significant time without jeopardizing the corporate mission.

58.3.4.4 Operational Impact, Ranking Factor, and Number of Users.
The *Operational Impact*, recorded in the seventh column, is an automated result that is a function of the criticality. Individuals within the enterprise will express their biases in the criticality ratings they assign to various functions. One employee may say that a function has a criticality rating of 7 and another may say 6 or 8. The operational impact

Criticality	Impact	Description
10–9	1	Critical operational impact or fiscal loss
8–7–6	2	Significant operational impact or fiscal loss
5–4–3	3	Some operational impact or fiscal loss
2–3	4	No short term impacts or fiscal losses

EXHIBIT 58.13   Transformation of Criticality to Operational Impact

measure lowers the granularity of the estimates by transforming a scale of 10 levels to a scale of 4 levels. In this way, individual biases can be normalized and the estimates adjusted to achieve a 4-level assessment of functional criticalities and impacts.

Operational impact is derived through a many-to-one mapping that transforms criticality to operational impact as shown in Exhibit 58.13. This transformation achieves a data-smoothing function that removes discontinuities caused by individual or organizational biases. It also reverses the order of importance, making 1 the highest impact and 4 the lowest impact. Criticality measurements are transposed; where earlier a higher number meant higher criticality to a system, now a lower number means greater impact and higher priority. This provides a mathematical convenience for combining survival time and criticality into a single measure.

The eighth column is the *Ranking Factor*, which is the combination of survival time and operational impact, and hence criticality. The ranking factor is the product of the survival time in days and the operational impact. A function with short survival time and high operational impact receives the highest-priority (lowest-number) ranking factor. For example, a function with a one-day survival time and level 1 operational impact receives a ranking factor of 1. Another function with seven-day survival time and operational impact of 3 earns a ranking factor of 21.

The purpose of the ranking factor is to provide a single measure that ranks all corporate functions from highest priority to lowest priority for recovery planning purposes. The compilation of all functions listed in ascending order of ranking factor will show functions in their order of priority for disaster recovery and restoration.

The ninth column of the matrix shown in Exhibit 58.10 is the *Number of Users*. This column simply records the number of employees involved in each function. Note that in most cases, individual employees perform multiple functions and, therefore, will be counted as users in several functional areas. As a result, the sum of users in this column may exceed the total employees of the enterprise. This duplication is acceptable and accounted for in the detailed plans.

58.3.4.5 Category.

The tenth column is used to record the *Category* of the function. This column summarizes the analysis achieved through the assessment of survival time, identification of criticality, and computation of ranking factors. The category is simply a way of grouping functions with similar recovery periods. Once sorted by ranking factor in ascending order, the functions are then classified into several categories based on natural groupings.

Using heuristic techniques or more formal graphical ones, the survival times of the functions can be traced or mapped as they proceed from highest priority to lowest priority. The functions will naturally fall into groups or clusters. Often one category consists of functions requiring recovery within one to three days, which can be assigned Category I, and which form the foundation of functions requiring quick recovery. Another group, which can be assigned Category II, often consists of functions requiring recovery or resumption in one to two weeks. These are the highest-priority recovery functions, once all of the Category I items have resumed. Other categories are similarly assigned.

Exhibit 58.14 shows a sample translation of functions to a graph and the subsequent assignment of categories. Each function is represented by one "tick" mark on the horizontal axis, the x-axis. The corresponding survival time is the height, graphed on the y-axis. In the exhibit, there are four categories: Category I functions have survival periods of from 1 to 3 days. Category II functions have survival times of 7 to 14 days. Category III functions have survival times of 30 days, and Category IV have survival times of 60 days. Although there are usually more functions than those shown on the exhibit, the process is the same.

58.3.4.6 System Elements.
The twelfth and final column is really a series of columns each representing a system element. The system elements consist of hardware, software, communications systems, and operating units. The purpose of these columns is to record which functions make use of which system elements. For each function, the disaster recovery planner marks the appropriate system element used in performing that function.

Columns may correspond to hardware devices or to a functional hardware description, such as an imaging system. Major software systems may be column headings, especially for custom-built or custom-tailored software systems, such as material requirements planning (MRP) or accounting systems. Office software systems such as word processors, spreadsheets, presentation software, databases, communication software, and many other software packages may each form column headings as well. Software packages that are always installed as a group may be described that way in the column. Several system elements may constitute one functional system. For example, the time-keeping and recording function may use electronic punch clocks, communication links between the clocks and a computer, and software to translate the electronic punch clock data into time sheets. This entire system may be labeled as the time-keeping system and be consolidated into one column.

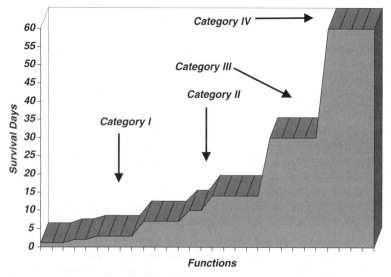

EXHIBIT 58.14   Category Assignment Curve

This column also functions as a check and balance against the defined scope of the recovery plan. If columns are necessary for systems that are out of scope, then either the scope must be changed or important statements must be made regarding the limited recovery posture for those system elements not included in the plan.

58.4 BUSINESS IMPACT ANALYSIS MATRIX ANALYSIS.   The BIA matrix forms the heart of the business impact analysis. The matrix provides the basic information needed to establish recovery requirements and timelines, and to estimate costs of outages. The matrix can be manipulated to help the recovery planner perform the analyses required for translating the business objectives defined earlier in the process into the business continuity plan objectives.

58.4.1 Listing the Functions Organizationally.   The major matrix manipulations that the planner will perform are a special set of sorts. Exhibit 58.15 shows a sample BIA matrix. This sample BIA matrix is representative of a corporate headquarters facility with some production and warehousing capabilities. The matrix shown is for illustrative purposes only and therefore is composed of only a selected subset of the columns found in an operational matrix. It also shows only a few of the many corporate functions that would normally comprise a full matrix.

This matrix is sorted alphabetically by department. Within departments, it is sorted first by survival time of functions, starting with shortest survival. When the survival time of functions is equal, functions are sorted by criticality so that the most critical functions are listed first. This matrix sort, called the organizational sort because it follows corporate structures, frequently is the first one used, and is most useful for summarizing interviews and results. This sort is also the one that is most useful when meeting with department managers, for their concerns center on their own departments.

58.4.2 Finding Cross-Department Functions.   A second useful view emphasizes similar functions across departmental boundaries. In this view, shown in Exhibit 58.16, functions that cross departments are grouped together. This matrix, which for simplicity is a subset of the matrix shown in Exhibit 58.15, provides facility for uncovering functions with similar titles performed by different departments. In the exhibit, there are three sets of functions with similar names but different departments.

The corporate accounting and human resources departments both perform functions named *Benefits*. However, the two departments describe the survival time and criticality of these functions very differently. Human resources considers this function a minor inconvenience with virtually no fiscal impact and an allowable downtime of more than two weeks. The accounting department tags this function with a downtime of only one day and a greater inconvenience with fiscal impact. The ranking factors of these two functions, both called Benefits, are widely different in value, showing at a glance that there is a discrepancy here. The planner must determine whether this discrepancy is the result of inconsistent descriptions, and therefore a problem, or the result of different functions with a similar name.

The other two sets of cross functions are the *Payroll* function, another overlap between the corporate accounting and human resources departments, and *Production Scheduling*, which is performed by both the materials department and customer service. In both cases, the survival time and criticality measures were assessed to be similar by both departments, with ranking factors that are close or the same.

The matrix makes apparent the existing overlaps, but the planner must determine whether the overlaps are similar, overlapping functions, or different functions with

Department	Functions	Survive Days	Criticality	Ops Impact	Ranking Factor	No. of Users	Category
Corp Accounting	Cash Management	1	10	1	1	2	
Corp Accounting	Benefits	1	5	3	3	1	
Corp Accounting	Payroll (Mgt)	2	9	1	2	2	
Corp Accounting	A/P	2	6	2	4	3	
Corp Accounting	Financial Planning	30	7	2	60	4	
Corp Accounting	Income Tax	30	7	2	60	2	
Corp Accounting	A/R	30	6	2	60	3	
Corp Accounting	G/L	30	5	3	90	2	
Corporate Services	Auto Fleet Mgt	30	6	2	60	1	
Corporate Services	Travel Administration	30	2	4	120	2	
Corporate Services	Facilities	1	10	1	1	2	
Customer Service	Order Entry	1	8	2	2	1	
Customer Service	Production Scheduling	2	9	1	2	1	
Human Resources	Payroll (Union)	1	10	1	1	2	
Human Resources	Workers Comp	10	8	2	20	1	
Human Resources	Benefits	15	3	3	45	1	
Human Resources	OSHA Compliance Programs	90	N/A	N/A	N/A	1	
Human Resources	Rideshare Program	90	1	4	360	1	
Marketing	Pricing Strategies	2	10	1	2	3	
Marketing	Strategic Product Development	14	9	1	14	5	
Marketing	Account Targeting	30	6	2	60	3	
Marketing	Advertising	90	3	3	270	2	
Materials	Production Scheduling	1	8	2	2	2	
Materials	Purchasing	1	8	2	2	3	
Materials	Bill & Materials	3	6	2	6	1	
Materials	Materials Planning	7	4	3	21	2	
Materials	Invoice I/F	14	8	2	28	2	
QA	Inspection Records	7	3	3	21	1	
QA	Project Tracking	14	4	3	42	4	
QA	Reporting	30	3	3	90	1	
R&D	CAE	1	7	2	2	4	
R&D	General Research	14	4	3	42	2	

EXHIBIT 58.15   Sample BIA Matrix

similar names. In the first example, the function named *Benefits* is quite different. The human resources department views this function as a regular record-keeping function with occasional changes, and it includes tracking and managing employee health plan choices, usually offered annually. Short processing delays are usually inconsequential to the enterprise and its employees. For the corporate accounting department, however, the same named function includes making matching funds payments, exercising stock options, and calculating other financial disbursements based on existing benefits packages and agreements. The functions are similarly named but different in meaning.

Department	Functions	Survive Days	Criticality	Ops Impact	Ranking Factor	No. of Users	Category
Corporate Services	Auto Fleet Mgt	30	6	2	60	1	
Corp Accounting	Benefits	1	5	3	3	1	
Human Resources	Benefits	15	3	3	45	1	
Customer Service	Order Entry	1	8	2	2	1	
Human Resources	OSHA Compliance Programs	90	N/A	N/A	N/A	1	
Corp Accounting	Payroll (Mgt)	2	9	1	2	2	
Human Resources	Payroll (Union)	1	10	1	1	2	
Marketing	Pricing Strategies	2	10	1	2	3	
Materials	Production Scheduling	1	8	2	2	2	
Customer Service	Production Scheduling	2	9	1	2	1	
QA	Project Tracking	14	4	3	42	4	

EXHIBIT 58.16   Emphasizing Cross Departmental Functions

The other two examples are similar functions with the same meanings but performed from different perspectives. *Payroll* for management and union personnel is performed differently due to union rules and regulations. Therefore, corporate accounting can calculate regular salaries and benefits for management employees and produce payroll checks. However, the human resources department must be involved in calculating pay for unionized, hourly employees to make certain that all rules and regulations are followed precisely.

Production Scheduling, performed by customer service and by materials, is a similar function with different perspectives. For customer service, production scheduling means setting requirements for customer deliveries and, thereby, determining production schedules. *Materials* finalizes the schedules to reconcile possibly conflicting production requirements for different customers by advancing or delaying schedules within corporate policy constraints.

The planner must understand the meaning of each function and recognize the differences between similarly named functions so that all recovery capabilities meet the true needs of the corporate users and customers.

58.4.3   Using the Ranking Factor.   A third view, which is the most important part of the matrix analysis, is the ranking factor view. In this sort, shown in Exhibit 58.17, functions are listed in ascending order according to their ranking factor first and then in ascending sequence according to survival days. The purpose of this view is to assign *Category* designations to all functions and to establish specific timelines for the categories. These timelines become the disaster recovery plan *technical* objectives. Exhibit 58.17 consists of the same data as the previous exhibits but sorted differently.

A useful function of the ranking factor is to list functions in a reasonable priority order for recovery timeline planning. The primary purpose of the *Category* designation is to group functions by recovery requirement or timeline, as a function of short-term importance to the enterprise. Therefore, the ranking factor sort is ideal for determining functional categorizations. All Category I functions for this organization must be

Department	Functions	Survive Days	Criticality	Ops Impact	Ranking Factor	No. of Users	Category
Human Resources	Payroll (Union)	1	10	1	1	2	I
Corporate Services	Facilities	1	10	1	1	2	I
Corp Accounting	Cash Management	1	10	1	1	2	I
R&D	CAE	1	7	2	2	4	I
Materials	Production Scheduling	1	8	2	2	2	I
Materials	Purchasing	1	8	2	2	3	I
Customer Service	Order Entry	1	8	2	2	1	I
Marketing	Pricing Strategies	2	10	1	2	3	I
Customer Service	Production Scheduling	2	9	1	2	1	I
Corp Accounting	Payroll (Mgt)	2	9	1	2	2	I
Corp Accounting	Benefits	1	5	3	3	1	I
Corp Accounting	A/P	2	6	2	4	3	I
Materials	Bill & Materials	3	6	2	6	1	I
Marketing	Strategic Product Development	14	9	1	14	5	II
Human Resources	Workers Comp	10	8	2	20	1	II
QA	Inspection Records	7	3	3	21	1	II
Materials	Materials Planning	7	4	3	21	2	II
Materials	Invoice I/F	14	8	2	28	2	II
R&D	General Research	14	4	3	42	2	II
QA	Project Tracking	14	4	3	42	4	II
Human Resources	Benefits	15	3	3	45	1	II
Marketing	Account Targeting	30	6	2	60	3	III
Corporate Services	Auto Fleet Mgt	30	6	2	60	1	III
Corp Accounting	Financial Planning	30	7	2	60	4	III
Corp Accounting	Income Tax	30	7	2	60	2	III
Corp Accounting	A/R	30	6	2	60	3	III
QA	Reporting	30	3	3	90	1	III
Corp Accounting	G/L	30	5	3	90	2	III
Corporate Services	Travel Administration	30	2	4	120	2	III
Marketing	Advertising	90	3	3	270	2	III
Human Resources	Rideshare Program	90	1	4	360	1	III
Human Resources	OSHA Compliance Programs	90	N/A	N/A	N/A	1	III

EXHIBIT 58.17   Ranking Factor View

recovered in less than 3 days. For most of these functions, the criticality is high and the survival time is low. Category II functions begin when the survival time jumps to 14 days.

This type of orderly grouping is not exceptional; it occurs in most organizations. The natural organizational activity is to perform functions, generally in a regular, repeating pattern. Many functions are critical and performed almost daily. Other functions are performed weekly, monthly, quarterly, or annually. The ranking factor is a good tool for viewing functions according to their natural cycle. It works because this factor measures

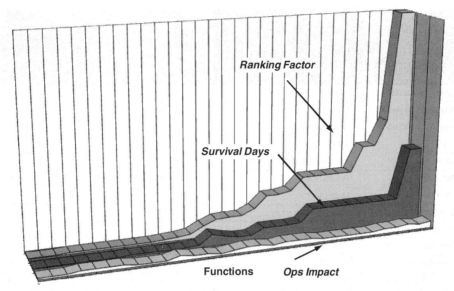

EXHIBIT 58.18   Graphing the Three Measures

both cycles and relative importance. Either measure alone would be insufficient. Exhibit 58.18 graphs three basic measures: survival days, operational impact, and ranking factor. This graphical representation is based on the data contained in Exhibit 58.17.

Each item on the horizontal (x) axis represents one function from the matrix. The height of each of the three curves represents their numerical values. The ranking is an increasing curve because the data are presented according to the ranking factor view. The survival days is mostly increasing but does drop near the middle of the graph and then rises again. This dip corresponds to the two functions with 7-day survival times The rankings of the operational impact curve begin at fairly low values, corresponding to high levels of effects such as criticality 10 or 9, and end with fairly high values, corresponding to lower levels of effects which are typically less than 5 or 6. This curve rises and falls but follows a generally increasing pattern.

Sorting this information according to operational impact would not yield sufficient information upon which to base recovery timelines. Some functions with great detrimental effects only begin to have an effect after a longer time. Similarly, a simple sort of survival time may erroneously include functions as high priority whose operational impacts are too low to merit the quick recovery and expense associated with Category I functions. In both cases, the timeline would not be accurate because the sorting criteria exclude either levels of impact or time. Only the ranking factor is reliable since it reflects both time and effect simultaneously.

58.5   JUSTIFYING THE COSTS.   One of the most difficult aspects of the planning process is justifying the costs of the planning process, the reserve equipment, and the contract services. The cost justification is performed best and most efficiently using the generalized cost consequence model rather than the quantitative risk model. Both models are described in the sections that follow.

58.5.1   Quantitative Risk Model.   The quantitative risk model is a formal and rigorous methodology for analyzing expected losses that will be incurred over a predetermined time period. This procedure requires a significant amount of analysis and research. The model consists of three main factors: probability of loss, cost of loss, and annual loss expectancy (ALE). The probability of loss is really a sum of the probabilities of different catastrophic events that range from partial outages to severe interruptions. The cost of loss depends on the level of interruption. For example, a partial building loss affecting computer systems but leaving phone systems in operating condition has a much lower cost than a complete building destruction. Therefore, the cost of loss is dependent on the type of disaster.

A simplified risk model considers the probability of loss and the cost of the loss. The annual loss expectancy is the product of the probability and the cost. For example, let us assume there is a 5 percent probability (annual) of a major power failure. Stated differently, this means that the facility will experience a major power failure once in 20 years. Let us further assume that the power failure will cause a 72-hour outage, which will cost the enterprise $1,250,000. The ALE is calculated as 5% × $1,250,000, or $62,500. This number is compared to the baseline cost of the recovery plan and the cost of capital. For example, say the cost of the recovery plan is $2,000 per month and the cost of capital is $25,000. Then the baseline cost or comparison figure is (12 × $2,000) + $25,000, or $49,000. Since the comparison figure is lower than the ALE, recovery planning is justified.

There are some serious shortcomings in this simplified approach. First, the cost of the outage depends on the level of loss. A 72-hour power outage is significantly costlier than a 24-hour outage. Therefore, the ALE must reflect the difference in probabilities of different levels of impact. Another problem is defining the probability of occurrence for an aggregation of events.

The more acceptable risk model must consider the different levels of loss and sum the probabilities of all disasters that can cause that level of loss to define the true probability of loss for that loss level. This is accomplished for each loss level. First, a series of disaster events is defined. Each event is then refined into levels. For example, office buildings are susceptible to loss due to fire. Data on numbers of fires and amount of destruction (in predefined ranges) are available from various fire protection services. For a given facility, the total number of such buildings in the geographical vicinity is considered. Then the frequency or probability of a fire causing a range of damage is calculated. This calculation is performed for each defined range of damage. The level of loss for each range of damage is assessed, then the ALE is calculated for each range of damage by multiplying the probability of a fire causing that range of damage with cost of the loss if there is such a fire. All the ALE values are summed to calculate the total fire ALE. This calculation must be performed for all types of disasters that can affect the facility to determine the grand total ALE. For each level of impact for all disasters, the baseline costs also must be calculated. These figures are also summed to form a total baseline cost. The grand total ALE is then compared with this baseline cost figure.

This analysis is a complex process that requires great effort to generate and even greater patience to explain. However, there are two more important problems with the quantitative risk model.

1. Calculating all the outage costs is very difficult and subject to debate. Moreover, once the cost figures are finalized, they are subject to constant change due to the changing business climate and practices.

2. Calculating the probabilities is also very difficult and often requires many subjective conclusions. For example, what is the effect of modernizing the sprinkler

system based on the level of damage experienced by a particular type of fire? Each countermeasure can significantly alter both the cost and the probability. Moreover, the probability of any particular event tends to be quite small, often less than 1 percent.

While the quantitative risk model is an interesting actuarial exercise, it is of marginal use in modern business continuity planning.

58.5.2 Generalized Cost Consequence Model.   The generalized cost consequence (GCC) model (developed by this author between 1990 and 1995) does not consider probabilities of specific disaster events. Instead, it estimates the total cost of outages as a function of time after an event. This model is significantly simpler than the quantitative risk model: It is easier to build and simpler to explain. The GCC estimates the cost of an outage for each function and applies that cost to the total disaster cost after the maximum allowable down time has been exceeded.

For instance, assume the cost of delaying the treasury department's bank management function is $25,000 per day after the first day. Let us also assume that the cost of delaying the law department's general contract review is $5,000 per day after seven days. For the bank management function, the cost to the enterprise is calculated as $25,000 per day beginning on the second day. For the contract review function, the cost is calculated as $5,000 per day beginning on the eighth day. Therefore, the contract review function does not contribute to loss during the first seven days. This calculation is performed for each function, and then the costs are collected by category. This category cost summary is used to develop and present a graph that shows the total cost losses for each category level once they are activated and the total for all categories over time.

A sample graph of the contribution of functions aggregated by category level is shown in Exhibit 58.19. In this example, Category I functions cause slightly more than $120,000 of loss on a daily basis once the maximum allowable downtime has been exceeded. Category II functions contribute slightly under $60,000 in this example. It is likely that different functions will commence their loss contribution at various times after the disaster event. Therefore, the true Category I loss contribution may begin at a lower level and increase to its full level. That distribution of effect will occur beginning on the first day any function exceeds its allowable downtime and continues to grow until the last day any function exceeds its downtime, at which point the effect will have achieved its full loss contribution. Since categorizations cluster functions with similar

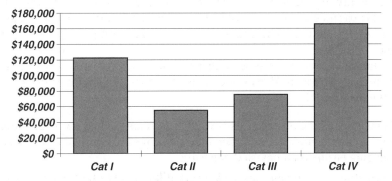

EXHIBIT 58.19   Summary of Loss Contribution

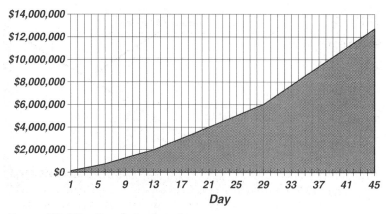

EXHIBIT 58.20 Cumulative Loss Summary

downtimes, the loss can be presented as a single, or point, value rather than as a value that varies over time.

The bars indicate that Category I has a higher value than Categories II and III. Category IV is also high. The U-shape is characteristic of this graph. No matter how many categories are used, the Category I functions tend to be quite high in their contributions. The next one or two categories are lower, but increasing in values until the lowest-priority category, which tends to be quite high. This shape results from the manner of the categorizations. The Category I functions are highly critical with great effects on corporate operations. Category I functions tend to be few in number, with each function contributing significantly. The middle categories tend to be larger in number than Category I, with the number increasing with each succeeding category, although still small compared to the overall set of organizational functions. The final category tends to contain the largest number of functions, each of which contributes less on a daily basis than the Category I functions, but the sheer magnitude of this set often causes it to be the largest overall contributor to loss. Of course, Category I functions begin their effects quickly, while loss of Category IV functions may be insignificant for weeks.

Exhibit 58.20 presents a sample graph showing the accumulation of losses from all categories following a disaster. This exhibit uses the same values as in Exhibit 58.19 but presents them in a different format and represents the losses accumulated after 45 days. Neither exhibit measures physical losses such as real property, capital equipment, and the like. Physical losses are not issues that affect the planning process; they affect the cost to recover and are independent of continuation measures. The horizontal (x) axis represents the number of days since the disaster event caused damage and cessation of corporate functions. The vertical (y) axis represents the total losses the enterprise will have sustained on the corresponding day represented on the x-axis.

At the time of the disaster occurrence, no losses will have accumulated. Thereafter, the accumulated loss is increased each day by the cost contribution of the category whose earliest start time has already been surpassed. Assume that Category I functions begin to contribute to corporate losses of $120,000 on the first day, that Category II functions begin to contribute losses of $60,000 on the seventh day, and that Category III functions contribute $80,000 daily beginning on the fourteenth day. In this case, the cumulative loss begins at zero and grows by $120,000 per day for the first six days. On the seventh day, the Category II functions begin to contribute $60,000 per day along

EXHIBIT 58.21   Cumulative Loss Summary With and Without Planning

with the ongoing contribution of the Category I functions. Therefore, beginning on the seventh day, the cumulative loss grows by the sum of $120,000 and $60,000, which is $180,000 daily. On the fourteenth day, the daily loss increases by another $80,000, representing the Category III contribution. This brings the total daily loss to $240,000, which is the sum of the contributions of Categories I, II, and III.

The cumulative loss summary shows at a glance the loss that an enterprise will experience over time following the disaster, if no recovery planning is performed. The active simplifications of this model are the grouping of functions by category and the subsequent representation of each category as a single value beginning at a fixed point in time. This may render the estimate slightly inaccurate at some local points, but the overall values are as accurate as the underlying estimates.

The generalized cost consequence model summarizes at a glance the effects of loss of functions. These loss figures can be affected by insurance reimbursements, legal liabilities, and overall management objectives.

A second model can be developed if the recovery planning is in place, showing the residual loss proposed. That model would be developed in a similar manner but with the assumption that certain functions are restored within established time parameters. There would be residual loss only if the restoration occurs later than the allowable downtime, which will almost certainly be the case for some functions. Exhibit 58.21 presents a graph that shows cumulative losses with and without a disaster recovery plan in place. The Without Plan curve is similar to the previous exhibit. The With Plan curve reflects the residual loss that would occur even if a plan were in place. This loss is normally dramatically lower but is seldom zero. Typically, a reduction to zero residual loss would require extraordinary and prohibitively expensive measures. Most organizations can benefit more from a substantial lowering of residual losses than from a full reduction to zero losses.

The estimation process itself is much simpler than for the quantitative risk model. For each function, the loss estimate is based on three criteria, or types of losses:

1. Tangible and direct losses
2. Tangible and indirect losses
3. Intangible losses

The tangible and direct losses are the easiest to calculate. These losses can be traced to specific revenue-producing functions. The results are direct because the loss occurs as a first-order effect, meaning that revenue stops because the function cannot be performed. The results are tangible because they can be measured easily. An example of such a function is automated production control of an assembly line. If the systems exceed their allowable downtime, then production will cease. The cost is the resultant loss of sales after inventory is depleted. Another example is loss of order entry functions. In this case, the result is similarly calculable: Lost sales after in-stock items are depleted and existing orders are produced. Tangible, direct losses include lost sales, lost manufacturing, lost deliveries, and other lost opportunities.

The tangible and indirect losses are the most common, although slightly more difficult to estimate. Support functions generally produce tangible results whose deprivation would cause a financial loss indirectly. For example, a public corporation issues quarterly earnings reports that, if late, could have significant consequences on the company's stock value. Although this is not a direct loss resulting from cessation of sales or other production, the loss can be calculated using accounting standard practices. The internal accounting personnel are in the best position to provide this estimate to the disaster recovery planner. Tangible, indirect losses include penalties, fees, fines, market share, and other issues that can be directly calculated, or at least estimated with some degree of confidence.

Intangible losses are the most difficult to calculate. The intangible effects include reduced public confidence, compromised customer satisfaction, promises not kept, damaged reputation, and other losses that are general in nature and not easily calculable. Sometimes these losses are not translated into specific financial losses and are, therefore, not represented in the cost graphs. In such cases, prominent notations should be made explaining the additional but not quantified losses.

According to a study by Contingency Planning Research in their 2001 Cost of Downtime Study, hourly losses by major companies can range from a low of $12,000 for service-oriented organizations to over $7 million for a major brokerage firm. There are no strict rules for estimating losses. The timeline can be specified in increments of days, as shown in the preceding examples. It also can be as fine as hours or minutes. Some industries, such as hospitals and other acute care facilities, must measure loss in finer increments.

The generalized cost consequence model can solve the problem of cost justification. This model shows the potential, possibly catastrophic, losses without engaging in the analysis paralysis that can stem from a detailed quantitative risk model development effort.

58.6 PLAN PRESENTATION.   The development of a business continuity plan is an involved and somewhat complex process. Though there is the simplifying technique of the generalized cost consequence model, there is still significant work required to devise and implement a workable and resilient plan.

The complexity of the development process, however, must give way to simplicity in the final plan that is presented to the enterprise. Complex analyses and detailed descriptions must give way to simple and easy-to-read flows and action plans, for even after significant training, the people responsible for carrying out the plans need simple documentation to help them along.

Exhibit 58.22 provides on example of how to present the overall recovery flow. This one diagram can form the basis for a set of sections that describes each of the specific steps to be followed. Each decision point requires information and decision guidelines; the BCP document can describe each of these steps and can provide guidance for which

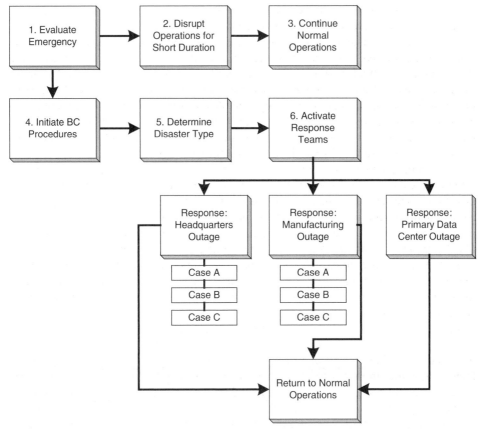

EXHIBIT 58.22   Recovery Flow

path to follow. In this diagram, some recovery responses have *cases* that further define the steps to take. In this example, the cases are parameterized by the expected outage period or the actual outage duration.

Exhibit 58.23 illustrates the meaning of the cases in the preceding exhibit. This illustration draws from the previously described concepts of function categories and lays those categories against their specific timeline requirements. The cases overlay time periods and make it clear which functions must be recovered and in which of the three cases they reside. The diagram intends to clarify that categories of functions

EXHIBIT 58.23   Cases and Categories

continue across time boundaries, and new categories are activated at their designated times.

In this example, Case A represents the time period from 1 hour after an event to 1/2 day after the event. In Case A, only Category 1 functions are activated. If the event lasts longer than 1/2 day, up to 2 days, then after the 1/2-day period, the organization enters Case B and activates Category 2 functions but leaves Category 1 functions active. If the event duration is greater than 2 days, then Case C shows that Category 1 and 2 functions continue, and Category 3 and 4 functions are activated at the 2- and 3-day points.

58.7 CONCLUDING REMARKS.   This chapter has introduced a methodology for analyzing mission-critical functions in an organization and for structuring business continuity plans that reflect organizational needs and resources. Chapter 59 in this *Handbook* continues the discussion with details of how to recover full functionality should a disaster occur.

58.8 FURTHER READING

Barnes, J. C. *Business Continuity Planning and HIPAA: Business Continuity Management in the Health Care Environment.* Brookfield, CT: Rothstein Associates, 2004.

Barnes, J. C. A *Guide to Business Continuity Planning.* Hoboken, NJ: John Wiley & Sons, 2001.

Butler, J. G., and P. Badura. *Contingency Planning and Disaster Recovery: Protecting Your Organization's Resources.* Charleston, SC: Computer Technology Research Corp., 1997.

Fulmer, K. L. *Business Continuity Planning: A Step-by-Step Guide with Planning Forms on CD-ROM*, 3rd ed.. Brookfield, CT: Rothstein Associates, 2004.

Gregory, P., and P. J. Rothstein. *IT Disaster Recovery Planning for Dummies.* Hoboken, NJ: John Wiley & Sons, 2007.

Hiatt, C. J. A *Primer for Disaster Recovery Planning in an IT Environment.* Hershey, PA: Information Science Reference, 1999.

Hiles, A. *Business Continuity: Best Practices—World-Class Business Continuity Management*, 2nd ed. Brookfield, CT: Rothstein Associates, 2003.

Hiles, A. ed. *The Definitive Handbook of Business Continuity Management*, 2nd ed. Hoboken, NJ: John Wiley & Sons, 2008.

Myers, K. N. *Manager's Guide to Contingency Planning for Disasters: Protecting Vital Facilities and Critical Operations*, 2nd ed. New York: John Wiley & Sons, 1999.

Rothstein, P. J., ed. *Disaster Recovery Testing: Exercising Your Contingency Plan.* Brookfield, CT: Rothstein Associates, 2007.

Sayed, A., and A. Sayed. *Business Continuity Planning Methodology.* Mississauga, Ont.: Sentryx, 2003.

Schreider, T. *Encyclopedia of Disaster Recovery, Security & Risk Management.* Norcross, GA: Crucible Publishing Works, 1998.

Snedaker, S. *Business Continuity and Disaster Recovery Planning for IT Professionals.* Norwell, MA: Syngress, 2007.

Toigo, J. W. *Disaster Recovery Planning: Preparing for the Unthinkable*, 3rd ed. Englewood Cliffs, NJ: Prentice-Hall, 2002.

Wallace, M., and L. Webber. *The Disaster Recovery Handbook: A Step-by-Step Plan to Ensure Business Continuity and Protect Vital Operations, Facilities, and Assets.* New York: AMACOM, 2004.

CHAPTER **59**

DISASTER RECOVERY

Michael Miora

59.1 INTRODUCTION. In Chapter 58 in this *Handbook*, the importance of a business impact analysis (BIA) and the method of preparing one were described. Once the preliminary groundwork is finished and the BIA analysis is complete, the next step is to design specific strategies for recovery and the tasks for applying those strategies. In this chapter, we discuss the specific strategies to recover the Category I functions, the most time-critical functions identified during the BIA, as well as the remaining lower-priority functions. We examine the traditional strategies of hot sites, warm sites, and cold sites as well as a more modern technique we call reserve systems. We describe how to make good use of Internet and client/server technologies, and of high-speed connections for data backup, for making electronic journals and for data vaulting. We develop the recovery tasks representing the specific activities that must take place to continue functioning, and to resume full operations. These tasks begin with the realization that there is, or may be, a disaster in progress, continue through to full business resumption, and end with normalization, which is the return to normal operations. We examine a set of tasks taken from a real-world disaster recovery plan to illustrate how each task fits into an overall plan, accounting for anticipated contingencies while providing flexibility to handle unforeseen circumstances.

59.2 IDENTIFYING THREATS AND DISASTER SCENARIOS. Threat assessment is the foundation for discovery of threats and their possible levels of impact.

Threat assessments can vary from rigorous analyses of natural events and the probabilities associated with them, to informal surveys of recent disasters and their regional characteristics. The rigorous analysis will yield detailed results but will require significant effort to perform the required research and to interpret the results. The informal survey can yield sufficient information for the disaster recovery planner, and it requires significantly less effort.

59.2.1 Threats. Local fire, police, and other emergency response services can provide the data needed for an informal survey. Flood district management agencies can provide data regarding floods of all types, whether caused by storms, draining, or other factors. Police departments can provide information about building or neighborhood closures due to man-made catastrophes, whereas city and county governments can provide information about emergency declarations over a period of years.

Compiling this list of threats accomplishes two objectives: It helps define the different levels of impact, and it helps to develop a risk mitigation plan. The mitigation techniques outlined in the plan are intended to lower the damage caused by the likeliest disasters. For example, an area prone to seasonal flooding can reduce the risk of computer outages by placing computer installations and important equipment above the flood level. Facilities located in areas prone to power failures can install UPS (uninterruptible power supply) equipment with higher capacities than usual for the type of equipment being protected.

Many threats can have important consequences to information-processing systems. Physical security risks stand out among them as the highest-profile disasters. These are also the most highly dependent on geography and include events such as fire, flood, and earthquake.

Exhibit 59.1 lists a large number of threats to help the disaster recovery planner begin the process of listing threats that apply to specific facilities.

EXHIBIT 59.1 List of Threats

Accidents	Denial-of-service attacks	Kidnapping/hostages
Acts of God	Disgruntled employees	Labor disputes
Aircraft accident	Drug abuse	Local area disaster
Alcohol abuse	Dust storms	Malicious damage
Area evacuation	Earthquakes	Mass illness
Arson	Elevator failure	Municipal service failure
Asbestos	Embezzlement	Nuclear accident
Boiler explosion	Environmental controls fail	Postal strike
Bomb threat	Evacuation	Power failure
Brownout	Falling object	Regional disaster
Building inaccessible	Fire	Sabotage
Chemical spill	Flood	Sanctions
Civil unrest riots	Fraud	Sandstorm
Cold weather	Hacker attack	Snowstorm
Communications failure	Hardware failures	Strike
Computer virus	Heat	Terrorism
Construction disturbance	Humidity	Tornado
Crime	Hurricane	Utility failure
Data diddling	Ice storms	Volcano
Delivery interruptions	Industrial espionage	Water damage
Demonstrations	Information compromise	Water supply failure

59.2.2 Disaster Recovery Scenarios.

Each of the threats described in Exhibit 59.1 causes specific damage, with the scope of damage and damage characteristics well known and predefined. Once the characteristics of specific threats are known, then mitigation measures can be applied. One of the important mitigation techniques is the application of survivable technologies to mission-critical functions. Survivable technologies applied to the most critical of the functions (Category I) can prevent outages or at least significantly lower the probability and duration of the outage. For example, client/server and distributed architectures can be implemented with geographic data distribution, so that the loss of a single data center will not disrupt operations but may only degrade them. One such strategy is the geographically dispersed placement of two computers operating on a single main network with functionality shared between them. If backup data are regularly logged from one machine to another, then both systems maintain current databases. If one system is disrupted, then the other can assume full functions; the response times may degrade, but the functionality will not be lost. Replicated architectures with automatic failover are an even better alternative. The desirability of such measures was amply demonstrated by the catastrophe of September 11, 2001, again by Hurricane Katrina, and yet again in the Southern California fires of 2007.

Escalation scenarios are mechanisms that map the expected duration of failures against the requirements for operational continuity. With well-known threats as described, and the ensuing and defined outage durations that can be characterized, disaster declaration and escalation points can be calculated and presented. Timelines must be carefully constructed to leave little room for doubt.

Exhibit 59.2 provides an example of an escalation timeline. Note that the figure is based on data from Chapter 58, and from Exhibit 58.17 in particular. In this exhibit, the top, horizontal row of boxes corresponds to recovery time estimates. For each column, specific initiation parameters are established. The operators and engineers can, at a glance, determine whether this particular situation requires a disaster declaration. For example, an estimated downtime of less than one day requires no recovery since in Exhibit 58.17, there are no functions requiring recovery in less than one day. The key factors are that the operations personnel must be trained in the use of the procedures and must have ready access to contact information for disaster recovery declaration authorities.

Disaster recovery scenarios and activities are dependent on the scope of the damage. Therefore, it is necessary to group specific events according to a classification of the damage they inflict on a facility. Once this is accomplished, the disaster recovery planner can identify declaration, escalation, and recovery activities based on the specific threats and their resulting disaster scenarios. Classifications of damage include the duration of an outage and the scope of its effects.

Exhibit 59.3 summarizes some threat durations and provides some sample classifications of damage. The first column of the exhibit lists a sampling of threats, and

EXHIBIT 59.2   Escalation Timeline

Exhibit 59.3   Sample Classifications of Damage

Event Description	Possible Scope of Effect	Potential Duration of Effect
Aircraft accident	Building to local area	Hours to days
Asbestos	Partial to full building	Days to weeks
Bomb threat	Building to local area	Hours to days
Chemical spill	Building to lacal area	Hours to days
Civil unrest/riots	Local to regional	Days to weeks
Cold weather	Local to regional	Days
Communications failure	Building to regional	Hours to days
Computer virus	Systems	Hours to days
Data diddling	Systems	Hours to days
Earthquakes	Local to regional	Days to weeks
Environmental controls fail	Partial to full building	Hours to days
Fire	Partial to full building	Days to weeks
Flood	Local to regional area	Days to weeks
Hardware failures	Systems	Hours to days
Hurricane	Local to regional area	Days to weeks
Ice storms	Local to regional area	Days to weeks
Municipal service failure	Local	Hours to days
Nuclear accident	Regional area	Days to weeks
Snowstorm	Local to regional area	Days to weeks
Volcano	Regional area	Weeks
Water damage	Building to local area	Hours to days

the second column classifies each threat according to the possible scope of its effect. The set of possibilities contains systems only, partial or full building, local area, and regional area.

A systems-only disaster leaves the facility unaffected but partially or fully disables the system's operations. Breaches of logical security usually affect only systems, as do hardware failures. The exhibit does not attempt to differentiate between types of systems and number of systems affected, but the disaster recovery planner must do that classification for each facility and for the interactions of facilities. A characteristic of systems-only disasters is that sometimes they can travel across physical boundaries, such as when the incident involves a security breach, a connectivity disruption, or a software failure.

As an example of a system disaster, in 2007, one major company experienced just such a failure during the testing of a dry pipe sprinkler system. When the system was pressurized, the pipes burst. The data center was not serviced by the sprinkler system; it had its own system in place. However, one pipe crossed over the data center, a fact thereto unknown to the systems management personnel. When that pipe burst, the entire data center, which included a raised floor, was quickly flooded, making all the equipment wet from top and bottom. Fortunately, this company had prepared for the loss of any one of its data centers by building a load-balanced system, so that the loss of any one data center would cause only minimally reduced response times.

Partial- or full-building disasters consist of events that cause physical damage to a building. Fires usually affect only one building at a time. Even detection of asbestos, which most often occurs during building maintenance or improvement, is seldom a multibuilding affair. Local and regional area disasters are difficult to distinguish from each other. Generally, a disaster that affects a single geographic area, such as a city or neighborhood, is a local area disaster, whereas a disaster affecting more than one geographic entity is a regional disaster. The importance of this demarcation is that local area disasters at a company site may affect some of the employees personally, although most will be unaffected, except as it relates to company business. A regional disaster usually affects most employees' homes and families as well as the organizations that employ them. A municipal services failure clearly affects a single geographic entity, and employees living outside of that municipality are unlikely to be affected. Conversely, a major storm resulting in floods, or a large earthquake, will affect residents and businesses over a wide area, probably leaving employees at work concerned with the health and safety of their families and homes. The availability of employees to handle a disaster is much greater when the disaster is local, or of smaller scope, than during a regional disaster.

The third column in Exhibit 59.3 estimates the duration of the effect, ranging from hours to days to weeks. These are inexact and somewhat vague guidelines only. Although fire is listed as having a duration ranging from days to weeks, a very small fire may be managed and the building reoccupied in only a few hours. Similarly, an earthquake is listed as having a duration of days to weeks, yet a major earthquake may have large impacts lasting many months. After the 1994 Northridge earthquake in Southern California, for example, major highway arteries were closed for many months, requiring employees to telecommute or spend hours per day traveling. This affected the operations of many companies, forcing them to redesign their workflows. The Seattle earthquake of February 2001, however, had no such long-term effects. Many companies initiated disaster recovery procedures to handle the commuting problem, even when there had been no physical damage to the corporate facilities. The terrorist destruction of the World Trade Center twin towers in New York on September 11, 2001, is perhaps the most obvious example of how the destruction or closure of major roads and other transportation means affected operations of companies not otherwise affected by the terrorist act itself.

The disaster recovery planner must analyze enough specific threats against the corporate operations and physical plant to build a series of disaster scenarios, which become the guiding forces of the recovery activity definitions. Some planners design disaster recovery scenarios to suit each disaster threat. Floods call for one set of activities, fires another. This can result in an extensive set of scenarios, each requiring training, testing, and maintenance. This technique may be too complex. Another similar approach uses active scenarios chosen from a set of only five possible levels of disasters: systems only, partial building, full building, local, and regional. Each organization should try to reduce the number of disaster scenarios, generally to no more than three, and many can handle emergencies adequately using only two scenarios. For most organizations, a systems-only disaster is not restricted to computer systems, but may include phone systems and telecommunications systems. Systems-only cases must be defined in the context of the organization's unique structure.

For example, a manufacturing facility may require three scenarios: systems only, partial building, and full building. Perhaps for the manufacturer, a loss of systems can be handled with a hot site for computers and a fast, high-bandwidth connection to the shop floor. A partial building disaster, affecting only office space, can be handled similarly, but with additional office space for support functions. A full-building disaster that damages or destroys manufacturing capability requires a completely different set of continuation and recovery procedures. As another example, a corporate office facility may require just two scenarios—systems only and building disaster—where the building disaster is a combined building, local, and regional scenario. The systems hot site can handle the systems-only disaster. The building disaster scenario will require that all functions be restored at a hot site that provides full office functions from phone to fax to desks and copiers in addition to computer systems and networks.

The planner defines the sets of disasters and develops recovery scenarios for those sets. This defines the number of scenarios required; then the disaster recovery activities can be designed.

59.3   DEVELOPING RECOVERY STRATEGIES.   The BIA defines the timeline for recovery for each category of functions. The recovery strategies depend on factors such as: the complexity of the functions, the amount of information required to carry them out, the number of people involved in performing the function, and the amount of interaction between this function and other functions. The strategy of choice for each function is based on the timeline and the specific factors relating to it. The tasks required to activate the function immediately after a disaster follow directly from the BIA timeline and from the various factors that have been described.

Recovery strategies are defined differently from continuation strategies. The recovery strategy is the overall plan for resuming a function, or set of functions, in a near-normal work mode. The continuation strategy is the plan for immediate or nearly immediate operations of a key function, even if it results in significantly degraded performance or limited capability. The continuation strategy is most often applied to a small set of functions rather than to a more complete set, and it is often only temporary. Although the recovery strategy may be used for several weeks or longer, the continuation strategy typically survives for hours or days.

Traditional recovery strategies include hot sites, warm sites, and cold sites. The most common recovery strategy uses a commercial service provider to maintain an on-demand operating capability for well-defined systems. There are a variety of such companies, some of which provide a standby mainframe or midrange system, along with selected peripherals and telecommunications facilities on a first-come, first-served basis. Others guarantee availability by providing a dedicated facility.

The operating capability required is defined at the outset. Processor type is specified down to the model level. Required disk space, hard drives, tape drives, ports, connectivity, and all other required elements must be specified explicitly. Timeline requirements must be stated precisely, with rehearsal, practice, and drill times negotiated in advance. Geographic location of the backup systems is often determined at the time of disaster declaration, and connectivity is usually provided to corporate fixed facilities. The obvious advantage of this strategy is ready access to maintained systems and environments. The principal disadvantage is cost.

A continuation strategy usually depends on internal resources rather than on commercially available providers. Continuation strategy requires that equipment be available instantly, with current data. "Instant availability" means that the systems must be local, or at least connected, yet survivable. The continuation strategy is becoming more common as microcomputer-based systems assume greater roles in corporate computing structures. The continuation strategy often relies on reserve systems, a concept pioneered over the past five years. This strategy, described in Section 59.3.2.8, uses high-performance microcomputers residing off site at homes, branch offices, and other locations easily accessible to employees.

The reserve system provides immediate, but limited, functionality so that operations can be continued after a disaster while awaiting full restoration or recovery.

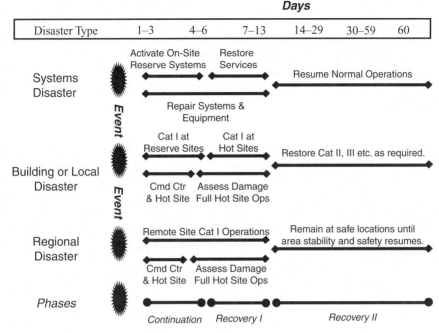

Days

| Disaster Type | 1–3 | 4–6 | 7–13 | 14–29 | 30–59 | 60 |

Systems Disaster
Activate On-Site Reserve Systems — Restore Services — Resume Normal Operations
Repair Systems & Equipment

Building or Local Disaster
Cat I at Reserve Sites — Cat I at Hot Sites — Restore Cat II, III etc. as required.
Cmd Ctr & Hot Site — Assess Damage Full Hot Site Ops

Regional Disaster
Remote Site Cat I Operations — Remain at safe locations until area stability and safety resumes.
Cmd Ctr & Hot Site — Assess Damage Full Hot Site Ops

Phases
Continuation — Recovery I — Recovery II

Event

EXHIBIT 59.4   Recovery Phases

59.3.1 Recovery Phases.

Orderly recovery requires organized processes and procedures. The BIA uncovers the time sensitivity and criticality of functions, so that continuation and recovery strategies can be designed. Activation of these strategies is performed systematically in time-phased increments.

Exhibit 59.4 shows an example of such phasing. The figure is based on Exhibit 58.17, and illustrates a common schema that consists of three scenarios. Each scenario represents a collection of disasters according to their effects on the company. The first, a systems disaster, represents an effect that has interrupted computer and related systems but has left basic services such as heating and air conditioning, water, power, and life safety intact. The second scenario is the building or local disaster. In this case, a major portion of the building, the entire building, or even several surrounding buildings are rendered unfit for occupancy. This may be due to a problem with the building or with the local area, including fire, toxic spills, minor flooding of surrounding areas, terrorist action, and other such events. The third scenario is the regional disaster, in which some calamitous event affects a wider geographic area. Examples of such catastrophes are earthquakes, hurricanes, floods, large fires or firestorms, and heavy ice and snowstorms.

Each of these scenarios requires different recovery strategies and tasks. However, the overall recovery phases remain similar. The exhibit shows that there are three basic phases: continuation of critical (Category I) functions, recovery of critical functions, and recovery of other functions. These are labeled near the bottom of the figure as "Continuation," "Recovery I," and "Recovery II."

The Continuation phase begins at the time of the disaster. For each scenario, the goal of the continuation phase is to support the Category I functions as best as possible, and within the time frames defined by the BIA. In this example, the BIA timeline for Category I functions is one to three days. For the systems disaster and the building or local disaster scenarios, the Continuation phase depends on the local or on-site reserve

EXHIBIT 59.5   Spread of Functions across Categories

systems. For the regional disaster, where local functioning may be impossible, the Category I functions must be supported by remote sites.

The recovery phase is further divided into two subphases. Recovery I phase restores full or nearly full functionality to the Category I functions that were partially supported by the reserve systems. In the example, the Recovery I phase begins after all continuation functions have been stabilized. In practice, it is more common for the Recovery I phase to begin shortly after the disaster event in order to minimize the duration during which the Category I functions must operate in a degraded fashion. The Recovery II phase is used to recover other functions in the order they are needed, as defined by the BIA. Exhibit 59.5 shows the typical spread of functions across categories. Typically, Category I functions constitute approximately 10 to 15 percent of the functions performed in a facility or campus. The Category II functions consist of functions that are very important and time critical but can be delayed for a short time. These functions significantly outnumber the Category I functions, sometimes reaching 20 to 35 percent of facility functions. Category III and, if applicable, Category IV functions are much greater in number, often comprising more than half of the facility functions performed.

The BIA process assessed the cost contribution of each category of functions to the total losses the company would sustain after a disaster without a plan. Exhibit 59.6 compares the number of functions per category to the total impact of the functions in each category on operations in a typical organization. Although Category I functions number the fewest of all categories, their impact is the greatest. The Category III functions typically rank second in contributions to losses, with Category II third in rank. The critical functions that constitute Category I are ranked first precisely because of their high impact and time criticality. Category III is typically the largest group, so that even though the impact of each function may be small, the large number of functions increases the total effect of that group. Category IV tends to be a fairly small set of functions, so typically it is small in number and last in impact.

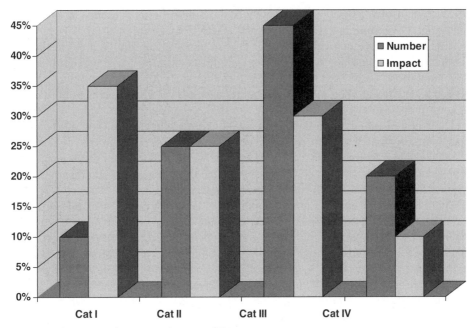

EXHIBIT 59.6 Number versus Impact of Functions

In the example, the systems disaster phases reflect certain assumptions. The Continuation phase begins at the time of the disaster and continues for up to three days. The Recovery phase is scheduled to begin no later than the fourth day, with full recovery by the seventh day, at which time a return to normal operations is expected. The underlying assumption is that the off-site reserve systems have been replicated on site. This is shown by the caption "Activate On-Site Reserve Systems" on Exhibit 59.4. An additional assumption in this example is that the system can be recovered in less than seven days. Some analysis would have been performed to show that new equipment or equipment repairs could be obtained fairly early during the first seven days, leaving enough time for service restoration, including data recovery, to be completed by the seventh day. In this example, it is also clear that the Category II functions are required beginning on the seventh day. This is illustrated by the building or system disaster Recovery II phase, which begins on the seventh day and is labeled as restoring Category II, III, and other functions.

59.3.2 Range of Strategies. Three general areas of traditional recovery strategies address the needs of mainframes, midrange systems, and PC LAN systems. There is a rich history and many years of experience in providing recovery for large, mainframe systems, with strategies that include hot sites, cold sites, reciprocal or mutual aid agreements, and commercial recovery facilities, as will be described.

Strategies for recovery of midrange systems, including distributed systems, minicomputers, and workstations, include all the same strategies as those used for mainframe systems, along with mobile data centers, internal redundancy, failover arrangements, and agreements with manufacturers for priority shipping of replacement equipment.

PC LAN system recovery strategies are the newest of the three areas. They typically make use of combinations of capabilities, including quick replacement, off-site equipment storage (equipment sparing), and hot sites.

59.3.2.1 Cold Sites. A cold site is a room or set of rooms in a "ready-conditioned" environment. It is a fully functional computer room with all of the required facilities, including electrical power, air conditioning, raised floors, and telecommunications, all in operating condition and ready for occupancy. Missing from this fully functional room, because of high costs, is the computer equipment, including the processors and all required peripherals. Cold sites can be owned by one company or shared by several companies.

The major advantage of a dedicated cold site, somewhat diminished in the shared case, is simply that for a relatively low acquisition or leasing cost, the site is guaranteed to be available over the long term to the owner or lessee of the site. To be effective, a cold site must be distant enough from the main facility so that a disaster that makes the primary facility unusable will likely not affect the cold site.

There are several disadvantages to cold sites. First and foremost is that ordering, receiving, installing, and powering up the computer system can take many days. Once the system is functional, the cold site becomes a dedicated facility ready to perform all functions in a controlled environment, but the time required to achieve this state can stretch into a week or more. Few organizations can rely on a cold site as their primary vehicle for disaster recovery. A secondary disadvantage of cold sites is the inherent inability to test the recovery plan. An untested plan is an unreliable plan—testing a cold site would require obtaining all of the requisite equipment, installing the equipment, and performing operations on the new equipment. Few organizations can afford the costs associated with such testing. There are also hidden pitfalls with this strategy. Key equipment may be unavailable for immediate delivery. Communication lines may be untested and unreliable. This strategy is generally not a desirable first line of defense. It can, however, be a part of a larger overall strategy that includes other types of sites.

59.3.2.2 Hot Sites. A hot site is a facility ready to assume processing responsibility immediately. The term usually refers to a site that contains equipment ready to assume all hardware functions, but requiring massive restoration of data and an influx of personnel to operate the equipment. The hot site cannot, therefore, begin total processing instantaneously. In actuality, the site is only warm, with an ability to get hot fast. A hot site can be dedicated to one organization, shared by several organizations, or leased from a specialty company, called a commercial recovery service provider. The provider option is described in a later section.

The primary advantage of a hot site is the speed of recovery. The time to resume processing is defined as the time to reach the facility with people and backup media, plus the time to restore data and programs from the backup media, to test the operations, and to go live with a fully functional system. For larger systems, this period can range from less than two days to almost a week.

The primary disadvantage of a hot site is the cost associated with acquiring and maintaining the fully equipped site. For this reason, most organizations choose to share the cost of a hot site with other organizations, which may be sister companies or only neighbors. In any event, there is a large cost associated with maintaining the site and ensuring that it is updated with every change to each of the participant's requirements, while still maintaining compatibility with all of them. One of the most common solutions to this problem is to use a service provider.

59.3.2.3 Reciprocal Agreements. Reciprocal agreements were often used in the earlier decades of disaster recovery planning but are uncommon today. A reciprocal agreement is an arrangement between two or more companies in which each agrees to make excess capacity available to the others in case of a disaster. The major advantage is the apparent low cost of this solution. The major disadvantage is that these arrangements rarely provide the needed computing power. A major issue with these arrangements is maintaining compatible systems. If one company changes a processor, it may find that its partners' systems cannot perform adequately, even in degraded mode. If the host company faces a crisis or deadline of its own, a reciprocal company may find itself with no computer power at all. These arrangements are seldom testable, because it is the rare company willing to shut down operations to help a partner perform a disaster recovery test.

59.3.2.4   Internal Redundancy.   A strategy of internal redundancy requires that a business have multiple facilities, geographically dispersed, with similar equipment in each site. If there are data centers at several sites, then the alternate data centers may be designed with excess capacity to support a potential failure at another site.

The major advantage of internal redundancy is that the organization maintains complete control of all equipment and data, without relying on any outside company to come to its aid. The excess capacity at the various alternate sites must be carefully protected, and management must exercise diligence in budgeting and operations. Careful intracompany agreements must be crafted to ensure that all parties are aware of, and agree to, the backup arrangements. Internal redundancy can be an effective solution in cases where temporarily degraded processing still can provide sufficient support to meet timeline requirements. If degraded performance is not an acceptable option, then the cost of the excess capacity will probably be too high. If reasonable degradation is acceptable, then those costs can be manageable.

Internal redundancy can also be difficult to test. Testing requires that processing be shifted to a recovery mode. Unlike external, separate computers, all of these redundant systems would be operational. Testing one disaster recovery plan requires affecting a minimum of two corporate locations. A failed test that causes a system crash or other problem can have damaging consequences.

Internal redundancy can overcome its difficulties if the redundancy is part of a load-balanced system with automatic or semiautomatic failover. In such cases, normal processing is already split between the primary and backup system so that both systems are fully operational at all times. The recovery requirements add an additional dimension to the nominal load-balancing configuration. Namely, there can be no system or system component that is unique to only one site. The most common load-balancing implementations may still rely, for example, on a database housed at only one site. This is insufficient for recovery purposes. If full duplication can be achieved, then the sudden loss of one of the systems causes degradation rather than loss of functionality. There are, however, often technical issues that many organizations must overcome prior to the implementation of such load balancing with full redundancy. For example, some legacy systems do not support multiple points of processing; some modern implementations may require a single database instead of multiple, overlapping databases, as is required for full load balancing with redundancy.

59.3.2.5   Mobile Data Centers.   Mobile data centers are transportable units such as trailers outfitted with replacement equipment, air conditioning, electrical connections, and all other computer requirements. Mobile data centers are used most often for recovery of midrange and PC LAN systems. The primary advantage of the mobile data center is that it can be activated quickly at reasonably low cost. The primary disadvantages are the expense of testing such a facility and the possibility that a local or regional disaster will prevent successful activation. Deploying a mobile data center requires careful planning. Land must be available to accommodate the transportable units, with outside parking lots as the most common resource. Local government and municipal regulations must be researched in advance to ensure that such units do not violate ordinances, and can arrive as certified for immediate occupancy. External power and communications hookups also must be available.

59.3.2.6 Priority Replacement Agreements.

Some computer vendors support priority equipment replacement agreements. These are arrangements in which the vendor promises to ship replacement equipment on a priority basis. For midrange systems, this is often an agreement to send the next-off-the-line system to the priority customer. The major advantage of this strategy is its low cost. However, if the vendor is not currently manufacturing the required system, or if the assembly line is down for any reason, and if equipment stocks are depleted, there may still be a significant delay in receiving the equipment. This is the major disadvantage. This strategy also assumes the disaster recovery plan makes an alternate facility available in case the primary facility is damaged along with the equipment being replaced.

59.3.2.7 Commercial Recovery Services.

Commercial recovery service providers can support a combination of the strategies just discussed. These companies generally provide three major benefits: cost sharing, reduced management needs, and diminished risk of obsolescence. First, they spread facility costs across multiple subscribers so that each subscriber saves as compared with building and maintaining a comparable, privately held capability. Because all subscribers share the same physical space, each pays less than would be needed to maintain such a site independently.

The second major benefit of using a commercial provider is that these companies eliminate the need for the subscriber to manage backup resources. Management and maintenance of such a site by an individual business could be a heavy burden, but the provider's primary focus is on managing, maintaining, and upgrading the equipment and sites. The subscriber company can be assured that the equipment is exercised and serviced regularly and that peripheral equipment, power systems, and facility support structures are properly maintained. A properly run site will also provide security, safety, compliance with evolving rules and regulations, and competent staffing. The provider assumes full responsibility for these functions during normal operations and continues support during times of crisis. The subscriber brings its technical personnel, while the provider leaves its facilities staff in place.

The third major benefit centers around today's fast pace of hardware evolution. A subscriber company typically leases a hot site or other service for a five-year period. During that time, hardware platforms will evolve. The subscribing company can protect its lease investment by ensuring that system upgrades are reflected in the leased equipment configuration for reasonable extra charges. A business that provides its own hot site must upgrade the hot site whenever hardware, and sometimes software, changes are made to the operational systems.

The disadvantage of commercial recovery services is in the obvious risk that the hot site may not be available in an emergency. Indeed, if a local or regional disaster affects numerous subscribers, there could be significant contention for the provider's resources. To address this issue, providers typically maintain hot sites in geographically dispersed areas. Although it is likely that in the case of a local or regional disaster a

EXHIBIT 59.7   Strategy Overview

Strategy	Activation	Cost	Testability	Availability	Reliability
"Ideal strategy"	Fast	Low	Excellent	High	Excellent
Reserve systems	Fast	Low	Excellent	High	Excellent
Internal redundancy	Fast	Medium	Poor	Medium	Good
Commercial providers	Fast	Varies	Excellent	High	Excellent
Hot site	Fast	High	Excellent	High	Excellent
Mobile data centers	Medium	Low	Medium	High	Good
Reciprocal agreements	Slow	Low	Poor	Low	Poor
Priority replacement	Slow	Low	Poor	Low	Poor
Cold site	Slow	High	Poor	High	Poor

subscriber would need to use a hot site farther away than planned, it is unlikely that the subscriber would be left completely without the prearranged resources.

59.3.2.8   Reserve Systems.   The newest of strategies is the reserve system, which is a small replica of a portion of an operational system meant for use during the first few days following a disaster. The reserve system provides continuation of key functions for short durations, although in degraded mode. The reserve system usually resides off site at an employee's home or at another corporate office. Another version of the reserve system is also kept on site. A reserve site may be equipped with a microcomputer or a minicomputer ready to assume functioning in case the primary system becomes unavailable. This meets the important criteria of a reserve system, which must be fast and easy to activate, simple to move, low in cost, testable, available, and highly reliable.

The reserve system concept was not feasible until client/server technology emerged and telecommuting with high-speed communications became accepted and readily available. Many large organizations provide employees the option of telecommuting on a regular basis so that they work at home sometimes and in the office at other times. Web-centric processing and remote application server technologies can provide powerful reserve systems for disaster recovery.

Proper security precautions must be taken to protect proprietary, confidential, and critical information stored on these reserve systems. Strong encryption protects against theft, while redundant systems protect against other losses. The reserve system is a quick-response, short-term solution intended to solve the problem of immediate continuation, even in the case where employees may be unable to travel outside their immediate residence areas. See Exhibit 59.7 for an overview of different recovery strategies.

59.3.3   Data Backup Scenarios and Their Meanings.   Data backup is a key function in all system installations. The best recovery strategy, chosen to meet recovery timelines according to the BIA, is useless without a backup from which to restore and resume operations. Data backup is perhaps the single most critical element of a disaster recovery plan, yet only 31 percent of U.S. companies have backup plans and equipment. See Chapter 41 in this *Handbook* for details of backup scenarios.

59.4   DESIGNING RECOVERY TASKS.   The disaster recovery plan becomes an operating document when the strategies and reserve capabilities are translated into specific actions to be performed during the disaster recovery process. These are the actions required to protect assets, mitigate damage, continue partial operations, and resume full operations. Most tasks begin with actions to evaluate the disaster and then to initiate recovery procedures. The example recovery task flow (Exhibit 59.8) lists a series of steps to evaluate the situation. These steps, numbered 1 through 5, determine whether to declare a disaster or not. The second set of steps, numbered 6 through 10, is used to initiate recovery procedures. These first two sets of steps are called the beginning sequence.

The beginning sequence leads to full activation of a disaster recovery effort. The next set of activities, called the middle sequence, institutes the actions necessary to perform business continuation and recovery. Usually multiple choices for the middle sequence correspond to the disaster scenarios developed. Each path in the middle sequence is executed for a particular scenario. At the end of the middle sequence, full operations are resumed as specified in the disaster recovery plan. In the exhibit, the middle sequence includes two distinct paths. The first path includes steps numbered 11 through 20, and the second path includes steps numbered 21 through 30.

The end sequence begins with damage assessments and continues through resumption of normal operations in the original facility, a semipermanent facility, or a new facility. The end sequence may begin while the middle sequence is still unfolding. The timing is dependent on the requirements specific in the BIA. The end sequence consists of two sets of activities performed in sequence. The first set consists of steps 31 through 38, and the second set consists of steps 39 through 59.

59.4.1 Beginning Sequence.

The beginning sequence (Exhibit 59.9) helps the disaster recovery team in its first two major actions: evaluation of the emergency and initiation of the recovery procedures. Box 1, labeled "Disaster Evaluation," begins the process with a set of actions whose end goal determines what actions to take to meet the upcoming emergency. In step 2, the disaster recovery team determines which course of action to take: continue normal operations, disrupt operations for a short while and then resume normal operations, or initiate a full- or partial-scale disaster recovery. The decision is based on a set of predetermined criteria.

Box 2 is labeled "Evaluate Emergency." This is the step in which the disaster recovery team assesses the expected duration and extent of the upcoming or existing outage. Using a set of criteria developed as part of the BIA, and based on the assessment of the outage, the team determines which course of action to take. For example, if the emergency is a power outage, the disaster recovery team will likely call the power utility to determine the cause. If the outage is expected to last less time than the shortest recovery requirement, then it may make the most sense simply to disrupt operations for a short time without initiating recovery procedures. The comprehensive disaster recovery procedures provide sufficient guidance in a simple form to support the team's decision-making process while leaving room for real-time evaluation and decision making.

If the decision is to initiate disaster recovery procedures, then the flow proceeds through box 5, "Initiate DR Procedure," to the initiation phase represented by the actions in boxes 6 through 9. In step 6, the disaster recovery team determines which of the disaster scenarios applies; the team formally declares that type of disaster in step 7, and notifies, in step 8, the disaster recovery team and others, as required, of the decisions made and the next steps to take. All members of the team are pretrained and equipped with written procedures that anticipate each of these potential decisions. The only remaining step in the beginning sequence is box 9, "Manage Legal Issues." From the moment a disaster situation is considered, the team must document its decisions.

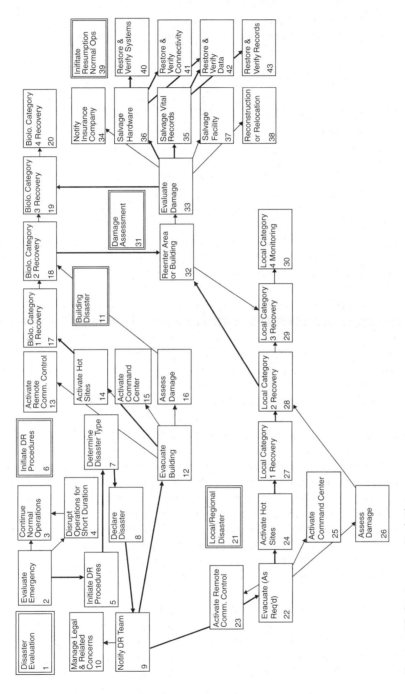

Exhibit 59.8 Recovery Task Flow

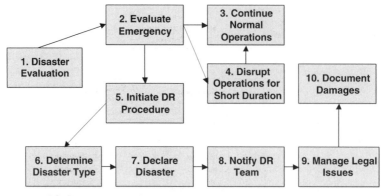

Exhibit 59.9 Beginning Sequence

In some industries, this is required by regulatory agencies; in public companies, it may be required for reporting to a board of directors' committee meeting. For all companies, it is important to maintain a clear record of the diligence used in planning and implementing recovery.

In addition to legal concerns, there are insurance concerns. Typically, money spent during the recovery process is reimbursable by insurance policies. This includes out-of-pocket expenditures by staff; the cost of travel, food, and lodging vouchers; and other allowed expenditures for meeting disaster recovery needs. In its haste to restore damaged systems, the team may neglect to document specific damages; once repaired, it is difficult to submit an insurance claim unless the damage is documented properly. Box 10 represents a step that begins early and continues throughout the disaster recovery process.

59.4.2 Middle Sequence.   The middle sequence represents the activities that begin once the disaster recovery procedures are under way. In our example, there are two possible paths for the middle sequence to follow. The steps are labeled similarly, but the specific actions taken are quite different. There is an advantage to using a schematic representation of the steps and their relationships: The overall structure or shape can show at a glance the complexity or simplicity of the plan. It is best to be as uncomplicated as possible, even if the form and structure require larger content. Exhibit 59.10 describes the middle sequence, "Building Scenario."

The first step listed in the middle sequence, Building Scenario, is to evacuate the building. Although this is clearly performed as early as possible, perhaps even early in the beginning sequence, it is presented here for completeness. Human safety is the primary concern of any recovery plan—no employee should ever be allowed to delay evacuation or reenter a building, except in the case of a qualified individual who is helping others evacuate or attempting a rescue attempt. The next four activities occur in parallel. They are represented by boxes 3 through 6, and include activation functions for remote communications, the hot sites, and the command center. These four steps also include a first effort at damage assessment.

Box 3 is labeled "Activate Remote Communications Control." This is the activity that reroutes digital and analog communications from their normal patterns to their emergency routes. This may include telecommunications lines, call center toll-free lines, normal business lines, data lines, and other communications media. Typically, arrangements are made in advance with the various telecommunications carriers so that

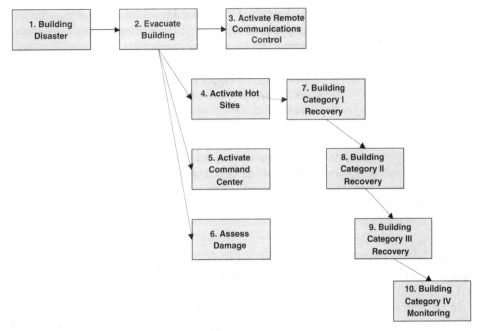

EXHIBIT 59.10 Middle Sequence, Building Scenario

a series of short phone calls can initiate the rerouting. If arrangements were not made in advance, then the rerouting will not meet timeline requirements, and may significantly impair the efficiency of the disaster recovery team members.

Box 4, "Activate Hot Sites," represents the sets of actions required to inform the hot site provider that a disaster is in progress. Hot site activation must be performed at the earliest moment, so that the hot site can be available as soon as possible and so that, in cases of contention, the preferred hot site will be available.

Hot site activation usually obligates the company to pay certain activation costs and occasionally a minimum usage cost. If the disaster requires the hot site, then insurance often reimburses the company for related expenses, but if the declaration was erroneous, the company will suffer a financial loss.

The major hot site providers' services are quite reliable. There are few instances of hot site providers failing to meet their obligations, and many stories of near-heroic feats performed to meet customer needs. One provider even abandoned its own operations so that a client suffering from a regional disaster could occupy the provider's corporate space to continue its own operations. Hot site contracts usually include a proviso that in cases of contention, where more than one company is seeking the same disaster recovery space, the provider can send the late declarer to another, equivalent site. This means that the disaster recovery plan must include instructions for multiple hot sites. All maps, directions, instructions, and delivery requirements must be consistent with the assigned hot site location. Clearly, it is in the company's best interest to declare early so that the hot site of choice is obtained. It would be prudent to err on the side of early declaration rather than late declaration, especially in cases of regional disasters.

Boxes 7 through 10 represent recovery of the various categories of functions. It is seldom possible or desirable to recover all functions simultaneously. The BIA determined and documented the timelines for all functions needing recovery. The procedures must reflect that analysis so that functions are in fact recovered "just in time." These four boxes are labeled Building Category Recovery I to IV. Each box represents the full set of procedures required to bring all the functions in each category into operational mode. For example, if there are seven functions in the Category I group, then there will be seven sets of procedures required to implement Box 7. Category I functions usually require special efforts, such as reserve systems. Therefore, each Category I function may require two sets of activation procedures: the first for the reserve system and the second for the hot site.

At the conclusion of the middle sequence, all required functions would have been recovered. It may be that during the beginning sequence a determination was made that the disaster would require only recovery of a subset of functions. A small-scale power failure, for example, may require only Category I functions to be recovered. A weather disaster with no lasting effects may require Category I and Category II functions. This decision is made during the early phases of the recovery, and reevaluated continually throughout the recovery process.

59.4.3   End Sequence.

The end sequence represented in Exhibit 59.11 is the long path back to normal operations. The end sequence consists of two major phases. The "Damage Assessment" set of activities comprises the first phase and includes boxes 2 through 8. The "Initiate Resumption of Normal Operations" set of activities constitutes the second phase and includes boxes 10 through 13. Although there is an assess damage activity at the beginning of the middle sequence, that activity is a quick assessment of damage for the purpose of determining what recovery options need to be activated. This damage assessment activity is a comprehensive evaluation of damage to equipment, facilities, and records.

Box 2 is labeled "Reenter Area or Building." This activity needs supporting procedures to guide disaster recovery team members on what regulatory, municipal, state, and federal authorities control access into damaged facilities. Often access is restricted for long periods of time even when there is little or no apparent damage. For example, following an earthquake, structural engineers may tag a building as uninhabitable pending further analysis. As another example, after a fire, the fire marshal may prohibit entry pending analysis by chemical engineers to determine whether the fire produced

Exhibit 59.11   End Sequence

hazardous materials. Fires often cause chemical reactions that transform normal, benign office materials into toxic chemicals. The procedures for box 2 should provide contact information for each major agency that may control the facility after a disaster.

Box 3 leads to five parallel activities. The first, "Notify Insurance Company," is related to the "Manage Legal and Other Concerns" activity in the beginning sequence. In this case, the various insurance carriers will need to send their own adjusters and engineers to help assess the damage.

The procedures for box 4 should provide the disaster recovery team with specific contact information for all insurance carriers with which the company has policies in force. The insurance company must be given the opportunity to investigate the premises before any salvage, repair, or cleanup operations begin. Unlike the period immediately following a disaster, when some cleanup may be required for safety and health reasons, the insurance company will look very unfavorably at any attempt to disturb the scene prior to it inspections. This does not mean that facility repairs must await a leisurely investigation and inspection by the insurance company; there are immediate steps to take to make preparations for salvage and repair. The procedure for box 4 will aid the disaster recovery team in deciding what they can do immediately, how they can document status prior to repairs, and what must await the approval of the insurance company and others.

Boxes 5 through 7 are the control procedures for salvaging hardware, records, and the facility. The procedures for "Salvage Hardware" must contain all the contact information for hardware vendors, including computer, communications, reproduction, and others. Each type of equipment requires different salvage operations; the best procedure for a computer may, for example, be the worst procedure for a magnetic tape drive. The salvage procedures should provide general guidelines and contact information for quick access to salvage experts. The same is true for facility salvage procedures.

Salvaging vital records is a complex and unpredictable process. For some records, drying is the top priority; for others, getting them into oxygen-free containers is far more important. The procedures supporting the "Salvage Vital Records" activity must provide contact points, general instructions, and guidance for making decisions about salvage possibilities. Unlike hardware, where the salvage decision is usually driven by cost considerations alone, salvaging vital records and legacy materials may be driven by other factors, such as corporate legacy and history considerations or legal issues. The salvage decision is often much more subjective in this area.

Box 8 is labeled "Reconstruction or Relocation." This task differs from the other tasks in three important ways. First, it is likely that the members of the disaster recovery team will not have the required authority to make this decision but will play an important role in presenting analyses to the decision-making top management people. Second, there are no specific company-external contacts to be made by the disaster recovery team as a part of this process. Although a real estate agent may be contacted for information, it is not likely that the disaster recovery team will undertake that task. The third difference is that the result of this activity is not some specific observable process but a set of recommendations made to top management. The procedures built to support this activity should provide guidance to the disaster recovery team so that they can develop the analyses and present the results in a timely fashion.

Box 9 represents the last phase of the disaster recovery process, initiating the process that returns operations to a normal operating environment. At the time the plan is written, there is no way to predict whether by following this step the company will be relocating to a new facility, or making minor repairs or none, and returning to the existing facility. The importance of these last steps is that they confirm the operability of the newly restored and operational systems. Each of these activities needs to be supported by a set of procedures that guide qualified personnel in their tasks of restoring and verifying systems, networks, data, and records.

59.5   IMPLEMENTATION AND READINESS.   The final steps in preparing the disaster recovery plan are proving that the plan works and ensuring that the people understand their roles. This is performed through rehearsals, walk-throughs, and testing. Once the plan is completed and all of the reserve systems and capabilities have been installed, it is time to test whether these backup systems work as planned. There are a variety of testing phases, starting with extremely limited tests performed separately from ongoing operations and proceeding through full tests using live data.

The first set of tests is intended to prove that specific functions and capabilities are in place and available for use. These are the on-site and off-site limited tests, whose goal is to segregate tasks into small groups of related functions. With only a few functions per tests, there can be many tests that, in the aggregate, prove that each required function is successfully represented in the suite of recovery capabilities. The on-site portion of these tests will "disconnect" the users from normal operating capabilities such as LAN, WAN, and support staff.

This is best accomplished by setting up a testing room within the facility, but away from operations. Users are given the tools and instructions they would receive during a real disaster, and they attempt to perform their designated disaster recovery functions. An example of such a function is emergency payroll operations, where the outsource company is notified that this is only a test or the backup company facility is put on notice that a test is in progress. The tests would determine whether off-line systems were able to process and transfer data as expected. It also may demonstrate that manual procedures work as written. In this testing, the keys are to set test objectives in advance, monitor test progress, ensure that users have only the expected disaster recovery tools at their disposal and no others, and document the results. After the on-site tests prove satisfactory, these same basic, limited procedures should be followed off-site as they would be during an actual emergency. This requires some employees to stay away from the office, so the tests should be planned to avoid periods of expected high activity.

Once the functions have been tested, the next set of tests is intended to prove that the technical systems can be made operational in the planned time frame and that the systems can support users as expected. Two types of tests accomplish this: off-site network tests and hot site tests. These are discussed together because they are often overlapping capabilities performed at the same time. The off-site network and large-system hot site tests demonstrate that the systems and networks can each be restored within the time allotted and that the interface between them survives the transition to hot site operations. One of the primary advantages of performing the off-site network and hot site tests concurrently is that connectivity and intersystem functionality can be demonstrated.

The last test is a full operations test that attempts to show that all of these elements will work together. Just as in a real emergency, the test will focus on a subset of normal operations. Critical functions are tested first, and other functions are added according to the recovery timeline. For these operations, a test disaster is declared. Employees are notified that this is a test and that they are to cease normal operations and immediately implement their recovery procedures.

Most disaster recovery tests use simulated data or backup data that are real but are not the operational data. Changes made and transactions recorded during such tests are never brought back into the operational environment. Processing performed during the test is based on simulated business operations, with "representative" transactions rather than real ones. In the past decade, there has been a trend toward making final full operations tests online, using actual backup sites, systems, and procedures for processing real transactions. This makes the test process significantly more exciting, with a corresponding increase in stress, for employees and management. Mistakes made in this type of testing can cost the company dearly, but success can assure the company of a recovery plan that is much more likely to succeed during a real crisis.

Employees participating in full operations tests, using real data, are going to be much more serious, but employee rewards are also greater. There is more of a feeling of accomplishment if the test processed live data rather than simulated data. After the test, employees can return to work without needing to catch up on missed work. Management is also more likely to be directly involved in a live test than in a simulated test—because in a real test, management will be called on to make real decisions. They are more likely to be present, just as they would be during a real emergency. Not all organizations are structured in such a way as to make live tests possible. When they can be used, they are the most valid test of the recovery plan. However, they should never be attempted until the plan has been proven using multiple instances of the full complement of tests that should precede the live test.

59.6 CONCLUDING REMARKS.   Over the past three decades, the very nature of the threats we considered, and the preparations we made, have changed dramatically. In the early days, major fears included equipment failures and minor geographic events, such as storms and small floods. In the event of a major catastrophe, we felt confident that our plans would unfold as well as those of our neighboring companies; perhaps there would even be some cooperation between companies.

In the decade of the 1990s, however, the criticality of systems combined with an upsurge in man-made disasters forced us to rethink our practices, scenarios, and procedures. The first bombing of the New York World Trade Center in 1993, the bombing of the Murrah Federal Building in Oklahoma City in 1995, the damage to the Pentagon and the heinous destruction of the World Trade Center twin towers in 2001, as well as attacks and failed attempts worldwide since then have finally led us to the point where we must include "artificial" disasters in our planning as well as natural ones. The disaster recovery planner must now consider disasters and recovery scenarios that include terrorism as well as tornadoes. The task is difficult, but the techniques and technologies are the same as before.

59.7 FURTHER READING

See Chapter 58 in this *Handbook* for a list of suggested readings.

CHAPTER **60**

INSURANCE RELIEF

Robert A. Parisi, Jr. and Nancy Callahan

60.1 INTRODUCTION. This chapter presents an overview of traditional insurance products and discusses how they may or may not provide coverage for the risks associated with intellectual property and with computer and network security. It also addresses the new types of coverage that have been developed expressly for those risks.

60.1.1 Historical Background. Historically, people have responded to the risks associated with commerce by finding ways to lessen their impact or severity.

- Around 3000 BCE, Chinese merchants cooperated by distributing cargo among several ships prior to navigating dangerous waterways, so that the loss of one ship would not cause a total loss to any individual.

- Around 1700 BCE, Babylonian merchant caravans were constantly imperiled by bandits. In addition to any risk management practices they might have employed similar to those of Chinese merchants, the Babylonians opted for a risk transfer approach:

  > Babylonian king Hammurabi developed a code of law, known as the Code of Hammurabi, which codified many specific rules governing the practices of early risk-sharing activities. For instance, the code dictated that traders had to repay merchants who financed trading voyages unless thieves stole goods in transit, in which case debts would be cancelled.[1]

- In addition to the well-known Colossus, the people of Rhodes created the *general average*—an insurance construct that survives to this day. The people of Rhodes were a superstitious lot, and would often attribute the fact that a voyage was not going well to some aspect of the cargo being cursed; once identified, the "cursed" cargo was heaved overboard—much to the chagrin of its owner. In response to this practice, which apparently became a burden on trade, Rhodes developed the general average, whereby all the noncursed stakeholders on the voyage contributed pro rata to making the unlucky soul whole—at least economically.

- Similarly, as Venice rose to power in the thirteenth century CE and began to venture farther afield in pursuit of commercial and political gain, Venetians encountered such diverse problems as spoilage, pillage, and piracy. The clever Venetians established the practice of pooling their funds and then indemnified any losses from that fund—essentially creating the first mutual insurance company.

- Finally, during the late seventeenth century in London, as international commerce grew, there developed the modern approach to risk transfer, whereby disinterested third parties put up financial capital against the likelihood of a loss of a ship or cargo. The third parties, who frequented Edward Lloyd's coffeehouse, were called underwriters because they would literally write their names on posted pieces of paper under the names of the ships they desired to insure.

60.1.2 Growing Recognition of the Need for Insurance.

Network security is not a product, a software application, or a corporate edict. It is a process—a living entity that must evolve and adapt to meet increasing and ever-changing threats. There is no substitute for the combination of a comprehensive security policy and the employment of best-of-breed technology applications.

What has become painfully apparent, to both board members and chief information officers, is that the only network that can be maintained inviolate is one user on one computer—in other words, no network at all. If legitimate business can be done across a real network, then so too can malicious business be done across that network. This awareness is critical to an entity's network security. It should lead the entity to look beyond its technology to the more traditional ways that businesses have employed to manage the risks of simply doing business. A company does not decline to buy fire insurance because it relies on its new sprinkler system; a bank does not refrain from purchasing crime coverage because it has the best locks and guards.

Changes in accounting rules over the past decade have served to bring computer and network security to the fore. More and more companies now have an increasing percentage of their balance sheet assets represented by ones and zeroes in their databases. Companies traditionally have bought insurance to protect against damage or loss of their principal assets: their plant, their fleet of vehicles, and so on. Where do they turn now that these principal assets are the data and information stored in their networks?

The last few years have also seen a proliferation of laws, regulations, and industry practices that affect not just privacy and computer security but corporate governance as well. A company cannot be in compliance with the Sarbanes-Oxley Act (SOX) if it cannot make a definitive statement that its systems are providing accurate financial information—and yet SOX makes no mention of computer security per se.

60.1.3 General Liability Issues. Businesses traditionally have managed the risks they face through the purchase of insurance, principally commercial general liability (CGL) and property policies. The additional risks faced by financial institutions and professional services firms usually were addressed through a mix of fidelity/surety bonds and specialty insurance products, for example, errors and omissions insurance. What they have in common, however, is the fact that all these lines of coverage were created before the widespread, commercial use of computers and networks, especially the Internet. Not surprisingly, these policies often fall short of addressing the complex computer and network security exposures that companies face in the New Economy.

The CGL policy is the most fundamental component of a corporation's insurance portfolio and, not surprisingly, the coverage that receives the most attention upon the prospect of an Internet loss. Originally called *comprehensive general liability*, such policies provide a wide range of coverage for the liability of an insured, because of bodily injury or property damage suffered by a third party as a result of the insured's action or inaction. This coverage, which is explored in greater detail, in Section 60.3 is the situs of coverage for intellectual property (IP) infringement claims—an issue of critical importance today, when so much of a company's worth, even its existence, is based on its rights under patents, copyrights, or trademarks.

The basic CGL policy provides coverage for all sums the insured is legally obligated to pay as a result of bodily injury, property damage, or personal and advertising injury. However, the potential bodily injury associated with information technology is limited.

60.2 INTELLECTUAL PROPERTY COVERAGE. Of critical importance to a company dealing with new technologies is the potential that its new innovation is a variation on existing and protected intellectual property. In such cases, the innovator may be forced to cease production, to obtain a license from the entity that owns the IP at issue, or to seek to have the legal protections of the applicable area of IP invalidated through the courts. Alternatively, the company in possession of protected technology, created through the expenditure of millions of dollars for research and development (R&D), may suddenly find that such technology has been incorporated in the new product of a competitor. The victimized company is faced with loss of market share and, possibly, with a threat to its very existence. It must enforce its legal property rights—either through a license to the offender or by seeking to preclude the use of the technology. In both situations, all parties will be subject to significant legal fees to resolve the issue.

In CGL policies, coverage generally exists (on a defensive basis) for the infringement of a third party's intellectual property. However, the coverage is neither a broad grant nor a particularly effective one. In order to trigger coverage, the infringement must be deemed an offense under the policy's Personal and Advertising Injury section. Even then, coverage is limited by the applicable definitions, exclusions, and the restrictive insuring agreement.

The most current International Organization for Standardization (ISO) language for the ISO CGL form CG 00 01 (July 1998) provides:

COVERAGE B. PERSONAL AND ADVERTISING INJURY LIABILITY.

1. Insuring Agreement.

   a. We will pay those sums that the insured becomes legally obligated to pay as damages because of "personal injury" or "advertising injury" to which this insurance applies. We will have the right and duty to defend the insured against any "suit" seeking those damages . . ..

By virtue of the use of the defined term—"advertisement"—the form is clear that advertising injury liability coverage is applicable solely to offenses committed in the course of advertising the insured's business.

This grant of coverage is conditioned by caveats that are restrictive in the old economy of brick-and-mortar commerce and all the more troublesome when viewed in context of the Internet. In order to comprehend fully which coverage provisions may or may not exist, it is first necessary to understand how the policy defines the operative terms.

The current CGL policy includes the key term:

"Personal and Advertising Injury" means injury arising out of one or more of the following offenses:

f. The use of another's advertising items in your "advertisement"; or

g. Infringement upon another's copyright, trade dress, or slogan in your advertisement.

As identified herewith, the grant of coverage is limited. There is no coverage for an infringement if it does not satisfy the three-pronged test outlined in *New Hampshire Insurance Co. v. Foxfire:*[2]

1. Advertising activity of the policyholder

2. A claim that falls within one or more of the enumerated advertising injury offenses

3. Causal nexus between the offense and the advertising activity

This test is merely one of several threshold requirements that must be satisfied before coverage will apply. The policy requires that the advertising injury arise out of the covered offense and that the claim seeks damages recoverable under the policy. The question of coverage is further limited by several exclusions that serve to drive home the limited scope of coverage.

Ambiguity in the language of the CGL has created some confusion in the marketplace. The situation worsens when applied to the Internet. More specifically, the exclusion regarding "an offense committed by an insured whose business is advertising, broadcasting, publishing or telecasting" makes the coverage particularly problematic.

If the policyholder specifically operates in the media business, the exclusion's applicability is clear and unequivocal. However, what happens in the more likely scenario where the policyholder is not a multimedia service provider, but merely an e-tailer or someone who maintains an informational Web site? Not surprisingly, there are two schools of thought.

One group, championed by the plaintiff's bar, argues that, unless the policyholder is actively engaged in the business of advertising, broadcasting, publishing, or telecasting as those industries have been traditionally defined, the exclusion is not applicable. This logic rests on the argument that computers and the Internet do not alter the fundamentals of how the world does business.

The second school of thought looks to the way that computers and the Internet have blurred the line between traditional media activities and a company's online presence. By maintaining any presence online, the policyholder's activities now fall within the parameters defined by the exclusion. This position is not readily understood and bears further exploration.

It is rare for a Web site not to contain a banner advertisement, hyperlink to a third party's site, or material imported from sources other than the policyholder's cache of copyrights and trademarks. The presence of such content clearly places the policyholder in the shoes of an advertiser, broadcaster, or publisher. Even the most literal policy interpreter is hard-pressed to differentiate between the newspaper or television network that accepts advertisements and the e-tailer that carries a banner ad.

The applicability of the exclusion becomes less clear when a business carries no banner ads or hyperlinks and contains no material beyond that which has sprung from the corporate mind of the policyholder. The question then becomes one not involving misuse of a third party's content. Does the simple maintenance of a Web site presume a business of advertising, broadcasting, publishing, or telecasting? The logic behind that position argues that the insured, by maintaining a Web site, is effectively sidestepping the services of publishers and broadcasters and doing the job itself.

Finally, another argument considers the manner, speed, and magnitude with which business is conducted via the Internet. The medium of the Internet was never contemplated when the insurance industry drafted the CGL policy. Similarly, premiums charged for CGL policies do not reflect any actuarial data related to the Internet. In fact, the very nature of the Internet lies in direct opposition to most assumptions an insurance underwriter formulates when calculating a premium.

For instance, when a business contemplates launching an advertising campaign, a concept traditionally goes through some preliminary review or in-house analysis. That concept is then taken to an advertising agency, where, among other things, it would be reviewed for general propriety (whether it infringed another's copyright, trademark, etc.). The final product then would be marketed to either the print or broadcasting media, where the publisher would review the advertisement. In granting advertising injury/personal injury coverage, the insurance underwriter assumes the content has gone through similar independent reviews. On the World Wide Web, however, such levels of scrutiny are typically nonexistent.

It is unlikely that this coverage ambiguity will be resolved definitively until more cases reach the courts. Even then, there will be issues surrounding the applicability of boilerplate policy. Several carriers have either clarified the intent of the policy by expressly excluding Internet activity or simplified it by not offering such coverage to those entities that have an Internet exposure. Finally, several companies have addressed the issue by creating a policy that affirmatively covers the risks associated with a company presenting information, be it substantive content or just a banner advertisement.

60.2.1 Loss/Damage to Intangible Assets.
Property damage is generally defined as physical injury to tangible property including all resulting loss of use of that property and loss of use of tangible property that is not physically injured.

Several cases have looked at the nexus between the virtual world and property damage. In a recent case, a large assembler of personal computers purchased disk drives from a manufacturer and subsequently alleged that the disk drives were defective. It did not, however, allege that the defective drives caused any harm to the other components, nor did it claim any loss of use. The manufacturer presented the claim to its CGL carrier, which later denied the claim. In the resultant coverage litigation, the court ruled the claim did not involve property damage because "physical incorporation of a defective product into another does not constitute property damage unless there is a physical harm to the whole."[3] The implication is clear: The mere fact that a piece of hardware or application is defective will not trigger coverage based on an argument of property damage. The importance of this distinction cannot be underestimated. This issue will be emphasized further in Section 60.2.10 when first-party coverage is explored as a result of similar direct loss.

The more critical and interesting issue is whether damage to or loss of computer data is property damage. Generally, courts that have looked at the issue have held that loss of data in isolation does not constitute damage to tangible property.[4] This position is under attack.

60.2.2 Intellectual Property Policies.
As a result of the emerging importance of technology and the increased financial recognition of intangible assets, various insurance products have been developed to fill the void.

These policies fall within three general types:

1. Third-party liability
2. Prosecution or abatement
3. First-party liability/loss

The most common forms of insurance coverage available for IP are third-party liability policies, including policies offering errors and omissions or professional liability coverage. In these policies, coverage can be found for an insured's liability to a third party for infringing on that party's IP rights. There is a limitation on this coverage, though. Coverage usually is conditioned on the infringement being part and parcel of the insured rendering the service that is the basis (or trigger) of the coverage. Additionally, coverage usually is restricted to claims for copyright or trademark infringement and generally carries express exclusions for trade secrets and patents.

This sort of coverage is written either on a claims-made or occurrence basis. Traditionally, firms that provide content (e.g., advertising agencies, media firms, and publishing companies) have found coverage copyright and/or trademark infringement in multimedia liability policies that are written on an occurrence basis. The policy covers an insured for claims arising out of wrongful acts that occur during the policy period. In contrast, most other errors and omission/professional liability policies are written on a claims-made basis. They provide coverage for claims made and reported to the carrier during the policy period. The two types of policies can be distinguished further by the fact that claims-made policies may provide coverage for wrongful acts of the insured that occurred prior to the policy period, often dating back several years.

Firms looking for more explicit coverage for IP infringement claims, including coverage for trade secrets and patents, must look to policies with the sole purpose of providing such coverage.

60.2.3 Claims Made versus Occurrence Coverages.
Insurance policies generally fall into one of two types: claims-made or occurrence based. The differences in such policies are relatively simple to grasp.

An occurrence insurance policy provides coverage for claims that are made at any time so long as the wrongful acts that form the basis of the claim occurred during the policy period. As such, a one-year occurrence policy that was effective January 1,

2010, would respond to any claim relating to covered wrongful acts that occurred after January 1, 2010, and before January 1, 2011.

It generally does not matter if the claim is made long after the policy has expired. Traditionally, some CGL and most media liability policies have been written on an occurrence basis; this group of policies is often the first line of defense for claims of copyright and trademark infringement.

A claims-made insurance policy provides coverage for claims made during the policy period, regardless of when the wrongful acts giving rise to the claim occurred. Using the previous 1999–2000 example, a claims-made policy would respond to a claim made against the policyholder only during the policy period, even if the wrongful acts complained of occurred several years prior to the inception of the policy. Nearly all professional liability/errors and omissions policies and some CGL policies are written on a claims-made basis. Nearly all policies that offer express and specialized coverage for IP infringement liability are written on a claims-made basis.

How the occurrence/claims-made distinctions apply to the exposures created by the Internet is generally of interest only to insurance brokers and underwriters. Some insurance companies have taken the approach that the Internet is entirely a media risk and, as such, should be addressed by occurrence-based coverage. In contrast, other carriers view the exposure as entirely based in the services a Web site provides, even if those services are media related and offer only claims-made coverage to Internet businesses. Still another, smaller group of insurance carriers has taken the approach that the Internet presents risks that are best served by both types of coverage and have offered blended policies.

The benefits of occurrence versus claims-made policies really depends on whether the claimant is likely to discover and assert its claim soon after the wrongful act, and whether the policyholder has any existing insurance coverage that will respond to potential claims from its prior actions.

60.2.4 Duty to Defend versus Indemnity.   Those policies providing express coverage for IP are written on both a duty-to-defend and an indemnity basis. The differences between the two types of coverage are less subtle than the claims-made/occurrence distinction, although the two share some of the same history.

Generally, most third-party liability policies written by domestic insurance companies today obligate the insurance company to defend the policyholder so long as the asserted claim alleges facts that might reasonably be expected to result in coverage under the policy. Different jurisdictions take different views on how to interpret that duty and its trigger. The question is the subject of no small amount of case law and legal analysis. For the purposes of this discussion, it need merely be noted that the general duty to defend under the law is broader than the insurer's duty to indemnify the policyholder for damages. So long as a claim alleges arguably covered damages, the carrier will owe a defense.

Some older policies, as well as those offered through Lloyds' of London, are written on an indemnity basis. The practical effect of this is that the policyholder must incur the cost of defending itself and paying damages for which it is held liable. The insured then must seek indemnity or reimbursement, subject to any retention or deductible, from the carrier.

Whether a policyholder is better served by an indemnity or a duty-to-defend policy depends not only on its ability to fund a defense but also on its desire to maintain complete control over that defense. In a duty-to-defend policy, the carrier, subject to the deductible or retention, provides a defense for covered claims from day 1, including designating and appointing defense counsel.

Duty-to-defend policies usually are associated with a pay-on-behalf-of component. This element of coverage obligates the carrier to pay on behalf of the policyholder any covered damages for which the policyholder is held liable, subject only to the applicable deductible or retention.

In the case of an infringement liability policy, the duty to defend is triggered when a claim alleges that an insured has violated or infringed on the IP rights of another in the course of its business or, if more narrowly underwritten, in the course of the expressly designated covered activity. It is important to note that the validity of the claim is often irrelevant to the duty of the carrier to provide a defense.

60.2.5 Who Is Insured?   The typical policy generally provides coverage to the principal or named insured and to subsidiaries of the named insured; the named insured usually is the entity that applied for the insurance and completed the application. Subsidiary coverage traditionally has been limited to actions taken while a subsidiary of the named insured. Coverage also would be provided to any present or former partner, officer, director, or employee of the named insured or subsidiary, but only while acting in his or her capacity as such. Generally it includes the estates, heirs, legal representatives, or assigns of deceased persons who were insureds at the time that the IP infringement was alleged to have been committed, and the legal representatives or assigns of insureds in the event of the insured's incompetence, insolvency, or bankruptcy.

Persons qualifying as insureds under the policy are a potentially large and diverse group. Traditionally, IP infringement liability policies have focused not so much on the *who* but on the *what* of coverage. In this case, the *what* is the scope of the policyholder's business activity for which the insurance carrier has agreed to provide coverage. This can be anything from a single product or service to the entire breadth of the policyholder's operations.

60.2.6 Definitions of Covered Claims.   The value of IP coverage can best be viewed by how it defines a claim. As can be seen by current cases, more often than not, the first salvo fired by a plaintiff is not one seeking damages, but rather one seeking to enjoin the infringer from further infringement. Unfortunately, many policies require that the claimant seek monetary damages before coverage attaches. For coverage to be truly effective, a company should make sure that it would respond to actions seeking:

- A demand for money, services, nonmonetary, or injunctive relief *or*
- A suit(s), including a civil, criminal, or arbitration proceeding, for monetary or nonmonetary relief

Integral to a covered claim is how the policy defines claims expenses. Simply offering coverage for those expenses incurred in defense of an infringement action often gets to only half of an effective defense. To paraphrase the cliché, often the best defense is a strong offense. In order for defensive coverage to be effective, it needs to incorporate coverage for expenses incurred in seeking to challenge the validity of the patent that a company's product or service is allegedly infringing.

60.2.7 Prior Acts Coverage.   The question of prior acts coverage can be a crucial one when the coverage is written on a claims-made basis. A company must consider how long it has been doing what it is seeking to protect. Ideally, coverage should go back to the inception of the company; unfortunately, such broad coverage is not always available. Carriers often limit coverage to a discrete number of years prior to policy inception—the time when the policyholder instituted certain internal IP controls and/or when it began the activities for which coverage is sought.

Prior acts coverage is not an issue for policies written on an occurrence basis, since, by definition, they provide coverage only for acts that occur within the policy period.

60.2.8   Extensions of Coverage.   Most IP insurance policies currently available are written to cover only a specific type of IP infringement, chief among them the patent infringement policy. The typical company, assuming that such an entity even exists, does not have the luxury of being sued only for an isolated activity. It is more probable that a company, by its very existence, will create potential exposures across the entire spectrum of intellectual property. As such, companies need coverage that will respond to an allegation of more than just patent infringement.

Several insurance carriers offer coverage options that address this range of IP risks in a single policy form. Other carriers have addressed this issue by endorsing only that coverage that the company specifically requests. The most common coverage extensions available are for copyright and/or trademark infringement.

60.2.9   Common Exclusions.   The most common exclusions in third-party liability coverage generally relate to intentional or criminal activities. Several policies contain absolute exclusions when the infringement is willful or intentional. Other carriers soften the impact by providing a defense until the prohibited conduct is proven. Even then it is possible that coverage will apply to those insureds under the policy that did not know of or participate in the willful conduct.

Along similar lines is the exclusion for punitive or exemplary damages. Historically, such damages have been excluded as a matter of course. Recently, however, some carriers have offered coverage for awards of such damages to the extent that to do so is not against public policy or otherwise against the law.

Other common exclusions track with the principle that liability insurance is meant to cover fortuitous risks. They include claims arising out of breach of contract, antitrust activities, and infringements that existed prior to the inception of the policy. The policies are meant to cover unforeseen risks, not known claims or the cost of doing business.

60.2.10   First-Party Coverage and Other Key Provisions.   One breed of coverage differs by its very nature. This *first-party coverage* reimburses the policyholder for the loss of the value of its IP after it is declared invalid (patents) or misappropriated (trade secrets). In addition, coverage is available in the market for a policyholder's loss of a trade secret resulting from a computer attack.

At the moment, the number of carriers offering such coverage is very limited, and the underwriting is, in a word, intense. The first coverage is called patent validity coverage, which indemnifies buyers and/or sellers of patent rights for loss related to the patents subsequently being declared invalid or held unenforceable. Such coverage can be tailored to the premium that the company wants to pay. The basic coverage pays up to the purchase price of the patent rights. Expanded coverage pays for the loss of expected royalty income. This coverage is limited to patent only.

Another recent innovation provides first-party coverage for loss of a company's trade secrets. At least two Internet-focused policies also provide first-party coverage to a policyholder for the loss of its trade secrets. These policies provide coverage for the assets a policyholder has decided to treat as a trade secret. The policies generally require that the trade secrets be misappropriated through some deficiency in the security of the policyholder's computer system.

60.3 PROPERTY COVERAGE.   Of particular importance to any commercial entity that values its information is the protection, or lack thereof, afforded under existing property policy forms. Traditionally, such policies provide coverage for the direct financial loss suffered by the policyholder for *damage to or loss of use of* an entity's physical or tangible property as a result of such brick-and mortar-perils as fire, windstorm, theft, and the like. This form of property policy is referred to in the insurance industry as *all-risk*; while broader in the scope of the perils it covers, it is still subject to the brick-and-mortar restraint that what is damaged be of a tangible nature.

The realities of the how things work today, and the shift away from a company's worth being largely comprised of physical assets, suggests that such tangible property coverage is no longer adequate or sufficient, in and of itself. In today's economy, the lifeblood of an organization is generally not its buildings and equipment, although the events of September 11 demonstrate how vital such coverage may be. In fact, a fairly standard business model is for a company to have equipment provided to it only virtually, by its Web hosting company or by any number of application service providers. The latter often replace many of the systems that a company would have leased or purchased outright, only a few short years ago.

Such relationships create further problems for the traditional property policy. The typical policy provides coverage for tangible property at the physical locations of a business. As such, even if one overcomes the hurdle of whether intangible assets are or are not covered under the policy, it is likely that such property is not resident at the locations covered under the policy.

Often purchased in conjunction with the standard property policy is coverage for loss of income due to a business interruption. This coverage has the same *damage to or loss of use of* trigger, but whereas the basic property policy seeks to indemnify the policyholder for the actual lost or damaged property, business interruption coverage reimburses a policyholder for loss in the form of (1) the loss of net income plus normal operating expenses that continue during the covered interruption; and (2) the necessary extra expense incurred in the effort to continue normal business operations. In addition, coverage often is extended to include contingent or dependent business interruption. This provides coverage for a policyholder if a business that the policyholder depends on is interrupted by a peril covered under the policy, and subsequently causes the policyholder to suspend business as a result.

In today's world, most if not all businesses rely on third parties to maintain some element of their network or computer systems, from the obvious application service provider (ASP), or hosting company (ISP), to the less obvious, but equally vital, outsourcing of network security. The concept of weakest link applies not only to those allowed within a firewall—such as supply chain elements and extranets members—but also to the backbone and infrastructure suppliers. The network or site will be just as inoperative, whether the distributed denial-of-service attacks the business directly or brings down its hosting company or ASP, backup and business continuity plans notwithstanding.

A case in Arizona threw into question much of what the insurance industry felt was well settled on the issue of tangible versus intangible. In *American Guarantee & Liability Ins. Co. v. Ingram Micro, Inc.*,[5] a policyholder sought coverage under a property policy for loss of functionality of its computer systems resulting from the loss of programming information in random access memory due to a power outage. The judge, in finding for the policyholder, based his decision largely on federal computer crime law and his own stated belief that the continued distinction between *tangible* and *intangible* property was pointless.

Not surprisingly, the *Ingram Micro* case has had a galvanizing effect on the legal and insurance community. The policyholder bar has hailed it as a commonsense decision whereas the carriers and the legal community at large have pointed at the holes in the logic, personal opinion, and leaps of faith in the decision. What all can agree on, however, is that it has created an increasing awareness and sensitivity by companies as to their insurance portfolios. Since the *Ingram Micro* decision was never published, it is not binding precedent. In addition, subsequent case law has thrown the *Ingram Micro* decision into question.

The logical extension of increased interaction and dependencies between service providers and clients, as well as between coventurers and simple conversants, is that, increasingly, businesses will come to hold or touch more and more information assets besides their own in their computer system. Such property, like its electronic brethren, tortured judicial logic notwithstanding, will not rise to the level of *covered property*, which generally is limited to tangible property located in or on the policyholder's premises.

It has been suggested that coverage might be found under the property policy pursuant to the *valuable papers and records* extension. The only problem with this argument is that absent express endorsement to the contrary, valuable papers and records are defined as manuscripts and the like, not electronic data or the media used to store or record such data.

There also have been attempts to resurrect the notion that coverage might be found under the *sue and labor* aspect of coverage. This would afford coverage not for the loss itself but for the costs associated with fixing the problem. Much was made of this in numerous cases seeking coverage for year 2000 (Y2K) remediation efforts; these cases have begun to die quiet deaths due in large part to the *known* element of Y2K (the technological equivalent of a burning building in that programmers were well aware of the problem) and the nonevent that Y2K eventually proved to be. The analogy in network and computer security would be to look to one's insurance company to pay for the company's firewall and intrusion detection system.

60.4 CRIME/FIDELITY COVERAGE.   Traditional crime and fraud policies have provided, and do provide, a certain level of coverage for direct financial loss due to computer fraud. These policies, however, have usually been limited to indemnifying a policyholder for loss of *money, securities, and other property.* The policies also can contain limitations as to coverage involving both the intent and the identity of the thief, that is, whether an employee of the policyholder or a third party. However, these policies fall short in protection or indemnification for the theft or misappropriation of information and of intangible assets such as trade secrets, data, and technology—the essential elements of e-commerce.

The policies that do afford express coverage for the loss suffered by a policyholder as a result of a computer crime generally limit the coverage to the loss of intangible property or information assets. They also can include loss that is other than the deprivation of the information asset, such as situations where the crime involves the copying of data. In today's economy, a company can effectively suffer a loss where its information assets are only copied—for example, the disclosure of a client list, business plan, vendor relationship details, and the like.

60.5 E-COMMERCE POLICIES. In the time since the fourth edition of this *Handbook* was published in 2002, the marketplace for ecommerce policies has matured only slightly, with little or no uniformity between the competing products. One thing that the market does seem to agree on, though, is a focus on all industries as opposed to the technology, telecommunications, and financial sectors. The markets offering policies with definitive coverage for information technology, e-commerce, and network security have remained relatively static, though new entrants now come from established carriers as opposed to small start-up entities. What remains important to note is that all of these forms must, and will, continue to change with time as the technology to which they are tied changes and evolves. One need only look back to the early 1990s to find policies that spoke of the infinite channels of the Internet, and information security as part and parcel of the general content-related risks faced by publishers and broadcasters.

These e-commerce policies generally fall into two categories: (1) those that cover damage caused to others by the actions or failures of the policyholder's computer systems and (2) those that cover direct financial loss of the policyholder from certain specified cyber perils.

The most common e-commerce policy is that which would defend and indemnify a policyholder for claims made against it by others for damages allegedly suffered by those third parties. In addition to filling the gaps in traditional policies, such as the CGL policy, such policies also extend new coverage that is peculiar to the needs and exposures of information technology and computer system security.

Typical third-party exposures include the infringement of another's intellectual property, violation of privacy rights, content-based liability such as libel and slander, and professional malpractice. Claims alleging such suffered wrongs are more often than not attributable to acts of negligence by an insured. They also do not differ dramatically from their Old Economy cousins, with the exception of the myriad of privacy issues that recently have come to the fore in the form of general privacy, healthcare, and financial information.

The new exposures or risks that these policies respond to include the damage caused by the transmission of malicious code, the unwitting participation in a distributed denial of service attack as a zombie,[6] and others. These perils also are the triggers for coverage for the direct loss suffered by the policyholder itself in the form of stolen information assets, corrupted data, network interruption, cyber extortion, and so on.

The more robust e-commerce policies must, and will, adapt to the inherent differences between the Old and the New Economy. Policyholders risk finding themselves bare at worst or at best succeeding in forcing a settlement after protracted litigation, when they seek to shoehorn coverage for the unique risks of the Internet into hoary old policies from the days of black-and-white television and the Cold War. Just as new coverages developed around the new exposures of employment practices, so too have new coverages arisen to address the new exposures of a company Web-enabling its business practices.

As these new e-commerce policies cover new risks, the due diligence performed by the insurance carrier in underwriting the risk must break new ground. The few carriers that have taken the time to educate themselves about the risks inherent in computer and network security have turned to computer security professionals to assist in their due diligence. This due diligence generally takes the form of remote penetration testing, an online network security assessment, a full-blown on-site security audit, or some combination. What is important to note is that these activities basically are unrelated to insurance and that they focus exclusively on the computer and network security issues; as such, they represent a true value added to the applicant in the form of an additional set of eyes taking a critical look at its security without the applicant having to pay for it.

In addition, companies recently have begun to develop and market coverage that would allow individuals to cover the damages and costs associated with the loss and repair of their financial or credit identity. Such coverage also has been available to individuals under traditional personal lines policies, such as homeowners' insurance, although that capacity seems to be disappearing as the risks associated with such loss become more widespread and publicized.

Recent events, and like as not future events, will continue to highlight the vulnerability of even the most robust computer and network security. Apart from simply shutting down a business, the only way for a business to operate with the confidence that it will survive a successful computer attack and to instill that same confidence in its trading partners, be they customers or suppliers, is to have that traditional old risk-transfer vehicle, the insurance policy, sitting behind all that technology.

The issue of computer and network security is itself changing as well. Accounting changes, shifts in asset composition, and the leveraging of intangible assets have caused network and computer security to evolve from a technology issue into a management liability issue. That evolution requires that companies address both the efficacy of their technology and the completeness of their insurance portfolio. Of critical importance today, is the issue of privacy.

60.6 PRIVACY AND IDENTITY THEFT EXPOSURES.   Businesses of all sizes across all industries hold both confidential commercial, and personally identifiable, information in their care. Both businesses and consumers can take advantage of insurance to mitigate the consequences of breaches of confidentiality involving personally identifiable information.

60.6.1 Issues for Businesses.   Consumers, employees, clients, vendors, merger partners, and other constituents expect the businesses they entrust with confidential information to safeguard it. When a business fails to do so, the consequences can be severe.

60.6.1.1 Civil/Legal Liability.   Companies may be held legally liable for losses that consumers or other third parties incur if information in their care is compromised or identity theft occurs. Even if a business has sound security practices in place and is not negligent in handling private data, the cost of defending allegations of negligence, and the settlements that often result, can be significant. A few of the many recent scenarios that have put companies at risk follow.

- In June 2005, victims of a massive compromise involving millions of credit card accounts stolen from payment-processor CardSystems Solutions[7] filed a class-action lawsuit demanding damages. Plaintiffs included not only individuals but also retailers affected by the breach.[8] CardSystems was also charged by the Federal Trade Commission (FTC) and agreed to comply with strict standards for security improvements and audits.[9]

- After a hacker stole debit card information in 2006 from TJX Companies, Inc., owners of T.J. Maxx and Marshalls stores across the United States, approximately a dozen banks had to reissue thousands of new cards to customers.[10] The banks sued the retailer for the cost of reissuance and fraud.[11] This case was deemed the largest security breach in history to that date.[12] A settlement agreement was negotiated in 2008 that offered "vouchers, cash benefits, credit monitoring, identity theft insurance, and reimbursements to eligible people affected by the intrusion(s). TJX will also hold a one-time special event reducing prices 15% for one day at T.J. Maxx, Marshalls, T. J. Maxx'n More, Marshalls MegaStore, HomeGoods, A.J. Wright, Winners and HomeSense stores on a future date not yet determined."[13]

60.6.1.2 *Regulatory Issues.*   Various regulatory bodies may bring administrative actions against entities experiencing a privacy breach. Actions may be brought by the Federal Trade Commission (FTC), the Securities and Exchange Commission (SEC), the Commodity Futures Trading Commission (CFTC), state insurance authorities, federal banking agencies, and state attorneys general. Responding to these investigations can require significant managerial and legal expenses. In addition, companies may be forced to undertake lengthy, expensive corrective actions as a result of the investigations and settlements.

Illustrating the impact of a regulatory investigation is the widely publicized case of ChoicePoint, in which a major consumer data broker agreed to pay $10 million in civil penalties and $5 million for consumer redress in January 2006 to settle FTC charges arising from a data security breach. Under the terms of the settlement, the company was also required to implement new procedures to enhance information security and must undergo security audits by a third party every other year for decades. The breach compromised the personal financial records of more than 163,000 consumers and resulted in at least 800 cases of identity theft.[14]

Many states have enacted laws requiring companies to notify consumers if information has been compromised. These laws dictate when a company must give notice and what method of communication must be used. Although requirements vary state to state, costs of notification can run into hundreds of thousands of dollars.

On the federal side, a number of initiatives have been progressing through the House and Senate. At the time of writing (July 2008), the links to the Library of Congress *THOMAS* system[15] provided the following status for significant proposals with possible liability implications for holders of personally identifiable information:

- H.R. 516
  - Title: To increase the security of sensitive data maintained by the Federal Government.
  - Sponsor: Representative Jo Ann Davis [VA-1] (introduced 1/17/2007); Cosponsors (None)
  - Latest Major Action: 3/23/2007. Referred to House subcommittee. Status: Referred to the Subcommittee on Information Policy, Census, and National Archives.
- H.R. 3046
  - Title: To amend the Social Security Act to enhance Social Security account number privacy protections, to prevent fraudulent misuse of the Social Security account number, and to otherwise enhance protection against identity theft, and for other purposes.
  - Sponsor: Representative Michael R. McNulty (NY-21) (introduced 7/16/2007); Cosponsors (53)

- Latest Major Action: 9/24/2007 Placed on the Union Calendar, Calendar No. 210.
- H.R. 4175
  - Title: To amend title 18, United States Code, with respect to data privacy and security, and for other purposes.
  - Sponsor: Representative John Conyers, Jr. (MI-14) (introduced 11/14/2007), Cosponsors (7)
  - Latest Major Action: 12/18/2007 House committee/subcommittee actions. Status: Subcommittee Hearings Held.
- H.R. 4241
  - Title: To prohibit the transfer of personal information to any person or business outside the United States, without notice.
  - Sponsor: Representative Ted Poe (TX-2) (introduced 11/15/2007), Cosponsors (None)
  - Latest Major Action: 1/11/2008 Referred to House subcommittee. Status: Referred to the Subcommittee on Financial Institutions and Consumer Credit.
- S. 239
  - Title: A bill to require Federal agencies, and persons engaged in interstate commerce, in possession of data containing sensitive personally identifiable information, to disclose any breach of such information.
  - Sponsor: Senator Dianne Feinstein (CA) (introduced 1/10/2007), Cosponsors (None)
  - Latest Major Action: 5/31/2007 Placed on Senate Legislative Calendar under General Orders. Calendar No. 180.
- S. 495
  - Title: A bill to prevent and mitigate identity theft, to ensure privacy, to provide notice of security breaches, and to enhance criminal penalties, law enforcement assistance, and other protections against security breaches, fraudulent access, and misuse of personally identifiable information.
  - Sponsor: Senator Patrick J. Leahy (VT) (introduced 2/6/2007), Cosponsors (7)
  - Latest Major Action: 5/23/2007 Placed on Senate Legislative Calendar under General Orders. Calendar No. 168.
  - Senate Reports: 110-70
- S. 1208
  - Title: A bill to provide additional security and privacy protection for Social Security account numbers.
  - Sponsor: Senator Byron L. Dorgan (ND) (introduced 4/25/2007), Cosponsors (None)
  - Related Bills: H.R. 3271
  - Latest Major Action: 4/25/2007 Referred to Senate committee. Status: Read twice and referred to the Committee on Finance.
- S. 1814
  - Title: A bill to provide individuals with access to health information of which they are a subject, ensure personal privacy with respect to health related

information, promote the use of nonidentifiable information for health research, impose criminal and civil penalties for unauthorized use of protected health information, to provide for the strong enforcement of these rights, and to protect states' rights.

- Sponsor: Senator Patrick J. Leahy (VT) (introduced 7/18/2007), Cosponsors (2)
- Latest Major Action: 7/18/2007 Referred to Senate committee. Status: Read twice and referred to the Committee on Health, Education, Labor, and Pensions.

- S. 2454
  - Title: A bill to amend the Communications Act of 1934 to protect the privacy rights of subscribers to wireless communications services.
  - Sponsor: Senator Barbara Boxer (CA) (introduced 12/12/2007), Cosponsors (2)
  - Latest Major Action: 12/12/2007 Referred to Senate committee. Status: Read twice and referred to the Committee on Commerce, Science, and Transportation.

- S. 2859
  - Title: A bill to amend the Family Educational Rights and Privacy Act of 1974 to clarify limits on disclosure of student health records, and for other purposes.
  - Sponsor: Senator Jim Webb (VA) (introduced 4/15/2008), Cosponsors (1)
  - Latest Major Action: 4/15/2008 Referred to Senate committee. Status: Read twice and referred to the Committee on Health, Education, Labor, and Pensions.

60.6.1.3 *Damages to Brand Image, Consumer Confidence.* When private information in a company's care is compromised or stolen, the company can suffer damage to its reputation and a decline in customer and employee confidence. How a company communicates the problem to those affected and manages the aftermath of an incident is critical.

If a company responds to a security breach or a potential security breach with rapid, effective communications and proactive, practical assistance for victims, it can mitigate damage to its public image. Companies that handle private or confidential data must plan, and prepare to mount, an appropriate response, and they must consider the costs such a response will entail.

60.6.1.4 *Special Considerations.* All businesses that handle personal information are exposed to privacy- and identity theft-related liabilities. Certain businesses hold especially sensitive information, and have a particularly pronounced risk. This includes:

- Any company that holds confidential information under a confidentiality agreement.
- Financial services companies that hold information concerning an individual that would be considered *nonpublic personal information* as defined under Title V of the Gramm-Leach Bliley Act of 1999 (Public Law 106-102, 113 Stat. 1338). This definition encompasses all information on applications to obtain financial services, such as credit card or loan applications, bank or credit card account histories, and the fact that an individual is or was a customer of the financial institution.
- Healthcare companies that handle information that could be considered *protected health information* within the Health Insurance Portability and Accountability

Act of 1996 (HIPAA). HIPAA defines protected health information to encompass all *individually identifiable health information* held or transmitted by a covered entity or its business associate in electronic, paper or oral form.

60.6.1.5 Business Insurance for Identity Theft and Privacy Liability.
Specialized insurance allows businesses to manage the significant exposure associated with privacy breaches and identity theft. The insurance addresses the expenses and liability that can result when confidential information in a company's care, custody, and control is disclosed, compromised, or stolen. The same markets that provide e-commerce policies have responded with specialized coverage for privacy breaches. In evaluating this coverage, it is important to note that while the e-commerce policies generally require a computer malfunction of some sort, the privacy liability coverage responds to the claim however the privacy breach occurs—be it a computer glitch, Dumpster diving, or a rogue employee walking out the door with a laptop or paper file. A sound insurance program should provide coverage for:

- **Legal liability and defense costs.** This includes judgments, settlements, and defense fees incurred as a result of civil litigation initiated by consumers, clients, organizations or other businesses.

- **Regulatory action expenses.** This includes legal expenses that result from investigations, negotiation of consent orders, and formal adversarial proceedings instituted by government or regulatory agencies. This is a critical privacy coverage, since the regulatory action will often precede the civil suit. It is in the insured's and insurer's best interests to have a favorable resolution of the regulatory action.

- **Notification costs.** The costs incurred to notify individuals or businesses whose information was compromised or stolen, including costs of mail, e-mail, telephone, or advertising. This is an interesting coverage enhancement, not generally found in other policy forms. It is, however, of growing importance as relates to current and pending state and federal regulations.

- **Crisis communications management expenses.** This includes the cost of public relations counsel to help a company shield its reputation during a pivotal period.

- **Costs of recovery services for victims.** This includes the costs of education, assistance, and credit monitoring for customers, employees, or others whose information was stolen or compromised. Providing these services can help a company to retain customers, maintain employee satisfaction, and prevent costly legal actions in the wake of an incident.

60.6.1.6 Other Commercial Insurance Policies.
Many companies operate with the perception that traditional insurance policies, such as commercial general liability (CGL), directors and officers (D&O) liability, or errors and omissions (E&O) insurance, address privacy and identity theft exposures. However, traditional commercial insurance policies are generally not designed to address risks related to computer networks and electronic information. Citing just one example, CGL policies typically do not define *territory* to align with the global nature of the Internet and do not contemplate the various privacy laws worldwide. They would not normally include expenses associated with victim notification, crisis management, and identity theft recovery either.

In fact, company management and other professionals who rely solely on traditional insurance could be surprised to find they have little or no insurance when a privacy breach or identity theft incident occurs. The specialized privacy and identity theft insurance discussed previously was designed expressly to fill this significant coverage gap.

60.6.2 Issues for Consumers.   Identity theft, defined as the theft and fraudulent use of an individual's personal identification information, including a Social Security number, account numbers, or other personal data, is the fastest-growing financial crime in America. One of every eight adults, or a family member, has been a victim of identity theft.[16] More than 9.3 million individuals were victimized in the United States in 2004.[17]

Identity theft is not only widespread, but it is costly. Individuals use unlawfully obtained personal information to purchase goods and services or to obtain new mortgages, lines of credit, or additional credit cards. A criminal may use a stolen identity to commit employment fraud or to escape criminal prosecution.

60.6.3 Insurance for Consumers.   Consumers in the United States are well protected from the direct financial loss that can result from identity theft. If unauthorized credit card charges and electronic banking transactions are reported promptly, an individual has little financial liability. Still, individuals whose identities are stolen must undertake a time-consuming and often costly process to restore their names and credit. It can take six months to detect identity theft and up to 600 hours to recover from the crime.[18] In some cases, individuals must pay to dispute fraudulent debts and accounts opened by an identity thief.

Insurance can help individuals alleviate the costs associated with the compromise of their personal information and identity theft. This insurance is geared primarily to mitigate the costs of recovering from such incidents and to ease the recovery process. A typical policy might provide:

- **Expense reimbursement,** encompassing numerous fees and expenses required to recover from identity theft
- **Income protection,** which pays wages lost as a result of time off from work required to recover from identity theft
- **Identity restoration services,** including the services of a personal case manager to handle identity recovery work on the victim's behalf
- **Loss prevention and mitigation services,** such as access to a customer service center to assist in preventing identity theft and credit monitoring to promote early detection of problems

Many financial institutions, associations, employers, and service providers make this type of insurance available to customers, members, and employees.[19] Identity theft insurance may also be available to consumers in conjunction with homeowners' or business owners' policies.

60.7 CONCLUDING REMARKS.   The significant exposures resulting from intellectual property and privacy breaches that companies and individuals face today have become serious boardroom concerns. To mitigate against these exposures, a comprehensive insurance program should be a critical component of the risk management strategies put in place. Although insurance for information systems exposures was once considered novel and limited in scope, it has quickly evolved, and new products in the marketplace offer broad and effective protection.

60.8   FURTHER READING

Dionne, G. *Handbook of Insurance*, vol. 22. Huebner International Series on Risk, Insurance and Economic Security. Dordrecht, The Netherlands: Kluwer Academic Publishers, 2000.

Ostrager. B. R., and T. R. Newman *Handbook on Insurance Coverage Disputes*, 9th ed. New York: Aspen Law & Business, 1998.

Sutcliffe, G. S. *E-Commerce Insurance and Risk Management*, 2nd ed. Gainesville, GA: Shelby Publishing, 2001.

60.9   NOTES

1. Norma L. Nielson, "Insurance." *Microsoft® Encarta® 2008* [DVD]. Redmond, WA: Microsoft Corporation, 2007.
2. 820 F. Supp. 489 (N.D. Cal. 1993).
3. *Seagate Technology, Inc. v. St. Paul Fire & Marine Ins. Co.*, 11 F. Supp. 2d 1150 (N.D. Cal. 1998).
4. *Rockford Pharmacy, Inc. v. Digital Simlistic, Inc.*, 53 F. 3d 195 (8th Cir. 1995).
5. D. Ariz. 2000.
6. Zombies are computers that have been taken over by an attacker and used to transmit large volumes of traffic. See Chapters 18, 20, 30, and 41 in this *Handbook*.
7. R. Lemos, "MasterCard Warns of Massive Credit-Card Breach," *SecurityFocus*, June 17, 2005, www.securityfocus.com/news/11219.
8. J. Evers, "MasterCard Data Breach: Lawsuit Demands Damages," Silicon.com, July 7, 2005, http://software.silicon.com/security/0,39024655,39150141,00.htm
9. Federal Trade Commission, "CardSystems Solutions Settles FTC Charges," February 23, 2006, www.ftc.gov/opa/2006/02/cardsystems_r.shtm.
10. T. Lewis, "TJX Sued for Loss of Consumer Data," ConsumerAffairs.com, January 29, 2007, www.consumeraffairs.com/news04/2007/01/tjx_folo.html.
11. R. Lemos, "New England Bankers Sue TJX for Breach," *SecurityFocus*, April 26, 2007, www.securityfocus.com/brief/490.
12. J. Evers, "Revealed: World's Largest Security Breach," Silicon.com, March 30, 2007, www.silicon.com/retailandleisure/0,3800011842,39166613,00.htm.
13. United States District Court for the District of Massachusetts, "The TJX Companies, Inc. and Fifth Third Bancorp.," Case No. 07-10162, 2008, www.tjxsettlement.com/.
14. Federal Trade Commission, "ChoicePoint Settles Data Security Breach Charges; to Pay $10 Million in Civil Penalties, $5 Million for Consumer Redress: At Least 800 Cases of Identity Theft Arose From Company's Data Breach," 2006, www.ftc.gov/opa/2006/01/choicepoint.shtm.
15. Library of Congress THOMAS system for tracking legislation: http://thomas.loc.gov/.
16. K. Gilpin, "Identity Theft affects Millions, Survey Shows," *New York Times*, September 3, 2003.

17. M. T. Van Dyke, ed. "2005 Identity Fraud Report," Javeline Strategy and Research (January 2005).

18. L. Foley and J. Foley, "Identity Theft: The Aftermath 2003," Identity Theft Resource Center (September 2003).

19. M. E. Kabay, "Defending against Identity Theft: LifeLock." *Network World Security Strategies*, March 4, 2008, www.networkworld.com/newsletters/sec/2008/0303sec1.html, and "Defending against Identity Theft: Identity Guard." *Network World Security Strategies*, March 6, 2008, www. networkworld.com/newsletters/sec/2008/0303sec2.html.

CHAPTER **61**

WORKING WITH LAW ENFORCEMENT

David A. Land

61.1 INTRODUCTION. Today, working with law enforcement is likely one of the most important aspects of computer security, and of our collective need to protect our sites and our sites' information. The entire paradigm has shifted to one where you will need law enforcement, and they will most certainly need you. In times past, however, this was not the case. Understanding their needs before, during, and after the commission of a crime significantly enhances your organization's opportunity to come back online quickly, with, it is hoped, little or no disturbance to your users or customers. Likewise, conveying your needs to law enforcement prior to an incident will serve you well later on. Working with law enforcement is, however, not your opportunity to assume the role of law enforcement. You must know your limitations and at what point to engage your law enforcement contacts.

Most organizations, whether they support the corporate or the government sector (.com or .edu), will at some point have a need to meet, or otherwise collaborate with, a local, state, or federal law enforcement or intelligence agency. The term "intelligence agency" is included here to remind the reader that entities, such as the Federal Bureau of Investigation (FBI) and other government departments within the United States, have an intelligence role tied directly to computer incidents or cyber-related investigations. Furthermore, as cyber-related crimes know no geographical bounds, there is also the possibility that investigative agencies of other nations, such as the Royal Canadian Mounted Police and Interpol, might need to become involved. The need for collaboration with any of these agencies is driven by the inevitable reality that at some point, a computer or cyber-related crime will be committed where the computers or information of an organization are the targets of unwelcome attacks.

The goals of law enforcement tend to vary based on jurisdiction and the intended mission of an investigating organization. Where a computer or cybercrime may be of little or no prosecutorial value to one agency, another may find there is indeed value in pursuing. Keep that in mind when making that first contact. Also keep in mind that there is absolutely nothing wrong with selling your company's desire to pursue an investigation to law enforcement. It may be the case that you must do some of the initial investigative legwork to make it more attractive for law enforcement to pursue. Much will depend on the nature of the crime and any losses your organization may have experienced.

These threats may involve external threats from hackers, crackers, phreakers, and the like, or an internal threat involving a trusted employee(s) or a competitor attempting to steal, acquire, or otherwise damage information critical to your organization's viability. Even more likely are issues of fraud, waste, and abuse by an individual who has legitimate and authorized access to organizational networks or computing systems. To address these inevitabilities, it is prudent to examine your organization for potential vulnerabilities and to develop a logical path forward in addressing these vulnerabilities. In the planning process, identify your supporting law enforcement organizations and meet with them in order to put in place some form of memorandum of agreement (MOA). This memorandum should clearly articulate the responsibilities of each entity; creating this document will save everyone a substantial amount of time, avoid potential miscommunications, and ensure that organizational information and assets are handled in an appropriate manner.

61.2   RELEVANT LAWS.   In examining computer crime laws, it is worthwhile to understand which laws, and which law enforcement agencies, are responsible for responding to you or your organization. It is equally necessary to know when the need for law enforcement involvement is warranted and unwarranted. When does a computer crime break a federal, state, or local law? Exhibit 61.1 lists crimes that should be reported whenever they are discovered or when there is any uncertainty as to their status as a crime. Exhibit 61.2 presents a list of activities you should not report.

61.3   PLAN AHEAD.   When you know when and whom to call, dealing with any type of significant cyberincident can be manageable. Leaving things to chance or uncertainty, or assuming that someone else is responsible and will take care of things can leave your organization in a very precarious situation. Know who is responsible for the conduct of a computer-related investigation and, where possible, train for such likelihoods. These efforts can greatly reduce the time from discovery to prosecution.

Report intrusions or attacks on major networks, or those that deal with sensitive data.

If sensitive data such as client financial information, medical records, customer credit card information, social security numbers, and the like has been compromised, you should report it to the authorities. This is also true if the company has government/defense contracts or deals with other types of regulated information. The FBI's computer crime squad investigates major network intrusions and network integrity violations. You can report these types of attacks to federal, state, and local authorities and let them sort out the jurisdictional issues.

Report intrusions or attacks that result in large monetary losses.

The amount of monetary loss often determines whether a theft is considered a misdemeanor or felony. Felony offenses will get more attention from law enforcement agencies when they involve a bank or most any other type of financial institution. The following site enumerates the laws relative to financial institutions and the requirement to report: http://www.fdic.gov/news/news/financial/1997/fil97124.html

Report cases of suspected State-sponsored or Industrial espionage.

If an intruder goes after your company's trade secrets, or there are indications that individuals within your organization are the targets of a foreign intelligence service, this is a serious federal offense that will be investigated by the FBI who maintains the charter for all domestic counterintelligence investigations, and by other government and military agencies.

Report cases involving child pornography.

This is an offense that is taken very seriously by law enforcement. If child pornography was discovered on your company computers and was not promptly reported, you, as network administrator, may be implicated or held liable in a civil lawsuit. The possession of child pornography images on a computer, no matter who is in possession of the computer, is breaking the law and is subject to prosecution.

Report e-mailed or other digitally transmitted threats.

All states have laws against threatening and harassing communications. Physical threats against individuals, terrorist threats, bomb threats, blackmail, and similar electronic communications should be reported to security personnel and local police.

Internet fraud

If one of your users is a victim of "phishing" scams or other fraudulent activities perpetrated by an e-mail or unknown individuals on the Web, this information can be reported to one of many different Federal Agencies. Within the US you can report to the Federal Trade Commission, the FBI, the US Secret Service, the US Postal Service, the National Fraud Information Center, etc. A complete list of US Government and non-Government agencies as well as investigative organizations of other countries can be found at http://www.consumerfraudreporting.org/governments.php

Report suspected terrorist activities.

If you suspect that your network is being used for communications between terrorists, first and foremost do not attempt to investigate yourself. Report suspected activities to the U.S. Department of Homeland Security, or the FBI via the FBI's "tips" Web site.

Exhibit 61.1   Activities You Should Always Report

Source: http://i.i.com.com/cnwk.1d/i/tr/downloads/home/computer_crime_reporting_checklist.pdf.

They can also reduce the potential of having agencies involved that would otherwise not have a need to know (e.g., the local press). (See Exhibit 61.3.)

61.3.1   Federal Bureau of Investigation.   The Federal Bureau of Investigation (FBI) is responsible for the investigation and prosecuting of more than 200 federal statutes. Relative to the cyber world, the FBI has two primary responsibilities:[1] First, it is the lead law enforcement agency for investigating cyber attacks by foreign

▣ Don't report port scanning and similar "non–intrusive" activities.

Although port scanning is often a precursor to intrusion or attack, in most jurisdictions it's not, in itself, a crime. It's more like walking down a hallway in an apartment building and trying each door to see if it's locked. If you find an unlocked door and go inside, that is criminal trespass – but as long as you don't go in, you haven't committed a crime.

▣ Don't report viruses, Trojans, worms, and spyware—at least, not to law enforcement agencies, although there are exceptions.

Malicious software is a huge and ever growing problem that does a great deal of damage and costs companies millions of dollars. However, law enforcement agencies generally don't respond to individual malware reports. While those who release viruses and other malware can be prosecuted under Title 18 of the U.S. Code, prosecutors generally go after developers of malware that is widely distributed and causes a large amount of harm. If you encounter a new variety of malware, check the pages of popular anti-virus vendors and report to them if it isn't already listed. Remember that the sender of a virus often doesn't even know he or she is sending it. However, if you have evidence that a particular person wrote and intentionally released a piece of malware with the intent to cause harm or otherwise destroy data, you should contact local law enforcement or your local FBI cyber crime squad.

Exhibit 61.2   Activities You Should Not Report

Source: http://i.i.com/cnwk.1d/i/tr/downloads/home/computer_crime_reporting_checklist.pdf.

adversaries and terrorists. The FBI also works to prevent criminals, sexual predators, and others intent on malicious destruction from using the Internet and online services to steal from, defraud, and otherwise victimize citizens, businesses, and communities.

The FBI retains jurisdiction over cases involving national security, including counterintelligence and counterproliferation, terrorism, banking, and organized crime. The U.S. Secret Service retains jurisdiction where the Treasury Department is victimized or whenever computers are attacked that are not under the purview of the FBI. In certain federal cases, the Customs Department, the Commerce Department, or a military organization, such as the Air Force Office of Investigations, Naval Criminal Investigative Service, U.S. Army Intelligence, or U.S. Army Criminal Investigation Division, may also have jurisdiction.

In the United States, a number of federal laws protect against attacks on computers, misuse of passwords, electronic invasions of privacy, and other transgressions. The Computer Fraud and Abuse Act of 1986 is the statute governing most common

Exhibit 61.3   Computer Crime Reporting Checklist: Where to Report

---

- **Local/State Law Enforcement:** Call your local police department, county sheriff's agency. Do not call 9-1-1. Ask for the agency's high tech crimes unit or, its smaller investigation division.
- **FBI Computer Crimes Squad**: nccs@fbi.gov or 202-324-9164
- **FBI Tips site**: https://tips.fbi.gov/
- **US Secret Service Form 401—Cyber Threat/Network Incident Report**: http://www.secretservice.gov/net.intrusion_forms.shtml
- **Internet Fraud Complaint Center**: http://www.ifccfbi.gov/index.asp
- **National White Collar Crime Center (NW3C)**: http://www.nw3c.org/
- **FTC Identity Theft Web site**: http://www.consumer.gov/idtheft/index.html

---

Source: http://i.i.com/cnwk.1d/i/tr/downloads/home/computer_crime_reporting_checklist.pdf.

computer crimes, although prosecutions may take place under other laws. The Computer Abuse Amendments Act of 1994 expanded the 1986 act to address the transmission of viruses and other harmful code.

Many of the states within the United States have adopted their own computer crime laws.

According to the Federal Investigative Guidelines,[2] federal law enforcement can gather only proprietary information concerning an incident in four ways:

1. Request for voluntary disclosure of information
2. Court order
3. Federal grand jury subpoena
4. Search warrant

Statutes Relevant to Computer Crime
- Public Law 100-235 (aka Computer Security Act of 1987)
- Public Law 99-508
- Title 18 U.S.C. § 1030, Public Law 99-474
- Title 50 U.S.C. § 783 (b)
- Title 18 U.S.C. § 794 (a)

61.3.2 U.S. Postal Inspection Service.[3]   The U.S. Postal Inspection Service is the federal law enforcement arm of the U.S. Postal Service. Postal inspectors enforce over 200 federal laws in investigations of crimes that may adversely affect or fraudulently use the U.S. mail, the postal system, or postal employees. Many fraud schemes that originate over the Internet, such as auction fraud or multilevel marketing schemes, or that involve payment or delivery via the U.S. mail, are under the jurisdiction of the Postal Inspection Service.

61.3.3 U.S. Secret Service.[4]   The U.S. Secret Service began as a force investigating counterfeit currency; it still enforces all laws relating to "the counterfeiting of obligations and securities of the United States," which includes financial crimes, identity theft, computer fraud, and any computer-based attacks on the infrastructure of the United States. It is worth noting that the U.S. Secret Service is another investigative agency like the FBI. Both agencies work very well together and collaborate on many cyber-related investigations.

61.4 MEMORANDUM OF AGREEMENT.   A memorandum of agreement (MOA) between any organization and any law enforcement agency is a prudent measure. With an MOA in place, both sides of any investigation have a clear understanding of what to expect. Within the MOA, specific points enumerate the breadth and depth of responsibilities.

For those interested, the Department of Justice maintains a list of recent computer crimes cases and who was involved in the litigation: www.usdoj.gov/criminal/cybercrime/cccases.html.

Know your limitations. Know when to call the police or FBI and when to deal with a situation yourself. Discuss the inherent problems on both sides, such as public disclosure.

61.5   HANDLING EVIDENCE AND THE CHAIN OF CUSTODY.   Many different cyber-related investigative agencies and groups can be found on the Web. For seven years, I have been a member of the International Association of Computer Investigative Specialists (http://cops.org), which offers to the public a comprehensive set of directions relative to computer forensics and the collection of electronic evidence. A step-by-step process for the examination and collection of electronic evidence follows.[5]

1. Examine the media, logically and systematically, by starting where the data of evidentiary value is most likely to be found. These locations will vary depending on the nature and scope of the case. Examples of items to be noted might include:
   - If the media is a hard drive, the number and type of partitions should be noted.
   - If the media is an optical disc then the number of sessions should be noted.
   - File systems on the media should be noted.
   - A full directory listing should be made to include folder structure, filenames, date/time stamps, logical file sizes, and so on.
   - Installed operating systems should be noted.
   - User-created files should be examined using native applications, file viewers, or hex viewers. This includes such files as text documents, spreadsheets, databases, financial data, electronic mail, digital photographs, sound, and other multimedia files, and the like.
   - Operating system files and application created files should be examined, if present. This would include, but is not limited to, boot files, registry files, swap files, temporary files, cache files, history files, and log files.
   - Installed applications should be noted.
   - File hash comparisons may be used to exclude or include files for examination.
   - Unused and unallocated space on each volume should be examined for previously deleted data, deleted folders, slack space data, and intentionally placed data. Previously deleted filenames of apparent evidentiary value should be noted. Files may be automatically carved out of the unallocated portion of the unused space based on known file headers.
   - Keyword searches may be conducted to identify files or areas of the drive that might contain data of evidentiary value and to narrow the examination scope.
   - The system area of the volume (i.e., FAT, MFT, etc.) should be examined and any irregularities or peculiarities noted.
   - Examination of areas of the media that are not normally accessible, such as extra tracks or sectors on a floppy disk, or a host-protected area on a hard drive may be required.
   - To facilitate examination of data, including user settings and device and software functionality, the computer may be booted using either a copy of the boot drive or by using a protected program to determine functionality of the hardware and/or software.
   - The forensic software used during the examination should be noted by its version, and should be used in accordance with the vendors licensing agreement. The software should also be properly tested and validated for its forensic use by the examiner or the examiner's agency.

2. At the conclusion of the examination process, provide sufficient notation of any discovered material of an apparent incriminating or exculpatory evidentiary nature.

3. Provide sufficient documentation of all standard procedures and processes initiated, as well as detailed notation of any variations made to the standard procedures.

4. Properly mark any output of the recovered data with appropriate identifiers in accordance with policies from the examiner's agency.

61.6   ISSUES OF LIABILITY.   In examining any media or conducting any cyber-centric investigation, consideration should be given to these areas:

- Proprietary information
- Business-sensitive information
- Export-controlled information
- Downloading copyrighted music or videos
- National defense information

61.7   ASK LAW ENFORCEMENT TO GIVE BACK.   In many situations where law enforcement is notified of an event requiring further investigation, the agency may ask you for everything even remotely connected to the investigation. At the same time, most law enforcement agencies have the ability to give back. They can provide training to key personnel and information on various topics, including identity theft, espionage, equipment theft, access control, and so on.

61.8   THE KNOCK AT THE DOOR.[6]   What do you do if your first indication of a possible security incident is a law enforcement agent appearing at your office with a search warrant? In many cases, nothing could be more unnerving. However, if you have done your homework and you have an established rapport with this law enforcement agency, you have little to fear. You already have a plan in place for just such a situation, and you know the rights and obligations.

Although, under the best of circumstances, stress can still occur, it is important to remain unemotional and to express complete willingness to comply with the search warrant team. Avoid being defensive or giving the appearance that you are trying to hide anything. Offer all assistance possible and take these seven steps:

1. Read the warrant carefully and understand what the search warrant team wants to search or seize.

2. Notify both upper management and the legal department of current events.

3. If the authorities want to search a local machine, the impact on the organization may be minimal. Get the appropriate manager or supervisor to evaluate the impact and to assist the officers in securing the machine. In cases of child pornography, the police will take the entire computer. Work with them to see if backup copies can be made of critical data and programs prior to removal.

4. If a server is the target, see if copies of relevant portions of the hard drives will satisfy the requirements of the warrant. Where it is not possible to do this, involve your server and network administrators to bring down the server in

an orderly fashion. Your plan should also include bringing online any backup server.

5. Rarely will an entire network have to be taken down. Have your network administrator work with law enforcement to ensure orderly access to parts of the network described in the search warrant.

6. After the search and seizure, the team will leave you "an officer's return" regarding what property was seized. Retain this document for review by your legal staff. Make arrangements with the team to follow up with them on the status of your equipment. Offer whatever technical assistance to law enforcement that your legal department deems advisable.

7. Meet with your management, legal counsel, and technical staff after the team leaves to assess the impact of the seizures on your operations. Also, consider what actions need to be taken for continued operations.

61.9   KEEPING YOUR OPERATION RUNNING DURING AN INVESTIGATION.

Any investigation that involves a continued law enforcement presence requires time and resources of the organization to ensure support to clients or customers. In this regard, it is important to anticipate such an occurrence and to develop a plan on how to cooperate with law enforcement without shutting down your operation. For the most part, computer crime specialists can generate data dumps, make secure copies of files, and create logs without carting away all of your organization's computers. Administrators should, however, have a plan in place to allocate requisite resources in a manner that will avoid—or at least minimize—disruptions in business operations. Suggestions that will help to minimize the disruption caused by an on-site investigation follow.

- Schedule meetings with key organizational members of your information technology organization, as well as other key legal and management employees, and develop a plan that can be implemented should a significant event take place during either normal or noncritical work periods. Once your plan is developed, *test it!*

- If any part of the network needs to come down in support of investigative activities, arrange, where feasible, for this outage to take place during nonpeak hours. Your law enforcement counterparts may be of a different mind, with a greater sense of urgency to take down suspect systems. If possible, work out such details beforehand.

- Depending on the operating system environment your organization operates in, you will need to know where to acquire the necessary logs and audit files. These files should be identified now rather than during the heat of a significant investigation. Doing this up front will help minimize the amount of staff time necessary to retrieve the files when needed.

- Make sure law enforcement does not take software or database files for which no copy or backup exists. Prior to this, and as a matter of policy, ensure that all organizational employees and contractors are following required backup and copying procedures to avoid any unnecessary loss of vital data. Should any law enforcement agency show up with a warrant or subpoena, you are compelled to provide any and all information specified within those documents.

- Keep the investigation compartmentalized, on a need-to-know basis. This action will reduce the amount of staff involved and protect the investigation. The more people cognizant of an ongoing investigation, the greater the possibility that information central to the investigation may be compromised.
- Keep the lines of communication open with law enforcement. Knowing about the needs for records or access to information systems in advance can save staff time and system downtime. In short, do not wait for law enforcement to visit you, visit them, and do it frequently. This will establish good rapport and create trusts that may be needed at some future time.
- Encourage on-site copying of memory and any magnetic media rather than their removal. Computer forensics specialists possess this capability (aka: fly-away kits), and not all cases require the removal of equipment to a forensics lab. With law enforcement cooperation, you can schedule these procedures during nonpeak hours and keep your equipment on the premises and in service.

61.10 NONELECTRONIC RECORDS AND THE INSIDER THREAT

Insiders will not necessarily lose their special knowledge of internal controls when they switch roles from "insider" to "outsider." These persons may remain a threat to the information system for some time. The distinction becomes even cloudier when some access to information systems remains, without all of the formal controls applied to other employees.[7]

Paper records, video surveillance tapes, proximity card records, and any other means of tracking employee activity can all play a major role in the investigation of computer crimes and incidents. Admittedly, no one wants to assume the role of "Big Brother," but at the same time, an organization's livelihood may well depend on these methods of verifying access. No one metric exists that clearly demonstrates the true nature of insider threats. It is, however, reasonable to believe that greater than half of all computer crimes are committed by current or former insiders. To assess, and perhaps better to detect, this threat to organizational computing systems, internal documentation and monitoring become important evidence trails. For example, if video cameras monitor the entrances to the computer processing center or labs, the video surveillance tapes produced document the entrance and exit of any employee at a given time. If the entrances use access cards, the reports or databases containing the access records document employee traffic into sensitive areas. The use of conventional access tracking is not by itself foolproof and will not, for example, preclude "piggybacking."

Contradictions between access and video records can often document anomalies or possible misdeeds that will require further investigation. For example, if the access control report indicates John Jones entered the computer lab at 6:45 P.M. on 07-12-08, but the videotape for same time shows Sam Smith entering, there is clear indication that Sam has used John's card or access code. The question now remains: Why? Is there a need to call in law enforcement? At first blush, there is no apparent need to make such a call. Only after some initial investigation on the part of your security staff will this perhaps be necessary.

Paper files—personnel records, departmental documents, project logs, programming modification records, sign-out logs for software, and job assignment records—all tell a story. When you want to know who worked on what, or who had access to which project, paper records can often provide the needed history. Audit logs such as those stored on a UNIX or UNIX-type operating system within /var/log can provide even greater illumination.

To date, many information security professionals believe that computer crime usually emanates from an external source. The truth remains that most computer crimes are perpetrated by workers from within. Furthermore, a certain percentage of that crime will be cold cases, crimes that are discovered well after the fact. In investigating cold cases, investigators quickly discover that employees have left and that the pertinent software is no longer in use. To further exacerbate the problem, people's recollections rapidly fade, and remembering who did what, and when, is difficult. Paper records from projects, as well as any backed-up data, may be the best evidence available in cold cases. This is especially true looking well into the past, with a need to compare the new and the old.

When examining paper records, videotape, or any other media, maintain a database of what you have examined and any cross-references against other records. When any documented information is provided to law enforcement, your database will more easily support investigative activities and will further document the chain of custody of any evidence gleaned from these record sources. Such a record will prove to be an invaluable resource in quickly locating information in an investigation.

61.11   INFORMATION SHARING (THE HUMAN FACTOR).   After 9/11, all law enforcement officers will agree that the sharing of information between any organization and law enforcement is critical to the success of cyber-related investigations. Working with any law enforcement agency has both benefits and consequences. Benefits accrue because:

- Most law enforcement agencies have, or are quickly coming online with, a cyber-investigative capability. Many of the federal agencies have taken steps to train and educate investigators to ensure that the most comprehensive investigation is conducted with the least amount of disturbance to the victim agency.

- Law enforcement agencies are also being funded to establish, or better train officers in, cyber-investigative disciplines that, in most instances, facilitate the acquisition of personnel, equipment, and training.

- Working with law enforcement agencies can serve as a conduit to training and education for on-site first responders and cyber security personnel. The FBI or any other law enforcement agency benefits from better educating you as to what it wants and needs, as this helps to ensure that all evidence is properly collected and remains intact. Exhibit 61.4 is a draft example of how a memorandum of understanding (MOU) or an (MOA) between two or more entities might be constructed for the purpose of sharing law enforcement data.

One of the resources in the United States for forming good relations with law enforcement agencies is the InfraGard. The regional meetings of InfraGard members offer an excellent opportunity for sharing information with trusted members of critical infrastructure organizations and with law enforcement officials. The organization describes itself in this way on its home page:

InfraGard is an information sharing and analysis effort serving the interests and combining the knowledge base of a wide range of members. At its most basic level, InfraGard is a partnership between the Federal Bureau of Investigation and the private sector. InfraGard is an association of businesses, academic institutions, state and local law enforcement agencies,

EXHIBIT 61.4   Information-Sharing Example

Information-Sharing Initiative—Implementation Plan

Participating Sites

I. Objective

Implement a program to retrieve information of varying degrees of criticality from specified contributors for the purpose of establishing a repository of related data. This is to enable single search capability for the production of a single composite record. The record will be available as a tool to enhance operational needs of the participants. The record should support tactical operations as well as strategic, investigative, and analytical operations.

II. Participating Agencies

This should include, state, local, federal, and commercial law enforcement, investigative, and analytic entities.

Specific and detailed memorandums of understanding (MOU) will be entered into for each cooperating entity. The MOUs will specify the particular information and data for submission, the limitations or restrictions placed on the data by the subscribing entities, and the roles, responsibilities, and facts agreed upon. Each MOU will recognize and acknowledge the oversight and leadership responsibilities exercised by [your company or the agency taking lead responsibility].

III. Security and Location of Equipment

The system's "Data Warehouse" and IS equipment, including but not limited to computers, servers, printers, and peripherals, will be physically located in a secure facility on your location. The building should be a controlled and "Limited Access" facility, populated with data from three levels (described further below) of information from detailed investigative and analytical assessments.

   The security of the system will be controlled and accredited in accordance with the "Organization's" Master Security Plan. (Your site here) is a tenant of the Master Plan. Systems maintenance (updates, backups, etc.) and password control will be regulated by the "Organization's" technical security personnel, who will produce quarterly reports articulating the usage and administration of the system.

   The "Organization's" Accepted Use and Security banner will be displayed on all Web pages and sign-in screens.

   Access to the system will be restricted to member agencies and their described representatives; the total to be determined by the Executive Management Team. Access levels will be defined as follows:

Level 1: Federal, State, and Local Law Enforcement (L/E) Information

This category is primarily concerned with the identification of persons and normally relates to public safety. Included are sensitive but unclassified law enforcement information such as police and related investigative and field reports, arrest and conviction data, identification databases, and the like.

Level 2: Analytical Access Data

Users in this category will have access to all unclassified tactical incident information available from typical federal government sources for the purpose of analyses based on the data that have been manually collated. Examples of this level of data are I-94 Arr/Dpt Records, Visa Database accesses (Department of State), I-20 Student and Visitor records, Custom's Treasury Enforcement Communications System (TECS) data, unclassified federal investigative data (Foreign Access Central Tracking System/FACTS and Personnel Access System).

(Continued)

EXHIBIT 61.4   *(Continued)*

Information-Sharing Initiative—Implementation Plan

Level 3: Classified and Security Related Data Sources

Data not generally shared unless the inquiring entity maintains a clearance and a "need to know" the information. These data are normally derived from isolated databases in the control of the federal or contractor organization. Access to these systems will undergo a much higher screening and approval process. Examples of this level of data are the identity-sensitive documentation and classified systems within the FBI.

Sharing of Level 3 data is an additional phase for implementation after the initial system is operational. Submission of data concerning Levels 1 and 2 can be shared, based on the existing capabilities of joined database systems. However, Level 3 data loading presently can only be accomplished by stand-alone disk loading and by manual transport (sneaker net).

IV. Information to be Shared

Each participating Agency will provide current data relating to Intelligence, Counterintelligence, Counterterrorism, Terrorist Matrixes, Threat Assessments, Law Enforcement (L/E) alerts, and other L/E sensitive activity reports. All participants will be specifically tasked with providing the elements of Homeland Security effecting Energy, Banking and Finance, Agriculture, Food, Water, Public Health, Information Technology and Telecommunications, Transportation and Border Security, Postal and Shipping, Defense, Government and Emergency Services, and Maritime Security.

Queries of the system by participating agencies will enable access of data on violent criminal gangs, information on persons in jail or prison, searches of criminal records, and other data related to criminal activity (arrest, citation, and booking information, and field and investigative reports.) The Federal and DOE data available for review will consist of similar and related alerts, State Department Visa application data, Department of Commerce, Homeland Security data and assessments, as well as portions of the Personnel Access System (PAS) and defined Export Control data. Other initiatives include work authority statements and internal security reports concerning suspected attempts to breach security.

V. Proposed Date of Implementation

The time frame of implementation is best approximated to be a minimum of 6 months from date of contract.

VI. Administration Management

The Lead Agency [to be determined] will be responsible for overall management and administration of the system. Each individual agency will be responsible for day-to-day supervision and oversight of the review, as required to ensure the appropriate level of security of data submitted. Likewise, each participating site will ensure proper data integrity as outlined in MOU. This implies that each site will be responsible for ensuring that the data they upload is not infected with any form of virus or Trojan. While this may not be the most appropriate place for insertion, it must be covered.

The Lead Agency will coordinate with the other agencies the standards and compliance protocols, rules of access and operation, policies for dissemination of analytical reports, and security standards, and will specifically conduct periodic and cursory reviews, not less than monthly, to ensure appropriateness of participation and usage of system. Periodic audits will be conducted to ensure that the highest level of quality information is received, and that appropriate retrieval queries are being administered.

(Continued)

EXHIBIT 61.4 *(Continued)*

Information-Sharing Initiative—Implementation Plan

A management team of no less than the Lead Agency and (X) member agencies will be formed to execute the fundamental oversight operations described herein. Each participating agency will be represented by its Executive Manager (CIO or Organizational Investigator, Chief of Police, Sheriff, Commander, etc.) for all operations and decisions. Standards and protocols should be specified in any accompanying MOUs. However, full agency members will enjoy several perks. Most important is the notion of one agency, one vote, which covers development and structure processes relative to the oversight principals and directives.

The management team will define reporting processes to evaluate the program on a quarterly basis to ensure that system integrity is intact and to be cognizant of additional improvements that can be undertaken to provide a more thorough and user-friendly product and process.

---

and other participants dedicated to sharing information and intelligence to prevent hostile acts against the United States. InfraGard Chapters are geographically linked with FBI Field Office territories. Learn more about InfraGard.

There is, however, another side to any relationship with law enforcement that must be considered. Despite your efforts to be as forthcoming as possible with law enforcement, situations may arise that will cause you and your organization great angst. There may be times when an investigator is simply not able to fully disclose all information gleaned during the conduct of an investigation. There also may be times when your efforts and your methodologies in investigating, prior to involving law enforcement, will come under scrutiny. Probably the most disconcerting of all situations is where law enforcement is compelled to make public disclosure of an incident. It is during these times that you want to work with your own management and legal staff as well as with the law enforcement agency conducting the investigation. Everyone concerned wants to make the public aware of any known or suspected threats, but this must also be weighed against the potential harm that might result from a public release. Another concern from the company's point of view is public perception of security measures within the organization, and to what extent they can protect information and thus customer investments.

61.12 CONCLUSION. Trying to stay ahead of cybercriminals is not getting easier. Attempts to understand their intent or motivations are rarely successful. The best chance any organization has is to come to know local law enforcement agencies and to help them know you. Articulate your expectations in the event of a significant cyber event, and have them do the same. Working together is the only path to success. Given that not all computer security or cyber law enforcement entities are created equal, you have to be willing to share knowledge, all in pursuit of the same end goal.

61.13 FURTHER READING

Ballou, S., and K. Higgins, eds. *Electronic Crime Scene Investigation: A Guide for First Responders*. National Criminal Justice Reference Service of the Office of Justice Programs, U.S. Department of Justice, 2001. Available free from www.ncjrs.gov/pdffiles1/nij/187736.pdf.

Computer Crime and Intellectual Property Section. Criminal Division, United States Department of Justice. "Searching and Seizing Computers and Obtaining Electronic Evidence in Criminal Investigations," 2002. Available free from www.cybercrime.gov/s&smanual2002.htm.

InfraGard home page: www.infragard.net/.

61.14   NOTES

1. www.fbi.gov/cyberinvest/cyberhome.htm.

2. www.cert.org/tech_tips/FBI_investigates_crime.html.

3. www.ifccfbi.gov/aboutus/partners.asp.

4. www.bbc.co.uk/crime/fighters/ussecretservice.shtml.

5. www.iacis.com/iacisv2/pages/forensicprocedures.php.

6. www.securityfocus.com/infocus/1523.

7. http://abyss.usask.ca/~roebuck/threats.HTML.

INTRODUCTION TO PART VII

MANAGEMENT'S ROLE IN SECURITY

Management responsibilities include judgements of which resources can rationally be expended in defending against which threats. Managers must understand how to cope with the lack of quantitative risk estimates while using what information is available to guide investment decisions in personnel and technology. Their decisions are affected by regulatory and legal requirements and by the practical constraints of their relationships with other leaders within their organizations. This part includes chapters and topics that bear on information assurance managers' roles:

62. **Risk Assessment and Risk Management.** Which vulnerabilities warrant repair? Which threats must be taken seriously? How much expense is justified on specific security measures?

63. **Management Responsibilities and Liabilities.** Roles, responsibilities, due diligence, staffing security functions, and the value of accreditation and education

64. **U.S. Legal and Regulatory Security Issues.** For U.S. practitioners especially, this chapter reviews the Gramm-Leach-Bliley Act and the Sarbanes-Oxley legislation

65. **The Role of the CISO.** The chief information security officer as an agent of change and as a strategist working to ensure that security fits into the strategic mission of the organization, and that it is communicated effectively to other C-level executives

66. **Developing Security Policies.** Approaches to creating a culture of security where policies grow organically from the commitment of all sectors of the organization, instead of being imposed unilaterally by security staff

67. **Developing Classification Policies for Data.** The essential role of data classification and how to implement systems that conform to regulatory and legal requirements

68. **Outsourcing and Security.** Security of outsourcing and outsourcing of security

CHAPTER **62**

RISK ASSESSMENT AND RISK MANAGEMENT

Robert V. Jacobson

62.1 INTRODUCTION TO RISK MANAGEMENT

62.1.1 What Is Risk? There is general agreement in the computer security community with the common dictionary definition: "the possibility of suffering harm or loss." The definition shows that there are two parts to risk: the *possibility* that a risk event will occur, and the harm or *loss* that results from occurrences of risk events. Consequently, the assessment of risk requires consideration of both factors: the frequency of threat events that cause losses, and the loss each such event causes. The product of the two factors, frequency and loss, is a *quantitative* measure of risk; for example, we might express a risk as an *annualized loss expectancy* (discussed in Section 62.4.3) of, say, "$100,000 per year." Risk is managed by taking actions that recognize and reduce these two factors.

Management of risk is important to the design, implementation, and operation of information technology (IT) systems because IT systems are increasingly an essential part of the operation of most organizations. As a result, both the size of the potential harm or loss and the possibility of a risk event occurring are increasing. In extreme cases, a risk loss may be large enough to destroy an organization. If an organization's risk management program is deficient in some area, the organization may suffer excessive harm or loss, but at the same time, the organization may be wasting resources on ineffective, excessive, or misdirected mitigation measures in other areas.

62.1.2 What Is Risk Management?
This chapter discusses risk management with special emphasis on two aspects of risk management: risk assessment and risk mitigation. Exhibit 62.1 suggests that risk management can be thought of as a four-step process.

The first step in managing the risks to an IT system is to identify and assess the risks quantitatively. The second step is to use the product of the risk assessment to identify the *optimum* set of risk measures.[1] In this context, "optimum" means making mitigation the best use of the resources available. Because no organization has infinite resources, risk management requires allocating finite resources, by selecting from the broad range of IT risk mitigation measures, the *optimum* set. Since the resources being allocated are measured quantitatively in monetary terms, the risks must likewise be measured in monetary terms. A CIO can hardly expect to go to the CFO and announce that the risk assessment has identified a "High" risk, so a "High" security budget will be needed to address the risk. This issue is discussed in more detail in Section 62.4.3.

The third step, security operations, is to perform the ongoing, daily activities necessary for the effective functioning of the risk management measures. Finally, the fourth step, security auditing, is to evaluate the effectiveness of IT security operations and to detect changing conditions that require a reassessment of risks, the implementation of new mitigation measures, or modifications to the security management program. Daily

EXHIBIT 62.1 Four IT Risk Management Activities

security management tasks and IT auditing are discussed elsewhere in this *Handbook* (see, e.g., Chapters 23, 27, 40, 47, 52, 53, and 54), so this chapter will confine itself to the first two steps: *risk assessment* and *risk mitigation.*

62.1.3 Applicable Standards.

There are two widely cited standards that address IT system risks: ISO/IEC 17799[2] (ISO 17799) and GTAG Information Technology Controls[3] (GTAG-ITC).

In 1995 the British Standards Institute published BS7799 entitled *Information Security Management Systems—Specification with Guidance for Use.* It is described as defining a six-step process:

1. Define the scope of the information security management system (ISMS).
2. Define a security policy.
3. Undertake a risk assessment/analysis.
4. Manage the risk.
5. Select control objectives and the actual controls to be implemented/applied.
6. Prepare a statement of applicability.

In 2000 BS7799 became ISO 17799. Although ISO 17799 offers a wealth of advice, its treatment of risk is not sharply focused. *ISO 17799 Section 0.4—What Is Information Security?* defines information security as "the protection of information from a wide range of threats in order to ensure business continuity, minimize business risk, and maximize return on investments and business opportunities." Although the definition includes "business continuity" as an objective, it focuses on "information" while it ignores threats to the *operation* of IT facilities such as fire, hardware failures, power outages, and so on that may not directly affect information. Since both information *and* physical facilities are required to perform the IT functions that support the operation of the parent organization, it is essential to consider both to manage risks effectively. Here is a simple example: If physical access controls do not protect data storage devices against improper physical access, control over access to stored data is lost regardless of logical access controls (e.g., passwords that may be in place). Thus, when reading ISO 17799, one should mentally translate the phrase "information security" as "IT system risk management," and take note of missing topics.

Section 0.4—Assessing Security Risks makes these sound observations: "Expenditure on controls needs to be balanced against the business harm likely to result from security failures." and "The results of the risk assessment will help to guide and determine the appropriate management action and priorities for managing information risks, and for implementing controls selected to protect against these risks." In section 2.9, ISO 17799 replaces the dictionary definition of risk quoted in Section 62.1.1 with this: "[risk is the] combination of the probability of an event and its consequence." If the word "combination" means "product," then what is being defined is annualized loss expectancy (ALE), a far more accurate term. ISO 17799, *Section 4—Risk Assessment and Treatment,* begins with this assertion: "Risk assessments should identify, quantify, and prioritize risks against criteria for risk acceptance and objectives relevant to the organization." These two *qualitative* criteria, risk acceptance and corporate objectives, are incompatible with a *quantitative* risk assessment, and the assertion is at cross-purposes with section 0.4, as quoted. Finally, ISO 17799, *Section 14—Business Continuity Management,* similarly loses sight of cost-benefit as the only valid criterion for defining a business continuity program. In summary, although this ISO standard offers many security topics for consideration, its emphasis on *information* security results in a fuzzy treatment of risk management.

In October 2005, ISO 17799 became ISO 27001 as a part of an ISO plan to devote the 27000 series of standards for "information security matters." ISO 27001 is described as a "standard" for "information security management systems." Despite the name, it is not a standard. It is actually a guideline for IT system security management that covers all aspects of IT system operations. In effect, it spans the third and fourth boxes in Exhibit 62.1.

The GTAG-ITC guide (Global Technology Audit Guide—Information Technology Controls), published by the Institute of Internal Auditors, addresses risk management from the viewpoint of an internal auditor but is a useful source of information for IT risk managers because of its detailed discussion of roles and missions, and of IT controls. *Section 8—Analyzing Risk* discusses specifics of risk management. Section 8.1 includes this sensible comment: "However, each control has a specific cost that may not be justified in terms of cost-effectiveness . . . . Furthermore, no list of controls is universally applicable." This says very clearly that IT controls, even those recommended by auditors, should pass a cost-effectiveness test before being selected for implementation. *Section 8.2.4—Performing Risk Analysis* describes the risk management process succinctly but has the same conceptual error as ISO 17799 in that it refers to "assets" but ignores processes and the facilities needed to perform them.

The reference to risk management measures as "controls" may suggest that actions that are not "controls"—for example, insurance or business continuity plans—are not a part of the risk management program. This is the reason why we use the term "risk management measures" here, not "controls."

62.1.4   Regulatory Compliance and Legal Issues.

Increasing regulatory and legal issues are impacting risk management, most notably the Sarbanes-Oxley Act. More and more corporate officials are being sent to jail for infractions. As a result, it is not surprising that there may be an overreaction to compliance regulations with excessive measures being recommended by auditors. Whenever implementation of a compliance recommendation does *not* include a cost justification, and the implementation cost is material, it may be a candidate for a simple risk analysis like this:

1. What effect does the recommended measure have on the probability of noncompliance? In other words, what will be the difference in the likely loss experience with and without the recommended measure?
2. Does this difference compare favorably with the cost to implement and maintain the recommended measure?

There are several points to be made:

- If the cost-benefit is marginal or negative, consideration should be given to alternate (and lower cost) ways to achieve the same end result.
- If the cost-benefit is strongly negative, consideration should be given to dropping the recommendation.
- Under no circumstances should an organization deliberately break the law.

For more about these issues, refer to Chapter 65 in this Handbook.

62.2 OBJECTIVE OF A RISK ASSESSMENT.   This *Handbook* describes the pros and cons of a wide range of security measures that can be applied to an IT system. However, no organization has unlimited resources, and so it is necessary to decide which measures should be implemented.[4] It would be convenient if there were a set of security standards that applied equally to all IT systems, but as the GTAG-ITC guidelines cited in Section 62.1.3 note, this is not the case for two basic reasons:

1. Each IT system has its own particular risk environment.
2. Each IT system has a unique workload. Although two or more IT systems may perform the same list of functions, it is highly unlikely that the systems will have exactly the same level of activity for each of the functions, and so the cost of lost data and service interruptions will not be the same.

Because of these differences, each IT system will have unique security requirements.[5] These two factors correspond to the two elements in the definition of risk:

1. The risk environment determines the possibility of experiencing harm or loss.
2. The characteristics of the system workload, and the associated IT system assets, determine the magnitude of the harm or loss.

The objective of a risk assessment is to generate information about risk exposures and the potential for loss associated with the workload in order to estimate the ALE of the IT system under current conditions. This estimate is needed to optimize the subsequent risk mitigation decisions and to validate decisions about existing security measures. In this context, *optimize* means to allocate the organization's resources to those actions that will yield the best overall performance. It would be suboptimum to spend $10,000 to avert $1,000 in expected losses. To avoid such wasteful expenditures, one must be able to estimate quantitatively both expected losses[6] and the effect of proposed mitigation measures. For this reason, in all but the simplest situations, a risk assessment must produce a quantitative, monetary measure of risk, so that (1) risks can be compared with one another on a common basis and (2) the cost of risk mitigation measures can be related to the risks they are meant to address. Assessing a risk as "high," "unacceptable," or in other qualitative terms does not provide the information needed to support decisions to implement risk mitigation measures, which will always have *quantitative* implementation costs.

Exhibit 62.2 shows why a quantitative estimate of ALE is an essential element in the optimization of the strategy. A sum of money has been budgeted for IT risk management for next year. A risk management measure is selected and implemented, and so funds are expended. The implementation is expected to reduce one or more risk factors. As a result, we expect *future* risk losses will be reduced, and funds will be saved. By comparing the present values of the funds expended now and those saved in the future, we can estimate the return on investment (ROI) of the implemented measure. The goal is to maximize the ROI and to avoid risk management measures with small or negative ROIs. This is the essential character of businesslike IT system risk management. However, it is evident that we *must* be able to make credible estimates of expected risk losses under both current conditions and under the assumption that a proposed risk management measure has been implemented to optimize our risk management strategy. It may be suggested that quantitative assessment of risk is "too complicated" and so a simpler, qualitative method can be used instead. However, the complexity is

EXHIBIT 62.2 Evaluating an IT System Security
Strategy

inherent in risk itself, and any "simple" assessment technique will be inherently weak
and potentially misleading. This topic is discussed in more detail in Section 62.4.3.

62.3 LIMITATIONS OF QUESTIONNAIRES IN ASSESSING RISKS.   One
may be tempted to think of a "security questionnaire" or checklist as a valid risk assessment, but even if the checklist seems to be authoritative because it is automated, this is
not the case. Typical questionnaires evaluate, to some extent, the risk environment but
not expected loss. At best, a questionnaire can only compare the target of the questionnaire with a security standard implicit in the individual questions. Questionnaires do
not meet the objective of a risk assessment, because the answers to a questionnaire will
not support optimized selection of risk mitigation measures. The most a well-designed
questionnaire can do is to identify potential risk areas, and so it can be of help in
scoping and focusing a quantitative risk assessment.

Questionnaires suffer from several other shortcomings:

- The author of a question and the person who is answering the question may have
  different understandings of the meanings of key words. As a result, an answer
  may not match the intent of a question.

- Questions tend to be binary, but most answers are inherently quantitative. For
  example, consider the binary question "Do users comply with password policy?"
  Although the anticipated answer is either yes or no, a meaningful answer is likely
  to be much more complicated because each user will have a unique pattern of
  compliance. Some users will make every effort to be 100 percent compliant, some
  will make every effort to circumvent the policy, and the remaining users will
  comply to a greater or lesser extent. Note also that the question does not attempt
  to evaluate the appropriateness of the policy.

- Because questionnaires are inherently "open loop," and because of the binary
  answer issue just discussed, questionnaires tend to miss important information

		Consequences	
		Low	High
Occurrence Rate	Low		
	High		

Exhibit 62.3   "Jacobson's Window," A Simple Risk Model

that would be elicited by a risk analyst who interacts directly with respondents and responds to a quantitative answer with a new question.[7]

Questionnaires are appealing because they appear to relieve the risk assessor of the need to probe into the business system being assessed, but something better is needed for a valid risk assessment. The remaining sections of this chapter build a model of risk and then show how to apply quantitative parameters to the model. Although a greater effort is required, far superior results are achieved.

62.4   MODEL OF RISK.   Exhibit 62.3 is a simplified model of threats and consequences devised by the author of this chapter. The model takes the first steps toward quantification of risks. In this very simple model, all risk events are assumed to have either a low or high rate of occurrence, and all consequences of risk event impacts are assumed to be either low or high. William H. Murray, at the time an executive consultant at Deloitte and Touché, referred to this risk model as Jacobson's Window. Let us now consider the implications of the model.

62.4.1   Two Inconsequential Risk Classes.   The two-by-two empty matrix model implies that there are four classes of risk: low-low, high-low, low-high, and high-high. Exhibit 62.4 suggests that two of the classes can be ignored. The low-low class can be ignored because these risks do not matter. As an extreme example, it is obvious that a risk event that occurs at about 10,000-year intervals and causes a $1 loss each time can be ignored safely. Experience suggests that the high-high class can be assumed not to exist in the real world. If 50-ton meteorites crashed through the roofs of computer rooms every day, there would be no attempt to use computers. In practice, high-probability, high-loss risks just do not exist. Catastrophic events do occur, but not frequently.

62.4.2   Two Significant Risk Classes.   This analysis suggests that there are only two significant risk classes: high-low and low-high. Data entry keystroke errors are an example of a high-low risk: a high probability of occurring and usually a low resulting loss. A major fire that destroys the building housing an IT system is an example of a low-high risk: a low probability of occurrence and a high consequential

		Consequences	
		Low	High
Occurrence Rate	Low	Do not care	
	High		Does not happen

EXHIBIT 62.4 Two Inconsequential Risk Classes

loss. However, we know that real-world risks do not fall into just these two classes. Instead there is a spectrum of risks from high-low to low-high.

62.4.3 Spectrum of Real-World Risks.

Exhibit 62.5 illustrates the distribution of representative risks from high-low (keystroke errors) to low-high (major fires). Conceptually, there is little difference between the high-low and low-high threats. Experience suggests that averaged over the long term, the high-low and low-high threats will cause losses of similar magnitude to an organization. This concept is quantified by the notion of annualized loss expectancy. The ALE of a risk is simply the product of its rate of occurrence, expressed as occurrences per year, and the loss resulting from a single occurrence expressed in monetary terms, for example, dollars per year.

Here is a simple example of ALE: Assuming that 100 terminal operators each work 2,000 hours per year and make 10 keystroke errors per hour, the occurrence rate of keystroke errors would be 2 million per year. Next, assuming that 99.9 percent of the errors are immediately detected and corrected at an insignificant cost, then 2,000 errors slip by each year, a high occurrence rate risk, and must be corrected later at a cost estimated to be $10 each, a low consequence for each occurrence. Thus, the ALE of the high-low risk: Keystroke error is estimated to be 2,000 occurrences per year × $10 per occurrence, or an ALE of $20,000/year.

		Consequences	
		Low	High
Occurrence Rate	Low	cash	"low–high" major fire flooding fraud
	High	power failure software bug key error "high–low"	

EXHIBIT 62.5 Spectrum of Real-World Risks

Continuing our example, assume that the probability of a major fire in any one year is 1/10,000 (in other words the annualized probability of occurrence of a major fire is estimated to be 0.0001), and if the loss resulting from a major fire would be $200 million, then major fire is a low-high risk. These assumptions lead to an estimate of $20,000/year for the ALE of major fires.

Thus, the two risks from opposite ends of the risk spectrum are seen to have ALEs of about the same magnitude. Of course, we have manipulated the two sets of assumptions to yield similar ALEs, but the results are typical of the real world. However, note that we are assured of having a loss of $20,000 *every year* from keystroke errors, but a loss of $200 million in only one of the next 10,000 years.

Exhibit 62.6 is a computer-generated[8] plot of threat occurrence rates and consequences (total single-occurrence loss) taken from an actual quantitative risk analysis of a facility. Each of the numbered boxes represents a threat type. Because the two scales are logarithmic, the contours of constant ALE are diagonal straight lines. As expected there are no threats in the high-high (doesn't happen) and low-low (trivial) zones.

Although the ALEs span a range of about four orders of magnitude, (from about $50 per year to about $500,000 per year), frequencies and consequences each span about seven orders of magnitude. This result is typical of the real world and illustrates the fundamental flaw in high-medium-low risk models like the matrix in Exhibit 62.7. These models attempt to simplify risk assessments by defining a very limited range of values, three each, for frequency and consequence. As a result, threat event ALEs that

Exhibit 62.6   Plot of Actual Threat Frequencies and Consequences

		Threat Occurrence Rate		
		Low	Medium	High
System Impact	High	Medium	High	Very High
	Medium	Low	Medium	High
	Low	Very Low	Low	Medium

EXHIBIT 62.7   Typical Risk Matrix

differ by as much as two orders of magnitude, as illustrated in Exhibit 62.5, are given the same ranking when assessed using a high-medium-low matrix.

Proponents of this risk model are silent about the details. First, as Exhibit 62.6 shows, the "Very High" and "Very Low" risks are meaningless in the real world. Second, the matrix requires users to compress numerical values with a range of almost seven orders of magnitude (e.g., from 100/year to 1/20,000 years) into only three values: Low, Medium, and High. In other words, two risks with same consequence but occurrence rates that differ by a factor of 100 might receive the same evaluation. Likewise, because of the arbitrary boundaries between low, medium, and high, two risks with the same consequence but with occurrence rates that differ by 1 percent could receive different ratings. These considerations defy common sense and make it clear that rating a risk as high, medium, or low cannot be the basis to cost-justify a proposed risk management measure.

62.5   RISK MITIGATION.   Exhibit 62.6 shows that the effect of risk exposures on IT systems can range from trivial to catastrophic, and it is not always immediately obvious which risk exposures are the most dangerous. For this reason, it is essential to base the selection of risk mitigation measures on a quantitative assessment of risks. In this section, we consider the practical considerations in generating quantitative assessments and applying them to risk mitigation decisions.

62.5.1   ALE Estimates Alone Are Insufficient.   As noted, ALE is a useful concept for comparing risks, but we recognize intuitively that ALE alone is not a sufficient basis for making risk mitigation decisions about the low-probability high-consequence risks. There are two reasons for this.

1. The difficulty in generating a credible estimate of occurrence rate for low-probability risks. As a rule, one can generate credible estimates of the consequences of a low-probability risk, but the same is not true of its occurrence rate. Risks that flow from human actions such as fraud, theft, and sabotage are also difficult to quantify credibly.

2. A common human trait that this writer has postulated as Jacobson's 30-Year Law:

   People (including risk managers) tend to dismiss risks that they have not *personally* experienced within the past 30 years.

Why 30 years? It is not clear, but it may be related genetically to human life expectancy, which until just a few generations ago was about 30 years. Possibly people who were able to suppress anxiety about rare events were more successful than those who worried too much. Numerous instances of Jacobson's 30-Year Law can be found. For example, the U.S. Government has had a major fire at about 28-year intervals beginning in 1790, most recently at the Military Records Center. Presumably, each new generation of federal property managers must relearn the lessons of fire safety by direct experience. The Northeast power blackout of 2003 followed a similar event in 1976, 27 years earlier.

It seems to be common for senior managers, particularly public officials, responding to a calamity (e.g., Hurricane Katrina), to say something like this: "Who could have imagined that such a thing would happen? However, we have taken steps to see that it will never happen again." This is an imprudent statement for two reasons. First, prudent managers will anticipate potential disasters. Second, saying "never" implies that perfect security is the goal. This is nonsensical since perfect security is infinitely expensive and so cannot be achieved.

62.5.2 What a Wise Risk Manager Tries to Do.   Unlike the senior managers just quoted, an organization's risk manager should be trying to imagine every possible *material* risk the organization faces, even those not personally experienced, and developing estimates of the impact of these risks. Next, the risk manager should strive to identify the optimum response to each material risk by identifying security measures that have a positive ROI. Potentially fatal low-occurrence/high-consequence threats require treatment irrespective of ALE and ROI as discussed in Section 62.5.4.

Consider this example of cost-effectiveness: The ALE for keystroke errors was estimated in the Section 62.4.3 example as $20,000 per year, or $200 per operator. This estimate is credible because presumably there has been ample past experience with both the occurrence rate and impact cost of the keystroke-error risk. The risk manager considers how to treat this risk. Imagine that experience suggests that spending $100 each year on keyboard skills training for each operator would reduce the undetected error rate by 30 percent. Because the $100 per operator expense would yield a benefit of $60 in reduced ALE (30 percent of $200, the per-operator ALE), the ROI[9] of training would be –40 percent, clearly not a cost-beneficial mitigation measure. In effect, we would be spending $10,000 to achieve a $6,000 loss reduction. However, if the error rate were reduced by 90 percent instead of 30 percent, the training would appear to be a good investment; spending $100 each to train operators, would produce a reduction in ALE per operator of $180, an ROI of +80 percent. The goal of the risk manager is to find the package of risk management measures that yields the greatest overall ROI.

62.5.2.1 *Three Risk Management Regions.* Basing risk management decisions on ROI estimates, as described, does not work for the low-probability, high-consequence risks because of two negative factors: (1) the credibility of risk estimates and (2) management's concern about the risk consequences. End users commonly have a higher level of concern about risks than IT system managers, but as a rule it is the IT system managers who make the decisions about security measures. An IT system manager generally has no difficulty choosing between buying a faster server and a more reliable server. The benefit of higher throughput is immediately evident. The benefit of higher reliability is not as obvious. Thus, although a risk manager may identify a significant low-occurrence, high-cost risk before it has occurred, an organization's senior managers probably would be unaware of these low-high risks and would be genuinely

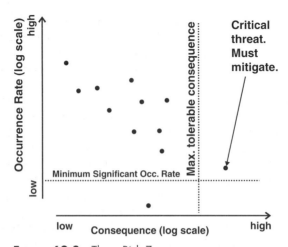

EXHIBIT 62.8 Three Risk Zones

Copyright 2002 International Security Technology, Inc.

surprised were a major loss to occur. Hence, the "Who could have imagined. . ." press releases. In other words, simply identifying an exposure might be thought to be enough to justify adoption of a mitigation measure to address the exposure. This suggests that the risk manager needs additional criteria for selecting risk mitigation measures. The next section presents an overview of mitigation measures to clarify the selection criteria.

It will help risk managers to understand that the universe of risk events to which an organization is exposed by dividing the total risk space into the three regions shown in Exhibit 62.8. The two axes are logarithmic, and the dots represent individual threats.

These regions help define appropriate risk management actions. The boundaries of the regions are defined by two senior management decisions.

1. The first decision is to define the *minimum significant threat event occurrence rate*. The concept is that it is reasonable to simply ignore the risk of threat events for which we have estimated occurrence rates less than some minimum rate. For example, senior management may decide to ignore risks with occurrence rates estimated to be less than once in 20,000 years (i.e., the probability of an occurrence of the threat next year is estimated to be less than 0.00005).

2. Senior management may also identify a loss level (consequence) that is *intolerably high*. Risk events of this type will appear in the lower right of Exhibit 62.6, and 62.8. The occurrence rate of these events is immaterial as long as they exceed the minimum consequence criterion and the minimum occurrence rate. If we estimate that the loss caused by an occurrence of a threat event (commonly referred to as the single-occurrence loss [SOL]) exceeds the loss threshold *and* the occurrence rate exceeds the minimum material occurrence rate, then we *must* take steps to reduce the loss, perhaps by transferring the risk with an insurance policy or by reducing the estimated occurrence rate to a value below the minimum material occurrence rate.

It is instructive to consider where to plot an unusual risk event like the attack on the World Trade Center (WTC) on September 11, 2001. It is likely that many organizations have facilities that would generate losses in excess of their maximum tolerable loss if totally destroyed by a similar terrorist attack. This implies that such organizations should take steps to protect these facilities against terrorist attacks. However, we should also take into account the estimated rate of occurrence before making a decision. How can we make a credible estimate of such a rare event? We can begin by estimating how many such events will occur next year in the United States. For example, based on past experience, we might assume that there will be about two such attacks each year. Then we estimate the likelihood that, of all the facilities in the United States, our facility would be selected for attack. This will depend on the "attractiveness" of our facility to a terrorist group when compared with all other potential targets in the United States. For example, assume that there are 100 "attractive" buildings that are as widely recognized and as vulnerable as the WTC. If our facility is one of the 100, then we might estimate the occurrence rate as $1/100 \times 2$, or a probable occurrence rate of 0.02/year. If, however, our building is *not* one of the 100 high-profile buildings, then we might estimate that if there are 200,000 similar buildings in the United States, our occurrence rate is $1/200,000 \times 2$, or an occurrence rate of 1/100,000 years. In this latter case, our senior management probably would choose to ignore the risk.

The remaining portion of the Exhibit 62.6 graph, the mid- to upper-left-hand corner, is the zone where the risk manager attempts to find cost-beneficial risk management measures, as discussed in the next sections.

62.5.2.2 Where ROI-Based Risk Management Is Effective.
ROI-based mitigation works well for high-probability, low-consequence risk exposures for two reasons: The manager who approves the expenditure (1) believes that the risk exists and should be addressed and (2) believes further that the parameters used to generate estimates of ALE and the reduction in ALE, used to estimate ROI, are reasonable and credible.

62.5.2.3 Four Reasons for Adopting a Risk Management Measure.
There are four general tests of the utility of a risk management measure.

1. **The measure is required by law or regulation.** In effect, a governing body has determined (one hopes) that the measure makes good public policy because it will always meet one of the remaining three tests. Exit door signs in public buildings are a good example. Sarbanes-Oxley may be an example of a bad (not cost-effective) law.

2. **The cost of the measure is trivial but its benefit is material.** For example, a little-used door that compromises physical access controls is not being kept locked. One can institute a procedure and install security hardware to keep the door locked at very low cost.

3. **The measure addresses a low-high risk that has an intolerable single-occurrence loss, as discussed in Section 62.5.2.1.** For example, it would be intolerable for a corporation to experience an SOL that exceeded owner equity or net worth. The failure several years ago of a prominent British merchant bank following unwise speculation by a staff member is a tragic example of an organization that failed to identify and address an intolerable SOL exposure.

4. **The cost of the measure will be more than offset by the reduction in future losses (ALE) that it will yield.** In other words, the mitigation measure has a positive ROI. This reason is commonly used to justify protection against the high-low risks. Operator keyboard training described in Section 62.5.2 is an example.

Procedures for managing the last two risk categories follow.

62.5.3   How to Mitigate Infrequent Risks.   After the high-low threats have been addressed using an ROI analysis, the risk manager considers all imaginable low-high risks, one by one, and makes for each such risk an estimate of the SOL and the rate of occurrence. The report of this analysis should describe for each threat the confidence level of the estimates of its SOL and occurrence rate. These estimates are arranged in descending order of SOL. The list is presented to senior management, who draws a line somewhere on the list and says, "The risks above the line are intolerably high. Do something about them." The risk manager then considers each of the unacceptable risks in two ways.

62.5.3.1   *Reduce the Magnitude of High Single-Occurrence Losses.*
Sometimes the magnitude of an SOL can be reduced. There are several possibilities:

- **Transfer the risk by obtaining insurance against it.** The premium will depend in part on the amount of the loss that is deductible. For example, one might obtain insurance against a $100 million SOL with a $10 million deductible to minimize the insurance premium. In effect, the intolerable $100 million SOL has been reduced to a tolerable $10 million SOL at the cost of the insurance policy premium.

- **Disburse the risk exposure.** For example, replace a single IT center with an intolerable SOL of $500 million of catastrophic physical damage, and service interruption losses, with three centers having SOLs of about $167 million each. The centers should be sufficiently isolated from one another to rule out shared disasters. The cost will be the incremental cost of the less efficient operation of three facilities.

- **Reduce the vulnerability of the IT system to the risk.** For example, implementing an enhanced business resumption plan, at some additional cost, can speed up recovery off site. This will reduce the SOL associated with catastrophic service interruption losses. Notice that this an example of a risk mitigation measure that affects more than one threat.

The risk manager also may strive to reduce the occurrence rate of a high SOL. Because of the uncertainty of the estimates of low occurrence rates, this is less satisfactory. Nonetheless, even the uncertain occurrence rate estimates can be useful. If two risk exposures have the same SOL but differ by an order of magnitude in estimated occurrence rate, it is reasonable to assume that the risk with the lower occurrence rate represents a lesser danger to the organization.

62.5.3.2   *Risk Management Measures Selection Process.*   Assume that the risk manager has presented a risk assessment/risk mitigation report to senior management as described. The report lists the low-high risks with one or more strategies for treating each risk.[10] The senior manager is responsible for selecting the mitigation measures for implementation because, as noted, ROI-based justification is inappropriate for this class of risks.

1. If the risk manager is able to identify a relatively low-cost mitigation measure that reduces the rate of occurrence of a risk to a low enough value, senior management may elect to adopt the mitigation measure.

2. There is some rate of occurrence below which the senior manager is willing to ignore a risk, even if the estimate is low confidence. Typically this applies to

very low occurrence rate events. Extreme examples are a nuclear detonation or a crashing meteorite.

3. Risk transfer by insurance, or one of the other techniques listed earlier, reduces the SOL to a tolerable level, and the senior manager is willing to accept the cost of the insurance coverage.

A complete tabulation of occurrence rates and the costs of mitigating actions for all the high-SOL risk exposures will help senior management to prioritize the implementation of the mitigation measures.

62.5.4   ROI-Based Selection Process.   After the potentially fatal risks have been addressed as described, the risk manager can turn to selection of measures to address the remaining high-low risks. A five-step procedure for selecting strategies on the basis of ROI is straightforward.

1. For each of the threats, identify possible risk management measures. As noted, some measures will affect more than one threat. There are four possible strategies:

    a. **Threat mitigation.** Measures to reduce the occurrence rate and/or the impact of one or more of the threats.

    b. **Risk transfer.** Use an insurance policy or other contractual means to transfer some or all of the risk to another party.

    c. **Business resumption plans.** Take steps in advance of threat occurrences to decrease the time required to resume business operations. This type of strategy applies to non-IT business systems that are included in the scope of the risk management project.

    d. **IT system recovery plans.** Take steps in advance of threat occurrences to decrease the time required to resume operation of the IT system and to reduce the amount of stored data lost. (See Section 62.6.3.3 for details.)

2. For each strategy, estimate the present value of the *cost* to implement and maintain the measure, taking into account the remaining life of the facility, the useful life of the measure, and the applicable time value of money. The organization will not enjoy the full benefit of a measure with a high initial cost and a low annual support cost if the life of the facility is less than the life of the measure.

3. For each strategy, estimate the effect of the measure on the occurrence rate and consequence of the threat(s) that the strategy addresses. Use these data to calculate total ALE assuming the measure is implemented. Calculate the present value of the *reduction in total ALE* the strategy is expected to yield. This is the *benefit* of the measure. Note also that in addition to reducing risks, a strategy may reduce operational costs. This cost saving should be added to the ongoing benefit (ALE reduction) of the strategy.

4. Using the values of cost and benefit, calculate ROI:

$$\text{ROI} = ((\$\text{Benefit} - \$\text{Cost})/\$\text{Cost}) \times 100\%$$

For example, using the data in Section 62.5.2, ROI is calculated as:

$$\text{ROI} = ((\$6{,}000 - \$10{,}000)/\$10{,}000) \times 100\%$$
$$= (-\$4{,}000/\$10{,}000) \times 100\%$$
$$= 0.4 \times 100\% = -40\%$$

This equation normalizes the ROI and expresses it as a percentage. Zero percent represents a neutral ROI (benefit equals cost). One hundred percent would represent a very beneficial measure, and 1,000 percent would probably be a no-brainer. If the measure generates a cost saving, the saving is added to the ALE reduction benefit when calculating the ROI. Note that the ROI analysis of a risk mitigation measure *will understate its benefit* if the risk assessment does not include all the risk events that the measure will address.

5. Make a list of the strategies in descending order of ROI after discarding the strategies with a negative ROI.

Presumably, management now selects for implementation the strategies in descending order of ROI until all available resources are allocated. However, if two or more strategies impact the same threat, it is possible that their effects may be partially overlapping. The risk manager can investigate this possibility in this way. Begin by assuming that the most attractive strategy has been implemented and recalculate the "baseline ALE." Next, verify the parameters for the remaining strategies, taking into account the effect of the measures assumed to have been implemented. Recalculate their ROIs as described, and repeat the selection process. It would be convenient if there were an analytic way to do this, but this author has been unable to devise a practical way to do so because of the wide range and complexity of potential interactions.

62.5.5 Risk Assessment/Risk Management Summary.   The risk model illustrated by Jacobson's Window leads to five conclusions.

1. Risks can be broadly classified as ranging from high-probability, low-consequence to low-probability, high-consequence events. In general, risk events in this range cause losses over a relatively narrow range of loss values when expressed as an annual rate or ALE.

2. Because of IT operating staff familiarity with the high end of the high-low risks, all available measures may already have been taken such that there may not be any cost-beneficial way to further reduce the ALE of some of these threats.

3. Midrange risks can be addressed by selecting mitigation measures with a positive ROI, based on the relationship between the cost to implement a mitigation measure and the reduction in ALE it is expected to yield.

4. Treatment of low-high risks requires the judgment of senior management, based on estimates of SOL and, to a lesser extent, estimates of rate of occurrence. Mitigation measures or risk transfer may reduce single-occurrence losses to acceptable levels or decrease occurrence rates to the level at which risks can be ignored.

5. To be effective, the risk management function must be:
   - Performed by properly qualified persons.
   - Independent of IT line management.
   - Reported to senior management to ensure that all risks are recognized and that resource allocation is unbiased.

62.6 RISK ASSESSMENT TECHNIQUES.   The first step in performing a risk assessment is to define the scope and focus of the assessment. The scope will define the IT functions or business processes, the physical assets, the intangible assets, and the liability exposures that are to be included in the assessment. The focus means the kinds of risk events to be included in the analysis. Risk events may include failures of the IT hardware and software, software logical errors, deliberate destructive acts by both insiders and outsiders, and external events such as earthquakes, hurricanes, river floods, and so forth. Sometimes the focus is determined by the desire to evaluate a specific class of risk management measures.

62.6.1   Aggregating Threats and Loss Potentials.   Aggregation is a key concept of quantitative modeling, and refers to the practice of combining related items to keep the model at a manageable size. For example, one can define a single risk event (IT server failure) or two risk events (Server01 failure and Server02 failure) under the assumption that the two servers support different systems with different loss potentials), and so on in ever-increasing detail. The more risk events defined for a risk assessment, the greater will be the effort required to establish the risk parameters and perform the calculations. However, *the individual risk events will not all have the same impact on the results of the assessment.* Indeed, some risk events will be found to be completely inconsequential, so the time expended to estimate their parameters will have been wasted. In other words, an appropriate degree of detail will not be immediately obvious.

This suggests that one should begin an assessment using highly aggregated risks, functions (typically business processes), and assets, perhaps no more than 10 to 15 of each in a typical situation, together with roughly prepared estimates of the risk parameters. This preliminary analysis will show which elements are important to the results. One can then add details to the important elements as appropriate and refine the material estimates to improve the validity of the model. This approach works to concentrate the effort on the important issues and avoids wasting time refining unimportant input data.

62.6.2   Basic Risk Assessment Algorithms.   It is generally accepted that ALE, in dollars (or other currency as appropriate) per year, is calculated as:

ALE = Threat Occurrence Rate (number per year)×
Threat Effect Factor (0.0 to 1.0) × Loss Potential (in monetary units)

The term "threat occurrence rate" (TOR) is used to designate the estimate of the probability of occurrence of a threat event during a risk management planning period, typically one year. Thus the TOR is the probability of occurrence at an annualized *rate.* The functions and assets are characterized by their potential to trigger a loss when impacted by one or more of the threats. The term "potential for loss" or simply "loss potential" is used specifically to designate the worst-case loss a function or asset can generate. This implies that there is at least one threat event (the worst-case threat) that will trigger a loss equal to the loss potential. Other threats will cause lesser losses because they have a lesser effect on the function or asset. The threat effect factor is used to quantify the relationship between a threat event and a function or asset. If the threat event has no impact on the function or asset, the corresponding threat effect factor will be zero. If the threat event triggers the worst-case loss (the loss potential), the threat effect factor will be 1.0. Threat effect factors will range from zero to 1.0 for all threats.

	Process #1	Process #2	Process #3	Process #4
Threat #1	TEF_{11}	TEF_{12}	TEF_{13}	TEF_{14}
Threat #2	TEF_{21}	TEF_{22}	TEF_{23}	TEF_{24}
Threat #3	TEF_{31}	TEF_{32}	TEF_{33}	TEF_{34}
Threat #4	TEF_{41}	TEF_{42}	TEF_{43}	TEF_{44}

EXHIBIT 62.9   Threat Effect Factors Connect Threats and Processes, Functions, and Assets

Exhibit 62.9 illustrates how each threat-function or threat-asset pair includes a threat effect factor. The single-occurrence loss, expressed in monetary units for each function or asset with respect to a given threat event, is calculated as:

SOL = Threat Effect Factor (0.0 to 1.0) × Loss Potential (monetary units)

The terms "loss potential" and "threat effect factor" are as defined. The sum of the SOLs for all the functions and assets with respect to a given threat is the consequence of an occurrence of the threat.

From these two definitions, we can see that:

ALE = SOL × Threat Occurrence rate ($/year).

The sections that follow discuss these two equations in more detail and describe techniques for estimating values for TOR, loss potential, and threat effect factor.

62.6.3   Loss Potential.   There are four basic kinds of losses that contribute loss potential:

1. **Property damage losses.** Property damage losses occur when a threat event impacts an asset of the organization. The asset may be physical property damaged, for example, by a fire or flood, or the asset may be an intangible asset, such as a trade secret or a proprietary database, the improper disclosure, modification, or destruction of which causes a loss to the organization.

2. **Liability losses.** The operation of an IT system may expose the organization to liability for damage or injury. For example, improper operation of an IT-controlled process might release a toxic gas. Improper disclosure of personal information may cause the individual to sue the organization for damages. If third parties place reliance on data generated or maintained by an IT system, there may be an exposure to damage suits if the data are incorrect as a result, for example, of flaws in the IT system.

3. **Service interruption losses.** Service interruption losses occur when IT system services or other business functions are interrupted or are not initiated in a timely manner because of the action of a threat event. In general, the longer the duration of an interruption, the greater will be the amount of the loss. This means that service interruption loss potential must be estimated in the form of

a table of values appropriate to the expected range of interruption durations the threats are expected to generate. As a consequence, each threat that causes service interruptions must be defined in terms of the percentage of the threat's occurrences that result in each of the interruption durations used to define service interruption loss potential.

4. **Lost data losses.** IT systems typically require stored data to function. If the primary copy of the stored data is lost, the data are recovered from the most recent backup copy or reconstructed from paper records, if they exist, of prior transactions. The magnitude of the data loss will depend on the rate at which the stored data change, the frequency with which a backup copy is made, the accuracy of the backup copy process, and the frequency of the occurrences of the threat events that require data recovery of the stored data. The stored data used by some IT systems do not change continuously, and so a complete backup copy can be made after each update phase, and data loss thus avoided.

Loss potentials, as described in the next three subsections, are based on estimates of the worst-case losses with respect to the list of risk events.

62.6.3.1 *Property and Liability Losses.*

Property and liability losses are treated the same way, so they can be discussed together. It is advisable to begin consideration of property damage losses by making an aggregated list of possible sources. For example, the initial list might consider together all the hardware in an IT facility and all of the databases needed to operate each of the principal IT applications. For each such asset,[11] an estimate is made of the worst-case loss that the organization could experience with respect to that asset. For example, the worst-case loss for a set of stored data would be the cost to reconstruct the data from backup copies and the cost to recover any missing or corrupted data. There will be other losses resulting from interruptions to IT services that require the availability of the data, but these losses are described separately in the next subsection.

Liability[12] loss potentials, if included in the scope of the risk management project, should be estimated in the same way. The first step is to determine which liabilities should be included in the risk assessment. The organization may already have a mechanism for addressing liability exposure, possibly through a risk transfer mechanism. However, the liability exposures that are unique to the IT operations should be included and the worst-case loss potential estimated as described.

62.6.3.2 *Service Interruption Losses.*

Service interruption (sometimes referred to as denial of service[13]) losses refer to the losses experienced by end users of an IT system when the service is not performed on time. The first step in estimating service interruption losses is to construct a list of the IT services for which there is a significant interruption loss potential. Here, too, it is desirable to aggregate individual applications in basic service areas. Examination of a wide range of functions suggests that there are six different classes of service interruption losses. Since each class of loss may begin after a different interruption duration, it is unlikely that there will be a single loss rate that begins at the instant the interruption begins and has a fixed rate per hour of interruption duration into the indefinite future. Reviewing the causes with the persons most familiar with each service, typically the line-of-business managers, will determine which classes apply and what the loss potential factors are. By tabulating the losses associated with each of the classes, one can generate an overall loss potential for a suitable range of service interruption durations.

1. **Reduced productivity.** Would people be idled if there were a service interruption? If yes, how many and how soon? What, approximately, is their total pay, including benefits? If substantial production facilities would be idled, what is the approximate hourly cost of ownership of the facilities, computed as the total life-cycle cost of ownership divided by the total operating life in hours?

2. **Delayed collection of funds.** Does the IT system application trigger collection of funds for the organization (e.g., a billing system or a loan-notes-due collection system)? If yes, determine the average amount collected each business day that would be affected by a service interruption. Because in most cases it will be possible to do some manual processing of the high-value items, the affected amount may be less than the full daily processing dollar volume. Determine a suitable cost-of-money percentage for use in present-value calculations by consulting the organization's treasurer or controller. Alternatively, the current commercial bank prime rate plus one or two percentage points can be used. The total loss does not increase linearly with the duration of the interruption. For example, assume that the one-day loss is $100 due to delayed collection. After a two-day outage, the loss would be $300: $200 from the first day and $100 from the second day. A three-day outage would cost $600: $300 of accumulated losses for the first day, $200 for the second day of delayed collections, and $100 for the third day, and so on.

3. **Reduced income.** Will an interruption of the application impact sales revenue or other income receipts? If yes, estimate the amount of income lost both immediately, and over the long term, for a range of service interruption durations appropriate to the risk events included in the risk assessment. It may be difficult for the end user to make an estimate, unless it is possible to remember the last major service interruption and to describe what happened. What would the organization do if a major competitor had a service outage? How would the outage become known, and how would it be exploited to increase income? These questions may help to determine the amount of reduced income to be expected.

   Along with reduced income, there would probably be a reduction in operating expenses, such as cost of sales, caused by the decreased activity. When the reduction in operating costs is subtracted from the reduced revenues, the result is the net loss. Estimates should be made for the shortest service interruption duration that the user believes would cause significant lost business; in addition, planning should include provisions for one or more service interruptions of greater duration.

4. **Extra expense.** How would the user respond to an outage? Would it be necessary to hire temporary help or to work overtime? Could an outside service be used? Would there be an increased error rate, which would increase error research and correction expenses? Might there be increased fraud loss and fraud investigation costs? The cost to catch up, after the outage ends, is often a major extra expense factor. Beginning with the shortest significant duration, several estimates should be made, including a worst-case scenario.

5. **Lateness penalties.** If the application entails any lateness penalties, contractual, regulatory, or legal, an estimate should be made of the amount of the penalties

that would be triggered by an outage, and the outage duration that would trigger the penalties.

6. **Public perception.** Public perception, as a catchall term, refers to the indirect effects of a service interruption. Staff morale and customer attitudes may be affected negatively by the impression that the organization's risks are not being effectively managed. The value of publicly traded stock may be adversely affected, and pending mergers or stock offerings may be derailed. The cost of borrowing may increase.

This procedure does not involve asking end users to estimate the maximum "tolerable" service interruption duration. This is *not* a useful question. An attempt by end users to establish the value of *tolerable* is simply an opinion or subjective judgment call. The basic risk assessment will establish the expected annualized losses. Then an evaluation of the cost-benefit or ROI of alternative risk mitigation measures, implemented to reduce the number and duration of service interruptions, will identify the optimum IT system configuration, including measures to control service interruptions.

62.6.3.3 IT Systems Interruption Mitigation.

IT system service interruption mitigation is a special case because of the effect of lost-data losses. This is why.

The performance of IT system continuity plans is often characterized using two parameters referred to as recovery time objective[14] (RTO) and recovery point objective (RPO). RTO is the maximum service interruption duration that will result from the action of threats on an IT system. The RTO of the continuity plan in place for an IT system will determine the expected losses of an IT system that result from the impact of the service interruption threats. Decreasing the RTO will decrease the expected loss but will increase the cost to implement and maintain the IT system continuity plan.

The RPO is a measure of the frequency with which an IT system backs up stored data. The more frequently data are backed up, the lower will be the lost data losses but the greater will be the cost to install and maintain the backup provisions.

The risk management task is to pick the IT system continuity plan (RTO-RPO combination) that has the most favorable cost benefit. The *cost* is the cost to install and maintain a given RTO-RPO combination. The *benefit* is the reduction in expected loss the RTO-RPO combination will achieve, compared with the RTO-RPO combination currently in use. This is why the question "What is your maximum 'tolerable' outage duration (i.e., RTO)?" is worthless. A rational selection depends on both cost and benefit, not the subjective appeal of any particular RTO.

Typically, there is an interaction between RTO and RPO. For example, tape is probably less expensive as a backup storage medium than disk, so we would expect a tape-based IT system continuity plan to be cheaper than a disk-based plan. However, tape will restrict the range of RPOs that can be implemented and may control the best achievable RTO, both of which will increase expected loss. There is another important point: There is no inherent connection between the service interruption loss potential of an IT system and the cost of RTO-RPO combinations for the system.

For example, a small inexpensive system (one with low RTO and RPO costs) might be running a very time-critical, high-value function (e.g., currency trading), while a large system with high RTO and RPO costs might be analyzing the works of William Shakespeare for the local college, a low-criticality task.

62.6.4   Risk Event Parameters.   As noted in the prior section, during the determination of loss potential, a list of significant risk events can be constructed. The list should be examined critically to determine if additional event types should be added to it, bearing in mind the aggregation considerations discussed earlier and the defined scope of the project.

Once the risk events list has been completed, two parameters are estimated for each event:

1. **Occurrence rate.** There are several ways to estimate occurrence rates. If the event has had a relatively high occurrence rate in the past, typically more than once in 10 years, the organization is likely to have records of those events, from which the occurrence rate can be inferred with high confidence. However, there are two cautions.

   a. Consideration must be given to any changes in the environment that would affect the occurrence rate. For example, the root cause of some system crashes may have been corrected, so that one would expect the future rate to be lower than in the past.

   b. It is important to avoid double counting. For example, a system outage log may lump electric power failures into a catchall category: hardware failure. If electric power failure is included in the risk assessment as a separate risk event, its occurrences may be inadvertently counted twice.

      If the risk event is external to the IT facility—for example, river flooding and earthquake—one can usually find external sources of information about past occurrences. For example, one could use the Web page www.nhc.noaa.gov/pastint.html to determine if a given U.S. location has ever been impacted by a high-intensity hurricane. Numerous Web sites can support a risk assessment. One also may find that past copies of local publications can help to determine the past local history. In some cases, there will be no meaningful past history for a risk event, particularly if the event is of recent origin, such as e-business fraud and terrorism. In these cases, it may be possible to reason by analogy with other similar risk events to develop a reasonable estimate.

2. **Outage duration.** The range of outage durations for each threat must be estimated in order to be able to estimate service interruption losses. If the outage duration is not the same for all the IT systems that the risk event impacts, one may either use an average value or define a separate risk event for each of the systems, keeping in mind the aggregation considerations just discussed.

Until an initial overall risk assessment, such as Exhibit 62.6, has been generated, analysts do not know which of the input data are important. Consequently, it is counterproductive to devote effort to refining initial data. The wide range of values encountered in a typical risk assessment makes it clear that rough initial estimates of the risk parameters will be sufficiently accurate to identify the critical parameters.

62.6.5   Threat Effect Factors, ALE, and SOL Estimates.   From the basic risk assessment algorithms, it is possible to determine the risk event/loss potential pairs for which the threat effect factor is greater than zero (see Section 62.6.2), and having done so, to estimate the value of the factor. It is then possible to use the risk data discussed earlier and the algorithms to calculate an estimate of the ALE and SOL for each of the pairs, and then to tabulate the individual ALE and SOL estimates to obtain a complete risk assessment for the IT organization. This is useful as a baseline because it provides an assessment against which to evaluate potential risk mitigation measures. In other words, the benefit of a risk management measure is the amount by which it reduces this baseline or current expected loss estimate.

In order to validate the assessment, it is necessary to identify the threat event/loss potential pairs that account for the majority of the expected losses. Typically, about 20 percent of the pairs cause 80 percent of the total expected loss. Reviewing the details of each input item, these questions should be asked: Were source data transcribed correctly? Are the assumptions reasonable? Were calculations made correctly? Does any threat event/loss potential pair account for so much of the expected losses that it should be disaggregated from other data items? Once the validation process is complete and indicated changes have been made, it is feasible to consider risk mitigation, but first one must gain acceptance of these data.

Field experience has disclosed a very powerful technique for gaining acceptance of estimates used in the risk assessment. First we gather data from knowledgeable people in the organization: line-of-business managers, IT specialists, audit, security, and the like. We use these data to make a preliminary baseline estimate of risks as described. We then convene a round table meeting of all the people who provided the data. We show them the results and the input data. This results in a useful discussion of the data and tends to identify inputs based on faulty assumptions, personal biases, and misinformation. It is rather like an instant peer review. The agreed changes to the input data are then used to make a final estimate of risks, which can be used to evaluate proposed mitigation measures.

62.6.6 Sensitivity Testing.   The preceding discussion implies that a single value is to be estimated for each of the risk parameters included in the risk assessment. However, it may be thought that a parameter should not be limited to a single value and that a Monte Carlo technique should be used to generate a set of ALE and SOL estimates. In a Monte Carlo approach, one generates random inputs into a model following specified probability distribution functions for each of the variables being studied. The outputs of the model then generate frequency distributions that allow one to evaluate the sensitivity of critical outputs to the precision of specific inputs. There are two obstacles to using this approach. Apart from the big increase in the complexity of the calculations, there is still a requirement to select a *single* risk mitigation strategy based on the set of ALE and SOL estimates. It is not feasible to install a range of performance value for a given mitigation measure to match a range of loss estimates. As described previously, cost-beneficial risk mitigation measures are selected by calculating the baseline ALE and then recalculating the ALE, assuming that the proposed mitigation measure has been installed. The difference between the two ALE estimates is taken to be a reasonable estimate of the return in the ROI calculation. Assuming two sets of 1,000 ALE estimates (without and with a proposed mitigation measure) generated by a Monte Carlo simulation, calculating all possible differences produces a set of 1 million returns. Which one should be selected to calculate ROI?

Using the most likely value for each risk parameter and generating only two ALE estimates, the difference between the two may be used to calculate ROI. Because the ROI typically flows from a relatively large number of parameters, the overall result will tend to average out any individual departures from the average values used, and so will be a fair representation of the actual risk losses that will occur.

However, if confidence in the accuracy of an estimate is extremely low, estimates using low, median, and high values of the parameters should be used to evaluate the effect on the overall results. Whenever a risk assessment includes a material low-confidence parameter, full disclosure should be made to the managers who review and act on the results. Risk analysts should bear in mind that almost all other decisions about resource allocations that senior managers are regularly called on to make are based on uncertain estimates of future events. There is nothing unique about the uncertainties surrounding risk mitigation decisions.

62.6.7 Selecting Risk Mitigation Measures. The objective of the risk mitigation process is to identify the optimum set of mitigation measures. The first step is to address the intolerable SOL exposures as discussed in Section 62.5.3. The risk assessment and the evaluation of potential risk mitigation measures provide the raw material on which to base an implementation strategy for the risk exposures in the midrange. Considerations include:

1. The mitigation measures with negative ROIs can be discarded.
2. The remaining mitigation measures can be tabulated in three ways:
   a. In descending order of net benefit: ALE reduction minus the implementation cost.
   b. In ascending order of implementation cost.
   c. In descending order of ROI.
3. Based on other considerations, senior management selects mitigation measures from one of the three lists. Two other considerations include:
   1. The availability of resources for risk mitigation may be limited, in which case some mitigation actions must be deferred until the next budgeting period. In extreme cases the lowest-cost measures may be selected.
   2. The mitigation of risk exposures that have a particularly undesirable effect on marketing considerations, as compared with other loss categories, may be given priority.

62.7 SUMMARY. This chapter has shown the tremendous advantage of having a detailed, quantitative assessment of the risk exposures leading to a quantitative evaluation of prospective mitigation measures. Senior managers will appreciate the advantage of using rational business judgment in place of seat-of-the-pants guesswork.

62.8 FURTHER READING

Berg, A., and S. Smedshammer. *Cost of Risk—A Performance Vehicle for the Risk Manager*. Linköpings, Sweden: Linköpings University, 1994.
Gordon, L. A. *Managerial Accounting—Concepts and Empirical Evidence*. McGraw-Hill, 2000.
Hamilton, G. *This Is Risk Management*. Studentlitteratur: Chartwell-Bratt, 1988.
Jacobson, R.V. "Operational Risk Management: Theory and Practice." Symposium of Risk Management and Cyber-Informatics, Orlando, FL, 2004.
Jacobson, R. V. "What Is a Rational Goal for Security?" *Security Management* (December 2000).
Lalley, E.d P. *Corporate Uncertainty & Risk Management*, Risk Management Society Publishing, 1982.

Murray, W. H. "Security Should Pay: It Should Not Cost." In: *Proceedings of the IFIP/Sec '95*. Chapman & Hall, 1995.

National Institute of Standards and Technology. *Guideline for the Analysis of Local Area Network Security*. Federal IT Standard Publication 191 (November 1994).

Reiss, R. D., and M. Thomas. *Statistical Analysis of Extreme Values*, Birkhäuser Verlag, 2001.

Ropeik, D. *Risk—A Practical Guide for Deciding What's Really Safe and What's Really Dangerous in the World Around You*. Houghton Mifflin, 2002.

Sunstein, C. R. *Risk and Reason*. Cambridge University Press, 2002.

62.9 NOTES

1. The term "mitigation measure" is used here broadly to refer to all actions taken to manage risks, and may include logical controls over access to data, physical controls over access to IT hardware, facilities to monitor operations, selection and supervision of IT personnel, policy and procedures to guide operations, and so forth— in short, all of the security techniques described in this *Computer Security Handbook*.

2. The full reference is: ISO/IES 17799-2005(E) Information Technology—Security techniques—Code of Practice for Information Security Management available in the United States from ANSI.

3. The full reference is: Global Technology Audit Guide—Information Technology Controls. It is published by the Institute of Internal Auditors.

4. Another way of expressing this concept is: Perfect security is infinitely expensive, and so it is not a rational goal of a risk management program.

5. As a practical matter, it may become obvious that in some situations, the differences between the members of a group of like IT systems are too small to be significant and that a single set of security measures can be adopted for all of the systems.

6. "Expected loss" is a shorthand term for the losses an organization can reasonably expect to experience, given its risk environment and the potential for loss of its functions and assets. It is the sum of the individual ALEs.

7. This author has made it a practice at the end of each interview to ask: "Is there something I should have asked about?" or words to that effect. In most cases new information emerges as a result.

8. The plot was generated automatically by CORA® (Cost-Of-Risk Analysis), a risk management software system.

9. Return on investment is the ratio of the return received from an investment to the investment itself. If a bank pays back $1.05 one year after $1.00 has been deposited in the bank, the ROI is roughly 5 percent. To determine ROI accurately, one must take the ratio of the present value of the return to the present value of the investment.

10. A given measure may address more than one threat, so the total of the individual reductions in expected loss is used to evaluate the ROI of the measure.

11. This is an example of the advantage of aggregation. Rather than estimating the loss potential for individual physical item, it is much more efficient to aggregate the items into large classes. It may also be feasible to estimate loss potential on the basis of replacement cost per unit area.

12. The term "liability" is used here as a shorthand for "exposure to liability." For example, an IT service performed for others might expose the organization to a liability action if the service was performed incorrectly, resulting in a client loss. This potential risk exposure is referred to here simply as a liability.

13. The term "denial of service" implies that service interruptions are the result of deliberate attacks on an IT system, but, of course, there are many other threats that cause service interruptions. For this reason, the term may cause misunderstanding, and so should not be used.

14. The use of the word "objective" is unfortunate in this context. It would be more precise to use a term like "provision" of "performance" to make clear that the quantity is what a contingency plan is expected to achieve, not a vague goal. However, the terms "RTO" and "RPO" are widely used so we use them here.

CHAPTER **63**

MANAGEMENT RESPONSIBILITIES AND LIABILITIES

Carl Hallberg, M. E. Kabay, Bridgitt Robertson, and Arthur E. Hutt

63.1 INTRODUCTION. This chapter reviews the critical roles of management in establishing, implementing, and maintaining information security policies in the modern enterprise. It also reviews some of the risks to management personnel in failing to ensure adequate standards of information security.[1]

63.1.1   Role of Management.   Organizations are unequally affected by the risk of loss. In certain government computer installations, matters of national security are at stake, and the measures required to protect such facilities are elaborate and costly. At the other end of the spectrum are computers used exclusively for word processing of unclassified materials, and which are not connected to networks; these require few security precautions except for file backup and antivirus software. This chapter and this *Handbook* do not address either of these extremes, but rather the bulk of user organizations in business, government, and universities, where concentrations of information assets and dependence on computers create an exposure to loss, and managers must balance security with cost effectiveness and common sense while convincing colleagues with a superficial knowledge of security to pay attention to their recommendations.

Management provides the essential framework for accomplishing technical work. Whether it is drawing up a security policy, enforcing such policies, training the individuals who will implement and enforce those policies, or proposing a budget to get all this done, management plays an essential role. Information technology (IT) managers ensure the consistent functioning of the organizational computing environment. Ideally, they also provide insights and guidance to upper management in strategic planning to take advantage of new opportunities.

Many organizations, regardless of size and history, have heterogeneous networks with many different operating systems running different applications and serving many purposes and clients. Web servers sit next to e-mail servers, which connect to outside networks, which then rely on connections to more than one third-party corporate network. The rapid pace of technological change impedes the IT manager's ability to keep the enterprise IT infrastructure running smoothly.

A key function of IT managers is loss avoidance by managing risk intelligently, in order to reduce the likelihood of trouble in the IT sector and to reduce the costs of coping with such trouble.[2] In a broader sense, this entire *Handbook* is designed to support management in these efforts.

IT managers must focus constantly on enabling business functions. Given that most enterprises do not consider security as their main task, IT managers must ensure that information security policies and technology support, rather than hinder, the principal business of the enterprise. It is equally important to impress this philosophy of service to the strategic and operational goals of the enterprise on all members of the security staff. Many of these members may have developed their careers entirely in the technical sectors, and they may not have developed a service orientation towards their nontechnical fellow workers, and toward the enterprise itself.

63.1.2   CISO.   In recent years, information security has been growing in visibility as a major business concern. IT managers are now being joined by information security managers. For example, a major bank responded to infiltration of its systems in the 1990s by naming a CISO, a chief information security officer reporting at the same level as officers such as the CIO (chief information officer), CFO (chief financial officer), COO (chief operations officer), CTO (chief technology officer), and CEO (chief executive officer). Together, the CIO and the CISO face complex responsibilities, and are increasingly visible in the corporate infrastructure.

Today, CISOs are increasingly found in all types of corporations. They may report to the CIO, or they may have a position on an equal level with the CIO. Some of the functions in a security organization are suggested in the hierarchy that follows. (These functions do not imply one team or one person per function but simply illustrate the range of functions a CISO must coordinate.)

- CISO
  - Security policy team
    - Development
    - Awareness
    - Education
    - Update management
  - Access controls
    - Data classification functions
    - Identification, authentication and authorization functions
  - Intrusion detection and prevention
    - Outward-facing intrusion detection systems
    - Gateway security devices
    - Malware control team
  - Security assessment
    - Security auditing
    - Penetration team
  - Engineering coordination
    - Software quality assurance coordination
    - Patch management review
    - Network security oversight
    - Control systems and logging management
  - Security Incident Response Team
    - Planning and rehearsals management
    - First line response
    - Data gathering and forensic analysis
    - Coordination with internal functions (legal, public relations, human resources, etc.)
    - Coordination with law enforcement

One of the factors in this increased visibility of the CISO is the rapid growth in the popular press of technology issues coverage and of information security breaches in particular. For example, distributed denial-of-service attacks, malware infestations, breakdowns of privacy policies, theft of credit card numbers, loss of control of large volumes of personally identifiable information, identity theft, Web site defacements, spam, phishing, and the other forms of abuse to information systems, described in several chapters of this *Handbook,* have kept the public aware of information security and its breaches.[3]

In some sense, publicity has helped the IT world because some IT managers now have increased ammunition with which to argue for management support of the security function. Publicity has increased visibility, however, so that even a minor breach of security may spark an overreaction in the upper echelons of the enterprise. Indeed, in

California, it is now law (SB 1386) that companies that suffer from some forms of information security breaches must quickly advise their customers of these events.[4]

63.1.3 Information Security Integrating into Strategic Vision.   IT security managers are now able to help their businesses achieve strategic goals and to further their responsibilities by showing that security involves more than just protecting assets, it is also potentially a business enabler. In the absence of a secure IT infrastructure, businesses may be slow to enter a given market for fear of losses and liabilities resulting from security breaches. However, with security integrated into the corporate culture, these enterprises can confidently enter new arenas and convince their potential clients that their data will be safe. The authors have personal experience from consulting assignments in which clients stated that their own potential customers were reluctant to do business with them because their security measures were inadequate.

George Lin describes the benefits of a business-focused IT organization:

> In a business-focused IT organization...IT staff are more interested in understanding the business—and the people, processes, and organization that make up the business—than they are in the technology for its own sake. These staff members possess a balanced set of soft skills, and business acumen as well as analytical and technical skills. They think about business processes first and technology second. The solutions they propose tend to be more complete, often involving people, process, and organization as well as technology, which is seen as simply a tool. Interacting with such an organization yields an experience similar to that expected from Big Four consulting firms, but with the added intimacy and insights only an internal organization can provide.
>
> More importantly, IT/business alignment becomes a nonissue because it is natural to a business-focused IT organization, the very DNA of its staff. There is no need to expend effort specifically on IT/business alignment because the business-focused IT organization thinks and acts like the business that it serves, and is an integral part of that business.[5]

In this framework, information security becomes not an afterthought, preventing loss, but part of the design strategy, which will help realize gain. This is a much more powerful, and positive, view of information security's role in the business world than is the traditional one. Using information security principles in the design of a product or service generally helps to create a more robust product or service, one that will be less prone to risk.

The National Institute of Standards and Technology has articulated a roadmap for integrating security considerations into the system development life cycle (SDLC)[6] (with addition of three more security objectives in compliance with the Parkerian hexad described in Chapter 8 in this *Handbook*):

> A general SDLC includes the following five phases: *initiation, acquisition/development, implementation/assessment, operations/maintenance, and sunset (disposition)*. Each of these five phases includes a minimum set of security tasks needed to effectively incorporate security in the system development process. Including security early in the information SDLC will usually result in less expensive and more effective security than adding it to an operational system.
>
> The following questions should be addressed in determining the security controls that will be required for a system:
>
> • How critical is the system in meeting the organization's mission?
> • What are the security objectives required by the system, e.g., integrity, confidentiality, and availability [and control, authenticity, and utility]?

- What regulations and policies are applicable in determining what is to be protected?
- What are the threats that are applicable in the environment where the system will be operational?

Integrating a security methodology into a product or service helps to defines roles and responsibilities and helps to manage expectations.

63.1.4   Net Present Value of Information Security.   A paper from the late 1990s articulated the positive value of information security in a competitive economy. The summary included these conclusions:

> The news is that we can now go beyond gibbering and fist shaking. In today's e-commerce environment, effective information security can actually increase business and increase profits, not merely reduce risk. . . .
>
> Tom Nelson, VP and Chief Strategy Officer of AtomicTangerine, has defined the Net Present Value of Information Security (NPVSec) as follows: "NPVSec is the value protection and value creation that is realized when barriers to e-Business are removed through mechanisms that ensure business integrity, service availability, and customer/consumer confidentiality and privacy. Value creation examples include: new distribution channels, new revenue streams, new business models, among others."
>
> In other words, instead of viewing information security solely as a risk-avoidance measure—like a kind of insurance policy that never actually pays anything back—we are forced by the nature of e-business to accept that security actually *supports* and *enables* e-business.
>
> As we have seen . . . e-business has brought security to the forefront of strategic thinking for successful businesses. Business leaders can no longer tolerate the view that security is an add-on feature relegated to the end of the design process. Security is a process, not a product or a state; security affects every e-businesses bottom line in a positive way. Security is no longer a cost center; it's part of your repertoire for meeting the legitimate needs of your public. Instead of seeing security as solely the purview of the technical staff in your organization, you should ensure that your marketing and public relations departments are well versed in the principles of information security and can communicate effectively to an anxious public about the measures you are taking to safeguard your customers' privacy and their money.[7]

Another perspective on the value of integrating information security into a corporate culture argues that "the responsibility for protecting the organization's information assets is no longer restricted to the CSO [chief security officer]. Every employee has a responsibility to help protect the proprietary data they are entrusted with."[8] The authors write that:

> This approach
>
> - Improves individual leadership through collaboration and team building.
> - Strengthens corporate allegiance
> - Helps to provide a sense of community
> - Builds an intelligent workforce where every employee is recognized and watched by their peers for their individual contribution to the team's strength. . . .
>
> In addition, embedding security deep into every process of the corporation, starting at the executive level, is an extremely effective method of taking one problem and leveraging the success of that solution to correct other problems.

63.1.5 Case Study: Veterans Affairs.   The next summary of a specific case of management failures will serve to help readers think about the management responsibilities for information assurance.[9]

63.1.5.1 Announcement without Taking Responsibility. In March 2007, *Network World* writer Jon Brodkin wrote an excellent analysis of 10 letters informing victims of data theft or loss of control of personally identifiable information (PII) that their data might be compromised.[10] He pointed out that almost all of the letters failed to express any responsibility for the loss of control over data stored on unencrypted disks that were lost or stolen or for poorly secured Web sites that posted PII without protection, or with poor protection. Perhaps staff attorneys warned the public relations officials to avoid any implication of responsibility to avoid contributing anything that would exacerbate their liability in potential lawsuits. Passive voice is often used to shift responsibility from specific agents to the great gaseous cloud of the unnamable and unblamable. The classic example is "Mistakes were made."

In 2007, this letter was sent to physicians affected by a security breach.

DEPARTMENT OF VETERANS AFFAIRS

1615 Woodward St.

Austin, TX 78772

——, MD

Dear ——, MD:

I am writing to you, as the Director of the Veterans Integrated Service Network (VISN) 7 in Atlanta, Georgia, to inform you that I have been notified that a portable computer hard drive used by an employee of the Birmingham Veterans Affairs (VA) Medical Center is missing. This portable hard drive was used to back-up information contained on a VA employee's office computer, related to research projects with which the employee was involved. A file on the portable hard drive included information from the Unique Physician Identification Number (UPIN) Directory dated 2004, which includes demographic information and identifiers, such as the UPIN, dates of birth, state license numbers, business addresses, and employer identification numbers (EIN). In the case of your information, we believe the EIN was your Social Security Number. This file was obtained by VA from the Centers for Medicare & Medicaid Services (CMS) for the purpose of conducting research on veterans' health care.

The Birmingham VA Medical Center has conducted extensive physical searches and has involved local police and Federal investigative resources, and a reward is being offered; however, the hard drive remains missing. To prevent further security breaches or losses, we have taken immediate measures to protect the integrity and security of all personally identifiable information including prohibition of the use of external drives and the required encryption of personally identifiable information when authorized distribution is required.

An independent risk analysis was conducted as required by law, and risk mitigation recommendations are being implemented immediately. VA will contact you shortly by mail to offer a credit monitoring service at no cost to you. In the mean time, one precaution we recommend is for you to request a free credit report from one or more of the three national credit bureaus by calling the toll free number 1-877-322-8228. The credit bureaus may also be contacted at:

Equifax

P.O. Box 740241

Atlanta, GA 30374

1-800-685-1111

Experian

P.O. Box 9554

Allen, TX 75013

1-888-397-3742

TransUnion

P.O. Box 2000

Chester, PA 19022

1-800-916-8800

More information about credit protection, including placing a "fraud alert" on your accounts, is available by calling the Federal Trade Commission at its toll free number, 1-877-438-4338, or by visiting its website, http://www.ftc.gov/

If you have questions concerning this letter, the Birmingham VA Medical Center has established a dedicated call center to answer your questions. Please contact us toll free at 1-877-xxx-xxxx from 6:00 am to 9:00 pm CT, or e-mail us at < address suppressed >.

We at VA take information security and privacy very seriously. We apologize for any inconvenience or concern this situation may cause, but we believe it is important for you to be fully informed of any potential risk to you.

Sincerely,

[digitized signature]

Lawrence A. Biro

Network Director, VISN 7

63.1.5.2 *Initial Problems.* On May 3, 2006, a career civil servant at the Department of Veterans Affairs (VA) violated official policy by taking computer disks containing PII about 26.5 million veterans home with him. The disks were stolen from his home.[11] Two weeks after officials learned of the theft, the VA disclosed the incident to the public and set up a Web site and an 800-number to provide veterans and with information and a channel for reporting possible identity theft.[12]

The USA.gov Web site put up a page called "Latest Information on Veterans Affairs Data Security"[13] with answers to frequently asked questions; the VA itself also continued issuing press releases.[14]

In early June 2006, the VA announced that the stolen data might include PII about up to 1.1 million active-duty troops, 430,000 members of the National Guard, and 645,000 members of the reserves.[15] Reactions from a coalition of veterans groups were immediate: They launched a class-action lawsuit demanding full disclosure of exactly who was affected by the theft and seeking $1,000 in damages for each victim.[16]

The VA struggled to cope with the bad publicity and potential legal liability resulting from the May theft. On May 26, 2006, Secretary of VAR James Nicholson issued a Directive to all VA supervisors in which he wrote:

Having access to such sensitive information brings with it a grave responsibility. It requires that we protect Federal property and information, and that it shall not be used for other than authorized activities and only in authorized locations. As managers, supervisors, and team leaders it is your responsibility to ensure that your staff is aware of and adheres to all Federal and VA policies and guidelines governing privacy protected material. I also expect each and every one of you to know what sensitive and confidential data your subordinates, including contractors, have access to and how, when and where that data is used, especially in those cases where it is used or accessed off-site."[17]

On May 30, 2006, the VA fired the analyst "responsible for data loss" and announced changes in the administration of information security in the organization.[18] The press release made no mention of who was responsible for allowing anybody to store unencrypted PII on VA computers or media.

Coincidentally, at the end of May, the Government Accountability Office (GAO) issued a report: "GAO-06-612: Homeland Security: Guidance and Standards are needed for Measuring the Effectiveness of Agencies' Facility Protection Efforts."[19] The report specifically named the VA as requiring "guidance and standards for measuring performance in federal government facility protection."

On June 21, 2006, the VA announced that it would provide free credit monitoring for everyone affected by the data theft in May.[20]

But worse was yet to come.

63.1.5.3 *Systematic Management Failures.*   On June 14, 2006, Linda D. Koontz, Director, Information Management Issues, and Gregory C. Wilshusen, Director, Information Security Issues of the Government Accountability Office of the United States, offered testimony before the Committee on Veterans' Affairs, House of Representatives. The GAO report on their analysis and recommendations later appeared as GAO-06-866.[21] Highlights of their analysis included these comments:

> For many years, significant concerns have been raised about VA's information security—particularly its lack of a robust information security program, which is vital to avoiding the compromise of government information, including sensitive personal information. Both GAO and the department's inspector general have reported recurring weaknesses in such areas as access controls, physical security, and segregation of incompatible duties. The department has taken steps to address these weaknesses, but these have not been sufficient to establish a comprehensive information security program. For example, it is still developing plans to complete a security incident response program to monitor suspicious activity and cyber alerts, events, and incidents. Without an established and implemented security program, the department will continue to have major challenges in protecting its information and information systems from security breaches such as the one it recently experienced.

Two related reports appeared about a week later with specific comments about the May 2006 data breach[22] and about the overall challenges facing the VA and the Department of Defense (DoD) in protecting PII of active-duty and retired military personnel.[23]

At the end of June 2006, the laptop and external hard drive stolen on May 3 from the consultant's home were recovered. Forensic examination suggested that the data had not been accessed. This good news suggested that the disaster might blow over.

It was not to be.

The Inspector General (IG) of the VA, George Opfer, released a report on July 11 severely criticizing senior managers of the VA for their lackadaisical response to the original theft of unencrypted PII. The inadequate data security policies had not yet been corrected.[24] VA secretary James Nicholsen responded to the IG's report with assurances that the agency had "embarked on a course of action to wholly improve its cyber and information security programs."[25]

63.1.5.4 *Continued Problems.* On Monday, August 7, 2006, Secretary Nicholson announced that a Unisys subcontractor working for the VA offices in Philadelphia and Pittsburgh had reported that his desktop computer was missing. The computer contained PII for 18,000 and possibly up to 38,000 veterans.

A week later (August 14), the VA announced that it would spend $3.7 million on encryption software and would encrypt data on all the department's computers and external data storage media or devices. Installation would begin Friday, August 18.[26]

In mid-September, the stolen Unisys desktop computer with VA data was located and a temporary employee working on subcontract to Unisys was arrested and charged in the theft.[27]

In October 2006, the Congressional Committee on Oversight and Government Reform published a report on data losses in U.S. government agencies since January 1, 2003.[28] There were 788 incidents in 19 agencies—in addition to hundreds of incidents at the VA. The report's findings included these bald assertions:

1. Data loss is a government-wide occurrence. . . .

2. Agencies do not always know what has been lost. The letters received by the Committee demonstrate that, in many cases, agencies do not know what information has been lost or how many individuals could be impacted by a particular data loss. Similarly, agencies do not appear to be tracking all possible losses of personal information, making it likely that their reports to the committee are incomplete. For example, the Department of Justice reports that, prior to the May 2006 Veterans Administration data breach, "the Department did not track the content of lost, stolen, or otherwise compromised devices."

3. Physical security of data is essential. Only a small number of the data breaches reported to the Committee were caused by hackers breaking into computer systems online. The vast majority of data losses arose from physical thefts of portable computers, drives, and disks, or unauthorized use of data by employees.

4. Contractors are responsible for many of the reported breaches. Federal agencies rely heavily on private sector contractors for information technology management services. Thus, many of the reported data breaches were the responsibility of contractors.

Alas, the best-laid plans of VA administrators gang aft agley, and on October 31, 2006, VA officials informed 1,400 veterans that their PII had been lost on unencrypted data disks sent by mail from the VA clinic in Muskogee, Oklahoma, on May 10, June 10, and July 10 were lost. A spokesperson for the hospital explained the three-month delay as being due to the "wait for officials in Washington to approve the wording of the letter." Approval arrived October 26. There was no explanation of why the data were unencrypted nor why two additional disks were mailed out after the May 10 disk was lost. A report on this incident dated November 3, 2006, by Rick Maze in the *Federal Times*[29] also indicated that a laptop computer from the VA hospital in Manhattan was stolen on September 8 from a computer locked to a cart in a locked room in a locked corridor—and that the data on the stolen machine was deliberately not encrypted despite policy because "a decision had been made not to encrypt data being used for medical purposes."

And more was to come in February 2007.

63.1.5.5   Analyses and Responses.   On Friday, February 2, 2007, Secretary of Veterans Affairs Jim Nicholson announced that a VA employee in the VA medical center in Birmingham, Alabama, had reported an external hard drive as missing on January 22. According to Representative Spencer Bachus (R-AL), the backup hard drive contained PII on up to 48,000 veterans—and despite VA regulations promulgated in 2006, as many as 20,000 of those records were not encrypted.[30] A week later, the VA admitted that the hard drive actually contained PII about 535,000 patients and 1.3 million doctors.[31] It was that loss that led to the letter quoted in the first part of this section.[32]

A few weeks later, the GAO released the closest thing to an exasperated blast of which government workers are capable. In testimony before the Subcommittee on Oversight and Investigations, Committee on Veterans' Affairs, House of Representatives on February 28, 2007, GAO Director of Information Security Issues Gregory C. Wilshusen presented a report entitled "Veterans Affairs Needs to Address Long-Standing Weaknesses."[33] The summary on page 2 of the PDF file includes this commentary:

> For many years, GAO has raised significant concerns about VA's information security—particularly its lack of a comprehensive information security program, which is vital to safeguarding government information. The figure below details information security weaknesses that GAO identified from 1998 to 2005. As shown, VA had not consistently implemented appropriate controls for (1) limiting, preventing, and detecting electronic access to sensitive computerized information; (2) restricting physical access to computer and network equipment to authorized individuals; (3) segregating incompatible duties among separate groups or individuals; (4) ensuring that changes to computer software were authorized and timely; or (5) providing continuity of computerized systems and operations. The department's IG has also reported recurring weaknesses throughout VA in such areas as access controls, physical security, and segregation of incompatible duties. In response, the department has taken actions to address these weaknesses, but these have not been sufficient to establish a comprehensive information security programs. As a result, sensitive information has remained vulnerable to inadvertent or deliberate misuse, loss, or improper disclosure. Without an established and implemented security program, the department will continue to have major challenges in protecting its systems and information from security breaches.

In early March 2007, the VA reacted to the January 22 loss of the portable hard drive. CIO Robert Howard promulgated a policy restricting the use of portable data storage devices. Only flash drives smaller than 2 GB—and only those issued by the VA's CIO office itself—would be permitted on the VA network or computers. Encryption would be used throughout the system, just like the assurance issued in August 2006 about spending $3.7 million on encryption tools.[34] In addition, the CIO announced sweeping changes in security administration, with promotion of five deputy CIOs to the rank of assistant secretaries for these functions: application development, information security, operations and maintenance, resource management, and strategic planning.

As of late May 2007, federal agencies announced that they would stop storing Social Security numbers and other PII wherever possible.[35]

For an extensive compilation of additional cases of interest, see the "Chronology of Data Security Breaches" managed by GuardianEdge.[36]

63.2   RESPONSIBILITIES.   Modern information processing philosophy transcends the boundaries of the computer room and demands the consistent delivery and collection of data to and from remote sections of the organization. Once this operating mode is extensively used, the company becomes dependent on its continued availability. Any shutdown or cutoff in service can be disastrous, unless the company is able promptly to revise operations, in order to continue vital activities. Central computers, local servers, workstations, and the network are essential to the operating environment.

Computer security includes the protection of confidentiality, control, integrity, authenticity, availability, and utility of information.[37] Computer security encompasses the total infrastructure for maintenance and delivery of information, including physical computer hardware, supporting equipment, communication systems, logical processes defined by software, and the human factors that support and possibly threaten this infrastructure.

Computer security is inseparable from the basic structure of the information processing system; one cannot and should not design a system without including security as an underlying strategy. The objectives and properties of secure systems must be considered collectively from their inception.

Software, systems, and networks should be designed to ensure information protection that corresponds to business needs. There are many steps that can be taken to do this, but managers must place a high priority on making it happen. Managers are in a position to see what the business needs actually are, much more so than the typical infosec analyst or engineer. A prime example is e-commerce Web site management. No reputable site allows transactions without minimal SSL encryption. A savvy information security manager will track all information from the setting up of the SSL tunnel, all the way through the shipping process, and beyond into the storage of information gathered during any transaction, and ensure that security is not lacking at any juncture in the process. If the data are not securely stored while sitting in a database, the whole process falls apart.

The ability of a system to ensure accuracy, reliability, and confidentiality is a basic building block. The collective system (hardware, software, communications, and people) must be able to maintain and process data correctly, and move traffic (transactions, inquiries, commands, etc.) from its origins to the intended destinations, without unauthorized modification or disclosure and without misrepresentation, forgery, or other breaches of authenticity. Reliable performance is essential. Any failures should be orderly and predictable, with adequate detection methods to provide timely evidence of failure and to permit prompt corrective actions. Hardware/software limitations should be known and documented, as should load limits. Bounds checking, at a minimum, should be implemented in all software to avoid buffer overflows. Any inputs that are not checked should be documented, and measures should be put in place to detect possible abuses.

Suspicious user activity should be detectable through appropriate analysis of logfiles. The network and its data should be protected from contamination or outside interference using appropriate gateway security devices and other intrusion prevention systems. Firewalls must be present, updated, and frequently reviewed, along with intrusion detection systems and intrusion prevention systems (IDS/IPS), and all logs should be centralized and scrutinized. Measures should be put in place to ensure that data transmitted are the same as the data received and that error correction is used wherever possible.

Service-level agreements should define goals for efficient response and adequate capacity, in order to support acceptable performance. Systems should be able to recover quickly from either short-term or long-term disruptions. Backup measures, including data backup and equipment backup[38] and tested incident response, contingency, and recovery plans, should be in place.[39] Appropriate cost recovery measures should also be in place.[40] Prevention of harm is of primary importance.

Single points of failures should be avoided. Avoid dependence on single equipment devices or single communications pathways. Web servers should be clustered, and databases should be replicated across various servers and placed in different geographic regions. Avoid overloading the network at peak activity periods. Provide environmental backup (redundant power, air-conditioning, heating and other support systems, limited equipment access, etc.) to reduce other exposures.[41]

Management should have the capability to limit who can access the systems, how much capacity can be used for each purpose or function, what purposes are allowed, what data are accessible and transmittable for each user, and what connections can be made. Technical measures include access control (system access, resource restrictions), logon password control, alternative identification methods (personal tokens, digital signatures, biometric authentication), callback connections, network isolation from public networks, firewalls, and physical security of system components.[42]

Administrative measures include publication of policies, standards, and guidelines; screening of personnel; security awareness training; system change control procedures, including security criteria in system design; and monitoring system activity and quality.[43]

In addition, management should use the audit function as an independent arbiter to measure compliance with policies, standards, and guidelines as well as to assess the adequacy of technical protection. The system and its network should preserve and display evidence of use, behavior, and content, and should record deviations from expected use.[44]

Managers are responsible for specific tasks or functions to the extent that they make decisions about business processes and suffer the consequences or reap the benefits of those decisions.

63.2.1 Policy Management.

Managers spend more time on people issues than on technical issues. The right people must be hired for each position. (See Chapter 45 for more on employment practices and policies.) Employees who do not work responsibly and competently must either be brought up to the proper standard or let go. Employees who do their jobs properly must be kept satisfied, lest they move to another organization. Management in the IT world must ensure compliance with corporate policies.[45] Compliance with policies includes motivation, supervision, judgment, and adaptation.

63.2.2 Motivation.

Employees need motivation to pay attention to information security policies, which often are perceived as a nuisance, interfering with the fundamental goals of the enterprise. Upper management, in particular, must set an example by following enterprise policies; when top managers are seen to ignore policies, the people reporting to them quickly imitate their behavior, and the problem spreads throughout the organization. For example, if the CEO refuses to wear a picture badge, the vice presidents (VPs) will quickly follow suit because they will associate *not* wearing badges with high status. Similarly, the directors reporting to VPs will start dropping their badges, and so within a few months the entire hierarchy will be convinced that no one but stock clerks should wear badges. Sometime later, the stock clerks will be resisting badges too.

According to *Computerworld* writer Mary Pratt, writing in 2006:

The risk that employees pose is significant. They can fall prey to social engineering, a fancy term for being conned. They can ignore company policy by failing to encrypt sensitive data. Or they might install unauthorized software that can corrupt the system.

Think you're well protected? Recent findings from the Computing Technology Industry Association might convince you otherwise. In this year's CompTIA information security study, 59% of the organizations surveyed indicated that their latest security breaches were the result of human error alone. That's up from 47% last year.[46]

A survey by NFO Prognostics highlighted that 66 percent of the companies surveyed believe that staff training or certification has improved their IT security through increased awareness and proactive risk identification.[47]

Since people can be the company's greatest strength against attacks, training employees should be a high priority in any organization. At Stop and Shop, in February 2007, employees noticed suspicious activity; they saw four people tampering with the keypads for credit/debit card authorization units. The employees notified police at once, and the suspects were arrested. That kind of quick thinking and commitment can make an enormous difference in the effectiveness of security systems of all kinds—and it depends on management support and motivation.[48]

Some managers think that punishment is the only motivation that can change behavior; but everything known about human psychology shows that reward is more powerful.[49] Reward is not limited to salary increases and bonuses; sometimes the most effective way to keep IT employees satisfied and productive is to provide training. The IT world is evolving, and the demand for competent staff has never been higher. Most employees want to feel that their employers value their services and that they are worth an investment to improve staff competence. Training employees, and providing challenging opportunities for the exercise of intelligence, serves the interests of both employer and employee. See Section 63.5.3 for more details about education.

Challenging employees in other ways can be highly motivating. For example, managers can encourage staff to prepare and deliver presentations at internal meetings and at security conferences. Some examples of useful conferences are SecureWorld-Expo, InfoSecWorld, and NetSec. Motivated employees can lead special interest group discussions at conferences (such as RSA, SANS, etc.) and so develop a web of relationships that promote sharing of knowledge, and that enhance their self-image. There are also security contests to test their skills, such as the Honeynet forensics contest.

The Honeynet Project provides archives of past security challenges that allow security staff to challenge their technical skills, as well as to learn and teach new tricks of the trade. The Honeynet Project posts these challenges on the Web,[50] and tasks would-be contestants to unravel what the hacks were and how they were performed. Along with finding out what had happened, judging was also based on how much information was uncovered and how this information was communicated. These challenges have been solved, but they are still valuable lessons for any infosec staff. Many other challenges pop up frequently and can easily be found using Google.

Many journals and Web-based magazines are ready to accept articles written by professionals in the field. Not only does writing solidify employees' knowledge and build their own confidence, but it also instills confidence in the entire team. Writing and teaching help the enterprise, as well as its clients and partners, to view the security team as a real benefit, at the same time that the organization develops a strong reputation for excellence in security.

Another way for management to make the security team more cohesive is to build camaraderie. A monthly pizza party or an occasional outing to a sports event can do a lot to ease stress and to help everyone to know each other. Having good friends at work can reduce turnover and motivate employees to do their best, not only for the rather abstract goal of doing good for the enterprise, but also because of a commitment to their colleagues.

To help encourage a higher level of expertise, and to establish a feeling of belonging, periodic "brown bag" lunch sessions can be effective. At each session, a different team member can be designated to present an informed talk or to lead a discussion on a topic of general interest. There could even be an informal call for papers, giving team members an opportunity to present valuable information in a professional manner.

At the same time, a little friendly competition can help as well. For example, if the enterprise has a training network that can be subdivided into several subnets, managers can organize a "tiger-team challenge." Each team will be responsible for securing a subnet or host and then given the opportunity to break into the subnet or host of another team. The winners would get both a reward and a responsibility. The reward can be as simple as pizza for the team or a modest trophy. The responsibility would be to present the exploits used and the ways to secure against them to the rest of the teams.

Another way to build the team is to support staff in choosing the areas in which they want to excel. There may be some overlap, but overlap can be good. Clearly, if there are two firewall experts, the enterprise is less vulnerable should one of them be absent. Furthermore, the firewall experts can provide better-quality assurance by discussing alternatives when planning a change and better-quality control by checking each other's work. It can also help to have the security team members switch roles periodically, both to ensure that no one gets into a rut and to contribute to the challenges presented when a change is made.

Last, almost nothing is more infuriating than being expected to accomplish a task without the necessary resources. Adequate time to get a task done is always an important issue, as many people have several tasks to do, and each of the tasks may be seen as critical by someone. A manager should be willing to give the team all of the resources it needs to complete a task in the allotted time, or it should be made clear to other departments, or to higher management, what the realistic expectations are for the completion of such tasks, if required resources are lacking. If expectations are properly managed, there should be less conflict and fewer problems.

It is useful to view management not as separate from the IT security team, but as an integral part of it. This allows management to contribute directly toward the employees' enthusiasm as well as to detect early warning signals of impending trouble. A manager who does not spend time listening to the team members, or who does not understand what their jobs involve at a technical level, will not be respected by the team. Lack of respect will block communication and keep the department from becoming a solid, effectively functioning unit.

63.2.3 Supervision.   What we know about damage to computer systems indicates that errors and omissions are a major source of harm. Poorly trained employees make mistakes, but so do trained employees who have become careless. Managers should examine performance records as a normal part of their supervision of the security team. In particular, every incident that damages production systems should be analyzed to identify the *reasons* for the event. Careful technical support records and log files can help the team spot the crucial weaknesses, whether technical or human, that allowed compromise of the damaged systems.[51]

Analysis of security breaches of all kinds may reveal that certain employees are associated with unusually high or unusually low frequencies of particular problems.

Careful analysis of both types of extremes can be helpful in spotting weaknesses for remediation and strengths from which to learn, so that the knowledge can be spread across the entire unit. However, managers must not assume that disproportionate numbers of problems are necessarily caused by the employees involved; for example, low rates of penetration during the day shift may be associated with lower rates of attack from hackers, who often work in the evenings or nights. Similarly, higher rates of security breaches may, after detailed study, be found to have been caused by factors entirely outside the control of a particular employee.

In addition to monitoring performance, managers must ensure that all employees know that they are being monitored. Warning notices, pre-employment agreements, and yearly policy reviews can ensure that staff develops no unwarranted expectation of privacy about their work.[52]

One of the most effective supervisory practices an information security team leader, or any other manager, can use is *managing by walking around*.[53] Managers should set aside time every week to observe the conditions and to absorb the atmosphere of the working areas. Visiting team members, and hearing about their specific job experiences, both positive and negative, can only improve communications and motivation within the security team.

Not surprisingly, poor communication is a major enemy of effective team development. This poor communication can exist on multiple levels: among IT staff members, between staff members and IT management, and between IT and internal customers.[54]

Tools for enhancing communication include production control meetings, regular brief status review meetings, all-hands updates at which group members are required to give updates, and individual staff members to give technical updates, as well as establishing regular and thorough communication with internal customers and top management.

All members of the IT staff should be familiar with all lines of communication and with what behavior is expected of them in every scenario. Pushing communication awareness down through the organization appears to be an effective strategy.

63.2.4   Judgment and Adaptation.   Management must not permit policies and procedures to keep the work from getting done. The comic strip *Dilbert*[55] has become popular largely because it caricatures managers who apply policy unintelligently; for example, in one real company known to the authors, managers decided to give the marketing department new laptops because of all the traveling they had to do. The managers then decided that to prevent theft, the laptops should be so securely fastened to the employees' desks that they could not be moved at all.

When security policies interfere with productivity, the correct solution is rarely black and white. Usually, neither dropping the policy nor enforcing it without change is appropriate. A hospital security administrator, for example, might note that a workstation in the emergency room is always logged on for the entire day, using the ID and password of the first person who logged on. Clearly, this violates the principle that everyone using the system must be positively identified and authenticated. Piggybacking on the first user damages the credibility of log files and makes it impossible to ascertain exactly which person is retrieving and modifying data at any time during the day. However, cracking down insensitively on the emergency room staff is a bad idea; chances are that the harried medical and support personnel are simply racing to get their work done saving lives. Logging off and on repeatedly is not a good method of identification and authentication in that environment. A reasonable security manager would listen to the employees, understand their point of view and their functional needs, and then explore technical alternatives to the usual ID-password technique. For example, the security manager might find that proximity cards or smart cards could meet the requirements at reasonable cost.[56]

Management must concern itself with safeguarding the resources under its jurisdiction. Just as investors seek both a high rate of return and reasonable safety for their investments, so must managers seek a high rate of return through the effective use of resources under their command and take adequate steps to protect the value of the resources.

The manager's function is essentially the management of resources: human resources and capital resources. In a computer operations environment, capital resources are represented by the investment in equipment and operating programs. Human resources are represented by the skills needed to operate and control both hardware and software facilities. Human capital resources are also represented by complete operating programs. Information is another form of resource, one that is often created as a product of data processing or concentrated at the computer facility, in order better to utilize equipment resources.

63.2.5 Management Failures.   The most pervasive vulnerabilities in computer security are due to poor management. Efforts to contain or mitigate computer security exposures often fall short, or fail, because of management inadequacy, either of senior management or of operating management, or both. Sometimes the problem is simply inertia. Equally damaging is management lip service. In far too many instances, computer security is simply not taken seriously by senior management. Some of the most common management errors are listed next:[57]

- The belief that "if it hasn't been needed before, it probably will not be needed now." This is the default frame of mind, which is really self-insurance.
- Competition with other goals. Security measures use resources that are often needed for other activities. If security is regarded as an add-on burden rather than an integral part of the business process, it may be neglected or postponed.
- Lack of contribution to the bottom line. If security needs to be cost justified as an independent activity, it may be regarded as a target for elimination or reduction.
- Unwillingness properly to fund security activities. Far too often management is reluctant to commit all the resources needed for complete protection. A prime example is the lip-service contingency plan, published and display to the auditors, but never fully implemented.
- The explosive growth of the Internet and of the Web has increased the number of novice computer users into the hundreds of millions worldwide, cowering in fear at the latest hoax but cheerfully sending each other joke programs with embedded viruses. Some of these novices have taken on responsibilities for computer system management and have spread havoc within their organizations.
- The common occurrence of laptop theft has shown how vulnerable *any* kind of unencrypted removable media can be. Several companies have come under fire for not having a laptop encryption policy. This policy should be extended to any type of removable media (such as USB "thumb" drives) for certain types information.
- Cell phones and PDAs are other technologies that need to be controlled. They are frequently connected to company computers, on the company network, to sync

up with Microsoft Outlook e-mail and calendars. These provide another potential point of entry for malicious software.

- Adults such as teachers and parents (many of them violating software copyrights without realizing they are breaking the law) have too often failed to teach children in their care how to resist the wiles of criminal hackers, virus writers, pornographers, and pedophiles. Some of these children have now grown up and become young managers who tolerate, encourage, or demand illegal acts by their employees.

- Some Web sites are being managed by undertrained staff who know nothing about the years-old vulnerabilities they have left invitingly on their systems. These unfortunate people are stuck with inadequate resources and dismissive managers, who nevertheless blame them when the site is plastered with obscenities by teenagers with little or no conscience. Even worse, the Web site may be used in a for-profit scheme by the ever-increasing legions of highly skilled professional hackers.

- In addition to the old vulnerabilities, these undertrained (or simply overworked) staff may also be introducing new vulnerabilities to their Web sites, by using new tools or methodologies with no consideration of security, These new methodologies, such as the current AJAX (Asynchronous JavaScript and XML), may make use of old tools, but may do it in a new insecure way.

- Some Web designers assume that users should trust mobile application programs (Java applets, ActiveX controls) whose origins are uncertain, whose documentation is unavailable, and whose actions may be pathological. Technically incompetent managers who take credit for their corporate Web site may have no idea of what their Webmasters are doing—and failing to do—to protect their site.[58]

- Software makers, who ought to have known better, have blurred the distinction between document and program by adding automatic execution of macros to their word processors. E-mailed Trojan horses are activated automatically when the message is opened. Bloated programs are routinely so full of bugs that consumers now think it is normal to pay money for a service release that fixes what never ought to have been released. Some managers with inadequate training take this situation as a given.

- Not necessarily a failure on just the part of management, software is often written without thought to security at all. Buffer overflows continue to be the "lowhanging fruit" for software hackers. Unfortunately, secure coding has been slow to catch on, but is showing signs of gaining traction today.[59] SANS has announced it will offer courses in secure coding, and there is an expanding list of books and papers on the subject. Perhaps as it becomes mainstream, universities will start requiring full courses in secure coding practices for computer programming degrees.

- We collectively continue to use Internet protocols devised decades ago and which have no provision for packet authentication. Criminals forge mail headers and packet headers with impunity, and use them for denial-of-service attacks and e-mail spam. Network managers continue to avoid output filtering, which could reduce such attacks, because it is too low on their list of priorities, or because they have never considered their responsibility to other Internet users.

- Access control still relies largely on the outdated and ineffective use of passwords chosen by untrained users. Conveniently for criminal hackers, many users pick names of family members, people with whom they are having illicit romances, movie stars, pets, favorite sports teams, and the names of objects on their desks or visible from their windows. Some managers contribute to this situation by refusing to follow recommendations for better passwords and by refusing to consider better, or additional, authentication methods such as tokens and biometrics.

- Some managers are loyal neither to colleagues nor to employers. The boom in firings and job-hopping has led to a shortsighted emphasis on the quarterly bottom line that makes investments in corporate security seem pointless.

- Security specialists still lack reliable data on network and computer intrusions. Although there are now some resources for information sharing, such as CERT/CC, many managers resist contributing to the knowledge base for fear that they and their enterprise will be embarrassed by their victimization.

- Social engineering is still one of the largest weaknesses of the security realm. Hackers really do not need to spend much time trying to break through defenses when so many users are perfectly willing to give them free access to go right through. While it is debatable whether training programs will ever be sufficient to overcome this, managers need to pay close attention to the "phishing" attacks that are now becoming more popular, and more sophisticated.

Some organizations are taking steps to implement creative and memorable security awareness programs such as *Jeopardy*-style games, where workers compete to supply the right answers to security-related topics. Scavenger hunts on a company's Web site are used to find the answers to 10 security-related questions.[60]

63.2.6   Risk Management.   Part of the data processing management task is to protect information resources and to safeguard the human capital resources that are essential to the services provided. Top management must concern itself with adequate recognition of the risks and must be assured that protective measures relative to these risks are in effect.[61]

In addition to the problems caused by management failures discussed in Section 63.2.5, managers should be aware of other risks in their work such as:

- **Physical hazards.** The likelihood of threats, whether accidental or intentional, that can result in physical damage. Fire, water, power loss, explosions, vandalism, terrorism, and civil disorder are all within this category.

- **Equipment malfunction.** The possibility of failures in computers and supporting equipment, such as printers, disk drives, and air conditioners.

- **Software malfunction.** The likelihood of loss and failures caused by computer programs, including operating system software and application programs.

- **Human error.** The threat of disruption or loss due to accidental or intentional action or inaction by employees. Computer operators, programmers, maintenance engineers, and service personnel can all precipitate loss.

- **Misuse of data.** The capacity for intentional misuse of information or facilities by perpetrators of crime, such as fraud, espionage, misrepresentation, forgery, or theft of data or other assets controlled by the data.

- **Loss of data.** The intentional or unintentional loss of information through disruption of the physical media upon which the data resides, or the corruption or erasure of the data.

In addition to classifying risks by category of threats, it is useful to analyze risks by the magnitude of potential loss, the probability of loss, and the frequency and permanence of occurrence. Although magnitude of loss can be expressed in terms of time or dollars, it is more practical to use dollar cost as a common basis for measurement. Quantifications should be based on reasonable and supportable estimates of the costs associated with the actual occurrences of adverse events.

Threats must be evaluated in terms of probability or occurrence. True risk is difficult or impossible to measure, but a reasonable priority of risks may be established by evaluating the likelihood of occurrence in conjunction with the magnitude of potential loss for each threat. An aggregation of consequential costs for each threat, over a common time period, and based on the likelihood of occurrence for each threat, can serve to prioritize seemingly diverse risks.

Three convenient groupings for permanency of damage are disasters, solid failures, and transient failures. Disasters are serious and lengthy disruptions usually resulting in costly reconstruction of data, alternative off-premises processing, loss of business, and high cost. Solid failures are those that require shutting down part or all of the system in order to take corrective action. Costs of solid failures may range from simple inconvenience to substantial loss of business. Transient failures are defined as temporary disruptions that do not recur regularly and therefore may be difficult to correct. Like solid failures, their costs can vary widely.

Quantification of risk is imprecise at best and varies greatly from one organization to another, and even among computer installations in the same organization. Nevertheless, quantification affords the means of ordering the relative importance of various threats and of substantiating the need for expenditure to counteract threats. In summary, even though probability estimates for specific events may represent intuitive feelings about likelihood, rather than actuarial knowledge, they can nonetheless serve as a basis for focusing discussion and planning.

An effective computer security program requires a balance of rationality and prudence. It also requires a continuing management commitment. Absolute security is an impossible dream unless one has unlimited resources—and even then, many responses would still have to be post hoc reactions to new threats, vulnerabilities, and attacks. Surprisingly, however, even on a modest budget, it is usually possible to achieve reasonable security. Many basic safeguards can be implemented for modest expenditures of time and effort. Many chapters in this *Handbook* discuss such basic safeguards.

63.3 LIABILITIES.   As discussed, security managers focus on minimizing liability by a practice generally known as risk management. Risk management is the traditional model for information security; ideally, one determines risk by identifying the threats and vulnerabilities and then evaluating the associated costs and probabilities of each type of incident. The probabilities are difficult to define, and as a result, much of risk management is, in practice, an intuitive, nonquantitative process.

Security managers face many liabilities. Some of the possible negative consequences of inadequate security include:

- Loss of revenue
- Loss of reputation
- Loss of business partner confidence
- Loss of consumer confidence

- Loss of enterprise valuation
- Failure of the entire enterprise

Each of these types of loss also involves a loss of trust. Trust is easy to lose, especially in uncertain economic climates, and it is, unfortunately, harder to regain trust than to establish and maintain it. It is necessary for managers to understand that security and privacy are integral to the services and products offered by the enterprise. Security and privacy must apply to data from customers, business partners, employees, and every other individual or entity with whom the enterprise comes into contact.

63.3.1 Stakeholders. It is easy to think of only stockholders and customers when evaluating the potential costs of security breaches. However, it is useful to enumerate all of the people, and other entities, that are potentially affected by information security breaches. Such *stakeholders* can include:

- **Stockholders.** People and organizations owning stock in a privately held or publicly traded enterprise
- **Employees.** Managers and workers depending on an enterprise for their livelihood
- **Customers.** People and organizations depending on fulfillment of contractual obligations by the enterprise
- **Potential customers.** Those who might want to do business with the enterprise
- **Suppliers.** Those depending on the enterprise for acceptance of materials and services followed by payment as per contract
- **Data subjects.** People or other entities about whom an enterprise stores, manipulates, and reports data
- **Regulatory agencies and law enforcement.** People and organizations devoted to enforcing statutory regulations and laws
- **Users of other systems victimized by means of a compromised system.** Innocent bystanders who may be harmed, through no fault of their own, when a compromised system is used as an intermediary to launch attacks on an ultimate target

Managers must explore the potential consequences of specific types of security incidents with respect to all of the stakeholders. This wider analysis contributes significantly to effective risk management.

63.3.2 Due Diligence of Care. Due diligence of care in information security refers to the research and analysis carried out in establishing that risks have been minimized to an extent consistent with industry standards. Due diligence investigations, typically, are crucial in mergers and acquisitions, where unanticipated liabilities resulting can result in financial disaster and legal culpability.

Unfortunately, just as there is no sound basis for assertions about computer crime rates, there is not even the most rudimentary basis for asserting that any given level of security represents adequate care for information. What, precisely, is the right length for the asymmetric encryption key used in protecting confidential e-mail sent across the Internet? Does failing to update antivirus signatures daily constitute a violation of due diligence, or is once a week good enough? Does due diligence in securing a manufacturing system require installation of an intrusion detection system?

What about lacking an IDS in a hospital or a bank? Is a computer emergency response team a requirement to demonstrate due care in protecting information assets?

Attempts at defining security standards have not yet convinced more than a few enterprises to conform to their recommendations; the information security field is not yet at the point where quality assurance was a decade ago, when the International Standards Organization promulgated ISO 9000 certification, and it became widely used in manufacturing plants around the world.

Sensitivity to due diligence of care should, at a minimum, begin with consideration of legal and regulatory requirements for the protection of information. Contractual obligations with any and all stakeholders will determine the required degree of responsiveness to intrusion, and may help determine whether to cooperate with law enforcement authorities to investigate any breach of security.[62]

63.3.3 Downstream Liability.

In recent years, a growing number of security experts and attorneys have predicted that the doctrine of downstream liability would become a significant factor in pushing management toward better security. Downstream liability is an application of the legal theory of contributory negligence as it applies to information security. In turn, contributory negligence refers to reckless endangerment of others, "reckless" meaning without consideration of the consequences and endangerment resulting from putting others at risk of harm. The term "downstream" refers to the conventional model in which the source of data is viewed as being upstream of the recipient of those data; thus if someone compromises a university computer system and uses those computers to launch an attack on a bank, the bank is viewed as downstream from the university. Conceivably, the bank's attorneys could accuse the university administrators of negligence for allowing their computers to be compromised and therefore claim damages.

Keeping in mind that the authors are not attorneys, and that the information being discussed here is in no sense legal advice (for legal advice, consult an attorney), examples of what might be construed in a court of law as downstream liability include:

- Distributing virus-infected documents through e-mail because all antivirus mechanisms have deliberately been turned off
- Allowing a malefactor to install *zombie* software on a poorly configured system and involving that compromised system in a distributed denial-of-service attack[63]
- Failing to install patches for a well-known and years-old vulnerability, thus allowing a criminal hacker to attack a third party via a root compromise of the poorly secured system[64]
- Allowing private information such as credit card numbers belonging to thousands of people to be stolen and distributed on the Internet, for use in credit card fraud
- Providing an unsecured e-mail server that provides an open spam-relay point for junk e-mail, with a forged REPLY-TO address, to flood millions of mailboxes with unwanted e-mail, thereby causing thousands of bounce messages and angry accusations to clog the mail system of the innocent owner of the forged REPLY-TO address
- Having an employee who sends out thousands of fraudulent notices using the employer's e-mail system to libel a competitor, causing depression of that competitor's sales and stock price

- Configuring a *honey-pot* system on the enterprise network to attract the attention of criminal hackers—who then turn around and use the honey pot to attack a third party

It is important to note that *honey pots*, while used as security measures to attract a hacker to a specific server for the purpose of gathering data on an attack, do in fact introduce security holes. The honey pot is a live server, with intentional vulnerabilities built in, connected to a company's network. Once penetrated, an attacker may use it as a platform from which to launch future attacks. Special safeguards must be designed to prevent this.

One possible safeguard is to prevent any traffic that leaves the honey pot to actually go anywhere, or to trap it on what might be termed a "honey logger," a server designed to simply catch all the traffic for the purpose of analyzing it.

As of this writing, there appear to have been no cases in which a plaintiff has successfully sued an enterprise for damages on the basis of downstream liability linked to inadequate security. However, in December 2000, FirstNet Online (Management) Limited filed a lawsuit in the Court of Sessions in Edinburgh, Scotland, against Nike, Inc., apparently an innocent victim. The incident began in June 2000, when someone hacked the DNS (Domain Name System) by filing incorrect data for resolution of the nike.com domain with Network Solutions, Inc., which is charged with the responsibility of managing acquisition and retention of certain classes of domain names. All subsequent attempts to reach nike.com were redirected to the s11.org domain, an activist site devoted to fighting globalization. The redirection allegedly caused serious harm to the Web-hosting service for s11.org; according to the plaintiffs, FirstNET Online "experienced an 1800% increase of traffic over the 46 hours it took to correct the problem completely."[65] Blaming Nike administrators for failing to protect the password required for updating the DNS records at Network Solutions, the plaintiffs demanded compensation for the expenses incurred. Nike officials rejected such accusations and blamed Network Solutions for allowing the redirection of Internet traffic to the s11.org site. Readers will want to search the Web for later developments in this interesting case.

63.3.4 Audits. As managers attempt to manage security according to nebulous principles of due care, they must remember that in many enterprises, IT and information security departments are seen as being equivalent to the police. Many people in these departments have privileged access to other people's secrets; for example, they can read all e-mail, and can often tell exactly what Web sites employees have been visiting. In some environments, network monitors allow administrators and security personnel to activate keystroke monitoring and to view in real time the appearance of any given terminal or workstation on the network. Because of the enormous power of these people, managers must ensure that their levels of access are not abused.

Information systems auditors are responsible for keeping the technical and security staff honest. In some larger enterprises, there is a department of internal audit whose director reports to the same level as other officers, such as the CEO and CFO. In other cases, third-party auditors monitor adherence to policy, standards, and procedures.[66]

Security audits are often feared, and with good reason. In general, many audits are performed with the focus of finding fault. This approach is counterproductive and unnecessarily stressful. The point of an audit should not be to find the maximum number of offenses but rather to assess the level of compliance. The most important outcome of an audit is finding areas of potential improvement. A nonadversarial style facilitates positive results; thus an auditing team should provide constructive suggestions for improvement wherever possible.

An auditing team also needs to listen to those being audited. Although a particular network may not be configured to full compliance with security policy, there may be reasons for this apparent failure. For example, suppose a specific patch was required by security policy to have been installed on a Solaris server, but a particular Solaris server did not comply. An auditor might report a failure without further investigation even though, in reality, the patch might have been installed but found to be incompatible with a critical application. Just like managers, audit teams need to see the big picture, not just the rules and procedures. The main point is that all audits must be done with the needs of the business in mind. It does no good to have a process that gets in the way of the business at hand. Instead, to enable the business, alternative measures must be found. That is the job of the auditor—to help ensure compliance and to provide another set of eyes that can see to it that all needs are taken care of.

To prove due diligence, auditing is a must. Generally, third-party audits create more trust, as a third party has no bias about the findings. However, it is important to ensure that a third-party audit firm maintains its independence. It can be risky to use a small firm that bases more than a modest fraction of its revenue on income from any one client. However, it may be undesirable to have the same large firm perform accounting or auditing functions while also serving as security consultants.

63.4 COMPUTER MANAGEMENT FUNCTIONS.   The job of the manager is to provide leadership, and it must be provided in an organized and creative manner. Management is dynamic, not static, and the manager must deal with change—change in the organizational environment, change in people, and change in the methods of management. Unfortunately, the laws of inertia apply to management as to physics, and change will often be resisted. The challenge to the manager is to manage change.

Even a successful security program will usually result in higher costs, as well as in changes in the organizational structure and in the working environment. To compound the problems, the benefits of the security program are not highly visible. Security is essentially preventive and is often regarded as capital expenses and overhead of questionable value. Too often, upper managers dismiss proposals for better security by pointing out that there have been no breaches of security in the last year; thus the more successful the security program, the less evidence there is to support its usefulness. To counteract this circular and destructive reasoning, security managers should compile evidence of the numbers and types of attempted penetrations identified by intrusion detection systems[67] and attempted malfeasance by authorized users identified by system and application logging.[68]

The tools of the manager include planning, organizing, integrating, and controlling. These are not independent activities that can be completely separated; rather they represent a matrix. Taken as an interrelated process, they achieve balance and direction.

63.4.1 Planning for Computer Security.   The planning function of management includes the determination of objectives, policies, priorities, schedules, standards, and strategy.

It is important to define the scope and purpose of a computer security program in terms of objectives. There should be a clear statement of results to be achieved within a given period of time. Security objectives must be balanced with other organizational objectives, because conflicts may arise. As an example, the need for controlled access will naturally conflict with desires for user flexibility and convenience. Objectives should be imaginative and responsive to change and conflict.

Planning for computer security requires the participation of top management, so that security objectives can be reconciled with general organizational objectives and with financial priorities. It is also necessary to coordinate security activities between data processing and all the other areas of the organization. Auditing, insurance, legal, financial, and other groups are affected by, and should contribute to, a computer security program.[69]

The objectives, policies, schedules, and standards that result from the planning process need to be communicated throughout the organization. While this is generally true for all planning, it is especially crucial to the success of a security program, which may conflict with existing corporate culture.[70] Finally, feedback is essential to permit recognition of failures and departures from plans. Only by monitoring results is it possible to take corrective action or to readjust the objectives, policies, plans, schedules, and standards to the practicalities of the real world.

63.4.2 Organizing.   Organization is the process of marshaling resources, grouping activities and responsibilities, and establishing relationships that will enable people to work together most effectively in determining and accomplishing the objectives of an enterprise.

The important elements of organization for computer security include:

* Obtaining resources of personnel, money, and facilities adequate to accomplish the assigned mission
* Fitting responsibly into the organizational pattern
* Assigning responsibility and authority to individuals
* Formulating supporting methods and procedures
* Measuring organizational effectiveness

Traditionally, the organizing function is concerned with grouping activities into manageable components and grouping human resources into logical relationships to accomplish the desired results. It would be unusual to find an enterprise that was designed with an optimum structure to achieve security at the expense of other goals. Security is not an independent activity, nor does it represent the primary goal of a data processing organizational element. Data processing departments are usually organized into units that reflect the nature of the work performed, or user relationships, or some other structure designed to achieve an adequate service level for the end user. Security measures quite often conflict with the service objectives. That conflict is all the more reason why security must be managed in order to be effective. It is also motivation for creating a separate functional activity, particularly in large organizations, so that information security can be administered independently of competing activities.

63.4.3 Integrating.   Computer security is frequently an afterthought to the organization of the data processing function. Security is also perceived as a passive activity. As a result, responsibility for security is often assigned haphazardly. Security should not merely be superimposed but, instead, should be carefully fitted into the organizational structure. Some important considerations are:

- Accountability for specific security tasks should be included in formal job definitions of every job level.

- Training programs should include a complete review of security objectives and policies, as well as details relating to assigned security tasks.

- Supervisory and management personnel should be assigned responsibility for both performance and attitude of staff with respect to security.

- Certain line or staff positions could include responsibility for overall security, or a grouping of security tasks, or measurement and monitoring of security. It may be convenient to combine security and control of data processing into a single function. Monitoring of security effectiveness is sometimes assigned to the data processing auditor.

- Primary responsibility for information security should not be assigned to those with inherently conflicting priorities; for example, it is a bad practice to assign major responsibility for security to the chief of operations, the director of software development, or the vice president of finance.

- Information systems security should be coordinated and reviewed with security specialists in other areas of the organization. In a manufacturing concern the plant security personnel, or in a bank the bank security officer, should be consulted. It may be desirable to assign monitoring responsibility for security housekeeping tasks to these specialists.

- Whenever possible, policies should be translated into written guidelines and procedures to provide the detailed requirements for each task. Standards for performance of each activity must be formulated and applied.

Initiating and monitoring the accomplishment of objectives according to established plans requires skillful leadership. The integration function has a direct bearing on the success of a security program. Without effective leadership, security can become a farce. With leadership, a security program can overcome its basic passivity and truly enhance the utility of information systems. Management must embrace and inspire the concept of security as an everyday fact of life. But beyond transmitting a positive attitude of acceptance, management must also be concerned with testing and improving security. The security program is dynamic rather than static. Management's role must be one of continued concern in order to identify, adopt, and adapt better methods to accomplish corporate security objectives.

63.4.4 Controlling.   The final process in the management cycle is measuring and controlling. It is the function that is concerned with achieving cost-effective results, and includes establishing standards, improving methods, examining results, and adjusting the organizational mechanism for corrective action.

The basis for effective control is the use of consistent techniques for measurement and the application of standards for comparison and interpretation. Results should be analyzed promptly, as feedback to effect corrective action. Control systems need not be burdensome or elaborate, but they should be consistent, and they should allow for flexibility and adjustment. Management action is the end product of control. Mistakes in original objectives and plans are forgivable, but failure to recognize and react to mistakes can only compound the problem, add to costs, and undermine the effective use of valuable resources.

63.5   SECURITY ADMINISTRATION.   In large organizations, an independent security administration function is often the most effective method for accomplishing the overall objective of improved information security.

63.5.1   Staffing the Security Function.   The importance of information security has given rise to a new management specialty, consisting of professionals involved in the planning and administration of protection for the integrity and security of automated information assets. Titles such as information security administrator, computer security manager, information systems security officer, and chief information security officer have been used to describe these roles.

Coordination of the information security function requires a combination of managerial and technical talents. The successful administrator must be a superior communicator capable of selling the concept of security and maintaining security awareness at all levels of the organization. Sufficient technical knowledge is important, so that the information security administrator can evaluate and initiate appropriate technological solutions to meet corporate information security policies and to counteract threats. While technical skill, in the form of a data processing background, is important, a broader range of capabilities is needed for maximum effectiveness. The ideal security administrator should possess the ability to communicate with all levels of management and should have good knowledge of related functions such as auditing, internal control, and general security. It is also important to have some knowledge of the industry within which the organization operates.

The administration of information security can be centralized or decentralized, depending on the needs of the organization. Where multiple data center locations are involved, the decentralized approach may be more appropriate to accomplish the details of administration. However, it is important to have one focal point for overall coordination of information security policy. It is also essential to understand that responsibility for information security rests with all members of the organization, and not just the security personnel. Security is a shared responsibility, and this concept must be widely promoted by the security administrator, and strongly backed by senior management.

63.5.2   Authority and Responsibility.   As in all management areas, information security administrators (ISAs) need not only specific responsibilities but also the authority to carry out their duties. Those duties are listed next:

- **Establish policy statements and guidelines for information protection.** Although policy is the primary responsibility of senior management, it is appropriate for the ISA to participate in the delineation of a formal policy statement covering this important organizational goal and to prepare appropriate guidelines.
- **Identify vulnerabilities and risks.** The ISA serves as a consultant and coordinator in the process of risk analysis. The sensitivity of data resources must be decided by senior management, but with full consensus and agreement by all affected sections of the organization. The ISA has a special responsibility to identify specific risks that affect the automated data resources. The ISA should then coordinate the process of quantifying or otherwise prioritizing the value of the vulnerable data, in order to establish a basis for selection and economic justification of protective measures.

- **Recommend protective measures.** Major responsibility for identification of economic solutions to information security vulnerabilities is usually assigned to the ISA. Requiring a combination of technical knowledge and management analysis, this process entails the evaluation of protective solutions for technological, operational, and economic effectiveness. Appropriate recommendations must be coordinated with other affected sections of the organization, including audit, data processing operations, software development, legal counsel, human resources, facilities security, public relations, and others. Implementation plans must also be developed, and there must be a management commitment to the implementation.

- **Control the implementation of protective measures.** Whether the final administration of the day-to-day security procedures is centralized or decentralized, the coordination and control of implementation for major protective measures should be centralized. A prerequisite for implementation is the development of standards for information security to ensure consistency in the application of protection. Important areas for standardization are security design for application systems, programming development, data sensitivity criteria, database access, and program maintenance. In general, security standards cover the entire systems life cycle.

- **Measure effectiveness of security precautions.** Feedback is essential to assess how effectively policies are being followed. Since the nature of information security is defensive, the measures adopted can easily fall into disuse unless there is ongoing confirmation of effectiveness. The ISA should have primary responsibility to conduct security audits for operational systems as well as for systems under development. Backup protection and disaster-recovery procedures are especially sensitive plans that must be tested periodically. Monitoring of variances in security procedures is also important, and is best controlled through the ISA function. In many organizations these activities are coordinated with the auditors. Finally, the ISA should provide senior management with reports on the effectiveness of security policy, with identification of weaknesses, and with recommendations for improvement.

- **Promote security awareness and security education.** Another important area of responsibility for the ISA is security education and awareness. The concept of security must be actively communicated to all members of the staff to maintain awareness of its importance. An effective program should achieve a workable balance between security and the utility of computer resources.

- **Ensure security awareness across cultures.** In today's global economy, many companies are located in various geographic regions. As a result, security professionals must understand the role that culture plays in the global enterprise. Different cultural perspectives exist regarding security, and these must be taken into consideration when developing a security awareness program. Understanding the impact of culture on business operations will be very beneficial for the organization. For example, how should global enterprises create cross-border awareness strategies? How might the laws and regulations in various countries help or inhibit the creation of an awareness program?

  Although English is still a widely used language of business, U.S. security professionals are well advised to understand the cultural nuances of their foreign counterparts in order to protect their organization against increasing threats. The growing economic power of the European Union, and of China, and India, should prompt U.S. professionals to begin expanding their language competencies to match those of their global competitors.

63.5.3 Professional Accreditation and Education.

Professional accreditation can provide managers with a basis of assurance that a common body of knowledge is applied to the requirements of information security in their enterprise. There are several professional societies and organizations that offer specialized certification to information security personnel. Such certification is voluntary, since there are no specific licensing requirements for information security practitioners. However, certification does signify serious professional intent on the part of the individual to acquire and maintain the needed knowledge and skills. In most cases, the certification process requires a combination of education, experience, and knowledge; knowledge is evaluated through written examinations. Once achieved, a professional certificate requires continuing education in the field to maintain its validity.

Unfortunately, some managers fear that after they provide training or support advanced education, their employees will leave and use their new skills to benefit some other organization—perhaps even a competitor. In reality, some employees are more likely to walk out if the investment is *not* made. Numerous studies have shown that if employees feel valued, they will be more willing to stay. For example, a summary of changing contributions to employee satisfaction specifically states that:

- Although money is clearly an important consideration, cash is not the primary factor that keeps people in their current job or attracts them away to a new job.

- Opportunity to grow and learn at work is emerging as a primary determinant of attracting and retaining employees....

- Although employees consistently indicate that education and training are key aspects of their willingness to stay at or leave their current job, employees also typically rank the quality of their employer's education and training function as low.[71]

Training need not be expensive, excessively time consuming, or difficult.[72] Online security training can be taken anytime and is self-paced. Training videos are also an excellent tool for stimulating employee knowledge and interest. The simplest way to locate such resources is to search on the Web with a good search engine using keywords such as "security training." A particularly helpful site is CCCure.org, which includes a wealth of self-study materials as well as links to many vendors.[73]

Another alternative is to have the employer use obsolete equipment for training, equipment that would otherwise lie idle in a storage area. Even small departments may have old PCs lying around dormant, as well as hubs and possibly router/switches. These can be used to create a network for testing and learning at little cost. Companies that do not have spare equipment can buy used equipment for less than the cost of a one-week intensive course. For an employee who wants to learn the basics of firewalls, Linux is a cheap (and even free) operating system that has just recently started supporting firewalls. Setting up a Linux firewall requires no expensive software or appliances. It can provide an effective way of encouraging employees to learn the practical details of configuring firewalls—a valuable skill set in any security department—while rewarding loyal employees by showing confidence in their commitment to learning, and to their continued employment in the enterprise.

Once the firewall is set up, other employees can use the testing and training network to learn about penetration testing, intrusion detection, and other security elements. Different operating systems can be installed, with various applications, all for a minimal investment. As technology, techniques, and tools change, this training network will be valuable in keeping skills up to date.

External, college-level undergraduate and graduate education also provides re-sources for employees and managers. Universities and colleges are increasingly rec-ognizing the value and validity of educational programs centering on information assurance, both at the technical and managerial levels. Some offer noncredit courses or certificate courses in addition to degree programs. Some offer online programs that support the needs of working adults. Managers can take advantage of these opportuni-ties to improve the knowledge base within their organizations and to increase employee loyalty and retention by supporting employees who want to further their careers in in-formation assurance. Some programs include case studies that may, with permission, center on fieldwork within the students' own work environments, resulting in extensive analysis and recommendations of immense value to their employers.[74]

63.6   CONCLUDING REMARKS.   Society needs the insights of information assurance specialists. Managers with daily opportunities to think about the strategic implications of vulnerabilities, exploits, and, above all, about the business processes for which they are responsible are in an excellent position to contribute not only to the success of their own enterprises but also to the future of their societies. As Adam Shostack and Andrew Stewart have written in their future-pointing treatise, it is time for a new school of information security—one that involves:

- Learning from other professions, such as economics and psychology, to unlock the problems that stymie the security field. . . .
- Sharing objective data and analysis widely. . . .
- The embrace of the scientific method for solving important security problems. Analyzing real-world outcomes is the best way for information security to become a mature discipline.[75]

Readers should embrace every opportunity to bring their experience and wisdom to a wider audience, and by speaking and writing they should share their insights with each other, and with the general public.

63.7   FURTHER READING

Laplante, P., and T. Costello. *CIO Wisdom II: More Best Practices*. Upper Saddle River, NJ: Prentice-Hall, 2005.
Patterson, T. *Mapping Security*. Upper Saddle River, NJ: Prentice-Hall, 2005.
Swiderski, F., and W. Synder. *Threat Modeling*. Redmond, WA: Microsoft, 2004.

63.8   NOTES

1. Because this entire *Handbook* in a sense provides the underlying details for the management of information assurance, most cross-references to other chapters have been relegated to endnotes to avoid cluttering the text.
2. See Chapters 60 and 62 in this *Handbook*.
3. For an extensive discussion of the role of the CISO, see Chapter 65 in this *Handbook*.
4. California State Legislature (2002) Senate Bill SB 1386, http://info.sen.ca.gov/pub/01-02/bill/sen/sb_1351-1400/sb_1386_bill_20020926_chaptered.html.
5. G. Lin, "The Tao Perspective," in D. Lane, ed., *CIO Wisdom* (Upper Saddle River, NJ: Prentice-Hall, 2003), Chapter 4.
6. NIST, "Information Security System in the Systems Development Lifecycle," 2004 [Brochure], http://csrc.nist.gov/groups/SMA/sdlc/index.html.

7. M. E. Kabay, "The Net Present Value of Information Security: A Paradigm Shift for INFOSEC and E-commerce," vol. 17 (2006), www2.norwich.edu/mkabay/infosecmgmt/npvsec.pdf.

8. J. Bassett and D. Rothman *A Seat at the Table for CEOs and CSOs: Driving Profits, Corporate Performance & Business Agility* (Bloomington, IN: AuthorHouse, 2007), p. 111.

9. This section is based on the paper by M. E. Kabay, "The VA Data Insecurity Saga," 2008, www2.norwich.edu/infosecmgmt/vasaga.pdf.

10. J. Brodkin, "Deep Regrets, from TJX to ChoicePoint, about Data Leaks," *Network World,* March 14, 2007, www.networkworld.com/news/2007/031407-wider-net-apologies-letters.html?page=1.

11. G. Gross, "U.S. Agency Loses Data Containing 26 million IDs," *Network World,* May 22, 2006, www.networkworld.com/news/2006/052206-us-agency-loses-veterans-data.html?brl.

12. G. Gross, "Lawmaker Calls on VA Head to Resign after Data Theft," *Network World,* May 25, 2006, www.networkworld.com/news/2006/052506-lawmaker-calls-on-va-head.html?inform.

13. U.S. Government Veterans Information, "Latest Information on Veterans Affairs Data Security," www.usa.gov/veteransinfo.shtml.

14. Using keyword "data" in the search field at www1.va.gov/opa/pressrel/index.cfm provides a reasonable chronology.

15. U.S. Department of Veterans Affairs, "Secretary Nicholson Provides Update on Stolen Data Incident: Data Matching with Department of Defense Providing New Details," June 6, 2006, www1.va.gov/opa/pressrel/pressrelease.cfm?id=1134.

16. "Data on 2.2M Active Troops Stolen from VA," *USA TODAY,* June 7, 2006, www.usatoday.com/news/washington/2006-06-06-veterans-data_x.htm.

17. U.S. Department of Veterans Affairs "Directive by the Secretary of Veterans Affairs R. James Nicholson to All VA Supervisors on Information Security," May 26, 2006, www1.va.gov/opa/pressrel/pressrelease.cfm?id=1128.

18. U.S. Department of Veterans Affairs "VA Secretary Inserts New Leadership in Policy & Planning Office," May 30, 2006, www1.va.gov/opa/pressrel/pressrelease.cfm?id=1129.

19. U.S. Government Accountability Office, "Homeland Security: Guidance and Standards are Needed for Measuring the Effectiveness of Agencies' Facility Protection Efforts," Report GAO-06-612, May 2006, www.gao.gov/cgi-bin/getrpt?GAO-06-612.

20. U.S. Department of Veterans Affairs "VA Secretary Inserts New Leadership in Policy & Planning Office," May 30, 2006, www1.va.gov/opa/pressrel/pressrelease.cfm?id=1129.

21. U.S. Government Accountability Office, "Veterans Affairs: Leadership Needed to Address Information Security Weaknesses and Privacy Issues," Report GAO-06-866T, June 14, 2006, www.gao.gov/cgi-bin/getrpt?GAO-06-866T.

22. U.S. Government Accountability Office, "Information Security: Leadership Needed to Address Weaknesses and Privacy Issues at Veterans Affairs," Highlights of GAO-06-897T, 2006, www.gao.gov/highlights/d06897thigh.pdf.

23. U.S. Government Accountability Office, "Information Technology: VA and DOD Face Challenges in Completing Key Efforts," Highlights of GAO-06-905T, 2006, www.gao.gov/highlights/d06905thigh.pdf.

24. Department of Veterans Affairs Office of Inspector General, "Review of Issues Related to the Loss of VA Information Involving the Identity of Millions of Veterans," Report No. 06-02238-163, July 11, 2006, www.va.gov/oig/51/FY2006rpts/VAOIG-06-02238-163.pdf.

25. "Personal Data for 38,000 Veterans Missing, VA Says," *USA TODAY,* August 7, 2006, www.usatoday.com/tech/news/computersecurity/infotheft/2006-08-07-veterans-data_x.htm?csp=34.

26. G. Gross, "VA to Spend $3.7M on Encryption Tools: The Move Follows the Theft of a VA Laptop in May," *Computerworld,* August 14, 2006, www.computerworld.com/action/article.do?command=viewArticleBasic&articleId=9002447.

27. R. McMillan, "Unisys Contractor Arrested in VA theft: Investigators Do Not Believe 21-year-old Suspect Sought Agency's Data," *InfoWorld,* September 15, 2006, www.infoworld.com/article/06/09/15/HNunisyscontractorarrested_1.html.

28. H. A. Waxman, "Committee Report Finds Data Breaches Throughout Federal Government," Committee on Oversight and Government Reform, 110th Congress, October 13, 2006, http://oversight.house.gov/story.asp?ID=1127.

29. R. Maze, "VA Reports Two More Data Security Lapses," *Federal Times,* November 3, 2006, www.federaltimes.com/index.php?S=2331714.

30. A. Broache, "Hard Drive Vanishes from VA Facility," *C|Net News,* February 5, 2007, http://news.com.com/2100-1029_3-6156386.html.

31. G. Keizer, "Lost VA Hard Drive May Have Held 1.8M IDs: Initially, the Agency Said Just 50,000 Were Potentially Affected," *Computerworld,* February 13, 2007, www.computerworld.com/action/article.do?command=viewArticleBasic&articleId=9011218.

32. M. E. Kabay, "PIIssed Off Yet?" *Network World Security Strategies,* June 12, 2007, www.networkworld.com/newsletters/sec/2007/0611sec1.html.

33. U.S. Government Accountability Office, "Information Security: Veterans Affairs Needs to Address Long-Standing Weaknesses," Report GAO-07-532T, February 28, 2007, www.gao.gov/new.items/d07532t.pdf.

34. G. Gross, "VA to Spend $3.7M on Encryption Tools: The Move Follows the Theft of a VA Laptop in May," *Computerworld,* August 14, 2006, www.computerworld.com/action/article.do?command=viewArticleBasic&articleId=9002447.

35. J. Vijayan, "OMB Sets 120-day Deadline for Fed Breach-Notification Plans: Agencies have the summer to develop and implement first phases of policies," *Computerworld,* May 29, 2007, www.computerworld.com/action/article.do?command=viewArticleBasic&articleId=9021544.

36. GuardianEdge, "Chronology of Data Security Breaches," www.guardianedge.com/news/recent-data-breaches/.

37. See Chapters 1 and 3.

38. See Chapter 57.

39. See Chapters 56, 58, and 59.

40. See Chapter 60.

41. See Chapters 22 and 23.

42. See Chapters 24 through 37.

43. See Chapters 43 through 50.

44. See Chapters 51 through 55.

45. Policy issues are discussed in detail in Chapters 44, 45, 47, 48, 49, and 50 of this *Handbook*.

46. M. K. Pratt, "Employee Security Training: Beyond Posters." *Computerworld* (2006), www.computerworld.com/action/article.do?command=viewArticleTOC &specialReportId=100&articleId=110494.

47. G. G. Gross, "Study: Human Error Causes Most Security Breaches," *Computerworld* (2003), www.computerworld.com/careertopics/careers/training/story/ 0,10801,79485,00.html.

48. E. Dickson, "Could the Arrests in the Stop and Shop Data Breach Indicate a Tie to Armenian Mobsters?" Fraud, Phishing and Financial Misdeeds Blog (2007), http://fraudwar.blogspot.com/2007/02/could-arrest-in-stop-and-shop-data.html.

49. See Chapter 50 for more information about using social psychology to motivate compliance with security policies.

50. http://honeynet.org/misc/chall.html.

51. For more about log files, see Chapters 52 and 53; on postmortem analysis, see Chapter 56.

52. See Chapters 49 and 50.

53. T. J. Peters and R. H. Waterman, *In Search of Excellence: Lessons from America's Best-Run Companies* (New York: HarperCollins, 1983). See also H. K. Jones, "Does MBWA (Management By Wandering Around) Still Work?" (2007), Self-Growth.com, www.selfgrowth.com/articles/Jones6.html.

54. B. J. Fox, "Communications: Communication Excellence in IT Management," in D. Lane, *CIO Wisdom,* ed. (Upper Saddle River, NJ: Prentice-Hall, 2003), Chapter 5.

55. S. Adams, "Official Dilbert Website" (2008), www.dilbert.com/.

56. See Chapter 28.

57. M. E. Kabay, "A Rant about InfoSec: A Security Veteran in a Bad Mood Dumps on Everyone" (2004); www2.norwich.edu/mkabay/opinion/rant.pdf.

58. See Chapter 30.

59. See Chapter 38.

60. For more security-awareness ideas, see Chapter 49.

61. Chapter 62 of this *Handbook* discusses risk management in more detail.

62. See Chapter 61.

63. See Chapter 18.

64. See Chapters 15 and 40.

65. See www.nikesucks.org.

66. See Chapter 54.

67. See Chapter 27.

68. See Chapters 53 and 54.

69. See Chapter 56 for a more extensive discussion of these principles in connection with the computer emergency response team.

70. See Chapter 50 for a discussion of the psychology of implementing security policies.

71. L. J. Basai, "Employee Retention." Learning in the New Economy," *LineZine* (Summer 2000), www.linezine.com/3/themes/hardtalk.htm.

72. M. R. Farnum, "Security Awareness Training Does Not Have to Be Hard," Hitting the Security Nerve—*Computerworld* Blogs (2006), http://blogs.computerworld .com/node/4175.

73. http://cccure.org/.

74. For more details of certification and education in the security field, see Chapter 75 for the United States and Chapter 76 for Europe.

75. A. Shostack and A. Stewart, *The New School of Information Security* (Upper Saddle River, NJ: Addison-Wesley, 2008), p. xiv.

U.S. LEGAL AND REGULATORY SECURITY ISSUES

Timothy Virtue

64.1 INTRODUCTION. The regulatory requirements facing today's business leaders can strengthen the overall business environment while offering increased safeguards to stakeholders such as consumers, suppliers, shareholders, employees, and other interested parties transacting with today's businesses. Although regulatory requirements vary from institution to institution and across different industries, the recurring theme is that management must be proactively involved and fully accountable for the actions of its organization.

Compliance is an ongoing process that can be achieved successfully only when the organization's senior leaders support compliance from both a cultural and operational perspective. In other words, the right attitudes (integrity, honesty, transparency, etc.), also known as *tone at the top*, must be exemplified in all facets of the organization while working in tandem with operational processes to create a comprehensive compliance environment. A culture of compliance must be integrated throughout the organization and must be seamlessly built into all operational facets of the business.

Many organizations are restructuring independent and isolated operational units (sometimes described as *silos*) and focusing on coordinated strategic risk management for the enterprise. Such changes support business values, achieve compliance, and reduce risk.

Another recurring theme of today's regulatory environment is accountability for, and protection of, sensitive or private information. Specific regulatory requirements and how an organization addresses the requirements will vary, based on industry, organizational structure, and internal processes. However, an effective enterprise-wide regulatory-governance model should incorporate two common elements:

1. The senior management team must create a compliance-driven culture by actively exercising leadership by example.

2. The team must actively support this culture of compliance by enabling computer security strategies, tactics, and technologies as discussed throughout this *Handbook*.

Compliance with regulatory requirements must include, but is not limited to, these computer security fundamentals:

- Program management
  - Policy and procedure design and implementation
- Risk assessment and management
  - Prevention
  - Detection
  - Response
- Implementation of safeguards
  - Administrative controls
  - Physical controls
  - Technical controls
- Awareness and training

Although there are a number of regulations that today's business leaders may be accountable for, these requirements vary from industry to industry. This chapter focuses on two important U.S. regulations: the Sarbanes-Oxley and the Gramm-Leach-Bliley acts. These particular acts require a significant level of management involvement in order to validate that the organization adequately addresses the regulatory requirements.

64.2   SARBANES-OXLEY ACT OF 2002.   Although a comprehensive discussion of the Sarbanes-Oxley Act of 2002 (SOX) is outside the scope of this text, a high-level understanding of the key components is required so that management may adequately fulfill its responsibilities under this act. SOX is made up of 11 titles and is administered by the Securities and Exchange Commission (SEC). The main goal of the legislation, also sometimes referred to as the Public Company Accounting Reform and Investor Protection Act of 2002, is to protect the public and shareholders from accounting errors and fraudulent practices by requiring that companies monitor and record any access to sensitive financial data. They must provide reports on their controls, and must respond in a timely and appropriate manner should an incident occur.[1]

Exhibit 64.1 offers each title within SOX with a brief description added by the author.

EXHIBIT 64.1 Eleven Titles of SOX with Descriptions

Title #	Name	Description
I	Public Company Accounting Oversight Board	Establishment of a private nonprofit board. Duties of the board include establishing auditing, quality control, and independence standards for public accounting firms.
II	Auditor Independence	Prohibits certified public accountants from simultaneously performing audit and nonaudit services.
III	Corporate Responsibility	Requires that the Securities and Exchange Commission (SEC) order the national security exchanges and associations to bar the listing of an issuer that does not comply with the specific requirements set forth in Title III.
IV	Enhanced Financial Disclosures	Sets forth various requirements to validate the accuracy of financial statements and supporting disclosures.
V	Analyst Conflicts of Interest	Defines a code of conduct for security analysts and includes a measure to help restore confidence in their reporting.
VI	Commission Resources and Authority	Authorizes the SEC to hire staff to provide additional oversight of auditors and audit services. Also outlines the conditions a person can be prohibited from practicing as a broker, advisor, or dealer.
VII	Studies and Reports	Provides for research to be conducted for the enforcement of actions against violations by SEC registrants and auditors.
VIII	Corporate and Criminal Fraud Accountability	Defines penalties for the destruction of audit reports and the willful destruction, manipulation, or falsification of documents in federal investigations and bankruptcy proceedings.
IX	White Collar Crime Penalty Enhancements	Increases the penalties for white-collar crimes and requires that both the CEO and CFO of a corporation certify periodic financial statements.
X	Corporate Tax Returns	Requires that the CEO sign the corporation's federal income tax return.
XI	Corporate Fraud and Accountability	Establishes penalties for persons who manipulate or destroy documents or impede an official proceeding.

All of the individual components from Exhibit 64.1 that specify the requirements for SOX must have the support and involvement of an organization's senior leadership team. It is important to note that no single component of SOX is more important than any other component. In fact, SOX derives its strength and effectiveness because this is truly a case where the whole is greater than the sum of its parts.

Although all of the components to SOX are important and require active participation by management at both a strategic and operational level, the remaining discussion focuses on the part of the act that affects computer security the most, Section 404.

The passage of SOX in 2002 led the way for an important change in how business leaders in today's public companies look at information security. This change has caused significant impact on today's information systems, the security that supports them, and management's perception of how the systems affect financial reporting. Although SOX was primarily intended to enhance the integrity of financial reporting, it has broader implications. Specifically, the integrity of financial reporting can be accomplished only by ensuring the integrity of the source information used to complete financial reporting requirements. Management must therefore support the design, implementation, and continuous management of strong controls over the information systems that are the primary source for today's financial reporting requirements.

64.2.1 Section 404 of SOX.   Since compliance with SOX is supported by the organization's ability to develop, implement, and manage a combination of business reporting requirements and management controls, many of the organization's information systems are directly or indirectly involved in the SOX compliance process. The breadth and depth of the impact will vary among different organizations but can range from end user computing applications (e.g., spreadsheets) all the way to the data center, as well as anything in between. For this reason, business leaders must address these issues and must provide adequate support to achieve continuous compliance with SOX. As referenced earlier, SOX addresses a number of areas requiring senior executive leadership and support. However, Section 404 of SOX is most relevant to information security programs, and requires businesses to:

- Evaluate the adequacy of internal controls that impact financial reporting
- Implement new controls as necessary
- Annually test and report on the assessment results of internal controls

Section 404 requires the business to implement a comprehensive internal control framework sustainable throughout the enterprise. Furthermore, these controls must not only directly protect the integrity of financial data and indirectly protect the systems that support the data, but the business is also required to show that these controls are operational and are functioning as intended. Since compliance with SOX affects the organization at an enterprise-wide level, information security protections should be designed, implemented, and managed from a holistic perspective supported by management as part of an overall business strategy, rather than as a single compliance activity. When this approach is taken, the business is better positioned to comply with SOX, to achieve compliance sustainability, and to validate that compliance is integrated throughout the entire organization.

In most organizations, almost all corporate information, including financial information, is linked to enterprise information systems. Many systems feed or share information with each other. Therefore, the organization must look at data origins, data flows, and data output to validate that they have adequately identified all of the information that could impact financial reporting. Management must provide the appropriate level of support for robust controls to protect the data resources of critical corporate information systems, which ultimately act as the primary data source the business must rely on when delivering and validating the integrity of the organization's financial statements.

With today's modern technologies pervasively deployed in business environments, organizations are likely to face a variety of SOX compliance challenges. These challenges result from the vast number of information systems, the associated supporting infrastructure, highly connected and communication intensive networks, and in many cases externally facing Web-based applications that are highly susceptible to exploitation.

Additional challenges come from the inside as well. The insider threat is quickly becoming one of the most difficult security challenges to overcome, and causes the majority of security problems for many organizations (see Chapter 45 in this *Handbook*). Internal data protection challenges are further complicated by the increase in *privileged users* such as database administrators, system administrators, and a variety of other users with powerful access to critical information systems. Such users often unknowingly create significant SOX compliance risks for their organization. These powerful privileges are often overused, and ultimately can be the pathway to noncompliance or malicious activity within the organization. Furthermore, many of these privileged users can manipulate system log files so that their malicious activity goes unnoticed or in some cases becomes untraceable (see Chapter 53).

64.2.2 Management Perspectives on SOX.   Properly administered compliance initiatives must strike a balance between information security and system usability, to support business and compliance objectives without creating an environment of distrust. Although the insider threat is a significant threat to many businesses, the senior leadership team must accept that employees are a critical component of business operations. Since management controls are intended to protect sensitive system data, and not to create a hostile work environment, SOX-related corporate policies and standards must support the spirit of the act by ensuring that organizations closely monitor and control access to critical business systems while not impeding employee productivity. Achieving this balance is not always an easy task.

Regardless of the specific strategies organizations employ to design, implement, and manage, there are some fundamental operational policies and processes that should be put in place to protect the integrity of both the data and ultimately the organization's financial reporting.

Fortunately, many organizations may find they already have a majority of the required controls in place, because many of the control requirements can be accomplished through traditional information security best practices. Some of the more common examples include controls that address segregation of duties (e.g., among development, test, and production environments) and appropriate data-security controls and safeguards.

A list of more common database safeguard components that senior management should focus on when complying with Section 404 of SOX follows.

- Monitor database access by privileged users.
- Monitor changes in privileges.
- Monitor access failures.
- Monitor schema changes.
- Monitor direct data access.

In order to get a better grasp on all of the complexity associated with database compliance challenges, senior leadership teams in many organizations elect to take a back-to-basics approach. One of the most effective strategies to deploying such a simplified approach is to use the traditional five Ws. Specifically, organizations should be asking these questions in terms of database compliance:

1. Who did something to the database?
2. What did they do?
3. Which specific data component?
4. When was the activity performed?
5. Where was the information accessed?

When members of the organization's senior leadership team approach the SOX compliance issue in this manner, they are in a better position to understand, and ultimately to assume the responsibility for, the data security and integrity for which they are accountable.

The requirement of having an organization's senior management work with an external auditor to report on the internal control program is, unfortunately, the most costly requirement of SOX and requires an enormous effort.

However, organizations should also take note that there are a number of benefits from designing, implementing, and managing effective compliance strategies, beyond initial SOX compliance. Establishing a comprehensive internal controls program not only aids in SOX compliance but also forms a foundation for operational improvements. Anytime the organization's senior management team can institute an effective internal controls program, it is not only taking steps to compliance, but also building a solid foundation on which enterprise-wide data governance programs can follow.

64.3   GRAMM-LEACH-BLILEY ACT.   One of the most significant pieces of legislation to affect the financial services industry was the Financial Services Modernization Act of 1999, commonly referred to as the Gramm-Leach-Bliley Act or GLBA.[2] It was enacted in response to the standardization of the U.S. banking and insurance industries in the late 1990s. The financial services industry was undergoing substantial change during this period. Since financial institutions and insurance companies were allowed to merge and consolidate their operations, legislators and industry observers were concerned about providing adequate protection of consumer rights and data protection. Specifically, significant concerns developed over the consolidation of consumer data. There was substantial fear that sensitive consumer data would be openly shared among financial organizations and their subsidiaries. This open environment would likely threaten consumer rights and the security of sensitive and personal financial data. The consolidation and reform within the financial services industry was enabling the creation of new financial services holding companies that could offer a full range of financial products. Prior to the passage of GLBA, some major financial institutions were selling personal and sensitive detailed customer information to business partners. This type of disclosure often included the disclosure of account numbers and other highly sensitive data to telemarketing firms. These telemarketing agencies often used the account numbers to charge customers for products and services they did not want and that had no value to customers.

64.3.1   Applicability.   GLBA applies to U.S. domestic financial institutions; it defines financial institutions as "companies that offer financial products or services to individuals, like loans, financial or investment advice, or insurance." GLBA coverage includes but is not limited to organizations that provide insurance, securities, payment settlement services, check cashing services, credit counselors, and mortgages.

GLBA is intended to address the proper handling of nonpublic financial information. However, senior management teams of financial institutions must acknowledge that the act also includes a wide range of information that is not obviously financial in nature. This additional coverage is intended to offer further protections to the consumer and properly align with the spirit of the law. Specifically, the additional types of information that must be protected include the consumer's name and address. However, protection may extend to:

- Information given to a financial institution in order to receive a financial product or service
- Information generated or remaining as a result of a transaction between a financial institution and a consumer
- Information obtained by the financial institution while providing a financial product or service to a consumer

As mentioned, GLBA requires financial institutions to safeguard nonpublic personal information (such as a Social Security Number, credit-card details, or a bank account number) provided by a consumer under various privacy rules or resulting from a transaction or other service performed on behalf of the consumer. This information is not necessarily considered financial information. For example, under GLBA, a consumer's name identifying a recipient of services from a specific institution is also considered nonpublic information that must be protected under GLBA. Specifically, GLBA mandates:

- Secure storage of consumer personal information
- Providing adequate and sufficient notice to consumers regarding how the financial institution shares their consumer personal and financial information
- Providing consumers with the choice to opt out of sharing their personal and financial information

64.3.2 Enforcement.   GLBA is enforced by the Federal Trade Commission (FTC), various financial industry regulators, and state attorneys general. More stringent requirements may be placed on the financial institutions by individual states, because GLBA does not preempt state law.

Although current legislation does not offer a remedy of civil action, a financial institution's failure to comply with notice is considered a deceptive trade practice by both state and federal authorities. Some states do have specific legislation that offers a private right of action for consumers.

Title V of the act provides that financial institutions may share practically any information with affiliated companies but may share information with nonaffiliated companies for marketing purposes only after providing an opportunity for the consumer to *opt out* of the information sharing process. Management needs to play a proactive role in providing administrative, managerial, and technical support to achieve compliance with Title V of the Act. Consumers must be provided with easy-to-understand and easy-to-use opt-out choices. Organizations that make opting out difficult, or that otherwise appear to be duplicitous, are likely to be viewed as noncompliant with Title V of GLBA.

The provisions of Title V do not preempt or supersede state law. If organizations are conducting business in a state that has more stringent requirements, then those state requirements must be met, in addition to GLBA. Section 505 requires that the act and its associated regulations be enforced by various federal and state regulatory agencies having jurisdiction over financial institutions. This requirement of GLBA offers federal enforcement authority to a variety of enforcement agencies. The more common enforcement agencies include:

- Office of the Comptroller of the Currency
- Federal Reserve Board
- Federal Deposit Insurance Corporation
- Securities and Exchange Commission

An organization's senior leadership team should also note that the Federal Trade Commission has general enforcement authority for any financial institution that does not fall within the jurisdiction of any of the specific enumerated regulatory agencies.

As previously stated, the intent of GLBA is to offer adequate protection to consumers conducting business with financial services firms. Although the hope is that organizations will comply with GLBA on goodwill, the act was created with some serious repercussions to financial institutions that do not comply. GLBA does not include a private right of action, but financial institutions are required to give consumer notice, and they could face liability under deceptive trade practice statutes if the notices are determined to be deceptive or inaccurate. Furthermore, financial institutions that fail to comply with GLBA may also be subject to penalties under the Financial Institution Reform Recovery and Enforcement Act (FIRREA). FIRREA contains and offers penalties that range from up to $5,500 for violations of laws and regulations; up to $27,500 if violations are unsafe, unsound, or reckless; and up to $1.1 million for knowing violations. Given the consequences of noncompliance, organizations need to take the appropriate actions to obtain consumer protection and compliance with GLBA.

64.3.3   Consumers and Customers.   One common misconception of GLBA is the interpretation of the legislation as it relates to the nonconsumer customers of financial institutions. This is likely to occur since the term "consumer" and "customer" are often used interchangeably. However, in the context of GLBA, the critical distinction must be made. GLBA defines a *consumer* as "an individual who obtains, from a financial institution, financial products or services which are to be used primarily for personal, family, or household purposes, and also means the legal representative of such an individual." A *customer* is a type of consumer who has established some sort of ongoing relationship with an institution accountable to GLBA. An example of a customer would be an individual who has received credit financing to purchase a car. This individual would need to make monthly payments to a financial institution and hence has established an ongoing relationship. Under this definition, a business could not be defined either as a customer or as a consumer (since a business is not an individual) and therefore does not fall under the protections of GLBA.

64.3.4 Compliance. Compliance with GLBA signifies that financial institutions must comply with a number of the act's provisions. From a high-level perspective, organizations must adhere to these points when seeking compliance with GLBA:

- Organizations must provide consumers with clear and conspicuous notice of the financial institution's information-sharing policies and practices.
- This notice must be given at the start of a new customer relationship and maintained on an annual basis.
- Organizations must provide customers with the right to opt out of having their nonpublic personal information shared with nonaffiliated third parties (unless the activity falls under one of the GLBA exceptions).
- They must refrain from disclosing to any nonaffiliated third-party marketer, other than a consumer reporting agency, an account number or similar form of access code to a consumer's credit card, deposit, or transaction account.
- Financial institutions must comply with the regulatory standards established to protect the security and confidentiality of customer records
- Financial institutions must also protect against security threats and unauthorized access to such protected customer information.

64.3.5 Privacy Notices. As a part of GLBA, financial institutions are required to disseminate privacy notices to their consumers explaining what information the financial institution will collect about the consumer, whom the information may be shared with, and how the financial institution protects that information. The information the notice must refer to is the consumer's nonpublic personal information (such as a Social Security number, bank account number, or credit card number) collected, for example, during an application for auto financing. In an effort to help companies comply with this requirement in a consistent and effective manner, the Federal Trade Commission (in conjunction with various other financial regulators) established a GLBA privacy notice standard. Under this standard, financial institutions must provide a privacy notice at the inception of a relationship with a consumer and once a year for as long as the relationship persists. Furthermore, this notice must provide consumers with the option to declare within 30 days after the receipt of the notice that they do not want their information shared with the third parties mentioned in that privacy notice. Financial institutions must also mandate that the privacy notice itself be written in such a way that it is a clear and accurate statement of the company's privacy practices. Provided these requirements are met by the financial institution's privacy notice, the institution may share consumer information with its affiliated companies.

A financial institution may also share consumer information with nonaffiliated organizations provided it has clearly disclosed what information will be provided, to whom, and how it will be protected, and provided that consumers have a method of opting out clearly described in their privacy notices. However, GLBA prohibits financial institutions from disclosing consumer account numbers to nonaffiliated companies for purposes of telemarketing, direct-mail marketing, (including through e-mail), even if the consumer has not opted out of sharing the information for marketing purposes. There will be special circumstances in which consumers will not have the option to require that their information not be shared. Some of the more common occurrences of these special circumstances are:

- When a financial institution is required to share information with an outside organization as part of fulfilling its customer obligations (e.g., data processing services)
- When a financial institution is legally required to share the information
- When the information is shared with an outside service provider that market the products or services of the financial institution

64.3.6   GLBA Safeguards Rule.   A significant component of GLBA is the *GLBA Safeguards Rule.* The Safeguards Rule is intended to support the privacy and protective rules within GLBA. In many organizations, it is the operational driver supporting the other components of GLBA. If the other components of GLBA are the *why* of the legislation, then the Safeguards Rule is the *how.*

GLBA contains specific requirements and safeguards that are applicable to both electronic and paper records. Management must protect records in both formats, even though the widespread use of electronic data processing makes it easy to overlook sensitive consumer information in hardcopy format because an increasing number of employees work almost exclusively with electronic representations of the data. GLBA requires financial institutions to develop, implement, and continuously manage a *comprehensive* information security program, which it defines as including administrative, technical, and physical safeguards to protect the security of customer information.

64.3.7   Flexibility.   GLBA covers a broad array of financial institutions, and therefore mandates that an information security program be appropriate to the size, complexity, nature, and scope of the activities of each specific financial institution. This level of flexibility offers an organization's management team the flexibility to balance consumer protection against business objectives. However, it is critical that this flexibility not be abused and that the intent of the act be addressed. Furthermore, an organization's senior leadership team must not interpret the lack of specific safeguards as an opportunity for noncompliance with GLBA, but rather as an opportunity to provide consumer protection without impeding business operations.

Flexibility aside, certain key requirements must be followed to be compliant with the Safeguards Rule. The foundational security practices include having at least one designated employee to audit systems; determine risks; and develop, implement, and manage procedures to address information security. Specifically, a financial institution must provide three levels of security:

1. **Administrative security.** Includes program management of workforce risks, employee training, and vendor oversight
2. **Technical security.** Includes technical controls for computer systems, networks, applications, access controls, and encryption
3. **Physical security.** Includes safeguarding facilities, corresponding environmental protection, and disaster recovery protections

In order for financial institutions to be fully compliant with the Safeguards Rule, they need to create comprehensive internal controls for strong administrative, technical, and physical safeguards. To help guide an organization's senior leadership team toward

GLBA compliance, some of the major requirements that financial institutions must keep in mind when building an organizational culture founded on consumer protection and GLBA compliance are listed next:

- Validate that consumer information is kept secure and confidential.
- Validate that consumer information is protected from likely threats to its security and integrity.
- Validate that consumer information cannot be accessed by any unauthorized entities, or accessed in a way that would result in substantial loss or in a way that would inconvenience the consumer.[3]

Fortunately, for many organizations, implementing the Safeguards Rule does not usually require significant structural changes to their information security program. This occurs because the principle of the Safeguards Rule requires compliance with basic information security program elements. These elements are based on best practices that should already be a part of an effective information security program.

Specifically, each financial institution must designate an employee to manage the programs safeguards. Depending on financial institution's size, culture, and organizational structure, the actual title and responsibilities of the position will vary significantly. However, at a high level, this function typically requires the identification and assessment of the organization's risk as it relates to consumer information. Furthermore, the organization's risk management must be carried out diligently, so that each relevant area of the institution's operation successfully completes a comprehensive evaluation of the effectiveness of its safeguards. In most cases, the effectiveness of the organization's safeguards can be measured by the organization's ability to manage risk successfully by designing, implementing, and managing adequate information security controls. This activity should further be supported by senior management's ability successfully to monitor and test the information risk management program on a regular basis.

Finally, it is important that the financial institution's senior leadership team proactively protect customer information, even when working with third parties. Under GLBA, financial institutions must also select the appropriate service providers to support their GLBA requirements and to enter into security-minded agreements. Simply utilizing third parties does not free financial institutions from their GLBA obligations. The organization's senior leadership team must establish agreements in a manner that adequately protects consumer information and that requires the service provider to implement appropriate and GLBA relevant safeguards. GLBA stresses that, at a minimum, the safeguards performed by the third party must be equal to the protections offered internally by the financial institution's senior leadership team.

64.4 EXAMINATION PROCEDURES TO EVALUATE COMPLIANCE WITH GUIDELINES FOR SAFEGUARDING CUSTOMER INFORMATION.   The Office of the Controller of the Currency of the United States Department of the Treasury has published a useful table of recommended evaluation procedures that will help readers apply the principles discussed in this chapter.[4] A simplified and edited representation of the procedures is supplied in Exhibit 64.2.

64.5 CONCLUDING REMARKS.   The U.S. legal and regulatory security issues facing today's businesses are best exemplified by the Sarbanes-Oxley Act of 2002 and the Gramm-Leach-Bliley Act. The significant increase of today's regulatory-driven business environment mandates that an organization's senior leadership team

EXHIBIT 64.2   Recommended Evaluation Procedures

Key Questions or Considerations

I.   Determine the involvement of the board.

A.   Has the board or its designated committee approved a written Corporate Information Security Program that meets the requirements of the Information Security Guidelines?

B.   If the board has assigned responsibility for program implementation and review of management reports to an individual or to a committee, is the necessary knowledge, expertise, and authority to perform the task available?

C.   Does the program contain the required elements?
   1. If more than one information security program exists for the institution, are the programs coordinated across organizational units?

D.   Are the reports from management to the board (or its designated committee) useful? Does the report adequately describe the overall status of the program, including material risk issues, risk assessment, risk management and control decisions, service provider oversight, results of testing, security breaches and management's response, and recommendations for program changes?
   1. How often does the board (or its designated committee) review reports?

E.   Overall, do management and the board (or its designated committee) adequately oversee the institution's information security program?

II.   Evaluate the risk assessment process.

A.   Review the risk assessment program.
   1. How does the institution assess risk to its customer information systems and nonpublic customer information?
   2. Has the institution evaluated the risk to the entire customer information system?
   3. Has the institution used personnel with sufficient expertise to assess the risk to its systems and customer information on an enterprise-wide basis?
   4. Is the risk assessment part of a formal risk assessment process with timelines and milestones? If not, how will management ensure timely completion?
   5. Does the institution have a process for identifying and ranking its information assets (data and system components) according to sensitivity? How does it use this process in its risk assessment?

B.   Assess adequacy and effectiveness of the risk assessment process.
   1. Does the institution identify all reasonably foreseeable internal and external threats that could result in unauthorised disclosure, misuse, alternation, or destruction of customer information, or of customer information systems?
   2. Does the institution support its estimate of the potential damage posed by various threats?
   3. Review the institution's existing controls to mitigate risks. Does the institution's analysis consider the current administrative, physical, and technical safeguards that prevent or mitigate potential damage?
   4. Does the institution use test results to support its assessment of the adequacy and effectiveness of those controls?

C.   Does the institution identify and prioritize its risk exposure, decide on the risks it must mitigate, and create a mitigation strategy? Is the decision to accept risks documented and reported to the appropriate management levels?
   1. Does the institution promptly act to mitigate risks that pose the immediate possibility of material loss?
   2. How does the institution demonstrate that the mitigation strategy was reviewed by appropriate officials?
   3. Does the risk assessment provide guidance for the nature and extent of testing?
   4. Does the risk assessment include vendor oversight requirements?

EXHIBIT 64.2 *(Continued)*

Key Questions or Considerations

III. Evaluate the adequacy of the program to manage and control risk.

A. Review internal controls and policies. Has the institution documented or otherwise demonstrated, at a minimum, that it considered the following controls, and adopted those it considered appropriate?
  1. Access controls, such as controls to authenticate and permit access to customer information systems to authorized persons only.
  2. Access restrictions at physical locations, such as buildings and computer facilities, to permit access to authorized persons only.
  3. Encryption of electronically transmitted and stored customer data.
  4. Procedures to ensure that systems modifications are consistent with the approved security program.
  5. Dual control procedures, segregation of duties, and employee background checks.
  6. Monitoring systems and procedures to detect actual and attempted attacks on, or intrusions into, customer information systems.
  7. Response programs specifying actions to be taken by specific individuals when the institution suspects unauthorized access (i.e., incident response).
  8. Measures to protect against destruction, loss, or damage of information from potential environmental hazards, such as fire and water damage or technological failures.
B. Is staff adequately trained to implement the security program?
  1. Obtain from management a listing of the training provided to all users of the institution's system.
C. Determine whether key controls, systems, and procedures of the information security program are regularly tested by independent third parties, or by qualified independent staff, in accordance with the risk assessment.
  1. Assess whether the nature and frequency of testing is consistent with the risk assessment.
  2. Assess whether tests are conducted or reviewed by independent third parties or qualified staff independent of those that develop or maintain the security program.
  3. Assess whether management reviews test results promptly. Assess whether management takes appropriate steps to address adverse test results.

IV. Assess the measures taken to oversee service providers.

A. Determine whether the institution exercises due diligence in selecting service providers.
B. Determine what information is supplied to service providers.
C. Obtain a copy of the contract(s) with the service provider(s). Determine whether contracts require service providers to implement appropriate measures to meet the objectives of the guidelines.
D. If the institution's risk assessment requires monitoring a service provider, then perform the following steps for each applicable service provider.
  1. Determine whether the service provider contract provides for sufficient reporting from the service provider to allow the institution to evaluate appropriately the service provider's performance and security, both in ongoing operations, and when malicious activity is suspected or known.
  2. Determine whether the institution's actions adequately control information supplied to service providers, ensuring that the information is managed and secured properly.
  3. Review financial condition of service provider.

EXHIBIT **64.2**   *(Continued)*

Key Questions or Considerations

V. Determine whether an effective process exists to adjust the information security program.

A.   Does the institution have an effective process to adjust the information security program as needed? Is the appropriate person assigned responsibility for adjusting the information security program?

B.   Review procedures that are in place to ensure that when the institution makes changes in technology, and in its business functions, the requirements of the guidelines are also considered. These changes can include:

1. Technology changes (e.g., software patches, new attack technologies, and methodologies).
2. Sensitivity of information.
3. Threats (both as to nature and extent).
4. Upcoming changes to the institution's business arrangements (e.g., mergers and acquisitions, alliances and joint ventures, outsourcing arrangements).
5. Upcoming changes to customer information systems (e.g., new configurations or connectivity, new software).

C.   Determine whether appropriate expertise is applied to evaluate whether changes to the information security program are necessary.

D.   Determine whether appropriate controls exist to ensure that changes to the information security program are properly implemented in a timely, risk-minimized manner.

VI. Summarize and communicate your findings.

A.   Discuss issues, conclusions, and potential violations with executive in charge.

B.   Discuss findings with institution management. If you have identified material issues, obtain and document management commitments to address those Issues.

C.   Complete work papers.

D.   Detail findings with support in a Summary Comment.

---

take a proactive role in compliance. This involvement must be approached from both a strategic ("tone at the top") and operational (designing, implementing, and managing information security controls that enable enterprise level regulatory compliance) perspective.

Although many of today's existing regulatory requirements are very comprehensive and have a significant impact on many business environments, organizations will likely face challenges related to both existing and forthcoming regulatory requirements on a continual basis. Additionally, new regulatory requirements will be enacted to address any issues that develop from emerging technologies. Although the extent and specific requirements the future will bring are difficult to pinpoint, it is likely that regulatory requirements will continue to grow. The specific requirements will present themselves in the future, but the overall intent of the regulations will be to continue to address any emerging issues and protect consumers, shareholders, and data from abuse.

Regardless of what the future brings, an organization's senior leadership team must adequately address regulatory requirements in order to protect the interests of both their customers and their company. Organizations that take a strategic enterprise-wide governance approach, have senior management actively involved, and create a compliance-driven culture will position themselves for successful regulatory compliance.

64.6 FURTHER READING

Anand, S. *Essentials of Sarbanes-Oxley*. Hoboken, NJ: John Wiley & Sons, 2007

Bianco, K. M., J. Hamilton, K. R. Benson, A. A. Turner, and J. M. Pachkowski. *Financial Services Modernization: Gramm-Leach-Bliley Act of 1999 Law and Explanation*. Washington, DC: CCH Inc., 1999.

Cohen, H. R., and W. J. Sweet. *After the Gramm-Leach-Bliley Act: A Road Map for Banks, Securities Firms, and Investment Managers*. New York: Practising Law Institute, 2000.

Dunham, W. B. *After the Gramm-Leach-Bliley Act: A Road Map for Insurance Companies*. New York: Practising Law Institute, 2000.

GeoTrust. "Meeting SOX and GLBA Compliance: A Guide to Automating User Authentication and Document Integrity." White paper, 2006, www.geotrust.com/resources/white_papers/pdfs/WP_SOX_0206s.pdf.

Greene, E. F., D. M. Becker, and L. N. Silverman. *Sarbanes-Oxley Act: Analysis and Practice*. New York: Aspen Law & Business, 2003.

Hermann, D. S. *Complete Guide to Security and Privacy Metrics: Measuring Regulatory Compliance, Operational Resilience, and ROI*. Boca Raton, FL: CRC Press, 2006.

Miles, B. L. *The Canadian Financial System*. Huntington, NY: Nova Science Publishers, 2004.

64.7 NOTES

1. American Institute of Certified Public Accountants Center for Audit Quality, AICPA Sarbanes-Oxley Home Page, 2008, http://thecaq.aicpa.org/Resources/Sarbanes+Oxley/.

2. Gramm-Leach-Bliley Act: 15 U.S.C. SubChapter 1, §§ 6801–6809, www.ftc.gov/privacy/glbact/glbsub1.htm.

3. Federal Trade Commission, "Standards for Safeguarding Customer Information: Final Rule," May 23, 2002, 16 CFR § 314 ¶1a, www.ftc.gov/os/2002/05/67fr36585.pdf.

4. U.S. Department of the Treasury, Office of the Controller of the Currency, "GLBA Examination Procedures," 2001, www.occ.treas.gov/ftp/bulletin/2001-35a.pdf.

ROLE OF THE CISO

Karen F. Worstell

65.1 CISO AS CHANGE AGENT.   The title of chief information security officer (CISO) has evolved because of the realization that the function of the chief information officer (CIO) is so broad as to require another person to focus specifically on the *security* elements of information. Another motivation derives from the fact that the CISO can perform functions that are not usually associated with the CIO. Our approach to information security needs to change in response to the disruptive events affecting the network and the boardroom. CISOs should be the change agents to make this happen. This is a shift from the majority of CISOs' emphasis today as senior managers of information technology (IT) security.

Today, CISOs are in the trust business due to the need to create and maintain a network of trust among all the people, business processes, and technology of an enterprise and its partners. The interconnected ecosystem that developed since the commercialization of the Internet has seen dramatic shifts of trust: Consumers are thinking twice before conducting business transactions online, governments have intervened with regulations to improve the trust environment. The shift has between toward less trust each time we encountered a "disruptive event"— an event that awakened us to the fact that things were not as they seemed and made us aware that protection of networked information and systems needed to address something we had not anticipated. The timeline of disruptive security events that began in 1986 with the promise of productivity by Macs and PCs worsened with the Brain virus (1986). Trust continued to decline with the Morris Worm (1988) and the Concept.A macro virus (1995). Our world became flatter,[1] and security became an entirely new kind of problem with the commercialization of the Internet and the introduction of the Web. In 1995 we still trusted the networked ecosystem. We saw the malicious works of nefarious individuals and groups, and we saw the future threat, but still did not fully realize how bad it would get.

Throughout this chapter, the author refers to "information security" and the "CISO." This is not to the exclusion of aspects of security that do not deal directly with information systems; rather, it is intended in the broadest possible sense to address the interdependent disciplines that are required successfully to protect information in all its forms. It is in this context that the title "CISO" is used, inclusive of "CI" and "CSO" rather than exclusive.

In 2001, the horrific events of 9/11 rocked the planet, Enron collapsed, trust plummeted with Slammer (2002) and the insidious stealthy vectors that utilize port 80 to steal everything from personal identities, to bank accounts, and company data. The networked ecosystem has provided no end of new material for our profession while making "computer security," "spyware," and "identity theft" household terms.

Mark Twain once said the definition of insanity is to do the same thing over and over and expect different results. It is clear that we will need to apply a different way of thinking and new roles and responsibilities to the discipline of information security if we are to make progress in enabling the kind of protection that is required by businesses and agencies while enabling business agility and competitiveness. This is the opportunity of the CISO.

Trends reveal that we are just past the cusp of a new kind of "disruptive event" worldwide—the introduction of legislative and regulatory mandates to ensure effectiveness of controls for protection of consumers, critical infrastructures, and shareholder value. We deal today with a myriad of high-impact networked-based crimes: extortion, corporate espionage, and massive fraud. Many experienced CISOs believe that a "cyber–Pearl Harbor" scenario is plausible. Since 2001, we are acutely aware of the vulnerability of critical infrastructures, at least 85 percent of which are owned and maintained by the private sector. Recent figures[2] indicate that new home PCs are compromised with anything from spyware to Trojans within 5 minutes of connecting to the Internet (it takes up to 60 minutes to download protective software). Although corporate PCs may enjoy a relative degree of protection, as many as 90 percent of personal home PCs have some kind of spyware. Corporations with the resources to address information security have doubled the use of IT security standards and guides since 2003. But the insidious attack on the home user is winning a game with serious stakes: Consumer confidence in the Internet is waning. Once "computer security" was the domain of techies and "geeks"; it is now pervasive enough to be a household concern.

"Security" has definitely reached the awareness of the C-level offices (chief executive officer, chief financial officer, etc.) on mahogany row, and there are articles in the popular press on a daily basis concerning information security around the world. This visibility ensures that no one can hide behind a plea of ignorance of security problems. Legislators and regulators are more concerned than ever, and new statutes, codes, regulations, and guidelines have proliferated. In the face of huge threats and the need for a corporate duty of care, network security remains a concern, but compliance to regulations and statutes and the ability to demonstrate adherence have become mandatory.

Penalties for noncompliance to these recently established governing rules are setting breathtaking precedents: $1.2 billion for a large U.S. financial institution, $15 million for another. The U.S. Veteran's Administration admitted to the compromise of personal information, including Social Security numbers, of 26.5 million living American veterans.[3] It may be noted that even New Zealand was for sale on eBay® recently—reportedly the efforts of an unknown party in Queensland—and was taken off line after 22 bids had reached A$2,000.[4] The reserve, if any, was probably not met. We live in a new world. Trust is no longer assumed; it is easily broken in the most inadvertent to the most imaginative ways. The case law for settlements and summary judgments in information security matters is providing the basis for the best potential dollar-based impact analysis on business and information security risk since Basel II, which is the second set of international guidelines on banking laws and regulations recommended by the Basel Committee on Banking Supervision.[5]

Companies, and clearly U.S. Government agencies, do not have control of intellectual property, employee data, or consumer data. The need to retain corporate records in the event of litigation regarding business matters, and to produce such information on demand under discovery, is infeasible for many firms with petabytes or more of structured and unstructured data. Recent legislation, regulations, and case law will drive the need for information security programs to solve this enormous data management and security problem and to demonstrate a level of effectiveness to a standard of care that will stand up to the scrutiny of opposing counsel. It is the role of the CISO to understand fully the implications of these new burdens and to incorporate them into a strategy along with the business strategy of each enterprise. Where information security spending was benchmarked by Gartner Group at 1 to 3 percent of overall IT budget in the mainframe days, and 5 to 7 percent at the dawn of distributed computing, the spending to resolve problems created by past failures to address solid controls, and to be prepared for the threats of the future to any degree, should well exceed 10 percent of an overall IT budget. This does not include the special allowances that will be required to treat some of the worst offenses. According to the 2004 Information Security survey conducted by PricewaterhouseCoopers and *CIO* magazine, the best practices group spent 14 percent of their IT budgets on information security each year.[6] Companies must plan for these expenditures; the role of the CISO will be to help clarify obligations, business necessities, and strategic spending.

65.2 CISO AS STRATEGIST. Information is the prize that motivates wrongdoers, perpetrators, and miscreants who tamper with, destroy, and penetrate systems that process, store, and transmit digital information. Phil Condit, former chairman of The Boeing Company, said it well at his keynote to the International Information Integrity Institute in 1995: "Information is the business."[7] His statement was visionary at the time. Indeed, since 1995, it is safe to say that information is the foundation of business, but it is the way it is used, combined, mined, shared, represented, accessed, and manipulated for business logic's sake that creates competitive advantage. And each of these areas of application logic and information requires rules-based protection to ensure that the business is basing decisions on sound knowledge.

There are three main drivers for CISOs to define a new strategy for information security:

1. Systems are inherently insecure as a result of enormous variations in configuration, sheer complexity, and volume of vulnerabilities. A risk-based approach using conventional methods is no longer valid (if it ever was).

2. The reach of global business processes, personnel, and business systems introduces new considerations into an already complex security problem.

3. The playing field between the "protectors" and the "interlopers" is dramatically uneven. There are literally hundreds of thousands, if not millions, of interlopers with a follow-the-sun $7 \times 24 \times 365$ factory of attacks. Companies cannot afford any such investment to counter the attacks, even if it were possible with a combination of people and automation. The attack vectors change too quickly to be able to get ahead of the curve on the protection side of the equation. Nation-states, organized crime, terrorist organizations, fraudsters, and identity thieves are continuously developing ingenious models to attack, steal, and destroy precious assets of individuals as well as of enterprises.[8] Worse, professionals continue to consider trusted insider as the most significant threat. With a globally distributed workforce of contractors, employees, and suppliers, it is necessary to have an approach to information protection controls that enables a reasonable assurance that both the external and insider threats are appropriately addressed.

The CISO as a strategist will be successful adopting and integrating new methods into the business, such as a rules-based standard of care and due diligence to that standard of care. This will necessarily include existing methods of network protection, data classification, and so forth—the standard of ISO/IEC 17799:2005 provides an excellent framework. It is the decision-making process about priorities that must change.[9]

As a strategist, the CISO will need to look at the security problem as an executive businessperson would. Adopting the kinds of strategic thinking described in classics such as *The Art of the Long View* is a key success factor.[10] A partial list of things to consider includes the reliance on information, why protection is important, the insecurity of systems, the futility of risk-based security, and world trends.

65.2.1   Reliance on Digital Information.   Digital information is the lifeblood of our commerce, financial infrastructure, healthcare, transportation, energy, and even our very identities as citizens. In the United States alone there are 15 distinct critical infrastructures, vital to the interests of the country and to national security:

1. Information technology
2. Telecommunications
3. Chemicals
4. Transportation systems
5. Emergency services
6. Postal and shipping services
7. Agriculture and food
8. Public health and healthcare
9. Drinking water/water treatment

10. Energy
11. Banking and finance
12. National monuments and icons
13. Defense industrial base
14. Key industry/technology sites
15. Large gathering sites[11]

Eight-five percent of the systems that make up these critical infrastructures are owned by private enterprise. The systems that interconnect to deliver services require integrity, availability, the trusted relationships, and confidentiality. If we cannot trust the systems, we cannot trust the information. If we cannot trust the information, we cannot trust decisions based on that information. Information security also now requires us to be able to demonstrate digital ownership and even chain of possession. We have to maintain digital information in such a way that we know where our IP is at all times, what records our company must maintain, and how to store, label, and retrieve them. The definition of information security as CIA—confidentiality, integrity, and availability—is too simplistic.

65.2.2 Inherent Insecurity of Systems.   Systems include hardware, software, utilities, scripts, and transport media, all of which are ultimately created by humans with scheduled deadlines and constrained budgets, and installed by organizations with scheduled deadlines and constrained budgets. It is all flawed. The vulnerabilities that exist today, let alone the ones we are going to learn about tomorrow and the next day, cannot all be addressed. Perfect security is a myth, unattainable, and arguably a waste of time to try. Risk-based methods for identifying required security tactics do not scale, nor is there meaningful data that describe probability and ALE (annualized loss expectancy) realistically for information security.[12]

65.2.3 World Trends.   Our world is changing. Based on a report titled "Ten Trends to Watch in 2006" published by McKinsey and Company,[13] trends that will have significant implications for security professionals include:

- Dramatic geographic shifts in centers of economic activity, particularly in IT services, where labor and talent are increasing globally. Worldwide, distributed, and devolved security models will be required, as the supply chain and internal processes in a company's value chain are widely distributed. The implications of physical security, information systems protection, personnel practices, and the diversity of governing regulations and statutes require a much broader, business-based view of asset protection. Use of company-owned, leased, and outsourced facilities will prove to be a challenge to asset protection.

- Technological connectivity will transform the way we live and interact and will completely disrupt current security infrastructures. Enhanced connectivity and mobility using smaller (i.e., less observable), highly capable Internet-enabled devices requires access to enterprise information resources from anywhere, at any time, putting an enormous strain on rule sets designed to filter incoming and outgoing information, and where it travels. Peer-to-peer networking, tiny mass storage devices, blending of personal and enterprise computing on common devices—these are just a few of the near-term changes that will completely alter the way enterprise rules are handled for information protection. Grid computing, virtual machines, work from home—all are issues that challenge the notion of comprehensive asset protection, both physical and logical.

- New models of in-the-cloud knowledge, including production, access distribution, and ownership are emerging, and fundamental trust models remain to be defined or even described. "Software as a service" [SAAS] is already enabled for consumers and small businesses, and, probably enterprise services will follow. The download and introduction of software over the Web, and access to proprietary information in an anywhere-computing environment, requires redefinition of the way we think about intellectual property and data management.

A coordinated, interdisciplinary management approach to a proper set of controls based on business risk is essential to deal effectively with the enormous requirements to protect information in business today. Whether the enterprise is private or public, regardless of nationality, "the world is flat," and a solid information protection strategy must recognize the implications of that.

To summarize, successful use and management of information is the business. Setting priorities that demonstrate due diligence to a properly business-driven standard of care for the confidentiality, integrity, availability, ownership, and proper possession of information is the charge of the CISO. It is essential that the CISO function at the level of executive management and as a business strategist, participating with the executive leadership team to enable the integration of due diligence to a standard of care into all business streams.

65.3   STRATEGY, GOVERNANCE, AND THE STANDARD OF CARE.   Recognizing the information security changes that drive the role of the CISO, what should be done to be successful? What are the key focus areas that should define the role of a CISO?

Success for information security professionals will depend on several key factors in this new world:

- Standard of care (e.g., rules-based) strategy
- Governance and accountability
- Clear roles and responsibilities
- Metrics, reporting, and executive visibility

The remainder of this section examines each of these more fully. For a general discussion of management's role in information assurance, see Chapter 63 in this *Handbook*.

65.3.1   Standard of Care.   A CISO has one vision statement that drives strategy: to establish due diligence to a standard of care for the business; that is to say, to put in place the mechanisms (controls, oversight, monitoring, metrics, and reporting) that will enable the business to demonstrate due diligence to that standard of care.[14] Instead such a standard of care is rules based, but it is not prescriptive in itself. The standard of care is the set of documented business risks from an information protection perspective, and the declaration of a set of rules in policy, that effectively mitigate those business risks. The standard of care declares "what" will be done. It is the governing book of policy to be reviewed and monitored by the executive leadership team, the audit committee of the board of directors, and senior management. It is the set of rules with which all internal standards and desktop procedures must comply.

Although a complete treatment of the identification of business risk is outside the scope of this chapter, it can be summarized in this way: Prior to identifying the controls within a standard of care, steps must be taken to qualify business risk relatively as "high," "medium," or "low" based on magnitude of potential business impact and perceived exposure. It does not use quantitative risk analysis methods such as those found in Octave, FAIR, or any other popular risk-based quantitative methodology. It does not use ALE. It does enable the business to defend the design of the standard of care, the controls of which are derived from the business risk analysis.

The standard of care derives its meaning from two primary sources: internationally accepted standards and the risk analysis that defines the business risks.

The basic set of internationally accepted standards is summarized in Exhibit 65.1. For more detailed analysis of security standards, see Chapters 44 and 51 in this *Handbook*.

It is important for these standards to be used as a foundation for the policy, to ensure that security policy is recognized by the larger body of security professionals, and to serve as an interchangeable trading partner agreement in the communication and enforcement of security expectations.

It is not in the scope of this chapter to go into the risk assessment methodology in detail; however, a general description will serve to indicate that this is not a vulnerability assessment. The risk assessment process is one used not to identify system vulnerabilities but to identify potential areas relating to people, process, and technology that could result in an exposure that reaches a defined threshold of business impact. For example, in a technology firm, one might align three major areas of concern: major inaccuracies in financial reporting (the domain of the Sarbanes-Oxley Act of 2002), failure adequately to control IP, and the subsequent risk to trade secrets, patents, or copyrights, and failure adequately to protect customer data. Each of these "slices" of business risk can be the foundation for the questions in the risk assessment to ascertain major systems exposure, business process exposure, or exposure caused by people doing things incorrectly, such as human error or even malfeasance. Risk rankings will need to be on the basis of assumptions and figures acceptable to the senior leadership team; the wildcard in any risk ranking is probability. The business impact threshold will vary widely with each business. Thresholds may be set using the financials of the company. A company that has a *materiality threshold* (i.e., the minimum level of loss that matters significantly to the organization), for example, of $5 million that defines a material weakness in Sarbanes-Oxley compliance will prioritize its risks differently than a firm for which the materiality threshold is on the order of $500 million.[15]

With the risk analysis to use as a rationale, the road map to tailoring a book of policy derived from the international standards becomes a series of steps to take for each risk, to define the mitigating control, and to map that control to a control statement in, for example ISO/IEC 17799:2005. Repeating this for all the risk categories and all the risk areas, one will have a foundation to demonstrate to any trading partner or outside party why the standard of care is relevant and appropriate to the company.

The next step is to help provide the translation of the high-level standard of care policy statements into action. Creating a set of implementation standards for the various controls described in the standard of care gives clear direction to all parties charged with ensuring that the needed controls are in place. The implementation standards also provide the foundation for a set of measurements and tests to determine that the controls are working as intended. This is the critical element that enables the executive team and the CISO to demonstrate that the controls are not only the right ones, but that they are working properly.

Basic set of internationally accepted standards includes	Useful in this context:
BS 7799	Replaced —see ISO/IEC 27001.
ISO/IEC 17799:2005 — Information technology. Security techniques. Code of practice for information security management.	This universal standard provides a complete set of guidelines for an effective Information Security Management System (ISMS). It is essential guidance to help manage an effective information security policy. It offers a common language and a common understanding to enable an organization to develop, implement and measure effective security management practice, providing confidence in intercompany trading. ISO/IEC 17799 details a number of individual security controls, which may be selected and applied as part of the ISMS. ISO/IEC 17799, again based on a British standard, is scheduled to become ISO/IEC 27002 in a couple of years.
BS 7799-2:2005 (ISO/IEC 27001:2005) Information technology. Security techniques. Information Security Management Systems. Requirements.	ISO/IEC 27001 specifies the requirements for the security management system itself. It is this standard, as opposed to ISO/IEC 17799, against which certification is offered. ISO/IEC 27001 has also been harmonized to be compatible with other management systems standards, such as ISO/IEC 9001 and ISO/IEC 14001. Organizations already certified under BS 7799-2:2002 need to prepare for transition to ISO/IEC 27001 in order to meet its requirements.
BS ISO/IEC 13335-1:2004 Information technology. Guidelines for the management of IT security. Concepts and models for information and communications technology security management	This standard is useful to: • Define and describe the concepts associated with the management of IT security. • Identify the relationships between the management of IT security and management of IT in general. • Present several models that can be used to explain IT security. • Provide general guidance on the management of IT security.
IT Governance Institute's *Control Objectives for IT* (CoBIT®)	CoBIT® is a way to implement governance. It provides a tailorable set of controls.
ITIL—IT Infrastructure Library	ITIL® provides a cohesive set of best practice, drawn from the public and private sectors internationally. It is supported by a comprehensive qualifications scheme, accredited training organizations, and implementation and assessment tools. The best practice processes promoted in ITIL® support and are supported by the British Standards Institution's standard for IT service Management (BS15000). (OGC - ITIL)

EXHIBIT 65.1   International Standards for Information Security Governance

The CISO does not get involved in monitoring firewall rules or router configurations. This is work that is the domain of an operations security manager who is carrying out the standards established by the CISO. The CISO should review the reporting (once it is established) to ensure that the controls described for all Internet connectivity are in place and working, and to ensure that the handling of technical details is delegated to specialized technical staff and management.

65.3.2 Governance and Accountability.   A recent research project completed by Booz Allen Hamilton reveals several factors that are changing the face of protecting enterprise assets, and ultimately adjusting the roles of the security profession. The information protection strategy is undergoing "convergence," defined by ASIS International as "the identification of security risks and interdependencies between business functions and processes within the enterprise and the development of managed business process solutions to address those risks and interdependencies."[16] The role of the successful CISO is not only converging into an interdependent set of security specialties; it is also blending into business functions, intertwined into the fabric of decision-making processes throughout the life cycle of business strategy, plans, and execution.

Given the need for managing all the complexity recently introduced, security professionals must also adopt a different outlook—a more business-oriented than a protectionist position. Tim Mather, CISO of Symantec Corporation, describes it this way:

> For many information security professionals, the urge is to promote information security—zealously. Many times too zealously. We often come to believe that security awareness equates to zealous promotion of information security objectives, especially the deployment of (information) security technology—often at the "expense" of people, and policies and processes. However, that zealous promotion of information security objectives tends to cloud our judgment as to the business considerations of the risks involved. Our information security-colored glasses are polarized to security and tend to filter out business unit considerations. This leads to a loss of credibility with business unit personnel, hindering our ability to accomplish our information security goals.
>
> Our challenge is to articulate our information security objectives in terms of business risk that business unit personnel can understand and appreciate. That being said, it does not mean being "soft" on our objectives. We are not paid to install the "speed bumps" in enterprise hallways, but that articulation does mean translating information security objectives into "business-speak." Only the combination of articulate translation and polite but firm emphasis on our information security objectives will gain us the credibility that we need to accomplish our enterprise information security goals. And that effort has to begin, and continue, at the top of the enterprise—with its executives.

Part of the reason security managers have had to take such hard positions in the past is that information security practices have had a strong tendency to be in organizational silos: executive protection, IT, physical security, local business practices, policy management, HR investigations, fraud, and so on. Each of these practice areas is a specialty, to be sure, and will continue to require specialization. Independence can no longer be effective. Privacy, information security, data management, mobility, supply chain management, workforce management, and human resources, facility management—the protection elements of these business domains, and so much more, must be coordinated to avoid weak links in the protection strategy that could prove disappointing if not devastating to a business, or to individuals.

With the need for an interdisciplinary approach at an executive level, with a broad reach across an enterprise, one might argue that the centralization of primary information security functions under a CISO would be one way to ensure that all information security practice would be consistent and easily measured; on the contrary, the temptation to ensure the fidelity of an organizational mission through assembling affected functions under a single manager should be resisted. In a successful information security strategy, it is far too easy for all enterprise management to think of security as "security's business" or as "the CISO's job." In fact, the function of security should be emphasized as a business function, with accountability distributed in the business across all business unit executives, led by an executive-level security team. This has five advantages.

1. There will never be a security organization large enough to do the entire job of securing information assets in the new world. Security truly has to be everyone's job, in ways that are measured and tracked. Putting security accountability into the business units will leverage resources effectively.

2. Accountability is a good way to get someone's attention. Management is attentive to scorecards that are read at the top, with expectations for improvements that have been assigned to a responsible individual or group.

3. The interdisciplinary approach needed for the rapidly emerging challenges and competing priorities can best be addressed by an interdisciplinary team, including functions such as supply chain management, that have no reason to be merged into a security organization.

4. Being closely tied to the business allows for upstream integration into business processes, allowing security to be "built in" [versus an afterthought] when new business initiatives, strategies, and ventures are being designed.

5. The funding for proper protection of information assets is no longer a security problem or an IT problem, but it is a business problem, with the proper business visibility of what is and is not getting done, and what is the residual risk from funding decisions.

A simple policy-driven governance structure has been effective in many large-scale organizations to establish the necessary linkages with the business, to ensure consistency in strategy and approach, to gain executive buy-in on strategy through collective priority setting, and to gain visibility of progress and of unresolved issues on an ongoing basis. A basic governance structure can be tailored to fit corporate culture such as the number of representatives, and the layers of working groups. What is essential is the creation of a governance body to ensure corporate due diligence and to avoid conflicts of interest such as are described further in Section 65.5.5.

A policy-driven approach to security and disaster recovery governance includes these components:

- Senior Leadership Team (C-level executives)
  - Authority for policy
  - Governance body
  - Program oversight
- Policy
  - Establishes accountability
  - Establishes programs and program authority
  - Establishes governance processes
  - Publishes under authority of the senior leadership team
- Principles
  - Five to six high-level statements at a descriptive level
  - Separate from policy
  - Establishes guidance for business unit standards

- Business Unit Team
  - Provides staff support
  - Facilitates governance process
  - Provides technical leadership for security across business units
  - Consists of representatives from each business unit plus audit
  - CISO is chair
  - Coordinates policy principles for senior leadership team approvals
  - Establish standards at the prescriptive level
  - Implements standards
  - Monitors effectiveness of implementation (provides metrics and reports to senior leadership team)
  - Coordinates key initiatives for security and recovery improvement across business units

In this structure, the CISO can function as an agent of change for driving broad, funded, prioritized initiatives with true business impact.

Joel Scambray, coauthor of *Hacking Exposed* and senior security strategist at Microsoft, sees the need for CISOs as change agents:

> Information security is now such a very broad topic, the role of the senior security professional has to move away from implementation of the security technology to the role of change agent. Network issues are diminishing: so much can go through port 80 inbound and then by proxy to the application, the themes in the attack community are shifting and will always continue to do so as technology evolves. Attackers will strike a business through the path of least resistance and that is going to be throughout the business, not just in the network and applications. It is essential to have business group accountability to address risks in all areas, for each executive to think about risk and ensure they are taking informed steps to bring it to within acceptable levels.
>
> The CISO has to move up in the corporate structure—it's a revenue-protecting job and has to be supported at the highest levels of the company to get the company to focus on the right risks.[17]

65.3.3 Roles and Responsibilities.   In general terms, there are a set of roles and responsibilities that support accountability that have been shown effective in practice. Some would require substantial change in the organizational responsibilities within a company or agency. That ISO is the change agent to make things better; once the foundation for security governance is in place, this should be a discussion topic. Outside professional opinions can be solicited. Refer to the practices documented at Institute of Internal Auditors (IIA), Information Security and Control Association (ISACA), and IT Governance Institute (ITGI). Evaluate them in the context of your company; you may not be able to implement all ten of these principles for accountability and reporting, but even some of them would demonstrate progress. The 10 principles for effective information security control follow. For each item involving security, the CISO is the leader, or receives and acts on reports, or merely a participant and observer.

1. The CISO does not "own" IT assets but manages them on behalf of the business. Governance processes are in place for effective business management of IT.

2. An independent third party regularly reviews the implementation of each of these principles to verify control design and control effectiveness.

3. The expenditures on IT security are justified in terms of business value according to parameters established between the CISO and the business units.

4. IT security is actively monitored by an IT governance board consisting of IT, business management, and the CFO, and adjusted according to business needs.

5. Security, information assurance, and cybersecurity rules are tied to business rules in ways that are traceable, understandable, and agreed to by the business.

6. All IT security change is authorized by specifically designated IT management change boards.

7. Application development processes verify that applications perform only as intended, throughout the life cycle of the application, under the supervision of IT governance boards.

8. All IT security operations and processes are standardized, documented, and reviewed regularly for consistency by IT management and independent third parties.

   a. New processes are developed to accommodate business change.

   b. Existing processes are reviewed regularly for update, to accommodate business change. Consider having legal counsel review the documentation to determine if the records present unexpected legal risks or if they can provide legal advantage in any dispute over the standard of care.

9. All information systems assets (data, infrastructure, applications, processes, and services) have clear business owners with accountability to ensure:

   a. Assets are used only as intended.

   b. Assets are accessed only by those who are authorized according to defined business rules. (Access is defined as ability + opportunity.)

   c. Assets are available for use according to defined business rules.

10. Business and IT employees, contractors, vendors, and third parties have necessary documentation and training on a regular basis to carry out these principles in an effective, verifiable manner for the businesses in which they are engaged, and they have proof of training on a timely basis.

Generally, the business does not want to "own" IT. They see IT as a utility, the domain of "IT staff" and too much work to understand. This is the major hurdle to be overcome in the change agent role of CISO. Remember, IT is the business. That is to say, IT today governs the systems that process the information that is the lifeblood of the business. Without the information, the business will stop. The logic applied to the information on behalf of the business should be owned by the business. It is worth the effort; once the business realizes its own accountability for the confidentiality, availability, integrity, ownership, and possession of business information, as well as for information security practices and improvements, it will enjoy a whole new level of interest in, and responsibility for, the enterprise.

65.3.4 Reporting.   With the governance structure established, the ability exists to assign accountability to the right places in the organization. The senior leadership team should identify how management will be held accountable. This is not a choice of "if" but of "how." Without clear accountability, governance and policy will mean nothing because they will not be implemented or enforced effectively. The primary tools for enabling executive accountability are reporting, monitoring, and metrics.

65.3.5 Monitoring.   Monitoring in the context of the standard of care is the set of processes, human resources, and automated and manual tools needed to ascertain how well the controls established by the standard of care are functioning. Key to monitoring success is to monitor meaningfully—monitor to determine that the set of controls established is, or is not, working as intended. This is a function that can easily be coordinated and shared with internal audit, and care must be taken to ensure that the monitoring is appropriate for the applicable standard of care rules. Monitoring should be done with an objective degree of proof—hearsay is not adequate monitoring. Monitoring will usually need to be automated to handle the scale and frequency required in most information systems environments.

65.3.6 Metrics.   Metrics have been a difficult challenge for all CISOs. The generic advice is this: Choose metrics for reporting that are essential to (a) give the business a set of key performance indicators and (b) make a difference in a needed control area. We often measure something in security just because we can. This is a mistake. Measuring the number of viruses or number of penetration attempts is not meaningful because they are high-volume certainties. The measurement system has to ensure that good results could not be achieved from failing to look; a decline in security incidents from outside attacks may be truly declining, based on 100 percent visibility of the problem, or the problem may have shifted to a space that is not monitored. In most cases it is probably, the latter, given the changing vectors in the network attack space.

65.3.7 Executive Visibility.   For executive visibility, experience indicates that a CISO executive scorecard, published with the support of the CEO, CFO, COO or other executive sponsor, will drive behavior according to the metrics that are chosen and reported. Reporting should be at least quarterly—more frequent would be desirable, but may be difficult to achieve. Quarterly frequency allows for continuity of program management in making security improvements that require executive support for implementation.

65.4 SUMMARY OF ACTIONS.   In summary, the strategy for information security has to balance vulnerability management with a standard of care that is appropriate to all stakeholders. These stakeholders include business owners, trading partners, consumers, regulators, auditors, shareholders, and information owners whose membership in the interconnected community puts them at risk if any member has a breach. This requires coordination among diverse specialists and organizations. Security as a state of being is not feasible; due diligence to a standard of care is the approach CISOs should adopt.

The CISO has to develop a standard of care that answers to many demands. The Federal Information Security Management Act of 2002, EU Data Protection Act, Gramm-Leach-Bliley, HIPAA, Sarbanes-Oxley Act of 2002, Senate Bill 1386, BS 7799 certification, FIPS 199 and 200, as well as various NIST publications, and a host of local codes and statutes around the world greatly complicate the compliance function. It is best to adopt a standard-of-care approach that provides, based on international standards, a single comprehensive response to all queries. Expectations of records management, compliance with e-discovery, business continuance, disaster prepared-ness, IP and trade secret protections, sanctions for unfair information practices or advertising, and a burgeoning library of case law in matters related to security and privacy have become the drivers to which information security professionals must re-spond. Clearly, information security has become a risk management role worthy of a C-level executive, working in a structured governance role to involve the business. Today, the transition from security director or even from today's CISO is not complete to the C-level role that the CISO name implies. The points made thus far indicate a real need to pursue this as a professional group, and to adopt some generally accepted prin-ciples and standards so that businesses and agencies can enjoy the level of information protection that is required in this "new world."

65.5   RECOMMENDATIONS FOR SUCCESS FOR CISOs.   For all the inter-views that I did at RSA in 2006, only one quote made it into the press. Under the title "Microsoft CISO Has a Sense of Humor," the reporter indicated that I had answered all their detailed questions with serious thoughtfulness. But when they asked me what would be the best advice to someone who aspires to be a CISO, they quoted, "Have a stiff drink until the feeling goes away." I actually said, "Have a lie-down somewhere," but no matter—the quip hit the papers.

It was seen as funny, but there is also a real need to consider the demands made on an individual who aspires to a C-level role in security, where there is so much at stake. Many technical security managers are chosen to fill the role but are ill equipped to transform into executive management. Even worse, a CISO who does understand the executive role and moves to perform it in an organization where CISO roles are not understood can easily fail. To quote Machiavelli:

> Let it be noted that there is no more delicate matter to take in hand, nor more dangerous to conduct, nor more doubtful in its success, than to set up as a leader in the introduction of changes. For he who innovates will have for his enemies all those who are well off under the existing order, and only lukewarm supporters in those who might be better off under the new.[18]

In this section, several pointers based on input from various CISOs are offered to help you assess whether an organization is ready for a CISO and whether you are ready. The areas include:

- Education and experience
- The "culture" of security in the business
- The alliance with corporate and outside counsel
- The partnership with internal audit
- The tension with IT and dealing with the potential conflict of interest
- Organizational structure
- Responsibilities and opportunities outside of CISO internal responsibilities

65.5.1   Education and Experience.   First and foremost, do you have appro-priate background to be able to lead with wise counsel and appropriate judgment? Do you feel you are better at tactical detail, or do you prefer "the big picture"? In a panel during a plenary session at RSA 2005, LJ (Lisa) Johnson, CISO of Nike, related that her MBA degree was very helpful in her role as CISO, and this sentiment echoes across others in similar positions; however, successful leaders in this space do not all have advanced degrees—life experience is a significant contributor. Reading the wealth of books on various aspects of business management, information systems, and information security is also a good way to expand one's background. Conferences are beginning to focus on the role of CISOs as the role is described in this chapter, but, for the most part, conferences are best at keeping up with technical or auditing trends.

One way to evaluate the background that is necessary, whether it be by experience, reading, or the classroom, is to evaluate the various stakeholders with whom a CISO must effectively communicate to one degree or another. Internal audit, legal counsel, business executives, and IT staff are the core stakeholders. Within the business units, finance, supply chain, and HR are areas with which the CISO will have frequent discussions. Do you know your company's value chain? Do you understand the major business processes? Have you read the company's disclosure statements, and annual report? Do you understand the major cost concerns and the revenue streams? What are the key risks, outside of security, that occupy the executive team's time? If you know the answers to these questions, you are in the minority of security professionals. If you do not create your own action plan to network with key individuals, then read, take a course, and create a career plan that will give you experience in these areas. Do not be afraid to admit that you are learning and interested in getting more information from the experts in a particular area.

Whether your education is a BS in computer science, a MBA, or high school, you can get a great education on the job in preparation to taking a leadership role in information security. Evaluate what it will take for success, and then make your plan to get that information on the job or in school.

Each company is unique, so each CISO job will have unique elements built on the basic CISO job description. A word of warning: As a new CISO, take the time to absorb the culture before launching major changes or initiatives. Remember Machiavelli—people need to know you care before they care what you know.

65.5.2 "Culture" of Security in the Business.   The culture of security can be very difficult to ascertain. In a centralized security model that lends itself to top-down management, one at least knows where to look. In a company where security may be part of the company's core business, and many think of themselves as CISOs, the role is much more challenging. The culture can be defined as the set of attitudes toward accepting direction, allowing time and resources to be used in order to put proper controls in place. The next points will help you take a pulse check on culture and could be used for some due diligence prior to accepting a CISO role:

- **Risk appetite.** What is the materiality threshold (minimum significant loss) for risk management? It is important to understand this so that you can properly ascertain the importance of the issues you will encounter and thereby know whether they require an FYI or escalation as an urgent matter.

- **Cultural norms and attitudes.** Is the workforce dynamic, high rate of job turnover, low threshold of tolerance for change, autonomous? You would work with this kind of workforce and the culture it engenders much differently than a company with a "by the rule-book," policy-driven bureaucracy. There is no "right" answer, but you need to know how people receive security direction; most people favor a "carrot" over a "stick"; it is a question of what kind of carrot.

- **Relevant regulations and statutes.** You will need an inventory and at least a basic understanding of the way regulations and statutes affect information security. If the company is multinational, this requires an understanding of local jurisdictions, local statutes, and local regulations as well. Find the people who can share with you what they know about this area.

- **Influence and awareness of the "court of public opinion."** The court of public opinion is essentially a form of reputation risk and the impact that it can have on the organization. A decision about security, such as fixing a security bug in an online application, may not be governed by specific laws, but it could definitely create the perception of poor security practices in a way that influences other security issues that the company may have in the public eye. This area may be a major influence for highly visible companies, or less of a concern for others.

- **Influence of risk to reputation.** With consumer confidence at an all-time low for Internet security, this is an element of the company's risk profile that it is essential to define explicitly as much as possible. Would the company go so far as to achieve full transparency of its security controls and privacy statements as an approach to building trust as a competitive advantage? Or is it willing to take more reputation risk by obscuring the privacy statement because the security controls are not quite what they should be? As you discover security issues, knowing the company's posture relative to transparency and associated reputation risk will be useful to determine what to escalate.

- **Who else manages various aspects of risk?** Make it a point to build and maintain an active network of peers in these areas:
  - Financial
  - Legal
  - Corporate strategy and planning
  - Marketing
  - Other areas of security (consulting, product, customer support)

- **How is your role seen in relationship to those managers?** Who else should you be talking to? Keep asking the questions.

65.5.3   Alliance with Corporate and Outside Counsel.   There are a few roles that merit special mention. Corporate counsel and outside counsel are becoming increasingly interdependent with the information security team. Historically, company policy, investigations, contracts, and incidents have all (or should be) coordinated with counsel. New developments in records management, e-discovery, third-party management, privacy, and case law relating to information security breaches and losses have created a new role for counsel in defining protection of consumer and employee data and company IP. Counsel will be necessary to navigate the rule of law as it pertains to information, information systems, and associated business practices. This is an organization with which the CISO needs to be close.

65.5.4   Partnership with Internal Audit.   While it is not uncommon to find IT personnel who assume that what audit does not know cannot hurt them, this attitude is a grave mistake. Internal audit is another special relationship for the CISO. A close IT-audit partnership is essential for these key reasons, and it should be the responsibility of the CISO to ensure that this partnership is in place and working smoothly:

- The rules for standard of care require demonstration that the controls are working effectively as designed. There is no better organization to provide clarity on what that entails than internal audit.

- Internal audit can collaborate with information security on the standard of care monitoring and reporting, thus effectively extending information protection resources.

- The CISO is accountable to ensure that control processes and policies that pertain are in place and working well. Internal audit should have full access to information security processes to ensure compliance and to provide independent assurance against potential conflict of interest.

- By cultivating a close partnership (yet maintaining the arm's-length relationship), the CISO and an organization can exchange information, set priorities for the audit and security improvement programs, and provide support for each other on core issues to escalate.

65.5.5 Tension with IT.   Many CISOs report to IT, and therein lies a potential for conflict of interest, or the appearance of conflict of interest. This is an area of increasing concern. The issue resides with the CISO needing to identify the security concerns and strategies for the company, including scope that extends beyond IT control, but doing so may be perceived as reflecting poorly on the IT management chain. Also, having a CISO report to the CIO creates an impression that the CISO is the IT security manager. Further, IT budgets are often calculated on the basis of run rates, assuming that it is an operational utility. Funding all the security effort out of an IT budget is a mismatch in two ways: Security is not a run-rate type of function, and taking what amounts to 10 percent or more of the IT budget for security is generally a significant hardship on other parts of IT that are critical to the business.

To address the conflict of interest concern, one could move the CISO role out of IT and have it reporting at the CFO, COO, or CEO level. The CISO in this regard would be a peer of the CIO. This has an advantage of removing the conflict of interest and the impression of IT security manager, but it also introduces the possibility of the CISO losing touch with the IT organization. Another alternative, if the CISO reports to the CIO, is to establish the governance structure and provide dotted-line relationships to the senior leadership on the governance board. Internal audit can monitor the relationships and processes to ensure that conflicts of interest are not developing. Politics being what they generally are, the latter choice seems the most difficult to implement well.

65.5.6 Organizational Structure.   Organizational structure for the CISO will, of course, be heavily influenced by the company. We have already discussed some independent factors that argue against the CISO reporting to the CIO. Companies are moving away from the traditional model of having the senior information security manager, or in some cases CISO, report directly to the CIO, opting instead to have the CISO report to the CEO, COO, or, in some cases, the CFO. In addition, a cross-functional, dotted-line relationship to key stakeholders may be required for adequate reporting and oversight.[19]

Aside from the question of to whom should the CISO report, what should the CISO manage? How should that be structured? The CISO's role as an executive should be focused on governance, policy management, and compliance monitoring and reporting. The CISO should establish parameters for IT security operations, information security investigations, forensics and incident handing, identity and access management, business continuance, records management and e-discovery but need not necessarily handle the day-to-day oversight of those functions. The CISO could also be responsible for physical security and executive protection or have oversight of those roles with other security managers.[20] The role has grown to become more than any single person can track if all these functions report directly to the CISO. It is incumbent upon the CISO to set the strategy and the structure for all these related security functions and to monitor their progress against predefined performance objectives.

65.5.7 Responsibilities and Opportunities outside of CISO Internal Responsibilities.

In this chapter, we have described CISOs as change agents and strategists, adopting a standard of care, and strategies that implement that standard of care, and that demonstrate due diligence to it. Such individuals have much to contribute to the profession, to the community at large, to the technical community, and even to the definitions being established by governing bodies at the local, state, federal, and international levels.

It would be unreasonable to try to prescribe what CISOs should do outside of their direct internal responsibilities. Suffice it to say that CISOs should subscribe to a professional ethic to share what they have experienced, to codify security practice, and to bring about a better understanding of the problem space, so that defined problems can be solved with best practices that ultimately become standard protocols. Make it a practice to participate in professional organizations, to write, and to speak to community, professional, and trade organizations. Get the word out. Work to eliminate confusion. Define the role. There is much at stake for those who choose to wear this mantle—in the words of Theodore Roosevelt, "It behooves every man to remember that the work of the critic is of altogether secondary importance, and that in the end, progress is accomplished by the man who does things."

65.6 CONCLUDING REMARKS.

CISOs are strategic, executive agents of change for the protection of information that is the lifeblood of critical infrastructures and private enterprise. The realm of disciplines that CISOs must manage is expanding as the scope of security has broadened—an interdisciplinary approach that involves all aspects of the business to provide digital, physical and personnel security is required with input from vital stakeholders.[21]

This role is different from that of technical security management in the near past, and involves tools that are different. The complexity and sheer insecurity of the interconnected ecosystem requires that we adopt a standard of care and that we be able to demonstrate due diligence to that standard of care—this is the mission of CISOs.

CISOs to be successful, depend on strong governance, roles and responsibilities, management accountability, and strong reporting practices (including monitoring, metrics, and executive visibility) to be successful. CISOs would necessarily provide oversight, direct or indirect, of functional roles such as technical security management functions.

CISOs are a rare breed and need to make their contributions to their respective organizations as well as to the larger set of professional, community, and industry groups that need guidance, clarity, and judgment in their movement forward to a trusted, interconnected ecosystem.

The challenge is huge—that is why CISOs like it. It is ever-changing, touches every part of business and technology, and is ultimately a people job. It is a very difficult job and, under the right circumstances, is a very rewarding one. It is a high position of trust and responsibility, and it finally has come into its own.

65.7 NOTES

1. Thomas L. Friedman, *The World Is Flat: A Brief History of the Twenty-First Century* (New York: Farrar, Straus and Giroux, 2005).

2. Eugene Spafford, "Information Security: Insanity Rules," AusCERT2006, AusCERT, Royal Pines Resort, Gold Coast, Australia, May 24, 2006.

3. Larry Greenemeier, "VA Had Many Security Warnings before Its 26.5 Million-Person Breach," *Information Week,* www.informationweek.com/news/showArticle.jhtml?articleID=188500807&subSection=All+Stories.

4. P. Colgan, "New Zealand Not for Sale: eBay," News.com.au, May 12, 2006, www.news.com.au/story/0,10117,19112037-29277,00.html.

5. Bank for International Settlements, "Basel II: Revised International Capital Framework." (2006), ww.bis.org/publ/bcbsca.htm.

6. Scott Berinato, with Lorraine Cosgrove Ware, "Six Secrets of Highly Secure Organizations," *CIO Magazine,* September 15, 1005; http://findarticles.com/p/articles/mi_kmcio/is_200409/ai_n6833335.

7. P. Condit, Keynote Speech, International Information Integrity Institute Forum 25, The Boeing Company, Seattle, WA (January 1995).

8. United States, Office of the National Counter-intelligence Executive, Annual Report to Congress on Foreign Economic Collection and Industrial Espionage—2004 (Washington, DC: ONCIX, 2005).

9. Donn Parker, "Making the Case for Replacing Risk-Based Security," *ISSA Journal* (May 2001): 6–10.

10. P. Schwartz, *The Art of the Long View: Planning for the Future in an Uncertain World* (New York: Doubleday, 1991).

11. P. W. Parfomak, "Guarding America: Security Guards and U.S. Critical Infrastructure Protection," Congressional Research Service Report for Congress, November 12, 2004, Order Code RL32670; http://ftp.fas.org/sgp/crs/RL32670.pdf.

12. Parker, "Making the Case for Replacing Risk-Based Security."

13. Ian Davis and Elizabeth Stephenson. "Ten Trends to Watch in 2006," *McKinsey Quarterly,* www.mckinseyquarterly.com/article_page.aspx?ar=1734&L2=18&L3=30.

14. 498. S.W. 2d 388, 391.

15. The concept of materiality threshold is widely used in accounting. For example, see the "Accounting Terminology Guide" from the New York State Society of CPAs, www.nysscpa.org/prof_library/guide.htm.

16. Booz Allen Hamilton, "Convergence of Enterprise Security Organizations," *ASIS* (Alliance for Enterprise Security Risk Management) *International,* November 8, 2005; www.asisonline.org/newsroom/alliance.pdf.

17. Stuart McClure, Joel Scambray, and George Kurtz, *Hacking Exposed,* 5th ed. (Emeryville, CA: McGraw-Hill Osborne, 2005).

18. Niccolo Machiavelli, *The Prince* (1513), Chapter VI, Para 5.

19. Berinato with Cosgrove Ware, "Six Secrets of Highly Secure Organizations."

20. See, for example, Fran Howarth, "The Convergence of Physical and IT Security," IT-Director.com, September 11, 2006, www.it-director.com/business/regulation/content.php?cid=8743.

21. Friedman, *The World Is Flat.*

CHAPTER **66**

DEVELOPING SECURITY POLICIES

M. E. Kabay and Sean Kelley

66.1 INTRODUCTION. This chapter reviews methods for developing security policies in specific organizations. Some of the other chapters of this *Handbook* that bear on policy content, development, and implementation are listed next:

- Chapter 23 provides an extensive overview of physical security policies.
- Chapter 25 discusses local area network security issues and policies.
- Chapter 39 reviews software development policies and quality assurance policies.

- Chapter 44 presents resources and standards for creating effective security policies.

- Chapter 49 looks at methods for enhancing security awareness.

- Chapter 45 provides guidance on employment policies from a security standpoint.

- Chapter 47 makes explicit recommendations about operations management policies.

- Chapter 48 reviews specific recommendations for e-mail and Internet usage.

- Chapter 50 presents concepts and techniques from social psychology to make security policy implementation more effective.

- Chapter 52 discusses the policies that apply to application design.

- Chapter 72 looks at censorship and content filtering on the Internet.

66.2   COLLABORATING IN BUILDING SECURITY POLICIES.   Policies are the foundation of effective information security, but the task of policy creation is complicated by human and organizational resistance. Technology alone does not work. In changing human behavior, rationality and substance are not enough: The *process* of development affects how people feel about policies and whether they see these rules as needless imposition of power or as an expression of their own values.

Security is always described as being everyone's business; however, in practice, security *interferes* with everyone's business. For example, network managers work hard to make networks user friendly. They do everything they can to make life easier for users; they provide network access routines with a graphical user interface, client/server systems with hot links between local spreadsheets and corporate databases, and a gateway to the Internet for their users. Superficially, one might think that implementing network security would simply involve defining access controls, applying encryption, and providing people with handheld password generators. Unfortunately, as discussed in Chapter 50, security policies offend deep-seated self-conceptions. People form close-knit work groups in which they trust each other; they do not lock their desks when they leave them for a few minutes, so why should they obey the network security policy that dictates locking their sessions? They even lend people car keys in an emergency; why should it be such a terrible breach of security to lend access codes and passwords to trusted colleagues in an emergency?

Security policies challenge users to change the way they think about their own responsibility for protecting corporate information. Attempting to impose security policies on unwilling people results in resistance, both because more stringent security procedures make people's jobs harder and because people do not like being told what to do—especially by security officials perceived as being outside the chain of command.

The only approach that works in the long run is to present security to everyone in the organization in a way that causes recognition that each one, personally and professionally, has a stake in information protection. Security managers, to be successful, must involve employees from throughout the enterprise in developing security policies. Users must justifiably feel that they own their security procedures; employees with true involvement in the policy development process become partners, rather than opponents, of effective security.

66.3   PHASE 1: PRELIMINARY EVALUATION.   Studies of the extent to which information security policies are in place consistently show that relatively few of the respondents have adequate policies in place. For example, the 2007 Global Security Survey run by *CIO Magazine* and PricewaterhouseCoopers was based on interviews and questionnaires involving 7,200 executives, security professionals, and technology managers "across all industries and more than 100 countries" about their organization's security and privacy policies and practices. According to the summary on page 2 of the report:

1. Only 6 out of 10 respondents worldwide (57 percent) say their organization has an information security strategy in place. Only another 13 percent, however, consider putting one in place a "top priority."

2. Almost half of all respondents worldwide (48 percent) say their organization does not actively engage both business and information technology decision makers in addressing information security.

3. More than 7 out of 10 security managers, administrators, and technicians worldwide believe that their organization's security policies and spending can be improved.[1]

In what follows, it is assumed that a specific officer or manager (or group of officers or managers) in the enterprise has taken on the task of developing security policies. The group will be called the *policy development group*.

Before attempting to formulate policies, the policy development group needs formal authorization to use corporate resources in such a project. It should not be too difficult to obtain a short memorandum from top management to everyone in the organization that lays out the reasons for asking for their time and energy in gathering information about the current state of security. Such authorization and continuing top-level support are essential tools in convincing people to cooperate with the policy development group.

In the absence of existing or adequate security policies, a preliminary inventory is the first step in providing upper management with the baseline information that will justify developing a corporate information security policy. The preliminary evaluation should be quick and inexpensive—perhaps days of work by a few people. There is no point in wasting time in expensive detail work before getting approval, support, and budget from upper management.

The goal of the preliminary evaluation is to ask the people who work with information resources what they believe are their most important security needs. Even though they may not be conscious of security as a distinct need, in practice, employees and managers do have valuable insights that transcend theory and generalizations. Data entry clerks may tell the security staff about security violations that no one else has observed or even thought about; for example, they may observe that a bug in a particular program makes the previous operator's data entry screen available for unauthorized entries when the shift changes and a new operator sits at the same terminal.

The policy development group should work closely with human resources (HR) personnel in developing the research instruments for interviewing staff. HR members are likely to know the key managers to contact in each department. The managers have to be convinced to support the effort so researchers can interview willing staff. Some of the HR people are likely to have the professional skills and experience required to provide accurate and cost-effective evaluations of beliefs, attitudes, and behavior affecting security. They may be able to help construct unbiased questionnaires, organize focus groups, and guide interviews.

However, if the security staff and the HR staff are not confident about being able to handle this preliminary data collection, the policy development group should see if it can obtain authorization to hire a consultant with proven expertise in collecting and analyzing social attitudes. The policy development group might want to discuss such a study with a firm specializing in security audits and organizational analysis. If no one knows where to start looking for such resources, the policy development group can contact information security associations, security magazines, security Web sites, and local universities and colleges to ask for suggestions.

These key issues should be part of the preliminary study:

- Introduction to the study
- State of current policy
- Data classification
- Sensitive systems
- Critical systems
- Authenticity
- Exposure
- Human resources, management, and employee security awareness
- Physical security
- Software development security
- Computer operations security
- Data access controls
- Network and communications security
- Antimalware measures
- Backups, archives, and data destruction
- Business resumption planning and disaster recovery

The next sections suggest some typical questions that would be helpful in gathering baseline data about the current state of security. All these questions (and more site-specific topics) should be asked of all the respondents in the preliminary evaluation. Applicable questions are not necessarily repeated in each section; instead, questions in the earlier parts of this list may be adapted for use in later sections. These suggestions are not intended to limit creativity but rather to stimulate development of more questions that would be particularly useful for a specific enterprise.

66.3.1 Introduction to the Study. Employees may perceive many of the questions as threatening. The preamble or introduction to the study, whether it is by survey or by interviews, should make it clear that this is *not an audit* and that its purpose is to establish the framework for an appropriate set of security policies—policies suited to the needs of the organization and its stakeholders. The information should be anonymized so that no person will be targeted for reprisal if the study discovers problems. Every effort should be made to reassure employees that the study is designed to learn about the facts of security with a view to improvement, rather than a search for culprits who will be punished.

66.3.2 State of Current Policy. The questions that follow not only gather baseline information about security policies but also determine whether employees have any idea about who is responsible for formulation of those policies.

- Does the enterprise have any security policies at all?
- Who developed them: an individual? a group?

- Where and how are the security policies available (paper, electronic)?
- When were the policies last updated? Last disseminated?
- Who, if anyone, has explicit responsibility for maintaining security policies?
- Who implements security policy at the enterprise level?
- To whom does the chief information security officer report within the enterprise?
- Who monitors compliance with security policies, standards, and compliance?

66.3.3 Data Classification.   Questions to ask include:

- Are there levels of security classification that apply to your work? If so, what are they called?
- Are there rules for determining whether information you handle should be classified at a particular level of confidentiality?
- Are documents or files labeled to show their security classification?
- What is your opinion about the value of such classification?
- Do people in your group pay attention to security classifications?
- Do you have any suggestions for improvement of how data are classified?[2]

66.3.4 Sensitive Systems.   The questions in this section focus on information that ought to be controlled against unauthorized disclosure and dissemination.

- In your work, are there any kinds of information, documents, or systems that you feel should be protected against unauthorized disclosure? If so, name them.
- How do you personally protect sensitive information that you handle?
- How do others in your department deal with sensitive information? No names, please.
- To your knowledge, have there been any problems with release of sensitive information in your department?
- Do you have any suggestions for improving the handling of sensitive data in your area?

66.3.5 Critical Systems.   The questions in this section focus on information that requires special attention to availability and correctness.

- In your work, are there any kinds of information, documents, or systems that you feel are so critical that they *must* be protected against unauthorized modification or destruction? If so, name them.
- Are there any special precautions you use, or know of, to safeguard critical data in your area?

66.3.6 Authenticity.   Questions to ask include:

- Do you know of any cases in which anyone has used someone else's identity in sending out messages such as letters, faxes, or e-mail? If so, were there any consequences?
- Does everyone in your group use digital signatures on electronic documents?

- Does anyone in your group make or use unauthorized copies of proprietary software? If so, do you think there is any problem with that?

66.3.7 Exposure.   Questions to ask include:

- What are the worst consequences you can realistically imagine that might result from publication in the newspapers of the most sensitive information you control?
- What might happen, in your opinion, if key competitors obtained specific confidential information that you use or control in your area?
- Can you estimate monetary costs associated with the scenarios you have just described?
- What would be the worst consequences you can foresee if critical information you work with were to be altered without authorization, or through accidental modification?
- What might happen if you could not access critical information quickly enough for your work?
- Can you estimate the costs of such breaches of data integrity and data availability?
- Could there be trouble if someone forged documents in your name, or in the enterprise's name? Can you sketch out some scenarios and associated costs resulting from such breaches of authenticity?

66.3.8 Human Resources, Management, and Employee Security Awareness

- As far as you know, who is responsible for developing security policies?
- Do you know where to find the security policies that apply to your work?
- When, if ever, did you last sign any documents dealing with your agreement to security policies?
- Who is responsible for monitoring compliance with security policy in your workgroup? In the enterprise as a whole?
- Have you ever received any training in security policies? If so, when was the last time?
- Have you ever seen any written materials circulating in your workgroup that discuss information security?
- Do you think of protecting corporate information as one of your official responsibilities?[3]

66.3.9 Physical Security

- Does anyone check your identity when you enter the building where you work? Always?
- Are there any electronic access-control systems limiting access to your work area? What are they?
- Do people hold a secured door open to let each other into your work area? Do you let people in after you open a secured door?

- Have you ever seen a secured door into your area that has been blocked open (e.g., for deliveries)?
- Do people leave your work area unlocked when everyone leaves?
- Do staff members wear identity badges at work? Are they supposed to? Do you wear your badge at work?
- Do visitors wear badges?
- Have you ever seen strangers in your area who are not wearing visitor badges?
- What would you do if you saw a stranger in your area who was not wearing a visitor's badge?
- Do you lock any parts of your desk when you leave your workspace?
- What would you do if you heard the fire alarm ring?
- Where is the nearest fire extinguisher?
- Who is the fire marshal for your floor?
- What would you do if someone needed emergency medical attention?
- Is there an emergency medical station in your area or on your floor?
- Do you know who is qualified in cardiopulmonary resuscitation (CPR) in your group or on your floor? Do such people wear identifying pins?
- Have you had recent training in what to do in the event of an emergency? Have you been trained in how to evacuate the building?
- Is there anything that comes to mind that you would like to see to improve physical security and safety in your work area?[4]

66.3.10 Software Development Security.   These questions would be asked only of the software development team:

- Are there any security policies that apply to your work? What are they?
- Have you ever discussed security policies in your group?
- Is security viewed positively, neutrally, or negatively in your group? And by yourself?
- Do you and your colleagues discuss security during the requirements analysis and specification phases when developing software?
- How do you see quality assurance as part of the development process?
- Do you use automated software testing tools?
- Do you use automated version control software? If not, how do you exercise control?
- How do you document your systems?
- Do you think that your source code is adequately protected against unauthorized disclosure and modification?
- What is your opinion about Easter eggs (unauthorized code for an amusing picture or game)?
- Could anyone plant an Easter egg or a logic bomb (unauthorized, harmful functions) in code being developed in your group?

- Have you ever seen an Easter egg or a logic bomb in code from your group? Did it get through to production?
- Can you think of ways you would like to see better security in your work?[5]

66.3.11 Computer Operations Security.   These questions would be asked only of the computer operations team:

- How long do you wait after initial release before installing new operating system versions on your production machines?
- How do you put new software into production?
- Can development personnel access production software? Production data?
- How do you handle problem reports? Do you have an automated trouble-ticket system?
- Can people from outside the operations group enter the operations center?
- Are contractors, including repair technicians, allowed to circulate in operations without being accompanied?
- Does the cleaning staff ever circulate within the secured areas of operations without operations staff present?
- Are system components labeled?
- Is there an emergency cutoff switch for main power to the entire data center? Does it include air conditioning?
- Are there uninterruptible power supplies for critical components of your systems?
- Do you keep records of system downtime? What is your downtime over the last three months? The last year?
- What accounts for most of the downtime? Have remedies been implemented?
- Who monitors system resource utilization? Are there automated reports showing trends in disk space usage? CPU utilization? Network bandwidth usage?
- What improvements in security would you like to see in operations?[6]

66.3.12 Data Access Controls

- Do you have to identify yourself to the computers and networks you work with?
- Do you have a user name (ID) that no one else shares?
- Are you required to use a password, passphrase, or personal identification number (PIN) as part of your routine when starting to use your computer?
- Have you ever shared your unique user ID and password or PIN with someone else? Or have you borrowed someone else's user ID and password to get some work done? If so, how often does this happen?
- Do you use a token, such as a physical key or a smart card, to prove who you are to the computer system? If so, have you ever lent or borrowed such tokens? What for? How often?
- In your work, are there any limitations on the data you are allowed to see, modify, add to, or delete?
- Are there data you can see but not change?
- Do you use encryption on any of the data you work with?

- Do you or members of your group use laptop computers? If so, do you encrypt sensitive data on the disks of those portable systems?

- Do you or anyone in your group take work home? If so, do you put corporate data on your own, personal (noncompany) computers? Does anyone else have access to those computers? Are there any controls on accessing corporate data on the home computers?[7]

66.3.13 Network and Communications Security.   Most of the next questions would be appropriate only for network managers, administrators, and technicians. However, some of the questions are suitable for everyone.

- As a user, do you know what the rules are about using your employer's e-mail system and Internet access?

- Do you know anyone who regularly violates system usage restrictions? No names, please.

- Have you ever seen pornography on corporate systems? Child pornography? Racist and other objectionable materials? If so, did you know what to do? And what did you do?

- Has anyone ever discussed rules for secure e-mail with you? Do you know how to encrypt sensitive messages? Do you ever encrypt messages?

- As a network manager, do you have up-to-date network diagrams, or can you produce them on demand?

- Do you know which services are running on your Internet-connected systems? Are all of the running services needed?

- How do you determine which patches are appropriate for installation on your systems? How often do you check? Who is responsible for managing patches? How long does it take between notification of a vulnerability and installation of an appropriate patch?

- Does your security architecture include firewalls? If so, what determines the security policies you instantiate in the filtering rules?

- Do you have egress filtering enabled on your firewalls?

- Do you have intrusion detection systems? If so, who responds to apprehended intrusions? How are the responsible people notified of an intrusion?

- What are the procedures for responding to an intrusion?

- If your organization uses passwords, how do you handle requests for new passwords?

- Do you have centralized remote-access controls?

- Do remote users use virtual private networks (VPNs) to access corporate systems from outside the firewalls?

- Are your users supposed to use encryption for sensitive e-mail that traverses the Internet? Do they? How do you know?

- Do your users apply digital signatures to all communications?

- Are your Web servers protected against intrusion and vandalism?

- Have you kept sensitive information off your Web servers?

- Do you encrypt all sensitive information stored on your Web servers?

- How long would it take you to recover a valid version of the Web site if it were destroyed or vandalized?
- Do your telephone voicemail boxes have unique, nonstandard passwords? How do you know?
- How do you find out if an employee is being fired or has resigned? How long does it take between termination of employment of such an employee and deactivation of all system and network access?

66.3.14   Antimalware Measures

- Do you and all of your users have antimalware products installed on every workstation?
- How often are antimalware products updated? How are they updated?
- How long does it take for all vulnerable systems to be brought up to date?
- Do you or your users open unexpected, unsolicited e-mail attachments?[8]

66.3.15   Backups, Archives, and Data Destruction

- How often do you do backups of your electronic data?
- Where do you store backup media? Are current copies retained off site as well as on? How do you know which media to use to restore a specific file?
- How long do you keep different types of backups? Why?
- How do you prevent unauthorized access to backup media?
- If you keep data backups for several years, how do you ensure that the old media will be readable and that the data developed for old applications will be usable?
- How do you dispose of magnetic and optical storage media after their useful life is over? Are the discarded media readable?
- Do you make backup copies of paper documents? Where are these copies kept? How would you locate a specific document you needed?
- How long do you keep various types of papers? Why?
- When you dispose of paper documents, does their content influence how they are destroyed? How do you dispose of sensitive paper documents?[9]

66.3.16   Incident Response

- Do you know what to do if you see a security problem such as strangers without badges in secured areas, threats of violence arriving by e-mail, damaged company Web pages, bad data in files you use, missing files or data, or forged messages?
- Is there a specific team dedicated to responding to computer security breaches?
- Are you part of a computer security incident response team (CSIRT)? If so:
  - Is this a long-term assignment?
  - Do you have documentation and training on how to respond to specific types of incidents?
  - How are out-of-hours incidents handled?
  - Does your CSIRT hold practice drills?

- Are there incident postmortems?
- Do you have relations with local law enforcement officials? If so, which levels (municipal, state, federal)?
- Have you ever experienced pressures from management to suppress incident reports of criminal activity to law enforcement?[10]

66.3.17   Business Resumption Planning and Disaster Recovery

- Do you have business resumption planning (BRP) or disaster recovery plans (DRP)? If so, where are they kept?
- Who is responsible for keeping BRP and DRP up to date?
- Have you ever participated in a BRP or DRP testing? If so, how long ago was the last one? When is the next scheduled test?
- During BRP and DRP tests, does anyone use video cameras or tape recorders to keep track of critical steps in the recovery?
- After a test, have you participated in analyzing the results of the tests to improve the plans?[11]

66.4   PHASE 2: MANAGEMENT SENSITIZATION.   Support from upper management is essential for further progress. The goal in this phase is to get approval for an organization-wide audit and for a policy formulation project. In conjunction with the rest of the information security project team, the responsible managers should plan on a meeting that lasts no more than one or two hours. The meeting should start with a short statement from a senior executive about the crucial role of information in the organization's business.

Professional aids, such as management-oriented training videos, are helpful to sensitize managers to the consequences of poor information security. For an up-to-date list of such videos, enter the keywords "information security training video" into a search engine such as Google. After the video film, the team can present its findings from the preliminary evaluation. The immediate goal is to constitute an *information protection working group* to set priorities, determine an action plan, define a timetable and milestones, and formulate policies and procedures to protect corporate information resources. The presenters should name the people you want to see in your working group; all of these people should be contacted before the meeting to be sure that they have agreed in advance to participate in the working group.

The presenters should provide estimates of the time involved and the costs of in-house, and consulting, services and software. To end the briefing, it is useful to offer upper managers a range of background reading about security. Some managers may be intrigued by this field; the more they learn, the more they will support security efforts. One of the best resources for such sensitization is "Managing Risk from Information Systems: An Organizational Approach."[12] This 67-page summary provides "guidelines for managing risk to organizational operations and assets, individuals, other organizations, and the Nation resulting from the operation and use of information systems." The authors state: "The guidelines provided in this special publication have been broadly developed from a technical perspective to be generally useful across a wide range of organizations employing information systems to implement mission and business processes." They also provide extensive cross-indexing to other public documents issued by the National Institute of Standards and Technology (NIST), all of which are freely available online.[13]

66.5   PHASE 3: NEEDS ANALYSIS.   The information protection working group should include representatives from every sector of the enterprise. As the group investigates security requirements, the participants' wide experience and perspective will be crucial in deciding which areas to protect most strongly. More important, their involvement is a concrete expression of corporate commitment to a fundamental attitude change in the corporate culture: Security is to be an integral part of the corporate mission.

For example, in a manufacturing firm, the team would include managers and staff from the factory floor, the unions, engineering, equipment maintenance, shipping and receiving, facilities management (including those responsible for physical security), administrative support, sales, marketing, accounting, personnel, the legal department, and information systems. Each of these members of the working group will help improve enterprise security.

If the organization is very large, the group may have to set up subcommittees to deal with specific sectors. Each subcommittee evaluates to what degree the systems and networks are vulnerable to breaches of security. For example, one group could focus on local and campus communications, another on wide area enterprise networks, and a third on electronic data interchange with clients and suppliers.

A typical audit covers the facilities, personnel policies, existing security, application systems, and legal responsibility to stakeholders (owners, shareholders, employees, clients, and the surrounding community). Based on the findings, the subcommittees formulate proposals for improving security. This is where the specialized knowledge obtained from information security specialists and information security courses will prove especially useful.[14]

66.6   PHASE 4: POLICIES AND PROCEDURES.   Once the information protection working group has built a solid floor of understanding of enterprise information security needs, the members are ready to construct the policies and procedures that meet those needs. The process should start from existing templates and normally takes weeks to months to complete a workable draft.[15]

Genuine participation by all the representatives from every sector of the enterprise is a critical element of success; without a thoroughgoing sense of ownership of the policies, working group members will fail to internalize the new policies. All the members of the working group must become enthusiasts for their collective efforts; in some sense, these people become missionaries engaged in the long-term conversion efforts of phase 5, the implementation of the policies.

66.7   PHASE 5: IMPLEMENTATION.   Once the working group members have defined the new or improved security policies, they are about halfway to their goal. The hardest part is ahead: explaining the need for security and the value of the new policies to fellow employees and convincing them to change. Even if they agree intellectually, there is a good chance that their ingrained social habits will override the new rules for at least months and possibly years. The challenge is to overcome these habits.

Chapter 50 shows in detail how to use the insights of social psychology to change corporate culture by working on beliefs, attitudes, and behavior. In addition to the suggestions in that chapter, the information protection working group should organize and deliver awareness and training sessions for all levels of the enterprise:

- Upper management
- Technical support
- Lower-level staff
- Other technical staff

The next sections offer some simple agendas for such preliminary sessions.

66.7.1 Upper Management.   Security policies and procedures require management support and sanctions. The transformation of corporate culture should begin at the top. Although it is difficult to coordinate the presence of top executives, the working group should try to organize a half-day executive briefing session on enterprise security. In practice, the group may be able to convince upper management to attend for one or two hours. The focus should be intensely practical, and should show executives how to protect themselves and the enterprise against common dangers. Suggested topics:

- **A review of the business case for improving security.** Industrial espionage, natural and man-made disasters, vandalism
- **Network security.** Protection against eavesdropping and tampering
- **Access controls.** Tokens, biometrics, passwords
- **Encryption.** E-mail, laptops, provision for emergency data recovery
- **Backup policies** for PCs, networks, and mainframes
- **Security agreements.** Summaries of the policies and procedures to be read and signed annually
- **Need for total support** to convince other staff to comply with security policies

66.7.2 Technical Support.   The next target is the technical support group, the people who help explain security policies to users. In a one-day training session, the presentations can cover:

- Everything covered in the executive briefing
- Operating system security provisions
- Security software features
- Changes in operations to comply with new procedures

66.7.3 Lower-Level Staff.   Lower-level staff need a half-day session that answers these questions in terms that apply directly to their own work:

- Why should I care about information security?
- What are my obligations as an employee?
- How do I protect the PC I am responsible for against viruses?
- How do I back up my data?
- How do I manage my passwords?
- What must I do if I see someone violating our security policies?

The class ends with participants signing the security agreement.

66.7.4   Other Technical Staff.   More intensive training and education are needed for technical staff, such as members of the software development, operations, and network administration groups. More in-depth, specific material will have to be incorporated into their training; however, such training can be spread over a longer time than that for the groups already discussed, because of the rhythm of work and the crucial importance of technical competence for implementation of the policies. Most enterprises rely on outside trainers, specialized off-site or online courses, and certification programs to raise their staff to the appropriate levels of competence.

66.8   PHASE 6: MAINTENANCE.   Once the enterprise has begun to integrate a concern for security into every aspect of its work, the issue must be kept fresh and interesting. As described in Chapter 49, successful security awareness programs include amusing posters, interesting videos, occasional seminars on stimulating security topics such as recent frauds or computer crimes, and regular newsletters with up-to-date information. Finally, every employee should regularly reread and sign the annual security agreement. This practice ensures that no one can argue that the organization's commitment to security is a superficial charade.

66.9   CONCLUDING REMARKS.   For a secure installation, three things are essential:

1. Sound policies that have been developed with the cooperation of everyone concerned and that are updated periodically
2. Widespread dissemination of those policies, with ongoing observation of their implementation and with frequent training and continual reinforcement
3. Commitment to security on the part of everyone, from top management on down

When these essential elements are in place, the entire organization will function at a more productive level, one at which the possibilities of disruption and damage will have been reduced to a minimum. Nothing less is acceptable.

66.10   NOTES

1. PricewaterhouseCoopers (2007), "2007 Global State of Information Security Study," http://tinyurl.com/4sq5b6.
2. See Chapter 67 in this *Handbook.*
3. For additional ideas in framing questions about security awareness, see Chapter 49. For ideas on appropriate questions dealing with employment practices and policies, see Chapter 45.
4. For more detail about physical security and additional ideas on appropriate questions, see Chapters 22 and 23.
5. For much more information suitable for devising questions about development security, see Chapters 38 and 39.
6. For more information suitable for devising questions about operations security, see Chapter 47.
7. For additional ideas on looking at identification and authentication, see Chapters 28 and 29.
8. See Chapter 41 for more ideas on checking for appropriate levels of antimalware precautions.

9. For additional suggestions to help in framing questions about data backups, see Chapter 57.

10. See Chapter 56.

11. For more ideas on questions that are appropriate in quickly evaluating the state of business resumption planning and disaster recovery, see Chapters 58 and 59.

12. R. Ross, S. Katzke, A. Johnson, M. Swanson, and G. Stoneburner, "Managing Risk from Information Systems: An Organizational Perspective," National Institute of Standards and Technology NIST SP 800-39, Second Public Draft (April 2008), http://csrc.nist.gov/publications/drafts/800-39/SP800-39-spd-sz.pdf.

13. The Further Reading sections of chapters in this *Handbook* (as well as sections of the chapters themselves) provide a wealth of material for management sensitization.

14. Chapters 54, 62, and 63 have information that will help the information protection working group develop an evaluation plan.

15. Chapter 44 contains many practical suggestions and resources for the content and style of security policies.

CHAPTER **67**

DEVELOPING CLASSIFICATION POLICIES FOR DATA

Karthik Raman and Kevin Beets

67.1 INTRODUCTION. A figure appears from the bushes on a dark and stormy night and silently slips past two guards. Inside the building, a flashlight flickers to life and begins a slow dance around a cluttered office. The beam freezes. It illuminates an envelope that is stamped with large red letters: "TOP SECRET."

The top secret label is likely the most popularly recognized part of an example of a data classification (DC) scheme. DC labels information so that its custodians and users can comply with established data protection policies when organizing, viewing, editing, valuing, protecting, and storing data.

Historically, DC has been used by the government and military. Today, however, it has increasingly become a necessity for businesses because of the competitive value of information, because of the legal requirements for maintenance of sound financial and operational records, and because of the demands of privacy-protection laws.

This chapter explains why DC is necessary, how it relates to information security, common laws and standards associated with DC, its design and implementation in an enterprise, hardware and software solutions that can assist in performing DC, and some practical recommendations to consider when implementing DC.

67.2   WHY DATA CLASSIFICATION IS PERFORMED.   Information life cycle management (ILM) is a combination of processes and technology that allows for the control of data throughout its life cycle.[1] ILM ensures that data storage professionals can manage data from creation through destruction. DC is an important part of ILM.

Consider an audit on a business for compliance with the requirements of the Health Insurance Portability and Accountability Act (HIPAA). If a data administrator has not established a DC scheme, not only will the audit take longer than it should, but the company may be fined for lacking controls on sensitive data; indeed, the company may not understand or be able to describe the nature of its data. For example, in the absence of DC, someone in the organization could conceivably post patient records on a public Web site with no conception of the seriousness of such an error. Without having clear standards and procedures for classifying data, employees cannot reliably know what to protect and how to disseminate information securely.

Although legal requirements and compliance fines are major reasons for implementing DC, a business can also gain from increased productivity and cost savings through DC. Allowing data to flow in a free yet secure manner is critical to the carrying out of business objectives. DC is one of the steps in risk analysis that helps to estimate and justify rational protection costs.

As this chapter is being written in 2008, energy costs are rising rapidly. DC can help analysts identify information that may have outlived its usefulness and that can be purged from active data storage systems, thus increasing the efficiency of data access and reducing some of the wasted energy involved in maintaining large data stores.[2]

In summary, DC can bring an organization these benefits:

- Compliance with data standards and legal requirements
- Streamlined and secure sharing of data
- More efficient data storage and retrieval
- Tracking of data through the ILM

67.3   DATA CLASSIFICATION'S ROLE IN INFORMATION SECURITY.

Guidelines such as those from the Federal Financial Institutions Examination Council (FFIEC) highlight the need to secure data as an integral part of DC.[3]

Classifying data allows the institution to ensure consistent protection of information and other critical data throughout the system. Classifying systems allows the institution to focus its controls and efforts in an efficient and structured manner. Systems that store or transmit data of different sensitivities should be classified as if all data were at the highest sensitivity. Classification should be based on a weighted composite of all relevant attributes.[4]

DC supports risk analysis and helps security analysts determine the degree of protection required for data during transport and storage; classification allows clear definition of what types of users may be able to access or modify the data. Investment in encryption (see Chapter 7 in this *Handbook*) and physical controls (see Chapters 22 and 23) are affected by data classification.

DC plays a central role in business continuity planning (see Chapter 58) and in disaster recovery planning (see Chapter 59).

Legal requirements and compliance standards may make the marriage of DC and security a *mandatory* step for some businesses. A brief overview of such standards and compliance codes follows.

67.4 LEGAL REQUIREMENTS, COMPLIANCE STANDARDS, AND DATA CLASSIFICATION.   The amount of data that passes through an average-size enterprise's computers and networks daily can run into terabytes. Regulations and compliance standards may make it necessary that the enterprise's IT staff be able to manage all of these data. The use of DC to meet legal requests, and for compliance, has been hastened by the advent of the "paperless" office. Just 20 years ago, an enterprise could reasonably manage its data for compliance if its (physical) filing systems were well organized. In today's digital office however, an enterprise's data can be scattered over any number of hosts, in several geographic locations, across storage area networks in offsite data centers, or any combination of each of these. Without a concerted enterprise-wide automation and DC implementation, meeting regulatory requirements will be nearly impossible.

Compliance with a number of laws and standards is facilitated by DC. For more extensive discussion of privacy laws, see Chapter 69 in this *Handbook*. For more extensive discussion of intellectual property laws, see Chapter 11.

67.4.1 Legal Requirements.   This section summarizes key provisions of several U.S. laws that bear on DC.

67.4.1.1 Privacy Act of 1974.   The Privacy Act of 1974 aims to regulate the disclosure of records by government agencies. The Computer Matching and Privacy Protection Act of 1988 was grafted into the Privacy Act of 1974, and introduced provisions for

> agencies to follow when engaging in computer-matching activities; provide matching subjects with opportunities to receive notice and to refute adverse information before having a benefit denied or terminated; and require that agencies engaged in matching activities establish Data Protection Boards to oversee those activities.[5]

67.4.2 Family Educational Rights and Privacy Act.   Educational institutions that receive U.S. government funding have to contend with the requirements of FERPA, which regulates the handling of educational data. Many sections of FERPA on information disclosure are relevant to DC. Here are some examples:[6]

99.12 What limitations exist on the right to inspect and review records?

99.33 What limitations apply to the redisclosure of information?

99.34 What conditions apply to disclosure of information to other educational agencies or institutions?

99.35 What conditions apply to disclosure of information for federal or state program purposes?

99.36 What conditions apply to disclosure of information in health and safety emergencies?

99.37 What conditions apply to disclosing directory information?

67.4.2.1 Health Insurance Portability and Accountability Act.   One of the most important regulations that medical organizations must consider is the Health Insurance Portability and Accountability Act of 1996. Title II of HIPAA, "Preventing Health Care Fraud and Abuse; Administrative Simplification; Medical Liability

Reform," mandates a set of standards for the management of health information. The contents of Part C of Title II, "Administrative Simplification," address security:[7]

Sec. 1171. Definitions.

Sec. 1172. General requirements for adoption of standards.

Sec. 1173. Standards for information transactions and data elements.

Sec. 1174. Timetables for adoption of standards.

Sec. 1175. Requirements.

Sec. 1176. General penalty for failure to comply with requirements and standards.

Sec. 1177. Wrongful disclosure of individually identifiable health information.

Sec. 1178. Effect on state law.

Sec. 1179. Processing payment transactions.

67.4.2.2   *Gramm-Leach-Bliley Act.*   The Gramm-Leach-Bliley Act (GLBA) of 1999 introduced reform for the financial sector. Title V of GLBA imposes privacy requirements on the handling of information by financial organizations:

> It is the policy of the Congress that each financial institution has an affirmative and continuing obligation to respect the privacy of its customers and to protect the security and confidentiality of those customers' nonpublic personal information.

The contents of "Title V—Privacy" are:[8]

Subtitle A—Disclosure of Nonpublic Personal Information

Sec. 501. Protection of nonpublic personal information.

Sec. 502. Obligations with respect to disclosures of personal information.

Sec. 503. Disclosure of institution privacy policy.

Sec. 504. Rulemaking.

Sec. 505. Enforcement.

Sec. 506. Protection of Fair Credit Reporting Act.

Sec. 507. Relation to state laws.

Sec. 508. Study of information sharing among financial affiliates.

Sec. 509. Definitions.

Sec. 510. Effective date.

Subtitle B—Fraudulent Access to Financial Information

Sec. 521. Privacy protection for customer information of financial institutions.

Sec. 522. Administrative enforcement.

Sec. 523. Criminal penalty.

Sec. 524. Relation to state laws.

Sec. 525. Agency guidance.

Sec. 526. Reports.

Sec. 527. Definitions.

67.4.2.3 Sarbanes-Oxley Act. The Sarbanes-Oxley (SOX) Act was introduced in 2002 in the wake of a slew of accounting scandals involving a few large U.S. corporations. The scope of SOX is broad, and many of its sections may have relevance for DC. For example, Section 404, "Management assessment of internal controls," makes "establishing and maintaining an adequate internal control structures and procedures for financial reporting"[9] the responsibility of management.

67.4.2.4 Federal Rules of Civil Procedure. The Federal Rules of Civil Procedure (FRCP) are a set of rules for the trial of noncriminal cases in federal courts in the United States. The most recent editions of the FRCP include sections that address electronically stored information (ESI).[10]

Rule 26, "General Provisions Governing Discovery; Duty of Disclosure," states that a party should be able to provide:

> a copy of, or a description by category and location of, all documents, electronically stored information, and tangible things that are in the possession, custody, or control of the party and that the disclosing party may use to support its claims or defenses, unless solely for impeachment.[11]

Rule 34, "Production of Documents, Electronically Stored Information, and Things and Entry Upon Land for Inspection and Other Purposes," states:

> Any party may serve on any other party a request (1) to produce and permit the party making the request, or someone acting on the requestor's behalf, to inspect, copy, test, or sample any designated documents or electronically stored information.

Further, Rule 34 states:

> [A] party who produces documents for inspection shall produce them as they are kept in the usual course of business or shall organize and label them to correspond with the categories in the request.

67.4.3 Compliance Standards. For more detailed discussion of security standards, see Chapter 51 in this *Handbook*. This section summarizes key elements of widely used security standards that bear on DC.

67.4.3.1 U.S. Federal Government's Executive Order 12958. On March 25, 2003, President George W. Bush issued "Further Amendment to Executive Order 12958, as Amended, Classified National Security Information."[12] The preamble sates that this order describes "Classified National Security Information" and stipulates:

> This order prescribes a uniform system for classifying, safeguarding, and declassifying national security information, including information relating to defense against transnational terrorism. Our democratic principles require that the American people be informed of the activities of their Government. Also, our Nations progress depends on the free flow of information. Nevertheless, throughout our history, the national defense has required that certain information be maintained in confidence in order to protect our citizens, our democratic institutions, our homeland security, and our interactions with foreign nations. Protecting information critical to our Nations security remains a priority.

The order provides extensive policies and procedures for classifying and maintaining the security of information affecting the national security of the United States. In particular, the well-known classifications used in U.S. Government circles are defined in this way:

> Sec. 1.2. Classification Levels. (a) Information may be classified at one of the following three levels:
>
> (1) "Top Secret" shall be applied to information, the unauthorized disclosure of which reasonably could be expected to cause exceptionally grave damage to the national security that the original classification authority is able to identify or describe.
>
> (2) "Secret" shall be applied to information, the unauthorized disclosure of which reasonably could be expected to cause serious damage to the national security that the original classification authority is able to identify or describe.
>
> (3) "Confidential" shall be applied to information, the unauthorized disclosure of which reasonably could be expected to cause damage to the national security that the original classification authority is able to identify or describe.

67.4.3.2 ISO/IEC 17799.

ISO/IEC 17799 of 2005 "establishes guidelines and general principles for initiating, implementing, maintaining, and improving information security management in an organization."[13] It makes it the responsibility of an organization's security management to design and implement DC according to confidentiality and importance. It suggests a five-point labeling system for data, in order of increasing confidentiality and importance requirements: public documents, internal use only, proprietary, highly confidential, and top secret.[14]

67.4.3.3 Control Objectives for Information and Related Technology.

Control Objectives for Information and related Technology (CoBIT) is a set of standards and tools for IT management. The Web site of Information Systems Audit and Control Association (ISACA), the organization that maintains CoBIT, states:

> COBIT enables clear policy development and good practice for IT control throughout organizations. COBIT emphasizes regulatory compliance, helps organizations to increase the value attained from IT, enables alignment and simplifies implementation of the COBIT framework.[15]

The CoBIT 4.1 standard states in section PO2, titled "Define the Information Architecture," that "the establishment of an enterprise data model that incorporates a data classification scheme to ensure the integrity and consistency of all data" is part of the Planning and Organizing phase of the CoBIT strategic information technology (IT) plan.[16]

A well-written article by Rafael Etges, CISA, CISSP, and Karen McNeil in the ISACA's *Information Systems Control Journal* points out that sections DS5.8 (primarily); DS5, "Ensure Systems Security"; DS11, "Manage Data"; and DS13, "Manage Operations"; are relevant to DC.[17]

67.4.4 Other Standards.

Other regulations may apply to a specific field of business or as part of working with businesses in other fields:

Defense contracting. Department of Defense (DoD) issuances

Finances. Federal Financial Institutions Examination Council (FFIEC) regulations

Life sciences. Food and Drug Administration (FDA) regulations

Media, telecom. Federal Communications Commission (FCC) regulations

67.5   DESIGNING AND IMPLEMENTING DC.   In this section, we outline how a business can design and implement DC. Both tasks should be carried out by IT or information security staff with the support of management. These tasks should be iterative.

The process to design DC can be modeled in this way:[18]

Obtain Management Approval

1. Study the organization's Business Continuity Plan (BCP) and note the organization's current IT assets and storage-management processes.

2. Present the benefits of DC to the heads of business units (BU).

3. Survey users in various BUs about how they store, retrieve, and edit data and how they would like to see their data organized and labeled.

4. List the revenue-generating and mission-critical usage of each BU's data. Understand how each unit uses and manipulates data specific to its needs, and how those data may be shared across other units.

Once these steps are undertaken, the DC team can devise a data-labeling scheme that takes into account all BUs and their interactions.

The process of implementation of DC can be modeled as in this way:

1. Obtain management approval.

2. Map data-labeling scheme to available hardware, networks, systems, and storage.

3. Apply automation or DC tools where relevant.

4. Guide users through adoption of new DC scheme and solicit feedback.

Finally, the DC team should report the results of DC design and implementation to management. A refined data classification report would include a service-level agreement (SLA) for data usage as well as a comprehensive model of costs.[19] One of the major costs to announce would be for new hardware, networks, storage, or software needed to implement DC.

For more details of developing security policies in general, see Chapter 66 in this *Handbook*.

67.5.1   Data Classification Solutions.   Software solutions for DC have been driven mostly by the advances in data-storage optimization. Some examples of the storage advances that helped to spark these solutions include:

- Virtualization—the ability to logically organize multiple physical locations
- De-duplication technology to reduce duplicate data
- Cheaper storage media

As stated earlier, knowing the type of data being managed is imperative when deciding how to secure it, store it, and manage its information life cycle. This process can be involved and extremely time consuming. Several vendors provide software solutions to assist in this classification process. Most of these solutions run on rack-mounted appliances. The information and classification management (ICM) market provides tools and consultation for DC.

Some of the features that a data custodian may want to consider when making a software solution decision include:

- **Policy-based data-type discovery.** DC based on the policies outlined by the data custodian. These policies can later be used to enforce automatically a business's storage policies.
- **File metadata classification.** DC using a file's metadata and file content.
- **Multiple file system management.** Seamless classification across multiple file system types.
- **Compliance and legal considerations.** DC that includes usage of legal metadata, retains file ownership chains, and uses pattern-matching for sensitive data such as Social Security numbers.
- **Report style.** DC based on the utility of the reports on data that have been discovered, labeled, and classified.

One example of a software data classification system is Titus Labs' Document Classification[TM] for Microsoft Office.[20] The product:

- Classifies and labels Office documents
- Applies document markings that clearly identify the existence of confidential and private information
- Helps stop information leaks of hidden content in Microsoft Word documents
- Encourages proper handling of sensitive information for compliance.

RSA Data Security's Data Loss Prevention (DLP) Suite is described by the company as providing

- Centralized policy management
- Enterprise performance and scalability
- Highest levels of accuracy
- Flexible incident workflow, audit, and reporting[21]

67.5.2 Examples of Data Classification Schemas.   Security policy and practice can vary widely in design and implementation across different organizations. So too can DC design and implementations. For example, here are some differences in the implementation of DC in three major U.S. universities:

- The George Washington University's Data Classification Security Policy states:

    Data is a critical asset of the University. All members of the University community have a responsibility to protect the confidentiality, integrity, and availability of data generated, accessed, modified, transmitted, stored or used by the University, irrespective of the medium on which the data resides and regardless of format (such as in electronic, paper or other physical form).

    Three categories of data are defined, *Public*, *Official Use Only*, and *Confidential*. The policy gives examples of each category.[22]
- Stanford University's Data Classification Guidelines Webpage states the case for the classification of the university's data clearly and concisely. It defines three

categories of data, *Public*, *Sensitive*, and *Restricted*, and tabulates some legal requirements, reputation risks, other risks, access restrictions, and examples of these categories.[23]

- The University of Missouri's DC policy outlines the case for DC and defines four categories of data, *Public*, *Confidential*, *Restricted*, and *National Security Interest*. It lists three network zones, each with its own security requirements. It tabulates various setup and usage requirements for each data category.[24]

For each of the three examples, the DC policies and procedures can vary based solely on the labels chosen. Those entities that use fewer labels will most likely have fewer policies and procedures across a broader spectrum of data, as opposed to those that choose to divide their data into more categories. For example, if a business chooses to label all data as *Confidential*, a single policy would be in place that all users would need to follow, as opposed to a business that chooses to label data with many different labels. In practice, the number of labels or categories would most likely be somewhere between three and six.

67.6 CONCLUDING REMARKS.   In conclusion, here are some important points to remember when dealing with DC:

- A complete solution will most likely not be achieved by using software solutions alone. Since DC is still evolving, these solutions may require customization to fit what a business must accomplish. Thorough research will be required to find a best-fit solution.[25]
- In order to determine what type of data is used across an entire business, it is imperative to interview users from all segments of the business using surveys.
- Locations of data must be written into a DC policy. Since data can reside in many different locations, a policy must be drafted to account for geography and to allow for proper storage and retrieval of these data from varied locations.
- An educational policy for users will need to be created for the "Important" data type (or equivalent) level and above. Creators and users of valuable data types must be educated about the policies and procedures that are put into place for the storage, retrieval, and use of their data.
- A complete DC solution will take some time to implement. Because of the complexity of DC, a complete and well-designed implementation will not happen overnight. A realistic estimate should be provided to management when undertaking a DC project.
- Compliance and legal requirements need to be understood well for each particular business. Several compliance standards make a business legally liable for certain data types. It is imperative to understand which of those standards apply to the business's data when taking on the DC task. Remember, too, that legal requirements may also cover investigations that require these data, so understanding data-handling laws is also important. For further information, see Chapter 55 in this *Handbook*.

67.7   NOTES

1. S. Duplessie, N. Marrone, and S. Kenniston. "The New Buzzwords: Information Lifecycle Management," *Computerworld*, March 31, 2003, www.computerworld.com/hardwaretopics/storage/story/0,10801,79885,00.html.

2. D. Hill, "Storage Tip: Increase Energy Efficiency of Stored Data," *IT World*, April 9, 2007, http://storage.itworld.com/5002/nlsstorage070410/page_1.html.

3. Federal Financial Institutions Examination Council, Information Security Booklet (July 2006), www.ffiec.gov/ffiecinfobase/booklets/information_security/information_security.pdf.

4. Federal Financial Institutions Examination Council, 2006.

5. 5 U.S.C. § 552a, U.S. Congress, The Privacy Act of 1974, December 31, 1974, www.usdoj.gov/oip/04_7_1.html.

6. 20 U.S.C. § 1232g, U.S. Congress, Family Educational Rights and Privacy Act (FERPA), August 21, 1974, www.access.gpo.gov/nara/cfr/waisidx_04/ 34cfr99_04.html.

7. 42 U.S.C. § 201 *et seq.*, U.S. Congress, Health Insurance Portability and Accountability Act of 1996, August 21, 1974, www.cms.hhs.gov/HIPAAGenInfo/Downloads/HIPAALaw.pdf.

8. 15 U.S.C. § 6801 *et seq.*, U.S. Congress, Text of the Conference Report of Gramm-Leach-Bliley Bill, November 12, 1999, http://banking.senate.gov/conf/somfinal.htm.

9. 15 U.S.C. § 7241, 18 U.S.C. § 1350, U.S. Congress, Sarbanes-Oxley Act of 2002, July 30, 2002, http://frwebgate.access.gpo.gov/cgi-bin/getdoc.cgi?dbname=107_cong_bills&docid=f:h3763enr.tst.pdf.

10. Kahn Consulting, "The Federal Rules of Civil Procedure: Meeting the IT and Legal Challenges of the New E-Discovery Rules," May 1, 2007, www.law.com/jsp/legaltechnology/detailWP.jsp?id=1190797378589 (registration required).

11. Committee on the Judiciary, 109th Congress, Federal Rules of Civil Procedure, December 1, 2006, http://judiciary.house.gov/media/pdfs/printers/109th/31308.pdf.

12. G. W. Bush, Executive Order, March 25, 2003, www.whitehouse.gov/news/releases/2003/03/20030325-11.html.

13. ISO, *ISO—FAQs—Information Security* (2005), www.iso.org/iso/support/faqs/faqs_widely_used_standards/widely_used_standards_other/information_security.htm.

14. ISO, *ISO17799 News,* No. 6 (2006), http://17799-news.the-hamster.com/issue06-news2.htm.

15. ISACA, "COBIT 4.1 Is Available!" (2008), www.isaca.org/Template.cfm?Section=COBIT6&Template=/TaggedPage/TaggedPageDisplay.cfm&TPLID=55&ContentID=7981.

16. IT Governance Institute, *CoBIT 4.1: Framework, Control Objectives, Management Guidelines, Maturity Models* (Rolling Meadows, IL: Author, 2007), www.isaca.org/AMTemplate.cfm?Section=Downloads&Template=/MembersOnly.cfm&ContentFileID=14002 (registration required).

17. R. Etges and K. McNeil, "Understanding Data Classification Based on Business and Security Requirements," *Information Systems Control Journal* 5 (2006),

www.isaca.org/Template.cfm?Section=Home&CONTENTID=35620&TEMP LATE=/ContentManagement/ContentDisplay.cfm.

18. IT Governance Institute, *CoBIT 4.1.*

19. K. Langdon and J. Merryman, "Data Classification: Getting Started," July 1, 2005, http://searchstorage.techtarget.com/magazineFeature/0,296894,sid5_gci1258224 ,00.html (registration required).

20. Titus Labs, Document Classification™ for Microsoft Office, www.titus-labs.com/software/DocClass_default.html.

21. RSA Data Loss Prevention (DLP) Suite, www.rsa.com/node.aspx?id=3426.

22. Chief information officer, George Washington University, "Data Classification Security Policy: George Washington University," December 6, 2005, http://my.gwu.edu/files/policies/DataClassificationPolicy.pdf.

23. Stanford University. "Classification of Data: Stanford University," November 6, 2007, www.stanford.edu/group/security/securecomputing/dataclass_chart.html.

24. Curators of the University of Missouri, "MU Data Classification System," August 3, 2007, Division of Information Technology, University of Missouri, http://doit.missouri.edu/security/data-classification/.

25. B. Reed, "Data-Classification Best Practices," January 18, 2007, www.networkworld.com/news/tech/2007/012207-techupdate-data-classification.html.

OUTSOURCING AND SECURITY

Kip Boyle, Michael Buglewicz, and Steven Lovaas

68.1 INTRODUCTION. The term "outsourcing" has come to identify several distinct concepts, each requiring a different risk management strategy. In this chapter, we examine today's practice of outsourcing and the effects and considerations it has, or should have, on the work of information assurance professionals.

Organizations (companies, nonprofits, government agencies, etc.) outsource to gain efficiencies and effectiveness. The efficiencies gained, however, do have consequences. An outsourcing strategy of *implement-it-and-forget-it* is unwise, as the outsourcing environment can change quickly and dramatically.

Michael Cooney points out some of the significant considerations and problems facing the outsourcing world at end of the first decade of the 21st century:

- Security problems
- China's rise
- India's growth
- India's turmoil
- Blunders
- H-1B visa trials
- Small business outsourcing
- Managed services[1]

Despite the negative overtones that sometimes accompany the practice of outsourcing, there can be great benefits. Here are a few:

- A corporation's self-knowledge improves dramatically when it is compelled to articulate, explain, and define its corporate mission to others.
- Outsourcing clarifies and institutionalizes roles, goals, and measures of success.
- One of the largest and most important aspects is that outsourcing done successfully demands risk identification and formalized mitigation activities that might otherwise not occur within the corporation.
- Outsourcing allows a company to focus on corporate core competencies, thus making gains in:
  - Effectiveness (i.e., doing the tasks for which you have the potential to produce the desired results)
  - Efficiencies (i.e., using an optimal amount of time and energy to complete a task)
  - Focus (i.e., concentrating on key business objectives)
  - Discipline (i.e., holding the corporation accountable for corporate objectives, and holding the vendor to clearly and contractually defined objectives)
- An organization gains or intends to gain financial improvements by moving work to vendors that can perform the work at a lower cost and/or at a greater level of specialization.

68.1.1 Definitions

Vendor or contractor—an arm's-length entity providing an outsourced service

Organization or business—the entity contracting for its products or services with a vendor

Outsourcing—the fulfillment of a specific business function or functions by contracting with a vendor to perform within the vendor's own facilities

Insourcing—the commonplace use of contract or noncompany employees to fulfill certain business functions within the physical and logical corporate boundaries

68.1.2 Distinctions.

The risks and considerations of outsourcing an inbound call center, outsourcing a corporate IT function, insourcing a corporate finance function, insourcing an HR function, or a combination of insourcing and outsourcing of a corporate security function all require different perspectives and tactical activities. Despite the commonalities among outsourcing functions (e.g., connectivity, user management, definition of task, measurements of effectiveness, goals and objectives), the same outsourcing blueprint for an inbound call center would not serve for outsourcing corporate security. The objectives, rules, policies, risks, and rewards for each scenario are distinct and require customized attention.

Outsourcing decisions depend on which functions an organization decides it should perform for itself to maintain effectiveness and which functions would be performed more efficiently or more effectively by a vendor. Outsourcing also implies that an organization does not have, does not want to have, and cannot or will not have a specific expertise as part of its core business missions.

68.1.3 Insourcing.

Insourcing is an accepted business practice; the government and many of today's large corporations hire contractors who work as insourcers within the physical and logical boundaries of their organization.

Insourcing poses risks to an organization because the place of work for the insourcer (vendor) is often within the physical boundaries of the organization—well within the physical perimeter, and in many cases, inside the logical perimeter defenses of the corporation. The contract worker is not an employee, but in most cases the contractor enjoys the same accesses as employees for the duration of the contract.

The defenses used for external protection are not as effective (if at all) against an insider with malicious intent. Security considerations regarding an insourced contractor require a different approach, more similar to layered security strategies employed for internal company resources.

Besides traditional IT security concerns, for these outsiders with insider access, the problems of human error, omissions, or complete bungling must be addressed. Security from external sources does not normally include internal human-error considerations. Before considering insourcing, an organization should already have a formal risk management strategy (quality control) for internal human errors as well as for insider espionage and other insider threats.

An insourced contractor is not a full-fledged member of an organization and frequently resides somewhat outside of internal controls, thus requiring a separate and recognized classification and specific handling appropriate to the role. The General Accounting Office recently conducted a study of four federal agencies that rely on contractors to collect certain data on American citizens. The study found that "[a]gencies often do not limit the collection or use of information as required by the Privacy Act of 1974, . . . agencies don't ensure the accuracy of information. . .[and] contractors are not bound by those fair information practices and they often don't comply with all of them."[2]

Sound risk management requires acknowledgment and recognition that significant and substantial risks exist when insourcing. Attention to detail, a reality-based risk assessment, clearly articulated risks, attainable observations, and concrete audit points are all essential to manage successfully the insourced contractors and their mission. (See Chapters 13 and 45 in this *Handbook*.)

68.1.4 Nearshoring. *Nearshoring* is the outsourcing of a specific discrete business function to a vendor located within the same, a nearby, or a bordering geographic region.

In some cases, an international outsource vendor will place components of its business in a specific country to acquire work within that country. For example, a U.S.-based outsource vendor will often position its operations in the United States to fulfill contracts from companies in the United States. Nearshoring can also include outsourcing to a bordering or regional country that shares a common cultural knowledge and understanding, as when a U.S. organization outsources to a group in Canada or Mexico.

Many of the largest technology companies in the world are some of the largest nearsourcing vendors. "Productized offerings from the large outsourcers include service desks, desktop management and specialized network offerings. Examples include EDS Agile, HP SMB Services, and IBM Express Advantage."[3]

During the opposition to outsourcing that occurred in the first few years of the 21st century, the negative connotations of outsourcing were sometimes blunted, when organizations nearshored their outsourcing work. The move toward globalization, and the painful lessons it taught certain nation-centric IT organizations, seemed easier to comprehend and accept if those jobs went to vendors located within relative proximity.

68.1.5 Offshoring. *Offshoring* is the outsourcing of specific, discrete business functions to a vendor whose corporate headquarters, or employees who fulfill the outsourced function, reside and work on another continent, as when a European company outsources to a company based in India.

Perhaps the most controversial kind of outsourcing, offshoring evokes a strong response, both in countries that move work offshore and in offshoring destinations. Nationalism, job security, self-interest, and a host of other emotions, both rational and irrational, seem to be part of every discussion. Those concepts, along with many others, are examined in Thomas Friedman's cornerstone book on outsourcing, *The World Is Flat*.[4] Friedman's perspective organizes the many disparate elements converged to "flatten the world" and to create a truly global work environment.

Regardless of the reasoning behind the decision, offshoring involves different considerations from insourcing and nearshoring. Fundamental business tasks taken for granted in a single geopolitical environment require different considerations when offshoring. Many of the questions should be asked and answered long before addressing the ability of the offshore vendor and its employees simply to do the job.

Despite all of these complications, offshoring is an established business practice and successfully accomplished every day. However, the rules that make offshoring successful will make any other business successful:

- Clearly understand your business.
- Clearly articulate your outsourcing (insourcing, nearshoring and offshoring) goals.
- Possess a razor-sharp understanding of all risks, and managing those risks in an effective and reasonable manner.

68.2 WHY OUTSOURCE? There are two main drivers behind the growth of outsourcing today: the never-ending quests for greater organizational *effectiveness* and for greater *efficiency*. These drivers have come to the forefront of our economy because of the shift in strategic business thinking, begun in the 1990s, that is still affecting the way organizations are managing their businesses and serving their customers.

68.2.1 Effectiveness versus Efficiency. Being *efficient* implies using an optimal amount of time and energy for getting a task done. In contrast, being *effective* means accomplishing the intended consequences of the task.

68.2.2 Being Effective. Historically, management has been primarily interested in increasing the efficiency of important business processes. But since the late 1980s, enlightened managers have realized that it can be very wasteful to try to optimize a process that does not lie within the core competency of the organization.

What are an organization's core competencies? A core competency is a *mission-critical* task or function that an organization is good at. "Mission-critical" refers to functions that are directly related to the strategic goals of the organization; for example, a hospital or a restaurant will consider cleanliness a mission-critical goal, whereas an automobile repair facility probably would not. Examples of core competencies may include reliable processes (e.g., Procter & Gamble's consumer brand management or Toyota's mantra of continuous improvement); a unique way of relating to customers (Nordstom's superior retail service) or to suppliers (Boeing's supply chain management); or the particular look and feel of products or services (Apple's computers and iPods). A core competency also must meet these three conditions:

1. It can be used to develop entirely new products and services.
2. It provides significant customer benefits.
3. It is difficult for competitors to duplicate.[5]

If all three conditions are met, then a core competency can provide an organization with a true competitive advantage, which is a highly prized organizational asset, and which must be continuously guarded lest the competitive advantage be lost. A corollary is that all other functional areas, which are not within the core, are candidates for outsourcing.

By delegating tasks to vendors, an organization's management may concentrate more fully on its core business. Ideally, this will allow the organization to use its limited financial, talent, and other resources in the most productive manner. Knowing which activities an organization should perform, and which it should not, is the heart of being effective.

68.2.3 Being Efficient. Assuming one is doing the right things (i.e., being effective), the next logical question is whether one is doing them as efficiently as possible? Is the organization using the optimal amount of resources while still achieving quality and quantity goals? This question is important to both outsourcing organizations and to vendors performing outsourced work.

How can one measure efficiency? An often-sought-after outcome of efficiency is direct cost minimization. The idea of using outsourcing to achieve direct cost cutting is attractive. For example, according to a 2005 article appearing in *Mortgage Strategy*, British companies can save up to 40 percent by outsourcing all kinds of jobs to India. These companies report savings of a minimum £10 million pounds each year for every 1,000 jobs they outsource.[6]

In addition to direct cost reduction, other financial benefits of outsourcing to increase efficiencies include:

- **Decreased capital expenditure.** Because vendors utilize their own tools and infrastructure, there is no need for organizations to borrow money to purchase these items.

- **Decreased fixed costs.** Fewer fixed, lower, recurring payments allow an organization to manage its cash more easily because it would need less of it; fixed costs must be paid even when sales decrease, which may lead to a shortage of cash that could eventually bankrupt an organization.

- **Increased variable costs versus fixed costs.** If an organization pays a vendor based on units of work performed, then the costs of production become more variable, which is easier to manage as costs rise or fall based on the volume of goods or services required.

Another positive outcome of outsourcing is increased speed or work cycle time. By hiring a vendor located in India to test the quality of software written in the United States, an organization can perform software development work nearly 24 hours per day. Each morning upon return to work, U.S. programmers would have the results of testing in India and could begin making corrections right away. By using this "follow the sun" approach, an organization can gain a speed advantage over its rivals.

Possibly the greatest aspect of efficiency that outsourcing can deliver is management focus. There can be great value in focusing a company's management team directly on those activities that differentiate it from the competition. Whenever a management team is focusing on noncore functions, it is usually operating not from a position of strength but from one of weakness. By definition, the team is not expert at noncore activities. In these cases, the team can spend too much time trying to understand and manage something that does not differentiate the organization from its competitors. If the noncore activities require too much management time and attention, there is a real risk that the core competencies of the organization may decrease in value. In the most serious of cases, an organization can lose its competitive edge completely, driving down sales, revenue, and profits.

68.3   CAN OUTSOURCING FAIL?   Yes, outsourcing can fail. For example:

> In 2004, J.P. Morgan Chase & Co. reassumed main technology functions following its merger with Bank One Corp., abandoning a U.S.$5 billion pact with International Business Machines Corp. The same year, Electronic Data Systems Inc. abandoned a U.S.$1 billion deal to run Dow Chemical Co.'s phone and computer networks.[7]

Deloitte Consulting's 2005 study, "Calling a Change in the Outsourcing Market," offers evidence that large organizations do not always achieve great efficiencies from outsourcing. The study, based on personal interviews with 25 of the largest organizations across eight industry sectors, reveals that:

- Seventy percent of participants have begun looking more cautiously at outsourcing after having negative experiences with outsourcing projects.

- One in four respondents have brought functions back in-house when outsourcing failed to deliver on promises of lower cost and more efficient operations.

- Forty-four percent of participants saw no cost savings as a result of outsourcing.[8]

68.3.1 Why Does Outsourcing Fail?   There are many risks to outsourcing, but direct cost reduction, often a top goal of outsourcing, can create the greatest risk of all. Indeed, "outsourcing deals most frequently stumble when they focus primarily on reducing costs."[9] Despite this observation, in a set of recent surveys, the rate of cost reduction as a driver for offshoring has been growing. From 2004 to 2006, the rate went from just over 70 percent of respondents to just over 80 percent.[10]

Total expenditure on outsourcing can meet or exceed the baseline of spending established prior to outsourcing. Although this may not be an inherently bad situation, management may perceive the experiment as a failure if the organization approaches outsourcing opportunities primarily to cut costs. However, if seen from a perspective of effectiveness rather than simply of efficiency, the outsourcing activities may be quite successful.

There are many other business reasons why outsourcing can fail. Looking more closely at the organization's perspective within the typical loss scenarios, in many cases the failure occurs because of one or more of these reasons:

- Monitoring and evaluating the performance of an outside vendor is a difficult task for many reasons, often due to inadequate selection, and to monitoring of performance metrics.
- The outsourcing organization did not work hard enough to create a "win/win" opportunity for both itself and the vendor.
- Aligning the goals and priorities of the outside vendor with the organization's goals and priorities is rarely easy.
- Outsourcing requires an organization to master new and more complicated forms of communication, especially when outsourcing to a vendor in another country.
- It is challenging for an organization to ensure that the vendor's employees maintain sufficient knowledge and skill levels to do the work that has been delegated.
- Outsourcing usually introduces insecurity to the workforce and to the unions, as fear of job losses dominates their thinking. Terminating a contract usually requires a disruption in service continuity, and the quality of service can suffer, sometimes visibly to customers.[11]

Even when outsourcing appears to succeed from an operational perspective, there may be hidden inefficiencies in information protection that can decrease the overall value of the activity.

68.3.2 Universal Nature of Risk.   Risk is inherent in virtually every human activity. One of the distinct advantages of an organized society is the ability of that society to distribute risk. Thus, not every member of society need manage every single risk.

When outsourcing, the greatest cost is that of ignorance, and the ultimate price is failure. Poorly defined expectations and poor planning, resulting from a fundamental ignorance of a business, will doom any corporate project, including outsourcing.

During early planning phases of the outsourcing project, it is prudent for the information assurance team to assess the entirety of the outsourcing project. However, information assurance does not have to own all aspects of the project; it is enough that the information assurance group should possess an end-to-end perspective, so that it can appropriately assess risk.

To relegate information assurance only to technical security tactics and practices is a serious error. Regardless of the vendor, the ultimate accountability (referred to as *responsibility*) stays with the firm. "One thing that can't be outsourced—responsibility.... Everything from employee policies to customer satisfaction to ethical and legal issues roots back to the impact on shareholder value. These responsibilities stay with the firm regardless of the functions that have been outsourced."[12]

The vendor, however, is accountable for carrying out all elements of the contractual agreement.

Thus at the earliest planning stages, an information assurance review includes the overall scope of the outsourcing project. Questions should include:

- What information assets are at risk?
- What is the value and sensitivity of those assets?
- What current and future "risk shadow" will the outsourcing project cast on those corporate information assets?

The responses to these questions provide the foundation for the outsourcing project as well as the degree of involvement from the information assurance community after that preliminary review.

Planning complex endeavors normally proceeds by careful identification and examination of concepts that move from general to specific. The sections that follow include broad categories for consideration at the onset of the outsourcing project. These categories require in-depth examination, as they relate to the specifics of each unique outsourcing project.

68.3.3   Clarity of Purpose and Intent.   To outsource, one must possess the ability to articulate the task and to focus on creating a mutually beneficial vendor relationship. Poorly defined tasks lead to frustration and to unstructured attempts to meet inchoate needs instead of to measurable objectives—limitations that cause both organization and vendor to fail.

Corporations depend on current employees to articulate the soon-to-be-outsourced task. Ironically, those employees best suited to articulate the task are frequently those whose jobs are most at risk after the successful implementation of the outsourcing project. This conflict of interest is a risk consideration that must be addressed. Several phases of outsourcing include, but are not limited to, the collection and documentation of task knowledge for outsourced functions, vendor solicitation such as the request for information (RFI) or the request for proposal (RFP), vendor selection, and training.

Vendor selection is itself a key and integral part of the risk management of outsourcing, hence the importance of identifying, articulating, and quantifying the outsourcing goals. Once vendor selection occurs, corporate employees train vendor personnel on the outsourced functions. When the vendor personnel are trained and functional, most outsourcing results in the redeployment or release of corporate employees who fulfilled the specific task prior to outsourcing.

Risks related to clarity of purpose and intent include:

- Poor identification and definition of the outsourced task results in an ineffective outsourcing program.
- Employees involved in the outsourcing project are aware that in many cases they are training their replacements.

- A reduction in force regardless of the cause is a traumatic corporate event bringing unease and unrest to other employees.

- Unease and unrest can translate into lost productivity, poor morale, and corporate insider sabotage, all of which ultimately cause lost revenue.

68.3.4 Price. One of the largest risks of outsourcing is the formation of an unstable relationship with the vendor. When margins are paper thin, security of corporate data often becomes the first victim. Recent findings from IT research firm Gartner indicate that a significant number of CIOs still look at outsourcing in terms of near-term profitability.

As a result, they're setting themselves up for failure.... By 2008, more than 2.3 million offshore service workers will be employed by U.S. companies. But according to a recent Dun & Bradstreet survey, 20% of those outsourcing relationships will fail in the first two years, and 50% within five years.[13]

Risks related to price issues include:

- The vendor's culture must at least absorb, if not improve on, the originating company's corporate culture and do so in a fiscally responsible way.

- Defining outsourcing success by cost reduction alone introduces ongoing and increasing risk throughout the outsourcing relationship.

68.3.5 Social Culture. The vendor must understand and address the social culture of the outsourced task, and the differences from its own. Vendors must understand, absorb, and fulfill the outsourced task, under the same social norms as the sponsor organization. Cultures around the world have different societal norms, expectations, and nuances regarding confidentiality, possession, integrity, authenticity, availability, and utility. Vendors must be able to respond, react, and live within both the social culture they serve and their home culture.
Risks related to social culture include:

- Failure of the vendor to adapt to the social culture of the society served can result in lost money, wasted effort, potential legal issues, and customer dissatisfaction.

- Failure of organizations and vendors to anticipate, recognize, and mitigate problems arising from cultural differences regarding security, whether insourced or outsourced, poses a potentially catastrophic risk.

68.3.6 International Economics. The organization not only needs to understand its corporate and customer economics; it also must have a very deep and forward-looking view into the economic horizon of the vendor's geopolitical economy.
There are many willing vendors in emerging and low-cost labor markets. Without a clear understanding of the economic future of the vendor's country, a corporation can easily find itself tied to a vendor in an eroding or imploding economy.
Risks related to economic issues include:

- When the economy of a country collapses, any contractual relationship to an outsourcing vendor in that country will not survive.

- Forced into an evanescent relationship, a corporation may not have the ability to pull the outsourced task in-house, or to another vendor, quickly enough to save its own business.

68.3.7 Political Issues.   Regardless if the vendor is nearshore or offshore, the organization must have a very clear understanding, perspective, and acceptance of the political nuances in the vendor's country.

Political nuances and practices differ in every country. Acceptable behavior in one country may be reprehensible in another. Corporations must consider how political nuances intertwine with corporate objectives and policies.

Corporations must also be aware of and acknowledge the new risks and instabilities of the new century, and factor them into every nearshoring and offshoring outsourcing effort.

> The terrorist attacks Tuesday on trains in the western India city of Mumbai appeared unlikely to dampen investments and outsourcing to India. . . . The government also found evidence from terrorists killed in an encounter last year that they were targeting India's successful outsourcing industry.[14]

Risks related to political issues include:

- Are graft and bribery accepted or expected within the local political system? If so, how will such practices accord with national restrictions on the contracting organization? Will the outsourcing entity need to sponsor or participate in the political system of the vendor's country? How will such involvement be perceived nationally and internationally?
- Is the country politically stable? What are the opposing forces, and how do they see outsourcing vendors?
- Does the nearshoring or offshoring country possess an environment compatible with terrorist activities? What assurances of business continuity can the vendor make under such circumstances?

68.3.8 Environmental Factors.   Site selection is one of the fundamental building blocks in any outsourcing project and a topic worthy of careful examination by itself. (For additional details, see Chapter 23 in this *Handbook*.)

Risks related to environmental factors include:

- If nearshore or offshore, will the vendor's regional infrastructure predictably and reliably support the expected and required service levels for the outsourced task?
- How susceptible is the nearshore/offshore location to natural disaster?
- Could a natural disaster trigger debilitating political or economic events in the host country?
- Does the host country possess the ability to recover from an environmental disaster?

68.3.9 Travel.   Whether nearshore or offshore, outsourcing will likely, and with regularity, send employees to the vendor for training, quality control, and other management functions. Important travel considerations focus on the costs of travel as well as on employee safety and health, addressing such issues as travel safety, food safety, medical preparations (immunizations, malaria pills, etc.), and locally available medical care.

Risks related to travel include:

- Will foreign workers be able to obtain required travel documents (e.g., exit permits from their home country, working visas for the outsourcing organization's country) allowing them to work in the client's organization?
- Extensive travel is grueling, takes a toll on employees' personal lives, and can cause productivity and management issues.
- Travel is expensive. Failure to budget for appropriate amounts of travel to the vendor will result in budget overruns.
- In the post-9/11 world, the risks and stresses to travelers have increased. Depending on the vendor's location, exposure of corporate employees to terrorist threats, or the fear of terrorist threats, is a significant consideration.

68.3.10 Labor. Labor and workforce risks occur everywhere from Detroit, Michigan, to the Philippines and Bangalore, India. Without a clear understanding of the risks particular to the vendor's region, a corporation could find itself in a quagmire of constant turnover, escalating wages, work stoppages, and unfettered cost growth.

Careful examinations of current and forecasted workforce trends are core to the vendor selection process. As outsourcing sites gain in popularity, wages escalate driven by competition for workers. Once a corporation moves key functions to a vendor, if workforce conditions negatively change, previous cost savings could be lost. Important considerations include current and forecasted worker supply, the vendor's ability to retain employees (as evidenced by annual turnover rates), a propensity for collective bargaining in the vendor's country, as well as the stability of the government and the opposition's tactics.

Additionally, understanding the history of strikes or work stoppages in the vendor's location is a necessary preparation. For example:

> Political strife led to a shutdown Oct. 4 of most major outsourcing companies in Bangalore. . . . In April, Bangalore shut down for two days when citizens rioted following the death of Indian film icon Rajkumar. Published reports said the country's software companies lost $40 million in revenue.[15]

As mentioned in Section 68.3.6, the economic conditions in the offshore location should be followed carefully. Some countries suffering inflation may push workers toward collective action. For example, in April 2008, 20,000 Vietnamese workers at a factory making shoes for Nike went on strike to demand increased wages to keep pace with inflation.[16]

Another issue is whether worker exploitation (e.g., wages below a reasonable minimum, child labor, slave labor, unhealthful working conditions) exsist in the offshore location, or is practiced by the outsourcing vendor. Do such practices pose a threat to morale and reputation of the outsourcing organization?[17]

68.3.11 Additional Risks. Although the preceding lists may seem expansive, there are still many other fundamental and significant elements that must be part of any outsourcing decision-making process. Other complex and, in some cases, deeply fundamental considerations are:

- Loss of corporate expertise over tasks
- Loss of direct control
- Internal changes in corporate purpose (i.e., moving from a company of doers to a company that manages those who are doers)
- Overhead of ongoing contract management issues

Understanding all of the risks allows the prepared organization to knowingly accept, mitigate, transfer, or ignore risks associated with the outsourcing project.

68.4　CONTROLLING THE RISKS.　Outsourcing is an area in which the motto "Security transcends technology"[18] holds particularly true. Almost none of the threats to information itself, or information technology, is unique to an outsourced environment, although perhaps some may grow more dangerous in far-removed or foreign locales. Outsourcing does involve some serious security issues, but most—at first glance—might appear indirect threats to information assurance.

68.4.1　Controls on What?　Most of the security issues of outsourcing involve people, corporations, societies, and governments. Security controls to mitigate the risks of outsourcing have little to do with technology such as computers and a great deal to do with organizational behavior. Since contractors perform crucial tasks but often are geographically far removed from those ultimately accountable for the tasks, the policies, contracts, agreements, and trust relationships that the organization has set up in advance will dictate the success of the endeavor. In particular, the organization's information technology security policy takes on a much more visible role. The technological controls involve the assurance of interpersonal notions like trust and accountability, and are perhaps overshadowed by concern with legal matters, site selection, contractual obligations, politico-economics, and separation of duties.

68.4.2　Controlling Outsourcing Risk.　Many of the risks described in Section 68.4 transcend the boundaries of individual risk types but are similar to other risk areas in the way they map to the six security foundation elements.[19] It seems appropriate, then, to couch the discussion of controls in terms of the security foundations. This section focuses on controls that mitigate, for instance, confidentiality concerns in outsourced environments, touching on how the controls might affect the risk classes differently. Since part of the scope of this chapter is the outsourcing of security functions, some of the controls mentioned do not immediately appear to relate to information assurance but may affect other success metrics.

68.4.3　Availability Controls.　When resources are local, the primary source of problems that can lead to a loss of availability has to do with physical and logical infrastructure. When resources are remote, the infrastructure issues are still important, and can indeed be more problematic. A good example of this difference is the February 2007 trans-Pacific cable cut that made much of Asia inaccessible over the Internet. The farther the vendor from the home company, the more difficult and expensive it can be to acquire an alternate route for communications.[20]

Mitigation of availability risk revolves around planning. Sound backup strategies and business continuity plans should already be in place for the organization; the outsourcing project should also have these plans, both for the vendor site and for the staff at the home organization responsible for vendor communications. Given the economic, political, and environmental concerns that could lead to total (and possibly permanent) unavailability of the outsourced site, a backup vendor should be in place for disasters. These kinds of controls would be appropriate for natural disasters, labor strikes, terrorism, and a variety of other risks to availability. (For much greater detail on backups, business continuity planning and disaster recovery, see Chapters 57, 58, and 59 in this *Handbook*.)

If the vendor is in a foreign country where laws and contracts are enforced differently (or not at all), a service-level agreement incorporated into disaster planning might turn out to be a hollow, unenforceable contract.[21] Part of the evaluation of any outsourcing decision should be a visit to the site, including inspection of policy documents and physical tours of facilities. The organization needs to be sure that controls at the vendor site really do mirror the vendor's policy and contract documents.

Beyond making sure that plans are in place against unavailability, the organization must be able to check up on the performance of the vendor. The agility required to switch to a backup vendor becomes much more possible with advance notice for at least some of the possible outages. For instance, if the availability of a site relates to escalating economic problems causing workforce shortages, a periodic analysis of the regional news media, and of the vendor's work performance, might give hints of problems on the horizon. Automated checking is appropriate as well, especially to keep track of network resources when access traverses the public Internet. Ultimately, for both people and technology, mitigating the risks of outsourced availability comes down to planning and monitoring.

68.4.4   Utility Controls.   The utility of information (and of remote resources) hinges mostly on communication—both format and process. Careful version control avoids incompatible data. Encryption recovery agents can avoid the loss of utility if a user forgets a decryption password, but national and international restrictions on encryption must be kept in mind when planning the use of encryption across national borders.[22] These utility issues are common to any organization. With outsourcing, incompatible formats become more of a problem, especially with offshoring. If an application written in the United States uses ASCII encoding, but the vendor has applications that use Unicode, format issues can arise that need to be accounted for and solved. Although these problems may not become apparent immediately, planning for them must occur well in advance.

Human communication is also an issue with outsourcing. Even if the organization's native language is spoken by employees in the outsource vendor's site, it may not be their first language. Spoken communication (e.g., at a help desk) can suffer greatly if a technician's accent is too difficult for employees and customers of the outsourcing organization to understand. Similarly, written documentation and regular reports can lead to misunderstandings if language skills are not adequate. Either of these situations becomes manageable through advance planning for workforce training and through on-site liaison from the home organization, especially early in the relationship.

68.4.5   Integrity and Authenticity Controls.   The risk that the organization's data might be changed unknowingly, or replaced with other data, hinges on trust. Any time crucial business functions are given to an outside entity, trust issues arise. The organization must understand how much information is being shared, and with whom. Role-based access control and the principle of least privilege are appropriate here: Based on its role of supporting a particular business function, what is the minimum amount of privilege the vendor needs to do its job? Nevertheless, to be an effective support organization, the vendor may need access to corporate information that could prove damaging if misused.

From the perspective of integrity and authenticity controls, the decision to outsource must be accompanied by a decision about levels of trust. This trust should include an analysis of the vendor's history and reputation as well as a visual inspection of the site. The "trust infrastructure," which would include access control mechanisms as well as division of labor and delegation of responsibilities, must be designed by the organization. Importantly, the vendor must not be able to make changes in this structure. Changes to trust relationships must be driven by the organization.

Given fluctuation of economies, job markets, and international relations, the decision to trust the outsourced personnel and processes should not be a one-time event. Ongoing monitoring could reveal occasional lapses that might grow into bigger problems. How easy is it for the home organization to check up on the integrity and authenticity of data? Where are logs kept? Are backup copies of the logs (or the originals) sent to the home organization? What about change tracking on servers? Each of these questions should be addressed, and the answers should be written into the contractual language.

68.4.6   Confidentiality and Possession Controls.   Merely by making the decision to outsource partially compromises confidentiality and possession of corporate information, just as the strength of a secret is decreased as soon as it is shared with a trusted confidant. The home organization must decide whether the loss of confidentiality and possession is balanced by the benefits of outsourcing. Within the United States, and in many countries with strong legal systems, laws protecting physical and intellectual property can help support this decision. The penalties enforced by the legal system serve as a deterrent to thieves, and also serve to compensate damages in the event of a successful compromise. In countries where laws protecting intellectual property are weak (or absent), this level of deterrent and compensation is not available, and the balance of risk shifts.

In June 2006, an employee at the HSBC bank call center in Bangalore, India, was arrested and charged with hacking into the bank's computers, breaching confidentiality agreements and privacy laws, and helping to steal £233,000. The accused was discovered to have been hired on the basis of forged school transcripts. According to news reports, the only criterion for hiring personnel into that call center was English-language skills.[23]

In the absence of strong legal backing, the organization can replace some of the deterrent, normally provided by laws, with language in the contract linking contractual compliance with payments and ongoing business relationships. The vendor should be required to meet security expectations, and the contract should specifically state that parts of the agreement (or the entire agreement) might be voided if security proves inadequate. Coupled with ongoing monitoring to catch problems before they become habitual or endemic, contractually tying security performance to the future of the relationship might prevent a damaging, large-scale loss of confidentiality or possession. And, while this kind of contractual language might not help in a foreign court, it should help protect the organization if the vendor manages to bring suit against the organization in the organization's home jurisdiction.

68.4.7 Making the Best of Outsourcing.

Controlling the risks of outsourcing any function involves planning and careful implementation, primarily focused on trust and monitoring. The advice to "trust, but verify" applies particularly to outsourcing situations, in which a vendor necessarily gains at least some level of access to the organization's internal information and systems. Planning for risks to availability requires adequate business continuity and disaster recovery planning. Training, liaison, and careful planning well in advance of the outsourcing move are required to mitigate risks to utility. Integrity and authenticity controls, as well as confidentiality and possession controls, hinge on monitoring and enforcement, which can become problematic in different legal climates. Making contracts include business consequences for falling short of security requirements can help control the shortfalls of foreign jurisdictions.

68.5 OUTSOURCING SECURITY FUNCTIONS.

Delegating security functions to an outside vendor can increase the quality of an organization's overall security posture. This is done by leveraging the vendor's security expertise and perspective, which presumably it has acquired by providing a number of in-depth services to a large number of organizations.

Despite the media attention surrounding the outsourcing of some IT security functions, the use of a contracted guard force by organizations has been a common practice for years. As mentioned in Section 68.1.3, this is an example of insourcing: the use of contract or noncompany employees to fulfill certain business functions within physical and logical corporate boundaries.

In the last few years, organizations such as financial institutions have been nearshoring complex and costly IT security functions. This work is very challenging for any organization, as the goal is to guard production networks against a never-ending stream of continuously changing threats. Also, these security functions usually do not pass the core competency tests described in Section 68.2.2, meaning they are good candidates for outsourcing. A leading example would be 24-hour-per-day monitoring and management of firewalls and intrusion-detection systems.

A new twist on a mature outsourcing tactic is offshoring software testing for security vulnerabilities. Assuming the vendor has the necessary tools and talent, outsourcing this function appears to make sense for many of the same reasons that organizations outsource quality assurance testing for any software development project. Not only is it an opportunity to gain effectiveness, but the efficiencies (e.g., faster cycle time and lower cost) can be compelling as well.

68.5.1 Who Outsources Security?

In 2004, organizations with annual revenues over US$1 billion outsourced IT security twice as often as smaller ones. In contrast, only 9 percent of small and 8 percent of midsize companies say that outsourcing IT security is a business priority.[24]

But outsourcing IT security functions is making a big market even bigger. For example, Gartner forecasted the North American market for security services to grow from US$4.1 billion in 2001 to US$9.0 billion in 2006. Consulting will be the largest IT security-services segment, at 40 percent of the projected market in 2006.[25] North American revenues for managed-security service providers (MSSPs), such as Counterpane (IDS monitoring) and Postini (anti-spam), will have grown about 20 percent a year from US$950 million in 2004, to US$1.7 billion in 2007.[26]

68.5.2 Why Do Organizations Outsource Security?

According to Levine, the top two reasons why organizations outsource network security are as a strategy for dealing with staffing challenges (effectiveness) and a desire for financial savings (efficiency).[27]

68.5.2.1   Staffing Challenges.   Getting the most value from a security staff is an enduring challenge. Not only must talented people be found and retained, but they must be deployed so as to gain the greatest benefits. The highest value work for a security team includes those tasks that must be done from deep within the business context such as policy setting, architecture, design, and risk management. These tasks require in-depth knowledge of a business's strategies, strengths, weaknesses, organizational structure, and culture. They are the core competencies of the corporate security team.

Given this situation, one of the best ongoing exercises a security officer or manager can perform to maximize the value of their team is to regularly ask: Are my people exclusively working on tasks that cannot be delegated to anyone else? Another way to ask this is: Are my people doing any tasks that someone with less experience and organizational knowledge could perform at the same level of competency?

An example of a situation that can benefit from outsourcing security is protecting the network in an organization with limited technical resources.

Protecting the organizational network is a demanding job. Securing network connected digital assets (i.e., information systems) requires robust defenses against malicious hackers, viruses, worms, spyware, keystroke loggers, and denial of service attacks, just to name a few specific online threats. It may be difficult or impossible to find and employ enough security staff members who are both effective and efficient at dealing with all these threats.

In addition, understanding and defending against the latest threats requires constant education of staff, proactive monitoring, maintenance, and patching of the organization's network defenses. The capital expenditure for the "care and feeding" of specialized software and equipment can be very high.

Due to the nature and rapid pace of the threats, and a chronic shortage of talented people, there is an ongoing need to replace security staff. This adds additional expense for contract workers, decreased productivity, and increased risk of mistakes. Keeping information assurance specialists around after you have trained them is not easy; other organizations want and need them too. Outsourcing offers one way to transfer the burden of staff training and retention to another organization.

Finally, security service providers offer competent handling of routine security activities (i.e., monitoring and maintenance of hardware and software), and they can prepare the many reports required to document compliance with corporate policies and outside regulations. With these tasks being taken care of by a vendor, organizations can focus their internal efforts and personnel on more critical, high-value IT security functions.

68.5.2.2   Financial Savings.   Despite our admonition in Section 68.4.4 to avoid outsourcing as a primary means to achieve direct cost reduction, an MSSP can offer tremendous economic efficiencies. For example, full-time security monitoring can be outsourced for significant cost savings.

A substantial challenge for all but the largest organizations is monitoring IT security 24 hours per day, seven days a week. For financial institutions in particular, this level of monitoring has become the de facto standard of due care. But providing that kind of constant vigilance is nearly impossible for many small organizations, such as community banks.

To provide 24-hour-per-day coverage with internal staff, organizations have to hire at least three full-time professionals, but would likely require twice as many to prevent staff burnout and a high turnover rate over the long term. Having backup coverage in place would require even more employees.

Managing an "average" week of 24-hour-per-day monitoring and response takes a minimum of five fully trained people. To begin with, you need one person for each of the three 8-hour shifts during the week. For weekends, the most economical approach is to have one person for each of two 12-hour shifts. Realistically, due to sickness, vacation, holidays, training, and other demands on staff, there would need to be between 8 and 10 employees to provide reliable coverage.

The economics of this situation are straightforward. In the United States, a nearshore vendor can be hired to manage a small organization's firewalls, as well as run host intrusion detection and perimeter intrusion detection, for between US$25,000 and $50,000 a year.[28] In contrast, any organization in the United States would likely spend at least six times that amount on salaries alone to perform those functions with minimal staff. It is common for a highly skilled, in-house security professional to be paid between US$70,000 and US$100,000 a year in salary alone.[29] Add money for benefits (20 to 50 percent of base salary) as well as facilities, equipment, and other employment costs (80 to 150 percent of base salary), and the fully burdened cost for each employee can be almost two times what they are paid in direct salary.

At one of our organizations, the fully burdened cost of all employees is calculated every quarter by taking their direct salary and adding 184 percent.[30] Using this formula, the fully burdened cost of a security professional paid US$100,000 a year in direct salary is US$284,000.

68.5.2.3 Threat Intelligence and Additional Perspectives. An organization is best positioned to make decisions regarding IT security when it has the freshest, most complete intelligence (information concerning an enemy or possible enemy[31]) about emerging threats.

However, the tremendous volume of threat data being released every day can overwhelm all but the largest organizations. Even national governments struggle to keep up, and they usually have dozens or hundreds of people dedicated to gathering and analyzing data. Beyond problems of volume, there is the question of scope: It is difficult to know how any given vulnerability will be applicable to a specific system, if at all. A software maker's estimation of vulnerability severity is generic in nature; it may be more or less severe within the context of another organization. This is where a MSSP can really help.

MSSPs typically have the ability to gauge severity and spot trends based on what is happening to its other customers. One MSSP advertises that it

> process[es] over a billion security events every day across more than 7,000 devices, giving our security research group unprecedented internal and external threat visibility across the globe. Using this visibility, [this vendor] maps the latest vulnerabilities and real-world threats to your infrastructure, enabling your team to prevent attacks.[32]

In Section 68.3.11, "the loss of corporate expertise over tasks" was mentioned as one of the risks of outsourcing. If your organization takes advantage of an MSSP's intelligence capability, and you have the opportunity and resources, a valuable provision in an outsourcing contract would be to transfer the vendor's intelligence-gathering skills to one or more employees of your organization. However, vendors may view such knowledge as proprietary.

68.5.3 What Are the Risks of Outsourcing Security?   Trust is at the heart of the question of outsourcing risks. Can you trust the vendor to whom you are outsourcing, and its employees? Internal employees cannot typically gain the kind of intimacy with these people that they can with each other. This is a barrier to the human desire and tendency to build trust with others through direct interaction and observation.

There are, of course, specific risks in outsourcing security functions. Certainly, total control of an organization's security should never be transferred to an outside vendor. Although it may be possible to delegate (i.e., outsource) some operational duties, most companies find that keeping control of critical functions is vital to a successful security program. Examples of critical functions include firewall administration, direct control over all administrative/root accounts, and direct control over security logging. However, depending on your ability to manage the risk to your organization, you may feel comfortable delegating any of these functions. At the end of the day, outsourcing IT security is a very personal decision.

Some specific risks for IT security outsourcing include:

- An IDS monitoring vendor is more profitable as the number of events it responds to decreases. If the vendor is also responsible for tuning your IDS, will your vendor tune the devices to produce the least number of events?

- How can you ensure that in a significant customer-wide event, your organization will not be ignored or placed at a lower priority by your vendor?

- Is the vendor paid by "event" rather than by alert? If the answer is yes, what safeguards are in place to monitor potential abuse?

- Where are the outside vendor's personnel located: onshore, nearshore, offshore? Each would require specific contract language to accommodate language, cultural, and legal distinctions.

- Is the vendor vigilant about the background and expertise of its personnel?

- Who is monitoring the activities and behavior of the vendor's employees when they access your organization's data?

- Some countries are known as hotbeds of corporate espionage. Do you have strong control of your source code, to ensure that the vendor's employees do not share the code with any other persons or entity?

68.5.4 How to Outsource Security Functions.   Although not very different from outsourcing any business process, there are some unique aspects to outsourcing IT security functions. This section describes what is different and provides specific examples. We encourage you to consult with your contracting office or other reputable and knowledgeable sources for a more thorough treatment.

68.5.4.1 Where to Begin.   As with any outsourced work, first gather your business requirements and use them to define the outcomes you expect the vendor to deliver. Normally, this information is delivered to the vendor as a statement of work (SOW). Include in your SOW only those functions that do not require intimate knowledge and experience of the specific, mission-critical functions of the organization. As discussed in Section 68.2, outsourcing should allow management to focus on its mission-critical functions; thus it is inappropriate to outsource functions that require great experience and insight in those areas.

68.5.4.2 Brief Case Study I.   One author of this chapter recently delegated responsibility for resetting passwords and creating user accounts to an outside vendor. The business driver to delegate was the result of an analysis of effectiveness of his internal team: There was just too much work to do for the number of employees authorized. In addition to asking whether a less experienced (i.e., less expensive) team could accomplish certain tasks, the security team also considered the risks to the organization if the work were not done correctly.

In a team decision meeting, we determined that resetting passwords and creating accounts for nonadministrative users was of sufficiently low risk that we could delegate those tasks. In contrast, we determined that performing these tasks on administrative and service accounts was too risky to delegate, so we continued to do that work. the fact that the daily volume of administrative account work was relatively low compared to nonadministrative accounts helped justify keeping those tasks in house.

68.5.4.3 Determining Desired Outcomes.   When defining outcomes for operational IT security tasks, focus on the urgency and severity levels of the responses. This is typically driven by the response times required by the organization.

68.5.4.4 Brief Case Study II.   Once we decided to delegate resetting passwords and creating user accounts, we then asked operational business leaders what responsiveness they required. Based on their input, we assigned password resets as severity level 1, requiring no more than four hours to complete upon receipt of request. User account creation is severity level 2, requiring no more than one business day to complete upon receipt of request.

68.5.4.5 Choose a Reliable Vendor.   Once your SOW is complete, choose a reliable IT security vendor. Consider these points before you make your final decision:[33]

- Financial health (e.g., annual revenues, longevity)
- Reliable infrastructure (e.g., state-of-the-art tools; disaster resistant)
- Competent staff (e.g., sufficient experience; appropriate credentials; access to global intelligence)
- Satisfied customers (e.g., talk with MSSP references; ask what they like the least about the MSSP)
- Vendor independence (e.g., no hidden financial motives to sell you solutions that are not appropriate for your organization; third-party attestations of effectiveness)
- Appropriate service-level agreement (e.g., contains requirements, outcomes desired, response times, roles and responsibilities, and metrics)
- Legal safeguards (e.g., recourse for your organization in the event of vendor breach of contract; if offshored, the applicable laws in the host country that might prevail in a contractual issue, or in a government "nationalization" situation)

68.5.4.6 Service-Level Agreements.   Once a reliable vendor is chosen, a strong, precise service-level agreement (SLA) is required. The SLA must specify outcomes desired, response times, roles and responsibilities, metrics, and other requirements. Ideally, the SLA should be written to remain relatively stable over time. Realistically, an SLA needs reliable provisions for change and conflict resolution because the requirements will change over time, no matter how much homework you do.

68.5.4.7 Metrics.   Include metrics in the SLA that will allow you to measure outcomes; install an independent monitoring system to validate reported metrics and to detect unauthorized behavior by vendor staff. Periodically (weekly at first, then monthly if performance warrants), review the metrics and activities with the vendor's management to ensure that work performed matches the requirements of the SLA; adjust the SLA as necessary to drop metrics that are not useful and add new metrics that are.

68.5.4.8 Brief Case Study III.   We monitor the vendor response times for resetting passwords and creating user accounts by examining the timestamps in the vendor's ticketing system correlated with the events written in the system logs. To ensure the vendor does not tamper with the system logs, we have many events immediately forwarded to a centralized logging server to which the vendor has no access.

68.5.4.9 Gaining Maximum Efficiency.   Unless you have a good reason not to do so, allow the vendor to determine how it will deliver your desired outcomes. This gives the vendor the ability to determine how to achieve maximize efficiency. Of course, a vendor is inherently motivated to do this in order to be competitive and maximize profits. Be aware that this also means the vendor has incentives to cut corners, which could result in security incidents for you.

68.5.4.10 How the Vendor Does the Work.   Once the vendor has created its procedures, be sure to review and approve how the vendor will do the work. After all, security is based not just on what things you do but how you do them. The ultimate authority in the matter will be your organization's information security policy. Be careful, though, not to criticize vendors just because they do not do things the way your team would. Your priorities are to get the right outcomes with the least risk at an affordable price. Be very careful not to upset your priorities over nothing more than personal preferences.

68.5.4.11 Brief Case Study IV.   In outsourcing password resets and account creation, we allowed the vendor to devise its own procedures. In our case, it made sense to permit this level of freedom because the vendor had tools and know-how that our team did not. For instance, we did not have an incident ticketing system, and the vendor already had one up and running. This allowed the vendor to receive, log, and assign work more efficiently than we could.

   However, after some time one of the risks we noted in Section 68.6.3.10 reared its ugly head. We found that the vendor sometimes placed passwords in the ticketing system because doing so saved time (it did not have to reset the passwords every time it went into an account) and allowed the ticket to be closed more quickly. Clearly, we were not as motivated by their profit motive as by preserving our security posture. This is why we regularly monitored the vendor's ticketing system by having a console installed directly in our work area.

68.5.4.12 Holding the Vendor Accountable.   Finally, be sure to include a strong penalty provision in your SLA to deter careless mistakes by the vendor. If your monitoring tools are effective, you will know about mistakes before the vendor does.

Be thoughtful, though, because you do not want to deter the vendor from reporting those mistakes. The point of discussing a mistake should not be to punish as a first recourse, but to correct the vendor in the hope that it will grow in competence and become a better steward of your security work.

68.5.5 Controlling the Risk of Security Outsourcing. Organizations should consider their decision to outsource security in terms of their organization's overall outsourcing strategy, and should determine if their organization has the skill sets and tools necessary to manage the outsourcing relationship. Also, they must realize that contract management skills will be the primary management tool, not IT management expertise.

Ongoing monitoring by the outsourcer will be required. Organizations cannot take for granted the presence and effectiveness of monitoring activity. Provisions must be made to ensure that organizations get the services they are paying for. Should the vendor fail to deliver the services, the organization should be prepared to perform the work once again, quickly and effectively. Once confidence in an IT security vendor has been lost, the vendor's administrative access should be revoked as soon as possible.

Refer to Section 68.4 of this chapter, controlling the risks of IT outsourcing, for more advice.

68.6 CONCLUDING REMARKS. Outsourcing is a new term for an old concept: We humans have always liked to do what we are good at doing, relying on the skills of others to fill in the gaps in our competencies. We outsource tasks to concentrate on being more effective at our core skills, and we hope to become more efficient as a result. Types of outsourcing—insourcing, nearshoring, offshoring—differ based on how far from the parent organization the outsourcing vendor operates, but there are other much more significant differences when evaluating the risks of outsourcing.

Many organizations have saved significant amounts of money by outsourcing some functions. Hindsight, however, shows that many organizations that outsource solely to save money find themselves with significant problems caused by a lack of careful evaluation of outcomes and risks. Proper planning should include:

- Being clear about the purpose of the outsourcing
- Avoiding the tendency to focus too much on the bottom line
- Adequately understanding social culture
- Accounting for differences in politics and economics
- Analyzing potential problems in infrastructure and environment
- Anticipating travel and labor issues

Any organization that looks at all these issues well in advance of an outsourcing decision stands a good chance to succeed, despite the potential pitfalls.

The keys to mitigating risks in any outsourcing project—careful planning and constant vigilance—are particularly applicable if security functions are the subject of an outsourcing decision. Depending on the security stance and regulatory environment of the home organization, some security functions may be able to be outsourced in a way that does not put the organization at unacceptable risk. In the end, the great care required to outsource security functions properly has the potential to improve security throughout the organization, and perhaps even make security easier to do well at a vendor site than at the home organization.

68.7   FURTHER READING

Axelrod, C. W. *Outsourcing Information Security*. Norwood, MA: Artech House, 2004.

Carmel, E., and P. Tjia. *Offshoring Information Technology: Sourcing and Outsourcing to a Global Workforce*. Cambridge, UK: Cambridge University Press, 2005.

Cohen, L., and A. Young. *Multisourcing: Moving Beyond Outsourcing to Achieve Growth and Agility*. Cambridge, MA: Harvard Business School Press, 2005.

Cooney, M. "Can You Trust China for Outsourcing?" *Network World*, May 29, 2006. http://www.networkworld.com/columnists/2006/052906edit.html.

Cullen, S. *Intelligent IT Outsourcing: Eight Building Blocks to Success*. Woburn, MA: Butterworth-Heineman, 2003.

Dara, N. "Cyber Crime Comes of Age as Foreign Plugs Sell Secrets," *DNA India*, October 19, 2005; http://dnaindia.com/report.asp?NewsID=6411.

Greaver, M. F. *Strategic Outsourcing: A Structured Approach to Outsourcing Decisions and Initiatives*. New York: AMACOM, 1999.

Koulopoulos, T. M., and T. Roloff. *Smartsourcing: Driving Innovation and Growth Through Outsourcing*. Avon, MA: Platinum Press, 2006.

Power, M. J., K. Desouza, and C. Bonifazi. *The Outsourcing Handbook: How to Implement a Successful Outsourcing Process*. London, UK: Kogan Page, 2006.

Sood, R. *IT, Software and Services: Outsourcing and Offshoring*. Austin, TX: AiAiYo Books, 2005.

Stees, J. *Outsourcing Security: A Guide for Contracting Services*. Woburn, MA: Butterworth-Heineman, 1998.

Vashistha, A. *The Offshore Nation: Strategies for Success in Global Outsourcing and Offshoring*. New York: McGraw-Hill, 2006.

68.8   NOTES

1. M. Cooney, "Outsourcing Bonanza 2006: 8 Outsourcing Trends You Need to Know About," *Network World,* December 13, 2006; www.networkworld.com/news/2006/121306-outsourcing-trends.html.

2. M. Cooney, "Government Agency Outsourcing Firms Don't Respect Private Data, GAO Reports," *Network World,* April 5, 2006; www.networkworld.com/news/2006/040506-gao-outsourcing.html.

3. Dan Twing, "10 Reasons Why Small Businesses Should Consider Outsourcing," *Network World,* July 5, 2006; www.networkworld.com/newsletters/asp/2006/0703out1.html?page=1.

4. T. L. Friedman, *The World Is Flat: A Brief History of the Twenty-first Century* (New York: Farrar, Straus and Giroux, 2006), pp. 48–172.

5. G. Hamel and C. K. Prahalad, "The Core Competence of the Corporation," *Harvard Business Review* 68, No. 3 (May-June 1990): 79–93.

6. "Tempted by the Call of the East," *Mortgage Strategy,* August 22, 2005, p. 3.

7. S. Thurm, "Behind Outsourcing: Promise and Pitfalls," *Wall Street Journal,* February 27, 2007.

8. D. E. Levine, "Farming Out Network Security: Outsourcing might save you money if you choose your provider with care," *Security Technology & Design* (May 2005); www.securityinfowatch.com/print/Security-Technology-and-Design/Network-Security/Farming-Out-Network-Security/4256SIW2 or http://tinyurl.com/5fshta.

9. Levine, "Farming Out Network Security."

10. Duke University/Archstone Consulting LLC Offshoring Research Network 2004 and 2005 surveys; Duke University/Booz Allen Hamilton Offshoring Research Network 2006 survey. As reported by Mary Brandel, "Offshoring Grows Up," *Computerworld*, March 12, 2007; www.computerworld.com.au/index.php/id;1922874537 or http://tinyurl.com/5zw7ph.

11. D. Winkelman, D. Dole, L. Pinkard, J. Molloy, D. Willey, and M. Davids, "The Outsourcing Source Book," *Journal of Business Strategy* 14, No. 3 (May-June 1993): 52.

12. D. Twing, "Reviewing the Security Aspect of Outsourcing," *Network World Outsourcing Newsletter,* September 7, 2005.

13. K. Evans-Correia, K., "Outsourcing on Verge of Cultural Evolution," *SearchCIO.com* April 18, 2006; http://searchcio.techtarget.com/news/article/0,289142,sid182_gci1179791,00.html or http://tinyurl.com/65blch.

14. "Mumbai Blasts Should Not Affect Investments to India." *IDG News Service,* July 12, 2006; http://www.itworld.com/Man/2701/071206mumbai/pfindex.html

15. M. Cooney, "No Outsourcing Today: Strike Closes India's Tech Center," *Network World,* October 5, 2006; www.networkworld.com/news/2006/100506-strike-closes-india-tech-center.html or http://tinyurl.com/55pcpx.

16. Associated Press, "20,000 Vietnamese Workers Go on Strike at Nike Contract Factory," April 1, 2008; www.iht.com/articles/ap/2008/04/01/news/Vietnam-Nike-Strike.php or http://tinyurl.com/6jeru8.

17. F. Fallone, "Overview Child Laborers," *IHS Child Slave Labor News*, 2005; http://ihscslnews.org/view_article.php?id=54.

18. (ISC)^2, International Information Systems Security Certification Consortium: www.isc2.org

19. We owe a lot to Donn Parker for this new way to look at information assurance. See Chapter 3 in this *Handbook* for his description of these security elements.

20. H. Timmons, "Cut Cable Disrupts Web and Phones in India and Middle East," *International Herald Tribune,* January 31, 2008; www.iht.com/articles/2008/01/31/technology/net.php.

21. See, for example, A. Eunjung Cha, "New Law Gives Chinese Workers Power, Gives Businesses Nightmares," *Washington Post,* April 14, 2008; www.washingtonpost.com/wp-dyn/content/article/2008/04/13/AR2008041302214.html or http://tinyurl.com/6x7zzn.

22. See, for example, J. Markoff, "Encryption Tool Rekindles Security Debate," *International Herald Tribune,* May 21, 2006; www.iht.com/articles/2006/05/21/business/privacy.php.

23. K. V. Subramanya, "HSBC Scam: U.K. recipient of data is of Indian origin," *The Hindu,* June 30, 2006; www.hindu.com/2006/06/30/stories/2006063002920700.htm or http://tinyurl.com/45u23s.

24. G. V. Hulme, "Job Security Curtails Security Outsourcing," *InformationWeek,* July 28, 2003; www.informationweek.com/news/software/showArticle.jhtml?articleID=12803139 or http://tinyurl.com/6cb3kk.

25. C. Costanzo, "Internet Security: Outsource or go it alone?" *Community Banker* 14, No. 6 (June 2005); http://findarticles.com/p/articles/mi_qa5344/is_200506/ai_n21373311/pg_1 or http://tinyurl.com/6n7c2m.

26. Costanzo, "Internet Security."

27. Levine, "Farming Out Network Security."

28. Costanzo, "Internet Security."

29. Costanzo, "Internet Security."

30. This calculation was current in March 2007. The formula described and the 184 percent figure are the result of our consultation with the finance department at one of the author's employers. The name of the employer is being withheld to protect their confidentiality.

31. *Merriam-Webster's Collegiate Dictionary*, 11th ed. 2004, p. 650. Also online at www.merriam-webster.com/dictionary/intelligence.

32. Secure Works, "Threat Intelligence Service," www.secureworks.com/services/ threat_intelligence.html.

33. J. Mears, "Is Security Ripe for Outsourcing?" *Network World,* August 23, 2004; www.networkworld.com/news/2004/082304outsecure.html or http:// tinyurl.com/6yc3tl.

INTRODUCTION TO PART VIII

PUBLIC POLICY AND OTHER CONSIDERATIONS

This edition of the *Handbook* ends with compelling issues in information security. Part VIII provides a basis for vigorous discussion about important and controversial topics such as:

69. **Privacy in Cyberspace: U.S. and European Perspectives.** With increasingly frequent losses of control over personally identifiable information, the public is ever more concerned about privacy

70. **Anonymity and Identity in Cyberspace.** How individuals are representing themselves in Internet-mediated communications; the social and legal consequences of completely anonymous interactions, and of untraceable but stable identifiers

71. **Medical Records Protection.** How the special requirements of high availability coupled with extreme sensitivity of medical information poses complex problems for security specialists in medical environments

72. **Legal and Policy Issues of Censorship and Content Filtering.** How corporations and governments around the world regulate access to information that violates social norms, or is perceived as a potential threat to state power

73. **Expert Witnesses and the *Daubert* Challenge.** How security specialists should prepare for their day in court

74. **Professional Certification and Training in Information Assurance.** Benefits and costs of education, professional certifications, examinations, and commercial training

75. **U.S. Undergraduate and Graduate Education in Information Assurance.** Initiatives in the United States have added information assurance to the curriculum of many programs at institutions of higher learning

76. **Undergraduate and Graduate Education in Information Assurance.** Perspectives on information assurance education at the baccalaureate and advanced levels in Europe and the United States

77. **The Future of Information Assurance.** A giant in the field of information assurance reviews the foundations of IA, best practices, and risk reduction and applies his expertise to computer-aided voting as a case study in applied security

CHAPTER

CHAPTER **69**

PRIVACY IN CYBERSPACE: U.S. AND EUROPEAN PERSPECTIVES

Henry L. Judy, Scott L. David, Benjamin S. Hayes, Jeffrey B. Ritter, and Marc Rotenberg

69.1   INTRODUCTION: WORLDWIDE TRENDS.   As information technology continues to develop, increased opportunities and incentives are created to collect information about individuals and to use that personal information for diverse and lucrative purposes. Some believe that, in a global information economy, the most economically valuable electronic asset will be aggregations of information on individuals. For over two decades, concerns regarding the privacy of the individual and cross-border movement of personal information have been reflected in international policy frameworks, such as the Organization for Economic Cooperation and Development (OECD) Privacy Guidelines. In recent years, these concerns have escalated in Europe, the United States, and other economies, particularly due to the rapid commercialization of the Internet and the development of new and more powerful information technologies. There are also significant developments with DNA databases, RFID technologies, and electronic health records. These concerns have accelerated the growth of privacy law, with recent enactments in the United States, Europe, and other areas of the world.[1] At the same time, new policy frameworks have emerged, most notably in the Asia-Pacific region.

69.1.1   Laws, Regulations, and Agreements.   Across the emerging body of global privacy law, which varies substantially from jurisdiction to jurisdiction, general patterns are beginning to emerge. Virtually any piece of information related to an individual is defined as "personal information" and, therefore, potentially subject to regulation with respect to its collection, storage, use, and transfer. Different types of personal information, and different uses of personal information, are subject to different levels of regulation. Typically, the collection and use of medical and other highly sensitive data, such as data revealing the subject's race, religion, political affiliation, sexual orientation, or data relating to children, is most highly regulated.

What conduct is regulated? Privacy laws are structured on the essential principle that the individual person—a "data subject"—should retain some control over the information about himself or herself that is collected or used by a person or organization, whether a business, a nonprofit organization, or a government. Privacy laws impose obligations that are intended to prevent the collection or use of information in any manner that is inconsistent with the expectations of the data subject. In effect, the data subjects' control of their own personal information cannot be circumvented or denied, except with their consent. Privacy laws impose obligations on organizations that collect personal information, and empower the data subject and the state to enforce the data subject's rights under that agreement.

In addition, across different legal systems and, particularly in the United States, across different regulatory schemes governing different industries, privacy laws embrace comparable core principles, commonly referred to as "fair information practices."[2] These practices include the concept of control by the data subject but also may embrace rules that prohibit or limit certain data practices regardless of the consent of, or other involvement by, the data subject.

For chief information officers, security officers, risk managers, general counsels, systems designers, and consultants of any company charged with assuring compliance with privacy laws, new technologies and new business practices are raising new challenges for the enforcement of privacy rules. Regulatory controls that target information assets such as personal information are transforming how information systems are designed and managed. Technology executives are required to assume increased responsibility for legal compliance across divergent legal regimes; business executives and legal officers are required to acquire significant new understandings of the technologies deployed in information management and the business relationships through which personal information is collected, used, and transferred in support of the execution of business relationships. In some circumstances, information technology is both a source and a means of addressing privacy issues.

What makes privacy law important to all of these participants is not the imposition of yet another set of regulations requiring compliance. Instead, privacy law tests companies in their ability to truly integrate business, law, and technology into the coherent planning and execution of their information systems. As the world's economy continues its remarkable transformation into a global environment in which information in electronic form is a significant measure of economic wealth, those companies that master privacy as a competitive opportunity, rather than as a regulatory cost without economic benefit, will be best positioned to safeguard the data of their customers and avoid the growing concerns about security breaches and identity theft.

However, although attention is increasingly paid to overcoming inadequate protection of personal privacy, there is a corresponding increase in the attention paid to the policy issues raised by the impact of new privacy practices. A few examples will suffice. Law enforcement and national security agencies are concerned about how increased privacy protection, including encryption and anonymizer techniques, will weaken their ability to detect crime and terrorism. Medical researchers are concerned about their ability to conduct statistically valid medical research. At the same time, the absence of effective privacy safeguards has led to growing concerns about identity theft and security breaches, particularly in the United States.

69.1.2 Sources of Privacy Law. The legal structures governing personal information use have developed along different lines concerning public and private entities. Typically, governments and other public sector entities are restrained from undue intrusion into citizens' private lives by constitutional mechanisms.[3] Citizens typically are provided access to government-held personal information by statutes, although there has been an increase in constitutionally mandated access rights to personal information as formerly oppressive regimes give way to more democratic governments. The converse is equally true.[4]

By contrast, restraints and obligations placed on private uses of personal information derive almost exclusively from statutory law. However, the recent adoption of the European Charter of Fundamental Rights requires that nation-states treat personal data protection as a basic human right. Such a requirement will stand as a prerequisite for any new potential member of the European Union.[5]

This development suggests a new trend: that data protection may be enshrined into constitutions or supranational law. Indeed, certain developing nations that have recently enacted new constitutions have created bases for their private-sector data protection laws in them. Also, the new member states of the European Union have all adopted data protection rules to comply with the EU Data Directive. As a result, any attempt to master what privacy law is all about will demand, regrettably perhaps, complex legal analysis.

69.2 EUROPEAN APPROACHES TO PRIVACY

69.2.1 History and Organization for Economic Cooperation and Development Principles. Interest in the right of privacy increased in the 1960s and 1970s with the advent of information technology and new data processing techniques for records concerning the individuals. The surveillance potential of computers prompted public demands for specific rules governing the collection and handling of personal information. The genesis of legislation in this area usually is traced to the first modern data protection law, enacted in the German state of Hesse in 1970. That enactment was followed by national laws with differing objectives and scope in Sweden (1973), the United States (1974), Germany (1977), and France (1978).[6]

Two highly influential international instruments emerged following these enactments. The Council of Europe (COE) passed the Convention for the Protection of Individuals with regard to the Automatic Processing of Personal information[7] (the COE Convention) in 1981. In the same year, the Organization for Economic Cooperation and Development (OECD) issued Guidelines Governing the Protection of Privacy and Transborder Data Flows of Personal information (the OECD Guidelines).[8] Both instruments articulate specific rules regarding the handling of personal information. Both present a comparable set of principles for fair information use that have since become the framework for the data protection laws of dozens of countries. These principles recognize personal information as data to be afforded legal protection at every step of their "life cycle" of collection, processing, storage, use, transfer, and destruction.

To date, over 40 countries have adopted the COE Convention, and another 3 have signed it but not adopted it into law.[9] In addition to being relied on by OECD nations to create data protection laws, the OECD Guidelines have been relied on by other nations that are not OECD members.[10] The OECD has continued to be involved in privacy issues and, indeed, makes available a privacy policy statement generator on the privacy page of its Web site.[11]

69.2.2   European Union Data Protection Directive 95/46/EC.   In 1990, both to (1) ensure that member states protected "fundamental" privacy rights when processing personal information, regardless of the national citizenship of the data subjects, and (2) prevent member states from restricting the free flow of personal information within the European Union (EU), the European Commission proposed the EU Directive on Data Protection. On October 24, 1995, following years of discussion and debate, the Council and Parliament of the EU adopted the final version of Directive 95/46/EC.[12] The directive became effective on October 25, 1998.

The directive is not self-executing. Instead, it requires EU member states to pass national legislation that transpose its terms. It is important to realize that the national laws that have been enacted in each of the EU member states are not identical. Indeed, there are fairly significant differences among these laws. Thus, having an understanding of the directive by no means guarantees that a business understands all of the steps it must take to comply with each national law.

69.2.2.1   European Union Directive Requirements.   The EU Directive applies to all commercial uses of personal information. The directive establishes limitations and obligations on "controllers" (entities directing the collection, use, or transfer of personal information) and "processors" (those utilizing personal information at another party's direction) with respect to the "processing" (virtually any collection, use, transfer, or destruction of personal information) of "personal information" (any information that is readily traceable to a particular individual). The directive, like other privacy laws, is organized around certain key principles of information use. These can be summarized as follows:

> *Notice.* Data subjects, individuals to whom personal information relates, must be informed of:
>
> - The identity of the collector of the information;
> - The uses or purposes for which it is collected;

- How they may exercise any available choices regarding its use;
- Where and to whom it may be transferred; and
- How data subjects may access information relating to themselves by an organization.

Consent. Data subjects have the right, except under certain exceptions, not to have their personal information used without their consent, the right to opt out of having personal information used for direct marketing purposes, and the right not to have any "sensitive information" collected or used without express permission. Sensitive information includes information relating to race, religion, health, union membership, beliefs, and sex life.

Consistency. Organizations may use personal information only in strict accordance with the terms of the notice given to the data subjects and any choices with respect to its use exercised by them.

Access. Organizations must give data subjects access to the personal information held about them and must allow them to propose corrections to inaccurate information.

Security. Organizations must provide adequate security, using both technical and other means, to protect the integrity and confidentiality of personal information. The sufficiency of such means is measured with respect to the state of the art.

Onward Transfer. Personal information may not be transferred to a third party unless that third party has been contractually bound to use the data consistently with the notice given to data subjects, any choices they have exercised, and applicable law.

Enforcement. The directive grants a private right of action to data subjects where organizations do not follow the law. In addition, each EU country has established a Data Protection Authority—a regulatory enforcement agency—that has the power to investigate complaints, levy fines, initiate criminal actions, and demand changes in information-handling practices of businesses.

69.2.2.2 International Data Transfer Restrictions. While the directive governs much of the interaction between a business and its data subjects (i.e., its customers and employees), it also regulates how companies operating in multiple jurisdictions worldwide may move personal information within themselves and among their various affiliates or subsidiaries.

Transfers of personal information relating to EU-based data subjects to non-EU countries are *prohibited* unless the country of destination has "adequate" legal protections for privacy. Many countries, including the United States, are not considered by the EU to have "adequate" legal protection. Transfers to such countries may take place only with the consent of the data subject, or where other "guarantees" exist that personal information will be treated according to the EU standard. EU regulators have the legal authority to prohibit transfers of personal information where such guarantees cannot be demonstrated. This requirement is very problematic for many businesses and may require significant technological, organizational, and/or contractual changes.

One possible solution to the directive's transfer restrictions is the U.S./EU "Safe Harbor." This arrangement is discussed in Section 69.3.3.5.

69.2.2.3   *State of Implementation.* All 27 member countries of the European Union, including the new members states, have passed legislation fully implementing the directive.[13]

69.2.3   Harmonization of Non–EU European Countries to the EU Directive.

Largely due to the EU Directive's prohibition on the transfer of personal information to countries with lesser degrees of legal protection, and the fear in many countries of the potential adverse economic impact that could result from the interruption of data flows from EU countries, a number of other countries have passed essentially identical national legislation so as to assure "adequate" levels of legal protection. These countries can be roughly divided into two categories: EU trading partners that wish to ensure that data flows will not be interrupted[14] and countries actively conforming their national legislation to the EU model in hopes of gaining membership to the EU.[15]

69.2.4   European Union Telecommunications Directive.

In addition to the general Data Protection Directive, the EU has enacted a second directive, imposing specific privacy-protective obligations on communications service providers. The Telecommunications Directive[16] obliges carriers and service providers to ensure technologically the privacy of the communications carried on their systems, including e-mail and other Internet communications. This directive also restricts access to billing information, places limitations on marketing, allows for per-line blocking of caller ID, and requires that information gathered during a communication be deleted upon the termination of the communication.[17] A new proposal would replace the Telecommunications Directive with a broader version affecting all "electronic communications" in the European Union.[18]

69.2.5   Establishment of the European Data Protection Supervisor.

In 2002, the European Parliament and the European Council established the office of the European Data Protection Supervisor as "the independent supervisory body entrusted with monitoring the application to Community institutions and bodies of Community instruments relating to the protection of natural persons as regards the processing of personal data and the free movement of such data." In 2003, Mr. Peter Hustinx and Mr. Joaquin Bayo Delgado were appointed for a term of five years as European Data Protection Supervisor and Assistant Supervisor.[19]

69.3   UNITED STATES

69.3.1   History, Common Law Torts.

The concept of privacy as a tort is a twentieth-century phenomenon. The framers of the U.S. Constitution did not recognize an explicit right to privacy, perhaps because privacy was intrinsic to an agrarian society. But the necessity for privacy protection under law gradually became apparent with urbanization and industrialization in the late nineteenth and early twentieth centuries. The concept of a "right to be left alone" was posited by Charles Warren and Louis Brandeis in a seminal 1890 article in the *Harvard Law Review*.[20] Today, virtually every state recognizes a common law or statutory right of privacy.[21]

Like most common law torts, privacy law matured in a piecemeal fashion at the state level because there was no federal law on point. In 1960, the *Restatement of Torts* defined four "subtorts" that are generally held to comprise the common law of privacy. These are:[22]

1. **Intrusion.** The unreasonable intrusion, by physical or other means, upon the seclusion of another, if the intrusion is substantial and would be highly offensive to a reasonable person.

2. **Revelation of private facts.** The unauthorized and unreasonable publicity of facts about a person's private life, if the matter publicized is of a kind that would be highly offensive to a reasonable person, and which is not of legitimate concern to the public. These facts must be communicated to more than a single person or a small group in order to trigger this tort.

3. **"False light."** Publicity that unreasonably places the other in a false light before the public. Essentially, a photo or story cannot be used if that photo or story conveys a false impression of someone. Note that this tort can be used if the person is cast in either a negative or *positive* false light.

4. **Misappropriation.** The unauthorized appropriation of another's name or likeness for benefit or gain. Misappropriation actions are most commonly brought by celebrities whose image is used without authorization in connection with advertising or promotion.

69.3.2 Public Sector.   In the United States, government traditionally has been restrained from undue intrusion into the private lives of citizens by various provisions of the U.S. Constitution and similar provisions in the constitutions of many of the states of the Union. The Fourth Amendment to the U.S. Constitution, for instance, prohibits "unreasonable search and seizure" by the government. Fourth Amendment protection is also made applicable to the states by operation of the Fourteenth Amendment to the U.S. Constitution, which provides that "[n]o state shall make or enforce any law which shall abridge the privileges or immunities of citizens of the United States." Yet, except in certain state constitutions, there is no explicit right of privacy. Thus, many of the rules regarding how government may collect, maintain, and use personal information relating to citizens has been defined by case law and statutes. In the public sector, state governments may have greater privacy protection obligations to their employees than private sector businesses in the same states have to their employees.

69.3.2.1 *Privacy Act of 1974 (Including the Freedom of Information Act).*   The most comprehensive privacy legislation in the United States, the Privacy Act of 1974,[23] placed limitations on how the federal government may use and transfer personal information, and gave individuals a right, subject to certain exceptions, to know what information is held about them by the federal government.[24] The Privacy Act incorporates the Freedom of Information Act (FOIA), which allows access to federal government records, except in certain situations.

The act is intended to:

- Permit individuals to determine what records pertaining to them are collected, maintained, used, or disseminated by federal agencies
- Permit individuals to forbid records that are obtained by an agency for one purpose to be used for another purpose without consent
- Permit individuals to obtain access to agency records pertaining to them and to correct or amend such records as appropriate

- Ensure that agencies collect, maintain, and use personal information in a manner that ensures that the information is current, adequate, relevant, and not excessive for its intended use
- Create a private right of action for individuals whose personal information is not used in accordance with the act[25]

All provisions of the act are subject to certain exceptions, such as criminal investigations or national security concerns. In addition, the act protects each individual, so access to certain information can be limited where providing such information would compromise another individual's privacy.

69.3.2.2 Electronic Communications Privacy Act of 1986. The Electronic Communications Privacy Act (ECPA),[26] which amended the federal wiretap law of 1968, generally prohibits unauthorized and intentional "interception" of wire, oral, and electronic communications during the transmission phase, and unauthorized "accessing" of electronically stored wire or electronic communications. It is applicable in many connections. For example, it establishes standards for capturing telephone numbers through the use of pen registers and trap-and-trace devices. Pen registers record telephone numbers of outgoing calls; trap-and-trace devices record telephone numbers from which incoming calls originate, much like common caller ID systems. Although telephone numbers are not protected by the Fourth Amendment,[27] ECPA requires law enforcement agencies to obtain court orders to install and use these devices. Rather than the strict probable cause showing the necessity for wiretaps, pen register orders require only certification from a law enforcement officer that "the information likely to be obtained is relevant to an ongoing criminal investigation."[28] It is also relevant to workplace invasions of privacy by electronic means (see Section 69.3.3.6).

69.3.2.3 Right to Financial Privacy Act of 1978. Under the Right to Financial Privacy Act,[29] the federal government is prohibited from obtaining the financial records of an individual, or information contained therein, from a financial institution without giving notice to the individual. Where the disclosure is sought via a subpoena, the required disclosure normally must be made within 90 days after the subpoena is served on the financial institution. Where the disclosure is sought by all other means, the required notice normally must be given prior to, or contemporaneously with, the disclosure request.

69.3.2.4 Driver's Privacy Protection Act. The Driver's Privacy Protection Act[30] marked the first time the U.S. Congress passed a law limiting how state governments may use personal information. Specifically, the act prohibits disclosures of personal information obtained in connection with a motor vehicle record by state governments, except in order to facilitate legitimate government activities, facilitate recalls, and the like. This act provides civil and criminal penalties as well as a private right of action. The act survived a challenge to its constitutionality, brought by the state of South Carolina, by a 9-to-0 vote in the U.S. Supreme Court.[31]

69.3.2.5 Law Enforcement and National Security Surveillance. As technology has developed, crime and criminal activities have become increasingly sophisticated. Yet the same developments of technology have greatly facilitated information gathering and surveillance by law enforcement and national security organizations.

Law enforcement agencies have used technology to investigate crimes such as money laundering, narcotics trafficking, insider trading, and fraud. The technology used can be divided roughly into two categories: monitoring and surveillance. Monitoring technology is used to search for indicia of criminal behavior, without focusing on the activities of particular individuals. Examples of monitoring technologies used to detect crime online include:

- **Packet sniffers.** Programs that monitor all traffic flowing through a network, looking for keywords, phrases, e-mail addresses, and the like. When a packet sniffer finds the type of data it is looking for, it saves the communication for later review.

- **"Black boxes."** Hardware installed by law enforcement agencies at Internet service providers (ISPs) in order to monitor communications or Web traffic. Typically, but not always, black boxes use packet-sniffing technology. In the United States, the Federal Bureau of Investigation (FBI) is currently promoting the use of its "Carnivore" system, a black box that it wishes to install at all ISPs and whose name has been described in the press as a colossal public relations blunder. At least one ISP has refused to install Carnivore;[32] currently the program is under review. In February 2001, the FBI renamed its software DCS1000.

Surveillance technology, by contrast, is used to eavesdrop on the communications or transactions of particular individuals. Monitoring technologies often are used or usable for this purpose. In addition, audio listening devices (bugs) and closed-circuit television (CCTV) are increasingly in use.[33]

National security agencies worldwide conduct monitoring and surveillance of communications, to varying degrees. The United States, United Kingdom, New Zealand, Australia, and Canada are reputed to have an integrated global surveillance system known as Echelon. Although details of the Echelon system's capabilities are closely guarded state secrets, some reports indicate that the system is able to intercept virtually any electronic communication on earth.[34] Telecommunications operators in the United States should be aware that the Communications Assistance for Law Enforcement Act of 1994 (CALEA)[35] mandates certain technical standards for telecommunications networks in order to facilitate law enforcement interception of communications. Recent court decisions may, however, ultimately limit CALEA's application.[36]

In 2001, the Council of Europe is developed, in consultation with the U.S. Department of Justice, an international Convention on Cyber-Crime which entered into force in 2004.[37] The Convention is controversial. Although 22 countries have ratified the treaty, 22 counties that were signatories at the outset have not ratified the treaty.[38] Privacy advocates have also criticized this convention for being unduly intrusive.[39]

69.3.3 Private Sector. Compared to other nations, the United States has been fairly slow to pass privacy laws affecting the private sector, preferring instead to rely on industry self-regulation (see Section 69.4.1). Nonetheless, the development of the Internet and electronic commerce, the integration of the financial services industries, and the integration of healthcare services have all spawned new private-sector legislation. Thus far, this legislation has concentrated on particular business sectors rather than regulating uses of personal information generally and has generally emphasized online business practices.

69.3.3.1 Financial Services Sector (Gramm-Leach-Bliley Act).   The Gramm-Leach-Bliley Act (GLB), enacted in 1999, requires every "financial institution" to protect the security and confidentiality of its customers' nonpublic personal information, disclose its privacy policies to consumers, and provide consumers with an opportunity to direct that the institution not share their nonpublic personal information with unaffiliated third parties.[40] Violations of the privacy provisions of GLB are subject to enforcement by various federal regulators; the specific sanctions that may be imposed vary according to the regulatory agency that has jurisdiction in a particular case.

Eight federal agencies have issued regulations enacting the privacy provisions of GLB.[41] The Federal Trade Commission (FTC), among others, has acted aggressively to apply GLB as broadly as possible. Specifically, the FTC defines "financial institution" by reference to a variety of other regulations. This has the effect of causing a number of businesses not traditionally thought of as "financial institutions," such as career counselors,[42] real estate settlement services, and property appraisers,[43] to be subject to GLB's privacy regulations.

Another example of the broad application of these regulations is how "nonpublic personal information" is defined. In the case of certain agencies, it is defined as *any* personal information given by a consumer to an institution, whether the information is otherwise publicly available or not.

The regulations went into effect on July 1, 2001. All affected companies were required to have systems in place to comply with the regulations by that date. A list of the critical aspects of the GLB regulations follows.

- "Customers,"[44] and in some instances "consumers,"[45] must receive initial and annual notices of how their personal information will be used by the financial institution and to which nonaffiliated third parties, other than service providers, it may be transferred.

- Where personal information is to be shared with nonaffiliated third parties other than service providers, the "customer" or "consumer" must be given an opportunity to opt out of having the personal information transferred.

- Appropriate security controls must be maintained, and specified procedures must be followed, for the adoption and testing of information security protocols.

- Sharing of personal information among affiliates remains unaffected.

Some of the effects of GLB that businesses should be aware of include:

- Systems must be created to capture a reliable record of a customer's opt-out (where applicable) at any time and to adopt controls to prevent that customer's personal information from being transmitted outside of a company or its affiliates.

- Systems must be created to deliver the appropriate notices to customers.

- Credit bureaus will no longer be legally able to sell "credit header" information.

- Banks and other financial institutions may become limited in their ability to sell or transmit lists of customers.

- Banks and other financial institutions must draft and execute, in most cases, detailed written information security policies.[46]

- Contract provisions governing the security of information transferred from financial institutions to other entities should be reviewed and may need to be amended.

- Where a particular company may be subject to GLB regulation by more than one federal agency, particular care should be used to establish any differences in the different agencies' regulations and any provisions that may defer to a different agency's rules in such a situation.

69.3.3.2 *Children's Online Privacy Protection Act.* The Children's Online Privacy Protection Act of 1998 (COPPA) prohibits the collection, use, or disclosure of personally identifiable information from and about children under the age of 13 on the Internet without prior "verifiable parental consent."[47] Obtaining "verifiable parental consent" has proven technologically challenging for some organizations. Violations of COPPA are enforced as "unfair or deceptive" trade practices by the Federal Trade Commission.[48] Web site operators should refer to the FTC's informational Web site[49] for more information.

69.3.3.3 *Health Insurance Portability and Accountability Act.* The Health Insurance Portability and Accountability Act of 1996 (HIPAA) mandated the establishment of standards to protect the privacy and confidentiality of individually identifiable health information.[50] Under HIPAA, the Department of Health and Human Services has adopted rules to implement the legislative mandate.[51] Both civil and criminal penalties can be assessed for violations.

The HIPAA regulations present significant challenges to "covered entities." A number of the key concepts embodied in the regulations are not clearly defined. The obligations created by the regulations will require significant changes in the systems infrastructure and business processes of many affected entities. HIPAA is likely to dramatically affect any business dealing with personal information gathered in a healthcare setting. Compliance with the HIPAA privacy rules became mandatory for covered entities in April 2003, while the compliance deadline for small health plans was April 2004. The first such interpretive guidance has now been published by HHS.[52] Additional interpretations are expected. At the time of publication, legislation was pending in the United States Congress that would create new privacy requirements for electronic health records.

The key features of the HIPAA privacy regulations include:

- Providers and health plans are required to give patients a clear written explanation of how they will use, keep, and disclose information.
- Covered entities must provide patients with access to their health records.
- Permitted uses and disclosures of personally identifiable health information must, subject to certain exceptions, be limited to the "minimum amount necessary to accomplish the purpose for which the information is used or disclosed."[53]
- Disclosure logs must be kept that record each entity to which personally identifiable health information has been disclosed, and individuals must have a right to access these logs.
- A provider or payer generally is not able to condition treatment, payment, or coverage on a patient's agreement to the disclosure of health information for other purposes.
- Federal criminal penalties will apply to obtaining health information under false pretenses, and knowing and improper disclosures of health information, with penalties set higher if the violation is done for "monetary gain."

- States are not preempted from further regulation of health information, so long as an affected entity could comply with both the federal and the state requirements.
- Violations of the regulations will be subject to substantial fines.

The HIPAA regulations are complex with respect to privacy and electronic data transactions.[54] For more information on medical records security, see Chapter 71 in this *Handbook*.

69.3.3.4   Cable and Video Acts.   Although the United States has been very hesitant to pass private-sector legislation regulating how businesses use personal information, it has not altogether shied away from doing so. Two important exceptions to that general policy stance are in the form of federal legislation: the Cable Communications Policy Act[55] and the Video Privacy Protection Act.[56]

The Cable Communications Policy Act of 1984, section 551, governs the "protection of subscriber privacy." This section requires that cable television companies give their customers initial and annual notice of what personal information the companies collect, to whom it is distributed, how customers may access it, and what other limitations the act places on the companies. Cable companies are prohibited from using their cable systems to collect personal information without prior consent of customers. Companies are also prohibited from retransferring any personal information without customers' prior consent. Companies may retransfer names, addresses, and telephone numbers to other companies, but only after offering customers the chance to opt out of such disclosures. Law enforcement may obtain personal information from cable companies by court order. The act creates a private right of action for customers, which includes the ability to recover punitive damages and attorneys' fees from companies that violate it. An ongoing question concerns the application of these privacy provisions to new services offered by cable companies.

The Video Privacy Protection Act of 1988 prohibits the transfer of videotape rental and sales records except for certain narrow exceptions, including permission of the customer. Transfers of such records may be made to law enforcement agencies enforcing a warrant. Customers may bring civil suits against violators of this act. A recent case involving the social network service asserted that Blockbuster violated the act when it disclosed video purchases to Facebook subscribers.

69.3.3.5   United States/European Union Safe Harbor.   The EU Directive restricts the export of personal information to only those nations with laws offering "adequate" privacy protection.[57] Since, as of 1998, no official body in the EU had determined U.S. law to be "adequate," ongoing data transfers from Europe to the United States across a wide number of significant industries (airlines, entertainment, credit cards, retailing) were in jeopardy of disruption.

In April 1998, U.S. and European Commission officials entered into negotiations to create a "Safe Harbor" for American companies desiring to import from Europe personal information relating to European citizens, by which American companies (and their trading counterparts) would not be required to prove the "adequacy" of American law as a condition to the execution of data transfers. Difficult negotiations ultimately produced, in July 2000, an arrangement under which transfers of personal information from the European Union to the United States will be allowed for those companies willing to comply with the "Safe Harbor" principles.[58] In substance, the principles are similar to the requirements of the directive. Under those principles, in the absence of committing to the jurisdiction of European officials, an American company importing personal information on European citizens must:

- Comply with the Safe Harbor principles, according to the guidance offered in the FAQs (see http://www.export.gov/safeHarbor/ for more details).
- Self-certify, on a voluntary basis, with the U.S. Department of Commerce its adherence to principles for the protection of personal information that are consistent with European legal principles, which adherence must be publicly announced.
- Provide for independent third-party verification that the company adheres to the Safe Harbor principles. This step can be accomplished by joining a self-regulatory privacy program that adheres to the Safe Harbor. Joining such an organization can, by itself, also qualify the company for the Safe Harbor. Examples such as TRUSTe or BBBOnline have been cited as representative of the types of programs contemplated; in effect, the U.S. and EU governments are encouraging self-regulation, deferring to nongovernment programs to enforce suitable standards on participating companies.[59]

Companies subject to explicit federal regulations regarding the privacy of personal information (e.g., HIPAA)[60] may in the future be eligible to self-certify their compliance with the applicable laws and gain the Safe Harbor recognition that would permit their transactions with European data to occur.[61] In the meantime, companies must be subject to the jurisdiction of the Federal Trade Commission for unfair or deceptive trade practices, under the U.S. Federal Trade Commission Act, or subject to the jurisdiction of the U.S. Department of Transportation in order to be eligible to join the Safe Harbor.[62] Failure of a company that has joined the Safe Harbor to abide by its stated privacy policy is actionable under the FTC act as an unfair or deceptive trade practice.[63] In addition, companies would be subject to sanctions under other applicable laws.[64]

Currently, European officials in those nations that have enacted laws responsive to the EU Directive are authorized to enforce those laws against American companies, or their trading partners, involved in exporting personal information. To date, few conspicuous actions have been taken (largely as a result of an informal "standstill" agreed on during the pendency of the Safe Harbor negotiations).[65] As of May 22, 2008, there are 1,461 organizations on the Safe Harbor List. However, 284 organizations are designated "not current" with respect to certification status. There is no indication on the Commerce Department Web site that any organization has received a noncompliance letter for "persistent failure to comply" with Safe Harbor.

69.3.3.6 *Workplace Privacy.*   Software has been developed, and is increasingly used, to monitor employee e-mail, voicemail, and Web usage. Some software can record every keystroke made by an employee,[66] or allow an employer to see what Web page the employee has on the screen in real time.

The area of workplace privacy presents an especially difficult Hobson's choice for employers. Monitoring gives rise to assertions of invasion of privacy, and the failure to monitor gives rise to claims of negligence in failing to detect and act on claims of maintaining a discriminatory work environment.

In the United States, the common law is fairly well established that because employers own the computer equipment and networks used by their employees, and particularly where employees have been given explicit notice that their Web usage or e-mail may be subject to monitoring, employers may monitor such computer usage.[67]

The Electronic Communications Privacy Act (ECPA) (see Section 69.3.2.2) is the only federal statute relevant to claims of workplace invasions of privacy by electronic means. ECPA prohibits unauthorized and intentional "interception" of wire, oral, and electronic communications during the transmission phase and unauthorized "accessing" of electronically stored wire or electronic communications. An e-mail is an "electronic communication."[68]

ECPA contains two important exceptions. The first is the "system provider" exception. There is considerable debate whether an employer who provides a company system for e-mail and/or Internet access is covered by this exception. The second is the "consent" exception. Under this exception, an employer may intercept electronic communications if the prior consent of *one* of the parties to the communication has been obtained.[69] Hence, an employer needs the implied or express consent of *only* the employee. An employee probably will be considered to have given consent if he or she continues to use a communications system after having been advised of the employer's monitoring policy, although evidence of explicit consent through a signed writing, a returned e-mail, or other technique is clearly preferable. For this reason, many companies require that employees agree to the company monitoring policy in writing as a condition of employment.

While voicemail is subject to employer monitoring by the same rules that apply to e-mail, live employee telephone calls, even when made from company phones on company time, are subject to different rules. ECPA's prohibition on the "interception" of telephone calls during the transmission phase requires that employers not monitor employees' *non–work-related* telephone calls. Although it is awkward, the rule requires employers to cease monitoring of employees' telephone calls upon the first indication that the call is made for personal purposes.[70]

In Florida and Maryland, state law requires that *both* parties to a communication consent to the monitoring of that communication.[71] Obtaining only an employee's consent therefore is unlikely to be legally sufficient to allow such monitoring in these states. In addition, other state laws governing the monitoring and interception of communications may apply. As of the publication deadline date of this chapter, however, there were no laws at either the state or the federal level prohibiting workplace e-mail or Web usage monitoring in the United States.

In the European Union, all workplace monitoring is considered to be the collection of personal information and is subject to the terms of the Data Protection Directive, discussed earlier.

69.3.3.7   Anonymity of Internet Postings and "Cybersmearing."   Internet chat rooms, forums, and message boards have been used increasingly by disgruntled employees, customers, competitors, and others to attempt to damage or artificially elevate the stature of companies in the marketplace. Postings may include personal attacks; assertions about a company's business practices, the quality of its goods and services, or the worth of its stock. Such postings may be highly offensive to particular individuals, may result in intangible changes of perception about a company in the marketplace, or may result in a very real and measurable impact on the company's stock price. Understandably, companies that find themselves subject to such postings may wish to take action.

Options that a company may wish to consider when faced with negative or harmful Internet postings follow.

- **Do nothing.** Posters of negative messages may feed on the attention created by a public response. If ignored, they may become disinterested in pursuing the activity.
- **Utilize investigators to identify the poster.** If the poster's identity is known and the person is contacted by the company's counsel, the poster may cease the offending activity.
- **Contact law enforcement.** This option is appropriate where postings seem to have been intended to manipulate stock prices or where messages threaten or suggest harm to individuals or property.
- **File suit against "John Doe" and subpoena the relevant ISP to discover the identity of the poster.** This option is not as straightforward as it may seem. Many "John Doe" defendants have vigorously challenged such subpoenas,[72] and a recent court decision ruled that an ISP did not have to reveal the poster's identity.[73]

For a more detailed review of anonymity in cyberspace, see Chapter 70 in this *Handbook*.

69.3.3.8 Online Monitoring Technology. Much of the public concern surrounding privacy has derived from the use of various technologies to monitor Internet usage and compile information about users, often without clear notice to consumers. This section gives a brief description of the most prevalent technologies currently in use for online information gathering.

"Cookies" are small text files that are placed by a Web server onto the hard drive of an Internet user when that user visits a Web site. Cookies allow Web servers to "recognize" computers bearing their cookies when users revisit Web sites. Web sites can use cookies to monitor what pages users view, what sites they come from to the Web site, and where they go when they leave the site; cookies also can be used to trigger stored user settings and preferences at the Web site. The use of cookies is almost ubiquitous on commercial Web sites. Users have the ability, through browser software, to view and delete cookies or to set their browsers to reject them or warn them each time a cookie is placed.

"Web beacons," also called "Web bugs," "single-pixel Graphics Interface Formats," (GIFs) or "clear GIFs," are extremely small graphics files, invisible to the naked eye, that are used by online advertisers to gather marketing data. Web beacons function by recognizing cookies. When a user visits a Web site bearing a company's Web beacon, that company can now learn that this is the same user who visited that company's own site earlier. Or, if the cookie was placed by an advertising company, the company can identify each site that the user visits that bears the company's Web beacons. This allows company to know more about users' exact Internet usage and surfing patterns than were possible using only cookies. Unlike the case with cookies, browsers do not readily detect the presence of Web beacons, nor do Web site privacy policies typically disclose the use of Web beacons.[74] Their use has provoked increasing consumer uneasiness; therefore, companies should proceed with care when electing to use or host Web beacons.

69.3.3.9 Location Privacy. An explosion in the use of wireless devices, many of which are equipped with Global Positioning System (GPS) devices that allow for the identification or monitoring of the location of the device, has spurred corresponding public concern over how to protect the privacy of location information. Great marketing opportunities are envisioned, such as being able to extend special offers to consumers who are in the physical vicinity of a store or restaurant, but many people also have identified the potential for abuses. Great concern has been expressed by privacy advocates that information about individuals' every move will become available before any clear rules are established concerning the protection or use of that information.

Because the technology that allows for the collection and use of this information is so new, industry best practices have not yet developed, and little legal guidance is available. It is expected, however, that location privacy will be the subject of intense policy and legislative debate over the next several years. Location-based advertising raises particular concerns when consumers are expected to pay the cost of incoming messages. There are also questions about the appropriate legal standards to access location information for law enforcement purposes. Because of consumer and media sensitivity to issues of location privacy, companies should carefully consider the legal and public relations aspects of collecting, using, or transferring such information.

69.3.3.10   Genetic Discrimination.   The collection and use of genetic information raises particular privacy concerns because this information can be used to determine whether individuals are prone to certain illnesses. This has implications for both employment and health insurance determinations. Among the most significant privacy bills recently enacted in the United States is the Genetic Information Nondiscrimination Act. The act prohibits discrimination on the basis of genetic information with respect to health insurance and employment. From introduction to final passage, the bill took almost a dozen years.

69.3.3.11   Social Network Sites and Privacy.   Among the most closely watched new areas of concern are the privacy impact of social network sites, such as Facebook and MySpace.[75] Concerns arise with respect to both the amount of personal information, particularly of minors, that is made available over the Internet, and also the advertising techniques that involve the collection and use of personal information. When Facebook introduced a revised News Feed service in 2006, the company was accused of invading the privacy of users and facilitating stalking. Over 700,000 users signed an online petition demanding the company discontinue the feature, stating that this compromised their privacy. Subsequently, Mark Zuckerberg, the CEO of Facebook, published an open letter apologizing for not having consulted with users prior to changing the service.

In 2007, the European Network and Information Security Agency issued a report on social networks and privacy. The paper concludes that social networks are a clear benefit to society; however, the study warns of the danger that new technologies pose in a world where there may be a false sense of intimacy created by social networks. The paper recommends government and corporate policy changes, increasing transparency of data handling practices, and encouraging social networking education rather than the banning of social networking sites in schools.[76] In 2008, the International Working Group on Data Protection in Telecommunications released a report and guidance on privacy in social networking services. The report identifies risks to privacy and security, and provides guidance to regulators, service operators, and users to counter these risks. Risks include the large amount of data collection; the misuse of profile data by third parties; insecure infrastructure and application programming interfaces. Regulators should ensure openness and require data breach notification. Providers must be transparent, live up to promises made to users, and use privacy friendly defaults. Privacy and consumer groups are also encouraged to raise the awareness of regulators, providers, and the general public.[77]

69.3.4 State Legislation.   As noted in other sections, most federal privacy laws and regulations in the United States do not preempt state law. Most often, federal statutes set a "floor" upon which states may create stricter rules. This approach to legislating is important because it reflects the federalism form of government that grants states significant power. It also allows the states to develop new approaches to emerging privacy challenges and to operate as "laboratories of democracy." Not surprisingly, in the absence of substantial federal legislation, U.S. states have acted aggressively to pass new legislation regarding personal information.

The important point regarding state privacy laws is that such laws are numerous and often organized by industry or commercial sector. A company always should research the laws of the state(s) in which it operates to determine whether there are state-level laws that affect its use of personal information.

States already have passed legislation concerning emerging privacy issues, such as DNA databases, RFID tags, and other new technologies. Examples of significant privacy state laws follow.

- California passed an influential security breach notification in 2003. SB 1386 requires "any person or business that conducts business in California, and that owns or licenses computerized data that includes personal information, [to] disclose any breach of the security system . . . to any resident of California whose unencrypted personal information was, or is reasonably believed to have been, acquired by an unauthorized person." The statute imposes specific notification requirements on companies in such circumstances. The statute applies regardless of whether the computerized consumer records are maintained in or outside California. Many states subsequently passed security breach laws similar to California, and California subsequently extended the legislation in 2007 to cover medical records.

- California also enacted strong consumer privacy legislation in 2003. The California Financial Information Privacy Act provides the strongest financial privacy protections in the United States. Among the key provisions, the law gives consumers greater control over their personal information held by businesses, requires simple and understandable notices, and includes strong penalties.[78]

- According to the National Conference of State Legislatures, the majority of state legislatures have taken steps to safeguard genetic information beyond the protections provided for other types of health information. The state of New Mexico, for example, grants the individual the right to access genetic information, requires consent for a wide range of purposes, and establishes specific penalties for violations of genetic privacy.[79]

- Several states have passed laws to regulate the use of RFID. Washington State passed a law in 2008 that makes it a felony to intentionally scan another person's identification remotely without his or her knowledge and consent, for the purpose of fraud, identity theft, or some other illegal purpose.[80] A 2006 law in Wisconsin prevents the forcible implementation of RFID tags into humans.

69.4 COMPLIANCE MODELS.   Responding to the challenges presented by rapidly developing privacy laws and the threats posed by hackers, requires the confrontation of complex new issues. A number of different paradigms are emerging. Each is interrelated, but for purposes of explanation, it may be best to consider each individually. Real-world solutions to privacy issues will, in almost every case, involve the use of multiple overlapping compliance models. This section illustrates, by providing a broad overview, the various models that are emerging as themes of privacy law compliance.

69.4.1 U.S. Legislation.   The primary compliance model for privacy protection is the enactment of law that makes clear the obligations of organizations that collect and use personal information and the rights of individuals who provide personal information. Privacy legislation is typically based on Fair Information Practices that are intended to promote the flow of personal data but to do so in a way that makes clear the purposes for which personal information is collected and will be used. Privacy legislation typically includes a variety of enforcement mechanisms, including a private right of action that allows an individual, or group of individuals, to file a lawsuit when a provision of the law has been violated; enforcement by the state of attorney generals, which can be particularly important when there is a pattern or practice of violation; as well as action by the Federal Trade Commission, which has the power to investigate unfair and deceptive trade practices.

69.4.2 U.S. Federal Trade Commission Section 5 Authority.   The United States Federal Trade Commission has authority to investigate unfair or deceptive trade practices under Section 5 of the FTC Act. The FTC has applied this authority in a varity of privacy cases, involving primarily negligent security practices.

69.4.3 Self-Regulatory Regimes and Codes of Conduct.   Self-regulatory regimes, including industry codes of conduct, are emerging as a means for achieving compliance with fair information practices among businesses. Self-regulation has two appealing aspects: (1) it minimizes the need for government to devote resources to enforcement, and (2) it allows the greatest degree of flexibility of business practices—important to those who stress that overregulation will stunt the growth of electronic commerce.

At the same time, self-regulatory approaches have come under increasing scrutiny from privacy officials, consumer organizations, and political leaders, particularly in the European Union. The EU national data protection commissioners (the Article 29 Committee) opposed the Safe Harbor proposal as inadequate. The Trans Atlantic Consumer Dialogue found that there was insufficient enforcement.[81] The European Parliament challenged the adequacy of the Safe Harbor Arrangement with the United States.[82]

Codes of conduct are explicitly contemplated by the EU Data Protection Directive as one means of compliance. The directive encourages EU member states to foster codes of conduct within self-policing industries as a means of ensuring compliance with data protection laws across entire business sectors.[83]

69.4.4 Contract Infrastructure.   Several privacy laws contemplate the use of contracts to define how personal information will be collected, used, and/or transferred. Although the specific uses of contracts vary from law to law, an underlying trend is emerging: The rules governing the entire "life cycle" of personal information will be supplemented and maintained by a network of contracts.

Personal information, under most privacy laws, is collected from an individual subject to the terms of how that information will be used and to whom it may be transferred. In the absence of law, industry standards, or other guidelines, the rules for how personal information may be used are defined by the policies given to the data subject. Preferably, these policies will incorporate all of the elements of fair information practices. Once a company has collected personal information, it must process and use the data pursuant to the rules. Since personal information often passes from the collecting company to its affiliates, service providers, and others, additional contracts must be executed among and between all of these entities to ensure that the rules originally defined in the notice are followed.

Companies should begin to think about a "chain of contracts" that starts with fair information practices for the data subject—essentially a contract between the company and the individual. The terms of that contract are then enforced, by means of other contractual relationships, as personal information moves to different business entities, across national boundaries, and to third-party businesses.

69.4.5 Synthesis of Contracts, Technology, and Law. Contracts alone are not a complete solution to privacy issues. Although indemnity provisions and contractual warranties may, on paper, ensure that personal information has been properly collected, used, and transferred, the practical realities of the situation may be otherwise. Some points to consider:

- Policing such contracts may be beyond the means or the inclinations of many businesses.
- Most businesses are not likely to sue their trading partners to enforce these contracts, except in the most grievous cases.
- Most consumers do not perceive themselves as having enough at stake to bring actions on an individual level, but the possibility of class-action lawsuits may exist.
- The security of personal data, once compromised, is difficult to resecure—it is hard to unring the bell.
- Finally, given the massiveness of the data files typically involved, the speed with which data can be moved, and the multiplicity of jurisdictions into which it can be sent, governmental enforcement may face a larger challenge than governments will be willing to pay for.

Accordingly, technological controls on the collection, processing, access, storage, and transfer of personal information become a key element in the management of personal information.

Technology can be used to enforce the contract infrastructure (see Section 69.4.2). For instance, when a customer makes a choice not to be included on a mailing list, it is technology that will segregate that person's information and ensure that the choice is honored. It is technology that will ensure that information relating to all the people who opted out of a proposed use of their data is not transferred to a third party for marketing uses. And it is, therefore, technology that ensures that the third party receiving personal information for marketing uses can use the information in those ways without incurring regulatory or public relations damage. Even simple policing techniques, such as the use of dummy names to detect unauthorized uses by onward transferees, can be administered more effectively using modern information technology. In this example, contracts and technology combine to add value. Contracts set terms of use for personal information that eliminate legal risk; technology ensures that the terms are followed. The end product is a valuable asset—usable personal information, the currency of the new economy.

It is vital that technological infrastructures embody both the specific legal rules that a company must observe with respect to personal information and the contracts created to manage that compliance process. Likewise, it is vital that the contracts themselves embody the legal requirements, the needs of the business, and the limitations of available technology. Business processes must adapt to the realities of the law, but must utilize technology and contractual relationships in order to maximize profits. To manage personal information assets effectively, technologists and businesspeople must begin to think about law, while lawyers must become familiar with technology and business.

69.4.6 Getting Started: A Practical Checklist.

An outline of some of the practical steps that must be taken for an organization to begin to implement effective personal information management practices follows. This checklist is not all-inclusive but is designed to illustrate how the core privacy principles and different compliance models begin to interact in the management process.

- Achieve buy-in, at the highest level of the organization, to the idea that personal information management must be part of an organization's critical infrastructure.
- Perform due diligence to identify *all* types of personal information collected and the routes by which the data travel in and out of the organization.
- Identify all of the uses to which the information is put during its life cycle through collection, processing, use, transfer, storage, and destruction.
- Identify each law affecting the collection, use, and transfer of personal information to which the company is subject.
- Create an institutional privacy policy that accurately considers both a commitment to abide by various legal requirements and the legitimate business activities of the organization.
- Create supporting materials that educate employees and instruct on policy implementation.
- Implement consistent data transfer agreements with all data-trading partners, vendors, service providers, and others with whom personal information is acquired or transferred.
- Build privacy management into the organization's strategic planning, providing sufficient resources for personnel, training, technology, and compliance auditing.
- Hold employees accountable for implementation and compliance with the privacy policy and contract requirements.
- Consider innovative approaches to privacy protection and business development that limit or eliminate the collection of personally identifiable information.
- Periodically audit compliance.

69.5 FURTHER READING

Agre, P. E., and M. Rotenberg. *Technology and Privacy: The New Landscape.* Cambridge, MA: MIT Press, 1998.
Bennett, C. J. and C. D. Raab. *The Governance of Privacy: Policy Instruments in a Global Perspective.* Cambridge, MA: MIT Press, 2006.

Bygrave, L. A. *Data Protection Law: Approaching Its Rationale, Logic and Limits.* The Hague: Kluwer Law International, 2002.

Garfinkel, S., and B. Rosenberg. *RFID Applications, Security, and Privacy.* Upper Saddle River, NJ: Addision-Wesley, 2006.

Nora, S. and A. Minc. *The Computerization of Society.* Cambridge, MA: MIT Press, 1981.

Rosen, J. *The Unwanted Gaze: The Destruction of Privacy in America.* New York: Random House, 2000.

Rotenberg, M. *Privacy and Human Rights 2006.* Washington, DC: Electronic Privacy Information Center and Privacy International, 2006.

Rotenberg, M. *The Privacy Law Sourcebook 2004.* Washington, DC: Electronic Privacy Information Center, 2006.

Solove, D. J., M. Rotenberg, and P. J. Schwartz. *Information Privacy Law.* New York: Aspen, 2006.

WEB SITES

- Department of Commerce, Safe Harbor: http://www.export.gov/safeHarbor/
- Electronic Privacy Information Center: www.epic.org
- European Commission, Justice and Home Affairs, Data Protection: ec.europa.eu/justice_home/fsj/privacy/index_en.htm
- Federal Trade Commission, Privacy Initiatives: www.ftc.gov/privacy/
- National Conference of State Legislatures, NCSL 50—State Legislative Tracking Resources: www.ncsl.org/programs/lis/lrl/50statetracking.htm
- Privacy, Business and Law—Pandab is an online newsletter summarizing the top news articles on privacy, law and business: www.pandab.org
- Privacy Exchange—a global information resource on consumers, commerce, and date protection worldwide: www.privacyexchange.org
- Privacy International—Privacy International (PI) is a human rights group formed in 1990 as a watchdog on surveillance and privacy invasions by governments and corporations: www.privacyinternational.org

69.6 NOTES

1. In this context, various non-U.S. legal systems, especially European law, tend to use the term "data protection," while the law in the United States tends to use the term "privacy." This chapter uses the terms interchangeably, although readers should be aware that "privacy" often is considered to be a broader concept than "data protection."

2. An excellent summary of these emerging principles is found in "National Principles for the Fair Handling of Personal Information," issued by the Office of the Privacy Commissioner, Australia (revised ed., January 1999), available at: www.privacy.gov.au/business/index.html.

3. E.g., the Fourth Amendment to the U.S. Constitution.

4. The U.S. Freedom of Information Act typifies the former trend; the constitutions of Argentina and South Africa typify the latter.

5. See Draft Charter of Fundamental Rights of the European Union, Charter 4487/00, Brussels, September 28, 2000: Article 7 ("Respect for Private and Family Life")

of the charter states: "Everyone has the right to respect for his or her private and family life, home and communications." Article 8 ("Protection of Personal Data") states: "1. Everyone has the right to the protection of personal data concerning him or her. 2. Such data must be processed fairly for specified purposes and on the basis of the consent of the person concerned or some other legitimate basis laid down by law. Everyone has the right of access to data that has been collected concerning him or her, and the right to have it rectified. 3. Compliance with these rules shall be subject to control by an independent authority."

6. Sweden: The Data Act of 1973, found in Svensk Författningssamling (SFS; Swedish Code of Statutes) 1973: 289, amended at SFS 1982: 446; United States: The Privacy Act of 1974, P.L. 93-579, 5 U.S.C. §552a; Germany: The Federal Data Protection Act (BDSG), available in English in Ulrich Dammann, Otto Mallmann, and Spiros Simitis, eds., *Data Protection Legislation: An International Documentation* (Frankfurt am Main: [West] Germany, 1977); France: Loi No. 78-17 du 6 janvier 1978 relative à l'informatique, aux fichiers et aux libertés, *Journal Officiel de la République Française*, January 7, 1978.

7. ETS No. 108, Strasbourg, 1981. Available at: www.coe.fr/eng/legaltxt/108e.htm.

8. Paris, 1981. An important distinction in the activities of the OECD (as opposed to the activities of the COE) is the involvement and support of the U.S. government. The OECD is supported by nearly 30 governments. For more information, see: www.oecd.org.

9. Council of Europe, Convention for the Protection of Individuals with regard to Automatic Processing of Personal Data (ETS No. 108): conventions.coe.int/Treaty/Commun/ChercheSig.asp?NT=108&CM=1&DF=&CL=ENG (status May 18, 2008).

10. For example, Hong Kong, Estonia, and Lithuania seem to have based their privacy laws, in part, on the OECD Guidelines. Brazil and Malaysia are currently considering passage of privacy laws based on the OECD Guidelines.

11. See www.oecd.org/privacy.htm.

12. Directive 95/46/EC of the European Parliament and of the Council of October 24, 1995, on the protection of individuals with regard to the processing of personal information and on the free movement of such data, text available at: europa.eu.int/eur-lex/en/lif/dat/1995/en_395L0046.html.

13. Justice and Home Affairs—Data Protection—the law—Status of implementation of Directive 95/46: ec.europa.eu/justice_home/fsj/privacy/law/implementation_en.htm

14. Hong Kong, New Zealand, Chile, Argentina, and Canada have passed such laws; Japan, India, Brazil, and Australia, among others, have proposed new conforming legislation.

15. The Czech Republic, Hungary, Poland, Latvia, and Estonia have already passed national legislation that mimics the EU model. Romania, Turkey, and Russia, among others, have proposed such legislation.

16. Directive Concerning the Processing of Personal Data and the Protection of Privacy in the Telecommunications Sector (Directive 97/66/EC of the European Parliament and of the Council of December 15, 1997), available at: www.ispo.cec.be/legal/en/dataprot/protection.html.

17. See David Banisar, *Privacy & Human Rights 2000*, EPIC and Privacy International; available at: www.privacyinternational.org/survey/phr2000/threats.html.

18. European Commission, "Proposal for a Directive of the European Parliament and of the Council Concerning the Processing of Personal Data and the Protection of Privacy in the Electronic Communications Sector," available at: europa.eu. institutionalize/comm/information_society/policy/framework/pdf/com2000385_en .pdf.

19. Justice and Home Affairs—Data Proection—European Data Protection Supervisor, ec.europa.eu/justice_home/fsj/privacy/eusupervisor/index_en.htm.

20. Charles Warren and Louis Brandeis, "The Right of Privacy," 4 *Harvard Law Review* 193 (1890).

21. See, e.g., *Cox Broadcasting v. Cohn*, 420 U.S. 469 (1975); *Time, Inc. v. Hill*, 385 U.S. 374 (1967).

22. See Restatement (2d), Torts, § 652.

23. 5 U.S.C. § 552a. 5 U.S.C. § 552 incorporates the Freedom of Information Act (originally passed in 1966).

24. The Fair Credit Reporting Act of 1970 (15 U.S.C. § 1681 *et seq.*) was arguably the first sweeping privacy law.

25. P.L. 93-579, congressional finding and statement of purpose, paragraph (b).

26. 18 U.S.C. § 3121 et seq.

27. See *Smith v. Maryland*, 442 U.S. 735, 742–45 (1979).

28. 18 U.S.C. § 3122(b)(2).

29. See 12 U.S.C. §§ 3401–22.

30. 18 U.S.C. § 2721 (1994).

31. See *Reno v. Condon*, 528 U.S. 141 (2000).

32. "Earthlink Says It Refuses to Install FBI's Carnivore Surveillance Device," *Wall Street Journal*, July 14, 2000.

33. For more details on monitoring and surveillance, see Banisar, "Privacy & Human Rights."

34. See "Interception Capabilities 2000" (Part 2/5: "The State of the Art in Communications Intelligence [COMINT] of the Automated Processing for Intelligence Purposes of Intercepted Broadband Multi-language Leased or Common Carrier Systems, and Its Applicability to COMINT Targeting and Selection, Including Speech Recognition"), European Parliament, PE 168. 184 Vol. 2/5.

35. 47 U.S.C. §1001 et seq.

36. See *United States Telecom Ass'n v. FCC*, 227 F.3d 450 (D.C. Cir. 2000).

37. Council of Europe, Convention on Cybercrime, CETS No. 185: conventions. coe.int/Treaty/Commun/QueVoulezVous.asp?NT=185&CM=8&DF=5/19/2008 &CL=ENG.

38. Council of Europe, Convention on Cybercrime, CETS No. 185, Status of May 19, 2008 conventions.coe.int/Treaty/Commun/ChercheSig.asp?NT=185& CM=8&DF=5/19/2008&CL=ENG.

39. See, e.g., www.cdt.org/international/cybercrime/001211cdt.shtml.

40. Signed into law on November 12, 1999; to be codified at 15 U.S.C. § 6801 *et seq.*

41. The Federal Deposit Insurance Corporation (FDIC), the Office of the Comptroller of the Currency (OCC), the Office of Thrift Supervision (OTS), and the Federal Reserve Board issued joint regulations. The Securities and Exchange Commission (SEC), the National Credit Union Administration (NCUA), the Commodity Futures

Trading Commission (CFTC), and the Federal Trade Commission (FTC) have each issued separate sets of regulations.

42. See 47248 *Federal Register*, Vol. 61, No. 174, Friday, September 6, 1996.

43. See 12 CFR Ch. 11 § 211.5(d).

44. Individuals with whom a "financial institution" has an ongoing relationship.

45. All individuals who seek financial products or services for personal, family, or household purposes, whether or not those products or services are ever actually obtained.

46. A degree of variation has emerged concerning required information security standards under GLB. The SEC and CFTC regulations set forth very general requirements; the OTS, OCC, FDIC and Federal Reserve Board jointly issued detailed information security guidelines (66 *Federal Register* 8615, February 1, 2001); the NCUA also issued guidelines paralleling those issued by the banking agencies (66 *Federal Register* 8152, January 29, 2001); the FTC issued a proposed regulation that represents a significant simplification of the banking agencies' guidelines (66 *Federal Register* 46112, August 7, 2001).

47. 15 U.S.C. § 6501 *et seq.*

48. 16 CFR § 312.9.

49. See: www.ftc.gov/bcp/conline/pubs/buspubs/coppa.htm.

50. P.L. 104-191, August 21, 1996.

51. The final rule was published December 28, 2000, at 65 *Federal Register* 82,461 (2000).

52. Available at: www.hhs.gov/ocr/hipaa/finalmaster.html.

53. See 45 CFR § 164.506

54. More information about HIPAA's privacy regulations can be obtained at: www.hhs.gov/ocr/hipaa or at hipaadvisory.com.

55. 47 U.S.C. § 551 (1984).

56. 18 U.S.C. § 2710 (1988).

57. See Section 69.2.1.2.2 for more details.

58. The full text of the Safe Harbor Principles is available at www.ita.doc.gov/td/ecom/menu.html.

59. Additional information on TRUSTe and BBBOnline can be obtained at www.truste.org and www.bbbonline.org. Note that neither organization offers certification of offline privacy practices and is therefore not available as a complete solution to any company that engages in any type of offline collection or use of the personal information of EU residents.

60. The European Commission has deferred a review of whether the privacy provisions of GLB are "adequate" pending implementation and possible further legislative action in the United States.

61. Although the Safe Harbor principles allow for "adequacy" determinations for U.S. business sectors that are subject to particular sectoral privacy laws, no determination has yet been made of the adequacy of any particular law.

62. See Introduction and Annex to Safe Harbor Principles: 15 U.S.C. § 45. Note that banks, savings and loans, and entities such as stockyards and meat packers are excluded from the scope of the FTC act and are therefore not eligible for Safe Harbor membership.

63. See draft Safe Harbor FAQ No. 11: Dispute Resolution and Enforcement, available at: www.ita.doc.gov/td/ecom/RedlinedFAQ11Enforc300.htm. Note that entities that are eligible for Safe Harbor membership because they are subject to the jurisdiction of the Department of Transportation may be subject to enforcement actions brought by the department.

64. See draft Safe Harbor FAQ No. 11: Dispute Resolution and Enforcement.

65. The "Safe Harbor" came into effect in early November 2000. The informal stay of enforcement by EU Data Protection Authorities against U.S. companies was due to end in June 2001. Some enforcement actions have been brought against U.S. companies already; for instance, American Airlines was forced to change its practices with respect to passenger information by the Swedish authority and Microsoft was fined $60,000 in Spain.

66. During 2001, such keystroke monitoring was the subject of increasing controversy. In the first case testing the use of such technology for law enforcement purposes, a federal judge in New Jersey recently ordered the U.S. government to reveal how it had performed keystroke monitoring of an alleged criminal. See Opinion and Order, August 7, 2001, *United States v. Nicodemo Scarfo et al.*, available at: www2.epic.org/crypto/scarfo/order_8_7_01.pdf. In another recent incident, judges of the Ninth U.S. Circuit Court, based in San Francisco, ordered their information technology personnel to remove keystroke-monitoring software that had been installed on their computers by order of the Judicial Conference of the United States. See Neil Lewis, "Rebels in Black Robes Recoil at Surveillance of Computers," *New York Times*, August 8, 2001.

67. See, e.g., *Smyth v. Pillsbury Co.*, 914 F. Supp. 97 (E.D. Pa. 1996).

68. 18 U.S.C. § 2510.

69. 18 U.S.C. § 2511(2)(d).

70. See *Watkins v. L.M. Berry & Company,* 704 F.2d 577 (11th Cir. 1983); *Ali v. Douglas Cable Communications,* 929 F. Supp. 1362 (D. Kan. 1996); *U.S. v. Murdock,* 63 F.3d 1391 (6th Cir. 1995); *Deal v. Spears,* 980 F.2d 1153 (8th Cir. 1992).

71. Fla. Stat. 934.03-934.09; Md. Cts. & Jud. Proc.Code Ann. Sec. 10-402 (1980). The Maryland law was the basis for the criminal investigation into Linda Tripp's recording of her conversations with Monica Lewinsky regarding then-president Clinton.

72. See www.johndoes.org for more information.

73. See *Dendrite International, Inc. v. John Does 1-14, et al.*, New Jersey Superior Court (Morris/Sussex Vicinage), November 28, 2000, docket no. MRSC-129-00.

74. Free software that allows users to identify Web beacons on websites is available at: www.bugnosis.com.

75. EPIC, Social Networking Privacy, epic.org/privacy/socialnet/default.html.

76. ENISA, Security Issues And Recommendations for Social Networks (October 2007): www.enisa.europa.eu/doc/pdf/deliverables/enisa_pp_social_networks.pdf.

77. International Working Group on Data Protection in Telecommunications, Report and Guidance on Privacy in Social Network Services, "Rome Memorandum" (March 2008): www.datenschutz-berlin.de/attachments/461/WP_social_network_services.pdf?1208438491.

78. Privacy Rights Clearinghouse, "California Financial Information Privacy Act: Senate Bill 1 (Speier & Burton): www.privacyrights.org/ar/SB1Info.htm.

79. National Conference of State Legislatures, "State Genetic Privacy Laws," updated January 2008): www.ncsl.org/programs/health/genetics/prt.htm.

80. "First of Its Kind RFID Law Prohibits Malicious Spying on Consumers," www.prweb.com/releases/2008/03/prweb803114.htm.

81. Submission of the TACD, March 30, 2000 at: www.ita.doc.gov/td/ecom/Comments400/TACDComments1.htm.

82. European Parliament resolution on the Draft Commission Decision on the adequacy of the protection provided by the Safe Harbor Privacy Principles and related Frequently Asked Questions issued by the U.S. Department of Commerce (C5-0280/2000–2000/2144(COS)): epic.org/privacy/intl/EP_SH_resolution_0700.html.

83. Directive 95/46/EC, Article 27. The International Commercial Exchange provides an example of such an industry initiative. See www.icx.org for more information.

ANONYMITY AND IDENTITY IN CYBERSPACE

M. E. Kabay, Eric Salveggio, and Robert Guess

70.1 INTRODUCTION. As electronic communications technology becomes widespread among increasingly international populations of computer users, one of the most hotly debated questions is how to maintain the benefits of free discourse while simultaneously restricting antisocial communications and behavior on the Net. The debate is complicated by the international and intercultural dimensions of communications today; what is viewed as freedom in some parts of the world is perceived as license in other communities. Conversely, what are conceived by some as attempts to impose civility on international discourse are sometimes rejected as gross interference in freedom of speech by others.

At the heart of much of the debate over the advisability and possibility of imposing limits on behavior in cyberspace is the question of identity. Some of the most egregious abuse of cyberspace seems reasonably to be attributable in part to the ease of concealing identity; using no names or false names, malefactors can often escape almost all of the consequences of their actions. The FBI and other U.S. federal agencies consider identity theft a serious issue for law enforcement and national security: "Identity theft not only victimizes the individuals whose identity is stolen, but it can also pose a public safety and national security risk. . . . It is imperative that law enforcement know the true identity of the individuals they encounter while protecting our communities."[1]

Corporations and individuals can suffer serious damage to their interests from abuse of anonymous communications. For example, denial-of-service (DoS) attacks depend on concealing the origins of the streams of spurious data. The availability of anonymous, highly critical postings to discussion groups about specific companies has resulted in problems in hiring new staff and depression of stock prices.[2] Anonymous abuse of individuals can cause great personal distress; in 1997, for example, an Annapolis, Maryland, woman was mail-bombed after she warned other writers about extortionate fees from an author's agency; her name, phone number, and address were posted on alt.sex groups on the Usenet and resulted in floods of offensive phone calls.[3] A woman in Atlanta was appalled when someone posted a photograph of an unknown anonymous woman with the victim's name and contact information; she received calls from men who told her the announcement claimed she was offering free sex. A victim of such anonymous harassment founded WHO@ (Working to Halt Online Abuse) to help victims fight this oppression.[4] The CyberAngels, an offshoot of the Guardian Angels vigilante group, claim to be willing and able to help victims.[5]

In Florida, two students posted a picture of one of their high school classmates on a Web site. The boy was pictured dancing with his prom date—but the girl's head was replaced by the picture of one of their male teachers. An electronic voice on the site announced that the teacher "must die." The student was profoundly disturbed by the intimations of homosexuality, as were the teacher and his colleagues. However, the state attorney's office reluctantly concluded that there is no valid state statute making it illegal for someone to publish libelous information anonymously on the Net. Although Florida does have a law forbidding "anonymous publication of material that holds a person up to ridicule or contempt," legal experts concluded that such a limitation on speech is unconstitutional.

One of the biggest issues facing law enforcement is how to deal with cyber threats, especially anonymous threats. Many of the current laws, while similar in nature, are defused in court over technicalities by shrewd lawyers. It has been stated that new laws covering these new threats are sorely needed, but that the system is about five years behind the times.[6]

In an early case of cyber-harassment, an innocent Florida businessman, Bruce Hovland, was harassed in 1997 by thousands of phone calls from angry strangers who complained about junk e-mail that threatened to bill their credit cards for almost $200 in return for nonexistent pornographic videos they had never ordered and did not want. Hovland was the victim of a deliberate smear campaign, probably by a malefactor who had refused to pay rent at Hovland's marina and who had lost his boat in a seizure as a result. The anonymous malefactor spammed the Net in Hovland's name and suggested that people call his business number collect. Hovland guessed that he lost about two weeks of business because his phones were ringing off the hook. Hovland pointed out that his case was relatively minor; he imagined the mayhem if an emergency number were posted on the Net in such a fraud. The case illustrates the difficulty for victims in finding an agency willing to receive and follow up on complaints about such outrageous and dangerous attacks.[7]

Anonymity is fundamental to the abuse of the Net practiced by many spammers. Almost all spam contains forged headers in an attempt to escape retribution; in some cases the forgeries name real domains. One of the most significant early cases began in May 1997, when Craig Nowak, a college student, chose flowers.com at random as the fraudulent return address for his first attempt at junk e-mail.[8] In so doing, he was merely following the suggestions of the unscrupulous purveyors of spam-distribution programs, who usually advise their naive users to forge the headers of their junk e-mail. Unfortunately for his victim, flowers.com is a legitimate business whose owner received 5,000 bounced messages and plenty of abuse for supposedly spamming the world. The enraged owner of flowers.com, Tracy LaQuey Parker, launched a lawsuit for damages and was supported by the Electronic Frontier Foundation (Austin chapter) and the Texas Internet Service Providers Association. In late September 1997, the plaintiffs won a temporary injunction against Nowak and his company, preventing him from further use of the appropriated domain name. In November 1997, Judge Suzanne Covington imposed a fine of over $18,000 on the defendants and added a particularly significant passage in her judgment that clearly enunciates the damages caused by forgery of return addresses:

> The Court additionally finds that the Plaintiffs have suffered, and will continue to suffer if [the defendant is] not enjoined, irreparable harm in the form of diminution in value of Plaintiffs' domain name; the possibility that Plaintiffs' reputation will be damaged forever by unauthorized use of a domain name associated with them in the controversial and hated practice of Internet spamming; and service disruptions. The potential harm to the Plaintiffs cannot be adequately valued in damages, and therefore the Plaintiffs have no adequate remedy at law. . . . The Court further finds that Plaintiffs . . . suffered actual damages from the unauthorized actions of the Defendants, including lost time, lost income, lost business opportunities and lost use of their respective computer systems.[9]

In light of the seriousness of these abuses of inadequate identification in cyberspace, system managers and others concerned with the continued success of the Internet as an effective communications medium should consider the reasons for abusive behavior of anonymous individuals. Is such abuse an aberration particular to cyberspace, or are there precedents in history and in other areas of life that can provide insights to shape public and corporate policy toward identification in cyberspace?

This chapter reviews some of the findings of social psychology that show how anonymity has generally been associated with antisocial behavior. It appears that anonymity on the Net will inevitably continue to spawn antisocial behavior in cyberspace and that we must somehow integrate this kind of abuse into plans for the further development of the Internet. The chapter then presents some practical ways system managers can encourage employees in their own organizations to use the Net responsibly. Some practical suggestions on how different degrees of tolerance for anonymity can be integrated into a cyberspace polity are discussed.

70.2 DEFINITIONS. Before exploring anonymity in cyberspace, it is helpful to establish some common vocabulary. What is cyberspace? What are identity and its absence? What is pseudonymity?

70.2.1   Cyberspace.   In this chapter, "cyberspace" means the totality of electronic data storage and transmission; this chapter focuses on communications using the Internet. On the Internet, there are users of specific domains defined in the Domain Naming System (DNS), such as companies (those using addresses ending in *.com*), universities and other educational institutions (*.edu* addresses), U.S. government agencies and departments (*.gov*), the U.S. military (*.mil*), and network service providers (*.net*) among others.[10] There are many geographical domain names, such as those ending in *.de* (Germany) or *.uk* (United Kingdom), which include users from commercial, educational, government, and military organizations. In addition, there are many Internet Service Providers (ISPs) in the *.net* and *.com* domains in the United States, and others throughout the world in geographical domains, whose members communicate through the Internet. Customers of value-added networks (VANs) such as America Online (AOL) and CompuServe (CS) communicate through the Internet as well as having restricted areas within their VANs where only members can post messages and files. All Internet users can post messages in public discussion lists on the Usenet or through remailing lists, which broadcast all inbound e-mail to participants. Henceforth, for convenience, "the Internet" or "the Net" will include any of these users. Users of direct-dial bulletin board systems and modem-to-modem direct links are explicitly excluded from this discussion.

70.2.2   The Real World.   As used here, "the real" world refers to the material, physical, atomic, and molecular world of everyday human interactions. Using "real world" in this way is not intended to imply that cyberspace is less significant, less useful, or even less real than the planetary level on which we interact; it is merely a convenient reference to distinguish the physical from the electronic.

70.2.3   Identity in the Real World.   The key meanings of the noun "identity" for our purposes are defined as:

- The collective aspect of the set of characteristics by which a thing is definitively recognizable or known
- The set of behavioral or personal characteristics by which an individual is recognizable as a member of a group
- The distinct personality of an individual regarded as a persisting entity; individuality

70.2.4   Anonymity and Pseudonymity in the Real World.   Clarke summarizes the importance of personal identification in this way:

> The purposes of the interchange of identification include
>
> - to provide a gesture of goodwill,
> - to develop mutual confidence, and
> - to reduce the scope for dishonesty;
> - to enable either person to initiate the next round of communications; and
> - to enable either person to associate transactions and information with the other person.[11]

In line with these points, apparently ancient knights would tip their visor up for two reasons: for recognition as friend or foe, and out of respect for those being met.

"Anonymity" can be defined simply as being without a name or with an unknown name. "Pseudonymity" is the use of a false name. These terms are imbued in English with a negative connotation; nonetheless, anonymity has an honorable history in world philosophy and politics. In the United States, for example, the seminal *Federalist Papers*, which appeared in 1787 under the pen name "Publius," is a publication held up as an outstanding example of anonymous contribution to political thought.[12]

Anonymity is protected in some government-sponsored monitoring programs such as those supported by the Occupational Safety and Health Administration (OSHA) of the U.S. Department of Labor, where regulations stipulate for example that "Completed NETS Cards [hazard reports] can be given to a department manager or deposited, anonymously, into one of the drop boxes located throughout the facility."[13]

Clarke explores the concepts and history of human identity in a section of his paper on management and policy issues relating to human identification. Individuality has been a central concept in Western civilization since the Renaissance, says Clarke.[14] However, individuals can adopt more than one identity; for example, some women use their husband's surname in private life but maintain their original family name in their professions. Some people have several identities; for example, novelists with different styles sometimes use various pen names. The Danish philosopher Sørren Kierkegaard wrote under 16 pseudonyms; Charles Dodgson wrote as Lewis Carroll; Eric Blair wrote as George Orwell. As the work of these writers illustrates, anonymity and pseudonymity are not inherently linked to antisocial behavior.

70.3 SOCIAL PSYCHOLOGY OF ANONYMITY.   Technological change can have profound consequences on social behavior. For example, the development of mass-produced automobiles made possible the development of suburban shopping malls in the United States, which in turn have led to an adolescent mall culture unimaginable in the 1920s.[15] Most of us have observed that driving an automobile can alter a person's behavior from civility to incivility; in some cases, otherwise normal people become violent when they are behind the wheel of a car.[16]

It seems quite likely that the pervasive spread of the Internet will have equally profound effects on social organization and interactions. We should study what is already known about the effects of anonymity as we analyze anonymity in cyberspace. The sections that follow review some well-established information on anonymity and social behavior from the social psychology literature. The implications of these principles for individuals, corporate policy makers, ISPs, and governments are discussed in the final section.

70.3.1 Deindividuation Theory.   What do scientists know about the behavior of anonymous people? In general, the findings are not encouraging for the future of cyberspace unless we can somehow avoid the known association of antisocial behavior and anonymity.

Early work on people in groups focused on anonymity as a root of the perceived frequency of antisocial behavior.[17] The anonymous members of a crowd show reduced inhibition of antisocial and reckless, impulsive behavior. They are subject to increased irritability and suggestibility. One wonders if the well-known incidence of flaming (rude and largely *ad hominem* communications through e-mail and postings on the Usenet and other public areas) may be traceable to the same factors that influence crowd behavior.

Later social psychologists formulated a theory of deindividuation[18] in which they proposed that one's personal sense of identity can be overwhelmed by the sense of belonging to a group.

Zimbardo suggested that anonymity, diffusion of responsibility, and arousal contributed to deindividuation and antisociality.[19] He noted that deindividuated people display reduced inhibitions, reduced reliance on internal standards that normally qualify their behavior, and little self-awareness.

70.3.1.1 *Deindividuation and Technology.*

As mentioned briefly earlier, there is some reason to suppose that technology can contribute to the deindividuation of its users.

Anonymity has been postulated to account in part for the strong contrast between normal behavior and the behavior of those who become aggressive and hostile when driving cars.[20] It seems intuitively plausible that being isolated in a tight personal space, a cocoon of glass and metal, gives some drivers a feeling of power precisely because of their (possibly temporary) anonymity. In addition, the anonymity of the other drivers may lead to a kind of dehumanization of the other. It would be interesting to study how many angry drivers refer to "that car" instead of "that driver" when they rail against some random act of road rudeness. Similarly, it may be that the isolation of an Internet user also may contribute to aggressivity; the object of wrath may, much like the driver of another car, be dehumanized. Sometimes it seems that e-mail flamers are engaged in their version of a video game; they give the impression of losing sight of the real human beings on the other end of their verbal aggression.

Writers of computer viruses and others in the criminal computer underground may also focus so intensely on the challenge of defeating machines that they lose sight of their human victims. Criminal hackers have expressed themselves as attacking systems, not people. At a hacker conference, comments were heard such as "Oh, I would never steal anything from a person, but if I found a radio in an office and it were labeled with a company sticker I wouldn't think twice about taking it." A commonplace informal interpretation of the insouciance of hackers and virus writers is that they are subject to what is laughingly called the "video-game syndrome": They seem to focus on their actions as if they were part of a game with only computers on the receiving end.

Chapter 12 of this *Handbook* provides more detail on deindividuation theory.

70.3.1.2 *Anonymity and Aggression.*

Sometimes, anonymous people go beyond verbal abuse and seem willing to inflict harm on others. Experimental work by Zimbardo suggested that anonymity can significantly increase aggression.[21] For example, when women were asked to deliver electric shocks to victims, those who agreed to wear white lab coats and hoods administered what they thought were longer shocks to the supposed victims compared with women who wore their own clothes and nametags.

In a cross-cultural study, Watson analyzed the correlations between the ritual, anonymizing costumes and war paint of warriors and their style of battle and their postbattle treatment of prisoners.[22] He found a strong positive relationship between anonymity and brutality.

Violent soccer fans seem to be disinhibited in part because of the anonymity of the crowd.[23] In a personal undercover investigation, a journalist found that anonymity and pseudonymity are integral components of the antisocial behavior of soccer hooligans.[24] These findings suggest that so-called dark-side hackers may be influenced significantly in their willingness to cause damage to computer systems and networks precisely because their very anonymity influences them to cross normal behavioral boundaries. These people may not be the permanently, irremediably damaged human beings they sometimes seem; they may, instead, be relatively normal people responding in predictable ways to the absence of stable identification and identity.

70.3.1.3 Anonymity and Dishonesty.
Does anonymity increase the likelihood that people will transgress rules and laws? Apparently yes.

In an experiment involving children, young trick-or-treaters were asked to take only one candy from a bowl and then left alone or in groups, supposedly unobserved. Those children who had given their names to adults were observed to be far less likely to take extra candy or to steal coins than those who had remained anonymous, even when the adults were apparently away.[25] (If these effects of anonymity on youngsters are consistent and widespread, they may contribute to the problems of system administrators who are under siege by underage hackers.)

70.3.1.4 Deindividuation and Self-Awareness.
Why does anonymity change people's normal inhibitions and influence them to behave abnormally? It seems that the deindividuation of anonymous people lowers their self-reflective propensities.

Exploration of the inner world of deindividuated people suggests that they are less aware of themselves and may even enter a state of altered consciousness.[26] Prentice-Dunn and Rogers studied the behavior of college men who, as in the work of Zimbardo cited earlier, were asked to administer what they thought were electric shocks to confederates of the experimenters who were masquerading as victims. Some subjects were subjected to dim lighting and loud background noise; their names were not used; and they were told that the levels of the shocks they gave would not be recorded. These subjects were thought to be deindividuated. Other subjects experienced bright lights in quiet rooms; they were called by name; and they were told that the shock levels they delivered would be monitored. The deindividuated subjects administered more severe shocks to their victims than did the individuated students.

These observations may tie into the work on autotelic experiences.[27] Autotelic experiences are deeply satisfying activities that result in a temporary loss of self-awareness; they typically occur in repetitive, challenging, feedback-rich activities such as programming (or perhaps virus writing) and criminal computer hacking. Csikszentmihalyi studied people in a variety of work environments and in their home life and hobbies. The subjects reported on their attainment of a state of timelessness, where the passage of time was insensible. Many who have programmed know how easy it is to forget to eat or to go home when deeply involved in work; similarly, writers and musicians can lose track of time. The research suggested that some of the key attributes of an activity that leads to this autotelic experience are rapidity of feedback (e.g., seeing an article grow as one writes or running an increasingly complex program under development) and being at the limits of one's abilities. In contrast, challenges that are too easy or too hard tend not to result in the loss of self-awareness that defines the autotelic state.

Several recent popular books dealing with criminal hackers have mentioned the ability of legendary hackers to stick to their hacking for hours on end as if they were entranced. Combine the autotelic nature of hacking with the deindividuation associated with anonymity, and we have a prescription for trouble.

70.3.1.5 Anonymity and Prosocial Behavior.
The picture is not necessarily all bad, however. Sometimes a different environment actually can liberate anonymous subjects from their counterproductive inhibitions. For example, in some cases,

it can be shown that anonymity has an unusual effect: It increases prosocial behavior instead of increasing antisocial behavior.[28] Gergen, Gergen, and Barton put people into brightly lit chambers or in totally dark chambers and monitored the behavior of the strangers they had put together; in the dark room, there was much more uninhibited and positive expression of physical contact such as hugs and of emotional openness such as discussions of personal matters.[29] However, directionality of these effects may be affected by the demand characteristics of the situation. That is, the way the experimental objectives were described could cause significant differences in the subjects' behavior.

The constructive, supportive communications often seen in discussion groups dealing with substance abuse, abusive relationships, and other personal and interpersonal problems illustrate the possible benefits of anonymity in a positive context.

70.3.2   Identity in Cyberspace.

What exactly is meant by "identity" when using electronic communications? Is one's e-mail address an identity? Could a made-up name be an identity?

Identity on the Internet is primarily the e-mail address.[30] The e-mail address sometimes provides crude and unreliable information about affiliation (e.g., domain names *.gov, .mil, .edu*) and geographic location (e.g., *.ca, .uk, .fr*).[31] Roger Clarke, a scholar with a long professional interest in questions of identity, identification, and privacy in cyberspace, has written an excellent introduction to these questions.[32] For discussions of information technology, Clarke defines "identification" as "the association of data with a particular human being."[33]

70.3.2.1   *Theory of* Nymity.

There has been considerable discussion on the Net about the kinds of identity (sometimes called *nymity* in these discussions) that people assume in cyberspace. One of the best-known writers on this subject was "L. Detweiler." It is still not known whether this is a real name. Detweiler suggested that identity on the Internet is amorphous and unstable because there is no one-to-one relationship between a person and an e-mail address. One person may use multiple e-mail addresses, and many people may share a single address.[34]

Detweiler conducted a vigorous battle against what he perceived as a sinister and deceptive practice he called *pseudospoofing*. Pseudospoofing, in Detweiler's conception, is the use of multiple aliases by an individual or a conspiracy; these aliases allow the perpetrators to deceive observers into misjudging the number of people agreeing or disagreeing over specific positions.[35] One of the literary sources for such a practice is the science-fiction book *Enders Game* by Orson Scott Card.[36] Card posits a galactic political debate in which two individuals distort political debate by engaging in erudite polemics using pseudonyms; but they also invent subsidiary personae who agree or disagree with the main pseudonyms. These subsidiary personae lend credibility to the desired winning side by offering support for their chosen position or by deliberately posting poor arguments and attitudes to discredit the opposing side. The spurious numbers of these constructed personalities convinces politicians to pay attention to the debates.

A current illustration of the problems of pseudospoofing is the widespread difficulties experienced in online voting. The ease with which identity can be created, coupled with the ease of automatically scripting multiple votes, leads to unreliable tallies in almost all online polls. The only way to avoid such abuses is to enforce some tight coupling of real-world identity with the electronic identity registered for voting. Eventually, biometric identification may be the only acceptable form of authentication for voting online.[37]

70.3.2.2 Types of Anonymity and Pseudonymity. To understand the problem of anonymity and pseudonymity, it is useful to define varying degrees of the behavior. Froomkin distinguishes among four forms of imprecise or absent identification:

1. **Traceable anonymity,** Any anonymous remailer that keeps a record of the relation between the original message and the anonymized message allows tracing.
2. **Untraceable anonymity.** No record is kept or available showing the origin of an anonymized message.
3. **Untraceable pseudonymity.** A continuous identity or persona allows communication with a correspondent but there is no way to link the pseudonym to the correspondent's real-world identity.
4. **Traceable pseudonymity.** Someone, somewhere has the information required to complete the link between a pseudonym and a real-world identity.[38]

The "anonymizing" remailer *anon.penet.fi* was actually a *traceable pseudonym remailer*. When a message was received by the server, its headers were stripped and it was assigned a fixed random pseudonym. In order to allow replies to the pseudonym to be forwarded to the original sender, every pseudonymous identity was linked in a table to the original e-mail address. When Finnish police ordered Johan Helsingius in 1995 to identify the pseudonymous poster of copyrighted Scientology texts on the Usenet, Helsingius felt obliged to reveal the link.[39] Traceable online anonymity allows people to maintain their privacy by using screen identities, but many ISPs will furnish the real-world identity to law enforcement officials with a warrant or to tort lawyers with a subpoena. AOL, for example, furnished subscriber details to the lawyers for a Caribbean resort considering a lawsuit for defamation based on postings by "Jenny TRR."[40] All ISPs that charge money for access inherently provide traceable pseudonymity even when they permit false screen names.

Larry Lessig, David Post, and Eugene Volokh also distinguish between anonymity, pseudonymity, and traceability in their Internet course on cyberspace law.[41] They emphasize that private organizations, such as Internet service providers, can freely set terms of service that allow or forbid anonymity, but they may be required in the United States to provide traceability if the courts require it for individuals.[42] In general, it is difficult to see how the rule of law can apply to cyberspace without some form of traceability. Whether civil law or the criminal law is involved, the defendant must be found for court proceedings to have any effect. Untraceable anonymity and untraceable pseudonymity preclude justice for the aggrieved parties. Clarke points out that privacy interests are always to be balanced with other interests such as the public good, commercial interests, and the interests of other individuals.[43] For example, the desire to post anonymous libel (construed as privacy of personal behavior) conflicts with the desire of the victim to be free from libel; anonymity makes it impossible to use the civil law for redress.

70.3.2.3 Why Anonymity and Pseudonymity Are Commonplace in Cyberspace. Surely anonymity and pseudonymity are possible using older means of communication: People have thrown rocks through windows, sent anonymous vituperation through the mail, and harassed people with anonymous phone calls for millennia, centuries, and decades respectively. Historically, such behavior has been of relatively minor importance. How is it that anonymity and pseudonymity seem so important in cyberspace?

One factor is the ease with which one can be untraceably anonymous in cyberspace. Many ISPs allow users to define screen names or aliases; some ISPs, such as AOL, have distributed millions of trial subscription disks that allow one to create an identity and then dispose of it after 50 hours online. Spammers often use disposable free accounts from such services as Hotmail, even defeating methods designed to stop them from abusing the services.[44]

Anonymous remailers permit users to send e-mail to a central address where all identifying information is stripped, and the original text is then retransmitted to the desired destination. In the wake of the tragic events of September 11, 2001, when terrorists killed thousands of people in attacks on the World Trade Center in New York City and on the Pentagon in Washington, D.C., commentators expressed doubts about the future of anonymizing services. "Using anonymizers at all raises all sorts of red flags," said John Young, operator of the Cryptome Web site (www.cryptome.org), which covers intelligence matters. Even before the terrorist attacks, the well-respected Freedom Network operated by Zero-Knowledge Systems had experienced financial difficulties; that service shut down on October 22, 2001.[45]

Some moderated Usenet groups and e-mail–based mailing lists require a "real" name, but there is little effort or even possibility, as things currently stand, for authentication of such names. Unmoderated groups, by definition, do not require real names at all; such groups allow postings by anyone. Almost all contributions to countercultural or frankly criminal Usenet groups and distribution lists are anonymous or at best pseudonymous.

In addition, some people systematically forge the headers of their e-mail, often introducing completely false addresses for their origin but occasionally picking real addresses, whether by accident or design.[46] Forging e-mail headers can conceal the true origin of a message.[47] Junk e-mail almost always includes false return addresses. Another way to generate false header information is to compromise someone's e-mail account. If security on an e-mail address is compromised, messages can be forged with a false ID.

The other factor that makes anonymity and pseudonymity especially significant in cyberspace is the ease of replication of messages. An anonymous communicator could hope to reach at best a few dozen or hundred people in a day with the phone system or by mail; in most areas, each phone call or letter would cost something to send. In contrast, outbound electronic mail and postings to Usenet groups generally cost the originator nothing.

70.4   BALANCING RIGHTS AND DUTIES.   Is there a basis for evaluating the ethics of using anonymous and pseudonymous communications? Are these modes of communications protected by principles of privacy, for example?

70.4.1   Benefits of Anonymity and Pseudonymity.   Historically, anonymity has been recognized as a benefit for acts of charity for those wishing to remain nameless for political, social, or personal reasons. Maimonides, the great 12th-century rabbi, defined anonymous giving to anonymous recipients as the second-highest level of charity.[48]

In discussions of whether society ought to restrict anonymity and pseudonymity, a common argument is that these modes of communication are necessary to fight tyrannical corporate and political institutions. Anonymity and pseudonymity are, in this view, expressions of the right to privacy. Abuses are the price society has to pay to preserve the benefits of these tools of expression. The next sections examine the concepts of privacy and the resulting benefits of anonymity and pseudonymity.

70.4.1.1 Privacy in Cyberspace.

If privacy rights are claimed to protect anonymous and pseudonymous communications, it is important to understand the concepts of privacy.

Clarke defines privacy as "the interest that individuals have in sustaining a 'personal space,' free from interference by other people and organizations." He analyses the concept further, naming four dimensions of privacy:

1. **Privacy of the person.** Freedom from compulsory tampering with one's body
2. **Privacy of personal behavior.** Freedom in such matters as sexual preferences, religion, and politics
3. **Privacy of personal communications.** Freedom from routine monitoring of interpersonal communications
4. **Privacy of personal data.** Control over who can obtain and what can be done with personal information[49]

Political discussion groups, resistance to totalitarian regimes, and discussions of socially embarrassing or traumatic problems are made easier for many people by the use of pseudonyms or of anonymity. Anonymity permits unrestricted political speech, whistleblowing with reduced likelihood of retaliation, and public or private discussions of potentially embarrassing personal problems.[50] Ubois writes:

> Anonymous communications are helpful in many ways. They've long been a tool of suicide prevention hotlines, suggestion boxes, and personal ads. Anonymity assures privacy, confidentiality and security for individuals, but it also highlights the clash of interests between the individual and the community. Under a repressive government, it is a vital tool for keeping discourse alive. Just consider that Tom Paine would have landed in prison shortly after the publication of Common Sense if his identity hadn't been kept a secret.[51]

In chat rooms and multiuser dungeons, anonymity permits a flowering of imaginative departures from the strictures of a participant's real-world identity, social status, personality, gender and gender preferences, political affiliation, national origin, and religion. Multimedia environments such as WorldsAway (www.worldsaway.com/home.shtml) provide an imaginative pseudonymity by allowing players to select a name and a pictorial representation of themselves (an avatar) with amusing and fanciful features, such as various imaginary animal heads, skin colors, body shapes, and so on. Players adopt personae that can be quite different from their real-world identities, yet there is a consistent identity within the virtual world. Because of this consistency, social mechanisms have arisen in these worlds; for example, avatars can be invited to join parties if they are perceived as friendly or excluded and shunned if they have violated the norms of the imaginary world.

Anonymous, invisible electronic personalities can escape some of the damaging effects of intolerance and prejudice.[52] Everyone probably knows of Peter Steiner's famous *New Yorker* cartoon showing two dogs at a terminal, one of whom is saying "On the Internet nobody knows you're a dog."[53] Another current example is the country music video "Online" by Brad Paisley in which he sings "I'm much cooler online" and boasts about completely illusory qualities.[54]

For example, some professors may spend more time and effort in discussions with undergraduate students if they do not realize with whom they are corresponding.[55] At an intellectual level, stripping the authors of published materials of all details of their age, sex, race, national origin, and other attributes can reduce the effects of prejudice and focus discussion on substance. Absent such details, correspondents must perforce focus on the texts rather than on personalities.[56]

In electronic commerce, anonymity is a prerequisite for successful implementation of some trading systems.[57] All electronic or digital cash schemes (e-cash) emphasize the value of anonymous transactions for safeguarding consumer privacy.

In a legal sense, anonymity and pseudonymity are analogous to limited liability—a concept familiar from the business world. In business, people pool their assets into a limited liability partnership or other form of collectivity to prevent seizure of all their private assets if their collective entity becomes liable for debts or penalties.[58] Perhaps cyberspace anonymity and pseudonymity can encourage collective publications in an analogous way; for example, Post and others have formed the Cyberspace Law Institute. Some members would be reluctant to participate if their real-world identities were known to the public.

Thus, anonymity and pseudonymity cannot reasonably be forbidden without the loss of important benefits to individuals, corporations, and society at large.

70.4.2   Privacy and Freedom in Virtual Worlds.   With the increasing growth of global access to the Internet, millions of people have joined virtual communities or virtual worlds where they can interact—often anonymously or pseudonymously. At the time of writing (July 2008), one list of virtual worlds included summary details of 28 of the most popular platforms for electronic social interactions for participants from young children through adults:

Active Worlds	Playdo	Virtual Magic Kingdom
Coke Studios	Second Life	Voodoo Chat
Cybertown	Sora City	VPchat
Disney's Toontown	The Manor	VZones
Dreamville	The Palace	whyrobbierocks
Dubit	The Sims Online	Whyville
Habbo Hotel	There	Worlds.com
Mokitown	TowerChat	Yohoho! Puzzle Pirates
Moove	Traveler	
Muse	Virtual Ibiza[59]	

As of June 2008, there were an estimated 137 million users of virtual worlds; by 2017, according to some industry analysts, there would be a billion users.[60]

The freedom from discrimination based on physical, cultural, gender, and sociological attributes has proven liberating for many members of these virtual worlds; many participants have formed strong friendships that may even extend into the "real world."[61]

70.4.2.1   Defeating Dataveillance.   Another area where anonymity and pseudonymity have marked benefits is in preventing intrusive monitoring of individual behavior in cyberspace. Clarke has defined dataveillance as surveillance using electronically compiled information about a person.[62] The growth of some kinds of electronic commerce will increase pressures for strong identification and authentication;[63] anonymity serves to protect privacy in a world of electronic commerce. For example, without anonymous digital cash, it would be easy to accumulate detailed records of every electronic purchase made by an individual. Complete knowledge of purchasers' interests can be unfair for customers; for example, knowing that a user is addicted to fantasy simulation games, a retailer may neglect to offer that person a discount—or may even increase the price of the next game.[64] Froomkin summarizes the issues well in his magisterial review of the challenges of anonymity in cyberspace:

> Anonymity lies at the heart of three interrelated problems arising from computer-aided communications over distributed networks (which I will call "the Internet" for short). First, communicative anonymity is an issue in itself: the Internet makes anonymous communication easy, and this has both good and bad consequences. . . .
>
> Second, the availability of anonymous electronic communication directly affects the ability of governments to regulate electronic transactions over the Internet (both licit and illicit).
>
> Third, anonymity may be the primary tool available to citizens to combat the compilation and analysis of personal profile data, although data protection laws also may have some effect. The existence of profiling databases, whether in corporate or public hands, may severely constrict the economic and possibly even the political freedoms of the persons profiled; although profiling may not necessarily change the amount of actual data in existence about a person, organizing the data into easily searchable form reduces her effective privacy by permitting "data mining" and correlations that were previously impossible.[65]

Froomkin discusses digital cash as an application of electronic anonymity and emphasizes the potential for abuse by "the Argus State" if anonymity is not guaranteed for readers. For example, he points out, in the absence of anonymous digital cash, reading texts on the Internet using micropayments for each access could provide a traceable record of a person's interests. Such records would be a gold mine for repressive regimes worldwide.

Again, trying to ban anonymity and pseudonymity would have serious disadvantages for everyone, not just the benefits of impeding abuse by a minority of antisocial users.

Finally, police forces and intelligence agencies always recognize anonymity and pseudonymity as potentially important tools in specific investigations. Undercover or covert operations and agents can provide critically important evidence in anticrime and antiterrorist work. Even organizations such as the FBI-sponsored InfraGard recognize the value of anonymized information-sharing about attacks on computer systems.[66]

70.4.3 Disadvantages of Anonymity and Pseudonymity. Several commentators have reviewed the abuses of anonymous and pseudonymous modes of communication.

In considering the benefits of having a professor communicate with an anonymous student, misrepresentation of identity by such an undergraduate in one sense manipulates a professor into a decision based on a falsehood.[67] Contrary to the beliefs of many supporters of anonymity, social interactions are not necessarily equivalent to isolated streams of data interchange; conversing with a student can be enriched by having a sense of previous conversations, a picture of shared knowledge based on a relationship. Anonymity strips interactions of the deeper communication that is enhanced by such relationships.

Widespread use of untraceable e-cash may lead to increased fraud, tax evasion, money laundering, extortion, blackmail, and kidnapping.[68] Some crimes where solicitation leads to potential blackmail—for example, hiring a murderer—may become easier with anonymity and untraceable e-cash. Industrial sabotage by anonymous publication of trade secrets can damage organizations; for example, the publication of RC4 encryption algorithms from the respected company RSADSI has lowered the monetary value of the algorithm. Froomkin writes, "[The] inability to redress legitimate claims is, I believe, the strongest moral objection to the increase in anonymous interaction."

Jurisprudence in the United States has generally supported claims to a right of anonymity in political speech. However, there have been several precedents where anonymity used to cloak socially harmful acts has been stripped from the perpetrators. Perfect (untraceable) anonymity prevents society from bringing sanctions to bear on malefactors.[69] Detweiler suggested "that Internet anonymity is a bad thing [and] that all user accounts should lead back to real users in the hopes of improving online behavior, especially in chat systems and the like." He responded to critics who claimed that "anonymity is an important part of life and ought to be part of the Internet as well" by pointing out that in real life, anonymous people cannot engage in such activities as opening a bank account, getting a driver's license, getting telephone service, or buying insurance coverage. He concluded, "So grow up and accept responsibility for what you do on the Internet."[70]

Rose, well known in cyberspace law circles, writes scathingly of the seamier applications of online anonymity:

> People can anonymously transmit all sorts of illegal and injurious materials into public areas: copyright infringements, obscenity, stolen credit information, lies and slander, and so on. Individuals with a bone to pick against anyone else can get their licks in without fear of reprisal. Anonymous remailers are great for cowards. People who want to spread messages of hate and misunderstanding, but are unwilling to stand behind their views in public, can operate behind a wall of complete anonymity and inject a strong dose of thought pollution into the public arena.[71]

Another argument supporting disclosure of the origins of speech is quoted by Froomkin, ironically from an anonymous author: "'Disclosure advances the search for truth,' because when propaganda is anonymous it 'makes it more difficult to identify the self interest or bias underlying an argument.'"[72] Libel on the Internet is particularly pernicious, since once anything has been circulated via the Net, it becomes impossible in practice to destroy all, or even many, of the copies that may reside on numberless computers around the world.

The imaginary Good Times virus supposedly destroys hard disks as soon as the victim reads an e-mail message; Craig Shergold was once a sick child in England who asked for postcards—and is now heartily sick of the bagsful of cards he receives daily; and the "Jessica Mydek" hoax claims to be an appeal on behalf of an unfortunate girl, but she never existed.

The resurgence of hoaxes and rumors such as the Good Times virus[73] and the pathetic stories of Craig Shergold[74] and Jessica Mydek[75] illustrate the persistence of undated, unsigned, and untrue messages in Cyberspace. These unfounded, exaggerated, or obsolete stories, threats, and appeals circulate endlessly among the gullible on the Net. There is no reason to suppose they will ever stop.

One of the significant lessons from e-mail hoaxes and chain letters is that unsigned, undated correspondence is always to be treated with skepticism. This principle of devaluing anonymous or pseudonymous communications will be used later in this chapter in a model for categorizing and sequestering communications as a function of their traceability.

70.5 SYSTEMS ANALYSIS OF ANONYMITY.   Why can the usual protections of the criminal and civil law not deal with anonymous and pseudonymous communications? This problem is addressed by David Post and David Johnson.

Post and Johnson argue that geographically defined nation-states cannot reasonably cope with a virtual, boundaryless communications medium.[76] In the real world, geographical clustering combines with basic concepts of consent of the governed through some form of representation to legitimize the exercise of state power. Without the consent of the governed, state power fades insensibly into state tyranny. In their requirements analysis of possible systems of governance of cyberspace, they add that wherever possible, those affected by the conduct to be regulated have some say in framing the regulations.

However, in cyberspace, argue Post and Johnson, there is no geographical clustering. There is no "here" or "there" in cyberspace. "Location is indeterminate because there is no necessary relationship between electronic addressing . . . and the location of the addressee (machine or user) in physical space."

Post and Johnson applied the work of the scientist Stuart Kauffman on self-organizing systems to study the nature of rule-making in a complex system that can model the interactions among users in cyberspace.[77] Research on self-organization of complex systems suggests that optimum configurations of constraints (regulations) can evolve when there is some degree of aggregation (they refer to "patches") in the population. These aggregates represent groups where individuals sacrifice some of their preferences in return for overall improvement in the way the whole society works. Members of a patch share responsibility for governing their behavior.

One of the most striking findings of Post and Johnson's research is that systems where most of the effects of an individual's actions are felt by others, outside its decision-making unit, lead to chaos or to suboptimal configurations of rules. Contrariwise, a balance between bringing consequences to bear on individuals in a "patch" and allowing effects to propagate through the larger population leads to more optimal results in the system.

As a result of the experiments, Post and Johnson suggest that one of the most powerful tools for rebuilding comity in cyberspace is grouping users by their Internet Service Providers. Each ISP can develop its own rules governing the behavior of members; sanctions for transgression of these local rules would include banishment from the ISP.

The authors examine the case of unsolicited commercial e-mail ("spam"). As long as each ISP enforces technical measures against allowing fraudulent origination addresses, everyone in cyberspace can decide whether to filter out messages from any given ISP or not. ISPs that allow behavior judged harmful by others will limit the range of communication of their members.

Those that are viewed as restrictive will self-select their own members accordingly. Thus without any global legislation, simply allowing individuals to choose ISPs that have published rules they like could lead to an effective self-regulation of communications. In essence, loudmouthed rumormongers would end up talking only to each other; junk e-mail could be identified simply from its provenance; and even copyright violations could be punished by collective banning of communications from the offending ISPs.

Such a model is an instance of the ideal "market of ideas" in that objectionable ideas are not forbidden, they are just ignored. Of course, admirable and desirable ideas may also be ignored, but at least there is a choice involved. Access for communication becomes a form of currency in such a model—perhaps appropriate for the governance of cyberspace, the realm of electronic communications.

70.6   IMPLICATIONS AND DISCUSSION.   Any attempt to restrict anonymity on the Internet would inevitably affect pseudonymity as well.[78] Anonymity and pseudonymity make law enforcement difficult enough, but these difficulties are exacerbated by the jurisdictional problems caused by a thoroughly decentralized communications medium like the Internet; "[W]ho should be setting the rules that apply to this new global medium?"[79] What, then, are some of the practical measures we can individually and collectively take to preserve the benefits of anonymity and pseudonymity without suffering the consequences of abuse?

70.6.1   Individuals, Families, and Schools.   Absorbing and applying normative behavior begins in earliest childhood and continues throughout the development of the child's capacity for rationality and ethical judgement. Children should be taught that anonymity and pseudonymity are not acceptable under normal circumstances. The same methods that parents, teachers, and other adults use to teach children a visceral dislike of antisocial behaviors such as lying, cheating, stealing, and bullying should be applied to behavior in cyberspace.

It takes time to integrate morality into our technological universe. Twenty years ago, many drivers felt that driving under the influence of alcohol was adventurous. Today most people feel that it is stupid and irresponsible. Smoking in public is becoming rare. Many of us in northern cities have witnessed exiled smokers huddled together in the cold outside buildings where they once lit up with impunity.

Similarly, we need a consensus on good behavior in cyberspace.

Criminal hackers who break into computer systems and roam through users' private files should be viewed as peeping Toms. Criminals using computers to steal services should be recognized as thieves. Those who destroy records, leave logic bombs, and write viruses should be viewed as vandals. Hackers who smear obscenities in source code should be seen as twisted personalities in need of punishment and therapy. Government agencies proposing to interfere in electronic communications should be subject to scrutiny and intense lobbying.

Beyond such prohibitions and inhibitions of taboos, cyberspace needs the electronic equivalent of Emily Post. We need to discuss the immorality of virus writing, the ethical implications of logic bombs, and the criminality of electronic trespassing. We should teach children how to be good citizens of cyberspace, and not just in schools. We should sit down with computer-using youngsters and follow them through their adventures in cyberspace. Parents should ask their teenage whiz kids about hacking, viruses, software theft, and telephone fraud. We must bring the perspective and guidance of adult generations to bear on a world that is evolving faster than most of us can imagine.

The adolescent confraternity of criminal hackers and virus writers has already begun developing totems: the personae of Dark Avenger and Acid Phreak loom over youngsters much as Robin Hood once did for another generation.

What we need now are taboos to match the totems.[80]

70.6.2   Ethical Principles.   How do people make judgements about a course of action when there are no explicit guidelines? There are several kinds of principles that people use in reasoning about a new situation (see Chapter 43 of this *Handbook* for a more extensive discussion of ethical decision making).

70.6.2.1   *Rights and Duties (Deontology).*   The concepts of rights ("Something that is due to a person or governmental body by law, tradition, or nature") and duties ("An act or a course of action that is required of one by position, social custom, law, or religion," according to the 1992 edition of the *American Heritage Dictionary*) should influence one's decisions.

Are any rights abridged by anonymity? For example, the right to know the source of a warning so that we may judge the motives and credibility of the statement is infringed when such a message is posted anonymously or pseudonymously.

Personal duties at issue in a decision on posting anonymous warnings about a competitor's product include notions of trust, integrity, and truthfulness, all of which are violated by such an act. We lower the trust of technical advice when we use anonymous postings; we damage the integrity of an entire profession; and we implicitly betray truthfulness by failing to identify the source of such information.

Professional duties or responsibilities also apply. We are expected to maintain appropriate professional relationships, but anonymous posting does not further a web of trust among colleagues. Posting anonymous messages casts doubt on the goodwill of all the innocent people who are perceived as possibly being the author of such messages. In terms of maintaining efficacy, anonymous postings reduce the flow of information among professionals by aborting the possibility of private communication with the authors of the anonymous messages.

70.6.2.2   *Consequentialism (Teleology).*   One approach to evaluating the ethical dimensions of a proposed act is to look at the possible consequences of the act. Does the action minimize actual and potential harm? Egoism looks at what is good for me or does the least harm to me. Anonymous posting of critical information about a competitor's product offers the potential of benefits to one's employer with minimal direct consequences. However, such behavior opens up the organization to less obvious consequences, such as the risk of blackmail, degradation of trust within the group, lowered morale, and departure of employees whose moral sensibilities are outraged by what they see as unethical behavior.

Utilitarianism views decisions in terms of what is good for the group or does the least harm for the group. The question here is the inclusivity of the "group." If the group includes all users and potential users of the defective product, then posting the information serves a good purpose; the decision on whether to post anonymously resolves to the same questions as those raised in discussions of the consequences for an organization of having an employee post messages anonymously. The climate of trust, the credibility of warnings in general, and respect for the entire industry can be harmed by anonymous postings of warnings.

An altruistic approach to decisions accepts that what is good for all may be worth doing even if there is some harm to one's self. By this yardstick, posting a warning with full attribution is definitely the preferred way of communicating information about a problem. Another altruistic approach, however, would be to inform the competitor of the flaw in its product via private communications. The hope here is that such altruism will be reciprocated and that the industry as a whole can benefit from improvement in all products.

70.6.2.3   *Kant's Categorical Imperative.*   At a different level, Immanuel Kant's principles for judging the ethical dimensions of an act are immensely useful in all aspects of life. The principle of consistency asks, "What if everyone acted this way?" In our example, if everyone posted anonymous warnings, the credibility of all warnings would be damaged. In the absence of a mechanism of redress, unscrupulous people would contaminate the alerts with false information, making it difficult to trust any warning. Since some people would retaliate for fraudulent postings about their products by posting equally fraudulent attacks on their competitors, the system of alerts would collapse, causing harm to users and to producers.

Another principle Kant enunciated was that of respect: Are people treated as ends rather than means? The author of an anonymous message may not be thinking about the people affected by that message; they remain ciphers—amorphous, unknown entities of no importance. In contrast, an empathic and ethical person remembers that every group consists of individual human beings with pretty much the same range of feelings as anyone else. Using them as a means of increasing market share is not respectful.

70.6.3 Corporations and Other Organizations.

How can organizations contribute to the reduction of harmful anonymous or pseudonymous communications?

Every corporation, government department, nonprofit organization, educational institution, healthcare facility, banking or financial services organization, and so on should explicitly address the question of anonymity and forgery on the Net. Some practical guidelines to consider in setting organizational policy follow.

- No user of a corporate user ID should ever forge headers or use pseudonyms when communicating using corporate resources.
- Corporate firewalls should be configured to prevent all TCP/IP packets from passing outward through the firewall with forged IP addresses.
- SMTP servers should be configured to prevent any e-mail from leaving a site with forged headers.
- All corporate e-mail outbound from a site should be signed digitally by its author(s) to provide a basis, when necessary, for repudiation of unsigned and fraudulent e-mail.

In addition, discussions of the ethical framework for making decisions about the use of technology should be integrated into employee training at all levels. Managers, in particular, ought to be cognizant of the principles of ethical decision making so that they can fluently guide their staff in practical problem solving.

70.6.4 Internet Service Providers.

Because many users send e-mail or post to Usenet groups, through accounts with ISPs, these services have an obligation to become involved in preventing abuses of anonymity and pseudonymity. Except for some free services that are independently funded or that derive revenue from advertising rather than from user fees, ISPs must establish a relationship with their users in order to be paid; most use credit card accounts for this purpose. This method of billing inherently provides a link to the real-world identity of a user through the credit card issuers. Thus for most ISPs, it is possible to enforce traceable anonymity and pseudonymity. Faced with a subpoena, for example, most ISPs will be able to provide authorities with all the information needed to track down the person whose account was used to send a message. Whether the owner of the account is the author of a particular message depends on the security of identification and authentication mechanisms in use. Passwords, for example, are unlikely to be considered strong authentication because there are too many ways passwords can be compromised. Biometric authentication, however, may provide for strong authentication if error rates are considered sufficiently low to warrant the imputation of authorship based on biometrics.

One of the most interesting suggestions about the role of ISPs in governing anonymity and pseudonymity—and behavior in general—in cyberspace comes from Lewis.[81] Lewis suggested that those interested in banning anonymity online could support ISPs requiring traceable identity for all their customers. Let individuals choose what kind of ISP they want to use, but control access to their communications according to the degree of strong identification and authentication in use by the ISP. This suggestion is remarkably close to Post and Johnson's work on model systems in that ISPs can play a pivotal role in determining the future of the Internet without having to involve governments.[82]

Some practical suggestions for ISPs:

- ISPs could automatically sign every outbound message using their Public Key Cryptosystem secret key.[83] With today's fast parallel processors, it should be possible to sign outbound traffic without inordinate interference with transmission speed and at acceptable cost.

- Every e-mail message could be verified instantly as authentically coming from the specified ISP; forgeries would be practically impossible as long as the security of the ISPs secret keys was maintained.

- The next step would be publication of every ISP's terms of service in a public forum, signed by its secret key; these summaries would allow ISPs to sort themselves out immediately according to how restrictive their policies on anonymity and pseudonymity were.

- The SMTP would have to be modified to provide for verification of digital signatures, but given such changes, any ISP could automatically block incoming mail from ISPs whose policies were unacceptable.

For example, suppose the Truthful ISP insisted on maintaining records of exactly who was registered for any given ID and blocked outbound forged e-mail and unsolicited commercial e-mail. Truthful ISP might want to block mail from the CyberSleaze ISP, where forgeries and floods of spam were commonplace.

70.6.5 A Free Market Model for Identity in Cyberspace.
What might happen over time as a result of allowing communications only with selected ISPs, depending on their terms of service? Eventually there would likely be an equilibrium in which those users who wished to send and receive anonymous, untraceable e-mail could subscribe to those ISPs supporting that kind of communication. Others could automatically block e-mail from unwanted ISPs. Furthermore, individuals who wished to use anonymity or pseudonymity sometimes could subscribe to more than one ISP and take advantage of their different policies. Computer systems managers who wanted to deal only with other professionals at work could use a restrictive ISP; however, they also could use a different ISP to post and read messages in a highly charged, free-wheeling discussion group about the politics of gun control, without having to reveal their real names or fear that they could ultimately be traced through a pseudonym.

As the forces of the marketplace continued to work on ISPs, there might be further evolution toward different degrees and types of communication blockage. ISPs with a reputation for harboring miscreants who libel and defame others without cause could find themselves being shut out of an increasing number of reputable communities of users. Those whose users exercised moderation and responsibility might find themselves being received by a widening circle of ISPs.

The advantage of this model is that individuals could exert power over their electronic environment by voting with their subscriptions, but no one would be censored by bureaucrats or tyrants. Just as Hyde Park in England allows both geniuses and crackpots to speak yet forces no one to listen, the electronic Hyde Park would provide a mechanism for shutting out the lunatics while letting the loonies talk to each other as they wish.

What this model would not permit is the imposition of unwanted communications on powerless victims. This model would spell the end of unsolicited commercial e-mail. If digital signatures indicating the source ISP from which executable code was first distributed became commonplace, the same mechanism could seriously interfere with the distribution of viruses and other harmful programs. ISPs that became known for harboring virus writers or distributors would see their credibility as communications partners eroded. This model does not require individuals to sign their product or messages; the only constraint is that the ISP do so.

What about individuals who own their own domain on the Net? The same principles would apply. The modified SMTP software would automatically sign all output from their sites. Any site that refused to provide digital signatures could be excluded by any ISP that chose to apply such an exclusionary rule.

70.6.6 Governments.   The role of governments in cyberspace is complex. On one hand, several governments—notably that of the United States—have contributed to the development of the Internet through legislation and funding. On the other hand, many governments, especially totalitarian regimes, are intolerant of unfettered communications. Under the communist regimes, most countries in the Soviet Union and its satellites made ownership of unregistered spirit duplicators, photocopiers, fax machines, and modems illegal. Today, Burma, in the grip of the tyrannical State Law and Order Restoration Committee, still does. See Chapters 51 and 52 in this *Handbook* for more details of government constraints on speech in cyberspace.

No matter how carefully crafted they are, attempts to apply legal constraints on anonymity in cyberspace will be undermined by inconsistent government regimes throughout the globe. The least restrictive geographical entities will subvert more restrictive jurisdictions.[84] If, say, Restrictopolis were to impose strictures on anonymous Internet use, its anonymity-seeking citizens might be able to use the ISPs in Liberalopolis, where the rules would be much freer.

On a less practical, more philosophic level, there are profound objections to any government regulation of the Internet. As Lewis writes: "We do not outlaw wig shops or Halloween masks just because some people use them for illegal or immoral purposes. We do not require caller-ID services for everyone just because some people make obscene or harassing phone calls. Nor should we strip the cloak of online anonymity from everyone, including those who legitimately need privacy, just to prevent sickos from abusing it."[85]

In the United States, the government would likely run up against strong constitutional guarantees of speech, especially political speech—and including anonymous political speech—if it tried to ban anonymity outright.[86] A particularly significant setback for government attempts to control anonymity in the United States came in June 1997. The case began in January 1997.[87] As Declan McCullagh described the judgment:

> In Georgia, Judge Marvin Shoob ruled that a state law forbidding anonymity online is unconstitutional since it violates free speech and free association rights. The law is so broadly

written, the judge indicated, that even America Online screen names could be considered illegal. Judge Shoob "understood clearly the very strong need for our plaintiffs to communicate anonymously," the ACLU's Ann Beeson says. Both judges [in Georgia and in a similar case in New York] issued preliminary injunctions barring the state attorneys general from enforcing the laws. . . .

Georgia's Judge Shoob, in a 21-page opinion, ruled that the law—that the Democrat-controlled legislature passed in haste last year to muzzle a dissident Republican representative—violated the First Amendment.

This echoes a recent Supreme Court case, McIntyre v. Ohio, in which the justices ruled that the right to anonymity extends beyond political speech; that requiring the author's name on a leaflet is unconstitutional; that writing can be more effective if the speaker's identity is unknown.[88]

Democratic governments worldwide would do better to stay out of cyberspace and allow users to develop their own transnational solutions for governing behavior, including the use of anonymity and pseudonymity.

70.7 CONCLUDING REMARKS. Readers of this brief review of anonymity and pseudonymity are urged to consider these key observations and recommendations:

- Anonymous and pseudonymous communications are inherently associated with an increased incidence of antisocial behavior through deindividuation.
- There are circumstances where anonymity and pseudonymity are useful tools in the defense of liberty and justice.
- Anonymous and pseudonymous electronic communications have already been used to harass victims, damage commercial interests, and launch hoaxes and rumors into cyberspace.
- The major problems of anonymity and pseudonymity in cyberspace can be avoided by the use of traceable identification.
- Making ISPs responsible for enforcing their chosen level of strong identification and authentication will allow a nongovernmental, nonlegalistic approach to reducing abuse by anonymous and pseudonymous Internet users.
- All electronic communications ought to be tagged with unforgeable authenticators of identity.
- Individuals, families, and schools have a role to play in integrating cyberspace into the moral universe of children.
- Corporations and other organizations ought to integrate ethical decision making into their management procedures.
- Governments will continue to fail in their efforts to govern cyberspace because electronic communications networks are inherently divorced from geographical jurisdictions.

70.8 SUMMARY. The growth of the Internet has increased the use of anonymity and pseudonymity in electronic communications. Internet users must be able to preserve the benefits of privacy while fighting the abuses of anonymous and pseudonymous people. In the real world, identity resides in the ways that individuals are recognized and held responsible for their actions; in cyberspace, identity is potentially just a user ID. Social psychologists have found that anonymity can contribute to deindividuation—a state of loss of self-awareness, lowered social inhibitions, and increased impulsivity.

This chapter suggests practical applications of these insights from social psychology for managers concerned with reducing abusive behavior by their own employees. In addition, the chapter addresses the wider problem that, given the social psychology of anonymity, abuses of the Internet are certain to continue. There must develop a collective response to incivility and irresponsibility, without falling into authoritarian strictures on speech. This chapter further suggests that a free market approach using accessibility to communications as a kind of currency may help the Net evolve toward a more civil society. By blocking e-mail from ISPs that fail to enforce acceptable standards for a given community of users, Net users can sort themselves into groups that tolerate or welcome different levels of anonymity and pseudonymity. No government intervention would be required under such a system.

In addition, this chapter suggests a framework for reaching into the early years of the educational system to help integrate cyberspace into the moral universe of children worldwide. In addition to being a moral imperative to support educational efforts on computer ethics, such programs are in the best economic interests of industry, academia, and government systems managers.

70.9   FURTHER READING

Boellstorff, T. *Coming of Age in Second Life: An Anthropologist Explores the Virtually Human.* Princeton, NJ: Princeton University Press, 2008.

Federrath, H., ed. Designing Privacy Enhancing Technologies: International Workshop on Design Issues in Anonymity and Unobservability, Berkeley, CA, July 25–26, 2000. *Proceedings.* Springer.

Griffin, R. J. *The Faces of Anonymity: Anonymous and Pseudonymous Publication from the Sixteenth to the Twentieth Century.* New York: Palgrave Macmillan, 2003.

Nicoll, C., J. E. J. Prins, and M. J. M. van Dellen eds. *Digital Anonymity and the Law: Tensions and Dimensions.* Asser Press, 2003.

Robbins, S. and M. Bell. *Second Life for Dummies.* Hoboken, NJ: John Wiley & Sons, 2008.

70.10   NOTES

An asterisk (*) in notes marks a secondary reference drawn from D. G. Myers, *Social Psychology,* 4th ed. (New York: McGraw-Hill, 1993); R. A. Lippa, *Introduction to Social Psychology,* 2nd ed. (Pacific Grove, CA: Brooks/Cole Publishing, 1994); or D. O. Sears, L. A. Peplau, and S. E. Taylor, *Social Psychology,* 7th ed. (Englewood Cliffs, NJ: Prentice-Hall, 1991).

1. "Identity Theft Working Group Increases Federal Prosecutions: Maryland Crime Victims' Resource Center to Assist Victims," U.S. Department of Justice, United States Attorney's Office for the District of Maryland, February 21, 2008; http://baltimore.fbi.gov/dojpressrel/pressrel08/ba022108.htm.

2. R. Abelson, "By the Water Cooler in Cyberspace, the Talk Turns Ugly," *New York Times,* see http://query.nytimes.com/gst/fullpage.html?res=9F04E6D81039F93AA15757C0A9679C8B63

3. M. E. Kabay, "The INFOSEC Year in Review 1997"; see: www2.norwich.edu/mkabay/iyir/1997.PDF.

4. WHO@ home page: www.haltabuse.org/.

5. CyberAngels home page: www.guardianangels.org/cyberangels.php.

6. R. D. Clifford, *Cybercrime: The Investigation, Prosecution and Defense of a Computer-Related Crime*, 2nd ed. (Carolina Academic Press, 2006).

7. J. Kornblum, "Net Crime Begs Questions: Who to Call?" *C|Net News,* August 5, 1997; http://news.cnet.com/2102-1023_3-202141.html.

8. J. Kornblum "Antispam Efforts Heat Up," C|Net News, November 14, 1997; http://news.cnet.com/Antispam-efforts-heat-up/2100-1023_3-205363.html.

9. S. Covington, No. 97-06273 of the District Court of Travis County, Texas, 345th Judicial District; see: www.mids.org/nospam/judgment.html.

10. Internet Corporation for Assigned Names and Numbers (ICANN) "Top-Level Domains (gTLDs)," 2008, www.icann.org/tlds/.

11. R. Clarke, "Human Identification in Information Systems: Management Challenges and Public Policy Issues," *Information Technology & People* 7, No. 4 (1994): 6–37; www.anu.edu.au/people/Roger.Clarke/DV/HumanID.html.

12. A. M. Froomkin, "Anonymity and Its Enmities," *Journal of Online Law*, 1995, article 4; www.wm.edu/law/publications/jol/95_96/froomkin.html.

13. OSHA, "Milliken & Company VPP Star Site." OSHA Voluntary Protection Programs, Success with VPP, 2006; www.osha.gov/dcsp/success_stories/vpp/reg4_ss_milliken_elm.html

14. Clarke, "Human Identification in Information Systems."

15. Froomkin, "Anonymity and Its Enmities."

16. C. Free, "Make Their Day: Fury at the Wheel Turns Frustrated Drivers into Outlaw Dirty Harrys with a Rage for Revenge," *People Weekly* 48, No. 9 (1997): 59.

17. G. Le Bon, *The Crowd: A Study of the Popular Mind* (New York: Macmillan, 1896).*

18. L. Festinger, A. Pepitone, and T. Newcomb, "Some Consequences of Deindividuation in a Group," *Journal of Abnormal and Social Psychology* 47 (1952): 382–389.*

19. P. G. Zimbardo, "The Human Choice: Individuation, Reason and Order versus Deindividuation, Impulse, and Chaos," in W. J. Arnold and D. Levine, eds., *Nebraska Symposium on Motivation* (Lincoln: University of Nebraska Press, 1970).*

20. Free, "Make Their Day"; J. J. Russell, "The New Menace on the Road," *Good Housekeeping* 224, No. 4 (1997): 100–110.

21. Zimbardo, "The Human Choice."

22. R. I. Watson Jr, "Investigation into Deindividuation Using a Cross-Cultural Survey Technique," *Journal of Personality and Social Psychology* 25 (1973): 342–345.*

23. J. H. Kerr, *Understanding Soccer Hooliganism.* Buckingham: Open University Press, 1994.*

24. B. Buford, *Among the Thugs* (London: Mandarin Paperbacks, 1991).

25. E. Diener, S. C. Fraser, A. L. Beaman, and R. T. Kelem, "Effects of Deindividuating Variables on Stealing by Halloween Trick-or-Treaters," *Journal of Personality and Social Psychology* 33 (1976): 178–183.*

26. S. Prentice-Dunn and R. W. Rogers, "Effects of Deindividuating Situation Cues and Aggressive Models on Subjective Deindividuation and Aggression," *Journal of Personality and Social Psychology*39 (1980): 104–113*; E. Diener,

"Deindividualtion, Self-Awareness, and Disinhibition," *Journal of Personality and Social Psychology* 37 (1979): 1160–1171.*

27. M. Csikszentmihalyi, *Flow: The Psychology of Optimal Experience* (New York: Harper & Row, 1990).

28. C. B. Spivey and S. Prentice-Dunn, "Assessing the Directionality of Deindividuation: Effects of Deindividuation, Modeling, and Private Self-Consciousness on Aggressive and Prosocial Responses," *Basic and Applied Social Psychology*11 (1990): 387–403.*

29. K. J. Gergen, M. M. Gergen, and W. H. Barton, "Deviance in the Dark," *Psychology Today* (October 1973): 129–130.*

30. L. Detweiler, "Anonymity on the Internet FAQ" (1993), www.webster.edu/~bumbaugh/net/anonfaq.html; L. Detweiler, "The Joy of Pseudospoofing" (1993), http://cypherpunks.venona.com/date/1993/10/msg01172.html.

31. Detweiler, "Anonymity on the Internet FAQ."

32. R. Clarke "Introduction to Dataveillance and Information Privacy, and Definitions of Terms" (1999), www.anu.edu.au/people/Roger.Clarke/DV/Intro.html.

33. Clarke, "Human Identification in Information Systems."

34. Detweiler, "Joy of Pseudospoofing."

35. Detweiler, "Joy of Pseudospoofing."

36. O. S. Card, *Ender's game* (New York: Tor Books, 1985).

37. For current resources on electronic voting issues, see the Electronic Privacy Information Center's files at http://epic.org/privacy/voting/.

38. Froomkin, "Anonymity and Its Enmities."

39. Froomkin, "Anonymity and Its Enmities."

40. C. Johnson, "Anonymity On-line? It Depends on Who's Asking," *Wall Street Journal*, November 24, 1995, p. B1.

41. L. Lessig, D. Post, and E. Volokh (1997). *Cyberspace Law for Non-Lawyers*. Lesson 23—Privacy 11: Privacy: Self-Help: Anonymity, Part 1 (1997); www.ssrn.com/update/lsn/cyberspace/lessons/priv11.html.

42. L. Lessig, D. Post, and E. Volokh, *Cyberspace Law for Non-Lawyers*. Lesson 24—Privacy 12: Privacy: Self-Help: Anonymity, Part 2 (1997); www.ssrn.com/update/lsn/cyberspace/lessons/priv12.html.

43. Clarke, "Introduction to Dataveillance and Information Privacy."

44. E. Mahyuni, "Gone in 6 Seconds: Hotmail CAPTCHA Hacked by Spammers," Tech.Blorge, April 16, 2008; http://tech.blorge.com/Structure:%20/2008/04/16/gone-in-6-seconds-hotmail-captcha-hacked-by-spammers/.

45. W. Rodger, "Zero-Knowledge to Close Anonymity Service" (2001), www.securityfocus.com/news/262.

46. C. Pappas, "The A to Z of Internet Sleaze," *Home Office Computing* 15(8): 70.

47. Detweiler, "Anonymity on the Internet FAQ."

48. "Maimonides' Eight Levels of Charity." Mishneh Torah, Laws of Charity, 10: 7–14. Chabad.org Library, www.chabad.org/library/article_cdo/aid/45907/jewish/Eight-Levels-of-Charity.htm.

49. Clarke, "Introduction to Dataveillance and Information Privacy."

50. Froomkin, "Anonymity and Its Enmities"; A. M. Froomkin, "Flood Control on the Information Ocean: Living with Anonymity, Digital Cash and Distributed

Databases," *University of Pittsburgh Journal of Law and Commerce* 15 (1996): 395; http://osaka.law.miami.edu/~froomkin/articles/ocean1.htm.

51. J. Ubois, "Anonymity Has Its Place," *MIDRANGE Systems* 8, No. 8 (1995): 28.

52. Detweiler, "Anonymity on the Internet FAQ."

53. P. Steiner, "On the Internet, Nobody Knows You're a Dog." *New Yorker*, July 5, 1993; www.cartoonbank.com/item/22230.

54. B. Paisley, "Online" (2008), YouTube video of performance in Nashville: www.youtube.com/watch?v=W7RDTVZ1NWs.

55. Detweiler, "Anonymity on the Internet FA."

56. Froomkin, "Flood Control on the Information Ocean."

57. Froomkin, "Flood Control on the Information Ocean."

58. D. Post, "Knock Knock, Who's There?: Anonymity and Pseudonymity in Cyberspace" (1995), *www.cli.org/DPost/X0012_KNOCK.html*

59. Virtual Worlds Review: www.virtualworldsreview.com/.

60. Anonymous (2008). "Interview: Strategy Analytics' Barry Gilbert—137M Virtual Worlds Users Now; 1B by 2017," *Virtual Worlds News,* June 3, 2008; www.virtualworldsnews.com/2008/06/strategy-analyt.html.

61. G. Stringer, "The Internet" course notes, Creative Media and Information Technology course MIT 2114/2214, 2005. University of Exeter (UK), Chapter 8: Virtual Communities, www.services.ex.ac.uk/cmit/modules/the_internet/webct/ch08.html#d0e4833.

62. Clarke, "Introduction to Dataveillance and Information Privacy."

63. Detweiler, "Anonymity on the Internet FAQ."

64. Froomkin, "Anonymity and Its Enmities."

65. Froomkin, "Flood Control on the Information Ocean."

66. InfraGard home page: www.infragard.net/.

67. Detweiler, "Anonymity on the Internet FAQ."

68. Froomkin, "Anonymity and Its Enmities."

69. Post, "Knock Knock, Who's There?"

70. Detweiler, "Anonymity on the Internet FAQ."

71. L. J. Rose, *NetLaw: Your Rights in the Online World* (New York: Osborne/McGraw-Hill, 1994), pp. 183–184.

72. Froomkin, "Flood Control in the Information Ocean."

73. Good Times Virus Hoax FAQ: www.cityscope.net/hoax1.html; but see also the satirical version at http://ifaq.wap.org/computers/goodtimesfaq.html.

74. B. Mikkelson, "Craig Shergold," Snopes.com (2007): www.snopes.com/inboxer/medical/shergold.asp.

75. B. Mikkelson, "American Cancer Society Hoax." Snopes.com (2006); www.snopes.com/inboxer/medical/cancer.asp.

76. D. Post and D. R. Johnson, "The New Civic Virtue of the Net: Lessons from Models of Complex Systems" (1997), www.cli.org/paper4.htm.

77. Post and Johnson, "New Civic Virtue of the Net"; S. A. Kauffman, *The Origins of Order: Self-Organization and Selection in Evolution* (Oxford: Oxford University Press, 1993).

78. Post, "Knock Knock, Who's There?"

79. Post and Johnson, "New Civic Virtue of the Net."

80. M. E. Kabay, "Totem and Taboo: Civility and Vandalism in Cyberspace." Proceedings of the 17th National Computer Security Symposium, Baltimore, MD, October 11–14, 1994. Reprinted in NCSA News (June 1995): 4; online at: www2.norwich.edu/mkabay/ethics/totem_taboo_cyber.pdf.

81. P. Lewis, "Cloaks and Daggers: Online Anonymity Is a Blessing and a Curse," *Home Office Computing* 14, No. 7 (1996): 133.

82. Post and Johnson, "New Civic Virtue of the Net."

83. See Chapters 7 and 37 in this *Handbook*.

84. Froomkin, "Anonymity and Its Enmities."

85. Lewis, "Cloaks and Daggers."

86. Lessig et al., *Cyberspace Law for Non-Lawyers*, Lesson 24.

87. D. McCullagh, "Brick by Brick," *The Netly News* (editorial), 1997.

88. D. McCullagh, "Courts Strike Down New York and Georgia Net-Censorship Laws," sent Friday, June, 1997, 13:49:06 -0700 (PDT), on fight-censorship-announce@ vorlon.mit.edu mailing list.

CHAPTER 7

MEDICAL RECORDS PROTECTION

Paul J. Brusil

71.1 INTRODUCTION. U.S. regulatory compliance forces increased attention on information protection. Regulations such as SOX 404 (Sarbanes-Oxley), FISMA (Federal Information System Management Act), GLB (Gramm-Leach Bliley), HIPAA (Health Insurance Portability and Accountability Act), and others are establishing floors of due diligence regarding information protection in specific public and private sectors. They are requiring attention to information protection policy and procedures development, business process changes, technology enhancement, and other factors related to establishing and to maintaining information protection.

From a healthcare provider's perspective, there is tradition regarding the privacy and security of a patient's medical information. Indeed, the central concept of HIPAA privacy and security requirements arises from Hippocrates and his oath. Abusers of this oath, personnel outside the purview of this ethical oath, hackers, and criminals represent the people problems that HIPAA privacy and security regulations address.

This chapter identifies and examines the issues pertaining to privacy and security of personal medical records. The term "medical record" is used here to mean all types of healthcare information, be it dental records, therapist records, physician notes and records, medical claims, and so on. Medical records contain personally identifiable, confidential information, the protection of which is the subject of HIPAA and other privacy and security regulations.

Medical records are critical for a variety of healthcare delivery and healthcare business purposes, including diagnosis, preventive and curative treatments, research, administration, and numerous other activities. Medical records are crucial to the operations and survival of healthcare entities; they require stringent security measures.

The roles of information and technology in healthcare are considered in Section 71.2. Technical drivers for healthcare information privacy and security are examined in Section 71.3. Other drivers for healthcare information protection are summarized in 71.4. Applicable United States laws and regulations are identified in Section 71.5. Section 71.6 considers in some detail the most significant U.S. law regulating medical information: HIPAA.

71.2   INFORMATION AND INFORMATION TECHNOLOGY IN HEALTH-CARE

71.2.1   Medical Record Information Is Key to Healthcare.   Medical records are the lifeblood of healthcare entities, whether they are individual healthcare providers, small physician office practices, large medical hospital complexes, healthcare insurance companies, or insurance claims clearinghouse intermediaries.[1] Without patient data, research data, financial data, billing data, human resources, administrative data, and so on, healthcare entities can be crippled.

Care suffers if medical records are unavailable. Healthcare delivery after natural disasters has been devastated because of the unavailability of medical records. Other potential widespread events (disease outbreaks, cyberterror, etc.) may similarly impact connectivity to medical records and thus the delivery of healthcare services.

Healthcare information is essential to several organizations[2] for various purposes, some of which are identified here. Healthcare entities need information to meet obligations to customers, personnel, payers, (e.g., insurance companies or employers), and others. Historical personal medical record information is essential to all care providers who treat a specific patient. Information associated with current diagnoses and treatment plans supports payment of healthcare provider fees by government (e.g., Medicare/Medicaid) and/or private health insurance carriers. Personal records of hospital discharges, outpatient encounters, treatments, births, deaths, immunizations, and so on, are of interest to state and federal disease control agencies. Some healthcare information may also be needed by social service or law enforcement agencies.

Personal healthcare information also exists on commercial databases. Some are obvious: those maintained by pharmacies, rehabilitation facilities, and medical supply stores. Others are less obvious: databases derived from catalog orders, warranty registrations, and consumer questionnaires.

Other organizations need data aggregated across several personal medical records. Aggregated information provides actuarial data needed by healthcare administrators for cost trend analyses and insurance companies for insurance policy price setting. Other aggregated healthcare information facilitates epidemiological research, analyses of treatment efficacies, identification of long-term public health trends, or tuning of healthcare resource allocation plans.

71.2.2 Role of IT in Healthcare.   To cope with expansions of health care information, many healthcare entities must use information technology (IT) for acquiring, processing, storing, and conveying medical records and for measuring and improving the quality of care. Healthcare has been quick to adopt IT-enhanced medical technology to improve diagnoses, treatments, and patient care. However, it has been slower to embrace IT-assisted e-business principles for automating and improving business operations and efficiency. This has been surprising given the information-intensive nature of the business. It was not until the early 2000s that healthcare IT growth reached levels comparable to other IT-centric industries. Evidence shows IT is lowering healthcare cost escalation.[3]

Desire for IT-enabled, real-time, medical records access and handling is growing.[4] For treatment purposes, patients benefit when healthcare providers have rapid access to accurate information to assist in personalized decision making. For healthcare researchers, cures may lurk in evidence-based analysis of population-wide volumes of medical records. For healthcare business purposes, healthcare costs can be lowered when service claims and associated payments are exchanged in real time. Healthcare system improvements may arise when oversight bodies can analyze population-wide diagnoses and treatment regimens. Needs for rapid access to healthcare information drives the push for electronic medical records that can be exchanged readily among multiple parties, healthcare systems, healthcare entities, jurisdictions, and states.

Benefits accompany increased reliance on electronic medical records and associated IT to provide services, to conduct day-to-day business, and to share medical records. Estimates indicate over $80 billion will be saved annually with wide-scale IT adoption by care providers.[5]

But unwanted consequences accompany IT proliferation. Their likelihood is increasing. IT vulnerabilities and risks can lead to healthcare information exposure, misuse, abuse, or alteration and to delivery of potentially inappropriate healthcare services and treatments. As sensitive healthcare information is accumulated, aggregated, and made accessible to more parties, there is a greater chance of massive disclosures of personal information, breakdowns of medical services, and catastrophic personal and economic losses.

71.3 INFORMATION PRIVACY AND SECURITY ARE IMPORTANT IN HEALTHCARE.   Privacy and security of medical records started drawing attention in the 1990s. HIPAA and PDD-63 (Presidential Decision Directive 63) focused national attention on healthcare information protection. Section 71.3.1 identifies technological risks and vulnerabilities associated with medical records. Needs and challenges of healthcare information protection are considered in Ssection 71.3.2. Section 71.3.3 summarizes a core model for healthcare information protection.

71.3.1   Increasing Healthcare Information Technology Risks and Vulnerabilities.   As new networking and IT capabilities, devices, applications, and systems are introduced to the healthcare field, risks and vulnerabilities accompanying electronic medical records increase.

Incidences of medical record breaches are increasing. An emergency room patient attempted suicide after being called by a prankster who stole patient contact information and wrongfully informed the patient of pregnancy and HIV infection. Over 100 hospital employees pried into the medical records of a renowned athlete receiving treatment. A governor's health record and numerous voters' medical records were retrieved from a database of state employee health insurance claims, using birth date and ZIP code data obtained from a voters' database.

Over a six-month period in 2006,[6] privacy breaches rose at 45 percent of healthcare payers to nearly two-thirds of payers. Most payers experienced up to five privacy breaches. Over a third of providers and payers experienced at least one, and up to 11, data security incidents. Military employee personal health information was not immune to breaches.[7] At the Department of Veterans Affairs, disclosure of up to 29 million personal records containing healthcare information is among the largest privacy breaches.[8] Even the agency that promulgated HIPAA was not immune; a General Accounting Office review of the Department of Health & Human Services (HHS) concludes HHS is behind in incorporating security into everyday operations. Significant security weaknesses could lead to breaches of personal health information from millions receiving Medicare and Medicaid coverage.[9]

Medical identity theft is a looming crisis.[10] Stolen care provider identities can be used to post false prescriptions and to submit fraudulent billing claims. Stolen patient identities can be used to steal healthcare services and prescription drugs. Stolen services lead to potentially harmful, bogus additions to legitimate patients' medical records. Fraudulent claims can lead to false patient copays, false provider back-billing of patients, and inappropriate exhaustion of patient lifetime benefits. Nearly 500,000 yearly victims may exist.[11]

Use of emerging technologies for acquiring, processing, storing, and communicating healthcare information escalates security breech opportunities and susceptibility to ever-newer attack vectors. Increasing numbers of unsavory individuals plying the Internet escalate potentials for breaching medical records: more cads exploiting vulnerabilities in more healthcare networking gear and in integrated healthcare IT systems and applications.

For example, Web technology allows healthcare entities to set up personal electronic medical records that can be accessed, managed, amended, and corrected online, both through portals for healthcare providers and portals for healthcare consumers. Attackers thus have more potential entry points to attempt healthcare information breaches. Furthermore, undetected spyware and keystroke loggers can transmit recorded keystrokes of sensitive personal patient information to the unintended.

New data warehousing and mining tools supporting healthcare information fusion, convergence, and analysis bring new information protection problems. Information cross-referencing and merger across private and public databases can create highly confidential, cradle-to-grave personal medical information profiles by aggregating distributed snippets of less sensitive data. Potential merger of medical records with other personal information databases housing shopping and credit card information can create data warehouses with disturbing amounts of aggregated personal and medical information. As sensitive healthcare information is merged, the greater is its value as a potential target for cyber malcontents.

As new technologies are fielded in healthcare environments, more vendor implementations of new technologies need to be trusted both for their ability to be implemented correctly and for assurance that they can minimize new risks and exposures. Trust must be established (see, e.g., Chapter 51 in this *Handbook*) that there are no vendor implementation flaws that allow unauthorized information to be entered into or extracted from medical records.

71.3.2 Healthcare Information Privacy and Security Needs and Challenges.   Medical records protection is essential not only for protection of personally confidential information but also for success, stability, and survival of healthcare entities' care delivery, operations, and businesses.

Privacy and security policies, procedures, and mechanisms are needed for various reasons. They are needed to facilitate safe access to, and distribution of, patient history data to support both local treatment planning and remote treatment planning (e.g., by off-site specialists or telemedicine service providers). They are crucial to real-time payment for rendered healthcare treatments and prevention of falsified billing claims. They enable the business side of healthcare to leverage electronic commerce paradigms. Healthcare entities can benefit from real-time healthcare service provisioning and business operations models while controlling attack costs.

From the patient perspective, healthcare information privacy is paramount, along with ensuring reliability of data used in medical decisions. Healthcare consumers do not want cyberterrorists making deadly changes to electronic medical records and treatment orders. Both personal safety and population safety demand protection of healthcare information.

Some of the challenges associated with medical records protection may be unique to healthcare; for example:

- Wireless communication of orders and patient information to and from the hospital bedside, or among healthcare provider's offices, can be prone to disclosure, modification, and eavesdropping by medical services and information thieves, busybodies, and paparazzi.

- Errors or deliberate alterations associated with billing charges may be criminal; but they can be deadly in the case of healthcare histories, treatment orders, or prescriptions. Survivability of both patients and healthcare entities is at stake.

- Many healthcare providers are attaching to the Internet to submit billing claims or to access patient medical records.

- Electronic commerce with supply-chain partners provides other potential points of entry to healthcare IT systems. Healthcare entities must establish trust in the security provided by parties that may never be seen or met.

- Many factors increase the likelihood that medical information will be accessed by the unauthorized and used improperly. They include proliferation of government, institutional, and commercial databases housing medical information, large numbers of people involved in settling health insurance claims, and the number of people, authorized and unauthorized, who can access a person's medical records.

- Multiple replications of healthcare data and multiple data users elevate risks of data exploitation.

- Multiparty needs for medical records lead to pressure on legislatures for legal restraints on access to personal information by different parties.

- Because the healthcare industry is so fragmented with different players and stakeholders, it literally takes an act of Congress to coordinate the industry in matters such as IT, privacy, and security.

- As the healthcare industry is a latecomer to embracing IT, it tends to lack experience in IT privacy and security strategies, mechanisms, and procedures.

- With immaturity of information assurance (IA) experiences and knowledge of IA issues in the healthcare sector, the it-won't-happen-to-us mentality is prevalent and medical records protection issues are downplayed.

71.3.3 Core Privacy and Security Model in Healthcare.   The model of medical records privacy shifted with the advent of HIPAA. Patients now own their own private healthcare information. All other healthcare entities and individuals must protect that information from intentional or unintentional disclosure. Security procedures, measures, and mechanisms are used to protect and to maintain privacy of patient information.

The classic model of information security, built on healthcare entities striking acceptable balances among availability, confidentiality, integrity, and accountability, applies. These attributes are essential for establishing trust in healthcare information during its capture, processing, storage, transmission, and sharing.

- **Availability.** Information has to be available to those who are entitled to see it or to process it, at the time when they need it. Those who do not need specific information in the performance of their duties must be denied access. Threats to availability arise from denial of service attacks and from deliberate or accidental infrastructural damage to networks, hardware, and software.

- **Integrity.** Information needs to be defended against accidental or deliberate corruption and modification. Threats include viruses, malware, worms, emerging Internet-borne threats, unauthorized or accidental modification, errors in structural integrity, logical corruption, and fraudulent misuse.

- **Confidentiality.** Information should not be available to those who are not entitled to see or to process it. Threats include unauthorized access and disclosure by hackers or by careless disregard for the rights of privacy.

- **Accountability.** Healthcare entities must establish and control who is responsible for what. Nonrepudiation mechanisms must safeguard against denials of specific actions. Also, security incidents may be nobody's fault but may be big problems if prevention is nobody's *job*. Individual responsibility must be a matter of record so that appropriate remedial action may be taken, including assignment of blame and additional training.

Trade-offs exists among these attributes. Emphasizing one may adversely impact others. For example, emphasis on confidentiality may impact availability (physical and electronic access controls tend to complicate legitimate access). In combination with other factors (e.g., human error, or hardware or software failure) preserving confidentiality may result in less accessible data.

Medical records protection measures need to be tailored to the precise privacy and security requirements of each specific healthcare entity. Therefore, government regulations should not prescribe specific protection mechanisms universally applicable to all healthcare entities.[12]

**71.4 NONMEDICAL DRIVERS FOR HEALTHCARE INFORMATION PRO-
TECTION.**   Medical records protection is not just a technical issue. It is also subject
to nontechnical, social, administrative, and regulatory pressures both outside and inside
healthcare entities.

71.4.1 Political Pressure.   Many healthcare services are the responsibility of
state or federal governments. Being under governmental auspices assures tensions
created by political pressures. Many politicians focus on requiring healthcare administrative simplification (and presumed cost-cutting) and extending publicly funded
coverage to different population groups. Issues surrounding the privacy and security
of medical information may not appear as rallying points for elections. They can unite
political factions, as was the case for passing HIPAA legislation. But the cost burdens
of complying with HIPAA may act to increase political tensions and factions.

71.4.2 Public Pressure and Media Pressure.   Public sensitivity about
medical records seems related to possible embarrassment if sufferers' maladies were
known. Some medical conditions carry emotional baggage or taboos. If disclosed, they
can significantly impact a patient's everyday life. They can impact job or promotion
prospects. They can impact appraisal of fitness as parents. They can upset eligibility for
insurance or quality of life rights. Creditworthiness or financial status can be affected.

There is concern of intrusive sales efforts targeted on the basis of healthcare information. Such tactics are seen as an invasion of privacy.

Public opinion seems indeterminate as to how significant a priority is medical record
privacy during the heat of a medical emergency.[13]

Media have their own political or socioeconomic agendas, but all are interested in
"good" stories. Bureaucratic incompetence is newsworthy, as are medical or computer
malefactors. Maladies of celebrities, misdiagnoses, or surgical mistakes receive wide
coverage.[14]

71.4.3 Patient Expectations.   Patients often perceive their personal information as confidential and expect that anyone who works with their data has a "duty of
confidence." Americans overwhelmingly favor strong protection of their healthcare
information.[15]

- Computerization is seen as the greatest threat to privacy; over 50 percent believe
  the shift from paper to computer-based systems makes protection of their medical
  information more difficult.

- Patients are reluctant to divulge their medical records to anyone other than their
  care providers; 60 percent prefer not to grant access to prospective employers. Seventy percent do not want drug companies to use personal data in pharmaceutical
  sales and marketing databases.

- Most patients do not trust private and government health insurers to maintain
  confidentiality; only a third trust such entities to maintain confidentiality.

- Many patients worry that the privacy of their medical information will be violated.
  About 15 percent even withhold information when asked for medical history. They
  also may provide false information, pay medical fees personally even if insured,
  change doctors, ask doctors not to keep a record of their condition, or avoid
  medical care altogether.[16]

Interestingly, despite concerns about medical record protection, many patients feel such protection is under control by technology vendors or healthcare entities even in light of the rash of large personal information breeches at many institutions.

Patient expectations in other countries, such as the United Kingdom, are similar. For example, the National Health Service of the United Kingdom includes this reassuring language in its "Core Principles":

> The NHS will respect the confidentiality of individual patients and provide open access to information about services, treatment and performance.
>
> Patient confidentiality will be respected throughout the process of care. The NHS will be open with information about health and healthcare services. It will continue to use information to improve the quality of services for all and to generate new knowledge about future medical benefits.[17]

71.5 UNITED STATES LAWS AND GOVERNMENT POLICIES.

Healthcare entities are impacted by numerous statutes, some specific to the healthcare industry, some more general. Some U.S. laws that pertain to the privacy and security of healthcare information are identified in the sections that follow.

71.5.1 Federal Laws

- **Privacy Act.** One of the earliest laws covering medical databases is the Privacy Act of 1974. Without written individual consent, this law forbids disclosure of personally identifiable health information, such as Medicare treatment records, collected by the U.S. government. In addition to Privacy Act provisions, the HHS Centers for Medicare & Medicaid Services are required to follow specific additional Privacy Act Regulations.[18]

- **False Claims Act.** Healthcare providers submitting fraudulent claims can be punished with triple damages, penalties of $5,000 to $10,000 per wrongful billing, and exclusion from government insurance programs. Many of the accused settle out of court because it is often more expensive to win such legal cases and much more costly if they lose. Without adequate security, electronic billing can open doors to malicious attacks on healthcare claims so that they appear to be wrongful, prosecutable billing claims.

- **HIPAA.** HIPAA is a massive and comprehensive law pertaining to several areas of healthcare. HIPAA includes a section on Administrative Simplification, which includes provisions for privacy and security for healthcare information. HIPAA's Administrative Simplification section amended the Social Security Act title XI and has been added—in total—as Part C of Title XI. HIPAA is discussed in detail in Section 71.6.

- **Electronic Signature Act of 2000.** The Electronic Signatures in Global and National Commerce (E-Sign) Act provides for an e-signature to have the same legally binding weight as a written signature. There appears to be movement on the part of healthcare providers toward use of electronic signatures on treatment and prescription orders.

- **FISMA.** Certain government agencies that deal with healthcare information need to comply with both HIPAA and the Federal Information Security Management Act of 2002 (FISMA).[19] FISMA requires all federal agencies to adopt and to demonstrate use of NIST-specified IT security processes and procedures that include categorizing risks associated with IT systems, developing and maintaining minimum controls to protect information systems, verifying and monitoring the effectiveness of their security controls via a specified certification and accreditation framework, and taking corrective actions when necessary. The private sector might benefit by using the NIST framework together with HIPAA (and also ISO 17799) requirements to "assess, measure, track, and deliver a more secure and user-friendly [information handling environment] and in the process achieve [HIPAA] compliance."[20]

71.5.2 State Privacy and Security Laws.

Several states have applicable laws. For example, California's Security Breach Information Act (Senate Bill 1386) requires any company—including those that are entities covered under HIPAA—to disclose potential security breaches. This is the seminal law that establishes a new paradigm for combating personal information disclosure breaches. The law targets disclosure offenders rather than imposing burdensome regulations on all. It leverages data custodians' desires to sustain their images as reliably safe repositories of personal information. As such, having sufficient information protection safeguards is essential. As of 2006, 23 states had similar laws.[21] The corresponding New York law extends provisions to apply to state government agencies.

Although these laws maybe intended to be used when "consumer" personal data are compromised, it is not hard to imagine patients as consumers (of healthcare).

Observers have noted that the existing state laws are overlapping, inconsistent, and incomplete.[22] Accordingly, federal legislation may establish a uniform, national solution that supersedes the mosaic of state laws.

71.5.3 Government Policies.

Various government policies relate to medical record protection. Policies try to enhance or to fill gaps in existing laws, or to establish rules in lieu of applicable laws. Some policies may be overtaken by events or are of uncertain precedence priority with respect to laws. As such, the examples that follow may no longer be applicable at the time of the reading of this chapter. Readers should investigate what policies may be in effect when reading this material.

- **Presidential administrations** issued policies,[23] plans,[24] and positions[25] wherein the healthcare sector is deemed a critical national infrastructure. It needs to be protected. It needs to continue operating because the nation and economy depend on it.
- **The Health Care Finance Agency (HCFA)** established policy[26] for incorporating security functionality and for appropriately using the Internet to convey healthcare information protected by the Privacy Act as well as other sensitive HCFA information.
- **The Office of Management and Budget** promulgated policy recommending all federal agencies, including those operating as healthcare entities for which HIPAA is also applicable, to implement protection mechanisms including encrypting all data stored in mobile devices and establishing database access logging.[27]
- **The National Security Telecommunications and Information Systems Security Committee** representing the aggregate of major federal agencies issued a policy directive[28] pertaining to the purchase and use of IT products. The policy looks to the purchase and use of products evaluated according to the Common Criteria. It is felt that such evaluations increase trust in the security features

implemented in IT products. This policy applies to federal agencies that act as entities covered under HIPAA.

- **The Federal Acquisitions Regulation Council** issued a rule specifying that procurement officers at all federal agencies are required to incorporate IT security requirements in their IT acquisition planning. This policy applies to federal agencies that act as entities covered under HIPAA.

- **The Executive Branch** issued the Homeland Security Presidential Directive/ HSPD-12[29] requiring government employees and contractors working at government agencies—including those operating as entities covered under HIPAA regulations—to use specific government IDs issued by trusted authorities only to identity-proved individuals.

71.5.4 Emerging Legislation.   Pertinent legislative activities constantly emerge. HIPAA started a chain reaction of new legislation related to IT-oriented privacy and security. New laws and regulations are likely, especially given that many feel extant laws are insufficient.[30] Advocacy and lobbying groups, such as the Consumer Privacy Legislative Forum,[31] form to help drive legislation that may impact healthcare in unpredictable ways.

Although it is impossible to identify legislation emerging when this chapter is published, readers should be vigilant about what looming legislation may be adopted and may impact their medical records privacy and security situations.[32] In the mid-2000s legislative activities were high, examples of which follow. Some proposed legislation is specific to healthcare. Others are generic but have definite potential to impact healthcare. Certainly even more legislation will follow.

At the time of going to press (July 2008), the THOMAS database[33] reported 120 bills before the 110th Congress with floor action (i.e., that had been reported from committee for action by the House or Senate)[34] that included the term "health information." Some of the key legislation under consideration at that time included:

- Dignified Treatment of Wounded Warriors Act
- Free Flow of Information Act of 2007
- Genetic Information Nondiscrimination Act of 2007
- Health IT Promotion Act
- Healthcare Information Technology Enterprise Integration Act
- Medicare Improvements for Patients and Providers Act of 2008
- Wired for Health Care Quality Act

Some look to affirm HIPAA. Others look to fix gaps and inconsistencies in HIPAA or to address privacy issues from the perspective of nationwide sharing of all healthcare information.

As for generic privacy legislation, the rash of privacy breaches sparked interest in passing consumer-oriented, personal data protection legislation.[35] If adopted, enterprising attorneys will likely look to establish precedent that patients are also covered "consumers" (of healthcare services). There is interest in updating the Privacy Act. Other efforts that readers can track[36] included:

- Consumer Notification and Financial Data Protection Act
- Data Accountability and Trust Act

- Electronic Health Information Privacy Act
- FISA Amendments Act of 2008
- Identity Theft Enforcement and Restitution Act of 2007
- Personal Data Privacy and Security Act
- Personal Data Privacy and Security Act of 2007
- Safeguarding America's Families by Enhancing and Reorganizing New and Efficient Technologies Act of 2007
- Social Security Number Privacy and Identity Theft Prevention Act of 2007

Other federal legislation pertains to privacy on wireless transmissions. Such legislation may impact use of personal digital assistants (PDAs), other bedside devices, and portable ambulatory care devices used for medical record information capture and retrieval, and treatment order entry. Other legislation is looking to establish a government commission to investigate privacy issues in the United States. Other legislation includes a potential amendment to financial security laws to restrict the use of healthcare information when making credit and financial decisions.

Federal legislation is accompanying the government's desire to design and to implement a National Health Information Infrastructure with associated Electronic Health Records. Legislation may be needed to reconcile differences in state-specific healthcare information standards and pertinent state-specific information protection regulations. As input to this legislation, a multistate National Health Information Privacy and Security Collaboration has been formed to identify and to propose resolutions to state-by-state differences in privacy and security practices and laws.[37]

At the state level, California is looking to enhance SB1386 to notify individuals if their personal information is stolen from paper records or backups of computer-stored data. There has also been discussion of adding safe harbor provisions to such laws to protect organizations from liability and to absolve them of notification responsibilities if they encrypt personal data.

While governments are looking to expand information protection regulations, the private sector wishes to address IT security through incentives such as government-funded R&D and tax breaks, not through regulatory obligations.[38]

Despite industry's desires, it appears that development of regulations will only intensify. Emerging legislation is also spreading into other IT-powered national infrastructure industries, such as telecommunications, energy, and power that support the healthcare industry. It appears legislative interest in IT privacy and security that may impact the healthcare sector will be present for years.

71.6 HEALTH INSURANCE PORTABILITY AND ACCOUNTABILITY ACT.
HIPAA[39] establishes federal regulations for several areas of healthcare and its administration. It is the most sweeping change to the healthcare industry since the introduction of Medicare. It is moving the industry toward widespread use of technology, electronic information, and a single, common electronic transaction environment for electronic billing.

An overview of regulations relevant to electronic medical records and their protection appears in Section 71.6.1. The HIPAA strategy for addressing protection is given in Section 71.6.2. Summaries of the specific HIPAA regulations that pertain to medical records protection appear in Sections 71.6.3 and 71.6.4. Section 71.6.5

provides overviews of penalties for HIPAA violations. Observations pertaining to fielding HIPAA regulations appear in Section 71.6.6.

71.6.1 HIPAA Administrative Simplification Overview. HIPAA does not just focus on patient data privacy and security matters. HIPAA goals include (a) improving portability and continuity of healthcare insurance when a patient changes jobs, (b) minimizing waste, fraud, and abuse in healthcare insurance and healthcare delivery, and (c) simplifying healthcare insurance administration.

Administrative Simplification (Title II, Subtitle F of HIPAA) looks to improve the efficacy and reliability of the healthcare system and to reduce its costs. It looks to minimize so-called protected health information (PHI), consisting of deliberate or inadvertent access, alteration, loss or deletion, transmission, disclosure, or misuse of personally identifiable patient healthcare information. These may occur during the acquisition, processing, storage, and transmission of such information within, or between, specific healthcare entities called "covered entities."

To effect these intents, Administrative Simplification mandates development and use of several so-called standards, which are the regulations containing requirements that pertain to conveying and to protecting personal healthcare information. Several regulations have been developed; others are yet to be developed.

71.6.1.1 Electronic Transaction Regulations. Specific EDI (Electronic Data Interchange) transactions with standardized content are specified for use among covered entities such as healthcare payers, healthcare providers, and others. The transaction types pertain, for example, to health claims submissions, claims status checks, care encounters reports, health plan eligibility/enrollment/de-enrollment, care payments, plan premium payments, treatment authorization, and so on.

Specific standard content is stipulated for these transactions. Unique identifiers must be used to represent covered entities and employers[40] so that any entity that touches or adds/modifies healthcare information can be uniquely identified. Unique code sets must be used as transaction data elements to represent, for example, encounter descriptions, diagnoses, billing, and so on.

Healthcare providers can choose whether to use the stipulated electronic transactions or to continue using paper-based transactions. Healthcare payers are required to accept transactions both in standard electronic form and in paper-based form.[41] The largest U.S. healthcare payer, Medicare, mainly deals with electronic transactions and accepts paper-based billing transactions only under limited circumstances.

Additional HIPAA transaction standards are constantly under development. For example, one established in 2006[42] pertains to HIPAA standard transactions for electronic attachments to electronic healthcare claims.[43] Attachments may convey clinical and administrative data useful to adjudicating payment for an electronic billing claim.[44] The popular and trade press continue to monitor HIPAA developments.[45]

71.6.1.2 Information Protection Regulations. Administrative Simplification specifies regulations[46] for privacy and security[47] applicable to PHI while it is in the custody of covered entities, in transit between covered entities, and in transit from covered entities to others. Regulations include developing, documenting and implementing privacy and security policies and procedures (P&P), implementing security technology addressing specified security requirements, training staff about HIPAA requirements, guaranteeing patient rights regarding their PHI, and appointing privacy and security directors to monitor and to enforce privacy and security matters. The privacy and security provisions are amplified in Sections 71.6.3 and 71.6.4.

71.6.1.3 Compliance Regulations.   HIPAA includes a strategy to enforce compliance to its rules by officers and employees of covered entities. It stipulates penalties (Section 71.6.5) for violations including intentional and unintentional disclosure of PHI.

71.6.2 Privacy and Security Strategy.   The HIPAA approach for healthcare information protection focuses on stipulating privacy and security requirements—not on specifying privacy and security solutions.

The privacy and security requirements are applicable under two basic conditions. The requirements apply to (a) "covered entities" and (b) to all personally identifiable, patient healthcare information—precisely and legally defined as PHI—associated with such covered entities.

Covered entities of all types and sizes must meet these requirements. Covered entities are stipulated and include:

  a. Health insurance carriers (sometimes referred to as "health plans," including government agencies such as the Centers for Medicare and Medicaid Service that act as insurance carriers)

  b. Healthcare billing clearinghouses (entities between providers and payers that can, if necessary, translate covered entities' transactions between HIPAA standard formats and nonstandard/proprietary, payer-specific or provider-specific formats)

  c. Healthcare providers (institutions like medical centers, private physicians, and government agencies that provide healthcare services such as the Federal Employee Health Benefits Program, and DoD's TriCare Program), if they conduct certain specified transactions

  d. Business associates of covered entities (including government contractors such as those contracted for processing Medicare claims).

Contrary to some perceptions,[48] not every organization that generates, processes, or holds personally identifiable health information is a "covered entity" that must abide by HIPAA information protection regulations.[49] Tools to determine whether any specific entity is a "covered entity" are available.[50]

The privacy requirements stipulate how PHI is controlled. Legally authorized uses and disclosures are defined. Privacy requirements pertain to PHI created, stored, or conveyed in any form. For PHI in electronic form, privacy protection largely depends on HIPAA-stipulated security requirements.

The security requirements apply only to PHI in electronic, "computerized" form.[51] By securing electronic transactions that convey PHI between healthcare IT systems and by securing storage and processing of electronic PHI, abuse and fraud can be minimized and privacy of such information can be increased. The security requirements can be met by common, generally accepted, widely used security principles and practices.

HIPAA does not specify a one-size-fits-all privacy and security solution, applicable to all situations. Although every covered entity that electronically receives, maintains, processes or transmits PHI must comply with applicable HIPAA privacy and security requirements, HIPAA does not specify how to meet these requirements. Privacy and security requirements may be met by covered entities by appropriate combinations of P&P, measures, security technology, and other ways deemed appropriate by each covered entity.

By focusing on privacy and security *requirements* rather than *solutions*, HIPAA offers flexibility, scalability, and technology neutrality; different covered entities can meet HIPAA information protection requirements by whatever strategy is reasonable and appropriate to each covered entity at any given point in time. Particular solutions may vary from situation to situation, but each solution must meet the HIPAA requirements. Some healthcare enterprises may need to implement more sophisticated information protection solutions than others. Small, less complex healthcare provider offices may have more limited privacy and security P&P and training requirements than those of large, more complex medical centers. Healthcare enterprises may need to change aspects of their information protection strategy as they change in size.

HIPAA's information protection requirements are:

- **Scalable,** so that they work for both small practices and large healthcare enterprises, at reasonable cost

- **Technology-neutral,** so that as technology changes, covered entities are not bound to outdated solutions, and efficacies of new technologies can be leveraged without having to change HIPAA's information protection regulations[52]

- **Flexible,** so that different covered entities and their business partners can use policies, procedures, methods, and technologies appropriate to their situations—as long as they meet HIPAA's information protection requirements

HIPAA provides a national floor for the protection of PHI; state and other federal laws may provide even stronger protections. In some cases, HIPAA may enhance the protections afforded by other laws. In other cases, other laws may deal with privacy and security more stringently than HIPAA. In circumstances where HIPAA and other jurisdictionally applicable laws are in conflict, HIPAA specifies that stronger information protection laws prevail.[53] If HIPAA is the most stringent applicable law, covered entities are free either to use HIPAA privacy and security requirements or to adopt even more protective requirements.

Covered entities must each assess their own potential risks to the PHI they handle. They must develop, document, implement, and maintain appropriate information protection P&P and measures to address their unique risks and situations. They can use risk management techniques to help decide what strategy of potentially overlapping safeguards is reasonable and appropriate to their situations. All analyses, decisions, and rationale for decisions must be documented. HIPAA allows covered entities to select industry-acceptable, best-practice information protection strategies for the situation at hand.[54] Covered entities need periodic assessments to ensure continuing appropriateness and adequacy of their solutions to meet HIPAA requirements.

HIPAA does not specify how compliance to HIPAA information protection requirements is achieved. Each covered entity decides how it will achieve compliance with HIPAA requirements. Guidance from the HHS Centers for Medicare & Medicaid Services (CMS)[55] and the HHS Office of Civil Rights (OCR),[56] or neutral, third-party guidance such as that provided by the National Institute of Standards and Technology (NIST),[57] the Industry Advisory Council,[58] and others[59] may be useful to help covered entities architect appropriate protection strategies compliant with HIPAA requirements. Further, when implementing an architected strategy, it may be useful to consult some of the solution-specific and/or HIPAA-compliant product lists[60] published by the trade press to identify potential procurement options. Other implementation assistance may become available via the efforts of the Certification Commission for Health IT (CCHIT) chartered to develop criteria[61] and processes for certifying security measures of IT products associated with the emerging U.S. Electronic Health Records initiative.[62]

71.6.3   Privacy Regulations.   Privacy regulations[63] establish requirements pertaining to safeguarding privacy of PHI in any form[64] from inappropriate or unauthorized disclosure or use. Regulations apply to PHI created, stored, processed, used, transmitted, or received by covered entities (and certain of their associated contractors and service providers). They limit sharing of PHI by covered entities. They also establish requirements pertaining to rights of patients with regard to their healthcare information.

The strategic concept associated with these requirements is simple: to ensure patients' personal information is adequately protected and kept private without unduly disrupting the flow of healthcare information needed to provide, to oversee and to pay for care, to assist healthcare research, and to improve the quality of the healthcare system. These requirements strike a balance between providing patients with greater peace of mind versus the public responsibility to support national medical priorities. Such priorities include protecting public health, identifying public health trends, conducting medical research, improving the quality of care available for the nation, and fighting healthcare fraud and abuse.

Given the massive extent, diversity, and complexity of the healthcare sector, the privacy requirements are comparably comprehensive—and appropriately flexible—to cover the plethora of uses of healthcare information by various covered entities and others outside the healthcare sector. Only a brief introduction and summary of the privacy requirements is given here.

The privacy regulations provide patients with rights to inspect and to correct their personal healthcare information, and otherwise to control how their health information is used and shared. The regulations require written patient consent for each covered entity to use a patient's PHI. Disclosure of PHI without patient consent is allowed for only a few, specified reasons. The regulations require business partners of each covered entity—via contracts or other similar mechanisms—to maintain the privacy of any patient information that is provided to them by the covered entity.

The regulations define the generally accepted set of information to be protected and kept private. It includes patient demographic information, common identifiers, insurance billing and payment information, symptoms, examination and test results, diagnoses, treatment, and future care plans that can be associated with or used to identify a patient, and so on. This information may be oral or recorded in any form or medium, such as paper, magnetic tape, computer drive, and so on. There are no privacy requirements that apply to healthcare information that is de-identified via specified ways.

A sampling of the privacy requirements follows.[65] As readers' needs dictate, more detailed synopses[66] or the full HIPAA Privacy Regulations should be consulted for increasingly more detailed descriptions of privacy requirements.

- **General use and disclosure requirements.** Other than information that is specifically permitted or under the written consent of the applicable patient, a covered entity cannot use or disclose PHI.

- **Specific permitted use and disclosure requirements.** Covered entities may share certain PHI without a patient's formal signed consent only under certain specified situations, including, for example, among healthcare providers involved in a patient's treatment, with third-party payers (e.g., insurance carriers), with the patient, with parties involved with medical reviews assessing the quality of patient care, with parties involved with assessing the performance of care providers and healthcare operations, and with regulatory and public health agencies, ethical researchers, and auditors. For certain specified reasons, a covered entity may share certain PHI with only informal patient permission not involving a signed, formal consent authorization.

- **Required use and disclosure requirements.** Covered entities are permitted—but not required—to share PHI without a patient's consent or permission for 12 national priority purposes outside a patient's healthcare context. Examples of these purposes include public health activities, law enforcement, legal proceedings, protecting victims of abuse, workers' compensation, and so on.

- **Authorization requirements.** A patient-signed, written consent authorization with certain specified conditions and constraints is required by covered entities for any use or disclosure of PHI that is not for treatment, payment or healthcare operations or otherwise permitted or required.

- **Minimum necessary data requirements.** Covered entities are required to develop and to use P&P to ensure that no more PHI is used or disclosed than the minimum amount needed for each purpose for which information is used or disclosed.

- **Privacy practices notice requirements.** Covered entities are required to develop privacy practice notices, to post these notices, and to collect individual patient acknowledgments of their receipt. These entities must abide by clearly stated procedures that (a) protect the privacy of patients' information, (b) describe how PHI is used and disclosed, and (c) describe how patients can access their PHI.

- **Patient access and control rights requirements.** Covered entities are required to give individual patients the rights to receive a copy of the entity's privacy practices notice and to specify how the entity should communicate with the patient. Patients have the right to inspect, and to obtain copies of, any disclosures and distributions of healthcare information about themselves. Patients have the right to get an accounting of the disclosures and to amend, correct, and restrict the uses, disclosure, and distribution of healthcare information about themselves.

- **Administrative requirements.** Covered entities are required to develop and to implement appropriate privacy P&P consistent with the HIPAA privacy regulations and tailored to fit their size and complexity, to train and to discipline employees regarding privacy P&P, and to designate a privacy official responsible for the entity's privacy practices and activities.

- **PHI safeguards requirements.** Covered entities are required to have reasonable and appropriate administrative, technical, and physical safeguards to prevent intentional or unintentional use or disclosure of PHI in violation of the HIPAA privacy regulations and to otherwise abide by all the allowed and disallowed uses and disclosures of PHI. The HIPAA security regulations (see Section 71.6.4) stipulate such safeguards for electronic PHI.

71.6.4 Security Regulations. These regulations[67] establish requirements for safeguarding confidentiality, integrity, and availability of electronic PHI created, received, processed, and/or stored by covered entities. PHI must be protected against reasonably expected threats, vulnerabilities, and hazards as well as against disclosures and inappropriate use not permitted by HIPAA's privacy regulations. The requirements also establish an organizational culture that facilitates the provisioning and maintenance of security safeguards.

There are linkages between HIPAA privacy requirements and HIPAA security requirements.[68] Some requirements overlap or complement each other. For example, privacy and security regulations both contain awareness-training requirements. They can be combined so that employees of covered entities stay aware of both the importance of protecting PHI and the means by which PHI is protected. In other cases, a specific security requirement may need to be implemented to address a specific privacy requirement.

As outlined below, the security regulations stipulate various categories of administrative, technical, and physical security requirements as well as organizational, P&P, and documentation requirements. They require covered entities to assess risk and to provide for the safeguarding of electronic PHI at risk. For each covered entity, there must be fully auditable procedures for controlling access to PHI and for protecting PHI against compromise and misuse.

71.6.4.1 Administrative Safeguards Requirements. These requirements pertain to administrative P&P and actions targeted to manage (a) selection, deployment, and maintenance of security safeguards to protect electronic PHI and (b) roles of employees in protecting PHI. The requirements categories include:

- **Security management process.** Implement P&P for preventing, detecting, containing, and correcting security violations.
- **Assigned security responsibility.** Identify an individual responsible for developing and implementing security-oriented P&P.
- **Workforce security.** Implement P&P for ensuring appropriate employee access to, or denial of access to, PHI.
- **Information access management.** Implement P&P for authorizing access to PHI consistent with privacy access requirements.
- **Security awareness and training.** Implement a security awareness and training program for all employees.
- **Security incident procedures.** Implement P&P for handling incidents that impact systems associated with PHI.
- **Contingency plan.** Establish and implement P&P for responding to emergencies that damage systems containing PHI.
- **Evaluation.** Periodic assessments that the security P&P address the security requirements.
- **Business associate contracts and other arrangements.** Establish legally binding, chain-of-trust agreements with business partners for protecting PHI conveyed to such partners.

71.6.4.2 Physical Safeguards Requirements. These requirements pertain to physical measures and associated P&P to protect IT systems, facilities, and applicable equipment from physical hazards, unauthorized physical access, and unauthorized intrusions. The requirements categories include:

- **Facility access controls.** Establish and implement P&P to control physical access to IT systems, related equipment, and the facilities that house them.
- **Workstation use.** Implement P&P regarding physical location and use of computers to access electronic PHI.
- **Workstation security.** Implement physical safeguards to control physical access to computers used to access electronic PHI.
- **Device and media controls.** Implement P&P regarding receipt, reuse, and disposal of hardware, software, and electronic media that handle electronic PHI.

71.6.4.3 Technical Safeguards Requirements.   These requirements pertain to technological measures and associated P&P to protect and to control access to electronic PHI created, maintained, and communicated to and from electronic healthcare systems. The requirements categories include:

- **Access control.** Implement technical P&P for controlling access by people and software to IT systems that handle electronic PHI.
- **Audit controls.** Implement technical and procedural mechanisms that examine and record activities and accesses to IT systems that handle electronic PHI.
- **Integrity.** Implement P&P to ensure the validity of electronic PHI.
- **Person or entity authentication.** Implement procedures to verify legitimacy of people and software attempting to access electronic PHI.
- **Transmission security.** Implement technical security measures to control unauthorized access to electronic PHI in transit over computer networks.

71.6.4.4 Organizational Requirements.   These requirements pertain to using business associate contracts or other official arrangements to establish trust that third parties associated with, or providing services to, covered entities will maintain HIPAA provisions.

71.6.4.5 Policies and Procedures and Documentation Requirements.   These requirements pertain to developing all the requisite P&P (as outlined earlier), to developing and using all required documentation and documentation configuration control measures, and to implementing the P&P to comply with HIPAA security regulations.

71.6.4.6 Implementation Specifications.   Each stipulated security requirement summarized above must be met by a defined implementation specification stipulated in the HIPAA security regulations, or, if no implementation specifications exist, by measures documented and implemented by each covered entity. NIST Special Publication 800-66 identifies (in Table 2) implementation specifications accompanying each security requirement.

For security requirements met by HIPAA-stipulated implementation specifications, such implementation specifications are individually identified as either being "required" or "addressable."[69] Covered entities must comply with all 13 *required* implementation specifications. Covered entities must document how they assessed and decided whether each specific *addressable* implementation specification is appropriate, or not, and whether it applies, or does not, to their specific environment, and whether the covered entity implemented, or not, each addressable implementation (or some equivalent alternative measures). NIST SP 800-66 Table 2 also summarizes which implementation specifications are required and which are addressable.

For example, to meet HIPAA's contingency plan requirement, a covered entity is *required* to establish and to implement data backup, disaster recovery, and emergency mode operations plans; and it must also *address* procedures for testing and revising such plans.

71.6.5 Enforcement, Penalties, and Liabilities.   Unlike other government regulations, such as SOX, HIPAA depends on weaker, non-proactive enforcement strategies. It does not include yearly comprehensive audits and compliance standards that must be met. There are no "HIPAA police" to seek out HIPAA violators. There is no government willingness to fine violating organizations millions. It does not have the teeth or effectiveness of proactive regulations like SOX.

Instead, the focus is strictly on complaint-driven enforcement. PHI disclosure victims must initiate triggering complaints and take on liability of uncertain legal outcome.

Specific HHS offices receive and investigate complaints. They decide about the interpretation, implementation, and enforcement of certain HIPAA regulations.[70] Security regulations enforcement rests with HHS CMS. Enforcement of privacy regulations rests with HHS OCR.[71] Procedures for filing PHI complaints are available.[72] Evidence[73] suggests HIPAA complaint handling is nontrivial for the involved HHS offices.

In response to a complaint, these HHS offices can impose civil (monetary) and criminal (prison) penalties for certain HIPAA violations. Initial track records suggest these offices have not been inclined to impose penalties and would rather work with implicated covered entities to fix situations that may have led to complaints. When HIPAA complaints are not resolved, covered entities can be penalized $100 per violation, up to $25,000 per year per HIPAA requirement not met. HIPAA specifies relatively small penalties on the officers and/or employees of healthcare-relevant organizations that fail to address HIPAA requirements.

However, there are large criminal penalties—fines and imprisonment—for those who wrongfully handle confidential PHI. Any person who knowingly obtains, uses, causes to use, intends malicious harm, tries to sell or to transfer or to gain from, or discloses, patient information inappropriately faces penalties.[74] Penalties range from $50,000 to $250,000 and up to 10 years imprisonment, depending on seriousness of the offense.

Although penalties can be stiff, some argue the real dangers of HIPAA enforcement may instead arise from loss of confidence in the implicated entity and possible litigation under contract law. When disclosure of personal information causes damage and the legal system is engaged, HIPAA penalties—especially the criminal penalties—can mean the difference between business failure and business survival for implicated entities. PHI disclosures, whether wrongful or unintentional, have potentials to be devastating. Some argue potential consequences of HIPAA litigation should be considered when developing disaster plans.

It may not be only directly implicated, covered entities that are at risk for PHI disclosure penalties. The "linked liability" concept may extend HIPAA-relevant liabilities and penalties to others. Covered entities forced into litigation for PHI privacy or security breaches may try to share blame or to pass it to others, such as the communications provider used to connect covered entity offices. Such other parties may also try to spread blame to yet others, such as negligent vendors of IT products with implementation errors, vulnerabilities, and less than adequate security. The ultimate assignment of liability may be legally tortious.[75] To minimize liability exposure, firms linked in even obtuse ways to covered entities are wise to be able to show (a) they exercised due diligence in establishing normal and customary privacy and security measures within their enterprises, services, or products; (b) their measures are in line with industry best practices and HIPAA requirements, and (as required by HIPAA) anticipate and address new threats; and (c) they made correct decisions regarding their privacy and security measures.

Some argue employers offering health insurance also have implicit liabilities linked to HIPAA. They argue, first, that employers have a duty to ensure healthcare plans and associated care providers offered to employees are compliant with HIPAA. Second, when insurance carriers send enrollment and benefits data to employers, employers are acting as business associates subject to provisions that business associates of covered entities must also be HIPAA compliant.

71.6.6   Realities in Fielding HIPAA Information Protection Regulations.   Many believe HIPAA makes good business sense. They feel HIPAA's information protection regulations are generally what any protection-conscious organization would do on its own. They feel healthcare-accrediting organizations should include HIPAA regulations in their accrediting criteria. As such, it would seem reasonable to expect large voluntary compliance rates. However, although many who are knowledgeable in information protection say HIPAA protection regulations are a necessity given the risks of growing and evolving threats, the real-world impact of HIPAA currently appears mixed.

Surveys indicate HIPAA has prompted increased procurement of IT and security technology, especially by large care provider entities and especially those with supportive executives.[76] However, HIPAA is not just technology and cash poor; nonprofit providers struggle to find staff and resources to undertake HIPAA compliance efforts. Many feel that the burdens of demonstrating compliance to many applicable regulatory laws—not just HIPAA—are excessive.

At the time of this writing, HIPAA has not reached the level of panacea that was hoped for by the law's authors (Senators Kennedy and Katzenbach). Both cost savings and ubiquity seem difficult to realize, although some analysts claim to find measurable return on investment.[77]

The next sections examine HIPAA's acceptance, benefits, shortcomings, and future impacts.

71.6.6.1   Benefits Are Appearing.   Like the sister law GLB applicable to the financial sector, HIPAA fosters in the healthcare sector a fundamental new paradigm in the way electronic information of a personal type is handled and protected both of these laws extend to personal electronic information the rigorous legal control traditionally applied only to paper documents.

Anecdotally, many "soft" benefits are accruing as a result of HIPAA. Entities in the healthcare industry are being tied together better. With shifts away from paper-based healthcare information and transactions, productivity and efficiency seem to be increasing.[78] Administrative and back-office costs appear lower because of diminished error rates in creating insurance claims, less opportunity to commit fraud, and reductions in sizes of accounts receivable queues. Staff easily adjust to stronger authentication procedures when accessing PHI.

Of significant benefit is that patient privacy sensitivity is elevated, and there has been improvement in privacy and security awareness, practices, and measures.

71.6.6.2 Compliance Trends Are Mixed.
Attempts to comply with HIPAA have seemed inconsistent and in some cases slow.[79] Even though many regulation compliance dates have passed, the rate of compliance of covered entities is not total.

In 2006 (three years after the mandatory standard transaction compliance date), about three-fourths of healthcare providers and payers indicated they *could* exchange HIPAA transactions; but only about two-thirds said they *are* exchanging some HIPAA standard transactions.[80] There are reasons that HIPAA standard transactions use has been emerging slowly. There appears to be much finger pointing.[81] Providers say they are ready but their payers are not. Payers report they are ready but their providers are not.

As for privacy requirements compliance, in 2006 (three years after the mandatory privacy compliance date) about 80 percent of providers and carriers claimed they were "mostly" compliant to HIPAA privacy requirements. The apparent inverse observation that perhaps up to one-fifth of covered entities are unable or unwilling to comply with privacy requirements is eye opening. Furthermore, evidence exists that the number of (even partly) compliant covered entities may be dropping somewhat year-to-year.

As for security requirements compliance, in 2006 (one year after the mandatory security compliance date), only 55 percent of large healthcare providers and about 70 percent of insurance companies were in complete compliance with security regulations. Although the initial rate[82] of achieving compliance for security requirements appears greater than the initial rate[83] of achieving privacy compliance, the compliance numbers reported for insurance carriers may be misleading and may be lower.

The compliance evidence for small providers anecdotally suggests HIPAA compliance can be a tremendous, uncertain burden. (See Section 71.6.6.3 for examples.)

It is not clear whether continuation of the above, less-than-stellar compliance rates will trigger disciplinary actions by HHS OCR and CMS HIPAA enforcement bodies.

71.6.6.3 Compliance Status by Covered Entities.
Large care providers (e.g., hospitals and medical centers) generally are complying in large numbers. The compliance story for other entities is dubious. Small care providers (single doctors and small offices of care providers) tend to be overwhelmed. Insurance carriers are often not changing their systems and procedures to adapt to HIPAA. Clearinghouses are trying to provide interfaces between providers and carriers, but these intermediaries are having troubles too.

Large Providers Status.   Large healthcare providers are often well equipped with staff and resources to adopt, and to maintain compliance with, HIPAA provisions. Many are already set up with appropriate staff to handle compliance to other laws (e.g., SOX in the case of publicly traded provider entities) and other regulations including periodic accreditation reviews (e.g., potential security and privacy audits conducted by the healthcare sector's Joint Commission on Accreditation of Healthcare Organizations, JCAHO). Some feel HIPAA regulations are too burdensome, require unreasonable funding rates, and in some cases are too difficult or too much of an impact on legacy healthcare procedures. Many others, on their own and before HIPAA was conceptualized, instituted many[84] of the good practices now required by HIPAA. Some did not understand they were already doing the right things for privacy and security until they audited their information protection procedures, process, and technology relative to HIPAA requirements. These were well positioned to comply fully and quickly. For them, it is clear HIPAA-promulgated standards, processes, and regulations are reasonable precautions, make organizations more credible, and make good business sense. Perhaps the greatest problem facing large providers was to identify all the data element instances with HIPAA-defined PHI associated with a specific patient.

Insurance Carriers Status.   Insurance entities appear to have difficulties adapting to HIPAA.[85] Surveys indicating high compliance rates may be misleading. Some carriers retain old, noncompliant business, computing, and communication strategies and rely on clearinghouses to provide HIPAA-compliant interfaces to providers. Interactions between clearinghouses and carriers may still be the same as before HIPAA was instituted. Why? Because such carriers may be unwilling to change their operational claims and payments systems. Much as for the Y2K situation, carrier systems may be old, minimally documented, legacy systems written in old computer languages by code designers who are long since gone. Carrier executives fear changing or replacing their systems that "work." Furthermore, defining need-to-know rules to accompany claims processing, coverage provisioning, and communications with providers has been problematic.

Depending on the extent of their businesses, some insurance carriers must conform to several other major government regulations, such as SOX and GLB, for which enforcement of regulations is certain. With perceived lack of HIPAA enforcement, and lack of desire to change working systems critical to their business, the HIPAA compliance story may be clouded.

Clearinghouse Status.   For intransigent carriers, clearinghouses translate between HIPAA-compliant transactions, with accompanying protection measures, and carrier-specific methods of interacting. Sometimes carriers incorrectly claim they "outsource" their HIPAA compliance needs to clearinghouses.

Interactions between clearinghouses and large providers seem to have become HIPAA compliant with more regularity. Why? Perhaps because large providers that are already set up for electronic claim submissions with electronic PHI are led to believe they will not get payments if they are not HIPAA compliant, and they do not want to jeopardize their primary flow of income, namely carrier payments for their services rendered. Perhaps, in an attempt to lower their own HIPAA-compliance liabilities, clearinghouses may put pressure on providers to comply with HIPAA regulations.

In short, it appears most claims interactions between clearinghouses and large providers are HIPAA compliant while some are not, and claims interactions between clearinghouses and carriers are often not HIPAA compliant because carrier systems have not been modified to receive or send HIPAA transactions and to address HIPAA protection requirements.

Small Providers' Status.   For small providers, the situation is much different. Many still bill via paper claims and some (especially in the dental community) do not have computers in their practices. For them, HIPAA transaction and security regulations do not apply, and their flow of income is not dependent on changing to electronic PHI and electronic claims transactions. However, many—but not all—of the HIPAA privacy and security requirements still apply, along with a multitude of other government-imposed regulations. Small providers may feel less pressure because they perceive large hospitals are more tempting HIPAA enforcement targets.

Some insurance carriers are providing Web interfaces for direct billing interaction with care providers. But for small care providers, there are substantial logistical and pragmatic problems. Batch submission of claims via browsers is not supported, and the practice management software used in small care provider offices is generally written to interface to a specific clearinghouse and not via a browser. It is also not clear that carriers' Web interfaces support HIPAA-stipulated EDI transactions.

Confusion as to what is or is not required for small providers to comply is the norm. Most do not have people on their staffs dedicated to compliance issues; and they are working "flat out" trying to delivery patient care. Many are already running with substantial non–revenue-generating overhead without even considering adding staff for HIPAA matters.

They receive constant barrages of HIPAA guidance and newsletters from vendors, provider professional societies, and others. They receive solicitations from consultants whose credibility is unknown and who purport to be able to tell them what to do for HIPAA compliance. Equipment vendors tell them their products are "HIPAA compliant." Vendors do not necessarily tell them to what parts of HIPAA their products comply, nor what procedures buyers need to follow to meet other associated HIPAA requirements. They do not know exactly what they must do regarding HIPAA compliance. Professional societies send books on how to comply, but small providers cannot take the time and financial loss of ceasing to deliver services in order to read the books to determine how to deal with HIPAA information protection regulations and how to prove whether they comply with HIPAA.

Many suspect that handing out generic HIPAA privacy forms is sufficient. But they do not necessarily know what all the sentences mean or what to do if a patient does not sign the form. The more proactive ones make staff more aware of privacy and security, alter some procedures, and appoint individuals (typically, IP-naive) as responsible privacy and security officials (who typically do not have the clout of management).

In short, dealing with HIPAA is often a mess for the smallest care providers. Confusion and uncertainty abound.

71.6.6.4 Other Potential Reasons for Noncompliance.   Additional anecdotal reasons have been cited for why privacy compliance rates may be stagnant or dropping. Such reasons also abound for why other HIPAA compliance rates are not higher.

Some surveys cite difficulty in accounting for all PHI disclosures, increased costs, and diminished management support—despite threat of personal penalties.[86]

Others argue there is innate difficulty to make holistic IA approaches as espoused in HIPAA work, because of organizational and corporate cultural difficulties. These may arise when trying to converge IT security, physical security, and the various other aspects of IA.[87] Still others argue[88] that HIPAA regulations are too voluminous, and insufficient staff is available to manage regulatory information protection requirements.[89]

Some feel a more effective way to make sure privacy and security of personal information is enhanced is to move away from a regulatory environment toward an "image-oriented" environment (akin to that associated with California law SB1386). They feel PHI custodians will be motivated if they must notify affected individuals when a PHI breach is believed to have occurred. The image-oriented strategy may have merit given the importance that many organizations, including healthcare organizations, place on brand image, perceived community status, the perceived criticality of data privacy to brand image or status,[90] and the plausible assumption that fear of unflattering publicity will force enterprises to strengthen their information protection measures.

Some covered entities may not yet realize that HIPAA compliance is an ongoing business process—not a one-time event—that must continue forever after the initial push to verify initial compliance with HIPAA. It must be a continuous commitment and process that needs to be sustained as new threats, new IT, and new security technology strategies emerge.[91] Some feel technology is changing so quickly it is hard to discern whether products based on newer technology are covered by and, if so, comply with HIPAA regulations.

With issued HIPAA noncompliance penalties being few and far between, and with lack of HIPAA policing bodies, some say the "stick" associated with enforcing HIPAA violations does not seem a significant deterrent to noncompliance. They have no fear of legal or publicity retribution.

To date, experience has borne out the reality of this lack of concern.[92] As of 2006, there have been about 20,000 privacy violation complaints. Of these, only 300 were refered to the Justice Department for criminal consideration. There has been only one conviction where the defendant, not the covered entity, was fined $9,000 and sentenced to 16 months in prison.[93]

Many feel government enforcement is matched to the context within which a PHI complaint is reported. Legal recourse would be used only to prosecute deliberate and flagrant violations. For covered entities showing a good-faith effort to resolve situations that led to PHI breach complaints, the government will not adopt an adversary prosecutorial stance.

However, other factors may counterbalance a laissez-faire attitude toward HIPAA violation prosecution. HIPAA enforcement is not the only recourse for personal information disclosure associated with medical records. Monetary penalties have been significant when other avenues were pursued. For example, while not necessarily related to HIPAA infractions per se, in 2005 the California Department of Managed Health Care fined a division of a health insurance carrier (Kaiser Permanente) $200,000 for exposing the PHI of over 100 individuals.[94] In one of the larger privacy breaches in the United States, in 2006 the unauthorized discloser of personal information—albeit not PHI—from 6 million people was ordered to pay New York State over $1 million.[95]

71.6.6.5 Cost Examination.
The government hopes strategic cost savings and competitive pressures are strong motivators for HIPAA to be promulgated throughout the healthcare sector.

However, the cost picture regarding HIPAA compliance is complex and has not yet been well researched. It includes factors such as costs to upgrade extant policies and procedures, technology, processes, and staff training so as to attain initial HIPAA compliance. It includes HIPAA-compliance maintenance costs. It must reflect the savings (or cost growth retardation) generated by using HIPAA's electronic business model. It must reflect the savings generated by minimizing the cost to recover from numerous information breaches. Only anecdotes related to costs are currently available, and opinions about cost factors are mixed.

Aggregate costs to attain initial HIPAA privacy compliance are estimated at $17.5 billion over 10 years.[96]

Costs to attain initial HIPAA security compliance vary dramatically among covered entities. Many have in-place information protection measures, and the gaps between what they have fielded and what HIPAA requires, tempered by the risk-assessment–determined value of closing each gap, will vary substantially from entity to entity. It will also depend on factors such as entity size. For large carriers with old legacy business, computing, and communication strategies, questions arise as to whether the costs of undertaking an uncertain conversion for the sake of achieving HIPAA compliance may far exceed the benefits of such compliance.

Although the government understands many of the factors that drive the cost to achieve initial security compliance,[97] it is difficult for the government to predict with certainty what the aggregate of these costs may be across all covered entities. Certainly, because HIPAA applies to over 2 million covered entities, the overall impact of HIPAA information protection compliance will easily exceed the $100 million threshold the government uses to label a major economic impact. Privately, senior HHS officials have indicated the aggregate financial impact just from achieving initial HIPAA compliance will rival the $8 billion cost of fixing the Year 2000 problem.

The actual recurring annual costs associated with HIPAA have been large. At about $4 billion[98] annually, they are similar to the costs to achieve and maintain compliance with SOX 404. Although aggregate costs appear high, start-up and annual costs devoted to HIPAA compliance for any given covered entity do not seem unreasonable.[99]

The government estimates the combined impact of all HIPAA regulations will save[100] the healthcare sector $29.9 billion over 10 years.[101]

For now, the jury is still out regarding the cost picture associated with HIPAA. Some believe that HIPAA privacy and security regulations do not simplify health-care administration and instead impose significant new administrative burdens on the healthcare sector. Others believe it is inappropriate to put a price on personal privacy. Is the cost of implementing HIPAA nationwide exceeding the predicted costs? Probably. Is HIPAA lowering the costs (or slowing the rate of cost increases) of healthcare by lowering the funds spent on billing paperwork and by increasing efficiencies on the business side of healthcare? Perhaps. Is HIPAA requiring healthcare entities to spend more money on HIPAA-compliant IT and compliance maintenance processes? Absolutely. Does this lead to spending less on patient care? Unlikely. Will the savings incurred by complying with HIPAA offset the costs of converting to and maintaining compliance with HIPAA? Perhaps not. Are the costs of maintaining compliance with HIPAA less than the savings that could be incurred if health-care sector automation greater than that specified within HIPAA is adopted? No one knows.

But HIPAA compliance activities have certainly raised awareness of privacy and security issues; staff and management are more conscious and conscientious about patient privacy. What price is reasonable for maintaining protection of one's private PHI? Evidence shows it can be high.[102] Some argue it is priceless. Perhaps the hindsight of time will shed light on the various potential cost/savings factors.

71.6.6.6 *Potential Future Impacts.*   There are many impacts of HIPAA that are yet to be considered fully. Examples follow.

The precedence between privacy and security requirements of state laws and the federal HIPAA law can have problematic consequences. Interoperability issues can arise between parties that have stronger protection methods and those that have the common, minimal level of protection stipulated by HIPAA. Some argue that HIPAA is not particularly appropriate for emerging healthcare IT models based on nationally networked, electronic healthcare records.[103] Development and exchange of electronic healthcare records is hampered by inconsistencies and variations in privacy and security policies and regulations between jurisdictions. Furthermore, there may be legal questions regarding how patient data can be shared across state lines. Some argue that HIPAA needs to be modified to provide more comprehensive national information protection standards that form a consistent, mandatory uniform ceiling above the growing hodge-podge of similar but inconsistent state laws. Studies of these potential problems just began at the time of writing this chapter.

Along another vein, government information protection regulations may be having some adverse effects. Information protection compliance matters are now visible to senior executives and boards. Organizations focus efforts on updating P&P and mechanisms to comply with regulations. But there is evidence that organizations may be so fixated on initial compliance efforts as to pay little attention to emerging security threats and emerging IT technologies.[104]

Other complaints are arising from healthcare research efforts that rely on evidence-based medicine and longitudinal studies of patients. Such research may require some sort of patient identifying mechanism to correlate several different disclosed medical records associated with the same individual. HIPAA creators are aware of this concern.[105] The HIPAA privacy regulations allow for covered entities to use institutional review boards or privacy boards to waive individual authorization to disclose and to use PHI for research purposes.[106] Such provisions can add costs to research studies. Other solutions have been proposed.[107,108]

Of some concern are increased efforts by a growing number of countries to develop national electronic health record infrastructures that rely on patient-perceived confidence in PHI protection assurance.[109] Growing patient concern about privacy seems to be occurring in parallel with a corresponding decreased rate of compliance with information privacy and security regulations.[110] These dichotomies portend potentially troubling, clashing trends.

Signals from other economic sectors relying on Internet-supported capabilities currently seem mixed. The rash of breaches of personal data nationwide has been massive,[111] smacks of complete ineptitude, and still appears to be increasing.[112] Consumer resistance has started slowing the growth of online banking. Complaints associated with other mandates such as SOX have increased. Such factors have the potential to impact negatively on HIPAA endorsement within the healthcare sector.

On the brighter side, increased awareness of healthcare privacy and security issues brought about by HIPAA has led to positive efforts in the healthcare sector.

Covered entities banded together in 2006 to form the eHealth Vulnerability Reporting Program.[113] This was an alliance focused on collaboratively finding, publicizing, and fixing vulnerabilities in healthcare application software, especially those software packages that are large and for which software development errors would be more numerous, on average. This group evolved into HITRUST, the Health Information Trust Alliance, which has established a Common Security Framework (CSF) for health information security.[114]

Traditional healthcare accreditation organizations, such as the Electronic Healthcare Network Accreditation Commission (EHNAC) and the Utilization Review Accreditation Commission (URAC), which conduct, independent, third-party accreditations of covered entities, are expanding foci to examine healthcare information protection. For example, EHNAC Healthcare Network Accreditation Program examines privacy/security/PHI matters.[115] URAC is looking to HIPAA privacy accreditations[116] and HIPAA security accreditations.[117]

71.7   SUMMARY.   Medical records are at the heart of proper healthcare, but there are innumerable threats to their security and privacy. Although many government and industry initiatives are aimed at protecting these data, their success has been somewhat limited. Expansion of existing efforts and potential new directions may be necessary before the problems can be resolved, and the opportunities and benefits realized.

71.8 FURTHER READING

Amatayakul, M., ed. *Handbook for HIPAA Security Implementation*. American Medical Association, 2003.

Beaver, K., and R. Herold. *The Practical Guide to HIPAA Privacy and Security Compliance*. Auerbach, 2003.

Hoyt, R., M. Sutton, and A. Yoshihashi. *Medical Informatics: Practical Guide for the Healthcare Professional*. Lulu.com, 2007.

Krager, C., and D. Krager. *HIPAA for Health Care Professionals*. Delmar Cengage Learning, 2008.

Wu, S. S. *A Guide to HIPAA Security and the Law*. American Bar Association, 2007.

71.9 NOTES

1. HIPAA calls such entities "covered entities."

2. Some organizations considered here are not HIPAA-specified "covered entities." They may not be impacted by HIPAA.

3. N. Ferris, "Insurers Tout Efforts to Promote Health IT," *Government Health IT Newsletter,* December 13, 2005; www.govhealthit.com/online/news/91712-1.html.

4. M. K. McGee, "A Pill, a Scalpel, a Database," *InformationWeek,* February 13, 2006; www.informationweek.com/news/management/showArticlejhtml?.articleID=179103437 or http://tinyurl.com/5laupl.

5. M. K. McGee, "No Quick Cure for Healthcare System," *InformationWeek*, October 24, 2005; www.informationweek.com/news/management/showArticle.jhtml?articleID=172303129 or http://tinyurl.com/5v5hqs. See also M. K. McGee, "Putting the Pressure on Providers" InformationWeek, October 24, 2005; www.informationweek.com/news/management/showArticle.jhtml?articleID=172303130 or http://tinyurl.com/5a96pp.

6. HIMSS/Phoenix Health Systems, "US Healthcare Industry HIPAA Compliance Survey Results: Winter 2006," www.hipaadvisory.com/action/surveynew/results/winter2006.htm.

7. D. Onley, "Intrusion Detected in DoD Server," *Government Computer News,* May 1, 2006; http://appserv.gcn.com/cgi-bin/udt/im.display.printable?client.id=gcn_daily&story.id=40626 or http://tinyurl.com/6hgqql.

8. Health Privacy Project, "Data Security Breach Discloses Veterans' Medical Information," May 24, 2006; www.healthprivacy.org/info-url_nocat2303/info-url_nocat_show.htm?doc_id=374199 or www.healthprivacy.org/info-url_nocat2303/info-url_nocat_show.htm?doc_id=374199 or http://tinyurl.com/5tvds6.

9. J. Appleby, "Security of Medicare Info Questioned," *USA Today,* March 23, 2006; www.usatoday.com/tech/news/computersecurity/2006-03-23-medical-data_x.htm or http://tinyurl.com/5euctm.

10. C. Heun, "E-health Initiatives Could Lead to New Forms of ID Theft," *InformationWeek,* June 16, 2006; www.informationweek.com/news/showArticle.jhtml?articleID=189500020 or http://tinyurl.com/5qs9pj.

11. P. Dixon, "Medical Identity Theft: The Information Crime that Can Kill You," *World Privacy Forum,* May 3, 2006; www.worldprivacyforum.org/pdf/wpf_medicalidtheft2006.pdf.

12. The HIPAA law uses this strategy of not precisely and universally specifying what security mechanisms are required throughout all covered entities.

13. Electronic Frontier Foundation, "Medical Privacy," 2008, http://epic.org/privacy/medical/.

14. See, for example, K. C. Jones, "Prying in Britney Spears' Medical Records May Cost Employees' Jobs," *InformationWeek*, March 17, 2008; www.informationweek.com/news/management/compliance/showArticle.jhtml?articleID=206904141 or www.informationweek.com/news/management/compliance/showArticle.jhtml?articleID=206904141 or http://tinyurl.com/6go99g.

15. J. Lemieux, D. Nicholson, D. Lansky, and C. Shirky, "Connecting Americans to Their Health Care: A Common Framework for Networked Personal Health Information," Connecting for Health Personal Health Technology Council (December 2006); www.connectingforhealth.org/commonframework/docs/P9_NetworkedPHRs.pdf.

16. Princeton Survey Associates for the California HealthCare Foundation, "Confidentiality of Medical Records: National Survey," http://admin.chcf.org/.

17. UK National Health Service, "About the NHS: NHS Core Principles," (2008), www.nhs.uk/aboutnhs/coreprinciples/Pages/NHSCorePrinciples.aspx.

18. Department of Health and Human Services, Title 45, Public Welfare, Subtitle A, Part 5b, Privacy Act Regulations, www.access.gpo.gov/nara/cfr/waisidx_02/45cfr5b_02.html.

19. Federal Information Security Management Act of 2002, H.R. 2458, Public Law 107-347, 44 USC 35 Subchapter III §3541 *et seq.*; www4.law.cornell.edu/uscode/html/uscode44/usc_sup_01_44_10_35_20_III.html or http://tinyurl.com/5pfn93.

20. G. McKee, J. Faraone, and M. E. Kabay, "The Problem with Compliance, Part 2," *Network World Security Strategies Newsletter*, March 23, 2006; www.networkworld.com/newsletters/sec/2006/0320sec2.html.

21. E.g., Washington State's Breach Disclosure law (SB 6043), wwwleg.wa.gov/pub/billinfo/2005-06/Htm/Bills/Session%20Law%202005/6043-S.SL.htm or http://tinyurl.com/dwqbf.

22. W. Eazel, "Microsoft Urges U.S. Government to Revamp Data Privacy Laws," *SC Magazine*, November 4, 2005; www.scmagazine.com/us/news/article/526269/.

23. W. J. Clinton, "Presidential Decision Directive/NSC-63: Critical Infrastructure Protection," May 22, 1998, The White House, Washington, D.C.; www.fas.org/irp/offdocs/pdd/pdd-63.htm.

24. W. J. Clinton, "Defending America's Cyberspace: National Plan for Information Systems Protection, Version 1.0," January 11, 2001, The White House, Washington, D.C.; www.fas.org/irp/offdocs/pdd/CIP-plan.pdf.

25. G. W. Bush, "The National Strategy to Secure Cyberspace," The White House, February 2003; www.whitehouse.gov/pcipb/.

26. United States Department of Health and Human Services, "HFCA Internet Security Policy" (1998), http://csrc.nist.gov/groups/SMA/fasp/documents/policy_procedure/internet_policy.pdf or http://tinyurl.com/6bouzn.

27. "OMB Lays Down Federal Security Law," Dark Reading newsletter, *TechWeb*, June 29, 2006; www.darkreading.com/document.asp?doc_id=98316,

28. National Security Telecommunications and Information Systems Security Committee Secretariat, National Security Agency, "National Security Telecommunications and Information Systems Security Policy (NSTISSC) No. 11, Revised Fact Sheet. National Information Assurance Acquisition Policy," July 2003. Ft. Meade, MD; http://www.niap-ccevs.org/cc-scheme/nstissp_11_revised_factsheet .pdf

29. G. W. Bush, "Policy for a Common Identification Standard for Federal Employees and Contractors," Homeland Security Presidential Directive/HSPD-12, The White House, August 27, 2004; www.whitehouse.gov/news/ releases/2004/ 08/20040827-8.html. See also: W. Jackson, "Ready or Not, Here's HSPD-12," *Government Computer News,* October 26, 2005; www.gcn.com/online/ vol1_no1/37426-1.html.

30. Cyber Security Industry Alliance, "Digital Confidence Index" (May 2006), www.csialliance.org/publications/surveys_and_polls/index.html.

31. D. Kaplan, "IT Leaders Team Up to Lobby Congress for Privacy Law," *SC Magazine,* June 20, 2006; www.scmagazine.com/us/ newsletter/dailyupdate/ article/20060621/565405/. See also "Tech Heavyweights Join Effort for Federal Privacy Law," TechWeb, June 21, 2006; www.darkreading.com/ document.asp?doc_id=97668.

32. Interested readers may track emerging legislation via several Web sites: "Legal & Regulatory Topics: Legislation" portal of Dark Reading Security Insider, TechWeb Business Technology Network, www.darkreading.com/topics. asp?node_id=1678

33. A powerful tool for tracking U.S. legislation is the Library of Congress THOMAS database (http://thomas.loc.gov/), which provides various search tools including keyword entry and bill number selection.

34. Library of Congress THOMAS: About Floor Actions, http://thomas.loc.gov/ home/floor.html.

35. Information about emerging privacy-oriented legislation can be gleaned from tracking services such as the Electronic Privacy Information Center (EPIC) Bill Track, www.epic.org/privacy/bill_track.html.

36. To locate the current status of a bill, use the "Search Bill Summary & Status" for the current Congress available from the "Bills, Resolutions" page of THOMAS at http://thomas.loc.gov/home/bills_res.html.

37. M. Mosquera, "States to Assess Privacy Laws for HHS Health IT Effort," *Government Computer News,* May 23, 2006; www.gcn.com/online/vol1_no1/ 40850-1.html. See also: "22 States Join National Health Information Privacy and Security Collaboration," *HIPAAdvisory,* May 25, 2006; www.hipaadvisory. com/news/newsarchives/2006/0525rti.htm.

38. C. Carlson, "Industry Lobbies against Cyber-Security Mandates." *Enterprise News & Reviews,* September 27, 2005; www.eweek.com/article2/ 0,1895,1864330,00.asp.

39. 104th Congress of the USA, "Health Insurance Portability and Accountability Act of 1996," Public Law 104-191, Code of Federal Regulations (CFR) Title 45 Part 164, August 21, 1996; http://frwebgate.access.gpo.gov/cgi-bin/ getdoc.cgi?dbname=104_cong_public_laws&docid=f:publ191.104.pdf or http:// tinyurl.com/5z4csd.

40. A patient ID requirement is also part of the HIPAA law; however, because of expected widespread controversy, a solution has not yet been specified.

41. In practice, as a continuing stimulus to migrate toward cheaper, e-business models, many healthcare insurance carriers are charging providers a per-transaction premium for submitting paper-based transactions.

42. United States Department of Health & Human Services, "HIPAA Administrative Simplification: Standards for Electronic Health Care Claims Attachments," September 23, 2005. Proposed Rule, 45 CFR Part 162, *Federal Register* 70, No. 184 (2005): 55989–56025; http://a257.g.akamaitech.net/7/257/2422/01jan20051800/edocket.access.gpo.gov/2005/05-18927.htm or http://tinyurl.com/5fng7e.

43. J. Spencer and M. L. Bushman, "The Next HIPAA Frontier—Claims Attachments," *HIPAAdvisory* (March 2006); www.hipaadvisory.com/action/tcs/nextfrontier.htm.

44. Many more transaction types will be standardized under additional HIPAA rules.

45. For example, see D. Heffley, "Under the Microscope: Health Insurance Applications," *HealthNews,* July 9, 1008; www.healthnews.com/blogs/dan-heffley/health-related-products/under-microscope-health-insurance-applica-tions-1333.html.

46. Any questions concerning interpretations of the HIPAA regulations issued by the Department of Health and Human Services can be submitted via e-mail to: askhipaa@cms.hhs.gov.

47. The initial HIPAA draft security regulations included an electronic signature standard, which according to the final HIPAA security rule will be finalized later. The intent of the electronic signature standard was to require a reliable method for ensuring message integrity, nonrepudiation, and user authentication for HIPAA-specified transactions by verifying the identity of the person signing a transaction and the authenticity of the PHI included in the transaction.

48. The Health Privacy Project maintains a list of several other myths (and truths) about the HIPAA privacy regulations. See: www.healthprivacy.org/info-url_nocat2303/info-url_nocat_show.htm?doc_id=173435 or http://tinyurl.com/q6hx.

49. This does not mean to imply that such an organization that is not a covered entity, but nonetheless has such healthcare information, should not abide by the types of requirements—that is, typical, industry, best practice requirements—articulated in HIPAA regulations. It just does not need to do so legally under the purview of HIPAA law.

50. United States Department of Health and Human Services Centers for Medicare & Medicaid Services, "Are You a Covered Entity?" December 14, 2005; www.cms.hhs.gov/HIPAAGenInfo/06_AreYouaCoveredEntity.asp.

51. Analog forms of information such as paper-to-paper fax, voice telephony, mail, and so on are not within HIPAA's scope.

52. In effect, technology neutrality acts to increase the longevity of the HIPAA law by allowing healthcare entities to use the latest and most promising, emerging information protection solutions and tools.

53. There may be situations wherein precedence priorities between jurisdictional laws can cause problems (see Section 71.6.6).

54. In some situations, for example, covered entities may need to replace older IT systems that may not be able to meet HIPAA requirements (such as, e.g., maintaining transaction logs with detailed information about each data exchange involving personally identifiable patient information).

55. United States Department of Health and Human Services Centers for Medicare & Medicaid Services, "Security Information Series" (7-part series), December 12, 2007; www.cms.hhs.gov/EducationMaterials/04_SecurityMaterials.asp.

56. United States Department of Health and Human Services Centers, "Standards for Privacy of Individually Identifiable Health Information," April 3, 2003; www.hhs.gov/ocr/hipaa/guidelines/guidanceallsections.pdf.

57. The NIST reference helps provide an introductory level understanding of HIPAA security concepts and activities useful to implementing an information security program. Examples of acceptable ways to meet HIPAA requirements are given. It also provides cross-mapping of HIPAA requirements to other government standards, such as other NIST publications and FISMA. It is especially useful to government agencies that must comply with both HIPAA and FISMA. See also NIST Special Publication 800-100, "Information Security Handbook: A Guide for Managers" (March 2007), http://csrc.nist.gov/publications/nistpubs/800-100/SP800-100-Mar07-2007.pdf.

58. American Council for Technology and Industry Advisory Council: Security & Privacy Shared Interest Group (SIG) Compliance Committee, "Federal Regulatory Compliance Guide and Matrix," November 3, 2005; www.actgov.org/actiac/documents/051018FedRegComplianceMatrix.pdf.

59. WPC, HIPAA EDI Implementation Guides (2008); www.wpc-edi.com/hipaa. (Complete set of PDF downloads $2000.)

60. See, e.g., "HIPAA Academy Certified Solutions," www.hipaaacademy.net/consulting/certified_solutions.html; "Healthcare Intelligence Network," www.hin.com/hipaacomply.html; and E. Chickowski, "Roundup 2006: A Health Approach," *SC Magazine,* December 14, 2006; www.scmagazineus.com/Roundup-2006-A-healthy-approach/article/34262/ or http://tinyurl.com/4fqemv.

61. Certification Commission for Healthcare Information Technology, "Final Criteria: Security & Reliability for 2006 Certification of Ambulatory Electronic Health Records," May 1, 2006; www.cchit.org/files/Ambulatory%20Domain/Final%20Criteria%20-%20SECURITY-RELIABIL-ITY%20-%20Ambulatory%20EHRs%20-%202006.pdf or http://tinyurl.com/4ystb7.

62. The long-term viability of this publicly funded, private organization and its initiatives is uncertain. Other similar efforts have not survived.

63. United States Department of Health and Human Services, Office of the Secretary, "45 CFR Parts 160, 162, and 164 Health Insurance Reform: Security Standards; Final Rule," *Federal Register* 68, No. 34 (2003): 8334–8381; www.cms.hhs.gov/SecurityStandard/Downloads/securityfinalrule.pdf or http://tinyurl.com/eyl7k.

64. The HIPAA privacy requirements apply to protected health information in any form, including, for example, paper form, whereas the HIPAA security requirements apply only to protected health information in electronic form.

65. For many of the privacy requirements, the HIPAA privacy regulations law may specify certain exceptions that apply to a specific requirement as summarized in general terms herein.

66. U.S. Department of Health and Human Services, Office of the Secretary, "45 CFR Parts 160, 162, and 164 Health Insurance Reform."

67. U.S. Department of Health and Human Services, Office of the Secretary, "45 CFR Parts 160, 162, and 164 Health Insurance Reform."

68. S. Weil, "The HIPAA Security and Privacy Rules—Intersections and Dependencies," *HIPAAdvisory,* ND; www.hipaadvisory.com/action/security/intersect-depend.htm.

69. United States Department of Health & Human Services, Centers for Medicare & Medicaid Services, "Security Standard Overview" (2007); www.cms.hhs.gov/SecurityStandard/.

70. United States Department of Health & Human Services, Centers for Medicare & Medicaid Services, "Enforcement Overview" (2005); www.cms.hhs.gov/Enforcement/.

71. United States Department of Health & Human Services, Office for Civil Rights, "Medical Privacy—National Standards to Protect the Privacy of Personal Health Information" (2008); www.hhs.gov/ocr/hipaa/.

72. States Department of Health & Human Services, Office for Civil Rights, "How to File a Health Information Privacy Complaint with the Office for Civil Rights" (2008); www.hhs.gov/ocr/privacyhowtofile.htm.

73. M. McGee, "Computers with Patient Data Stolen on Eve of HIPAA Security Rules," *Information Week,* April 13, 2005; www.informationweek.com/story/showArticle.jhtml?articleID=160702270.

74. Whistleblowers have safe harbors.

75. N. R. Mead, "Who Is Liable for Insecure Systems?" *Computer* (IEEE Computer Society) 37, No. 7 (July 2004): 27–34. (Membership or purchase required.) http://csdl2.computer.org/persagen/DLAbsToc.jsp?resourcePath=/dl/mags/co/&toc=comp/mags/co/2004/07/r7toc.xml&DOI=10.1109/MC.2004.69 or http://tinyurl.com/4wzf92.

76. B. Brenner, "Are Hospitals Gaining on HIPAA?" *SearchSecurity,* May 16, 2005; http://searchsecurity.techtarget.com/originalContent/0,289142,sid14_gci1088594,00.html or http://tinyurl.com/4xvbao.

77. America's Health Insurance Plans, "Electronic Processing of Health Claims Speeds Payments, Cuts Costs," May 25, 2006; www.ahip.org/content/pressrelease.aspx?docid=16454.

78. There are potential pitfalls in ready, electronic availability of patient information. For example, while insurance carriers are able to run their businesses more effectively (and presumably cheaper) with electronic claims conveying electronic PHI, might some carriers use PHI to profile patients against actuarial data and to tailor insurance premiums to each patient?

79. J. Vijayan, "Progress Is Slow on HIPAA Security Rules: Data Mandates Aren't Driving Health Care Companies to Comply," *Computerworld,* September 12, 2005; www.computerworld.com/securitytopics/security/story/0,10801,104543,00.html or http://tinyurl.com/4c3nmg.

80. HIMSS/Phoenix Health Systems, "US Healthcare Industry HIPAA Compliance Survey Results: Winter 2006," HIPAAction; www.hipaadvisory.com/action/surveynew/results/winter2006.htm. A conflicting survey indicates that, in 2006, hospital and insurance executives were reporting serious problems in processing electronic claims and had to revert to paper in many cases: G. Fest, "Medical Banking: Paper Processing Is No Rx For Payments," *Bank Technology News* (May 2006); www.americanbanker.com/$nocookies$/btn_article.html?id=20060501SPFRIPK6 or http://tinyurl.com/4fgl7h.

81. D. Guerin Gue and R. Upham, "The HIPAA Prescription for Healthcare—Why Isn't It Working?" *Health Management Technology* (September 2004); www.healthmgttech.com/archives/0904/0904the_hipaa.htm.

82. F. Fogarty, "Stitching Up Health Records: Privacy Compliance Lags," *eWeek*, April 16, 2006; www.eweek.com/c/a/Health-Care/Stitching-Up-Health-Records-Privacy-Compliance-Lags/ or http://tinyurl.com/4u6o3d.

83. M. L. Baker, "Study: Providers Come Up Short on HIPAA Privacy Compliance," *Enterprise News & Reviews*, Ziff Davis Internet, April 14, 2005; www.eweek.com/article2/0,1895,1787237,00.asp.

84. At about the time that HIPAA's Security Regulations went into effect, it was estimated that large organizations were already typically 70 to 90 percent compliant: Shari Weiss, "It's a Slow Cure, But Healthcare Gets a Grip on HIPAA," *Information Week,* June 6, 2005; www.informationweek.com/news/showArticle.jhtml?articleID=164300712.

85. Bill Brenner, "March to HIPAA: The Best Insurance Policy," SearchSecurity.com news service, March 15, 2005; http://searchsecurity.techtarget.com/originalContent/0,289142,sid14_gci1067093,00.html.

86. N. Ferris, "Privacy Rule Compliance Said to Be Diminishing," *Government HealthIT,* April 19, 2006; www.govhealthit.com/online/news/94120-1.html.

87. Cath Everett, "Red Tape Binds Virtual, Physical Security," *Infosecurity Today* (May/June 2005); www.infosecurity-magazine.com/features/mayjune05/redtape_mayjun.html.

88. Rob Preston, "Opinion: Overregulation Isn't the Answer to Security Breaches," *InformationWeek*, July 15, 2005; www.informationweek.com/story/showArticle.jhtml?articleID=165702843.

89. Marcia Savage, "Companies Lack Resources to Meet Privacy Requirements," *SC Magazine,* August 31, 2005; www.scmagazine.com/uk/news/article/493030/companies+lack+resources+meet+privacy+requirements/.

90. Everett, "Red Tape Binds Virtual, Physical Security."

91. Compliance assessment automation tools may help reduce costs and inefficiencies associated with ongoing compliance monitoring and with managing the associated ongoing documentation and processes.

92. www.eweek.com/article2/0,1759,1949646,00.asp.

93. On the other hand, handling PHI misuse charges involving business associate covered entities can become a legal quagmire involving court suits based on contract law violations.

94. "Governance," *Security Watch Email Newsletter*, July 11, 2005.

95. D. Kaplan, "Settlement Reached on Huge N.Y. Privacy Breach," *SC Magazine*, March 13, 2006; www.scmagazine.com/uk/news/article/546177/settlement+reached+huge+ny+privacy+breach/.

96. S. C. Withrow, "HIPAA Compliance: Where Are the Savings?" January 15, 2002, Withrow, McQuade & Olsen, LLP, Atlanta, GA; www.wmolaw.com/hipaasavings.htm#N_4_.

97. See, e.g., page 8373 of the HIPAA security regulations, www.cms.hhs.gov/SecurityStandard/Downloads/securityfinalrule.pdf.

98. Predicted to be $3.7 billion, nationwide, for 2005. See S. Marlin, "Add It Up: Compliance Doesn't Come Cheap," *InformationWeek*, March 21, 2005; http://www.informationweek.com/news/management/showArticle.jhtml?articleID=159902182.

99. See current HIPAA compliance surveys, such as follow-on surveys to www.hipaadvisory.com/action/surveynew/results/winter2006.htm.

100. This estimate only takes into effect one-time costs such as system conversion/upgrade costs, start-up costs of automation, and training costs. It does not take into account recurring costs to monitor and to maintain HIPAA compliance.

101. HHS, Health Care Financing Administration, "Health Insurance Reform: Standards for Electronic Transactions, 45 CFR Parts 160 and 162, *Federal Register* 65, No. 160 (August 17, 2000): 50351; www.njha.com/hipaa_section/pdf/hipaa-fr-standards.pdf.

102. With regard to the 2006 data breach of 29 million personal records at the Veterans' Affairs administration, recovery cost just "to pay for credit reports, monitoring and potential damage" was estimated at $250 million.

103. H. Hayes, "HIPAA: Best if Used by...," *Government HealthIT,* June 12, 2006; www.govhealthit.com/print/3_12/news/94795-1.html.

104. K. Young, "IT Security Weakened by Compliance Issues: Red Tape Driving the Security Agenda, Says Report," vnunet.com, November 2, 2005; www.vnunet.com/vnunet/news/2145330/regulatory-red-tape-ties.

105. http://privacyruleandresearch.nih.gov/.

106. See HIPAA privacy regulations, Section IV, Final Regulatory Impact Analysis, subsection 5. Research, p. 53258. www.hhs.gov/ocr/hipaa/privrulepd.pdf.

107. M. E. Kabay, "Unexpected Consequences of HIPAA," Security Strategies Newsletter, *Network World*, June 6, 2006; www.networkworld.com/newsletters/sec/2006/0605sec1.html.

108. Methods for de-identifying medical records are being investigated. See. e.g., Ferris, N. (2006). "Hidden Keys to Health," *GovernmentHealthIT*, February 13, 2006; www.govhealthit.com/print/3_1/features/92279-1.html.

109. B. Brewin, "Privacy, Security Keys to HER Adoption Globally," *Government HealthIT* June 29, 2005.

110. Ferris, "Privacy Rule Compliance Said To Be Diminishing."

111. Tony Kontzer and Larry Greenemeier, "Sad State of Data Security," *InformationWeek*, January 2, 2006; http://www.informationweek.com/news/security/cybercrime/showArticle.jhtml?articleID=175800226.

112. Paul McDougall, "High Cost of Data Loss," *InformationWeek,* March 20, 2006; http://www.informationweek.com/news/security/cybercrime/showArticle.jhtml?articleID=183700367&pgno=2.

113. PR Newswire, "Health Care Industry Leaders Convene to Address Security Vulnerabilities in Health Information Systems," June 6, 2006; www.prwebdirect.com/releases/2006/6/prweb395154.php.

114. www.hitrustalliance.org/.

115. EHNAC Products, HNAP, www.ehnac.org/content/view/145/203/.

116. HIPAA Privacy Accreditation Program, www.urac.org/programs/prog_accred_HIPAAP_po.aspx.

117. HIPAA Security Accreditation Program, http://www.urac.org/programs/prog_accred_HIPAAS_po.aspx?navid=accreditation&pagename=prog_accred_HIPAAS.

LEGAL AND POLICY ISSUES OF CENSORSHIP AND CONTENT FILTERING

Lee Tien, Seth Finkelstein, and Steven Lovaas

72.1 INTRODUCTION

> Everyone has the right to freedom of opinion and expression; this right includes freedom to hold opinions without interference and to seek, receive, and impart information and ideas through any media and regardless of frontiers.[1]

One might think that the Internet will make this ringing proclamation a reality. Like no other technology, the Internet transcends national borders and eliminates barriers to the free flow of information. Governments, however, are trying to control speech on the Internet.

72.1.1 Scope of This Chapter: Government Intervention.   Many nations protect rights of free speech and free expression. The First Amendment to the U.S. Constitution provides that "Congress shall make no law . . . abridging the freedom of speech or of the press." The Canadian Charter of Rights and Freedoms protects freedom of speech and press in article 2 as fundamental rights. While Great Britain has no formal constitution, the Magna Carta of 1215, the 1512 Privilege of Parliament Act, the 1689 Bill of Rights, and the 1911 Parliament Act all protect the freedom of speech.[2]

Despite such constitutional protections, speech is regulated everywhere. Article 1 of the Canadian Charter of Rights and Freedoms permits "demonstrably reasonable" limitations on freedom of expression. Great Britain and Canada have promulgated legislation regulating racially defamatory speech, group defamation, or speech that incites racial hatred. Although American law is far more protective of speech, some expression is deemed "unprotected" by the First Amendment, and even protected speech can be regulated in a variety of circumstances.

Accordingly, some governments have enacted laws prohibiting certain content on the Internet and have sought to prosecute users and service providers. Others have tried to control access by insisting on the installation of national "proxy servers" and requiring the blocking of targeted Web sites. Governments also have encouraged "self-regulation" intended to enlist service providers to control customer behavior.

72.1.2 Whose Laws? Whose Standards?   It is often thought that governments cannot successfully censor the Internet. After all, one nation's laws may be unenforceable elsewhere. But national laws can be applied to communication intermediaries like Internet service providers (ISPs), blocking access by people in that country.

Moreover, just as speech originating in one nation can reach a worldwide audience, one nation's laws can have powerful effects in other nations. As commentators have put it, "[t]he reach of the Internet multiplies both the number of laws and the number of jurisdictions applicable to speech transmitted on-line."[3] Indeed, "[b]ecause content posted on the Internet is instantaneously transmitted worldwide, Internet users and providers almost automatically face potential liability in any country to which the Internet is connected—not just the nation where the speech was created or where the author lives."[4]

The most prominent example is a recent case in which a French court ordered the U.S.-based Yahoo to "take all necessary measures to dissuade and make impossible any access via Yahoo.com to the auction service for Nazi merchandise as well as to any other site or service that may be construed as an apology for Nazism or contesting the reality of Nazi crimes."[5] The French court held that "the simple act of displaying [Nazi artifacts] in France violates Article R645-1 of the Penal Code and therefore [is] a threat to internal public order."[6] It described the mere availability of such information to be "a connecting link with France, which renders our jurisdiction perfectly competent to rule in this matter."[7] After the French order was handed down, Yahoo filed suit in the United States seeking a judgment that it need not comply with the French order.[8] The French parties moved to dismiss the U.S. case for lack of personal jurisdiction, but the U.S. district court denied the motion, allowing Yahoo to proceed.[9] In 2004, however, the U.S. Appellate Court overturned the district court's decision, ruling that the district court judge lacked the authority to hear the case, but also noting that Yahoo should not expect both to benefit from the worldwide availability of its product and to avoid the possible consequences of that availability.

Resolving international jurisdiction in cyberspace is one of the most difficult and important issues for the Internet, but it is beyond the scope of this chapter. Moreover, the ways in which the laws of one nation may affect Internet speech in another extend beyond the topic of this chapter, state-backed censorship. Even when governments do not themselves target particular kinds of speech, their laws may give private parties legal rights against expression originating overseas, as in the area of defamation.[10] Laws relating to commerce also may raise free speech concerns, as in the areas of intellectual property[11] and privacy regulation. For instance, the 1995 European Union Data Protection Directive generally restricts all "processing" of "personal data," giving data subjects legal rights quite different from those found in the United States.[12]

72.1.3 Defining Objectionable Material: International Differences.

For most countries, the major concerns stem from the increased availability of "objectionable" content over the Internet. This section focuses on how the meaning of "objectionable" differs from country to country.

72.1.3.1 *Sex.*

A common type of objectionable material is speech about sex. In the United States, a series of attempts have been made to regulate the availability of sexually oriented speech over the Internet, although with little success.[13] Several Middle Eastern nations also block pornographic sites.[14]

In 1995, the Bavarian Justice Ministry informed CompuServe that senior company officials could face prison terms for violation of German antipornography laws. German police provided CompuServe a list of the discussion groups that contained potentially objectionable material.[15] In February 1997, Germany indicted Felix Somm, head of CompuServe's German subsidiary, for failure to prevent the dissemination of illegal material on its online service; with this Germany became the first western democracy to prosecute an official of an online service for illegal Internet content.[16] German prosecutors argued that because CompuServe had access to screening software, the company had the opportunity to block the offending material but failed to do so. Soon thereafter, Germany enacted its Information and Communications Services Act of 1997 (ICSA). The ICSA, however, has been sharply criticized for failing to resolve the uncertainties faced by ISPs.[17]

72.1.3.2 *Hate.*

Another major category of objectionable speech is what might loosely be called "hate speech."[18] American hate sites include sites promoting white supremacy, Nazi or neo-Nazi views, "skinheads," and the Christian Identity Movement.[19] Internet content that promotes Nazi views and Holocaust denial has attracted considerable international attention.

For instance, the German constitution, known as the Basic Law, incorporates freedom of expression as a fundamental individual right. But Article 5, the main provision concerning free speech, expressly provides that the government may limit an individual's expressive right if it conflicts with other people's rights, public order, or criminal laws. Thus, under Germany's general laws and the laws protecting youths, publishing or distributing neo-Nazi or Holocaust denial literature is a criminal offense.[20]

In February 1996, German prosecutors in Mannheim investigated several ISPs, including America Online, regarding alleged distribution of neo-Nazi material on the Internet in violation of anti-Nazi laws.[21] More recently, German-born Frederick Toben, who uses the Web site of his Australian-based Adelaide Institute to advocate Holocaust denial, was found guilty of offending the memory of the dead.[22] The lower court had ruled "that German law against inciting racial hatred could not be applied to content on a foreign website."[23] Germany's Federal Court of Justice, the Bundesgerichtshof, overturned the lower court ruling and found that German law applies to Internet content that originates outside the country's borders, so long as people inside of Germany can access that content.[24] In a 2002 study, Harvard Law School professor Jonathan Zittrain found that Google was systematically excluding search results containing banned content in the French and German versions of its site and that this was apparently "because of pressure applied or perceived by the respective governments."[25]

Canadian law directs courts to balance an individual's free speech rights with societal equality interests. Thus, Canadian courts have upheld hate speech convictions under laws that criminalize the willful promotion of hatred.[26] The Canadian Supreme Court held the statute constitutional.[27] The Court defined hate speech as including a requirement that "the accused 'promote' hatred against an identifiable group, indicating more than simple encouragement or advancement and rather required that the hate monger intend or foresee as substantially certain a direct and active stimulation of hatred against an identifiable group."[28]

The Internet has raised new issues in Canada regarding hate speech. Bernard Klatt runs the Fairview Technology Center out of his home in British Columbia, and about a dozen neo-Nazi, white supremacist, and skinhead clients have used his server to publish material against immigration and homosexuality while celebrating Hitler's accomplishments and "Euro-Christianity." The Canadian government has attempted to shut down Klatt, but he and his clients have insisted that they had not broken any laws.[29]

The Zündelsite, a multilingual archive and news service, may be the most prominent Holocaust denial Web site run by an individual. Its administrator, German Canadian Ernst Zündel, became one of the denial movement's martyrs when he was convicted in Canada for his Holocaust denial pamphlets.[30] The Canadian Supreme Court later overturned his conviction.[31] Zündel's U.S.-based Web page then became the target of an official inquiry by the Canadian Human Rights Commission.[32] Zündel was deported from the United States to Canada in 2003. The Canadian government determined that he represented a risk to national security, and deported him to Germany, where he was sentenced in 2007 for the maximum term of five years on outstanding charges of incitement for Holocaust denial.[33]

72.1.3.3 Politics and Culture.
Various countries also regulate Internet content that generally threatens the government or political, social, and cultural values.

72.1.3.3.1 China. At the end of 2006, there were approximately 137 million Internet users in China, an increase of 34 million over the previous year.[34] The Chinese government, although eager to capitalize on the Internet, feels that the "Internet is a very real threat to the hold their dictatorial regime has over the country."[35] Accordingly, China severely restricts communication via the Internet, including much dissent and the free reporting of news. The so-called Measures for Managing Internet Information Services prohibit private Web sites from publishing "news" without prior approval from communist officials.[36]

A major obstacle for would-be Chinese Internet users is the registration process required to get online. One must pick an ISP and provide identification. One must also fill out a Police File Report Form that will be sent to the ISP, the local Public Security Bureau (PSB), and the provincial-level PSB Computer Security and Supervision Office. In addition, users must complete a Net Access Responsibility Agreement, pledging "not to use the Internet to threaten state security or reveal state secrets" or to read, reproduce, or transmit material that "endangers the state, obstructs public safety, or is obscene or pornographic."[37] The ISP application itself requests information such as employer's address, home address, and profession; home, office, cell phone, and pager numbers;

as well as details about the computer, the modem type, and permit number, which is assigned by the PSB.[38]

In January 2000, the Chinese newspaper the *People's Daily* published new Internet regulations issued by China's State Secrecy Bureau. These laws "ban the release, discussion, or transfer" of "state secret information" on bulletin board systems, chat rooms, or Internet news groups. E-mail users were banned from sending or forwarding state secrets by e-mail. In addition, all Web sites are required to undergo a security check. A provision requiring that anyone using encryption technology register with the government was later rescinded.[39]

In May 2000, after the China Finance Information Network, a financial Web site, republished a Hong Kong newspaper about corruption by a provincial official, Chinese public security officials suspended the site for 15 days and fined the site 15,000 yuan (US $1,800).[40] On August 3, 2000, state security officials forced a Chinese ISP to shut down the Xinwenming (New Culture Forum) site run by a group of dissidents in Shandong Province for posting "reactionary content."[41]

The following month, China's State Council passed Internet laws that limited foreign investment and imposed strict surveillance requirements on Internet content by mandating that Internet content providers monitor both the material they publish and the people who access that material, including the times users log onto the Internet, their account numbers, their Internet addresses, and the phone numbers they are dialing in from.[42]

On November 7, 2000, the Ministry of Information Industry and the Information Office of the State Council released new laws banning commercial media organizations from setting up independent news sites; prohibiting commercial portals from carrying news items based on their own sources; and requiring China-based Web sites to obtain permission from the State Council Information Office before linking to overseas news sites or carrying news from overseas news media. The new Internet laws also restrict the content of online chat rooms and bulletin boards.[43]

In December 2000, the National People's Congress passed a new law to foster Internet safety. This law criminalizes several forms of online political activity, including using the Internet to "incite the overthrow of state power, topple the socialist system, or . . . destroy national unity," promote "cults," or support the independence of Taiwan.[44]

The Ministry of Public Security announced on February 27, 2001, that it released Internet filtering software called Internet Police 110 on February 26. The software comes in three versions for households, Internet cafés, and schools that can monitor Web traffic and delete or block messages from sources deemed "offensive." According to a news report published in the China Securities News, it can send text or voice warnings to[45] network administrators about any unauthorized Internet surfing.[46]

On March 20, 2001, official Chinese media reported that China is developing a surveillance system to monitor activities on the Internet, which will be similar to the data-recording "black box" installed in commercial airplanes. According to Hong Kong *iMail*, it will be able to record all communications through the Internet.[47]

In April 2001, the official Chinese news agency Xinhua reported that China would impose a three-month ban on the opening of new Internet cafés. This is part of "a major offensive against unchecked use of the Internet. Xinhua said authorities are to conduct a massive probe into existing Internet outlets, which it views as potential hotbeds of dissent and vice."[48]

In addition, since January 2000, the Chinese government has been arresting individuals who use the Internet in a manner they deem dangerous, often for online political or religious activity. Qi Yanchen, sentenced to four years in prison on

September 19, 2000, is the first Chinese convicted of subversion for material he wrote that was published on the Internet. Qi was officially charged for writing articles in the May 6, 1999, and May 17, 1999, U.S.-based Chinese dissident e-mail publication *Dacankao* (V.I.P. Reference).[49] Guo Qinghai, a freelance writer, was arrested in September 2000 for "subverting state power." Guo published articles on the Internet that discussed Qi Yanchen's case. He also posted, on overseas online bulletin boards, essays promoting political reforms in China. He was sentenced to four years in prison.[50]

Zhang Haitao, creator of the only China-based Web site on the outlawed Falun Gong, was charged with subversion on October 11, 2000, and is accused of establishing a site promoting Falun Gong and of posting an online petition urging followers to protest the government ban on the group.[51] Zhang Ji, a college student in Heilongjiang Province, was charged on November 8, 2000, with "disseminating reactionary documents via the Internet." Authorities say Zhang had e-mailed information to U.S. and Canada-based Web sites of the Falun Gong religious group as well as downloaded news about the group and shared it with others in China.[52]

Google recently has had a rocky relationship with the Chinese government, with its entire service being blocked several times for serving information critical of government policy. In January 2006, Google agreed to block a list of search terms that would be provided by the Chinese government and limit searches from within China to this partial set of results at google.cn. The independence of Taiwan and the 1989 Tiananmen Square massacre remain on the list of forbidden topics. Given the history of outright bans, Google seems to have decided that some content was better than none.[53]

72.1.3.3.2 The Middle East.   According to Human Rights Watch, the United Arab Emirates (UAE) is "the regional leader in advocating censorship of the Web through the use of high-tech means."[54] Dial-up users in the UAE do not access the Internet directly; they dial into a proxy server maintained by Etisalat, the state telecommunications company, in collaboration with a U.S. firm that is contracted to maintain and update the software. Although UAE officials have insisted that the proxy server's sole purpose is to block pornographic sites, at least one nonpornographic site, that of the Gay and Lesbian Arabic Society (www.glas.org) is blocked. When asked about the site, an Information and Culture Ministry official explained that there had been complaints about it.

Saudi Arabia bans publishing or even accessing various types of online expression, including "[a]nything contrary to the state or its system"; "[n]ews damaging to the Saudi Arabian armed forces"; "[a]nything damaging to the dignity of heads of states"; "[a]ny false information ascribed to state officials"; "[s]ubversive ideas"; and "[s]landerous or libelous material."[55]

All 30 of the country's ISPs are linked to a ground-floor room at the Riyadh Internet entranceway, where all of the country's Web activity is stored in massive cache files and screened for offensive or sacrilegious material before it is released to individual users. The central servers are configured to block access to "sensitive" sites that might violate "the social, cultural, political, media, economic, and religious values of the Kingdom."[56]

According to Human Rights Watch, although official Saudi explanations of Internet censorship focus on materials deemed offensive to conservative Muslim sensibilities, Saudi blocking apparently extends to political sites. In early 1999, the site of at least one exiled dissident group, the Committee against Corruption in Saudi Arabia (www.saudhouse.com), was reportedly blocked.

Yemen's telecommunications service provider, Teleyemen, told Human Rights Watch that there is a "general requirement... to limit information which is considered to be undesirable in terms of causing offenses against social, religious, or cultural standards" and that Teleyemen uses the Surfwatch censorware program in conjunction with a proxy server.

More recently, controversies have erupted when Middle Eastern Islamic groups or nations have protested content offensive to Islam that was hosted outside their own borders. In 2005, a Danish newspaper published caricatures of the prophet Muhammad, which many Muslims found to be offensive. The cartoonist, the newspaper, and the Danish people as a whole were targeted with boycotts and death threats. Imams in Denmark brought suit to have the government punish the newspaper but had no success in the courts. In 2007, Turkey briefly blocked all access to YouTube in protest of a video insulting the nation's founder, Mustafa Kemal Atatürk. Google, which had purchased YouTube earlier that year, quickly removed the video in question, and Turkey revoked the ban.[57]

72.1.3.3.3 Myanmar/Burma.   In 1988, a new military clique called the State Law and Order Restoration Council (SLORC) took power in the country formerly known as Burma, now known as Myanmar. They managed to achieve cease-fires with 15 armed organizations, but they refused to step down, asserting that only "the military can ensure national unity and solidarity,"[58] even after the National League for Democracy's overwhelming victory in the 1990 election. In 1997, the SLORC was renamed the State Peace and Development Council (SPDC), but the membership remained largely unchanged.

SLORC/SPDC maintains power partly by controlling access to information. In January 2000, the Myanmar Post and Telecommunication (MPT), then the only ISP in Myanmar, passed a measure that forbids Internet users from posting political speech on the Web, such as writings "detrimental to the interests of the Union of Myanmar" or "directly or indirectly detrimental to the current policies and secret security affairs of the government of the Union of Burma."[59] Only the person granted an Internet account may use it, and the account holder is held responsible for all use of that account. Web pages may not be created without government permission, and violation of any regulation is subject to legal action.[60] In 2005, Myanmar's only private ISP, Bagan Cybertech, was nationalized under the control of the MPT, and the government has entered into an agreement with U.S. Web content filtering company Fortinet in order to better control Web access from within Myanmar.[61]

The Burmese military has been effective at "warding off any Internet revolution by limiting the rights of its citizens."[62]

72.2   U.S. CONTEXT: FIRST AMENDMENT RIGHTS.   The First Amendment of the U.S. Constitution strongly protects freedom of speech in the United States. In several ways, the right to speak is the most powerful of all U.S. constitutional rights. First Amendment scrutiny can be much stricter than in other areas of constitutional law. It is usually easier to get in front of a court when "speech" is at issue, and to win, because many technical legal requirements are relaxed.

Thus, although the right to speak is not constitutionally absolute, and may be restricted by government, several basic principles limit governmental authority to restrict freedom of speech, more than it is limited from restricting other activities. These principles have been articulated through a variety of legal doctrines.

72.2.1 What Does the First Amendment Protect?   Today, the First Amendment generally protects all forms of communicative or expressive activity[63] from "state action" or governmental interference.[64] Courts generally presume that linguistic acts or visual depictions are covered by the First Amendment but require litigants to show that nonlinguistic acts are speech unless the law has already so held.[65]

Nevertheless, the coverage of the First Amendment is quite broad. It includes not only the right to speak but also the right *not* to speak, or against "compelled" speech,[66] the right to speak or associate anonymously,[67] and the right to read or to receive information.[68] Often activity that is not necessarily communicative is protected because it enables or facilitates expression. Highly discretionary city licensing of newsstands was found to be an invalid scheme of licensing that affected liberty of circulation.[69] Money is not speech, but election campaign contributions and expenditures are protected as speech.[70]

In addition, the First Amendment requires that the government observe some degree of neutrality in its treatment of speakers[71] and speech media;[72] it cannot arbitrarily prefer one speaker or one medium to another.

72.2.2 Basic First Amendment Principles.   There is no consensus or accepted theory underlying U.S. protection of free speech. The different rationales for freedom of speech can be categorized as more or less "positive" or "negative." Positive justifications identify speech as related to some special moral, social, or political value. For example, the "marketplace of ideas" theory is based on the notion that "the best test of truth is the power of the thought to get itself accepted in the competition of the market."[73] Courts also have defended the right to free expression as embodying the value of "speaker autonomy,"[74] thus "putting the decision as to what views shall be voiced largely into the hands of each of us, in the hope that use of such freedom will ultimately produce a more capable citizenry and more perfect polity, *and in the belief that no other approach would comport with the premise of individual dignity and choice upon which our political system rests.*"[75]

Negative theories presume the value of speech and focus instead on the dangers of government regulation of speech. The main idea here is that speech is as vulnerable to threats of punishment as to punishment itself. "It is characteristic of freedoms of expression in general that they are vulnerable to gravely damaging yet barely visible encroachments."[76] This fear of "chilling effects" on speech sometimes is associated with the possibility that juries may not treat unpopular speakers or unorthodox ideas fairly, but it also reflects a concern that individuals may censor themselves. Such self-censorship can harm public debate while being almost "invisible" to the courts because it occurs through many small individual choices.[77]

72.2.2.1 Harm/Causation.   Perhaps the most important First Amendment principle is that the government has the burden to show that the speech it wishes to regulate truly causes significant harm. This principle was not accepted for many years; in the early days of First Amendment law, speech could be punished as an "attempt" if the natural and reasonable tendency of what was said would be to bring about a forbidden effect. Thus, for instance, individuals who had mailed circulars to draftees arguing that conscription was unconstitutional and urging them to assert their rights were convicted for conspiring to attempt to obstruct the draft.[78]

Today, courts are far more skeptical about government claims of harm. If speech could be restricted merely because the mathematical expectation of harm were significant, speech would be easier to restrict as it were more widely disseminated. Such a result is inconsistent with the First Amendment's protection of open, public discourse. As a classic opinion stated, "no danger flowing from speech can be deemed clear and present, unless the incidence of the evil apprehended is so imminent that it may befall before there is opportunity for full discussion. If there be time to expose the evil by the processes of education, the remedy to be applied is more speech, not enforced silence."[79]

The concern here is not only for the speech itself; it includes a concern that the speaker can properly be held responsible for harm. The modern approach is exemplified by a case where a speaker was convicted for advocating violence. The Supreme Court reversed the conviction because the law did not require the government to show both that the speaker intended to produce "imminent lawless action" and that the speech was "likely to incite or produce such action."[80] The requirement of intent helps protect speakers from being held responsible for the acts of others. As one court put it, "Much speech is dangerous. Chemists whose work might help someone build a bomb, political theorists whose papers might start political movements that lead to riots, speakers whose ideas attract violent protesters, all these and more leave loss in their wake."[81] Without careful attention to harm and causation, the right to speak would mean little.[82]

72.2.2.2 *Neutrality.*

Not all reasons that government might use to restrict speech are valid. Thus, a second basic First Amendment principle is governmental neutrality as to speech content. Government is likely to have illegitimate reasons for wishing to restrict speech, such as the desire to suppress political criticism, but it may be able to disguise such hostility by claiming that less selfish interests, such as "public order" or the civility of discourse, are truly at stake.[83] Also, because public officials may have a strong self-interest in stifling dissent, they are likely to ignore or undervalue the social interest in free speech. Such motivations may lead to regulation that skews or distorts public debate. In general, then, government may not regulate speech based on its substantive content or the message it conveys.[84]

72.2.2.3 *Precision.*

Third, all speech regulation must be precise. "Because First Amendment freedoms need breathing space to survive, government may regulate in the area only with narrow specificity."[85] Much of the First Amendment's force stems from this principle. Imprecise regulation not only chills speech but also gives officials too much discretion to discriminate on the basis of content. Without clearly stated standards, courts cannot easily ferret out content-based discrimination.[86] Insisting on precision also allows courts to avoid assessing the importance of the legislature's goals; they need only say that the means are too blunt.

72.2.2.4 *Background Doubt-Resolution Principles.*

Adding to the strength of First Amendment protection for speech are several principles for resolving uncertainty. Speech regulation generally requires knowledge or intent on the speaker's part, which protects bookstores and others that "carry" others' speech.[87] Moreover, the factual burden of proof is usually on the person or entity seeking to restrict speech.[88] Finally, speech that in itself might be disfavored receives "strategic" protection in order to protect undue chill to public discourse; for instance, while false statements of fact may be considered of little First Amendment value, permitting the punishment of mere falsehood would overly burden speakers.[89] Put simply, doubts generally are called in favor of speech.

72.2.3   Limitations on Government Interference with Speech

72.2.3.1   *Distinction between Substantive Tests and Procedural Safeguards: Example of Prior Restraints.*   A critical distinction in First Amendment (and other) law is between substantive and procedural review. The difference is best explained by reference to "prior restraints," which are presumed unconstitutional.

Most people are familiar with prior restraints as judicial orders preventing speech or publication. In such cases, government "carries a heavy burden of showing justification for the imposition of such a restraint."[90] For instance, the Supreme Court required the government to demonstrate that publication of the *Pentagon Papers* "will surely result in direct, immediate, and irreparable damage to our Nation or its people."[91] Judicial "gag orders" on press publication are subject to similarly searching scrutiny.[92] In these cases, courts are concerned with whether the particular restraint on speech is sufficiently justified.

A second line of prior restraint doctrine illustrates procedural scrutiny. American hostility to prior restraints is a reaction to English press licensing systems under which nothing could be printed without the prior approval of government or church authority. The fear is that discretionary permit schemes make freedom of speech "contingent upon the uncontrolled will of an official."[93] Thus, the law authorizing such a licensing scheme must provide "narrowly drawn, reasonable and definite standards for the [administering] officials to follow."[94] Thus, licensing schemes, such as for screening obscene movies, are constitutional only if accompanied by procedural safeguards necessary "to obviate the dangers of a censorship system."[95] There must be a "prompt final judicial decision" reviewing any "interim and possibly erroneous denial of a license." Moreover, "because only a judicial determination in an adversary proceeding ensures the necessary sensitivity to freedom of expression," the censor must, "within a specified brief period, either issue a license or go to court."[96] In such cases, the particular restraint is relatively unimportant: The issue is whether the statute itself contains sufficient procedural safeguards.

72.2.3.2   *Levels of Substantive Scrutiny and the Issue of Content Neutrality.*   First Amendment cases typically feature three levels of substantive scrutiny, turning mainly on how the statute regulates the meaning of speech: by subject, by viewpoint, or without reference to meaning at all. In general, strict scrutiny applies to laws that attempt to stifle "speech on account of its message."[97] In such situations, the government must demonstrate both that there is a compelling interest in restricting the speech and that it has chosen the least restrictive means of furthering that compelling interest.

When the government targets not subject matter but particular views taken by speakers on a subject, the violation of the First Amendment is all the more blatant.[98] Viewpoint discrimination is thus an egregious form of content discrimination. The government must abstain from regulating speech when the specific motivating ideology or the opinion or perspective of the speaker is the rationale for the restriction.[99] Such scrutiny is so stringent that it applies to otherwise "unprotected" speech.[100]

However, the government often regulates speech without reference to its meaning or communicative impact. So-called content-neutral speech regulation is subject to intermediate rather than strict scrutiny "because in most cases they pose a less substantial risk of excising certain ideas or viewpoints from the public dialogue."[101] Such laws "do not pose such inherent dangers to free expression, or present such potential for censorship or manipulation, as to justify application of the most exacting level of First Amendment scrutiny."[102]

Intermediate scrutiny comes in two main flavors. Content-neutral regulation of the time, place, or manner of speech must be narrowly tailored to serve a significant government interest and leave open ample alternative channels for communication.[103] Content-neutral regulation in other contexts must further a substantial government interest and not burden substantially more speech than necessary to further that interest.[104]

A third type of intermediate scrutiny is the "secondary effects" doctrine, which operates as an exception to the general rule that content-based speech regulation is subject to strict scrutiny. The doctrine asks whether the harm is attributable to the communicative aspects of the speech; if not, the regulation is said to be aimed not at speech but rather at its "secondary effects," and the regulation is deemed content-neutral.[105] Thus, city zoning ordinances have been upheld even though they applied only to theaters that showed adult films because their purposes of preventing crime and protecting property values and the quality of urban life were deemed unrelated to speech content. This doctrine has been criticized for permitting speech suppression "whenever censors can concoct 'secondary' rationalizations for regulating the content of political speech."[106] The main limit on the doctrine is the rule that "listeners' reaction to speech is not a content-neutral basis for regulation."[107]

72.2.3.3 Types of Procedural Scrutiny: Vagueness and Overbreadth.

Laws generally may not "set a net large enough to catch all possible offenders, and leave it to the courts to step inside and say who could be rightfully detained, and who should be set at large."[108] This hostility to vague laws is greater when speech is concerned; courts will assume that ambiguous legal language will be used against speech.[109] The void-for-vagueness doctrine emphasizes both fair notice to citizens of what conduct is prohibited and clear standards for law enforcement to follow.[110]

A closely related doctrine is that of overbreadth. A law is overbroad when it "does not aim specifically at evils within the allowable area of [government] control, but . . . sweeps within its ambit other activities that constitute an exercise" of First Amendment rights.[111] The danger is "not merely the sporadic abuse of power by the censor" but the "continuous and pervasive restraint on all freedom of discussion that might be reasonably regarded as within its purview."[112] Accordingly, the overbreadth doctrine permits facial[113] invalidation of laws that inhibit speech if impermissible applications of the law are substantial, when "judged in relation to the statute's plainly legitimate sweep."[114] Both doctrines exemplify the basic precision principle.

72.2.4 Exceptions Where Speech Can Legally Be Limited. The government can restrict speech both directly and indirectly. Roughly speaking, the government is more limited in direct regulation of speech than in indirect regulation. First Amendment law also contains many subdomains with their own special rules, such as over-the-air broadcasting,[115] government enterprises,[116] and government subsidies.[117]

72.2.4.1 Neutral Laws of General Applicability. Many laws, in some sense, restrict speech to an extent. Absent special circumstances, "generally applicable" laws can be applied to speech without triggering First Amendment scrutiny. Classic examples are laws against speeding applied to a news reporter hurrying to file a story or taxes that apply to books and newspapers as well as other goods.

The "generally applicable" doctrine contains its own limits. Courts will look to see whether the law appears to be a pretext for targeting speech and whether it was based on perceived secondary effects.[118] If so, then there will be some level of First Amendment scrutiny.

72.2.4.2 *Constitutionalization of Crimes and Torts: Advocacy of Illegality, Threats, and Defamation.*   Another major category of First Amendment doctrines relates to crimes and torts directed at speech. In general, the First Amendment does not prevent the application of criminal law to speech simply because it is speech. Although agreeing to participate or assist in doing an unlawful act is usually accomplished through "speech," the larger course of conduct in which that speech is integrated overrides any potential First Amendment applicability.[119] Even so, there can be concern for speech-suppressive effects.

Criminal laws that are likely to involve speech "must be interpreted with the commands of the First Amendment clearly in mind."[120] As discussed in Section 72.2.2.1, laws that criminalize incitement to unlawful action must require proof of both intent and harm. Similarly, threatening may be criminally punished if the law is carefully defined and applied to "true threats" but not "political hyperbole."[121] Recently, the Supreme Court held that federal law prohibiting the disclosure of unlawfully intercepted communications could not be applied to those who had innocently acquired the information of public concern.[122]

Tort laws that target speech also must be construed and applied in light of First Amendment concerns. The prime example is libel or defamation law. For many years, the First Amendment simply did not apply to libel suits. In 1967, however, the Supreme Court held that libel suits were a form of government action because courts must enforce libel judgments, and thus imposed First Amendment restrictions on such lawsuits.[123]

72.2.4.3 *"Fighting Words," Obscenity, and Child Pornography (So-Called Unprotected Speech).*   Certain categories of speech, such as obscenity, child pornography, "fighting words," and so on, are considered "unprotected" even though they are linguistic or pictorial. Here the issue is not that the speech is not communicative but that its value is low; "fighting words," for instance, are deemed "utterances [that] are no essential part of any exposition of ideas, and are of such slight social value as a step to truth that any benefit that may be derived from them is clearly outweighed by the social interest in order and morality."[124]

Even so, the definition of "fighting words" is closely limited. First, the words must "by their very utterance inflict injury or tend to incite an immediate breach of the peace."[125] Second, they must be "directed to the person of the hearer."[126]

The Supreme Court defines obscenity as works that, (1) taken as a whole, appeal to the prurient interest of the average person in sex, (2) portray sexual conduct in a patently offensive way, and (3) taken as a whole, lack serious literary, artistic, political, or scientific value.[127] This definition illustrates how the Supreme Court has sought to ensure that even laws that target unprotected speech do not reach too far. In particular, the first prong of the obscenity test is evaluated with reference to "contemporary community standards." As the Supreme Court observed, "It is neither realistic nor constitutionally sound to read the First Amendment as requiring that the people of Maine or Mississippi accept public depiction of conduct found tolerable in Las Vegas, or New York City."[128] Moreover, any statute regulating obscenity must define the "sexual conduct" at issue.

Child pornography is defined generally as works that visually depict sexually explicit conduct by children below a specified age.[129] As with obscenity, the statute must clearly define the conduct that may not be depicted[130] and must require some element of knowledge or intent. Unlike obscenity, however, legally regulable child pornography need not appeal to the prurient interest of the average person, need not portray sexual conduct in a patently offensive manner, and need not be considered as a whole.[131] Child pornography is the least protected type of speech. Note that *virtual* child pornography is not regulated. The U.S. Supreme Court clarified the distinction, noting that in actual child pornography, the perpetrator commits child abuse in the creation of the pornography; no such abuse is present in the virtual version.[132]

But even "unprotected" speech is not entirely invisible to the First Amendment. Regulations that target such speech must be based on the reason why the speech is categorized as unprotected; thus, even though "fighting words" may be regulated because of their potential to generate violence, regulating only "fighting words" that relate to race, color, creed, religion, or gender would "impose special prohibitions on those speakers who express views on disfavored subjects," amounting to unconstitutional viewpoint discrimination.[133]

72.2.4.4 *Less-Protected Speech, Media, and Recipients.* Other categories of speech are protected by the First Amendment but may be regulated more easily. The main examples are commercial speech, broadcast speech, and speech that is "indecent" or "harmful to minors."[134]

Commercial speech is defined as speech that proposes a commercial transaction; the main example is advertising. Originally, such speech was considered unprotected, but today its regulation is subject to a form of intermediate scrutiny.[135]

Broadcast speech is also subject to a form of intermediate scrutiny.[136] The Supreme Court has long adhered to the view that different media of expression may require different First Amendment analyses. The standard for regulating the speech of cablecasters is not entirely clear.[137]

With regard to sexual content, there are three forms of less-protected speech. First, although nonobscene sexual expression is in a sense "fully" protected, cities may rely on "secondary effects" analysis to regulate the location of bookstores and theaters that sell "adult" material or offer "adult" entertainment like nude dancing.[138]

Second, the Supreme Court has permitted substantial regulation of "indecent" speech over the airwaves[139] and on cable TV.[140] Indecency regulation is closely tied to the interest of preventing minors' access to sexual material. As that interest varies, so does the latitude for regulation. For example, the regulation of indecent speech delivered telephonically was not permitted.[141] Thus, indecency is an odd speech category that is regulated primarily with respect to the audience: The government has a strong interest in regulating minors' access to indecency, but it has no such interest in regulating adults' access.

Closely related to the category of "indecency" is materials judged "harmful to minors" (HTM). Roughly speaking, this category is like obscenity, but geared to those under the age of 17.[142] This category has become increasingly important in the censorware context given the "full" protection accorded to speech over the Internet. Courts have narrowly tailored HTM-based access restrictions to their constitutional boundaries. This point was made clear in *Reno v. ACLU*, where the Supreme Court held unconstitutional a general prohibition of indecent speech on the Internet. The Court found:

- Parents may disseminate HTM speech to their children.[143]
- The HTM concept applies only to commercial transactions.[144]
- The government may not simply ban minors' exposure to a full category of speech, such as nudity, when only a subset of that category can plausibly be deemed HTM.[145]
- The government interest is not equally strong throughout the HTM age range.[146]

72.2.5 Legislation and Legislative Initiatives in the United States.

Since the advent of the Internet, there have been many attempts to regulate access to Internet speech. Such legislation can be divided into two basic categories. In the first category, the law imposes liability for communicating certain kinds of material over the Internet. Such laws did not require the use of software to block Internet sites or to filter their content because they focused on the conduct of the speaker or publisher. In the second category, the law requires or encourages the use of filtering software by those who make Internet content available.

In 1996, Congress enacted the Communications Decency Act (CDA), which sought to regulate the communication of "indecent" material over the Internet. The CDA prohibited Internet users from using the Internet to communicate material that, under contemporary community standards, would be deemed patently offensive to minors under the age of 18. In holding that the CDA violated the First Amendment, the Supreme Court explained that without defining key terms, the statute was unconstitutionally vague. Moreover, the Court noted that the breadth of the CDA was "wholly unprecedented" in that, for example, it was "not limited to commercial speech or commercial entities" but rather embraced "all nonprofit entities and individuals posting indecent messages or displaying them on their own computers."

In response to the Supreme Court's invalidation of the CDA, Congress in 1998 enacted the Child Online Protection Act[147] (COPA). The COPA scaled down the restrictions of the CDA by using the "harmful to minors" category of speech. The COPA was found unconstitutional by a district court because it failed the strict scrutiny test for content-based regulation of speech.[148] That holding was affirmed on appeal although on a different rationale—that because "harmful to minors," like obscenity, must be defined by reference to discrete, diverse, geographically defined communities, COPA's attempt to promulgate a national "harmful to minors" standard was necessarily unconstitutional.[149] States also have attempted to control access to Internet speech by using the "harmful to minors" concept, but these attempts have proven similarly unsuccessful.[150]

The second category is exemplified by the Child Internet Protection Act (CIPA),[151] which, roughly speaking, requires all schools and libraries that receive certain types of federal funding to adopt and implement an Internet safety policy and to use "technology protection measures" on all computers that offer Internet access. Such measures must block or filter Internet access to visual depictions that are obscene, child pornography, or harmful to minors. Libraries must also regulate access by minors to "inappropriate material." Thus, the CIPA effectively requires the use of filtering software, sometimes referred to as "censorware."

72.2.6 Attempts to Control Access: Case Law. The American Library Association has taken a firm stance against censorware in libraries[152] and has committed itself to challenging federal censorware requirements. To date, though CIPA applies to both libraries and schools, the legal battle over the use of censorware to control access to speech on the Internet has primarily involved libraries. The plaintiffs in these cases have library and librarian associations, including the American Library Association, library patrons and users, and entities and individuals whose Web sites are likely to be blocked by censorware.

72.2.6.1 Public Libraries. On one hand, public libraries must be concerned that, by implementing censorware, they violate patrons' First Amendment right to receive information. On the other hand, public libraries also face liability for encouraging a hostile workplace for their employees by not implementing censorware on library Internet terminals.

As to the first concern, libraries face a conflict between not censoring adults' access to constitutionally protected material on the Internet and protecting children from inappropriate content. In a 1998 case involving a Virginia library, a federal district court found the library's blocking policy unconstitutional.[153] The challenged policy required that "site-blocking software . . . be installed on all [library computers]" so as to block child pornography, obscene material, and harmful-to-minors material.[154] The defendants implemented the policy by installing the commercial filtering software X-Stop on all public library terminals in the county.

The court first concluded that the public libraries were limited public forums and then subjected the defendants' indisputably content-based filtering policy to strict constitutional scrutiny.[155] Assuming that the library's interests were compelling, the court found that its policy was not the least restrictive means of furthering those interests. First, the court held that the library had not even considered less restrictive means, including privacy screens, library staff monitoring of Internet use (which had been used to enforce other library policies), and filtering software installed only on Internet terminals used by minors or only when minors are using them.

More important, the court found that the censorware-based policy violated the First Amendment because censorware is both overbroad and overinclusive. On one hand, the X-Stop censorware blocked more speech than that targeted by the policy.[156] On the other hand, even if censorware could somehow be tailored to exclude only restricted materials, it unconstitutionally "limit[s] the access of all patrons, adult and juvenile, to material deemed fit for juveniles."[157]

Finally, the court found that the library policy violated the doctrine barring prior restraints. Mandatory filtering policies that rely on commercial blocking software arguably constitute prior restraints because, as in *Mainstream Loudoun*, they "entrust all . . . blocking decisions . . . to a private vendor" whose standards and practices cannot be monitored by the filtering library.[158]

In a more recent and notable departure from this line of argument, the U.S. Supreme Court found in a 2003 case from Pennsylvania that CIPA was constitutional because the library's interest in preventing minors from accessing obscene material "outweighs the free speech rights of library patrons and website publishers."[159]

As to the second concern, libraries are unlikely to face liability from patrons for failing to use censorware. For example, in *Kathleen R. v. City of Livermore*,[160] a woman sued a public library, complaining that her 12-year-old son was able to view and download pornography at a public library in Livermore, California. The plaintiff sought an injunction that would prohibit the library "from maintaining any computer system on which it allows people to access…obscene material or on which it allows minors to access … sexual material harmful to minors." The plaintiff also claimed that the library had a constitutional duty to "protect" library patrons from unwanted and "harmful" sexually explicit materials. The California court of appeals rejected all of the plaintiff's claims.

A different concern here is library liability to employees for failing to use censorware under sexual harassment "hostile work environment" theories. Federal civil rights laws and many states' parallel civil rights laws afford employees the "right to work in an environment free from discriminatory intimidation, ridicule and insult."[161] Arguably, access to materials over the Internet that are offensive due to their sexually explicit nature or messages regarding race, religion, or ethnicity may subject a library to liability for a hostile environment under these laws. In 2001, employees of a Minnesota library brought a successful complaint before the Equal Employment Opportunity Commission claiming that the library failed to prevent a hostile work environment by failing to prevent the viewing of objectionable material on library computers.[162]

72.2.6.2 Public Schools.   There are no cases involving the use of censorware in public schools. Schools traditionally have been considered places where the government has a strong interest in regulating speech,[163] particularly with respect to curricular materials.[164] Prevailing cases emphasize the importance of inculcating values and maintaining civility in schools, along with the risk that the viewpoints expressed by student speech would be attributed to the school. Moreover, most public school students are too young to enjoy the same constitutional rights as adults.

Nevertheless, the First Amendment should place significant limits on public schools' use of censorware. In general, students do not "shed their constitutional rights to freedom of speech or expression at the schoolhouse gate."[165] Thus, while schools have maximum authority over curriculum and school-sponsored activities and substantial authority to regulate student speech, they have less authority to regulate students' right to receive information. Despite schools' "comprehensive authority" to prescribe and control student conduct, "students may not be regarded as closed-circuit recipients of only that which the State chooses to communicate."[166]

Moreover, the extent of governmental power to regulate conduct of minors not constitutionally regulable when committed by adults is a "vexing" question, "perhaps not susceptible of precise answer."[167] Although the government has a general interest in regulating schools, the interest in regulating students' access to "objectionable" extracurricular information is of uncertain pedigree. For instance, the Supreme Court has characterized the government interest in protecting children against "harmful to minors" material as derivative of or secondary to parents' interests.[168] Thus, "[s]peech that is neither obscene as to youths nor subject to some other legitimate proscription cannot be suppressed solely to protect the young from ideas or images that a legislative body thinks unsuitable for them."[169] This characterization suggests that the state has no interest in blocking a minor's access to HTM material to which parents do not object.[170]

Moreover, the state's interest is not uniformly strong across all minors. In general, minors' fundamental rights, including the right to receive information, strengthen as they grow older; "constitutional rights do not mature and come into being magically only when one attains the state-defined age of majority."[171] Moreover, some high school students are 18 or 19 and thus not minors for HTM purposes.

The Electronic Freedom Foundation published a report in 2003 that examined the issue of Internet content filtering in public schools. Based on the state of current filtering technology, which significantly underblocks material that would be considered harmful to minors and significantly overblocks some material that would be considered protected by the First Amendment, the EFF recommended that schools should use other, less restrictive methods.[172]

72.3   PARENTAL INVOLVEMENT/RESPONSIBILITY.   Although the technical issues of censorware are identical regardless of whether it is being applied by government, employers, or parents, the parent-child case generates much of the political discussion. Two conflicting mental models are at work in the debate.

The primary impetus for censorware arises out of an idea that might be called the "toxic material" theory, under which viewing certain information has a toxic effect, akin to a harmful drug or a poison. As was stated in a lawsuit seeking an injunction against a library with unrestricted Internet access: "Children such as Brandon P. who view obscenity and pornography on the library's computers can and have sustained emotional and psychological damage in addition to damage to their nervous systems. It is highly likely that such damage will occur given the library's policy."[173] The outcome of the toxic material threat model has been legislation such as the CIPA.

In contrast, theoretical discussion typically takes place in a model that can be termed the "control-rights" theory. This is concerned primarily with authority relationships within some framework. One paper submitted to a government commission stated:

> [T]he decision by a third party that a person may not use a computer to access certain content from the Internet demands some sort of justification. The burden should be on the filterer to justify the denial of another person's access. The most plausible justifications for restricting access are that the third party owns the computer or that the third party has a relation of legitimate authority over the user.[174]

However, the control-rights discussion does not address the assumptions and threat model inherent in the toxic material theory. A belief in harmful information logically requires restrictions to be as extensive and widespread as possible. In fact, this is an instance of typical security practices, where the potential attack is viewed along the lines of dangerous contamination. All possible environments where the subject may be located then need to be secured to the greatest extent possible. This social need is similar to the technical requirement regarding banning privacy, anonymity, and even language-translation Web sites. It is all a matter of security holes.

72.4   SUMMARY.   Although the Internet has the technological potential to create a global forum for free expression, one must not underestimate the political and technological barriers at work.

Internet-specific laws. Some governments have criminalized certain types of Internet speech. Such criminal penalties may come in the form of laws intended to protect minors from "harmful" material. Under U.S. law, however, requiring Internet speakers to shield certain populations from their speech has been found to effect a ban on that speech.[175]

Application of existing laws. Governments need not specifically enact laws targeting Internet-based speech. For example, the German government action against CompuServe for providing access to illegal material merely applied existing laws to the Internet.

Content-based license terms applied to Internet users and service providers. Some countries have established licensing systems that require Internet users and/or service providers to agree to refrain from certain kinds of speech or that block access to speech as a condition of having, or using, or providing access to the Internet. For instance, China has issued rules requiring anyone with Internet access to refrain from proscribed speech.

Compelled use of computerized censorship, rating, or content labeling tools, Various techniques can prevent individuals from using the Internet to exchange information on topics that may be controversial or unpopular, may enable certain governments to enforce their own ratings systems, and may (through overblocking by overly broad filtering techniques) inappropriately block access to significant amount of nonobjectionable content.

72.5   FURTHER READING

Electronic Privacy Information Center, Filters and Freedom 2.0 (2001): http://epic.org/bookstore/filters2.0/default.html.

Semitsu, Junichi P. "Note, Burning Cyberbooks in Public Libraries: Internet Filtering Software vs. the First Amendment," 52 *Stan. L. Rev.* 509 (2000).

Lessig, Lawrence. *Code and Other Laws of Cyberspace.* New York: Basic Books, 1999.

OpenNet Initiative. Documenting Internet Content Filtering Worldwide. http://opennet.net/.

Sullivan, Kathleen M. "First Amendment Intermediaries in the Age of Cyberspace," 45 *UCLA L. Rev.* 1653 (1998).

Weinberg, Jonathan. "Rating the Net," 19 *Hastings Comm. & Ent. L.J.* 453 (1997).

72.6   NOTES

1. Universal Declaration of Human Rights, art. 19, G.A. Res 217A, U.N. GAOR, 3d Sess., U.N. Doc. A/810 (1948).
2. Thomas D. Jones, "Human Rights: Freedom of Expression and Group Defamation Under British, Canadian, Indian, Nigerian and United States Law—A Comparative Analysis," 18 *Suffolk Transnat'l L. Rev.* 427, 428 (1995) (footnotes omitted).
3. Samuel Fifer and Michael Sachs, "The Price of International Free Speech: Nations Deal With Defamation on the Internet," 8 *DePaul-LCA J. Art & Ent. L.* 1, 2 (1997).
4. Samuel Fifer and Michael Sachs, "The Price of International Free Speech: Nations Deal With Defamation on the Internet,"
5. Order of the County Court of Paris, at 2, in *La Ligue Contre Le Racisme Et L'Antisemitisme v. Yahoo! Inc.*, No. RG: 00/05308 (Nov. 20, 2000) (translated).
6. Order of the County Court of Paris, at 4.
7. Order of the County Court of Paris, at 4.
8. www.cdt.org/jurisdiction/010607yahoo.pdf.
9. *Yahoo! Inc. v. La Ligue Contre le Racisme et L'Antisemitisme, et al.,* 145 F. Supp. 2d 1168 (N.D. Cal. 2001).
10. *See* note 3 generally.
11. Jane Ginsburg, "Copyright Without Borders? Choice of Forum and Choice of Law for Copyright Infringement in Cyberspace," 15 *Cardozo Arts & Ent. L.J.* 153 (1997).
12. Peter Swire, "Of Elephants, Mice, and Privacy: International Choice of Law and the Internet," 32 *Int'l Law.* 991 (1998).

13. *See* text at Section 72.2.5.

14. *See* text at Section 72.1.3.3.2.

15. John T. Delacourt, "Recent Development: The International Impact of Internet Regulation," 38 *Harv. Int'l L. J.* 207, 212 (1997).

16. Kim Rappaport, Note, "In the Wake of Reno v. ACLU: The Continued Struggle in Western Constitutional Democracies with Internet Censorship and Freedom of Speech Online," 13 *Am. U. Int'l L. Rev.* 765, 791 (1998).

17. Kim Rappaport, Note, at 795–799.

18. Some observers reported that the Internet seems to foster "hate" sites. Laura Leets, "Responses to Internet Hate Sites: Is Speech Too Free in Cyberspace?" 6 *Comm. L. & Pol'y* 287, 288 (2001) (noting that watchdog groups have documented about 2,800 hate sites).

19. *Id.* at 291–294.

20. *See* note 16, at 785–786 (footnotes omitted).

21. *Id.* at 789 (footnotes omitted).

22. Steve Kettmann, "German Hate Law: No Denying It," December 15, 2000: www.wired.com/news/politics/0,1283,40669,00.html.

23. www.wired.com/news/politics/0,1283,40669,00.html.

24. www.wired.com/news/politics/0,1283,40669,00.html.

25. J. Zittrain and B. Edelman, "Localized Google Search Result Exclusions" (2002); http://cyber.law.harvard.edu/filtering/google/.

26. Canadian Criminal Code § 319(2), R.S.C. 1985, c. C-46 (willful promotion of hatred against an identifiable group); see *id.* at § 181 (willful publication of false statements likely to injure a public interest).

27. *R. v. Keegstra*, 3 S.C.R. 697 (1990).

28. *See* note 27.

29. Robert Cribb, "Canadian Net Hate Debate Flares," March 25, 1998: www.wired.com/news/news/politics/story/11195.html ("Cribb").

30. Zundel was charged with spreading "false news" in violation of § 181 of the Canadian Criminal Code.

31. *R. v. Zündel* [1992] 2 S.C.R. (Can.) 731.

32. Credence Fogo-Schensul, "More Than a River in Egypt: Holocaust Denial, the Internet, and International Freedom of Expression Norms," 33 *Gonz. L. Rev.* 271, 245 n.32 (1997–1998) (citation omitted).

33. "Ernst Zundel Sentenced to 5 Years in Prison for Holocaust Denial," *Winnipeg Free Press,* February 15, 2007, online edition: www.winnipegfreepress.com/breakingnews/world/story/3881650p-4489229c.html.

34. Internet World Stats, March 24, 2007: www.internetworldstats.com/asia/cn.htm.

35. "China Again Seeks to Control the Internet," December 6, 2000, www.bizasia.com/gen/articles/stand_art.htm?ac=EKBGN-Y.

36. Managing Internet Information-Release Services, P.R.C. Ministry of Information Industry Regulation, November 7, 2000; see also "China Issues Regulations on Managing Internet Information-Release Services," China Online, November 13, 2000; www.chinaonline.com/issues/Internet_policy/NewsArchive/Secure/2000/November/C00110604.asp. Other restrictions target a variety of disfavored groups, particularly supporters of the Falun Gong spiritual movement.

See "China Passes Internet Security Law," China Online, December 29, 2000; www.chinaonline.com/issues/Internet_policy/NewsArchive/Secure/2000/December/C00122805.asp.

37. Geremie R. Barme and Sang Ye, "The Great Firewall of China" (June 1997), www.wired.com/wired/archive/5.06/china.html?person=bill_gates&topic_set=wiredpeople.

38. www.wired.com/wired/archive/5.06/china.html?person=bill_gates&topic_set=wiredpeople.

39. Digital Freedom Network, "Attacks on the Internet in China," April 30, 2001: www.dfn.org/focus/china/netattack.htm.

40. www.dfn.org/focus/china/netattack.htm

41. www.dfn.org/focus/china/netattack.htm

42. www.dfn.org/focus/china/netattack.htm

43. www.dfn.org/focus/china/netattack.htm

44. www.dfn.org/focus/china/netattack.htm

45. www.dfn.org/focus/china/netattack.htm

46. www.dfn.org/focus/china/netattack.htm

47. www.dfn.org/focus/china/netattack.htm

48. www.dfn.org/focus/china/netattack.htm

49. www.dfn.org/focus/china/netattack.htm

50. www.dfn.org/focus/china/netattack.htm

51. www.dfn.org/focus/china/netattack.htm

52. www.dfn.org/focus/china/netattack.htm

53. Michael Liedtken, "Google Agrees to Censor Results in China," January 24, 2006; www.breitbart.com/article.php?id=D8FBCF686&show_article=1.

54. Human Rights Watch, "The Internet in the Middle East and North Africa: Free Expression and Censorship," hrw.org/advocacy/internet/mena/.

55. Saudi Internet regulations, Saudi Arabia Council of Ministers Resolution, February 12, 2001, www.al-bab.com/media/docs/saudi.htm.

56. Human Rights Watch World Report 1999, "Freedom of Expression on the Internet," www.hrw.org/hrw/worldreport99/special/Internet.html.

57. "Turkey Revokes YouTube Ban" The Age.com, March 10, 2007; www.theage.com.au/news/Technology/Turkey-revokes-YouTube-ban/2007/03/10/1173167025391.html.

58. Christina Fink, Burma: "Constructive Engagement in Cyberspace?" (1997), www.burmafund.org.

59. Digital Freedom Network, "The New Net Regulations in Burma," January 31, 2000, www.dfn.org/voices/burma/webregulations.htm.

60. www.dfn.org/voices/burma/webregulations.htm.

61. Alison Hunter, "Burma's Internet Censorship Worsening," October 12, 2005; www.mizzima.com/mizzima/archives/news-in-2005/News-in-Oct/12-Oct-05-40.htm.

62. Digital Freedom Network, "Burma Wards Off the Internet Revolution," January 31, 2000; www.dfn.org/focus/burma/Web-crackdown.htm.

63. The notion of "unprotected" speech is discussed in Section 72.2.4.3.

64. In the context of the right to speak, the requirement of state action is somewhat relaxed compared to other constitutional rights. For example, when private persons—not the government—use the courts against another private person's speech, "state action" is usually found. E.g., *New York Times Co. v. Sullivan*, 376 U.S. 254 (1964) (defamation); *Hustler Magazine, Inc. v. Falwell*, 485 U.S. 46 (1988) (intentional infliction of emotional distress).

65. *Texas v. Johnson*, 491 U.S. 397, 403 (1989).

66. *W. Va. Bd. of Educ. v. Barnette*, 319 U.S. 624, 632 (1943).

67. *McIntyre v. Ohio Elections Comm'n*, 514 U.S. 334 (1995).

68. *Lamont v. Postmaster General*, 381 U.S. 301, 307 (1965) (invalidating law requiring willing recipient to request that certain, state-defined materials be sent to him); *Virginia Pharmacy Bd. v. Virginia Consumer Council*, 425 U.S. 748, 756 (1974).

69. *City of Lakewood v. Plain Dealer Publishing Co.*, 486 U.S. 750 (1988).

70. *Buckley v. Valeo*, 424 U.S. 1, 19 (1976).

71. *Simon & Schuster, Inc. v. Members of N.Y. State Crime Victims Bd.*, 502 U.S. 105, 117 (1991).

72. *City of Ladue v. Gilleo*, 512 U.S. 43 (1994).

73. *Abrams v. United States*, 250 U.S. 616, 630 (1919) (Holmes, J., dissenting).

74. *Hurley v. GLIB*, 515 U.S. 557 (1995).

75. *Cohen v. California*, 403 U.S. 15, 24 (1971) (emphasis added).

76. *Bantam Books, Inc. v. Sullivan*, 372 U.S. 58, 66 (1963).

77. *Thornhill v. Alabama*, 310 U.S. 88, 97 (1940). ("It is not merely the sporadic abuse of power by the censor but the pervasive threat inherent in its very existence that constitutes the danger to freedom of discussion.")

78. *Schenck v. United States*, 249 U.S. 47, 52 (1919).

79. *Whitney v. California*, 274 U.S. 357, 377 (1926) (Brandeis, J., concurring).

80. *Brandenburg v. Ohio*, 395 U.S. 444, 447 (1969).

81. *American Booksellers Assn., Inc. v. Hudnut*, 771 F.2d 323, 333 (7th Cir. 1985), *aff'd.* mem. 475 U.S. 1001 (1986).

82. See also *Planned Parenthood v. American Coalition of Life*, 244 F.3d 1007 (9th Cir. 2001).

83. *New York Times Co. v. Sullivan*, 376 U.S. 254, 292 (1964).

84. *Police Dept. of Chicago v. Mosley*, 408 U. S. 92, 96 (1972).

85. *NAACP v. Button*, 371 U.S. 415, 433 (1963).

86. *See* note 69.

87. *Smith v. California*, 361 U.S. 147 (1959).

88. *Speiser v. Randall*, 357 U.S. 513 (1958).

89. *Gertz v. Robert Welch, Inc.*, 418 U.S. 323 (1974).

90. *Organization for a Better Austin v. Keefe*, 402 U.S. 415, 419 (1971).

91. *New York Times Co. v. United States*, 403 U.S. 713, 729 (1971) (Stewart, J., concurring).

92. *Nebraska Press Ass'n v. Stuart*, 427 U.S. 539 (1976).

93. *Staub v. Baxley*, 355 U.S. 313, 322 (1958).

94. *Niemotko v. Maryland*, 340 U.S. 268, 271 (1951).

95. *Freedman v. Maryland*, 380 U.S. 51, 58 (1965).

96. *Id.* at 58–59.

97. *See, e.g., United States v. Playboy Entertainment Group, Inc.*, 120 S. Ct. 1878, 1880 (2000); *Reno v. ACLU*, 521 U.S. 844 (1997).

98. *R.A.V. v. St. Paul*, 505 U. S. 377, 391 (1992).

99. *Perry Ed. Assn. v. Perry Local Educators' Assn.*, 460 U. S. 37, 46 (1983).

100. *R.A.V., supra* (government may not regulate otherwise unprotected "fighting words" based on viewpoint).

101. *Turner Broadcasting System, Inc. v. FCC*, 512 U.S. 622, 642 (1994) (citations omitted).

102. *Id.* at 661.

103. Clark v. Community for Creative Non-Violence, 468 U.S. 288, 293 (1984).

104. *United States v. O'Brien*, 391 U.S. 367, 376–77 (1968)

105. *City of Renton v. Playtime Theatres, Inc.*, 475 U.S. 41, 47 (1986)

106. *Boos v. Barry*, 485 U.S. 312, 335 (1988) (Brennan, J., concurring).

107. *Forsyth County v. Nationalist Movement*, 505 U.S. 123, 135 (1992).

108. *United States v. Reese*, 92 U. S. 214, 221 (1876).

109. *NAACP v. Button*, 371 U.S. at 337.

110. *Kolender v. Lawson*, 461 U.S. 352, 357–358 (1983).

111. *Thornhill v. Alabama*, 310 U.S. 88, 97 (1940).

112. *Id.* at 97–98.

113. Often, laws are struck down only "as applied," that is, the particular application of the law to a particular person is found to violate the Constitution. Facial invalidation, on the other hand, is not limited to the particular application but to the entire law, roughly speaking. *See, e.g.,* Richard H. Fallon, Jr., "As-Applied and Facial Challenges and Third-Party Standing," 113 *Harv. L. Rev.* 1321 (2000).

114. *Broadrick v. Oklahoma*, 413 U. S. 601, 612–615 (1973).

115. *Red Lion Broadcasting Co. v. FCC*, 395 U.S. 367 (1969).

116. *Int'l Soc'y for Krishna Consciousness, Inc. v. Lee*, 505 U.S. 672, 678 (1992).

117. Legal Services Corporation v. Velazquez, 531 U.S. 533, (2001).

118. *Arcara v. Cloud Books, Inc.*, 478 U.S. 697, 707 n.4 (1986).

119. *Giboney v. Empire Storage & Ice Co.*, 336 U.S. 490, 502 (1949).

120. *Watts v. United States*, 394 U.S. 705, 707 (1969).

121. *Watts v. United States*, 394 U.S. at 707–8.

122. *Bartnicki v. Vopper*, 121 S.Ct. 1753, 1765 (2001).

123. *New York Times Co. v. Sullivan*, 376 U.S. 254 (1964).

124. *Chaplinsky v. New Hampshire*, 315 U.S. 568, 571 (1942).

125. *Chaplinsky v. New Hampshire*, at 572.

126. *Cohen v. California*, 403 U.S. 15, 20 (1971).

127. *Miller v. California*, 413 U.S. 15, 24 (1973).

128. *Miller v. California*, 413 U.S. at 32.

129. *New York v. Ferber*, 458 U.S. 747, 764 (1982).

130. The federal child pornography statute reaches "any visual depiction" of a minor under 18 years old engaging in "sexually explicit conduct," which includes "actual

or simulated" sexual intercourse, bestiality, masturbation, sadistic or masochistic abuse, or "lascivious exhibition of the genitals or pubic area." 18 U.S.C. § 2256.

131. *Ferber*, 458 U.S. at 764–765. Notably, the rationale for regulating child pornography is not content-based. Instead, it is based on the harm to children from being subjects of sexual performances, as well as the harm from the distribution of such photographs.

132. *Ashcroft v. The Free Speech Coalition*, 122 S. Ct. 1389 (2002).

133. *R.A.V. v. City of St. Paul*, 505 U.S. 377, 391 (1992).

134. *Ginsberg v. New York*, 390 U.S. 629 (1968).

135. *Liquormart, Inc. v. Rhode Island*, 517 U.S. 484 (1996).

136. *Red Lion Broadcasting Co. v. FCC*, 395 U.S. 367 (1969).

137. Speech on the Internet, however, is entitled to "full" First Amendment protection.

138. *City of Erie v. Pap's A.M.*, 120 S.Ct. 1382 (2000).

139. *FCC v. Pacifica*, 438 U.S. 726 (1978).

140. *Denver Area Educ. Telecom. Consortium v. FCC*, 518 U.S. 727 (1996); but see note 97.

141. *Sable Communications v. FCC*, 492 U.S. 115 (1989).

142. Speech is "harmful to minors" if it (i) is "patently offensive to prevailing standards in the adult community as a whole with respect to what is suitable . . . for minors"; (ii) appeals to the prurient interest of minors; and (iii) is "utterly without redeeming social importance for minors." *Ginsberg v. New York*, 390 U.S. 629, 633 (1968) (upholding conviction of magazine vendor for selling adult magazine to 16-year-old).

143. *Reno*, 521 U.S. at 865.

144. *Reno*, 521 U.S.

145. *Erznoznik v. City of Jacksonville*, 422 U.S. 205, 212–214 (1975).

146. *Reno*, 521 U.S. at 878. Lower courts have held that "if a work is found to have serious literary, artistic, political or scientific value for a legitimate minority of normal, older adolescents, then it cannot be said to lack such value for the entire class of juveniles taken as a whole." *American Booksellers Ass'n v. Webb*, 919 F.2d 1493, 1504–5 (11th Cir. 1990) (quoting *American Booksellers Ass'n v. Virginia*, 882 F.2d 125, 127 (4th Cir. 1989) (other citations omitted).

147. Pub. L. No. 105-277, 112 Stat. 2681 (1998) (codified at 47 U.S.C. § 231).

148. *ACLU v. Reno*, 31 F. Supp. 2d 473 (E.D. Pa. 1999).

149. *ACLU v. Reno*, 217 F.3d 162, 177 (3d Cir. 2000), cert. granted sub. nom. *Ashcroft v. ACLU*, [121 S.Ct. 1997] (2001), argued Nov. 28, 2001.

150. E.g., *ACLU v. Johnson*, 194 F.3d 1149 (10th Cir. 1999) (affirming injunction against enforcement of New Mexico statute criminalizing dissemination by computer of material harmful to minors); *American Libraries Ass'n v. Pataki*, 969 F. Supp. 160 (S.D. N.Y. 1997) (enjoining a New York statute similar to the CDA that criminalized the use of a computer to disseminate sexually explicit materials to minors)

151. Codified at 47 U.S.C. § 254(h) and 20 U.S.C. § 9134.

152. The ALA's Resolution on the Use of Filtering Software in Libraries is available from the ALA Office for Intellectual Freedom.

153. *Mainstream Loudoun v. Bd. of Trustees of the Loudoun County Library,* 2 F. Supp. 2d 783 (E.D. Va.1998) (*Mainstream Loudoun I*); *Mainstream Loudoun v. Bd. of Trustees of the Loudoun County Library,* 24 F. Supp. 2d 552 (E.D. Va. 1998) (*Mainstream Loudoun II*).

154. *Mainstream Loudoun I*, 2 F. Supp. 2d at 787.

155. *Mainstream Loudoun II*, 24 F. Supp. 2d at 564–565.

156. *Id.* at 556 ("undisputed" that "sites that do not contain any material that is prohibited by the Policy" were blocked).

157. *Mainstream Loudoun II*, 24 F. Supp. 2d at 567.

158. *Mainstream Loudoun II*, 24 F. Supp. 2d at 569.

159. Electronic Freedom Foundation, "Supreme Court Supports Library Internet Blocking Law," June 23, 2003; www.eff.org/Censorship/Censorware/20030623 _eff_cipapr.php

160. 87 Cal. App. 4th 684 (1st Dist. 2001).

161. *Meritor Savings Bank FSB v. Vinson,* 477 U.S. 57, 65 (1986).

162. "EEOC Determination that Net Porn Leads to Library Hostile Working Environment," May 23, 2001; www.eff.org/Censorship/Censorware/20010523_eeoc_ determination.html.

163. *Bethel School District No. 403 v. Fraser*, 478 U.S. 675 (1986) (upholding suspension of high school student for making sexually suggestive speech at school assembly).

164. *Hazelwood Sch. Dist. v. Kuhlmeier*, 484 U.S. 260 (1988) (upholding teacher's censorship of articles destined for newspaper prepared by journalism class).

165. *Tinker v. Des Moines Indep. Community School Dist.,* 393 U.S. 503, 506 (1969).

166. *Id.* at 511. Schools may [, however,] regulate students' First Amendment rights if the prohibited speech would "materially and substantially interfere with the requirements of appropriate discipline in the operation of the school." *Id.* at 509. This burden cannot be satisfied by "undifferentiated fear or apprehension of disturbance"; the school must show "something more than a mere desire to avoid the discomfort and unpleasantness that always accompany an unpopular viewpoint." *Id.* at 508.

167. *Carey v. Population Servs. Int'l*, 431 U.S. 678, 692 (plurality opinion) (1977).

168. *Reno v. ACLU*, 521 U.S. 844 (1997); *Ginsberg v. New York,* 390 U.S. 629 (1968); *Prince v. Massachusetts,* 321 U.S. 158, 166 (1944).

169. *Erznoznik,* 422 U.S. at 213–214.

170. In other contexts, schools often accommodate or try to accommodate parental wishes as to the exposure of their children in school to undesired material, even when the material is part of the school's chosen curriculum. Catherine J. Ross, "An Emerging Right for Mature Minors to Receive Information," 2 *U. Pa. J. Const. L.* 223, 247 n.119 (1999) ("nearly every school district in the country allows parents 'to opt their own children out of sexuality and AIDS education, as well as out of specific activities or assignments that conflict with their religious beliefs.'"), *quoting* People for the American Way, *A Right Wing and a Prayer: The Religious Right and Your Public Schools* 60 (1997). In some states, such accommodation with respect to all or specified categories of curricular materials is required. *Minn. Stat. Ann.* § 126.699 (West 1994) (schools must allow parents to review curricular materials and must provide alternative materials to replace

those that parents find objectionable for any reason); *Mass. Gen. Laws Ann.* ch. LXXI 32A (West 1998) (requiring that school districts notify parents of the content of any curriculum primarily involving "human sexual education or human sexuality" and afford parents a flexible way of exempting their children from such curricula upon written notice to the school); *Va. Code Ann.* § 22.1-207-2 (Michie 1998) (giving public school parents the right to review "the complete family life curricula [sic], including all supplemental materials").

171. *Planned Parenthood of Cent. Mo. v. Danforth*, 428 U.S. 52, 74 (1976) (minors' right to abortion).

172. Electronic Freedom Foundation, "Internet Blocking in Public Schools," June 23, 2003; www.eff.org/Censorship/Censorware/net_block_report/.

173. *First Amended Complaint in Kathleen R. v. City of Livermore*, www. techlawjournal.com/courts/kathleenr/19981103.htm.

174. Members of the Information Society Project at Yale Law School, "Filtering the Internet: A Best Practices Model," September 15, 1999; www.copacommission. org/papers/yale-isp.pdf.

175. *Reno v. ACLU*, 521 U.S. 844 (1997).

CHAPTER **73**

EXPERT WITNESSES AND THE *DAUBERT* CHALLENGE

Chey Cobb

73.1 INTRODUCTION. Whenever science or technology enters the courtroom, there must surely be an expert who can give clear and proper explanations of the subject matter to the judge and jury. As new sciences and technologies have emerged, the courts have had to decide if a person is, indeed, an expert and whether or not the science is real and admissible.[1]

In 1923, the United States courts began accepting scientific evidence based on a new rule. That rule used the "general acceptance" test to determine if evidence was legitimate. This test was based on the rulings in *Frye v. United States*, which declared that if a scientific practice was generally accepted among the scientific community in which it was practiced, it could be admitted in court. This has become generally referred to as the *Frye test*.[2]

In 1975, the federal government made the scientific assertions a bit stronger by issuing the Federal Rules of Evidence No. 702 (FRE 702), which states in part:

> If scientific, technical, or other specialized knowledge will assist the trier of fact to understand the evidence or to determine a fact in issue, a witness qualified as an expert by knowledge, skill, experience, training, or education, may testify.[3]

About the same time that FRE 702 was created, various states started changing laws to include the "theft of computer services" as a punishable offense, but it was not until 1984 that the Counterfeit Access Device and Computer Fraud and Abuse Law (18 U.S.C. § 1030) was created, officially making it a federal offense to play fast and loose with computer systems of any kind.[4]

Computers had been accepted as a science, crimes could be committed on or with a computer, and someone would be needed to explain computers and their workings to the courts. Enter the digital expert witness. Although it is difficult to say when the first computer expert was used as a witness in a computer crime trial, it is fair to say that such experts soon began playing an important part in the judicial process.

Since computer crimes became "official" in 1984, computer experts are often needed in trials in which the examination of a computer or computer component is crucial to proving the case. For example, in 1991, Special Agent Jim Christy of the Air Force Office of Special Investigations (OSI) became involved in a murder case on an air force base where the suspect had physically destroyed two floppy disks by cutting them into many pieces. Agent Christy and a deputy played with the pieces like a jigsaw puzzle until they eventually recovered 95 percent of the data on the disks. Those data were key to obtaining a conviction.[5] Following that case, computer forensics became a hot topic and a new industry soon followed.

The computer crime laws have been updated many times in the ensuing decades, evidence rules have changed, and computer forensics are considered a solid science, but it was *Daubert v. Merrell Dow Pharmaceuticals* case in 1993 that really began to have an effect on expert witness testimony in cases where a computer or related technology is involved.[6]

73.2   *DAUBERT*.   In 1974, a boy name Jason Daubert was born with a severely disfigured right arm and hand. His mother had taken Bendectin, an antinausea medication, made by Merrell Dow Pharmaceutical, to combat the morning sickness she experienced while pregnant. This particular drug had been taken by tens of millions of women over the course of more than two decades, and a considerable number of children were born with significant birth defects. Many thousands of families took Merrell Dow to court over this problem, but Daubert's case was not decided until 1993.

73.2.1   Expert Witnesses' Testimony.   Merrell Dow stated that the drug was not the problem, and worked to get the case thrown out of court. Merrell Dow presented the court an affidavit, given by a medical doctor, stating that he had reviewed many studies that indicated that the drug offered no risks in *humans* when taken during the first trimester of pregnancy. The Daubert family countered with eight affidavits from other experts that indicated there was a significant risk of birth defects in *animal* tests.

Sadly, the court did dismiss the case. In simple terms, the court felt that the Dauberts' affidavits did not compare apples to apples (i.e., animal studies were not the same as human studies). More important, however, the court also said that Dauberts' experts' findings were not admissible because they were neither published nor had they been subjected to peer review.

73.2.2 *Daubert* **Challenge.** The *Daubert* decision was heralded by many in the legal system as one of the most important findings by the Supreme Court in decades, because it went straight to the heart of the question of expert witnesses and testimony concerning science of one type or another. Many attorneys felt that juries were not capable of understanding new sciences or able to find flaws in scientific methods. With the *Daubert* case, however, the judges become "gatekeepers" of admissible evidence and, as gatekeepers, they decide whether scientific evidence could be admissible at all, based on these considerations:

- Whether the theory or technique used by the expert has been tested or *can* be tested
- Whether the theory or technique has ever been published and subjected to peer review
- Whether there is a known or potential rate of error for the method used
- The degree of acceptance within the relevant scientific community
- Whether standards exist for the method or technique used

73.3 WHETHER THE *DAUBERT* CHALLENGE IS APPLICABLE: REFINING *DAUBERT*. It is hard to imagine any legal ruling in a U.S. court ever going unchallenged for very long, and so it went with *Daubert*. When lawyers refer to a *Daubert* challenge today, they are more likely making reference to the *Daubert* Trilogy, which are the rulings in *Daubert* plus two other subsequent cases: *General Electric Co. v. Joiner*[7] and *Kumho Tire Co. v. Carmichael*.[8] In these cases, the judges made rulings that were an attempt to further define and refine the original *Daubert* rulings.

73.3.1 General Electric Co. v. Joiner. The 1997 Joiner case was one concerning product liability. Experts were called up to testify to the cancer-causing abilities of a certain fluid that Mr. Joiner came in contact with on a daily basis. Ultimately, the ruling made changes to the original *Daubert* ruling by adding that the *Daubert* challenge should be used not just for scientific testimony but for *all* testimony that could be described as "scientific, technical or other specialized knowledge" under FRE 702.

Additionally, in *Joiner* it was ruled that the judge's scrutiny is not limited to methodology but can extend to the expert's analysis. This puts another strain on expert witnesses because the science, technology, and methodologies of collecting the evidence can be fine, but the interpretation of that evidence can be called into question.

73.3.2 Kumho Tire Co. v. Carmichael. Last in the *Daubert* trilogy is *Kumho Tire*, which was another product liability case tried in 1999. The science in question here revolved around tire failure, and *Daubert* challenges abounded. The final ruling in this case decreed that a trial judge is vested with broad authority to determine whether and to what extent the enumerated *Daubert* factors are applicable to a case.

To clarify: Technical and nontechnical testimony can be challenged, the expert witness's findings can be challenged, and, finally, the judge can decide that all, some, or none of the *Daubert* challenges apply.

Computers are sometimes easier to understand than U.S. law.

73.4 DIVIDED WE FALL? Since *Joiner* and *Kumho Tire,* there have been other decisions concerning *Daubert*, admissibility of evidence, and expert witnesses, but the *Daubert* trilogy seems to be the standard—at least for federal courts. (*Daubert* and subsequent decisions were made in federal courts.) State courts, however, seem to have a lot more leniency in deciding what rules to use to determine admissibility. If you are an expert witness in a federal trial, there is a good chance you may have to face a *Daubert* challenge. If the case is at the state level or lower, you will likely experience an unusual mix of rules and challenges. The next list shows which standards apply in different states of the United States.

States Accepting *Daubert*	States Accepting *Frye*	States with Their Own Rules
Connecticut	Alaska	Arkansas
Indiana	Arizona	Delaware
Kentucky	California	Georgia
Louisiana	Colorado	Iowa
Massachusetts	Florida	Military
New Mexico	Illinois	Minnesota
Oklahoma	Kansas	Montana
South Dakota	Maryland	North Carolina
Texas	Michigan	Oregon
West Virginia	Missouri	Utah
	Nebraska	Vermont
	New York	Wyoming
	Pennsylvania	
	Washington	

If you are called as an expert witness in any case, it is best to know what rules and challenges the court may be considering in the case. Leave no doubt; talk to your attorney and, if he or she has not considered a possible *Daubert* (or other) challenge, it could mean a tough road ahead. A competent attorney will be able to give you guidance on what testimony is likely to be challenged, and an excellent attorney will spend a long time with you going over your questions and concerns.

73.5   BEING THE BEST YOU CAN BE.   Being an expert witness in a trial means more than just sitting in the stand and letting your expertise and knowledge flow. You need to be on the top of your game and know absolutely all you can possibly know about the subject matter in which you are to give testimony. One court recently dismissed an expert witness's opinion in digital forensics because he had *heard* of a certain book but had not personally read it.[9]

Although there are no hard-and-fast guidelines to being a good expert witness, you can use some general stratagems that have worked well for others. Certainly, if the list of books in online bookstores is any indication, the market for expert witnesses is strong.[10]

73.5.1   Prepare Your Résumé.   The first step in becoming an expert witness is to have a very strong résumé that is completely and totally factual. The résumé will be entered in the trial records, so this is no time for elaboration of the facts. Expert testimony is allowed only if the court declares a witness to be an expert in a specified field, and your résumé will help establish the facts of the matter.

Highlight these items in your résumé to indicate your areas of expertise:

* Education
* Training
* Certificates
* Licenses
* Employment
* Lists of published articles, books, opinions
* Lists of speaking engagements and titles of talks

Once the court has examined your résumé, oral examination by the attorneys and the judge will likely follow. This can be quite easy, or it can be long and arduous.

73.5.2 Find Out Exactly What Testimony Is Expected.

When contacted by an attorney to be an expert witness, do not be too fast to accept or decline. Most likely the attorney will be fishing at this point and will discuss things only in broad, general terms. It is also likely that your contact has limited knowledge of the subject matter. Find out as much as you can about the charges and what the attorney needs (or wants) to make the case.

Once you have reached an understanding with your contact, get everything in writing and make it a contract. This will be a statement of what is expected of you and what expertise is required to give the testimony. Your contract should also list your fees and payment schedule. This is where TV and reality take different roads. You have probably seen televised courtroom dramas where the opposing counsel undermines an expert witness by asking "How much were you paid for your testimony today?" Although that makes good television, in reality the courts *expect* that an expert witness is paid, and a fee actually lends credibility to the witness.

Also look for any legal protections you will be offered for your testimony. You might be asked to do or say something that is a potential breach of ethics or confidentiality, and this could result in a loss of certain types of certification.

73.5.3 Examine the Paperwork.

As soon as you are under contract, review the paperwork. If you discover there have been misrepresentations and you no longer want the job, you can back out at this point with no hard feelings. Of course, you may want to remain on the case, but you will need to discuss any concerns or questions with the attorney and possibly make an amendment to your contract.

Go over the paperwork as many times as you can until you are completely familiar with all aspects of the case. If the trial is particularly contentious, your familiarity with the case will certainly come into question.

73.5.4 Start Reading.

Now is a good time to start brushing up on your knowledge base. Dig into your library of industry standard books and give them a review. Look for recent books on the subjects and articles in reputable journals. The more you are able to quote facts and figures, the better you will look on the stand.

73.5.5 Prepare a Written Report.

Whether or not a written report is required should be a condition of your contract, but it is always a good idea to write up a report, even if it is just for your own use. While on the stand, you will be allowed to refer to your notes and to your report, although the court may want to examine them. Notes prepared at the time observations were made have stronger evidentiary value than statements from memory. This is a good strategy and makes you look very professional, and strong in your opinions.

It is a good idea to list all your sources and resources in your report, as well as your methodologies. This is an area where the *Daubert* challenge can get sticky, and the veracity of your opinion, based on what you have used and how you have used it, may come into question.

73.5.6 Ask for Pretrial Meetings.
It is always a good idea to practice what you need to say, especially when it is to be delivered to a large group of people. Just as you would practice giving a lecture or speech, you should practice what you are going to say on the stand. You will need to appear to be confident at trial, so ask the attorney for assistance in preparing for trial. There is always the possibility that new questions or concerns may arise during the pretrial meeting, but it is better that these come up in the meetings than in front of the court.

73.5.7 Be Professional.
Everyone is familiar with the geek stereotype: long hair, torn jeans, T-shirt, and sandals, but that is totally inappropriate. Dress professionally for court. When giving your testimony, use language that the layperson can understand. Do not let your ego show, and certainly contain your temper.

73.5.8 Accept the Oddities.
No one expects you to understand everything that happens in a court proceeding. Simply answer the questions directly, and do not be afraid to say you do not know. (If you do not know because it cannot be known, however, that is important to relate.) You do not have to justify anything you say unless you are asked to. If an objection is raised, stop speaking and wait for the judge to ask you to continue. Last, do not be afraid to ask questions yourself if you are unclear on questions or procedures.

73.6 SUMMARY.
It is certainly an ego boost to be considered enough of an expert in your field to be called as an expert witness, and some people have made successful careers of it. If you do make a career of being an expert witness, however, you cannot justify being an expert if you do not continually upgrade your expertise through industry experience. In any case, whether you are an expert, or whether your testimony is acceptable, is ultimately up to the court.

If you are called to be an expert witness and agree to the job, you do not really need to know the legal ins and outs of the *Daubert* challenge (or any other challenge); that is the attorney's job. The best plan is to know your subject matter better than anyone else and to be completely firm in your opinions and conclusions. If there is a challenge, do not take it personally. More often than not, the challenge has more to do with the methodology used in coming to your conclusions or to the science itself. To be prepared, it is best to keep detailed notes of everything you read and every step you take in coming to your opinions.

73.7 FURTHER READING

Computer Fraud and Abuse Act of 1986 (amended 1994, 1996, and 2001).

United States Department of Justice, Computer Crime & Intellectual Property Section, Scott Eltringham, editor in chief. *Prosecuting Computer Crime*, www.usdoj.gov/criminal/cybercrime/ccmanual/index.html.

73.8 NOTES

1. The author is not a lawyer, and the facts presented here are a layperson's interpretation of the laws concerning digital evidence and expert witnesses.

2. *Frye v. United States,* 293 F. 1013 (D.C. Cir. 1923); www.daubertontheweb.com/frye_opinion.htm.

3. Federal Rules of Evidence, www.law.cornell.edu/rules/fre/rules.htm.

4. Counterfeit Access Device and Computer Fraud and Abuse Act of 1984, www.answers.com/topic/counterfeit-access-device-and-computer-fraud-and-abuse-act-of-1984.

5. *Wired* article on SA Jim Christy, www.wired.com/wired/archive/15.01/cybercop.html.

6. *Daubert v. Merrell Dow Pharmaceuticals,* 509 U. S. 579 (1993); http://supct.law.cornell.edu/supct/html/92-102.75.html.

7. *General Electric v. Joiner,* 522 U. S. 136 (1997); www.law.cornell.edu/supct/html/96-188.ZO.html.

8. *Kuhmo Tire v. Carmichael,* 526 U. S. 137 (1999); www.griffithlaw.net/research.database/uploads/DAUBERT%20CHALLENGES%20IN%20GOVERNMENTAL%20LITIGATION%20final%20draft.pdf.

9. Daniel J. Ryan and Gal Shpantzer, "Legal Aspects of Digital Forensics," http://www.danjryan.com/Legal%20Issues.doc.

10. Malack Amenya, "Recovering, Examining and Presenting Computer Forensic Evidence in Court," http://209.85.165.104/search?q=cache:dubQuXkv3YkJ:www.csam.montclair.edu/~robila/SECURITY/F2004_P/P6/finalcomputerforensics.doc+daubert+challenge+digital+forensics+witness.

PROFESSIONAL CERTIFICATION AND TRAINING IN INFORMATION ASSURANCE

Christopher Christian, M. E. Kabay, Kevin Henry, and Sondra Schneider

74.1 BUILDING SKILLS THROUGH PROFESSIONAL EDUCATION. Perhaps one of the most critical decisions an organization has to make today is how to invest in its staff. Technology, policies, and well-defined processes are all important elements of an organization's infrastructure, but the most valuable and versatile asset that any company has today is its personnel.

How do we recruit, develop, and maintain a skilled and professional staff, with other organizations competing for our trained experts, and how do we maintain their level of proficiency despite the rapid changes in technology and the many pressures of keeping the business operating?

Many companies struggle with the need to provide opportunity for their staff, while realizing that training and educating their staff makes these people attractive to other organizations.

Government regulations and legislation as well as increasing expectations from customers, suppliers, and business partners require information technology (IT) staff who are up to date with the latest technologies and who can provide assurance of reliable and stable IT operations. In most cases, a company is required either to develop internal resources to meet these demands or to pay a large price to recruit such people from external sources. More and more organizations are building relationships with universities and technical colleges to ensure that a ready supply of new graduates is available for their use. However, to retain good employees, it is necessary to make expensive investments in their further education. This is money and time that is hard to justify in some cases, and there are numerous options when it comes to registering for a professional training or educational program.

74.1.1   Training and Education.   There is a significant difference between training and education. In this chapter, the emphasis is on training; in Chapter 75 of this *Handbook*, it is on education. When a company invests in a technology such as a firewall or intrusion prevention system, it often has to provide training to the people responsible for managing the device. Such training is best provided through official sources because the product vendors can often arrange for training as a part of the purchase price, and there is a certain assurance that the training materials are up to date if they are provided by an official source.

One common mistake that companies make is to send only one person to the official training program and then trust that person to pass the knowledge gained to their peers. What usually happens is that the person who attends the course provides a 10-minute overview to the rest of the staff when she returns. In part, this kind of slipshod knowledge transfer occurs because many organizations have no systematic way of evaluating a training program and ensuring that they receive value for their investment, and they put no thought into knowledge sharing.

All worthwhile education and training programs should go beyond merely passing on information passively; they should provide the students with some form of practical work—whether through labs, a case study, or the need to prepare for and pass a difficult project or an extensive examination. It is too easy to have programs that are not really effective—the students can easily slip into a state of "lecture hypnosis" where they are following along with the program but not really absorbing or digesting the material. It is only when they are asked to answer questions about the material, or use it in a practical manner, that most people will truly grasp and retain the information.

One factor to consider is the location of the class. Far too many students do not gain the expected benefit from a class due to its location. Ideally, a student should not be continuously distracted or pulled from the program to address issues back at the office or to handle e-mail during the class. Although it is possible to multitask, distraction makes what is being said in the class difficult to absorb. Lack of concentration causes the sponsoring organization to lose the investment it made in the class; students may ask questions that were addressed earlier and thus frustrate other students; and distracted students may do poorly in the lab work or examinations and cause conflict by blaming the course or the instructor. While a student is assigned to a training class, he should not participate in activities back at the office except in an emergency. As for holding classes in a resort or holiday location, the distractions may make it even harder for the students to focus on the course—especially if they are busy late into the evenings. Training should be held at facilities that enable serious study and learning. The courses themselves should not be just interesting hot topics but rather those that will directly benefit employees in their work–and as soon as possible. Avoid educating someone in skills they will not use for several months: since they will probably have forgotten most of the information by the time they try to use it.

Education and training are sometimes seen as a reward for an employee or a measure of respect for the staff. Although reward and respect are important, it is inappropriate to hand out training assignments as if they were perquisites of rank or signs of management favor. Courses should be focused on meeting specific objectives. In addition, to emphasize that learning is legitimate work and not a perk, employees who take assigned courses on weekends or outside their normal work shifts should be assigned compensatory time to make up for the use of their personal time.

74.1.2 Certificates, Certification, and Accreditation.

Sometimes students, professionals, and marketers use the terms "certificate" and "certification" interchangeably. In addition, academics and professionals sometimes differ in their interpretation of "accreditation."

- A *certificate* is a "document providing official evidence: an official document that gives proof and details of something such as personal status, educational achievements, ownership, or authenticity."[1]
- *Certification*, in this context, is the process (thus, a verb) of examining the work experience, knowledge and trustworthiness of a candidate for a particular certificate; confusingly, the certificate granted for qualified applicants is often referred to as a particular *certification* (and thus, a noun).
- "Accreditation" refers to the process of "officially recogniz[ing]" a person or organization as having met a standard or criterion. In information assurance, accreditation is carried out by official, industry- and government-recognized bodies.

The next sections explain the three of the most important accreditation organizations and processes for information assurance: ANSI/ISO/IEC 17024, NOCA/NCCA, and IACE.

74.1.3 ANSI/ISO/IEC 17024 Accreditation of Personnel Certification.

The International Organization of Standardization (ISO) and the International Electrotechnical Commission (IEC) have developed a global, voluntary benchmark for organizations responsible for certification of personnel. Fully enacted as of April 1, 2003, this international standard (ANSI/ISO/IEC 17024) was designed to harmonize the personnel certification process worldwide and create more cost-effective global standards for certifying workers in a wide range of fields.

This accreditation process involves both a review of a paper application and the performance of an audit (on-site visit) to validate information provided by each applicant organization. The use of an on-site audit for accreditation of personnel-certification agencies is unique to ANSI. More than 300,000 professionals held certifications from organizations accredited under ANSI's ANSI/ISO/IEC 17024 Accreditation Program at the time of writing (July 2008).

74.1.4   NOCA/NCCA.   The National Organization for Competency Assurance (NOCA), founded in 1977, promotes excellence in credentialing worldwide through these services:

- Education
- Research
- Advocacy
- Standards
- Accreditation[2]

The organization provides annual conferences, webinars, and publications. In 1987, NOCA created the National Commission for Certifying Agencies (NCCA) to formalize the process of accreditation of certification programs and organizations.

NCCA uses a peer review process to:

- Establish accreditation standards
- Evaluate compliance with the standards
- Recognize organizations/programs that demonstrate compliance
- Serve as a resource on quality certification

Certification organizations that submit their programs for accreditation are evaluated based on the process and products, not the content, and are therefore applicable to all professions and industries.

NCCA-accredited programs certify individuals in a wide range of professions and occupations including nurses, automotive professionals, respiratory therapists, counselors, emergency technicians, crane operators, and more. As of July 2008, NCCA has accredited over 190 programs representing 78 organizations.[3]

74.1.5   IACE.   The Information Assurance Courseware Evaluation (IACE) Program of the National Security Agency (NSA) provides consistency in training and education for the information assurance skills that are critical to the security of the United States. Focused on meeting the needs of U.S. Government requirements for specific levels of competence in IA, the IACE process ensures that certified institutions meet the minimum national training and education standards for the duties and responsibilities of:

- Information Systems Security (INFOSEC) Professionals, NSTISSI 4011
- Senior Systems Managers, CNSSI 4012
- System Administrators (SA), CNSSI 4013
- Information Systems Security Officers, CNSSI 4014
- System Certifiers, NSTISSI 4015
- Risk Analyst, CNSSI 4016[4]

The certification process involves detailed mapping of curricula to these standards and is a prerequisite for application for certification as a Center of Academic Excellence

Exhibit 74.1   Comparison of Certification and Certificates

Certification	Certificate
Results from an assessment process that recognizes an individual's knowledge, skills, and competency in a particular specialty	Results from an educational process
Typically requires professional experience	For newcomers and experienced professionals
Awarded by a third-party, standard-setting organization, typically not for profit	Awarded by educational programs or institutions often for profit
Indicates mastery/competency as measured against a defensible set of standards, usually by lab, application, and exam	Indicates completion of a course or series of courses with a specific focus (different from a degree-granting program)
Standards set through a defensible, industry-wide process (job analysis/role delineation) that results in an outline of required knowledge and skills	Course content determined by the specific provider or institution, not standardized
Typically results in credentials to be listed after one's name (QISP, CISSP, QIAP, SSCP, GIAC)	Usually listed on a resume detailing education
Has ongoing requirements in order to maintain; holder must demonstrate he/she continues to meet requirements	Demonstrates knowledge of course content at the end of a set period in time

in Information Assurance Education (CAEIAE), which is limited to colleges and universities.[5]

Institutions must apply for recertification every five years after their IACE certification.

74.1.6 Summary of Accreditation, Certification, and Certificates.
Certification differs from a certificate program, which is usually an educational offering that confers a document at the program's conclusion.

Accreditation of a certification involves a voluntary, self-regulatory process established by defined organizations and using published standards. Accreditation is granted when stated quality criteria are met.

By submitting to accreditation and enforcing documented, verified standards for professional certification, organizations such as (ISC)[2], SANS, CompTIA, and Security University seek to protect the public and consumers against meaningless claims of professionalism. ANSI has evaluated and accredited (ISC)[2]'s CISSP, CompTIA's Security +, and SANS' GIAC certifications; Security University's Q/ISP, Q/IAP, Q/WAD and Q/SSE's certifications were awaiting NOCA and ANSI approval at the time of writing (July 2008). See Exhibit 74.1 for a comparison of certification and certificates.

74.2 INFORMATION SECURITY CERTIFICATIONS.
Information systems security (ISS) has grown into one of the most important and sought after fields in the job market today. This is not a market saturated with professionals. Security professionals are well paid right out of college. This means that there is still a large demand for ISS practitioners.

Persons responsible for a company's information security are given a lot of power. With this in mind, a company should hire only those whom it can trust to do the job right, and who are ethical. Certifications provided by security groups and societies support management's quest for trustworthy, competent employees. Through rigorous examinations, adherence to approved protocols and standards of ethics, a security professional can achieve one or many professional security-related certifications.

What follows are brief summaries of some of the key security-related certifications. They are similar to each other in the way that they are obtained, and many ask that a candidate follow a strict code of ethics. The differences lie in the areas of focus of each certification. Some may be for more managerial roles, while others may cater to security architects. In the end, these certifications all try to communicate to potential employers that the certified professionals are trustworthy and that they stand out from the larger mass of uncertified candidates.

In the 2007 *SC Magazine/EC-Council Salary Survey*, a key finding was that "[w]hile not a mainstream occurrence, many companies are striving to ensure they're viewed as being proactive about securing digital assets by asking that new hires have a certification."[6] Indeed, there has been a steady increase in the acceptance of certification as a credible indicator of professional competence in the information assurance field. For example, even by 2003, the information technology industry had recognized the value of the Certified Information Systems Professional (CISSP)® designation. A writer for the prestigious *SC Magazine* wrote:

> The CISSP designation from the International Systems Security Certification Consortium—or (ISC)² —is often referred to as the de facto standard when it comes to information security certifications. It is described as the "International Gold Standard," according to (ISC)². But companies and government agencies also place importance on more technical certifications, such as the SANS Institute's Global Information Assurance Certification (GIAC).[7]

In June 2004, the CISSP designation was accredited by the International Standards Organization under the ISO/IEC 1702 standard, making it a globally recognized security-professional certification.[8]

In August 2004, the United States Department of Defense issued DoD Directive 8570.1. The *DoD Fact Sheet* from (ISC)² is provided in full as an appendix to this proposal.[9] The key points of this development are:

- ". . . requires any full- or part-time military service member, contractor, or foreign employee with privileged access to a DoD information system, regardless of job or occupational series, to obtain a commercial information security credential accredited by ANSI or equivalent authorized body under the ANSI/ISO/IEC 17024 Standard. . . ."
- The CISSP designation was recognized at the highest levels of both the technical and management categories.

The *Fact Sheet* continues with a discussion of "the significance of this mandate and of commercial certification in general." The authors write:

> This mandate will have far-reaching implications, including:
>
> - The Directive is viewed as a government endorsement of the effectiveness and cost-efficiency of commercial certification.
> - It provides military and civilian personnel with a certification that is professional, internationally recognized and vendor-neutral (not tied to any agency, technology or product).

- It provides a portable certification that is recognized in both the public and private sectors.
- It mandates and endorses a global standard (ANSI/ISO/IEC 17024).
- It positions the information security profession as a distinct job series.

In a 2008 survey sponsored by (ISC)^2, analysts found that "[t]he clear differentiator in terms of career advancement and professional growth lies in certifications such as the CISSP. 'Certifications are a measure of experience and knowledge, and businesses increasingly like to see that certification....'"[10]

The next sections review key certifications:

- CIA: Certified Internal Auditor
- CISA: Certified Information Systems Auditor
- CISM: Certified Information Security Manager
- CISSP: Certified Information Systems Security Professional
- GIAC: Global Information Assurance Certification

74.2.1   Certified Internal Auditor (CIA).   The Certified Internal Auditor (CIA$^®$) is the standard certification among professionals working in the auditing field. A CIA certification recognizes that the individual has achieved a level of standards that enforces "competency and professionalism"[11]

This certification and three other certifications within the auditing field— *Certification in Control Self-Assessment* (CCSA), *Certified Government Auditing Professional* (CGAP), and *Certified Financial Services Auditor* (CFSA)—are offered through the Institute of Internal Auditors (IIA), which is globally recognized as a leader, authority, and principal educator for auditing professionals. The Institute of Internal Auditors was founded in 1941 in Altamonte Springs, Florida, and is made up of over 108,000 members found worldwide. The IIA has set the standard for all professionals by giving them the opportunities to get certified, continue their education and research, provide technological guidance, and enhance their reputation as professionals.[12]

The criteria for eligibility to take the CIA exam are described next.

74.2.1.1   Education.   Candidates require a suitable background in education. The candidate must have a bachelor's degree (or its equivalent) from an accredited college-level institution. No specific degree is mentioned. Experience within the workforce is not accepted by the IIA as a proper substitute in place of a degree. The only exception for those without degrees is for student candidates within their senior year in an undergraduate program or in a graduate program. If a candidate is using this substitution, it is required that she be a full-time student (12 credit hours—undergraduate or 9 credit hours—graduate). Once this is approved, the student candidate is then eligible to register and take the CIA exam. Once the students have taken the exam and passed, their certification will be withheld until they have achieved their diplomas.[13]

74.2.1.2   Character Reference.   Each candidate is expected to uphold and represent high standards, proper moral conviction, and show a good professional attitude. A character-reference form must be submitted by the candidate to recognize the fact that she has met all criteria to become a certified CIA and that she meets the standards applied by the code of ethics established by the IIA.[14] The form must be completed by one of the following: a certified CIA, a supervisor, a manager, or an educator.

74.2.1.3 *Professional Experience.* Another prerequisite to becoming a CIA candidate is having professional experience. The minimum is 24 months of internal auditing or its equivalent. By definition of "equivalent," the other form of work that can be done is two years of work within the disciplines of auditing (internal/external), quality assurance, compliance, and internal control. However, a candidate can substitute the for one year's credit toward the required experience:

- A master's degree
- Work experience in a related professional discipline (accounting, law, or finance)

The candidate is allowed to take the CIA qualification before completing the professional experience requirements. However, the certification will be withheld until such a time as the required work hours are completed.[15]

74.2.1.4 *Code of Ethics.* All CIAs and CIA candidates must adhere to the IIA written and approved code of ethics. "This code is a standard for all professionals within the auditing field or related working fields."[16] It is of the utmost importance that the code be followed. The introduction of the code of ethics states: "The purpose of The Institute's code of ethics is to promote an ethical culture in the profession of internal auditing."[17] It also defines four disciplines of ethical behavior: integrity, objectivity, confidentiality, and competency.[18]

74.2.1.5 *Continuing Professional Education.* Once a person is certified as a CIA, her requirements are never completed. A CIA is defined as a person who maintains an ever-growing knowledge and skills base. It also means that CIAs are up to date on all new improvements and developments within their fields of work, relating to internal auditing standards, procedures, and techniques. To make sure that this is being done, all CIAs must send out a report listing 80 hours of continuing professional education (CPE) every two years. The report is analyzed at the IIA headquarters in Altamonte Springs, Florida.

74.2.1.6 *The Exam.* The examination for a CIA consists of four parts:[19]

1. The Internal Audit Activity's Role in Governance, Risk, and Control
2. Conducting the Internal Audit Engagement
3. Business Analysis and Information Technology
4. Business Management Skills

Each part consists of 100 multiple-choice questions with an allowance of 2 hours 45 minutes each. The overall exam focuses on the candidate's knowledge of current auditing practices, understanding of internal audit issues, risks, and remedies. A candidate can take each exam at any time in any order.

In addition, candidates may take IIA specialty exams:

- Certification in Control Self-Assessment (CCSA)
- Certified Government Auditing Professional (CGAP)
- Certified Financial Services Auditor (CFS)[20]

All these exams are offered throughout the world under the auspices of local chapters of the Institute of Internal Auditors. The standard fees for the United States are listed in the current *CIA Candidate Handbook*.[21]

74.2.2 Certified Information Systems Auditor (CISA). Sponsored by the Information Systems Audit and Control Association (ISACA®), the Certified Information Systems Auditor (CISA) is considered a serious primary certification "for all information systems (IS) audit, control, and security professionals."[22] The CISA certification Web site boasts that "the mark of excellence for a professional certification program is the value and recognition it bestows on the individual who achieves it."[23] Having a CISA opens many doors and opportunities for professionals working in the information systems discipline. The CISA is a recognized certification within all industries worldwide, and it is highly recommended that professionals in the IS field become certified with this designation. More than 40,000 people are currently recognized as certified CISAs.

The next requirements are standard for becoming a CISA.

74.2.2.1 *Successful Completion of the CISA Examination.* The exam is open to anyone willing to take the test. Those who wish to embark on this path need to show an interest in information security, audit, and control. This examination is offered twice a year in June and December. The CISA Certifications Board administers the test and grades it. They then give the candidate information, upon success, about the remaining requirements to becoming a CISA. The board ensures that each exam is up to date. Each question and area is reviewed by a panel of CISA officials. The exam contains 200 multiple-choice questions to be answered, and can be taken in any number of languages. A number of CISA study guides are available through the ISACA® CISA Web site. Once the exam is successfully completed, the next steps need to be taken to become fully certified.

74.2.2.2 *Experience as an Information Systems Auditor.* A minimum of five years of professional information systems auditing, control, or security work experience are needed for certification; certain equivalencies are available:

- A maximum of one year of information systems experience or one year of financial or operational auditing experience can be substituted for one year of information systems auditing, control or security experience.
- 60 to 120 completed college semester credit hours (the equivalent of an associate or bachelor degree) can be substituted for one or two years, respectively, of information systems auditing, control, or security experience.
- Two years as a full-time university instructor in a related field (e.g., computer science, accounting, information systems auditing) can be substituted for one year of information systems auditing, control, or security experience

These substitutions must be completed within 10 years of applying for the CISA application or within 5 years of taking the exam.

74.2.2.3 *Code of Professional Ethics.*[24]   All CISA members and candidates must submit to the standards applied by the code of professional ethics. This code was written and approved by the ISACA®. It is a small document with seven tenets. It can be viewed at the corresponding link in the index, or a copy can be viewed in the appendix at the end of this chapter.

74.2.2.4 *Continuing Professional Education (CPE) Policy.*   Member maintenance fees and a minimum of 20 hours of CPE are annually required. Over a three-year period, a total of 120 hours of CPE is required. By request, the ISACA will provide information and criteria for each member's personal CPE. The complete CPE policy can be seen on the ISACA Web site.[25] It contains these sections:

- Audits of Continuing Professional Education Hours
- Revocation, Reconsideration and Appeal
- Retired and Non-practicing CISA Status
- Calculating Continuing Professional Education Hours, Certification Requirements
- Verification of Attendance Form
- Code of Professional Ethics
- Qualifying Educational Activities

74.2.2.5 *Information Systems Auditing Standards.*   All CISA members and candidates must adhere to the information systems auditing standards also adopted by the ISACA.[26]

Once the exam has been taken and successfully passed, CISA candidates must fill out an Application for Certification detailing that they met the requirements for full certification.[27] This must be done within five years of passing the exam. Annual membership fees are part of the requirement. The continuing professional education policy must be followed to assure that all CISA members are up to date with all auditing practices and policies within the fields of information systems auditing, control, and security.

74.2.3 *Certified Information Security Manager (CISM).*   The Certified Information Security Manager (CISM) is achieved similarly to that of the CISA. The Information Systems Audit Control Association (ISACA) administers and monitors this certification. CISM was created for experienced information security managers. Thus, CISM is a more specialized certification for a more defined role in the information security and assurance field.[28] This qualification is for individuals who manage, design, oversee, or assess a company's information security.[29] A CISM member is more of a leader in the discipline of information security, in control of other individuals who would be more suited to be qualified with a CISA certification or the like. The assurance given to employers is that they are hiring experienced professionals with the proper knowledge and ethical standing to run a secure management operation, and who have the additional ability to provide consulting advice. Like the CISA, the CISM is recognized worldwide as a top certification within the IS field.[30] There are four steps required in order to achieve recognition as a CISM.

74.2.3.1 *Successfully Pass the CISM Exam.*   The CISM candidate must pass the exam. This exam can be taken at any time, even prior to completing necessary work experience requirements. A passed test will be valid for only five years. The rest of the requirements to become a CISM must be completed within the five-year validation period. However, once all the criteria are met within the time limit, the test does not have to be taken again. The exam is available twice a year: December and June.

The exam consists of five parts:

1. Information Security Governance
2. Risk Management
3. Information Security Program Management
4. Information Security Management
5. Response Management[31]

More information regarding the CISM exam can be found at the CISM Exam Overview Website.[32] Information can be obtained including:

- Bulletin of Information (BOI),[33] which provides information on the exam
- Exam dates
- Instructions on registration
- Membership in ISACA
- Exam locations
- *Candidate's Guide*
- Content area (a description of certification and examination)
- Test center locations
- Exam registration
- Preparation
- Frequently asked questions

74.2.3.2 *Code of Professional Ethics.* Like CISA members, all CISM members and candidates must adhere to ISACA's Code of Professional Ethics.[34] This guide is to promote professionalism and standards of personal conduct. ISACA requires standards to be set for each of their members and for those nonmembers who have certifications through their program.

74.2.3.3 *Continuing Education Policy.* The Continuing Education Policy for CISMs works like that for CISAs. Member maintenance fees and a minimum of 20 hours of CPE are annually required. Over a three-year period, at least 120 hours of CPE are required. By request, the ISACA will provide information and criteria for each member's personal CPE. The objectives of the CISM CPE policy are:

- Maintain an individual's competency by requiring the update of existing knowledge and skills in the areas of information systems auditing, management, accounting, and business areas related to specific industries (e.g., finance, insurance, business law, etc.)
- Provide a means to differentiate between qualified CISMs and those who have not met the requirements for continuation of their certification

- Provide a mechanism for monitoring information systems audit, and control, and for security professionals' maintenance of their competency
- Aid top management in developing sound information systems audit, control, and security functions by providing criteria for personnel selection and development[35]

74.2.3.4 Work Experience.   The last requirement before becoming a fully certified CISM is work experience. At least five years of experience in information security management are required and must include the five areas specified in the exam. Substitutions for this requirement can be completed by conducting two years of work as a certified CISA or CISSP in good standing, or by completing a postgraduate degree in information security or in a related field. Another credit toward the requirement can be obtained for a year of work as an information systems manager while holding a skill-based security certification (GIAC, MCSE, or CompTIA Security +).[36]

Once these requirements are met, a CISM Application for Certification must be completed and sent in for review by members of a CISM board through ISACA. Annual certification maintenance fees apply.[37]

74.2.4 Certified Information Systems Security Professionals (CISSP).
The International Information Systems Security Certification Consortium, the (ISC)[2] established the *Certified Information Systems Security Professional* (CISSP) designation in the 1990s as a result of intense committee work by security experts. They consulted many texts and used their own experience in defining the *Common Body of Knowledge* (CBK) on which the examinations are based. In the decade since the certification was introduced, over 50,000 professionals have been certified.

According to (ISC)[2], a CISSP is typically responsible for "developing the information security policies, standards, and procedures and managing their implementation across an organization."[38]

The main requirements for being a certified CISSP are that the candidate must have at least four years of work experience in the discipline of information systems security within one or more of the 10 test domains in the ISS Common Body of Knowledge (CBK) or at least three years of such experience if the candidate has a four-year college degree. "Additionally, a Master's Degree in Information Security from a National Center of Excellence can substitute for one year toward the four-year requirement."[39]

The CISSP member or candidate must subscribe to the (ISC)[2] code of ethics. Like all codes of ethics, this standard is set to ensure that all members of this esteemed certification meet the highest standards of professionalism and adhere to a strict code of moral ethics.[40]

As with other certifications, a candidate must pass an exam; in this case, it is a six-hour exam consisting of 250 multiple-choice questions. The exam covers topics such as Access Control Systems, Cryptography, and Security Management Practices. The test is administered by the (ISC)[2]. The exam cannot be taken until all prerequisite requirements are completed. To obtain certification the candidate must[41] :

- Pass the CISSP exam with a scaled score of 700 points or better.
- Submit a properly completed and executed Endorsement Form.
  - The candidate must have a CISSP application endorsed by another credentialed CISSP.

- If required, the candidate must pass an audit that asserts professional experience.
  - A percentage of CISSP candidates will be chosen randomly for audit of their professional experience.
  - If the candidate is up to spec, then certification will be received within seven days.

All CISSP members must then recertify their credentials every three years by completing least 120 CPE credits and a paying a fee.

74.2.4.1   CISSP Concentrations.   There are three certified concentrations within CISSP:

1. Information Systems Security Architecture Professional (ISSAP)
2. Information Systems Security Engineering Professional (ISSEP)
3. Information Systems Security Management Professional (ISSMP)

Each credentialed certification allows a CISSP to deepen his concentration and specialty into a specified field.

Each concentration stresses a number of domains in regard to each individual field. These domains define what is expected of a candidate or member of each concentration and what professional expertise is expected.

74.2.4.1.1   *ISSAP*[42].   ISSAP concentration focuses in the direction of security architecture and security planning:

- Access Control Systems and Methodology
- Telecommunications and Network Security
- Cryptography
- Requirements Analysis and Standards, Guidelines, Criteria
- Technology Related Business Continuity Planning (BCP) and Disaster Recovery Planning (DRP)
- Physical Security Integration

74.2.4.1.2   *ISSEP*[43].   The ISSEP concentrates more heavily on national security and works particularly well with government branches such as the NSA:

- Systems Security Engineering
- Certification and Accreditation
- Technical Management
- U.S. Government Information Assurance Regulations

74.2.4.1.3   *ISSMP*[44].   As the name implies, the ISSMP concentration focuses on security management and regulations:

- Enterprise Security Management
- Enterprise-Wide System Development Security
- Overseeing Compliance of Operations Security
- Understanding Business Continuity Planning (BCP), Disaster Recovery Planning (DRP), and Continuity of Operations Planning (COOP)
- Law, Investigations, Forensics, and Ethics

74.2.4.1.4 Obtaining Certification.   All three of the CISSP concentrations are obtained in the same manner. The candidate must be a CISSP in good standing, must pass an exam (ISSAP, ISSEP, or ISSMP specific), and must subsequently maintain the credential in good standing.[45] The (ISC)^2 organization proctors these exams.

For those interested, the (ISC)^2 offers concentration review seminars that can be found on their Web site (www.isc2.org). These seminars can be found throughout the United States and Europe. Any information regarding time, place, and price can be found at the (ISC)^2 Web site.

74.2.5 Systems Security Certified Practitioner (SSCP).   The Systems Security Certified Practitioner (SSCP) certification is designed for a group of acknowledged professionals within the network and security administration discipline who may not yet qualify for the CISSP designation. The focus of this certification is based upon seven test domains[46]:

1. Access Controls
2. Administration
3. Audit and Monitoring
4. Risk, Response, and Recovery
5. Cryptography
6. Data Communications
7. Malicious Code/Malware

The SSCP certification is provided and authorized by the International Information Systems Security Certification Consortium (ISC)^2. Candidates and members are required to adhere to the (ISC)^2 code of ethics. They must have a minimum of one year of work experience in any one of the above-mentioned test domains. Also, an SSCP specified exam must be taken and passed.

This exam is made up of 125 multiple-choice questions in which all seven test domains are covered.

The American Society for Industrial Security International (ASIS) Certified Protection Professionals are considered to be in the top tier of professional practitioners of information security with an emphasis on protecting people, property, and information. Becoming a CPP is actually an award granted based on experience, education, and the passing of an exam. As of 2007, there were 10,000 people recognized as professional CPPs.

Candidates wishing to obtain this certification must meet these security and educational requirements[47]: Either

- Nine years of security experience, with a minimum of three years in a managerial role in charge of security *or*
- A BA or higher with seven years of experience in the security field and a minimum of three years in a managerial role in charge of security

Candidates who believe they meet these requirements stated must send in an application to ASIS, where it will be reviewed and notification will given if the applicant is eligible to take the CPP exam.

74.2.6 Global Information Assurance Certification.   In 1989, the SysAdmin, Audit, Network, Security Institute (SANS) began working to provide research and education resources in security.

> The Global Information Assurance Certification (GIAC) was founded in 1999 to validate the real-world skills of IT security professionals. GIAC's purpose is to provide assurance that a certified individual has practical awareness, knowledge and skills in key areas of computer and network and software security. GIAC currently offers certifications for over 20 job-specific responsibilities that reflect the current practice of information security. GIAC is unique in measuring specific knowledge areas instead of general purpose information security knowledge.[48]

74.2.6.1 GIAC Overview.   The GIAC is a valuable addition to any other certification. Whereas other certifications provide that the member is knowledgeable and capable in her role as an information security expert, and is someone who lives up to a standard of ethics, the GIAC compounds these qualifications with a set of usable skills assuring any potential employers that the persons they are looking at are capable of carrying out information security needs. The GIAC is a good certification by itself, but it works well with any other certification such as the CISSP.

What makes GIAC a unique certification compared to other certifications is its scope and focus. The GIAC is more concerned with a variety of skill sets whereas other certifications focus on general-purpose security knowledge.[49] These skill sets are:

- Security Administration
- Management
- Audit
- Software Security

GIAC certification lasts for four years, thus ensuring that all GIAC members stay current with rising concerns, new skill sets, and an evolved course base.

74.2.6.2 GIAC Certifications and Certificates.   A GIAC designation is not a set standard of practiced and learned protocols. Instead SANS offers a number of certifications and certificates that are dedicated to different areas that require information security and different skill sets. Divided into divisions—Audit, Legal, Management, Operations, Security Administration—the certificates are further divided into levels (basic to more advanced skill sets). In order to attain a GIAC certification, a five- or six-day SANS Training course must be taken followed by an exam. The exam can be taken within a six-month period from the end of the course.

74.2.6.2.1 Silver Certification.   The exam is taken online and consists of 50 to 100 multiple-choice questions and must be completed within 60 to 90 minutes. The cost of a GIAC certification is the same whether the candidate chooses self-study or conference training. Upon successful completion of the exam, a Silver certification is given to the candidate.

74.2.6.2.2 Gold Certification.   The Silver certification can be further upgraded to a Gold certification two years or more after completing the Silver certification process. Upgrading requires completion of a technical paper related to the candidate's Silver certification. The paper must be completed in a six-month period, although a three-month extension can be added for an extra fee. When the paper is submitted, it is reviewed using a number of criteria:

- Technical—errors
- Education—clarity of thought and advanced knowledge of subject matter
- Extension—a topic outside the box of normal course studies
- Organization—paper clarity, setup, and professional work[50]

74.2.6.2.3 Certificates.   Certificates are also offered by SANS as part of the GIAC certification. Certificates are different from certification in that they are based on shorter classes (one to two days), shorter tests that must be completed sooner (no more than 10 weeks after the completion of the course). Most important, a certificate is more focused on a particular topic area than a certification. With certificates, GIAC candidates can modify their direction and knowledge base toward the topics in which they are particularly interested or that are directly related to their work. The certificates fall into the same five categories as certifications—Audit, Legal, Management, Operations, and Security Administration—and have varying knowledge levels (introduction to advanced).

74.3   PREPARING FOR SECURITY CERTIFICATION EXAMINATIONS.
The key to passing the security certification exams is daily attention to expanding one's exposure to interesting and thought-provoking information and ideas in the field. Cramming does not work; it is not possible to remember what is learned in a rush for very long. Indeed, all students should learn to use SQ3R (survey/question, read/recite, review) a well-established study method that pays off with long-term integration and retention of knowledge. Readers may want to use a one-page summary of this technique.[51] Granted, some test takers enroll in short courses (boot camps) devoted to preparing for specific certifications, but without long-term commitment to professionalism, such efforts result in a certificate that raises eyebrows among employers and clients when the crammer fails to display an ingrained understanding of soon-forgotten concepts and terminology.

Anyone committed to professionalism and long-term success in a field should read a wide range of reputable publications and participate in serious discussion groups.

74.3.1 Newsletters.   Some of the electronic newsletters useful for anyone preparing for certification exams are listed next:

- *Computerworld*   newsletters: www.computerworld.com/action/member.do?command=registerNewsletters
  - Disaster Recovery
  - Infrastructure & Control
  - Networking Security
  - Security: Issues and Trends
  - Virus and Vulnerability Roundup
- *CRYPTO-GRAM* from Bruce Schneier: www.schneier.com/crypto-gram.html
- Department of Homeland Security resources: www.dhs.gov/xinfoshare/programs/
  - Homeland Security Advisories and Information
  - Daily Open Source Infrastructure Report

- *EFFector* from the Electronic Frontier Foundation: www.eff.org/effector/
- *EPIC Alert* from the Electronic Privacy Information Center: www.epic.org/alert/
- *Network World* Newsletters: www.networkworld.com/newsletters/
  - Security: Identity Management Alert
  - Security: Network Access Control Alert
  - Security: Threat Alert
  - Security Strategies Alert
- *ITL Computer Security Bulletins* from the National Institute of Standards and Technology Information Technology Laboratory Computer Security Division's Computer Security Resource Center keep readers abreast of new documents issued by NIST: http://csrc.nist.gov/publications/nistbul/index.html
- *RISKS FORUM DIGEST* from the Association for Computing Machinery Committee on Computers and Public Policy: http://catless.ncl.ac.uk/Risks/
- SANS newsletters: www.sans.org/newsletters/?ref=1701
  - @RISK: The Consensus Security Vulnerability Alert
  - NewsBites
- ZDNet UK newsletters: http://community.zdnet.co.uk/account/manage.htm
  - "IT White Papers"
  - "Security"

74.3.2 Web Sites.   The National Institute of Standards and Technology Information Technology Laboratory Computer Security Division's Computer Security Resource Center has a several good resources for review by anyone taking security certifications.

First, the NIST Special Publications (SP) page—http://csrc.nist.gov/publications/PubsSPs.html—has a wealth of valuable papers for anyone interested in reviewing and extending security knowledge, especially security-management knowledge.

A related page is the NIST ITL CSD CSRC Draft Publications list, http://csrc.nist.gov/publications/PubsDrafts.html, which offers even more recent documents plus the opportunity for certification preparers to apply their analytical skills to improving proposed documents. Some of the drafts are also linked from the previously mentioned SP page, but on the draft page each is described in a one-paragraph summary that includes the deadlines for comments.

Even if certification candidates are not currently working in the U.S. federal government, they would do well to read many of the Federal Information Processing Standards (FIPS) available from the NIST ITL CSD CSRC (http://csrc.nist.gov/publications/PubsFIPS.html).

A collection of interesting white papers on security-related topics is maintained by Entrust: www.entrust.com/resources/whitepapers.cfm. At latest count, there are over 100 papers freely available from that source (some of them in German) without having to sign up for anything. Some of the papers readers may find valuable in stimulating their thinking about security fundamentals:

- AITE Online Banking Security: FFIEC Deployment Experiences
- An Introduction to Cryptography and Digital Signatures v2.0
- Authentication: The Cornerstone of Secure Identity Management

- Best Practices for Choosing a Content Control Solution
- Common Criteria Evaluation
- Countering On-Line Identity Theft: New Tools to help Battle Identity Theft on the Internet
- Did Security Go Out the Door with Your Mobile Workforce?
- Enhanced Online Banking Security—Behavioral Multi-Factor Authentication
- Entrust Internet Security Survey—European Survey Overview and Report Methodology
- GIGA Report: Total Economic Impact of Entrust TruePass and Token-based Authentication
- Information Security Governance: Toward a Framework for Action (BSA white paper)
- Myths and Realities in Content Control for Compliance
- Protecting Information on Laptops and Mobile Devices
- Quantum Computing and Quantum Cryptography
- Security in a Web Services World
- Trends in Outbound Content Control: A White Paper by Ferris Research
- Trusted Public-Key Infrastructures
- Understanding Secure Sockets Layer (SSL): A Fundamental Requirement For Internet Transactions
- Using a PKI Based Upon Elliptic Curve Cryptography
- Web Portal Security Solution
- Web-Services Security Quality of Protection.

74.3.3 CCCure.org.   The CCCure.Org site run by Clément Dupuis and Nathalie Lambert—www.cccure.org—is rich in resources for anyone preparing for a security-certification exam.

The Web site started in 2001 when Clément was working in Montréal, Canada, after a 20-year career in military communications and security in the Canadian Army. He was certified as a CISSP in 1999. Clément and his friend Chris Hare decided to create study guides for several of the domains from the Common Body of Knowledge (CBK), www.isc2.org/cgi/content.cgi?category=8; they then put them on the Web for anyone to use. That was the birth of what became CCCURE.ORG. It became so popular that it was kicked off several hosting sites because it generated too much traffic for a free service. Clément and his wife, Nathalie Lambert, a mechanical engineer who became an expert in programming and networking, had to convert it into a commercial venture. However, in addition to monetary contributions by a few carefully selected advertisers, it is supported by the work and enthusiasm of thousands of volunteers.[52]

The CCCure home page is extensive; it includes a great deal of material for anyone to soak up, lots of interesting knowledge and ideas, and the ability to contribute insights. In particular, the Quiz section has an excellent review tool that generates questions for several certifications including the CISSP, CISA, SSCP, and GSEC; readers can choose the domain(s), topics, difficulty level, whether to include related questions, and the number of questions. The quiz generator creates a unique, randomized quiz at every iteration. It is a valuable tool because it forces active recall and application of the knowledge you are trying to consolidate. Indeed, a recent article in *ScienceNow* from the American Association for the Advancement of Science indicates that testing improves retention not only of the material tested but of other information being learned at the time of the test.[53]

The CCCure.org site features a list of suggested readings and a forum where participants can engage in spirited discussion of technical issues relating to their exam preparation.

74.3.4   Books and Free Review Materials.   Some of the most useful books for overall coverage of the field are:

- *The Official (ISC)^2 Guide to the CISSP® Exam* by Susan Hansche, CISSP, John Berti, CISSP, and Chris Hare, CISSP (ISBN: 0-8493-1707-X) is available from the (ISC)^2 Company Store,

- *Information Security Management Handbook on CD-ROM, 2006 Edition* (a classic in the field) by Harold F. Tipton and Micki Krause,

- *Handbook of Information Security*, 3-volume set (chosen as a textbook for the master's program in information assurance at Norwich University) by Hossein Bidgoli, http://tinyurl.com/yf2549 or www.networkworld.com/newsletters/sec/20 06/0410sec2.html

- *Computer Security Handbook, 5th edition* edited by Bosworth, Kabay, and Whyne, which you are currently reading

In addition, the (ISC)^2 provides a slightly disorganized list of books at www.isc2.org/cgi-bin/content.cgi?category=698.

Ideally, people preparing for any exam do best if they can study in teams. For example, they can use lecture slides as review material to quiz each other—they should be able to speak intelligently about every point on every slide. The files thus serve as one of the ways to check for holes in coverage of the material and also as a way of consolidating and strengthening knowledge. Searching on "security course slides" in a Web search engine brings up many possible sites for such materials. These are intended for educational purposes in college and university courses, but they serve admirably as preparatory and review materials for professionals approaching exams. Security-course slides available from the Web site of one of the authors include:

- I340 Intro to IA lectures: www2.norwich.edu/mkabay/courses/academic/norwich/ is340/lectures.htm. The course covers some of the subjects in Volume I of this *Handbook* (although the chapter headings refer to the fourth edition).

- IS342 Management of IA: www2.norwich.edu/mkabay/courses/academic/ norwich/is342/Lectures/index.htm. This course covers many of the topics in Volume II of this *Handbook* (again, the chapter headings refer to the fourth edition).

- CJ341 Cybercrime & Cyberlaw: www2.norwich.edu/mkabay/courses/academic/ norwich/cj341/Lectures/lectures.htm. This course is taught for the Department of Criminal Justice at Norwich University by Professors Kabay, Stephenson, and Towers. The course materials offer a detailed look at intellectual property, defamation, computer trespass, and how law enforcement has to deal with digital evidence, including the specific laws relating to computer crimes of all sorts. "Legal, Regulations, Compliance and Investigations" is one of the 10 domains of the CBK (Common Body of Knowledge) for the CISSP: www.isc2.org/cgi/content.cgi?category=8.

In addition to all of this free knowledge, it is also possible to enroll in a wide range of preparatory courses. However, one should be leery of taking a short course *instead* of reading and thinking for a long time about any subject beyond the purely technical. The most important aspect of learning is thinking, not memory. Take a course if you like, but not just before your exam. Use the course as a form of review and verification—a tool for strengthening what you already know, but above all for identifying what you have to think and learn about at greater length.

74.4   COMMERCIAL TRAINING IN INFORMATION ASSURANCE.   There are many courses offered in information assurance at different levels; most of them concentrate on technical subjects. In this section, we review some of the best-known offerings.

74.4.1   Security University Classes and Certifications.   Security University is setting a new Security certification standard by being "Qualified" to competently complete a job or task with skills validation. Security University is grouping SU Security Certifications into exam-based and education-based (skills validation) certifications.

> **Exam-based certifications.** A person is certified as being able to competently complete a job or task, usually by the passing of an examination, which can also be learned by self-study with no classroom requirement.
>
> **Education-based certifications** are instructor-led sessions, where each course has to be passed and hands-on labs must be competently completed to provide skills validation.

Tactically trained security professionals are in demand. CISSPs armed with a Q/ISP (Qualified/ Information Security Professional) can prove they know the "how to" of the computer security business as well as risk mitigation. The founder, Sondra Schneider, offers a perspective on her philosophy of hands-on security education and training.[54]

Not only is it important to seek courses with direct benefit to daily activities but it is also critical to invest in tactical security skills. Tactical security skills are the "how to" security skills such as how to provide defense in depth through technical diversity, incident response, security awareness, hack, code analysis, write secure software and applications and lastly how to do black-box testing (assessments) of wired and wireless networks, software and applications.

How does one learn tactical security skills? Security University provides highly focused *Tactical Security* training for one or many tactical security skills. Security University Qualified/ Information Security Professional (Q/ISP) certification consists of completing four classes and one workshop that transfer a multitude of tactical security skills to the student. From the moment students enter a class, they are working on the practice and are challenged by qualified instructors who have mastered their Tactical Security skills to the highest degree.

The new Qualified/ Software Security Expert (Q/SSE) certification sets the new standard in developing new active skills that can be immediately applied to the workplace. The Q/SSE boot camp uncovers exactly how coding can and will become the next hacking frontier.

Hacking is an art and a science. Creating exceptions in live systems yields unauthorized access to networks and applications. Armed with any one of the Tactical Security skills, students exceed general theories. Generalized training sets a foundation. Combining a foundation, like that of the CISSP, with the capability to apply skills helps candidates achieve career goals and success while learning how a hacker thinks.

In the next years, more companies will discover that black box testing only reveals 15% of their vulnerabilities. Only through tactical code analysis and software testing skills can you elevate your level of assurance that you have done what is necessary to keep the hackers off your networks. Security University's Qualified Training programs work because they make the student produce work, so they leave with new usable skills. Security University's training provides excellent return on investment because it is methodology driven. Specific technology may become outdated; however by learning methodologies the tactical security skill set can be automatically transferred to replacement technologies since the student truly understands what to do and where to go in any related situation.

Security University offers a wide range of computer security classes, exams, and education certifications:

- Qualification & Certification Tracks
  - SU Q/ISP Qualified/ Information Security Professional (four classes, one workshop)
    - QISP001 ECSA Prep & Qualified/ Security Analyst Penetration Tester
    - QISP002 LPT & Qualified/ Penetration Tester License Workshop
    - QISP003 CEH Prep & Q/EH Qualified Ethical Hacker/Network Defender
    - QISP004 Q/EP Qualified Edge Protector
    - QISP005 CHFI Prep and Q/FE Qualified/ Forensic Expert
  - SU Q/IAP Qualified Information Assurance Professional (three classes)
    - QIAP001 Q/AAP Qualified Access, Authentication & PKI Professional
    - QIAP002 Q/NSP SOA Qualified Network Security Policy Administrator and Security Services Oriented Architect
    - QIAP003 Q/CA Qualified/ Certification and Accreditation Administrator class
- Computer Security Introduction classes
  - QSAP001 Qualified Internet Threat Security Awareness Training and Compliance for MGT
  - QSAP002 Qualified Security Awareness Training
  - SSCP001 Security + and SSCP Bootcamp
  - SSCP002 SSCP System Security Certified Professional
  - QISP006 Catching the Hackers—Introduction to Intrusion Detection
  - QSAP003 Qualified Security Awareness Defender Certificate for Managers
- SU CWNP Wireless Certifications
  - CWNP001 Certified Wireless Network Administration CWNA
  - CWNP002 Certified Wireless Security Professional CWSP

- CWNP003 Qualified Wireless Analyst and Defender Bootcamp QWAD
- CWNP004 Wireless CWNA/CWSP Bootcamp
- SU EC-Council Certifications
  - EC001 CEH Prep—Ethical Hacking Certification
  - EC002 ECSA Prep EC—Council Security Analyst
  - EC003 LPT License Penetration Tester
  - EC004 CHFI Prep—Computer Hacking Forensic Investigator
- Specialty Security Classes
  - ISC2001 CISSP ISC2 Certification Review Class
  - QIAP004 DoD Information Technology Security Certification and Accreditation Process DITSCAP
  - QIAP005 Mission Critical Planning (Hands On)
  - QISP007 Linux/UNIX Security
  - QISP008 Catching the Hackers II: Systems to Defend Networks
- SU QSSE Qualified Software Security Expert
  - QSSE001 Qualified Software Security Expert 5 Day Bootcamp
  - QSSE002 Qualified Software Security Penetration Tester
  - QSSE003 Software Testing Bootcamp
  - QSSE004 How to Break & FIX Web Security
  - QSSE005 How to Break & FIX Software Security
  - QSSE006 Fundamentals of Secure Software Programming
  - QSSE007 Qualified Software Hacker/Defender
  - QSSE008 Qualified Software Tester Best Practices
  - QSSE009 Introduction to Reverse Engineering

74.4.2 Getronics Security University[55].   Another resource for professionals looking for security education is Getronics Security University. Working with (ISC)^2 as a registered provider of CPEs for CISSP and SSCP holders, the company offers 38 short online courses lasting from 15 minutes to 5 hours.[56]Courses include:

- 010 Information Security Essentials (15 minutes)
- 028 Laptop Security Essentials (15 minutes)
- 081 Information Privacy Essentials (20 minutes)
- 082 Identity Theft Essentials (20 minutes)
- 101 Introduction to Computer Crime (2 hours)
- 110 Introduction to Information Security (1.3 hours)
- 112 Risk Management (1 hour)
- 113 Information Ownership, Valuation, and Classification (1 hour)
- 114 Social Engineering (1 hour)
- 115 Information Security Policies (1 hour)
- 119 eCommerce Security Fundamentals (1 hour)
- 128 Information Security for Remote Users (2 hours)

- 130 Access Control (1 hour)
- 142 Networks and Telecommunications (1 hour)
- 147 Introduction to Wireless Security (1 hour)
- 150 Business Continuity Planning (1 hour)
- 160 Incident Response (1 hour)
- 161 Malware Basics (1 hour)
- 163 Introduction to Computer Investigations (1 hour)
- 170 Introduction to Cryptography (1 hour)
- 171 Basic Concepts of Cryptography (1 hour)
- 177 Introduction to Public Key Infrastructure (2 hours)
- 181 Information Privacy (1 hour)
- 182 Identity Theft (1 hour)
- 184 Cybersafety (1 hour)
- 191 Computer Room Security (1 hour)
- 231 Network Access Controls (2 hours)
- 232 Firewalls (2 hours)
- 233 Virtual Private Networks (2 hours)
- 243 Database Security (2 hours)
- 244 Introduction to Web Application Security (5 hours)
- 247 Wireless Network Security (5 hours)
- 261 Intrusion Detection in Networks (5 hours)
- 262v2 Fighting Malware (3 hours)
- 277 Intermediate Public Key Infrastructure (PKI) (5 hours)
- 282 Understanding Due Care, Due Diligence, and Negligence (2 hours)
- 382 Executive Review GLBA, SOX, SB1386 (15 minutes)
- 482 NIST SP800 50 (building awareness & training programs) (4 hours)

Per-student and institutional licenses are available for these courses.

74.4.3   CEH Franchise.   The International Council of Electronic Commerce Consultants (EC-Council) was created to "support and enhance the role of individuals and organizations who design, create, manage or market Security and E-Business solutions."[57] The EC-Council has established a number of certifications:[58]

- Entry-Level Security Certifications
  - Security 5
  - Network 5
  - Wireless 5
- IT Security Professional Certifications
  - C|EH Certified Ethical Hacker
  - C|HFI Computer Hacking Forensic Investigator
  - E|CSA EC-Council Certified Security Analyst

- C|NDA Certified Network Defense Architect
- L|PT Licensed Penetration Tester
- E|CVP EC-Council Certified VOIP Professional
- EC-Council Network Security Administrator
- EC-Council Certified Computer Investigator
- Disaster Recovery and Business Continuity
  - EC-Council Disaster Recovery Professional
- Programming Certifications
  - E|CSP EC-Council Certified Secure Programmer
  - C|SAD Certified Secure Application Developer
- Graduate-Level Certifications
  - Fundamentals in Computer Forensics
  - Fundamentals in Information Security
  - Fundamentals in Network Security
  - E|CSS EC-Council Certified Security Specialist
- E-Business Certification
  - C|EP Certified e-Business Professional

The EC-Council has licensed its courses to dozens of organizations around the world. Readers will have no difficulty finding resources by contacting the organization directly.[59]

74.5 CONCLUDING REMARKS.   This chapter cannot provide an exhaustive listing of training and certification resources. Practitioners should monitor the trade press for indications of trends in acceptance of new certifications and should judge how to keep themselves at the forefront of the field through continued professional development. In addition, professionals may find it satisfying, personally educational, and even moderately lucrative to involve themselves in training and certification as teachers. At the least, holders of professional certifications should consider serving as proctors for examinations so that their associations can continue offering these valuable indicators of professional knowledge without having to depend on government and industry handouts.

74.6 NOTES

1. Microsoft® Encarta® Dictionary 2008.
2. NOCA general information: www.noca.org/GeneralInformation/AboutUs/tabid/54/Default.aspx.
3. NCCA Accreditation: www.noca.org/Resources/NCCAAccreditation/tabid/82/Default.aspx
4. IACE Program: www.nsa.gov/ia/academia/iace.cfm.
5. Centers of Academic Excellence: www.nsa.gov/ia/academia/caeiae.cfm.
6. I. Armstrong, "Money Matters: SC Magazine/EC-Council Salary Survey 2007," *SC Magazine,* April 1, 2007; www.scmagazineus.com/Money-matters-SC-Magazine EC-Council-Salary-Survey-2007/article/34874/.

7. M. Savage, "Get Qualified: Certification—That's the Name of the Game," *SC Magazine,* November 1, 2003; http://scmagazine.com/asia/news/article/419631/get-qualified-certification-thats-name-game/.

8. A. Saita, "The CISSP Receives International Standardization," SearchSecurity.com, June 23, 2004; http://searchsecurity.techtarget.com/original-Content/0,289142,sid14_gci989901,00.html.

9. (ISC)^2, DoD Fact Sheet, 2007: www.isc2.org/cgi-bin/content.cgi?page=949.

10. C. Hildebrand, "Forecast 2008: Information Security Goes Strategic." *InfoSecurity Professional* (Spring 2008): 4–7. https://www.isc2.org/cgi-bin/securedocument.cgi?id=15.

11. CIA Home Web Page: www.theiia.org/?doc_id=3.

12. CIA Home Web Page.

13. IIA Approved "Character Reference for CIA Candidate": http://www.theiia.org/download.cfm?file=10037

14. CIA Home Web Page.

15. NOCA general information: www.noca.org/GeneralInformation/AboutUs/tabid/54/Default.aspx.

16. IIA Approved "Character Reference for CIA Candidate."

17. IIA Approved Code of Ethics: www.theiia.org/?doc_id=604.

18. IIA Approved "Character Reference for CIA Candidate."

19. CIA Exam Content: www.theiia.org/certification/certified-internal-auditor/cia-exam-content/.

20. Specialty certifications: www.theiia.org/certification/specialty-certifications/.

21. *CIA 2008 Candidate Handbook:* www.theiia.org/download.cfm?file=75018.

22. ISACA® Web page, CISA Certification: www.isaca.org/Template.cfm?Section=CISA_Certification&Template=/TaggedPage/TaggedPageDisplay.cfm&TPLID=16&ContentID=4526.

23. Savage, "Get Qualified."

24. ISACA Code of Professional Ethics: www.isaca.org/Template.cfm?Section=Code_of_Professional_Ethics1&Template=/ContentManagement/ContentDisplay.cfm&ContentID=20454.

25. CPE Policy Guideline: www.isaca.org/Template.cfm?Section=Continuing_Education_Policy&Template=/TaggedPage/TaggedPageDisplay.cfm&TPLID=28&ContentID=20482.

26. Standards, Guidelines, and Procedures: www.isaca.org/Template.cfm?Section=Standards&Template=/TaggedPage/TaggedPageDisplay.cfm&TPLID=29&ContentID=6707.

27. Application for Certification and Maintaining Certification: www.isaca.org/Template.cfm?Section=CISA_Certification&CONTENTID=20473&TEMPLATE=/ContentManagement/ContentDisplay.cfm.

28. ISACA Homepage, CISM Certification Web page: www.isaca.org/Template.cfm?Section=CISM_Certification&Template=/TaggedPage/TaggedPageDisplay.cfm&TPLID=16&ContentID=4528.

29. IIA Approved "Character Reference for CIA Candidate."

30. B. Brenner, "Numbers: ISACA Says Survey Illustrates Benefits of CISM Cert: A Recent Survey Backs the Notion that CISMs Are in a Better Position to Deal

with a Growing Emphasis on Business Needs over Technology, an ISACA Official Says," *CSO Magazine,* June 5, 2008; www.csoonline.com/article/379914/Numbers_ISACA_Says_Survey_Illustrates_Benefits_of_CISM_Cert.

31. CISM Certification Content Area: www.isaca.org/Content/NavigationMenu/Security/CISM_Certification/Exam_Information1/Content_Areas1/CISM_Certification_Content_Areas.htm.

32. CISM Exam Overview: www.isaca.org/Template.cfm?Section=CISM_Certification&CONTENTID=20608&TEMPLATE=/ContentManagement/ContentDisplay.cfm.

33. CISM Bulletin of Information: www.isaca.org/Template.cfm?Section=Bulletin_of_Information1&Template=/ContentManagement/ContentDisplay.cfm&ContentID=20611.

34. Hildebrand, "Forecast 2008."

35. Requirements for CISM Certification: www.isaca.org/Template.cfm?Section=CISM_Certification&CONTENTID=20681&TEMPLATE=/ContentManagement/ContentDisplay.cfm.

36. IIA Approved "Character Reference for CIA Candidate."

37. CISM Application and Maintenance: www.isaca.org/Template.cfm?Section=Application_and_Maintenance1&Template=/ContentManagement/ContentDisplay.cfm&ContentID=20683.

38. CISSP, About Certification Web page: http://certification.about.com/od/certifications/p/cissp.htm.

39. CISSP Professional Experience requirement - https://www.isc2.org/cgi/content.cgi?category=1187

40. CISSP Code of Ethics: www.isc2.org/cgi/content.cgi?page=31.

41. CISSP Exam Information: www.cissp.com

42. ISSAP Information Page: www.isc2.org/cgi-bin/content.cgi?category=522.

43. ISSEP Information Page: www.isc2.org/cgi-bin/content.cgi?category=523.

44. ISSMP Information Page: www.isc2.org/cgi-bin/content.cgi?category=524.

45. (ISC)^2® Web site—ISSAP, ISSEP, ISSMP Credentials: www.isc2.org/cgi-bin/content.cgi?category=99.

46. SSCP Webpage: http://certification.about.com/od/certifications/p/sscp.htm.

47. ASISI Certified Protection Professional Web page: www.asisonline.org/certification/cpp/index.xml.

48. GIAC Home Web page: www.giac.org.

49. GIAC Program Overview: www.giac.org/overview/.

50. GIAC Gold Certification Web page: http://www.giac.org/gold.

51. www2.norwich.edu/mkabay/methodology/sq3r and in PDF www2.norwich.edu/mkabay/methodology/sq3r.pdf.

52. For more about the history and philosophy of CCCure.Org, see www.cccure.org/modules.php?name=News&file=article&sid=397.

53. J. Cutraro, "Testing Boosts Memory," *ScienceNow,* November 13, 2006; http://sciencenow.sciencemag.org/cgi/content/full/2006/1113/2.

54. Security University home page: www.securityuniversity.net/.

55. Getronics Security University home page: https://gsuonline.com/main.htm.

56. Getronics Security University course catalog: https://gsuonline.com/coursecatalog. htm.

57. EC-Council FAQ: www.eccouncil.org/faq.htm.

58. EC-Council certifications: www.eccouncil.org/certification.htm.

59. EC-Council Accredited Training Provider: www.eccouncil.org/atp.htm.

UNDERGRADUATE AND GRADUATE EDUCATION IN INFORMATION ASSURANCE

Vic Maconachy and Seymour Bosworth

75.1 INTRODUCTION. Information assurance has come to the forefront of the consciousness of the modern world. Recent events such as high-publicity breaches of security, as well as pervasive small-scale abuses of the technologies available at work and at home, have highlighted the need for trained professionals able to operate in the complex world of information assurance. Toward this end, recent initiatives in the United States and Europe have added information assurance into the undergraduate and graduate curriculum of more common degrees such as computer science, and have also identified information assurance as its own discipline worthy of its own curriculum. This chapter outlines some of the initiatives that have taken place in the United States and speculates about the future of the discipline.

75.2 U.S. INITIATIVES IN TRAINING AND EDUCATION OF INFORMATION ASSURANCE

75.2.1 TIE System. Any approach to information assurance (IA) education must be presented in a conceptual context. The Trusted Information Environment

Domain	Concept	Elements	Notes
Trusted	Information and information systems designed, developed, maintained, and retired to protect against intrusion, theft, disruption, denial of service, and data diddling	Life cycle management approach Risk management Known degrees of trust (common criteria)	Need to speak to implied versus real assurance
Information	Three states of information: being created, at rest, being transmitted	Information valuation Information in isolation Information in aggregation	Needs to address "flagging" of information and establishing classes of privileged users
Environment	Total context of protecting information and information systems in both enclave and shared environments	Defense in depth: • Technology • Operations • People Not just networks Risk assumed by one is assumed by all Five security services all operating in harmony: 1. Confidentiality 2. Integrity 3. Availability 4. Authentication 5. Nonrepudiation	Allow for trust between domains and domain boundaries and effective consequences management

EXHIBIT 75.1 Approach to TIE Together Information and Information Systems Security

(TIE) model shown in Exhibit 75.1 is a view of protecting information and information systems within the context of a trusted cyberspace.

While some refer to this approach as an enclave mentality, it does open the possibilities for secure cross-domain solutions (CDS). In the CDS environment, permissions are granted and revoked as access to shared information and information system space is allocated and adjudicated by the system owners. This will be the way of the future as more segments of our society desire to intercommunicate. Examples of this might be insurance companies gaining, or being granted access to, selected patient information.

In the TIE approach, educators can see two things immediately:

1. Understanding (and thus learning) of IA is surrounded by many interacting factors.

2. In the Environmental area, people development is a critical part of *defense in depth*.

The term "defense in depth" (DID) refers not just to a program or system, but to a way of thinking about information assurance. In this view, there are only three real

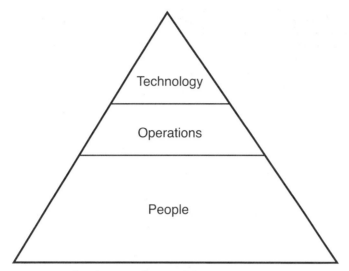

EXHIBIT 75.2   Three Fundamental Countermeasures to Protect Critical Information Infrastructures

broad classes of countermeasures in any information assurance arsenal, as shown in Exhibit 75.2.

1. The first countermeasure, technology, often comes to market with flaws.
2. The second countermeasure, operations, encompasses things such as best practices, policy, and so on. This countermeasure is necessary because of the flaws in the first countermeasure.
3. The third countermeasure, people, includes not just the education and training but also the development of people. The development takes many forms, running the gamut from seminars through personal certifications and career development. The people part of the countermeasures triad serves as the base or foundation for the other two countermeasures.

Intrinsic in this, or any IA model, is the concept of risk. In a trusted environment, risk assumed by one is assumed by all. Here, education has an important, fundamental, and critical role to play. A common understanding of risk (to include threat and vulnerability) among users, operators, maintainers, and designers of information systems can make the difference between a secure and an inherently insecure system. Thus, a risk-based approach to teaching information assurance lies at the very heart of preparing IA professionals.

The people part of an IA program is *not* just about education. It is about development of people for the IA profession. That development includes a full spectrum of learning and proficiency development. The learning portion includes a range of understanding from simple awareness (often referred to as *situational awareness*) through formal education. The proficiency part is the testing and formal credentialing that certain knowledge and skills have been mastered. The latter part of this equation has given rise to an entire suite of private sector certifications such as CISSP,[1] GIAC,[2] Security Plus,[3] and other commercial certification programs discussed in Chapter 74 in this *Handbook*. Some authors contend that certifications amount to "inferred professionalization" in the sense that certifications focus exclusively on easy-to-measure indicators of proficiency.[4] Those authors would argue that in contrast, *conferred professionalization* would assure an individual is not just competent but actually fully equipped to practice a discipline. In the conferred professionalization model, the individual is judged to be ready by recognized practitioners in that field. Most important, as Mike Whitman put it, "Policy must be communicated to employees. In addition, new technology often requires training. Training, Awareness and Education are essential if employees are to exhibit safe and controlled behavior."[5] The National Centers of Academic Excellence in Information Assurance Education serve as an excellent starting point to seek personal and employee education in IA.[6]

75.2.2   Growth of IA Education Programs in the United States.   In 2004, Drs. Matt Bishop and Deborah Frinke characterized the state of IA education: "Security and privacy education is, at its heart, driven by a compelling national and international need."[7] In the past several years, the study and research of information assurance has risen from an area of study of limited interest to an international rush for developing courses and research. In February 2003, the President of the United States reported

> In addition to the vulnerabilities in existing information technology systems, there are at least two other major barriers to users and managers acting to improve cybersecurity: (1) a lack of familiarity, knowledge and understanding of the issues, and (2) an inability to find sufficient numbers of adequately trained and/or appropriately certified personnel to create and manage secure systems.[8]

As part of a response to this need, the National Security Agency, in cooperation with the Department of Homeland Security, established national Centers of Academic Excellence in Information Assurance Education (CAE).[9] This program fosters the development and identification of universities that have reached a significant level of depth and maturity in building IA curriculum, and looks beyond curriculum to assess the long-term commitment of universities to IA education. The purpose and vision of the National CAE program is: "Reducing the vulnerability of our National Information Infrastructure by promoting higher education in information assurance and producing a growing number of professionals with IA expertise in various disciplines." This government-sponsored program does not attempt to accredit academic institutions that teach IA. Rather, the program stands as a way to recognize and encourage the study of IA. There are 10 multipart criteria for the program, which include such things as having faculty active in IA practice and research as well as declared concentrations in IA. At the time of writing (June 2008), only 93 universities have been formally recognized as CAEs.[10]

An interesting finding, after several years of the CAE program, is the documentation that the study of IA is truly interdisciplinary. Subjects in IA range from telecommunications through computer science and into policy and legal areas. The fact that the IA concentrations can be found in several disciplines gives further evidence to the pervasive nature of IA. IA programs are found in electrical engineering programs, computer science programs, business programs, and information technology programs. The growth in the recognition of IA as part of many career fields now finds elements of IA taught in medical schools, law schools, and, perhaps most important, schools of education, where teachers learn the importance of protecting students from the harm often found on the Internet.

The curricula at the CAEs are based on national education and training standards developed by the Committee for National Security Systems (CNSS).[11] Prior to those standards, there was neither research nor a generally accepted codified body of knowledge in the IA community. The CNSS standards were developed with the assumption that U.S. employers need IA professionals grounded in theory and principles and also able to implement changes. The standards serve to codify what IA knowledge, skills, and abilities (KSAs) IA professionals should know and what levels of performance they should be expected to exhibit.

The CNSS Training Standards are generally regarded as training road maps. However, at the higher cognitive levels of operation, those standards offer clear guidance to educators doing curriculum design. Using the Bloom Taxonomy of Learning,[12] one can see that the CNSS Standards cover the developmental range from awareness through literacy and training into education. For example, the CNSSI Instruction # 4016 includes the "Countermeasures IA functions" and "Analyzing Potential Countermeasures." In that section, these levels of performance are defined:

- **Entry level:** *Discuss* testing roles and responsibilities.
- **Intermediate level:** *Apply* discriminate approach variables and constants based on test procedures to gain acceptance for joint systems usage.
- **Advanced level:** *Analyze* applicability of network and vulnerability scanning tools.[13]

Note the increasing complexity of the requirements. Initial requirements are simply a broad understanding of IA countermeasures. At the advanced level, the student must put IA countermeasures into the context of network vulnerability scanning. This natural progression in difficulty helps us distinguish programs that provide awareness from those that are more training-oriented and from education-focused curricula. The need for the distinction among awareness, training, and education in IA was first recognized in 1989.[14] The debate at that time centered around compliance with the Computer Security Act of 1987 (PL 100-235), which required annual *training* in computer security "for all persons involved in management, use, or operation of Federal computer systems that contain sensitive information."[15] This delineation of levels also lends itself to developing career progression from entry level through journeyman to master.

75.2.3 Information Assurance as Part of a Learning Continuum.
The translation of ascending knowledge and skills can best be depicted by the Information Assurance Awareness, Literacy, Training, and Education Continuum as shown in Exhibit 75.3.[16] As a person becomes aware of information assurance (IA) and then becomes engaged with active learning about IA, he or she may well proceed through a continuum of ever-increasing complex knowledge. A classic example of this progression is illustrated using passwords as a topical area as shown in Exhibit 75.4.

As shown in Exhibit 75.4, using passwords progresses from recognizing a prompt to conducting evaluations by designers of password strength schema. When IA knowledge and skills are analyzed to this level, one can quickly see the difference between requirements for end users versus system administrators versus design engineers. The CNSS standards include a hierarchy of verbs used to discern differing levels of IA performance and complexity of understanding:

EXHIBIT 75.3 IA Awareness, Literacy, Training, and Education Continuum

Level of Understanding/Operation	Keyword	Performance Item
Awareness	Recognize	Password prompt on a computer screen
Literacy	Define	Password protection
Training	Implement	Password given basic instructions as to length, mix of characters, and expiration

EXHIBIT 75.4 Maturation of Password Handling

Entry-Level Verbs:
- Define
- Demonstrate
- Describe
- Identify
- Outline
- Use

Intermediate-Level Verbs:
- Design
- Manage

- Prepare
- Recommend
- Implement

Advanced-Level Verbs:

- Compare
- Evaluate
- Integrate
- Resolve
- Revise
- Verify

There are currently six CNSS Education and Training Standards. They are:

1. Information systems security professionals
2. Senior systems managers
3. System administrators
4. Information systems security officers
5. System certifiers
6. Risk analyst

Current plans call for the development of standards for information systems security engineers and end users. An area that is receiving considerable attention is the codification of best practices and required knowledge for personnel developing code. This area could be termed secure coding or software assurance, as discussed in Chapters 38 and 39 in this *Handbook*. These competencies should be taught to all those who do or practice coding. Developing a cadre of secure coding experts may not affect industry practices in this area as fast as teaching larger numbers of coders. In essence, security must become an essential core knowledge and competency for all coders.

An example of the information security training roles of various information technology workers can also be found in NIST Special Publication 800-16.[17] In that document, it is stressed that IT security training needs evolve or change over time. More important, the NIST publication recognizes the fact that information assurance is not the job only for IA professionals. Requirements for knowledge and skills in IA pervade the federal work environment. From the first-line supervisor to the local system administrator, IA skills are now minimal essential skills required to sustain the federal information networks and architectures. A more recent NIST publication[18] notes that, within the U.S. federal government, there is a mandate for IT security training. Specifically, the Federal Information Security Management Act (FISMA) of 2002 tasks the head of each agency with the responsibility to "ensure that the agency has trained personnel sufficient to assist the agency in complying with (the requirements) and related policies, procedures, standards, and guidelines." Thus, within the U.S. Government, there is a mandate to employee IA professionals in support of secure information technology operations.

The requirement for trained and educated IA professionals extends beyond the government sector and has been recognized as a need for many years. Steele[19] noted that 65 percent of hospitals with links to external computer systems did not have

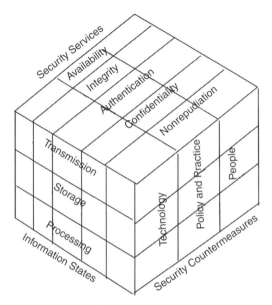

EXHIBIT 75.5 Information Assurance Model

adequate security measures and 80 percent had not properly defined who should have access to computer records." This condition probably extends into many other critical information infrastructures, such as transportation and water systems. A simplistic yet elegant paradigm for understanding the relationship between the states of information and various countermeasures can be found in Exhibit 75.5. In this model, understanding that security countermeasures must include a people dimension is critical to preserving and defending information systems.[20]

In a later article, further refining this approach, additional dimensions were added: An IA professional must also integrate the concepts of time and social context into this paradigm. "Time, when integrated into this model is not a causal agent of change, but a confounding change agent."[21] Further, as we have learned from recent physical calamities, the state of IA may be seriously affected by the social context of our times. For instance, after September 11, 2001, some U.S. Government homeland security initiatives were based on the assumption that citizens would willingly give up some personal and constitutionally guaranteed freedoms in return for measures described as leading to a more secure environment. In some nations, strong cryptography is forbidden on their telecommunications systems; similarly, Internet service providers in some areas of the world are expected to provide names of individuals who frequent certain Web sites.[22] All of these elements combine to present an ever-shifting international social climate for information assurance.

75.2.4 Time to Respond. In the words of U.S. Senator John Edwards when he introduced the Cybersecurity Research and Education Act of 2002: "We now live in a world where terrorists can do as much damage with a keyboard and a modem as with a gun or bomb . . . . Two choices are available: adapt before the attack or afterward."

Adaptation of a society begins with education and is born out of experience. Cybersecurity awareness, training, and education are the key to a safer cyberworld. This education must begin at early ages in order for cyber-security to become a part of every person's safe computing practices. Programs such as Stay Safe On-Line offer promise in reaching and preaching safe and ethical cyberbehavior.[23] Programs such as the National Information Assurance Training and Education Center at Idaho State University offer an amazing range of curriculum materials suitable for all levels of IA education.[24]

75.3   DISTANCE LEARNING IN HIGHER EDUCATION   Distance learning, or e-learning, whose most important element is the online course, provides a relatively new facility for education in Information Assurance and related subjects. A typical institutional set of principles, as stated by the American Distance Education Consortium, (ADEC), requires that "Distance learning programs should result in learning outcomes appropriate to the rigor and breadth of the degree/certificate awarded. Programs should be coherent, comprehensive, and developed with appropriate discipline and pedagogical rationale. Each program should provide for significant interaction, whether real-time or delayed interaction, between faculty and students and among students."[25]

To accomplish this, a superior mix of media, students, teachers, providers, and courses is necessary for both distance learning and distance teaching.

75.3.1   Media   In distance learning, the central medium for communications between teacher and students is usually a computer on the Internet, rather than face-to-face interactions. Other media include:

- Cassettes: audio or video, at home or in groups
- Computers: online or offline
- Conversations: e-mail, Instant Messaging, face-to-face, phone
- Disks: CD or DVD
- Distribution: hand-outs, USPS, delivery services, computers
- Electronic whiteboards and blackboards
- Fax: text, graphics
- Group Sessions: demonstrations, lectures, experiments
- Hand-helds: IP based, MP3, PDA
- Internet: text, graphics, VoIP
- Presentations: slides, movies, VCRs
- Print: textbooks, reports, surveys, workbooks, study guides
- Teleconferences: audio, video
- Wireless Communications: television, compressed video, radio

Unlike conventional classrooms, where communication between teacher and student are instantaneous and coordinated, in distance learning there may be large and random intervals between a statement or question and the response. Such media, and their methodologies, are often termed asynchronous.

75.3.2   Students   The importance of online learning is exemplified by the finding that almost 3.5 million students were taking at least one online course during the fall of 2006, and that nearly twenty percent of all U.S. higher education students were taking at least one online course. This represented a 9.7% annual growth rate over four years as compared with the overall higher education student population.[26]

The major advantages of distance learning from the students' point of view lie in overcoming the barrier imposed by conventional on-campus studies. Some of the obstacles that are likely to be overcome are scheduling or time constraints, inconvenient locations, disabilities, costs, and family and business commitments. The flexibility and innate characteristics of distance learning can lower or eliminate these barriers.

In a more positive sense, one of the advantages lies in integrating the Web as a convenient, easily accessed source of information. Another is the ability to organize thoughts before responding to a query. Threaded discussions provide a means for exploring a subject in detail, and over extended periods of time. One student commented:

> In a face-to-face class the instructor initiates the action; meeting the class, handing out the syllabus, etc. In online instruction, the student initiates the action by going to the Web, posting a message, or doing something. Also, I think that students and instructors communicate on a more equal footing where all of the power dynamics of the traditional face-to-face classroom are absent.[27]

To a teacher, of course, that may not represent an advantage.

75.3.3 Teachers From a teacher's viewpoint, many of the advantages that accrue to students may also benefit themselves. However, there are some difficulties to be overcome. From start to finish, a high degree of motivation must be maintained despite some or all of these disincentives.

- Old lecture skills may have to be discarded
- New multi-media presentation skills will have to be learned
- The teacher may cease to be the main font of wisdom, but only a pointer to where it resides
- Some technical skills will be required to operate new equipment, or to work with equipment operators
- More preparation time will be needed
- Students must be motivated, self-disciplined, and encouraged to participate
- Excessive use of e-mail may have to be restrained
- Course material provided online loses proprietary value, and makes replacement of the originator easier, even by low-paid, unskilled presenters
- Teaching conventional courses may be more higher regarded by administrators when deciding on tenure or promotions

In spite of these, and other problems, an increasing number of teachers find distance learning to be a rewarding application for their knowledge and skills.

75.3.4 Providers Why do institutions provide online offerings? Improving student access is the most often cited objective for online courses and programs. All types of institutions cite improved student access as their top reason for offering online courses and programs.

- Institutions that are the most engaged in online education cite increasing the rate of degree completion as a very important objective.
- Online is not seen as a way to lower costs; reduced or contained costs are among the least-cited objectives for online education.

Type of Course	Proportion of Content Delivered Online	Typical Description
Traditional	0%	Course with no online technology used—content is delivered in writing or orally.
Web Facilitated	1 to 29%	Course that uses web-based technology to facilitate what is essentially a face-to-face course. Uses a course management system (CMS) or web pages to post the syllabus and assignments, for example.
Blended/Hybrid	30 to 79%	Course that blends online and face-to-face delivery. Substantial proportion of the content is delivered online, typically uses online discussions, and typically has some face-to-face meetings.
Online	80+%	A course where most or all of the content is delivered online. Typically have no face-to-face meetings.

EXHIBIT 75.6   Type of Course

The appeal of online instruction is indicated by the high number of institutions which cite growth in continuing and/or professional education as an objective for their online offerings.[28]

75.3.5   Courses   The range of institutions providing online courses extends from the U.S. government to the most prestigious private universities, and from giant State universities to small, independent colleges. Even private, for-profit organizations have offerings in the field.

There are courses available online that offer baccalaureate, graduate, and post-graduate degree credits, along with others that provide associate degrees, or certificates. The courses may be grouped into several types as defined by the Sloan Consortium.[29]

75.3.6   Summary   Online learning is both widespread and rapidly proliferating. In higher education, it may well be the wave of the future because of its many advantages, and in spite of its significant problems. The present number of institutions is large and diverse, as are the courses available in information assurance and related subjects. Substantial growth in students, faculty, institutions, courses, and technology warrant substantial investments of time, money, and other resources in all aspects of this mushrooming phenomenon. Anyone seeking to advance a career, either as a student or as a teacher, but unable or unwilling to attend full-time classes, would benefit from distance and online educational opportunities.

75.4   BUSINESS CONTINUITY MANAGEMENT.   Events such as the bombings of 9/11 and Hurricane Katrina have brought business continuity management (BCM) into mainstream corporate practice. Businesses that had plans for continuity of service to customers during a business disruption survived those events, whereas those without plans often failed. As a result, organizations both large and small are implementing BCM systems. Once relegated to the margins of corporate practice as an aspect of information technology or corporate security, BCM has become recognized as a fundamental aspect of sound business practice.

The growth of continuity management has been further fueled by regulations requiring continuity programs in industries such as healthcare and finance. Insurance companies are also starting to require continuity programs as a condition of coverage. Moreover, with 85 percent of the nation's critical infrastructure, and nearly 100 percent of the economic infrastructure, in private hands, BCM is a national security priority. Recognizing the importance of securing the nation's economic infrastructure for national security, President Clinton issued Presidential Decision Directive Order 63 in 1997 to address critical infrastructure protection.[30] The federal government has extended this effort to support private-sector BCM programs. In August 2007, the federal government passed Implementing Recommendations of the 9/11 Commission Act of 2007, which mandates the Department of Homeland Security to actively encourage the development of continuity programs in the United States.[31]

Continuity of operations is as much needed in the public sphere as the private, as public sector agencies must have programs to ensure their own continuity of service during an emergency. In recognition of the public sector need for continuity programs, President Bush signed National Security and Homeland Security Presidential Directive 51, requiring continuity programs to "be incorporated into daily operations of all executive departments and agencies."[32]

The growth in BCM programs has fueled tremendous demand for professionals who understand risk management in the context of business operations. As a result, the number of business continuity professionals has exploded in recent years. CNN recently named Business Continuity Director one of the "Seven Trendy New Jobs," and membership in professional organizations in the field is growing rapidly.[33]

Norwich University in Northfield, Vermont, developed an online Master of Science in Business Continuity Management degree in 2008 to serve the education needs of private and public sector business continuity professionals.[34] We expect to see increased attention to this discipline at both undergraduate and graduate levels of education.[35]

75.5   CONCLUDING REMARKS.   Information assurance, with public and private sector development of educational and training initiatives, has secured a required focus of study for future employees. It is a constantly changing field, wide open for continued new research. The governmental support and mandate of such initiatives will ensure that if any companies or universities were to lag in their adoption, there would be unfavorable consequences, aside from the presence of a serious shortcoming in their educational curriculum.

We can expect to see continued growth in information assurance education in colleges and universities worldwide.

75.6   NOTES

1. www.isc2.org.
2. www.giac.org.

3. www.quickcert.com/security+.htm.

4. W. V. Maconachy, L. Figallo, and C. D. Schou, "INFOSEC Professionalization: A Road to be Traveled," *Forum for Advancing Software Engineering Education* 9, No. 1 (January 1999); www.cs.ttu.edu/fase/v9n01.txt.

5. Michael E. Whitman and Herbert J. Mattord, *Principles of Information Security*, 2nd ed. (Boston: Thompson Course Technology, 2005), p. 139.

6. www.nsa.gov/ia/academia/acade00001.cfm.

7. Matt Bishop and Deborah Frinke, "Joining the Security Education Community," *IEEE Computer Security*, 2004.

8. G. W. Bush "The National Strategy to Secure Cyberspace," The White House (2003); www.whitehouse.gov/pcipb/.

9. www.nsa.gov/ia/academia/acade00001.cfm

10. www.nsa.gov/ia/academia/caeiae.cfm.

11. www.nsa.gov/ia/academia/cnss.standards.cfm

12. www.officeport.com/edu/blooms.htm

13. Committee for National Security Systems Instruction No. 4016, National Information Assurance Training and Education Standard for Risk Analyst, Washington, DC, November 2005.

14. W. V. Maconachy, "Computer Security Education, Training and Awareness: Turning a Philosophical Orientation into Practical Reality," *Proceedings: 12th National Computer Security Conference,* p. 557A-I, National Computer Security Center (October 1989).

15. Computer Security Act of 1987, http://csrc.nist.gov/groups/SMA/ispab/documents/csa_87.txt.

16. W. V. Maconachy, Corey D. Schou, Daniel Ragsdale, and Don Welch. "A Model for Information Assurance: An Integrated Approach," *Proceedings of the 2001 IEEE Workshop on Information Assurance Security,* United States Military Academy, West Point, NY, June 5–6, 2001.

17. National Institute of Standards and Technology. *Information Technology Security Training Requirements: A Role and Performance-Based Model,* SP 800-16 (April 1998); http://csrc.nist.gov/publications/nistpubs/800-16/800-16.pdf.

18. National Institute of Standards and Technology. *Building an Information Technology Security Awareness and Training Program,* SP 800-50 (October 2003); http://csrc.nist.gov/publications/nistpubs/800-50/NIST-SP800-50.pdf.

19. H. Steele, "The Prevention of Non-consensual Access to Confidential Health Care Information in Cyberspace," *Computer Law Review, Technology Journal* (Spring 1997)

20. C. Schou, J. Frost, and W. V. Maconachy, "Information Assurance in Biomedical Informatics Systems. The Role of Literacy, Awareness, Training and Education in Protecting Healthcare's Critical Information Infrastructure," *IEEE Engineering in Medicine and Biology Magazine* (January 2004).

21. A Model for Information Assurance: An Integrated Approach. Proceedings, 2nd Annual IEEE Systems, Man and Cybernetics Information Assurance Workshop. West Point, June 2001.

22. See, for example, Associated Press, "House OKs Warrantless Wiretapping Bill: Senate is Also Expected to Approve Measure Providing Protection for Telecoms," CBS News, June 25, 2008; www.cbsnews.com/stories/2008/06/20/national/main4198400.shtml.

23. www.staysafeonline.info/.

24. www.niatec.org.

25. American Distance Education Consortium. www.adec.edu/admin/papers/GPfor
    DL.html.

26. Allen, I. E. and Seaman, J, Online Nation: Five Years of Growth in Online Learning,
    Needham, MA: Sloan-C, 2007. www.sloan-C.org/publications/survey/index.asp.

27. Teaching College Courses Online vs Face-to-Face. www.thejournal.com/articles/
    15358_4.

28. Allen, I. E. and Seaman, J, Online Nation.

29. Allen, I. E. and Seaman, J, Online Nation.

30. W. J. Clinton, Presidential Decision Directive/NSC-63: Critical Infrastructure Pro-
    tection (1998), http://fas.org/irp/offdocs/pdd/pdd-63.htm.

31. H. R. 1: Implementing Recommendations of the 9/11 Commission Act of 2007,
    www.govtrack.us/congress/bill.xpd?bill=h110-1.

32. G. W. Bush, National Security Presidential Directive 51, Homeland Security Presi-
    dential Directive/HSPD-20: National Continuity Policy (2007), www.whitehouse.
    gov/news/releases/2007/05/20070509-12.html.

33. J. Sahadi, "7 Trendy New Jobs: From Keeping BlackBerrys in Shape to Settling Mi-
    nor Divorce Disputes, Some Interesting New Positions Have Sprung Up in Recent
    Years," CNNMoney.com, April 21, 2006; http://money.cnn.com/2006/04/20/pf/
    new_jobs/index.htm.

34. See www.graduate.norwich.edu/business-continuity/.

35. This section was contributed by John Orlando.

EUROPEAN GRADUATE WORK IN INFORMATION ASSURANCE AND THE BOLOGNA DECLARATION[1]

Urs E. Gattiker

A fundamental fact in computer, information, and network security[2] is the impossibility of 100 percent assurance that a computer system is trusted.[3] How education can help in achieving the required level of trust considering various stakeholders (e.g., society, consumers, shareholders, and suppliers) is open to discussion. Some have suggested that certification is the answer; others support the notion that information assurance programs can fill the gap. In the latter case, advocates also hope that such programs will provide nations with the professionals required to reduce risks of possible disasters while improving security of critical infrastructure and information in particular.

This chapter focuses on undergraduate and graduate education efforts in the area of computer security in Europe. Specifically, we try to address three issues:

1. How the Bologna Declaration is influencing education in information security across Europe
2. What focus programs on information security currently have
3. How increasing convergence could help or stifle our efforts in better protecting information and critical infrastructure

First, this chapter outlines some of the recent developments in postsecondary education set in motion by the Bologna Declaration of 1999. Next, the chapter presents and discusses the development of the educational programs fitting this new framework. Finally, key findings are summarized, explaining where these efforts might lead us regarding education and training, and we highlight practical implications.

76.1   UNDERGRADUATE AND GRADUATE EDUCATION.   The next sections outline some of the most recent developments regarding undergraduate and graduate education. Space limitations make it impossible to be complete. At this stage, it is important to point out that until quite recently, the postsecondary education system of European countries has been quite diverse and sometimes outright incomprehensible for outsiders. In turn, with globalization and the European Union expanding from 15 member states to 27, some standardization has become necessary. This standardization will result in mutual acceptance of degrees, and make it easier for people wanting to move for work across national borders. Accordingly, Europe has embarked on a journey of convergence regarding undergraduate and graduate education since the Bologna Declaration[4] was signed in 1999. By the end of 2006, 45 countries had signed the Bologna accord. Although the accord is scheduled for implementation by 2010, it is unlikely that this deadline will be met. Some have suggested that having more countries and systems sign the accord, such as Asian and Pacific Rim countries, is more important than meeting the 2010 deadline.

76.2   CONVERGENCE OF EDUCATIONAL PROGRAMS.   The Bologna process has done much to move university and college education forward into a framework that is comparable across Europe. For instance, the Bologna Declaration enables both technical colleges and universities to offer undergraduate and graduate programs leading to undergraduate or graduate degrees, such as a master. The Bologna system has also resulted in countries requiring their universities to have their programs approved by accreditation agencies.

The European Commission has tried to make these programs and efforts more comparable for prospective students, employers, and policy makers by funding various projects including but not limited to Tuning Educational Structures in Europe.[5] This project focuses on developing tools that help in comparing educational structures and content of studies across universities and countries. Such work is intended to facilitate the comparability of curricula in terms of structures, programs, and actual teaching (e.g., workload, hours of study per week, type of assignments, etc.).[6]

In theory, it is estimated that there are about 30 hours of work per unit of credit. Considering 30 units are given per semester, using the European Credit Transfer and Accumulation System (ECTS) adds up to 900 hours a semester (30 credit points × 30 hours). If a semester lasts 16 weeks, the student has about 55 hours of school work per week, on average. Considering that many hold part time jobs as well, ranging from as little as 5 hours up to 20 hours a week, the work and study week would be long and intense. In reality, however, only a few prestigious institutions will be able to attract students who pass strict admission requirements.[7] Also, students submitting to such rigor and time demands will represent a relatively small group of the total undergraduate and graduate student populations.[8]

Much has been accomplished and many things more will be accomplished to ensure that program convergence occurs. A European Computer Education Association (ECEA) was supposed to be established with the help of funding from the European Commission. However, so far the association has been stillborn.[9] Moreover, as of this writing (August, 2008), a tuning assessment of computer science programs across Europe has yet to be begun.[10] The 2007 Bologna ministerial summit in London[11] indicated that Europe has accomplished quite a few important milestones. More must be accomplished, however, to reach the 2010 target date for Bologna Declaration implementation in full across most of the 46 countries that signed up by May, 2007. (Several countries outside of Europe have joined and signed the declaration as well.)

76.3 BACHELOR'S AND MASTER'S IN INFORMATION SECURITY.   This section addresses how the convergence in undergraduate and graduate education might affect training and education regarding computer science and information security in particular (see also Section 76.2 and Exhibit 76.1) for greater detail.

76.4 COMPUTER SCIENCE: DOES IT ENCOMPASS INFORMATION SECURITY, ASSURANCE, AND SECURITY ASSURANCE?   The scientific discipline of computer science is sometimes called informatics in Europe and may include but not be limited to such subfields as security engineering,[12] security assurance,[13] and information assurance.[14] In turn, acquiring a degree in security engineering might include skills, knowledge, and understanding in such areas as cryptography and access controls as well as the nuts and bolts of other protection technologies.[15]

Four challenges warrant special mention:

1. The term "information assurance" is a relatively recent usage and definitions provided for the term vary widely.
2. The term is not widely used in Europe in university or applied settings.
3. Regardless of the Bologna efforts for convergence, entrance requirements at leading engineering and science schools for studying information security still differ.
4. What is being taught in these programs is influenced by faculty and their particular expertise and interests.

The term "information assurance" is rarely used except in business, where the influence of globalization may have resulted in use of the term. Unlike the United States, with the Department of Homeland Security, Europe has no agency that is funding centers of excellence regarding IA or information security. Hence, the economic incentive to label a program accordingly does not exist.

The U.S. Department of Homeland Security provides a strong economic incentive with easy money for university programs or courses that accelerate the further commercialization of academia, by training in information security and related subjects. In spite of the lack of an economic incentive for universities in Europe, information security is of considerable interest to industry, policy makers, and society. As a result, ambitious curricula in these areas have sprung up. Some programs also have very specific entrance requirements. In particular, the mathematical knowledge that students entering a program must have is spelled out and generally tested.[16]

76.5   BOLOGNA BACHELOR'S DEGREE.   So what does the Bologna Declaration do for education at the university level in computer science and information security specifically? In short, the Bologna Declaration stipulates these requirements for the bachelor's degree:

1. A bachelor-level degree is earned at an institution of higher education and requires between three and four years of full-time study, or 180 to 240 ECTS credits.

2. The degree can be fulfilled at both traditional universities and at nonuniversity institutions of higher education.

3. The title of each degree program should note the details (profile) and its learning outcomes and should be included in the diploma supplement issued to the student.

4. Bachelor-type programs must prepare students for further study. Most important is that these programs should be freestanding and not regarded as part of a longer curriculum. This allows students to change disciplines and/or pursue graduate studies at another institution. Admission to second-cycle (graduate) degree programs requires successful completion of first-cycle (undergraduate) degrees.

Point 4 is of particular interest. It suggests, similar to North America, that the student can fulfill entrance requirements for a graduate program in information security by having acquired an unrelated undergraduate degree. It also points out that the institution can, however, demand proof of proficiency in certain areas. This could be demonstrated by having attended and attained ECTS credits in certain courses (e.g., mathematics) and by passing an exam before being allowed to register in the graduate program.

It is important to understand that to meet all graduation requirements for a bachelor's degree as part of the Bologna system, the student must have acquired 180 ECTS[17] credit points; some countries may require 240 ECTS. These are obtained over a three-year or four-year period using the semester system (i.e., 30 units according to the European Credit Transfer System each semester). Unlike a North American undergraduate degree, the first year with its general distribution requirements is not part of the university education in Europe, if 180 ECTS are required for graduation. In fact, students have taken and successfully passed these types of courses during their high school program (see Exhibits 76.1 and 76.2).

EXHIBIT 76.1 Information Assurance and Security Assurance: ECTS Credit Points Programs

Prerequisites or Focus of ECTS Credit Points Studies	ECTS Credit Points
Foundation courses in computer science	70
Foundation courses in mathematics and statistics	20
Specialization courses	40
Undergraduate thesis (minimum or higher)	10
Total number of ECTS in computer science or related fields out of 180 ECTS credits (could be higher)	140

Today, a majority of students will continue with their master's studies right after having completed their undergraduate program. Also, the master's program attended will most likely be at the same institution where they did their undergraduate studies (e.g., Denmark, Finland, France, Germany, Italy, Slovenia and Switzerland). The Bologna system allows for two broad types of master's programs:

1. Consecutive master programs offer a direct continuation from a corresponding bachelor's program (i.e., where one has specialized in computer science). Students have the option to choose specialization streams, whereby a major and minor focus can be attained. Ninety ECTS credit points are required of which about 30 ECTS are taken by a thesis project of about 6 months' duration. In total, the study program should take three semesters or 18 months. Sometimes more in-depth projects delay the student at the end so graduation requirements are met after 24 months.

2. Specialized master's programs offer interdisciplinary studies, and often students have not taken an undergraduate degree in exactly the same area. In such courses, 120 ECTS credit points are required of which about 30 ECTS are taken up by a thesis project of about 6 months' duration. Usually these programs take four semesters and last about 24 months.

76.6 MOVING FROM UNDERGRADUATE TO GRADUATE EDUCATION: BOLOGNA.   Based on point 4 in Section 76.5, a bachelor's program that the student attended full time for three or four years should not be regarded as part of a longer curriculum. Hence, the student should be allowed to change disciplines and pursue graduate studies in another discipline (see also Section 76.7).

This poses a challenge for developing curriculums that deal with computer science at the graduate level and information security or information assurance in particular. Depending on a student's undergraduate degree at a university, his or her education in computer science may differ substantially. For instance, following the Bologna system, the first year of study in a bachelor-type course exposes students to material that they require for successful completion of the program. For computer science, this might include courses in mathematics and introduction to computer science. The second year may require students to take several core courses in computer science.

Exhibit 76.2 Information Assurance and Security Assurance: Graduate Programs

Prerequisites or Focus of Undergraduate Studies	Consecutive[a] ECTS	Specialized[b] ECTS
Bachelor of Science degree is in the **same field**, such as computer science, with a major in computer/information security. Master studies require the student to do advanced work in computing security (i.e., concentration courses and master thesis address computer security issues)	90 or 120	
Bachelor of Science degree is in the same field, such as computer science, with a major in **software engineering**. Master studies offer the student advanced work in computing security (i.e., concentration courses and master thesis address computer security issues)	90 or 120	
Undergraduate studies may not have been in computer science but what is considered a **related discipline** (e.g., natural sciences, such as mathematics or physics), giving the student the skills and knowledge considered a prerequisite for admission (e.g., mathematics and programming). Master studies will be done in computer science with a concentration on information security (i.e., concentration courses and master thesis address computer security issues).	120	90 or 120
Undergraduate studies may have been in neither computer science nor a related discipline. However, student may be able to meet prerequisites (e.g., having attended and successfully completed several types of courses during undergraduate studies or passing a test demonstrating these skills before being fully admitted) or attend and successfully pass prerequisite courses before being fully admitted to the program (e.g., mathematics and computing). Master studies will be done in computer science with a concentration on information security (i.e., concentration courses and master thesis address computer security issues).	120	120
Student has **successfully completed a bachelor's degree.** Undergraduate studies may have been in neither computer science nor a related discipline. However, student may be able to meet **prerequisites** (e.g., having attended and successfully completed several types of courses during undergraduate studies) or else attend these courses before being fully admitted to the program (e.g., mathematics and computing). Master studies will be done in computer science with a concentration on information security (i.e., concentration courses and master thesis address computer security issues).		120

Exhibit 76.2 (Continued)

Prerequisites or Focus of Undergraduate Studies	Consecutive[a] ECTS	Specialized[b] ECTS
Student may have completed undergraduate studies in any subject.		120

[a]This table outlines some of the possible variations in programs. All other things being equal, a consecutive-type master's program provides students with more in-depth knowledge and understanding of the subject than a specialized master's degree. This is due in part to having had training of 180 ECTS during undergraduate studies as well as an additional 120 ECTS of graduate work in information security. Some universities offer only this type of program in information security (see the first entry under the "Prerequisites" column) to get a master of science degree. A graduate of such a program cannot be compared to one who acquired 120 ECTS in information security subjects while his or her undergraduate degree was taken in, say, modern languages.
[b]A student in a specialized program may already have a master's from a consecutive-type program, such as an engineer acquiring a master of business administration degree. Generally, specialized programs are offered to satisfy continuous education efforts and may be attended part time and are fee-based. Master of science programs in business using the consecutive structure are being offered throughout Europe (e.g., Aarhus School of Business; http://asb.dk/programmes/master.aspx).

As shown in Exhibit 76.1, some computer science programs define 70 ECTS for the foundation courses in computer science; a further 20 ECTS credits must be taken in the area of mathematics and statistics.[18] These are the minimum requirements.

The third year is taken up for specialization by taking courses as part of one's major (about 40 ECTS) as well as getting credit (about 10 ECTS or more) for doing an undergraduate thesis that focuses on a topic relevant to the major. Hence, after students have acquired all the basics in computer science and mathematics, they may then specialize in information security[19] or cryptography.[20] Naturally, specialization options, at least in part, depend upon the expertise and focus of the particular program and its staff and their research interests.

The undergraduate curriculum often entails a practical component, such as doing lab exercises (e.g., being an administrator of a Linux server and being asked to harden the server to protect it against simulated and real attacks from fellow students) as well as doing an internship at a company.

As also outlined in Exhibits 76.1 and 76.2, people who acquire a bachelor's diploma in computer science have successfully completed 140 ECTS credits in computer science, including courses in mathematics. A specialist in cryptography may have acquired 70 ECTS credits or more as well as writing a thesis on cryptography.

Students who decide to pursue a Consecutive Master's in cryptography at the University of Leuven or Aarhus will enter the program already having a good amount of knowledge in the field (i.e., at least 70 ECTS related to or directly covering cryptography). In contrast, students who take a Specialized Master in cryptography (see Exhibit 76.1) and study cryptography (i.e., likely 120 ECTS) do not have the same amount of knowledge and understanding about cryptography as those entering a Specialized Master's program in cryptography. In fact, unless the entering students bring a substantial background in mathematics, as demonstrated by having ECTS credits from undergraduate math courses and/or passing an entrance exam, the program cannot be as mathematics intensive as otherwise possible.

Put differently and as outlined in Exhibit 76.2, having 120 ECTS in cryptography or security engineering is surely different from bringing 270 ECTS to the table. In addition, programs offering courses for a Specialized Master accept students with vastly different backgrounds. This surely will not result in having a student population that is highly skilled in advanced mathematics, unless this is part of very specific prerequisites, without which students will not be accepted. Exhibit 76.2 suggests that a student may specialize in eight different types of programs of study leading to a Master in Information Security degree. Naturally, within each program, there are nuances and differences in the curriculum that affect the skills and knowledge that students will acquire. However, these go beyond the scope of this chapter.

76.7   EXECUTIVE AND SPECIALIZED MASTER'S DEGREES.   Specialized Master's degrees usually require students to complete the requirements for the degree within three years after starting the program. Most programs require full-time study. Funding requirements have resulted in quite a few executive-type master's programs being offered throughout Europe. Generally such programs (e.g., education, executive management, information security officer) require students to attend blocks of training. For instance, a block may start Wednesday night and finish late afternoon Saturday. Some parts of the program may be taught during evenings throughout the year. In addition, most of these programs charge hefty fees to allow universities to make a profit or at least recover costs, since public funding for such programs is nonexistent or very limited.

At this time, it is not possible to compare the quality of executive-type programs to specialized programs. Unless there is a calibration of some sort regarding assignments and readings, executive-type programs will always be perceived as watered-down Specialized Master's programs.

76.8   SIMILARITIES AND DIFFERENCES: ARTS AND SCIENCE.   The Bologna Declaration's greatest achievement so far has been the move toward a two-cycle structure of bachelor's and master's programs all in lieu of the traditional long program that resulted in students receiving a degree after four and a half to five years of study.

Earlier (see Exhibits 76.1 and 76.2) we pointed out that students may acquire an undergraduate degree and either enter the workforce immediately thereafter or continue toward a master's degree. Naturally, graduate study may also be undertaken after some work experience has been acquired. In most instances, students continuing with their studies right after graduation enter what is called a Continuous Masters program. This program enables students to further specialize in the discipline they majored in doing undergraduate work. Alternatively, students can choose to pursue a Specialized Master in an area different from computer science, such as business, to obtain an MBA.

Different paths in training involve different levels of complexity of the material, and of the know-how to be acquired. Moreover, lower complexity involves more procedural knowledge and skills while science requires abstract analytical thinking and declarative knowledge. Undergraduate and graduate education focuses on helping students learn and understand concepts, theories, and foundations of disciplines.

What makes things a bit more complex is that undergraduate degrees may be acquired at different types of institutions that are either more or less applied to the solution of practical problems. Exhibit 76.3 represents an educational pyramid, which separates the various stages based on complexity of the material to be learned. Procedural knowledge is acquired through learning to perform certain tasks whereby practice helps to make one better at these tasks. Declarative knowledge is defined as helping students better understand concepts and theories (the big picture).[21]

Exhibit 76.3 also shows that the level of complexity in the material to be covered in an educational program increases from vocational training to university-level education. Similarly, and as also outlined in Exhibit 76.2, science that addresses concepts, theories, and models needed to explain and understand phenomena is not necessarily the same as the art of hardening a UNIX box against attackers' efforts to compromise data stored in it.

As illustrated in Exhibit 76.3, a computer operator requires less declarative knowledge about computer science than does a systems administrator. The systems administrator's know-how is very much focused on the system or software he or she is required to work with. Hence, this person's procedural skills about the Microsoft Exchange server may be the basis for enabling him or her to harden that system against attacks. Most likely, this knowledge will not provide the person with the skills to be proficient enough to harden a UNIX or Linux box satisfactorily. Accordingly, skills taught in certification or vocational programs are very context and application specific. This is, of course, appropriate. After completing such training, the individual expects to be able to work with a Microsoft Exchange server, making sure the system runs smoothly and securely.

Exhibit 76.3 also indicates that a technical college or polytechnic offers programs whose primary focus is on application skills and transferability of acquired know-how

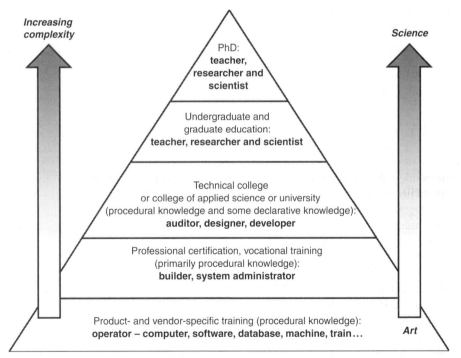

EXHIBIT 76.3 Information Security Education and Training: From Art to Science

from the classroom to the work setting. Most certainly, such programs also provide the student with some theoretical knowledge and concepts.

This more applied market niche is filled by what is called a university of applied sciences in Germany or Switzerland (called *Fachhochschulen*), technical colleges in the United Kingdom, and polytechnics (*hogeschools*) in the Netherlands. Here, subjects are taught that are tailored specifically to industry.

All things being equal, one would expect that the university-type program offers the greatest amount of general-type skills about a subject, including learning about theories and models. However, under pressure to prepare a well-trained as opposed to a well-educated workforce, university education has increasingly focused on practical application-oriented curricula. In turn, the differences in some areas between an undergraduate degree from an applied university compared to a university have become smaller.

76.9 WHAT DO PROGRAMS IN INFORMATION SECURITY TEACH STUDENTS?

As mentioned, environmental pressures have moved European universities to focus more on practical, application-oriented curricula. Hence, as in Canada or Australia, students wanting to embark on a career in information security may finish their bachelor's degree and leave their institution with a backpack of skills and factual knowledge, rather than with a way of thinking that might help one excel in a profession during one's entire work life. Unfortunately, such a skills and knowledge may be quite ephemeral and ever more quickly become obsolete.[22]

As an academic institution, a university has two primary tasks: education and research. The latter is usually defined as the free and unconstrained pursuit of knowledge. In contrast, applied universities are usually expected to focus on research that could be considered useful by someone else, which is in most cases industry. The result is that undergraduate education, and in some cases even master's programs, can be offered by applied universities and polytechnics or technical colleges. However, the curricula of these institutions have a different focus, as outlined in Exhibit 76.4.[23]

Exhibit 76.4 represents a rudimentary comparison between what could be and is most likely to be taught in a science program at a university and at more professionally

EXHIBIT 76.4 Information Security and Computer Science: Between Art and Science?

Science (Basic and Applied Research) Education	Art (Professional and Vocational) Education
Concepts	Practice—how to
Fundamental recurrences and patterns—generalization	Skilled performance of tasks
Discovery and presentation of ideas	Invention, new products and services
Analysis of the problem	Synthesis of the issues or opportunities
Dissection of the issues and questions	Construction
Theory and models	Principles-based standards—prescriptive or inherent rules of the trade

focused schools (or what may be called the *art* of information security). The exhibit suggests that science has different activities at center stage than does art. The latter does not refer to drawings or sculptures but to the useful practices of a field, such as information security. As the right-hand column indicates, professional-type schools are likely to teach more applied skills and knowledge regarding information security that could be grouped under the art of useful practices in the field. However, as Exhibit 76.3 suggests, more applied programs teach both: applied science and the art of the profession.

At the other end of this continuum between science and art is certification. For instance, ISACA's Certified Information Systems Auditor certification focuses on training students to follow best practices in the field while providing IS auditing, control, and security services.[24] There is surely no theory and science involved in this but only art, best practices, and standards.

Based on Exhibits 76.3 and Exhibit 76.4, one has to conclude that according to its mandate, education in an applied university will remain more applied than in the traditional university program. However, environmental realities have resulted in universities and polytechnics, as well as applied universities, offering some instruction about useful practices or what is called art in Exhibit 76.4.

This text presents an overview of what is happening in the educational landscape in Europe, without evaluating the programs or suggesting that either science or art in teaching information security is better than the other.

76.10 UNDERGRADUATE EDUCATION: POLYTECHNICS AND UNIVER-SITY.   Until now, Polytechnics or Universities of Applied Sciences taught the more application-oriented curricula. This made sense, because in some countries, students generally received nine years of formal schooling followed by a three- to four-year apprenticeship. Apprenticeship programs are offered throughout Europe in different forms. Some require attending school for two to three days a week (or in blocks of weeks) while the rest of the time, apprentices work in an organization in the field of the trade under close supervision. In turn, the apprentices acquire a "journeyman" certificate that qualifies them to attend a university of applied sciences to study for an undergraduate degree.[25]

The challenge here is in choosing between university programs and applied ones that are comparable. Thanks to the Bologna Declaration, students who have a bachelor's degree must ultimately be able to attend a Continuous Master program at a university of their choice. In some countries, Continuous Master and Specialized Master programs are offered at both polytechnics and universities. However, differences will remain because, for instance, the Netherlands has decided that Hogeschools (Polytechnics) will not offer education leading to a Continuous Master's degree. The master's degree can be acquired only at a university. In other countries, polytechnics are free to offer both Continuous Master's and Specialized Master's programs.

76.11 INFORMATION ASSURANCE: DEFINING THE TERRITORY.   Computer science can be described as a systematized body of knowledge together with predictions made by researchers with who validate and test those hypotheses in various contexts. But how does this relate to information assurance?

As mentioned, information assurance is hardly if ever part of a program taught at university level in Europe. The term as such, cannot be found in most curriculum descriptions and brochures. Outsiders could, however, conclude that this is simply a matter of semantics.

We believe that the difference is more than just one of semantics. For instance, the early attempts to define IA in the European context pretty much focused on protecting information assets from threats and attacks against a country's critical infrastructure.[26] In 1999, the term "information assurance" might only have *implied* information assurance of critical infrastructure, it is now widely accepted as such.[27] A comprehensive definition of information assurance as might be used in the United States and agreed to by computer science researchers[28] is not shared in Europe.

Sometimes less technically inclined individuals may feel that besides semantics, the terms "information assurance" and "security assurance" are synonymous. We do not agree. Information assurance focuses on the ability to access information and to preserve its quality and its security. Hence it centers on the threats to information and the mechanisms we can use to protect it.[29]

In contrast, security assurance focuses on the correctness, consistency, or completeness of the requirements and implementation of those mechanisms. It uses assurance techniques that provide justification for the mechanisms, and evidence that as implemented and operated, they do meet the security requirements as outlined in the security policy.[30] Formal mechanisms may use mathematical proofs to make their case that security requirements have been met.

Security assurance is alive and thriving, albeit under different names. Nonetheless, in Europe, undergraduate education in computer science with an emphasis on information assurance may entail a few courses that serve to cover the IA component, such as CS 447 Computer Forensics, CS 448 Fault Tolerance, CS 449 Survivability, or any CS 404 approved as an IA elective.

It is not clear how these courses relate to protecting systems serving a country's critical infrastructure. In fact, in Europe, infrastructure protection likely includes both computer security and network engineering.[31] In the United States, many of the centers of excellence for information security and assurance education offer master's-type programs that would be categorized as Specialized Master's program under the Bologna Declaration. In particular, looking at published entrance requirements for these centers, students attending such programs will most likely not have an undergraduate degree in computer science nor will they meet the stringent mathematics requirements that might be expected for those who enter a Continuous Master's program in information security.[32]

Research in the IA area indicates that skills and attributes taught in the curriculum of NSA Centers of Academic Excellence in Information Assurance Education may not have as much practical relevance as expected. A study assessing CISSP certification with what is being taught suggests that there is little if not zero association with the skills and attributes employed, or addressed, by information systems security professionals in an information systems security work environment.[33]

One might say that these programs are not intended to teach what might be called the plumbing trade. Instead, they are supposed to teach students to design, develop, and manage information systems that protect confidentiality, integrity, availability, and so on. Hence both programs and students must focus their attention on the threats to information and on the mechanisms we can use to protect it. In addition to IA, however, security assurance (i.e., focusing on the correctness, consistency, or completeness of the requirements and implementation of those mechanisms) is something one would expect a graduate of any of these programs to understand.

76.12   TEACHING INFORMATION SECURITY: THE MALWARE EXAMPLE.
Teaching students about malware is an area where arguments can get very heated. Undergraduate and graduate education focuses on helping students learn and understand concepts, theories, and foundations of disciplines. Malware epidemics are a clear example that not all may be up to standard regarding the correctness, consistency, or completeness of the requirements and implementation of those mechanisms. The use of code path analysis will surely help in reducing the number of vulnerabilities subject to zero-day exploits.

Training students regarding concepts and theories about malware means that instead of just focusing on how to do things right, university education also addresses how to avoid doing things wrong or what can happen if one does things wrong.

In North America, malware has entered the curriculum of computer science programs in various ways. Most famous is the recent example by the University of Calgary (U of C). There, fourth-year computer science majors meeting certain course prerequisites can apply to take a course addressing malware issues.[34] The U of C announcement in summer 2003 created a stir in antivirus vendor circles. Several vendors chose to misquote material and get excited about nothing spectacular. In fact, the teaching objectives in this course are very much in line with what one would expect from an advanced undergraduate course for computer science majors[35] in information security.

In reality, theory and practice are symbiotic. Business practices in the commercial world led to the development of several security policy models, such as the Clark-Wilson model. These models in turn help designers of security policies to better understand and evaluate the mechanisms and procedures required to secure their sites. Courses at university that teach virology in computer science focus on building virus-resistant systems that might help reduce the risk of new viruses spreading quickly in vulnerable systems.

The stir created because of the course taught at the U of C came as a surprise to many researchers in Europe, where teaching about virology is a common practice. For instance, most French computing science programs have a course that includes a virology component and/or require students to complete such a course.[36] Naturally, these courses are taught within the strict limits of the law and neither propagate virus writing nor allow students to spread viruses. Instead, course materials and exercises try to apply scientific principles to teach students how to engineer systems that could be less vulnerable to viruses. Additionally, such teaching and research also helps students and scientists discover if accepted practices in engineering can, or should, be changed. This teaching and research latter may foster better efforts for safeguarding systems, data, and information against future attacks and new forms of malware.

Although programs carrying the label MSc in information assurance are rare if not nonexistent in Europe, education preparing individuals for work in IA is available. While the U of C experience with the antivirus course may suggest that some vendors want universities to specify their curriculum according to what they think is appropriate, universities should resist these attempts.[37] In fact, we hope that in Europe and elsewhere, universities will continue to strive to teach their students higher-order learning and help advance science, theory, and practice and worry less about day-to-day issues that concern security software vendors.

76.13   CONCLUSION OF EUROPEAN INITIATIVES OVERVIEW.   Some have argued that the Bologna accord will herald unprecedented changes in higher education curricula. However, the biggest change the Bologna Declaration has brought to Europe is that it has replaced longer study for one diploma with a two-phase program. As a result, students get a bachelor's degree after three years of study and then can enter the field with a first degree if they wish. After receiving a first degree, students also have the choice to pursue further study in either a Continuous Master or a Specialized Master program.

The second big shift has been the increase in Specialized Master's degrees, which some universities perceive to be a major factor in maintaining their competitiveness in the market, partly because of growth predicted in the market for such degrees. These degrees offer students a chance to improve their knowledge and skills in a particular field. As Exhibit 76.1 illustrates, students entering these programs have a variety of backgrounds ranging from undergraduate degrees in engineering to fine arts, including possibly some work experience after receiving their bachelor's degree. This situation represents a challenge for getting all students to reach the same level of knowledge and skills.

In contrast, students entering a Continuous Master program tend to have an undergraduate degree in the same field (e.g., computing science) or a highly related one (e.g., mathematics). In the latter instance, specialization in information security may take 24 months instead of 18 months (see also Exhibit 76.2). It will be interesting to see if a Specialized Master's diploma will become the norm for chief security officers of larger corporations, or if a Continuous Master's will be preferred. Perhaps people with technical skills will acquire managerial know-how through a Specialized Master's program, such as an MBA program. This would be useful if they wanted to pursue a managerial career such as a C**-level type of executive, who might also be responsible for risk and IT security matters. The particular program that students attend will have a significant impact on their technical knowledge and on their understanding of risks, threats, programming vulnerabilities, and defenses, as well as of human resources.

Globalization has resulted in a convergence of standards,[38] and the Bologna Declaration is one of the many results thereof. However, when looking at postsecondary education and information security, convergence should not result in a shift from principles-based standards to prescriptive rules.[39] The same must apply for education. Hence, doing a good job in information security must surely be more than checking answers off a multiple-choice test.[40] In a recent study across Europe,[41] the authors pointed out that information security skills and know-how represent a moving target. The study also concluded that while training at university or technical colleges focuses on more general-type issues, the work in the certification and skills area clearly addresses vendor- and industry-specific concerns.

But not all differences will be eliminated with these efforts. For instance, it remains to be seen if the requirements of Bologna and national governments to have their university programs accredited will result in intellectually stricter criteria. Universities have already shown their adaptability to the new realities by choosing the accreditation agency that suits their needs best. A university may choose one accreditation agency over another for quite rational reasons (e.g., ISNM.de chose ZEvA over ASIIN[42] for accrediting its MSc.). ASIIN requires a higher mathematical and science component in the programs it evaluates than ZEvA does. This requirement applies regardless of whether a Continuous or a Specialized Master's degree is being assessed for possible accreditation by the agency. Hence, depending on the national accreditation agency's emphasis, programs it certifies may be similar in name but definitely not in content. Different levels of mathematics required as a prerequisite do change the focus of a master's program in information security quite a bit.

76.14   IMPLICATIONS FOR EDUCATION.   When schools receive accreditation for an MSc. program, they usually broadcast their results. However, the new educational landscape also means that marketing is becoming ever more important for securing additional research funding and scholarships. Hence it is to be expected that schools will avoid pointing out their incoming students' possible weaknesses in mathematical skills but instead focus on their strengths, whatever these might be.[43] However, for computer science and its subdomain of information security in particular, some basic knowledge of advanced mathematics can change the focus and depth of a postgraduate program dramatically.

Regardless of how far the Bologna Declaration will standardize university programs in the information security subdomain, vendor- and industry-specific concerns should be considered but not put center stage in education. Too much commercialization may have implications for society as well as for the profession that might not be desirable, nor would an elitist choice be the right one. However, it is clear that there are different types of education to prepare students and graduates for productive careers in information assurance or, as we prefer to call it, information security. Moreover, different types of education have different roles. Universities do not teach their students how to solve problems presented in a variety of job situations. To be ready for a journey that requires lifelong learning, students need to acquire the knowledge and understanding to see things from an original point of view.

Nonetheless, the expression "real world" hides a strong anti-intellectual bias. We have to define what an education focusing on practical application of information security in its curriculum entails. Moreover, information assurance focusing on problem solving might leave our students with piecemeal skills that become obsolete and outdated with the next version of software installed on the organization's servers.

A wonderful example of this issue is the comparison between *Viruses Revealed*[44] (of which this author is a coauthor) and *Computer Viruses: From Theory to Applications*.[45] The former is a practical tour de force for system administrators outlining the art of malicious code and fighting such attacks, while the second, by Filiol, is a gem as far as proofs, concepts, and theories are concerned. Naturally, without understanding some advanced mathematics to follow his case, one is lost after the first chapter if not before. Put differently, while Filiol's work does not advance a reader's quest for better using hands-on tools for protecting the server right now, it does help the reader in better understanding the issues regarding programming and malware. It especially advances comprehension of how viruses evolved and continue to evolve, including cryptoviruses.[46]

In conclusion, we could say that not every activity must have practical effects that are quantifiable, such as passing a multiple-choice test with 250 questions, to be able to know anything about information security (see the CISSP exam). If universities go too far in providing training that suits vendors, industry, and government, they may err too much on the side of providing students with piecemeal skills that soon become obsolete. Rapid changes in information and wireless technology pose new challenges. Moving toward ubiquitous computing in a nanotechnology environment, moreover, requires educated professionals who are curious and able to do some unorthodox thinking.

If information assurance will ever become an independent academic discipline[47] —which I do not feel is likely to happen in the European university setting—there must be room for work at different levels of intellectual rigor for the betterment of society.

76.15 IMPLICATIONS FOR MANAGERS. Information assurance is an important area for training as well as for upgrading the skills of security officers. Without considering security and dependability issues, and without also understanding the development of secure and dependable applications and networks when attending IA training, graduates will be unprepared for the ever-increasing complexity they encounter at work. Accordingly, training and education must also address the managing of risks, reliability, dependability, and security of ever-more complex systems and not focus only on certification based on passing multiple-choice tests. Understanding concepts and being able to transfer them into various settings may be a better preparation for doing well as a security officer than acquiring too many tools and knowledge of facts. Put differently, while we may have standards we should follow, it does not automatically mean that the certification process through an accreditation agency is standardized. In fact, it may differ substantially across agencies, and it may be subjective, according to and reflective of, the preferences held by a team of assessors used by a particular accrediting organization.

Ideally, security and dependability should be considered together and treated seamlessly from the first stages of any system design. However, the current reality is different. The development process for information and communications systems is focused mainly on functional features. Security analysis and secure and dependable development are trailing in professionalism and investment in many areas. This undesirable trend should not be further exacerbated by training that follows the same path. Long-term objectives should not be thrown overboard in the rush to realize an immediate gain.

Education and training tend to concentrate on "how to do things right" and too seldom address "how to avoid doing things wrong." But managers also have a tendency to focus on what certification the person has and too seldom consider whether candidates have the theoretical grounding to manage rapid change in technology.

Exhibit 76.5 provides a rudimentary checklist for managers and human resource experts to assess differences in candidates from various educational backgrounds who want to work in IT security and risk management.

As the exhibit shows, all else being equal, the more courses in mathematics that were taken in order to meet graduation requirements, the more likely a graduate will be

EXHIBIT 76.5 Checklist for the Recruiting Process of IT Officers

Prerequisites or Focus of Undergraduate Studies	Undergraduate Program	Graduate Program
Length of program (number of semesters required)		
Prerequisites required for entering program (e.g., mathematic skills by having attended and passed special courses or passing a subject-based entry exam before being admitted to a program)		
Specialization taken whilst studying computer science such as information security, information assurance, etc. (i.e., total number of ECTS credits taken in information security)		
Thesis topic (ECTS credits obtained)		

able to handle technical issues. Also, the more ECTS credits taken in a subdiscipline such as security engineering, the greater the in-depth understanding of this area that candidates will bring a new job.

Overemphasis on certification does not make the type and depth of courses taken easier to discover, and to address in the hiring process. But certification may be a globalization trend, whereby principle-based standards that follow commonsense rules are being replaced by prescriptive rules. The latter are preferred in litigious societies, because they outline what is wrong and what is right and can, in turn, be used to take another party to court, or as a regulator to impose a fine.

As Exhibit 76.5 suggests, the Bologna model does not necessarily make the job of recruiters and human resource specialists easier. At first glance, a degree in computer science with a specialization in information security or assurance from two universities may appear similar. In actuality, it is the ingredients of each that determines their relative excellence.

76.16   NOTES

1. The author would like to thank Eric Filiol (Ecole Supérieure et d'Application des Transmissions, France) for his important suggestions and comments made on an earlier draft of this paper.
2. The term *information assurance* is not widely used in Europe. Instead, we use the term *information security and computer science*. Our rationale for this choice is explained later in this chapter.
3. By *trusted* we mean that the system always operates as expected by design and policy.
4. The Bologna Declaration of June 19, 1999, Joint Declaration of the European Ministers of Education (www.bologna-bergen2005.no/Docs/00-Main_doc/990719BOLOGNA_DECLARATION.PDF). In short, it focuses on four issues:
   1. Developing a framework that helps increase mobility for learning and teaching while strengthening collaboration across Europe
   2. Accepting and accrediting degrees and training across national borders
   3. Structuring tertiary education using two levels based on undergraduate and graduate programs whose completion results in bachelor's and master's degrees
   4. Introducing the European Credit Transfer System (ECTS) that allows students to transfer credits to another institution in another country

   The declaration has resulted in the Bologna type of system distinguishing between graduate and undergraduate courses, thereby facilitating the comparison and mutual acceptance of degrees and certification across national boundaries.

   The agreement was launched by European countries and includes states that are not members of the European Union, such as Switzerland and Norway.
5. Tuning Educational Structures in Europe: Tuning Methodology, http://tuning.unideusto.org/tuningeu/index.php?option=content&task=view&id=172&Itemid=205.
6. Tuning Educational Structures in Europe: Student Workload, Teaching Methods and Learning Outcomes: The Tuning Approach, http://tuning.unideusto.org/tuningeu/index.php?option=content&task=view&id=179.
7. Most European countries try to make postsecondary education as affordable as possible by limiting tuition and other fees. In turn, the vast majority of university programs and institutions are government funded. In some cases, private support

from alumni, endowments, and third-party research funds can be considerable. For students, this means that tuition and fees may be a couple of hundred euros a semester for a local resident or EU citizen attending a public institution in Denmark. Attending the same program at a publicly funded institution in the United Kingdom may cost € 1,000 or more in fees and tuition per semester. However, with the Bologna Declaration, publicly funded institutions have launched graduate programs that are supposed to be self-financing. In practice, tuition and fees are needed to finance these privately funded programs. Here, a two-year master's program may cost €15,000 or more in tuition and fees, excluding living expenses.

8. Students who are not used to paying much to attend university are naturally suspicious of having to pay what they perceive as exorbitant tuition fees. Once students agree to pay such fees, they will challenge the program regarding services and teaching quality. In fact, similar to executive programs, independent learning may no longer be the primary focus. However, supplying students with presentation slides and as some say "chewing out the material for them" could become the key for getting above average teaching evaluations from students. Moreover, students want good grades to land the jobs they might feel they deserve. In such circumstances, grade inflation is just around the corner. As a result, no one wants to get a grade that indicates average performance; everyone expects to receive top grades. In turn, a grade-point-average will become more difficult to interpret because market pressures may in part result in grade inflation.

9. The association ECEA was launched in fall of 2003 (see http://ecet.ecs.ru.acad.bg/ecet/Docs/ireport_2003.pdf).

10. Tuning Educational Structures in Europe: Computing Science, http://tuning. unideusto.org/tuningeu/index.php?option=content&task=view&id=14&Itemid =37.

11. Bologna Process: Towards the European Higher Education Area, www.ond. vlaanderen.be/hogeronderwijs/bologna/.

12. For a definition of the term *security engineering,* see Urs E. Gattiker, "CyTRAP.eu/RiskIT Labs: Getting the Security Jargon Right—Security Engineering" (2006), http://cytrap.org/RiskIT/mod/glossary/view.php?id=2&mode= entry&hook=402 (requires free registration to log in).

13. For a definition of the term *security assurance,* see Urs E. Gattiker, "CyTRAP.eu/RiskIT Labs: Getting the Security Jargon Right—Security Assurance" (2006), http://cytrap.org/RiskIT/mod/glossary/view.php?id=2&mode= entry&hook=398 (requires free registration to log in).

14. The term *information assurance* is defined by Urs E. Gattiker, "CyTRAP.eu/RiskIT Labs: Getting the Security Jargon Right—Information Assurance" (2006), http://cytrap.org/RiskIT/mod/glossary/view.php?id=2&mode=entry&hook=396 (Accessed: May 23, 2006).

15. R. Anderson, *Security Engineering* (Hoboken, NJ: John Wiley & Sons, 2001).

16. Most of the universities that are members of the IDEA consortium have specific prerequisites regarding math courses. In fact, students may have to pass an entrance examination if they do not appear to have the required knowledge (see http://www. idea.ethz.ch) (Accessed: May 16, 2006).

In France, a prerequisite for most programs in this area is having passed education and exams reaching a certain level of mathematics (e.g., www.supelec.fr or www.cryptis.unilim.fr/). Students must have passed a specified set of courses in mathematics during high school to enter an undergraduate program in computing science or information security. Moreover, additional courses in mathematics must be completed successfully during undergraduate education to meet the prerequisites for a Continuous Master's type of education in computing science.).

17. European Credit Transfer System (ECTS) guarantees academic recognition of studies abroad by providing a way of measuring and comparing the student's learning achievements and transferring them from one institution to another.

18. For instance, as described by the University of Aarhus's degree requirements for a bachelor's in computer science, see www.nat.au.dk/default.asp?id=9213&la= DK.

19. The description is one for computer science students who are interested in taking an undergraduate major in information security at an institute of technology; see www.maturanden.inf.ethz.ch/studium/aufbau_struktur.

20. This description is for a three-year bachelor degree in informatics with a focus on cryptographic issues.

21. U. E. Gattiker, "Computer Skills Acquisition: A Review and Future Directions for Research," *Journal of Management* 18 (1992): 547–574.

22. S. Santini, "Determining Computing Science's Role," *IEEE Computer* 37, No. 12 (December 2004):126–127.

23. This table borrows from U. E. Gattiker, "W21—2005—Book Review— Introduction to Computer Security," *EU IST News,* May 25, 2005, http://casescontact.org/euist_view.php?newsID=3650, as well as from P. J. Denning, "Is Computer Science Science?" *Communications of the ACM*, 48, No. 4 (2005): 27–31.

24. A short description is provided at www.isaca-canberra.org.au/certification.

25. For instance, in Switzerland, attaining the journeyman certificate as electrician will enable the person to attend an undergraduate degree program in electrical engineering. If a person wants to do this at a university, however, he or she has to pass an entrance examination first.

26. For instance, E.A.M. Luiijf, "Information Assurance and the Information Society." In: U.E. Gattiker, ed., *EICAR Best Paper Proceedings* (1999), pp. 1–17.

27. For instance, E.A.M. Luiijf, "How to Prepare for the Next Waves of Information Assurance Issues?" Paper presented at the *Euro-Atlantic Symposium on Critical Information Infrastructure Assurance*. 23–24 March, Riva San Vitale, Switzerland; www.cimap.vt.edu/CIIA/Papers/Session2-5-luiijf.pdf.

28. Gattiker, "CyTRAP.eu/RiskIT Labs: Getting the Security Jargon Right— Information Assurance."

29. For instance, M. Bishop, *Introduction to Computer Security* (Boston: Addison-Wesley, 2005), pp. 303–316.

30. Gattiker, "CyTRAP.eu/RiskIT Labs: Getting the Security Jargon Right—Security Assurance."

31. This is certainly the case in these programs at ENSTA (France);

32. For example, George Mason University, http://www.ise.gmu.edu/academic_info/masters/ms-isa.html.

33. A. L. Fundaburk, "The Education of Information Security Professionals: An Analysis of Industry Needs vs. Academic Curriculum in the 21st Century" (PhD diss., 2004).

34. CPSC 527—Computer Viruses and Malware (was CPSC 599.48); see: http://pages.cpsc.ucalgary.ca/~aycock/virus-info.html. The University of Calgary described the course in summer 2003 (first being taught during fall semester 2003) in this way: "Once again, the University of Calgary's department of computer science explores new territory as it becomes the first institution in Canada to offer a course in computer viruses and malware as part of its undergraduate program. This course is unique—along with covering legal, ethical and computer security issues, it will focus on developing malicious software, such as computer viruses, worms and Trojan horses, that are known to wreak havoc to the tune of billions of dollars worldwide on an annual basis."

35. J. Aycock and K. Barker, "Viruses 101," ACM *SIGCSE Bulletin* 37, No. 1 (2005): 152–155.

36. U. E. Gattiker, "Virology—Preparing Our Students for the Future," Cytrap blog (December 2006); http://cytrap.eu/blog/?p=130.

37. During fall 2005, the University of Calgary also began teaching a course entitled CPSC 528—Spam and Spyware (was CPSC 599.63); http://pages.cpsc.ucalgary.ca/~aycock/spam-info.html.

38. For more information about this term, see: http://cytrap.org/RiskIT/mod/glossary/view.php?id=2&mode=entry&hook=391 (requires free registration to log in).

39. For more information about this term, see: http://cytrap.org/RiskIT/mod/glossary/view.php?id=2&mode=entry&hook=390 (requires free registration to log in).

40. Certified Information System Security Professional, www.isc2.org/cgi-bin/content.cgi?category=97.

41. P. Weiss, D. Dolan, W. Stucky, and P. Bumann, "ICT-Skills Certification in Europe" (2005), www.cepis.org/.

42. ASIIN is the only German accreditation agency specializing in accrediting degree programs from the fields of engineering, informatics/computer science, the natural sciences, and mathematics (www.asiin.de/english/newdesign/index_ex5.html). ZEva (Germany's first such agency) was launched by the universities of the state of Lower Saxony, with a particular focus in evaluating and accrediting programs with an international focus.

43. ISNM's Master of Science (M.Sc.) in Digital Media received international accreditation by ZevA. Evaluation team was particularly impressed by ISNM's cutting-edge research projects and unique 3 "i"—qualities put into practice on every day of a student's life: international, intercultural, interdisciplinary." Quoted from www.isnm.de/content/exploring/msc/msc.php.

44. D. Harley, R. Slade, and U. E. Gattiker, (2001). *Viruses Revealed* (Berkeley, CA: Osborne/McGraw-Hill, 2001).

45. E. Filiol, *Computer Viruses: From Theory to Applications* (Paris: Springer Verlag, 2005).

46. U. E. Gattiker, "Trend that Matters—Malicious Cryptography—Cryptoviruses Coming Your Way—Have You Paid the Ransom Yet?" *EU-Ist News,* May 11, 2006; http://casescontact.org/euist_view.php?newsID=4011.

47. Merely labeling something as information assurance does not make it a striving academic discipline. Instead, it could be a label that is needed to secure funding from whatever source funds programs labeled as such.

THE FUTURE OF INFORMATION ASSURANCE[1]

Peter G. Neumann

77.1 INTRODUCTION

Assurance is in the eye of the beholder.

Although this chapter is at the end of the *Handbook*, we are still only at the beginning of the quest for meaningfully trustworthy systems. We begin by asserting that there are no easy answers, although some potentially worthy approaches are outlined here. Nevertheless, the reader must bear in mind that the problems of obtaining trustworthy systems are inherently complex, and thus it is important to approach this complexity constructively rather than with conventional ad hoc approaches (which usually produces seriously flawed systems).

This chapter is more concerned with long-term issues than most of the rest of the *Handbook*. It is intentionally less of a hands-on guide than an assessment of what is possible. As such, it tends to open up many questions and possible future directions. It is intended to serve as a harbinger of what will be important in the future if the information assurance community is to contribute to the development and use of meaningfully secure computer systems, networks, and enterprise-based application software.

Webster's generic dictionary definition of *assurance* is relevant in the present context: "something that inspires or tends to inspire confidence." Assurance can mean many different things to different people, especially in the context of environments dependent on information systems—which historically have experienced many failures and unexpected deviations from expected behavior on the part of the technology, the people involved, and in some cases the natural environments in which those systems operate. Thus, useful notions of assurance should encompass all factors that are relevant in any particular enterprise.[2]

The first question that must be considered by a system developer or acquirer is this: With respect to what requirements, for which attributes, of which systems, is assurance desired? Without well-defined requirements, most considerations of assurance are relatively meaningless.

Requirements typically include local to enterprise-wide properties relating to system and network security, reliability, system survivability, human safety, system monitoring and accountability, guaranteed real-time performance, facile interoperability, ease of use, ease of system administration, ease of maintainability, and ease of long-term evolvability in the face of changing circumstances. These requirements may be generic or specific to particular enterprises, and they tend to be associated with particular layers of abstraction, such as hardware, operating systems, application software, networking, or total systems. In the absence of well-defined requirements for the desired attributes, any concept of assurance must be considered suspect, because it is likely to be ill founded.

Although this is ostensibly a handbook on security, a system that is not reliable is not likely to be secure. A system that is not secure is not likely to be safe or survivable. Thus, we stress the notion of trustworthiness that encompasses security as just one of its requirements. By focusing on trustworthiness with respect to the broader spectrum of requirements, it is likely that a system would be more likely to satisfy those requirements—rather than the usual approach of trying to add the other requirements retroactively.

Another fundamental question for system developers and users is this: What kind of assurance is required? A wide range of approaches to assurance is available. Consequently, the response in any particular application environment depends on the nature of the requirements and the criticality of the intended applications, as well as on many other considerations, such as cost, development schedules, and risks of producing systems whose failures result directly from the inability of those systems to satisfy their intended requirements. Those risks may themselves have associated costs and long-term implications.

What is desired here are some measures of assurance that a system will, with acceptable likelihood, satisfy its requirements under specified (and, we hope, realistic) assumptions. That is, a system should be demonstrably *trustworthy*—in other words, worthy of being trusted to satisfy the given requirements under the specified assumptions and not to do something too horrible if those assumptions are violated. Note that if a system is not reliable and its resources are not adequately available, it is also not likely to be secure, particularly in the presence of reliability failures. Therefore, it is typically not enough for a system merely to satisfy a set of requirements for integrity, confidentiality, and availability. For that reason, we prefer the more encompassing concept of *trustworthiness* when discussing assurance, presumably with respect to a more realistic and comprehensive set of requirements.

Assurance is a concept that is meaningful throughout the system life cycle. In particular, we want a priori assurance that stated requirements are complete, mutually consistent, actually relevant, and realistically implementable. Next, we need assurance that system architectures and detailed design specifications can satisfy the given requirements—ideally, before any software is written, and certainly before systems are deployed for any particular purposes. We then need assurance that hardware and software are consistent with their specifications, and indeed that the systems can do what is expected of them. In cases in which specifications are either inherently incomplete or indeed nonexistent, determining whether implemented systems actually can satisfy their given requirements with any meaningful assurance is very difficult, and likely to be unsatisfying. These concepts are generally static in nature, although we must potentially reevaluate them whenever changes occur. Further assurance could demonstrate dynamically that operational configurations and administrative practice are consistent with operational expectations.

Assurance can have widely varying degrees of rigor, from rough estimates based on vague assumptions at one extreme, through programming language annotations that can be interpreted by preprocessors, compilers, and static analysis tools, to system testing, and at the high end to detailed mathematically based formal methods that permeate the development cycle. Assurance can be qualitative or quantitative, objective or subjective, formal or informal. Unfortunately, informal analyses may inspire confidence without actually being trustworthy. Furthermore, even the most rigorous formal methods may give meaningful assurances only within the context of the assumptions implicit or explicit in the analyses, ignoring overall system vulnerabilities. Further details are given in Section 76.3.

As noted, we must reconsider assurance arguments whenever any changes are made. Clearly, changes in requirements can necessitate consequent changes in design and implementation. Similarly, even small changes in software or execution environments can invalidate previously sound assurance arguments and have harmful effects. As a consequence, assurance is typically a moving target.

77.2 VIEW OF THE FUTURE. Whether or not information systems are adequately trustworthy, we often must trust them. As our enterprises become increasingly dependent on information systems, it is imperative that we radically improve our collective ability to develop and operate trustworthy systems. As a consequence, greater emphasis must be placed on assurance that is pervasively integrated into the system development and procurement processes. This represents a significant change in the way computer systems and applications are developed, and creates challenges for everyone involved—conceptual thinkers, people who establish the requirements, system designers, implementers, development managers, and system administrators, as well as government and corporate personnel involved in procurement, legislation, oversight, and enforcement. User communities also need to be more aware of the myriad risks that result from the absence of assurance, and should be involved in assessing the viability of would-be systems. Improvements in education, training, and general awareness are also essential to foster a culture in which assurance is deemed much more important.

A primary goal is to achieve trustworthy systems and networks, with some demonstrably sound measures of assurance—that is, rigorously addressing how well the intended trustworthiness can be achieved. Measures of assurance can be sought in a variety of ways, throughout the development cycle, and thereafter as well. For example, they might involve analyses applied to requirements, architectures, and detailed system designs of operating system and application software, compilers, hardware, and operational practices.

Potentially important challenges relating to assurance suggest many fruitful areas for research and development. These span the entire development cycle from requirements, to system architecture, to detailed design, to implementation. Some approaches might involve relatively short-term development of analysis tools, whereas others might require major rethinking of how to design, develop, assure, procure, and use computer systems and networks.

Imagine a future world in which we have developed techniques and tools that enable us to build trustworthy systems. Further imagine that these techniques are cost effective, widely used in mainstream developments, and demonstrably capable of producing systems that satisfy well-defined requirements. This is the world that we need to attain.

Two possible paths toward this end come easily to mind.

1. Placing ill-founded trust in faulty, insecure, and fundamentally broken systems, society would experience failures with increasing frequency and negative repercussions, leading to a crescendo of disasters publicly viewed as completely unacceptable. At that point, perhaps, serious effort would be devoted to the challenges just discussed.

2. In a proactive alternative, placing emphasis now on research, education, training, cultural change, and recognized importance of a priori understanding of the consequences, we could build the systems of tomorrow that are trustworthy from the outset because of the way in which they are developed and operated.

Clearly, much greater commitment is needed to provide assurance of trustworthiness with respect to essential properties, especially for properties of entire systems rather than just of a few components in isolation.

At the higher ends of assurance, the potential benefits of formal methods remain considerable, particularly with respect to hardware and software. Their usefulness in the specification and analysis of critical system components remains enormous. Such methods have been adopted in recent years with respect to hardware development (particularly subsequent to the 1994 Intel Pentium Floating Divide processor problem, which resulted in Intel hiring a large group of formal methodists), where formal assurance techniques have had demonstrably tangible value in assuring that the hardware designs satisfy stringent criteria. Assurance applied to operational practice lags far behind either hardware or software assurance. In the light of past events—including rampant system flaws and detected vulnerabilities, system failures, experienced penetrations, flagrant system misuses, deaths and injuries, financial losses, and other problems—formal methods remain a potentially important part of the process of developing trustworthy systems with meaningful assurance. An ongoing effort to stimulate further advances in realistic uses of formal methods is found in "Verified Software: A Grand Challenge."[3]

With respect to software developments, formal analyses selectively applied throughout the development cycle can provide some significant levels of assurance, although informal techniques such as code inspection, testing, and red-teaming are complementary techniques that can also be useful. Of some potential help, but by no means sufficient by themselves, are measures of institutional goodness (as in the Capability Maturity Model) and individual programmer competence (as in certification of software engineers, such as the CISSP process described in Chapter 74.) Note that highly rated organizations and certified system developers can nevertheless produce bad systems. Overall, no single assurance technique is adequate by itself; each has inherent limitations that must be recognized and surmounted. Thus, a comprehensive combination of assurance techniques is highly desirable.

77.3 FOUNDATIONS OF ASSURANCE

If a program has not been specified, it cannot be incorrect; it can only be surprising.[4]

Several basic issues immediately come to mind in seeking increased assurance. This section considers some approaches that can contribute thereto.

77.3.1 Methodology.   The choices of methodologies, requirements, specification languages, programming languages, and assurance techniques are important to the success of a development effort. Many system development failures have been attributed to poorly defined requirements, an inappropriate system architecture, seriously incomplete system descriptions, or perhaps specifications that are too abstract, or badly overconstrained, or too low level. Thus, we may justify devoting considerable effort to establishing sound requirements and sound architectures.

However, there is also a danger that inappropriate choices of methodology, approach, and programming languages will lock the development into a path that will later require massive changes in the systems being developed. Thus, it is essential to consider all these factors wisely early in the system development process.

77.3.2 Guarantees.   Although one can make carefully couched conclusions based on tightly constrained assumptions about paper designs and software, there can never be any absolute guarantees with respect to the behavior of computer-communication technology in actual use. No matter how careful one may be, it is impossible to anticipate and compensate for all possible deleterious events, such as hardware malfunctions, software flaws, human mistakes, malicious human actions, and environmental disruptions. We should never use assurance techniques to create a *pretense* of perfection. Instead, these techniques should be used to identify imperfections and potential problems in requirements, architectures, and implementations, to reason about the implications of what might go wrong, and to iterate thereupon to transcend those obstacles.

77.3.3 Pervasively Integrated Assurance.   Techniques to provide assurance related to all relevant aspects of trustworthiness should be an integral part of the development cycle. The notion of building assurance into the system development process is akin to the classical notion of addressing security architecturally as a by-product of the development.[5] Such assurance techniques should be invoked persistently during operation, maintenance, administration, and long-term evolution.

77.3.4 Analysis of Requirements.   In general, efforts to increase assurance are meaningful only when meaningful requirements have been established. Having a well-defined relevant and extensive set of requirements is an important beginning to increasing developmental and operational assurance. Anything we can do to increase the soundness, completeness, and specificity of the stated requirements is likely to be valuable. In particular, assessing the realistic implementability of the requirements long before any development is undertaken can have significant payoffs later in development. Recognition of requirements that are likely to change over time can provide an impetus for more open-ended system designs.

Requirements are generally incomplete, erroneous, and even infeasible; developing a system based on such requirements is clearly counterproductive, costly, and time consuming. In contrast, detailed analyses of requirements (in particular, formal analyses where the requirements are formally defined) can be enormously beneficial.

77.3.5   Analysis of Compositions.   In the present context, the term "composition" has a range of meanings relating to how a system is constructed out of its components. It includes conventional computer science usage involving serial and parallel composition. It also includes the coexistence of multiple modules at a given layer of abstraction (horizontal composition) and the synergy among different layers of abstraction (vertical composition).

The concept of predictable composition is meaningful with respect to many entities, including requirements, specifications, protocols, implemented components, and proofs. Combinations of these entities often have surprising results. Consequently, as a result of a composition, analytic techniques can significantly increase assurance that existing properties will be preserved (*composability*), that existing properties will be suitably transformed, and that newly emergent properties will be acceptable (*compositionality*). It is desirable to be able to determine the existence of unspecified side effects, as well as the satisfaction of higher-layer properties resulting from composition, with respect to both designs and implementations of components and entire systems. Compositions can be evaluated with respect to many attributes, such as interoperability, sound information flow, the absence of covert channels, reliable and secure intercommunications, absence of deadlocks, serializability, and the avoidance of characteristic flaws. Resilience is also an important property, including identifying potential damage and confining it or otherwise remediating its effects.

In the vision of the future considered here, special-purpose and general-purpose systems and system applications might become routinely composable out of more or less compatible, demonstrably trustworthy components. To make such composition practical, a new type of analysis tool would be highly desirable. Such a tool would analytically determine the effects of composing software components (ideally, well designed and well specified), not just for the initial creation of a composed system, but also in subsequent reconfigurations, upgrades, and even in the installation of mobile code. Such an approach could, for example, take advantage of software formally shown to be consistent with its specifications, including descriptors relating to previously evaluated characteristics of the components, such as internal locks that might cause mutual deadlocks in certain contexts, assumptions regarding relative dependencies, identified interface limitations, and other attributes that might affect the effectiveness of the composition. Ideally, this approach could then be used iteratively: for example, initially pairwise or *n*-wise, and then over successively wider scopes, possibly ascertaining obstacles to the desired compositions or even potential failure modes that would suggest that a specific composition should not be permitted in certain types of environments because of the identified deficiencies. Other properties could also be included in the analysis, such as dynamic trustworthiness, configuration stability, and operational factors. There are practical difficulties with such an approach, but even small steps forward could be useful.[6]

77.3.6   Analysis of Property Transformations.

Composition may possibly alter the properties of the combined abstractions. Considerable value can accrue from transformations that demonstrably preserve desired properties—for example, transformations that maintain the consistency of specifications with requirements despite changes to requirements, or maintain the consistency of code to specifications despite the machinations of optimizing compilers, or maintain the satisfaction of evaluated properties after subsequent system modifications and reconfigurations. Demonstrating that a composition preserves certain essential properties, and that newly developed properties are satisfactory, can significantly simplify analysis of systems in the large. Transformations that result from nontrivial compositions, hierarchical layerings, and interpositions of mediators, such as trustworthy firewalls and guards, are of considerable value but may require further analysis because the resulting emergent properties may have unforeseen consequences. For example, joining two seemingly secure components via an unencrypted link may result in both of the components being compromisable. The analytic approach should also permit parametric architectural representations—for example, capable of being analyzed for what simplifications or complications might result when an architecture undergoes a particular change in design, such as making a file server multilevel secure instead of having multiple single-level file servers.

77.3.7   Analysis of Dependencies.

In any system, it is desirable to be able to identify explicitly all potential dependencies and, in particular, all potentially adverse dependencies—that is, components or subsystems that rely on other entities that are less trustworthy or of unknown trustworthiness. It is also useful to identify cyclic dependencies, especially those that can result in indefinite looping or deadlocks. Analysis of dependencies would be useful in avoiding many failures arising in large software systems, especially those with distributed control. The use of structured architectures with modular encapsulation that eliminates certain side effects can also avoid such problems in the first place, rather than having to rectify them later. Similar analytical techniques apply to undesired dependencies among policies, specifications, and assurance techniques themselves.

77.3.8   Detecting and Eliminating Vulnerabilities.

Assurance techniques in general, and formal methods in particular, are most fruitfully applied when they can dramatically improve the process of detecting and eliminating significant system flaws and vulnerabilities, and also improve the quality of the resulting systems. To this end, it is appropriate to ascertain that critical requirements soundly represent their intended purpose and to demonstrate, by formal, semiformal, or informal reasoning, that critical properties are satisfied by particular components or subsystems with respect to their specifications. It is also appropriate to examine critical aspects of the resulting system and of the implementation process itself, seeking to derive or prove properties of the system in terms of properties of its subsystems. The essence of this process is to provide cumulatively increasing confidence in the system design and its implementation by first *identifying* inadequate requirements, flawed designs, and bad implementations and then *overcoming* them. Steps that do not add substantively to this process are generally less effective. For example, if the requirements are flawed and the specifications are flawed, then attempting to carry out analyses that demonstrate consistency between code and specifications would be of questionable value. Once requirements are properly established, analyses and supporting tools can be helpful if they can identify certain types of flaws in designs, source code, and executables. In particular, formal techniques and other analyses can be useful in identifying flaws in authentication algorithms, access control mechanisms, network protocols, cryptographic embeddings, trustworthiness in general, and sets of requirements themselves.

77.3.9   Software and Hardware Consistency Analysis.

The term "correctness" is often used in a vague sense that raises the question of "correctness with respect to what?" Instead, this chapter refers to more precise statements such as "consistency of specifications with respect to requirements" or "consistency of code with respect to specifications" (assuming that there are any specifications!). It is generally unwise to overemphasize the process of trying to prove "correctness" of software and hardware: *Correctness* is meaningful only with respect to a set of presumed conditions that must be met—and those stated conditions themselves can often be wrong or incomplete. (The quote at the beginning of Section 76.3 is particularly pithy and also applies to requirements for trustworthiness as well as to specifications. It is also true of hardware.) Thus, efforts to increase the assurance that can be attained by an implementation should be up-front concerns, but not overly stressed, at least until the rate of discovery of flaws in requirements and design has dwindled to some agreed-on level of acceptability. However, at that point, code analyses can be valuable, especially if they are able to show the existence of design flaws and software bugs as well as the absence of certain types of harmful effects, such as Trojan horses or potential timing faults. In particular, formal methods in hardware implementations may prove effective—for example, in specifications, mask layouts, and fabrication, and especially for critical coprocessors or chips.

77.3.10   System-Oriented Analyses.

Overall, we need a system-oriented view of assurance that coherently encompasses temporal beginning-to-end life-cycle issues as well as analyses across and among layers of abstraction. Whether the analyses are linearly continuous (e.g., top to bottom, or bottom to top, or strictly beginning to end) or merely done piecewise and then joined together as appropriate is not so important as whether the separate analyses enable the pieces to fit together coherently. Higher-layer analyses, however, may be rendered useless if the integrity of the lower layers cannot be assured because of irreparable flaws.

Continuing on the subject of composition, horizontal (modular) composition and vertical (hierarchical abstraction) composition are both important subjects of analysis for the purpose of increasing assurance. Various past efforts are of considerable theoretical and practical interest.

Two relevant historical examples involve proving consistency within a successive refinement thread throughout the development effort, and proving consistency from top-level requirements through detailed design specifications to software implementation, and perhaps even subsequent operation and evolution, particularly when applied to large and complex systems and even when dealing with vertical and horizontal abstractions. One is the formally specified Provably Secure Operating System hardware/software design and analysis based on the Robinson-Levitt[7] Hierarchical Development Methodology approach. The second is the Moore-Hunt-Young CLInc stack.[8] Both showed the functionality of higher-layer abstractions to be related explicitly to the functionality of lower-layer abstractions, iteratively across all layers as desired—for example, from applications to hardware—as well as the relationships among different modules at the same layer. These techniques facilitate analysis of systems in the large, based on properties of the components. However, once again, those efforts must be considered as overkill unless there is proactive attention to requirements, system and network architecture, concise and complete specifications, and other good practices—in which case the comprehensive analysis can be compelling, even if labor intensive.

In an important sense, assurance is just as important an artifact as the code itself. Assurance is built in layers so that each layer is crafted from the assurance provided by the lower layers. Layering provides a way of isolating components from the effects of other components. Explicit assurance is also needed for managing incremental changes and adapting a system to new circumstances.[9]

77.3.11 Development Tools. Various development tools can be useful for the modeling and analysis of requirements, system and network architecture, testing, verification, source and object code, the various types of composability, configuration management, and operation. Some tools with interesting capabilities have been developed recently. However, they are too numerous and rapidly evolving to be itemized and contrasted here. A major challenge for their developers is to make these tools more general, more compatible with one another, and more rigorously based.

77.3.12 Measures of Assurance. To develop any concrete sense of assurance, it is necessary to establish well-defined standards and criteria against which requirements, architectures, specifications, software, tools, and operational practice can be evaluated. This is a complicated area. However, it is unrealistic to consider assurance without any *measures* of assurance itself. Above all, security—and even more so trustworthiness that encompasses other attributes such as reliability and human safety as well—is intrinsically multidimensional. Different applications may require different requirements, and evaluated systems typically do not satisfy all requirements equally. Reducing an evaluation to a single one-dimensional measure (e.g., a weighted average of the component measures) is clearly a bad idea unless the weights actually reflect the relative importance of the various attributes. Such a measure, however, may seem to be a wonderful idea for users and procurers, who seek (as in the case of system certification) simply a yes-or-no answer. With respect to trustworthiness, such measures are seldom black or white, especially if the requirements, the assumed range of threats and attacks, and evaluations are incomplete.

77.3.13 Risk Analysis and Risk Abatement. Allocation of resources devoted to security should generally have some logical basis related to the risks that can thereby be avoided. However, beware of overendowing quantitative risk analyses that are based on incorrect assumptions and inadequate analyses.[10]

The notion of risk management (see Chapter 62) is somewhat misleading, possibly suggesting that certain risks can be lived with or compensated for externally—for example, through legislation, liability, insurance, and penalties. That is often a dangerous concept when an alternative of simply avoiding those risks could be achieved, through a combination of sound system architecture, good software development practice, and other approaches discussed herein.

77.3.14 System Evaluation and Certification. The creation of comprehensive evaluation criteria (e.g., within the Common Criteria framework) and thorough independent and open evaluations can also significantly increase assurance levels. However, in the absence of well-defined requirements, standards, and evaluation processes, all such evaluations may be of questionable value: costly, time consuming, and ultimately not definitive.

Certification generally tends to be a black-and-white assessment of the evaluations, which means that the certification is more of a blessing than an assurance mechanism. With respect to systems that must be trust*worthy,* certification may give the appearance of goodness without any real substantiation. Beware of certifications without adequate evaluations. However, certifications based on detailed evaluations could be very useful, especially if accompanied by some sort of good-housekeeping seal that meaningfully attests to some measures of trustworthiness.

Evaluations should be conducted throughout a development process, not just when it supposedly is all done. Except in certain special-purpose dedicated systems, developments are seldom ever finished until the system is decommissioned.

A distinction must be made between total-system evaluations and partial evaluations that are done in the absence of the intended applications and enterprises that use those systems. This distinction suggests a need for the composability of evaluations of systems that can be extended incrementally to enterprises.

77.4   BEST PRACTICES FOR INCREASING ASSURANCE.   Providing meaningful assurance of trustworthiness is itself a complex problem, and needs to be spread out across the development process as well as into operational practice. Together with those concepts just outlined, these approaches can be used in combination with one another to enhance assurance:

- **Assurance-enhancing principles.** Disciplined adherence to certain useful assurance-enhancing principles[11] can be beneficial throughout system development. Some of these principles (such as modular abstraction and encapsulation, separation of concerns, hierarchical layering, least privilege, and minimization of what must be trustworthy) have been long established in academic communities, although they are not consistently used in practice.

- **Sound system architectures.** Considerable assurance can result directly from the establishment of an inherently sound conceptual architecture and analytic techniques for determining whether it is capable of satisfying its given requirements. One of the most fundamental but often ignored concepts involves architectures that effectively minimize what has to be trusted by suitably decomposing the system and ensuring that critical functions do not depend adversely on less trustworthy components. One example of that concept would be a high-assurance separation kernel on top of which a virtual machine monitor could be built. The monitor would allow multiple applications, possibly running on multiple virtualized operating systems, to execute simultaneously without interfering with one another.[12] Another approach involves creating systems that are more trustworthy than the subsystems out of which they are composed. This is a well-established approach for reliability, but also has some possibilities for security.[13] Such techniques can have enormous payoffs, as already noted, simplifying developments, reducing costs and overruns, further simplifying assurance analyses, and greatly increasing the likelihood of development success.

- **Sound software engineering.** Soundly based development methodologies with appropriate development tools can encompass techniques for many measures of assurance. Use of programming languages that systemically avoid characteristic flaws, together with supporting analytic tools that are formally based, and about which properties can be proven, are also desirable. It seems silly that we are still beset with buffer overflows, missing bounds checks, wild pointers, type mismatches, inadequate handling of exceptions, and other common bugs. Developments based on specific understanding of the risks to be prevented are likely to be more effective than other developments.[14]

- **Sound algorithms and protocols.** Analysis can determine consistency with requirements for trustworthiness (security, reliability, network resilience, and so on), with respect to both designs and implementations.

- **Robust system accountability.** Accountability is a broad topic that encompasses the collection of audit trails with appropriate accuracy, timeliness, and tamper-resistance, as well as dynamic analyses (in real time or post hoc) that can coherently detect system anomalies, misuse, and failures, and lead to intelligent remediation. Ideally, the audit trails should be sufficiently secure, robust, and tamper-resistant to permit their relatively indisputable evidentiary use in forensic applications. Thus, the assurance of the accountability mechanisms themselves can be important.

- **Analysis of properties.** Functional and nonfunctional properties of subsystems, systems, and networks are subject to analysis at different layers of abstraction. For example, subsystems, operating systems, application packages, and entire enterprises can all be modeled and analyzed, formally and informally, with respect to designs and implementations. Hierarchical dependence analyses can uncover design flaws, implementation bugs, and architectural inconsistencies in adverse trust relationships. Higher-layer properties—including emergent properties—can be analyzed hierarchically (e.g., as in the Robinson-Levitt approach).

- **Static and dynamic code analysis.** Ideally, the strategy of doing constructive design and analysis up front wherever it is advantageous suggests that discipline embedded in the software development process can have considerable payoff, augmenting what programming languages can do to encourage greater discipline. Compilers and related pre- and postprocessor tools that provide rigorous checking would also be useful. However, the integrity that can be provided by the best methodologies, programming languages, and compiler tools is potentially compromised by people involved in design and implementation, debugging, integration, maintenance, and evolution. Examples of relevant tools include checkers for buffer overflows and other types of flaws, as well as for dynamic configuration errors. In cases where static analysis is not effective, run-time checks may be desirable. Also of considerable interest is proof-carrying code[15] and cryptographic integrity seals that can detect and hinder undesired modifications of data and programs.

- **Code inspection, testing, and debugging.** The use of formally and informally based tools can also be highly beneficial for code inspection, testing, and debugging. Conventional uses of code inspection and testing are labor intensive, subjective, and very much dependent on the intelligence, education, training, and experience of the individuals involved; although those techniques can be aided by automated or semiautomated tools, there is always a risk that the weaknesses of the tools will interact with limitations of the people using those tools to result in a false sense of satisfactory results. Nevertheless, these approaches can be beneficial.

- **Red-teaming.** *Red teams* (penetration testers; see Chapter 46 of this *Handbook*) can also be used to increase assurance, if they provide truly independent and objective assessments. Although red teams have tended to be rather ad hoc in the past, the use of disciplined tool sets could actually be helpful (to the extent those tools are effective). The notion of pervasively integrated assurance suggests that the red-team concept should be substantially broadened to include pervasive interactive assessments throughout development rather than after premature decisions are cast in concrete. However, despite the desire for pervasive integration, it is important that the red team be independent of the development efforts, although still capable of providing valuable feedback.

- **Composability within the evaluation process.** Paul Karger and Helmut Kurth address the essential needs for cooperation and communication within various components of the evaluation process, particularly as it relates to the notion of composite evaluation within the Common Criteria.[16] (This is an important paper, and deserves considerable attention. One major point of the paper is that the results of hardware evaluations must flow unimpeded to the software developers and software evaluators, irrespective of proprietary constraints. The consequences of interfering with that information flow can be quite dire.) Note that the same conclusion also applies to red-teaming, where the red team needs to have effective communication paths to project management. Whether the concerns involve functional assurance, security assessments, quality assurance, or anything else, it is important that constructive feedback not be stonewalled.

- **Operational practice.** At present, system administration and operational practice seem generally less amenable to assurance techniques than to technical defense measures. However, there are some potential opportunities for progress in this area, particularly in handling software upgrades, in configuration management, in emergency recovery, and in planning for these activities in system design.

- **Research and development.** Consistent with the ability to analyze critical aspects of complex systems, research must continue to explore the frontiers of the technology, and development must be carried out with much greater discipline than is generally invoked today. Some readers will consider assurance issues to be pie in the sky, and unrealistic from the perspective of potential consequences of increased costs, project delays, and increased needs for education and training, the spectrum of assurance techniques does have something for everyone. At the low end, anything that reduces design flaws, implementation bugs, cost overruns, scheduling delays, and resulting operational risks at acceptable costs is beneficial. At the high end, judicious use of formal methods can add significantly to development and operation—but also can add complexity, delays, and cost overruns if used unwisely. Although formal models and specifications may seem to complicate the design process with delays, increased costs, and greater intellectual demands, they can also substantively improve assurance. Formal methods can also lead to earlier identification of problems that might otherwise be uncovered only in later stages of development and use. However, such methods need to be used with considerable care and applied primarily where they can accomplish things that design reviews, testing, and operational discipline cannot. Because errors in requirements, design, and specification are perhaps the most difficult and costly to repair, formalisms can be particularly valuable in the early stages of development.

- **Holistic approaches to systems.** Overall, assurance must be considered as an intrinsic part of the development cycle. Its costs and benefits must be evaluated not just locally and in the short term, but rather globally and in the long term—including costs of ongoing maintenance, administration, and system evolution. When considered holistically, the benefits may well eventually outweigh the shortcomings.[17]

77.5   ASSURANCE-BASED RISK REDUCTION.   Chapter 62 in this *Handbook* considers risk assessment and risk management. The assurance techniques summarized in the previous sections of this chapter can have significant effects in identifying and reducing risks, particularly with respect to the extent to which critical system requirements are likely to be satisfied by system designs and implementations. In general, it is better to anticipate the potential risks and avoid them through sensible system architectures and development, rather than to attempt to manage the risks in a badly designed and poorly implemented system. The techniques discussed in this chapter may be applicable in many different ways, all of which are potentially relevant here. In particular, analysis can contribute at all development stages and all layers of abstraction within a development. Furthermore, it is unwise to consider security in the absence of other requirements, especially where security interacts with reliability, safety, and other critical properties that are also encompassed by trustworthiness.

There have been many advances in assurance techniques over the past decades. Many of the pieces of the puzzles relating to the development and continued operation of trustworthy systems—including theories, methods, and tools—are now reasonably well understood and advancing in relevance. It is generally unwise to put all your eggs in one basket (such as a single development methodology of testing or penetrate-and-patch). Thus, a comprehensive combination of approaches is generally desirable, including many of the approaches discussed earlier, especially if the desired paradigm shifts are observed.

Several examples of past cases that caused serious risks are given in this section. These cases illustrate how assurance techniques might be applied to systems that must be trustworthy (particularly with respect to security, safety, and reliability). Even though these examples consider what might have been done to prevent effects that actually resulted, they are explicitly not intended as a "wise-after-the-fact" exercise in *hindsight*. Instead, consider them as explicit representations of what types of assurance might be applicable in *future* developments of a similar nature.[18]

77.5.1   Security.   The past and present are littered with security and integrity vulnerabilities and exploitations thereof, including privacy violations. Buffer overflows, erroneous or missing bounds checks, and other annoying types of security flaws that seem to recur much too frequently can be avoided with sensible system architectures, good programming practice, and a variety of static and dynamic assurance techniques. Similarly, the insertion and execution of malicious code such as Trojan horses, Web- and e-mail–based executables, and so on, need to be countered by sound architectures and operational practices that enforce isolation, confined execution, separation of concerns, and so on. Authentication can be made more trustworthy by incorporating demonstrably robust cryptography or possibly biometrically based authentication, and analyses that demonstrate the security of their embedding into systems, thus avoiding overreliance on porous perimeter defenses without additional security mechanisms. Real-time misuse detection and response can also increase assurance of trustworthiness, especially with respect to integrity violations, insider misuse, denial-of-service attacks, and other threats. Unfortunately, today's commercial systems tend to be rather limited; some of them could be supplanted by better system architectures and implementations. However, all of the problems and would-be solutions described in this *Handbook* are in need of some sort of assurance analysis.

77.5.2 Human Safety.   Historically, many seemingly easily avoidable accidents have occurred in healthcare, aviation, and other areas. Two examples are illustrative.

A computer-controlled therapeutic radiation machine called the Therac 25, manufactured by Atomic Energy of Canada Limited (AECL) and CGR MeV of France, was implicated in the deaths of six patients between 1985 and 1987 because of fundamental errors in management and systems engineering including inadequate code review, failure to analyze failure modes, and delays in responding to user complaints. This case is routinely used in systems engineering courses and papers as an example of the disastrous results of quality assurance failures in both the design and implementation phases of production. Testing a medical device such as the Therac 25 for an asynchronous time-dependent race condition (which resulted from poorly implementing the Therac 20 hardware interlock in software), and testing a heart pacemaker or defibrillator for electromagnetic interference would seem to be standard practice; yet these failure modes were not considered until after people had died.[19] Once again, better attention to requirements, architecture, and good software engineering practice could have avoided the problems altogether. Furthermore, electromagnetic interference problems clearly must be addressed through explicit requirements, threat models, and testing. However, testing generally cannot detect many failure modes, and needs to be supplemented with other assurance techniques.

On May 26, 1991, Lauda Air Flight 004, a B767, left Bangkok, Thailand, for Vienna, Austria, after a planned stop in its flight plan from Hong Kong to Vienna. Fifteen minutes into the flight, the plane disintegrated after reverse thrusters, normally used on landing, deployed in error. The death toll included 213 passengers and 10 crew members.[20] Design reviews and testing could have detected the missing interlock that allowed the Lauda Air thrust reverser to be deployed during flight, although more careful and proactive requirements, design, and implementation might have prevented the problem from occurring at all.

77.5.3 Reliability, Availability, and Survivability.   The ACM Risks Forum archives are full of reliability-related failures such as these:

- Excessive clock drift in the Patriot missile system caused the intended targets to be outside of the expected computational frame.[21] It is surprising that a demonstrably more robust clock algorithm was not used, irrespective of the requirements. Apparently the implementers tacitly assumed the launch platform would be moved frequently—perhaps once a day—to reduce the likelihood of its being targeted by the enemy. This design flaw could have been prevented through any of several assurance measures. For example, requirements could have explicitly demanded that the systems should operate correctly for several weeks, which would have necessitated a better clock mechanism. Alternatively, given the realization of an obviously unreliable clock, an operational fix could have required the launch platform computers to be rebooted daily.

- The Yorktown Aegis missile cruiser was disabled for 2.75 hours in September 1997 as a result of a divide-by-zero error in an application that crashed the operating system (Windows NT Smart Ship). This failure could have been prevented simply by observing the shrink-wrap disclaimers, which suggested that the software not be used in critical applications.[22] However, making the engine controls dependent on a system with recognizably poor survivability was an architecturally unwise decision. The implications should have been understood during requirement specification, development, and system certification. (One obvious approach to greater assurance is that critical applications need trustworthy operating systems that adhere to established principles, and that can inherently protect themselves against their own flaws. For example, the 1965 Multics ring-structured architecture effectively prevented this kind of flaws.)

- The backup computer synchronization problem on the very first Columbia Shuttle launch was apparently known to the designers, but not to the launch support team. The two-day launch delay could have been avoided by a simple retry that would have skipped over the 1-in-64 transient failure mode—if the documentation had noted this problem, or if the launch crew and the developers had been in closer contact. However, the synchronization problem could also have been prevented altogether by a more robust design, or explicitly diagnosed by a variety of analysis tools.[23]

Over the past five decades, there have been multiple cases of severe outages in which a single-point failure propagated widely, beginning with the 1965 Northeast power blackout. The 1980 ARPANET total network outage,[24] the 1990 AT&T long-distance collapse, and various electrical power outages—including the 2006 almost complete shutdown of Amtrak's New York–to–Washington corridor for an entire day—all share a common failure pattern: the propagation of a local failure into a widespread outage. In most of these cases, it had been widely believed by the developers and operators that single-point failures could not cause such propagating effects. At the least, some detailed modeling of the interactions among components could have demonstrated the possibility of mutual contamination and propagating outages, enabled further analysis to determine what conditions might trigger such effects, and inspired resulting architectural changes necessary to prevent such problems. Some combination of analysis techniques (such as fault-tree analysis and model checking) would presumably have detected specific failure modes that could trigger such outages. In the case of one of the extended AT&T System 7 telephone system outages, detailed laboratory simulation environments were normally invoked, but because a particular change affected only a few lines of code, it was not thought to be necessary to re-cycle through the entire analysis process.

77.5.4 Operational Assurances.   More careful analysis of human interfaces would be particularly valuable with respect to system administrators, both statically (e.g., leading to warnings before permitting certain questionable upgrades and configuration changes) and dynamically (in anticipating needs for emergency response). Furthermore, many of the concepts of this chapter could be applied to operational practices.

77.5.5 Sound User Interfaces.   Numerous serious accidents have resulted from poorly designed human interfaces, as well as from misguided internal system interfaces. Assurance techniques analyzing human interfaces could perhaps have avoided many of the cases noted in the ACM Risks Forum.

- Testing should have caught the sensor cross-wiring in maintenance of the British Midland 737, which caused the pilot to shut off the good engine rather than the failing one.[25]
- Testing might have detected the missing interlock in the F-16 landing gear that allowed retraction on the ground.[26]

- Sensible interface design might have proactively recognized the risk of using a GPS unit that after a battery change reset the coordinates of an intended Taliban target to the GPS unit itself, which killed the U.S. Special Forces launch crew. The designers of the weapons system might have anticipated the need for a warning to users.[27]

- Heart-monitoring devices should have had standards that could have prevented a developer from using an ordinary electrical plug as a connector that could mistakenly be plugged into an electrical socket, thus electrocuting the patient; in addition, the certification process should have prevented that device from being used.[28]

- A failure of a shuttle Discovery laser-beam experiment resulted from the target elevation over Mauna Kea being input in feet rather than miles (directing the laser up rather than down). That error could have been avoided by a human interface that explicitly insisted on an input in feet. Self-defining input types may seem like a low-assurance programming technique, but it would have avoided several past problems.[29]

This illustrative enumeration suggests the need for total-system development approaches and evaluations, with assurance as an integral factor throughout development and operation. Among the wide variety of assurance techniques (some almost obvious, some more subtle), each potential system risk can benefit from the application of some subset of the total collection of approaches to increasing assurance. Establishment of sound requirements, sensible architectures, and good software development practice would undoubtedly have avoided many of the problems discussed throughout this chapter, and could be significantly aided by careful requirements analysis, model-based design, model checking, formal test-case generation, static analysis, and so on. However, there is no one size that fits all; the particular techniques must be used in various coherent combinations, according to the circumstances, the development challenges and risks, and the competence of the developers and analysts. In addition, the amount of resources and the effort to be devoted to assurance need to be commensurate with the overall long-term and enterprise-wide risks. Unfortunately, most risk assessments relating to how much effort to devote to assurance tend to be shortsighted and locally scoped.[30]

77.6 ILLUSTRATIVE APPLICATION: COMPUTER-AIDED VOTING. To illustrate many of these concepts related to assurance, consider the election process as a specific application area, with particular emphasis on computer-based voting systems. Elections represent a problem area that involves technology, legislation, standards, independent evaluations, operational procedures, and people in many different capacities. Furthermore, they are in a sense a paradigmatic example of a system that must provide assurances to voters that their votes are correctly treated throughout. The security, integrity, and privacy requirements need to span the entire process in an end-to-end manner. Each step in the process typically includes many vulnerabilities, and each step is a potential weak link.

77.6.1 Election Process. The basic steps in the election process include:

- Registration of voters, ongoing throughout the year
- Preparation of ballot materials for a particular election

- Definition of ballot appearances for a particular election
- Preparation of voting machines for particular precincts
- Authentication of each voter for an election
- Authorization of each voter to cast his or her ballot
- Ballot-casting process
- Ballot-tabulation process
- Collecting local results into aggregate totals, including absentee ballots (see next list)
- Distributing the partial and final results as they emerge
- Verification and certification of the results
- Recounting in case of close or disputed elections

The basic steps associated with absentee ballots are these:

- Authentication and validity of absentee ballot requests
- Distribution of absentee ballots to voters
- Voter completion of absentee ballots and delivery as indicated
- Receipt, verification, and maintaining privacy of absentee ballots
- Counting of absentee ballots (different from mainstream ballots unless the same system is used for both)
- Merging the results into the mainstream aggregation (see list above)

There is no one-size-fits-all approach to elections. Some methods introduce additional complexities, such as preferential balloting that seeks to avoid runoff elections by iteratively discarding the candidate with the lowest totals and reranking accordingly. This method introduces its own set of problems.

Essentially, each step in the overall process has potential risks that must be addressed, detected, and remediated. The registration and voter certification processes need to be nondiscriminatory. Considerable care must be taken with voter registration databases.[31] The ballot appearance needs to minimize any potential voter confusion. Ballot-preparation systems must be unbiased. Ballot-casting systems must have sufficient independent audit trails to ensure that votes cast are consistent with voter intent and that recounts are meaningful in case of irregularities. Casting and processing ballots needs independent assurances of integrity. Today, instead of *strength in depth,* there is primarily only *weakness in depth.* Every step is a potential weak link. Clearly, assurance efforts throughout the process, from beginning to end, can help reduce computer-related risks. For example, a serious attempt to cast the computer-related voting part of the election process into the formulation of the Common Criteria is given by Rebecca Mercuri.[32] Significant risks are likely to be associated with failures to satisfy each of the next highly oversimplified illustrative sets of requirement topics, each of which would need much greater detail to be relevant to evaluation of a specific system and its intended uses.

77.6.2 Voting-Related Requirements. An extremely simplified enumeration of some of the main requirements for computer-based elections follows; of course, the requirements would actually be rather complex when fully explicated. (Some of these requirements would also be applicable to entirely paper-based methods.)

System Requirements

- **System integrity.** Tamper-resistance and tamper-evidence; absence of self-modifying code and run-time changes, trusted bootload; physical security of machines.

- **Data integrity and reliability.** Correct recording and processing of votes throughout; uncompromised voter inputs; detection of accidentally and intentionally altered votes; predictable and reproducible correctness.

- **System availability and survivability.** Availability of election systems during required periods of operation; ability to withstand denial-of-service attacks and other types of failures.

- **Voter anonymity and vote confidentiality.** Absence of associations between votes and specific voters; system-based protections against vote selling and voter coercion to the extent possible. Note that absentee ballots and voting remotely over the Internet or by telephone are typically subject to fraud and misuse.

- **Voter verifiability of individual votes.** Independent means of ensuring that each vote is correctly handled throughout; immediate disabling or alternative treatment of noncompliant systems.

- **Accountability.** Uncircumventable and definitive audit trails recording all pertinent information, with tamper resistance and tamper evidence of the audit process, sufficient for independent recounts based on demonstrably true input data.

- **Nonspoofability.** Nonspoofable identification and authentication of all personnel with any access to relevant computer systems; for example, shared passwords are a poor choice, especially if never changed. (Fixed cryptographic keys are similarly risky.)

- **Voter ease of use.** Usability is a serious concern for all voters, but especially for those with physical or other disabilities, or with language problems, and for election officials, subject to security constraints; avoidance of confusing and misleading ballot layouts.

System-Related Requirements

- **Chain of custody.** Provenance of equipment, software, and data throughout the end-to-end process, including system development, trustworthy software distribution, ballot image preparation, system initialization, preventive maintenance, final testing, configuration changes, actual operation, and post-mortem analyses. For example, insertion of malware and run-time changes must be prevented, and insider misuse must be detected when it occurs.

- **Testing, evaluation, and certification.** This is a huge problem area, and needs much greater attention to increase its relevance and value. The Election Assistance Commission's Voluntary Voting System Guidelines[33] are inherently incomplete. Testing is inherently incomplete. Evaluation does not adequately cover or prevent subsequent system changes, and the results in the past have generally been proprietary. Certification is based on incomplete knowledge. The California Secretary of State's Top-to-Bottom Review of voting systems in 2007[34] has inspired a much greater awareness of the depth of the existing problems, and is being emulated elsewhere as well.

- **System disclosability.** Considerable benefits can result if all relevant software, hardware, firmware, custom circuitry, election results, error indications, irregularities, and associated documentation are open for inspection and analysis, at least by unbiased qualified experts. Documentation must be truthful, and should include development practices, operational procedures, and testing procedures, all unambiguously and consistently described. Documentation must also elaborate on assurance measures that have been applied to each of the above system aspects.

Operational Requirements

- Evaluation of the competence, integrity, and trustworthiness of system developers and vendors

- Evaluation of the competence and integrity of election administrators and operators.

- Procedural and operational enforcement of requirements. For example, protections against tampering, loss of privacy, vote selling, voter coercion, adverse physical access, disenfranchisement, bias, conflicts of interest, preferential treatment of certain voters or votes, and so on, throughout the election process, within and beyond the purview of any computer-based systems.

- Detailed oversight on the satisfaction or violation of all of the above requirements.

Many assurance issues are relevant here, including essential functional components in the small and their compositions in the large—encompassing, for example, voting-specific software, operating systems, cryptography, and auditing functionality. It should be possible to reason about properties of the compositions of subsystems, interdependencies among the subsystems, and ultimately critical properties of the entire system and the end-to-end process.

The problems of election integrity are rapidly gaining public awareness and governmental visibility. For a more detailed view of the challenges in designing high-assurance voting machines, together with a system architecture that succeeds in considerably reducing what must be trustworthy in order to achieve high-assurance voter confirmation without having to trust the ballot-casting component, see Sastry, Kohno, and Wagner's analysis of how to design voting machines for verification.[35] Another approach pursues the principle of starkly minimizing what must be trustworthy, as exemplified by the remarkably small pVote system described in Ka-Ping Yee's doctoral thesis.[36] Another approach to confronting the requirements of privacy and integrity is that of-voter-verified audit trails proposed by Rebecca Mercuri,[37] which has now been adopted into several commercial systems. In addition, several novel approaches proposed by Ronald Rivest, David Chaum, and others satisfy almost all of the main functional requirements and could conceptually be used entirely without the use of computer systems.[38]

77.7 CONCLUSIONS. Perhaps the most important conclusion of this chapter with respect to developing and operating trustworthy systems and networks is that assurance must become a more integral part of the development cycle, subsequent operational use, and long-term evolution of systems and networks, and that it must become better able to deal with entire systems in the large. To this end, building security, reliability, and—more broadly—trustworthiness and its assurance into the entire life cycle is extremely important. Furthermore, usability must be considered as an integral part of the development process.

Attaining some nontrivial measures of assurance is seemingly a labor-intensive process, but then so is conventional software development, which includes testing, debugging, integration, red-teaming, maintenance, and evolution. Ideally, techniques for enhancing assurance should be incorporated into existing tools for software and hardware development. However, there are grave dangers in believing in the infallibility of technological solutions, procedures, automated tools, and assurance arguments that can be easily misused, compromised, or ignored. Once again, assurance ultimately depends on the integrity, intelligence, training, and experience of our system architects, designers, implementers, application system operators, system and network administrators, and—in many cases—end users themselves.

From a retrospective viewpoint, many of the approaches discussed in this chapter have their roots in the past, and indeed some of them could have been pursued more successfully years ago if there had been sufficient dedication. For example, stack overflows were essentially eliminated in Multics in 1965. Formal methodologies were available in the 1970s. Strongly typed safe programming languages have been developed. However, the disciplined use of such approaches in the development mainstream has been lacking.

Typically, there are enormous benefits from techniques that can be applied from the beginning of the development process, such as specifications for critical requirements, principled architectures, and formal, semiformal, or even informal design specifications. It is clearly preferable to prevent flaws early that would otherwise be detected only later on in the development process, or much worse, in operations. However, many flaws cannot be detected early—for example, those introduced during implementation, debugging, and maintenance—which can negate earlier assurance techniques. Consequently, assurance must be a distributed and temporal concept throughout development, maintenance, and operation, where constituent assurance techniques and isolated analyses must themselves be consistent, composable, and carefully coordinated. For example, careful documentation, disciplined development methodologies, coding standards, and thoughtful code inspection all have a place in helping increase assurance—as well as having secondary effects, such as reducing downstream remediation costs, and improving interoperability, system flexibility, and maintainability. However, there are of course risks in blindly believing in the results of specific assurance methods in isolation. Significantly greater emphasis needs to be devoted to developing and operating complex systems with appropriate assurance and to managing those activities. It follows that greater efforts need to be made to encompass the concepts of this chapter within mainstream university curricula and corporate training programs. It is always easy to speculate on what will happen in the future. It is also difficult to do so with any expectation of being accurate. Nevertheless, here are some glimpses of possible futures.

- In the absence of some significant cultural changes in education (at all ages), development practice, management awareness and training with respect to technical and nontechnical issues, legislation, enforced liability, social awareness and responsibility, altruism, and so on, it is likely that business as usual will continue more or less unabated, with the further prevalence of development failures, disasters, risks, unnecessary expenditures, and recriminations. Even a gradual evolution toward some improvements is not enough.

- In the presence of major cultural shifts, such as those outlined here, we might hope for some major improvements. Run-time errors could largely disappear, through carefully established parametric requirements, better system architectures, principled software engineering, use of sound programming languages, systematic uses of better analysis tools, fundamental attention to usability (especially with respect to security and system administration), and a pervasive commitment to higher assurance throughout. Predictable compositions utilizing libraries of trustworthy components could help significantly. The future is ready for great progress, but only with pervasive commitment to attaining it.

When it comes to providing meaningful assurance for security and other attributes of trustworthiness, the usual dictum applies: There are no easy answers. With respect to information security, trustworthiness, and assurance, nothing is absolutely certain (except perhaps this sentence). Some of the approaches discussed in this chapter may be mutually conflicting in some contexts. Some of them today are perceived (perhaps, in the long term, erroneously) to be impractical. Conventional wisdom often ignores assurance in the rush to market. Nevertheless, there are many critical applications that cry out for greater assurance, and we need to find ways to make it a pervasive, effective, and efficient part of the development process. If the critical needs of high-assurance systems cannot be used to drive system development, operation, and ongoing improvements more systemically, the overall development practice will continue to suffer seriously.

77.8 FURTHER READING

Neumann, P. G. "Reflections on Trustworthiness," In M. Zelkowitz, ed., *Advances in Computers*, vol. **70**, pp. 269–310, Academic Press imprint of Elsevier Science Publishers, 2007.

Neumann, P. G., and R. J. Feiertag. "PSOS Revisited," *Proceedings of the 19th Annual Computer Security Conference*, pp. 208–216. Available: http://www.acsac.org/ and http://www.csl.sri.com/neumann/psos03.pdf.

77.9 NOTES

1. The preparation of this chapter was supported by the National Science Foundation under Grant Number 0524111, with previous support from Douglas Maughan at DARPA under the Composable High-Assurance Trustworthy Systems program.

2. For some background on what typically can go wrong and what might be learned from past failures, see P. G. Neumann, *Computer-Related Risks* (New York: ACM Press, 1995).

3. See C. A. R. Hoare and J. Misra. "Verified Software: Theories, Tools, and Experiments," In *Proceedings of the Verified Software: Theories, Tools, Experiments Conference* Zurich, Switzerland, October 2005. For more recent items, see C. A. R. Hoare et al., "The Verified Software Initiative," 2007; ftp://ftp.csl.sri.com/pub/users/shankar/VSI/pdf.

4. W. D. Young, W. E. Boebert, and R. Y. Kain, Proving a Computer System Secure," *Scientific Honeyweller* 6, No. 2 (July 1985):18–27. Reprinted in M. D. Abrams and H. J. Podell, eds., *Tutorial: Computer and Network Security,* pp. 142–157 (New York: IEEE Computer Society Press, 1987).

5. E.g., G. McGraw, *Software Security: Building Security In* (Reading, MA: Addison-Wesley, 2006).

6. For a brief overview of some of the challenges, see P. G. Neumann, "Risks Relating to System Compositions," *Communications of the ACM* 49, No. 7 (July 2006), "Inside Risks" column. For a longer discussion from a research perspective, see P. G. Neumann, *Principled Assuredly Trustworthy Composable Architectures,* Technical report, Computer Science Laboratory, SRI International, Menlo Park, CA, December 2004; www.csl.sri.com/neumann/chats4.html, .pdf, and .ps. For a historical exemplar of this approach, P. G. see Neumann, R. S. Boyer, R. J. Feiertag, K. N. Levitt, and L. Robinson, *A Provably Secure Operating System, Its*

Applications, and Proofs, Report CSL-116, SRI International, Menlo Park, CA, 1980.

7. L. Robinson and K. N. Levitt, "Proof Techniques for Hierarchically Structured Programs," *Communications of the ACM* 20, No. 4 (April 1977): 271–283.

8. J. S. Moore, ed., "System Verification," *Journal of Automated Reasoning* 5, No. 4 (December 1989): 409–530. Includes five papers by Moore, W. R. Bevier, W. A. Hunt Jr., and W. D. Young.

9. See D. Jackson, M. Thomas, and L. I. Millet, *Software for Dependable Systems: Sufficient Evidence?* (Washington, DC: National Academies Press, 2007).

10. For example, see Section 7.10 of Neumann, *Computer-Related Risks,* pp. 255–257, attributed to Robert Charette.

11. For example, see J. H. Saltzer and M. D. Schroeder, "The Protection of Information in Computer Systems," *Proceedings of the IEEE* 63, No. 9 (September 1975): 1278–1308, and Neumann, *Principled Assuredly Trustworthy Composable Architectures,* which considers some additional principles and their relevance to trustworthiness. Also of interest is F. J. Corbató, "On Building Systems that Will Fail," *Communications of the ACM* 34, No. 9 (September 1991): 72–90, which considers approaches for developing secure systems.

12. Separation kernels stem from work by J. M. Rushby, "The Design and Verification of Secure Systems," Proceedings of the Eighth ACM Symposium on Operating Systems Principles, *ACM Operating Systems Review* 15, No. 5 (December 1981): 12–21, whose recent work further considers virtual-machine monitors and approaches to multilevel security that can be built thereupon.

13. See Neumann, *Principled Assuredly Trustworthy Composable Architectures.*

14. For example, see S. L. Pfleeger and J. L. Atlee. *Software Engineering: Theory and Practice,* 3rd ed. (Englewood Cliffs, NJ: Prentice-Hall, 2005).

15. G. C. Necula," Compiling with Proofs" (PhD diss., Computer Science Department, Carnegie- Mellon University, 1998).

16. P. A. Karger and H. Kurth, "Increased Information Flow Needs for High-Assurance Composite Evaluations," in IEEE Computer Society, *Proceedings of the Second International Information Assurance Workshop,* pp. 129–140, Charlotte, NC, May 2004.

17. P. G. Neumann, "Holistic Systems," *ACM SIGSOFT Software Engineering Notes* 31, No. 6 (November 2006): 4–5.

18. References to many of these cases can be found in Neumann, Computer-Related Risks, and in the ongoing P. G. Neumann, Illustrative Risks to the Public in the Use of Computer Systems and Related Technology, Index to RISKS Cases, Technical report, Computer Science Laboratory, SRI International, Menlo Park, CA. Updated regularly at www.csl.sri.com/neumann/illustrative.html; also in .ps and .pdf form for printing in a much denser format, which provides an index into the online ACM Risks Forum archives at www.risks.org and the ACM SIGSOFT Software Engineering Notes.

19. N. Leveson, "Medical Devices: The Therac-25," in *Safeware: System Safety and Computers* (Reading, MA: Addison-Wesley, 1995). Available: http://sunnyday .mit.edu/papers/therac.pdf.

20. H. Lauda Sogame, "Air B767 Accident Report," Aircraft Accident Investigation Committee, Ministry of Transport and Communications, Thailand, 1993. Available: www.rvs.uni-bielefeld.de/publications/Incidents/DOCS/ComAndRep/LaudaAir/LaudaRPT.html.

21. F. G. M. Roeber via S. Chow, "Some Details on Patriot Problem," *Risks Forum* 13, No. 35 (April 4, 1992). Available: http://catless.ncl.ac.uk/Risks/13.35.html#subj1.

22. "USS Yorktown Dead in Water after Divide by Zero," *ACM Risks Forum* 19, No. 88 (1988); http://catless.newcastle.ac.uk/Risks/19.88.html#subj1.

23. J. Garman, "The Bug Heard 'Round the World," *ACM SIGSOFT Software Engineering Notes* 6, No. 5 (October 1981): 3–10.

24. E. Rosen, "Vulnerabilities of Network Control Protocols," *ACM SIGSOFT Software Engineering Notes* 6, No. 1 (January 1981): 6–8.

25. R. Dorsett, "More on the British Midlands 737 Crash," ACM RISKS FORUM 8, No. 59 (April 18, 1989). Available: http://catless.ncl.ac.uk/Risks/8.59.html#subj1.

26. B. Janssen, "F-16 Problems," *ACM Risks Forum* 3, No. 44 (August 14, 1986); http://catless.ncl.ac.uk/Risks/3.44.html#subj1.

27. "Friendly Fire Deaths Traced to Dead Battery," *ACM SIGSOFT Software Engineering Notes* 27, No. 3 (May 5, 2002) and *ACM Risks Forum* 21, No. 98; http://catless.newcastle.ac.uk/Risks/21.98.html#subj1.

28. D. Fetrow, "Plug Compatible Modules; Criminal Encryption," *ACM Risks Forum* 4, No. 26 (December 10, 1986); http://catless.ncl.ac.uk/Risks/4.26.html#subj4.

29. "Discovery Laser-Beam Experiment," *ACM SIGSOFT Software Engineering Notes* 10, No. 3 (July 5, 1985).

30. P. G. Neumann, "Optimistic Optimization," *Communications of the ACM* 47, No. 6 (June 2004): 112, "Inside Risks" column.

31. P. G. Neumann, "Security and Privacy Risks in Voter Registration Databases," Computer Science and Telecommunications Board workshop, November 2007; www.csl.sri.com/neumann/cstb-vrdb07.

32. R. Mercuri, "Electronic Vote Tabulation Checks and Balances" (PhD diss., Department of Computer Science, University of Pennsylvania, 2001); www.notablesoftware.com/evote.html.

33. Online at www.eac.gov/vvsg.

34. The entire set of reports is available online: www.sos.ca.gov/elections/elections_vsr.htm and encompasses volumes of red-team, source code, documentation, and user accessibility analyses.

35. N. Sastry, T. Kohno, and D. Wagner, "Designing Voting Machines for Verification," in Proceedings of the 11th USENIX Security 2006, August 2006. San Francisco: USENIX.

36. K.-P. Yee, "Building Reliable Voting Machine Software" (PhD diss. University of California, Berkeley, 2007); http://zesty.ca/pubs/yee-phd.pdf.

37. Mercuri, "Electronic Vote Tabulation Checks and Balances."

38. For example, see R. L. Rivest and W. D. Smith, "Three Voting Protocols: ThreeBallot, VAV, and Twin," Electronic Voting Technology Workshop, Boston, MA, August 6, 2007; http://people.csail.mit.edu/rivest/publications.html See also D. Chaum's publications, www.chaum.com

INDEX

flaming, 48·3–48·4
forwarding, 48·15
Group Mail, 20·14
harvesting of addresses, 20·8
headers, 20·5, 48·2, 48·8, 70·10
hostile working environment, 48·3
HTML, 28·2, 48·19–48·20
impact of spam, 20·7–20·8
inefficient use of, 48·15–48·21
information about, obtaining, 20·5–20·6
and Internet hoaxes, 48·6–48·11, 48·43
junk e-mail. *See* Spam
list servers, 48·22
mail-bombing, 18·6–18·7, 48·3, 48·42
mail storms, 18·7, 48·21–48·23, 48·42–48·43
mass mailing, 20·13–20·16
monitoring, 69·13
multi-level marketing schemes, 48·10–48·11
opt-out choice, 20·17
overview, 48·2
and pedophiles, 48·12–48·13
permission issues, 20·16–20·17
Ponzi schemes, 48·9–48·10
private e-mail in the workplace, 48·21
reply all, 48·20
responsible practices, 20·15–20·16
Simple Mail Transfer Protocol (SMTP), 5·27,
    17·12–17·13
Simple Mail Transport Protocol (SMTP),
    20·3–20·5, 20·24
as source of phishing attacks, 19·8. *See also*
    Phishing
spam. *See* Spam
subject line, 48·15–48·16
and threats of physical harm, 48·12
transfer standards, 5·27
Unified Threat Management (UTM), 31·9
unsolicited commercial e-mail (UCE). *See*
    Spam
and viruses, 41·11
whitelists, 20·4, 20·18, 20·21–20·22
worms, 16·6
E-Sign Bill. *See* Electronic Signatures in Global
    and National Commerce Act (E-Sign Bill)
E-warfare. *See* Information warfare (IW)
Earthquakes and tsunamis, 22·17. *See also*
    Physical threats
Eavesdropping, 33·9, 33·17, 34·10–34·11
EBay, 48·25
Echo, 4·6, 5·23
Echo reply, 5·23
Edit checks, 47·15–47·16
EFF DES Cracker, 7·20, 7·37
Egress filtering, 18·12, 18·23, 18·25
Election process and computer-aided voting,
    77·16–77·19
Electrical EPROMs (EEPROMs), 4·9
Electrical power. *See* Power failures and
    disturbances

Electromagnetic pulse attack (EMP), 22·21
Electromagnetic pulses and magnetic fields and
    media storage, 57·20
Electromagnetic radiation (EMR), 25·5. *See also*
    TEMPEST (Transient ElectroMagnetic Pulse
    Emission Standard)
Electronic Communications Privacy Act (ECPA),
    11·30, 30·40, 34·4, 69·8, 69·14
Electronic Data Interchange (EDI), 32·13, 71·12
Electronic Health Records, 71·11, 71·15
Electronic Healthcare Network Accreditation
    Commission (EHNAC), 71·26
Electronic Signature Act of 2000 (E-Sign Act),
    71·8
Electronic Signatures in Global and National
    Commerce Act (E-Sign Bill), 42·14
Elliptic curve cryptography, 7·35–7·36
Embedded systems, 1·14
Emergency Management Assessment Program
    (EMAP), 22·10, 23·7
Emergency Operations Plan, 23·6
Emergency power, 23·38–23·44
Emergency response plans, 22·9–22·10. *See also*
    Business continuity planning (BCP);
    Disaster recovery; Physical site security
Emergency Support Functions (ESF), 23·54
Emerging technologies, 30·38
Employees:
    abuse, opportunities for, 45·4
    access issues, 13·2, 13·8, 45·4
    background checks, 13·2, 13·6–13·8, 16·9,
        45·2–45·3
    backup plans, 4·18
    behavioral changes, 45·7–45·9
    blogs, 48·5
    career advancement, 45·6–45·7
    and computer crime, 45·1–45·2
    confidentiality agreements, 45·14
    cross-training, 45·4–45·6
    dangerous insiders. *See* Insiders, information
        technology
    downloads, 19·18
    duty of loyalty, 11·3
    e-mail monitoring, 69·13
    employment agreements, 11·4, 45·3
    extranet services for, 32·13
    fiduciary duties, 11·3, 11·29
    health and safety issues, 22·3, 22·17,
        23·50–23·51, 58·14
    identification and authentication issues, 28·16
    indispensable, 45·4–45·6
    Internet use, policies on, 48·44. *See also*
        Internet
    key person and alternate, business impact
        analysis, 58·20
    and management practices, 45·3–45·10, 45·15
    mobility of, 26·2
    motivation, 63·12–63·14
    noncompetition agreements, 45·14–45·15

Endangerment, 3·2, 3·17–3·18
Enhanced Interior Gateway Routing Protocol
(EIGRP), 5·26
Ensconce Data Technology, 57·25
Enterprise applications, 26·2
Enterprise JavaBeans (EJB), 21·13
Enterprise resource planning (ERP) systems,
32·12
Enumerating, 55·13–55·14
Environment. *See* Physical threats
Equipment cabinets, 23·17–23·18,
23·31–23·35
Erasable, programmable read-only memory
(EPROM), 4·9
Errors:
attribution errors, 50·7–50·10
biometric authentication crossover error rate
(equal error rate), 29·15–29·16
calculation errors, 38·9, 39·8
codes and coding, 16·10, 21·7, 38·7–39·12,
38·8–38·13, 39·7–39·12
control (command) structure errors,
38·11–38·12, 39·11
functionality errors, 38·11, 39·10
initialization errors, 38·8–38·9, 39·7–39·8
input, 52·9
load condition errors, 38·10, 39·8–39·9
logic flow errors, 38·9, 39·8, 52·3
output format errors, 38·12–38·13,
39·11–39·12
parameter-passing errors, 38·9, 39·8
performance errors, 38·12, 39·11
performance (speed) errors, 38·12
program conflict errors, 38·10, 39·9
programming, 52·3
race conditions, 38·9–38·10, 39·9, 39·14,
52·4
resource exhaustion errors, 38·10, 39·9
software errors, types of, 38·8–38·13,
39·7–39·12
E.T. applications, 48·13
Ethereal, 25·4, 33·37–33·38
Ethernet, 1·10, 5·12, 6·3, 6·23
Ethernet II, 6·19–6·20
Ethics:
and computer crime, 12·12–12·15
consequentialism (teleology), 70·17
customer monitoring, 30·39
defined, 43·1–43·2
and dummy security devices, 23·19
importance of, 43·1–43·2, 43·7–43·8
Information Systems Audit and Control
Association (ISACA), 74·9–74·12
Institute of Internal Auditors (IIA) code of
ethics, 74·8
International Information Systems Security
Certification Consortium (ISC), 74·12,
74·14
and penetration testing, 46·9–46·10

principles, 43·2–43·7, 70·17–70·18
resources, 43·7
responsibility for, 43·7
rights and duties (deontology), 70·17
and surveillance systems, 23·29
and Web site management, 30·38–30·40
EU Data Protection Act, 65·13
EU Data Protection Directive 95/46/EC,
69·4–69·6
and codes of conduct, 69·18
implementation of, 69·4, 69·6
U.S./EU safe harbor, 69·5, 69·12–69·13,
69·18
EU Telecommunications Directive, 69·6
Europe, educational system:
applied universities (technical schools),
76·10–76·12
art and science, 76·8–76·11
bachelor's degree requirements, 76·4–76·5,
76·14
Bologna Declaration, 76·2–76·17
computer science terminology, 76·4
Continuous Masters program, 76·9,
76·11–76·12, 76·14–76·15
course credits, 76·3–76·8
declarative knowledge, 76·9
graduate programs, 76·5–76·8
implications of standardization,
76·15–76·17
information assurance, courses on, 76·13
information assurance, use of term, 76·4,
76·12
information security curriculum, 76·10–76·11,
76·13–76·14
information security degrees, 76·3
malware, courses on, 76·13–76·14
and mathematics, importance of, 76·8,
76·15–76·17
Specialized Master's degrees, 76·8–76·9,
76·11–76·15
European Credit Transfer and Accumulation
System (ECTS), 76·3–76·8
European Data Protection Supervisor, 69·6
European Union Data Protection Directive
95/46/EC. *See* EU Data Protection Directive
95/46/EC
Evaluation Assurance Levels (EALs), 51·20
Evanescent media, 42·10
Events, 8·4–8·11. *See also* Security incidents
Evidence. *See also* Cyber investigation
chain of custody, 55·12, 55·17, 61·7–61·8
collecting, 55·10, 55·16
corroboration of, 55·12, 55·17
and cyber investigation. *See* Cyber investigation
law enforcement agencies, cooperation with,
61·7–61·8
Exam preparation, 74·19–74·20
Exception reports, 53·23
Executive Order 12958, 67·5–67·6

and network operating systems, 6·27
packet sniffers. *See* Packet sniffers
and protecting Web applications,
21·6–21·7
Simple Network Management Protocol
(SNMP). *See* Simple Network Management
Protocol (SNMP)
and wiretapping, 15·10
TCP port 80, 15·22, 18·21, 30·32
TCP port 443, 30·32, 30·38
TCP (Transmission Control Protocol),
5·17–5·22. *See also* TCP/IP (Transmission
Control Protocol/Internet Protocol)
Tcpdump, 25·4
Teardrop, 25·14
Teardrop attacks, 18·9
Tebibytes, 4·4
Telecommunications Industry
Association/Electronic Industry Alliance
(TIA/EIA), Standard 606, *Administration
Standard for the Telecommunications
Infrastructure of Commercial Buildings,*
23·14
Telecommuting, 1·12
Telephone Consumer Protection Act of 1991,
11·29
Television, piracy, 42·8–42·10
Telnet, 5·27
Temperature:
and HVAC systems, 23·16–23·17,
23·44–23·46
as security hazard, 3·17, 4·11–4·12, 4·22,
22·23, 53·11, 57·20
TEMPEST (Transient ElectroMagnetic Pulse
Emission Standard), 15·13, 25·5
Temporal key integrity protocol (TKIP),
33·30–33·33, 33·36, 33·39, 33·47
Terms of use, 11·25–11·26
Terrorism and terrorists. *See also* September 11,
2001 attacks
computer crime, trends, 2·26
cyberterrorism, 12·3
information infrastructure, protecting against
threats, 23·49
physical threats, 22·4, 22·6, 22·20,
22·22–22·23, 22·26
reporting activities, 61·4
taxonomy, 8·16
Testimony, expert witnesses. *See* Expert witnesses
Testing:
automated, 39·15–39·16
backup plans, 4·20
best practices, 38·15
CC Testing Labs, 51·27–51·28
disaster recovery plan, 59·20–59·21
and internal controls, 54·13
penetration testing. *See* Penetration testing
race conditions, testing for, 39·14
regression testing, 39·15, 39·17

software development, 39·5–39·6,
39·12–39·16
software patches, 40·11–40·13, 40·15
and standards, 51·8–51·9. *See also* Standards
test-coverage monitors, 39·14
test data, 47·13–47·14
test libraries, 47·14
third-party commercial product assessments,
51·7, 51·11–51·12
Theft, 4·22, 19·6
Theft-of-service attacks, 34·10
Threat analysis, 3·14–3·18, 22·2, 22·9–22·15,
30·24, 51·21–51·22. *See also* Physical
threats; Risk assessment
Threats:
and business continuity planning, 58·4–58·6.
See also Business continuity planning
(BCP); Disaster recovery
classification of damage, 59·3–59·6
and disaster recovery, 59·1–59·2
list of, 59·2
malicious code threat model, 16·2–16·3
management awareness of, 63·16–63·19
physical threats. *See* Physical threats
threat occurrence rate, 62·17–62·18. *See also*
Risk assessment
understanding of and awareness programs,
49·19
unified threat management (UTM), 53·2
Voice over Internet Protocol (VoIP),
34·9–34·11
wireless local area networks, 33·9–33·14
Threats, assets, vulnerabilities model, 3·2,
3·20–3·22
Thumb drives. *See* Flash drives
Time, synchronous and asynchronous, 4·10–4·11
Time bombs, 2·10–2·11
Time sharing, 1·7
Time stamps, 47·14
TLS. *See* Transport Layer Security (TLS)
Token bus, 6·17
Token passing, 6·14
Token ring, 6·17, 6·20–6·22, 6·24
Token ring network, 6·14, 25·5
Tokens:
and authentication principles, 28·2–28·4
dongles. *See* Dongles
hardware, 7·30, 28·14
one-time password generators, 28·13–28·14
private key, 37·23
smart cards. *See* Smart cards
soft tokens, 28·14–28·15
types of, 28·3–28·4, 28·13
and virtual private networks, 32·5
Toolkits, 8·14, 15·20–15·21
Topology, local area networks, 6·3–6·7
TOR (the onion router). *See* Onion routing
Total quality management (TQM), 38·2
Touch cards, 23·22–23·23

DATE DUE